I0461270

A
Grammar
of
Meskwaki

Ives Goddard

Mundart Press

2023

Copyright © 2023 by Joshua Jacob Snider
Mundart Press, 807 Howard Street, Petoskey MI 49770

All rights reserved. No part of this book may be reproduced or
transmitted in any form or by any means, electronic or mechanical,
including photocopying, recording, or by any information storage
and retrieval system, without permission in writing from the publisher.

The publisher hereby grants such permission to the Sac and Fox Tribe
of the Mississippi in Iowa for any tribal educational or cultural purpose.

A publication of the Recovering Voices Program of the Smithsonian
Institution, supported in part by a gift from the Shoniya Fund.

Publisher's Cataloguing-in-Publication Data

Names: Goddard, Ives, 1941- author.
Title: A grammar of Meskwaki / Ives Goddard.
Description: Petoskey, MI : Mundart Press, 2023. | Includes bibliography.
Identifiers: ISBN: 9798986545035 | LCCN: 2023903051
Subjects: LCSH: Fox language--Grammar. | Fox language--Phonology. | Fox language--Inflection. | Algonquian
        languages--Grammar. | Algonquian languages--Phonology. | Algonquian languages--Inflection. | Fox
        language--Iowa--Tama County. | Sac & Fox Tribe of the Mississippi in Iowa--Languages--Grammar. | Sac
        & Fox Tribe of the Mississippi in Iowa-- Languages--Phonology. | Sac & Fox Tribe of the Mississippi in
        Iowa--Languages-- Inflection.
Classification: LCC: PM1195 .G63 2023 | DDC: 497/.314--dc23

Table of Contents

Preface

This grammar of the Meskwaki language is largely based on the extensive manuscript writings by native speakers that are in the National Anthropological Archives (Smithsonian Institution) and the fieldwork with speakers of the language undertaken to understand them. This work was made possible by the patient assistance of many members of the Meskwaki community, including especially Adeline Wanatee, Everett Kapayou, Horace White Breast, Leonard Young Bear, Frances Mitchell, Pearl Bear, Don Wanatee, Leo Keahna, Frank Pushetonequa, Helen Bullard, and Johnathan Buffalo. This book also owes much to work done on these manuscripts by Amy Dahlstrom and Lucy Thomason, including their own fieldwork and numerous publications, and their collegial discussions.

Meskwaki was earlier referred to as Fox, and the spelling "Mesquakie" was formerly used.

Meskwaki is the heritage language of the Sac & Fox Tribe of the Mississippi in Iowa.

Washington, January 2023

Abbreviations
(and Index)

Grammatical categories and conventions and miscellaneous (with references)

ABSTR	abstract (semantically empty)
acc.	accepted by
AI	animate intransitive (**§18.3**, ex. 2.3)
AI+O	AI taking a secondary object (transitivized AI) (**§22.3**)
AN, anim.	animate (**§19**)
anon.	anonymous
AOR	aorist (**§26.8**)
ast.	assertive (**§26.4**)
CC	changed conjunct (**§26.10**, **§30.11**)
cf.	compare
CH.PRET	changed preterite (**§26.25**)
CH.PRI	changed prioritive (**§26.18**)
compound (**§66**)	
con., CON	conclusive (**§26.3**)
CONJ	plain conjunct (**§26.7**)
conj.	conjunct (**§26.6-8**)
CV	consonant-vowel
dim., DIM	diminutive (**§25**)
dub., DUB	dubitative (**§26.2**)
ECM	exocentric compound member (**§60.4**)
e.g.	for example
EMPH	emphatic
EN	expressive-negative intonation (**§6.3**)
esp.	especially
ex., exx.	example, examples
exc.	exclusive (**§18.4**)
EXCLAM	exclamative (**§6.7**)
EXO	exocentric particle final (**§38.5**)
EXPR	expressive (**§6.4**)
ff.	and following
FUT	future (**§26.24**)
fut. imp., FUT.IMP	future imperative (**§26.19**)
HRSY	hearsay (see ex. 6.1)
IC	initial change (**§29.4**)
i.e.	that is
II	inanimate intransitive (**§18.3**, ex. 2.3)
imp., IMP	imperative (**§26.22**)
IN, inan.	inanimate (**§19**)
inc.	inclusive (**§18.4**)

IND	independent indicative (**§26.1**)
int., INT	interrogative (**§26.14-17**)
INTERJ	interjectional (**§6.8**)
INTS	intensive (**§6.6**)
irr.	irrealis (**§29.9(a)**)
iter., ITER	iterative (**§26.12, §30.13**)
lit.	literally
loc., LOC	locative (**§24, §28.15, §28.6**)
loc.obl	locative oblique (**§22.4(d,e)**)
ms.	manuscript
|N|	mutating /n/ (**§7.1**)
NAA	National Anthropological Archives, Smithsonian Institution
neg., NEG	negative (**§26.11, §30.12**)
NF	noun final (**§36**)
Ø	zero (not phonetically overt)
O	object
O2	secondary object (**§22.3**. ex. 2.85)
obl	oblique (**§22.4**)
obv., OBV	obviative (**§21**)
p.c.	personal communication
p, pl, pl.	plural (**§20**; ex. 2.1)
poss. th.	possessed-theme marker (**§28.5**)
pot., POT	potential (**§26.20**)
PPL	participle (**§26.13, §30.14**)
pret.	preterite (**§26.25, §30.15**)
PRI	prioritive (**§26.18**)
proh., PROH	prohibitive (**§26.19**)
prox.	proximate (**§21**)
PV	preverb (**§18.11**)
Q	interrogative intonation (**§6.2**)
RED1	one-syllable reduplication (**§39, §39.1-3**)
RED2	two-syllable reduplication (**§39, §39.4**)
rel., REL	relational (**§22.6**)
s, sg, sg.	singular (**§20**)
S	subject
|S|	mutating /s/ (**§7.1**)
subj., SUBJ	subjunctive (**§26.9**)
T (in a citation)	title
|T|	non-mutating /t/ (**§7.1**)
TA	transitive animate (ex. 2.9)
TA+O	TA taking a secondary object (**§22.3**)
th.	theme (**§28.5, §29.7**)
TI	transitive inanimate (ex. 2.9)
TI(1)	transitive inanimate of class 1 (ex. 2.10)
TI(2)	transitive inanimate of class 2 (ex. 2.10)
TI(3)	transitive inanimate of class 3 (ex. 2.10)

TI-O	objectless TI (**§22.3**)
TI-O+O	objectless TI taking a secondary object (ex. 2.87-88)
tr.	translated by
v	vowel
V	verb
w.s.	woman speaking
X	indefinite person (**§18.4**, **§53.3**)
X+number	anonymous (unidentified writer)
{...}	The gloss of the oblique complement of a relative root (**§22.4**).

Inflectional Persons

0	third person inanimate
0p	third person inanimate plural
0s	third person inanimate singular
0´	third person inanimate obviative
0´p	third person inanimate obviative plural
0´s	third person inanimate obviative singular
1	first person
1p	first person plural exclusive
1s	first person singular
12	first person plural inclusive
2	second person
2p	second person plural
2s	second person singular
3	third person animate
3p	third person animate plural
3s	third person animate singular
3´	third person animate obviative
3´p	third person animate obviative plural
3´s	third person animate obviative singular

Sources (Alphabetical by name and abbreviation.)

A	The Autobiography of a Meskwaki Woman. NAA 2999. Published with interlinear analysis and translation as Goddard (2006b).
Bill Leaf	
BL-OS	A Girl and a Little Boy (Otterskin). NAA 2794.50:1-24.
BL-RL	Red-Leggins. NAA 2794.68A:1-30 and NAA 2794.56:31-56. Edited by Lucy Thomason.
Charley H. Chuck	
C-FRS	The Frenchman and the Siouxs. NAA 2794.4.

C-FS   Fisherskin. NAA 2794.11.
C-G   Giants. NAA 2794.12.
C-Hist   Meskwaki History. Manuscript in the State Historical Society of Iowa, Iowa City.
            Published as: "A Collection of Meskwaki Manuscripts Prepared by
            Cha kä ta ko si ..." (1907). See Purcell (1974:52-54).
C-IW   When the Indian and the American First Met. NAA 2782.
C-L   [Ledger in Tama, Iowa; manuscript copy made May 1992.]
C-MWP   When Meskwakis Went on the Warpath. NAA 2658.14:1-17.
C-O   Otehkwa. NAA 2794:93. Edited by Lucy Thomason and Ives Goddard.
C-PB   What Some Potawatomis Did, Including One that was Blessed. NAA 2794.9(a).
C-PD   Prairie-Dog's Story. NAA 2794.46(a).
C-RP   Redstone-Pipe. NAA 2737.3.
C-RS   When Raccoon was Smart. NAA 2794.5.
C-SD   The Swan Dance. NAA 2739 ["Giant Butterfly"].
C-Ston   Has-a-Rock. NAA 2737.2.
C-UAN   The Uncle and Nephew. NAA 2737.1.
C-WH   Wampumhead: A Winter Story. NAA 2794.46(b).
C-YBB   The Youth that Fasted and the Manitou Big-Belly. NAA 2794.9(b).
C-YS   The Youth who was Smart. NAA 2737.4.
Frank Earle:
FE-Lang   The Meskwaki Language (1927). NAA 3005:1-120.
George Black Cloud:
GBC-BDB   [The Buffalo Dance of the Bear Gens.] NAA 2947 (Michelson 1930:8-35).
GBC-BHD   [The Buffalo Head Dance of the Thunder Gens.] NAA 2542 (Michelson
            1928:10-35).
GBC-Wapan   [The Wâpanôwiweni of the Bear Clan. Second Text.] NAA 2946 (Michelson
            1932:108-141).
Jack Bullard:
JB-BP   Ball-Player. NAA 1875.10.
JB-Meshq   Meshkwihowa. NAA 2677.1.
JB-RE   Red Eagle. NAA 2830.1(a).
JB-Tiger   The Winter Story of Tiger the Soldier. NAA 2838.
Jim Mamasaw:
JM-TMF   Two Meskwaki Friends. NAA 2835(e):32-38.
Joe Peters:
JoP-MortH   What those the Religion Dance Has Been Brought Here to Do When One of
            them Dies. NAA 3111-a(H) (Michelson 1925:464-471).
Jim Peters:
JP-Apay2   Apayashis [2]. NAA 2674-2. Edited by Lucy Thomason.
JP-BAB   The Boys who Avenged their Brothers. NAA 2664.9(i):71-79;
            Jim Peters (71A-78D) and Sam Peters (78E-79O).
JP-GTF   The Girl who Had Ten Friends. NAA 2794.47(3).
JP-HLOS   The Hunt Leader who Overcame a Spell. NAA 2664.9(h).
JP-KT   Kishko and Tohkan, and the Clans. NAA 1736,
JP-MC8D   What Happened When a Man Chased Eight Deer. NAA 2794.72(1).

JP-OPLA	What One Person Did Long Ago. NAA 1722a.
JP-SD	[The Sucking Doctor.] NAA 1831, Edited by Lucy Thomason.
JP-TO	[Turkey-Owner.] NAA 2724.2:53-93, 95-116. Edited by Lucy Thomason and Ives Goddard
JP-WMD	What Some Meskwakis Did Another Time. NAA 1722b.
JP-YMPE	The Young Man who Made Peace with the Enemy. NAA 1722:42-92.

James Poweshiek:

JPo-C	Postcard to Willie Poweshiek, March 21, 1918.

Alfred Kiyana:

K-Apay	The Apayashis (*apaya ši·haki*). NAA 2671.1. Edited by Lucy Thomason.
K-Auto	[The Autobiography of Alfred Kiyana.] NAA 1834.
K-B	The Story of the One who was Blessed by the White Buffalo. NAA 2062 (Michelson 1925:46-207).
K-BB	What they Do When a Baby is Born. NAA 2023.
K-BBD	Bear Bundle Dance. NAA 2154. Edited by Lucy Thomason.
K-BBWM	[The Boy Blessed by a Water Monster.] NAA 2230. Edited by Ives Goddard and Lucy Thomason.
K-BD	[Buffalo Dance.] NAA 2046.
K-Bene	Benesa Sacred Bundle Dance. NAA 2717.
K-BFF	A Certain Boy who was Afraid to Fast. NAA 2794.24.
K-BFS	One Blessed by the Spirit of Fire Way Long Ago. NAA 2026.
K-BH	The Medicine of the Bovid-Horns. NAA 2794.54(a).
K-BHD	The Buffalo-Head [Dance]. NAA 2525.
K-BHD2	The Buffalo-Head Dance of the Thunder Clan (Second Version). NAA 2196. Edited by Ives Goddard and Lucy Thomason.
K-BLI	The Buffalo who Lived with an Indian. NAA 2501. Edited by Ives Goddard and Lucy Thomason.
K-BLM	The Boys who Lived with their Mother. NAA 2777.15.
K-BR	Bear and Rabbit. NAA 2042.
K-BS	The Big Snake. NAA 2656.1.
K-CBFB	The Crazy Boy who Fought a Buffalo. NAA 2794.67. Edited by Ives Goddard and Lucy Thomason.
K-CDWP	[Ceremonial Dances, War Practices, and Traditions of the White Man.] NAA 2656.2. (Michelson's title: "South wind dance.")
K-CGB	[Commentary on the Green Buffalo Story.] NAA 2763 (1-49), 2952 (50-54, at the end).
K-CM	The Man who was Always Getting a Scare. NAA 2720.5. (Earlier title : "The Cowardly Man," based on Ida Poweshiek's title "Coward Man.") Edited by Ives Goddard and Lucy Thomason.
K-CWB	[Commentary on the White Buffalo Story.] NAA 2819.
K-ECRP	[The Eagle Clan Redstone Pipe Ceremony.] NAA 1850.
K-EGC	The Man who Had an Elm Tree Growing Out of his Chest. NAA 2720.6. Edited by Lucy Thomason and Ives Goddard.
K-F	Feather. NAA 2082.2. Edited by Lucy Thomason.
K-FASB	The Flying-Around Sacred Bundle Dance. NAA 2179.

K-FC   How the Fox Clan was Blessed. NAA 2957.1(1-6).

K-Fish   The Story of the Fish Clan. NAA 2667.

K-FM   What a Man and a Woman Do When they Get Married for the First Time.
            NAA 2432.2.

K-GBuff   Green Buffalo. NAA 1786. (Meskwaki title: "Wolf Clan. What Green
            Buffalo did when he bestowed a blessing.") Edited by Ives Goddard and Lucy
            Thomason.

K-GD   Ghost Dance: The One who was Blessed by Ghosts. NAA 2079. Edited by
            Ives Goddard and Lucy Thomason.

K-GF   The Girls who Were Friends. NAA 2794.44. Edited by Lucy Thomason.

K-HS   The Story of "Lady-Killer." NAA 2432.1. (Michelson's title: Homo
            Stuprator.)

K-ICH   When the Indians Captured Horses Long Ago. NAA 2433.2.

K-IFSB   When the Indians First Saw Blacks. NAA 2794.23.

K-ILM   The Indian Lead Miners of Long Ago, who Had a Lead Mine. NAA 1879.13.

K-JM   What Jealous Men Did Long Ago. NAA 2664.1.

K-K   Kashawiha. NAA 2664.7. Edited by Lucy Thomason and Ives Goddard.

K-Kin   Kinship Terminology and Archaic Vocabulary. NAA 2232 (1-40),
            2277 (41-72).

K-KK   Kawesahkweha and Kochipehkwaha. NAA 2764.10. Edited by Ives Goddard
            and Lucy Thomason.

K-Koch   Kochipehkwaha. NAA 2674.3. Edited by Lucy Thomason.

K-M   Masahkamikohkwêwa. NAA 2959. (Earlier referred to as "MAE," using
            Horace Poweshiek's translation "Mother-of-all-the-Earth.") Published in a
            bilingual edition as Thomason and Goddard (2022).

K-ManMa   A Manitou Man. NAA 2794.38a. Edited by Ives Goddard and Lucy
            Thomason.

K-MBGS   The Man who was Blessed by the Great Spirit. NAA 2794.74. Edited by
            Lucy Thomason and Ives Goddard.

K-MBT   The Indian Man who Became a Thunderer. NAA 2794.8.

K-Med   Words, Names, and Phrases: Medicines and Topical Vocabularies. NAA
            2841 (1:1-59), 2778 (2:1-48).

K-Mes   Mesoswa. NAA 2153(8).

K-MESB   What is Told about the One who Made the Eagle Sacred Bundle.
            NAA 1835.

K-MFWB   The One who Made Four War Bundles. NAA 2779.

K-MFS   The Man Whose Father was the Sun, and his Older Brother a Dog.
            NAA 2653.

K-MGL   The Man who Got Lost. NAA 2764. Edited by Ives Goddard and Lucy
            Thomason.

K-MGW   A Man of Long Ago who Had a Knack for Being Given Women.
            NAA 2794.87.

K-MHTW   The Man who Had Two Wives. NAA 2777.14.

K-MIM   The Man who was Indeed a Manitou. NAA 2794.32.

K-MKD   The Men who Knew How to Get a Drink. NAA 2794.22.

K-MLF	Mountain Lion and his Father. NAA 2794.60. Edited by Ives Goddard and Lucy Thomason.
K-MM	Maidens and Men. NAA 2794.92.
K-MMB	The Man who Made a Sacred Bundle. NAA 1879.9. Edited by Ives Goddard and Lucy Thomason.
K-MMD	The Man who Married his Daughter. NAA 2664.3.
K-MMDR	The Man who Married a Deer. NAA 2794.64. Edited by Ives Goddard and Lucy Thomason.
K-MME	The Man who Married Everything. NAA 2794.73.
K-MMGW	The Man who Married a Giant Woman. NAA 2655.1.
K-MND	Meskwaki Night Dances. NAA 1837.
K-MOR	The Man who Had Pet Raccoons. NAA 2794.91.
K-MortE	The Ghost Feast. NAA 1892.2. Edited by Lucy Thomason.
K-MortF	What People whose Child Dies Do. NAA 3111a-F. Edited by Lucy Thomason.
K-MP	Medicine Pack. NAA 2210. Edited by Lucy Thomason.
K-MP1	What is Called the White Buffalo's Left-Hoof Sacred Pack. NAA 2076.1. Edited by Lucy Thomason.
K-MP2	The White Tiny-Hoof Sacred Pack. NAA 2076.2. Edited by Lucy Thomason.
K-MP3	The Sacred Pack on the Right Front Hoof of the White Buffalo. NAA 2076.3. Edited by Lucy Thomason.
K-MWL	A Man who was a Warparty Leader and Warriors who were Great Fighters. NAA 2664.4.
K-MWS	The One who Made the Wailing Songs. NAA 2140. Edited by Lucy Thomason.
K-OBES	The Story of one Blessed by an Evil Spirit. NAA 2732.
K-OKUT	The One who Knew How to Use Things. NAA 1859.2. Edited by Ives Goddard and Lucy Thomason.
K-OMSP	The Story of One who Made a Sacred Pack. NAA 2766. Edited by Ives Goddard and Lucy Thomason.
K-ORF	The One who Runs Fast. NAA 2433.4. Edited by Ives Goddard and Lucy Thomason.
K-Owl	Owl. NAA 2153.1.
K-OWM	The Old Woman who Had Manitou Powers. NAA 2788.
K-Pach	Lazybones (*pačana*). NAA 2984.3. Edited by Amy Dahlstrom. (Dahlstrom 1996b:129-160.)
K-PBLA	People of Long Ago who Were Blessed. NAA 2794.86.
K-Pich	Pichishaha. NAA 2775. Edited by Lucy Thomason.
K-PKM	When People Killed One that had Manitou Powers. NAA 2720.4. Edited by Ives Goddard and Lucy Thomason.
K-PLA	The People of Long Ago. NAA 2664.5.
K-PMW	When Possum Married Woodchuck. NAA 2153(4).
K-RC	[Release Ceremony.] NAA 1892.1 (see Michelson 1925:361-364). Edited by Lucy Thomason.
K-RFB	When Raccoon was Friends with Badger. NAA 2153(5).

K-RMDW	When Raccoon Married Duck Woman. NAA 2654.
K-RP	Redstone Pipe. NAA 2720.1. Edited by Lucy Thomason.
K-RWD	What they Did When they Danced on Returning from War. NAA 2023.1.
K-RYL	Raccoon, who Yelled Loud. NAA 2764.9. Edited by Ives Goddard and Lucy Thomason.
K-S	Spider. NAA 2794.80. Edited by Lucy Thomason.
K-SBSB	Star-Bear Sacred Pack. NAA 2794.54(c).
K-SD	The Snail Dance. NAA 2606.
K-SF	When the Spirit of Fire was Made by the Manitous. NAA 1875.16
K-SGG	Shooter, and his Gandmother and Grandfather. NAA 2794.66. Edited by Ives Goddard and Lucy Thomason.
K-SH	The Summer Hunters. NAA 2720.3. Edited by Ives Goddard and Lucy Thomason.
K-SPC	Sacred-Pack Mask. NAA 2794.54(d).
K-Spot	The Spotted Cow Sacred Bundle. NAA .
K-SSB	Serpent Sacred Pack. NAA 2794.54(e).
K-SSP	The Sky Sacred Pack of the Eagle Clan. NAA 2273.
K-T	Turtle. NAA 2764.8. Edited by Ives Goddard and Lucy Thomason.
K-TCSB	The Story of the One who Made the Thunder Clan Sacred Bundle. NAA 1885.
K-TG	The Twin Girls. NAA 2155.
K-TM	Ten Men. NAA 2655.3. Edited by Ives Goddard and Lucy Thomason.
K-TO	Turkey-Owner. NAA 3065.
K-TYFB	The Two Youths who Fasted who Were Brothers. NAA 2433.3.
K-ULG	The Winter Story of an Unfortunate Little Girl. NAA 2794.6.
K-W	Wisahkeha, his Father, his Mother, his Younger Brother, and his Grandmother. NAA 2958.a. Edited by Amy Dahlstrom and Lucy Thomason.
K-Wap	Wapasaya. NAA 2122.
K-Wapes	Waterfowl Clan. NAA 2239.
K-WarD	War Dance. NAA 2433.5.
K-WB	When Wisahkeha Fed Bees to the Wolves. NAA 1879.3.
K-WC	What the War Chief Clan Did. NAA 1852. Edited by Ives Goddard and Lucy Thomason.
K-WD	[The Wisahkeha Dance.] NAA 2655.11, 8-10. Edited by Ives Goddard and Lucy Thomason.
K-Wewi	Wewipeha and his Wife. NAA 2794.88.
K-WF	[Wooden Figure.] NAA 2080. Edited by Ives Goddard and Lucy Thomason.
K-WKG	When the Cannibal Giant was Killed by Wisahkeha. NAA 2688.
K-WLB	The Woman who Loved her Brother. NAA 1875.11.
K-WLBS	[Wisahkeha's Younger Brother Slain.] NAA 2720.8. Edited by Ives Goddard and Lucy Thomason.
K-WM	A Woman who Had Manitou Powers. NAA 2794.38. Edited by Ives Goddard and Lucy Thomason.
K-WMB	The Wooden Manitou Buffalo. NAA 2221. Edited by Ives Goddard and Lucy Thomason.
K-Words	Words, Phrases, and Sentences on Various Topics. NAA 2841 and 2778.

K-WPGB	The Indian Woman Long Ago who was Pursued by a Grizzly Bear. NAA 2658.16.
K-Wpn	[Wâpanôwiweni, 1.] NAA 2833. Michelson (1932:20-107).
K-WSB	The Wolf Clan Sacred Pack Dance. NAA 2157.
K-WT	The Woman and the Toad. NAA 2764.6. Edited by Ives Goddard and Lucy Thomason.
K-WTS	Wisahkeha Traps the Sun. NAA 2311. Edited by Lucy Thomason.
K-WWB	The Married Couple: The Man Whose Wife was Wooed by a Bear. NAA 2153(2).
K-WYB	Wapasaya's Younger Brother Meskwasona. NAA 2121.
K-YC	The Youth who Became Corn, and the Indians of Long Ago that Grew as All Different Kinds of Things. NAA 1875.8.
K-YF	Youths who were Friends. NAA 2794.27.

Lucy Lasley and Jack Bullard

LLJB-Ksh	Keshakiwa. NAA 1875.13.
O	Alfred Kiyana, [The Owl Sacred Pack]. NAA 2693. Published with interlinear analysis and translation as Goddard (2007).

Sakihtanohkwewa

S-Apay	The Apayashis (apaya·ši·haki). NAA 2671.5.
S-IM	[The Ice Maidens.] NAA 2662.
S-OWA	When an Old Woman was Abandoned Long Ago. NAA 2777.4.
S-Pit	Pitishaha. NAA 2658.10.
S-RL	[Red-Leggins.] NAA 2700. Edited by Lucy Thomason.
S-RL2	Red-Leggins (2). NAA 1861. Edited by Lucy Thomason.
S-RSW	The Rolling Skull Woman. NAA 2794.81.
S-Shak	[Shahkanaha.] NAA 2659.
S-W	[Wisahkeha.] NAA 1875.7 and 1879.5. Edited by Lucy Thomason.
S-YMSG	The Young Man who Sailed across the Sea to Gamble. NAA 2794.49.

Shapochiwa

Sh-Buz	Buzzard. 2794.26. Edited by Lucy Thomason.
Sh-Elm	Has-an-Elm (Wêtanîpîmêha). 2664.8. Edited by Lucy Thomason.

Sam Peters

SP-BKWM	[When a Baby was Kidnaped by a Water Manitou.] NAA 2664.9(j):80-86.
SP-BPCS	[When the Berry-Pickers were Captured by the Siouxs.] NAA 2794.46(c).5.
SP-BSAB	[The Boy who was Set Adrift in a Bucket.] NAA 2794.85(e):27(part)-72.
SP-Fish	The Story of the Fish Clan. NAA 2005.1(a).
SP-FSSW	[A Family is Spared by Sioux Warriors.] NAA 2794.46(c).12.
SP-KCB	When Kwiyameha Chased Buffalo. NAA 2794.46(c).6. Ed. Lucy Thomason.
SP-Mak	[Makitoka.] NAA 2794.85(d):12(part)-27(part).
SP-MBW	[The Man Who was Blessed by a Wolf.] NAA 2741(b).2:45-55, 57-89.
SP-MortB	The Story of the First Beginning of When Anyone Dies. NAA 3111.a(B) (Michelson 1925:386-401).
SP-MRD	[The Man who Returned from the Dead.] NAA 2741(b).1.
SP-Net	Netawenechikeha. NAA 2794.46(c).9:39-43.
SP-PD1	Prairie-Dog's Story (1). NAA 2794.46(c):1-6.

SP-PD2   Prairie-Dog's Story (2). NAA 2005.4:67-103.
SP-Pich1   Pichishaha (1). NAA 2008-6:47-95. Edited by Lucy Thomason.
SP-RL   Red-Leggins. NAA 1860-3:20-42, 44-94. Edited by Lucy Thomason.
SP-SM   [The Suicide of Mehkohpeha.] NAA 2794.46(c).4:11-12.
SP-TF   True Friends. NAA 2664.9(k).
SP-Under   [The People of Under-Earth.] NAA 2012-3:40-46, 48-65. Edited by Lucy Thomason.
SP-WH   The Sacred Story of Wampumhead. NAA 2794.84(a).
X (Anonymous writers)
X2-SAR   The Singing-Around Rite. NAA 3002.A (Michelson 1925:541-611).
X5-EBE   The One Whose Eye was a Bear's Eye. NAA 2794.21. Edited by Lucy Thomason.
X5-RL   The Winter Story of Red-Leggins. NAA 2985:1-56. Edited by Lucy Thomason and Ives Goddard.
X6-MF   The Man who was Feared by the People. NAA 2794.36.
X6-MM   Bareshins (Mehchikahkwaha). NAA 2794.13. Edited by Lucy Thomason.
X7Sh-TO   (X7 and Shapochiwa.) Turkey-Owner. NAA 2794.63. Edited by Lucy Thomason and Ives Goddard.
X10-Met   [Metekopinisha.] NAA 2010:1-71. Edited by Ives Goddard and Lucy Thomason.
X10-PBW   The Pigs who Became White People. NAA 2794.45(d). Edited by LucyThomason
X10-TAN   [Tananohkya.] NAA 2010:72-100. Edited by Lucy Thomason.
X11-BG   [The Boy who Encountered a Grizzly Bear.] NAA 2664.9(g):52-56.

Speakers

AW	Adeline Wanatee	JoB	Johnathan Buffalo
BL	Bill Leaf	JoP	Joe Peters
C	Charley H. Chuck	JP	Jim Peters
EJ	Elsie Jones	JPo	James Poweshiek
EK	Everett Kapayou	K	Alfred Kiyana
FE	Frank Earle	LK	Leo Keahna
FM	Frances Mitchell	LL	Lucy Lasley
FP	Frank Pushetonequa	LYB	Leonard Young Bear
GBC	George Black Cloud	MM	Maggie Morgan
HL	Harry Lincoln	PL	Pearl Leaf
HP	Horace Poweshiek	S	Sakihtanohkweha
IP	Ida Poweshiek	Sh	Shapochiwa
JB	Jack Bullard	SP	Sam Peters
JM	Jim Mamasaw	TB	Thomas Brown
JMo	Jimmie Morgan	X	anonymous writer

Bibliography

Ackerman, Farrell, and Gert Webelhuth. 1998. *A Theory of Predicates.* Stanford: CSLI.

[Bartsch, Dick, translator.] 1996. *Me nwa tti mo ni E na tti me ko si tti TTi de da E ta be na so ta Ke tti Ma ne to na ki O tti E ne bye a ki Luke a. / The Gospel According to Luke from the Bible in the Meskwaki Language with Word List and Alphabet.* Colorado Springs, CO: The International Bible Society.

Bloomfield, Leonard. 1925-1927. Notes on the Fox Language. *International Journal of American Linguistics* [Part 1] 3:219-232 (1925), [Part 2] 4:181-219 (1927).

Brown, Thomas. 1926. [Translation of Alfred Kiyana's Buffalo-Head Dance.] NAA ms. no. 2943.

Cuoq, Jean-André. 1866. *Études philologiques sur quelques langues sauvages de l'Amérique.* Montreal: Dawson Brothers.

Dahlstrom, Amy. 1986. Weak Crossover and Obviation. *BLS* 12:51-60. Berkeley.

Dahlstrom, Amy. 1993. The Syntax of Discourse Functions in Fox. *BLS* 19: *Special Session on Syntactic Issues in Native American Languages*, pp. 11-21. Berkeley.

Dahlstrom, Amy. 1995a. *Topic, Focus and Other Word Order Problems in Algonquian. The Belcourt Lecture.* Winnipeg: Voices of Rupert's Land.

Dahlstrom, Amy. 1995b. Meskwaki syntax book. Online: https://lucian.uchicago.edu/blogs/adahlstrom/publications-2/selected-manuscripts/meskwaki-syntax-book/.

Dahlstrom, Amy. 1996a. Affixes vs. Clitics in Fox. *Contemporary Linguistics* 2:47-57. Chicago: Department of Linguistics, University of Chicago.

Dahlstrom, Amy. 1996b. Narrative Structure of a Fox Text. *nikotwâsik iskwâhtêm pâskihtêpayih! : Studies in Honour of H.C. Wolfart*, ed. by John D. Nichols and Arden C. Ogg. Algonquian and Iroquoian Linguistics Memoir 13. Winnipeg: University of Manitoba.

Dahlstrom, Amy. 2000. Morphosyntactic Mismatches in Algonquian: Affixal Predicates and Discontinuous Verbs. *The Proceedings from the Panels of the Chicago Linguistic Society's 36th Meeting*, ed. by Arika Okrent and John Boyle, 2:63-87. Chicago: Chicago Linguistic Society.

Dahlstrom, Amy. 2003a. Focus Constructions in Meskwaki (Fox). *Proceedings of the LFG03 Conference, University at Albany, State University of New York*, ed. by Miriam Butt and Tracy Holloway King, pp. 144-163. Stanford: CSLI Publications.

Dahlstrom, Amy. 2003b. Warrior Powers from an Underwater Spirit: Cultural and Linguistic Aspects of an Illustrated Meskwaki Text. *Anthropological Linguistics* 45:1-56.

Dahlstrom, Amy. 2004. External and Internal Topics in Meskwaki. Paper presented to the 36th Algonquian Conference, Madison, Wisconsin, October 30, 2004.

Dahlstrom, Amy. 2009. OBJ$_\theta$ without OBJ: a Typology of Meskwaki Objects. *Proceedings of the LFG09 Conference*, ed. by Miriam Butt and Tracy Holloway King, pp. 222-239. Stanford: CSLI Publications.

Dahlstrom, Amy. 2014. Multiple Oblique Arguments in Meskwaki. *Papers of the 42nd Algonquian Conference*, ed. by J. Randolph Valentine and Monica Macaulay, pp. 56-68. Albany: State University of New York Press.

Dahlstrom, Amy. 2015. Highlighting Rhetorical Structure through Syntactic Analysis: An Illustrated Meskwaki Text by Alfred Kiyana. *New Voices for Old Words: Editing Algonquian Languages*, ed. by David J. Costa, pp. 118-197. Lincoln: University of Nebraska Press.

Goddard, Ives. 1985. Paradigmatic Splitting by Morphological Regularization: The Fox Prohibitives. *International Journal of American Linguistics* 51:419-421.

Goddard, Ives. 1988a. Stylistic dialects in Fox Linguistic Change. *Historical dialectology*, ed. by Jacek Fisiak, pp. 193-209. Berlin: Mouton de Gruyter.

Goddard, Ives. 1988b. Post-Transformational Stem Derivation in Fox. *Papers and Studies in Contrastive Linguistics* 22:59-72.

Goddard, Ives. 1990a. Aspects of the Topic Structure of Fox Narratives: Proximate Shifts and the Use of Overt and Inflectional NPs. *International Journal of American Linguistics* 56:317-340.

Goddard, Ives. 1990b. Primary and Secondary Stem Derivation in Algonquian. *International Journal of American Linguistics* 56:449-483.

Goddard, Ives. 1991. Observations regarding Fox (Mesquakie) Phonology. *Papers of the 22nd Algonquian Conference*, ed. by William Cowan, pp. 157-181. Ottawa: Carleton University.

Goddard, Ives. 1993. Songs in Fox (Mesquakie) Texts: Linguistics and Philology. *Papers of the 24th Algonquian Conference*, ed. by William Cowan, pp. 212-239. Ottawa: Carleton University.

Goddard, Ives. 1994. *Leonard Bloomfield's Fox Lexicon: Critical Edition.* Algonquian and Iroquoian Linguistics Memoir 12. Winnipeg: University of Manitoba.

Goddard, Ives. 1995. Notes on Fox (Mesquakie) Inflection: Minor Modes and Incompletely Described Morphemes. *Papers of the 26th Algonquian Conference*, ed. by David H. Pentland, pp. 124-150. Winnipeg: University of Manitoba.

Goddard, Ives. 1996. Writing and Reading Mesquakie (Fox). *Papers of the Twenty-Seventh Algonquian Conference*, ed. David H. Pentland, pp. 117-134 (1996 [© 1997]).

Goddard, Ives. 2001. Contraction in Fox (Meskwaki). *Actes du 32e Congrès des Algonquinistes*, ed. by John D. Nichols, pp. 164-230. Winnipeg: University of Manitoba.

Goddard, Ives. 2002. Grammatical Gender in Algonquian. *Papers of the 33rd Algonquian Conference*, ed. by H.C. Wolfart, pp. 195-231. Winnipeg: University of Manitoba.

Goddard, Ives. 2004. Meskwaki Verbal Affixes. *Papers of the 35th Algonquian Conference*, ed. by H.C. Wolfart, pp. 97-129. Winnipeg: University of Manitoba.

Goddard, Ives. 2006a. The Proto-Algonquian Negative and its Descendants. *Actes du 37e Congrès des Algonquinistes*, ed. by H.C. Wolfart, pp. 161-208. Winnipeg: University of Manitoba.

Goddard, Ives. 2006b. *The Autobiography of a Meskwaki Woman: A New Edition and Translation.* Algonquian and Iroquoian Linguistics Memoir 18. Winnipeg: University of Manitoba. (Reprinted: Petoskey, Michigan: Mundart Press, 2022.)

Goddard, Ives. 2007. *The Owl Sacred Pack: A New Edition and Translation of the Meskwaki Manuscript of Alfred Kiyana.* Algonquian and Iroquoian Linguistics Memoir 19. Winnipeg: University of Manitoba.

Goddard, Ives, and Amy Dahlstrom. 2022. Meskwaki (Algonquian) Evidence against Basic Word Order and Configurational Models of Argument Roles. *Language Change and Linguistic Diversity*, ed. by Thiago Costa Chacon, Nala H. Lee, and W.D.L. Silva, pp. 242-259. Edinburgh: University Press.

Goddard, Ives, and Lucy Thomason. 2014. *A Meskwaki-English and English-Meskwaki dictionary, Based on Early Twentieth-Century Writings by Native Speakers.* Petoskey, Mich.: Mundart Press.

Howse, Joseph. 1844. *A Grammar of the Cree Language, with which is Combined an Analysis of the Chippewa Dialect.* London: J.G.F. & J. Rivington.

Jones, William. 1902. Fox and Sauk native texts and English translations of myths, traditions, parables, stories of fasting, visions, and dreams, Wisaka stories, and prayers. Three notebooks "obtained .. 1901 and 1902." NAA ms. no. 3022.

Jones, William. 1906. An Algonquian Syllabary. *Boas Anniversary Volume: Anthropological Papers Written in Honor of Franz Boas*, ed. by Berthold Laufer, pp. 88-93. New York: G.E. Stechert.

Jones, William. 1907. *Fox Texts.* Publications of the American Ethnological Society 1, New York.

Jones, William. 1911. Algonquian (Fox), ed. by Truman Michelson. *Handbook of American Indian Languages*, ed. by Franz Boas, pp. 735-873. Bureau of American Ethnology Bulletin 40, Part 1. Washington.

Jones, William, and Truman Michelson. 1915. *Kickapoo Tales.* Publications of the American Ethnological Society 9, New York.

Kinkade, M. Dale, and Anthony Mattina. 1996. Discourse. *Handbook of North American Indians, vol. 17, Languages*, ed. Ives Goddard, pp. 244-274. Washington: Smithsonian Institution.

Michelson, Truman. 1914. Algonquian Linguistic Miscellany. *Journal of the Washington Academy of Sciences* 4(14):402-409.

Michelson, Truman. 1921. *The Owl Sacred Pack of the Fox Indians.* Bureau of American Ethnology Bulletin 72. Washington.

Michelson, Truman. 1925. Accompanying papers. *Fortieth Annual Report of the Bureau of American Ethnology*, 1918-1919, pp. 21-658. Washington.

Michelson, Truman. 1928. *Notes on the Buffalo-Head Dance of the Thunder Gens of the Fox Indians.* Bureau of American Ethnology Bulletin 87. Washington.

Michelson, Truman. 1930. Notes on the Great Sacred Pack of the Thunder Gens of the Fox Indians. *Contributions to Fox Ethnology–II*, pp. 43-176. Bureau of American Ethnology Bulletin 95. Washington.

Michelson, Truman. 1932. *Notes on the Fox Wâpanōwiweni.* Bureau of American Ethnology Bulletin 105. Washington.

Purcell, L. Edward. 1974. The Mesquakie Indian Settlement in 1905. *The Palimpsest* 55(2):34-55.

Siebert, Frank T., Jr. 1967. Discrepant Consonant Clusters Ending in *-k in Proto-Algonquian, a Proposed Interpretation of Saltatory Sound Changes. *Contributions to Anthropology: Linguistics I*, ed. by A.D. DeBlois, pp. 44-59. National Museum of Canada Bulletin 214. Ottawa.

Skinner, Alanson. 1915. Societies of the Iowa, Kansa, and Ponca Indians. *Anthropological Papers of the American Museum of Natural History* 11(9):679-740.

Skinner, Alanson. 1928. Sauk [and Bûngi] Tales. *Journal of American Folk-Lore* 41:147-171.

The Sac & Fox Tribe of the Mississippi in Iowa. 1983. *Me skwa ki A to we ta ke. An Elementary School Text of the Mesquakie Language.* [Meshkwahkîhâtowêtâke. 'Let's speak Meskwaki!' Second title page: *Mesquakie Primer.*] Ann Arbor, Mich.: Karoma Publishers, Inc.

Thomason, Lucy. 1995. The Assignment of Proximate and Obviative in Informal Fox Narrative. *Papers of the 26th Algonquian Conference*, ed. by David H. Pentland, pp. 462-496. Winnipeg: University of Manitoba.

Thomason, Lucy. 2001. Participles of time in Meskwaki. Paper presented to the Thirty-Third Algonquian Conference, Berkeley, California, October 27, 2001.

Thomason, Lucy. 2003. The proximate and obviative contrast in Meskwaki. Ph.D. thesis, University of Texas, Austin.

Thomason, Lucy. 2004. Two, Three and Four Noun Phrases per Clause in Meskwaki. *Papers of the 35th Algonquian Conference*, ed. by H.C. Wolfart, pp. 407-430. Winnipeg: University of Manitoba.

Thomason, Lucy. 2005. Meskwaki Prenouns. *Papers of the 36th Algonquian Conference*, ed. by H.C. Wolfart, pp. 425-448. Winnipeg: University of Manitoba.

Thomason, Lucy. 2015. On Editing Bill Leaf's Meskwaki Texts. *New Voices for Old Words: Editing Algonquian Languages*, ed. by David J. Costa, pp. 315-452. Lincoln: University of Nebraska Press.

Thomason, Lucy, and Ives Goddard, editors. 2022. *Masahkamikohkwêwa (Grandmother Earth), a Synchretistic Meskwaki Cosmology.* Petoskey, Mich.: Mundart Press.

Trumbull, J. Hammond. 1877. The Algonkin Verb. *Transactions of the American Philological Association, 1876,* [7:]146-171. Hartford.

Valentine, J. Randolph. 2001. *Nishnaabemwin reference grammar.* Toronto: University of Toronto Press.

Voorhis, Paul H. 1971. New notes on the Mesquakie (Fox) language. *International Journal of American Linguistics* 37:63-75.

Voorhis, Paul H. 1974. *Introduction to the Kickapoo language.* Language Science Monographs 13. Bloomington: Indiana University.

Walker, Willard B. 1996. Native Writing Systems. *Handbook of North American Indians, Vol. 17, Languages*, ed. by Ives Goddard, pp. 158-184. Washington: Smithsonian Institution.

Whittaker, Gordon. 1996. The Sauk Language: A First Look. *Papers of the 27th Algonquian Conference*, ed. by David H. Pentland, pp. 362-401. Winnipeg: University of Manitoba.

Introduction

This book is a grammar of Meskwaki, an Algonquian language spoken today on the lands of the Meskwaki Settlement in Tama County, Iowa. There are two factors that make Meskwaki of particular interest and importance. It is arguably the most archaic language of the Algonquian family in preserving the word shapes of the ancestral Algonquian language that is reconstructed as Proto-Algonquian by linguists. And it is documented by a very large collection of texts written by numerous native speakers more than a century ago that is kept in the National Anthropological Archives (NAA) of the Smithsonian Institution in Suitland, Maryland.

This grammar describes phonology (sound system), grammatical categories, inflections, derivation of stems, sentence structure, and some aspects of how sentences are connected to form longer utterances and narratives (discourse). (It does not present a formal syntactic analysis, for which the papers of Amy Dahlstrom and her online grammar [Dahlstrom 1995] should be consulted.) Extensive reference is made throughout to textual sources. Examples for which an edition of the text is not yet published are cited by the manuscript page number. Examples in the "Autobiography" and "Owl" texts are sourced to the page and line of the interlinearized editions, using capital letters for the lines (Goddard 2006b, 2007). Examples in "Masahkamikohkwêwa" are sourced to the page and line of the running text of the edition as printed, using lower-case letters (Thomason and Goddard 2022).

Appendix 1 has notes on tangential and peripheral details, alternative analyses, cross-references, and information that may be of interest but is outside the descriptive narrative. Appendix 2 lists and analyzes all the inflectional endings in the "Autobiography" and "Owl" texts.

* * *

William Jones (1871-1909), a university-trained quarter-blood Meskwaki who had some speaking knowledge of the language, obtained texts and grammatical information from speakers in Iowa in 1901 and 1902 (Jones 1902, 1907, 1911; Bloomfield 1925-1927). After Jones was killed while making an ethnographic collection in the Philippines, Truman Michelson (1879-1938) helped to publish Jones's work on Algonquian languages and undertook the study of Meskwaki for the Bureau of American Ethnology of the Smithsonian (Michelson 1914, 1921, 1925, 1928, 1930, 1932, etc.). He took advantage of the fact the Meskwakis were literate in their language and hired many of them to write traditional narratives and ethnographic texts, paying them by the page. More recent work on Meskwaki has been undertaken by Paul Voorhis (1971), Ives Goddard (1985, 1988a, 1988b, 1990, 1991, 1993, 1994, 1995, 2001, 2002, 2004, 2006a, 2006b, 2007), Amy Dahlstrom (1993, 1995a, 1995b, 1996a, 1996b, 2003a, 2003b, 2004, 2009, 2014, 2015; Goddard and Dahlstrom 2022), and Lucy Thomason (1995, 2001, 2003, 2004, 2005, 2015; Goddard and Thomason 2014).

As the result of Michelson's efforts the NAA has over 26,000 pages of Meskwaki written by various speakers, along with English translations written by bilingual speakers for a good portion of them. The spelling used by them is that of a variant of the Great Lakes Algonquian Syllabary (Jones 1906; Walker 1996:168-172). This was learned from the Potawatomis, who appear to have adapted it from a writing by syllables that they must have been taught by French-speaking Roman Catholic missionaries. The writing of /š/ with ⟨d⟩ must have evolved from the French spelling of this sound with ⟨ch⟩, and the writing of /č/ with ⟨tt⟩ (which for some writers resembles ⟨ctt⟩) must go back to a French spelling with ⟨tch⟩. The syllabary does not write the contrast between short and long vowels and does not write /h/ (a sound that Potawatomi lacks), which occurs frequently before consonants in Meskwaki. As it thus omits the only details of pronunciation that might present a challenge to a writer, it can be written easily and relatively rapidly. The writings in the NAA document natural speech, and although there are occasional spelling errors, truly ambiguous or utterly obscure writing is extremely rare. False starts — starting sentences over again—are found, but they seem no more frequent than what might be expected in spontaneous speech. What is remarkable, rather, is the robust attestation of long sentences with extremely complicated word order.

The traditional spelling has continued in use in the community (The Sac & Fox Tribe of the Mississippi in Iowa 1983; Bartsch 1996).

[NOTE: The author and the publisher regret that the length mark (a raised dot) displays imperfectly in the italic font, being skewed too far to the right. This is a feature of the font, which it proved impractical to correct.]

Chapter 1.

§§1-16. Phonology, Writing, and Editing

PHONEMES

Segments

1. Meskwaki has nineteen segmental phonemes, eleven consonants (nine true consonants and two semivowels) and eight vowels (four short and four long).

(1.1) stops and affricate: *p, t, č, k*

fricatives: *s, š, h*

nasals: *m, n*

semivowels: *w, y*

short vowels: *i, e, a, o*

long vowels: *i·, e·, a·, o·*

The letters used have their usual linguistic values: *č* is like the "ch" of English "chip"; *š* is like the "sh" of English "ship."

The vowels have roughly the qualities they have in Spanish and Italian. Vowel letters followed by a raised dot (·) transcribe long vowels, pronounced somewhat like German "ih," "eh," "ah," and "oh." Short vowels are noticeably higher (more closed) than their long counterparts, except that geminate vowels, when they occur (**§1.1, §6.2**), are open. Long /e·/ may be raised after a post-consonantal /y/ and across some consonants before an /i/ in the following syllable. For example, for some speakers the /e·/ in *e·h=išawiči* 'he did {so}' is noticeably higher than the /e·/ of *e· šawiči* 'what he did', being influenced by the high vowel /i/ of the following syllable.

Phonemic transcriptions are in italics or between slashes: /../. Words that were not heard and were transcribed conjecturally are marked with a dagger (†).

Broad phonetic transcriptions, which give phonetic details, are enclosed between square brackets: [..].

Narrow transliterations of the Meskwaki syllabary are given between shallow-pointed angle brackets: ⟨..⟩.

Underlying forms are given between vertical bars: |..| (**§7**).

For the use of sharp-pointed brackets (<..>) in editing song texts see (**§16.6**).

Curly braces are used in English glosses to enclose the conventional glosses of oblique complements: {..} (**§22.4**).

1.1. Extrasystemic features. Expressive and imitative words contain some phonetic features not found in ordinary words. These include nasalized vowels ([ę], [ǫ]; often variable), vowel sequences, word-initial *h* and short *e*, word-final long vowels, and glottal stop ([ʔ]):

(1.2)   *ehę·he* 'yes' (also *ehe·he*)

(1.3)   *hao·ʔ* 'alright (I will)'; 'hello' (normalized as *hawo* in the edition of Alfred Kiyana's *Masahkamikohkwêwa* [Thomason and Goddard 2022])

(1.4)   *ǫ·hǫ·´* 'so <u>that's</u> it!' (also *o·ho·´*)

Words borrowed from English add some additional segments and sequences.

1.2. Variation in vowels and semivowels. Some lexical items have variants with different vowels used by different speakers. This discrepancy is kept in the editions of the texts as dialectal variation, as distinct from miswriting, which is emended (**§15**).

If a morpheme-internal short *o* follows a *t*, *n*, or *y* there may be a variant with short *a*:

(1.5)   *ma·nǫme·wa* 'he beats him in a contest' ~ *ma·nạme·wa*

(1.6)   *kepiškwe·nǫtwa* 'he choked on food' ~ *kepiškwe·nạtwa*

(1.7)   *nana·tǫhkwihe·wa* 'he picks a fight with him' ~ *nana·tạhkwihe·wa*

(1.8)   *pi·yǫhkwi* 'dry, rotten wood' ~ *pi·yạhkwi*

Alfred Kiyana consistently used the *a*-variants of these words, but other speakers seem to have been less consistent.

A few initials show a variation between short *a* and long *a·*:

(1.9)   *wạpaš-* (*wạpas-*) 'disparage, waste' ~ *wa·paš-* (*wa·pas-*)

   E.g., *wạpašihto·wa*, *wa·pašihto·wa* 'he treats it disrespectfully, wastes it'.

(1.10) *mạtakw-* 'cover' ~ *ma·takw-*

   E.g., *mạtakwišinwa*, *ma·takwišinwa* 'he lies covered up'.

For the editing of these, see **§16.2** (1.279, 280).

Some stems have alternative shapes with short *a* and *e*:

(1.11) *kạhkeše·wi* 'charcoal' (JB, JP, SP; Jones 1907:352) ~ *kẹhkeše·wi* (A, C, JP, K, S)

(1.12) *petẹsak-* 'obstructing' ~ *petạsak-*:

   petẹsakesi- AI 'face obstacles' (O 76G)

   petạsaki 'as an obstacle' (O 75I)

(1.13) *atẹška·ha* 'kingfisher' (K) ~ *atạška·ha* (Jones 1907:262, 264, AW)

In forms in which the modal suffix |-ehapa| con. does not lose the |e| by contraction or elision, one speaker has *-ahapa* instead of *-ehapa*:

(1.14) *na·na·na·pẹhapa=ča·hi·='niki.* (JB-Meshq 4)

   'Well, someone came and took them (I have learned)'

   (|CV+| RED1, |na·N-| TA 'go to get', |-a·pẹhapa| X–3/CON;

   |=ča·hi| 'so'; |i·niki| 'those (anim.)')

   nenahi-taneti·pạhapa '(it turns out) I <u>can</u> gamble' (C-RP 2)

   (|nahi| PV 'be given to', |taneti·-| AI 'gamble', |ne–pạhapa| 1s/CON)

These alternations between short *a* and *e* seem to involve optional assimilation to the quality of the vowel in the following syllable.

Other cases of variation seem more idiosyncratic.

(1.15) *=yẹpani* 'mind you, I expect, I warn you' ~ *=yạpani*

   e·mehkwa·hi (K, C, S, JB), *e·mehkwa·ni* 'spoon' (K, JB, SP)

   ~ *a·mehkwa·hi* (K, C), *a·mehkwa·ni* (SP)

These may show assimilation of *e·* to an *a* or *a·* later in the word.

Some stems show a secondary variation between intervocalic *w* and *y* (**§13.5**).

Clusters

2. Only a few combinations of true consonants occur, always preceded by a vowel:

(1.16) *h* + consonant: *hp, ht, hč, hk, hm*
(1.17) *š* + consonant: *šk, št*

Of these, *hm* and *št* are rare. Some additional clusters are found in English loanwords. The fricatives *s* and *š* (including *š* in clusters) are always preceded by a phonetic [h] after a vowel; this is analyzed as a predictable phonetic feature rather than as a segmental phoneme.

There are also sequences of true consonant and semivowel:

(1.18) consonant + *w*: *pw, tw, kw, sw, šw, hw, mw, nw*
(1.19) consonant + *y*: *py, ty, čy, ky, šy, my, ny*

The English loanword *čwiti·hi* 'treaty' adds *čw*.

These patterns may be combined, giving a sequence of two true consonants followed by a semivowel: e.g., *hky, škw*. Additional sequences arising from the addition of the prefixes *e·h=* AOR and *wi·h=* FUT (**§29.3**) and from the combination of words in sentences (**§4.2**) are *hn* and *hy*.

There are no vowel sequences in the deliberate pronunciation represented in the orthography (but see **§1.1**, **§16.2**; 1.284). Vowel sequences do occur in the colloquial style (**§3**), as a result of the loss of intervocalic semivowels. All ordinary words end in a short vowel, which before a pause is weakly articulated and usually devoiced. Ostensible word-final voiced vowels can probably be phonemicized as /-vhv/, but this is not written in *=iyo* 'For', in which the /-o/ is always voiced [-u], or in the final voicing on short words with interrogative or expressive intonation (**§6.2**, **§6.4**; 1.49, 51, 61). There are two monosyllabic preverbs, one ending in a long vowel and the other ending in *h*: *ki·* 'around' (beside more common *ki·wi*); *ki·h* PERF (beside more common *ki·ši*).

A *w* preceded by a consonant or in word-initial position is never followed by *o* or *o·*, and a post-consonantal or word-initial *y* never precedes *i*, *i·*, *o*, or *o·*. Word-initial *y* is found only in enclitics, words derived from babytalk, and expressive words.

Stylistic Registers

3. The syllabic orthography in which Meskwaki speakers write (§14) represents a deliberate style of pronunciation that contrasts with a colloquial (or casual) style or range of styles. The most noticeable feature of the colloquial styles is the loss of intervocalic semivowels with the concomitant shortening of long vowels that would, as a consequence, precede other vowels. This semivowel loss is maximal, but never universal, in allegro and relaxed styles and minimal, though always present, in the most formal contemporary styles. The resulting vowel sequences are usually retained and pronounced in distinct syllables, but short vowels of identical quality may coalesce into a single long vowel. Among other characteristics of colloquial style are a somewhat variable loss of *w* after a labial consonant and the replacement of *wi·h=* FUT by *i·h=*.

This grammatical sketch is based on written materials and hence describes the deliberate style almost exclusively. The styles are not, however, hermetically distinct, and some innovations of the colloquial style have been generalized to the deliberate style by some speakers and are hence reflected in writing. For example, some speakers occasionally or consistently write the equivalent of *i·h=* FUT. Also, the colloquial pronunciation of the negative preverb *pwa·wi* as *pai* gave rise to a new deliberate form *pa·wi* that appears commonly in writing.

Because shifting between the styles involves two-way adjustment strategies, vowels before semivowels in the deliberate style are sometimes pronounced with historically incorrect vowel length (either long for short or, less commonly, short for long). For example, the preverb *mawi* 'go and' (colloquial *mai*) was replaced by a new deliberate-style *ma wi* based on the pattern of *pa wi* NEG beside colloquial *pai*. The adoption of the new form *ma wi* had begun by 1900 and was universal in the 1990's, but because the texts show only *me wi* for this preverb with initial change (**§29.4**), which points to a basic shape with a short *a*, the editions write only *mawi*.

A very few morphemes have new deliberate forms that reflect colloquial-style semivowel loss and vowel contraction. For example, beside *na wanone hwe wa* 'he goes in pursuit of him' some speakers write only the equivalent of *na none hwe wa*, and a word like *ni šwawahi ne* 'two years' is occasionally written as if *ni šwa hi ne*.

Sentence Phonetics

4. When concatenated in a sentence words cluster in breath groups, between which there are often pauses and within which words are run together without pause, except in artificially slow speech. The breath groups serve as intonation units, providing a framework for the intonation contour of the sentence.

4.1. Enclitics. Enclitics are words that are always pronounced with no pause after the preceding word and hence never begin a sentence or breath group; they are always written with a preceding double hyphen (=), both in a sentence and when cited in isolation. Other words may optionally be cliticized (that is, pronounced as an enclitic) within the breath group; for these cliticized words, the clitic boundary is marked with a double hyphen only in the sentence, and not, for example, in the interlinear analysis.

When an enclitic or a cliticized word begins with a vowel, either this vowel or the final vowel of the preceding word is lost: the word-final vowel drops if the word-initial vowel that follows is anything but *i* or *i·*; word-initial *i-* drops after any vowel, the other vowel being retained; and word-initial *i·-* fuses with the preceding vowel giving a long vowel with the quality of the other vowel. The elision of word-initial *i-* or *i·-* is indicated by an apostrophe.

(1.20)   *kapo twe* 'at some point' + *=a pehe* 'usually' → *kapo tw=a pehe* (A 154C)

(1.21)   *i na* 'that (anim.)' + *ihkwe wa* 'woman' → *i na= 'hkwe wa* (Jones 1907:152.19)

(1.22)   *apeno he ha* 'baby' + *i ni* 'then' → *apeno he ha·='ni* (A 114E)

(1.23)   *kapo twe* 'at some point' + *i ni* 'then' → *kapo twe·='ni* (A 32C, etc.)

For consistency, the orthography assumes that final *-i* is treated like other vowels before *i-* and *i·-*; the first *i* is taken as retained and the second as elided or contracted, with transfer of length.

4.2. Elision of a word-final vowel after *h*. A final vowel may be elided before an enclitic or cliticized word if the preceding consonant is *h*. This elision regularly affects the final *-i* in particles (**§18.10**), including locative demonstratives, and in the inanimate interrogative pronoun *we kone hi* 'what?' and the inanimate indefinite pronoun *ke ko hi* 'something':

(1.24)   *i nina hi* 'that time' + *=ke hi* 'moreover' + *=meko* EMPH + *=wi na* 'but'
           → *i nina h=ke h=meko=wi na* (O 70B)

(1.25)   *we kone hi* 'what?' + *=ča hi* 'so' + *i nahi* 'with that'
           → *we kone h=ča hi·='nahi* (A 180C)

Elision of this type optionally affects the final vowel of the particle *me·kwe·he* 'I think' and the interrogative pronoun *we·ne·ha* 'who?':

(1.26) *me·kwe·he* 'I think' + *=ča·hi* 'so' → *me·kwe·h=ča·hi* (A 1B)

(1.27) *we·ne·ha* 'who?' + *=ča·hi* 'so' + *i·na* 'that (anim.)'
        → *we·ne·h=ča·hi·=·na.* 'Who's that?'

The author of A sometimes writes elision after *h* in other parts of speech, and this writing is kept in the edition.

(1.28) *kotakahi* 'others (obv.)' + *na·hka* 'and, also' → *kotakah=na·hka* (A 95G)

(1.29) *ne·wona·nehe* 'if I had seen you' + *=ke·hi* 'moreover' + *mo·hči* 'even'
        → *ne·wona·neh=ke·h=mo·hči* (A 144D)

In other cases the author of A does not indicate elision with a noun or verb:

(1.30) *se·nipa·hi=ke·hi* 'or ribbon appliqué' (A 60A)

(1.31) *o=wa·waneška·hahi=ke·hi* 'but as for the bad actors (obv.)' (A 80B)

(1.32) *ašihi=mana* 'make this (anim.)' (A 23C)

Rarely, the elision is not indicated for a particle:

(1.33) *we·nahi* 'I see now' + *ke·htena* 'truly' → *we·nahi=ke·htena* (A 127B)
        Cf. *we·nah=ke·htena* (all other occurrences, all other writers).

The elision of final vowels after *h* in nouns and verbs was generally rejected by speakers in the 1990's, however, and it is possible that the autobiography writer's spelling is an orthographic generalization of the citation forms of words. In all words final vowels preceded by *h* are subject to being dropped completely before a pause, and writers vary in the extent to which they write them:

(1.34) *neniwahi* 'men (obv.)' → *neniwah* (sentence-final; A 141B)

(1.35) *i·ni* 'that (inan.)' + *=ča·hi* 'so' → *i·ni=ča·h* (O 86E, 132E)

4.3. Contraction of *wi·-*. Words beginning with *wi·-* sometimes undergo elision as if they began with *i·-*. This elision is found with *wi·h=* FUT and between a preverb and its head verb or a prenoun and its noun. Kiyana writes it sparingly, and some writers only with *wi·h=* FUT, while some others write it much more frequently:

(1.36) *wi·h=pakami-wi·te·maki* → *wi·h=pakami·-'te·maki* 'for me to arrive with him'
        (A 85G)

(1.37) *ki·ši-wi·čawiwaki* → *ki·ši·-'čawiwaki* 'after I was married to him' (A 98A, 153D)

(1.38) *a·kwi* '(it is) not' + *wi·h=ni·šo·hpowa·či* 'that they would eat two-to-a-bowl'
        → *a·kwi·=·h=ni·šo·hpowa·či* 'they would not eat two-to-a-bowl' (O 4I and note)

This contraction is taken as lexicalized in some combinations:

(1.39) *ki·ši·seniya·ni* 'after I had eaten' (A 178G)

Although forms from uncontracted *ki·ši-wi·seniwa* 'he has finished eating' and contracted *ki·ši·seniwa* are both widely attested, *ki·ši·seniwa* seems to be commonly used by some writers who otherwise seldom if ever contract *wi·-* in compound stems.

4.4. Word-final echo vowel. Two-syllable words in which both vowels are short, including enclitics, have variants with an added final syllable consisting of a copy of the final vowel preceded by *h*:

(1.40) *=ipi* HRSY → *=ipihi* (O 57F; the only example in the text)

(1.41) *=meko* EMPH → *=mekoho* (O 4I; very common)

(1.42) *mani* 'this (inan.)' → *manihi* (O 78C)

These lengthened forms are optional variants used before a pause, but their frequency of use varies greatly for different lexical items and different speakers.

Uniquely, =*ihi* NEG (**§6.3**; 5.122*d*, 123*a*), which is always followed by an enclitic, has generalized an underlying shape |=ihi| in most contexts and in these cases retains the *h* when the final vowel is elided (1.53, 57). Before a few consonant-initial enclitics the underlying shape is |=i|, which is elided completely (1.54; 5.118*q*(3), 5.122*b*(11)).

Stress

5. Words do not have distinctive stress. Ordinarily there is a predictable stress and raised pitch on the second from the last syllable of a word that is by itself (as in a one-word sentence or a list), or of a word with fewer than four syllables which is preceded by another word, and on the fourth from the last syllable in an utterance of more than one phonological word. A preverb or prenoun of more than one syllable is treated as a separate phonological word for the purpose of assigning stress, even if the final vowel is elided (1.47). If a breath group ends in an enclitic, or a cliticized word of less that four syllables, the main stress falls on the syllable before the clitic boundary (=; 1.43-45) or, if there has been elision of an initial vowel (**§4.1**), on the second syllable before the clitic boundary (= '; 1.46).

In the phonetic transcriptions in the following sections the main stress is indicated by an acute accent ([´]) over the vowel, secondary stress by a grave accent ([`]), and voiceless vowels by a circle underneath. Where two successive syllables have vowels marked with grave accents these have relatively even stress and declining pitch. Raised high pitch is indicated by a double acute accent over the vowel ([˝]). Vowel qualities are written broadly.

(1.43) *ihkwe·wa* 'woman' + =*ke·hi* 'moreover'
    → *ihkwe·wa=ke·hi.* ([ihkwe·wáke·hi̥]) '.., as well as women.' (O 3D)
(1.44) *netekwa* 'she told me {something}' + *nekya* 'my mother'
    → *netekwa=nekya.* ([netekwánekyḁ]) '.. {so} my mother told me.' (A 122B)
(1.45) *i·ni* 'that' + =*ye·toke* 'it seems'
    → *i·ni=ye·toke.* ([i·níye·toke̥]) 'That seems to be so.' (O 130D)
(1.46) *i·ni* 'then' + =*meko* EMPH + =*ipi* HRSY
    → *i·ni=meko='pi* ([i·nimékopi̥]) 'Right away, they say, ...' (O 7H)

Initial =*i*- in enclitics is always elided, but its presence is guaranteed by the location of the preceding stress (1.46), and in some cases by its occurrence in non-cliticized doublets. There are no enclitics of more that three syllables, and a word of more than three syllables with elision before it is necessarily accented like an ordinary word, since the main stress cannot be more than four syllables from the end of the breath group.

Intonation

6. There are several patterns of sentence intonation. They differ in the location of main and secondary stresses, in overall pitch register, and in other features. The normal, interrogative, expressive negative, expressive, and emphatic intonations may appear on full sentences. The intonation contours of these five types are replicated on all breath groups, but the stress and pitch are most prominent on the last breath group of the sentence. The other patterns of intonation affect the final breath group or a single word.

6.1. Normal. The use of the ordinary second-from-last or fourth-from-last stress (**§5**) with low register characterizes the normal intonation. Sentences with this intonation are written with a final period. The normal intonation is used for non-emphatic positive and negative statements and commands and for question-word questions.

6.2. Interrogative. The interrogative intonation (Q) is transcribed by a sentence-final question mark (?), with a superscript question mark (?) after each breath group that replicates this intonation earlier in the sentence (A 192F). It is characterized by overall high pitch register, and by the placement of the greatest stress and highest pitch on the third syllable from the end in the last word (1.47), whether this is an independent word or an enclitic or cliticized word. (In phonetic transcriptions high pitch register is indicated by an up arrow [↑] at the beginning of the breath group.) When there is more than one breath group, the high pitches on each tend to be successively higher, with the last being especially prominent. If the last word in a breath group has only two syllables and its first syllable has a long vowel, this vowel is broken into a sequence of two short vowels with the high pitch and stress on the first of these (1.48, 50); if the initial long |i·| of such a word is elided (as in 1.22-23), the long vowel that replaces it is treated as if it were in the first syllable of the elided word. If the last word has only two short vowels, the final vowel is voiced, and the first vowel takes the high pitch and stress (1.49, 51).

A vocative form at the end of an interrogative sentence stands outside the scope of the interrogative intonation, which is therefore in such a case only indicated sentence medially, by one or more superscript question marks.

The interrogative intonation is used exclusively for yes-no questions. (Because question-word questions do not have interrogative intonation, they are not written with a question mark: A 145E, 147A, 180C.)

(1.47) *ni·h=maw-anenwi?* ([↑ni·hmawánenwį]) 'May I go swimming?' (A 14D, 15C)
        Cf. *ni·h=maw-anenwi.* ([ni·hmáwanenwį]) 'I'm going swimming.'

(1.48) *pye wa?* ([↑pyέɛwą]) 'Did he come?' (EK)
        Cf. *pye wa.* ([pyέ·wą]) 'He came.'

(1.49) *nekya?* ([↑nékya]) '(Was it) my mother?' (EK)
        Cf. *nekya.* ([nékyą]) '(The answer is,) my mother.'

(1.50) *i niki=ča·hi?* ([↑i·nikičáah(į)]) 'Is that them?' (EK)

(1.51) *ke waki=meko?* ([↑kɛ·wakiméko]) 'Still there?' (EK)
        Cf. *ke waki=meko.* ([kɛ·wakímekǫ]) 'Still, indeed.'

6.3. Expressive negative. The expressive negative intonation (EN), or "swing," is indicated by a sentence-final exclamation point and question mark (!?); each earlier breath group with this intonation is marked by superscript punctuation (!?) (A 92G, 131F, 183F, 190D, 192D; O 102D, 103D, 125F, 142C, 142F). It has overall high register, primary high pitch and stress on the fourth syllable from the last, and a prominent mid pitch and secondary stress on the second syllable from the last. Swing is used in several kinds of idiomatic expressions, typically giving the implication "Don't be ridiculous!" or "Of course not!" It is also used in gossipy speculation (5.129c). It is most often found with one of a small set of particles, especially if the expressive negative enclitic =ihi (5.122d), which surfaces as ='hi, ='h=, =ꞌ= (§4.4), is among them (1.53, 57). It may also be used without these (1.52, 55, 56).

(1.52) *wi·h=to tawaki!?* ([↑wi·htó·tawàkį]) 'What do I care about him?' (A 27C; O 143B)
        Cf. *wi·h=to tawaki* 'how I will treat him, what I will do to him'.
        ma mahka·či!? ([↑má·mahkà·čį]) 'it's not necessary; I don't have to, you don't have to' (AW, EK); 'We don't need that!' (JoB)
        Cf. *ma mahka·či.* ([ma·mahká·čį]) 'It's necessary.' (5.117f)

keše maneto wa wa wane nema·sa¹² wi·h=mi činikwe ni!? (K-M 4j [EK]; tr. HP)

"The Great Manitou surely knows what she [obv.] would eat."

(*keše maneto wa* 'God'; |wa·wane·nem-| TA 'fail to know', |–a·sa| 3s–3´/POT; |wi·h=| FUT, |mi·či-| TI(3) 'eat', |IC–nikwe·ni| 3´–0/INT.PPL; !? EN)

ki na=wi na¹² nana·ši ki·h=po ni-oškihoškinawe·hišine!? (K-M 151i [EK]; this is preferable to the transcription in the edition: *ki na=´h=wi na¹²..*)

'You're <u>never</u> going to get over your youthful indolence!'

(*ki na* EMPH/2s; =*wi na* 'but'; *nana·ši* '[not] ever'; |wi·h=| FUT, *po ni* PV 'cease', |CVCV+| RED2, |oškinawe·hišin-| AI 'lie as a young man', |ke–∅| 2s/IND; !? EN)

If a breath group with swing ends with an enclitic, the highest pitch and main stress are on the same pre-enclitic syllable where they would be with normal intonation; preceding syllables have a low pitch (within the high pitch register). (In all examples the enclitic begins with a consonant.) A three-syllable enclitic has the same pitch contour its syllables would have if they were part of an ordinary word, while a two-syllable enclitic has secondary stress and mid pitch on its first syllable:

(1.53)   *ki na=´h=we na!?* ([↑ki·náhwè·na̦]) 'What about you?' (EK)

       (*ki na* 'you (sg.)'; |=ihi| NEG; =*we na* 'in fact'; !? EN)

(1.54)   *i niki=ča·hi!?* (or *i niki=´=ča·hi!?*) ([↑i·nikíčà·h(i̦)]) 'What about them?' (EK)

       (*i niki* 'those (anim.)'; =*ča·hi* 'so'; !? EN; or with |=i| for |=ihi| NEG, indicated by /=´/)

On words of less that four syllables, the pitch contour is shortened and compressed to fit the available vowels, without long vowels being broken into two short vowels. In a three-syllable word with a long vowel in the first syllable, the pitch on this vowel combines the contour on the fourth-from-last and third-from-last syllables of longer words; the pitch falls from high to low on the first vowel and then rises to mid on the next-to-last vowel.

(1.55)   *me mye·hči!?* ([↑mê·myè·hči̦]) 'That's hardly necessary!' (K-ManMa 9 [AW])

       (*me mye·hči* 'it's required, it's unavoidable'; !? EN)

In words of less that four syllables that do not have a third-from-last syllable with a long vowel, the high pitch that begins the pitch contour on longer words is absent and the mid pitch that ends the contour falls at the end if the next-to-last vowel is long. In a two-syllable word with a long vowel in the first syllable, the pitch on this vowel combines the contour on the third-from-last and next-to-last syllables of longer words, including this final pitch fall: the pitch falls slightly to low, rises to high, and then falls to mid (indicated in the phonetic transcription with [˜]). If the final vowel is voiced, it is extra-short, low-pitched, and not part of the intonation contour:

(1.56)   *ta ni!?* ([↑tã·n(i̦)], [↑tã·nĭ(?)]) 'How could I?' (A 83F, 95B [AW])

       (*ta ni* 'how?'; !? EN)

The intonation on a two-syllable word with a short first vowel differs from normal only in being extra-high:

(1.57)   *pa wi-=´h=we na·=´ni¹²-isa!?* ([↑pa·wihwé·nà·ni ísa̦]) (EK)

       'He <u>said</u> it, didn't he?'; 'He wouldn't have <u>said</u> it otherwise!'

       (*pa wi* PV 'not', |i-| AI 'say {so}', |–sa| 3s/POT; |=ihi| NEG; =*we na* 'in fact'; |i·ni| 'that (inan.)'; !? EN)

6.4. Expressive. The expressive intonation (EXPR) is indicated by a sentence-final exclamation point (!). Generally, the highest pitch occurs on the fourth syllable from the end of the breath group and the pitch descends evenly and with relatively even stress over the last three non-final vowels, ending somewhat higher than the pitch would be with normal intonation. If the breath group ends with a non-cliticized three-syllable word, the highest pitch falls on the penultimate syllable of the preceding word, the fifth syllable from the end of the breath group; the first two vowels of the following three-syllable word then support the rest of the pitch template, in the usual way, but the final vowel of the preceding word is unstressed. The stress before an enclitic is merely raised in place, however, and thus may fall on the third vowel from the end. This intonation may be iterated on successive breath groups, in which case its occurrence sentence-medially is indicated by a superscript exclamation mark ('`).

Expressive intonation may indicate surprise or uncertainty, and when addressed to a second person it typically turns an ostensible statement into a non-insistent question, one that does not require an answer.

(1.58) *i·ni=ni·hka man=e·h=pya·či!* 'Hey, he has <u>arrived</u>!' (C-PD 18)
      ([i·níni·hka máne·hpyà·či̧])

ki·ši-=we·=meko -we·pe nemi·ke·ni' wi·h=nešiki! (C-PD 31)
      ([ki·šiwe·meko we·pe·némi·ke·ni, wí·hnèšiki̧])
      'I guess they must already be planning to kill me!'

ke·htena-'h=we·=meko' kemeškwahki·hi! ([ke·htenahwé·mekò keméškwàhki·hi̧])
      'You really ARE a Meskwaki, aren't you!' (SP-Wet 7)

ke·ko·h=meko=kena·te! 'You're getting <u>something</u>?' (EK)
      ([ke·ko·hmekókènà·tȩ])

ki·wa·tesihkani=ke·hi! ... ke·ko·h=ke·hi='šite·he·hkani! (X7Sh-TO 16)
      ([ki·wa·tesihkaníke·hi̧ ... ke·ko·hke·hišité·hè·hkàni̧]; two sentences)
      'Maybe you're lonesome. ... Or maybe you have something else on your mind.'

a·hkwamatakani=nekotahi! 'Maybe you're <u>sick</u> somewhere.' (C-O 26)
      ([a·hkwamatakaninékòtàhi̧])

asa·mi=we·=mana pehkiwa! 'This one is a whole lot different!' (C-YS 5)
      ([asa·miwe·mánă pèhkìwa̧])

A two-syllable word breaks an initial-syllable long vowel into two short vowels and has the secondary high pitch on the final vowel. In the attested example this intonation indicates emphatic agreement:

(1.59) *i·ni!* ([íinì]) 'Let's <u>do</u> that!' (Agreeing to suggestion.)

Additional patterns and functions and other treatments of enclitics are attested with intensive modification (**§6.6**).

No examples of this intonation were identified in the A and O texts.

6.5. Emphatic. The emphatic intonation (EMPH) in its most general use has scope over a single word at the end of a breath group, which need not be sentence-final. It is recognized as a separate intonation pattern in order to account for the occurrence of certain cases of shifted stress. It is transcribed by an acute accent on the stressed vowel.

One place where emphatic shifted stress is found is on enclitics that have stress and high pitch on their first syllable. This use of emphatic stress is closely associated with the enclitics it is found with and has specialized and highly idiomatic uses; it occurs only on the breath group that contains the enclitic.

(1.60) *i·ni=yá·pi ..* 'now here we go!' (A 33D, 40F; O 71C, 150E)

a·kwi=yá·pi. ([a·kwiyá·pi̧]) ''Tain't so!' (cf. 1.69)

i·ni=čá·hi. 'There it is.' (O 101G)
    (*i·ni* 'that (inan.)'; |=ča·hi| 'so'; ´ EMPH)

kekehke·neta=ké·hi. 'You <u>know</u> that.' (A 84B [AW])

In another pattern an utterance with otherwise normal intonation has an added stress on the final vowel. The stressed final vowel has a lower pitch than that of the syllable with the main stress, and if it is a high vowel (*i, o*) it is subject to being phonetically lowered. This pattern of intonation marks a statement as new and unexpected either to the speaker or, by presumption, the addressee. It may be iterated on successive breath groups.

(1.61)   *nenya·nanwihtó.* ([nenyá·nanwihtò]) 'I have <u>five</u> of them!' (EK)

   i·ni=ya·pi·='niní e·h=a·čimekočí. ([i·niyá·pi·ninè ɛ·ha·čímekočè]) (EK)

   '(Uh-Oh,) he (obv.) <u>told</u> on him!'

A special use of this intonation is to soften the abruptness of a warning, as when the social or kin relations of the speaker and addressee are such that normal intonation would sound inappropriately stern. In this use the added final stress may be replicated on all breath groups in the sentence.

(1.62)   *pe·hki=ya·pí sanakesiwá ihkwe·wa e·netá.* (C-FS 1; a woman, to her brother)

   ([pɛ·hkíya·pè, sanákesiwà, ihkwe·wáɛ·netà]; also [pɛ·hkíya·pì, ..])

   'Believe me when I tell you, one deserving to be called 'woman' is really hard to get.'

Emphatic stress is also written on two-syllable words extended by an echo vowel (**§4.4**) when they stress the first syllable against the usual rule:

(1.63)   *šewe·na mánihi:* ... 'But there's this: ...' (O 78C)

Before a pause and when not preceded by *=ihi* NEG (1.54) the enclitic *=we·na* optionally has emphatic intonation. Normal enclitic intonation seems to be found when *=we·na* means 'in fact, after all, it's only', and emphatic intonation in more idiomatic uses (O 67D; Michelson 1921:38.8), but the distinctions made in the editions should be considered tentative. The combination *='h=we·na* 'rather, I mean', used to indicate a correction of what the speaker or addressee has just said (5.123*a*), has normal pre-enclitic stress; occurrences of *=we·na* in this meaning without *='h* and with emphatic stress (O 66I, following Michelson 1921:38.4) are probably always editing errors. Emphatic intonation is also usual with *=ya·pi* 'here we go' (1.60, 68), but other intonations are found (1.62, 66).

6.6. Intensive. The normal (**§6.1**), interrogative (**§6.2**), emphatic (**§6.3**), and expressive (**§6.4**) intonations may occur with an intensive modification (INTS), which is indicated by a superscript exclamation point (ˈ) after the usual sentence-final punctuation. The intensive modification superimposes on the normal intonation an overall raised pitch register and a raised high pitch on the stressed syllable; in one-word utterances the fourth-from-the last syllable bears the high pitch.

The attested examples of the intensive normal and intensive interrogative intonations are in utterances with a single breath group:

(1.64)   *ki·na=wi·n=a·pehe.ˈ* ([↑ki·nawǐ·na·peh]) 'You're always doing stupid things!'

   (*ki·na* 'you (sg.)' + *=wi·na* 'but' + *=a·pehe* 'usually' + ˈ INTS)

(1.65)   *i·ni=ča·h=pe·hki.ˈ* ([↑i·ničă·hpɛ·hki̥]) 'That's too much!'

   Cf. *i·ni=ča·h=pe·hki* ... ([i·ničá·hpɛ·hki̥]) 'So then really ...'

(1.66)   *a·kwi=ya·pi.ˈ* ([↑a·kwǐya·pi̥]) '(But) it isn't supposed to be that way!'

   (Also *a·kwi=ya·pí.ˈ* ([↑a·kwǐya·pì]) with the same meaning; cf. 1.60.)

(1.67)   *wa·pake ki·h=na·kwa?ˈ* ([↑wa·pake kǐ·hna·kwa̧])

   'Are you <u>leaving</u> <u>tomorrow</u>?'

   Cf. *wa·pake ki·h=na·kwa?* ([↑wa·pake kí·hna·kwa̧])

   'Are you leaving tomorrow?'

The shifted stress of ordinary emphatic intonation (§6.5) may occur with intensive modification:

> (1.68) *we ̇kone ̇h=yá pi.*[!] ([↑wɛ·konɛ·hyǎ·pi̧]) 'What is it?' (Expression of concern.)
>
> Cf. *we ̇kone ̇h=yá pi.* ([wɛ·konɛ·hyá·pi̧]) 'What's going on?' (Astonished or wondering.)

The intensive expressive intonation is found with longer utterances, and when iterated on a breath group earlier in the sentence it is marked by a superscript exclamation point ('). It has an overall high pitch register, with the highest pitch on the fourth from the last syllable in ordinary words. The vowels in the two syllables following the high pitch are distinctly lower and nearly even in pitch, the middle vowel of the three having weaker stress than the third vowel and slightly higher pitch. The normal stress before an enclitic is raised in place to a raised high, and a two-syllable enclitic has the final vowel voiced (1.66, 69-70).

> (1.69) *a ̇kwi=ni ̇hka=meko*[!] *nahi- o ̇te ̇weneki -iha ye ̇kwini!*[!] (K-MGW 16)
>
> ([↑a·kwini·hkǎmèkò nahi o·tɛ·weneki ihǎ·yè·kwìni̧])
>
> 'You (pl.) never go to <u>town</u>!'

A three-syllable word breaks an initial-syllable long vowel into two short vowels (1.70):

> (1.70) *ke ̇htena=ni ̇hka=meko*[!] *te pwe wa!*[!] ([↑kɛ·htenani·hkǎmèkò tě̇epwè·wa̧];
>
> EK [tě̇epwèà]) 'He sure enough was right!' (K-BHD 46)

If the initial-syllable has a short vowel the following consonant is lengthened (1.71):

> (1.71) *ke ̇htena=ni ̇hka=meko*[!] *nepe wa!*[!] ([↑kɛ·htenani·hkǎmèkò něp·è·wa̧]; EK [něp·èà])
>
> 'He really did sleep!'

6.7. Exclamative. The exclamative intonation (EXCLAM) occurs on the last or only word of an utterance. The final vowel is stressed, with pitch falling from extra-high to mid, and is diphthongized: *-i* and *-e* become [ei] and *-o* and *-a* become [ou], with *-a* becoming [ao] after *kw*. The second component of the diphthong is optionally prolonged, corresponding to the degree of surprise, fear, or the like. The exclamative intonation is indicated unambiguously by a sentence-final diphthong (*-ei*, *-ou*, or *-ao*) followed by an exclamation point (!).

> (1.72) *nepa ̇kanei!* ([nepa·kaně̀i·]) '(My goodness!) It's a <u>bed</u>!'
>
> (Said as a bed was carried into the speaker's kitchen from outside.)
>
> Cf. *nepa ̇kani.* ([nepa·káni̧]) 'It's a bed.'
>
> (1.73) *i ̇nou!* ([i·nŏù····]) '(Run for your life!) It's <u>hi-i-im</u>!' (EK)
>
> Cf. *i ̇na.* ([í·na̧]) 'It's him.'

The exclamative intonation is only occasionally marked in syllabic writing, by spellings with word-final ⟨o⟩, ⟨ao⟩, or ⟨awo⟩ instead of *-a*, or with ⟨e⟩ instead of *-i*. If such spellings are used, they are transcribed in the editions as *-ou* (or *-ao* after *kw*) and *-ei*. Exclamative intonation can also be assumed for imperative forms punctuated with a following exclamation point (A 153E, 154B, 158C, 181G; O 25I).

6.8. Interjectional. The interjectional intonation (INTERJ) occurs inherently with interjections (1.74, 75) and is used optionally with certain particles in idiomatic expressions (1.76). It is realized as stress and high pitch on the final vowel; if the vowel is long the pitch falls. The highest pitch on the stressed vowel is the highest in the breath group. Interjectional intonation is transcribed with a prime mark (´) after the word on which it occurs:

> (1.74) *nahi´* 'Alright!', 'Now!' (A 21B; O 61I, etc.)
>
> (1.75) *ši·´* 'Say!', 'Hey!' (A 10F; O 63G, 65G)
>
> (1.76) *i ̇ni* 'that (inan.)' + *=kohi* 'certainly' + ´ INTERJ
>
> → *i ̇ni=kohi´* 'That's just the thing!', 'Excellent!' (O 88C, 88G).

An -*i*´ may be diphthongized as with exclamative intonation, though the diphthong is ordinarily relatively short.

MORPHOPHONEMICS

Types of Variation in the Shape of Elements

7. Morphemes (the meaningful elements that combine to make up words) usually keep the same phonemic shape in all their occurrences, but some have variant shapes when next to certain other morphemes. In most cases the variant phonemic shapes of a morpheme can be described as derived from a single, uniform underlying form by morphophonemic rules, with different rules applying, or not applying, depending on the shape or identity of the adjacent morpheme. Some morphophonemic rules are quite general, while others operate in only a small number of cases. Underlying forms and their constituent morphophonemes are written between vertical bars (|..|). There are underlying segments corresponding to each phoneme, and also three abstract underlying segments with special properties (**§7.1**).

Some variations in the phonemic shape of morphemes can be explained as resulting from the analogical extension of a pattern of variation from a form in which the variation arises by morphophonemic rules to another form with which it has a close paradigmatic relationship (**§11.1**, 1.123, 124; **§11.4**, 1.147, 150; **§13.1**, 1.205; **§28.15**, 3.105, 107).

Other, generally more extreme, variation is dependent on morphological context, rather than being phonological in nature. In effect, it involves the morphologically conditioned selection of different underlying forms. For suffixes, these variants are given in the list of endings (in **Appendix 2**). For stems, variations in the quality of the stem-final vowel are described in connection with the morphemes that condition them (**§29.10(a)**, 3.244, 245, 247; **§29.13**).

7.1. Abstract segments. Three abstract underlying segments are also set up: |N|, |S|, and |T|. These appear only as the final segment of morphemes of certain classes and are used to account for the ostensible dual treatment of certain consonants. Thus |s| and |S| are treated differently in the contexts for mutation (**§13.1**), but |s| and unmodified |S| are both pronounced *s*; |n| and |N| (pronounced *n* when unmodified) and |t| and |T| (pronounced *t* when unmodified) are also treated differently in mutation contexts, and |n| and |N| are treated differently before consonants (**§9.1**).

Connective Vowels

8. Because Meskwaki greatly restricts the possible sequences of consonants, if the combination of morphemes in a word would bring two consonants into contact, in most cases a connective vowel is inserted between them, except when the second consonant is a semivowel. When concatenated morphemes are separated by hyphens in underlying forms, the connective vowels, which belong to no morpheme, are italicized.

8.1. Connective *i*. In the formation of stems the connective vowel used is *i*:

(1.77) |we·p-| 'begin' + |-paho| 'run' (1.108) → *we pipaho*- AI 'start running' (O 52I)

Connective *i* is also found in endings:

(1.78) |-hk| proh. + |-če| 3,0 imp. → |-hk-*i*-če| → |+hk<u>i</u>če| 3,0/PROH

For most non-initial morphemes crucial evidence is lacking to determine whether the basic shape begins with a consonant (and adds connective *i*) or begins with *i* (which is deleted after a vowel; **§10.3**).

8.2. Connective *e*. When an intransitive or TI(3) verb stem ending in a consonant is followed by an ending beginning with a consonant (other than |w|), if the first consonant is not deleted or changed (by **§9.1**) the connective vowel inserted is usually *e*:

(1.79) |šekišin-| AI 'lie' + |+no| 2s/IMP → *šekišineno* 'lie down!' (A 110A)

(1.80) |makekiN-| AI 'be big' + |+no| 2s/IMP → *makekineno* 'get big!' (K-MFS 26)

(1.81) |mya·net-| II 'be bad' + |+kini| 0/NEG → *a·kwi .. mya·netekini* 'it is not evil' (O 73C)
(Cf. *we·wenehki* 'what is good' [K-M 289a] ← |we·wenet-| II + |+ki| 0/PPL(INsg))

A transitive animate theme sign ending in a consonant inserts connective *e*, always in the case of |-ekw| TA th. 2, and in the case of |-eN| TA th. 4 in all cases except before |-k| 3 (1.107):

(1.82) |-ekw| TA th. 2 + |-t| 3 → |-ekw-*e*-t| → |-ekot| (**§11.1**)
(as in |e·h=–ekoči| 3´–3s/AOR)

(1.83) |-eN| TA th. 4 + |-pwa| 2p → |-eN-*e*-pwa| → |+enepwa|
(in |ke–enepwa| 1s–2p/IND)

These same consonant-final morphemes add connective *e* word-finally as well:

(1.84) |na·t-| TI(3) 'go after' + |ke–∅| 2s–0/IND
→ |ke-na·t-∅| → *kena·te* 'you went after it' (cf. A 18G)

(1.85) |te·pičin-| AI 'fit (the space)' + |ke–∅| 2s/IND
→ |ke-te·pičin-∅| → *kete·pičine* 'you fit'

(1.86) |makekiN-| AI 'be big' + |ne–∅| 1s/IND
→ |ne-makekiN-∅| → *nemakekine* 'I am big'

(1.87) |-eN| TA th. 4 + |-∅| sg. → |-eN-*e*| → |+ene| (in |ke–ene| 1s–2s/IND):
keneškimene 'I forbade you' (A 73B)

8.3. Connective *o*. Some suffixes that ordinarily begin with |w|, |kw|, or |ko| insert |o| when they follow a consonant. These are: |-ko| 2p imp., |-w| irr., |-wa·| pl. (pluralizing animate third persons), |-wet| X rel., and |-kw| 3,0 irr., (← |-w| irr. + |-k| 3, |-k| 0; **§9.2**):

(1.88) |-am| TI(1) th. + |-ko| 2p imp. → |+amoko| 2p–0/IMP (O 134B, 140A)

(1.89) |-eN| TA th. 4 + |-kw| 3,0 irr. + |-e·ni| int. → |+enokwe·ni| 3s–2s/INT:
e nahina·čimohenokwe·ni 'whatever she used to tell you (sg.)' (A 139C)

(1.90) |-eN| TA th. 4 + |-w| irr. + |-akw| 12 + |-e·ni| int. → |+enowakwe·ni| 3,X–12/INT:
e·šimenowakwe·ni 'whatever we (inc.) were told to do' (O 103D)

(1.91)   *wi·h=* FUT + |na·t-| TI(3) 'go after' + |-wa·| pl. + |-t| 3 + |-i| conj.
→ *wi·h=na·towa·či* 'for them to go after it' (A 166B)

(1.92) |-am| TI(1) th. + |-wet| X rel. + |-ini| neg.-iter. → |+amowečini|
(in |IC–amowečini| X–0/REL/ITER):
me·ma·totamowečini 'whenever it is worshipped (with relation to him)' (O 114G)

The verb |i-| AI 'say {so}' appears before the suffixes that take connective |o| in the shape |iyo-|, as if |iy-| plus connective |o|:

(1.93) |i-| AI 'say {so}' + |e·h=–wa·či| 3p/AOR → *e·h=iyowa·či* 'they said {so}' (O 101G)

This stem is not found with |+ko| 2p/IMP in texts but was heard as regular *iko* 'say {so} (you pl.)!' in the 1990's. The diminutive stem is |iyo·hi-| (4.247*d*). The derived noun *iyoweni* 'what is said, the expression used' was heard with a short vowel (cf. 1.99), pointing to a stem |iyo-| AI.

The suffix |-wa·w| 2p,3p can be described as inserting |o|, but see **§11.1** (1.124, 125). Other suffixes beginning with |w| do not insert connective |o|: |-w| 3,0, |-w| sg., and |-wa·| 2p (pluralizing certain second person objects):

(1.94) |a·hči·šin-| AI 'lean' + |+wa| 3s/IND → *a·hči·šin̲wa* 'he leans' (cf. O 88D)

(1.95) |-eN| TA th. 4 + |-wa·| 2p + |-sa| 3,0 pot. → |+en̲wa·sa| 3–2p/POT

8.4. Connective o·. Some suffixes are preceded by connective |o·|: |-·hi| dim. (**§50.2**, 4.249, 4.252), |-hk| fut. imp. (3.226, 230), |-w| FORMTV (suffix making initials from AI stems and TI(1) themes; **§34.3**, 4.7, 4.8), |-wen| (suffix making nouns from AI stems and TI(1) themes; **§45.7**), |-ehka·no| AI 'pretend' (**§51.1**):

(1.96) |nep-| AI 'die' + |-·hi| dim. → |nepo̲·hi-| AI 'die (dim.)' (A 101B; O 35A)

(1.97) |-am| TI(1) th. + |-hk| fut. imp. + |-ani| 2s conj. → |+amo̲·hkani| 2s–0/FUT.IMP

(1.98) |nep-| AI 'die' + |-w| (initial-forming suffix) + |-e·nem| TA 'think about'
          → |nepo̲·we·nem-| TA 'think dead': *kenepo̲·we·nemi* 'you think that I am dead'

(1.99) |nep-| AI 'die' + |-wen| (noun-forming suffix): *nepo̲·weni* 'death'

Long *o·w* is well attested for derivatives of |nep-| AI 'die' (1.98, 99), but formations from other stems and themes were often heard with short *ow* (**§34.3**) in the 1990's.

8.5. Connective a. Some medials (**§32**) add connective |a| before the stem found in the corresponding dependent noun (**§22.1**):

(1.100)   Dependent noun |-pay| AN 'thigh, femur': *nepaya* 'my thigh, femur'
          Medial |-a̲pay-|: *wa·wa·kapaye·wa* 'he is bow-legged' (A 117A)

Replacement or Loss of a Consonant Next to Another Consonant

9. When a connective vowel (**§8**) is not inserted between consonants that would form an impermissible cluster, one of the consonants is changed or deleted.

9.1. Sequences of true consonants. The first of two true consonants is replaced or deleted. The nasals |m| and |n| are dropped:

(1.101) |-a̲m| TI(1) th. + |-k̲| 3 + |-e| subj. → |-a̲m-ke| → |+a̲ke| 3s–0/SUBJ:
          anwe·we·htake̲ 'if he blows it' (O 14B)

(1.102) |nana·hišin̲-| AI 'lie down' + |e·h=k̲i| 3s/AOR → |e·h=nana·hišin̲-ki|
          → *e·h=nana·hišiki̲* 'she lay down' (O 162E)

(1.103) |ašken̲-| II 'be raw' + |+n̲iwi| 0´s/IND → |ašken-n̲iwi|
          → *ašken̲iwi* 'it (obv.) is raw' (O 96K)

When a nasal is dropped before |-hk| proh., the *h* is also lost in the AI, the TI(1), and optionally the II (leaving just *k*), but the |h| may be kept in the II (leaving *hk*):

(1.104) |-a̲m| TI(1) th. + |-h̲k| proh. + |-ani| 2s conj. → |-a̲m-hkani| → |+a̲kani| 2s–0/PROH:
          ka·ta me·šena̲kani 'don't touch it' (A 48E)

(1.105) |šekišin̲-| AI 'lie' + |+h̲kiče| 0/PROH → |šekišin-h̲kiče|
          → *šekišiki̲če* 'he might be lying down'

(1.106) |mya·šiken̲-| II 'be bad' + |+h̲kiče| 0/PROH → |mya·šiken-h̲kiče|
          → *mya·šike̲hkiče* 'it might be bad' (Jones 1907:306.14)

Underlying |N| and |t| are replaced by *h*:

(1.107) |-eN̲| TA th. 4 + |-k̲| 3 + |-e| subj. → |-eN̲-k-e| → |+e̲hke| 3–2s/SUBJ:
          menwa·ko·me̲hke 'if he likes your ways' (A 160F)

(1.108) |iN̲-| 'to {somewhere}' + |-paho| AI 'run' → |ihpaho-| AI 'run to {somewhere}':
      e·h=ihpahowa·či 'they ran to {somewhere}' (O 160C)

(1.109) |išiso·mika̲t-| II 'be named {so}' + |IC–ki̲| 0/PPL(obl) → |IC-išiso·mika̲t-ki̲|
      → *e·šiso·mikahki* 'its name' (O 1A)

9.2. Sequence of |w| and |k|. The ostensible suffix |-kw| 3,0 irr., can be explained as resulting from the metathesis of |-w-k| to |-kw| (**§29.9(a)**, 3.220): |-w| irr. + |-k| 3 (replacing |-t| 3 [3.256]) → |-kw|; and |-w| irr. + |-k| 0 → |-kw| (e.g., in |–kwe·ni| 3,0/INT). When |-w| irr. is preceded by connective |o| (**§8.3**), the sequence |-ow-k| would give |-okw| by the same rule (1.89).

The same treatment is extended to |-amet| 3–1p; a preceding |-w| irr. combines with the last consonant of this suffix to give |kw| (**§29.9(e)**, 3.232).

9.3. Sequences of semivowels. The second of two underlying semivowels is deleted; the underlying sequences affected are |w-w| and |w-y|:

(1.110) |-ekw̲| TA th. 2 + |-w̲| sg. + |-a| anim. sg. → |-ekw̲-w̲-a| → |+ekwa|
      (e.g., |ne–ekwa| 3s–1s/IND)

(1.111) |takw̲-| 'together with' + |-we̲·we·k-esi| AI 'sound' → |takw̲-we̲·we·k-esi-|
      → |takwe·we·kesi-| AI: *takwe·we·kesiwa* 'he (drum) sounded in accompaniment'

(1.112) |mi·škaw̲-| 'powerful' + |-ya·| II 'be' → |mi·škaw-ya·| → |mi·škaw̲·-| II:
      mi·škaw̲a·wi 'it is powerful' (O 45E)

Treatment of Juxtaposed Vowels

10. Since vowel sequences are not permitted in words, if the combination of morphemes would bring two vowels together, either one vowel is dropped or a consonant is inserted.

10.1. Insertion of *y*. If two long vowels would come together in stem formation, a |y| is inserted between them in most combinations:

(1.113) |paka·-| 'into water' + |-a·šowi·| AI 'wade, ford' → |paka·-y̲-a·šowi·-|
      → |paka·ya·šowi·-| AI 'wade into the water' (O 54E)

(1.114) |CV+| RED1 + |a·čimoh-| TA 'instruct' → |a·-y̲-a·čimoh-|
      → |a·ya·čimoh-| TA 'instruct repeatedly' (A 45F)

Inserted |y| is also present in the reduplication of |i-| as |aya·-| (4.132*b*). A sequence |i·-i| inserts |y| but then contracts |i·yi·| to |i·| (4.78*b*; cf. 1.188); other sequences with |V·-i| do not seem to be found.

The first and second person AI conjunct central suffixes (3.239) begin with a vowel in their most abstract forms (|-a·n| 1s, |-an| 2s, |-a·k| 1p, |-akw| 12, |-e·kw| 2p). These suffixes insert |y| after a vowel, regardless of the length of either vowel. (The suffix |-amet| 3–1p, which is always preceded by |y| after |-i| TA th. 4, can be analyzed the same way.) The use of |y| with these suffixes can thus be accounted for by a variant of the *y*-insertion rule that operates regardless of vowel length. Nevertheless, because this rule is restricted to this one morphological context, the interlinear analysis writes underlying |y| in endings that are pronounced with *y*. Retaining consonant stems (**§18.3**) generalize connective |e| (**§8.2**) before these suffixes and insert |y| after it. These suffixes appear without the |y| after deleting consonant stems (**§18.3**) and suffixes ending in a consonant.

10.2. Insertion of *h*. In two-syllable reduplication (**§39.4**) an |h| is inserted before a vowel-initial stem:

(1.115) |CVCV+| RED2 + |eˑnikoweˑ-| AI 'make funny remarks' → |eˑni-h̲-eˑnikoweˑ-| AI
          → |eˑnih̲eˑnikoweˑ-| AI 'always make funny remarks' (A 71D)

10.3. Vowel elision. When juxtaposed vowels are not kept apart by |y|, if either vowel is long it is retained, and a preceding or following short vowel is lost:

(1.116) |ne̲+| 1 + |-i̲ˑk| 'lodge' + |-i| inan. sg. → *ni̲ˑki* 'my dwelling' (A 41H)

(1.117) |ayo̲ˑ-| TI(3) 'use' + |eˑh=e̲ki| X–0/AOR → *eˑh=ayo̲ˑki* 'it was used' (O 20A)

If both vowels are short the second one drops:

(1.118) |mi·či̲-| TI(3) 'eat' + |IC–e̲ki| X–0/PPL(INsg) → *mi·či̲ki* 'what is eaten' (O 12D)

In contrast to this treatment, |-pi| X and |-eˑni| int. drop |i| before the short vowel of suffixes (**§29.11(a)**, 3.252; **§29.11(d)**); this is taken to be the result of morphological variation in these specific elements.

Contraction

11. If the concatenation of morphemes brings together a semivowel and a following non-final short vowel, this sequence, together with any preceding vowel, may be contracted to a single vowel. The short vowel in question is usually |e|, but in some cases |a| or |i|. One-syllable contraction affects a post-consonantal semivowel and a following vowel and results in a short or long vowel; in one pattern the semivowel is retained before a long vowel. Two-syllable contraction involves two vowels and an intervening semivowel and always results in a long vowel.

All contraction may be considered morphologized. Although phonological in nature, it is not automatic: the identity of the juxtaposed morphemes determines whether it occurs and what form it takes. The same sequence of underlying segments may contract differently, or not at all, depending on the particular morphemes involved. For example, there are four possible treatments of |Vw-e|: no change (|Vwe|); contraction with the quality of the first vowel preserved (|Vˑ|); contraction with the vowel quality changed (always to |oˑ|); and no contraction but |e| treated like post-consonantal |we| (|Vwo|).

Some contraction is found in stem formation and within endings, but it mainly occurs in the inflection of nouns and TA verbs and in secondary derivation from stems of these two types. A detailed description of contraction is Goddard (2001).

11.1. Contraction of |w-e|. In most cases in inflection and primary stem derivation, and in all cases in secondary derivation, |w-e| between consonants contracts to -o-:

(1.119) |pepikweˑšk̲w-| IN 'whistle' + |-e̲ki| loc. → *pepikweˑšk̲oki* 'on the whistle' (O 42D)

(1.120) |tepahw-| TA 'pay' + |ne–e̲ko·pi| X–1s/IND → |ne-tepahw-eko·pi|
          → *netepaho̲ko·pi* 'I was paid' (A 62D)

(1.121) |ahkasw-| TA 'burn' + |eˑh=e̲meči| X–3´/AOR → |eˑh=ahkasw-emeči|
          → *eˑh=ahkaso̲meči* 'they (obv.) were burned' (O 149H)

(1.122) |aškw-| 'spare' + |-e̲n| TA, TI(1) 'act on by hand' → |aškw-en-|
          → |ašk̲on-| TA, TI(1) 'save' (O 5GF)

The regular contraction with |-ena·n| 1p,12 (1.123) is generalized to |-wa·w| 2p,3p (1.124), as if this also began with |e|:

(1.123) |-ški·šek̲w-| IN 'eye' + |ke–e̲na·nani| 12(INpl)
          → *keški·šek̲ona·nani* 'our eyes' (O 125J)

|-ek<u>w</u>| TA th. 2 + |-<u>e</u>na·n| 1p,12 → |-ek<u>o</u>na·n| (as in |ne–ek<u>o</u>na·na| 3s–12/IND):
   netene ˀnemek<u>o</u>na na 'he thinks {so} about us' (O 122B)

(1.124) |-ški·šek<u>w</u>-| IN 'eye' + |o–wa·wani| 3p(INpl)
   → *ošk<u>i</u> šek<u>o</u>wa wani* 'their eyes' (O 116D)

|-ek<u>w</u>| TA th. 2 + |-wa·w| 2p,3p → |-ek<u>o</u>wa·w| (as in |ke–ek<u>o</u>wa·wa| 3s–2p/IND):
   kenenehke ˀnemek<u>o</u>wa wa 'he thinks about you (pl.)' (O 83F)

In fact, whatever kind of contraction affects an |-ena·n| 1p,12 (1.123) is also ostensibly present in the form with |-wa·w| 2p,3p in the same paradigm (1.124; **§28.11**).

The |w| of |-ekw| TA th. 2 and |-w| (3,0) after a consonant contract with connective |e| and with the |e| of the independent order modal suffixes (|-etoke| dub., |-ehapa| con., |-epani| ast.) to long -*o·*:

(1.125) |-ek<u>w</u>| TA th. 2 + |-w| sg. (1.110) + |-etoke| dub. → |-ekw-w-etoke| → |-ek<u>w</u>-<u>e</u>toke|
   → |+ek<u>o·</u>toke| (as in |ke–ek<u>o·</u>toke| 3s–2s/DUB):
   kenenehke ˀnemek<u>o</u>toke 'it seems he thought of you' (O 66C)

|-ek<u>w</u>| TA th. 2 + |-pi| X → |-ek<u>w</u>-<u>e</u>-pi| → |+ek<u>o·</u>pi| (as in |ne–ek<u>o·</u>pi| X–1s/IND):
   netašamek<u>o</u> pi 'I was fed' (A 8E)

(1.126) |išiken-| II 'be {so}' + |-w| 3,0 + |-ehapa| con. → |išiken-<u>w</u>-<u>e</u>hapa|
   → *išiken<u>o</u>·hapa* 'so it must be {so}' (X2-SAR 198)

In primary stem formation, numeral initials and a few others in certain combinations contract |w-e| to long -*o·*:

(1.127) |ni·š<u>w</u>-| 'two' + |-<u>e</u>hkwe·w-| 'wife' + |-e·| AI ABSTR → |ni·š<u>w</u>-<u>e</u>hkwe·w-e·-|
   → |ni·š<u>o·</u>hkwe·we·-| AI 'have two wives': *ni ˀš<u>o</u>·hkwe we wa* 'he has two wives'

(1.128) |ahk<u>w</u>-| '{so} far' + |-<u>e</u>te·| 'be a room' → |ahk<u>w</u>-ete·-| → |ahk<u>o·</u>te·-| II 'be a room {so} long': *e ˀhk<u>o</u>·te ˀniki* 'the length of the lodge' (O 115E)

The initial |nye·w-| 'four' exhibits the same ostensible contraction as a numeral stem in |Cw|, in all patterns of contraction:

(1.129) |nye·w-| 'four' + |-ehkwe·w-| 'wife' + |-e·| AI ABSTR
   → *nye ˀw<u>o</u>·hkwe we wa* 'he has four wives'

An alternative to analyzing *o·* in cases like (1.127-129) as a special kind of contraction would be to consider it to be present in an underlying variant of these initials. The same holds for the apparent contraction by the same initials to *o·* in **§11.2** (1.136) and **§11.3** (1.141-143).

Three verb finals and a final pair begin with an |e| that does not undergo contraction with |w|: |-eka·| AI 'dance', |-etone·mo| AI 'talk', |-ehpo| II 'snow', and |-ešihw| TA 'chase' and |-eših| TI-O 'hunt':

(1.130) |pehk<u>w</u>-| 'bunched, lumped' + |-<u>e</u>ka·| AI 'dance' → |pehk<u>w</u>-<u>e</u>ka·-| AI:
   pehk<u>w</u>eke waki 'they dance in a bunch'

|ahk<u>w</u>-| 'end' + |-<u>e</u>tone·mo| AI 'talk' → |ahk<u>w</u>-<u>e</u>tone·mo-| AI:
   ahk<u>w</u>etone mowa 'he ends his talk'

|pehk<u>w</u>-| 'bunched, lumped' + |-<u>e</u>hpo| II 'snow' → |pehk<u>w</u>-<u>e</u>hpo-| II:
   pehk<u>w</u>ehpowi 'it snows large flakes'

|a·nw-| 'fail to' + |-<u>e</u>šihw-| TA 'chase (away)' → |a·n<u>w</u>-<u>e</u>šihw-| TA:
   a ˀn<u>w</u>ešihwe wa 'he fails to get him to go away'

|ana·k<u>w</u>-| 'evening' + |-<u>e</u>ših| TI(1)-O 'hunt' → |ana·k<u>w</u>-<u>e</u>ših-| TI(1)-O:
   ana ˀk<u>w</u>ešihamwa 'he goes on an evening hunt'

11.2. Contraction of |w-a|. Underlying |w-a| may contract to |o| or |o·|. Phonemic *wa* between consonants is, however, common, and |w-a| across a morpheme boundary is generally retained.

The inflectional morphemes beginning with |a| that are subject to contraction are the two-syllable suffixes of the set that marks nominal categories (§18.2, 2.2; §28) on nouns and in many verbal endings: |-aki| anim. pl., |-ani| obv. sg., |-ahi| obv. pl., |-ani| inan. pl.:

> (1.131) |mehtek<u>w</u>-| IN 'stick, tree' + |-<u>a</u>ni| inan. pl. → *mehteko̲ni* 'sticks, trees'
> (1.132) |ahkohk<u>w</u>-| AN 'kettle' + |-<u>a</u>ki| anim. pl. → *ahkohko̲ki* 'kettles'
> (1.133) |-ekw| TA th. 2 + |-w| sing. + |-<u>a</u>ki| anim. pl. → |-ek<u>w</u>-aki| (§9.2; 1.110) → |-eko̲·ki|
>   (as in |ne–eko̲·ki| 3p–1s/IND): *ki·h=tepa neko̲·ki* 'they'll be fond of you' (A 51E)

Most animate nouns with stems ending in |kw|, and a few others, do not have this contraction:

> (1.134) |mahk<u>w</u>-| 'bear' + |-<u>a</u>ki| anim. pl. → *mahk<u>w</u>aki* 'bears'

In stem derivation, underlying |Cw-ah| usually contracts to |Coh| with the finals |-ahw| TA, |-ah| TI(1) 'act on by tool' and |-ahwe·| AI+O 'use the supply':

> (1.135) |wi·šika·hk<u>w</u>-| 'firmly' + |-<u>a</u>h| TI(1) 'act on by tool'
>   → |wi·šika·hko̲h-| TI(1) 'fasten firmly' (A 149F)

Some stems do not show this contraction (e.g., 1.280), and some have both treatments.

With numeral initials, |w-a| contracts to long |o·| in most combinations:

> (1.136) |ni·š<u>w</u>-| 'two' + |-<u>a</u>piso| AI 'be tied' → |ni·šo̲·piso-| AI 'be tied together as a pair'

The medials |-ayak-| 'set' and |-awahi·m-|, |-awahi·n-| 'year' are exempt:

> (1.137) |ma·n<u>w</u>-| 'many' + |-<u>a</u>yak-| 'set' + |-e| ABSTR → *ma·n<u>w</u>ayaki* 'many kinds' (O 122B)
> (1.138) |ni·š<u>w</u>-| 'two' + |-<u>a</u>wahi·m-| 'year' + |-e| ABSTR → *ni·š<u>w</u>awahi·me* 'two years'
>   (A 61D)

11.3. Contraction of |w-i|. The sequence |Cw-iC| does not contract, with the following exceptions. The two suffixes of secondary derivation that begin with |iw| contract after |Cw| as if they had |ew|; these are |-iwe·| AI DETRANS (§52.3, 4.269) and |-iwi| AI, II 'be' (§47):

> (1.139) |pem<u>w</u>-| 'shoot (at)' + |-<u>i</u>we·-| AI DETRANS
>   → |pemo̲we·-| AI 'shoot (at people)': *pemo̲we·wa* 'he shoots'
> (1.140) |pek<u>w</u>-| 'ashes, dust' + |-<u>i</u>wi-| AI, II 'be' → |peko̲wi-| 'be dusty':
>   *peko̲wiwa, peko̲wiwi* 'he, it is dusty'

Numeral initials contract |Cw-iC| to |Co·C| in most cases:

> (1.141) |nes<u>w</u>-| 'three' + |-<u>i</u>šin-| AI 'lie' → |neso̲·šin-| AI 'sleep three to a bed':
>   *neso̲·šino·ki* 'the three of them slept together'
> (1.142) |tas<u>w</u>-| '{so many}' + |-<u>i</u>ke·-| AI 'dwell' → |taso̲·ke·-| AI 'live together as {so many}':
>   *e·ya·taso̲·ke·wa·či* 'as many as live in each lodge' (O 111B)

Again, |nye·w-| 'four' follows suit:

> (1.143) |nye·<u>w</u>-| 'four' + |-<u>i</u>ka·pa·-| AI 'stand' → |nye·wo̲·ka·pa·-| AI 'stand four together':
>   *nye·wo̲·ka·pa·waki* 'the four of them stand together'

Several non-initial morphemes are exceptions to this contraction, notably the medial |-ikamik-| 'family, household' and the final |-ih| TA, |-iht| TI(2) ABSTR:

> (1.144) |ni·š<u>w</u>-| 'two' + |-<u>i</u>kamik-| 'family, household' + |-esi-| AI ABSTR
>   → *ni·š<u>w</u>ikamikesiwaki* 'they occupy two houses, are two families'
> (1.145) |nes<u>w</u>-| 'three' + |-<u>i</u>h-| TA ABSTR → *nes<u>w</u>ihe·wa* 'he has, gets, kills three of them'

11.4. Contraction of |y-e|. The sequence |Cy-eC| always contracts to either |CiC| or |Ci·C|. All occurrences involve a noun stem ending in |Cy|; the suffix may be one of inflection or secondary derivation.

In noun inflection contraction to short |i| is rare. It is found in all forms of |-ky-| 'mother' (*nekya* 'my mother') and |-semy-| 'daughter-in-law' (*nesemya* 'my daughter-in-law'); in all forms except the locative of |-tay-| 'pet' (*netaya* 'my pet'), which is treated like a stem in |Cy|; and optionally in all forms except the locative of |ahky-| 'earth' (*ahki*). A few forms from other stems have been recorded with contraction to short |i|, but these were not accepted in the 1990's.

(1.146) |ne+| 1 + |-ky-| 'mother' + |-eki| loc. → |ne-ky-eki|
→ *nekiki* 'at my mother's; like my mother'

(1.147) |-ky-| 'mother' + |ne–ena·na| 1p(ANsg) → |ne-ky-ena·na|
→ *nekina·na* 'our (exc.) mother'

(1.148) |-tay-| 'pet' + |ne–ena·na| 1p(ANsg) → |ne-tay-ena·n-a|
→ *netayina·na* 'our (exc.) pet, dog, horse'

(1.149) |ahky-| 'land' + |ke–ena·nani| 12(INpl) → |ket-ahky-ena·nani|
→ *ketahkina·nani, ketahki·na·nani* 'our (inc.) gardens'

Patterned on the first-plural possessed forms are the corresponding second-plural and third-plural possessed forms (cf. §11.1; 1.123, 124):

(1.150) |-ky-| 'mother' + |ke–wa·wa| 2p(ANsg) → |ke-ky-wa·wa|
→ *kekiwa·wa* 'your (pl.) mother' (cf. 1.147)

The usual contraction of |Cy-eC| in inflection is to long |i·|:

(1.151) |ahky-| 'earth, land, dirt' + |-eki| loc. → |ahky-eki| → *ahki·ki* 'on earth' (O 87E)

The old short-vowel variant of the locative in (1.151) is lexicalized as *ahkiki* 'down below'.

In secondary derivation |Cy-eC| contracts to -*CiC*-:

(1.152) |wi·kopy-| 'basswood inner bark' + |-ehke·-| AI 'gather, obtain, make'
→ |wi·kopy-ehke·-| AI → *wi·kopihke·wa* 'she gathers and fixes basswood bark'

Stems with this contraction stem-internally are presumably lexicalized as separate words.

11.5. Contraction of |y-a|. When noun stems in |Cy| are followed by the endings subject to contraction after |Cw| (§11.2), the underlying |Cy-aC| always contracts to |Cye·C|; *netaya* 'my pet' is also treated like a stem in |Cy| (cf. 1.148).

(1.153) |ne+| 1 + |-ky-| 'mother' + |-ani| obv. sg. → |ne-ky-ani|
→ *nekye·ni* 'my mother (obv.)' (A 107B, 107H)
|o+| 3 + |-tay-| (as if |-tayy-|) 'pet' + |-ani| obv. sg. → |o-tayy-ani|
→ *otaye·ni* 'his pet (obv.)'

In stems with |čy| or |šy|, the |y| is optionally pronounced before *e·*, but it is not written in the syllabic texts.

(1.154) |ne+| 1 + |-škašy-| 'fingernail' + |-aki| anim. pl. → |ne-škašy-aki|
→ *neškašye·ki, neškaše·ki* 'my fingernails'

11.6. Contraction of |Vw-e| in nouns. Noun stems in |-Vw| generally contract |Vw-e| to a long vowel having the quality of the first vowel, both in inflection and in secondary derivation.

(1.155) |pešekesiw-| AN 'deer' + |o–emani| 3s(OBVsg) → |o-pešekesiw-emani|
→ *opešekesi·mani* 'his deer (obv.)' (O 155C)

(1.156) |-i·yaw-| IN 'body, self, life' + |ne–ena·ni| 1p(INsg) → |ne-i·yaw-ena·ni|
→ *ni·ya·na·ni* 'ourselves (exc.), our lives'

(1.157) |aškote·w-| IN 'fire' + |ne–emi| 1s(INsg) → |net-aškote·w-emi|
→ *neto·škote·mi* 'my fire' (§12.3; O 96E)

(1.158) |maneto·w-| AN 'manitou' + |-eki| loc. → |maneto·w-eki| → *maneto·ki* 'like a manitou'

(1.159) |meškwa·swa_w-| AN 'yarn belt' + |-ehke·-| AI 'make' → |meškwa·swa_w-ehke·-|
          → meškwa·swa_hke wa 'she makes a yarn belt'

The suffixes |-wa·w| 2p,3p and |-inaw| X are treated like noun stems before |-eki| loc., the only
contracting suffix that can follow them (3.105, 106; cf. 3.107):

(1.160) |-hkiwan-| IN 'nose' + |o-wa·w| 3p + |-eki| loc. → |o-hkiwan-wa·w-eki|
          → ohkiwanwa_ki 'on their noses' (K-CWB 85)

Two nouns do not show contraction in the texts, ni wa 'my wife' and no·ke·nawa, meno·ke·nawa
'soul':

(1.161) |-i·w-| AN 'wife' + |ne–ena·naki| 1p(ANpl) → |ne-i·w-ena·naki|
          → ni wena naki 'our (exc.) wives' (K-ILM 30)

(1.162) |no·ke·naw-| AN 'soul' → |ke–ena·naki| 12(ANpl) → |ke-no·ke·naw-ena·n-aki|
          → keno·ke·nawena naki 'our (inc.) souls' (K-FC 135)

Non-contraction increases in the more recent stages of the language.

11.7. Contraction of |Vw-e| in TA verbs. When a TA stem in |-Vw| precedes a suffix
beginning with |e|, either the sequence |Vw-e| is contracted to a long vowel, or there is no
contraction and the |e| is replaced by o. For contraction to take place both the stem and the suffix
must be subject to contraction. The TA stems in |-Vw| subject to contraction are the large
number in |-Caw| and the few in |-iw| and |-o·w|. The stems that never contract are |aw-| TA 'use'
and the small number in |-e·w| and |-a·w|. The suffixes that undergo two-syllable contraction are
|-ekw| TA th. 2 (and |-ekwi| TA th. 2a), |-eN| TA th. 4, |-eti·| AI RECIP, and |-etiso| AI REFL. The
suffixes and endings that never contract with |Vw| are |-et| X–3, |+ene·ha| X–3/POT, |-em| obv.,
and |+ehko| 2p–3/IMP. The stems that contract preserve the quality of the vowel that precedes the
|w|, except that |-Caw| contracts with |-eN| TA th. 4 to |-Co·N-| (1.166, 167).

Contracting stem with contracting suffix:

(1.163) |pye·notaw-| TA 'come to' + |+ekwa| 3´–3s/IND → |pye·notaw-ekwa|
          → pye nota_kwa 'he (obv.) came to her' (A 69B)

(1.164) |taši·hkaw-| TA 'be dealing with' + |-eti·| AI (reciprocal) → |taši·hka_ti·-| AI 'deal
          with each other': taši·hka_ti wa 'she's romantically involved' (A 96D)

(1.165) |ašihtaw-| TA 'make O2 for' + |-etiso| AI (reflexive) → |ašihta_tiso-| AI 'make O2
          for oneself': wi·h=ašihta_tisoyani 'for you to make them for yourself' (A 24D)

(1.166) |taši·hkaw-| TA 'be dealing with' + |ke–ene| 1s–2s/IND → |ke-taši·hkaw-ene|
          → ketaši·hko_ne 'I'm dealing with you' (A 84A)

(1.167) |to·taw-| TA 'treat {so}' + |IC–ehki| 3–2s/PPL(obl) (1.107) → |IC-to·taw-ehki|
          → e·to·to_hki 'how he treated you' (A 182B)

(1.168) |wi·čawiw-| TA 'be with' + |IC–ena·ni| 1s–2s/PPL(obl) → |IC-wi·čawiw-ena·ni|:
          nehki wi·čawi_na ni 'for as long as I've been with you' (A 159F)

(1.169) |ahko·w-| TA 'come behind, come next' + |-eti·| AI RECIP → |ahko·ti·-| AI:
          ahko_ti waki 'they followed each other'

Contracting stem with non-contracting suffix:

(1.170) |kepoškaw-| TA 'surround' + |e·h=–eči| X–3/AOR → |e·h=kepoškaw-eči|
          → e·h=kepoškawoči 'he was surrounded' (O 154D)

(1.171) |wi·čawiw-| TA 'be with' + |IC–emakini| 1s–3´/PPL(OBVsg)
          → |IC-wi·čawiw-emakini| → wi·čawiwomakini 'the one (obv.) I was with' (A 93D)

(1.172) |pesetaw-| TA 'listen to' + |-ehko| 2p–3/IMP → |pesetaw-ehko|
          → pesetawohko 'listen to him, them (you pl.)!'

Non-contracting stem with contracting suffix:

(1.173) |keša·w-| TA 'be envious of' + |ne–ekwa| 3s–1s/IND
→ |ne-keša·w-ekwa| → nekeša wokwa 'he is envious of me'

(1.174) |ne·w-| TA 'see' + |+ena·ne| 1s–2s/SUBJ → ne wona ne 'if I see you' (O 157E)

(1.175) |ne·w-| TA 'see' + |-eti·| AI (reciprocal) → |ne·woti·-| AI 'see each other':
e·h=ne woti ya·ke 'when we (exc.) saw each other' (A 149D)

After a non-contracting stem, |-iwe·| AI DETRANS is treated as if it had |ew| (§11.3):

(1.176) |ne·w-| TA 'see' + |-iwe·| AI DETRANS → |ne·w-iwe·-| → |ne·wowe·-|:
ne wowe wa 'he sees people'

11.8. Contraction of |V-w-e| in verbal suffixes. The suffixes |-w| 3,0 and |-w| irr. contract between the vowel of a stem or preceding suffix and the |e| of a following suffix.

(1.177) |ki·šiki-| AI 'grow up' + |-w| 3,0 + |-etoke| dub. [→ |+wetoke| 3s/DUB]
→ |ki·šiki-w-etoke| → ki šiki toke 'he must be grown up' (O 70B)

(1.178) |-i| TA th. 3 + |-w| irr. + |-ek| X + |-e·ni| int. → |-i-w-ek-e·ni| → |+i·ke·ni|
(as in |IC–i·ke·ni| X–1s/INT.PPL(obl)): wi·h=anemi-'ši-..-pemeni ke ni (O 93E)
'whether or not I will continue to be taken care of'

11.9. Contraction of |Vy-e|. Noun stems in |-ay| and |-iy| contract |ay-e| to |a·| and |iy-e| to |i·|:

(1.179) |asay-| AN, IN 'skin, hide' + |-eki| loc. → |asay-eki| → asa ki 'on, in a skin'
Cf. asaya AN 'small skin', asayi IN 'large skin'.

(1.180) |či·pay-| AN 'corpse, ghost' + |ne–ema| 1s(ANsg) → |ne-či·pay-ema|
→ neči pa ma 'my deceased relative'

(1.181) |o+| 3 + |-i·nwiy-| 'navel' + |-eki| loc. → |ow-i·nwiy-eki|:
owi nwi ki 'on his navel' (A 115E)

No verb stems end in |y|.

11.10. Contraction of |Vw-i| and |Vy-i|. Noun stems in |-Vw| and |-Vy| contract with two suffixes as if they began with |e| although they otherwise begin with i; these are the noun final |-ina·w| IN 'country of' (4.191b) and the secondary final |-ihka·h| IN 'place of':

(1.182) |neniw-| AN 'man' + |-ina·w-| 'country of' + |-eki| loc. → |neniw-ina·w-eki|
→ neni na ki 'among men, like men, on the male side'

(1.183) |maneto·w-| AN 'manitou' + |-ina·w-| 'country of' + |-eki| loc.
→ |maneto·w-ina·w-eki| → maneto na ki 'in the land of the manitous'

(1.184) |či·pay-| AN 'corpse, ghost' + |-ina·w| 'country of' + |-eki| loc. → |či·pay-ina·w-eki|
→ či pa na ki 'in the land of the dead'

(1.185) IC (§29.4, cf. §46.2) + |pene·w-| AN 'turkey' + |-ihka·h| IN 'place of'
→ IC + |pene·w-ihka·h-|: pe ne hka hi 'Turkey River'

There is similar contraction with inflectional |-inaw| X (indefinite possessor), assuming an additional irregularity (§28.10).

Replacement of Vowels

12. Some vowel alternations at the end of words (§12.1) or at the beginning of stems and words (§12.2) correlate with restrictions on the possible shapes that words may have. There are some additional cases of stem-initial vowel replacement in noun inflection (§12.3).

12.1. Shortening of word-final vowels. No word ends with a long vowel (with marginal exceptions: §1.1, §2), and if an underlying long vowel comes to occur in word-final position in the formation of a word, it is replaced by the corresponding short vowel:

(1.186) |anwa·či·-| AI 'be willing' + |ne–∅| 1s/IND → |net-anwa·či·-∅|
　　　　　　→ *netanwa·či* 'I was willing' (A 22E)

(1.187) |mayo·-| AI 'weep' |ne–∅| 1s/IND → |ne-mayo·-∅| → *nemayo* 'I wept' (A 163G)

When followed by |-i| inan. sg., noun stems in |-iy| contract |iy-i| to |i·| and then shorten this to |i|:

(1.188) |o+| 3 + |-i·nwiy-| 'navel' + |-i| inan. sg. → |ow-i·nwiy-i| → |owi·nwi·|
　　　　　　→ *owi·nwi* 'his navel' (A 114E)

12.2. Replacement of stem-initial |i| and suffix-initial |e|. Short *i* and short *e* do not contrast in initial syllables. Only *i*- occurs word-initially, and only *e* occurs in initial syllables that begin with a consonant. Stems that have *i*- after a word boundary have *e* after a prefix (§28.7, 3.41; §29.2, 3.143). Such stems are set up as having an underlying form with |i-|, matching their unprefixed shape; this *i*- is replaced by *e* after a pronominal prefix in the inflection of both nouns and verbs. Conversely, suffix-initial |e| (in |-ekw| TA th. 2, |-ekwi| TA th. 2a, |-eti·| AI RECIP, |-etiso| AI REFL) is replaced by *i*- when it comes to stand in word-initial position because of the dropping of the stem |iN-| TA 'say {so} to' before these suffixes (4.303, 4.304).

(1.189)　Alternation in stem-initial |i| and suffix-initial |e|

(a) |išitehka·so-| AI 'be named {so}' + |ne–∅| 1s/IND → |net-išitehka·so-|
　　　→ *netešitehka·so* 'I am called {so}' (O 72K)
　　　Cf. *išitehka·sowa* 'he is called {so}'.

(b) |iN-| 'say {so} to' + |-ekwa| 3´–3s/IND → |(iN)-ekwa|
　　　→ *ikwa* 'he (obv.) said {so} to him' (K-WYB 133)

(c) *pye·či* PV 'come and', |iN-| 'say {so} to' + |ne–eko·ki| 3p–1s/IND
　　　→ |ne-pye·či (iN)-eko·ki|
　　　→ *nepye·či-iko·ki* 'they came and said {so} to me' (K-FC 451)

(d) |iN-| 'say {so} to' + |e·h=-ekoči| 3´–3s/AOR → |e·h=(iN)-ekoči|
　　　→ *e·h=ikoči* 'he (obv.) said {so} to him'

(e) |iN-| 'say {so} to' + |e·h=-ekwiči| 0–3s/AOR → |e·h=(iN)-ekwiči|
　　　→ *e·h=ikwiči* 'it said {so} to him'

An |i-| preceded by a proclitic prefix (*e·h*= AOR or *wi·h*= FUT; §29.3) or two-syllable reduplication (**§39.4**) is treated as a word-initial vowel and realized as *i*- (1.189*de*, 1.193). The stem |i-| AI 'say {so}' is irregular (3.143).

12.3. Replacement of stem-initial vowels in nouns. Noun stems (but not verb stems) replace short *o*- with long *o·* after a pronominal prefix (1.190), and some replace *a*- with *o·* (1.157) or with *e* (1.191):

(1.190) |ke+| 2 + |ošehki·ta·kan-| IN 'clothing' + |-i| inan. sg. → |ket-ošehki·ta·kan-i|
　　　　　　→ *keto·šehki·ta·kani* 'your clothes' (A 178G)

(1.191) |ahkw-| AN 'louse' + |ke–ema| 2s(ANsg) → |ket-ahkw-ema|
　　　　　　→ *ketehkoma* 'your louse'
　　　　|aškwe·nečy-| IN 'little finger' + |ot–eki| 3s(loc) → |ot-aškwe·nečy-eki| →
　　　　　　→ *oteškwe·neči·ki* 'on his little finger' (also *otaškwe·neči·ki*)

12.4. Umlaut. The umlaut of stem-final |-a·| to *e·* and |-e·| to *a·* is found before certain morphemes. These replacements are not phonologically conditioned and hence are described as morphological processes (**§§29.7(a)** 3.190a; **29.10** 3.241, 243, 244; **29.13, 52.1**).

Replacement or Loss of a Consonant Before a Vowel

13. Under certain conditions a consonant at the end of a morpheme is replaced by another consonant or dropped entirely before the vowel of the following morpheme. The most common change of this type is MUTATION (**§13.1**). Much more restricted is the replacement of |t| by *s* (**§13.2**) or of |N| by *s* (**§13.3**). A semivowel after a consonant is lost before a vowel that would make an impermissible sequence (**§13.4**).

13.1. Mutation. Some initials, stems, and suffixes that end in *n, s,* and *t* have variants ending in *š*, or in the case of *t* more usually *č*, when followed by certain morphemes. These conditioned replacements are conventionally called mutation (Bloomfield 1925-1927, [1]:224-227). The consonants subject to mutation are written as underlying |N|, |S|, and |t| to differentiate them from underlying |n|, |s|, and |T|, which do not undergo mutation. (Because |T| is extremely rare compared to |t|, it is the non-mutating member of the pair that has the special notation in this case.) Mutation takes place before |i|, |i·|, and |y|, and also before the finals |-awi| AI 'be, do' and its transitive counterpart |-awiw| TA, and before |-awahi·m|, |-awahi·n|, the abstract noun final derived from the place-holder pronoun (**§18.1**, 2.15).

Mutation is found in particular categories of stem formation and inflection. Many instances occur with initials ending in |N| (> *š*) and |t| (> *č*):

(1.192) |iN̲-| '{so}' + |-im| TA 'tell, speak to' → |iN̲-im-| → |iši̲m-| TA:
  e·ši̲miki 'what I was told to do' (A 45A)

(1.193) |iN̲-| '{so}' + |-i·hta·| AI 'work, dress' → |iN̲-i·hta·-| → |iši·hta·-| AI:
  wi·h=iši·hta ya ni 'for me to work {so}' (A 11C)

(1.194) |mya·N̲-| 'badly, imperfectly' + |-ye·wi·| AI 'perform a task' → |mya·N̲-ye·wi·-|
  → |mya·šye·wi·-| → |mya·še·wi·-| AI: *nemya·še wi* 'I did a poor job' (A 3A)

(1.195) |kot̲-| 'try' + |-iht| TI(2) ABSTR → |kot̲-iht-| → |koči̲ht-| TI(2) 'try to make':
  koči̲hto no 'try to make it, them' (A 29C)

(1.196) |wi·t̲-| 'with' + |-awiw| TA 'have, get' → |wi·t̲-awiw-| TA → |wi·ča̲wiw-| TA 'be
  with': *wi ča̲wiwaka* 'the one I am with, my wife, my husband' (A 94B, 138D)

The initial |taN̲-| '{somewhere}; be engaged in' does not show mutation before |y| (cf. 1.194):

(1.197) |taN̲-| 'be engaged in' + |-ye·wi·| AI 'perform a task' → |taN̲-ye·wi·-|
  → |tan̲ye·wi·-| AI: *tan̲ye wi wa* 'he is working at the task' (stem: K-MDLA 8)

The only initial ending in a *t* that never undergoes mutation is |nekoT̲-| 'one':

(1.198) |nekoT̲-| 'one' + |-i| PF → |nekoT̲-i| → *nekot̲i* 'one'

(1.199) |nekoT̲-| 'one' + |-ih| TA ABSTR → |nekoT̲-ih-| → |nekot̲ih-| TA:
  nekot̲ihe wa 'he has, gets, kills one'

The initial |pi·t-| 'into' does not show mutation in the stem |pi·tike·-| AI 'enter' and its derivatives, including *pi·tike* P 'inside'; this is best taken as a frozen combination rather than a variant |pi·T-| 'into' + |-ik-| 'dwelling' + |-e·| AI ABSTR, since the words of this set are not restricted to referring to dwellings or structures.

The |t| in endings is always subject to mutation (> *č*):

(1.200) |-t| 3 + |-i| conj. → |-t-i| → |-či| (as in |e·h=–či| 3s/AOR)

(1.201) |-∅| TA th. 1 + |-aket| 1p–3 + |-ini| neg.-iter. → |-aket-ini| → |+akeči̲ni| 1p–3/NEG

This is the only type of mutation that affects suffixes.

The verb stems affected by mutation are the TA stems in |-N|, |-S|, and |-t| (all mutating to *š*):

(1.202) |mahkate·wi·N̲-| TA 'make fast' + |e·h=–iki| X–1s/AOR → |e·h=mahkate·wi·N̲-iki|
  → *e·h=mahkate·wi·ši̲ki* 'when I was made to fast' (A 8E)

(1.203) |neS-| TA 'kill' + |-iye·ka·ha| 1s–3/POT → |neS-iye·ka·ha|
        → *nešiye·ka·ha* 'I would kill him' (K-MMGW 11)

(1.204) |wi·h=| FUT + |wa·wi·t-| TA 'name, call by name' + |ke–i| 2s–1s/IND
        → |ke+wi·h=wa·wi·t-i| → *ki·h=wa·wi·ši* 'you (sg.) must call my name' (S-RL 69)

Some initials ending in a mutating consonant have generalized the variant with mutation within sets of related stems. Mutation is found in non-mutating contexts that have a close paradigmatic relationship with an element that regularly triggers mutation (1.205). These initials are analyzed as irregularly having additional, morphological environments for mutation.

(1.205) |wapaS-| 'disparage, waste' (1.9) + |-im| TA, |-ot| TI(1) 'speak about'
        → |wapašim-| TA, |wapašot-| TI(1) 'make fun of, say irreverent things about':
        wapašime·wa, wapašotamwa 'he speaks disrespectfully of him, it'

(1.206) |wapaS-| 'disparage, waste' + |-e·nem| TA 'think of' → |wapase·nem-| TA:
        ki·h=wapase·nemekowa·wa 'he will think you (pl.) foolish' (O 79F)

In (1.205) the *š* before *o* in the TI stem is analogical to the *š* before *i* in the TA stem; other environments retain unmutated *s* (1.206).

13.2. Replacement of |t| by *s*. In certain combinations of morphemes an underlying |t| is replaced by *s*. This takes place before certain finals beginning with |e| and |a·|, notably |-ehka·| AI, II 'proceed', |-ehkaw| TA, |-ehk| TI(1) 'act on by foot or body', |-ehtaw| TA, |-eht| TI(1) 'listen to', and |-a·pam| TA, |-a·pat| TI(1) 'look at'. The affected |t| may be separated from the vowel of the final by |aw|.

(1.207) |ot-| 'from {somewhere}' + |-ehka·| AI 'proceed' → |ot-ehka·-| → |osehka·-| AI:
        we·sehka·či 'where he originates from' (O 125E)

(1.208) |nawat-| 'pausing to' + |-ehkaw| TA 'act on by foot or body' → |nawat-ehkaw-|
        → |nawasehkaw-| TA: *nenawasehka·kwa* 'he invited me along' (A 69E)

(1.209) |na·t-| 'going after' + |-ehtaw| TA 'listen to' → |na·t-ehtaw-| → |na·sehtaw-| TA:
        e·h=na·sehtawa·wa·či 'they followed the sound of his voice' (O 61B)

(1.210) |pye·t-| 'coming' + |-a·pam| TA 'look at' → |pye·t-a·pam-| → |pye·sa·pam-| TA:
        e·h=pye·sa·pama·či 'he saw him coming' (X10-PBW 89)
        |na·kataw-| 'following' + |-a·pam| TA 'look at' → |na·kataw-a·pam-|
        → |na·kasawa·pam-| TA:
        e·h=na·kasawa·pama·wa·či 'they watched them all the way' (K-MGW 16)

In one case this replacement takes place instead of regular mutation:

(1.211) |mi·t-| 'defecate' + |-i·| AI ABSTR → |mi·t-i·-| → |mi·si·-| AI: *mi·si·wa* 'he defecates'
        (Cf. *mi·čitamwa* 'he defecates on it.)

13.3. Replacement of |N| by *s*. An underlying |N| in a TA stem is replaced by *s* before |-o| AI MID-REFL (**§53.5**):

(1.212) |kahkiN-| TA 'hide' + |-o| AI MID-REFL → |kahkiN-o-| → |kahkiso-| AI 'hide oneself':
        wi·h=kahkisoyani 'for you to hide yourself' (A 35B)
        (Cf. *kahkine·wa* 'he hid him'; *kahkiši* 'hide him!'.)

13.4. Loss of semivowels before vowels. A post-consonantal |w| drops before |o| or |o·|:

(1.213) |menw-| 'nicely' + |-ose·| AI 'walk' → |menw-ose·-| AI 'walk nicely':
        e·h=menomenose·niči "she [obv.] walked beautifully" (K-M 1137h; tr. HP)

(1.214) |wi·h=| FUT + |penaha·hkwaw-| TA 'comb the hair of' + |ke–ene| 1s–2s/IND
        → |ke-wi·h=penaha·hkwaw-ene| → |ki·h=penaha·hkwo·ne| (**§11.7**, 1.166)
        → *ki·h=penaha·hko·ne* 'let me comb your hair' (JM-TMF 34)

A post-consonantal |y| drops before |i| or |i·|:

(1.215) |ahk<u>y</u>-| 'earth' + |-i| inan. sg. → |ah<u>ky</u>-i| → ah<u>k</u>i 'earth'

A |y| ordinarily drops after |š| or |č|:

(1.216) |ne+| 1 + |-ška<u>šy</u>-| AN 'nail, claw' + |-a| anim. sg.

→ |ne-škaš<u>y</u>-a| → neškaša 'my nail' (1.154)

A |y| after |š| or |č| is optionally retained, however, if it is in a sequence *Cye·* that replaces |Cy-a| (§11.5, 1.154), and, at least for some speakers, in the finals |-ye·wi·| AI 'perform a task' and |-ya·| II ABSTR.

(1.217) |ki·š-| PERF + |-ye·wi·| AI 'perform a task' → |ki·<u>š</u>-<u>ye</u>·wi·-| AI:

ki <u>šye</u> wi wa, ki <u>še</u> wi wa 'he finishes the task'

(1.218) |me·neS-| 'shameful' + |-ya·| II ABSTR → |me·neS-<u>ya</u>·-| II:

me neš<u>ya</u> wi, me neš<u>a</u> wi 'it is shameful'

13.5. Replacement of |w| by *y*. In some cases |w| is replaced by *y* between a long front vowel and a back vowel:

(1.219) |ki·<u>w</u>-| 'around' + |-ose·| AI 'walk' → |ki·<u>w</u>-ose·-| AI → |ki·<u>yo</u>se·-| AI 'walk around':

we či-ki·ki <u>yo</u>se wa či 'the reason they go walking' (A 175D)

This replacement is variable, and there are doublets:

(1.220) *pi <u>ya</u> pehkwi, pi <u>wa</u> pehkwi* 'iron item'

This variability could stem from more than one factor, including dialectal variation in the original sound change, analogical reversal, and the variable presence of intervocalic semivowels in the two stylistic registers (**§3**).

ORTHOGRAPHY AND TRANSCRIPTION

Meskwaki Writing

14. The Meskwaki texts are editions of originals that were written in the vernacular writing system, a variant of the Upper Great Lakes Syllabary (Walker 1996:168-172; Kinkade and Mattina 1996:250; Goddard 1996). This is an alphabet-based syllabary that writes all the phonemic contrasts of the language except for vowel length and *h*. There is no capitalization or punctuation, except for a word divider, which is often omitted.

14.1. Transliteration. The narrow transliterations of the syllabary, given between shallow-pointed angle brackets (⟨..⟩), are phonetic. Thus the syllable that resembles "da" is transliterated ⟨ša⟩, apparent "tta" is ⟨ča⟩, and apparent "ga" is ⟨kwa⟩. As an exception to this, the graphic representation of *šk* is transliterated as ⟨sk⟩ when it consists of an ostensible ⟨s⟩ combined with ⟨k⟩ or ⟨kw⟩, and as ⟨šk⟩ when it is written with ⟨š⟩, or more precisely, with the beginning hook of the character that represents *š* attached to the second consonantal component to form a digraph.

14.2. Oral features in the written texts. The syllabary is easy to write, and the language as written generally flows along smoothly just the way the writer would have spoken it. Although some writers make corrections, one indication that the written texts are essentially spoken texts on paper is the fact that writers often correct themselves as they would in speaking. Thus, the repair particles =*we na* 'in fact, rather' and *ne pehe* 'I forgot' appear fairly often in written narratives. Sometimes repairs are unmarked and the mistake is left unretrieved in the written text, as it necessarily would be if spoken.

14.3. Writing conventions. Although sentence-level punctuation is not used, some writers occasionally employ devices in their writing to mark major sections of text. For example, in one place Kiyana places parentheses around the word *o ni* 'and then' to indicate the beginning of a major section (O 38I). At the end of O, Kiyana sets off a final oral colophon with a long space followed by an indentation (O 163E-F). In other texts he set off titles, speeches, and text-ending markers with fists or parentheses.

A word is continued from line to line and across page breaks with no indication of the split. Kiyana, however, adopted the practice of trying to end every page at a phonological word boundary. For example, in O there are 161 page breaks, but only three words run over from one page to the next.

Kiyana habitually writes ⟨ye⟩ not only for the syllables *ye* and *ye·*, but also for *yi* and *yi·*. Thus he writes *e yi·ki* 'also' as ⟨e ye ki⟩ (O 59F). This appears to be simply a personal writing habit and not the reflection of a unique pronunciation. Phonetic texts taken from Kiyana show [yi], and he occasionally writes ⟨yi⟩ as expected (O 8G, 133E). The editions normalize his writing of these syllables to *yi* and *yi·*, and the notes indicate the few cases where he uses ⟨yi⟩.

Writing Errors

15. Writers made relatively few spelling errors, and most that occur are the result of imperfect mechanical execution. Only a few writers are chronic bad spellers, who repeatedly mix up letters and syllables.

15.1. Wrong vowel or consonant. For all writers the commonest error is writing the wrong vowel or consonant. The single most frequent error is writing ⟨e⟩ for ⟨a⟩ (O 49G, 155A; A 52F), especially ⟨ne⟩ for ⟨na⟩ (O 100A, corrected; ⟨ne ne⟩ for ⟨na na⟩ [O 133E, corrected]) and ⟨me⟩ for ⟨ma⟩ (O 8F, 77A, 77E; corrected in O 9B, 78A). The reverse substitution is less common:

(1.221)   ⟨meskwakonanea⟩ for *meškwa·hkonene·ha* 'he would be painted red' (O 52B)

There is a word *meškwa·hkonane·ha* 'it would be painted red', the TI corresponding to the TA that is required, but since incorrect gender agreement is extremely rare the form in the manuscript is interpreted as a graphic error.

The most frequent consonant substitution is ⟨m⟩ for ⟨n⟩ (A 5D, 59F; O 104C, corrected), especially ⟨mo⟩ for ⟨no⟩ (O 7A; corrected in O 89H, 138B). Somewhat less common is ⟨n⟩ for ⟨m⟩ (A 57G).

A frequent pattern is the anticipation of the vowel or consonant of the following syllable, or the repetition (persistence) of the vowel or consonant of the preceding syllable. The first vowel anticipates the next vowel in:

(1.222)   ⟨pi si⟩ for ⟨pe si⟩ (O 115A, 123A)
(1.223)   ⟨ne no no⟩ for ⟨ne na no⟩ (A 56F)

The second vowel repeats the previous vowel in:

(1.224)   ⟨na kwa⟩ for ⟨na kwe⟩ (O 158A, corrected).

The consonant anticipates the consonant of the next syllable in:

(1.225)   ⟨mi mi⟩ for ⟨ni mi⟩ (O 21G, 80H)
(1.226)   ⟨te te⟩ for ⟨ke te⟩ (O 42A)
(1.227)   ⟨ta ta⟩ for ⟨na ta⟩ (O 55A)
(1.228)   ⟨to te⟩ for ⟨no te⟩ (O 96H)
(1.229)   ⟨ši ši⟩ for ⟨wi ši⟩ (O 67H)

(1.230) ⟨ya na ni⟩ for ⟨ya ya ni⟩ (A 71F)

(1.231) ⟨ka ki⟩ for ⟨a ki⟩ (A 98H)

Anticipation without substitution is found when an extra post-consonantal ⟨w⟩ occurs with a post-consonantal *w* in the next syllable:

(1.232) ⟨wi ke te mi no <u>nwa</u> kwe⟩ for *wiꞏh=ketemino <u>naꞏ</u>kwe* (O 84C)

(1.233) ⟨ki a ta <u>mwa</u> pwa⟩ for *kiꞏh=ata<u>ma</u>ꞏpwa* (O 90F)

The consonant repeats the one of the preceding syllable in:

(1.234) ⟨si so wi⟩ for ⟨si po wi⟩ (O 75G)

The anticipation and persistence of two-syllable sequences are seen in:

(1.235) ⟨ni sa ni sa⟩ for ⟨ni ka ni sa⟩ (O 108E)

(1.236) ⟨ni ka ni ka⟩ for ⟨ni ka ne ka⟩ (O 21E)

15.2. Omission of vowel or consonant. It is fairly common to find one of the consonantal components omitted in the writing of *šk*:

(1.237) ⟨i <u>se</u> se a⟩ for ⟨i <u>skwe</u> se a⟩ (*iškweꞏseꞏha* 'girl')

(1.238) ⟨i <u>kwe</u> se a ki⟩ for ⟨i <u>skwe</u> se a ki⟩ (*iškweꞏseꞏhaki* 'girls')

(1.239) ⟨ši⟩ for ⟨ški⟩ (A 65F, 115A)

Also not rare is the omission of ⟨w⟩ from a cluster:

(1.240) ⟨me sko <u>pa</u> ka na⟩ for *meškoh<u>pwa</u>ꞏkana* 'catlinite pipe' (O 91A)
         (Same, corrected, in O 45D.)

(1.241) ⟨pa⟩ for *-pwa* 2p (O 157J).

The omission of ⟨w⟩ in such cases as (1.240) and (1.241) conceivably reflects a pronunciation of the colloquial style (**§3**), but because writers sometimes add the omitted ⟨w⟩ later this omission is taken to be unintentional.

The omission of the vowel component of a syllable is rare. Perhaps the most frequent error of this type is the omission of ⟨a⟩ after a post-consonantal ⟨w⟩ (A 61D), but given the shapes of these elements this can be considered an instance of haplology. A few writers omit vowels from the final syllables of certain expressive and imitative words.

15.3. Omission of syllables. Because the syllable is the basic functional unit in the writing system, the omission of an entire syllable is actually more common than the omission of a vowel after a consonant or of a consonant that is not in a cluster:

(1.242) ⟨ma mi a ki⟩ for *mami<u>ši</u>ꞏhaki* 'ceremonial attendants' (O 5G)

(1.243) ⟨ki a ši pwa⟩ for *kiꞏh=aši<u>hto</u>ꞏpwa* 'you (pl.) shall make it' (O 62B)

(1.244) ⟨i i ši ke ke⟩ for *i<u>ši</u>hišikeke* 'if it keeps happening {so}' (O 91G; see note)

(1.245) ⟨<u>ne ne</u> ka pi so⟩ for *nenenekapiso* 'I was trembling' (A 65C)

(1.246) ⟨a kwa ma ta ni⟩ for *aꞏhkwamata<u>ka</u>ni* 'you might be sick' (A 108D)

(1.247) ⟨na i še wa⟩ for *nahi-<u>ši</u>ꞏšeꞏwa* 'he was a good hunter' (A 161E)

Syllables are often skipped at line ends (|) and at page breaks (‖):

(1.248) ⟨ma ni| ya wi⟩ for *ma<u>ni</u> niꞏyawi* 'this body of mine' (O 27G)

(1.249) ⟨ta ta ši mi‖ ka ni⟩ for *taꞏtašimi<u>ye</u>ꞏkani* 'don't talk about them' (A 53G)

(1.250) ⟨ki na na‖ ši so ya kwe⟩ for *ki na na e ꞏh=i<u>ši</u>soyakwe* 'our clan' (O 131G)

15.4. Writing extra syllables. Syllables are also sometimes written double:

(1.251) ⟨ne ka twe ne <u>ma ma</u> wa⟩ for *nekaꞏhtwe ne<u>ma</u>ꞏwa* 'I felt sorry for him' (A 163D)

In some cases an extra syllable or partial syllable appears to be a miswriting that was left unaltered in the flow of writing when the correct syllable was written after it:

(1.252) ⟨ka pw po twe ni⟩ for *ka<u>po</u>ꞏtwe ꞏ=꞊ni* 'then eventually' (A 163F)

(1.253) ⟨a kwi . ne se e <u>ne na</u> ki ni⟩ for *aʼkwi neʼseʼhena·kini* 'we didn't cure you' (O 120E)

15.5. Incorrect word dividers. Word dividers are sometimes inserted incorrectly in the middle of words:

(1.254) ⟨wi ši . ki⟩ for *wiʼšiki* 'firmly, loudly' (O 131F, 137F)

(1.255) ⟨e ta ši se se ki . e kwe⟩ for *eʼh=taši-seʼseʼkiheʼkwe* 'you were frightening him' (A 123F)

(1.256) ⟨či . na we ma či ki⟩ for *čiʼnaweʼmaʼčiki* 'those related to him' (A 165A)

(1.257) ⟨e ma wi . a či . mo a ki⟩ for *eʼh=mawi-aʼčimohaki* 'I went and told them' (A 166B)

Often inappropriate word dividers mark the end of what would be a possible word:

(1.258) ⟨wa pa ni ki . ni⟩ for *waʼpanikini* 'the next day (obv.; on repeated occasions)' (O 36C) Cf. the common word *waʼpaniki* 'the next day (obv.)'.

(1.259) ⟨i ni . ki| ke i.⟩ for *iʼniki=keʼhi* 'and those' (O 11H)
Cf. the common word *iʼni* 'that (inan.); then'.

In some cases it seems that the initial of a stem is marked as if it were the homophonous preverb:

(1.260) ⟨e ši . me na ko we⟩ for *eʼšimenakoʼwe* 'what I tell you (pl.) to do' (O 74A)

(1.261) ⟨ki ša ko či . te e ne a⟩ *kiʼšaʼkočiteʼheneʼha* 'one would feel terrible' (A 124A)

(1.262) ⟨wi ke ša či . e na ni⟩ for *wiʼh=kešaʼčihenaʼni* 'for me to be kind to you' (A 188B)

In the same way, a divider is sometimes added incorrectly before an enclitic:

(1.263) ⟨a kwi . me ko⟩ for *aʼkwi=meko* 'not indeed' (O36C)

(1.264) ⟨ma ni . ke i⟩ for *mani=keʼhi* 'and this' (O 21G)

(1.265) ⟨i ni . ča i⟩ for *iʼni=čaʼhi* 'so that' (O 86A)

This may happen even when there is elision:

(1.266) ⟨ši ši kwa na ni . na i⟩ for *šiʼšiʼkwanani·='nahi* 'and the gourds as well' (O 20A)

(1.267) ⟨ni na ke i .| ni⟩ for *niʼna=keʼhi·='ni* 'that's when I' (A 38B)

There is another example in (A 82E).

15.6. Wrong inflectional ending. Writing the wrong vowel or consonant sometimes results in ostensibly writing the wrong ending. Such cases are best taken as graphic errors, since the substitution of a wrong ending that differs by more than one written segment is extremely rare. The recognition of such errors is not automatic and may require consideration of the total context.

(1.268) ⟨e pi či ne se <u>ya</u> kwe⟩ as if 'as long as <u>we (inc.)</u> are living'
for *eʼhpiʼhči-neʼseʼ<u>ye</u>ʼkwe* 'as long as <u>you (pl.)</u> are living' (O 93C)

The form in (1.268) is in construction with the second plural emphatic pronoun; as written, with an ostensible first plural inclusive inflection, it does not make sense either in the clause or in the larger context (O 93D, 93G). These anomalies are eliminated by assuming that ⟨ya⟩ has been mistakenly written for ⟨ye⟩ and hence emending the text to have the second plural ending *-yeʼkwe* in place of the ostensible first plural inclusive *-yakwe*.

Similarly the writing of ⟨a⟩ instead of ⟨e⟩ (or ⟨o⟩) makes the ending of the common active form of the narrative aorist (|-a·či| 3s–3´) appear for the corresponding passive (indefinite-subject) form (|-eči| X–3, *-oči* after a stem in |-aw|). The interpretation in (1.269), made in the manuscript by a second hand, is required by the fact that the form is the complement of a verb with an indefinite subject:

(1.269) ⟨wi pwa wi me še ka <u>wa</u> či⟩
for *wiʼh=pwa wi-meʼšehka<u>wo</u>či* 'so that one does not touch them' (A 100A)

Graphic error is also the only reasonable interpretation in (1.270):

(1.270)   ⟨ma a ni . ki ke no wi . na ka mo na <u>ki</u>⟩
        for *ma·hani ki·ke·nowi-nakamo·na<u>ni</u>* 'these clan-feast songs' (O 19A)

Here the form as written would be *nakamo·naki*, with the animate plural ending *-aki* instead of the expected inanimate plural *-ani*, but there is no parallel for the word for 'song' being animate, and the correct gender is shown by the inanimate plural *ma·hani* 'these (inan.)' with which the noun in (1.270) forms a noun phrase.

The fact that the writers themselves sometimes correct errors of this kind supports the general validity of such emendations, where appropriate. For example, in (1.271) a form that would refer to 'your (pl.) singing' was changed by the writer to refer to 'our (inc.) singing' (cf. 1.268).

(1.271)   ⟨wi ne ne ne ki na we <u>me</u> kwe⟩, corrected to ⟨wi ne ne ne ki na we <u>ma</u> kwe⟩ (O 138C)
        wi·h=ne nenehkinawe <u>ma</u>kwe 'so that <u>our (inc.)</u> singing will make them mindful'

In (1.272) the writer corrected an ostensible active to the corresponding passive (cf. 1.269):

(1.272)   ⟨e a skwi <u>a</u> či⟩ changed to ⟨e a skwi <u>e</u> či⟩ *e·h=aškwihe<u>č</u>i* 'they were spared' (O 151G)

15.7. Whole word incorrect. Sometimes the wrong word is written, for example reversing opposites or substituting the wrong member of a set. This is, of course, a common type of slip of the tongue.

(1.273)   ⟨o ši se a ni⟩ (*ošise·hani* 'her uncle') for *o·sani* 'her father' (O 70E)

Sometimes the wrong word echoes another word in the context; the word intended may be a matter of conjecture:

(1.274)   ⟨ke ke ne me na kwe⟩, as if *kehke·nemena·kwe* 'if he knows you (pl.)',
        emended to *natawe·netamo·na·kwe* 'if he seeks them of yours (pl.)' (O 94H)

'If he knows you' makes no sense in the context; a stem is required that can form an appropriate higher verb for the complement clause *wi·h=nesa·či ki·hka·nwa wahi* 'for him to kill your friends', which the suggested emendation does. The stem of the form <u>*kehke·nemena·kwe*</u> that is represented in the manuscript presumably echoes that of *ki·h=<u>kehke·nema</u>·pwa* 'you (pl.) will know about him' (O 94F) occurring just previously; the inflection of the form is the appropriate one.

Occasionally an entire word is omitted:

(1.275)   <nehki> *wi·h=anemi-mehtose·neniwahkya·niwikwe·ni* (O 97A)
        'for however long the earth of mortals continues to exist'

The word *nehki* 'for {so} long a time' is not in the manuscript, but it is crucial to the meaning and present in other instances of the same construction (O 93G, 96B, 124G, 141F). Hence *nehki* can be supplied in (O 97A) with some confidence, but because an entire word has been added to what is in the manuscript, it is marked in the edition with the standard convention of pointed brackets. A possible explanation for the omission in this case is the fact the the previous word in the text ends with ⟨ni ki⟩; the writer presumably lost track of what he had written and after glancing back assumed that he had already written the word.

Conversely, an entire word may be repeated:

(1.276)   ⟨e a či mo a či . e a či mo a či⟩, as if *e·h=a·čimoha·či* 'he told her' twice (O 150D)

Although it sometimes happens that the same word is properly used twice in succession, in cases like (1.276) the correct interpretation is clearly to assume erroneous double writing.

Editing

   16. The editions aim to present a transcription of the spoken equivalent of what was written by the Meskwaki writer. Thus long vowels are marked, *h* is written, spelling errors are corrected, punctuation is added, and the text is broken into sentences and paragraphs. At the same time the information in the original text as written is preserved as far as practical. The omission of word dividers is indicated, and every change in the text of the manuscript is listed in the notes. In principle, then, the original text could be reconstructed by removing the added features and reversing the other changes.

   16.1. Editorial conventions. The representation of the manuscript text as an edited text entails the use of certain conventions. Several editorial symbols are used:

   (1.277)   Editorial symbols.

   Space ( ): a word boundary marked in the manuscript by a word divider.
   Hyphen (-): links or flags the parts of a compound stem;
       (1) used alone it indicates a manuscript word divider within a compound;
       (2) preceding part of a compound it indicates that another part or parts precede;
       (3) following part of a compound it indicates that another part or parts follow.
   Link (‿): a phonological word boundary with no manuscript word divider.
   Linked hyphen (⸗): equivalent to hyphen plus link.
   Bar (|): unmarked phonological word boundary at manuscript line end.
   Double bar (‖): manuscript page break (marked only if at a word boundary).
   Double hyphen (=): a clitic boundary, either
       (1) preceded by a proclitic prefix, or
       (2) followed by an enclitic or cliticized word.
   Apostrophe ('): the omission of either
       (1) a word-initial syllable in the variant forms of certain particles, or
       (2) an elided word-initial vowel in an enclitic or cliticized word.

The link, linked hyphen, bar, and double bar are not used in the citation of examples in this grammar. They are indicated in the editions.

   The use of the editorial symbols in (1.277) may be described by means of decision trees that determine the editorial treatment in each case:

   (1.278)   If a word divider is indicated,

           if it corresponds to a phonological word boundary,

               if neither preceded nor followed by part of a compound stem:
                   it is marked by a space.
               if preceded and followed by parts of a compound stem:
                   it is marked by a hyphen (-).
               if preceded by part of a compound stem:
                   it is marked by a hyphen plus a space (-).
               if followed by part of a compound stem:
                   it is marked by a space plus a hyphen (-).
           if it does not correspond to a phonological word boundary:
                   it is ignored in the edition and mentioned in the notes.

If a word divider is not indicated,
> but there is a phonological word boundary,
>> if it is neither preceded nor followed by part of a compound stem,
>>> if it is not at a manuscript line end:
>>>> it is marked by a linked space (‿).
>>> if it is at a manuscript line end:
>>>> it is marked by a vertical bar (|) and a space (or line break).
>> if it is both preceded and followed by parts of a compound stem,
>>> if it is not at a manuscript line end,
>>>> it is marked by a linked hyphen (͗).
>>> if it is at a manuscript line end,
>>>> it is marked by a vertical bar and hyphen (|-).
>> if it is preceded but not followed by part of a compound stem:
>>> if it is not at a manuscript line end,
>>>> it is marked by a hyphen and linked space (-‿).
>>> if it is at a manuscript line end,
>>>> it is marked by a vertical bar, hyphen, and space (|-).
>> if it is followed but not preceded by part of a compound stem:
>>> if it is not at a manuscript line end,
>>>> it is marked by a linked space and hyphen (‿-).
>>> if it is at a manuscript line end,
>>>> it is marked by a vertical bar, space (or line break), and hyphen (| -).
> but a proclitic prefix precedes:
>> it is marked by a double hyphen (=).
> but an enclitic or cliticized word follows,
>> if it is neither preceded nor followed by part of a compound stem:
>>> it is marked by a double hyphen (=).
>> if it is preceded by part of a compound stem and followed by an enclitic:
>>> it is marked by a hyphen and double hyphen (-=).
>> if it is followed by part of a compound stem elided with the preceding word:
>>> it is marked by a double hyphen and hyphen (=-).

If a manuscript page break occurs at a phonological word boundary it is indicated by a double bar (‖). This is preceded by a space (or hyphen) if there is a page-final word divider; it is preceded by no space (or a linked hyphen) if there is no word divider. Punctuation is placed inside a bar, double bar, or link. A word-internal manuscript page break is indicated in the notes.

16.2. Graphic ambiguities. The writing system is phonetically ambiguous on many points, and evidence not in the text must be used to determine the correct phonemic transcription.

In most cases the indication of vowel length and *h* is based on the pronunciation of native speakers as recorded by William Jones, Truman Michelson, James A. Geary, Paul H. Voorhis, and Ives Goddard. In a few cases comparative evidence from other languages may be used; the notes or the lexicon will specify the sources relied on. If a word or part of a word cannot be phonemicized it is written in a broad phonetic transcription of the syllabic text and placed between shallow-pointed angle brackets (⟨..⟩).

Morphemes attested with variable vowel length are transcribed to match the most common pronunciation, or the one less likely to be innovative. In some cases this is indeterminate (see the notes to O 78D, 84B, 98F). In the case of the variation between short *a* and long *a·* in initial syllables (§1.1) the usage of a particular writer can be determined from forms with initial change (§29.4), if they are attested. (Initial change replaces short *a* with *e·* but leaves long *a·* unaltered.) Thus in texts by Kiyana |wapaS-| 'disparage, waste' (1.9) is transcribed with a short vowel, since he always writes this initial with ⟨we⟩ in forms that have initial change:

(1.279)   *we·pašihto·ta* '(the one) who treats it disrespectfully' (K-SF 63)

On the other hand, *ma·takw-* 'cover' (1.10) is transcribed with a long vowel in Kiyana's texts, in light of his use of forms with virtual initial change that retain ⟨a⟩:

(1.280)   *ma·takwahamo·na·kwe* 'what they cloaked from you (pl.)' (K-Fish 70)

An additional problem is presented by stems beginning with the irregular reduplication ⟨a ya⟩, which was pronounced in the 1990's as *a·ya·-*. Forms with initial change on these stems are sometimes written with ⟨e ya⟩ and sometimes with ⟨a ya⟩:

(1.281)   *e·ya·taso·ke·wa·či* 'as many as lived in each lodge' (O 111B)

(1.282)   *a·ya·taso·ke·niči* 'as many (obv.) as lived in each lodge' (K-TCB 27, K-FC 695)

The editions normalize reduplicated stems of this type without initial change as having *a·ya·-*, since the frequent forms like (1.282) show that this variant was already established when the texts were written. The rarer forms with *e·ya·-* are taken as archaisms dating to a time when the stem without initial change had *aya·-*, which is given as the underlying form in the interlinears for just these forms.

The sequences *awo* (*awo·*, *a·wo*, *a·wo·*) and *e·wo* (*e·wo·*) are sometimes written ⟨a o⟩ and ⟨e o⟩; this is the only spelling used by some writers and is occasionally used by others:

(1.283)   *nye·wokoni* 'four days'

        Written ⟨nye wo ko ni⟩ (Kiyana), ⟨nye o ko ni⟩ (Sam Peters).

These writings are graphically ambiguous between a reading of the second syllable as *wo* or *wo·* and a reading as *ho* or *ho·*. Similarly ⟨a i⟩ may be written for *ayi* (*ayi·*). One word has never been found with ⟨y⟩ written and is phonemicized with a vowel sequence:

(1.284)   *nanai·hta, nanai·hta·wi* 'fortuitously'

        Written ⟨na na i ta⟩, ⟨na na i ta wi⟩.

Presumably (1.284) has generalized the colloquial pronunciation (§3) in which an intervocalic semivowel was dropped (cf. *šepawi·hta* 'luckily', usually pronounced *šepai·hta*).

Some contrasting grammatical forms cannot be distinguished in syllabic writing. For example, in inflections of the conjunct type first singular forms marked with |-a·n| 1s and second singular forms with |-an| 2s are always homographs. In a dialogue it may be unclear without analysis of the entire context whether a given form is a statement or a question and which one of the interlocutors it refers to. The ambiguity may persist over several sentences:

(1.285)   *e·h=pwa·wi-ki·ši-kehke·netamani* 'because you don't yet know it' (A 105F)

        Michelson: *e·hpwa·wiki·šikehke·netama·ni* "though I did not know about this"

In editing (1.285) Michelson followed his translator's rendition as first singular rather than the dictated phonetic text, which has the second singular. In his edition the same error continues through the following four lines (A 106A, 106B, 106C).

Similarly, the conjunct endings |-ena·kw| 3,X–2p and |-enakw| 3,X–12 are homographs.

(1.286)   *ki·ši-mama·či·hena·kwa* 'the one who has created you (pl.)' (O 83D)

        Or: *ki·ši-mama·či·henakwa* 'the one who has created us (inc.)'

The form with the second plural object in (1.286) is adopted in the edition because it is in a section of a formal speech in which the man speaking consistently uses the second plural, disassociating himself from the people he is addressing. Some speakers, however, feel that only the inclusive form in (1.286) is appropriate in discourse between human beings.

Other common endings that are homographs are those with |-at| 2s–3 and |-a·-t| 3s–3´:

    (1.287)   *či nawe mačiki* 'your (sg.) relatives'
               či nawe ma či̵ki 'his (obv.) relatives'

Stems that make initial change by prefixing *e·-* to the initial *t* of the stem (**§29.4**) have oblique-headed participles that are homographs of the corresponding aorist forms with *e·h=*:

    (1.288)   *e·to·tawa wa či* 'how they treated them (obv.)' (O 152D)
            Or: *e·h=to·tawa wa či* 'they treated them (obv.) {so}'.

The second, aorist reading of (1.288) is the one in Michelson's edition (Michelson 1921:62.18-19); it is a possible alternative.

Some cases of graphic ambiguity are inherently unresolvable since the homographs are grammatically equivalent; only the general context can be used to deduce the reading intended by the writer:

    (1.289)   *owi·kewa wi* 'their house' (O 106B)
            Or: *owi·ke·hwa wi* 'their little house'.
    (1.290) |ke–ekowa·wa| 3s–2p/IND
            Or: |ke–eko·hwa·wa| 3s–2p/DIM/IND.

Because the diminutives in (1.289) and (1.290) cannot be distinguished in syllabic writing, their use cannot be documented by written texts.

If there seem to be two plausible ways to edit the same syllabic sequence the alternative reading is given in the notes, but in almost all cases one of the possible readings is preferable to the other. An alternative in the earlier edition of Michelson is always given:

    (1.291)   ⟨ni na yo ma ni⟩: edited as *ni na= 'yo=mani* 'in my case, for example' (O 146F)
            Michelson: *ni n=ayo·h=mani* 'as for me here present'

In (1.291) the reading with *=iyo* 'for, for example' fits the context, while Michelson's reading with *ayo·h=mani* 'here, in the present case' is not quite right.

16.3. Word boundaries. Word dividers are often not written in the manuscripts, especially at the end of a manuscript line. Writers vary greatly in the consistency with which they use them. Decisions must thus be made about whether and how to mark various kinds of word boundaries in the edition.

Some free particles and pronouns are often cliticized, especially to the complex of enclitics that follows the first word of a sentence. This cliticization appears to be at least partly optional, to judge by the occasional use of word dividers and the readings of native speakers. Thus it is often arbitrary, at least at the current state of knowledge, whether to indicate such a particle as cliticized in cases where no word divider is written at a line end:

    (1.292)   ⟨o ni| ma ni⟩ edited as: *o ni=mani* 'and this' (O 16C)
    (1.293)   ⟨i ni ki me ko| še ski⟩ edited as: *i niki=meko=še ški* 'it was only that those' (O 32F)
    (1.294)   ⟨ma na| wi na⟩ edited as: *mana=wi na* 'this (anim.), however' (O 81C)
    (1.295)   ⟨a kwi| ta ta ki⟩ edited as: *a·kwi=ta taki* 'in a way not' (O 96G)
    (1.296)   ⟨ma ni| na ka⟩ edited as: *mani=na·hka* 'and this' (O 98B)
    (1.297)   ⟨na ka mo na ni| ki na na⟩ edited as: *nakamo nani=ki na na* 'songs us' (O 138F)

Similarly, some particles are used with verbs both as preposed free particles and as preverbs (**§38.3**). It can therefore be arbitrary whether or not to mark them as part of a compound:

    (1.298)   *a·kwi aya pami-pya ničini* 'they (obv.) did not come back' (O 18D)
            Or: *a·kwi aya pami pya ničini.*

In (1.298) the edition takes *aya·pami* 'back again' to be a preverb and links it with a hyphen. But *aya·pami* is attested with *pya·-* 'come' as a free particle (4.101*a*) as well as a preverb, so either editorial treatment is possible.

16.4. Constituent boundaries. Clause and sentence demarcation can also present challenges, given the absence of punctuation. In addition to the requirements of meaning, characteristic patterns of word order provide the best evidence for where syntactic units begin and end. One common problem arises with particles that may occur at either the beginning or the end of a sentence. Determining which sentence to place them in sometimes depends on evaluating slight differences of meaning between the two possibilities. The editions of A and O differ from those of Michelson in many such cases (e.g., in A 89A, 155D, 164A; O 58G, 78E, 97F, 101E, 115I, 117I, 133B). Similarly, a noun phrase or a more complex collocation may make sense either at the end of one sentence or at the beginning of the following one (e.g., in A 41H, 164A, 166A, 172A, 172E; O 56I, 68G, 72I, 122B, 122D).

Dependent clauses may also be hard to place. In (O 156F) *wa·wo·či wa·čini* 'the places where they came from' would presumably be a syntactically permitted locative complement to either the higher verb or its complement. It is translated with the former since that seems to give a better overall reading. Another such example is in (A 7B).

16.5. Emendation. Even though the texts are the autograph originals of the authors, they contain writing errors, like any spontaneous writing (§15). Emendation is therefore necessary. The goal of the editions has been to identify and correct these errors, with full annotation. The greatest danger in emending a text is always that a rare but genuine form or usage will be expunged as an error. The approach taken, therefore, is one of minimal emendation, giving the benefit of the doubt to unusual forms and variants where a case can be made that they are plausible.

Common, easily explained errors can, in general, be reliably emended. The best support for the validity of an emendation is evidence that the writing in question was changed elsewhere by the same writer. For example, in one text Kiyana writes a derivative of *nakamo·ni* 'song' with ⟨nekamo⟩ instead of the expected ⟨nakamo⟩. Given that cognate forms in related languages (like Cree *nikamon* 'song', Menominee *neka·mon*) reflect Proto-Algonquian **nekamo-* 'sing a ritual song', the writing ⟨nekamo⟩ is conceivably an archaism that should be retained in the edition. Against this, however, is the more immediate fact that in the same text the writer wrote this stem 45 times with ⟨na⟩, and the two other times he wrote it with ⟨ne⟩ he changed this to ⟨na⟩. The best explanation is, therefore, that Kiyana simply wrote ⟨ne⟩ for ⟨na⟩, a writing habit that was not uncommon for him. There are thus several lines of argument that support the emendation.

In some cases there is uncertainty whether a written form is a genuine archaism or a simple error:

(1.299)   *a·kwi .. otehči-nepwa·ya·nini* 'I was not catching on' (manuscript; O 103B)
          Or: *a·kwi .. otehči-nepwa·hka·ya·nini* (Michelson 1921:48.15).

The form in the manuscript was not accepted by the native speakers consulted by Michelson and me. There was agreement that a syllable ⟨ka⟩ should be added, making the ordinary stem *nepwa·hka·-* 'be smart'. There is, however, other evidence for the existence of a short stem *nepwa·-* 'be smart', as written in the manuscript to O 103B (1.299), in particular after preverbs like *otehči* 'getting'. Meskwaki has the same short stem in the compound *tahpi-nepwa·-* 'to catch on, realize things', with preverb *tahpi* 'through'. Because it seems distinctly possible that the short stem in (1.299) was correct as written, it was accepted in the edition. On the available evidence, however, proof is impossible; Michelson and the speakers who rejected this form may well have been correct.

In some cases where the written text is clearly defective it may not be clear what was intended.

> (1.300)   *i na ka=ke ·h=na ·hkači* 'And over at the other place .. also .. that (anim.)' (O 61A), emending manuscript ⟨inaka͟kanakači⟩.
>
> Or: *i na ka na ·hkač(i)* "Likewise yon .." (Michelson 1921:36.8).

The edition takes the second ⟨ka⟩ in the manuscript as an error for ⟨ke⟩ that repeats the preceding vowel; Michelson assumed that it was dittography of the preceding syllable. The emendation to *=ke ·hi* 'moreover' gives a smoother transition, but the effect is idiomatic and subtle.

Some emendations rely heavily on editorial judgment:

> (1.301)   *e ·h=one mowen͟ihena ·kwe* 'that he gave it to you to be your breath' (O 84A), emending manuscript ⟨eonemowienakwe⟩.
>
> Or: *e ·h=one mowihena ·kwe* (Michelson 1921:42.29).

Kiyana's written form in (1.301), without *-en-* after the *w*, was accepted by speakers consulted by Michelson and me, but such a form would be morphologically unique. The stem is the complex result of several layers of secondary derivation which literally means 'to cause' (*-h*) 'to have as one's breath' (*one moweni-*); *one moweni-* 'have breath' is a verb of possession regularly formed from the noun *ne mowen-* 'breath', which is derived from *ne mo-* 'breathe'. The stem Kiyana wrote is superficially plausible if one loses track of the layers of derivation, but it is not well formed. It might be defended as the equivalent of a slip-of-the-tongue nonce formation, but this does not seem a sound enough basis for accepting it in the edition. Instead its virtual existence is acknowledged in the textual notes and in this paragraph.

Some ostensible emendations restore an original text that was interfered with by earlier readers:

> (1.302)   *wi ·h=ki wi-a čimo ·hiyani* 'for you to go around telling your little tale' (O 157I), following manuscript ⟨wikiwiačimo͟iyani⟩, as originally written.
>
> Cf. *wi ·h=ki wi-a čim͟oyani* (Michelson 1921:64.11-12).

In (1.302) the syllable ⟨i⟩ (corresponding to *-·hi-*), which makes the stem diminutive, was erased in the manuscript, but as it was not written over this was presumably done by a second hand. This change may have been made by someone who, on first reading, took this form as the contextually inappropriate homograph *wi ·h=ki wi-a čimo͟hiyani* (with short *o*) 'for you to go around telling me'. The edition restores Kiyana's original text.

16.6. Editing song texts. Special conventions are used in editing song texts. Songs often contain unusual forms, and in addition the words may be sung with phonetic distortion. (An extended discussion and analysis of Meskwaki song texts is in Goddard [1993]).

The edition of the songs in "The Owl Sacred Pack" presents two versions of the Meskwaki text. The first line, enclosed in square brackets, is a broad phonetic transcription of the text as sung; this follows closely Michelson's phonetic rendition, with the symbols updated and normal sub-phonemic variation ignored. The sung text recorded by Michelson is often followed when it differs from the text as written by Kiyana. Michelson's line breaks are also generally followed, except where the syllable count or other factors point to an alternative.

The second line is a phonemic, spoken-word equivalent of the first line; because many song words do not exist as ordinary spoken words this is necessarily an analytical reconstitution. Also on the second line, syllables and inflectional affixes that are absent from the sung words are restored in pointed brackets (<..>) to the extent necessary to make complete spoken words (as in 1.275).

The interlinear morphemic analysis supplies additional missing elements, in particular omitted aorist preverbs.

Chapter 2.

§§17-26. Grammatical Categories

INTRODUCTION

Grammatical Categories and Morphological Processes

17. Meskwaki distinguishes a large number of grammatical categories. Some categories are basic properties that word stems have in the abstract, along with their meanings. Other categories are specified only within sentences. Both kinds of categories, and their combinations, are indicated by morphological processes. Viewed statically, the morphological processes are the formal patterns of the language, and the grammatical categories comprise the content expressed by these formal patterns.

For example, the stem |nakamo·n-| has the inherent properties that it means 'song', that it is a noun (**§18.2**), and that it is of inanimate gender (**§19**). To be used in a sentence, however, it must minimally undergo the morphological process of suffixation. Specifically, it must add (or, to put it differently, occur with) one of a small set of inflectional endings that its categorization as an inanimate noun permits. For instance, the process of suffixing |+ani|, the plural ending for inanimate nouns (2.2), to the stem |nakamo·n-| 'song' produces the word *nakamo·nani* 'songs' (2.1, 2).

17.1. The Marking of Categories. The morphological processes express the grammatical categories and to some extent provide an index to them, but the correspondence between content and formal expression is inexact. Plural is a single grammatical category present in words of many kinds, but there is no single morpheme that marks it. Every morpheme that marks plural also marks one or more other grammatical categories as well and is restricted to use with certain other morphemes or types of stem:

(2.1) Plural marking
   (a) *nakamo·ni* 'song', *nakamo·nani* 'songs' (|+ani| inanimate plural, nouns)
   (b) *neniwa* 'man', *neniwaki* 'men' (|+aki| animate plural, nouns)
   (c) *e·h=pya·či* 'he came', *e·h=pya·wači* 'they came' (|-wa·| third plural, conjunct verbs)
   (d) *newi·seni* 'I ate', *newi·senipena* 'we (exc.) ate' (|-pena| first plural, indicative verbs)
   (e) *na·kwa·no* 'go (you sg.)', *na·kwa·ko* 'go (you pl.)' (|+ko| second plural, imperative)

At the same time, an identical morphological process may mark different categories in different circumstances. The noun ending |+ani| marks the plural when added to an inanimate noun, but it marks the obviative singular when added to an animate noun (2.2). The identical shape of |+ani| INpl and |+ani| OBVsg does not point to the existence of a single grammatical category.

In fact, the grammatical categories expressed by an inflected word cannot be read directly off the morphemes that compose that word. What grammatical categories are expressed by a word depends on the category of the stem, the inflectional morphemes, and the paradigmatic relationships of the inflected form, that is, the contrasts with other minimally different forms. For example, the word *kemiˑnenepwa* means 'I gave it (or him or them) to you (pl.)'. Its component parts are a stem |miˑN-| TA+O 'give O2 to' (2.85) and the inflection |ke–enepwa|, which consists of the second-person prefix |ke+| 2 (3.137), a theme sign |-eN| (→ |-ene|) that indicates that the primary object (here, the recipient) is second person (**§29.7(d)**), and a suffix |-pwa| that marks second person plural (3.186). This form unambiguously makes pronominal reference to a first person singular subject, even though it contains no morpheme that marks first person singular (or first person or singular separately). This is because, in the particular paradigm this form occurs in, second-person objects of third persons and indefinites are not marked with the theme sign |-eN|; hence the use of |-eN| here means that the subject can only be first person. Also, it is a general feature of the inflection of transitive verbs in all categories that first and second persons (regardless of which is the subject and which the object) cannot both be pluralized, and the rule established by the rest of the paradigm is that if the first person is plural it is marked as plural, and the second person is then ambiguously either singular or plural. Therefore, since in *kemiˑnenepwa* the second person is pluralized, the first person must be singular. This form also makes pronominal reference to a secondary object (here, the thing given), which may be of either gender and either number, even though there is no overt morpheme marking this argument. This pronominal reference is, however, required by the stem |miˑN-| TA+O 'give O2 to', which always takes both a primary and a secondary object.

Still, even though the inflectional morphology does not correspond in a simple way to the categories it marks, it provides a guide to the categories that function in the language and is useful as an organizational framework for description.

PARTS OF SPEECH

Parts of Speech and their Inflection

18. There are four parts of speech: nouns, verbs, pronouns, and particles. Nouns and verbs are defined by the patterns of inflection they take, which have several subtypes. Pronouns have a number of different inflectional patterns and function as various kinds of substitutes and stand-ins for nouns and the pronominal categories of inflection. Particles, which are not inflected, fall into crosscutting syntactic and functional categories.

18.1. Types of inflection. The inflection of a word may be either an ending or a combination of a prefix and an ending. Patterning as a prefix there is also initial change (IC; **§29.4**), a morpheme of vowel ablaut that replaces the first vowel of the stem (or compound stem), affecting a few stems irregularly; with two exceptions, it has no effect on long vowels.

In the explanation of examples and in the interlinear analysis of texts, endings (that is, suffix complexes) are written with a preceding |+|, and prefixes are written with a following |+| or |=|.

When the combined inflection of a prefix and an ending is cited, a dash (–) is placed between them to indicate the position of the stem, and the |+|'s are omitted as redundant; a dash with no prefix makes it explicit that what follows is the entire inflection, not just an ending. In interlinear analysis the label for the combined inflection, incorporating the component of meaning contributed by the prefix, is placed beneath the ending, except that the prefix |wi·h=| FUT is only glossed separately.

All endings occurring in the "Autobiography" and "Owl Sacred Pack" texts are given in the *List of endings* (**Appendix 2**). The occurring inflectional combinations are listed separately, and the endings are analyzed into their constituent suffixes, which are distinguished from endings by being cited with a preceding hyphen (-).

18.2. Nouns and nominal categories. The core inflection of nouns defines the nominal categories: gender (animate or inanimate; **§19**), number (singular or plural; **§20**), and obviation (proximate or obviative; **§21**). These categories do not have separate inflectional labels but are expressed in inflection by unitary suffixes that indicate a combination of two or three of them together. In (2.2) the core inflection is given for a noun of each gender, animate (a) and inanimate (b). Following the gloss of each form is a full specification of the combination of categories indicated; the ending and its abbreviated label; and the abbreviated label (or labels) used for the corresponding pronominal inflections on verbs.

(2.2) Core Inflection of Nouns

	Inflected nouns	Endings	On verbs
(a)	*neniwa* 'man' (animate proximate singular)	|+a| ANsg	(3s)
	neniwaki 'men' (animate proximate plural)	|+aki| ANpl	(3p)
	neniwani 'man (obv.)' (animate obviative singular)	|+ani| OBVsg	(3´s)
	neniwahi 'men (obv.)' (animate obviative plural)	|+ahi| OBVpl	(3´p)
(b)	*nakamo ni* 'song' (inanimate singular)	|+i| INsg	(0s, 0´s)
	nakamo nani 'songs' (inanimate plural)	|+ani| INpl	(0p, 0´p)

The nominal categories are distinct from the pronominal categories on verbs that show agreement with them and hence are labeled differently.

Gender is an inherent (lexical) property of each noun, while number and obviation are ascribed in connection with the use of nouns in particular utterances. A noun may also be marked as vocative by different endings that distinguish only number (**§23**). Nouns have a secondary inflection for pronominal possessor (**§22.1**), and they may also be inflected for the locative (**§24**). The suffixes marking the core inflection and the locative suffix are mutually exclusive, but one or the other must be marked on every noun that is not a vocative, following any inflection for possessor. Different patterns of inflection for possession distinguish two classes of nouns, each with two subsets (2.67-70).

18.3. Verbs. An inherent property of every verb is its specification as taking from one to three core arguments. In addition to subject (**§22.2**), which every verb takes, the other core arguments are primary object and secondary object (**§22.3**). Verbs are inflected for pronominal reference to subject and primary object, and for mode and tense. Verbs may also be specified for taking obliques (**§22.4**).

There are four major categories of verb stems, each specialized for use with an intransitive subject or a primary object of one of the two genders (**§19**). Corresponding to each of these four categories is a distinct set of inflectional paradigms. The basic division is into intransitive and transitive verbs, which are subdivided according to gender.

Intransitive verb stems are specialized for use with subjects of a particular gender. Animate intransitive (AI) verbs are used with animate subjects, and inanimate intransitive (II) verbs are used with inanimate subjects:

(2.3)   AI: *meškosiwa* 'he (anything of animate gender) is red' (stem |meškosi-| AI 'be red')

              II: *meškwa·wi* 'it (anything of inanimate gender) is red' (stem |meškwa·-| II 'be red')

Typically, as in (2.3), the contrast in gender is indicated both in the verb stems (|meškosi-| AI, |meškwa·-| II) and in the inflections (|–wa| 3s/IND, |–wi| 0s/IND).

There are three formal classes of AI verbs: vowel stems, deleting consonant stems, and retaining consonant stems. These inflect differently with some suffixes. The deleting consonant stems are those ending in underlying |n|; the |n| is deleted before |č|, |s|, |k|, |hk| (which becomes |k|), and |-ni| obv. but is retained with inserted |e| before |t|, |p|, and |-no| 2s/IMP. The retaining consonant stems are those not ending in underlying |n|, including those that retain surface *n* in all forms, which are analyzed as having underlying |N|. All consonant stems add |e| word-finally and between a retained stem-final consonant and the consonant of a suffix (**§8.2**), except when the suffix is one that inserts connective |o| (**§8.3**).

Intransitive verbs typically come in pairs, with different stems for each gender (2.3), but some are used for only one gender (2.4; 2.82), and some have the same stem for both genders (2.5).

(2.4)   *mayo·wa* 'he weeps' (|mayo·-| AI 'weep')

(2.5)   *nepiwiwa* 'he is wet', *nepiwiwi* 'it is wet' (|nepiwi-| AI, II 'be wet')

AI verbs that lack a corresponding II may be used with inanimate subjects in either of two ways. In an archaic pattern, attested only in ritual songs, the AI is used with II inflections:

(2.6)   *mayo·wi* 'it weeps' (|mayo·-| AI 'weep', |–wi| 0s/IND) (song; O 34D, 34G)

In the productive pattern, an II stem is derived from the AI by a secondary final (**§52.1**), usually |-·mikat| II ABSTR (2.7) but in one class of forms |-ya·| II ABSTR.

(2.7)   *mayo·mikatwi* 'it weeps' (|mayo·mikat-| II 'weep', |–wi| 0s/IND)

This final is paired with |-·mikesi| AI ABSTR, which may be used in similar circumstances when the subject is a non-sentient animate or otherwise not in control of what would normally be a conscious act for a person (2.8; 4.268).

(2.8)   *wi·h=peno·mikesiyakwe* 'when we (inc.) shall depart this earth' (K-WYB 200)

              (|peno·mikesi-| AI ← |peno·-| AI 'depart, go home' + |-·mikesi| AI ABSTR)

Transitive verb stems are specialized for use with primary objects of one gender: transitive animate (TA) verbs are used with animate primary objects, and transitive inanimate (TI) verbs are used with inanimate primary objects:

(2.9)   TA: *mehkawe·wa* 'he found him, them (anything of animate gender)'

              (|mehkaw-| TA 'find')

              TI: *mehkamwa* 'he found it, them (of inanimate gender)' (|mehk-| TI 'find')

Here again there is a contrast in both the verb stems (|mehkaw-| TA, |mehk-| TI) and the inflections (|–e·wa| 3s–3ʹ/IND, |–amwa| 3s–0/IND).

Within the TI category there are three formal subclasses: TI(1), TI(2), and TI(3). The endings used with TI(1) stems always include a theme sign |-am| (realized as *-am-*, *-a*, *-a·-*); those used with TI(2) stems have a theme sign |-o·| (realized as *-o·-*, *-o*); and those used with TI(3) stems have no theme sign:

(2.10)   *ne·tamwa* 'he saw it' (|ne·t-| TI(1) 'see', |–amwa| 3s–0/IND)

            pye·to·wa 'he brought it' (|pye·t-| TI(2) 'bring', |–o·wa| 3s–0/IND)

            mi·čiwa 'he ate it' (|mi·či-| TI(3) 'eat', |–wa| 3s–0/IND)

All TI(2) stems end in |t| or |ht|. There are only a small number of TI(3) stems.

Transitive verbs almost always come in pairs, though for one large set the TA and TI stems are homophonous.

The correlation between transitive and intransitive stems and transitive and intransitive syntax is not absolute. Some formally TI stems occur sometimes or always without an object, and some formally AI stems occur sometimes or always with an object (**§22.3**).

Participles (**§26.13**) add to a verb a pronominal reference to the head of a relative clause, which need not be an argument otherwise represented in the inflection and, in fact, is not restricted as to its syntactic role.

The numerous verbal modes fall into three orders, defined by their different patterns of inflection: the independent (**§26.1-5**), conjunct (**§26.6-21**), and imperative (**§26.22**). The conjunct has several major sub-orders.

18.4. Emphatic pronouns and pronominal categories. The emphatic pronouns are listed in (2.11). Following the gloss of each form is the full descriptive name and the abbreviated label used in analysis:

(2.11)				
	ni na	'I'	first person singular	(1s)
	ki na	'you (sg.)'	second person singular	(2s)
	wi na	'he, she'	third person singular	(3s)
	ni na na	'we (exc.)'	first person plural, exclusive	(1p)
	ki na na	'we (inc.)'	first person plural, inclusive	(12)
	ki nwa wa	'you (pl.)'	second person plural	(2p)
	wi nwa wa	'they'	third person plural	(3p)

These seven emphatic pronouns are the only independent personal pronouns. They refer only to people or personified beings. They always add some degree of emphasis, focus, or contrast to the bare pronominal notion. Two of them may not be used together to emphasize two arguments of the same verb.

The emphatic pronouns define the seven basic pronominal categories, or persons (2.11). The nominal categories (2.2) intersect the pronominal categories in the animate third persons ("3") and supply further differentiation, to include animate obviatives ("3′"), inanimates ("0"), and inanimate obviatives ("0′"), none of which have pronouns in the emphatic set. An abstract third person category that includes both animate and inanimate can be recognized in some suffixes that mark both genders ("3,0"). For most purposes, however, it is more useful to consider the third person animate and third person inanimate to be separate basic categories.

An eighth pronominal category, the indefinite ("X"), which has no corresponding independent pronoun, also implies human or human-like agency. A verb may be inflected for an indefinite subject, and a noun may be inflected for an indefinite possessor (**§22.1**). Indefinite objects are indicated by AI secondary derivatives of TA verbs (**§53.1, 3**). When more than one indefinite-person form is used in a sentence, all the indefinites usually refer logically to the same person or people (A 4B, 16E, 44F, 63F, 98F-101E, 102F, 103BC). The indefinite may be translated as 'we', 'you', 'they', 'one', or 'people', in the indefinite senses these words have; a transitive verb with an indefinite subject is often equivalent to an English passive.

A third-person animate singular pronoun in actual use may be translated by any third-person English pronoun or by an indefinite expression like 'some', 'one', or 'any'. In examples cited without regard to a specific context, however, this pronominal category is, by convention, ordinarily glossed simply as 'he' ('him', 'his'), except where biology or cultural norms call for a feminine pronoun. The gloss 'it' outside a specific context refers only to something of inanimate gender, and not to living things that might be referred to as 'it' in English.

The first person exclusive excludes 'you' (the person or people spoken to), and the first person inclusive includes 'you'. The exclusive is also used in thoughts and soliloquies.

18.5. Demonstrative pronouns. Demonstrative pronouns indicate the nominal categories of the noun they modify (2.12) or substitute for and add the specification of several types and degrees of real or pragmatic distance.

(2.12) Agreement of demonstrative and noun

> *i·na neniwa* 'that man' (animate proximate singular)
> *i·niki neniwaki* 'those men' (animate proximate plural)
> *i·nini neniwani* 'that man (obv.)' (animate obviative singular)
> *i·nihi neniwahi* 'those men (obv.)' (animate obviative plural)
> *i·ni mi·ša·mi* 'that sacred bundle' (inanimate singular)
> *i·nini mi·ša·mani* 'those sacred bundles' (inanimate plural)

The seven demonstrative sets, as exemplified by the animate singular of each, are: *mana* 'this (near at hand, well known, or here presented)' (§31.2, 3); *i·na* 'that (present but away, or referred to before)' (§31.2, 4); *i·ya·ka* 'that (other, elsewhere nearby)' (§31.2, 5); *i·na·ka* 'that (other, elsewhere at a distance, or previously discussed)' (§31.2, 6); *ma·hiya* 'that (going away, or recently departed)' (§31.2, 7); *i·niya* 'that (gone, or referred to yet earlier)' (§31.2, 8); *anika·na·ka* 'that (further on)' (§31.2, 9).

18.6. Indefinite pronouns. The indefinite pronouns have different stems for the two genders: *owiye·ha* 'someone, anyone', *ke·ko·hi* 'something, anything'.

One use of these pronouns is in statements of absence; it is only in this construction that the indefinite pronouns have plural forms:

(2.13)   *nekya a·k=owiye·ha.* 'My mother was not at home.' (K-Auto 152)
　　　　(*nekya* 'my mother; *a·kwi* 'not'; |owiye·h-| 'anyone', |+a| ANsg)
　　　　pešekesiwaki a·k=owiye·haki 'there are no deer (any more)' (K-Auto 271)
　　　　(*pešekesiwaki* 'deer (pl.)'; *a·kwi* 'not'; |owiye·h-| 'anyone', |+aki| ANpl)
　　　　a·kwi=ke·ko·hani owa·wanani 'the eggs are gone' (K-M 772c)
　　　　(*a·kwi* 'not'; |ke·ko·h-| 'anything', |+ani| INpl; *owa·wanani* 'eggs')

Beside the indefinite pronouns there are also homophonous nouns derived from them: *owiye·ha* 'a person, some creature, a (large) animal', with diminutive *owiye·he·ha* 'a (small) animal'; *ke·ko·hi* 'thing, things', diminutive *ke·ko·he·hi*. These inflect like nouns, except that the inanimate is generally used only in the singular. The stems of the indefinite pronouns may also enter into the derivation of stems or parts of stems of other types.

18.7. Interrogative pronouns. The interrogative pronouns also have different stems for the two genders: *we·ne·ha* 'who?', *we·kone·hi* 'what?'. Interrogative as a semantic category cuts across several parts of speech, including also verbs of being derived from the interrogative pronouns (*we·ne·hiwa* 'who is he?'), question words that are formally part of the demonstrative system (*ta·na* 'which one is he?; where is he?'), and various particles (*kaši* 'how? what?'; *ke·swi* 'how many?'; *ta·ni* 'how? what?'; 2.153).

18.8. Place-Holder pronoun. The place-holder pronoun is inflected for nominal category or for the locative. It is used as a hesitation substitute for a name or a noun that cannot be recalled, or which is treated as too obvious in the pragmatic context to require explicit specification: *awahi·ma, awahi·na* 'what's-his-name'; *awahi·mi, awahi·ni* 'whatchamacallit'; *awahi·meki* 'at you-know-the-place'. (The different stems are dialectal variants.)

The place-holder pronoun is also used together with a noun or name in a naming construction that marks the introduction into the conversation of someone or something presented as new and unexpected (2.14; 5.164*b*).

(2.14)   *awahi·ma e·yi·ki i·nahi tana·čimoha·pi pešekesiwi-owi·wi·na.* (O 64J)
          'The one called Deer Horn was instructed there as well.'
          (*awahi·ma* (placeholder, anim.); *e·yi·ki* 'as well'; *i·nahi* 'there';
          |tana·čimoh-| TA 'instruct {somewhere}', |–a·pi| X–3/IND; *p.-o.* 'Deer Horn')

Example (2.14) shows the typical construction: the place-holder pronoun *awahi·ma* and the introduced name *pešekesiwi-owi·wi·na* 'Deer Horn' form a discontinuous noun phrase with the pronoun in sentence-initial position and the name on the other side of the verb.

The stem of the place-holder pronoun is also used as a default noun final in derived nouns (2.15) and in exocentric locative constructions (2.16; 4.113*j*); the preceding element is subject to mutation, as if it were the first member of a compound that had its final |-i| always elided:

(2.15)   *kehčawuhi·ma* 'great one; highly regarded person' (cf. *kehči* PN 'great')
          neniwawahi·ma 'male (animal)' (cf. *neniwi* PN 'of men' ← *neniwa* 'man')

(2.16)   *či·kawahi·ne, či·kawahi·me* 'nearby, on the side(s) or edge(s)' (cf. *či·ki* 'near, beside')

18.9. Alternative pronoun. Also classifiable as a pronoun is *kotaka* 'other (anim.)', *kotaki* 'other (inan.)', which is similar to demonstratives in syntax and in adopting its nominal categories from the noun it substitutes for or modifies.

18.10. Particles. Particles may be classed formally as free particles, enclitics, or interjections. Free particles typically occur as independent words, though if they have fewer than four syllables they (like other short words) may be cliticized (§4.1). Enclitics are always cliticized to the preceding word, with which they may or may not have a syntactic or semantic relationship. Interjections occur alone or in sequence, either by themselves or preceding a sentence. An interjection is syntactically independent of the sentence that follows it, but it may be linked to it semantically and even phonetically.

The particles that are not interjections may also be classified according to the types of constructions they form, whether with sentences, verbs, nouns, or other particles. Several kinds of syntactic function and semantic type may also be distinguished.

18.11. Prewords. Prewords are formed like particles and are, in fact, often formally identical to free particles, but they do not have the syntax of particles. A preword is part of a compound stem; depending on the kind of stem it enters into, it may be a prenoun, preverb, or preparticle. Since prewords are thus parts of words, rather than parts of sentences, they do not fall into the grammatical category of particles, despite having their morphology.

18.12. Proclitic preverbs. The proclitic preverbs |e·h=| AOR and |wi·h=| FUT are structurally part of verbal inflection. They share some formal attributes with reduplicating syllables (which are parts of stems) and with pronominal prefixes (which are parts of inflected words). For convenience, however, and because they are also in some ways separate words, like preverbs, they are set off with a double hyphen (=)

Major Grammatical Categories

Gender

19. The two genders are conventionally called the animate and the inanimate. The animate is the high gender, and the inanimate the low gender. Animate nouns end with the animate singular suffix *-a*, and inanimate nouns have the inanimate singular suffix *-i*. Gender is predictable only for the nouns in certain semantic categories; in many semantic fields nouns may be of either gender. The conventional names for the genders should not be taken too literally. There are actually a large number of non-sentient things, which are not believed to have ever had life or spiritual power, that are referred to by animate nouns.

19.1. Predictable animates. Predictably animate are all nouns for human beings, gods and spirits, personified beings, and animals:

(2.17)　　*neniwa* AN 'man'

　　　　　maneto·wa AN 'god, spirit, monster, snake'

　　　　　ahpene·wene·ha AN '(the Spirit of) Disease'

　　　　　mahkwa AN 'bear'

Dead people and animals remain animate:

(2.18)　　*či·paya* AN 'deceased person, corpse, ghost'

　　　　　ne·po·ha AN 'carcass'

The first person and second person exist only for the animate gender, and thus animate gender must be used in these categories even when what is speaking or spoken to is referred to by an inanimate noun, pronoun, or pronominal inflection, as in these (non-successive) sentences from a traditional story:

(2.19)　　*"kewe·ne·ha·hkowi," e·h=itaki.* (K-RYL 8)

　　　　　' "What kind of tree are you (anim.)?" he said to it (inan.).'

　　　　　(|we·ne·ha·hkowi-| AI 'be what kind of tree?', |ke-| 2s/IND;

　　　　　|it-| TI(1) 'say {so} to', |e·h=–aki| 3s–0/AOR)

(2.20)　　*"o·´, nemehtekomišiwi," e·h=ikwiči.* (K-RYL 8)

　　　　　' "Oh, I (anim.) am an oak," it (inan.) said to him.'

　　　　　(|mehtekomišiwi-| AI 'be an oak', |ne–Ø| 1s/IND;

　　　　　|iN-| TA 'say {so} to', |e·h=–ekwiči| 0–3s/AOR)

19.2. Predictable inanimates. Abstract nouns are always inanimate:

(2.21)　　*nepo·weni* IN 'death'

The inanimate is also the default gender used in constructions where there is no reference to any actual or potential noun that might determine the gender. These cases include pronominal designations of such things as events, actions, conditions, locations, and utterances:

(2.22)　　*mani e·h=keteminawesiya·ke* (K-SD 49)

　　　　　'this (inan.) (episode of) our (exc.) being blessed'

　　　　　(*mani* 'this (inan.)'; |keteminawesi-| AI 'be blessed', |e·h=–ya·ke| 1p/AOR)

(2.23)　　*mani e·h=apiwa·či.* 'This (inan.) is where they sit.' (A legend on a diagram.) (K-BD 3)

　　　　　(*mani* 'this (inan.)'; |api-| AI 'sit {somewhere}', |e·h=–wa·či| 3p/(loc.obl))

(2.24)　　*mani wi·h=iyani* 'This (inan.) is what you (sg.) must say.' (K-WLBS 21)

　　　　　(*mani* 'this (inan.)'; |wi·h=| FUT, |i-| AI 'say {so}', |–yani| 2s/PPL(obl))

The default status of the inanimate is also seen in its use for demonstratives that are in equational constructions with emphatic pronouns, which are not inflected for nominal categories (2.25):

>   (2.25)   *ni·na=ča·hi·=·'ni·=·'ni.* "I was the one." (K-M 361m; tr. HP) (Cf. 5.93*b*.)
>
>   (*ni·na* 1s/EMPH; *=ča·hi* 'so'; *i·ni* 'that (inan.)'; *i·ni* 'that (inan.)')

Also, the inanimate indefinite pronoun (**§18.6**) may be used for maximally indefinite reference to living things:

>   (2.26)   *e·h=pwa·wi- ke·ko·hi -nehto·či.* 'And he didn't kill anything (inan.).' (C-PB 1)
>
>   (|pwa·wi| PV 'not'; *ke·ko·hi* 'anything'; |neht-| TI(2) 'kill', |e·h=–o·či| 3s–0/AOR)

19.3. Consistent gender. Beyond these large categories of predictable gender there are some smaller sets that are consistently treated. All designations of corn and beans are animate (2.27), as are all corn preparations (2.28), except that ground-corn porridge is inanimate (2.29), like *nepo·pi* IN 'soup'. Nouns for squash (including pumpkins), rice, oats, and wheat are inanimate (2.30).

>   (2.27)   *ata·mina* AN 'corn (generic), uncooked corn'
>
>   *pi·wa·ha* AN 'extremely small variety of podded bean'
>
>   (2.28)   *papakena·wa* AN 'corncake'
>
>   (2.29)   *takwaha·ni* IN 'corn porridge'
>
>   (2.30)   *wa·pikoni* IN 'squash, pumpkin'
>
>   *mano·mini* IN 'wild rice; rice'

Sleds and drags, wagons, motorized vehicles, and two-wheeled vehicles are animate (2.31), while watercraft, trains, and aircraft are inanimate (2.32).

>   (2.31)   *šo·škwi·ha* AN 'sled, drag'
>
>   *ata·pya·na* AN 'wagon'
>
>   *pi·neši-pe·mipaho·ha* AN, *a·tamo·pi·na* AN 'automobile'
>
>   (2.32)   *anake·weni* IN 'bark canoe'
>
>   *ki·weške·wi·hi* IN 'passenger train'

19.4. Gender contrast. Some noun stems are used in both genders, with a difference of meaning. In one pattern the animate is a special variety of the generic inanimate:

>   (2.33)   Two-gender nouns: animate is special
>
>   (a)   *asenya* AN 'stone used in sweatlodge'
>
>   *aseni* IN 'stone'
>
>   (b)   *apehkwe·šimo·na* AN 'pillow'
>
>   *apehkwe·šimo·ni* IN 'head support'

In another pattern the inanimate has a collective meaning and the animate refers to the individual components of the set. In a few cases this pattern is even found for living things (2.34*b*). (Other collectives are animate; 2.27.)

>   (2.34)   Two-gender nouns: inanimate is collective
>
>   (a)   *šo·niya·ha* AN 'a coin, a bill'
>
>   *šo·niya·hi* IN 'silver, money'
>
>   (b)   *mi·čipe·ha* AN 'a game animal or game-bird'
>
>   *mi·čipe·hi* IN 'game (collective)'

In a third pattern a noun that is ordinarily animate is inanimate when used for something that is typically referred to with an inanimate noun, and even when a kinship term is used for an object.

>   (2.35)   Two-gender nouns: inanimate by attraction
>
>   (a)   *a·čimeko·ha* AN 'one told about, well-known character, hero of the tale' (4.229*a*)
>
>   *a·čimeko·hi* IN 'famous thing' (e.g., *ka·hpi·hi* 'coffee' [C-Hist 13])

(b)   *a·teso·hka·kana* AN 'myth, sacred story, "winter story" '
      a·teso·hka·kani IN 'written myth, manuscript of myth' (K) (cf. *mesenahikani* 'paper')

(c)   *panaša·ha* AN 'offspring, young of an animal or bird'
      panaša·hi IN 'interest (on a bank account)' (C) (cf. *šo·niya·hi* IN 'money')

(d)   *kemešo·mesena·na* AN 'our (inc.) grandfather'
      kemešo·mesena·ni IN 'our (inc.) grandfather' (cf. *mehtekwi* 'tree, stick', in this
      case used to refer to a ceremonial pole; K-ECRP 56; Goddard 2002:211)

Conversely, an inanimate noun sometimes appears to be attracted into the animate gender when it is in a construction that equates it explicitly or by implication with an animate noun.

(2.36) Two-gender nouns: animate by attraction

(a)   *kohpiči-nenoswayani=·yo=ke·hi e·h=opi·tanwa·niči.* (C-G 15)
      'Now, the quiver he had was of buffalo hide (obv.).'
      (*nenoswayi* IN 'buffalo hide', but here attracted to the gender of *pi·tanwa·na*
      AN 'quiver', which underlies |opi·tanwa·ni-| AI 'have a quiver')

(b)   *ki·yo·te·wayaki nemahkesenaki.* (K-ECRP 159; song)
      'Of serpent skins are my moccasins.'
      (|mahkesen-|, archaic form of *mahkese·hi* IN 'moccasin', attracted to the gender
      of *ki·yo·te·waya* AN 'snakeskin')

The attested examples do not permit a precise prediction of the direction of the gender attraction.

For most animate nouns outside the categories that are consistently animate the gender is not strictly predictable, but in many cases animate nouns refer to the special or unusual variety, in contrast to an inanimate noun that designates the generic or the ordinary in the same semantic field:

(2.37) *pi·tanwa·na* AN 'quiver'
        maškimote·hi IN 'bag'

(2.38) *wa·pi·wena* AN 'white clay' (used for face paint)
        ašiškiwi IN 'mud, clay'

Compare the uses of the nouns with two genders in (2.33). Perhaps as a special case of this pattern, large skins are inanimate (2.39) and small skins animate (2.40):

(2.39) *mahkwayi* IN 'bearskin'
        asayi IN 'skin of a larger animal'

(2.40) *mahwe·waya* AN 'wolfskin'
        asaya AN 'skin (of a smaller animal); buckskin'

In some semantic fields, notably trees (2.41) and body parts (2.42), nouns of both genders are found without a discernible overall pattern:

(2.41) *aša·šiko·ha* AN 'slippery elm (*Ulmus rubra*)'
        ani·pi IN 'American elm (*Ulmus americana*)'

(2.42) *neškaša* AN 'my fingernail'
        nete·hi IN 'my heart'
        ni·yawi IN 'my body, my life, myself'

When the word for 'body' (2.42) is used as a reflexive pronoun, it remains grammatically inanimate, even though what it refers to would otherwise be predictably animate:

(2.43) *e·h=nehto·či owi·yawi.* 'He (anim.) killed himself (inan.).' (C-L 110, C-Hist 36)
        (|neht-| TI(2) 'kill', |e·h=-o·či| 3s–0/AOR; *owi·yawi* 'his body, his life, himself')

This noun also furnishes non-third-person secondary objects and the third-person secondary objects in certain constructions. (Compare the treatment of the emphatic pronoun [2.25].)

Number

20. The contrast between singular and plural is variously marked on nouns, pronouns, and verbs.

20.1. Number in nouns and pronouns. Singular and plural number are distinguished for animate proximate nouns, animate obviative nouns, and inanimate nouns (2.2). Demonstrative, interrogative, place-holder, and alternative pronouns indicate the number of the nouns or noun phrases they agree with or substitute for (2.12).

Some nouns are used only in the singular:

(2.44) *nepi* 'water'

ako na 'snow'

(2.45) *mehtose neniwiweni* 'life'

nemehtose neniwiwenena ni 'our (exc.) lives'

(2.46) *ni yawi* 'myself' (2.42)

ni ya na ni 'ourselves (exc.)'

In the second forms in (2.45) and (2.46), the inflection |ne–ena·n-| marks the first plural exclusive possessor; the number of the noun itself is indicated by the inanimate singular ending *-i*. The indefinite pronouns (**§18.6**) are also only singular, except when used in negative existential statements or as nouns.

Some nouns are used only in the plural:

(2.47) *nemeso ta naki* 'my parents'

(2.48) *owi weti ·haki* 'the husband and wife, the married couple'

Like (2.48) are all such nouns that designate pairs or sets of people with a particular kin relationship to each other.

Some nouns may be used as representative singulars, referring to a large, non-specific class:

(2.49) *mehtose neniwa* 'a person', but also 'people (in general)'

A second person singular may refer to a collective second plural in similar cases (2.147*d*; 3.132, 133, 165, 184).

20.2. Number in verbs. Verbs distinguish number for most subjects and some animate primary objects using inflections for pronominal category (2.50) and for nominal category (2.51).

(2.50) *ni miyane* 'if you (sg.) dance' (|ni·mi-| AI 'dance', |–yane| 2s/SUBJ)

ni miye ·kwe 'if you (pl.) dance' (|–ye·kwe| 2p/SUBJ)

(2.51) *nene wa wa* 'I saw him' (|ne·w-| TA 'see', |ne–a·wa| 1s–3s/IND)

nene wa waki 'I saw them (anim.)' (|ne–a·waki| 1s–3p/IND)

In many verb forms, however, the distinction of number is neutralized. An obviative (2.52) or inanimate (2.53) argument distinguishes number only in certain endings of the independent order.

(2.52) Examples of number-marking for obviatives.

(a) *ni miniwani* 'he (obv.) dances' (|–niwani| 3´s/IND)

ni miniwahi 'they (obv.) dance' (|–niwahi| 3´p/IND)

(b) *ni minite* 'if he (obv.) dances; if they (obv.) dance' (|–nite| 3´/SUBJ)

(c) *ne we wa* 'he sees him (obv.) or them (obv.)' (|–e·wa| 3s–3´/IND)

(2.53) Examples of number-marking for inanimates.

(a) *po ·hkya wi* 'it has a hole in it' (|po·hkya·-| II 'have a hole', |–wi| 0s/IND)

po ·hkya wani 'they have holes in them' (|–wani| 0p/IND)

(b)   *po·hkya·niwi* 'it (obv.) has a hole in it' (|–niwi| 0´s/IND)
       po·hkya·niwani 'they (inan. obv.) have holes in them' (|–niwani| 0´p/IND)

(c)   *e·h=po·hkya·ki* '(that) it has a hole or they (inan.) have holes' (|e·h=–ki| 0/AOR)

(d)   *e·h=po·hkya·niki* '(that) it (obv.) has a hole or they (inan. obv.) have holes'
       (|e·h=–niki| 0´/AOR)

An animate third-person object is differentiated for number if the subject is obviative (2.54) and in non-diminutive independent indicative forms with a first singular or second singular subject (2.55):

(2.54)   *ne·wokosa* 'he (obv.) or they (obv.) would see him' (|–ekosa| 3´–3s/POT)
         ne·wokowa·sa 'he (obv.) or they (obv.) would see them' (|–ekowa·sa| 3´–3p/POT)

(2.55)   *ni·h=na·na·wa* 'I'll go after him'
         (|wi·h=| FUT, |na·N-| TA 'go after', |ne–a·wa| 1s–3s/IND)
         ni·h=na·na·waki 'I'll go after them (anim.)' (|ne–a·waki| 1s–3p/IND)

Other third-person objects do not distinguish number:

(2.56)   *ni·h=na·na·pena* 'We (exc.) will go after him or them (anim.)'
         (|ne–a·pena| 1p–3/IND)
         ni·h=na·te 'I will go after it or them (inan.)'
         (|na·t-| TI(3) [i.e., |na·t(e)-|] 'go after', |ne–∅| 1s–0/IND)

A second-person subject or object does not distinguish number if the verb is also inflected for a first person plural as the other argument.

(2.57)   *ketasemihenepena* 'we (exc.) help you (sg. or pl.)'
         (|asemih-| TA 'help', |ke–enepena| 1p–2/IND)

(2.58)   *ketasemihipena* 'you (sg. or pl.) help us (exc.)' (|ke–ipena| 2–1p/IND)

20.3. Other indicators of number. Plurality may also be indicated by stem reduplication and stem selection:

(2.59)   *e·h=kenwa·ki* '(that) it is long' (|kenwa·-| II 'be long (sg.)', |e·h=–ki| 0/AOR)
         e·h=kaka·nwa·ki '(that) they (inan.) are long'
         (|kaka·nwa·-| II 'be long (pl.)' [← |Ca_a·+| RED1, |kenwa·-| II 'be long (sg.)'],
         |e·h=–ki| 0/AOR)

Obviation

21. Nouns, pronouns that inflect for nominal categories, and third persons are either proximate or obviative. These are categories that relate more to the structure of discourse than to the morphology and semantics of words or the syntax of individual sentences. A proximate contrasted with an obviative is presented as primary, more central to the discourse; the obviative is secondary, more peripheral.

If there is only one third person in a context, the proximate is used as the default category. If there is more than one third person, only one can be proximate, except that conjoined nouns, if not both obviative, may be either both proximate (O 53G) or one proximate and the other obviative (2.60). A conjoined proximate and obviative show agreement as a proximate plural:

(2.60)   *ma·haki=na·hkači mešihke·ha mahkwa·hke·hani* (O 2I)
         'also this snapping turtle (prox.) and mud turtle (obv.)' (*ma·haki* 'these (prox.)')

But the extent of the context within which there is a single proximate is variable. Someone or something referred to in the obviative may be shifted to proximate, or another, new proximate may be introduced, or re-introduced. Speakers can manipulate the length of the span of discourse between these proximate shifts, and spans vary in length depending on genre, speaker, and other factors. Also, heightened topicality may result in something that is, or is expected to be, obviative being treated as a proximate.

Nouns and pronouns of both genders distinguish proximate and obviative in verbal agreement, but only animate nouns and demonstratives have distinct obviative inflections (2.12). Verbal agreement for obviation in part patterns like agreement for singular and plural (**§20.1**). Some inflectional forms, however, including some that distinguish number, do not distinguish proximate and obviative; for example, although obviatives may be the possessors of nouns, there is no distinct inflection for an obviative possessor in contrast to a proximate possessor. Conversely, in some cases where obviative is marked, it does not distinguish number. Also, some speakers use some obviative singular forms also as obviative plurals; this is most common for demonstrative pronouns (5.32*gh*).

As befits the discourse function of obviation, the choice of which of two nouns to make proximate and which obviative is usually undetermined by grammar and entirely up to the speaker. Thus for any verb with animate subject and object, there are two possibilities and two distinct inflectional forms, one for proximate acting on obviative and one for obviative acting on proximate. Obviation is morphologically determined in only one case: a noun possessed by an animate third person must be obviative. Obviation is also determined in the case of nouns or pronouns of different gender: the animate is always proximate and the inanimate obviative. If there are two inanimates in a context one may be proximate and the other obviative, but this probably reflects differential realization of the usual patterns of obviation.

Pronominal Reference

22. Nouns may be inflected for pronominal reference to a possessor (**§22.1**). Verbs are obligatorily inflected for pronominal reference to a subject (**§22.2**), and for pronominal reference to a primary object if one is present (**§22.3**). Pronominal reference is made to the eight pronominal categories (**§18.4**; 2.11) and, in the third person, to the intersecting nominal categories of gender, number, and obviation (**§18.2**; 2.2).

Some verbs make pronominal reference to a secondary object or an oblique, but these are not indicated in inflection. There are also some particles that take oblique complements.

The pronominal inflections on nouns and verbs may function as agreement with overtly expressed nouns, demonstrative pronouns, or other noun phrases:

    (2.61) Agreement with object
      (a)   *ki·h=kehke·nema·wa i·na* 'you (sg.) will know that one (anim.)' (K-BHD2 10)
         (|wi·h=| FUT, |kehke·nem-| TA 'know', |ke–a·wa| 2s–3s/IND; *i·na* 'that (anim.)')
      (b)   *ni·h=na·na·waki i·niki.* 'I will go after those (anim.).' (K-ECRP 45)
         (|wi·h=| FUT, |na·N-| TA 'go after', |ne–a·waki| 1s–3p/IND; *i·niki* 'those (anim.)')
    (2.62) Agreement with subject and object
      nese·waki nekye·ni ma·haki. 'These [people] killed my mother.' (S-APAY 21)
      (|neS-| TA 'kill', |–e·waki| 3p–3´/IND; *nekye·ni* 'my mother (obv.)';
      ma·haki 'these (anim.)')

(2.63) Agreement with possessor

        i·na owi·wani 'his wife, that one's wife' (K-BH 1)

        (*i·na* 'that (anim.)'; |o–∅–| 3s, |-i·w-| AN 'wife', |-ani| OBVsg))

The verb in (2.61*a*) has inflection for an object that is third-person animate singular (3s), agreeing with the animate singular demonstrative, while the verb in (2.61*b*) has inflection for an object that is third-person animate plural (3p), agreeing with the animate plural demonstrative. Animate singular and plural are overtly marked on these verbs with the suffixes *-a* and *-aki*, which correspond to the *-a* and *-iki* in the demonstratives.

    The form in (2.62) is inflected for a third-person animate plural acting on an animate obviative object, agreeing with an overt animate plural demonstrative (*ma·haki* 'these (anim.)') and an overt obviative singular noun (*nekye·ni* 'my mother (obv.)'). The animate plural subject is overtly marked on the verb by the suffix *-aki*, but although the verbal ending |+e·waki| 3p–3´/IND as a whole specifies an obviative object it does not include an overt obviative suffix that corresponds to this meaning. In fact, it is often the case that the inflection on a verb lacks a specific element indicating one of the pronominal categories to which the inflection as a whole unambiguously refers (§17).

    The possessed noun in (2.63) is inflected for a third singular possessor (prefix |o+| 3 and no plural suffix). This functions here as agreement with the animate singular demonstrative *i·na* 'that (anim.)'.

    Verbal inflections that do not distinguish number may show agreement with a noun or pronoun that is either singular or plural:

    (2.64)   *mi·hkemake owiye·ha* 'if I court someone' (K-SF 7)

            (|mi·hkem-| TA 'court', |–ake| 1s–3/SUBJ; *owiye·ha* 'someone (anim. sg.)')

        mehkawake neno·te·waki 'if I find some Indians' (C-O 25)

            (|mehkaw-| TA 'find', |–ake| 1s–3/SUBJ; *neno·te·waki* 'Indians (anim. pl.)')

When the pronominal inflections on possessed nouns and verbs are not functioning as agreement with words that are overtly present in the clause (as they are in 2.61-64), they have the syntactic status of pronouns (as in 2.51-56, 59, 73-75). In the case of forms that do not distinguish number, the pronominal reference may then be to either a singular or a plural:

    (2.65)   *newa·pata* 'I looked at it or them (inan.)'

            (|wa·pat-| TI(1) 'look at', |ne–a| 1s–0/IND)

        newa·pama·pena 'we (exc.) looked at him or them (anim.)'

            (|wa·pam-| TA 'look at', |ne–a·pena| 1p–3/IND)

        ne·wake 'if I see him or them (anim.)'

            (|ne·w-| TA 'see', |–ake| 1s–3/SUBJ)

        anetokwe·ni 'it or they (inan.) must be rotten'

            (|anet-| II 'rot', |–kwe·ni| 3s,0/INT)

A plural pronominal inflection may function pronominally for one of the component arguments and as agreement for the other:

    (2.66) Plural inflection combining pronoun and agreement

      (a)   *nemawi-manese·pena nenekwanesa.* 'I'm going to cut wood with my nephew.' (LK)

            (|mawi| PV 'go and', |manese·-| AI 'cut wood', |ne–pena| 1p/IND;

            nenekwanesa 'my nephew')

(b) *e·h=tašihečini nekya* 'the places where he and my mother were slain' (K-MFWB 54)
(|taših-| TA 'kill {somewhere}', |e·h=–ečini| X–3/PPL(loc.obl.pl);
nekya 'my mother')

(c) *kapo·twe e·h=nesapiwa·či okwisani.* (K-BFS 3)
'One time he and his son were home alone.'
(*kapo·twe* 'at some point'; |nesapi-| AI, 'stay home', |e·h=–wa·či| 3p/AOR;
okwisani 'his son (obv.)')

In (2.66a) the inflection is for first plural exclusive, the semantic components of which are first singular and, in this case, third singular. The third singular component functions as agreement with *nenekwanesa* 'my nephew', while the first singular component functions pronominally. In (2.66b) the verbal suffix |-et| X–3 is for third person undifferentiated for number, but the inanimate plural suffix |-ini| (referring to more than one place) and the preceding and following context show that the reference is to the speaker's father and mother, both. In (2.66c) the verb is inflected for third person proximate plural, so the obviative singular noun must be conjoined with a proximate argument that is only present as a component of the inflection functioning as a pronoun.

22.1. Possessor. The grammatical marking of possession indicates a relationship between a possessor and a possessed noun. The kinds of relationship that may be indicated this way include not only literal possession or ownership, but also kinship, affinity, authority, whole-to-part, and so forth. Most nouns occur freely in possessed form:

(2.67) *pi·tanwa·na* 'quiver' → *nepi·tanwa·na* 'my quiver'
ma·tesi 'knife' → *nema·tesi* 'my knife'

(2.68) *apeno·ha* 'child' → *netapeno·hema* 'my child'
šo·niya·hi 'money' → *kešo·niya·hemi* 'your (sg.) money'
ahkani 'bone' → *neto·hkanemani* 'my bones'

Many nouns of each gender add a possessed-theme marker |-em| in possessed forms (2.68), while many others do not (2.67). The sets defined by the use of this suffix do not seem to correlate consistently with any other characteristic of meaning, form, or use, though some patterns are discernible.

Some nouns, called dependent nouns, always specify information about a possessor. One set of these contains kinship terms and the like (2.69), and the other has words for most body parts and a few personal possessions (2.70).

(2.69) *nekwisa* 'my son'

(2.70) *nenehki* 'my hand'

It is not necessary, however, for a dependent noun to be marked for a specific possessor. There is an inflection for indefinite possessor (|o–inaw-| X) that may be used on both non-dependent nouns (2.71) and dependent nouns (2.72):

(2.71) *ni·ča·pa* 'doll' → *oni·ča·pinawaki* 'one's dolls' (A 4B)

(2.72) *o·šisemani* 'his grandchild (obv.)' → *o·šiseminawa* 'one's grandchild' (K-M 1065m)
onehki 'his hand' → *onehkinawi* 'one's hand' (O 48E)

Distinct from the forms inflected for indefinite possessor are the unpossessed forms of dependent nouns, which are formed three different ways. Kinship terms make a secondary derivative with |o–ema·w-| (2.73; §45.6), while body-part terms and the like use an inflection with |me+| X (2.74; 3.25, 27) or |o+| 3 (2.75; 3.26, 27), or in some cases either one:

(2.73) *okwisani* 'his son (obv.)' → *okwisema·wa* 'the son' (A 75E)

(2.74)   *onešiwayahi* 'his testicles (obv.)' → *menešiwaki* 'testicles' (K-MWL 29)
         onehki 'his hand' → *menehki* 'a hand' (K-CDWP 13, K-OKUT 45)
(2.75)   *onamaškayani* 'his skin (obv.)' (K-GD 29) → *onamaškaya* 'skin' (K-Words 20)
         owiˑši 'his head; a head'

For an inanimate dependent noun the unpossessed form with |o+| 3 is identical with the third-singular-possessed form, marked by the same prefix (2.75: 'head'). In the unpossessed form, however, the prefix lacks pronominal reference. The distinction is overt in animate nouns (2.75: 'skin'), which require an obviative ending (|+ani| OBVsg, |+ahi| OBVpl; 2.72-75) if possessed but have proximate endings (|+a| ANsg, |+aki| ANpl) if unpossessed, like unpossessed nouns with the prefix |me-| (2.74).

The unpossessed forms corresponding to some dependent nouns are synonymous dependent (2.76) or non-dependent (2.77) nouns, which often show an irregular formal resemblance.

(2.76)   *mehkoneˑweni* 'a blanket' (*nehkoneˑhi* 'my blanket')
(2.77)   *wiˑkiyaˑpi* 'house' (*niˑki* 'my house')

Participles cannot be possessed. For at least one common word, possession of a lexicalized participle is made on a virtual agent noun derived from the underlying verb (**§46**):

(2.78)   *aˑhkwahki* 'weaponry' (participle of *aˑhkwatwi* 'it is dangerous')
         ketaˑhkwatomi 'your (sg.) weapons' (as if with *aˑhkwatwi 'dangerous thing')

In (2.78) the semantic specialization of the possessed form shows that it is paradigmatically linked to the participle.

Other constructions may be used to indicate possession in cases where there are gaps in the system of possessor-marking on nouns. For example, possessors must be people or personified beings. Possession by others can only be indicated using other constructions, such as participles of verbs of possession (2.79), nominal compounds (2.80), and nominal adjuncts (5.172*d*):

(2.79)   *weˑwiˑpičiˑmikahki* 'its tooth' (*lit.*, 'what it (inan.) has as a tooth') (C-Ston 27)
         (|owiˑpiči-| AI+O 'have O2 as a tooth' → |owiˑpičiˑmikat-| II, |IC-ki| 0/PPL(INsg))
(2.80)   *mahkwi-owiˑpitani* 'bear's teeth' (*lit.*, 'bear teeth') (K-FM 17)
         (*mahkwa* AN 'bear' → *mahkwi* PN 'pertaining to bear'; *owiˑpitani* 'teeth'
         [cf. 2.75])

Participles of verbs of possession also supply forms that function syntactically as proximate nouns possessed by an obviative third person, which are not furnished by the inflection of nouns for possessor:

(2.81)   *weˑwiˑwita* 'her (obv.) husband (prox.)' (K-SGG 207, etc.)
         (*lit.*, 'the one (prox.) who has her (obv.) as wife')
         (|owiˑwi-| AI+O 'have O2 as a wife', |IC–ta| 3/PPL(ANsg))

22.2. Subject. All verbs are inflected for pronominal reference to a subject. The subject is the one that is or does what the verb specifies. Depending on the meaning of the verb, it may have any of a variety of semantic roles, including actor or agent, initiator, perceiver, experiencer, possessor of an attribute or thing, bearer of a relationship, and so forth. The subject of a derived passive verb (**§53.6**) may have the semantic role of any primary object (**§22.3**).

The gender of the subject determines the selection of the stem variant of an intransitive verb (2.3). A TA verb may have a subject of either gender, but with an inanimate subject the object must be a person or a personified being. Also, an inanimate cannot be the subject of a TI verb that is inflected for an inanimate object. Other constructions must be used to indicate an inanimate acting on an inanimate or a non-sentient animate (**§52.2**).

With some II verbs the subject only functions pronominally, lacks any definite reference, and is only singular. These are impersonal verbs, referring to time, environment, or events:

(2.82) Impersonal verbs (II)

(a) *ana·kwiwi* 'it's evening'

(b) *anakwe·wiwi* 'there's a rainbow' (← *anakwe·wa* 'rainbow')

(c) *we·pikenwi* 'it's starting to happen'

AI verbs that occur with a unique or prototypical subject are sometimes used without the subject (2.83) or with only a demonstrative (2.84):

(2.83) *anemi-pa·šisa·te* (SP-MRD 24)

'after noon has come and gone' (*lit.*, 'after he has flown past')

(2.84) *mana katawi-ahkwisa·te* 'before the end of this month' (JPo-C)

(*lit.*, 'when this (anim.) has almost gone to the end')

In both (2.83) and (2.84) the noun *ki·šeswa* 'sun, moon, month' is omitted. The AI's used this way resemble impersonal II verbs, but the option of using a demonstrative shows that the subject is present syntactically as a pronoun.

22.3. Object. All transitive verbs are inflected for pronominal reference to a primary object. The primary object corresponds to the direct object of an English verb with one object, to the indirect object of an English verb with two objects, and to the subject of an English passive verb if it corresponds to either of these kinds of objects. Its semantic role may include undergoer or patient, beneficiary, recipient, perceptual object or source, and so forth.

The gender of the primary object determines the selection of the stem variant of a transitive verb (2.9).

Some verbs have one object more or less than what is called for by the basic formal categorization of the stem (2.85). AI and TA verbs may make pronominal reference to a secondary object (O2), of either gender and either number, but this is not indicated by any overt addition to the verbal inflection (unless it is the head of a participle). The secondary objects of AI's and TA's correspond to English direct objects. These transitivized AI verbs are called AI+O ("AI plus O") verbs, and the double-object TA's are called TA+O ("TA plus O"). For some verbs the secondary object is optional. A transitivized II verb (II+O) may be derived from an AI+O with |-·mikat| II (2.7).

(2.85) *we·pa·hke·wa* 'he threw him, it, them (anim., inan.)'

(|we·pa·hke·-| AI+O 'throw O2', |-wa| 3s/IND)

kemo·twa 'he stole; he stole him, it, them (anim., inan.)'

(|kemo·t-| AI 'steal', AI+O 'steal O2', |-wa| 3s/IND)

kemi·nene 'I gave him, it, them (anim., inan.) to you (sg.)'

(|mi·N-| TA+O 'give O2 to', |ke–ene| 1s–2s/IND)

kekemo·temekwa 'he stole him, it, them (anim., inan.) from you (sg.)'

(|kemo·tem-| TA 'steal O2 from', |ke–ekwa| 3s–2s/IND)

Some verbs with the form and inflection of a TI are used, optionally or always, without pronominal reference to an object. These objectless TI's are called TI-O ("TI minus O"), or if distinguished for subclass: TI(1)-O, TI(2)-O, and TI(3)-O:

(2.86) *sesotamwa* 'he coughed' (|sesot-| TI(1)-O 'cough', |-amwa| 3s(-0)/IND)

In the analysis of verbs with this syntax, the label for the pronominal inflection has "(-0)" instead of "-0," signaling that the inanimate object is only formally present.

A few TI's are used either without an object or with an object of either gender; these may be thought of as formal objectless TI's that can optionally take a secondary object. Their distinctness appears clearly when they are used with animate syntactic objects:

(2.87)   *a·hkwamatake* 'if he is sick'
   (|a·hkwamat-| TI(1)-O 'be sick, have a pain', |–ake| 3s(-0)/SUBJ)
   ihkwe·wa ohketenani a·hkwamatake (K-Kin 65)
   'if a woman has a pain in her vagina (obv.)'
   (*ihkwe·wa* 'woman'; *ohketenani* 'her vagina (obv.)')

(2.88)   *e·h=ki·ši- .. -pečihto·či omehte·hani.* 'He had cached his bow (obv.).' (C-FRS 14)
   (|pečiht-| TI(2)-O 'cache things to be picked up later', |–o·či| 3s(-0)/AOR;
   omehte·hani 'his bow (obv.)')

These TI's can be classified as TI-O+O. They cannot be analyzed as AI+O's that happen to resemble TI themes, since, for one thing, the irregularities of the TI(1) theme sign |-am| are unique to that morpheme (as in 2.87, where the |m| is dropped in |–ake| 3s(-0)/SUBJ; **§29.7(f)**).

Some TA verbs may be used without specification of the objects that they prototypically take. This is freely done with verbs containing |-isah| TA '(cause to) move fast' when they refer to riding a horse:

(2.89)   *mani e·ši-kečisahakeči* (SP-KFC 24)
   'as soon as we (exc.) rode (our horses) out into the open'
   (*mani* 'this (inan.)'; |iši| PV '{so}' ['like this'; idiom: 'immediately, as soon as'],
   |kečisah-| TA 'cause to move fast into the open', |IC–akeči| 1p–3/CC)

While such verbs resemble TI-O's, their objects are present as syntactic pronouns. This is also the case in the idiomatic use of |mi·či-| TI(3) 'eat' without an overt object to mean 'take part in a peyote ceremony':

(2.90)   *e·h=taši-mi·čiwa·či* 'where they had a peyote meeting' (C-L 116)

If this were an objectless TI its meaning would be identical with |wi·seni-| AI 'eat'.

For some stems with the shape of double-object TA's (**§55.1**) a secondary object is not specified (2.91) or is optional (2.92):

(2.91)   *wi·tamawe·wa* 'he told him the facts' (4.353*h*)

(2.92)   *še·ški ki·h=sahkahamawa·pwa.* (K-WM 5; cf. O 107F)
   'You (pl.) must only make an offering of tobacco to it (anim.).' (*še·ški* 'only';
   |wi·h=| FUT, |sahkahamaw-| TA 'offer tobacco to', |ke–a·pwa| 2p–3/IND)
   nese·ma·wani ki·h=sahkahamawa·pwa (K-FC 102)
   'you (pl.) must make an offering of tobacco to him'
   (with *nese·ma·wani* 'tobacco (obv.)')

The verb in (2.92) would literally mean 'set fire to O2 for' but in its idiomatic use it can refer to sprinkling and tossing tobacco as well as to burning it.

22.4. Oblique. Some stems take an oblique complement, either obligatorily or optionally, as part of their argument structure. An oblique is not indicated in inflection, unless it is the head of a participle.

The largest class of stems that take obliques are those that contain a RELATIVE ROOT. The relative roots appear overtly as a set of six widely used initials. In addition, some stems that do not have one of these six initials function as if they did; these can be considered to contain a virtual relative root. In the glosses of relative roots the characterization of the oblique complement is enclosed in curly braces ({...}), indicating that this is a variable or place-holder and not a literal translation.

Some relative roots and some stems with virtual relative roots may also occur without an oblique complement. In the systematic cases the root or stem is described as having two variants with different meanings and different syntax. Some apparent cases of the absence of an oblique complement can be interpreted as having the oblique complement present pronominally, but this is not common. Still other cases seem idiomatic.

Distinct from the obliques that are complements of overt or virtual relative roots are instrumental obliques (**§22.4(g)**). Distinct from locative obliques (**§22.4(d,e)**) are locative adjuncts (**§22.5**; 5.89).

(a) The relative root |ahkw-| '{so} far, {so} long' (*ahkw-, ahko-; ahkwi* P,PV) takes an oblique that designates linear or temporal extent:

(2.93) *peno či=meko e·h=ahkwi-akwiškahkiwiniki.* (K-B 211)
'The land was covered with mud for a long distance.'
(*peno či* 'far'; *=meko* EMPH;
|ahkwi| PV '{so} far', |akwiškahkiwi-| II 'be muddy land', |e·h=—niki| 0´/AOR)

(2.94) *awita=·pi nana·ši ihkwe·wa oči·kwaneki ahkomi·sa.* (O 54F)
'They say the woman would never be in water up to her knees.'
(*awita* 'not (pot.)'; |=ipi| HRSY; *nana·ši* 'ever'; *ihkwe·wa* 'woman';
oči·kwaneki 'her knees (loc.)'; |ahkomi·-| AI 'be {so} far in water', |–sa| 3s/POT)

(2.95) *ayo nina·hi keye·či·hi wi·h=ahkwi-ketemino·nako·we* (O 92C)
'for me to bless you (pl.) for just a little while into the future'
(*ayo nina·hi* 'at the present time'; *keye·či·hi* 'soon';
|wi·h=| FUT, |ahkwi| PV '{so} far',
|ketemina·w-| TA 'bless', |e·h=—enako·we| 1s–2p/AOR)

Without an oblique this initial is |ahkw-| 'end':

(2.96) *e·h=ahkwahkamikahki* 'when the world ends' (O 128B)
(|ahkwahkamikat-| II 'be the end of the world', |e·h=—ki| 0/AOR)

(b) The relative root |ahpi·ht-| 'to {such} a degree or extent' (*ahpi·ht-, ahpi·hč-; ahpi·hči* P,PV) takes an oblique that specifies age, speed, intensity, and the like:

(2.97) *meše=mekoho ahpi·hčikiwa i·na ihkwe·wa.* (K-FC 31; tr. TB)
"The woman is some what past middle age."
(*meše* 'freely, middlingly'; *=mekoho* EMPH;
|ahpi·hčiki-| AI 'be {so} old', |–wa| 3s/IND; *i·na* 'that (anim.)'; *ihkwe·wa* 'woman')

(2.98) *i·ni=mekoho aye·niwe e·h=ahpi·htose·wa·či.* (K-FC 309)
'They kept walking at that same pace.'
(*i·ni* 'that (inan.)'; *=mekoho* EMPH; *aye·niwe* 'always the same';
|ahpi·htose·-| AI 'walk at {such} a speed', |e·h=—wa·či| 3p/AOR)

(2.99) *e·škami=meko netanemi-ahpi·hči-tepa·na·wa* (A 157A)
'I came to love him more and more'
(*e·škami* 'increasingly'; *=meko* EMPH; |anemi| PV 'go on',
|ahpi·hči| PV 'to {such} a degree', |tepa·N-| TA 'love', |ne–a·wa| 1s–3s/IND)

Without an oblique this initial is |ahpi·ht-| 'be in the process of':

(2.100) *e·h=ahpi·hči-=ke·h=wi·na=meko -nesekowa·či.* (K-BHD 39)
'What's more, they were constantly being killed by them (obv.).'
(|ahpi·hči| PV 'be in the process of'; |=ke·hi| 'moreover'; *=wi·na* 'but'; *=meko* EMPH;
|neS-| TA 'kill', |e·h=—ekowa·či| 3´–3p/AOR)

(c) The relative root |iN-| '{so}, {some} way, to {somewhere}' (*in-, iš-, ih-, -en-, -eš-, -eh-*; *iši* P,PV) takes a manner or goal oblique:

(2.101)   *aše <u>ino</u>weʾtoke* 'he's probably just kidding' (O 156A)

(*aše* 'just'; |inoweʾ-| AI 'tell people {so}', |–wetoke| 3s/DUB)

(2.102)   *weʾta paki <u>iši</u>-anweʾweʾhtaʾpi* 'it (a whistle) was blown to the east' (O 20C)

(*weʾta paki* 'east'; *iši* PV '{so}', |anweʾweʾht-| TI(1) 'blow', |–aʾpi| X–0/IND)

This initial may also take as a complement an utterance or a thought, expressed as either direct or indirect discourse.

(2.103)   "...," *eʾh=<u>ina</u>ʾčimohaʾtehe.* 'She had told him, "..." ' (A 119D-120D)

(|inaʾčimoh-| TA 'inform {so}', |eʾh=–aʾtehe| 3s–3´/AOR.PRET)

(2.104)   "*neketemaʾkihekwa,*" *ke<u>te</u>šiteʾhepetoke.* (A 26H)

'You (sg.) probably think I'm being cruel to you.'

(*Lit.*, 'You probably think, "She's being cruel to me." ')

(|ketemaʾkih-| TA 'treat badly', |ne–ekwa| 3s–1s/IND;

|išiteʾheʾ-| AI 'think {so}', |ke–petoke| 2s/DUB)

(2.105)   *wiʾh=naʾni miyani eʾh=<u>ine</u>nemenaʾni* 'because I wanted you (sg.) to dance' (A 160B)

(|wiʾh=| FUT, |CV+| RED1, |niʾmi-| AI 'dance', |eʾh=–yani| 2s/AOR;

|ineʾnem-| TA 'think about {so}', |eʾh=–enaʾni| 1s–2s/AOR)

Stems with virtual |iN-| '{so}' include: |i-| AI 'say {so}' (2.141); |ihaʾ-| AI 'go {somewhere}' (2.106); |pyaʾ-| AI 'arrive {somewhere}' (2.194), 'come, come back' (2.139, 208); |pyeʾčihaʾ-| AI 'come {some} way' (2.238; also the other stems with |-ihaʾ| AI 'go {some} way'); |iN-| TA, |it-| TI(1) 'say {so} to' (2.19, 20, 142); |it-| AI, II 'be {so}'; *nehki* 'for {so} long' (2.242, 281*c*):

(2.106)   *iʾtepi <u>iha</u>waʾči.* 'And they would go there.' (O 52C)

(*iʾtepi* '(to) there'; |ihaʾ-| AI 'go {somewhere}', |–waʾči| 3p/CONJ)

The initial |iN-| '{so}' is not common on verbs without an overt oblique complement. An apparent example with a pronominal oblique is:

(2.107)   *aʾkwi=keʾhi <u>ina</u>ʾhpawaʾyaʾnini.* 'What's more I didn't dream it.' (O 65I)

(*aʾkwi* 'not'; =*keʾhi* 'moreover'; |inaʾhpawaʾ-| AI 'dream {so}', |–yaʾnini| 1s/NEG)

Also, stems with the initial |iN-| '{so}' are used without any oblique in certain idioms:

(2.108)   *<u>iši</u>teʾheʾyane, niʾšihkakoha.* (K-Words 3)

'If you (sg.) want to, we (inc.) could be together.'

(|išiteʾheʾ-| AI 'think {so}', |–yane| 2s/SUBJ);

|niʾši-| AI 'be two' |–hkakoha| 12/POT)

Abstract nouns made from verb stems with the initial |iN-| '{so}' or with virtual |iN-| '{so}' systematically lack an oblique:

(2.109)   *ne<u>te</u>šiteʾhaʾkani* 'my plan' (O 75D)

(|išiteʾhaʾkan-| IN 'thought, plan' [← |išiteʾheʾ-| AI 'think {so}'], |ne–i| 1s(INsg))

Two derived initials contain |iN-| '{so}': |inehp-| '{so} high' (*inehp-, -enehp-*), which takes an oblique that specifies how high up something is or extends; and |inekihkw-| '{so} large, to {such} extent' (*inekihkw-, -enekihkw-, inekihko-, -enekihko-*), which takes an oblique that indicates size, specifically two-dimensional horizontal extent:

(2.110)   *nanoʾpehka=mekoho eʾh=<u>ine</u>hpaʾkwasowaʾči* (K-FC 531)

'there was a great pile of them (anim.)'

(*nanoʾpehka* 'very much, a great many'; =*mekoho* EMPH;

|inehpaʾkwaso-| AI 'be piled {so} high', |eʾh=–waʾči| 3p/AOR)

(2.111) *a·kwi i·ni wi·h=inekihkwa·kini* 'it will not be that big' (K-FC 167)
(*a·kwi* 'not'; *i·ni* 'that (inan.)';
|wi·h=| FUT, |inekihkwa·-| 'be {so} large', |–kini| 0/NEG)

(d) The relative root |ot-| 'from {something, somewhere}, because of {something}, toward {some direction}, through {some hole}, oriented {so}' (*ot-, oč-, os-; oči* P,PV) takes an oblique that designates a source, point of origin, reason, or direction:

(2.112) *a·kwi mana nekotahi <u>oči</u>kičini* 'this (anim.) is not from someplace else' (O 125D)
(*a·kwi* 'not'; *mana* 'this (anim.)'; *nekotahi* 'someplace';
|očiki-| 'originate from {something, somewhere}', |–čini| 3s/NEG)

(2.113) *we·či-kesi·ya·ki <u>ota·</u>hkwe* 'on the north side' (O 13B)
(*we·či-kesi·ya·ki* 'north'; *ota·hkwe* 'in, toward, or facing {some direction}')

(2.114) *ohka·twa·ki <u>oči-</u>ni·kiwaki* 'they are born feet-first' (A 100C)
(*ohka·twa·ki* 'their feet (loc.)';
|oči| PV 'oriented {so}', |ni·ki-| AI 'be born', |–waki| 3p/IND)

(2.115) *i·nahi <u>ota·</u>nakwe·wa·te* 'if they have their nesting hole there' (K-W 127)
(*i·nahi* 'there'; |ota·nakwe·-| AI 'have a burrow {somewhere}', |–wa·te| 3p/SUBJ)

(2.116) *a·kwi .. wi·h=owi·wiwa·či <u>oči-</u>taši·hkawa·wa·čini.* (A 80C)
'It's not in order to marry them that they're after them.'
(*a·kwi* 'not'; |wi·h=| FUT, |owi·wi-| AI+O 'have O2 as wife', |e·h=–wa·či| 3p/AOR;
|oči| PV 'because of {something}',
|taši·hkaw-| TA 'be dealing with', |–a·wa·čini| 3p–3´/NEG)

The initial |ot-| 'from {something}' is fairly common with no overt complement, either with a pronominal oblique (2.117*a*) or without any oblique as |ot-| 'off, away' (2.117*b*).

(2.117) |ot-| without an overt complement
(a) *ki·h=<u>otena·</u>pwa .. mehtose·neniwiweni* 'you (pl.) will get life from it' (O 143H)
(*mehtose·neniwiweni* 'life';
|wi·h=| FUT, |oten-| TI(1) 'get from {something}', |ke–a·pwa| 2p–0/IND)
(b) *e·h=<u>ota·</u>ška·či* 'he fell off' (K-RFB 6)
(|ota·ška·-| AI 'fall from {somewhere}; fall off', |e·h=–či| 3s/AOR)

(e) The relative root |taN-| '{somewhere}' (*tan-, taš-, tah-; taši* P,PV) takes a locative oblique complement:

(2.118) *nekotah=<u>taši</u>* 'someplace else' (A 9D)
(|nekotahi| 'somewhere'; *taši* '{somewhere}')

(2.119) *i·nah=meko e·h=<u>tanehkwe·</u>šimeči* 'it (anim.) was laid with its head next to it' (O 2E)
(|i·nahi| 'there'; =*meko* EMPH;
|tanehkwe·šim-| TA 'lay with head {somewhere}', |e·h=–eči| X–3/AOR)

(2.120) *i·nahi e·<u>taši</u>-nakamočiki* 'those (anim.) who sang there' (O 11I)
(|i·nahi| 'there';
|taši| PV '{somewhere}', |nakamo-| AI 'sing', |IC–čiki| 3/PPL(ANpl))

Many stems contain a virtual |taN-| '{somewhere}'. For a few stems (e.g., |awi-| AI 'be, live {somewhere}') this is always present, as they always occur with a locative oblique:

(2.121) *a·kwi i·nahi awiwa·čini* 'they were not there' (O 11H)
(*a·kwi* 'not'; *i·nahi* 'there'; |awi-| AI 'be {somewhere}', |–wa·čini| 3p/NEG)

Typically, however, stems that refer to an inherently localized action or state may be used with or without a locative oblique. When a locative oblique is present they function as if they contained a virtual |taN-| '{somewhere}'. The stems of this type are the positional stems (those for sitting, standing, and lying), verbs of having and being, and a few others, e.g. |ki·wita·-| AI 'stay ({somewhere}); be living {somewhere}', |tako-| AI,II 'exist ({somewhere}); be found {somewhere}', |nepa·-| AI 'sleep ({somewhere})', |aS-| TA, |aht-| TI(2) 'have ({somewhere}); put {somewhere}'.

(2.122)   *i·nahi e·pičiki pi·tike* 'those who sat inside there' (O 12A)
   (*i·nahi* 'there'; |api-| AI 'sit {somewhere}', |IC–čiki| 3/PPL(ANpl); *pi·tike* 'inside')
  i·nahi .. ase·waki nese·ma·wani 'they had tobacco there' (O 7I)
   (*i·nahi* 'there'; |aS-| TA 'have, put {somewhere}', |–e·waki| 3p–3´/IND;
   nese·ma·wani 'tobacco (obv.)')

The construction with virtual |taN-| '{somewhere}' also seems to be preferred when the oblique complement indicates a removed location where something is designated, described, or perceived as occurring or happening.

(2.123)   *neniwa i·nahi e·h=ne·wotisoči* 'the man saw himself in it' (K-WD 65)
   (*neniwa* 'man'; *i·nahi* 'there'; |ne·wotiso-| AI 'see oneself', |e·h=–či| 3s/AOR)

Except in these cases stems must have an added, overt |taN-| '{somewhere}' (in some form) when they take a locative oblique as a complement (2.119-120) or as the head of a participle (2.125, 253-255).

Without an oblique complement this initial appears as |taN-| 'be engaged in':

(2.124)   *owiye·hani taši-a·hkwe·nite* 'if anyone (obv.) is in a berserk rage' (O 14G)
   (*owiye·hani* 'someone (obv.)';
   |taši| PV 'be engaged in', |a·hkwe·-| AI 'be angry', |–nite| 3´/SUBJ)

Beside the extremely common use of |taN-| 'be engaged in' (2.124; 3.167c; 4.102h, 140abc, 141c, 157a), the occurrence of |taN-| '{somewhere}' with an unexpressed oblique complement construed as pronominal is rare; in the known cases the intended oblique is present overtly with the immediately preceding verb.

(2.125)   *e·h=ki·ška·pehkatenikini pye·ya·wa·čini, ahpene·či=meko e·h=tašiha·wa·či*
   maneto·wahi, ... (S-Apay 61)
   'Every time they came to places where there were cliffs they killed monsters there, ...'
   (|ki·ška·pehkaten-| II 'be a steep cliff', |e·h=–nikini| 0´/PPL(loc.obl.pl);
   |pya·-| AI 'come {somewhere}', |IC–wa·čini| 3p/ITER; *ahpene·či* 'every time';
   =*meko* EMPH; |taših-| TA 'kill {somewhere}', |e·h=–a·wa·či| 3p–3´/AOR;
   maneto·wahi 'monsters (obv.)')

(f) The relative root |taS-| '{so much, so many}' (*tasw-, taso·-; taswi* P; |taši| AI, |tasen-| II 'be {so much, so many}') takes an oblique that specifies an amount:

(2.126)   *a·pehtawapahkwe=meko wi·h=taso·seno·ni ta·htapako·ni.* (LL-LH 13)
   'Let the leaves on the ground be halfway up the sides.'
   (*a·pehtawapahkwe* 'halfway up the wall of the lodge'; =*meko* EMPH;
   |wi·h=| FUT, |taso·sen-| II 'be {so} many lying', |-wani| 0p/IND;
   ta·htapako·ni 'leaves')

In many constructions, 'one' (1.197; 2.241), 'two' (1.38, 127, 136, 138, 144; 2.108, 169), 'three' (1.141, 145), 'four' (1.129, 143, 279), 'five', and 'ten' are specified with initials, but other numbers appear as free particles used as oblique compliments to |taS-| '{so many}':

(2.127)   *no·hika e·h=taswipepo·nwe·ya·ni* 'when I was seven years old' (A 2F)
   (*no·hika* 'seven'; |taswipepo·nwe·-| AI 'be {so many} years old',
   |e·h=–ya·ni| 1s/AOR)

(2.128) *šwa·šika ta̱šiwaki* 'there are eight of them (anim.)' (S, JP, JB)

> (*šwa·šika* 'eight'; |taši-| AI 'be {so much, so many}', |–waki| 3p/IND)

The initial |taS-| '{so much, so many}' occurs without an oblique in certain constructions and idiomatic uses (2.214, 215, 247).

(g) Obliques of a second class have semantic functions that may be collectively referred to as instrumental. In explicit glosses an instrumental oblique is indicated as '{something}' to distinguish it from a secondary object.

(2.129) *wi·kopye·ni= 'pi so·kiha·pi.* 'He was tied with basswood strings.' (K-ECRP 37)

> (*wi·kopye·ni* 'cords of basswood inner bark'; |=ipi| HRSY;
> |so·kih-| TA 'tie (with {something})', |–a·pi| X–3/IND)

(2.130) *o·ni kehči-mehtekwina·kani=meko e·h=ahkwa·wiseki pene·wi·pemi.* (K-WYB 122)

> 'And then a great wooden bowl was filled with the turkey grease.'
>
> (*o·ni* 'and then'; *kehči-mehtekwina·kani* 'great wooden bowl'; *=meko* EMPH;
> |ahkwa·wisen-| II 'fill, be filled (with {something})', |e·h=–ki| 0/AOR;
> *pene·wi·pemi* 'turkey grease')

(2.131) *e·h=atame·heči meškohpwa·kanani* (O 119E)

> 'they were given a smoke from the catlinite pipe'
>
> (|atame·h-| TA 'cause to smoke (using {something})', |e·h=–eči| X–3/AOR;
> *meškohpwa·kanani* 'catlinite pipe (obv.)')

(2.132) *kwa·škwina·te·niki e·h=ča·kesowa·či ke·hkya·haki.* (S-Apay 50)

> 'The old folks were scalded to death by the boiling water.'
>
> (|kwa·škwina·te·-| II 'boil', |IC–niki| 0´/PPL(INsg);
> |ča·keso-| AI 'be burnt, scalded', |e·h=–wa·či| 3p/AOR; *ke·hkya·haki* 'old people')

(2.133) *owi·paškwahi e·h=ašiha·či ni·ča·pahi* 'he made dolls from corncobs' (K-M 691c)

> (*owi·paškwahi* 'corncobs (obv.)'; |aših-| TA 'make' + |e·h=–a·či| 3s–3´/AOR;
> *ni·ča·pahi* 'dolls (obv.)'
>
> *mi·ša·mi=ke·hi ni·h=ašihto pena i·ni owi·ši.* (K-TG 47F)
>
> 'And we're going to make a sacred pack with that head'
>
> (*mi·ša·mi* 'sacred pack'; *=ke·hi* 'and';
> |wi·h-| FUT, |ašiht-| TI(2) 'make', |ne–o·pena| 1p–0/IND;
> *i·ni* 'that (inan.)'; *owi·ši* 'head')

The initials |kek-| 'with, having {something}' (2.134*a*), |takw-| 'along with {something}', and |wa·wa·t-| 'mutually' (5.9*k*), especially as preverbs, and *wa·wiya·ki* PV 'mixed with' take an instrumental oblique. At least with |takw-| the oblique may be pronominal (2.134*b*), and with |wa·wa·t-| it is optional (5.8*n*).

(2.134) Initials and preverbs taking an instrumental oblique

> (a) *mi·ša·mi e·h=keko·mye·piniči* 'he sat with the sacred pack on his back' (O 160E)
>
> > (*mi·ša·mi* 'sacred pack';
> > |keko·mye·pi-| AI 'sit having {something} on one's back', |e·h=–niči| 3´/AOR)
>
> (b) *e·h=takwi-mešeneči* 'he was captured along with them' (O 149F)
>
> > (|takwi| PV 'along with {something}', |mešen-| TA 'catch', |e·h=–eči| X–3/AOR)
>
> (c) *a·kwi·ke·hi= 'pi·= 'nah neniwahi wa·wiya·ki-menowa·čini nepi ihkwe·waki.*
>
> > 'The women did not drink the water at the same time as the men.' (K-MP3 42)
> >
> > (*a·kwi* 'not'; *=ke·hi* 'moreover'; *=pi* HRSY; *i·nahi* 'there, in that case';
> > *neniwahi* 'men (obv.)'; |wa·wiya·ki| PV 'mixed with {something}';
> > |meno-| AI+O 'drink O2', |–wa·čini| 3p/NEG; *nepi* 'water'; *ihkwe·waki* 'women')

There is no oblique complement of |kek-| when it would be the same as the subject (O 90J), or when what functions as the oblique complement is a component of the same simple or compound stem (§38.3, 4.113*e*; §58, 4.370).

22.5. Adjunct. An adjunct is a noun phrase (or a particle functioning as a noun phrase [5.47]) that is linked either to a second noun phrase or to a sentence and specifies what the other noun phrase or the sentence relates to. In some cases an adjunct provides an attribution, a narrowing of reference, or a standard of reference for a comparison, such as might be glossed 'of', 'vis-à-vis', or 'compared to'. The link of an adjunct to more inclusive structures is unilateral and parasitic, being entirely due to its status an adjunct. Adjuncts are not licensed by the pronominal inflection or lexically specified argument structure of other words, and in this narrow sense they have no syntactic link to what they qualify.

The adjuncts linked to noun phrases (adnominal adjuncts) may be either partitive or attributive. Partitive adjuncts occur with quantifiers, either preceding (2.135*ab*) or following (2.135*cde*), and may be discontinuous (2.135*e*).

(2.135) Partitive adjuncts

(a)   *ma·haki a·neta* 'some of these (people)' (O 113A)

(b)   *neto·kima·mena·naki ni·šwi* 'two of our (exc.) chiefs' (K-Auto 286)

(c)   *a·neta=ma·haki* "some of these" (K-ECRP 72 2x; tr. TB)

(d)   *ni·šwi osi·me·hwa·wahi* 'two of their younger brothers' (K-G 5)

(e)   *a·kwi owiye·ha nekotahi wi·h=a·čini wi·nwa·wa.* (K-FC 310)
      'No one of them will go anywhere.'
         (*a·kwi* 'not'; *owiye·ha* 'someone, anyone'; *nekotahi* 'somewhere, anywhere';
         |wi·h=| FUT, |iha·-| AI 'go {somewhere}', |–čini| 3s/NEG;
         wi·nwa·wa 3p/EMPH [adjunct])

Attributive adjuncts also may either precede (2.136*abd*) or follow (2.136*c*) the noun phrase they are linked to and may be discontinuous.

(2.136) Attributive adjuncts

(a)   *nenoswi-owi·wi·naki na·tawino·ni* 'Buffalo-horn medicine.' (K-BH 1, title)
      (*nenoswi* PN 'of buffalo'; *owi·wi·naki* 'horns [adjunct]'; *na·tawino·ni* 'medicine')

(b)   *omehte·hwa·wahi='pi mehtekwa·pye·ni* 'the strings of their bows, they say'
      (S-Apay 63)
         (*omehte·hwa·wahi* 'their bows (obv.)'; |=ipi| HRSY; *mehtekwa·pye·ni*
         'bowstrings')

(c)   *nakamo·nani ki·ke·no·ni* 'clan-feast songs' (O 78F)
      (*nakamo·nani* 'songs'; *ki·ke·no·ni* 'clan feast [adjunct]')

(d)   *mano·ne·ha oškinawe·hani kepakamekwa?* (S-RL 42)
      'You mean Manoneha has a young man (obv.) (at her place) that hit you?'
         (*mano·ne·ha* 'Manoneha [adjunct]'; *oškinawe·hani* 'young man (obv.)';
         kepakamekwa 'he hit you'; *?* Q)

A locative noun or pronoun may serve as an attributive adnominal adjunct.

(2.137) Locatives as attributive adjuncts

(a)   *ohka·či onemači·neki* 'his left (rear) hoof' (K-MP1 14)
      (*ohka·či* 'his foot'; *onemači·neki* 'on his left side (loc.)' [adjunct])

(b)   *i·ya·h=owiye·he·hani* 'the animals (obv. sg.) up there' (K-WD 151)
      (*i·ya·hi* 'yonder' [adjunct]; *owiye·he·hani* 'animal (obv. sg.)')

The adjuncts linked to sentences (sentential adjuncts) indicate a point of reference (which may be internal or external) or a point of view. An internal point-of-reference adjunct indicates the source or focal point of what the verb denotes, especially an entity that is implicated in the action of the verb.

(2.138) Internal point-of-reference adjuncts

(a) *eˑh=wiˑškweˑweˑkahki meˑyoˑčiki* 'there was a din of people weeping' (O 160I)
(|wiˑškweˑweˑkat-| II 'be a great noise', |eˑh=-ki| 0/AOR;
|mayoˑ-| AI 'cry', |IC–čiki| 3/PPL(ANpl) [adjunct])

(b) *eˑh=mehčaˑki owiyeˑha pemehkaˑyane* (K-SSP 24)
'when you (sg.) walk in plain view of someone'
(|mehčaˑ-| II 'be open, clear {somewhere}', |eˑh=-ki| 0/PPL(loc.obl);
owiyeˑha 'someone' [adjunct]; |pemehkaˑ-| AI 'walk', |–yane| 2s/SUBJ)

Corresponding to the status of the adjuncts in (2.138) as internal is the fact that they do not cause the inanimate intransitive verbs to be obviative (since the adjunct participle and the verb are, in some sense, both aspects of the same thing; 6.26), unlike the external adjunct in (2.139a).

An external point-of-reference adjunct indicates the entity that is affected or relevant in any of a wide range of ways, including most generally that for which, that in the case of which, or that in connection with which the verbal state or action obtains or takes place.

(2.139) External point-of-reference adjuncts (generic function)

(a) *sanakateniwi niˑšoˑhkweˑwaˑčiki.* (K-MHTW 12)
'It's hard for those who have two wives.'
(|sanakat-| II 'be difficult', |–niwi| 0´/IND;
|niˑšoˑhkweˑwe-| AI 'have two wives', |IC–čiki| 3/PPL(ANpl) [adjunct participle])

(b) *eˑh=pyeˑči-mamaˑtomeˑči noˑšaˑničini* (K-Bene 93)
'a message came requesting their (medical) aid for (a woman) who was in childbirth'
(*pyeˑči* PN 'come and, to', |mamaˑtom-| TA 'entreat', |eˑh=–eˑči| X–3/AOR;
|noˑšeˑ-| AI 'give birth', |IC–ničini| 3´/PPL(OBVsg) [adjunct participle])

(c) *iˑni=mekoho wiˑh=oči-miˑškawesiwaˑči owiˑčiˑškweˑhwaˑwahi.* (K-FC 708)
'Because of that they will be mighty against their enemies.'
(*iˑni* 'that (inan.)'; *=mekoho* EMPH; |wiˑh=| FUT, |oči| PV 'from {something}',
|miˑškawesi-| AI 'be strong', |IC–waˑči| 3s/PPL(obl),
owiˑčiˑškweˑhwaˑwahi 'their enemies (obv.)' [adjunct])

One particular type of external adjunct states the standard of comparison with 'only', superlatives, and the like.

(2.140) External point-of-reference adjuncts: standard of comparison

(a) *mehtenoˑh=meko okyeˑni keˑški-neˑwokočini ihkweˑwahi.* (K-WSB 47; tr. HP)
"His mother was the only one of the women who could see him."
(|mehtenoˑhi| 'only'; *=meko* EMPH; *okyeˑni* 'his mother (obv.)';
|kaški| PV 'be able to', |neˑw-| TA 'see', |IC–ekočini| 3´–3s/PPL(OBVsg);
ihkweˑwahi 'women (obv.)' [adjunct])

(b) *kiˑči-anemi-mehtoseˑneniwa kiˑh=maˑwači-=meko -miˑškawesi.* (K-BBWM 40)
"you shall be the most powerful among your fellow people" (tr. HP)
(*kiˑči-anemi-mehtoseˑneniwa* 'your (sg.) fellow human being [adjunct]';
|wiˑh=| FUT, |maˑwači| PV 'of all'; *=meko* EMPH;
|miˑškawesi-| AI 'be powerful', |ke–| 2s/IND)

Very common is an adjunct outside a direct quotation that explains the pronominal reference of a verb inside the quotation:

    (2.141) Adjunct specifying the reference in a quotation

        (a)   *"ki·h=wača·hipwa=ča·hi," e·h=iniči i·nini kwi·yese·hani, i·nini ke·nwa·sowe·wani.*
               (K-BHD 7; tr. TB)
               " 'You [pl.] will now cook it for me,' the boy [obv.] said about that cougar [obv.]."
               (|wi·h=| FUT, |wača·h-| TA+O 'cook O2 for', |ke–ipwa| 2p–1s/IND; =ča·hi 'so';
               |i-| AI 'say {so}', |e·h=–niči| 3´/AOR; *i·nini* 'that (obv.)'; *kwi·yese·hani* 'boy (obv.)';
               i·nini 'that (obv.)'; *ke·nwa·sowe·wani* 'mountain lion (obv.)' [adjunct])

        (b)   *kotaka·='ni, "ki·h=ona·pe·mi," e·h=išiki.* (A 155C)
               'I was then told there was another (guy) that I was to marry.'
               (*kotaka* 'other (anim.)' [adjunct]; *i·ni* 'then';
               |wi·h=| FUT, |ona·pe·mi-| AI+O 'have O2 as husband', |ke–∅| 2s/IND;
               |iN-| TA 'say {so} to', |e·h=–iki| X–1s/AOR)

An adjunct is occasionally used to specify the agent of a passive verb; the verb may be inflected for an indefinite subject or be a derived passive.

    (2.142) Adjunct as agent of passive

        (a)   *i·na e·h=ne·woči apeno·ha kotakahi* 'that child was seen by others' (K-BHD 1)
               (*i·na* 'that (anim.)'; |ne·w-| TA |e·h=–eči| X–3/AOR; *apeno·ha* 'child';
               kotakahi 'others (obv.) [adjunct]' [i.e., not its parents])

        (b)   *i·ni='p=a·pehe·='na neniwahi, "nahi´, po·ni-mahkamahkate·wi·ši kekwisa,"*
               e·h=ineči. (K-MESB 13)
               'Then, they say, that (man) would be told by the (other) men, "Stop making your
                son fast." '
               (*i·ni* 'then'; |=ipi| HRSY; |=a·pehe| 'always'; |i·na| 'that (anim.)';
               neniwahi 'men (obv.) [adjunct]'; *nahi´* 'alright'; |po·ni| PV 'cease',
               |CVCV+| RED2, |mahkate·wi·N-| TA 'cause to fast', |–i| 2s–3/IMP;
               kekwisa 'your son'); |iN-| TA 'say {so} to', |e·h=–eči| X–3/AOR)

        (c)   *i·noki e·h=takwaho·soči e·škote·wi·hi.* (C-Hist 37)
               'Today somebody was run over by a train.'
               (*i·noki* 'today'; |takwaho·so-| AI 'be run over', |e·h=–či| 3s/AOR;
               e·škote·wi·hi 'train [adjunct]')

Point-of-view sentential adjuncts specify someone or something that plays no role in the named action but perceives or experiences it.

    (2.143) Point-of-view adjuncts

        (a)   *kapo·twe wi·nwa·wa e·h=we·pi-pya·niči neniwahi.* (K-FC 555)
               'Suddenly they had men arriving.'
               (*kapo·twe* 'at some point'; *wi·nwa·wa* 3p/EMPH [adjunct];
               |we·pi| PV 'begin', |pya·-| AI 'come' |e·h=–niči| 3´/AOR; *neniwahi* 'men (obv.)')

        (b)   *pe·hki=meko e·h=we·wenesiniči ihkwe·wa i·nini e·si·hani.* (K-WD 66; tr. HP)
               "The woman saw a beautiful clam shell."
               (*pe·hki* 'really'; =*meko* EMPH; |we·wenesi-| AI 'be pretty', |e·h=–niči| 3´/AOR;
               ihkwe·wa 'woman' [adjunct]; *i·nini* 'that (obv.)'; *e·si·hani* 'bivalve shell (obv.)')

    (c)   *we·wenesiniwani=ke·hi=·'pi oškinawe·haki.* (K-CM 9)
        'What's more, they say young men thought she was pretty.'
            (*we·wenesiniwani* 'she (obv.) is pretty'; *=ke·hi* 'moreover'; *=ipi* HRSY;
            oškinawe·haki 'young men' [adjunct])

    (d)   *o·ni neniwa kapo·twe e·h=ča·ki-=mekoho -onahona·pe miniči i·nihi še·škesi·he·hahi.*
        'And in time the man saw all those girls take husbands.' (K-FC 529)
            (*o·ni* 'and then'; *neniwa* 'man'; *kapo·twe* 'at some point'; *ča·ki* PV 'all',
            |CVCV+| RED1, |ona·pe·mi-| AI '(woman to) marry', |e·h=–niči| 3´/AOR;
            =mekoho EMPH; *i·nihi še·škesi·he·hahi* 'those young teenage girls (anim. obv.)')

Locative adjuncts specify a location but are not complements of a relative root (5.89).

22.6. Relational. A few non-third person verbal inflections may be replaced by distinct relational endings if there is an animate third person in the immediate context. Relational counterparts exist for certain conjunct, interrogative, prioritive, and potential endings that mark first singular or indefinite subjects. The use of the relational resembles the more automatic uses of the obviative, such as the forced obviation of inanimates and possessed nouns under similar circumstances.

    (2.144)   *e·h=ki·ke·noki* 'when a clan feast was given' (O 12D)
            e·h=ki·ke·no<u>we</u>či 'when a clan feast was given (rel.)' (O 11H)
    (2.145)   *me·ma·totamekini* 'whenever it is worshipped' (K-FC 182)
            me·ma·totamo<u>we</u>čini 'whenever it is worshipped (rel.)' (O 114G)
    (2.146)   *e·h=awi<u>ya</u>·ni* 'the place where I live'
            ke·hke·nemiči e·h=awi·hi<u>waki</u> (K-Auto 292) 'when he knew where I lived
            (dim., rel.)'

The relational endings partially resemble the corresponding TA endings added to a stem in *-w* TA. The relational cannot, however, be analyzed as a special TA formation for several reasons: the formal details differ (**§29.10(b)**); the relational is not freely made for all persons, as a derived TA would be; and the relational does not make pronominal reference to the third person that triggers it and cannot take an overt argument.

Vocative

23. Nouns and participles may be inflected for vocative forms, which announce who the utterance is addressed to.

    (2.147) Vocatives
        (a)   *oškinawe* 'young man!' (cf. *oškinawe·ha* 'a young man')
        (b)   *neni·tike* 'men!' (cf. *neniwaki* 'men')
        (c)   *nemešo·mesena·te* 'O grandfather of ours!'
            (cf. *nemešo·mesena·na* 'our (exc.) grandfather')
        (d)   *e·hkwe·wiyane* 'O women!' (|ihkwe·wi-| AI 'be a woman', |IC–yane| 2s/PPL(VOC))
            (*lit.*, 'O you (sg.) who are a woman', representative singular)

Vocatives do not occur with demonstratives or other determiners. They are syntactically independent of sentences, but they may cliticize to other words.

Inanimate nouns make singular and plural vocatives with the same inflections as animates:

    (2.148) Vocatives of inanimate nouns
        (a)   *mehtekwa·pye* 'O bowstring!' (Sh-Buz 25) (cf. 3.112)
        (b)   *nehka·tetike* '(O) my feet!' (Sh-Buz 28) (cf. 3.111)

Presumably, as with second-person verb forms, inanimate nouns must transfer to the animate gender to be inflected as vocatives.

Locative

24. Nouns have a locative form, which uses the same suffix |-eki| loc. for both genders. In the locative the contrast of number is neutralized, and obviation is not marked. The range of meanings is illustrated in (2.149).

    (2.149) Meanings of the locative

                aseni·ki 'at, on, or in the rock or rocks' (cf. *aseni* 'rock', *asenye·ni* 'rocks')

                okiki 'at, to his mother's; like his mother' (cf. *okye·ni* 'his mother')

The meaning 'like' appears to lie behind the use of the locative for a standard of comparison, which sometimes is found with *mehto·či* 'like':

    (2.150) Locative for standard of comparison

       (a)   a·wasi=meko pa·škesikaneki e·h=ahkwa·ška·niki owi·pwa·wani. (K-PLA 13)

            'Their arrows shot further than guns.'

                (*a·wasi* 'more'; *=meko* EMPH; *pa·škesikaneki* 'gun(s) (loc.)';

                |ahkwa·ška·-| II 'fall, fly {so far}', |e·h=–niki| 0′/AOR;

                owi·pwa·wani 'their arrows')

       (b)   *a·wasi=meko mehto·či e·h=ahpi·hte·neta·kosiči we·ta·se·ki.* (K-MIM 31)

            'He was thought of more highly than a warrior.'

                (*a·wasi* 'more'; *=meko* EMPH; *mehto·či* 'like'; |ahpi·hte·neta·kosi-| AI

                'be thought {so much} of', |e·h=–či| 3s/AOR; *we·ta·se·ki* 'warrior (loc.)')

Some nouns make derived collective forms that may be used for locatives with an explicitly plural reference (2.151, 4.191):

    (2.151) Locatives of collective nouns

       (a)   *wi·kiya·pihki·ki* 'in the houses, in the settlement'

                (Locative of *wi·kiya·pihkiwi* 'collection of houses', from *wi·kiya·pi* 'house'.)

       (b)   *aša·hina·ki* 'in the Sioux country'

                (Locative of *aša·hina·wi* 'the Sioux country', from *aša·ha* 'Sioux'.)

            neni·na·ki 'among men, like men, on the male side'

                (Derived from *neniwa* 'man'; compare *neni·ki* 'like a man'.)

Forms like those in (2.151) are really the locatives of distinct words derived from the simplex nouns (**§44**), rather than inflectional forms of the nouns. They are made on only a few nouns and have a much narrower range of use than ordinary locatives.

    Particles of location sometimes incorporate |-eki| loc. without being based on nouns (4.115):

    (2.152) *ahpemeki* 'up aloft'

            mehči·ki 'on the ground'

Some derived exocentric particles and particle phrases function as locatives (4.113; 5.71, 5.72*b*, 5.72*c*(1), 5.72*c*(7), 5.72*g*(1), 5.73*cfgh*).

    There are also locatives of demonstrative pronouns and certain other pronouns, as well as locative demonstratives that are not part of a demonstrative set. These have |-ahi| loc. indicating location and |-tepi| indicating displacement.

(2.153) *i nahi* 'at, on, in, or with that; there' (cf. *i ni* 'that (inan.)')

i ya·hi 'over there, up there, down there (at a distal ending point)'

i tepi 'to him, it, there (that distal goal)'

ta nahi 'where?'

ta tepi 'where to?; where from?'

Some participles (**§26.13, 17**) function as locatives (2.249, 251-258, 270, 281*d*).

Diminutives

25. Diminutive forms are made for nouns (2.154), intransitive and transitive verbs (2.155, 2.156), and some types of particles (2.157) and pronouns (2.158), though not from demonstrative or emphatic pronouns. Several different suffixes mark this category, but they all include an |h| preceded by a long vowel. In addition to small size, the diminutive may indicate other kinds of diminution and attenuation or an attitude of endearment or pity on the part of the speaker. In a diminutive verb the diminutive effect may apply to the verbal notion or to the subject or the object, or both. With verbs denoting qualities that have a scalar value the diminutive provides a comparative.

(2.154) *okwise·hani* 'his little, dear, or pitiful son' (cf. *okwisani* 'his son')

(2.155) *e·h=ne·se·hiči* 'he (baby) was still alive' (cf. *ne·se·wa* 'he survives, recovers')

e·h=keno·si·hiči 'he was taller' (cf. *e·h=keno·siči* 'he was tall')

e·h=pehtawaso·hiči 'he made himself a little fire'

   (cf. *pehtawasowa* 'he makes a fire for himself')

e na·kwi·hiki 'when it was early evening' (cf. *e na·kwiki* 'when it was evening')

(2.156) *mehkawe·hiwa* 'the poor thing found him; he found the poor thing; the poor thing found the poor thing' (AW; cf. *mehkawe·wa* 'he found him')

(2.157) *ma ne·he* 'quite a few' (cf. *ma ne* 'many')

kenwe·ši me·hi 'for quite a long time' (cf. *kenwe·ši* 'for a long time')

no·te·wi me·hi 'a bit before' (cf. *no ta* 'too soon')

(2.158) *we ne·he·ha* 'who (is the little one)?' (cf. *we ne·ha* 'who?')

Mode and Tense

26. Verbs distinguish a large number of categories with the functions of mode, evidential, and tense. The two tenses are the future (**§26.24**) and the preterite (**§26.25**). The other categories are conveniently referred to collectively as modes (**§§26.1-23**). Modes may be used independently, or their use may be partly or wholly determined by the syntactic context.

Many modes are multiply marked, having a particular set of pronominal inflections, one or more modal suffixes, and in some cases a modal prefix. In general, however, the modular formal components do not correspond perspicuously to components of meaning. No consistent general meaning can be recognized in such purely formal morphological components as the aorist proclitic preverb *e·h=* AOR, the ablauting process of initial change (**§29.4**), or the modal suffix |-ini| neg.-iter. Thus, although the modes may, to some extent, be arranged in sets according to their forms and functions, for the most part each mode is best considered as a unitary category marked in a complex way.

At the same time some modal uses fall into functional sets that crosscut their formal classification. For example, there is a core set of modes that, in effect, define the basic syntactic and semantic classification of clauses, each being the prototypical mode of a particular core clause type. A clause of one of these core types may have a verb of another mode (or a verbless predication), in which case the core modal function of the prototypical mode is present with an added grammatical category specified, or in some cases with simply a different formal expression. The core set of modes and the clause types they define are: the indicative (**§26.1**), defining indicative clauses; the aorist (**§26.8**), defining subordinate clauses; the potential (**§26.20**), defining potential clauses; and the imperative (**§26.22**), defining imperative clauses.

Disparate modes also function in parallel fashion in a construction in which verbs in the same mode as the main verb of a clause function like participles to define the specific reference of an indefinite noun or pronoun. This construction is found with verbs in the independent indicative (2.163), aorist conjunct (2.177), and subjunctive (2.193).

Attributive temporal clauses (meaning generally 'when') may have the verb in the aorist conjunct (**§26.8**), subjunctive (**§26.9**), changed conjunct (**§26.10**), or iterative (**§26.12**), or, implying the more precise meaning 'at the time or times when', they may have the particle *na·hina·hi* 'time, distance' in construction with a verb in any of these modes or with the changed interrogative (**§26.15**) or aorist interrogative (**§26.16**). The use of *na·hina·hi* may reduce or alter the range of possible temporal relations to the main verb, and in fact the changed interrogative does not make temporal clauses without it.

Substantival temporal clauses ('the time when') are made with *na·hina·hi* 'time' or *i·nina·hi* 'the time, that time' and the aorist conjunct, changed conjunct, iterative, or aorist or changed interrogative.

Generic conditional and temporal clauses have the aorist conjunct, but they appear in the subjunctive if the higher clause is future, subjunctive, or potential. If the higher verb is subjunctive, complement clauses that would ordinarily be in the aorist are also attracted into the subjunctive.

In contrast to the morphology of the modes, the morphemes that mark the two tenses generally have a consistent semantic content, and in most cases they combine with the modes in a modular fashion, though the patterns of use of the two tenses differ. The future morpheme (**§26.24**) functions as a future tense only with the independent modes, the aorist, negative, iterative, and participle in the conjunct order, and the interrogative modes; used with the subjunctive, prohibitive, potential, and imperative it indicates intention rather than temporal futurity. The preterite (**§26.25**) is found only with core conjunct modes (**§26.6**). The two tenses may occur together.

26.1. Independent indicative. The independent order is characterized by the use of pronominal inflections that in some cases include a prefix as well as suffixes.

The independent indicative (or indicative, for short; IND) makes statements and, with the interrogative intonation (**§6.2**), questions:

(2.159)   *ma·haki kene·wa·pena* 'we (inc.) see these [people]' (O 112E)
          (*ma·haki* 'these (anim.)'; |ne·w-| TA 'see', |ke–a·pena| 12–3/IND)

(2.160)   *kekehke·neta?* "Are you conscious?" (K-FC 18; tr. HP)
          (|kehke·net-| TI(1)-O 'know, be aware of things, be conscious', |ke–a| 2s/IND; *?* Q)

(2.161)   *ni·h=pi·tike?* 'may I come in?' (K-FC 26)
          (|wi·h=| FUT, |pi·tike·-| AI 'enter', |ne–ø| 1s/IND; *?* Q)

With an indicative higher verb of acting, pretending, appearing, dreaming, reporting, or the like a complement clause is in the indicative if it would be in the indicative as a main verb.

(2.162) Indicative in complement clause

(a) *mehto·či= 'pi=mekoho pemwa·pi ahpi·hčawiwa.* (O 46C)
  'They say he acted just as if he were shot.'
  (*mehto·či* 'like, as if'; |=ipi| HRSY; =*mekoho* EMPH;
  |pemw-| TA 'shoot', |–a·pi| X–3/IND; |ahpi·hčawi-| AI 'act {so}', |–wa| 3s/IND)

(b) *nekwi·yese·he·hi neteši·we·pi·hka·no.* 'I pretended to be a little boy.' (K-BHD 58)
  (|kwi·yese·he·hi-| AI 'be a little boy', |ne–Ø| 1s/IND;
  |iši·we·pi·hka·no-| AI 'pretend {so}', |ne–Ø| 1s/IND)

(c) *mehto·či=mekoho ihkwe·wani wi·čihe·wa išina·kwateniwi e·h=owi·kiči.* (K-FC 523)
  'His place looked as if he had a woman living there with him.'
  (*ihkwe·wani* 'woman (obv.)'; |wi·čih-| TA 'live with', |–e·wa| 3s–3´/IND;
  |išina·kwat-| 'appear {so}' II, |–niwi| 0´/IND); *e·h=owi·kiči* 'where he lived')

(d) *nekano·nekwa=nekoti netena·hpawa.* (K-BHD2 9)
  'I dreamt that someone spoke to me.'
  (|kano·N-| TA 'speak to', |ne–ekwa| 3s–1s/IND; *nekoti* 'one';
  |ina·hpawa·-| AI 'dream {so}', |ne–Ø| 1s/IND)

(e) *nene·wa·wa= 'škwe netena·hpawa ke·kye·peša·ta.* (K-SSP 44)
  'I dreamt that I saw one who was deaf.'
  (|ne·w-| TA 'see', |ne–a·wa| 1s–3s/IND; |=iškwe| WOMAN'S.EXPL;
  |ina·hpawa·-| AI 'dream {so}', |ne–Ø| 1s/IND;
  |kekye·peše·-| AI 'be deaf', |IC–ta| 3/PPL(ANsg))

(f) *kašketiwa, ina·čimowa.* 'He was constipated, he said.' (K-SF 32)
  (|kašketi-| AI 'be constipated', |–wa| 3s/IND,
  |ina·čimo-| AI 'narrate {so}', |–wa| 3s/IND)

(g) *ketepa·ši=ke·hi mani, ketena·čimo.* 'You love me even now, you say.' (K-OBES 171)
  (|tepa·N-| TA 'love', |ke–i| 2s–1s/IND; |=ke·hi| 'moreover'; *mani* 'as it is now';
  |ina·čimo-| AI 'narrate {so}', |ke–Ø| 2s/IND)

An indicative verb may function like a participle to define the specific reference of an indefinite noun phrase in an indicative clause. Naming constructions may use the independent indicative this way even with an aorist verb, at least in narrative (2.163c).

(2.163) Indicative functioning as participle

(a) *nene·ta·pe·škone·wi·hi we·wenetwi.* 'I have seen a beautiful flower.' (K-BHD2 31)
  (|ne·t-| TI(1) 'see', |ne–a| 1s–0/IND; *pe·škone·wi·hi* 'flower';
  |we·wenet-| II 'be good, pretty', |–wi| 0s/IND)

(b) *e·na·čimoči nekoti 'makitoka' išisowa, i·tepi e·h=a·piha·či.* (SP-MortB 46)
  'It's what was reported by a certain (man) named Makitoka',
  when he had been there.'
  (|ina·čimo-| AI 'report {so}', |IC–či| 3s/PPL(obl); *nekoti* 'one';
  makitoka (name); |išiso-| AI 'have {such} a name', |–wa| 3s/IND;
  i·tepi 'there'; |a·piha·-| AI 'have been {there}', |e·h=–či| 3s/AOR)

(c) *o·ni e·h=natomeči we·škaši·ha= 'pi išisowa.* (K-M 593h; tr. HP)
  "And a person whose name was Nail was asked to come."
  (*o·ni* 'and then'; |natom-| TA 'ask to come', |e·h=–eči| X–3/AOR; *we·škaši·ha*
  'Has-a-Fingernail'; |=ipi| HRSY; |išiso-| AI 'have {such} a name', |–wa| 3s/IND)

The interpretation of sentences like those in (2.163) as having a single main clause and not two coordinate clauses follows translations by native speakers; compare the parallel construction in other modes (2.177, 194).

In narratives the indicative does not ordinarily appear in the narrator's voice, but it may be used for comments presented as asides, often for increased vividness or emphasis or because they stand outside the narrative proper (e.g., O 57EF; 6.1). Otherwise it is very rare in narrative and of uncertain function.

The indicative mode defines the indicative clause type. The other mode that is commonly found in indicative clauses is the negative, and verbless indicative clauses are also common. Other modes appearing in indicative clauses have various evidential functions; these are the other modes of the independent order (the dubitative, conclusive, and assertive; **§26.2-4**), the plain interrogative (**§26.14**), and the prohibitive when meaning 'might' (**§26.19**, 2.296-301).

26.2. Independent dubitative. The dubitative (DUB) indicates that a statement or question is based on supposition or conjecture:

(2.164) Examples of the dubitative

(a) *keketeminawesipetoke.* 'It seems you (sg.) have received a blessing.' (O 66E)
(|keteminawesi-| AI 'be blessed', |ke–petoke| 2s/DUB)

(b) *kya·we·toke.* 'She must be jealous.' (A 153F)
(|kya·we·-| AI 'be (sexually) jealous' (4.326e), |–wetoke| 3s/DUB)

(c) *te·pesi·hi·toke·hiki* 'they must be somewhat thankful' (O 123A)
(|te·pesi·hi-| AI 'be thankful (dim.)', |–wetoke·hiki| 3p/DUB)

(d) *ke·htena=tike=manaha maneto·wi·toke?* (K-FC 331; EK)
'I wonder if he's really a manitou.'
(*ke·htena* 'truly'; *=tike* MAN'S.EXPL; *manaha* 'this (anim.)';
|maneto·wi-| AI 'be a manitou', |–toke| 3s/DUB; *?* Q)

With the negative preverb *pwa·wi* (~ *pa·wi*), which is normally not used in the independent order, the dubitative makes expressions of wondering or being uncertain.

(2.165) *pwa·wi- wi·na -pye·toke.* 'Why doesn't he come himself, I wonder?' (K-MFS 6)
(|pwa·wi| PV 'not'; *wi·na* 3s/EMPH; |pya·-| AI 'come', |–wetoke| 3s/DUB)

A dubitative form may be used in a participial function similar to that of the indicative (2.163), to specify an indefinite noun phrase as unidentified or conjecturally described.

(2.166) Dubitative functioning as participle

(a) *i·nahi='yo·we nešise·ha ako·ne·wa owiye·hasayini·toke.* (K-W 856)
'One of my uncles hung some kind of a skin there.'
(*i·nahi* 'there'; |=iyo·we| PAST; *nešise·ha* 'my uncle';
|ako·N-| TA 'hang', |–e·wa| 3s–3'/IND;
|owiye·hasayi-| AI 'be some creature's skin', |–ni·toke| 3'/DUB)

(b) *netanohka·nekwa ke·ko·heni·toke.* (X10-PBW 49)
'He asked me to make something or other.'
(|anohka·N-| TA 'commission', |ne–ekwa| 3s–1s/IND;
|ke·ko·hen-| II 'be something', |–ni·toke| 0'/DUB)

(c) *.. mešise·wahkiwini·toke i·ya·hi e·h=ahte·niki.* (K-ILM 1)
'.. there was what seemed to be a prairie chicken lek there.'
(|mešise·wahkiwi-| II 'be a prairie chicken lek', |–ni·toke| 0'/DUB;
i·ya·hi 'over there'; |ahte·-| II 'be {somewhere}', |e·h=–niki| 0'/AOR)

The dubitative suffix occurs in the enclitic *=ye toke* 'it seems, apparently, presumably' (2.171, 345, 357, 358; 5.122*z*).

26.3. Independent conclusive. The conclusive (CON) is used for a conclusion or a realization of something not previously known to the speaker:

    (2.167) Examples of the conclusive

        (a)   *ke·htena=meko išikeno·hapa.* 'So it must be true.' (X2-SAR 198)

            (*ke·htena* 'truly'; *=meko* EMPH; |išiken-| II 'be {so}', |–wehapa| 0s/CON)

        (b)   *pe·hki=ni·hka wi·keno·hapaniki pešekesiwi-ohka·taki.* (K-M 952.l)

           'Deer feet turn out to be very good eating.'

           (*pe·hki* 'really'; *=ni·hka* MAN'S.EXPL;

           |wi·keN-| AI 'taste good', |–wehapaniki| 3p/CON;

           pešekesiwi-ohka·taki 'deer feet')

Horace White Breast translated conclusive forms with the tag "and I never knew that before."

The conclusive suffix occurs in the enclitic *=ye·hapa* 'it turns out; I have found out; as we now see' (A 193H) and in the free particle *keye·hapa* 'I later found out or realized; as it turned out' (2.354, 357).

26.4. Independent assertive. The assertive (AST) marks a strong assertion by the speaker:

    (2.168) *wi·teko·wi·pani* 'he does have the nature of an owl' (O 16D, 16F; song)

           (|wi·teko·wi-| AI 'be an owl', |–wepani| 3s/AST)

The assertive is quite rare in texts. Only two endings are attested that are not in third-person intransitive forms, one found once and the other in two identical words (**§29.11c**).

The assertive suffix occurs in the enclitic *=ye·pani* (younger form *=ya·pani*) 'mind you', which is used with assertions, warnings, and the like.

26.5. Independent potential. The independent order has an archaic and extremely rare potential mode (IND.POT) attested by a single ending appearing, with |wi·h-| FUT, on two verbs in a traditional mythic utterance (Goddard 1995:140-141 [there called "future potential"]; **§30.5**).

26.6. Modes of the conjunct order. The conjunct order has a distinctive pattern of pronominal inflection that uses only suffixes. The modes of this type fall into four different sub-orders, each with characteristic inflections: the core conjunct (comprising the core conjunct modes), the interrogative (interrogative and prioritive modes), the prohibitive (prohibitive and future imperative modes), and the potential. While some pronominal suffixes are used in only one mode or sub-order, there are also a number that are shared by some or all of the sub-orders.

The core conjunct and interrogative sub-orders each have numerous modes. These two sub-orders have largely identical pronominal suffixes that are always followed by a modal suffix and have some modes marked by the proclitic preverb |e·h=| AOR (**§18.12**) or initial change (**§29.4**), which are not used in the prohibitive or potential sub-orders. The endings of the interrogative sub-order differ chiefly in including the irrealis suffix |-w|, which generally precedes the pronominal suffix but combines irregularly with suffixes that mark third and indefinite persons and has some other secondary effects.

The modes of the core conjunct sub-order are the plain conjunct (**§26.7**), aorist conjunct (**§26.8**), subjunctive (**§26.9**), changed conjunct (**§26.10**), negative (**§26.11**), iterative (**§26.12**), and conjunct participle (**§26.13**). The plain conjunct and the negative are used for main clauses, while the rest of the core conjunct modes make various kinds of subordinate clauses, except for some idiomatic uses.

The interrogative modes are the plain interrogative (**§26.14**), changed interrogative (**§26.15**), aorist interrogative (**§26.16**), and interrogative participle (**§26.17**). The prioritive modes (§26.18) are the plain prioritive and changed prioritive. The plain interrogative is used in main clauses, and the other interrogative and prioritive modes in subordinate clauses, again with some idiomatic exceptions. The interrogative modes do not make questions, although the plain interrogative may appear in interrogative sentences; the name is conventional.

26.7. Plain conjunct. The plain conjunct (CONJ) is used after *a·mihtahi* POT to make potential clauses (§26.20) with *i·ni* 'then' and *o·ni* 'and then'; less commonly *a·mihtahi* is used with neither of these:

(2.169) Plain conjunct with *a·mihtahi*

    (a)   *i·n=a·mihtahi i·niki ni·šo·ka·pawiheči.* (O 52A)
        'Then they would be made to stand as a pair.'
           (*i·ni* 'then'; *a·mihtahi* POT; *i·niki* 'those (anim.)';
           |ni·šo·ka·pawih-| TA 'make stand as a pair', |–eči| X–3/CONJ)

    (b)   *i·n=a·mihtahi akwapineči, ...* (K-Med 12) 'Then he would be bandaged, ...'
           (*i·ni* 'then'; *a·mihtahi* POT; |akwapiN-| TA 'bandage', |–eči| X–3/CONJ)

    (c)   *a·mihtah=wi·na=meko nesa·či.* (K-WYB 187)
        "Then he himself would kill them indeed." (tr. TB)
           (*a·mihtahi* POT; *wi·na* 3s/EMPH; *=meko* EMPH; |neS-| TA 'kill', |–a·či| 3s–3´/CONJ)

Especially after the potential has been established in a passage, but sometimes independently, the plain conjunct is used alone with the same potential function:

(2.170)   *mawi-wa·pama·či.* 'And he would go and examine them.' (O 40A)
        (*mawi* PV 'go and', |wa·pam-| TA 'look at', |–a·či| 3s–3´/CONJ)

In the passage preceding (2.170) *a·mihtahi* POT is used in (O 39H) and the potential mood in (O 39I).

The plain conjunct is also used independently with an apparent expressive flavor in the apodosis of conditional sentences (2.171*ab*) and in certain kinds of expressive idioms (2.171*cd*). These cases presumably also have idiomatic uses of the potential function.

(2.171) Plain conjunct in expressive constructions

    (a)   *ki·hpene=meko pahkiwaki ne·wake, nepowa·či=meko.* (SP-Ogre 179)
        'If ever I see any partridges, they would die!' (A threatening vow.)
           (*ki·hpene* 'if ever'; *=meko* EMPH; *pahkiwaki* 'grouse (pl.)';
           |ne·w-| TA 'see', |–ake| 1s–3/SUBJ; |nep-| AI 'die', |–wa·či| 3p/CONJ)

    (b)   *ki·hpene=meko pwa·wi-=ke·ko·hi=-'ši-kehke·netama·tisoyaneh, / nepeyakwe.*
        (C-YBB 5)
        'Were it the case that you'd gained no knowledge of how to do anything,/ we'd die!'
           (*ki·hpene* 'if ever'; *=meko* EMPH;
           pwa·wi PV 'not'; *ke·ko·hi* 'something'; |iši| PV '{so}';
           |kehke·netama·tiso-| AI 'learn about self', |–yanehe| 2s/SUBJ.PRET;
           |nep-| AI 'die', |–yakwe| 12/CONJ)

    (c)   *pwa·wi-=ye·toke=meko me·nešite·he·weni' -ahto·yani!* (C-FS 12; EK)
        'Apparently you have no shame at all!' (as if: 'It seems you'd have no shame!')
           (*pwa·wi* PV 'not'; *=ye·toke* 'it seems'; *=meko* EMPH;
           me·nešite·he·weni 'shame'; |aht-| TI(2) 'have', |–o·yani| 2s–0/CONJ; ! EXPR)

    (d)   *pa·wi-=ye·toke=meko -me·nešite·he·yani.* 'Aren't you ashamed of yourself!' (C-FS 6)
           (*pa·wi* PV 'not', |me·nešite·he·-| AI 'be ashamed';
           |=ye·toke| 'probably'; |=meko| EMPH)

Expressive intonation (**§6.4**) was obtained for (2.171*c*) and is a likely possibility for the other examples in (2.171) and for (2.172).

The rare instances of the plain conjunct used independently outside such constructions also appear to have an expressive flavor:

(2.172) *si po ki= 'pi pi ta ška nici.* (C-PD 7) 'They would run into the river!'

(*si po wi* 'river', |-eki| LOC; |=ipi| HRSY; |pi ta ška -| AI 'run into', |–nici| 3´/CONJ)

The sentence in (2.172) expresses the welcome realization by a warparty that their fleeing enemies would be trapped.

26.8. Aorist conjunct. The aorist conjunct (AOR) is used for coordinate clauses that imply temporal succession, for conditional subordinate clauses, for temporal subordinate clauses indicating co-occurrence, and for nominalizations and objective sentential complements. Common translations are: 'and', 'when', 'as', 'because', and 'that'. (For the aorist combined with the future, see **§26.24**.)

(2.173) Examples of the aorist

(a) *e h=taši hka noya ni* 'when I played' (A 1E)

(|taši hka no-| AI 'play', |e h=–ya ni| 1s/AOR)

(b) *e h=wi naniha či* 'as he was butchering it' (O 154C)

(|wi nanih-| TA 'butcher', |e h=–a či| 3s–3´/AOR)

(c) *e h=mawi-mi ka ti nici* 'because they (obv.) were going off to war' (O 18C)

(*mawi* PV 'go and', |mi ka ti -| AI 'fight', |e h=–nici| 3´/AOR)

The aorist may be accompanied by the particle *na hina hi* 'time':

(2.174) *na hina h e h=pešekwa hiyani* 'at the time of your divorce' (A 168J)

(*na hina hi* 'time'; |pešekwa hi-| 'get divorced', |e h=–yani| 2s/AOR

In (A 1B) two aorists without *na hina hi* 'time', one the complement of *ociwe pi* 'from {then} on', are in what is virtually an equational construction.

The aorist conjunct is also the usual mode in main clauses that begin with *i ni* 'then', *o ni* 'and then', or *kaho ni* 'so then':

(2.175) Aorist after particles for 'then'

(a) *i ni=ke h=meko e h=po ni wa či.* 'And then they immediately camped.' (O 14A)

(*i ni* 'then'; |=ke hi| 'moreover'; =*meko* EMPH;

|po ni -| AI 'camp', |e h=–wa či| 3p/AOR)

(b) *kaho ni na hka e h=a čimohiki.* 'So then I was again given instructions.' (A 98C)

(*kaho ni* 'so then'; *na hka* 'again'; |a čimoh-| TA 'inform', |e h=–iki| X–1s/AOR)

The aorist is the mode regularly used in main clauses in narrative even without these particles:

(2.176) Aorist in narrative

(a) *e h=ašamekowa či.* 'And it (anim. obv.) fed them.' (O 61H)

(|ašam-| TA 'feed', |e h=–ekowa či| 3´–3p/AOR)

(b) *e h=ki we wa či ne nosohka čiki.* 'The buffalo hunters turned back.' (O 126I)

(|ki we -| AI 'turn back', |e h=–wa či| 3p/AOR;

|nenosohke -| AI 'hunt buffalo', |IC–čiki| 3p/PPL(ANpl))

In a clause having an aorist verb, a second aorist conjunct may be used with an indefinite participial function, in the same way as the indicative (2.163):

(2.177) Aorist functioning as participle

    (a)   *e·h=ne·tamowa·či pe·hki e·h=meša·niki kohkoseni.* (K-SSP 69)
           'They saw a really large boulder.'
                (|ne·t-| TI(1) 'see', |e·h=–amowa·či| 3p–0/AOR; *pe·hki* 'really';
                |meša·-| II 'be big', |e·h=–niki| 0´/AOR; *kohkoseni* 'boulder')

Apparently all examples of this construction have a narrative aorist.

    The aorist conjunct is sometimes used in main clauses outside of narrative (2.178, 6.22*b*).

    (2.178) Aorist in main clauses

    (a)   *e·h=pye·či-wa·pamena·ni, nešemi.* (A 168E)
           'I've come to see you, niece.' (Beginning of quotation.)
                (*pye·či* PV 'coming', |wa·pam-| TA 'look at', |e·h=–ena·ni| 1s–2s/AOR;
                nešemi 'my niece (voc.)')

    (b)   *wo·-o·´, e·h=nese·kwe!* 'WAA-HAA! Now you've KILLED him!' (C-Ston 34)
                (|neS-| TA 'kill', |e·h=–e·kwe| 2p–3/AOR; ! EXPR)

    (c)   *i·h=natawi-nepo·hiči| kekwisena·na.* 'Our son might die.' (K-OMSP 11)
                (*wi·h=* FUT; *natawi* PV 'seek to; be time to'; |nepo·hi-| AI 'die', |e·h=–či| 3s/AOR;
                kekwisena·na 'our (inc.) son')

    (d)   *wi·h=owi·weti·ya·ke=kohi.* 'We would very much like to get married.' (K-2 3H)
                (*wi·h=* FUT; |owi·weti·-| AI 'marry each other', |e·h=–ya·ke| 12/AOR;
                =kohi 'certainly')

While such sentences might be considered to have a special use of the narrative aorist, there is no discourse context that would account for this. In fact, as the examples show, the reference is not to a past event but variously to the present effect or outcome of an action or to a future circumstance.

    The proclitic preverb |e·h=| AOR is not realized overtly when it would occur with the proclitic preverb |wi·h=| FUT (2.328-332). Much less frequently, when |e·h=| AOR is present, |wi·h=| FUT may be replaced by |wi·hi| PV FUT (**§26.24**, 2.333). Otherwise the aorist conjunct is found without |e·h=| AOR only in songs (where such forms are normal and often main verbs) and in casual style:

    (2.179) *tepehkwi no·tama·ni* 'I carry night upon my back.' (song; O 19B)
                (*tepehkwi* 'night'; |no·t-| TI(1) 'carry on back', |<e·h=>–ama·ni| 1s–0/AOR)

    (2.180) *na·kwa·wa·či.* 'They left.' (oral narrative; Jones 1907:58.14)
                (|na·kwa·-| AI 'leave', |<e·h=>–wa·či| 3p/AOR)

    (2.181) *kehkawiči* 'when he specified me' (casual style; Voorhis 1971:75)
                (|kehkahw-| TA 'specify', |<e·h=>–iči| 3s–1s/AOR)

Aorists without |e·h=| AOR (like 2.180) are, however, extremely rare in written narrative texts.

26.9. Subjunctive. The subjunctive (SUBJ) indicates 'if' or 'when' conditions in statements about the future (2.182) or in generic accounts of customary behavior (2.183):

    (2.182) *i·ni išawiyane* 'if you (sg.) do that' (O 157B)
                (*i·ni* 'that'; |išawi-| AI 'do {so}', |–yane| 2s/SUBJ)
           wa·pake 'tomorrow' (A 42E)
                (|wa·pan-| II 'be morning', |–ke| 0/SUBJ)

    (2.183) *pema·mowa·te* 'if they ran away' (O 49E)
                (|pema·mo-| AI 'flee', |–wa·te| 3p/SUBJ)

menopye·ya·wi anenwi·ke. 'It is good water for swimming.' (K-Words 2.31)

    (|menopye·ya·-| II 'have good water', |–wi| 0/IND;

    |anenwi·-| AI 'swim', |–ke| X/SUBJ)

It may be accompanied by the particle *na·hina·hi* 'time':

(2.184) *na·hina·hi nepo·hiya·ke* 'at the time when we die' (K-FC 509)

    (*na·hina·hi* 'time'; |nepo·hi-| AI 'die (dim.)', |–ya·ke| 12/SUBJ)

ne·wake na·hina·hi 'at the time I see him' (K-TCSB 36)

    (|ne·w-| TA 'see', |–ake| 1s–3/SUBJ)

It is also used for conditions that are contrary to fact in the present, either inherently or as a result of the non-occurrence of something.

(2.185) *kotake·hite=wi·na, awita i·ni išawisa.* (K-Wpn 43)

    'If, however, he were another (sort of person), he wouldn't have done that.'

    (|kotake·hi-| AI 'be another', |–te| 3s/SUBJ; =*wi·na* 'but';

    awita 'not (pot.)'; *i·ni* 'that (inan.)'; |išawi-| AI 'do {so}', |–sa| 3s/POT)

ki·ši-=mi·ši·ke, we·pi-=mekoho ·na·nakamohka·ha. (K-Wpn 146)

    'If I had already been given them (the songs), I would indeed begin to sing.'

    (ki·ši PV PERF; =*ke·hi* 'moreover'; |mi·N-| TA+O 'give O2 to', |–ike| X–1s/SUBJ;

    |we·pi| PV 'begin'; =*mekoho* EMPH;

    |CV+| RED1, |nakamo-| AI 'sing', |–hka·ha| 1s/POT)

The subjunctive may be used in a main clause in certain idiomatic constructions. Used alone (2.186) or with *na·pi=wi·na* (literally 'but better'; 2.187) it makes a suggestion or polite request; presumably the older construction was with *na·pi* in a predicative function ('it would be a good idea if').

(2.186) *ase·ma·wani awatawate.* 'You should take tobacco to them.' (C-WH 21)

    (*ase·ma·wani* 'tobacco (obv.)'; |awataw-| TA+O 'take O2 to', |–ate| 2s–3/SUBJ)

nepo·pihka·so·hiye·kwe. 'You can make yourselves a little soup.' (C-WH 16)

    (|nepo·pihka·so·hi-| AI 'make one's soup (dim.)', |–ye·kwe| 2p/SUBJ)

wi·hpe·ti·yakwe. 'Let's sleep together.' (K-TYFB 53)

    (|wi·hpe·ti·-| AI 'sleep together', |–yakwe| 12/SUBJ)

owiye·ha=na·hkači ni·ka·ni·te. 'Someone else can take the lead.' (K-ECRP 51)

    (*owiye·ha* 'someone'; *na·hkači* 'again'; |ni·ka·ni·-| AI 'lead', |–te| 3s/SUBJ)

aška·powi=ke·hi ašihto·wa·te. 'That way they can make fresh soup.' (C-WH 16)

    (*aška·powi* 'fresh soup'; =*ke·hi* 'moreover';

    |ašiht-| TI(2) 'make', |–o·wa·te| 3p–0/SUBJ)

(2.187) *na·pi=wi·na natawisenye·yakwe.* 'Shall we go look for a meal?' (K-Words 45)

    (*na·pi* 'better'; =*wi·na* 'but'; |natawisenye·-| AI 'seek to eat', |–yakwe| 12/SUBJ)

After the particle phrase *ta·ni·='nahi* (rare variants *taya·nahi*, *tawa·nahi*) it expresses a wish:

(2.188) *ta·ni·='nahi anwa·či·te.* 'I wish she would consent.' (A 84D)

    (*ta·ni·='nahi* 'I wish'; |anwa·či·-| AI 'consent', |–te| 3s/SUBJ)

When subordinated to another subjunctive or to a future verb, the subjunctive also subsumes the subordinating functions of the aorist, making temporal clauses (e.g., O 92E) and objective complements:

(2.189)   *ki·ši-kehke·netame·kwe .. nahikeke* (O 88E)
          'when you (pl.) have come to know that it is right'
              (*ki·ši* PV PERF, |kehke·net-| TI(1) 'know', |–ame·kwe| 2p–0/SUBJ;
              |nahiken-| II 'be proper', |–ke| 0/SUBJ)
          ki·ši-=ke·h -nahikwa·soyane kehke·nemeneke (A 60C)
          'what's more, when people know that you've become good at sewing'
              (*ki·ši* PV PERF, |nahikwa·so-| AI 'know how to sew', |–yane| 2s/SUBJ;
              |=ke·hi| 'moreover'; |kehke·nem-| TA 'know', |–eneke| X–2s/SUBJ)
(2.190)   *wi·hpe·mate ina·hpawa·yane* (A 169G)
          'if you (sg.) dream that you're sleeping with him'
              (|wi·hpe·m-| TA 'sleep with', |–ate| 2s–3/SUBJ;
              |ina·hpawa·-| AI 'dream {so}', |–yane| 2s/SUBJ)
(2.191)   *ki·h=ne·wokona·naki ke·htena=mekoho keteminawakwe* (K-M 166cd; tr. HP)
          "[they] shall see .. that we shall really bless her"
              (|wi·h=| FUT, |ne·w-| TA 'see', |ke–ekona·naki| 3p–12/IND;
              ke·htena 'truly'; =*mekoho* EMPH; |keteminaw-| TA 'bless', |–akwe| 12–3/SUBJ)
          a·kwi wi·h=kehke·netamowa·čini aškote·winike. (K-SSP 31)
          'They will not know that there is a fire there.'
              (*a·kwi* 'not'; |wi·h=| FUT, |kehke·net-| TI(1) 'know', |-amowa·čini| 3p–0/NEG;
              |aškote·wi-| II 'be a fire, have a fire in it', |-nike| 0'/SUBJ)
          wi·h=iši-ke·keteminawa·wa·či išawinite mehtose·neniwahi (K-Mes 21C)
          'what they should bless people to do'
              (|wi·h=| FUT, |iši| PV '{so}',
              |CV+| RED1, |keteminaw-| TA 'bless', |IC–a·wa·či| 3p–3'/PPL(obl));
              |išawi-| AI 'do {so}', |–nite| 3'/SUBJ; *mehtose·neniwahi* 'people (obv.)'

Under similar conditions a subjunctive may even substitute for a locative oblique participle,
which is formed the same way as an aorist conjunct (**§26.13**, 2.251-252):

(2.192)   *nepa·te pemehka·yane* 'if you walk by where he's sleeping' (C-IW 27)
              (|nepa·-| AI 'sleep {somewhere}', |–te| 3s/SUBJ;
              |pemehka·-| AI 'walk by {somewhere}', |–yane| 2s/SUBJ)
          po·sehkahkiwinike awite 'if he is in a deep hollow in the ground' (K-SSP 203)
              (|po·sehkahkiwi-| II 'be deeply hollowed ground {somewhere}', |–nike| 0'/SUBJ;
              |awi-| AI 'be {somewhere}', |–te| 3s/SUBJ)
          mo·hči pi·kwa·ke pemi-'šisa·ya·ne 'even if I run through a thicket' (X2-SAR 52-53)
              (*mo·hči* 'even'; |pi·kwa·-| II 'be a thicket', |–ke| 0/SUBJ;
              |pemi| PV 'along', |išisa·-| AI 'run {so}', |–ya·ne| 1s/SUBJ)

A future complement of a subjunctive is usually a future aorist (A 146E, 179F), but it may also
be a future subjunctive:

(2.193)   *wi·h=kya·take išite·he·te* 'if he intends to keep it a secret' (O 134F)
              (|wi·h=| FUT, |kya·t-| TI(1) 'keep secret', |–ake| 3s–0/SUBJ;
              |išite·he·-| AI 'think {so}', |–te| 3s/SUBJ)
          oto·kima·mahi wi·h=ča·kihtawate ine·nemate (K-MFWB 84)
          'if you want to kill all their chiefs'
              (*oto·kima·mahi* 'their chiefs'; |wi·h=| FUT, |ča·kihtaw-| TA+O 'kill all O2 for',
              |–ate| 2s–3/SUBJ; |ine·nem-| TA 'think {so} of', |–ate| 2s–3/SUBJ)

In such cases the complement has the meaning of a future aorist conjunct, but it has the inflection of a subjunctive as a result of attraction to the mode of the higher verb. This construction may be compared to the future subjunctive without a higher verb, meaning 'if he wishes to' (2.339) and the like.

A subjunctive may be used in an indefinite participial function, in the same way as the indicative (2.163) and the aorist conjunct (2.177):

(2.194) *ki·hpene ne·wakwe wa·peškesite pešekesiwa* (K-ECRP 40)
'if we happen to see a white deer'
(*ki·hpene* 'in the event that'; |ne·w-| TA 'see', |–akwe| 12–3/SUBJ;
|wa·peškesi-| AI 'be white', |–te| 3s/SUBJ; *pešekesiwa* 'deer')

In (2.194) the word order precludes taking the second subjunctive form as constituting a separate clause.

26.10. Changed conjunct. The changed conjunct (CC) makes temporal clauses that specify completion before the time of the main verb; it can be translated 'when' or 'after'. In narratives it is often used with the perfective preverb *ki·ši*.

(2.195) *i·ya·hi pye·ya·či* 'when she arrived there' (O 70H)
(*i·ya·hi* 'yonder'; |pya·-| AI 'arrive {somewhere}', |IC–či| 3s/CC)
mani e·ši-pemi-nowi·wa·či 'as soon as they walked out' (O 116C)
(*mani* 'this (inan.)'; |iši| PV '{so}' [idiom; cf. 2.89],
|pemi| PV 'along', |nowi·-| AI 'go out', |IC–wa·či| 3p/CC)
ki·ši-wi·seniwa·či 'after they had eaten' (O 61I)
(*ki·ši* PV PERF, |wi·seni-| AI 'eat', |IC–wa·či| 3p/CC)

The changed conjunct also makes clauses that designate a time in an absolute sense rather than in relation to a later time. It may be used independently, to refer to a specific time (2.196) or, idiomatically, a recurring time (2.197), but more commonly it is used with one of the particles *na·hina·hi* 'time, the first time' or *i·nina·hi* 'that time' (2.198; 5.94), or with one of the initials |aye·N-| 'continue to' (*aye·ši* PV, *aye·hi* PV) (2.199) or |ahpi·ht-| 'be in the process of' (*ahpi·hči* PV) (2.200). Such temporal clauses in equational constructions pattern like participles and may be considered to be participles of time (Thomason 2001); as such they make a potential with *a·mi* PV POT, like other participles (2.269-270).

(2.196) *e·ški-kano·šiyameči* '(at the time) when he first spoke to us (exc.)' (O 123B)
(*aški* PV 'first', |kano·N-| TA 'speak to', |IC–iyameči| 3–1p/CC)

(2.197) *me·no·hkami·niki* 'in spring', i.e., 'each spring' (O 133G)
(|meno·hkami·-| II 'be spring', |IC–niki| 0´/CC)
e·tasenwi-=meko -pehkote·ki 'each successive night' (SP-MRD 13)
(*tasenwi* '{so many} times'; =*meko* EMPH; |pehkote·-| AI 'be night', |IC–ki| 0/CC)

(2.198) *na·hina·hi na·kwa·či* 'at the time he started off' (O 17A)
(*na·hina·hi* 'time'; |na·kwa·-| AI 'leave', |IC–či| 3s/CC)
i·nina·h=meko mehteno·hi we·ši·heči. (O 2G)
'It was only at that time that it (anim.) was painted.'
(*i·nina·hi* 'that time'; =*meko* EMPH; *mehteno·hi* 'only';
|we·ši·h-| TA 'paint', |IC–eči| X–3/CC)

i·nina·h=ča·h=mani a·mi-pya·či. (K-WYB 15; tr. TB)
"She would have come [by] now."
> (|i·nina·hi| 'that time'; |=ča·hi| 'so'; *mani* 'this (inan.)';
> *a·mi* PV POT, |pya·-| AI 'come (back)', |IC–či| 3s/CC)

(2.199)   *e·ye·ši-ašihto·či maškimote·hi* 'while she was making a bag' (O 69J)
> (|aye·ši| PV 'continue to', |ašiht-| TI(2) 'make', |IC–o·či| 3s–0/CC;
> *maškimote·hi* 'bag')

e·ye·h-wa·se·ya·ki 'while it's still light' (A 9C)
> (|aye·hi| PV 'continue to', |wa·se·ya·-| II 'be light', |IC–ki| 0/CC)

(2.200)   *e·hpi·htetone·moweči* 'while a talk was being given (rel.)' (O 9A)
> (|ahpi·htetone·mo-| AI 'be in the process of talking', |IC–weči| X/REL/CC)

e·hpi·hči-ne·se·ye·kwe 'as long as you (pl.) are still living' (O 93C)
> (|ahpi·hči| PV 'be in the process of', |ne·se·-| AI 'live on', |IC–ye·kwe| 2p/CC)

e·hpi·htose·či=meko kapo·twe 'at some point right while he was walking along'
(K-B 5)
> (|ahpi·htose·-| AI 'be in the process of walking', |IC–či| 3s/CC; *=meko* EMPH;
> *kapo·twe* 'at some point')

26.11. Negative. The negative (NEG) is used with the particle *a·kwi* 'not' to make negative indicative clauses (2.201a), including negative questions (2.201b).

(2.201) Negative with *a·kwi*

(a)   *a·kwi=na·hka atama·wa·čini.* 'And also they did not smoke.' (O 10E)
> (*a·kwi* 'not'; *na·hka* 'also'; |atama·-| AI 'smoke', |–wa·čini| 3p/NEG)

(b)   *a·kwi ne·we·kwini? meškwe·he·wa?* 'Have you (pl.) not seen a red swan?' (K-F 13)
> (*a·kwi* 'not'; |ne·w-| TA 'see', |–e·kwini| 2p–3/NEG; *meškwe·he·wa* 'red swan'; ? Q)

The use of the negative mode without *a·kwi* has been found only in a rare idiom meaning 'can never help doing (so)' that has the preverb sequence *kaški-pwa·wi* (always written without a divider; literally '(not) be able to not' [5.11*a*, 5.6*a*]):

(2.202) Negative without *a·kwi*

(a)   *kaški-pwa·wi-='pi=mek=a·pehe·-ki·wa·tesiwa·čini* (K-MND 7)
'they could never help feeling lonely (when ...)'
> (*kaški* PV 'be able to', *pwa·wi* PV 'not'; |=ipi| HRSY; |=meko| EMPH;
> |=a·pehe| 'usually'; |ki·wa·tesi-| AI 'be lonely', |–wa·čini 3p/NEG)

(b)   *kaški-pwa·wi-='pi=mek=a·pehe, "šihihwi·´," -iničini.* (K-MMGW 2)
'They (obv.) could never help exclaiming, "Wow!" '
> (*kaški* PV 'be able to', *pwa·wi* PV 'not'; |=ipi| HRSY; |=meko| EMPH;
> |=a·pehe| 'usually'; *šihihwi·´* 'wow!'; |i-| AI 'say {so}', |–ničini| 3´/NEG)

The negative supplies the negation only in indicative clauses (§26.1). In other types of clauses negation is indicated variously. The potential has its own negative particle (§26.20), as does the prohibitive when used as a negative imperative (§26.19). Other modes, and the prohibitive in non-imperative uses, use the preverb *pwa·wi* 'not' (younger variant *pa·wi*), which may also be used after any of the modally specialized negative particles.

(2.203)   *e·h=pwa·wi-nenoše·wa·či* 'because they didn't listen' (A 6B)
> (|pwa·wi| PV 'not', |nenoše·-| AI 'heed', |e·h–wa·či| 3p/AOR)

(2.204)   *a·kwi mo·hči nekoti pwa·wi-nakamočini.* (K-FC 117)
          'There wasn't even one of them that failed to sing.'
          (*a·kwi* 'not'; *mo·hči* 'even'; *nekoti* 'one';
          |pwa·wi| PV 'not', |nakamo-| AI 'sing', |–čini| 3s/NEG)

The preverb *pwa·wi* 'not' is not used for ordinary negative statements, though it may be used in an independent indicative, dubitative, or potential verb in certain idiomatic sentence types (2.205*ab*, 207, 208), or, for example, with a prohibitive in a question indicating uncertainty (2.205*c*).

(2.205) |pwa·wi|, |pa·wi| PV 'not' in indicative clauses

   (a)   *pa·w-a·hpeči-pi·tike·wa!* 'He should always just come in!' (C-FS 12; EK)
          (|pa·wi| PV 'not', |a·hpeči| PV 'permanently',
          |pi·tike·-| AI 'enter', |–wa| 3s/IND; ! EXPR)

   (b)   *pwa·wi-ašatiso·toke!?* (K-M 115g; tr. EK)
          'He obviously must've fed himself (before this)!'
          (|pwa·wi| PV 'not'; |ašatiso-| AI 'feed self', |–wetoke| 3s/DUB); !? EN)

   (c)   *pwa·wi-=ke·hi -še·škesi·hihkiče?* 'Is she possibly not a virgin?' (K-FM 13)
          (|pwa·wi| PV 'not', |še·škesi·hi-| AI 'be a virgin', |–hkiče| 3s/PROH;
          =*ke·hi* 'moreover'; ? Q)

Other negative preverbs are not so restricted: *po·ni* PV 'cease, no longer do', *a·nawi* PV 'fail to, be unable to'.

Negative main clauses with indicative or potential verbs are also made with the irregular enclitic |=ihi| NEG (**§§4.4, 68.2(d)**), which is always followed by one of a small set of enclitics. This takes the shape = '*hi* before |=iyo| 'for' (2.206); = '*h* before =*we·na* (variant =*we·* before some enclitics) 'in fact, after all' (2.207, 208; A 92G, 131F, 183F, 190D, 192D; O 142C, 142F) and =*ya·pi* 'here I go, here we go'; and zero before =*ča·hi* 'so' (A 139D) and =*ye·toke* 'it seems' (2.171). It indicates that the speaker considers the corresponding non-negative to be ridiculous. Expressive negative intonation (**§6.3**, 2.206) can be presumed, though for written texts confirmation of the intonation is often lacking.

(2.206)   *meči= 'hi= 'yo=ni·na¹?' neteneniwi!?* 'Well, gee, I'm not a man, after all!' (O 103E)
          (*meči* 'quite'; |=ihi| NEG; |=iyo| 'for'; *ni·na* 1s/EMPH;
          |ineniwi-| 'be man', |ne–∅| 1s/IND; !? EN)

The enclitic |=ihi| NEG is also used idiomatically with |pwa·wi| PV 'not' and a future indicative or potential verb to indicate conviction.

(2.207)   *ki·h=pwa·wi-= 'h=we·na ke·keya·hi -we·ta·se·wi.* (K-WYB 41)
          'You (sg.) no doubt will eventually become a warrior.'
          (|wi·h=| FUT, |pwa·wi| PV 'not'; |=ihi| NEG; |=we·na| 'after all';
          ke·keya·hi 'eventually'; |we·ta·se·wi-| AI 'be a warrior', |ke–∅| 2s/IND)

(2.208)   *pwa·wi-= 'h=we·na i·nina·hi ke·htena -pya·sa, wi·h=pya·te ke·htena.* (K-WYB 25)
          'She would actually have come back by now, if she were actually going to.'
          (|pwa·wi| PV 'not'; |=ihi| NEG; |=we·na| 'after all'; *i·nina·hi* 'by now';
          ke·htena 'truly'; |pya·-| AI 'come, come back', |–sa| 3s/POT;
          |wi·h=| FUT, |pya·-| AI 'come, come back', |–te| 3s/SUBJ; *ke·htena* 'truly')

A sentence with |pwa·wi| PV 'not', |=ihi| NEG, and the potential in A 192D was confirmed as having expressive negative intonation; expressive negative intonation is also likely in 2.207, 2.208, and A 139D (another example with the potential), but the intonation was not obtained for these sentences.

26.12. Iterative. The iterative (ITER) indicates a repeated condition without specifying the time relative to either the main verb or the speech event; it is typically translatable as 'whenever':

(2.209)   *e·nwe·we·htame·kwini* 'whenever (in the future) you (pl.) blow it' (O 80D)
         (|anwe·we·ht-| TI(1) 'blow audibly', |IC–ame·kwini| 2p–0/ITER)
         mani=ke·h=meko e·ši·pye·či·keči·ničini ki·šeso·ni (O 6E)
         'And another thing, right when the sun came up (each time), ...'
         (*mani* 'this (inan.)'; |=ke·hi| 'moreover'; =*meko* EMPH; |iši| PV '{so}' [idiom: 2.89],
         |pye·či| PV 'coming', |keči·-| AI 'come into the open', |IC–ničini| 3´/ITER;
         ki·šeso·ni 'sun (obv.)')
         ke·toničini 'when they (obv.) would hoot' (O 60E)
         (|keto-| AI 'hoot', |IC–ničini| 3´/ITER)

(2.210)   *pe·po·nikini* 'in winter' (O 10A, O 58F)
         (|pepo·-| II 'be winter', |IC–nikini| 0´/ITER)

(2.211)   *e·hpi·hčina·ke·yakwini* 'during the times when we're singing' (O 140B)
         (|ahpi·hčina·ke·-| AI 'be in the process of singing', |IC–yakwini| 12/ITER)
         še·ški=meko e·hpi·hči-mawi·-'seničini (A 43B)
         'for only as long as she went to eat each time'
         (*še·ški* 'only'; =*meko* EMPH; |ahpi·hči| PV 'in the process of',
         |mawi| PV 'go and', |wi·seni-| AI 'eat', |IC–čini| 3s/ITER)

The complement of an iterative verb may have iterative inflection by attraction:

(2.212)   *wi·h=na·kwa·čini e·šite·he·čini* 'whenever she thought of leaving' (K-M 120j,l)
         (|wi·h=| FUT, |na·kwa·-| AI 'leave', |IC–čini| 3s/ITER;
         |išite·he·-| AI 'think {so}', |IC–čini| 3s/ITER)

The iterative may appear with the particle *na·hina·hi* 'time' or with *taswi* '{so much, so many}' or *tasenwi* '{so many} times' used idiomatically as preverbs and without an oblique complement:

(2.213)   *na·hina·h no·še·kini* 'anytime one has a baby' (A 105B)
         (*na·hina·hi* 'time'; |no·še·-| AI 'give birth', |IC–ekini| X/ITER)

(2.214)   *e·taswi-ši·ša·yanini* 'every time you (sg.) hunt' (K-MESB 43)
         (*taswi* '{so much, so many}', |ši·ša·-| AI 'hunt', |IC–yanini| 2s/ITER)

(2.215)   *e·tasenwi-wa·panikini* 'every day (obv.)' (SP-RL 82)
         (*tasenwi* '{so many} times', |wa·pan-| II 'be day', |-nikini| 0´/ITER)

The iterative of the indefinite-subject form of AI and TI verbs makes expressions with the idiomatic meaning 'as if':

(2.216)   *ke·kye·pi·kwe·kini* 'as if blind' (K-B 270M)
         (|kekye·pi·kwe·-| AI 'be blind', |IC–ekini| X/ITER)

For TA verbs the derived AI reciprocal (**§53.7**) is used in this construction:

(2.217)   *mehči=meko kwe·seta·ti·kini ketešawi.* (K-ECRP 109; tr. TB)
         "You (sg.) seem to act as though you are bashful."
         (*mehči* 'openly, ostensibly'; =*meko* EMPH;
         |koseta·ti·-| AI 'be shy towards each other', |IC–ekini| X/ITER;
         |išawi-| AI 'act {so}', |ke–∅| 2s/IND)

With |wi·h=| FUT this construction has the meaning 'as if to' (2.338).

26.13. Conjunct participle. Participles (PPL) form relative clauses. A participle shows inflection that either refers to or agrees with the head of the relative (or participial) clause.

There does not appear to be any restriction on the syntactic role of the head of a participle. The head may be any argument, oblique, or sentential adjunct in the clause, including any in possessive phrases or dependent clauses. (In morpheme glosses the head is specified in the parentheses at the end of the label for the pronominal inflection of the participle.)

(2.218) Subject as head

  (a) *e nwe we ·hika ta* '(one, anim.) who drums' (O 137D)

    (|anwe·we·hike·-| AI 'drum', |IC–ta| 3/PPL(ANsg))

  (b) *pe minehkawa čiki* '(ones, anim.) who pursued them (obv.)' (O 53A)

    (|peminehkaw-| 'pursue', |IC–a·čiki| 3–3´/PPL(ANpl))

(2.219) First person as head (cf. 2.25)

  ni na=ča ·hi ·= 'ni ·= 'ni ke nwa ·sowe wikiho noya ni. (K-M 361m)

  'And so I was the one who turned myself into a mountain lion.'

    (*ni na* 1s/EMPH; *=ča ·hi* 'so'; *i ni* 'that (inan.)'; *i ni* 'that (inan.)';

    |ke·nwa·sowe·wikiho·no-| AI 'transform oneself into a mountain lion',

    |IC–ya·ni| 1s/PPL(1s))

(2.220) Second person as head

  e neniwiyane 'O men!' (*lit.*, 'O you (sg.) who are a man', representative singular)

    (|ineniwi-| AI 'be man', |IC–yane| 2s/PPL(voc))

(2.221) Primary object as head

  (a) *e yo wa čini* '(ones, inan.) they use' (O 37D)

    (|ayo·-| TI(3) 'use', |IC–wa·čini| 3p–0/PPL(INpl))

  (b) *me nwe nemačiki* '(ones, anim.) you (sg.) like' (O 157C)

    (|menwe·nem-| TA 'like', |IC–ačiki| 2s–3/PPL(ANpl))

(2.222) Secondary object as head

  ne ·he netamo na na '(one, anim.) I think is right for you' (A 77A)

    (|nahe·netamaw-| TA+O 'think O2 proper for', |IC–ena·na| 1s–2s/PPL(ANsg))

(2.223) Possessor of subject as head

  (a) *me ·so nwa nita ona pe mani* 'the one whose husband had a big penis' (K-WLB 24)

    (|meso·nwe·-| AI 'have a big penis', |IC–nita| 3´/PPL(ANsg);

    ona pe mani 'her husband (obv.)')

  (b) *ihkwe waki wi če wa ničiki ošise ·hwa wahi* (K-MWL 44)

    'women whose uncles had gone in the warparty'

    (*ihkwe waki* 'women'; |wi·če·we·-| AI 'accompany X', |IC–ničiki| 3´/PPL(ANpl);

    ošise ·hwa wahi 'their uncles (obv.)')

  (c) *okahkwanwa wani= 'yo we po ·hkote nikiki* (O 47B)

    '(ones) whose legs had been broken by gunshots'

    (*okahkwanwa wani* 'their legs'; |=iyo·we| PAST;

    |po·hkote·-| II 'be broken by gunshot', |IC–nikiki| 0´/PPL(ANpl))

(2.224) Possessor of object as head

  ne ·semečiki o ·swa wahi '(ones) whose fathers had been killed' (K-RWD 7)

    (|neS-| TA 'kill', |IC–emečiki| X–3´/PPL(ANpl); *o ·swa wahi* 'their fathers (obv.)')

(2.225) Possessor of locative oblique as head

  ani pi ohka ·hkeki sa ·kenika. (K-EGC 1)

  'The (man) who had an elm tree growing out of his chest.'

    (*ani pi* 'American elm'; *ohka ·hkeki* 'his chest (loc.)';

    |sa·ken-| II 'grow ({somewhere})', |IC–nika| 0´/PPL(ANsg))

(2.226) Instrumental oblique as head

    (a)   *nese·ma·wani wi·h=keki-nowi·wa·čini* (O 7I)

        'tobacco (obv.) that they would go out with'

        (*nese·ma·wani* 'tobacco (obv.)'; |wi·h=| FUT, |keki| PV 'having {something}',

        |nowi·-| AI 'go out', |IC–wa·čini| 3p/PPL(OBVsg))

    (b)   *so·kisowa·čini* 'the cords they were bound with' (K-Apay 83; K-Bene 5; LLJB-K 16)

        (|so·kiso-| AI 'be tied (with {something})', |IC–wa·čini| 3p/PPL(INpl))

(2.227) Adjunct as head

    (a)   *mehteno·h=meko wi·či·so·makiki i·niki·='ni wi·h=išikenikiki.* (K-B 242)

        'My fellow clansmen are the only ones for whom it will have that effect.'

        (|mehteno·hi| 'only'; *=meko* EMPH; *wi·či·so·makiki* 'my fellow clansmen';

        i·niki 'those (anim.)';

        i·ni 'that (inan.)'; |wi·h=| FUT, |išiken-| II 'be {so}', |IC–nikiki| 0´/PPL(ANpl))

(2.228) Indirect discourse complement as head

        o·sani e·šite·he·čini 'the one he thought of as his father' (X10-MET 31)

        (*o·sani* 'his father (obv.)'; |išite·he·-| AI 'think {so}', |IC–čini| 3s/PPL(OBVsg))

(2.229) Component of conjoined subject as head

    (a)   *ni·šiwa·čini* 'his companion (obv.)' (K-GD 1)

        (|ni·ši-| AI 'be two', |IC–wa·čini| 3p/PPL(OBVsg))

    (b)   *wi·h=ni·šwi-mami·ši·hiye·kwa* (K-SSP 273)

        '(one) who will be a ceremonial attendant with you (sg.)'

        (|wi·h=| FUT, *ni·šwi* PV 'as a pair', |mami·ši·hi-| AI 'be a ceremonial attendant',

        |IC–ye·kwa| 2p/PPL(ANsg))

    (c)   *če·w-ahpi·hčikičihi* 'the others (obv.) he was the same age as' (K-B 9)

        (|če·wi| PV 'equally', |ahpi·hčiki-| AI 'be {so} old', |IC–čihi| 3/PPL(OBVpl))

    (d)   *e·tanwe·we·ti·čini* 'the one (obv.) he quarreled with' (K-WYB 50)

        (|tanwe·we·ti·-| AI 'quarrel with each other', |IC–čini| 3/PPL(OBVsg))

    (e)   *ahpene·či=meko wi·h=wi·šiki-neške·neti·yakwiki* (K-B 237)

        'the ones with whom we (inc.) shall always have mutual strong hatred'

        (*ahpene·či* 'always'; *=meko* EMPH; |wi·h=| FUT, |wi·šiki| PV 'strongly',

        |neške·neti·-| AI 'hate each other', |IC–yakwiki| 1p/PPL(ANpl))

(2.230) Argument of subordinate verb as head

    (a)   *ki·šisenika wi·h=nepo·hiči* '(one) who is fated to die' (K-MESB 25)

        (|ki·šisen-| II 'be already fixed, set', |IC–nika| 0´/PPL(ANsg));

        |wi·h=| FUT, |nepo·hi-| AI 'die', |e·h=–či| 3s/AOR)

    (b)   *pwa·wi-po·nite·he·yana e·h=me·nawa·nači*

        'the one you couldn't stop thinking about being in love with' (C-FS 10)

        (*pwa·wi* PV NEG, |po·nite·he·-| AI 'stop thinking', |IC–yana| 2s/PPL(ANsg);

        |me·nawa·N-| TA 'be in love with', |e·h=–ači| 2s–3/AOR)

    (c)   *ahkwiya·h=meko apeno·ha pe·hki me·ma·tomena·ka wi·h=ki·šikiči=meko*

        wi·h=ine·neme·kwe. (K-SBSB 20B) 'Children especially are who we really pray to

        you to bless to complete their growth.'

        (*ahkwiya·hi* 'especially'; *=meko* EMPH; *apeno·ha* 'child (representative singular)';

        pe·hki 'really'; |mama·tom-| TA 'pray to', |IC–ena·ka| 1p–2/PPL(ANsg);

        |wi·h=| FUT, |ki·šiki-| AI 'grow up', |e·h=–či| 3s/AOR); *=meko* EMPH;

        |wi·h=| FUT, |ine·nem-| TA 'think {so} about', |e·h=–e·kwe| 2p/AOR)

(d)   *i·niki a·mi-=mekoho -wi·ša šinaniki wi·h=asemihehki* (K-M 1016h; tr. HP)
  "the ones you ought to have been anxious to have help you"
   (*i·niki* 'those (anim.)'; *a·mi* PV POT; =*mekoho* EMPH;
   |wi·ša·šin-| AI 'be anxious', |IC–aniki| 2s/PPL(ANpl);
   |wi·h=| FUT, |asemih-| TA 'help', |e·h=–ehki| 3–2s/AOR)

(2.231) Secondary object of verbal complement as head
   i·niki wi·h=wi·to·hko·na·niki wi·h=otepowe·neni·hemiyani (K-M 1011c)
   'the ones I will allow you (sg.) to have as your councilmen' (*i·niki* 'those (anim.)';
   |wi·h=| FUT, |wi·to·hkaw-| TA 'allow', |IC–ena·niki| 1s–2s/PPL(ANpl);
   |wi·h=| FUT, |otepowe·neni·hemi-| AI+O 'have O2 as councilor', |e·h=–yani| 2s/AOR)

(2.232) Secondary object of subordinate verb as head
   i·nihi=·pi te·pihečihi e·h=mi·neči. (K-BHD 38)
   'Those (obv.) are the ones, they say, that he was pleased to be given.'
   (*i·nihi* 'those (anim. obv.)'; |=ipi| HRSY;
   |te·pih-| TA 'please', |IC–ečihi| X–3/PPL(OBVpl);
   |mi·N-| TA+O 'give O2 to', |e·h=–eči| X–3/AOR)

Another example like (2.232) is in A 192F.

The oblique argument of a relative root (**§22.4**) may be the head of a participle.

(2.233) *e·hkwiči* 'how long he is' (O 163F)
   (|ahkwi-| AI 'be {so} long', |IC–či| 3s/PPL(obl))

(2.234) *e·hpi·hči-sanakahki* 'how hard it is' (A 105E, 106B)
   (|ahpi·hči| PV 'to {such} a degree', |sanakat-| II 'be difficult', |IC–ki| 0/PPL(obl))
   e·hpi·htamatameki 'how painful it is' (A 114B)
   (|ahpi·htamat-| TI(1)-O 'have pain to {such} degree', |IC–ameki| X(-0)/PPL(obl))

(2.235) *e·šikeki* 'what happens' (A 103F)
   (|išiken-| II 'be {so}, happen {so}', |IC–ki| 0/PPL(obl))

(2.236) *e·ya·ya·ni* 'where I'm going' (O 75G)
   (|iha·-| AI 'go {somewhere}', |IC–ya·ni| 1s/PPL(obl))

(2.237) *pye·čiha·ye·kwe* 'the way you (pl.) came' (O 64D)
   (|pye·čiha·-| AI 'come {some} way', |IC–ye·kwe| 2p/PPL(obl))

(2.238) *mani .. ki·šekwi e·nekihkwa·ki na·hkači e·nehpya·ki* (K-FC 122)
   'the extent and height of the sky here above us'
   (*mani* 'this (inan.)'; *ki·šekwi* 'sky';
   |inekihkwa·-| 'be of {such} extent', |IC–ki| 0/PPL(obl); *na·hkači* 'and';
   |inehpya·-| 'be {so} high', |IC–ki| 0/PPL(obl))

(2.239) *we·či-mayo·wa·či* 'the reason why they wept' (O 18C)
   (|oči| PV 'from {something}', |mayo·-| AI 'cry', |IC–wa·či| 3p/PPL(obl))

If the head of a participle is the oblique argument of a lower verb, the appropriate relative root is copied onto the higher verb as a preverb:

(2.240) *e·ši-no·tawaki e·šimiwa·či* 'what I heard them say to me' (K-FC 79)
   (|iši| PV '{so}', |no·taw-| TA 'hear speak', |IC–aki| 1s–3/PPL(obl);
   |išim-| TA 'speak {so} to', |IC–iwa·či| 3p–1s/PPL(obl))

mani=meko e·hkwi-kehkahamawi·nameki wi·h=ahkwi-ki·ki·yose·ya·ke (K-M 82h)
"we have been told that this is as far as we can walk" (tr. HP)
(*mani* 'this (inan.)'; *=meko* EMPH; |ahkwi| PV '{so} far', |kehkahamaw-| TA+O
'designate O2 to', |IC–i·nameki| X–1p/PPL(obl)); |wi·h=| FUT, |ahkwi| PV '{so} far',
|Ci·+| RED1, |ki·yose·-| AI 'walk around', |IC–ya·ke| 1p/PPL(obl))

A common idiom with numerals uses a participle headed by the oblique complement of |iši|
PV,PP '{so}' to mean 'the only one', 'the only two', etc.:

(2.241)   *i·ni=meko e·ši-nekotihiwa·či nemeso·ta·naki.* (K-WLB 23)
'I was the only child my parents had.' (*i·ni* 'that (inan.)'; *=meko* EMPH;
|iši| PV '{so}', |nekotih-| TA 'have one', |IC–iwa·či| 3p–1s/PPL(obl);
nemeso·ta·naki 'my parents')

In some cases the oblique is an argument of a free particle that is in construction with the
verb that bears the participial inflection:

(2.242)   *nehki pe·mi-a·hkwamatamowa·či* 'for as long as they were still injured' (O 45F)
(*nehki* 'for {so} long';
|pemi| PV 'along', |a·hkwamat-| TI(1)-O 'be sick', |IC–amowa·či| 3p(-0)/PPL(obl))

(2.243)   *taswi pi·tike e·piwa·či* 'as many as were seated inside' (O 29B)
(*taswi* '{so many}'; *pi·tike* 'inside';
|api-| AI 'sit {somewhere}', |IC–wa·či| 3p/PPL(obl))

(2.244)   *i·ni taswayaki ne·škiti·ki=ke·ko·hi.* (A 102E)
'That's all the kinds of things one is warned against.'
(*i·ni* 'that (inan.)'; *taswayaki* '{so many} kinds';
|neškiti·-| AI 'admonish each other', |IC–eki| X/PPL(obl);
ke·ko·hi 'thing(s)' [adjunct])

(2.245)   *tasenwi ke·taka·nowe·či* 'as many stripes as it (anim.) has on its tail' (K-B 28)
(*tasenwi* '{so many} times';
|ketaka·nowe·-| AI 'have a striped tail', |IC–či| 3s/PPL(obl))

This is the syntax used with the idiom in which |iši| '{so}' is compounded before a numeral to
mean 'only' (2.241) if the numeral is a free particle functioning as a determiner:

(2.246)   *i·ni=meko iši-nye·wi nakamo·nani e·yo·wa·či.* (O 37E)
'Those were the only four songs they sang.'
(*i·ni* 'that (inan.)'; *=meko* EMPH; |iši| PP '{so}'; *nye·wi* 'four';
nakamo·nani 'songs'; |ayo·-| TI(3) 'use', IC–wa·či 3p–0/PPL(obl))

Equivalent to the common construction in (2.243) are participles with a pronominal argument as
head and *taswi* as a free particle meaning 'as many as', with no oblique complement:

(2.247)   *taswi=mekoho wi·te·mena·kwiki* 'the full number that go with you (pl.)' (O 93B)
(*taswi* 'as many as'; *=mekoho* EMPH;
|wi·te·m-| TA 'accompany', |IC–ena·kwiki| 3–2p/PPL(ANpl))

The oblique heads that are arguments of relative roots are generally inanimate, even when the
reference is to an animate (2.248a), but some speakers inflect for an animate oblique head
(2.248bc).

(2.248) Oblique head referring to animate

  (a) *i·niki=ke·h=mekoho we·či-nenoše·yani kemešo·mesaki.* (K-SSP 36)
     'And those grandfathers of yours are the reason you (sg.) can hear.'
      (*i·niki* 'those (anim.)'; |=ke·hi| 'moreover'; =*mekoho* EMPH;
      |oči| PV 'from{something}', |nenoše·-| AI 'have hearing, listen',
      |IC–yani| 2s/PPL(obl); *kemešo·mesaki* 'your (sg.) grandfathers')

  (b) *ma·haki=ča·h na·nekoti ki·h=awana·pwa e·taši-wa·wočihena·kwiki.* (JB-BP 35)
     'You must each take home one of these who were the reason you were being
     waylaid.'
      (*ma·haki* 'these (anim.)'; =*ča·hi* 'so'; *na·nekoti* 'one each';
      |wi·h=| FUT, |awaN-| TA 'take home', |ke–a·pwa| 2p–3/IND; |taši| PV 'engage in',
      |RED1+|, |očih-| TA 'kill, etc. {because of}', |IC–ena·kwiki| 3,X–2p/PPL(ANpl))

  (c) *ma·haki·=·niki we·či-po·n-o·siyaniki.* (LL in LLJB-KSH 8)
     'These are (the ones that are) the reason you (sg.) no longer have a father.'
      (*ma·haki* 'these (anim.)'; *i·niki* 'those (anim.)';
      |oči| PV 'because of {some reason}', |po·ni| PV 'cease, no longer',
      |o·si-| AI 'have a father', |IC–yaniki| 2s/PPL(ANpl))

An inanimate oblique head may be pluralized with |-ini| INpl.

  (2.249) Oblique head pluralized

  (a) *wa·woči·wa·čini* '(the different places) where they came from' (O 156F, 157H)
      (|CV+| RED1, |oči·-| AI 'come from {something}', |IC–wa·čini| 3p/PPL(obl.pl))

In an oblique participle, |iN-| '{so}' may be used to mean 'to do {so}':

(2.250) Idiomatic use of |iN-| '{so}' in oblique participle

  (a) *e·ši-neškimikini* '(the things) that I had been forbidden to do' (A 8F)
      (|iši| PV '(to do) {so}', |neškim-| TA 'forbid' |IC–ikini| X–1s/PPL(obl.pl))

  (b) *mani=ča·h=e·ne·nemaki:...* "This is what I want to do with them." (K-FC 345; tr. HP)
      (*mani* 'this (inan.)'; =*ča·hi* 'so'; |ine·nem-| TA 'think {so} about'
      [|iN-| '{so}' + |-e·nem| TA 'think about'], |IC–aki| 1s–3/PPL(obl))

A stem that takes a locative oblique argument may make a locative oblique participle.
Locative oblique participles have *e·h=* AOR instead of initial change (except with *a·mi* PV POT;
2.270); they may be pluralized with |-ini| INpl.

  (2.251) *e·h=owi·kiye·kwe* 'your (pl.) house', *lit.*, 'where you (pl.) dwell' (A 83B)
      (|owi·ki-| AI 'dwell {somewhere}', |e·h=–ye·kwe| 2p/PPL(loc.obl))
    e·h=awiwa·či 'the place where they were' (O 151C)
      (|awi-| AI 'be {somewhere}', |e·h=–wa·či| 3p/PPL(loc.obl))

  (2.252) *e·h=owi·kiya·kini* '(the lodges) where we (exc.) dwelt' (A 5C)
      (|owi·ki-| AI 'dwell {somewhere}', |e·h=–ya·kini| 1p/PPL(loc.obl.pl))
    e·h=owi·kiwa·čini '(the lodges) where they dwell' (O 136A)
      (|owi·ki-| AI 'dwell {somewhere}', |e·h=–wa·čini| 3p/PPL(loc.obl.pl))
    e·h=po·si-=meko·-sasakanikini 'in the very thickest parts of the brush' (A 173D)
      (*po·si* PV 'extremely', =*meko* EMPH, |sasakan-| II 'be thicket {somewhere}',
      |e·h=–nikini| 0′/PPL(loc.obl.pl))

A stem that does not inherently take a locative oblique argument can make a locative oblique
participle by adding the relative root |taN-| '{somewhere}', either as *taši* PV (2.253, 254) or in a
derived stem (2.255):

(2.253) *e·h=taši-aški-ki·ke·noweči* 'the place where the clan feast was first held' (O 111B)
   (*taši* PV '{somewhere}', *aški* PV 'first', |ki·ke·no-| AI 'hold clan feast',
   |e·h=-weči| X/REL/PPL(loc.obl))

(2.254) *e·h=taši-=meko·-ahkwima·či·ničini* (O 53C)
   'right (in the places) where they (obv.) ran out of breath'
   (*taši* PV '{somewhere}', =*meko* EMPH,
   |ahkwima·či·-| AI 'be exhausted from running', |e·h=-ničini| 3′/PPL(loc.obl.pl))

(2.255) *e·h=tanwe·tama·ni* '(the place) where I'm hooting' (O 60I)
   (|tanwe·t-| TI(1)-O 'make voice sound {somewhere}' [← |taN-we·t-|],
   |e·h=-ama·ni| 1s(-0)/PPL(loc.obl))

With a verb that is used to specify where something is designated or perceived as occurring (e.g., 2.124), a locative oblique participle refers to that place and not to the location of the subject. Such forms may have |taN-| '{somewhere}' as part of the stem, but they do not take *taši* PV '{somewhere}'.

(2.256) *e·h=tanehtawa·či e·h=ihpahoči.* 'He ran to where he heard his voice.' (S-RL 70)
   (|tanehtaw-| TA 'hear {somewhere}', |e·h=-a·či| 3s–3′/PPL(loc.obl);
   |ihpaho-| AI 'run to {somewhere}', |e·h=-či| 3s/AOR)

(2.257) *e·h=ma·wači·niči e·h=kehkahaki* (K-FC 323)
   'they (obv.) gathered at the place he had named'
   (|ma·wači·-| AI 'assemble', |e·h=-niči| 3′/AOR;
   |kehkah-| TI(1) 'specify', |e·h=-aki| 3s–0/PPL(loc.obl))

(2.258) *e·h=ne·woti·wa·čini=mekoho e·h=tašiheti·wa·či.* (K-FC 789)
   'They killed each other wherever they encountered each other.'
   (|ne·woti·-| AI 'see each other', |e·h=-wa·čini| 3p/PPL(loc.obl.pl);
   =*mekoho* EMPH;
   |tašiheti·-| AI 'kill each other {somewhere}', |e·h=-wa·či| 3p/AOR)

In effect these verbs mean 'hear (object) to be {somewhere}' (2.256), 'specify (object) to be {somewhere}' (2.257), and 'see (object) to be {somewhere}' (2.258).

The formal equivalent of a locative oblique participle without *taši* PV '{somewhere}' may be used in a metaphorical sense, referring to a group or situation. The distributive plural with |-ini| INpl refers to multiple sets or groups.

(2.259) *e·h=išisowa·či* '(by) their clan' (O 32C)
   (|išiso-| AI 'have {such} name', |e·h=-wa·či| 3p/PPL(loc.obl))
   ne·nekoti=meko e·h=išisowa·čini 'one from each of their clans' (K-CDWP 2)
   (|CV+| RED1, |nekoti| 'one'; =*meko* EMPH;
   |išiso-| AI 'have {such} name', |e·h=-wa·čini| 3p/PPL(loc.obl.pl))

(2.260) *nekotenwi e·h=ina·towe·či* 'one tribe' (C-Hist 11)
   (*nekotenwi* 'once';
   |ina·towe·-| AI 'speak {such} language', |e·h=-či| 3s/PPL(loc.obl))

(2.261) *e·h=wi·čawi·ti·kini* 'in marriages' (A 136C)
   (|wi·čawi·ti·-| AI 'be with each other', |e·h=-ekini| X/PPL(loc.obl.pl))

(2.262) *e·h=owi·nemoti·ye·kwini* (K-TG 80)
   'in cases where you (pl.) are brother-in-law and sister-in-law to each other'
   (|owi·nemoti·-| AI 'have each other as opposite-sex siblings-in-law';
   |e·h=-ye·kwini| 2p/PPL(loc.obl.pl))

With first- and second-person subjects the non-distributive forms appear to be functionally indistinguishable from first- and second-person participles.

(2.263) *e·h=mo·hkoma niyani, e·h=mo·hkoma niwiyani* 'you American' (C-Hist 8, 9)
(|mo·hkoma·n(iw)i-| AI 'be an American', |e·h=–yani| 2s/PPL(loc.obl))

(2.264) *mani nekoti e·h=išisoyakwe* 'we (inc.) of this single clan' (O 142A)
(*mani* 'this (inan.)'; *nekoti* 'one';
|išiso-| AI 'have {such} name', |e·h=–yakwe| 12/PPL(loc.obl))
e·h=ineniwiyakwe 'we (inc.) (who are) men' (K)
(|ineniwi-| AI 'be a man', |e·h=–yakwe| 12/PPL(loc.obl))

(2.265) *e·h=ihkwe·wiye·kwe* 'you (pl.) (who are) women' (A 140; K, C)
(|ihkwe·wi-| AI 'be a woman', |e·h=–ye·kwe| 2p/PPL(loc.obl))

Occasionally expressions for kinds of things have an inflection that is a cross between that of an aorist and that of a participle (2.266). These can be thought of as participles, with the subject as the head, that have taken over the use of *e·h=* AOR rather than initial change from the ostensible locative oblique participles that refer to single and multiple groups (2.259-262). All examples have the relative root |iN-| as part of the stem. This hybrid mode is labeled AOR×PPL ('aorist crossed with participle').

(2.266) Hybrid mode blending aorist and participle

(a) *nekotayaki=meko e·h=išikenikini* '(ones, inan.) of each kind' (K-YC 9)
(*nekotayaki* 'one set'; *=meko* EMPH;
|išiken-| II 'be {so}', |e·h=–nikini| 0´/AOR×PPL(INpl)

(b) *meše=we·=meko·=·'nahi e·h=išikiničihi* 'in fact, all kinds of them (anim.)' (K-SSP 29)
(*meše=meko·=·'nahi* 'any'; |=we·na| 'in fact';
|išiki-| AI 'be {so}', |e·h=–ničihi| 3´/AOR×PPL(OBVpl))

The sentential complement of a participle may be inflected as a participle by attraction:

(2.267) *wi·h=ne·wa ničihi e·šite·ha ničihi* "those who wished to see it" (K-WC 26; tr. HP)
(|wi·h=| FUT, |ne·w-| TA 'see', |IC–a·ničihi| 3´–3´´/PPL(OBVpl);
|išite·he·-| AI 'think {so}', |IC–ničihi| 3´/PPL(OBVpl))

Although a participle may not be inflected for any other mode, modal categories may be marked on participles by the preverbs *pwa·wi* 'not' and *a·mi* POT.

(2.268) *pwa·wi-ki·ke·nočiki* '(ones) who were not hosts of the clan feast' (O 32G)
(|pwa·wi| PV 'not', |ki·ke·no-| AI 'hold clan feast', |IC–čiki| 3/PPL(ANpl))

(2.269) *a·mi-ayo·či* '(one, inan.) he would use' (O 16C)
(*a·mi* PV POT; |ayo·-| TI(3) 'use', |IC–či| 3s–0/PPL(INsg))

A locative oblique participle with *a·mi* PV POT has (invisible) initial change rather than *e·h=* AOR (cf. 2.251, 252).

(2.270) *a·mi-taši-petesakesiye·kwe* 'where you (pl.) would face obstacles' (O 76G)
(*a·mi* PV POT; *taši* PV '{somewhere}'; |petesakesi-| AI 'face obstacles',
|IC–ye·kwe| 2p/PPL(loc.obl))
a·mi-nana·hapiwa·či 'where they should sit' (GBC-BHD 28)
(*a·mi* PV POT, |nana·hapi-| 'sit down', |IC–wa·či| 3p/PPL(loc.obl))
ma·h=koh=meko·=ne·h=ni·na a·mi-tašisenye·henako·we=·'yo·we. (K-B 207; tr. HP)
"Yonder was where, I would have let you feast too"
(|ma·hi| 'over (here, there)'; |=kohi| 'certainly'; *=meko* EMPH; |=ne·hi| 'too';
ni·na 1s/EMPH; *a·mi* PV POT, |tašisenye·h-| TA 'make eat {somewhere}',
|IC–enako·we| 1s–2p/PPL(loc.obl); |=iyo·we| PAST)

26.14. Plain interrogative. The plain interrogative mode (INT) indicates probability inferred from evidence. It can be generically glossed 'must be, must have', but native speakers often translate it simply as a past tense. It is also used in yes-no questions based on inference.

(2.271)   *aseniwikwe ni* 'he (must have) turned to stone' (O 160G)

(|aseniwi-| AI 'be stone, become stone', |–kwe·ni| 3s,0/INT)

nešike wane ni? 'I take it you live alone?' (K-MLF 68)

(|nešike·-| AI 'live alone', |-wane·ni| 2s/INT; ? Q)

26.15. Changed interrogative. The changed interrogative (CH.INT) makes conditional clauses referring to past (2.272) or present (2.273) occurrences with present relevance.

(2.272)   *ke·htena ke·teminawikwe ni maneto wa* (O 112D)

'if it is true that a manitou blessed me' (*ke·htena* 'truly';

|keteminaw-| TA 'bless', |IC–ikwe·ni| 3s–1s/CH.INT; *maneto wa* 'manitou')

(2.273)   *nowi·no, e·škwe·se·hiwane ni.* 'Come out, if you (sg.) are a girl.' (A 113B)

(|nowi·-| AI 'go out', |–no| 2s/IMP;

|iškwe·se·hi-| AI 'be a girl', |IC–wane·ni| 2s/CH.INT)

ke·hke·nemikwe ni=ča·h=maneto wa 'well, if a manitou does know me' (O 112F)

(|kehke·nem-| TA 'know', |IC–ikwe·ni| 3s–1s/CH.INT; |=ča·hi| 'so';

maneto wa 'manitou')

It occurs with |wi·h=| FUT in the meaning 'want to' (2.274); such a verb may be the virtual complement of a verb of thinking also in the changed interrogative (2.275):

(2.274)   *meše·='nahi·='nahi wi·h=mawima·we·kwe ni, ki·h=mawima·pwa* (K-M 151b)

'now, if you want to mourn them, you may mourn them'

(|meše·='nahi| 'at will, you may'; |=i·nahi| 'with that, now'; |wi·h=| FUT,

|mawim-| TA 'mourn', |IC–a·we·kwe·ni| 2p–3/CH.INT and |ke–a·pwa| 2p–3/IND)

(2.275)   *wi·h=po·ni-=ke·hi·-mahkate·wi·wane ni e·šite·he·wane ni* (K-BFS 4)

'and if you wish to cease fasting'

(|wi·h=| FUT, *po·ni* PV 'cease'; |mahkate·wi·-| AI 'fast', |IC–wane·ni| 2s/CH.INT;

=ke·hi 'moreover'; |išite·he·-| AI 'think {so}', |IC–wane·ni| 2s/CH.INT)

The changed interrogative is also used with the particle *na·hina·hi* 'time' for temporal conditions set at an indeterminate time:

(2.276)   *na·hina·h e·nenwi·wane ni* 'at whatever (future) time you (sg.) bathe' (A 39E)

(*na·hina·hi* 'time'; |anenwi·-| AI 'swim', |IC–wane·ni| 2s/CH.INT)

na·hina·hi ne·sa·te ni 'whenever (it was that) it (anim.) was killed' (K-FASB 64B)

(*na·hina·hi* 'time'; |neS-| TA 'kill', |IC–a·te·ni| X–3/CH.INT)

26.16. Aorist interrogative. The aorist interrogative (AOR.INT) is typically used to make substantival temporal clauses referring to an uncertain or indefinite time.

(2.277)   *i·nini=ča·hi e·hkwe·nemena ni e·h=nešiwana·ča·kwe ni.* (K-FASB 75B)

'My plan for you (sg.) extends to whatever time they [i.e., the earth and the sky] are destroyed.'

(*i·nini* 'those (inan.)'; *=ča·hi* 'so';

|ahkwe·nem-| TA 'think of {so} far', |IC–ena·ni| 1s–2s/PPL(obl);

|nešiwana·ča·-| II 'be destroyed', |e·h–kwe·ni| 0/AOR.INT)

In this use it may be accompanied by *na·hina·hi* 'time' (2.278; 2.282d; O 92D).

(2.278)   *na·hina·h=meko e·h=ki·šikiwane ni* 'at whatever time you (sg.) are grown up' (O 64I)

(|na·hina·hi| 'time'; *=meko* EMPH;

|ki·šiki-| AI 'grow up', |e·h=–wane·ni| 2s/AOR.INT)

It is also used with |wi·h=| FUT (**§26.24**) for a complement that is speculative.

26.17. Interrogative participle. If the head of a participle is stated or implied to be unknown, an interrogative participle (INT.PPL) must be used. The interrogative participle may also indicate that something is unknown to the speaker. In other respects it generally functions like a conjunct participle (**§26.13**). It can be generically glossed as 'whoever or whatever (it may be)'.

(2.279) Subject as head

   (a)   *te pwe·htawikwe na* 'whoever believes me' (O 133C)
          (|te·pwe·htaw-| TA 'believe', |IC–ikwe·na| 3s–1s/INT.PPL(ANsg))

   (b)   *i ni pe pikwe škowikwe ni* 'the whistle, whatever that may be' (O 102E)
          (*i ni* 'that (inan.)';
          |pepikwe·škowi-| II 'be a whistle', |IC–kwe·ni| 3s,0/INT.PPL(IN)

(2.280) Primary object as head

   (a)   *wi·h=mi čikwe ni* 'what she would eat, what she could eat' (K-M 5h, 15d)
          (|wi·h=| FUT, |mi·či-| TI(3) 'eat', |IC–kwe·ni| 3s–0/INT.PPL(INsg))

   (b)   *"...," e ne nema wate na* 'whoever you (sg.) may think of as: ...' (A 140A)
          (|ine·nem-| TA 'think about {so}', |IC–a·wate·na| 2s–3/INT.PPL(ANsg))

(2.281) Oblique as head

   (a)   *a kwi kehke nemakini e hpi hči-me meta ča hikwe ni* (A 97F)
          'I didn't know how great a time he had'
          (*a kwi* 'not'; |kehke·nem-| TA 'know', |–akini| 1s–3/NEG;
          ahpi hči PV 'to {such} a degree',
          |CV+| RED1, |meta·ča·hi-| AI 'have a good time', |IC–kwe·ni| 3s,0/INT.PPL(obl))

   (b)   *e h=nana tohtawiči we či-pešekwa hiwa ne ni* (A 143G)
          'he asked me why I had become divorced'
          (|nana·tohtaw-| TA 'ask', |e·h=–iči| 3s–1s/AOR; |oči| PV 'from {something}',
          |pešekwa·hi-| AI 'get divorced', |IC–wa·ne·ni| 1s/INT.PPL(obl))

   (c)   *nehki=meko ši ka wiwane ni* (A 176D)
          'for however long you (sg.) may be in strict mourning for your husband'
          (*nehki* 'for {so} long'; *=meko* EMPH;
          |ši·ka·wi-| AI 'be a widow in strict mourning', |IC–wane·ni| 2s/INT.PPL(obl))

   (d)   *nehki i nahi wi h=ki wita wa ne ni* (K-M 60e; tr. HP)
          "(to ask me) how long I was going to be there"
          (*nehki* 'for {so} long'; *i nahi* 'there';
          |wi·h=| FUT, |ki·wita·-| AI 'stay {somewhere}', |IC–wa·ne·ni| 1s/INT.PPL(obl))

   (e)   *e h=menwahkiwinikwe ni* 'someplace where the land might be nice' (O 56B)
          (|menwahkiwi-| II 'be good land ({somewhere})',
          |e·h=–nikwe·ni| 0´/INT.PPL(loc.obl))

   (f)   *wi h=owi kiwane ni* "where you would like to live" (K-M 63b; tr. HP)
          (|wi·h=| FUT, |owi·ki-| AI 'dwell {somewhere}', |e·h=–wane·ni| 2s/INT.PPL(loc.obl))

An interrogative participle (2.282*abc*) or aorist interrogative (2.282*d*) used absolutely has the meaning 'I wonder'.

(2.282) Interrogative participle and aorist interrogative in absolute use

   (a)   *e šawikwe ni=ni hka.* "I wonder how she is getting along?" (K-M 38a; tr. HP)
          (|išawi-| AI 'do {so}', |IC–kwe·ni| 3s/INT.PPL(obl); *=ni hka* MAN'S.EXPL)
          [continued →]

(b) *wi·h=išawiwa·ne·ni·='nahi* "I wonder what will become of me?" (K-M 8m; tr. HP)
   (|wi·h=| FUT, |išawi-| AI 'do {so}', |IC–wa·ne·ni| 1s/INT.PPL(obl); |='i·nahi| 'with that')

(c) *a·mi·-'šawiwa·ne·ni·='nah=mani* (A 127C)
   'I wonder what would have become of me now'
   (*a·mi* PV POT, |išawi-| AI 'do {so}', |IC–wa·ne·ni| 1s/INT.PPL(obl);
   |='i·nahi| 'with that'; =*mani* 'as it is now')

(d) *na·hina·hi mani ayo·hi mehtose·neniwa wi·h=awikwe·ni.* (K-M 76d; tr. HP)
   "I wonder when people will inhabit this place."
   (*na·hina·hi* 'time'; *mani* 'this (inan.)'; *ayo·hi* 'here'; *mehtose·neniwa* 'person';
   |wi·h=| FUT, |awi-| AI 'be {somewhere}', |e·h=–kwe·ni| 3s/AOR.INT)

Additional textual examples of interrogative participles are in (**§30.18**).

26.18. Prioritive. The prioritive is only used with the preverb |me·hi| 'yet' or the initial |metw-| 'keep on (?)' (|metwi| PV). A prioritive with |me·hi| may occur with *a·kwi* 'not'.

The prioritive with |me·hi| PV makes 'before' clauses. Presumably, when the reference is to past events the verb has initial change, as in the changed conjunct, though this is always masked by the presence of |me·hi| as the first preverb (**§29.4**). Such verbs are categorized as being in the changed prioritive mode (CH.PRI):

(2.283) *me·h–=meko -keči·nikwe ki·šeso·ni* (O 13F)
   'before sunrise' (*lit.*, 'before the sun (obv.) emerged')
   (|me·hi| PV 'yet'; =*meko* EMPH; |keči·-| AI 'emerge', |IC–nikwe| 3´/CH.PRI;
   ki·šeso·ni 'sun (obv.)')

(2.284) *mo·hči me·h-ona·pe·miwane=meko* (A 144C)
   'even before you (sg.) were married' (*mo·hči* 'even'; |me·hi| PV 'yet',
   |ona·pe·mi-| AI 'have a husband', |IC–wane| 2s/CH.PRI; =*meko* EMPH)

Conversely, when the reference is to the future, there is presumably no initial change, as in the subjunctive. These verbs are analyzed as being in the plain prioritive mode (PRI):

(2.285) *wa·pake ma·maya, me·h–=meko -keči·kwe ki·šeswa* (K-BH 6)
   'early tomorrow morning, before sunrise' (*lit.*, 'before the sun emerges')
   (|wa·pan-| II 'be dawn, day', |–ke| 0/SUBJ; *ma·maya* 'early';
   |me·hi| PV 'yet'; =*meko* EMPH; |keči·-| AI 'emerge', |–kwe| 3s/PRI;
   ki·šeswa 'sun')

When the prioritive is used with |metwi| PV 'keep on (?)', this preverb is followed by |pwa·wi| PV 'not', |=ihi| NEG may be present or absent, and there is no initial change. Some speakers fuse |metwi-pwa·wi| to *metopwa·wi* PV and there is one example of *meti(-)pwa·wi* (C-WH 16). The construction has the idiomatic meaning 'why is it taking so long!':

(2.286) *metwi-pwa·wi·='hi·='yo -pasekwi·wa·kwe.* (K-M 729c; tr. HP)
   "Why are they so long in getting up!"
   (|metwi| PV 'keep on (?)', |pwa·wi| PV 'not'; |=ihi| NEG; |=iyo| 'for';
   |pasekwi·-| AI 'get up', |–wa·kwe| 3p/PRI)

The two attested prioritive forms with stem-initial |metw-| lack |pwa·wi| PV 'not' and have initial change; one was read with |=ihi| NEG, but this cannot be present with the other:

(2.287) *nahi·´, me·twitanekokwe metemo·ha.* (Jones 1907:358.8-9, 359)
   "Well, what makes the old woman so long at her work!"
   (*nahi·´* 'alright'; |metwitaneko-| AI 'keep on (?) working', |IC–kwe| 3s/CH.PRI;
   metemo·ha 'old woman')

me tose·hkwe wane=ʼh=we na. 'What's taking you so long to cook!' (C-RS 26)
(|metose·hkwe·-| AI 'keep on (?) cooking', |IC–wane| 2s/CH.PRI; |=ihi| NEG;
|=we·na| 'after all')

It is not clear how the idiomatic meanings of expressions like those in (2.286, 287) are constructed.

26.19. Prohibitive and future imperative. The prohibitive sub-order uses special endings, without either initial change or |e·h=| AOR. It only makes main-clause verbs. Despite its conventional name, it has non-negative as well as negative uses.

Functionally, two modes of the prohibitive sub-order may be distinguished, prohibitive (PROH) and future imperative (FUT.IMP), but these modes contrast formally only for certain second-person transitive subjects (as summarized in **29.9(b)**, 3.227). For other subjects, there is no formal contrast. In these cases, some non-distinctive prohibitive-mode endings function either as prohibitives (negative or non-negative) or as future imperatives, and some ostensible future imperative endings are used only with the functions of the prohibitive mode.

The prohibitive mode is used with the prohibitive negative particle *ka ta* 'don't' as a negative imperative. The subject may be any person except indefinite.

(2.288) *ka ta natawa pihkani.* 'Don't look around (you sg.).' (A 39G)
(*ka ta* 'don't'; |natawa·pi-| AI 'try to see', |–hkani| 2s/PROH)

(2.289) *ka ta owiye·ha ki we·hkiče.* 'Don't anyone turn back.' (K-FC 743)
(*ka ta* 'don't'; *owiye·ha* 'someone'; |ki·we·-| AI 'turn back', |–hkiče| 3s,0/PROH)

(2.290) *ka ta owiye·ha ta tašimiye kani.* 'Don't talk about anyone (you sg.).' (A 53G)
(*ka ta* 'don't'; *owiye·ha* 'someone';
|CV+| RED1, |tašim-| TA 'talk about', |–iye·kani| 2s-3/PROH)

(2.291) *ka ta a nwe·htawiye ke ko.* 'Don't fail to believe and obey him.' (O 161G)
(*ka ta* 'don't'; |a·nwe·htaw-| TA 'disbelieve', |–iye·ke·ko| 2p-3/PROH)

(2.292) *ka ta kwi natawi-išinawe·hiye ka ke.* (O 114F)
'Don't let us make them feel uneasy about what they should do.'
(*ka ta* 'don't'; |kwi·natawi| PV 'at a loss',
|išinawe·h-| TA 'make feel {so}', |–iye·ka·ke| 1p-3/PROH)

(2.293) *ka ta=ke·h me šenakani ki nesani.* 'And don't touch your hair (you sg.).' (A 48E)
(*ka ta* 'don't'; |=ke·hi| 'moreover'; |me·šen-| TI(1) 'touch', |–akani| 2s-0/PROH;
ki nesani 'your (sg.) hair')

(2.294) *ka ta nenehke netakiče owiye·ha* 'don't anyone think about it' (K-FC 796)
(*ka ta* 'don't'; |nenehke·net-| TI(1) 'think about', |–akiče| 3s-0/PROH;
owiye·ha 'someone')

With a third-person animate subject and an obviative object only endings that are formally of the future imperative mode are attested in this true prohibitive function:

(2.295) *ka ta owiye·ha nesa·hkiče* 'don't anyone kill him' (K-Spot 80)
(*ka ta* 'don't'; *owiye·ha* 'someone'; |neS-| TA 'kill', |–a·hkiče| 3s-3´/FUT.IMP)

This contrasts with the variation in the corresponding non-negative forms (2.302, 303).

Without *ka ta*, the prohibitive mode has the meaning 'might' or 'might have':

(2.296) *wa wa kapaye·hkiče* 'he might be bow-legged' (A 117A)
(|CV+| RED1, |wa·kapaye·-| AI 'have a bent femur', |–hkiče| 3s,0/PROH)

(2.297) *nešiwana čihiye kani* 'you (sg.) might ruin (things for) them' (A 33F)
(|nešiwana·čih-| TA 'ruin, destroy', |–iye·kani| 2s-3/PROH)

(2.298)   *me ʼme ʼnešimihki ʼke* 'people might say embarrassing things about me' (A 153E)
          (|CV+| RED1, |me·nešim-| TA 'shame by speech', |–ihki·ke| X–1s/PROH)

(2.299)   *a ʼšihenakiče* 'they might get you (sg.) into their bad habits' (A 7C)
          (|a·ših-| TA 'get into bad habits', |–enakiče| 3–2s/PROH)

(2.300)   *a ʼhkwamatakani.* '(I'm guessing) you (sg.) might be sick.' (A 168F)
          (|a·hkwamat-| TI(1)-O 'be sick', |–akani| 2s(-0)/PROH)

(2.301)   *wanimo ʼči nenehke ʼnetakiče e ʼšimaki.* (K-Auto 119)
          'It's possible he might think about what I tell him to do.'
          (*wanimo ʼči* 'perchance'; |nenehke·net-| TI(1) 'think about' |–akiče| 3s–0/PROH;
          |išim-| TA 'tell to do {so}', |IC–aki| 1s–3/PPL(obl))

If there is a third person animate subject and an obviative object, the ending used in this
non-negative function may be formally either of the prohibitive mode or of the future imperative
mode. In either case the imagined occurrence may be desirable or undesirable from the point of
view of the speaker. There is, however, evidence that some speakers prefer the prohibitive forms
for possible past events and the future imperative forms for potential undesirable events.

(2.302) Formally prohibitive endings for 3–3´

  (a)   *kehke ʼnemiye ʼkiče* 'he might know about her' (JP-SD 62)
        (|kehke·nem-| TA 'know', |–iye·kiče| 3s–3´/PROH)

  (b)   *nešiye ʼwa ʼhkiče* 'they might kill them' (JB-M 48)
        (|neS-| TA 'kill', |–iye·wa·hkiče| 3p–3´/PROH)

  (c)   *mawa ʼpamiye ʼkiče.* 'he might have gone to see it (anim.) (is it possible?)' (EK)
        (|mawa·pam-| TA 'go to see', |–iye·kiče| 3s–3´/PROH)

(2.303) Formally future imperative endings for 3–3´

  (a)   *na ʼpi=ke ʼh pesetawa ʼhkiče.* 'Maybe she'll (desirably) listen to her.' (A 58G)
        (*na ʼpi* 'for the better'; |=ke·hi| 'moreover';
        |pesetaw-| TA 'listen to', |–a·hkiče| 3s–3´/FUT.IMP)

  (b)   *ke ʼkeya ʼhi nešiwana ʼčiha ʼhkiče* (K-W 554)
        'in the end she might (undesirably) destroy them'
        (*ke ʼkeya ʼhi* 'eventually'; |nešiwana·čih-| TA 'destroy', |–a·hkiče| 3s–3/FUT.IMP)

  (c)   *mawa ʼpama ʼhkiče.* 'he might go to see it (anim.) (so don't tell him about it)'
        (LYB)
        (|mawa·pam-| TA 'go to see', |–a·hkiče| 3s–3/FUT.IMP)

The prohibitive and future imperative modes have formally distinct and functionally
contrasting endings only for second persons acting on animate third persons (theme sign |-a·| TA
th. 1), or second persons acting on inanimates if the verb is TI(1) (theme sign |-am| TI(1) th.). In
just these cases the future imperative endings have the function of future imperatives:

(2.304)   *mani e ʼšisočiki a ʼčimoha ʼhkani.* 'Tell those of this clan (you sg.).' (K-B 165B)
          (*mani* 'this (inan.)'; |išiso-| AI 'have {such} name', |IC–čiki| 3/PPL(ANpl);
          |a·čimoh-| TA 'inform', |–a·hkani| 2s–3/FUT.IMP) (cf. 2.290, 297)

(2.305)   *mahkwa ʼči=mekoho wi ʼtamawa ʼhke ʼko* 'tell them good-naturedly (you pl.)' (O 89B)
          (*mahkwa ʼči* 'quietly'; =*mekoho* EMPH;
          |wi·tamaw-| TA 'tell facts to', |–a·hke·ko| 2p–3/FUT.IMP) (cf. 2.291)

(2.306)   *nenehke ʼnetamo ʼhkani* 'you (sg.) must think about it' (K-FC 124)
          (|nenehke·net-| TI(1) 'think about', |–amo·hkani| 2s–0/FUT.IMP) (cf. 2.293, 300)

If there is no distinct future imperative ending, the corresponding second-person prohibitive
mode form is used in this function:

(2.307)   *wi ·šikapihkani i nah=awiyane* 'when you (sg.) are there sit firmly' (K-MP2 34)
   (|wi·šikapi-| AI 'sit firmly', |–hkani| 2s/PROH;
   |i·nahi| 'there'; |awi-| AI 'be {somewhere}', |–yane| 2s/SUBJ)
   i ni=mekoho išawihke ·ko 'do exactly that (you pl.) [after I die]' (O 161F)
   (*i ni* 'that (inan.)'; *=mekoho* EMPH; |išawi-| 'do {so}', |–hke·ko| 2p/PROH)

(2.308)   *po ni-košihkani* 'fear me no more' (K-GD 36)
   (*po ni* PV 'cease'; |koS-| TA 'fear', |–ihkani| 2s/PROH)

26.20. Potential. The potential (POT) also has distinctive endings and uses neither initial change nor |e·h=| AOR. It makes a single mode, appearing only in main-clause verbs. It can usually be translated 'would' or 'would have', either with an expressed or implied condition or in a generalized account referring to no specific event or time. Sometimes it denotes contingent possibility ('could') or advisability ('should').

(2.309)   *pepo ·kehe=mata, sanakihto ·hkapa.* (A 38H)
   'If it had been winter instead, you (sg.) would have had a hard time.'
   (|pepo·-| II 'be winter', |–kehe| 0/SUBJ.PRET; *=mata* 'alternatively';
   |sanakiht-| TI(2)-O 'have hard time', |–o·hkapa| 2s(-0)/POT)

(2.310)   *oni ·ča nesihkapa=meko* 'you (sg.) could indeed have children' (A 193C)
   (|oni·ča·nesi-| AI 'have child', |–hkapa| 2s/POT; *=meko* EMPH)

(2.311)   *še ·ški ki ·ki wita ·hkapa* 'you (sg.) should just stay single' (A 141F)
   (*še ·ški* 'only'; |Ci·+| RED1, |ki·wita·-| AI 'stay around', |–hkapa| 2s/POT)

The potential occurs in questions:

(2.312)   *ihkwe ·we, owi ·weti yakwe, anwa ·či ·hkapa?* (K-WWB 3)
   'Woman, what if we get married, would you be agreeable?'
   (*ihkwe ·we* 'woman (voc.)'; |owi·weti·-| AI 'get married', |–yakwe| 12/SUBJ;
   |anwa·či·-| AI 'be willing', |–hkapa| 2s/POT; *?* Q)

The potential is made negative with the particle *awita* 'not (pot.)':

(2.313)   *awita i ni išawihkapa* 'that wouldn't have happened to you (sg.)' (A 176A)
   (*awita* 'not (pot.)'; *i ni* 'that (inan.)'; |išawi-| AI 'do {so}', |–hkapa| 2s/POT)

(2.314)   *awita wi ·h=a ·hkwe ·hkapa?* 'You wouldn't be inclined to get mad?' (K-MOR 20)
   (*awita* 'not (pot.)'; |wi·h=| FUT, |a·hkwe·-| AI 'be angry', |–hkapa| 2s/POT; *?* Q)

Rarely *a ·kwi* 'not' (**§26.11**) is used with a potential verb:

(2.315)   *i noki=wi na a ·kwi=meko ke ·ko ·hi-iši nahi-'ši-te ·pwe ·hka ·ha.* (K-TG 85)
   'But now nothing I say would ever be true.'
   (*i noki* 'now'; *=wi na* 'but'; *a ·kwi* 'not'; *=meko* EMPH;
   ke ·ko ·hi 'something'; *iši* '{so}'; *nahi* PV 'given to', |iši| PV '{so}',
   |te·pwe·-| AI 'speak the truth', |–hka ·ha| 1s/POT)

(2.316)   *kaš=a ·kwi='h=we ·=meko owiye ·ha takosa² mi ·čipe ·he ·haki?* (C-PD 20)
   'Come on, now, is there really nothing around in the way of game animals?'
   (*kaši* 'why!'; *a ·kwi* 'not'; |=ihi| NEG; |=we·na| 'in fact'; *=meko* EMPH;
   owiye ·ha 'anyone'; |tako-| AI 'exist', |–sa| 3s/POT;
   mi ·čipe ·he ·haki 'game animals (dim.)'; *?* Q)

The potential mode defines the potential clause type. The verb in a potential clause may be in the potential mode or in the plain conjunct, with or without *a mihtahi* POT (**§26.7**). A participle adds the meaning of the potential mode with *a mi* PV POT (2.269, 270, 282). A temporal or conditional clause of the kind that would normally have an aorist or changed conjunct verb has the verb in the subjunctive when subordinate to a potential clause (O 39H, 49G, 52I, 56A).

26.21. Injunctive. The imperative mode (IMP), used for non-negative imperatives, comprises forms from two orders. For imperatives with third person subjects, forms of what may be called the injunctive mode of the conjunct order are used; these are characterized by |-če| 3,0/IMP where the corresponding forms of the potential sub-order have |-sa| 3,0/POT (as in 2.316).

> (2.317)   *nawači-či·tapiče* 'let her first sit up' (A 111G)
>
>   (*nawači* PV 'first, stop to', |či·tapi-| AI 'sit up', |–če| 3s,0/IMP)

The classification of these third person forms adopted here is functional. Alternatively, from a purely formal perspective, the injunctive forms could be classed as a defective sub-order of the conjunct type.

26.22. Imperative. For imperatives with second-person or inclusive subjects, forms of the imperative order are used; this uses suffixes that are distinct from those of the conjunct order.

> (2.318)   *na·kwa·no.* 'Go (you sg.).' (O 152H)
>
>   (|na·kwa·-| AI 'leave', |–no| 2s/IMP)
>
> (2.319)   *wi·seniko.* 'Eat (you pl.).' (O 25I)
>
>   (|wi·seni-| AI 'eat', |–ko| 2p/IMP)
>
> (2.320)   *wi·te·mi* 'go with him (you sg.)' (A 96B)
>
>   (|wi·te·m-| TA 'accompany', |–i| 2s–3/IMP)
>
> (2.321)   *ši·ša·ta·we.* 'Let's go hunting.' (K-SGG 224)
>
>   (|ši·ša·-| AI 'hunt', |–ta·we| 12/IMP)

26.23. Imprecative. The archaic and extremely rare imprecative mode is attested by a single ending, whose exact shape is uncertain (Goddard 1993:232-232). Given its unique and variable morphology, it is uncertain which order it should be classified in (§35).

26.24. Future. The future tense is indicated by the proclitic preverb |wi·h=| FUT (*wi·h=*, younger variant *i·h=*; after pronominal prefixes *-i·h=*) (§18.12, §29.3).

The future is used with modes of the independent order and participles for events that are intended or looked for (2.55-56, 61-62, 111, 322-324), and also for orders, injunctions, and requests (2.126, 325-327; O 82B, 90HI, 96AC).

> (2.322)   *ni·h=peno·ha·wa* 'I'm going to send him home' (O 156E)
>
>   (|wi·h=| FUT, |peno·h-| TA 'send home', |ne–a·wa| 1s–3s/IND)
>
> (2.323)   *ni·h=a·čimoheko·petoke* 'I must be going to be told.' (K-M 528d)
>
>   (|wi·h=| FUT, |a·čimoh-| TA 'inform', |ne–eko·petoke| X–1s/DUB)
>
> (2.324)   *i·ni wi·h=išite·he·yani.* 'That's what you will think.' (O 62F)
>
>   (*i·ni* 'that (inan.)'; |wi·h=| FUT, |išite·he·-| AI 'think {so}', |IC–yani| 2s/PPL(obl))
>
> (2.325)   *ki·h=a·čimo* 'you (sg.) must report' (O 152I)
>
>   (|wi·h=| FUT, |a·čimo-| AI 'report', |ke–∅| 2s/IND)
>
> (2.326)   *ki·h=nenehke·neta·pwa* 'I want you (pl.) to bear it in mind' (O 161E)
>
>   (|wi·h=| FUT, |nenehke·net-| TI(1) 'think about', |ke–a·pwa| 2p–0/IND)
>
> (2.327)   *i·ni=meko wi·h=išawiye·kwe* 'that's precisely how you must do it' (O 98E)
>
>   (*i·ni* 'that (inan.)'; *=meko* EMPH;
>
> |wi·h=| FUT, |išawi-| AI 'do {so}', |IC–ye·kwe| 2p/PPL(obl))

The future of the aorist conjunct makes future complements of various sorts:

> (2.328)   *i·ni wi·h=we·pina·ke·yakwe.* 'Now we (inc.) are going to begin singing.' (O 135C)
>
>   (*i·ni* 'then'; |wi·h=| FUT, |we·pina·ke·-| AI 'begin singing', |e·h=–yakwe| 12/AOR)

(2.329) *e·h=neškimeči=meko wi·h=keši penowa·či* (O 46A)
'they were expressly forbidden to scratch themselves'
(|neškim-| TA 'forbid', |e·h=–eči| X–3/AOR; =*meko* EMPH;
|wi·h=| FUT, |keši·peno-| AI 'scratch', |e·h=–wa·či| 3p/AOR)

(2.330) *wi·h=ketemino na·kwe e·h=išima·či.* 'when he told them to bless you (pl.)' (O 84C)
|wi·h=| FUT, |keteminaw-| TA 'bless', |e·h=–ena·kwe| 3,X–2p/AOR;
|išim-| TA 'speak {so} to', |e·h=–a·či| 3s–3′/AOR)

It also makes purpose clauses:

(2.331) *wi·h=kehke·nemenakwe e·h=ki·ke·noye·kwe* (O 136D)
'so that they will know that we're holding a clan feast'
(|wi·h=| FUT, |kehke·nem-| TA 'know (about)', |e·h=–enakwe| 3–12/AOR;
|ki·ke·no-| AI 'hold clan feast', |e·h=–ye·kwe| 2p/AOR)

(2.332) *wi·h=a·čimoči* '(in order for him) to report' (O 156E; continuation of 2.322)
(|wi·h=| FUT, |a·čimo-| AI 'report', |e·h=–či| 3s/AOR)

As seen in (2.328-332), the aorist proclitic *e·h=* AOR is not used when |wi·h=| FUT is present (though underlying |e·h=| AOR is always written analytically as a component of the aorist inflection). Another way to combine these elements, far less common but with some speakers not rare, is to convert |wi·h=| FUT into an otherwise unused preverb *wi·hi* FUT (usually elided to *wi·h*), before which *e·h=* AOR is retained:

(2.333) *e·h=wi·h-ni·sa·si·či e·h=iši-mama·toma·či.* (K-SGG 149)
'She begged him to be able to come down.'
(|wi·hi| PV FUT, |ni·sa·si·-| AI 'descend', |e·h=–či| 3s/AOR;
|iši| PV '{so}'; |mama·tom-| TA 'pray to, beg', |e·h=–a·či| 3s–3′/AOR;
a·neta e·h=ša·kwe·nemowa·či e·h=wi·hi-petekye·šiha·wa·či. (K-W 403)
'Some were unwilling to renege on them.'
(*a·neta* 'some'; |ša·kwe·nemo-| AI 'be unwilling', |e·h=–wa·či| 3p/AOR;
|wi·hi| PV FUT, |petekye·ših-| TA 'renege on', |e·h=–a·wa·či| 3p–3′/AOR)

The preverb *wi·h(i)* FUT differs from the proclitic |wi·h=| FUT in that, like other preverbs, it is separable from the rest of the compound verb stem and may be followed by an enclitic:

(2.334) *e·h=wi·h-=ke·hi -neniwiyani.* (K-MBGS 9)
'including for you (sg.) to become a man (i.e., a warrior).'
(|wi·hi| PV FUT, |neniwi-| AI 'be a man', |e·h=–yani| 2s/AOR; |=ke·hi| 'moreover')

The predicative particle phrase *a·kwi-kana·kwa* 'it's not possible' (younger variant *kana·kwa* [A 123D, 127A, 134A]) and *a·kwi* 'not' when used predicatively take complements in the future aorist conjunct:

(2.335) *a·kwi-kana·kwa no·ta nepi wi·h=menowa·či* (O 45F)
'it was not allowed for them to drink water too soon'
(*a·kwi-kana·kwa* 'it's not possible'; *no·ta* 'too soon'; *nepi* 'water';
|wi·h=| FUT, |meno-| AI+O 'drink O2', |e·h=–wa·či| 3p/AOR)

(2.336) *a·kwi=ke·h=ma·mahka·či wi·h=pana·ča·niki.* (O 14F)
'Moreover, it would not necessarily be that it was damaged.'
(*a·kwi* 'not'; |=ke·hi| 'moreover'; *ma·mahka·či* 'necessarily';
|wi·h=| FUT, |pana·ča·-| II 'be ruined', |e·h=–niki| 0′/AOR)

The future aorist may be used by itself for an order or strong admonition, and a first-person form may be used for a statement of intent framed as a polite suggestion or request.

(2.337) Future aorist in main clause

    (a)   *wi·h=kehči-ni·miwa·či=mekoho.* 'They must dance hard, indeed.' (O 148D)
        (|wi·h=| FUT, kehči PV 'greatly', |ni·mi-| AI 'dance', |e·h=–wa·či| 3p/AOR;
        =*mekoho* EMPH)

    (b)   *wi·h=na·kwa·ya·ke.* 'It's time for us to go.' (K-WKG 25),
        'We'd like to go back now.' (K-MMDR 9)
        (|wi·h=| FUT, |na·kwa·-| AI 'depart, go back, go on', |e·h=–ya·ke| 1p/AOR)

    (c)   *wi·h=nawači-na·kwa·ya·ni.* 'I have to go back for a while.' (K-MM 8H)
        (|wi·h=| FUT, *nawači* PV 'first, briefly', |na·kwa·-| AI 'go back', |e·h=–ya·ni| 1s/AOR)

Expressions like (2.337a) are the equivalent of: 'It's that they must dance hard, indeed'. Expressions like (2.337bc) occur in fuller form as complements of *i·ni* 'now' (K-TO 43, K-SSP 151, K-FC 71).

    The future iterative with indefinite subject has the idiomatic meaning 'as if to' (cf. 2.216, 217):

(2.338)   *mehto·či=meko wi·h=pakišinekini e·h=ki·wi-'šawiwa·či.* (JoP-MortH 3)
        'They acted as if they were (birds) about to land.'
        (*mehto·či* 'like'; =*meko* EMPH; |wi·h=| FUT, |pakišin-| AI 'land', |IC–ekini| X/ITER;
        |ki·wi| PV 'around', |išawi-| AI 'do {so}', |e·h=–wa·či| 3p/AOR)

|wi·h=| FUT is not used to make a future for the subjunctive, iterative, plain or changed interrogative, prohibitive, potential, or imperative. In the infrequent cases where |wi·h=| FUT occurs with these modes it has a non-temporal meaning like 'wish to' (2.339, 341, 342), 'dare to' (2.343), 'be going to' (2.208 second clause, 2.340), or 'be inclined to' (2.314).

(2.339)   *owiye·ha=ke·hi wi·h=kakano·take, wi·h=kakano·tamwa.* (K-ECRP 55)
        'If someone wishes to talk to it, he may talk to it.'
        (|wi·h=| FUT, |kakano·t-| TI(1) 'speak to', |-ake| 3s–0/SUBJ)

(2.340)   *wi·h=wi·seničini* 'whenever he was about to eat' (K-BHD2 22 and 23; tr. HP:
        "before eating a meal," and, "When time came for him to eat .. generally")

(2.341)   *ayo·h=ke·h=mekoho wi·h=awihawihkiče? nešihka?* (K-M 715h)
        'Might she wish to live here by herself?'
        (|ayo·hi| 'here'; |=ke·hi| 'moreover'; =mekoho EMPH; |wi·h=| FUT, |CVCV+| RED2,
        |awi-| AI 'be, live {somewhere}', |–hkiče| 3s,0/PROH; *nešihka* 'alone'; ? Q)

(2.342)   *awita=we·na maneto·wa wi·h=keteminawisa.* (K-Wap 127; tr. TB)
        "After all, no manitou would want to bless me."
        (*awita* 'not (pot.)'; =*we·na* 'after all'; *maneto·wa* 'manitou';
        |wi·h=| FUT, |keteminaw-| TA 'bless', |–isa| 3s–1s/POT)

(2.343)   *wi·h=komino* 'dare to swallow me (you sg.)!' (K-W 267; a challenge in a myth song)
        (|wi·h=| FUT, |kom-| TA 'swallow', |–ino| 2s–1s/IMP)

If the subjunctive is the result of modal attraction, however, the future has its normal function (2.193).

26.25. Preterite. There are preterite modes corresponding to all the core conjunct modes except the plain conjunct and the iterative: aorist preterite, subjunctive preterite, changed preterite, negative preterite, and preterite participle. Essentially the preterite modifies the meaning of a mode to refer to a removed past time, a time earlier than and distinct from the recent past that is currently relevant. It can often be translated by the English auxiliary 'had'. Some preterites have idiomatic uses with certain particles.

    Although five preterite modes can be distinguished functionally, however, there are only three distinct preterite inflections for each pronominal combination (excepting some rare participle forms): one with |eꞏh=| AOR, one with initial change, and one with neither. This is because the suffix that marks the preterite (|-ehe| pret.) displaces the modal suffixes used in the core conjunct modes. The preterite inflection with |eꞏh=| AOR makes the aorist preterite, the inflection with initial change makes the changed preterite and the preterite participle, and the inflection with neither makes the subjunctive preterite and the negative preterite. The labeling of the preterite forms as belonging to five different modes thus takes into account their distinct functions, largely paralleling those of the core conjunct modes, as well as their formal features.

The aorist preterite (AOR.PRET) has the subordinating and narrative functions of the aorist but refers to a removed past time:

(2.344) *eꞏh=mehkawatehe meꞏnwawita neniwa* (A 181F)
'as you had found a well-behaved man'
(|mehkaw-| 'find', |eꞏh=–atehe| 2s–3/AOR.PRET;
|menwawi-| AI 'do well', |IC–ta| 3/PPL(ANsg); *neniwa* 'man')
kekimesi=meko eꞏh=poꞏniꞏnitehe mehtoseꞏneniwahi. (K-WMB 45)
'Every one of the other people had camped in.'
(*kekimesi* 'every'; *=meko* EMPH; |poꞏniꞏ-| AI 'camp', |eꞏh=–nitehe| 3´/AOR.PRET;
mehtoseꞏneniwahi 'people (obv.)')

An aorist preterite in a subordinate clause may be the only indicator that the entire collocation, including the higher verb, refers to the removed past:

(2.345) *weꞏči-pwaꞏwi-pyaꞏyaꞏni wiꞏh=aꞏčimohenaꞏnehe* (A 171E)
'which is why I didn't come to instruct you'
(|oči| PV 'from {something}', |pwaꞏwi| PV 'not',
|pyaꞏ-| AI 'come', |IC–yaꞏni| 1s/PPL(obl);
|wiꞏh=| FUT, |aꞏčimoh-| TA 'inform', |eꞏh=–enaꞏnehe| 1s–2s/AOR.PRET)

The aorist preterite often appears for the aorist when *=ye toke* 'it seems' (**§26.2**) is present; for some speakers this is rare, for others it is almost automatic.

(2.346) *eꞏh=teꞏpweꞏhtawaꞏtehe=ye toke* 'he seems to have believed her' (A 120E)
(|teꞏpweꞏhtaw-| TA 'believe', |eꞏh=–atehe| 3s–3´/AOR.PRET; *=ye toke* 'it seems')

When *=ye toke* is used in this way, its scope may extend over the clause or sentence that follows, with the aorist preterite alone maintaining the same function:

(2.347) *eꞏh=pyeꞏči-natoneꞏhwitehe* 'and (it seems) she came looking for me' (A 37G)
(|pyeꞏči| PV 'coming', |natoneꞏhw-| TA 'look for', |eꞏh=–itehe| 3s–1s/AOR.PRET)

The clause preceding (2.347) has *=ye toke* with an aorist preterite (A 37F). Other examples of this pattern are in (A 168C) and (O 130E). In (A 174E) *=ye toke* has scope only over the objective complement clause that has an aorist preterite. It is not clear whether the preterite alone may have the function of *=ye toke* without an earlier contextual occurrence of this enclitic; an interpretation as a removed past is often equally plausible.

An aorist preterite with the negative preverb *pwaꞏwi* and *=ye toke* makes a polite rebuke with a meaning like 'why didn't you' or 'you should have'.

(2.348) *mahkwaꞏči=keꞏh=ye toke| kaꞏhkami eꞏh=pwaꞏwi-neškimiyanehe.* "You ought to have scolded me quietly before." (K-M 857k; tr. HP)
(*mahkwaꞏči* 'quietly'; *|=keꞏhi|* 'moreover'; *=ye toke* 'it seems';
kaꞏhkami 'right from the start';
|pwaꞏwi| PV 'not', |neškim-| TA 'scold', |eꞏh=–iyanehe| 2s–1s/AOR.PRET)

The aorist preterite is combined with the future to give meanings like 'was about to', 'was to have', 'was supposed to have'. This usage is found in main clauses (compare 2.337a), in both ordinary speech and narratives, and in subordinate 'when' clauses (2.350, K-M 591g):

(2.349) *še·ški=mata wi·h=ne·neškima·tehe.* (K-M 214h; quoted sentence)
'He was only supposed to have scolded them, rather.'
(*še·ški* 'only'; =*mata* 'alternatively';
|wi·h=| FUT, |CV+| RED1, |neškim-| TA 'admonish', |e·h=–a·tehe| 3s–3/AOR.PRET)

(2.350) *i·tepi wi·h=ihpahowa·tehe* 'when they were about to run to it' (K-M 52g)
(*i·tepi* '(to) there' (2.153);
|wi·h=| FUT, |ihpaho-| AI 'run to {somewhere}', |e·h=–wa·tehe| 3p/AOR.PRET)

The subjunctive preterite (SUBJ.PRET) makes contrary-to-fact conditions (2.309, 350, 351).

(2.351) *oni·ča·nesiya·nehe=wi·na* 'if I had had children' (A 187A)
(|oni·ča·nesi-| AI 'have a child', |–ya·nehe| 1s/SUBJ.PRET; =*wi·na* 'but')

(2.352) *o·siya·nehe, i·ni a·mi-'nahina·pata·niya·nehe.* (K-WSB 4)
'If I had a father, that could have been how I looked (i.e., was dressed).'
(|o·si-| AI 'have father (living)', |–ya·nehe| 1s/SUBJ.PRET; *i·ni* 'that (inan.)';
a·mi PV POT, |CVCV+| RED2, |ina·pata·ni-| AI 'have {such} appearance',
|IC–ya·nehe| 1s/PRET.PPL(obl))

It also provides the contrary-to-fact equivalent to the subjunctive in wishes expressed with *ta·ni·='nahi* and its variants (2.353; cf. 2.188). Idiomatically *ta·ni·='nahi* may be omitted, with or without the presence of *kana·hi* 'at least'.

(2.353) Subjunctive preterite in wishes
(a) *ta·ni·='nahi aniweka·ya·nehe.* 'I wish I had danced fast.' (K-MHTW 36)
(*ta·ni·='nahi* 'I wish'; |aniweka·-| AI 'dance fast', |–ya·nehe| 1s/SUBJ.PRET)

(b) *kana·h=mata i·ni pwa·wi-to·tawa·tehe.* (K-KK 5)
'At the least he shouldn't have done *that* to him.'
(*kana·hi* 'at least'; =*mata* 'rather'; *i·ni* 'that (inan.)';
|pwa·wi| PV 'not'; |to·taw-| TA 'treat {so}', |–a·tehe| 3s–3′/SUBJ.PRET)

(c) *mani=mata išawiyanehe: a·čiha·čimohiyanehe.* (K-Words 2.5)
'If only you had instead done *this*: if only you had told me.'
(*mani* 'this (inan.)'; =*mata* 'rather'; |išawi-| AI 'do {so}', |–yanehe| 2s/SUBJ.PRET);
|CVCV+| RED2, |a·čimoh-| TA 'tell', |–iyanehe| 2s–1s/SUBJ.PRET).

The changed preterite (CH.PRET) is used in certain idiomatic constructions. It does not function as a preterite of the changed conjunct. Perhaps its most commonly encountered use is in construction with the sentence particles *šepawi·hta* 'it's a good thing' (5.120b) and especially *keye·hapa* 'it turned out; I later realized' (2.354; 5.120a).

(2.354) *keye·hapa=ke·h=wi·na menwi-to·tawitehe.* (A 26C)
'I later realized, though, that she was being good to me.'
(*keye·hapa* 'it turned out'; |=ke·hi| 'moreover'; =*wi·na* 'but';
|menwi-to·taw-| TA 'treat well', |IC–itehe| 3s–1s/CH.PRET)

The changed preterite is also used with the future tense to make a temporal subordinate clause with the meaning of the future aorist preterite, with which it is homophonous (2.349):

(2.355) *wi·h=očisahotehe, / "...," e·h=ikoči.* (K-MIM 26)
'And as he was about to jump, / a voice said to him, "..." '
(|wi·h=| FUT, |očisaho-| 'jump (off)', |IC–tehe| 3s/CH.PRET)

In this use it may be combined with the idiom *mani iši* 'immediately, as soon as' (literally 'like this'; 2.89, 194, 209):

(2.356)   *mani wi·h=iši-pakametehe* 'just as he [a drum] was about to be struck' (K-Wap 89)
(*mani* 'this (inan.)'; |wi·h=| FUT, |iši| PV '{so}',
|pakam-| TA 'hit', |IC–etehe| X–3´/CH.PRET)

A clause with *keye·hapa* may have an aorist preterite (2.357) instead of a changed preterite, and an aorist preterite may appear without *keye·hapa* after the construction with this particle and a changed preterite has been established in an earlier clause or sentence (2.358; cf. 2.347).

(2.357)   *keye·hapa e·h=ki·wa·ni·tehe neniwa.* 'It turned out the man was lost.' (SP-PD 1)
(*keye·hapa* 'it turned out'; |ki·wa·ni·-| AI 'be lost', |e·h=–tehe| 3s/AOR.PRET;
neniwa 'man')

(2.358)   *"...," e·h=ina·čimoha·tehe.* ' "...," she had told him.' (A 120D)
(|ina·čimoh-| TA 'inform {so}', |e·h=–a·tehe| 3s–3/AOR.PRET)

The verb in (2.358) follows a long quote, before which *keye·hapa* occurs with a changed preterite verb (A 119C).

The negative preterite (NEG.PRET) combines with *a·kwi* 'not' (**§26.11**) to make a removed past tense for the negative mode:

(2.359)   *a·kwi paši=mekoho keteminawi·hitehe* (K-Spot 147)
'She took no pity on me at all.'
(*a·kwi* 'not'; *paši* 'at all'; *=mekoho* EMPH;
|keteminaw-| TA 'pity', |–i·hitehe| 3s–1s/DIM/NEG.PRET)

It may be used with *=ye·toke* 'it seems'.

(2.360)   *a·kwi=ye·toke kehke·nema·tehe e·ya·nikwe·ni.* (K-M 516g)
'It seems he didn't know where the other could have gone.'
(*a·kwi* 'not'; *=ye·toke* 'it seems';
|kehke·nem-| TA 'know', |–a·tehe| 3s–3´/NEG.PRET;
|iha·-| AI 'go {somewhere}', |IC–nikwe·ni| 3´/INT.PPL(obl))

(2.361)   *a·kwi=ye·toke ne·watehe?* 'Didn't you see him?' (K-B 154)
(*a·kwi* 'not'; *=ye·toke* 'it seems'; |ne·w-| TA 'see', |–atehe| 2s–3/NEG.PRET; ? Q)
a·kwi=ye·toke i·ya·h=taši·seniyanehe. 'You didn't *eat* over there.' (shocked inference; K-MM 18C [AW])
(*a·kwi* 'not'; *=ye·toke* 'it seems'; *i·ya·hi* 'over there';
|taši·seni-| AI 'eat {somewhere}', |–yanehe| 2s/NEG.PRET)

The preterite participle (PRET.PPL) is a conjunct participle referred to a removed past time. It also appears by attraction in contrary-to-fact statements marked by the subjunctive preterite (2.250-351). Except for a few archaic forms (2.363, 364), the head is not marked overtly in inflection.

(2.362)   *i·na= 'pi·= 'na wi·h=ne·ya·pi-okima·wihetehe.* (K-ECRP 39)
'He is the one who would have been made chief again.'
(*i·na* 'that (anim.)'; *=ipi* HRSY; *i·na* 'that (anim.)';
|wi·h=| FUT, *ne·ya·pi* PV 'as before',
|okima·wih-| TA 'make chief', |IC–etehe| X–3/PRET.PPL)

(2.363)   *wi·h=penonitehepaniye·ne* 'the one (obv.) who was going to go home'
(K-WLB 11)
(|wi·h=| FUT, |peno-| AI 'go home', |IC–tehepaniye·ne| 3s/PRET.PPL(OBVsg))

(2.364)   *wiʔh=pyeʔtoʔtehepaniyeʔne* 'the ones (inan.) she was going to bring' (K-BHD 125)

         (|wi·h=| FUT, |pye·t-| TI(2) 'bring', |IC–o·tehepaniye·ne| 3s–0/PRET.PPL(INpl))

(2.365)   *iʔni eʔšawiwaʔtehe.* 'That is what they used to do.' (O 11C)

         (*iʔni* 'that (inan.)'; |išawi-| AI 'do {so}', |IC–wa·tehe| 3p/PRET.PPL(obl))

(2.366)   *eʔh=apihapinitehe* 'where he (obv.) had been sitting' (O 101D)

         (|CVCV+| RED2, |api-| AI 'sit {somewhere}',

         |e·h=–nitehe| 3′/PRET.PPL(loc.obl))

(2.367)   *eʔhpi·hči-tepaʔnakehe netapenoʔhema* 'as much as I had loved my child' (A 125B)

         (|ahpi·hči| PV 'to {such} a degree',

         |tepa·N-| TA 'love', |IC–akehe| 1s–3/PRET.PPL(obl); *netapenoʔhema* 'my child')

After *keyeʔhapa* 'it turned out' a participle with an oblique head appears as a preterite participle in (A 15E).

Chapter 3.

§§27-31. Inflectional Morphology

Expression of Grammatical Categories

27. The grammatical categories of Meskwaki (**Chapter 2**) are expressed, for the most part, by the inflection of words. The inflectional morphemes that are used comprise a small set of pronominal prefixes, a modal prefix, a tense prefix, a morpheme of vowel ablaut, and a very large number of suffixes. The patterns of occurrence of these morphemes and the correspondence between these formal patterns and the grammatical categories they express constitute the inflectional morphology of the language.

27.1. Inflection for nominal and pronominal categories. The inflections on nouns and verbs for nominal and pronominal categories employ morphemes that fall into three major sets: prefixes, central suffixes, and peripheral suffixes. A central suffix, in some cases operating in tandem with a prefix, marks pronominal category (**§18.4**), and a peripheral suffix marks nominal category (**§18.2**). The morphological opposition between central and peripheral suffixes has different functions in the two parts of speech.

NOUN INFLECTION

28. The prefixes and suffixes used in noun inflection are arranged as shown in (3.1, next page). Each column represents a position either before or after the noun stem. There is one prefix position and three inflectional suffix positions. The diminutive is a derivational category (**§41**), but it is marked by a morpheme that occurs among the inflectional suffixes (**§28.13**), making a fourth suffix position. The morphemes in each position are mutually exclusive.

In word-final position are the peripheral suffixes, which categorize the noun itself, marking core inflection, vocative, or locative. A peripheral suffix is present in every noun form, allowing for the zero variant of the vocative singular which is realized only by stem modification. The vocative endings in effect substitute for the animate core-inflectional suffixes. The locative categorizes the noun as syntactically an oblique.

(3.1)   Inflectional template (nouns)

prefix		STEM	thematic suffix	DIM	central suffix	peripheral suffix
pronoun |ne+| 1 |ke+| 2 |o+| 3 |me+| unposs.			theme sign |-em| poss. th.		pronoun |-∅| sg. |-ena·n| 1p,12 |-wa·w| 2p,3p |-inaw| X	core inflection |-a| ANsg, |-aki| ANpl |-i| INsg, |-ani| INpl |-ani| OBVsg, |-ahi| OBVpl
						vocative |-e| VOCsg, |-etike| VOCpl
						locative |-eki| loc.

The prefixes and the central endings jointly add an indication of a possessor (**§22.1**, **§28.5**); some non-dependent nouns add this inflection for possessor to a possessed theme, formed by the theme sign. The three prefixes that make pronominal reference mark person: |ne+| 1, |ke+| 2, |o+| 3. The inflections for indefinite possessor and for unpossessed dependent nouns have the prefixes |o+| 3 (without pronominal reference) and |me+| unposs. The central endings indicate the number of the possessor (|-∅| sg.; |-ena·n| 1p,12; |-wa·w| 2p,3p) or an indefinite possessor (|-inaw| X). With the first person pluralizer (|-ena·n| 1p,12), |ke+| 2 differentiates the inclusive from the exclusive (which has |ne+| 1). With the second and third person pluralizer (|-wa·w| 2p,3p), |ke+| 2 differentiates the second plural from the third plural (which has |o+| 3).

Not included in (3.1) is the ending |+ena·te|, which is analyzed as the combination of |-ena·n| 1p,12 with either |-e| VOCsg or |-etike| VOCpl (**§28.20**).

The core inflection of nouns

28.1. Suffix paradigm. The core inflection of nouns (**§18.2**) comprises six mutually exclusive suffixes, two of them homophonous. They mark number (singular or plural), gender (animate or inanimate), and for animate nouns obviation (proximate or obviative):

(3.2) Core inflectional suffixes of nouns

	Animate		Inanimate
	Proximate	Obviative	
Singular	|-a| ANsg	|-ani| OBVsg	|-i| INsg
Plural	|-aki| ANpl	|-ahi| OBVpl	|-ani| INpl

The animate obviative suffixes are referred to unambiguously as obviative (OBV), as there are no inanimate obviative noun suffixes, and animate proximate (non-obviative) suffixes are referred to simply as animate (AN).

When these suffixes follow the noun stem directly they constitute the complete ending, given as |+a| ANsg, etc.; a full paradigm of examples is in (2.2). They may also follow the central suffixes that mark certain possessed forms (3.1, 19, 38, 39).

28.2. Singular. The one-syllable endings (|+a| ANsg, |+i| INsg) show no variation. Their occasional absence after an *h* reflects a phonetically conditioned optional pronunciation, or for some writers merely a matter of orthography (**§4.2**). In some cases noun stems are modified when one of these endings follows. Stems in |-Cy| drop the |y|: (1) before |+a| ANsg if the preceding consonant is |š| or |č| (cf. 1.213); and (2) before |+i| INsg after all consonants (1.212):

> (3.3)   *neškaša* 'my fingernail' (cf. *neškaš(y)e·ki* 'my fingernails'; 1.154)
>
> (← |ne-škašy-a| ← |ne+| 1, |-škašy-| AN 'fingernail', |+a| ANsg)

> (3.4)   *nepi* 'water' (cf. *nepi·ki* 'in the water')
>
> (← |nepy-i| ← |nepy-| IN 'water', |+i| INsg)

> (3.5)   *pe·škiti* 'basket' (cf. *pe·škitye·ni* 'baskets'; also 3.98)
>
> (← |pe·škity-i| ← |pe·škity-| IN 'basket', |+i| INsg)

Stems in |-iy| lose this syllable before |+i| INsg:

> (3.6)   *owi·nwi* 'his navel' (A 114E) (cf. *owi·nwi·ki* 'on his navel'; 3.109)
>
> (← |ow-i·nwiy-i| ← |o+| 3, |-i·nwiy-| IN 'navel', |+i| INsg)

Before |+i| INsg some stems replace |t| with *č*:

> (3.7)   *ni·piči* 'my tooth' (cf. *ni·pitani* 'my teeth')
>
> (← |ne-i·pit-i| ← |ne+| 1, |-i·pit-| IN 'tooth', |+i| INsg)

The other nouns that have been found in the texts with this variation are: *nehka·či* 'my foot' (stem |-hka·t-|), *okehtanasiči* 'his big toe' (|kehtanasit-|), and *oče·hči* 'sinew' (|oče·ht-|). Stem-final *t* is retained in loanwords: *ko·ti* 'coat', *wi·ti* 'wheat'; these can be set up as having underlying |T|: |ko·T-| IN 'coat', |wi·T-| IN 'wheat' (**§13.1**).

28.3. Plural and obviative. The first vowel in a two-syllable ending may contract with a stem-final semivowel that follows a consonant.

Stems in |-Cy| always replace the following |a| with *e·* (**§11.5**; 3.3):

> (3.8)   *ahpenye·ki* 'potatoes' (cf. *ahpenya* 'potato')
>
> (← |ahpeny-aki| ← |ahpeny-| AN 'potato', |+aki| ANpl)

If this contraction produces a sequence *šye·* or *čye·*, the *y* is optionally dropped in pronunciation and apparently never written (1.154; 3.3).

Stems in |-Cw| in most categories contract underlying |Cw-aC| to |Co·C| (**§11.2**):

> (3.9)   *matepo·ni* 'lodge frames' (cf. *matepwi* 'abandoned lodge frame')
>
> (← |matepw-ani| ← |matepw-| IN 'lodge frame', |+ani| INpl)

> (3.10)   *neški·šeko·ni* 'my eyes' (cf. *neški·šekwi* 'my eye')
>
> (← |ne-ški·šekw-ani| ← |ne+| 1, |-ški·šekw-| IN 'eye', |+ani| INpl)

> (3.11)   *nenoso·ki* 'buffalos, cows' (cf. *nenoswa* 'buffalo, cow')
>
> (← |nenosw-aki| ← |nenosw-| AN 'buffalo, cow', |+aki| ANpl)

> (3.12)   *ahkohko·ki* 'kettles' (cf. *ahkohkwa* 'kettle')
>
> (← |ahkohkw-aki| ← |ahkohkw-| AN 'kettle' + |+aki| ANpl)

This contraction does not take place in most animate noun stems ending in |-kw| and, at least optionally, in the names of two mythological characters with stems in |-sw| and |-nw|:

> (3.13)   *šeka·kwaki* 'skunks' (← |šeka·kw-aki| ← |šeka·kw-| AN 'skunk', |+aki| ANpl)

> (3.14)   *meso·swani, meso·so·ni* 'Mesoswa (obv.)'
>
> (← |meso·sw-ani| ← |meso·sw-| AN 'Mesoswa', |+ani| OBVsg)

28.4. Irregular plural and obviative. The stem of *netaya* 'my pet (esp. dog, horse)' is treated before all suffixes like a stem in |-Cy|:

    (3.15)   *netaya* 'my pet': *netayeˑki* 'my pets'

Elicited forms of *nepaya* 'my thigh, femur' have the same treatment (AW, FM).

Some stems have two stem shapes before suffixes, either as synonymous variants or in different inflectional forms. In all cases the variation is between stem-final |-C| and |-Cy|:

    (3.16)   *niˑtoˑša* 'my co-wife, my rival' (stem |-iˑtoˑš-| and |-iˑtoˑšy-| AN 'rival'):
        owiˑtoˑšani, owiˑtoˑšeˑni 'his or her rival'

    (3.17)   *wiˑkiyaˑpi* 'house, lodge, wickiup' (usual stem |wiˑkiyaˑp-| IN 'house'; cf. 3.97):
        wiˑkiyaˑpyeˑni 'houses' (plural stem |wiˑkiyaˑpy-| IN 'house', |+ani| INpl)

Participles used as male names have obviative singulars made either like an ordinary participle or like a noun (cf. 3.136):

    (3.18)   *neˑnyeˑškwiˑta* 'Nenyeskwi (the older brother of Apayashi)'
        Participial obviative: *neˑnyeˑškwiˑničini* 'Nenyeskwi (obv.)' (Sh, S)
        Nominal obviative: *neˑnyeˑškwiˑtani* 'Nenyeskwi (obv.)' (JP)

Possessor

28.5. Inflections. The inflection for possessor (§22.1; 3.19) uses combinations of pronominal prefixes and central suffixes. In addition, some non-dependent nouns add the possessed-theme marker |-em| immediately after the stem. The peripheral suffixes, which pertain to the possessed noun (3.2), follow the suffixes that pertain to the possessor.

    (3.19) Inflection for possessor

1s	|ne–∅-|	or |ne–em-|	(|ne+| 1 ± |-em| poss. th. + |-∅| sg.)
2s	|ke–∅-|	or |ke–em-|	(|ke+| 2 ± |-em| poss. th. + |-∅| sg.)
3s	|o–∅-|	or |o–em-|	(|o+| 3 ± |-em| poss. th. + |-∅| sg.)
1p	|ne–enaˑn-|	or |ne–em-enaˑn-|	(|ne+| 1 ± |-em| poss. th. + |-enaˑn| 1p,12)
12	|ke–enaˑn-|	or |ke–em-enaˑn-|	(|ke+| 2 ± |-em| poss. th. + |-enaˑn| 1p,12)
2p	|ke–waˑw-|	or |ke–em-waˑw-|	(|ke+| 2 ± |-em| poss. th. + |-waˑw| 2p,3p)
3p	|o–waˑw-|	or |o–em-waˑw-|	(|o+| 3 ± |-em| poss. th. + |-waˑw| 2p,3p)
X	|o–inaw-|	or |o–em-inaw-|	(|o+| 3 ± |-em| poss. th. + |-inaw| X)
none	|me–|		(|me+| unposs.)

Third-person obviative possessors are marked the same way as third-person proximates.

For a few nouns the use of |-em| poss. th. is optional or variable:

    (3.20)   *otašaˑtiˑhemani* 'his headed arrows' (O 154G) (cf. *ašaˑtiˑhi* 'headed arrow')
        otašaˑtiˑhani 'his headed arrows' (K-HS 27; JB-BP 6)

    (3.21)   *onenoˑteˑwiˑhemani* 'his Indian tobacco' (K-GF 11)
        (cf. *nenoˑteˑwiˑha* 'Indian tobacco')
        onenoˑteˑwiˑhani 'his Indian tobacco' (Sh-Elm 36, 40)

The possessed forms of *ahki* 'land, earth' with and without |-em| poss. th. have different meanings:

    (3.22)   *ketahki* 'your garden, your planting field' (A 10F)
        ketahki(ˑ)mi 'your land' (K-B 77); *otahki(ˑ)mi* 'his land, his (a deity's) earth' (3.40)

A few nouns that take |-em| poss. th. show a stem in either |-C| or |-Cy| before it (cf. §28.4):

(3.23)   *šama·kaneša* 'soldier', *šama·kanešaki* 'soldiers' (stem |šama·kaneš-| AN 'soldier'):
          ošama·kanešemahi 'his soldiers' (S-YMSG 65)
          ošama·kaneši·mahi 'his soldiers' (S-YMSG 63, 67) (stem |šama·kanešy-|; **§28.9**)

When a noun is combined with |-i·t-| 'fellow', generally in the form |-i·či| PN, the resulting stem is a dependent noun. A noun that normally requires |-em| poss. th. does not use it in this derived stem:

(3.24)   *kemehtose·neni·ma* 'your (sg.) people' (representative singular)
          (← |ke-mehtose·neniw-em-a| ← *mehtose·neniwa* 'person' + |ke–em-| 2s)
          ki·či-mehtose·neniwa 'your (sg.) fellow people' (representative singular)
          (← |ke-i·či mehtose·neniw-a|
          ← |-i·či| PN 'fellow', *mehtose·neniwa* 'person' + |ke–Ø-| 2s)

Dependent nouns do not occur without an inflection from the paradigm in (3.19). For kinship terms in unattributed use a secondary derivative is made which functions as a non-dependent noun (2.73; 4.208*defg*). Other dependent nouns make unpossessed forms with the unpossessed prefix |me+| (2.74; 3.25), or with the third-person prefix |o+| (2.75; 3.26), or with either prefix (3.27):

(3.25)   *ote·hi* 'his heart' (← |o-te·h-i| ← |-te·h-| IN 'heart', |o–Ø-| 3s, |-i| INsg)
          mete·hi 'a heart' (← |me-te·h-i| ← |-te·h-| IN 'heart', |me+| unposs., |-i| INsg)

(3.26)   *owi·ši* 'his head' (← |ow-i·š-i| ← |-i·š-| IN 'head', |o–Ø-| 3s, |-i| INsg)
          owi·ši 'a head' (← |ow-i·š-i| ← |-i·š-| IN 'head', |o+| 3, |-i| INsg)

(3.27)   *osowa·nowi* 'his tail' (← |o-sowa·now-i| ← |-sowa·now-| IN 'tail', |o–Ø-| 3s, |-i| INsg)
          osowa·nowi 'a tail' (← |o-sowa·now-i| ← |-sowa·now-| IN 'tail', |o+| 3, |-i| INsg)
          mesowa·nowi 'a tail'
          (← |me-sowa·now-i| ← |-sowa·now-| IN 'tail', |me+| unposs., |-i| INsg)

A few nouns are optionally dependent: *no·ke·nawa* (cf. A 175D), *meno·ke·nawa* (K-FC 135) 'soul'; (3.130).

Some dependent nouns that do not refer to people or body parts lack a non-possessed form. The non-possessed equivalent may be made from a derived stem that is otherwise unused (3.28, 29), or supplied suppletively by an ordinary noun (3.30, 31).

(3.28)   *nehkone·hi* 'my blanket', *ohkone·hi* 'his blanket' (no non-possessed form)
          Cf. *mehkone·weni* 'a blanket'.

(3.29)   *neko·te·hi* 'my dress, skirt', *oko·te·hi* 'her dress, skirt' (no non-possessed form)
          Cf. *meko·te·weni* 'a dress, skirt'.

(3.30)   *ni·ki* 'my house', *owi·ki* 'his house' (no non-possessed form)
          Cf. *wi·kiya·pi* 'a house', which is not used with possessive inflection.

(3.31)   *ni·pi* 'my arrow', *owi·pi* 'his arrow' (no non-possessed form)
          Cf. *anwi* 'an arrow' (possessed forms most often mean 'shot, wizard's missile').

An unpossessed dependent noun may itself be possessed. Usually such forms are made on the unpossessed form with non-pronominal |o+| 3 functioning as a derivational prefix:

(3.32)   *keto·wi·šemena·nani* 'our (trophy) heads, our (trophy) scalps' (JP-MAF 22)
          (← |ket-owi·š-em-ena·n-ani|
          ← *owi·ši* 'head' [3.26] + |ke–em-ena·n-| 12, |-ani| INpl)
          neto·hka·temaki 'my (deer) feet' (K-M 955c)
          (← |net-ohka·t-em-aki| ← *ohka·taki* 'animal's feet (as food)', |ne–em-| 1s)

Such forms can also be found with no apparent difference in meaning from the usual dependent noun:

(3.33)   *oto·te·hemi* 'his heart' (K-W 418) (beside *ote·hi* 'his heart' [K-W 417])
           (← |ot-ote·h-emi| ← *ote·hi* 'heart' [cf. 3.25] + |o–em-| 3s)
           oto·sowa·nakowa·wani 'their tails' (K-BLI 16) (← |ot-osowa·nakw-wa·w-ani|
           ← *osowa·nako·ni* 'tails' [← |osowa·nakw-ani|] + |o–wa·w-| 3p)
           Cf. *osowa·nakowa·wani* 'their tails' (K-BLI 17)
           (← |-sowa·nakw-| 'tail' IN, |o–wa·w-| 3p, |-ani| INpl).

The noun *owi·šehkwayi*, *mi·šehkwayi* 'scalp' makes possessed forms on both unpossessed forms.

(3.34)   *oto·wi·šehkwa·mani* 'his (trophy) scalps' (K-MWL 33)
           (← |ot-owi·šehkway-em-ani| ← *owi·šehkwayani* 'scalps' + |o–em-| 3s)
           omi·šehkwa·mwa·wi 'their (trophy) scalp' (JP-MAT 33)
           (← *mi·šehkwayi* 'scalp' + |o–em-wa·w-| 3p)

When the scalp is part of the possessor's own body, it may be inflected as a dependent noun or partly regularized, in more than one way:

(3.35)   *ni·šehkwayi* 'my scalp (someone else's intended trophy)' C-G 4)
           kewi·šehkwa·na·nani 'our scalps (someone's intended trophies)' (C-G 4)
           omi·šehkwayi 'his (a dead enemy's own) scalp' (K-FC 274)

Some non-dependent nouns beginning with *ow-* optionally omit |o+| 3 in possessed forms, treating the stem-initial |o-| as a prefix:

(3.36)   *owa·wanwa·wani* 'their eggs' (K-FC 584)
           oto·wa·wanwa·wani 'their eggs' (K-FC 584)
           (← |(ot-)owa·wan-wa·w-ani| ← *owa·wanani* 'eggs' + |(ot)–wa·w-| 3p)

Beside the regular locative *ni·šeki* ([ni·hšékị]) 'on my head' (K-ECRP 16, K-WPGB 4; JP-MAF 11) from *ni·ši* 'my head', some speakers prefer the altered form *newi·šemeki* (A 112B) in order to avoid the homonymy with *ni·h=šeki* (also [ni·hšékị]) 'I must urinate'.

An animate noun possessed by a third person is always obviative, since the prefix makes pronominal reference to a possessor that is proximate (or construed as proximate). But when the third-person prefix is used as the default inflection on an unpossessed form it does not have pronominal reference and does not force the obviation of the noun:

(3.37)   *onamaškayani* 'his skin (obv.)' (← |-namaškay-| AN 'skin', |o–∅-| 3s, |+ani| OBVsg)
           onamaškaya 'skin' (← |-namaškay-| AN 'skin', |o+| 3, |+a| ANsg)

Inanimate dependent nouns that do not take |me+| cannot show this contrast, and the unpossessed form is identical to the form with third-singular possessor (3.26-27).

28.6. Regular paradigms. Noun stems that begin with a consonant and do not end with a semivowel take the inflections for possessor without phonological modification:

(3.38) Possessed forms of *ni·ča·pa* AN 'doll'

	sg.	pl.	obv. sg.	obv. pl.
1s	*neni·ča·pa*	*neni·ča·paki*	*neni·ča·pani*	*neni·ča·pahi*
2s	*keni·ča·pa*	*keni·ča·paki*	*keni·ča·pani*	*keni·ča·pahi*
3s			*oni·ča·pani*	*oni·ča·pahi*
1p	*neni·ča·pena·na*	*neni·ča·pena·naki*	*neni·ča·pena·nani*	*neni·ča·pena·nahi*
12	*keni·ča·pena·na*	*keni·ča·pena·naki*	*keni·ča·pena·nani*	*keni·ča·pena·nahi*
2p	*keni·ča·pwa·wa*	*keni·ča·pwa·waki*	*keni·ča·pwa·wani*	*keni·ča·pwa·wahi*
3p			*oni·ča·pwa·wani*	*oni·ča·pwa·wahi*
X	*oni·ča·pinawa*	*oni·ča·pinawaki*		

(3.39) Possessed forms of *mi·ša·mi* IN 'sacred bundle'

	sg.	pl.
1s	*nemi·ša·mi*	*nemi·ša·mani*
2s	*kemi·ša·mi*	*kemi·ša·mani*
3s	*omi·ša·mi*	*omi·ša·mani*
1p	*nemi·ša·mena·ni*	*nemi·ša·mena·nani*
12	*kemi·ša·mena·ni*	*kemi·ša·mena·nani*
2p	*kemi·ša·mwa·wi*	*kemi·ša·mwa·wani*
3p	*omi·ša·mwa·wi*	*omi·ša·mwa·wani*
X	*omi·ša·minawi*	*omi·ša·minawani*

Obviatives of indefinite-possessed forms are presumably possible, but they are not attested.

28.7. Prefixes with vowel-initial noun stems. When the prefixes are added to a stem that begins with a vowel they always undergo modification, and the stem-initial vowel is often modified as well.

With a non-dependent noun the prefixes add |t| before a vowel:

(3.40)   *netapeno·hema* 'my child' (← |ne-*t*-apeno·h-em-a| ← *apeno·ha* 'child' + |ne–em-| 1s)

After the |t| of a prefix, |i| is always replaced by |e|, and |o| is always replaced by |o·|:

(3.41)   *nete̱šite·ha·kani* 'my plan' (O 75D)
(← |ne-*t*-e̱šite·ha·kan-i| ← *išite·ha·kani* 'thought' + |ne–∅-| 1s)

(3.42)   *keto̱·kima·mena·na* 'our (inc.) chief' (O 107G)
(← |ke-*t*-o̱·kima·w-em-ena·n-a| ← *o̱kima·wa* 'chief' + |ke–em-ena·n-| 12)

Stem-initial |a| is most often retained (3.40), but in many stems it is replaced by |o·|:

(3.43)   *oto̱·hkanemi* 'his bone' (O 77H) (← |o-*t*-o̱·hkan-em-i| ← *a̱hkani* 'bone' + |o–em-| 3s)

Some stems attest both treatments:

(3.44)   *ota̱hki(·)mi* (K-FC 148; SP-Fish 25), *oto̱·hki(·)mi* (C-Hist 11) 'his land, his earth'
(← |o-*t*-a̱hky-em-i|, |o-*t*-o̱·hky-em-i| ← *a̱hki* 'earth, land, dirt' + |o–em-| 3s)

A few stems replace initial |a| with |e|. This is a recessive pattern found consistently with one noun and in the usage of some speakers with three others:

(3.45)   *kete̱hkoma* 'your louse' (← |ke-*t*-e̱hkw-em-a| ← *a̱hkwa* 'louse' + |ke–em-| 2s)

(3.46)   *ote̱škwe·neči·ki* (C-FS 8; SP-RL 84), *ota̱škwe·neči·ki* (Sh-PS 14) 'on his little finger'
(← *a̱škwe·neči* 'little finger' + |o–∅-| 3s + |+eki| LOC)

(3.47)   *ote̱neno·te·wi·hemani* 'his Indian tobacco' (SP-PD 86; cf. 3.21)
ota̱neno·te·wi·hani 'his Indian tobacco' (LL-Auto 111)
(← *aneno·te·wi·ha* 'Indian tobacco' + |o–em-| 3s or |o–∅-| 3s)

(3.48)   *ote̱ša·ti·hi* (K-ICH 6, K-SH 8), *ota̱ša·ti·hi* (K-TG 6) 'his headed arrow'
(← *aša·ti·hi* 'headed arrow' + |o–∅-| 3s)

Before the stem of a dependent noun that begins with a vowel, |ne+| 1 and |ke+| 2 drop the |e|, and |o+| 3 is replaced by |ow-|. If this underlying |ow-| precedes a stem-initial |o·|, the sequence |ow-o·-| contracts to |o·-|:

(3.49)   *ni̱yawi* 'my body, myself' (← |ne-i·yaw-i| ← |-i·yaw-| IN 'body', |ne–∅-| 1s, |+i| INsg)
owi̱yawi 'his body, himself' (← |ow-i·yaw-i| ← |-i·yaw-|, |o–∅-| 3s, |+i| INsg)

(3.50)   *no̱·sa* 'my father' (← |ne-o·s-a| ← |-o·s-| AN 'father', |ne–∅-|, |+a| ANsg)
o̱·sani 'his father' (← |ow-o·s-ani| ← |-o·s-|, |o–∅-|, |+ani| OBVsg)

28.8. Prefixes with compound nouns. When a compound noun is possessed, the pronominal prefix may appear on the prenoun alone, on the head noun alone, or on both, depending on several factors.

If the head noun of a compound is dependent, it necessarily has a pronominal prefix, and there is usually one on the prenoun as well:

(3.51)   *ketahtakwi-kemešo mesena naki* 'the grandfathers of all of us' (K-TCSB 92)
            (*tahtakwi* 'together' PN, |-mešo·mes-| AN 'grandfather', |ke–ena·naki| 12(ANpl))
            okaka či-osekwisani 'his "teasing" aunt, his mother's brother's wife' (K-Kin 4)
            (*kaka či* PN 'teasing', |-sekwis-| AN 'father's sister', |o–ani| 3s(OBVsg))

(3.52)   *neme neti hi-no hkomese ha* 'my harlot of a grandmother' (K-M 359c)
            (*me neti hi* PN 'fornicating' [← *me neti ha* 'fornicator, screw-up'],
            |-o·hkomese·h-| AN 'grandmother', |ne–a| 1s(ANsg))

Less commonly the prenoun has no prefix:

(3.53)   _*nehpen-okwisani* 'his stepson' (S-RL 1)
            (*nehpeni* PN 'step-', |-kwis-| AN 'son', |o–∅-| 3s, |+ani| OBVsg)

(3.54)   _*meškwahki hi-ona pe mani* 'her Meskwaki husband' (X5-EBE 21)
            (*meškwahki hi* PN 'Meskwaki', |-na·pe·m-| AN 'husband', |o–∅-| 3s, |+ani| OBVsg)

If the dependent noun has a third-person prefix that has no pronominal reference but merely marks the noun as unpossessed (3.26-27), the prefix is not repeated before the prenoun:

(3.55)   *anemo hi-owi ši* 'dog's head' (K-BD 14)

If the whole compound is a dependent noun because it contains the dependent prenoun |-i·či| PN 'fellow', only the prenoun has the prefix (3.24).

If the head noun of a compound is non-dependent, the prefix may appear on the prenoun as well as the head noun, or only on the prenoun:

(3.56)   *kekehči-kena tawino nena ni* 'our (inc.) great medicine' (K-MESB 91)
            (*kehči* PN 'great', |na·tawino·n-| IN 'medicine', |ke–ena·ni| 12(INsg))

(3.57)   *okehči-oni miwenwa wi* 'their main dance' (K-WarD 31)
            (*kehči* PN 'great', |ni·miwen-| IN 'dance', |o–wa·wi| 3p(INsg))

(3.58)   *kemešenahkye wi-kepi ša kanemi* 'your (sg.) prisoner strap' (K-BHD 19)
            (*mešenahkye wi* PN 'capturing', |pi·ša·kan-| IN 'strap, thong', |ke–emi| 2s(INsg))
            omešenahkye wi-pi ša kanemi 'his prisoner strap' (K-BHD 22)
            (same, with |o–emi| 3s(INsg))

(3.59)   *netahtakwi-nese ma na na* 'our (exc.) jointly offered tobacco' (K-BHD2 198)
            (*tahtakwi* PN 'together', |nese·ma·w-| AN 'tobacco', |ne–ena·na| 1p(ANsg))

If the prenoun is functionally the preverb in a compound verb stem from which the compound noun is derived as a unit, the prefix most commonly appears only on the prenoun, but two prefixes may also be used:

(3.60)   *kepwa wi-=mekoho -nenoše wenwa wi* 'your (pl.) disbelief indeed' (K-FC 453)
            (|pwa·wi| (PV)PN 'non-'; =*mekoho* EMPH; |nenoše·wen-| IN 'listening',
            |ke–wa·wi| 2p(INsg); compound noun stem:
            |pwa·wi nenoše·wen-| IN 'disbelief' ← |pwa·wi nenoše·-| AI 'not listen')
            opwa wi-onenoše wenwa wi 'their disbelief' (K-WD 149)
            (|pwa·wi| (PV)PN 'non-'; |nenoše·wen-| IN 'listening', |o–wa·wi| 3p(INsg))

Note that even though the noun in (3.60) is derived as a unit from a compound verb stem, the internal word boundary is retained and the prenoun (ex preverb) may be followed by an enclitic.

If a compound with two prenouns is possessed the prefix most often appears on both prenouns:

(3.61)   o̲čaki-o̲nehpen-o šisemani 'his step-great-grandchild' (K-Kin 1)
         (čaki PN 'little', nehpeni PN 'step-', |-o·šisem-| AN 'grandchild',
         |o–ani| 3s(OBVsg))

(3.62)   ne̲mi·ša·či-ne̲mačowiye·hi-no̲·hkomese·ha (K-W 582)
         'my dressed-up cranky-old grandmother'
         (mi·ša·či PN 'dressed-up', mačowiye·hi PN 'cranky' [← mačowiye·ha 'cranky
         one'], -o·hkomese·h-| AN 'grandmother', |ne–a| 1s(ANsg))

(3.63)   o̲kehči-o̲kehkinawa·či-ni·miwenwa·wi 'their main, distinctive dance' (K-WarD 32)
         (kehči PN 'great', kehkinawa·či PN 'distinctive',
         |ni·miwen-| IN 'dance', |o–wa·wi| 3p(INsg))

The prefix appears on only the first of two prenouns when they form a constituent:

(3.64)   ke̲ma·wači-kehči-ke̲mešo·mesena·na 'our greatest grandfather' (K-GBuff 164)
         (ma·wači-kehči PN-PN 'greatest [← ma·wači PN 'of all', kehči PN 'great'],
         |-mešo·mes-| AN 'grandfather', |ke–ena·na| 12(ANsg))

28.9. Contraction with |w| and |y|. A stem-final |w| or |y| almost always contracts with non-final |e| in suffixes, such as |-em| poss. th. and |-ena·n| 1p,12.

Stems in |-Cy| contract |y-e| to long |i·| or, less commonly, short |i| (**§11.4**):

(3.65)   neto·seni̲·mi 'my stone' (← |net-aseny-em-i| ← aseni 'stone' (|aseny-|) + |ne–em-| 1s)

(3.66)   neki̲na·na 'our (inc.) mother'
         (← |ne-ky-ena·n-a| ← |-ky-| AN 'mother', |ne–ena·n-| 1p)

Here and below (**§28.15**) the distinction between contraction to long /i·/ and contraction to short /i/ is made on the basis of what was observed in the 1990's, since short and long vowels are not distinguished in the written texts.

Stems in |-Cw| always contract |w-e| to |o| (**§11.1**):

(3.67)   oki·šeko̲mi 'his sky' (K-FC 181)
         (← |o-ki·šekw-em-i| ← ki·šekwi 'sky' + |o–em-| 3s)

(3.68)   keški·šeko̲na·nani 'our (inc.) eyes' (O 125J)
         (← |ke-ški·šekw-ena·n-ani| ← |-ški·šekwi-| IN 'eye', |ke–ena·n-| 12, |-ani| INpl)

Stems in |-Vw| almost always contract |Vw-e| to |V·|, with the quality of the vowel kept (**§11.6**; 3.24):

(3.69)   ni·ya̲·na·ni 'ourselves (exc.), our lives' (2.46)
         (← |ne-i·yaw-ena·n-i| ← |-i·yaw-| IN 'body', |ne–ena·n-| 1p, |-i| INsg)

(3.70)   ni·či-mehtose·neni̲na·naki 'our (exc.) fellow people'
         (← |ne-i·či mehtose·neniw-ena·n-aki|
         ← |-i·či| PN 'fellow', mehtose·neniwaki 'people' + |ne–ena·n-| 1p)

(3.71)   neto·škote̲·mi 'my fire' (O 96E)
         (← |net-aškote·w-em-i| ← aškote·wi 'fire' + |ne–em-| 1s)

(3.72)   nenese·ma̲·na·na 'our (exc.) tobacco'
         (← |ne-nese·ma·w-ena·n-a| ← nese·ma·wa 'tobacco' + |ne–ena·n-| 1p)

(3.73)   ki·či-maneto̲·na·naki 'our (inc.) fellow manitous'
         (← |ke-i·či maneto·w-ena·n-aki|
         ← |-i·či| PN 'fellow', maneto·waki 'manitous' + |ke–ena·n-| 12)

Stems in |-Vy| (i.e., |-ay| or |-iy|) similarly contract |Vy-e| to |V·| (**§11.8**):

(3.74)   kepene·siwa̲·mena·na 'our (inc.) (sacred) raptor skin' (O 125D)
         (← |ke-pene·siway-em-ena·n-a| ← pene·siwaya 'raptor skin' + |ke–em-ena·n-| 12)

28.10. Contraction before |-inaw| X. Stems in |-Vw| and |-Vy| contract with |-inaw| X (3.19) as if it began with |e|, and the full suffix |-inaw| also appears uncontracted after the |Vn| that results from the contraction. In other words, it is as if the suffix |-inaw| X took the shape |-eninaw| after stems in |-Vw| and |-Vy|:

(3.75)   *owiya̱ninawi* 'oneself, one's life' (A 44BF)
           (← |ow-i·yaw-inaw-i| ← |-i·yaw-| IN 'body', |o–inaw-| X, |-i| INsg)

(3.76)   *onamaška̱ninawa* 'one's skin' (FE-Lang 81)
           (← |o-namaškay-inaw-a| ← |-namaškay-| AN 'skin', |o–inaw-| X, |-a| ANsg)

(3.77)   *ohtawaka̱ninawani* 'one's ears' (FE-Lang 83)
           (← |o-htawakay-inaw-ani| ← |-htawakay-| IN 'ear', |o–inaw-| X, |-ani| INpl)

28.11. Special treatment before |-wa·w| 2p,3p. Before the suffix |-wa·w| 2p,3p (3.19) stems take the same surface shape that they have when contracted before |-ena·n| 1p,12:

(3.78)   *okiwa̱wani* 'their mother (obv.)' (K-TYFB 2; C-O 37; S-Shak 1) (cf. 3.66)
           (← |o-ky-wa·w-ani| ← |-ky-| AN 'mother', |o–wa·w-| 2p,3p, |-ani| OBVsg)

(3.79)   *oški·šeko̱wa̱wani* 'their eyes' (O 116D) (cf. 3.68)
           (← |o-ški·šekw-wa·w-ani| ← |-ški·šekw-| IN 'eye', |o–wa·w-| 3p, |-ani| INpl)

(3.80)   *owiya̱wa̱wi* 'themselves, their lives' (O 114E) (cf. 3.69)
           (← |ow-i·yaw-wa·w-i| ← |-i·yaw-| IN 'body', |o–wa·w-| 3p, |-i| INsg)

(3.81)   *ki·či-mehtose·neni̱wa̱wa* 'your (pl.) fellow man' (O 73G) (cf. 3.70)
           (← |ke-i·či mehtose·neniw-wa·w-a|
           ← |-i·či| PN 'fellow', *mehtose·neniwa* 'person' + |ke–wa·w-| 2p)

(3.82)   *onese·ma̱wa̱wani* 'their tobacco (obv.)' (O 111E) (cf. 3.72)
           (← |o-nese·ma·w-wa·w-ani| ← *nese·ma·wa* 'tobacco' + |o–wa·w-| 3p, |-ani| OBVsg)

(3.83)   *ki·či-maneto̱wa̱waki* 'your (pl.) fellow manitous' (K-B 301) (cf. 3.73)
           (← |ke-i·či maneto·w-wa·w-aki|
           ← |-i·či| PN 'fellow', *maneto·waki* 'manitous' + |ke–wa·w-| 2p)

In forms like (3.82-83), in which the vowel preceding the semivowel is long to begin with, the normal simplification of |w-w| to |w| (**§9.2**) would have produced the same result, but forms like (3.78-79), in which a semivowel is replaced by a vowel, or (3.80-81), in which an underlying short vowel becomes a long vowel, are not accounted for by otherwise occurring phonological processes.

The dependent noun |-i·k-| IN 'house' has this same property without contraction; |-wa·w| 2p,3p takes the unique shape |-ewa·w|, matching the vowel of |-ena·n| 1p,12:

(3.84)   *owi·ke̱wa̱wi* 'their lodge' (O 106B) (cf. *ni·ke̱na̱ni* 'our (exc.) lodge')
           (← |ow-i·k-ewa·w-i| ← |-i·k-| IN 'house', |o–wa·w-| 3p, |-i| INsg)

28.12. Non-contracting stems. There are two nouns with stems in |-Vw| that never have contraction in the texts, *ni·wa* 'my wife' and *no·ke·nawa, meno·ke·nawa* 'soul' (1.161-162).

(3.85)   *ni·we̱na̱naki* 'our (exc.) wives' (K-ILM 30) (cf. 3.104)
           (← |ne-i·w-ena·n-aki| ← |-i·w-| AN 'wife', |ne–ena·n-| 1p, |-aki| ANpl)

(3.86)   *keno·ke·na̱wena̱naki* 'our (inc.) souls' (K-FC 135) (← |ke-no·ke·naw-ena·n-aki|
           ← |(-)no·ke·naw-| AN 'soul', |ke–ena·n-| 12, |-aki| ANpl)

28.13. Possessed diminutives. If a stem that takes |-em| poss. th. is both possessed and diminutive, the diminutive suffix |-e·h| follows the suffix |-em|. In other words, the possessed form of a diminutive noun is formed by making the diminutive of the possessed noun. As a consequence, the pieces of the diminutive stem (single underline in the underlying forms in 3.87) and the pieces of the possessive inflection (double underline) are interdigitated.

(3.87)   *keše·šketo·heme·hena·na* 'our (inc.) little kettle' (← |ke-še·šketo·h-em-e·h-ena·n-a|
      ← *še·šketo·he·ha* 'little kettle' [← |še·šketo·h-| 'kettle', |-e·h| DIM] + |ke–em-ena·n-| 12)
      Cf. *neše·šketo·hema* 'my kettle' ← |ne-še·šketo·h-em-a| (|ne–em-| 1s).

28.14. Irregular possessed forms. For a very few nouns the shape of the stem before |-em|
poss. th. is different from that in unpossessed forms (see also §28.7). The regular possessed form
of *ihkwe·wa* 'woman' has a specialized meaning (*netehkwe·ma* 'my sister (man speaking)'), and
the possessed form with the general meaning is uniquely irregular:

(3.88)   *ketehkwe·yo·ma, keto·hkwe·yo·ma* 'your woman, a woman of your group'
      (← |ke-t-| + |ihkwe·w-| + |-em-a| ← *ihkwe·wa* 'woman' + |ke–em-| 2s)

mese·hi 'a piece of firewood' (pl. *mese·hani* 'firewood') always occurs with -*e·h* when
unpossessed, but the possessed forms either lack the -*e·h* (using the stem |mes-|) or treat it
formally as the diminutive suffix |-e·h| and hence separable (§28.13, 3.87):

(3.89)   *omesemani* 'his firewood' (K-OBES 103, K-WSB 49)
      omeseme·hani 'his firewood' (K-WT 7, K-OBES 156)
      (← |o-mes-em-(e·h-)ani| ← *mese·hani* 'firewood' + |o–em-| 3s)

oškinawe·ha 'young man' and *ke·hkya·ha* 'old person' make possessed forms from shortened
stems (cf. 3.129):

(3.90)   *neto·škinawe·maki* 'my young men' (C-FRS 3)
      (← |ne-t-o·škinawe·-em-aki| ← *oškinawe·haki* 'young men' + |ne–em-| 1s)
      oke·hkya·mahi 'his old folks (obv.)' (K-Wap 203)
      (← |o-ke·hkya·-em-ahi| ← *ke·hkya·haki* 'old people' + |o–em-| 3s, |-ahi| OBVpl)

neniwa 'man' always makes possessed forms from the longer, less common stem variant |ineniw-|:

(3.91)   *netẹneni·maki* 'my men'
      (← |ne-t-eneniw-em-aki| ← *neniwaki, ineniwaki* 'men' + |ne–em-| 1s)

metemo·h-a 'old woman' makes a possessed form with a specialized meaning using a stem
|metemos-| and the separable diminutive suffix:

(3.92)   *ometemoseme·hani* 'his old lady, his wife (obv.)' (K-SGG 208; C-RS 13; SP-P 36)
      (← |o-metemos-em-e·h-ani| ← *metemo·h-a* 'old woman' + |o–em-| 3s)
      (Cf. *metemo* 'O wife!')

Locative

28.15. The locative (§24) suffix |-eki| appears without other suffixes as the ending |+eki| LOC.
This suffix displaces the core inflectional suffixes (§28); hence locative forms do not distinguish
gender (3.93-94), number (3.95-96), or obviation (3.99).

(3.93)   *še·šketo·heki* 'in the kettle' (A 91I) (← |še·šketo·h-eki|; *še·šketo·ha* 'kettle')
(3.94)   *ošehkeki* 'on his belly' (A 115F) (← |o-šehk-eki|; *ošehki* 'his belly')
(3.95)   *maškimote·heki* 'to the bag' (O 48B) (← |maškimote·h-eki|; *maškimote·hi* 'bag')
      maškimote·heki 'in bags' (A 93A) (← |maškimote·h-eki|; *maškimote·hani* 'bags')
      (Here a reduplicated verb makes it clear that there is more than one bag.)
(3.96)   *nepwa·meki* 'on my thighs' (A 56G) (← |ne-pwa·m-eki|; *nepwa·mani* 'my thighs')

wi·kiya·pi 'house' has the stem |wi·kiya·p-|, without |y| (cf. 3.17):

(3.97)   *wi·kiya·peki* 'in, to the house' (A 35C) (← |wi·kiya·p-| IN 'house', |+eki|)

Most stems in |-Cy| before |-eki| LOC contract |y-e| to long |i·| (§11.4):

(3.98)   pe·škiti_ki 'in a basket' (A 93E) (← |pe·škity-eki|; pe·škiti 'basket',
               stem |pe·škity-|; 3.5)

Only the stem |-ky-| (nekya 'my mother') has contraction to short |i| in the locative (compare 3.66):

(3.99)   okiki 'at his mother's; like his mother' (← |o-ky-eki|; okye ni 'his mother',
               stem |-ky-|)

Stems in |-Cw| always contract |Cw-e| to |o|:

(3.100)   pepikwe škoki 'on the whistle' (O 42D) (← |pepikwe·škw-eki|;
               pepikwe škwi 'whistle')

Stems in |-Vw| contract |Vw-e| to |V·|, with the quality of the vowel kept (§11.6), except for a handful of non-contracting stems (3.104; cf. §11.6, 1.161-162; §28.12).

(3.101)   neni_ki 'like a man' (K-FM 1) (← |neniw-eki|; neniwa 'man')

(3.102)   aškote_ki 'in the fire' (A 176B) (← |aškote·w-eki|; aškote wi 'fire')

(3.103)   si po_ki 'to the river' (A 55G) (← |si·po·w-eki|; si po wi 'river')

(3.104)   owi weki 'at, to his wife's' (K-MLF 13) (← |ow-i·w-eki|; owi wani 'his wife')
               osoweki 'on the tail' (S-Apay 26) (cf. osowani 'tails' [archaic])

The possessive pluralizer |-wa·w| 2p,3p and the indefinite-possessor marker |-inaw| contract like noun stems (1.160):

(3.105)   ohka twa_ki 'their feet (loc.)' (A 99F)
               (← |o-hka·t-wa·w-eki| ← ohka twa wani 'their feet' + |-eki| LOC)

(3.106)   onehkina_ki 'on one's hands' (K-WD 165)
               (← |o-nehk-inaw-eki| ← onehkinawi 'one's hand' [O 48E] + |-eki| LOC)

The possessive pluralizer |-ena·n| 1p,12 (in 3.106) has the same ostensible contraction as |-wa·w| 2p,3p (in 3.105; see also 3.250, 3.277):

(3.107)   ni kena_ki 'in our (exc.) lodge'; ki kena_ki 'in our (inc.) lodge'
               (← |ne-i·k-ena·n-eki| ← ni kena ni 'our (exc.) lodge' + |-eki| LOC);
               (← |ke-i·k-ena·n-eki| ← ki kena ni 'our (inc.) lodge' + |-eki| LOC)

(Historically this was the regular contraction of the inclusive possessive pluralizer *-enaw.)

Stems in |-Vy| regularly contract |Vy-e| to |V·| (§11.8):

(3.108)   ohtawaka_ki 'in his ears' (K-Owl 6)
               (← |ohtawakay-eki| ← ohtawakayani 'his ears' + |-eki| LOC)

(3.109)   owi nwi_ki 'on his navel' (A 115E)
               (← |ow-i·nwiy-eki| ← owi nwi 'his navel' [3.6] + |-eki| LOC)

Monosyllabic stems in |-ay| are treated differently; the only example in the texts is an uncontracted form from nepaya 'my femur, front of thigh':

(3.110)   opayeki 'on his lap' (S-RL2 18)

This form was rejected by FM (in 2001), who gave a locative made like that of a stem in |-Cy| (cf. 3.15, 3.98): nepayi ki 'on my thigh or thighs'. There are no textual examples of a locative of netaya 'my pet', but the elicited locative was also made like this: netayi ki (AW in 1990).

Vocative

28.16. The regular vocative (§23) paradigm has the singular ending |+e| VOCsg and the plural ending |+etike| VOCpl:

(3.111)   *ni·hka·ne* '(O) my friend!'
          ni·hka·netike '(O) my friends!'
Inanimate nouns have vocative suffixes identical with those of animate nouns (2.148, 3.127).

28.17. Vocative singular. There is no contraction when |-e| VOCsg is added to a stem ending in a semivowel:

(3.112)   *mahkwe* '(O) bear!' (cf. *mahkwa* 'bear')
          netawe·ma·we '(O) my brother (w.s.)' (cf. *otawe·ma·wani* 'her brother')
          nesemye '(O) my daughter-in-law' (cf. *nesemya* 'my daughter-in-law')

Nouns with stems in |-h| regularly drop the |h| and shorten the vowel that precedes it instead of adding |+e| VOCsg. These are analyzed as having an ending |-∅| VOCsg and a phonological treatment that deletes the word-final |h| (as word-final consonants are not permitted) and shortens the resulting word-final long vowel (**§12.1**).

(3.113)   *mami·ši* '(O) ceremonial attendant!'
          (← |mami·ši·h-∅|; *mami·ši·ha* 'ceremonial attendant')
          mešwe '(O) rabbit!' (cf. *mešwe·ha* 'rabbit')
          wa·waneška '(O) naughty one!' (cf. *wa·waneška·ha* 'misbehaver')
          nemešo '(O) grandfather!' (cf. *nemešo·ha* 'my grandfather')

One kinship term adds |+e| VOCsg after |h|:

(3.114)   *neki·he* '(O) mother's sister, (O) stepmother!'
          (cf. *neki·ha* 'my mother's sister, my stepmother')

Irregularities found in the vocative singular of kinship terms include: the addition of *a-* before |ne+| 1 (3.115-117); hypocoristic shortening of the stem (3.116-121; **§40.4**); the addition (to the truncated form) of |-·h| followed by the short counterpart of the vowel that precedes the |h| (3.117-118, 120-121); and non-final vowel shortening (3.121). Beside the vocatives that have truncation but do not add *a-* there are also regular vocatives, though these are much less common (3.118-121).

(3.115)   *ano·se* '(O) father!' (cf. *no·sa* 'my father')
(3.116)   *ano·hko* '(O) grandmother!' (cf. *no·hkomesa* 'my grandmother')
(3.117)   *ane·he* '(O) mother!' (cf. *nekya* 'my mother')
(3.118)   *nene·he, nenekwa* '(O) nephew!' (cf. *nenekwa·ha* 'my cross-nephew')
(3.119)   *nesekwi, nesekwise* '(O) father's sister!' (cf. *nesekwisa* 'my father's sister')
(3.120)   *nesi·hi, nesi·me* '(O) younger sibling!'
          (cf. *nesi·ma, nesi·me·ha* 'my younger brother or sister')
          nekwi·hi, nekwise '(O) son!' (cf. *nekwisa* 'my son')
          neta·ha, neta·nese '(O) daughter!' (cf. *neta·nesa* 'my daughter')
(3.121)   *noši·hi, no·šiseme* '(O) grandchild!' (cf. *no·šisema* 'my grandchild')

Beside the irregular vocatives ending in *-hi* and *-ha* (3.120-121) there are younger, partially regularized forms ending in *-he*:

(3.122)   *nesi·he* '(O) younger sibling!'
          neta·he '(O) daughter!'
          noši·he '(O) grandchild!'

The vocative *noši·hi* '(O) grandchild!' also has an explicit diminutive *noši·he·he*. The largely ceremonial term *nenekwanesa* 'my nephew' (especially used for the Culture Hero) has the vocatives *nenekwanese* and *nenekwaneseme*.

Three stems in |-V·w| make the vocative singular as if they ended in |-V·h| (cf. 4.172, 4.179c):

(3.123) *naha·kanihkwe* '(O) daughter-in-law!'

(cf. *naha·kanihkwe·wa* 'co-resident daughter-in-law')

(3.124) *ošineke* '(O) son-in-law!' (cf. *ošineke·wa* 'son-in-law')

(3.125) *ni·hta* '(O) brother-in-law!' (JB-WMD 21) (cf. *ni·hta·wa* 'my brother-in-law')

28.18. Vocative plural. Stems in |-Vw| contract regularly with |+etike| vocpl:

(3.126) *neni_tike, ineni_tike* '(O) men!' (cf. *neniwa* 'man')

ihkwe_tike '(O) women!' (cf. *ihkwe·wa* 'woman')

ni·hta_tike '(O) my brothers-in-law!' (cf. *ni·hta·wa* 'my brother-in-law')

ni·či-maneto_tike '(O) my fellow manitous!' (cf. *maneto·wa* 'manitou')

Only one vocative plural is attested from a stem in |-Cw|:

(3.127) *neški·šekotike* '(O) my eyes!' (Sh-Buz 27) (cf. *neški·šekwi* 'my eye')

The only vocative plural attested for a stem in |-ay| lacks contraction:

(3.128) *wa·pikayetike* '(O) wolverines!' (SP-WH 5)

Some stems have variation or other irregularities in the vocative plural:

(3.129) *oškinawe·tike* '(O) youths!' (cf. *oškinawe·ha* 'young man'; 3.89)

(3.130) *šato·hetike, nešato·hetike, nešato·hemetike* '(O) (my) friends!' (cf. *šato* '(O) friend!')

The noun in (3.130) is attested as a non-vocative only in *kešato·hwa·wa* 'your (pl.) friend' (C-Hist 36), an ironic nonce-form effectively meaning 'I, who you (pl.) call your friend'.

28.19. Vocative participles. Vocative participles have |-e| in the plural as well as the singular, differentiated by the pronominal inflection:

(3.131) *po·hkipo·hki·kwa·yane* '(O) one-eyed one!' (C-WH 6, SP-WH 3)

(|CVCV+| RED2, |po·hki·kwe·-| AI 'have one eye', |IC–yane| 2s/PPL(voc); §29.13)

po·hkipo·hki·kwa·ye·kwe '(O) one-eyed ones!' (C-WH 17, SP-WH 11)

(|CVCV+| RED2, |po·hki·kwe·-| AI 'have one eye', |IC–ye·kwe| 2p/PPL(voc))

(3.132) *'maneto·wa·'e·neneke* '(O) you called manitous!' (representative singular) (K-SF 52)

(*maneto·wa* 'manitou'; |iN-| TA 'say {so} to', |IC–eneke| X–2s/PPL(voc))

(3.133) *we·wi·hka·nemena·ne* '(O) my friends!' (representative singular) (K-W 482)

(|owi·hka·nem-| TA 'have as friend', |IC–ena·ne| 1s–2s/PPL(voc))

(3.134) *nekya·ne·htamawiyane* '(O) you (sg.) who killed my mother!' (song; K-W 267)

(*nekya* 'my mother';

|nehtamaw-| TA+O 'kill O2 for, of', |IC–iyane| 2s–1s/PPL(voc))

Participles that are lexicalized (including those with or without initial change that are used as male names) usually make a vocative singular as if they were nouns, replacing |-a| ANsg with |-e| VOCsg:

(3.135) *we·šinetake* '(O) son-in-law!' (cf. *we·šinetaka* 'son-in-law', participle of *ošinetamwa* 'he has in-laws, is married into a family')

pawišike '(O) Poweshiek!' (cf. *pawišika* 'Poweshiek', obv. *pawišiničini*)

Regular participial vocatives (with verb morphology) are archaic and optional (cf. 3.18):

(3.136) *ne·nye·škwiyane* '(O) Nenyeshkwiha!' (JP-Apay 73)

Also: *ne·nye·škwi·te* (JP-Apay 53), *ne·nye·škwi* (JP-Apay 67)

(Cf. *ne·nye·škwi·ta, ne·nye·škwi·ha* 'Nenyeshkwiha'.)

28.20. Vocative with |-ena·n| 1p,12. The possessor pluralizer |-ena·n| 1p,12 combines with |-e| VOCsg and |-etike| VOCpl as |+ena·te| 1p(VOC). The same form is used for singular and plural addressees, though its use for a singular addressee is much more common:

(3.137) *nemešo mesena te, aškote ne siwe* 'O our Grandfather, Spirit-of-Fire!'
       (K-ECRP 126)
      nemami ši hemena te '(O) our ceremonial attendant!' (K-FC 303)
      ni kena te '(O) our house!' (K-W 104)
      ni hka nena te '(O) our friends!' (K-GBuff 226)

These forms can be described as made from nouns inflected for first-person exclusive possessor. Only one example is attested that is based on an irregular vocative singular with first-person possessor:

    (3.138) *ane hena te* '(O) our mother!' (S-RL 84) (cf. 3.117)

VERB INFLECTION: PREFIXES AND SUFFIXES

29. Verbs are inflected with a small set of prefixes (**§29.1-4**) and a very large set of suffixes (**§18.1, 3; §26; §29.5-13**).

Verbal Prefixes

29.1. Verbs may have from zero to two prefixes. For convenience of reference the morpheme of vowel ablaut called initial change (IC), which patterns like a prefix, can be included as a prefix in general statements.

The sequence and patterns of co-occurrence of the prefixes are shown in (3.139).

(3.139) Prefix template (verbs)

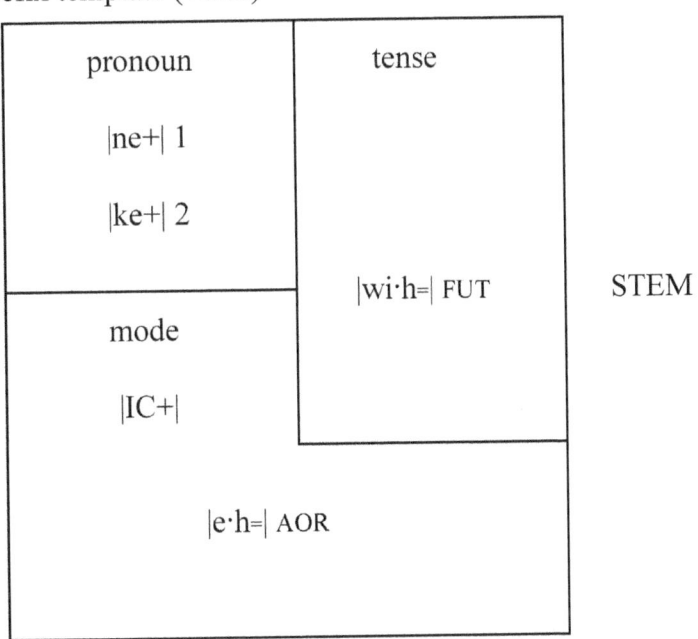

As seen from (3.139), the pronominal prefixes and initial change are mutually exclusive but may occur with the future morpheme, while the aorist marker does not occur with any other prefixal element (see, however, 2.329). Also, because of how these elements combine (3.140, 152), the prefix complex that occurs in actual words never has more than one syllable.

29.2. Pronominal prefixes. The pronominal prefixes on verbs are also found on nouns (§27.1, §28.5-8), but there is no third-person or indefinite prefix on verbs, and there are fewer formal irregularities than in the case of nouns. They are used only in the independent order. As with nouns, they combine with central suffixes to mark pronominal reference for a first or second person, differentiating first singular (|ne+| 1) from second singular (|ke+| 2), and first plural exclusive (|ne+| 1) from first plural inclusive (|ke+| 2). In the forms for a first person acting on a second person and for second person acting on first, the prefix does not operate in tandem with a pronominal suffix; the prefix is always |ke+| 2, and all information on the identity of the arguments is in the ending.

When a pronominal prefix occurs with |wi·h=| FUT fusion takes place:

(3.140) Pronominal prefixes combined with |wi·h=| FUT

|ne+| 1 + |wi·h=| FUT → *ni·h=* 1.FUT

|ke+| 2 + |wi·h=| FUT → *ki·h=* 2.FUT

As a result of the fusion of the prefixes with the future proclitic preverb (3.140), future paradigms in the independent indicative are as in (3.141):

(3.141) *ni·h=wi·seni* 'I will eat' (K-FC 216) (← |wi·h=| FUT, |wi·seni-| AI 'eat', |ne–∅| 1s/IND)

ki·h=wi·seni 'you (sg.) must eat' (K-TYFB 5)

(← |wi·h=| FUT, |wi·seni-| AI 'eat', |ke–∅| 2s/IND)

wi·h=wi·seniwa 'he will eat' (K-WarD 16)

(← |wi·h=| FUT, |wi·seni-| AI 'eat', |–wa| 3s/IND)

When a pronominal prefix occurs before a stem beginning with a vowel, a |t| is inserted:

(3.142) *netapi* 'I am, sit {somewhere}'

(← |ne-*t*-api| ← |api-| AI 'sit {somewhere}', |ne–∅| 1s/IND)

apiwa 'he is, sits {somewhere}'

(← |api-wa| ← |api-| AI 'sit {somewhere}', |–wa| 3s/IND)

Following this inserted |t|, a stem-initial |i| is replaced by |e| (§12.2):

(3.143) *netešite·he* 'I think {so}'

(← |ne-*t*-ešite·he·-| ← |išite·he·-| AI 'think {so}', |ne–∅| 1s/IND)

išite·he·wa 'he thinks {so}'

(← |išite·he·-wa| ← |išite·he·-| AI 'think {so}', |–wa| 3s/IND)

The other types of stem-initial vowel replacement after prefixes in nouns (§28.7) are not found in verbs.

A few stems have idiosyncratic treatments. After either of the prefixal morphemes in (3.139), |iha·-| AI 'go {somewhere}' has the shortened stem |a·-| (3.144, 150, 159, 161). The pronominal prefixes are added to this short stem in the usual way:

(3.144) *i·tepi=meko neta·* 'I go right there' (O 75F)

(*i·tepi* 'there'; |ne-*t*-a·-| ← |iha·-| AI 'go {somewhere}', |ne–∅| 1s/IND)

The verb |i-| AI 'say {so}' combines irregularly with the pronominal prefixes; the |i| is retained and |s| is inserted before it:

(3.145) *iwa* 'he says {so}' (← |i-wa| ← |i-| AI 'say {so}', |–wa| 3s/IND)

nesi 'I say {so}' (← |ne-*s*-i-| ← |i-| AI 'say {so}', |ne–∅| 1s/IND)

On a compound verb a prefix or prefix complex attaches only to the first or only preverb, even when it is separate from the head verb:

(3.146) *neta·hpeči-ki·wi-nešawi* 'I go around all the time by myself' (A 187D)

(|a·hpeči| PV 'permanently', |ki·wi| PV 'around', |nešawi-| AI 'be alone', |ne–∅| 1s/IND)

(3.147) *neki ši-= 'yo=ke·h -anehka·ti·pena* (A 143F)

   'of course, we had already become acquainted'

    (|ki·ši| PV PERF; |=iyo| 'for'; |=ke·hi| 'moreover';

     |anehka·ti·-| AI 'be acquainted with each other', |ne–pena| 1p/IND)

Compound verbs do not have the optional and multiple attachment of prefixes found with compound nouns (**§28.8**).

29.3. Tense and mode prefixes. After |wi·h=| FUT and |e·h=| AOR vowel-initial stems retain the shape they have word-initially, rather than taking any different shape they may have after the pronominal prefixes; to capture this distinction conveniently, tense and mode prefixes are designated as proclitic preverbs, and hence set off by a double hyphen (=), though they have the word-internal syntax of inflectional prefixes:

(3.148) *ni·h=išite·he* 'I will think {so}'

   e·h=išite·he·či 'he thought {so}'

(3.149) *ki·h=i* 'you must say {so}'

   e·h=iči 'he said {so}'

After the tense and mode prefixes, |iha·-| AI, |ihe·mikat-| II 'go {somewhere}' (cf. 3.161) and the derived applicative |ihe·notaw-| TA 'go {somewhere} to' (← |iha·-| AI + |-notaw| TA [**§54.6**]) have the same shortening that |iha·-| has after the pronominal prefixes (3.144):

(3.150) *i·tepi e·h=a·či.* 'She went there.' (O 70G)

   (*i·tepi* 'there'; |iha·-| AI 'go {somewhere}', |e·h=–či| 3s/AOR)

  e·h=awiči ni·h=a 'I will go to where he lives' (O 70E)

   (|awi-| AI 'be, live {somewhere}', |e·h=–či| 3s/PPL(obl);

   |wi·h=| FUT, |iha·-| AI 'go {somewhere}', |ne–∅| 1s/IND)

(3.151) *i·tep e·h=e·notawa·či* 'she went there to him' (K-ILM 23C)

   (*i·tepi* 'there'; |ihe·notaw-| TA 'go {somewhere} to', |e·h=–a·či| 3s–3´/AOR)

  i·tepi=meko ki·h=e·notawa·waki. "You must go straight to them." (K-WYB 21; tr. TB)

   (*i·tepi* 'there'; =*meko* EMPH;

   |wi·h=| FUT, |ihe·notaw-| TA 'go {somewhere} to', |ke–a·waki| 2s–3p/IND)

By convention the tense and mode prefixes are written out in full before *s* and *š*, even though *h=s* and *h=š* are pronounced the same as postvocalic *s* and *š*, respectively ([hs] and [hš]), with non-distinctive preaspiration (**§2**; see the examples after 3.36).

29.4. Initial change. Initial change is a morpheme of abstract function realized as a phonological change that affects the first vowel of a stem or compound stem. It is a process of ablaut, a morpheme consisting solely of the replacement of a vowel. In inflection, initial change marks some modes of the core conjunct and interrogative sub-orders, specifically the changed conjunct, iterative, and conjunct participle, and the changed interrogative, interrogative participle, and changed prioritive. It is also used in derivation (3.185; 4.221; **§46.2-3**).

Most stems use the regular set of vowel replacements, which affect short vowels only:

(3.152) Regular initial change

   |i| → *e·*

   |e| → *e·*

   |a| → *e·*

   |o| → *we·*

   long vowel → same long vowel

The changed form of all short vowels is |e·| or contains |e·|:

(3.153)   *e̲šiso mikahki* 'what its name is' (O 1A)
          (|išiso·mikat-| II 'have {such} a name', |IC–ki| 0/PPL(obl))
          Cf. *i̲šiso mikatwi* 'its name is {so}' (O 1B).
          (|išiso·mikat-| II 'have {such} a name', |–wi| 0s/IND)

(3.154)   *pe̲po nikini* 'in winter, in wintertime, in the winters (obv.)' (O 10A; A 23A)
          (|pepo·-| II 'be winter', |IC–nikini| 0′/ITER)
          Cf. *pe̲po kehe* 'if it had been winter' (A 38H).
          (|pepo·-| II 'be winter', |–kehe| 0/SUBJ.PRET)

(3.155)   *me̲hkwa tesičiki* 'ones that are quiet' (A 131C)
          (|mahkwa·tesi-| AI 'be quiet, reserved', |IC–čiki| 3/PPL(ANpl))
          Cf. *e·h=ma̲hkwa tesiwa·či* 'they were quiet-natured' (O 69A).
          (|mahkwa·tesi-| AI 'be quiet, reserved', |e·h=–wa·či| 3p/AOR)

(3.156)   *nwe̲wi wa·čini* 'whenever they went out' (O 8B)
          (|nowi·-| AI 'go out', |IC–wa·čini| 3p/ITER)
          Cf. *no̲wi no* 'come out (you sg.)' (A 112H, 113B).
          (|nowi·-| AI 'go out', |–no| 2s/IMP)

Although long vowels remain unaltered, the initial change is nevertheless described as present in the abstract morphology of the form rather than as completely absent.

(3.157)   *wa̲paniki* 'the next day', *lit.* 'when it was morning (obv.)' (O 162H)
          (← |IC+wa·pan-niki| ← |wa·pan-| II 'be morning', |IC–niki| 0′/CC)
          Cf. *wa̲pake* 'tomorrow', *lit.* 'when it is morning' (A 42E)
          (|wa·pan-| II 'be morning', |–ke| 0/SUBJ).

Such forms may be referred to as having invisible initial change.

A few verbs have overt initial change on long vowels. Two common, semantically similar verbs have |e·ya·| as the change of |a·|, and in related forms |e·ye·| as the change of |e·|. The verb |pya·-| AI 'come ({somewhere})' makes |pye·ya·-|:

(3.158)   *i̲ya·h pye̲ya ya·ni* 'when I arrived over there' (A 91A)
          (|i·ya·hi| 'yonder'; |pya·-| AI 'come ({somewhere})', |IC–ya·ni| 1s/CC)
          Cf. *pya̲no* 'come (you, sing.)' (A 9B)
          (|pya·-| AI 'come ({somewhere})', |–no| 2s/IMP).

The verb |iha·-| AI 'go {somewhere}' has |e·ya·-|, made on the shortened stem |a·-| (3.144, 150):

(3.159)   *e̲ya ya·ni* 'where I'm going' (O 75G)
          (|iha·-| AI 'go {somewhere}', |IC–ya·ni| 1s/PPL(obl))
          Cf. *wi·h=a̲ya·ni* 'for me to go {somewhere}' (A 96A; O 162C)
          (|wi·h=| FUT, |iha·-| AI 'go {somewhere}', |e·h=–ya·ni| 1s/AOR).

The corresponding II verbs have the same irregularity with |e·|, the umlaut of the stem-final |a·| in derivation (**§52.1**):

(3.160)   *kehčine pye̲ye mikateniki* 'when it (inan. obv.) got near' (K-SBSB 11)
          (*kehčine* 'near'; |pye·mikat-| II 'come ({somewhere})', |IC–niki| 0′/CC)
          Cf. *pye̲mikatwi* 'it (inan.) came {somewhere}' (K-ECRP 47)
          (|pye·mikat-| II 'come ({somewhere})', |–wi| 0s/IND).

(3.161)   *i̲ni mani e̲ye mikateki* 'that is how far this extends' (K-Bene 149)
          (*i̲ni* 'that (inan.)'; *mani* 'this (inan.)';
          |ihe·mikat-| II 'go {somewhere}', |IC–ki| 0/PPL(obl))
          Cf. *e·h=e̲mikateki* 'it (inan.) went {somewhere}' (K-BBD 39)
          (|ihe·mikat-| II 'go {somewhere}', |e·h=–ki| 0/AOR).

The applicative |ihe·notaw-| TA 'go {somewhere} to' (3.151) retains this peculiarity:

(3.162) *i ŧepi e ye notawačini* 'whenever you (sg.) go over there to them' (K-BBWM 44)

(*i ŧepi* 'there'; |ihe·notaw-| TA 'go {somewhere} to', |IC–ačini| 2s–3/ITER)

Cf. *i ŧepi e·h=e notawa·či* 'he went there to him' (K-FC 268)

(*i ŧepi* 'there'; |ihe·notaw-| TA 'go {somewhere} to', |e·h=–a·či| 3s–3´/AOR).

The applicative from |pya·-| AI 'come' (|pye·notaw-| TA, |pye·not-| TI(1) 'come to') is regular, showing no modification with initial change:

(3.163) *i nihi= 'pi pye nota ko̱čihi* 'those (obv.) who came to him' (K-FC 467)

(*i nihi* 'those (anim. obv.)'; |=ipi| HRSY;

|pye·notaw-| TA 'come to', |IC–ekočihi| 3´–3s/PPL(OBVpl))

Verbs of possession formed from the three dependent nouns beginning with |o·-| have |we·yo·-| as the change of this:

(3.164) *ki šeso ni we yo·sita neniwa* 'the man whose father was the sun' (K-MFS 1)

(*ki šeso ni* 'sun (obv.)'; |o·si-| AI+O 'have O2 as father', |IC–ta| 3s/PPL(ANsg);
neniwa 'man')

(3.165) *we yo·šisememena·ne* '(O) my grandchildren!' (K-W 482)

(*lit.*, 'O you (representative singular) whom I have as grandchild')

(|o·šisemem-| TA 'have as grandchild', |IC–ena·ne| 1s–2s/PPL(voc))

(3.166) *we yo·hkomesita* 'the one whose grandmother she was' (K-MMD 22)

(|o·hkomesi-| AI+O 'have O2 as grandmother', |IC–ta| 3s/PPL(ANsg))

Stems beginning with |t-| that contain an overt or virtual relative root, with or without an oblique valence (**§22.4**), make initial change as if they began with |it-|:

(3.167) Initial change with |taN-| '{somewhere}; be engaged in' (*taši* PV)

(a) *i ya·hi e ŧana·hkonika·čiki* '(those) making the rules down there' (K-FC 592)

(*i ya·hi* 'over there';
|tana·hkonike·-| AI 'make rules {somewhere}', |IC–čiki| 3/PPL(ANpl))

(b) *i nahi e ŧaši-nakamočiki* '(those) who sang there' (O 11I)

(*i nahi* 'there';
|taši| PV '{somewhere}', |nakamo-| AI 'sing', |IC–čiki| 3/PPL(ANpl))

(c) *e ŧaši-nana·hi·hkawičiki* '(those) who were attending to me' (A 110I)

(|taši| PV 'be engaged in',
|nana·hi·hkaw-| TA 'attend to', |IC–ičiki| 3–1s/PPL(ANpl))

(3.168) Initial change with |taS-| '{so much, so many}'), |tasw-| '{so many}' (*taswi* PV)

(a) *e ŧašinikwe ni* 'as many as there may have been of them (obv.)' (O 39B)

(|taši-| AI 'be {so many}', |IC–nikwe·ni| 3´,0´/INT.PPL(obl))

(b) *e ŧaswa·kwapiwe·kwe ni* 'as many of you as may sit together' (O 90A)

(|taswa·kwapi-| AI 'sit together as {so many}', |IC–we·kwe·ni| 2p/INT.PPL(obl))

(c) *e ŧaswi-ne·wakini* 'every time I saw him' (A 82E)

(|taswi| PV '{so many}', |ne·w-| TA 'see', |IC–akini| 1s–3/ITER; cf. 2.214)

(3.169) Initial change with |tako-| AI,II 'exist ({somewhere}); be found {somewhere}'

nepi·ki e ŧakočiki na·mepye·ki 'those that inhabited the waters' (K-Wap 148)

(*nepi·ki* 'in the water';
|tako-| AI 'exist {somewhere}', |IC–čiki| 3/PPL(ANpl); *na·mepye·ki* 'under water')

Cf. *wi·h=takowaki* 'they will exist' (K-SGG 110).

(3.170) Initial change with |to·taw-| TA, |to·t-| TI(1) 'treat him, it {so}'

      e to to na ni 'the way I treat you' (A 17C, 27E)

          (|to·taw-| TA 'treat {so}', |IC–ena·ni| 1s–2s/PPL(obl))

      Cf. *ka ta ke ko hi to tawiye ke ko* 'don't do anything to him' (O 156D).

These stems have a scattering of other forms made as if on stems beginning with |it-|. All make reduplicated forms from such longer stems (4.138-140; cf. 4.141-142). |to·taw-| TA 'treat {so}' has an alternate shape |ito·taw-| TA attested a number of times:

(3.171)   *ke ko hi ito tawiyane* 'if you do anything to me' (X10-MET 38)

      (*ke ko hi* 'something'; |ito·taw-| TA 'treat {so}', |–iyane| 2s–1s/SUBJ)

(3.172)   *a kwi we činowi wi h=ito to na nini* 'I won't give you an easy time of it' (K-BHD2 75)

      (*a kwi* 'not'; *we činowi* 'easily';

      |wi·h=| FUT, |ito·taw-| TA 'treat {so}', |–ena·nini| 1s–2s/NEG)

(3.173)   *meše=ča h=meko e to tawiwane ni ki h=ito tawi*

      'So, feel free to do whatever you want to me.' (X8-MFS 6)

      (*meše* 'freely'; |=ča·hi| 'so'; =*meko* EMPH;

      |ito·taw-| TA 'treat {so}', |IC–iwane·ni| 2s–1s/INT.PPL(obl);

      |wi·h=| FUT, |ito·taw-| TA 'treat {so}', |ke–i| 2s–1s/IND)

The stem |(i)t(o)-| AI,II 'be {so}, fare {so}', which lacks the |i-| after |e·h=| AOR (3.176*a*), and sometimes after |wi·h=| FUT (3.176*bc*; cf. 3.175*a*) or a word boundary (3.176*d*), takes initial change (3.174), the pronominal prefixes (3.175*b*), and reduplication (4.137*b*) only on the shape |it-|:

(3.174) Initial change on |it-| AI,II 'be {so}, fare {so}'

  (a)   *ta ni e teyani.* 'What has happened to you (sg.)?' (K-M 133i)

        (*ta ni* 'how?'; |it-| AI 'fare {so}', |IC–yani| 2s/PPL(obl))

  (b)   *i ni e teki* 'that's how it is, what it's like' (K-BD 25)

        (*i ni* 'that (inan.)'; |it-| II 'be {so}', |IC–ki| 0/PPL(obl))

(3.175) Other forms with |it-| AI 'be {so}, fare {so}'

  (a)   *wi h=iteyakwe* 'what was going to happen to us (inc.)' (K-CWB 79)

        (|wi·h=| FUT, |it-| AI 'fare {so}', |IC–yakwe| 12/PPL(obl))

  (b)   *kaši=ča h=ketete.* 'What's the matter with you (sg.)?' (JP-GTF 6)

        (*kaši* 'what?'; |=ča·hi| 'so'; |it-| 'fare {so}', |ke–∅| 2s/IND)

(3.176) Forms with |t-|, |to-| AI,II 'be {so}, fare {so}'

  (a)   *kaši=ča h=e h=teki.* 'How come?' (Jones 1907:138.18; K-BLM 26; JP-TF 5; 5.122*b*(6))

        (*kaši* 'what?'; |=ča·hi| 'so'; |t-| II 'be {so}', |e·h=–ki| 0/AOR)

  (b)   *ta ni=ča h=wi h=teyakwe* 'what will happen to us (inc.)' (JP-MAF 30)

        (*ta ni* 'how?'; |=ča·hi| 'so'; |wi·h=| FUT, |t-| AI 'fare {so}', |IC–yakwe| 12/PPL(obl))

  (c)   *kaši=meko wi h=towi.* 'What difference would it make? Why not?' (K-K 9)

        (*kaši* 'what?'; =*meko* EMPH; |wi·h=| FUT, |to-| II 'be so', |–wi| 0s/IND)

  (d)   *i ni towa sa* 'that would have happened to them' (K-WM 7)

        (*i ni* 'that (inan.)'; |t-o-wa·sa| ← |t-| AI 'fare {so}', |–wa·sa| 3p/POT)

Participles of some stems with one-syllable reduplication that have the reduplicating syllable as |Ca-| (4.120, 132) are found with the initial change realized as both |Ce·-| and |Ca·-|. With consonant-initial stems there is sometimes a semantic differentiation between the participle with |Ce·-|, used descriptively (3.177), and the one with |Ca·-|, used with or without a head noun as a name or to designate a type (3.178).

(3.177) Reduplication |Ca+| with initial change as |Ce·-|

　　　　ni·šwi e·h=pi·tikato·či me̲·ma·ka·hkwatenikini mese·hani. (K-FC 602G)

　　　　'He brought in two large logs.'

　　　　　　(*ni·šwi* 'two'; |pi·tikat-| TI(2) 'bring in', |e·h=-o·či| 3s–0/AOR;

　　　　　　|Ca_a·+| RED1, |maka·hkwat-| II 'be large stick, tree', |IC–nikini| 0´/PPL(INpl);

　　　　　　mese·hani 'logs')

(3.178) Reduplication |Ca+| with initial change as |Ca·-|

　　(a)　*meše·='nah=meko ma̲·ma·ka·hkwahkini e·h=ki·waki·wa·kwate·ki.* (K-B 311)

　　　　'Even large trees were down all over.'

　　　　　　(*meše·='nah(i)* 'as may be'; *=meko* EMPH;

　　　　　　|Ca_a·+| RED1, |maka·hkwat-| II 'be large stick, tree', |IC–kini| 0/PPL(INpl);

　　　　　　|CVCV+| RED2, |ki·wa·kwate·-| II 'lie around destroyed', |e·h=-ki| 0/AOR)

　　(b)　*po·čani ka̲·ka·nwisenikini* 'high boots (obv.)' (C-RS 5)

　　　　　　(*po·čani* 'boots'; |Ca_a·+| RED1, |kenwisen-| II 'be long', |IC–nikini| 0´/PPL(INpl))

　　(c)　*mehteko·ni ka̲·ka·nwa·nikini* 'poles (obv.)' (K-Fish 9, WYB 18)

　　　　　　(*mehteko·ni* 'sticks';

　　　　　　|Ca_a·+| RED1, |kenwa·-| II 'be long', |IC–nikini| 0´/PPL(INpl))

This distinction is not consistently observed, however:

(3.179) Reduplication |Ca+| with initial change as |Ca·-| and |Ce·-|

　　　　ka̲·ka·no·te·nikini, ke̲·ka·no·te·nikini 'longhouses (obv.)' (K-YF 16; K-YF 16, 17)

　　　　　　(|Ca_a·+| RED1, |keno·te·-| II 'be a long house', |IC–nikini| 0´/PPL(INpl))

Stems with one-syllable reduplication have |a·| as the initial change of |a| also in noun derivation (4.221*a*).

　　The participles of vowel-initial stems have the same variation, but they cannot be shown to make the same distinction. Such stems have either |aya·N-| as the reduplication of |iN-| '{so}' (including in derived initials that include this; 2.110-111; 4.132*b*) or |aya·taS-| as the reduplication of |taS-| '{so much, so many}' (treated as |itaS-|) (cf. 3.168; 4.138), but all such stems with |aya·-| have younger variants with |a·ya·-| (1.281-282; 4.133*cd*, 4.139). Hence participles with *a·ya·-* from these stems may have underlying |a·ya·-| (4.133, 4.139) rather than the special initial change seen in (3.178):

(3.180)　*atena·wi e̲·ya·nekino·hičiki* 'the smaller ones' (K-K 19)

　　　　　　(*atena·wi* 'less';

　　　　　　|Ca_a·+| RED1, |inekino·hi-| AI 'be {so} big (dim.)', |IC–čiki| 3/PPL(ANpl))

(3.181)　*na·htaswa·hkwe=meko a̲·ya·taswi-pepo·nwa·čiki* (K-WYB 65F; tr. TB)

　　　　"those who were several hundred years of age"

　　　　　　(*na·htaswa·hkwe* 'several hundred'; *=meko* EMPH; |a·ya·+| RED1,

　　　　　　|taswi(-)pepo·nwe·-| AI 'be {so many} years old', |IC–čiki| 3/PPL(ANpl))

　　The verb of being derived from *owiye·ha* 'someone' often has *e·-* as the initial change of |o-|, beside regular *we·-* (3.182-183); this is an archaism (cf. Kickapoo a(w)ieeha 'someone').

(3.182)　*meše=meko·='nahi e̲·wiye·hikwe·na* 'anyone whoever' (K-Kin 55);

　　　　　meše=meko we̲·wiye·hikwe·na 'anyone whoever' (K-Kin 61)

　　　　　　(*meše* 'freely'; *=meko* EMPH; |=i·nahi| 'with that' [→ *meše=meko·='nahi* 'any'];

　　　　　　|owiye·hi-| AI 'be someone, some animal', |IC–kwe·na| 3/INT.PPL(ANsg))

(3.183)　*e̲·wiye·hinikwe·hini* 'unidentified person or creature (obv.)' (JB-BP 1);

　　　　　we̲·wiye·hinikwe·hini 'unidentified person or creature (obv.)' (JB-BP 5)

　　　　　　(|owiye·hi-| AI 'be someone, some animal', |IC–nikwe·hini| 3´/INT.PPL(OBVsg))

The verb of being made from *tohka·na* 'member of the Tohkan division' may lack overt initial change. (The noun is the only one beginning with /to-/ and is a loanword from Siouan.)

(3.184) Initial change on |tohka·niwi-| AI 'be a Tohkan'

(a) *ki·na=na·hka tohka·niwiyane* 'and you Tohkans (representative singular)' (C-SD 8)
(*ki·na* 'you (sg.)'; *na·hka* 'also';
|tohka·niwi-| AI 'be a Tohkan', |IC–yane| 2s/PPL(voc))

(b) *taswi=mekoho twe·hka·niwiči* 'everyone who was a Tohkan' (K-M 388d)
(*taswi* '{so many}'; *=mekoho* EMPH;
|tohka·niwi-| AI 'be a Tohkan', |IC–či| 3s/PPL(obl))

Whether the contrast between (3.184a) and (3.184b) reflects a consistent distinction between the animate participle made on this stem and other forms with initial change is not known.

Initial change is used in primary derivation to form some particles from initials. Long vowels (|a·| and |e·|) are subject to initial change in this function: |a·| → |e·ya·|; |e·| → |e·ye·|. The change may apply twice: |a| → |e·| → |e·ye·| (3.185b).

(3.185) Particles derived by initial change

(a) *ne·ya·pi* 'as before' ← |na·p-| 'replacing' (cf. *na·pi* 'instead, rather, better')

(b) *te·ye·htakwi* 'collectively' ← |tahtakw-| ← |Cah+| RED1 + |takw-| 'with'
(cf. *tahtakwi* PV 'all together')

Verbal Suffixes

29.5. Verbs usually have at least one suffix and may have as many as five. An overt suffix is absent only in two inflections, which have a pronominal prefix and the zero variant of a suffix that appears overtly elsewhere: |ne–∅| 1s/IND, |ke–∅| 2s/IND. (In other modes of the independent order the corresponding forms have |-p| sg. instead of |-∅| sg. before the modal suffix.)

The verbal suffixes are shown in (3.186), assigned to positions according to the sequence in which they follow each other. Seven suffix positions are recognized for the inflectional suffixes (1-2, 4-8), and the diminutive suffix, a morpheme of stem derivation (§41), occurs amidst them in position 3. The suffixes in (3.186) do not account for two rare endings whose analysis is uncertain, each the unique representative of an otherwise unattested mode (§30.5).

There are pronominal suffixes in positions 1, 4, 6, and 8; thematic suffixes in position 2; and modal suffixes in positions 5 and 7. The pronominal suffixes in position 6 are the central suffixes, and those in position 8 are the peripheral suffixes. The suffix in position 1 correlates with those in position 8, and the ones in position 4 go with those in position 6. The suffixes in each position are mutually exclusive, but in a few cases a central pronominal suffix of position 6 (3.186, lower left) is followed by a combined pronominal and modal suffix of positions 6 and 7 (3.186, lower right).

Some suffixes may be analyzed as the fusion of two or more suffixes; it is often arbitrary whether to treat such ostensibly fused morphemes as derived from their parts before their concatenation in inflection or as resulting from processes of fusion that take place after all inflectional suffixes have been strung together in sequence in the word. The combined pronominal and modal suffixes given under positions 6 and 7 in (3.186) are pronominal suffixes specialized for use in certain modes but lacking a recurring, clearly segmentable modal suffix.

(3.186) Suffix template (verbs)

	(1)	(2)	(3)	(4)	(5)	(6)	(7)	(8)
STEM	pronoun (with 8) |-em| obv.	theme sign |-a·|, |-Ø| TA th. 1 |-ekw| TA th. 2 (|-ekwi| 2a) |-i| TA th. 3 |-eN| TA th. 4 |-am| TI(1) th. |-o·| TI(2) th.	DIM	pronoun (with 6) |-ni| obv. |-wa·| pl. |-wa·| 2p	mode |-w| irr. |-hk| proh. |-hk| fut. imp.	pronoun (central) (SEE LOWER LEFT)	mode, tense |-etoke| dub. |-ehapa|, |-ahapa| con. |-epani| ast. |-e·ni| int. |-ehe| pret.	pronoun (peripheral) |-a|, |-Ø| ANsg |-aki|, |-iki| ANpl |-i|, |-Ø| INsg |-ani|, |-ini| INpl |-ani|, |-ini| OBVsg |-ahi|, |-ihi| OBVpl |-e| VOC

|-i| conj.

|-e| subj.

|-ini|
neg.-iter.

---

(6) pronoun (central)

independent order

    |-Ø|, |-p| sg.; |-w| 3,0; |-pena| 1p,12; |-pwa| 2p;

    |-pi| X; |-w| sg.; |-ena·n| 1p,12; |-wa·w| 2p;

    |-na·| sg. ast.; |-na·wa·| 2p ast.

core conjunct, interrogative

    |-a·n| 1s; |-wak| 1s rel.; |-t|, |-k| 3; |-k| 0; |-ek| X;

    |-wet| X rel.; |-ak| 1s−3; |-at| 2s−3; |-et| X−3;

    |-aket| 1p−3; |-ako·w| 1s−2p

core conjunct, interrogative, prohibitive

    |-an| 2s; |-a·kw| 3,X−2p

core conjunct, interrogative, potential

    |-e·kw| 2p

conjunct order (all sub-orders)

    |-a·k| 1p; |-akw| 12;

    |-amet| 3−1p; |-namek| X−1p

---

pronoun and mode (combined)

prohibitive

    |-a| 1s; |-e·ko| 2p; |-i·ke| X;

    |-a·wa| 1s−2p

potential

    |-a·ha| 1s; |-apa| 2s; |-sa| 3,0;

    |-ene·ha| X; |-wene·ha| X rel.;

    |-a·wa·hi|, |-a·wa·ha| 1s−2p

imperative order

    |-no| 2s; |-ko| 2p; |-če| 3,0;

    |-ta·we|, |-ta·ne|, |-ta·ke| 12;

    |-i| 2s−3; |-ehko| 2p−3;

    |-na·ke| 2−1p

Other ostensible suffixes, that <u>are</u> analyzed as the combination of two suffixes, are not given in (3.186). The ways these suffixes combine are described in the discussion that follows and in **Appendix 2**.

The suffixes in the different position classes and their general patterns of occurrence are discussed in **§§29.6-12**. The inflections used for each mode are then described, and illustrated with paradigms or partial paradigms, in **§30**.

29.6. Position 1. The sole suffix in position 1 is |-em| obv. This usually precedes the direct theme sign (|-a·|, |-∅| TA th. 1) and marks the object as obviative when the subject is not third person:

(3.187) Obviative object marked by |-em| obv.

(a) *nesa·pi* 'he (prox.) was killed, they (prox.) were killed' (K-MLF 48; K-ECRP 45)
(|neS-| TA 'kill', |–a·pi| X–3/IND [← |-a·| TA th. 1, |-pi| X])
nesema·pi 'he (obv.) was killed, they (obv.) were killed' (cf. K-Wap 24; K-SSP 310)
(|neS-| TA 'kill', |–ema·pi| X–3´/IND [← |-em| obv., |-a·| TA th. 1, |-pi| X])

(b) *e·h=nese·či* 'he (prox.) was killed, they (prox.) were killed' (K-K 17, K-CDWP 10)
(|neS-| TA 'kill', |e·h=–eči| X–3/AOR [← |-∅| TA th. 1, |-et| X–3, |-i| conj.])
e·h=nesemeči okye·ni 'his mother (obv.) was killed' (K-Wap 27)
(|neS-| TA 'kill', |e·h=–emeči| X–3´/AOR [|+emeči| ← |-em-∅-et-i|
← |-em| obv., |-∅| TA th. 1, |-et| X–3, |-i| conj.]; *okye·ni* 'his mother (obv.)')

(c) *owiye·ha wi·čawiwake* 'if I am with someone' (K-FC 524)
(|wi·čawiw-| TA 'be with, marry', |–ake| 1s–3/SUBJ
[← |-∅| TA th. 1, |-ak| 1s–3, |-e| subj.]; *owiye·ha* 'someone')
wi·čawiwomake ihkwe·wani 'if I marry a woman (obv.)' (K-TO 15)
(|wi·čawiw-| TA 'be with, marry', |–emake| 1s–3´/SUBJ [← |-em-∅-ak-e|
← |-em| obv., |-∅| TA th. 1, |-ak| 1s–3, |-e| subj.]; *ihkwe·wani* 'woman (obv.)')

(d) *ne·saka* 'the one I killed' (K-Spot 38)
(|neS-| TA 'kill', |IC–aka| 1s–3/PPL(ANsg)
[|+aka| ← |-∅-ak-a| ← |-∅| TA th. 1, |-ak| 1s–3, |-a| anim. sg.])
ne·semakini 'the one (obv.) I killed' (K-WB 9; JB-Tiger 39)
(|neS-| TA 'kill', |IC–emakini| 1s–3´/PPL(OBVsg)
[|+emakini| ← |-em-∅-ak-ini| ← |-em| obv., |-∅| TA th. 1, |-ak| 1s–3, |-ini| obv. sg.])

In one archaic form |-em| obv. precedes the fourth theme sign (|-eN| TA th. 4) and indicates an obviative subject:

(3.188) *e·taswihemenakwe=meko keto·kima·mena·nani i·ni e·nekihkwimakwe,*
e·h=mama·tomakwe. (K-SSB 35)
'We (inc.) pray to them (deities, prox.) for as many of us as our chief (obv.) has.'
(*Lit.,* 'As many of us as our chief (obv.) has is the scope of our talk to
them (prox. [i.e., the deities]) when we pray to them (prox.).')
(|taswih-| TA 'have {so many}', |IC–emenakwe| 3´–12/PPL(obl); =*meko* EMPH;
keto·kima·mena·nani 'our (inc.) chief (obv.)'; *i·ni* 'that (inan.)';
|inekihkwim-| TA 'speak to with {such} scope', |IC–akwe| 12–3/PPL(obl);
|mama·tom-| TA 'pray to', |e·h=–akwe| 12–3/AOR)

In the independent order |-em| obv. is only used in indefinite-subject forms. In the interrogative sub-order it is only found in participles with indefinite subjects, except for one apparent nonce form. It is not used in the prohibitive or potential sub-orders or in the imperative order.

The |e| of |-em| obv. is not subject to contraction with stems in |-Vw|; it fuses with |-Cw| to |-Co| (**§11.1**, 1.121), and is replaced by |o| after the |w| of all stems ending in |-Vw| (**§11.7**, 1.171).

29.7. Position 2. In position 2 are the theme signs, which give information about the primary object of transitive verbs. The theme signs used with TA verbs contrast with each other, while those used with TI verbs are obligatorily selected according to the TI class. For the stems that are the same for both the TA and the TI, the TA and TI(1) theme signs are in some forms the only point of contrast, distinguishing the gender of the object. The inflectional forms of the TI(3) stems (2.10) are the only transitive verbs that have no theme sign; the endings used with TI(3) stems are identical to those used with AI stems.

a) |-a·| is the first TA theme sign (TA th. 1), called the direct theme sign. It indicates that the object is lower than the subject in the person hierarchy:

(3.189) Person hierarchy for subjects and objects (TA verbs): higher to lower

1,2 > X > 3 > 3´ > 3´´ > 0

In this hierarchy the first (1) and second (2) persons have the same rank, and the indefinite (X) and inanimate (0) appear only as subjects, since they cannot be objects of a TA. The animate third persons are differentiated as proximate (3), obviative (3´), and further obviative (3´´).

The theme sign |-a·| TA th. 1 has the automatic variant |-∅| before any vowel; this variant may be referred to for convenience as |-∅| TA th. 1, but it is not a distinct morpheme:

(3.190)   Retention and deletion of |-a·|, |-∅| TA th. 1

    (a)   *e·h=ina·či* 'he said {so} to him (obv.), them (obv.)' (O 25I, 66B)

                (|iN-| TA 'say {so} to', |e·h=–a·či| 3s–3´/AOR

                [|+a·či| ← |-a·-t-i| ← |-a·| TA th. 1, |-t| 3, |-i| conj.])

    (b)   *e·h=ineči* 'he was told {so}, they were told {so}' (O 41D, 58G)

                (|iN-| TA 'say {so} to', |e·h=–eči| X–3/AOR

                [|+eči| ← |-∅-et-i| ← |-a·| TA th. 1, |-et| X, |-i| conj.])

|-a·| TA th. 1 undergoes umlaut to *e·* before |-w| 3,0, whether contiguous (3.191*a*, 3.242*a*) or not (3.242*b*), but not before |-w| sg. (3.191*b*) or |-w| irr. (3.219).

(3.191) Treatment of |-a·| TA th. 1 before |-w| 3,0 and |-w| sg.

    (a)   *ne we̲ wa* 'he saw him (obv.), them (obv.)' (C-L 117; SP-Net 45)

                (|ne·w-| TA 'see', |–e·wa| 3s–3´/IND

                [|+e·wa| ← |-e̲·-w-a| ← |-a·| TA th. 1, |-w| 3,0, |-a| ANsg])

    (b)   *nene wa̲ wa* 'I saw him' (K-TO 4)

                (|ne·w-| TA 'see', |ne–a·wa| 1s–3s/IND

                [|+a·wa| ← |-a̲·-w-a| ← |-a·| TA th. 1, |-w| sg., |-a| ANsg])

|-a·| TA th. 1 combines with |-·hi| dim. to give |-e·hi| TA th. 1 dim.:

(3.192) |-a·| TA th. 1 + diminutive

    (a)   *či nawe me̲ hiyakwa* 'our poor relatives' (representative singular) (O 137I)

                (|či·nawe·m-| TA 'be related to', |IC–e·hiyakwa| 12–3/DIM/PPL(ANsg)

                [← |-e̲·hi-yakw-a| ← |-a·| TA th. 1, |-·hi| dim., |-yakw| 12, |-a| ANsg])

    (b)   *ke ško·hpenane̲ hiničihi* 'the few he (obv.) was able to kill' (X6-OS 28)

                (|kaško·hpenaN-| TA 'be able to kill', |IC–e·hiničihi| 3´–3´´/DIM/PPL(OBVpl)

                [← |-e̲·hi-ni-t-ihi| ← |-a·| TA th. 1, |-·hi| dim., |-ni| obv., |-t| 3, |-ihi| OBVpl])

The combined suffix |-e·hi| TA th. 1 dim. resembles the common diminutive suffix |-e·h| that is used after noun stems which end in a true consonant (**§41**, 4.166). It cannot be taken as having |-a·| TA th. 1 umlauted to |-e·| before |-·hi| dim., since |a·| in an AI stem that is subject to umlaut does not undergo umlaut before |-·hi| dim. (except when umlauted by a following |-w| 3,0).

|-a·| TA th. 1 also appears in secondary finals that derive nouns (4.206, 4.208) and verbs (**§53.6**) with a passive meaning.

b) |-ekw| is the second TA theme sign (TA th. 2), called the inverse theme sign. It indicates that the object is higher than the subject in the person hierarchy (3.189).

When |-ekw| TA th. 2 is followed by |p|, connective |e| is added (**§8.2**), and the resulting sequence |we| contracts to |o·| (**§11.1**; 1.125):

(3.193) |-ekw| TA th. 2 + |-pi| X → |-ekw-*e*-pi| → |+eko·pi|

(in |ne–eko·pi| X–1s/IND and |ke–eko·pi| X–2s/IND;

cf. |ne–eko·pena| X–1p/IND and |ke–eko·pwa| X–2p/IND)

As |-ekw| TA th. 2 is followed by |p| only in forms of the independent order with an indefinite subject and a first or second person object, the ostensible suffix -*eko*· that results from this contraction has the appearance of a variant of the theme sign specialized to mark passive forms:

(3.194)   *nemahkate·wi neko pi* 'I was made to fast' (A 7A)

(|mahkate·wi-N-| TA 'cause to fast', |ne–eko·pi| X–1s/IND [3.193])

When the subject is inanimate, the variant theme sign |-ekwi| TA th. 2a is used. This makes the TA inanimate-subject paradigms in all verbal modes. The object of a form with this inflection must, however, be a sentient being; if the object is a non-sentient animate a derived stem must be used (**§52**, 4.267).

(3.195) Contrast between |-ekw| TA th. 2 and |-ekwi| TA th. 2a

(a)   *netasemihekwa* 'he helped me' (K-Auto 135)

(← |ne-*t*-asemih-ekwa| ← |asemih-| TA, |ne–ekwa| 3s–1s/IND

[|+ekwa| ← |-ekw-w-a| ← |-ekw| TA th. 2, |-w| sg., |-a| ANsg])

(b)   *netasemihekwi* 'it (or they, inan.) helped me' (K-FC 247)

(← |ne-*t*-asemih-ekwi| ← |asemih-| TA, |ne–ekwi| 0–1s/IND

[|+ekwi| ← |-ekwi-∅| ← |-ekwi| TA th. 2a, |-∅| sg.])

Verbs with this theme sign take the inanimate subject as an argument, but they have the anomaly of allowing an indefinite object, as if the theme with |-ekwi| were actually a derived passive AI, a type of stem that takes the notional object as the subject.

(3.196)   *kehke nemekwipi e·ši-natawe netameki.* (K-M 247h)

'It (the water in Heaven) knows how one wants it to be.'

(|kehke·nem-| TA 'know', |-ekwipi| 0–X/IND;

|iši| PV '{so}', |natawe·net-| TI(1) 'want', |IC–ameki| X–0/PPL(obl))

The indefinite subject of the lower verb in (3.196) is copied as the indefinite object of the higher verb.

The |e| of |-ekw| TA th. 2 (and |-ekwi| TA th. 2a) contracts with the |-Vw| of contracting stems to |V·| (**§11.7**; 1.163), fuses with |-Cw| to |-Co| (**§11.1**), and is replaced by |o| after the |w| of a non-contracting stem (1.173).

|-ekw| TA th. 2 also appears, with a passive meaning, in the derivation of verbs (4.79-83) and a few nouns (**§46.2**, 4.229*a*).

c) |-i| is the third TA theme sign (TA th. 3). It indicates a first person object. Before |-i| TA th. 3, a stem-final |-N|, |-S|, or |-t| undergoes mutation to *š* (**§13.1**).

d) |-eN| is the fourth TA theme sign (TA th. 4). It indicates a second person object. In word-final position and before all true consonants except |k|, it adds connective |e| (**§8.2**; 1.83, 87), becoming |-ene|. Before |k| the |N| is replaced by |h|, giving |-ehk| (**§9.1**; 1.107). The |e| of |-eN| TA th. 4 contracts with a stem-final |-aw| to |o·| (**§11.7**; 1.166, 167), contracts with the |-Vw| of other contracting stems to |v·| (**§11.7**; 1.168), fuses with |-Cw| to |-Co| (**§11.1**), and is replaced by |o| after the |w| of a non-contracting stem (1.174).

The stem |iN-| TA 'say {so} to' optionally drops before |-ekw| th. 2 and |-ekwi| TA th. 2a (1.189*bcde*, 3.197). It always drops before |-eN| TA th. 4 if after the pronominal prefix (*ket-* 2):

> (3.197) *inekwa* and *ikwa* 'she (obv.) said to him' (K-MLF 50, after successive quotes)
> *ketene* 'I say {so} to you (sg.)' (← |ket-ene|
> ← |ke-*t*-iN-eN-*e*| ← |iN-| TA 'say {so} to' + |ke–ene| 1s–2s/IND)

This stem also always drops before |-eti·| AI RECIP (**§53.7**) and |-etiso| AI REFL (**§53.8**).

In the independent order and in some conjunct forms, the contrast between the third and fourth theme signs alone indicates whether second person is acting on first, or first person on second. In the independent order the prefix is always |ke+| 2 and hence does not contribute to distinguishing the meanings of the forms that have the contrasting theme signs.

> (3.198) Contrast between |-i| TA th. 3 and |-eN| TA th. 4
>
> Independent:
>
> (a) *kekehke nemi* 'you (sg.) know (about) me' (A 132H)
> (|kehke·nem-| TA 'know', |ke–i| 2s–1s/IND [|+i| ← |-i-∅| ← |-i| TA th. 3, |-∅| sg.])
> *kekehke nemene* 'I know (about) you (sg.)' (A 168J)
> (|kehke·nem-| TA 'know', |ke–ene| 1s–2s/IND
> [|+ene| ← |-eN-*e*-∅| ← |-eN| TA th. 4, |-∅| sg.])
>
> (b) *kekehke nemipwa* 'you (pl.) know (about) me' (K-BFF 10)
> (|kehke·nem-| TA 'know', |ke–ipwa| 2p–1s/IND
> [|+ipwa| ← |-i| TA th. 3, |-pwa| 2p])
> *kekehke nemenepwa* 'I know (about) you (pl.)' (K-IWF 6)
> (|kehke·nem-| TA 'know', |ke–enepwa| 1s–2p/IND
> [|+enepwa| ← |-eN-*e*-pwa| ← |-eN| TA th. 4, |-pwa| 2p])
>
> Conjunct:
>
> (c) *wi·h=nešiya·ke* 'that you will kill us' (K-WLB 38)
> (|wi·h=| FUT; |neS-| TA 'kill', |e·h=–iya·ke| 2–1p/AOR [with |-a·k| 1p])
> *wi·h=nesena·ke* 'that we will kill you' (X10-TAN 98)
> (|wi·h=| FUT; |neS-| TA 'kill', |e·h=–ena·ke| 1p–2/AOR [with |-a·k| 1p])

In other conjunct-order forms the central endings also differ:

> (3.199) *ne wiyane* 'if you (sg.) see me' (cf. A 25A)
> (|ne·w-| TA 'see', |–iyane| 2s–1s/SUBJ [← |-i| TA th. 3, |-an| 2s, |-e| SUBJ])
> *ne wona·ne* 'if I see you (sg.)' (O 157E)
> (|ne·w-| TA 'see', |–ena·ne| 1s–2s/SUBJ [← |-eN| TA th. 4, |-a·n| 1s, |-e| SUBJ])

In (3.198*a*) the central suffix is |-∅| sg., which is non-distinctive as it can mark either first or second singular. In (3.198*b*) the central suffix is |-pwa| 2p, marking the subject after the third theme sign and the object after the fourth theme sign. In (3.198*c*) the central suffix is |-a·k| 1p, which conversely marks the object after the third theme sign and the subject after the fourth theme sign. In (3.199) the central suffix agrees with the subject, either |-an| 2s or |-a·n| 1s.

e) The basic definitions of the TA theme signs (**§29.7(a-d)**) select |-ekwi| TA th. 2a if the subject is inanimate; they select |-a·| TA th. 1 or |-ekw| TA th. 2 when the object is third person (the choice depending on the hierarchy [3.189]), as long as the subject is not inanimate; they select |-i| TA th. 3 for a first person object when the subject is second person; and they select |-eN| for a second person object when the subject is first person.

For the combination of a first or second person object and a third person or indefinite subject, however, the definitions given for the theme signs would allow either the inverse theme sign or (depending on the person of the object) the third or fourth theme sign. In fact, different theme signs are selected in the independent order and in the other orders for just these combinations of arguments. It is as if the third and fourth theme signs were selected last in the independent order and were selected first in the other orders. Thus in the independent order the third and fourth theme signs have minimal use, appearing only in the forms that are not covered by the person hierarchy–those that involve a first and a second person as the subject and the object, in either combination. In contrast, in the other orders the third and fourth theme signs have maximal use, appearing in all forms with a first or second person object (except, as always, if an inanimate is the subject).

(3.200) Contrast in theme sign use in the independent and conjunct orders

(a)   *nekehke nemekwa* 'he knows (about) me' (K-FC 93)
  (|kehke·nem-| TA 'know', |ne–ekwa| 3s–1s/IND
  [|+ekwa| ← |-ekw| TA th. 2, |-w| sg., |-a| ANsg])
  e·h=kehke nemiči 'that he knows (about) me' (K-FC 55)
  (|kehke·nem-| TA 'know', |e·h=–iči| 3s–1s/AOR
  [|+iči| ← |-i| TA th. 3, |-t| 3, |-i| conj.])

(b)   *kekehke nemekwa* 'he knows you (sg.)' (K-CM 8)
  (|kehke·nem-| TA 'know', |ke–ekwa| 3s–2s/IND
  [|+ekwa| ← |-ekw| TA th. 2, |-w| sg., |-a| ANsg])
  e·h=kehke nemehki 'that he knows you (sg.)' (K-SPC 17)
  (|kehke·nem-| TA 'know', |e·h=–ehki| 3s–2s/AOR
  [|+ehki| ← |-eN| TA th. 4, |-k| 3, |-i| conj.])

(c)   *kekehke nemeko·pi* 'you (sg.) are known' (X10-PBW 48)
  (|kehke·nem-| TA 'know', |ke–eko·pi| X–2s/IND
  [|+eko·pi| ← |-ekw-e-pi| ← |-ekw| TA th. 2, |-pi| X])
  e·h=kehke nemeneki 'that you (sg.) are known' (S-Shak 5)
  (|kehke·nem-| TA 'know', |e·h=–eneki| X–2s/AOR
  [|+eneki| ← |-eN-ek-i| ← |-eN| TA th. 4, |-ek| X, |-i| conj.])

f) |-am| TI(1) th. is the theme sign for the TI verbs of class 1. It is replaced by *-a* in word-final position (3.201*b*) and before |k| (1.101; 3.201*c*), |s|, |n|, |č|, |hk| (1.104; 3.201*defg*), and |-ene·ha| X/POT (3.201*h*); it is replaced by *-a·* before |p| (3.201*i*).

(3.201) Variation in the shape of |-am| TI(1) th.

(a)   *ne tamakwe* 'if we see it' (O 147A)
  (|ne·t-| TI(1) 'see', |–amakwe| 12–0/SUBJ [← |-am| TI(1) th., |-akw| 12, |-e| subj.])

(b)   *nemata·kwe neta* 'I was fond of it' (A 14C)
  (|mata·kwe·net-| TI(1) 'enjoy', |ne–a| 1s–0/IND [← |-am| TI(1) th., |-∅| sg.])

(c)   *e·h=wa pataki* 'she looked at it' (A 92C)
  (|wa·pat-| TI(1) 'look at', |e·h=–aki| 3s–0/AOR [← |-am| TI(1) th., |-k| 3, |-i| conj.])

(d)   *mya ne netasa* 'he would think ill of it' (O 122G)
  (|mya·ne·net-| TI(1) 'dislike', |–asa| 3s–0/POT [← |-am| TI(1) th., |-sa| 3,0 pot.])

(e)   *ketenano* 'take it off' (A 178G)
  (|keten-| TI(1) 'take off', |–ano| 2s–0/IMP [← |-am| TI(1) th., |-no| 2s imp.])

(f)   *me·menata̲če* 'let her vomit' (K-W 96)

  (|me·menat-| TI(1)-O 'vomit', |–ače| 3s(-0)/IMP [← |-am| TI(1) th., |-če| 3,0 imp.])

(g)   *a·hkwamatak̲iče* 'she might get sick' (A 107E)

  (|a·hkwamat-| TI(1)-O 'be sick', |–akiče| 3s(-0)/PROH

  [← |-am| TI(1) th., |-hk| proh., |-če| 3,0 imp.])

(h)   *seswata̲ne·ha* 'it would be sprayed (with medicine) by mouth' (O 49B)

  (|seswat-| TI(1) 'spray (with {something}) by mouth', |–ane·ha| X–0/POT

  [← |-a-ene·ha| ← |-am| TI(1) th., |-ene·ha| X pot.])

(i)   *ki·h=kehke·neta̲ pena* 'we (inc.) will know it' (A 88B)

  (|wi·h=| FUT, |kehke·net-| TI(1) 'know', |ke–a·pena| 12–0/IND

  [|+a·pena| ← |-am| TI(1) th., |-pena| 1p,2p])

In secondary derivation from TI(1) stems the theme sign is in some cases absent and in other cases present (**§45.7**, 4.212; **§52.2**, 4.267; **§54.9**, 4.338; **§55.1**, 4.352). In one case |-am| TI(1) th. is replaced by *-a-* (**§54.9**, 4.337).

  g) |-o·| TI(2) th. is the theme sign for the TI verbs of class 2. It has no variants except for the automatic shortening of the vowel in word-final position (**§12.1**).

  (3.202) Variation in the shape of |-o·| TI(2) th.

  kočihto̲ no 'try to make them (inan.)' (A 29C)

  (|kočiht-| TI(2) 'try to make', |–o·no| 2s–0/IMP)

  netašihto̲ 'I made them (inan.)' (A 59D)

  (|ašiht-| TI(2) 'make', |ne–o·| 1s–0/IND)

In secondary derivation TI(2) stems always occur without the theme sign |-o·| (**§45**, 4.195; **§53**, 4.271*o*) except in a few cases where it could also be interpreted as connective |o·| (**§45.7**, 4.213; **§50.2**, 4.255; **§52.2**, 4.267*f*). In one formation |-o·| TI(2) th. appears to be replaced by |a·| (4.339).

  29.8. Position 4. The three suffixes in position 4 mark obviative and plural. They always occur with another pronominal suffix, either a central suffix of position 6 or a combined suffix of positions 6 and 7.

  a) |-ni| obv. specifies as obviative the third-person argument of any suffix of position 6 or positions 6 and 7 that indicates a single pronominal category:

  (3.203) Combination of |-ni| obv. and third-person suffixes

third person	obviative
|-w| 3,0	|-niw| 3´ and 0´ independent
|-t|, |-k| 3	|-nit| 3´ core conjunct
|-k| 0	|-nik| 0´ core conjunct
|-kw| 3,0 irr.	|-nikw| 3´ and 0´ interrogative and prioritive
|-hkiče| 3,0 proh.	|-nihkiče| 3´ and 0´ prohibitive
|-sa| 3,0 pot.	|-nisa| 3´ and 0´ potential
|-če| 3,0 imp.	|-niče| 3´ and 0´ imperative

In (3.203) |-kw| 3,0 irr. is the combination of |-w| irr. and both |-k| 3 and |-k| 0 (**§29.9(a)**, 3.220), and |-hkiče| 3,0 proh. is the combination of |-hk| proh. and |-če| 3,0 imp. (**§8.1**, 1.78).

  In addition, a single archaic form in a ritual prayer attests |-amenit| 3´–1p as the combination of |-ni| obv. and |-amet| 3–1p:

(3.204)   *neto·kima·mena·nani e·nekihkwišimiyameniči i·ni e·nekihkwi·natota·sakeči*
        pema·tesiweni. 'it's for all of us under the sway of our chief (obv.) that we pray to
        them (the deities, prox.) for life' (K-BHD 70)
        (*neto·kima·mena·nani* 'our chief (obv.)';
        |inekihkwišim-| TA 'have to {such} extent', |IC–iyameniči| 3´–1p/PPL(obl);
        i·ni 'that (inan.)'; |inekihkwi| PV 'to {such} extent',
        |natota·S-| TA(+O) 'pray to (for O2)', |IC–akeči| 1p–3/PPL(obl);
        pema·tesiweni 'life')

In the independent indicative an animate obviative marked by |-ni| obv. is also marked by an obviative peripheral ending of position 8 (3.205), and participles with obviative heads may also be doubly marked (3.302*a*), but otherwise |-ni| obv. is the sole mark of the obviative and number is not distinguished (3.206).

(3.205)   *nepo·hiwa* 'he (prox.) died' (K-ECRP 16)
        (|nepo·hi-| AI 'die (dim.)', |-wa| 3s/IND)
        oni·ča·nese·hani=·'pi nepo·hiniwani 'they say her child (obv.) died' (K-MBGS 14)
        (*oni·ča·nese·hani* 'her child (obv.)'; |=ipi| HRSY;
        |nepo·hi-| AI 'die (dim.)', |–niwani| 3´s [← |-ni| obv., |-w| 3,0, |-ani| OBVsg])
(3.206)   *e·h=penoči* 'he (prox.) went home' (O 7H)
        (|peno-| AI 'go off', |e·h=–či| 3s/AOR [|+či| 3 conj. ← |-t-i| ← |-t| 3, |-i| conj.])
        e·h=penowa·či 'they (prox.) left for home' (O 104G)
        (|peno-| AI 'go off', |e·h=–wa·či| 3p/AOR
        [|+wa·či| 3p conj. ← |-wa·| pl., |-t| 3, |-i| conj.])
        e·h=penoniči 'they (obv.) departed' (O 18B); also: 'he (obv.) departed'
        (|peno-| AI 'go off', |e·h=–niči| 3´/AOR [|+niči| 3´ conj. ← |-ni| obv., |-t| 3, |-i| conj.])

When |-ni| obv. follows a consonant there are three possible adjustments of the underlying consonant sequence. After |-am| TI(1) th. connective |i| (§8.1) is inserted:

(3.207)   *e·h=awato·taminiči* 'he (obv.) carried it home on his back' (O 161D)
        (|awato·t-| TI(1) 'carry off on back', |e·h=–aminiči| 3´–0/AOR
        [|+aminiči| ← |-am-i-ni-či| ← |-am| TI(1) th., |-ni| obv., |-či| 3 conj.])

After a retaining consonant stem (§18.3) or |-ekw| TA th. 2 connective |e| is inserted (§8.2):

(3.208)   *nehki=meko e·ne·teniči* 'for as long as they (obv.) were away' (O 16G)
        (← |IC-ine·t-e-niči| ← |ine·t-| AI 'be away {so} long', |IC–niči| 3´/PPL(obl))

The stem-final |n| of a deleting consonant stem (§18.3) is lost (§§9.1):

(3.209)   *ki·šišiniči* 'after he (obv.) lay down' (K-ECRP 25)
        (← |IC+ki·šišin-niči| ← |ki·šišin-| AI 'finish lying down', |IC–niči| 3´/CC)
        e·škikeniki 'which was new (inan. obv.)' (A 115A)
        (← |IC+aškiken-niki| ← |aškiken-| II 'be new', |IC–niki| 0´/PPL(INsg))

b) |-wa·| pl. pluralizes third person animates marked by the same third-person suffixes that are made obviative by |-ni| obv. (§29.8(a)), but except in interrogative participles it is not used when the third person is pluralized by a peripheral suffix (position 8). Hence it is not used in the independent order or in the interrogative modes other than the participle.

(3.210) Combination of |-wa·| pl. and third-person suffixes

third person	third plural
|-t|, |-k| 3	|-wa·t| 3p core conjunct
|-kw| 3 irr.	|-wa·kw| 3p prioritive, interrogative participle

[third person]   [third plural]

|-hki·če| 3 proh. |-wa·hki·če| 3p prohibitive

|-sa| 3 pot. |-wa·sa| 3p potential

|-če| 3 imp. |-wa·če| 3p imperative

Also, on the model of |-wa·-hk-*i*-če| 3p proh., |-wa·| pl. combines with |-iye·ki·če| 3–3´ proh. as |-iye·wa·hki·če| 3p–3´ proh. (**§29.9(b)**, 3.227).

Outside the interrogative participle, |-wa·| pl. is the only inflectional mark of the plural in the endings in which it occurs:

(3.211)   *nepo·hisa* 'he would die' (O 48H)

       (|nepo·hi-| AI 'die (dim.)', |–sa| 3s/POT)

       nepo·hiwa·sa 'they would die' (A 101B)

       (|nepo·hi-| AI 'die (dim.)', |–wa·sa| 3p/POT)

In the interrogative participle, |-wa·| pl. may be used redundantly together with |-iki| ANpl; this double marking makes the participial ending distinct from that of the corresponding changed interrogative.

(3.212) Optional |-wa·| pl. with animate plural interrogative participles

  (a)   *wi·h=anemi-mehtose neniwiwa·kwe·hiki* 'whatever ones are to live'

       (K-M 427a; |wi·h=| FUT, *anemi* PV 'go on',

       |mehtose·neniwi-| AI 'live', |IC–<u>wa</u>·kwe·hiki| 3p/INT.PPL(ANpl))

  (b)   *i·nahi e·tano·še·kwe·hiki* 'whatever ones were nesting there' (K-M 821g)

       (*i·nahi* 'there';

       |tano·še·-| AI 'give birth {somewhere}', |IC–kwe·hiki| 3p/INT.PPL(ANpl))

When |-wa·| pl. follows a consonant, connective |o| (**§8.3**; 1.91) is inserted:

(3.213)   *e·h=mama·totamowa·či* 'when they worshipped it' (O 9G)

       (|mama·tot-| TI(1) 'pray to', |e·h=–amowa·či| 3p–0/AOR

       [|+amowa·či| ← |-am-*o*-wa·či| ← |-am| TI(1) th., |-wa·| pl., |-t| 3, |-i| conj.])

(3.214)   *wi·h=na·towa·či* 'for them to go get it' (A 166B)

       (|wi·h=na·t-*o*-wa·či| ← |wi·h=| FUT, |na·t-| TI(3) 'go to get', |e·h=–wa·či| 3p–0/AOR)

c) |-wa·| 2p pluralizes the second person object in potential and imperative (injunctive) forms with a third person animate subject. It differs from |-wa·| pl. in not pluralizing a suffix of position 6 or positions 6 and 7 and in not inserting connective |o| after a consonant:

(3.215) |–enesa| 3–2s/POT (← |-eN-*e*-sa| ← |-eN| TA th. 4, |-sa| 3,0 pot.)

       |–en<u>wa</u>·sa| 3–2p/POT (← |-eN-wa·-sa| ← |-eN| TA th. 4, |-wa·| 2p, |-sa| 3,0 pot.)

(3.216) |–ene·če| 3–2s/IMP (← |-eN-*e*-če| ← |-eN| TA th. 4, |-če| 3,0 imp.)

       |–en<u>wa</u>·če| 3–2p/IMP (← |-eN-wa·-če| ← |-eN| TA th. 4, |-wa·| 2p, |-če| 3,0 imp.)

For example:

(3.217)   *nesenesa=meko i·niki anemo·haki* 'those dogs would kill you (sg.)' (K-RYL 5)

       (|neS-| TA 'kill', |–enesa| 3–2s/POT; =*meko* EMPH;

       i·niki 'those (anim.)'; *anemo·haki* 'dogs')

       ča·kihenwa·sa=meko 'she would have killed you all' (K-WKG 21)

       (|ča·kih-| TA 'kill all of', |–enwa·sa| 3–2p/POT)

29.9. Position 5. The three suffixes in position 5 are modal suffixes used in three of the conjunct sub-orders. Two are homophonous and overlap in function, but they combine in different ways with some theme signs. The two that occur with position 6 suffixes that mark first plural objects share the peculiarity of combining with these suffixes in irregular ways that suggest that the order of the suffixes is reversed (3.232-235).

a) |-w| irr. (the irrealis suffix) is one of the underlying constituent morphemes in all endings of the interrogative and prioritive modes of the interrogative sub-order. When it follows a consonant it is preceded by connective |o| (**§8.3**; 1.90), and it is subject to contraction with a following |e| (3.221-223).

The presence of |-w| irr. in interrogative and prioritive endings contrasts with its absence in the corresponding core conjunct endings:

(3.218)   *ona·pe·miyane* 'if you (sg.) marry him' (A 76B)

(|ona·pe·mi-| AI(+O) 'have (O2 as) husband', |–yane| 2s/SUBJ [← |-ane| (**§10.1**)])

me·h-ona·pe·miwane=meko 'even before you (sg.) got married' (A 144C)

(|me·hi| PV 'yet', |ona·pe·mi-| AI(+O) 'have (O2 as) husband',

|IC–wane| 2s/CH.PRI; =*meko* EMPH)

As a result, where core conjunct endings have |-∅| as the automatic variant of |-a·| TA th. 1 before a vowel (**§29.7(a)**, 3.190), the corresponding interrogative endings retain |-a·| TA th. 1 overtly before |-w| irr.:

(3.219) Retention of |-a·| TA th. 1 before |-w| irr.

(a)   *ne·wake* 'if I see him, them' (K-EGC 24)

(|ne·w-| TA 'see', |–ake| 1s–3/SUBJ

[← |-∅-ak-e| ← |-a·| TA th. 1, |-ak| 1s–3, |-e| subj.])

ne·wa·wake·na 'whoever I see' (C-FRS 15)

(|ne·w-| TA 'see', |IC–a·wake·na| 1s–3/PPL(ANsg)

[← |-a̲·-w̲-ak-e·ni-a| ← |-a·| TA th. 1, |-w| irr., |-ak| 1s–3, |-e·ni| int., |-a| ANsg]).

(b)   *wi·čawiwata* 'your husband' (A 96B)

(|wi·čawiw-| TA 'be with', |IC–ata| 2s–3/PPL(ANsg)

[← |-∅-at-a| ← |-a·| TA th. 1, |-at| 2s–3, |-a| ANsg])

wi·h=wi·čawiwa·wate·na 'whoever you (sg.) marry' (A 183F)

(|wi·h=| FUT, |wi·čawiw-| TA 'be with', |IC–a·wate·na| 2s–3/INT.PPL(ANsg)

[← |-a̲·-w̲-at-e·ni-a| ← |-a·| TA th. 1, |-w| irr., |-at| 2s–3, |-e·ni| int., |-a| ANsg])

When |-w| irr. is followed by the core conjunct third person animate suffix, it selects the post-consonantal variant |-k| 3 in place of |-t| 3 (3.256). This sequence |-w-k| (← |-w| irr., |-k| 3) metathesizes to |-kw| (**§9.2**). As a consequence of this, the third person animate *-t* of the core conjunct is ostensibly replaced in the interrogative sub-order by *-kw*:

(3.220)   *i·ni e·šawita* 'one like that' (K-FC 34)

(*i·ni* 'that (inan.)', |išawi-| AI 'do {so}', |IC–ta| 3/PPL(ANsg))

i·ni e·šawikwe·na 'whoever is like that' (K-FC 362)

(*i·ni* 'that (inan.)', |išawi-| AI 'do {so}', |IC–kwe·na| 3/INT.PPL(ANsg))

The combination of |-w| irr. and |-k| 0 also results in a sequence |-w-k| that metathesizes to |-kw|. In both cases, if |-w| irr. is preceded by connective |o| (**§8.3**) the result is |-okw|. The outcome of the metathesis of |-w-k| of both origins to |-kw| may be recognized for convenience as a distinct, combined suffix |-kw| 3,0 irr. which, like |-w| irr., takes connective |o| (**Appendix 2**).

When |-w| irr. is followed by a core conjunct indefinite subject suffix (|-ek| X or |-et| X–3) the sequence |-w-e| is always contracted:

(3.221)   *e·šawi·ke·ni* 'whatever it is that is done, what the rules may be' (JP-SMD 37)

(|IC+išawi·weke·ni| ← |išawi-| AI 'do {so}', |IC–weke·ni| X/INT.PPL(obl)

[|+w-ek-e·ni| ← |-w| irr., |-ek| X, |-e·ni| int.])

(3.222)   *wi·h=anemi- 'ši- .. -pemeni·ke ni* 'whether I will continue to be taken care of' (O 93E)
    (|wi·h=| FUT, *anemi* PV 'go on', *iši* PV '{so}',
    |pemen-| TA 'take care of', |IC–i·ke·ni| X–1s/INT.PPL(obl)
    [← |-i-w-ek-e·ni| ← |-i| TA th. 3, |-w| irr., |-ek| X–3, |-e·ni| int.])

(3.223)   *e ·šimeno ·ke ni* 'whatever you (sg.) are told to do' (K-Spot 236)
    (|išim-| TA 'speak {so} to', |IC–eno·ke ni| X–2s/INT.PPL [←
    |-eN-ow-ek-e·ni| ← |-eN-o-w-ek-e·ni| ← |-eN| TA th. 4, |-w| irr., |-ek| X, |-e·ni| int.])

(3.224)   *ke ·hkahwa ·te na* 'whoever is designated' (K-FC 138)
    (|kehkahw-| TA 'designate', |IC–a·te·na| X–3/INT.PPL(ANsg)
    [← |-a·-w-et-e·ni-a| ← |-a·| TA th. 1, |-w| irr., |-et| X–3, |-e·ni| int., |-a| ANsg])

As a result of this contraction, the presence of |-w| irr. after a stem or theme in a short vowel is indicated by the lengthening of the vowel (3.221, 222). With |-i| TA th. 1 there is thus an ostensible alternation between |-ik| X–1s (3.225*a*) and |-i·k| X–1s irr. (3.225*b*):

(3.225) First singular passive, core conjunct and interrogative
  (a) *e ·šimiki* 'what I was told to do' (K-ECRP 30)
    (|išim-| TA 'tell to do {so}', |IC–iki| X–1s/PPL(obl)
    [|+iki| ← |-i-ek-i| ← |-i| TA th. 3, |-ek| X, |-i| INsg])
  (b) *e ·šimi ·ke ni* 'whatever I may be told to do' (K-WKG 24)
    (|išim-| TA 'tell to do {so}', |IC–i·ke·ni| X–1s/INT.PPL(obl)
    [|+i·ke·ni| ← |-i-w-ek-e·ni| ← |-i| TA th. 3, |-w| irr., |-ek| X, |-e·ni| int.])

When |-w| irr. would be followed by |-wet| X rel. this sequence of morphemes is replaced by |-wa·t| X rel. irr., on the model of the TA endings, which have interrogative -*a t* X–3 irr. (3.224) beside conjunct |-et| X–3 (3.187).

(3.226)   *e ·h=peseše wa ·či wi ·h=iyowa ·te ni* (K-TYFB 17)
    'they were keen to hear whatever was going to be said'
    (|peseše·-| AI 'listen', |e·h=–wa·či| 3p/AOR;
    |wi·h=| FUT, |i-| AI 'say {so}' [1.93], |IC–wa·te·ni| X/REL/INT.PPL(obl)
    [← |-wa·t| X rel. irr. (for |-w| irr. + |-wet| X rel.), |-e·ni| int.])

b) |-hk| proh. is present in all endings of the prohibitive mode and some endings of the potential mode. When it follows certain other suffixes or stems of certain shapes it combines irregularly with them (3.227). A distinct suffix |-hk| fut. imp. is set up to account for certain endings in which the combination of a theme sign with |-hk| has a different, more regular outcome. These regularized endings constitute the future imperative mode of the prohibitive sub-order (**§26.19**).

(3.227) Combinations with |-hk| proh. and |-hk| fut. imp.

	|-hk| proh.	|-hk| fut. imp.
(AI in |-n|)	|-n| + |-hk| → -*k* (1.105)	
(II in |-n|)	|-n| + |-hk| → -*hk* (1.106) or -*k*	
(TA th. 1)	|-a·| + |-hk| → -*iye ·k*	|-a·| + |-hk| → -*a ·hk*
(+ |-wa·| pl.)	|-a·| + |-wa·| + |-hk| → -*iye wa ·hk*	|-a·| + |-wa·| + |-hk| → -*a wa ·hk*
(TA th. 4)	|-eN| + |-hk| → |-enak|	
(TI(1) th.)	|-am| + |-hk| → -*ak*	|-am| + |-hk| → -*amo ·hk*

Ostensibly, where core conjunct third person forms have |-t| 3 (followed by various modal suffixes), the corresponding forms in the prohibitive sub-order substitute -*hkiče*:

(3.228) Third singular, conjunct and prohibitive

    (a)   *wa·pamite* 'if he looks at me' (K-WLBS 20)

        (|wa·pam-| TA 'look at', |–ite| 3s–1s/SUBJ [← |-i| TA th. 3, |-t| 3, |-e| subj.])

    (b)   *ka·ta owiye·ha wa·pamihkiče* 'don't anyone look at me' (K-WLBS 20)

        (*ka·ta* 'don't'; *owiye·ha* 'anyone'; |wa·pam-| TA 'look at', |–ihkiče| 3s–1s/PROH

        [← |-i| TA th. 3, |-hk-*i*-če| 3,0 proh. (← |-hk| proh., |-če| 3,0 imp.; **§8.1**, 1.78)])

The prohibitive and future imperative modes contrast only when there is a second person subject and either a third person animate object (3.229*ab*) or an inanimate object of a TI(1) stem (3.229*cd*).

    (3.229) Contrast between prohibitive and future imperative

    (a)   Prohibitive 2s–3:

        ka·ta a·čimohiye·kani 'don't tell them (you sg.)' (S-YMSG 10)

        (*ka·ta* 'don't'; |a·čimoh-| TA 'inform', |–iye·kani| 2s–3/PROH

        [← |-iye·k| TA th. 1 proh. (for |-a·| TA th. 1 + |-hk| proh. [3.227]), |-an| 2s, |-i| conj.])

    (b)   Future imperative 2s–3:

        a·čimoha·hkani 'tell them (later) (you sg.)' (K-B 165B; 2.303)

        (|a·čimoh-| TA 'inform', |–a·hkani| 2s–3/FUT.IMP)

        [← |-a·| TA th. 1, |-hk| fut. imp. (3.227), |-an| 2s, |-i| conj.])

    (c)   Prohibitive 2s–0:

        ka·ta nenehke·netakani 'don't think about it (you sg.)' (K-FC 704

        (*ka·ta* 'don't'; |nenehke·net-| TI(1) 'think about', |–akani| 2s–0/PROH

        [← |-ak| TI(1) th. proh. (← |-am| TI(1) th., |-hk| proh. [3.227]), |-an| 2s, |-i| conj.])

    (d)   Future imperative 2s–0:

        nenehke·netamo·hkani 'you (sg.) must think about it' (K-FC 124; 2.305)

        (|nenehke·net-| TI(1) 'think about', |–amo·hkani| 2s–0/FUT.IMP

        [← |-am-*o*·-hkani| ← |-am| TI(1) th., |-hk| fut imp. (**§8.4**; 3.227), |-an| 2s, |-i| conj.])

Other second person forms use the undifferentiated prohibitive ending in both modal functions:

    (3.230) Homophony between prohibitive and future imperative

    (a)   Prohibitive function:

        ka·ta=mani išawihke·ko 'don't do this (you pl.)' (K-FC 162)

        (*ka·ta* 'don't'; *mani* 'this (inan.)'; |išawi-| 'do {so}', |–hke·ko| 2p/PROH)

    (b)   Future imperative function:

        mani išawihke·ko 'you (pl.) must do this' (K-FC 240)

With a third person animate subject and an obviative object, the functions of the prohibitive mode may be expressed either by endings that are formally of the prohibitive mode (|+iye·kiče| 3s–3′/PROH, |+iye·wa·hkiče| 3p–3′/PROH; 2.302) or by endings that are formally of the future imperative mode (|+a·hkiče| 3s–3′/FUT.IMP, |+a·wa·hkiče| 3p–3′/FUT.IMP; 2.295, 303). (The formally prohibitive endings are not found with *ka·ta* 'don't', but this is probably an accidental gap in attestation.) If the subject is third person and the stem is a TI(1), only endings that are formally of the prohibitive mode are found in prohibitive-mode functions (2.294, 301).

    c) The prohibitive and future imperative endings contain pronominal suffixes that follow the modal suffix. Some of these are combined pronoun and mode suffixes of positions 6 and 7 that are unique to the prohibitive sub-order (3.186). Other endings have the third person imperative suffix (|-če| 3,0) or a core conjunct pronominal suffix with the conjunct modal suffix, or in a few cases combinations of two pronominal suffixes. Prohibitive endings may also contain a suffix of position 4 (3.203, 210).

d) The endings of the potential mode contain |-hk| proh. if the subject is not third person or indefinite, or if the object with an inanimate subject is not third person. Following the |-hk| is either a combined pronoun and mode suffix (positions 6 and 7) or a core conjunct pronominal suffix (position 6) followed by the modal suffix |-ehe| pret. (position 7). In potential mode endings |-hk| proh. combines with other elements in the same way as in the prohibitive mode:

(3.231) *menwimenwišikakoha* 'we would lie there comfortably' (K-FC 507)

(|CVCV+| RED2, |menwišin-| AI 'lie comfortably',

|-hkakoha| 12/POT [← |-hk| proh., |-akw| 12, |-ehe| pret.])

e) The modal suffixes |-w| irr. and |-hk| proh. combine irregularly with the suffixes for first plural exclusive objects (|-amet| 3–1p and |-·namek| X–1p). The theme theme sign |-i| TA th. 3 (position 2) is not followed by the modal suffix (position 5) before one of these pronominal suffixes (position 6), in the otherwise universal sequence. Instead, these pronominal suffixes follow the theme sign directly and have their last consonant replaced on the model of the third person or indefinite subject endings of the same mode.

(3.232) Combination of |-w| irr. and |-hk| proh. with |-amet| 3–1p and |-·namek| X–1p

		with |-e| subj.	with |-w| irr.	with |-hk| proh.
|-t| 3s		*-t-e*	|-kw| *-kw-e ni*	*-hk-iče*
|-i-t| 3–1s		*-i-t-e*	|-ikw| *-i-kw-e ni*	*-i-hk-iče*
|-i-y-amet| 3–1p		*-i-y-amet-e*	*-i-y-amekw-e ni*	*-i-y-amehk-iče*
|-ek| X		*-(e)k-e*	|-w-ek| *-·k-e ni*	*-hk-i·ke*
|-i-k| X–1s		*-i-k-e*	|-i-w-ek| *-i-·k-e ni*	*-i-hk-i·ke*
|-i-·namek| X–1p		*-i-·namek-e*	*-i-·nami·k-e ni*	*-i-·namehk-i·ke*

In each of the interrogative and prohibitive endings for first plural exclusive object in (3.232) the final consonant of the core conjunct suffix is replaced on the same pattern as in the corresponding ending for first singular object. Like the surface alternation between *-t* 3 and *-kw* 3 irr. in third person animate endings (3.220), including those with first singular object (3.232), there is an ostensible replacement of core conjunct *-iyamet* 3–1p by *-iyamekw* 3–1p irr. as the combination of |-w| irr. and |-iyamet| 3–1p:

(3.233) *ki·šihiyameta* 'the one who created us (exc.)' (K-BR 9)

(|ki·ših-| TA 'finish making', |IC–iyameta| 3–1p/PPL(ANsg))

ki·šihiyamekwe na 'whoever created us (exc.)' (K-Fish 116)

(|ki·ših-| TA 'finish making', |IC–iyamekwe·na| 3–1p/INT.PPL(ANsg)

[← |-i| TA th. 3, |-amekw| (for |-w| irr. + |-amet| 3–1p), |-e·ni| int., |-a| ANsg])

Beside core conjunct *-ik* X–1s (|-i-ek|) the interrogative sub-order has the regularly formed *-i-·k* X–1s irr. (|-i-w-ek|; 3.225, 232). In the corresponding first plural exclusive ending, where the core conjunct has *-i-·namek* X–1p the interrogative has *-i-·nami·k* X–1p irr. (apparently copying the ostensible replacement of -Vk by *-i·k* in the first singular); this suffix functions as the (irregular) combination of |-w| irr. and |-i-·namek| X–1p.

(3.234) *e·h=pi·tahwi namekehe* 'we (exc.) had been buried' (K-K 7)

(|pi·tahw-| TA 'bury', |e·h=–i·namekehe| X–1p/AOR.PRET

[|-i-·namek-ehe| ← |-i| TA th. 3, |-·namek| X–1p, |-ehe| pret.])

pi·tahwi nami·ke ni 'we (exc.) must have been buried' (K-K 8)

(|pi·tahw-| TA 'bury', |e·h=–i·nami·ke·ni| X–1p/INT

[← |-i| TA th. 3, |-·nami·k| X–1p irr. (for |-w| irr. + |-·namek| X–1p), |-e·ni| int.])

Similarly in the prohibitive, what corresponds to core conjunct *-t* 3 is *-hk-i-če* 3 proh. (3.232), and, in parallel fashion, beside core conjunct *-i-y-amet* 3–1p there is *-i-y-amehk-i-če* 3–1p proh. functioning as the irregular combination of |-hk| proh. and |-amet| 3–1p before |-če| 3 proh.:

(3.235) *ke teminawiyameta* 'the one who blessed us (exc.)' (O 121F)

(|keteminaw-| TA 'bless', |IC–iyameta| 3–1p/PPL(ANsg)

[|+iyameta| ← |-i| TA th. 3, |-amet| 3–1p, |-a| ANsg])

ka ta kosetawiyamehkiče "They need not be afraid to approach us."

(K-WYB 195, tr. TB)

(*ka ta* 'don't'; |kosetaw-| TA 'fear to approach', |–iyamehkiče| 3–1p/PROH)

The ending |+i namehki ke| X–1p/PROH (3.232) is not citable from a text but was obtained in 1998 and 2003: *neši namehki ke* 'we (exc.) might be killed' (HWB); *wača hi namehki ke* 'they (indef.) might cook for us' (EK). Its formation beside core conjunct |-i namek| X–1p follows the pattern of the other endings for first plural exclusive object.

29.10. Position 6. In position 6 are the central pronominal suffixes, which mark pronominal category (§18.4). Their function contrasts with that of the peripheral pronominal suffixes of position 8, which mark nominal category (§18.2). The opposition between central and peripheral suffixes defines a morphological contrast between central and peripheral arguments. There is no such opposition, however, when the peripheral suffix in an ending specifies a third person central argument as plural or obviative; or when it marks the head of a participle; or when a first person and a second person are the arguments, and a central suffix alone is used to mark one of them as either subject or object. Conversely, the opposition between central and peripheral argument may be recognized as functionally present even when, as is often the case, the peripheral argument is not marked by a peripheral suffix.

There are two large classes of suffixes in position 6, the independent suffixes (§29.10(a)) and the conjunct suffixes (§29.10(b)). The independent suffixes are used in all modes of the independent order, except that the assertive mode has its own non-third person suffixes. The conjunct suffixes are used in all endings of the core conjunct and interrogative sub-orders, and in many endings of other conjunct sub-orders. Verbal endings that do not contain a central suffix of position 6 contain, or consist of, a combined pronoun and mode suffix of positions 6 and 7 (§29.10(c)). Some pronominal suffixes of the prohibitive and potential sub-orders and all pronominal suffixes of the imperative order are of this type.

a) The independent order has two principal sets of central suffixes, the objective suffixes and the absolute suffixes. There also are traces of a third set, used in the assertive mode. The central suffixes combine with the pronominal prefixes to form the central argument paradigms, which specify the central argument:

(3.236) Independent order: central argument paradigms

	prefix	absolute	objective	assertive mode
1s	|ne+| 1	|-Ø|, |-p| sg.	|-w| sg.	|-na·| sg. ast.
2s	|ke+| 2	|-Ø|, |-p| sg.	|-w| sg.	(unattested)
1p	|ne+| 1	|-pena| 1p,12	|-ena·n| 1p,12	(unattested)
12	|ke+| 2	|-pena| 1p,12	|-ena·n| 1p,12	(unattested)
2p	|ke+| 2	|-pwa| 2p	|-wa·w| 2p	|-na·wa·| 2p ast.
3,0		|-w| 3,0		
X		|-pi| X		

The plural objective suffixes match the central suffixes |-ena·n| 1p,12 and |-wa·w| 2p,3p used in the inflection of nouns for possessor (3.1, 18).

The objective suffixes are used when the ending contains a peripheral suffix (position 8), marking a peripheral argument, or is in a paradigm that uses peripheral suffixes to distinguish the number of the peripheral argument (**§29.11**). The absolute suffixes are used in endings with no peripheral suffix and no paradigmatically implied specification of the number of a peripheral argument, or when a peripheral suffix which is present does not mark a distinct, peripheral argument but rather specifies categories of the central argument.

The absolute central suffixes are used outside the central argument paradigm of (3.236) after |-i| TA th. 3 and |-eN| TA th. 4; the prefix is always |ke+| 2 and the central suffix marks either subject or object (3.197, 198, 312).

The absolute suffixes provide the only inflection for third person or indefinite central arguments and are used for most first and second person central arguments as well. The objective suffixes are used after |-ekw| TA th. 2 for all first or second person objects in all modes (except, presumably, the assertive). They are also used, with first and second singular subjects only, after |-a·| TA th. 1 in non-diminutive endings of the independent indicative. In the other independent modes, and even in the indicative if the diminutive suffix is present, only the absolute suffixes are used after |-a·| TA th. 1.

The absolute suffix |-∅|, |-p| sg. has the shape |-∅| if followed by no other suffix and |-p| before the modal suffixes |-etoke| dub. and |-ehapa| (|-ahapa|) con. For convenience this suffix is usually given as either |-∅| sg. or |-p| sg., depending on what shape it takes, but these are not distinct morphemes.

(3.237) *nenenehke·neta* 'I think about it' (K-WM 3)

(|nenehke·net-| TI(1) 'think about', |ne–a| 1s–0/IND

[|+a| ← |-a-∅| ← |-am| TI th. 1, |-∅| sg.])

kenenehke·neta petoke 'you (sg.) must remember it' (A 139C)

(|nenehke·net-| TI(1) 'think about', |ke–a petoke| 2s–0/DUB

[|+a·petoke| ← |-a·-p-etoke| ← |-am| TI th. 1, |-p| sg., |-etoke| dub.])

The absolute suffixes are added directly to AI and TI(3) vowel stems and TI(2) themes; when a long vowel comes to stand in word-final position, followed only by |-∅| sg., it is shortened (**§12.1**, 1.106, 107). Consonant-final stems add |e| word-finally (before |-∅| sg.) and before the |p| of a suffix (**§8.2**; 3.313).

After |-ekw| TA th. 2, |-w| 3,0 and |-w| sg. drop (**§9.3**; 1.110):

(3.238) *asemihekwa* 'he (obv.) helped her' (A 69D)

(|asemih-| TA 'help', |–ekwa| 3´–3s/IND

[|+ekwa| ← |-ekw-w-a| ← |-ekw| TA th. 2, |-w| 3,0, |-a| ANsg])

(3.239) *neki·šikenekwa* 'she raised me' (A 17B)

(|ki·šiken-| TA 'raise', |ne–ekwa| 3s–1s/IND

[|+ekwa| ← |-ekw-w-a| ← |-ekw| TA th. 2, |-w| sg., |-a| ANsg])

The underlying presence of |-w| 3,0 and |-w| sg. after |-ekw| TA th. 2 is, however, evident from the corresponding diminutive endings, in which these suffixes are retained after |-·hi| dim.:

(3.240) *ketemina·ko·hiwa* 'he (obv.) had blessed her (our dear one)' (K-FC 387)

(|keteminaw-| TA 'pity, bless', |–eko·hiwa| 3´–3s/DIM/IND

[|+eko·hiwa| ← |-ekw-o·-hi-w-a| ← |-ekw| TA th. 2, |-·hi| dim., |-w| 3,0, |-a| ANsg])

(3.241) *nekoseko·hiwa* "he rather fears me" (K-FC 331, tr. HP)

(|koS-| TA 'fear', |ne–eko·hiwa| 3s–1s/DIM/IND

[|+eko·hiwa| ← |-ekw-o·-hi-w-a| ← |-ekw| TA th. 2, |-·hi| dim., |-w| sg., |-a| ANsg])

The homophonous suffixes |-w| 3,0 and |-w| sg. are morphophonemically distinct in one environment. A preceding |-a·| TA th. 1 undergoes umlaut to -e· before |-w| 3,0, whether contiguous (3.242a) or non-contiguous (3.242b), but is unchanged before |-w| sg. (3.243).

(3.242) Umlaut of |-a·| TA th. 1 before |-w| 3,0

(a) *ine̲wa* 'she said {so} to her (obv.)' (A 107E)

(|iN-| TA 'say {so} to', |–e̲·wa| 3s–3′/IND

[← |-e̲·-w-a| ← |-a·| TA th. 1, |-w| 3,0, |-a| ANsg])

(b) *kotakahi=meko mehto·či menwe̲ neme̲niwani.* (K-CWB 77)

'it seemed (to her [prox.]) that he (1st obv.) liked others (2nd obv.)'

(*kotakahi* 'others (obv.)'; *=meko* EMPH; *mehto·či* 'as though';

|menwe·nem-| TA 'like', |–e̲niwani| 3′s–3″/IND

[← |-e̲·-ni-w-ani| ← |-a·| TA th. 1, |-ni| obv., |-w| 3,0, |-ani| OBVsg])

(3.243) Lack of umlaut before |-w| sg.

netena̲wa 'I told her (obv.) {so}' (A 58C)

(|iN-| TA 'say {so} to', |ne–a̲·wa| 1s–3s/IND

[← |-a̲·-w-a| ← |-a·| TA th. 1, |-w| sg., |-a| ANsg])

The stem-final |a·| of some AI and II stems also undergoes umlaut to e· before |-w| 3,0, whether contiguous or non-contiguous:

(3.244) Umlaut of AI stem-final |a·| before |-w| 3,0

(a) *neši·ša̲pena* 'we (exc.) hunted' (JB-LR 14)

(|ši·ša̲·-| AI 'hunt', |ne–pena| 1p/IND)

(b) *ši·še̲wa* 'he hunted' (K-Med 58)

(|ši·ša̲·-| AI 'hunt', |–wa| 3s/IND [← |-w| 3,0, |-a| ANsg])

(c) *ši·še̲niwahi* 'they (obv.) hunted' (cf. K-FC 221)

(|ši·ša̲·-| AI 'hunt', |–niwahi| 3′p/IND [← |-ni| obv., |-w| 3,0, |-ahi| OBVsg])

(d) *pye·hiwaki* 'they (little ones) have come' (S-Apay 48)

(|pya·-| AI 'come' + |-·hi| dim. + |–waki| 3p/IND [← |-w| 3,0, |-aki| ANpl])

(3.245) Umlaut of II stem-final |a·| before |-w| 3,0

e·h=keta·ška̲ki 'it gushed out' (K-W 47)

(|keta·ška̲·-| II, |e·h—ki| 0/AOR)

wi·h=keta·ške̲wi 'it shall gush out' (K-W 829)

(|wi·h-| FUT, |keta·ška̲·-| II, |–wi| 0s/IND [← |-w| 3,0, |-i| INsg])

In other AI and II stems ending in |a·|, including all those with the finals |-ka·pa·| AI 'stand' and |-ya·| II ABSTR, this vowel does not undergo umlaut before |-w| 3,0:

(3.246) *nepwa·hka̲wa* 'he is smart, wise' (K-Wap 13)

wa·wa·ta·samika̲pa̲wa 'he stood face-to-face' (O 17B)

meša̲wi 'it is big' (K-ECRP 100)

po·hkya̲wi 'it has a hole in it' (K-GBuff 22)

Before the modal endings |-etoke| dub., |-ehapa| con., and |-epani| ast., |-w| 3,0 contracts with a preceding vowel, which is lengthened if short and umlauted if subject to umlaut:

(3.247) *ka·htosi̲toke* 'she seems to grieve' (A 167B)

(|ka·htosi-wetoke| ← |ka·htosi-| AI 'be sorrowful over loss', |-wetoke| 3s,0s/DUB

[← |-w| 3,0, |-etoke| dub.)

či˙nawe me˙toke 'she seems to be related to him' (A 167B)

(|či˙nawe˙m-| TA 'be related to', |–e˙toke| 3s–3´/DUB

[← |-e˙-w-etoke| ← |-a˙| TA th. 1, |-w| 3,0, |-etoke| dub.)

(3.248) *maneto˙wi˙hapa* 'what do you know, he has the nature of a manitou' (K-Wap 39)

(|maneto˙wi-wehapa| ← |maneto˙wi-| AI 'be a manitou', |–wehapa| 3s,0s/CON

[← |-w| 3,0, |-ehapa| con.)

(3.249) *wi˙teko wi˙pani* 'he does have the nature of an owl' (O 16D)

(|wi˙tekowi-wepani| ← |wi˙tekowi-| AI 'be an owl', |–wepani| 3s,0s/AST

[← |-w| 3,0, |-epani| ast.)

The suffix |-w| 3,0, if after a consonant, and the |w| of |-ekw| TA th. 2 contract with the |e| of the modal suffixes to |o˙| (§11.1, 1,125, 126).

The suffixes |-pena| 1p,12 and |-pwa| 2p lengthen the |a| before the modal suffixes, and the suffixes |-ena˙n| 1p,12 and |-wa˙w| 2p contract in the same environment, in the same way that the corresponding suffixes in noun inflection contract before |-eki| loc.: the non-first plural undergoes regular contraction, and the first plural matches it (cf. 3.105, 107 [with an historical note]).

(3.250) *neki˙wa˙ni˙pena˙toke* 'we (exc.) have probably made a mistake' (K-FC 183)

(|ki˙wa˙ni˙-| AI 'go astray, be lost', |ne–pena˙toke| 1p/DUB

[← |-pena˙-etoke| ← |-pena| 1p,12, |-etoke| dub.])

kepesetawipwa˙toke 'you (pl.) must have heard what I said' (K-FC 108)

(|pesetaw-| TA 'listen to', |ke–ipwa˙toke| 2p–1s/DUB

[← |-i-pwa˙-etoke| ← |-i| TA th. 3, |-pwa| 2p, |-etoke| dub.])

(3.251) *nene˙wokona˙toke* 'he must have seen us (exc.)' (K-SSP 147)

(|ne˙w-| TA 'see', |ne–ekona˙toke| 3s–1p/DUB

[← |-ekw-ena˙(n)-etoke| ← |-ekw| TA th. 2, |-ena˙n| 1p,12, |-etoke| dub.)

kekaka˙čihekowa˙toke 'he must have been playing a joke on you (pl.)' (K-W 103)

(|kaka˙čim-| TA 'play a joke on', |ke–ekowa˙toke| 3s–2p/DUB

[← |-ekw-wa˙w-etoke| ← |-ekw| TA th. 2, |-wa˙w| 2p, |-etoke| dub.)

The suffix |-pi| X loses the |i| before a modal suffix:

(3.252) *nesa˙petoke* 'he must have been killed' (K-PBLA 4)

(|neS-| TA 'kill', |–a˙petoke| X–3/DUB

[← |-a˙-pi-etoke| ← |-a˙| TA th. 1, |-pi| X, |-etoke| dub.])

Cf. *nesa˙pi* 'he was killed' (K-MLF 48).

(|neS-| TA 'kill', |–a˙pi| X–3/IND)

b) The conjunct central suffixes are those used in the endings of the core conjunct and interrogative modes. Some of them are also used in the prohibitive or potential sub-orders, or in both.

There are two distinct sets of conjunct central suffixes (3.253, next page): the AI suffixes, which are monovalent (indicating a single pronominal category), and the TA suffixes, which are specialized for use after specific theme signs and bivalent (indicating the pronominal category of both the subject and the object).

The AI suffixes are the default set, being used in all AI, II, and TI endings, and in some TA endings. On TA verbs they are the central suffixes used in the endings for inanimate subject (after |-ekwi| TA th. 2a); in the diminutive endings on theme 1 (after |-e˙hi| TA th. 1 dim.); in the inverse endings (after |-ekw| TA th. 2); and after themes 1, 3, and 4 in the cases where no bivalent TA suffix exists. When used after themes 3 and 4 to mark a first person acting on a

(3.253) Conjunct order: central suffix paradigms

subject	AI	TA th. 1	TA th. 3	TA th. 4
1s	|-aˑn| |-wak| rel.	|-ak| 1s–3		|-akoˑw| 1s–2p
2s	|-an|	|-at| 2s–3		
1p	|-aˑk|	|-aket| 1p–3		
12	|-akw|			
2p	|-eˑkw|			
3	|-t|, |-k|		|-amet| 3–1p	|-aˑkw| 3,X–2p
0	|-k|			
X	|-ek| |-wet| rel.	|-et| X–3	|-ˑnamek| X–1p	|-aˑkw| 3,X–2p

second person or the reverse, they are not strictly part of the central suffix paradigm, as they may mark either subject or object (3.198), as with the corresponding independent order suffixes (3.197b).

There are relational suffixes (§22.6) only for first singular and indefinite subjects in the AI set. These begin with \|w\|, which does not contract or cause replacement of a following \|e\| by o. Before this \|w\| connective \|o\| is inserted after a consonant. Of the two suffixes, \|-wet\| X rel. is far more common; \|-wak\| 1s rel. is only attested in some core conjunct modes. A relational suffix may be used on a TA verb if the suffix would otherwise be from the AI set, which is the case if it follows \|-i\| TA th. 3 or \|-ˑhi\| dim.

(3.254) Relational suffixes on TA verbs

(a) *iˑni=ye toke noˑsa a miˑ-'ši-=mekoho -menwi-toˑtawiweči.* (K-FC 349)
    'I suppose that for my father that would be kind treatment for me.'
      (*iˑni* 'that (inan.)'; *=ye toke* 'it seems'; *noˑsa* 'my father' [adjunct]; *a mi* PV POT,
      \|iši\| PV '{so}'; *=mekoho* EMPH; \|menwi\| PV 'well', \|toˑtaw-\| TA 'treat {so}',
      \|IC–iweči\| X–1s/REL/PPL(obl) [← \|-i\| TA th. 3, \|-wet\| X rel., \|-i\| conj.])

(b) *ihkwe wahi či nawe meˑhiwakihi meše ˑ='nah=mek=a pehe netakwimekwa.*
    (Anonymous letter written in 1923, copied in C-L 306)
    'She would go so far as to claim I was going with women that I was somewhat related to.'
      (*ihkwe wahi* 'women (obv.)'; \|činawem-\| TA 'be related to',
      \|IC–eˑhiwakihi\| 1s–3/DIM/REL/PPL(OBVpl)
      [← \|-eˑhi\| TA th. 1 dim. (for \|-aˑ\| TA th. 1 + \|-ˑhi\| dim.), \|-wak\| 1s rel., \|-ihi\| OBVpl];
      \|meše\| + \|iˑnahi\| P-P 'freely'; \|=meko\| EMPH; *=a pehe* 'always';
      \|takwim-\| TA 'put with {someone} by speech', \|ne–ekwa\| 3s–1s/IND)

A relational inflection is also attested for one TA indefinite-subject form.

(3.255) *'manetowa' e nema wa teˑhini* 'whoever (obv.) was called "manitou" ' (K-MortC 6)
    (*maneto wa* 'manitou'; \|iN-\| TA 'say {so} to', \|IC–emaˑwateˑhini\|
    X–3′/REL/INT.PPL(OBVsg) [← \|-em-aˑ-waˑt-eˑh-ini\| ← \|-em\| obv., \|-aˑ\| TA th. 1,
    \|-waˑt\| (for \|-w\| irr. + \|-wet\| X–3 rel. [3.226]), \|-eˑh\| (← \|eˑni\| int.), \|-ini\| OBVsg])

The ending in (3.255) is in effect marked as relational by the insertion of \|-waˑ\| after the \|-aˑ\| TA th. 1 in the usual, non-relational ending \|-emaˑteˑhini\| X–3′/INT.PPL(OBVsg) (K-Bene 72, S-YF 11), on the model of other indefinite-subject relational interrogative endings (AI \|+waˑteˑni\|, TI(1) \|+amowaˑteˑni\|), which have \|waˑ\| after the stem vowel or theme sign.

After any vowel, any conjunct central suffix that begins with an underlying vowel inserts |y| (**§10.1**), except that |-ek| X drops the |e| in this environment (**§10.3**, 1.117, 118). The suffix |-amet| 3–1p, which appears only after |-i| TA th. 3, is analyzed the same way. For third person animate, the suffix |-t| 3 is used only after a vowel and after |-ekw| TA th. 2 (|-ekw-t| → |-ekw-*e*-t| [**§8.2**, 1.82] → |-ekot| [**§11.1**]), while |-k| 3 (homophonous with |-k| 0) is used after a consonant-final stem (even when connective |e| is inserted; **§8.2**); after |-eN| TA th. 4 (with no |e| inserted; 1.107); and after |-w| irr. (with metathesis; **§9.2**; 3.220).

(3.256)   Conjunct order: variants of central suffixes after consonants and vowels

	after consonant	after vowel
1s	|-a·n|	|-ya·n|
2s	|-an|	|-yan|
1p	|-a·k|	|-ya·k|
12	|-akw|	|-yakw|
2p	|-e·kw|	|-ye·kw|
3	|-k|	|-t| (also after |-ekw| TA th. 2)
0	|-k|	|-k|
X	|-ek|	|-k|
3–1p	(citation form) |-amet|	|-yamet|

Retaining consonant stems add a stem-final |e| before any suffix that inserts |y| after a vowel and thus take the suffixes in the form used after vowels (3.258).

(3.257) AI vowel stem

   e·h=na·kwa ya·ni 'and I started out' (A 35H)

   (|na·kwa·-| AI 'leave', |e·h=—ya·ni| 1s/AOR)

(3.258) AI retaining consonant stem

   wi·h=nepeya·ni 'that I would die' (A 177D)

   (|wi·h=| FUT, |nep-| AI 'die', |e·h=—ya·ni| 1s/AOR)

(3.259) AI deleting consonant stem

   wi·h=šekišekišina·ni 'that I would lie around' (A 167D)

   (|wi·h=| FUT, |CVCV+| RED2, |šekišin-| AI 'lie', |e·h=—a·ni| 1s/AOR|)

Because the insertion of |y| is not strictly phonologically predictable, the underlying form of endings is given in either their post-vocalic or post-consonantal shape, as appropriate.

Despite the lack of complete phonological predictability, however, the selection of the suffixes in (3.256) is fundamentally governed by phonology rather than by the inflectional class of the stem. For example, the presence of a vowel-final suffix of position 4 selects a post-vocalic suffix of position 6, even after a consonant stem:

(3.260)   *e·h=šekišinitehe* 'where they (obv.) were lying' (K-FC 145)

   (|šekišin-| AI 'lie', |e·h=—nitehe| 3′/PPL(obl) [← |-ni| obv., |-t| 3, |-ehe| pret.])

   e·h=nana·hišinowa či 'they lay down' (K-FC 13) (← |e·h=nana·hišin-o-wa·či|

   ← |nana·hišin-| AI 'lie down', |e·h=—wa·či| 3p/AOR [← |-wa·| pl., |-t| 3, |i| conj.])

Conversely, a consonant-final suffix of position 5 selects a post-consonantal suffix of position 6 after a vowel stem:

(3.261)   *i·ni=meko išawihkani.* 'You (sg.) should do just that.' (O 104F)

   (*i·ni* 'that (inan.)'; *=meko* EMPH; |išawi-| AI 'do {so}', |—hkani| 2s/PROH

   [← |-hk| proh., |-an| 2s, |-i| conj.])

The |e| of |-et| X–3 is not subject to contraction with stems in |-Vw|; it fuses with |-Cw| to |-Co| (**§11.1**), and is replaced by |o| after the |w| of all stems ending in |-Vw| (**§11.7**, 1.170).

The suffixes |-t| (~ |-k|) 3, |-k| 0, |-amet| 3–1p, and |-·namek| X–1p combine irregularly with the position 5 suffix |-w| irr. (**§29.9(a)** 3.220; **§29.9(e)**, 3.232, 233, 234).

The suffixes |-k| 3 and |-ek| X are distinct after deleting consonant stems:

(3.262)   *a·kwi owiye·ha šekišik̲ini* 'no one lay down' (O 36A)

(*a·kwi* 'not'; *owiye·ha* 'anyone'; |šekišin-| AI 'lie', |–kini| 3s/NEG)

a·kwi nahi-wa·wa·čika·šinek̲ini 'one never lies with one's feet facing' (A 99E)

(*a·kwi* 'not'; *nahi* PV 'given to',

|wa·wa·čika·šin-| AI 'lie with feet facing (another's)', |–ekini| X/NEG)

Forms with these suffixes made on retaining consonant stems would be homophonous, but |-ek| X is unattested and apparently not used with such a stem.

In some prohibitive, potential, and injunctive endings a pronominal suffix of position 6 is followed by a combined pronoun and mode suffix of positions 6 and 7. In all such cases the second suffix is used for the third person (of either gender) but does not contain a segment that can be identified with any another third person suffix. Otherwise, the suffixes of position 6 are followed (except in the independent indicative) by a tense or mode suffix of position 7, a pronominal suffix of position 8, or both.

The first plural exclusive object suffixes |-amet| 3–1p and |-·namek| X–1p are treated irregularly before the combined suffixes |-sa| 3,0 pot. and |-ene·ha| X pot., respectively. The pattern of contrast between core conjunct |-t| 3 and potential |-sa| 3,0 pot. is replicated in |-i-y-amet| 3–1p and |–iyamesa| 3–1p pot., and the contrast between |-ek| X and |-ene·ha| X pot. is replicated in |-i-·namek| X–1p and |–i·namene·ha| X–1p pot.

(3.263)   *awita=mekoho ka·škehtawiyamesa* 'they would not be able to hear us' (K-FC 198)

(*awita* 'not (pot.)'; *=mekoho* EMPH; |ka·škehtaw-| TA 'hear', |–iyamesa| 3–1p/POT

[← |-i-y-amesa| 3–1p pot. ← |-i| TA th. 3, |-amet| 3–1p, |-sa| 3,0 pot.])

(3.264)   *taši-wačawača·hi·namene·ha* 'there would be someone to cook for us' (K-BLI 4)

(|CVCV+| RED2, |wača·h-| TA 'cook for', |–i·namene·ha| X–1p/POT

[← |-i| TA th. 3, |-·namek| X–1p, |-ene·ha| X pot.])

The suffix |-ako·w| 1s–2p has the peculiarity that it only occurs in the ending |+enako·we|, with |-eN| TA th. 4 and the default modal suffix |-i| conj. (here always *-e*). Contrasts of mode and of nominal category for participial heads cannot be indicated after this suffix (3.298, 299); the same ending is used in all functions, except that of the interrogative, which apparently lacks a form for this combination of pronominal arguments.

c) The combined pronoun and mode suffixes of positions 6 and 7 show sporadic patterns in small sets, but they are most conveniently treated as fused combinations.

(3.265) Selected conjunct suffixes of position 6 and combined suffixes of positions 6 and 7

	conjunct (6)	prohibitive (6+7)	potential (6+7)	imperative (6+7)
1s	|-a·n|	|-a|	|-a·ha|	
2s	|-an|		|-apa|	
2p	|-e·kw|	|-e·ko|		|-no|
				|-ko|
3	|-t|, |-k|		|-sa|	|-če|
0	|-k|		|-sa|	|-če|
X	|-ek|	|-i·ke|	|-ene·ha|	
X–3	|-et|	|-i·ke|	|-ene·ha|	
X rel.	|-wet|		|-wene·ha|	
1s–2p	|-ako·w|	|-a·wa|	|-a·wa·hi|, |-a·wa·ha|	

The potential suffixes |-a·ha| 1s and |-apa| 2s begin with the same vowels as the conjunct suffixes |-a·n| 1s and |-an| 2s; a suffix |-ha| might be identified in other potential endings, but |-a·wa·ha| 1s–2s pot. is apparently actually a younger variant of |-a·wa·hi|, and in any case a suffix |-pa| (in |-apa| 2s) would be unique. Subtraction of |-ha| or |-hi| from |-a·ha| 1s pot. and |-a·wa·hi|, |-a·wa·ha| 1s–2s pot., with regular word-final vowel shortening, yields the prohibitive endings |-a| 1s proh. and |-a·wa| 1s–2s proh. The |-wa·| in |-a·wa·hi|, |-a·wa·ha| 1s–2s pot. might be identified with the position 4 suffix |-wa·| 2p, but the order of the elements would be a problem and the residue would be isolated. Also, |-a·wa·ha| 1s–2p cannot be |-a·ha| 1s pot. combined with |-wa·| 2p if |-a·ha| is |-a·n| 1s plus a modal suffix |-ha|, since the |n| would not drop before |w|.

The prohibitive suffix |-e·ko| 2p proh. looks like a contamination of conjunct |-e·kw| by |-ko| 2p imp., a resemblance that might be captured by positing an imperative modal suffix |-o|, but the residues left after segmenting this |-o| from other endings do not recur.

A single three-part rule accounts for which pronominal suffix is used after the third or fourth theme sign in any ending that marks second person acting on first or the reverse in all the independent and conjunct modes and sub-orders: if the subject and object are both singular, the suffix marks the subject; if the subject or the object is plural and the other argument is singular, the suffix marks the argument that is plural; if both arguments are plural, the suffix marks the one that is first person (see also 3.312). This rule will account for the use of the various unique suffixes that appear in endings for first singular on second plural outside the independent order if these are taken to be monovalent second plural rather than bivalent suffixes (as in 3.265).

The four bivalent suffixes marking third person animate objects that are designated for use after the first TA theme sign in (3.253) are not found in prohibitive and potential endings. In these sub-orders an animate subject acting on a third person animate object is indicated with one of the same monovalent suffixes as in the AI and the TI, either a core conjunct AI suffix or a combined pronoun and mode suffix:

(3.266) Monovalent pronominal suffixes in prohibitive and potential TA direct endings

  (a) *nešiwana čihiye ̓kani* 'you (sg.) might ruin things for them' (A 33F)
        (|nešiwana·čih-| TA 'ruin', |–iye·kani| 2s–3/PROH
        [← |-iye·k| TA th. 1 proh., |-an| 2s, |-i| conj.])

  (b) *ka ̓ta kwi ̓natawi-išinawe ̓hiye ̓ka ̓ke.* 'don't let us make them feel uncertain' (O 114F)
        (*ka ̓ta* 'don't'; *kwi ̓natawi* PV 'at a loss', |išinawe·h-| TA 'make feel {so}',
        |–iye·ka·ke| 1p–3/PROH [← |-iye·k| TA th. 1 proh., |-a·k| 1p, |-i| conj.])

  (c) *awita=na ̓hka mehkawiye ̓ka ̓ha* 'I wouldn't find one again' (A 138A)
        (*awita* 'not (pot.)'; *na ̓hka* 'again'; |mehkaw-| TA 'find', |–iye·ka·ha| 1s–3/POT
        [← |-iye·k| TA th. 1 proh., |-a·ha| 1s pot.])

  (d) *wa ̓pamiye ̓kapa* 'you (sg.) should consider them' (A 139E)
        (|wa·pam-| TA 'look at', |–iye·kapa| 2s–3/POT
        [← |-iye·k| TA th. 1 proh., |-apa| 2s pot.])

The combined suffixes |-sa| 3,0 pot. and |-če| 3,0 imp. are used in the potential mode and in the injunctive forms of the imperative in an exactly parallel fashion. Neither suffix distinguishes gender or in fact even contains a segment that is otherwise found marking the third person categories. Uniquely, in |+enakosa| 3–12/POT and |+enakoče| 3–12/IMP they follow |-akw| 12, which is otherwise never followed by a suffix that has a pronominal reference. In the prohibitive, |-če| 3,0 imp. is used on a different pattern, following the modal suffix |-hk| proh. in precisely the endings that lack |-hk| proh. in the potential.

The imperative suffixes used in the TA do not match pronominal suffixes used elsewhere.

d) Some adjustments are made before certain combined suffixes of positions 6 and 7.

Potential |-sa| 3,0 and imperative (and prohibitive) |-če| 3,0 insert connective |e| after retaining consonant stems and the theme signs |-ekw| TA th. 2 (2.54) and |-eN| TA th. 4:

(3.267) *nepesa* 'he would die' (O 48F)

(|nep-*e*-sa| ← |nep-| AI 'die', |–sa| 3s,0/POT)

pema·mo·mikatesa 'it (inan.) would flee' (K-FC 159)

(|pema·mo·mikat-*e*-sa| ← |pema·mo·mikat-| II 'flee', |–sa| 3s,0/POT)

no·neče 'let him suckle' (Jones 1907:106.11)

(|no·N-*e*-če| ← |no·N-| AI 'suckle, nurse', |–če| 3s,0/IMP)

we·ta·paki=ʼna·nemateče. 'Let the wind blow to the east!' (C-Ston 31)

(*we·ta·paki* 'east'; |ina·nemat-| II 'wind to blow {so}', |–če| 3s,0/IMP)

wa·pameneče 'let them see you (sg.)' (K-WF 28)

(|wa·pam-| TA 'look at', |–eneče| 3–2s/IMP

[← |-eN-*e*-če| ← |-eN| TA th. 4, |-če| 3,0 imp.])

These suffixes do not insert a connective vowel after the |m| of |-am| TI(1) th. (3.201*df*) or the |n| of deleting consonant stems, which drop:

(3.268) *te·pišis̲a* 'he would have enough room to lie'

(← |te·pišin̲-sa| ← |te·pišin-| AI 'have room to lie', |–sa| 3s,0/POT)

menwikes̲a 'it would be good' (K-FC 371)

(← |menwiken̲-sa| ← |menwiken-| II 'be good', |–sa| 3s,0/POT)

manahka oteče̲. 'Let the wind blow from over that way!' (K-MMGW 3)

(*manahka* 'over yonder';

← |oten̲-če| ← |oten-| II 'wind to blow from {somewhere}', |–če| 3s,0/IMP)

After |-hk| proh., connective |i| is inserted before |-če| 3,0 imp. (3.228).

Imperative |-no| 2s inserts connective |e| after all consonants except the |m| of |-am| TI(1) th.; that |m| is dropped (3.201*e*) but the |n| of deleting consonant stems is retained:

(3.269) *šekišineno.* 'Lie down!' (A 110A)

(|šekišin-*e*-no| ← |šekišin-| AI 'lie down', |–no| 2s/IMP)

Connective |o| is inserted before |-ko| 2s imp. after all consonants:

(3.270) *ma·takwišinoko* 'lie covered up (you pl.)' (K-WLBS 20)

(|ma·takwišin-*o*-ko| ← |ma·takwišin-| AI 'lie covered', |–ko| 2p imp.)

wi·šikenamoko 'hold them firmly (you pl.)' (O 140A)

(|wi·šiken-| TI 'hold firmly', |–amo̲ko| 2p–0/IMP [← |-am| TI(1) th., |-ko| 2p imp.])

Following a TA stem the |e| of |-ehko| 2p–3 imp. fuses with |-Cw| to |-Co| (**§11.1**) and is replaced by |o| after the |w| of all stems ending in |-Vw| (**§11.7**, 1.172).

The texts attest three variants of the hortative suffix ('let's'). By far the most common is |-ta·we| 12 imp.; there are a few cases of |-ta·ne| 12 imp. in AI and TA endings, and two or three examples of |-ta·ke| 12 imp., all in AI verbs in texts by Kiyana. No consistent difference of meaning or distribution has been identified for these three variants. Before this suffix connective |e| is inserted after all stem-final consonants, and |-am| TI(1) th. is replaced by |-a·|:

(3.271) *tahka·šineta·we* 'let's cool ourselves in the breeze' (K-ECRP 108)

(|tahka·šin-*e*-ta·we| ← |tahka·šin-| AI 'be cooled by wind', |–ta·we| 12/IMP)

pemwa·ta·we 'let's shoot him' (JB-M 12)

(|pemw-| TA 'shoot (at)', |–a·ta·we| 12–3/IMP [← |-a·| TA th. 1, |-ta·we| 12 imp.])

mawa·pata·ta·we 'let's go see it' (K-ILM 25)

    (|mawa·pat-| TI(1) 'go to look at', |–a·ta·we| 12–0/IMP

    [← |-am| TI(1) th., |-ta·we| 12 imp.])

kemo·teta·ne ma·haki 'Let's steal these.' (LL-K 1)

    (|kemo·t-| AI+O 'steal O2', |–ta·ne| 12/IMP; *ma·haki* 'these (anim.)')

nepa·ta·ke 'Let's go to sleep.' (K-RYL 7, twice)

    (|nepa·-| AI 'sleep', |–ta·ke| 12/IMP)

Elicited forms indicate that |-ene·ha| X pot. has the shape *-ene·ha* after a deleting consonant stem, showing that underlying |e| is present in this suffix in the AI as well as the TA. This conforms to the general pattern whereby the pronominal suffixes used in potential endings are identical in the AI and TA direct. Hence |-am| TI(1) th, must be taken to have the variant *-a* not only before true consonants and word-finally but also irregularly before |-ene·ha| X pot. (3.201*h*).

When following a TA stem the |e| of |-ene·ha| X pot. fuses with |-Cw| to |-Co| (**§11.1**) and is replaced by |o| after the |w| of all stems ending in |-Vw| (**§11.7**).

29.11. Position 7. In position 7 are mode and tense suffixes used in the independent and conjunct orders. The three suffixes marking independent modes (|-etoke| dub., |-ehapa| con., |-epani| ast.), the suffix |-e·ni| int. that marks the interrogative mode, and archaically and rarely the preterite suffix |-ehe| pret. may be followed by a peripheral pronominal suffix of position 8; the resulting concatenations combine irregularly. The other three suffixes of position 7, those used in the core conjunct modes (|-i| conj., |-e| subj., |-ini| neg.-iter.), are never followed by any further suffix.

After the independent modal suffixes the only peripheral pronominal suffixes used are those for the non-obviative plurals, which have the variants beginning with |i| (|-iki| ANpl, |-ini| INpl). The corresponding singular suffixes do not appear after these modal suffixes. Nevertheless, the endings identical to those with |-iki| ANpl or |-ini| INpl except for lacking these plural suffixes are unambiguously indicated to be singular by not being marked as plural, and they show the same selection of objective suffixes (3.236) as in the corresponding plural and independent indicative endings, which have overt peripheral suffixes. The obviative peripheral pronominal suffixes are not used in these modes, and hence obviative singular and plural are not distinguished for animate subjects or objects. The inanimate plural suffix |-ini| INpl is attested only after the dubitative suffix |-etoke| dub. and is optional.

The dubitative and conclusive endings have the same structure; they are identical except for the difference in the modal suffixes. The assertive endings have different central pronominal suffixes in forms without a third person central argument; these are poorly attested but the central suffixes, at least, must have followed the same structural pattern as those of the other modes.

a) |-etoke| dub. marks the independent dubitative mode (**§26.2**). Before a peripheral pronominal suffix it has the underlying form |-etoke·h|. The |e| is subject to contraction (**§11.1**, 1.125; **§11.8**, 1.177; **§29.10**, 3.247; cf. 3.250, 251):

(3.272) *te·pwe·toke* 'she must have been right' (A 44D)

        (|te·pwe·-| AI 'speak the truth', |–wetoke| 3s/DUB

        [← |-w| 3,0, |-etoke| dub.])

      te·pesi·hi·toke·hiki 'they must be somewhat thankful' (O 123A)

        (|te·pesi·hi-| AI 'be grateful (dim.)', |–wetoke·hiki| 3p/DUB

        [← |-w-etoke·h-iki| ← |-w| 3,0, |-etoke| dub., |-iki| ANpl])

nešwa·šika taseno·toke·hini 'there must have been eight of them (inan.)' (C-SD 21)
    (*nešwa·šika* 'eight'; |tasen-| II 'be {so} many', |-wetoke·hini| 0p/DUB)
meše=ke·hi po·hkete·toke kehtawakayani (K-M 515g)
"probably .. and your ears will be opened by the heat" (tr. HP; edition: 'must have')
    (*meše* 'freely'; *=ke·hi* 'moreover';
    |po·hkete·-| II 'have hole made by heat', |−wetoke| 0/DUB;
    kehtawakayani 'your ears')
ča·kine·ni·toke omeso·ta·nahi. 'It seems both his parents had died.' (K-KK 1)
    (|ča·kine·-| AI 'all die', |−ni·toke| 3´/DUB [← |-ni| obv., |-w| 3,0, |-etoke| dub.];
    omeso·ta·nahi 'his parents (obv.)')

b) |-ehapa| con. marks the conclusive mode (**§26.3**). It has the underlying form |-ehapan|
before a peripheral pronominal suffix, which is only |-iki| ANpl in attested endings. The |e| is
subject to contraction (**§11.1**, 1.126; **§11.8**; **§29.10**, 3.248).

    (3.273)   *šihihwi·´, pe·hki=we·=meko ma·maya na·kwe·hapa.* (K-BHD2 53; tr. HP)
          "Oh my, but he certainly starts out early."
          (*šihihwi·´* (surprise); *pe·hki* 'really'; |=we·na| 'in fact'; *=meko* EMPH;
          ma·maya 'early'; |na·kwa·-| AI 'leave', |−wehapa| 3s,0s/CON)
    (3.274)   *we·nahi owiye·haki=mekoho tako·hapaniki* (K-M 763q)
          'It turns out there are some creatures, obviously.' (After the Flood.)
          (|we·nahi| 'I see now'; *owiye·haki* '(indefinite) creatures'; *=mekoho* EMPH;
          |tako-| AI,II 'exist ({somewhere})', |−wehapaniki| 3p/CON)
    (3.275)   *we·nah=sanakato·hapa ayo·hi.* (K-Wap 36; tr. TB)
          "It certainly does seem to be very hard down here."
          (|we·nahi| 'I see now'; |sanakat-| II 'be difficult', |−wehapa| 3s,0s/CON)
    (3.276)   *ši·´, we·nah=ma·hiya na·mahkwamye·sahe·hapa nekwisani.* (SP-SFT 68)
          'Gee, it looks like she shoved my son under the ice!'
          (*ši·´* (sudden thought); |we·nahi| 'I see now'; *ma·hiya* 'that one (going away)';
          |na·mahkwamye·sah-| TA 'shove under the ice', |−e·hapa| 3s–3´/CON;
          nekwisani 'my son (obv.)')
    (3.277)   *šehehye·´, ki·h=ča·kihekona·hapaniki.* (JB-Meshq 5)
          'Oh dear! Now they'll kill us all!'
          (*šehehye·´* (realization of problem); |wi·h=| FUT, |ča·kih-| TA 'kill all of',
          |ke–ekona·hapaniki| 3p–12/CON [for |-ena·| ← |-ena·n| 1p,12, see 3.251)])

In forms in which the |e| would not be removed by contraction or elision, one speaker assimilates
it to the following |a| (1.114); these forms are described as having the variant |-ahapa| con., which
is not attested before a peripheral suffix:
    (3.278)   *we·nah=pe·hki=we·=meko keketemaheko·pahapa.* (C-Hist 33)
          'But I've learned to my surprise that you are in fact seriously mistreated.'
          (|we·nahi| 'I see now'; *pe·hki* 'really'; |=we·na| 'in fact'; *=meko* EMPH;
          |ketemah-| TA 'mistreat', |ke–eko·pahapa| X–2s/CON
          [|+eko·pahapa| ← |-ekw-*e*-p-ahapa| ← |-ekw| TA th. 2, |-pi| X, |-ahapa| con.])

c) |-epani| ast. marks the assertive mode (**§26.4**). When followed by a peripheral pronominal
suffix (only |-iki| ANpl is attested) one of the |i|'s drops.
    (3.279)   *maneto·we·hi·pani* 'he sure is a little spirit' (S-Apay 48, 49)
          (|maneto·we·hi-| AI 'be a manitou (dim.)', |−wepani| 3s,0s/AST)

(3.280) *kiši-na wahkwe nikini tanahkye paniki.* (K-BHD 76; song)
  'In the afternoons they graze.'
  (*kiši* PV PERF, |na·wahkwe·-| II 'be noon', |IC–nikini| 0´/ITER;
  |tanahkye·-| AI 'graze', |–wepaniki| 3p/AST [← |-w| 3,0, -epani| ast., |-iki| ANpl])

(3.281) *sanakato pani* 'it sure is hard' (K-OWM 5; JP-YMPE 90)
  (|sanakat-| II 'be difficult', |–wepani| 3s,0s/AST)

Only two assertive endings are attested that do not mark third person intransitives. The vowel lengths are conjectured on the basis of comparative evidence.

(3.282) *i ni=ma·h=nesina pani.* 'See, I told you so!' (C-RS 18)
  (*i ni* 'that (inan.)'; *=ma·hi* 'you see'; |i-| AI 'say {so}' [here |si-| (3.145)],
  |ne–na·pani| 1s/AST [+na·pani| sg. ast. ← |-na·| sg. ast., -epani| ast.])

(3.283) *i ni=ma·h=ki na ketenena wa pani wi·h=anemi-to·to nakwe.* (C-WH 17)
  'See, I told you that's what he would do to us.'
  (*i ni* 'that (inan.)'; *=ma·hi* 'you see'; *ki na* EMPH (*lit.* 'you (sg.)');
  |iN-| 'say {so} to' (here deleted [3.197]), |ke–enena wa pani| 1s–2p/AST)
  [← |-eN-e-na wa·-epani| ← |-eN| TA th. 4, |-na·wa·| 2p ast., |-epani| ast.])

d) |-e·ni| int. marks the interrogative modes (§26.14-17). It may be followed only by a peripheral pronominal suffix. It takes the shape |-e·n| before |-a| ANsg, giving *-e na* (3.219, 220, 224, 233), and it has the shape |-e·h| before the two-syllable suffixes, which have the variants that begin with |i| (|-iki| ANpl, |-ini| INpl, |-ini| OBVsg, |-ihi| OBVpl; 3.286, 287, 303, 326).

All the peripheral pronominal suffixes are used to mark the heads of interrogative participles, but in contrast to the pattern in the core conjunct modes, the animate plural suffix is also used in the other interrogative modes to mark the central argument.

(3.284) *we nahi·='niya te pwe kwe ni* 'I see now that he must have been right' (O 59C)
  (|we·nahi| 'I see now'; |i·niya| 'that (anim. abs.);
  |te·pwe·-| AI 'speak the truth', |–kwe·ni| 3s,0/INT)

(3.285) *wi·h=nepo·hikwe na* 'whoever is going to die' (O 41D)
  (|wi·h=| FUT, |nepo·hi-| AI 'die (dim.)', |IC–kwe·na| 3s/INT.PPL(ANsg))

(3.286) *nehki=mekoho e nemi-mehtose neniwikwe·hiki* (O 96B)
  'for however long they go on living'
  (*nehki* 'for {so} long'; *=mekoho* EMPH; *anemi* PV 'go on',
  |mehtose·neniwi-| AI 'live', |IC–kwe·hiki| 3p/INT.PPL(obl))

(3.287) *na·hina·h=mekoho e·h=nepokwe·hiki* 'whenever they may die' (K-FC 497)
  (*na·hina·hi* 'time'; *=mekoho* EMPH; |nep-| AI 'die', |e·h–kwe·hiki| 3p/AOR.INT)

In interrogative endings outside of the participle, an animate plural subject is not distinguished from a singular subject if it is not marked in the corresponding conjunct ending; in other words, if the object is second person or first plural, the same ending is used for both singular and plural third person animate subjects.

The inanimate plural suffix |-ini| INpl is rare and, apparently, optional:

(3.288) *ni na=wi na a·kwi kehke netama nini i nini i ni e šitehka te·kwe·hini.* (K-FC 89)
  'I myself do not know what the things may be that are called that.'
  (*ni na* 1s/EMPH; *=wi na* 'but'; *a·kwi* 'not'; |kehke·net-| TI(1) 'know',
  |–ama·nini| 1s–0/NEG; *i nini* 'those (inan.)'; *i ni* 'that (inan.)';
  |išitehka·te·-| II 'be named {so}'; |IC–kwe·hini| 0/INT.PPL(INpl))

(3.289)　*e·h=pwa·wi-nenohtaki 'ši·ši·kwanani' e·tamowa·te·ni.* (K-B 166)
　　　　'He didn't understand what might be called "gourds".'
　　　　(|pwa·wi| PV 'not', |nenoht-| TI(1) 'understand', |e·h=–aki| 3s–0/AOR;
　　　　ši·ši·kwanani 'gourds';
　　　　|it-| TI(1) 'say {so} to, call {so}', |IC–amowa·te·ni| X–0/REL/INT.PPL)

Because |-ini| INpl appears to be optional and |-i| INsg would be undetectable after |-e·ni| int. (assuming the same treatment as |-a| ANsg), interrogative participles ending in *-e·ni* are not analyzed as marking the head with a peripheral suffix. The head is taken rather as unmarked, with a default interpretation appropriate to the stem, which may be singular, plural, or oblique.

(3.290)　*i·ni pe·pikwe·škowikwe·ni* 'the whistle, whatever that may be' (O 102E)
　　　　(*i·ni* 'that (inan.)';
　　　　|pepikwe·škowi-| II 'be a whistle', |IC–kwe·ni| 3s,0/INT.PPL)

In fact, this analysis is required for interrogative participles with inanimate or oblique heads that cannot be indexed overtly because of the presence of the peripheral suffix |-iki| ANpl pluralizing the central argument (3.286), and also for those construed with obviative heads but without an obviative peripheral suffix (3.305). These unexpressed heads may be noted in the analysis of endings as "(IN)," "(obl)," "(loc.obl)," or "(OBV)" to make the gloss explicit, but these notations do not correspond to any overt morpheme in these cases.

Occasionally, and not rarely with some speakers, interrogative forms are found with *-e* (as if |-e| subj.) for *-e·ni* (expected from |-e·ni| int.):

(3.291)　*e·h=tanwe·taminikwe* 'wherever the voice was coming from' (C-Ston 1)
　　　　(|tanwe·t-| TI(1)-O 'make vocal sound {somewhere}',
　　　　|e·h=–aminikwe| [for |e·h=–aminikwe·ni|] 3´/INT.PPL, functioning as (loc.obl))

e) |-ehe| pret. has two functions. It marks the preterite counterparts of most of the core conjunct modes (§26.25), and it marks potential endings that have |-hk| proh. followed by a first or second plural core conjunct central suffix, distinguishing them from the corresponding prohibitive endings. After a suffix ending in |-kw|, |-ehe| pret. has the underlying variant |-eha|, with regular contraction to |-koha|.

(3.292)　*i·ni wi·h=išawiyakoha.* 'That's what would have happened to us (inc.)' (K-FC 532)
　　　　(*i·ni* 'that (inan.)'; |wi·h=| FUT, |išawi-| AI 'do, fare {so}',
　　　　|IC–yakoha| 12/PRET.PPL(obl) [← |-y-akw-eha| ← |-akw| 12, |-ehe| pret.])

(3.293)　*i·ni=mekoho išawihkakoha* 'we (inc.) could have done that' (K-FC 569)
　　　　(*i·ni* 'that (inan.)'; *=mekoho* EMPH; |išawi-| AI 'do, fare {so}',
　　　　|–hkakoha| 12/POT [← |-hk-akw-eha| ← |-hk| proh., |-akw| 12, |-ehe| pret.])

The modal suffixes that differentiate the core conjunct modes cannot follow the preterite suffix, and the modal contrasts are correspondingly reduced. Except for two rare and archaic forms, the peripheral pronominal suffixes are also excluded from appearing after |-ehe| pret., but although the nominal categories of the heads of preterite participles are not formally differentiated, these participles may function as having a head with any categories of gender, number, and obviation.

In the two attested preterite participles that have peripheral suffixes, |-ehe| pret. occurs as |-ehepan|, and the peripheral suffixes take the shape |-iye·ne| OBVpl and |-iye·ne| INpl (the vowel lengths are conjectured), resembling the absentative demonstrative *i·niye·ne* 'that (obv., abs.); those (inan. abs.)'.

(3.294) *i·nini wi·h=penonitehepaniye·ne* (K-WLB 11)

'the one (obv.) who was going to go home'

(*i·nini* 'that (obv.)'; |wi·h=| FUT, |peno-| AI 'go home',

|-nitehepaniye·ne| 3'/PRET.PPL(OBVsg)

[|-ni-t-ehepan-iye·ne| ← |-ni| obv., |-t| 3, |-ehe| pret., |-ini| OBVsg])

(3.295) *ki·šiseto·čini wi·h=pye·to·tehepaniye·ne* (K-BHD 125)

'the things she had set out that she was going to bring'

(|ki·šiset-| TI(2) 'finish setting', |IC–o·čini| 3s–0/PPL(INpl);

|wi·h=| FUT, |pye·t-| TI(2) 'bring', |IC–o·tehepaniye·ne| 3s–0/PRET.PPL(INpl)

[|-o·-t-ehepan-iye·ne| ← |-o·| TI(2) th., |-t| 3, |-ehe| pret., |-ini| INpl])

f) |-i| conj. is the default modal suffix after the central pronominal suffixes in the conjunct order. It marks the plain conjunct, aorist conjunct, and changed conjunct modes (**§26.7, 8, 10**). It is also used after the core conjunct pronominal suffixes with no modal function when they are used in the prohibitive and potential sub-orders. No suffix ever follows it. It takes the shape *-e* after |-a·k| 1p, |-akw| 12, |-e·kw| 2p, |-ako·w| 1s–2p, and |-a·kw| 3,X–2p (2.8, 95, 176, 199, 291, 325, 327, 328; 3.188, 198, 264). The endings with *-e* for |-i| conj. are homophonous with the corresponding subjunctive endings that have underlying |-e| subj. The endings with |-i| conj. in either surface shape are homophonous with the corresponding participial endings that contain |-i| INsg.

Before |-i| conj., |t| undergoes mutation to *č* (**§13.1**, 1.200; 3.200*a*, 206, 213).

g) |-e| subj. marks the subjunctive (**§26.9**) and both prioritive modes (**§26.18**). It is always realized as a word-final *-e*.

(3.296) *ki·šikiyane* 'when you grow up' (A 27D)

(|ki·šiki-| AI 'grow up', |–yane| 2s/SUBJ [|-y-an-e| ← |-an| 2s, |-e| subj.])

(3.297) *i·ya·h=meko me·h-pya·wane* 'before you get there' (K-BBWM 44)

(*i·ya·hi* 'yonder'; =*meko* EMPH; |me·hi| PV 'yet',

|pya·-| AI 'come {somewhere}'; |–wane| 2s/PRI [← |-w| irr., |-an| 2s, |-e| subj.])

h) |-ini| neg.-iter. marks the negative mode (**§26.11**) and the iterative mode (**§26.12**). It is always a word-final *-ini*, except that it is replaced by |-i| conj. after |-ako·w| 1s–2p.

(3.298) '..., ' *a·kwi wi·h=inenako·we* 'I will not tell you (pl.), "..." ' (O 99G, 100B)

(*a·kwi* 'not'; |wi·h=| FUT, |iN-| 'say {so} to', |–enako·we| 1s–2p/NEG

[← |-eN| TA th. 4, |-ako·w| 1s–2p, |-i| conj.])

(3.299) *ne·wonako·we* "when ever I see you [pl.]" (K-OKUT 31; tr. HP)

(|ne·w-| TA 'see', |IC–enako·we| 1s–2p/ITER)

A preceding |t| undergoes mutation to *č* (**§13.1**, 1.201).

29.12. Position 8. In position 8 are the peripheral pronominal suffixes, which mark nominal categories (**§18.2**). In the independent indicative the two-syllable suffixes have the variants that begin with |a| (|-aki| ANpl, |-ani| INpl, |-ani| OBVsg, |-ahi| OBVpl); the |a| contracts with a preceding post-consonantal |w| (**§11.2**, 1.133). In all other cases they have the variants that begin with |i| (|-iki| ANpl, |-ini| INpl, |-ini| OBVsg, |-ihi| OBVpl).

There is also a vocative suffix |-e| VOC, used on singular and plural second person participles (**§23**, 2.147, 219; **§28.19**, 3.131-134), which has the same shape as |-e| VOCsg, the vocative singular suffix used on nouns. The head of a vocative participle may be either the subject or the object.

The suffix |-i| INsg has the shape *-e* following the suffixes after which |-i| conj. is *-e* (**§29.11(f)**). After |-ehe|, in the shape |-ehepan|, |-ini| INpl and |-ini| OBVsg are realized as *-iye ne* (**§29.11(e)**, 3.294, 295), the other suffixes being unattested.

A peripheral pronominal suffix, outside of participles, gives information about either a central argument or a peripheral argument. In some transitive forms it marks a peripheral argument, distinct from the central argument that is marked by the central suffixes of position 6 (3.300*ab*).

(3.300) Peripheral suffix |-aki| ANpl marking peripheral argument

(a) *kekosa·waki* 'you (sg.) were afraid of them' (A 79D)
(|koS-| TA 'fear', |ke–a·waki| 2s–3p/IN
[← |ke+| 2, |-a·| TA th. 1, |-w| sg., |-aki| ANpl])

(b) *kekehke·nemekona·naki* 'they know about us (inc.)' (K-FC 538)
(|kehke·nem-| TA 'know', |ke–ekona·naki| 3p–12/IND
[← |ke+| 2, |-ekw| TA th. 2, |-ena·n| 1p,12, |-aki| ANpl])

In (3.300*a*) the suffix |-aki| ANpl marks the object, while in (3.300*b*) the same suffix marks the subject. The contrast in the theme signs accounts for this difference in syntactic role.

In other transitive forms and all intransitive forms a peripheral suffix specifies categories of the central argument, which is also marked by the central ending (3.301*abc*).

(3.301) Peripheral suffix |-aki| ANpl specifying central argument

(a) *mya·hkose·waki* 'they limped' (O 47B)
(|mya·hkose·-| AI 'limp', |–waki| 3p/IND [← |-w| 3,0, |-aki| ANpl])

(b) *kehke·neme·waki* 'they know him' (K-FC 232)
(|kehke·nem-| TA 'know', |–e·waki| 3p–3´/IND
[← |-a·| TA th. 1, |-w| 3,0, |-aki| ANpl])

(c) *neškinamo·ki* 'they hate it' (A 34A)
(|neškin-| TI(1) 'hate', |–amo·ki| 3p–0/IND
[← |-am| TI(1) th., |-w| 3,0, |-aki| ANpl])

In (3.301*abc*) |-aki| ANpl specifies as animate plural the argument marked by the central suffix |-w| 3,0, which does not distinguish number or gender. The central argument is an intransitive subject in (3.301*a*) and a transitive subject in (3.301*bc*). In a form with |-w| 3,0 after the inverse theme sign |-ekw| TA th. 2, the peripheral suffix specifies a transitive object (3.238).

In participles the peripheral suffix specifies the nominal categories of the head, which may or may not be one of the arguments of the verb on which it is marked and may, in fact, be any noun or pronoun in the clause or a subordinate clause. The range of the possible syntactic roles of the heads of participles is illustrated in **§26.13**; the basic patterns of marking subjects and objects as heads are exemplified with the four two-syllable suffixes in (3.302-304).

(3.302) Peripheral suffix |-iki| ANpl specifying head of participle

(a) *me·hkwa·tesičiki* 'quiet ones' (A 131C)
(|mahkwa·tesi-| AI 'be quiet', |IC–čiki| 3/PPL(ANpl) [← |-t| 3, |-iki| ANpl])

(b) *či·nawe·ma·čiki* 'those related to him (obv.); his (obv.) relatives (prox.)' (A 93D)
(|či·nawe·m-| TA 'be related to', |IC–a·čiki| 3–3´/PPL(ANpl)
[← |-a·-t-iki| ← |-a·| TA th. 1, |-t| 3, |-iki| ANpl])

(c) *ke·teminа·kočiki* 'those they (obv.) blessed, those blessed by them (obv.)' (K-FC 407)
(|keteminaw-| TA 'bless', |IC–ekočiki| 3´–3/PPL(ANpl)
[← |-ekw-e-t-iki| ← |-ekw| TA th. 2, |-t| 3, |-iki| ANpl])

(d)   *či nawe makiki* 'those I am related to; my relatives' (A 152A)

　　　(|či·nawe·m-| TA 'be related to', |IC–akiki| 1s–3/PPL(ANpl)

　　　[← |-∅-ak-iki| ← |-∅| TA th. 1, |-ak| 1s, |-iki| ANpl])

(e)   *me nwe nema we kwe hiki* 'whatever ones you (pl.) like' (K-FC 527)

　　　(|menwe·nem-| TA 'like', |IC–a·we·kwe·hiki| 2p–3/INT.PPL(ANpl)

　　　[← |-a·| TA th. 1, |-w| irr., |-e·kw| 2p, |-e·ni| int., |-iki| ANpl])

In (3.302) the suffix |-iki| ANpl marks heads which are intransitive subjects (3.302a), transitive subjects (3.302b), and primary objects (3.302cde).

(3.303)   Peripheral suffixes |-ini| OBVsg and |-ihi| OBVpl specifying head of participle

(a)   *ne sapiničini* 'the one (obv.) who stayed home' (O 17B)

　　　(|nesapi-| AI 'stay home', |IC–ničini| 3´/PPL(OBVsg))

(b)   *či nawe ma čini* 'the one (obv.) he's related to; his (prox.) relative (obv.)' (K-FC 443)

　　　(|či·nawe·m-| TA 'be related to', |IC–ačini| 3s–3´/PPL(OBVsg)

　　　[← |-a·-t-ini| ← |-a·| TA th. 1, |-t| 3, |-ini| OBVsg])

(c)   *či nawe ma čihi* 'the ones (obv.) he's related to; his relatives (obv.)' (K-Kin 59)

　　　(|či·nawe·m-| TA 'be related to', |IC–ačihi| 3s–3´/PPL(OBVpl) [cf. |-ihi| OBVpl])

(d)   *ke temina kočini* 'the one (obv.) who blessed him (prox.)' (A 34A)

　　　(|keteminaw-| TA 'bless', |IC–ekočini| 3´–3s/PPL(OBVsg))

(e)   *'pene sa' e nema te hini* 'whoever (obv.) was called Penesa' (K-Bene 72)

　　　(*pene sa* [a name]; |iN-| TA 'say {so} to', |IC–ema·te·hini| X–3´/INT.PPL(OBVsg)

　　　[← |-em| obv., |-a·| TA th. 1, |-w| irr., |-et| X–3, |-e·ni| int., |-ini| OBVsg])

(f)   *ne kato kaše hahi e nema te hihi* 'what creatures (obv.) were called horses' (S-YF 11)

　　　(*ne kato kaše hahi* 'horses (obv.)';

　　　|iN-| TA 'say {so} to', |IC–ema·te·hihi| X–3´/INT.PPL(OBVpl) [cf. |-ihi| OBVpl])

In (3.303a) and (3.303d) |-ini| OBVsg marks the subject as the head, and in (3.303b) and (3.303e) it marks the object as the head; in (3.303c) and (3.303f) |-ihi| marks the object as head.

(3.304) Peripheral suffix |-ini| INpl specifying head of participle

(a)   *e škikekini* 'new ones (inan.)' (A 178H)

　　　(|aškiken-| II 'be new', |IC–kini| 0/PPL(INpl) [← |-k| 0, |-ini| INpl])

(b)   *e yo wa čini* 'the ones (inan.) they sing (*lit.*, use)' (O 37D)

　　　(|ayo·-| TI(3) 'use', |IC–wa·čini| 3p–0/PPL(INpl) [← |-wa·| pl., |-t| 3, |-ini| INpl])

(c)   *wi h=mi nakini* 'the ones (inan.) that I will give him' (K-GB 16)

　　　(|wi·h=| FUT, |mi·N-| TA 'give O2 to', |IC–akini| 1s–3/PPL(INpl)

　　　[← |-ak| 1s–3, |-ini| INpl])

(d)   *e ši-neškimikini* 'the things I had been forbidden to do' (A 8F)

　　　(|iši| PA '{so}', |neškim-| TA 'forbid', |IC–ikini| X–12/PPL(obl.pl)

　　　[← |-i| TA th. 3, |-ek| X, |-ini| INpl])

(e)   *e h=owi kiwa čini* 'in the (lodges) where they live' (O 136A)

　　　(|owi·ki-| AI 'dwell {somewhere}', |e·h=–wa·čini| 3p/PPL(loc.obl.pl))

The participial head marked by |-ini| INpl is the subject in (3.304a), the primary object in (3.304b), the secondary object in (3.304c), and different kinds of obliques in (3.304de).

Interrogative participles sometimes lack the peripheral suffix for an obviative (3.305 [cf. 3.183] or inanimate (3.289) head.

(3.305)   *we wiye hinikwe ni* 'an unidentified creature (obv.)' (C-O 12, X6-MM 7)

　　　(|owiye·hi-| AI 'be someone, some animal', |IC–nikwe·ni| 3´/INT.PPL)

29.13. Umlaut of |e·| in AI participles. In AI conjunct participles a stem-final |e·| undergoes umlaut to |a·| if the head is the subject (2.176, 218*a*; 3.167*a*, 181, 306-308) or the possessor of the subject (3.309). This umlaut is found with second person subjects in vocative participles (3.131).

> (3.306) *e·skepya·ta* '(one) that drowned' (A 102C)
>
> (← |aškepye·-| AI 'drown', |IC–ta| 3/PPL(ANsg) [← |-t| 3, |-a| ANsg])

> (3.307) *ke·kye·pi·kwa·čiki* '(ones) who were blind' (O 112B)
>
> (|kekye·pi·kwe·-| AI 'be blind', |IC–čiki| 3/PPL(ANpl))

> (3.308) *e·ša·ha·towa·ničini* '(one, obv.) who spoke Sioux' (O 155E)
>
> (← |aša·ha·towe·-| AI 'speak Sioux', |IC–ničini| 3´/PPL(OBVsg))

> (3.309) *i·niki=ke·hi a·pi-maya·wosa·ničiki ošise·hwa·wani* (K-MWL 44)
>
> 'and those whose uncle (obv.) had been the leader of the warparty'
>
> (*i·niki* 'those (anim.)'; =*ke·hi* 'moreover'; |a·pi| PV 'have gone and', |maya·wose·-| AI 'lead a warparty', |IC–ničiki| 3´/PPL(ANpl); *ošise·hwa·wani* 'their mother's brother, mother's brother's son (obv.)')

A stem-final |e·| undergoes this umlaut even if followed by |-·hi| dim.:

> (3.310) *a·hkwa·hita* 'those who were a little angry (representative singular)' (K-FC 677)
>
> (|a·hkwe·-| AI 'be angry', |-·hi| dim., |IC–ta| 3/PPL(ANsg))

The |e·| in a sequence |-e·hi| does not undergo umlaut, however, if it is not the final vowel of a corresponding non-diminutive stem but, for example, a replacement of AI stem-final |i| before |-·hi| dim. (§50.1; 3.311) or the |e·| in |-e·hi| TA th. 1 dim. (← |-a·| TA th. 1 + |-·hi| dim.) (3.192*b*).

> (3.311) *če·keši·he·hita* '(one, anim.) that is small' (A 23B)
>
> (|čakeši·he·hi-| AI 'be small (dim.)' [← |čakeši·hi-| AI 'be small' + |-·hi| dim.], |IC–ta| 3/PPL(ANsg))

This umlaut does not occur in interrogative participles (3.212*b*).

VERB INFLECTION: MODES AND PARADIGMS (§30)

27. In the following sections the inflection for each verbal mode is described, illustrated by complete or partial paradigms. The paradigms are constructed using the verbs *penowa* 'he goes home' (|peno-| AI), *ahte·wi* 'it is ({somewhere})' (|ahte·-| II), *pakame·wa* 'he hits him' (|pakam-| TA), and *pakatamwa* 'he hits it' (|pakat-| TI(1)). Distinct inflections with consonant-final intransitive stems are illustrated with *nepwa* 'he dies' (|nep-| AI), *šekišinwa* 'he lies {somewhere}' (|šekišin-| AI), *we·wenetwi* 'it is good' (|we·wenet-| II), and *wi·kanwi* 'it tastes good' (|wi·kan-| II).

Independent Order

30.1. General features. The suffixes used in the verbal inflections of the modes of the independent order are: |-em| obv. (position 1; §29.6), but only with an indefinite subject; the theme signs (position 2; §29.7), with |-ekw| TA th. 2 prioritized over |-i| TA th. 3 and |-eN| TA th. 4 (§29.7(e)); |-ni| obv. (position 3; §29.8(a)); the independent order central pronominal suffixes (position 6; §29.10(a)); the independent order modal suffixes (position 7; §29.11(a-c)); and the peripheral pronominal suffixes (position 8; §29.12) (3.186).

AI, II, and TI verbs mark a central argument using the absolute paradigm (3.236), except in the assertive mode, which has its own central suffixes. The central argument is the subject. All persons in the paradigm have an absolute pronominal suffix, and the first and second persons have a pronominal prefix. In the third person endings, in addition to the central suffix |-w| 3,0, there is a peripheral pronominal suffix that differentiates the third person categories, and |-ni| obv. marks an obviative of either gender.

TI(1) and TI(2) verbs have a theme sign in addition to the inflection for the central argument, but TI(3) verbs do not. Except for these two theme signs, TI verbs have no inflection for the object, which is hence undifferentiated for number, but they make unambiguous pronominal reference to an object (except for stems specified lexically as objectless; §22.3). TI(3) stems and TI(2) themes (the stems plus |-o·| TI(2) th.) are inflected exactly like AI stems. (TI(3) stems differ from AI+O stems paradigmatically in being paired with TA stems.)

TA verbs mark arguments in several ways:

(1) Third person and indefinite central arguments are marked as in the AI. The absolute central suffixes are used (|-w| 3,0 and |-pi| X), and a third person is further specified by the peripheral suffixes and, where appropriate, |-ni| obv. The absolute suffix indicates the subject in direct forms (those with |-a·| TA th. 1) and the object in inverse forms (those with |-ekw| TA th. 2 or |-ekwi| TA th. 2a), except in the indefinite-subject forms with first or second singular objects, which have |-pi| X instead of |-p| sg. TA endings with these central suffixes make pronominal reference to a peripheral argument but have no inflection for it, except that an obviative object with an indefinite subject is marked by |-em| obv.

(2) A peripheral argument (which is always third person) is marked by a peripheral pronominal suffix in non-diminutive direct forms of the indicative mode with a first or second singular central argument as subject, and in inverse forms having a first or second person (singular or plural) central argument as object. The peripheral suffix indicates the object in the direct forms and the subject in the inverse forms.

(3) A first or second person central argument is marked by an objective inflection (prefix plus objective central suffix) if there is a peripheral suffix and by an absolute inflection if there is no peripheral suffix. The central inflection indicates the subject in the direct forms and the object in the inverse forms.

(4) The forms for second person acting on first and for first acting on second use the prefix |ke+| 2 and an absolute central suffix, but these do not form a morphological constituent. The central ending is selected according to a rule of prioritization that applies also to the corresponding forms in the conjunct order. (Another way of stating this is in §29.10(c).)

(3.312) Selection of the central suffix in forms with both first and second person arguments

      1) If both are plural: First plural rather than second plural

      2) If one is plural: Plural rather than singular

      3) If both are singular: Subject rather than object

(The third term of the prioritization rule in (3.312) is not germane to the independent order, where both first singular and second singular are marked by |-∅|, |-p| sg., but it applies in the conjunct order (3.199).) Regardless of the person marked by the central suffix (following 3.312) and the universal presence of |ke+| 2, in forms with |-i| TA th. 3 the second person is the subject and the first person the object, and with |-eN| TA th. 4 the first person is the subject and the second person is the object.

30.2. Independent indicative. The independent indicative (§26.1) uses the full set of independent order inflections (§29) with no modal suffix. The diminutive paradigm differs from the non-diminutive paradigm in that the TA direct forms with a first or second singular central argument as subject do not have a peripheral pronominal suffix and hence use the absolute central suffix.

(3.313) Independent indicative paradigm

subject	AI and II	TI(1)	TA direct
1s	nepeno nešekišine	nepakata 1s–0	nepakama wa 1s–3s nepakama waki 1s–3p nepakame ·hi 1s–3 dim.
2s	kepeno kenepe kešekišine	kepakata 2s–0	kepakama wa 2s–3s kepakama waki 2s–3p kepakame ·hi 2s–3 dim.
1p	nepenopena nešekišinepena	nepakata pena 1p–0	nepakama pena 1p–3
12	kepenopena kešekišinepena	kepakata pena 12–0	kepakama pena 12–3
2p	kepenopwa kešekišinepwa	kepakata pwa 2p–0	kepakama pwa 2p–3
3s	penowa nepwa šekišinwa	pakatamwa 3s–0	pakame wa 3s–3´
3p	penowaki nepo ·ki šekišino ·ki	pakatamo ·ki 3p–0	pakame waki 3p–3´
3´s	penoniwani, šekišiniwani	pakataminiwani 3´s–0	pakame niwani 3´s–3´´
3´p	penoniwahi, šekišiniwahi	pakataminiwahi 3´p–0	pakame niwahi 3´p–3´´
X	penopi, šekišinepi	pakata pi X–0	
0s	ahte wi		
0p	ahte wani we weneto ni		
0´s	ahte niwi, wi ·kaniwi we weneteniwi		
0´p	ahte niwani, wi ·kaniwani		

object	TA inverse	TA indefinite subject	TA inanimate subject
1s	*nepakamekwa* 3s–1s	*nepakameko pi* X–1s	*nepakamekwi* 0–1s
	nepakameko·ki 3p–1s		
	nepakamekoniwani 3′s–1s		
2s	*kepakamekwa* 3s–2s	*kepakameko pi* X–2s	*kepakamekwi* 0–2s
	kepakameko·ki 3p–2s		
1p	*nepakamekona na* 3s–1p	*nepakameko pena* X–1p	*nepakamekwipena* 0–1p
	nepakamekona naki 3p–1p		
12	*kepakamekona na* 3s–12	*kepakameko pena* X–12	*kepakamekwipena* 0–12
	kepakamekona naki 3p–12		
2p	*kepakamekowa wa* 3s–2p	*kepakameko pwa* X–2p	*kepakamekwipwa* 0–2p
	kepakamekowa waki 3p–2p		
3s	*pakamekwa* 3′–3s		*pakamekwiwa* 0–3s
		pakama pi X–3	
3p	*pakameko·ki* 3′–3p		*pakamekwiwaki* 0–3p
3′s	*pakamekoniwani* 3′′–3′s		*pakamekwiniwani* 0–3′s
		pakamema pi X–3′	
3′p	*pakamekoniwahi* 3′′–3′p		*pakamekwiniwahi* 0–3′p
X			*pakamekwipi* 0–X

TA theme 3	TA theme 4
kepakami 2s–1	*kepakamene* 1s–2s
kepakamipwa 2p–1s	*kepakamenepwa* 1s–2p
kepakamipena 2–1p	*kepakamenepena* 1p–2

30.3. Independent dubitative. The independent dubitative uses the independent order inflections (**§31**) with the modal suffix |-etoke| dub. (**§26.2** and **§29.11(a)**). Like the indicative diminutive, the TA direct forms with first and second singular subjects have the absolute central suffix and no peripheral suffix. No forms are attested with some obviative subjects. After |-etoke| dub. the peripheral suffixes that consist of a single vowel are not used. The modal suffix takes the shape |-etoke·h| before the other peripheral suffixes; these have the variants beginning with |i| and are optional or not used in some cases. When the modal suffix follows |-w| 3,0, the sequence |-w-e-| contracts with a preceding vowel (which is thereby lengthened if short) and is replaced by |o·| after a consonant. The absolute and objective suffixes for first and second plural also contract with |-etoke| dub., replacing |a|, |a·n|, and |a·w| with |a·|.

(3.314) Independent dubitative paradigm

subject	AI and II	TI(1)	TA direct
1s	_nepenopetoke_	_nepakata petoke_ 1s–0	_nepakama petoke_ 1s–3
2s	_kepenopetoke_	_kepakata petoke_ 2s–0	_kepakama petoke_ 2s–3
1p	_nepenopena toke_	_nepakata pena·toke_ 1p–0	_nepakama pena toke_ 1p–3
12	_kepenopena toke_	_kepakata pena·toke_ 12–0	_kepakama pena toke_ 12–3
2p	_kepenopwa toke_	_kepakata pwa toke_ 2p–0	_kepakama pwa toke_ 2p–3
3s	_peno toke_	_pakatamo toke_ 3s–0	_pakame toke_ 3s–3´
	nepo toke		
3p	_peno toke·hiki_	_pakatamo toke·hiki_ 3p–0	_pakame toke·hiki_ 3p–3´
3´	_penoni toke_	_pakatamini toke_ 3´–0	
X	_penopetoke_	_pakata petoke_ X–0	
0s	_ahte toke_ (also 0p)		
	we weneto toke		
0p	_ahte toke·hini_		
0´s	_ahte ni toke_		
	we weneteni toke		
0´p	_ahte ni toke·hini_		

object	TA inverse	TA indefinite subject	TA inanimate subject
1s	_nepakameko toke_ 3s–1s	_nepakameko petoke_	_nepakamekwipetoke_
	nepakameko toke·hiki 3p–1s	X–1s	0–1s
2s	_kepakameko toke_ 3s–2s	_kepakameko petoke_	_kepakamekwipetoke_
	kepakameko toke·hiki 3p–2s	X–2s	0–2s
1p	_nepakamekona toke_ 3s–1p	_nepakameko pena toke_	_nepakamekwipena toke_
	nepakamekona toke·hiki 3p–1p	X–1p	0–1p
12	_kepakamekona toke_ 3s–12	_kepakameko pena toke_	_kepakamekwipena toke_
	kepakamekona toke·hiki 3p–12	X–12	0–12
2p	_kepakamekowa toke_ 3s–2p	_kepakameko pwa toke_	_kepakamekwipwa toke_
	kepakamekowa toke·hiki 3p–2p	X–2p	0–2p
3s	_pakameko toke_ 3´–3s		_pakamekwi toke_ 0–3s
		pakama petoke X–3	
3p	_pakameko toke·hiki_ 3´–3p		_pakamekwi toke·hiki_ 0–3p
3´		_pakamema petoke_ X–3´	

TA theme 3	TA theme 4
kepakamipetoke 2s–1	_kepakamenepetoke_ 1s–2s
kepakamipwa toke 2p–1s	_kepakamenepwa toke_ 1s–2p
kepakamipena toke 2–1p	_kepakamenepena toke_ 1p–2

30.4. Independent conclusive. The independent conclusive uses the independent order inflections (**§31**) with the modal suffix |-ehapa| con. (**§26.3** and **§29.11(b)**). The pattern of inflection is exactly the same as in the independent dubitative mode, and the suffixes and contractions are the same except for the modal suffix |-ehapa| con., instead of |-etoke| dub. This suffix takes the shape |-ehapan| before an overt peripheral suffix. When the |e| is uncontracted some speakers replace it with |a|; in these cases a variant |-ahapa| can be recognized, but this variant is only given in (3.315) for the ending that is textually attested. Fewer forms are found in texts than in the case of the dubitative. No endings are citable for obviative or inanimate plural intransitive subjects or inanimate transitive subjects.

(3.315) Independent conclusive paradigm

subject	AI and II	TI(1)	TA direct
1s	*nepenopehapa*	*nepakata pehapa* 1s–0	*nepakama pehapa* 1s–3s
2s	*kepenopehapa*	*kepakata pehapa* 2s–0	*kepakama pehapa* 2s–3s
1p	*nepenopena·hapa*	*nepakata pena·*hapa 1p–0	*nepakama pena·hapa* 1p–3
12	*kepenopena·hapa*	*kepakata pena·*hapa 12–0	*kepakama pena·hapa* 12–3
2p	*kepenopwa·hapa*	*kepakata pwa·hapa* 2p–0	*kepakama pwa·hapa* 2p–3
3s	*peno·hapa* *nepo·hapa*	*pakatamo·hapa* 3s–0	*pakame·hapa* 3s–3´
3p	*peno·hapaniki* *nepo·hapaniki*	*pakatamo·hapaniki* 3p–0	*pakame·hapaniki* 3p–3´
X	*penopehapa*	*pakata pehapa* X–0	
0s	*ahte·hapa* *we weneto·hapa*		

object	TA inverse	TA indefinite subject
1s	*nepakameko·hapa* 3s–1s *nepakameko·hapaniki* 3p–1s	*nepakameko pehapa* X–1s
2s	*kepakameko·hapa* 3s–2s *kepakameko·hapaniki* 3p–2s	*kepakameko pehapa* X–2s
1p	*nepakamekona·hapa* 3s–1p *nepakamekona·hapaniki* 3p–1p	*nepakameko pena·hapa* X–1p
12	*kepakamekona·hapa* 3s–12 *kepakamekona·hapaniki* 3p–12	*kepakameko pena·hapa* X–12
2p	*kepakamekowa·hapa* 3s–2p *kepakamekowa·hapaniki* 3p–2p	*kepakameko pwa·hapa* X–2p
3s	*pakameko·hapa* 3´–3s	
3p	*pakameko·hapaniki* 3´–3p	*pakama pehapa*, *pakama pahapa* X–3

TA theme 3	TA theme 4
kepakamipehapa 2s–1	*kepakamenepehapa* 1s–2s
kepakamipwa·hapa 2p–1s	*kepakamenepwa·hapa* 1s–2p
kepakamipena·hapa 2–1p	*kepakamenepena·hapa* 1p–2

30.5. Other independent modes. The few attested endings of the assertive mode are given in (§26.4) and (§29.11(c)).

For the archaic and rare independent potential mode only an AI inflection for third plural (|wi·h=–na·wa·hi|) is attested: *wi·h=pya na wa hi=’yo we* 'they would have been going to come back'; *wi·h=a pi-či pa na wa hi=’yo we* 'they would have been going to come back from the dead' (Goddard 1995:140-141). The pronominal marking in this ending matches the second-person plural suffix of the assertive mode (3.283), and the modal marking has a parallel in the potential order suffix |-aʾwaʾhi| 1s–2p. The future proclitic preverb may mask the historical presence of a the third-person prefix |w-| that survives in the emphatic pronoun (2.11; cf. 3.130).

The equally rare imprecative mode (Goddard 1993:231-233, 1995:141) is attested by only a single TA ending which appears to have the shape |–aʾta(y)ina| or |–aʾtahina|. The meaning is apparently 'Would that I might .. (him or) them'. One writer uses this ending with the prefix |ne+| 1, with and without |wiʾh=| FUT, hence as a mode of the independent order. Elsewhere it is found, in one text, without the prefix, and hence ostensibly as a conjunct or imperative mode. It occurs in variants of one myth song that has other obscurities as well, and in one text not in a song. There is no form with this that can be cited with any confidence.

Conjunct Order

30.6. Conjunct order and its sub-orders. Conjunct order inflections fall into four sub-orders: core conjunct, interrogative, prohibitive, and potential. Pronominal prefixes are not used, and all pronominal marking is by suffixes. For marking pronominal arguments, however, the peripheral pronominal suffixes (position 8; §29.12) are not used, except that |-iki| ANpl pluralizes central arguments in the interrogative modes. Otherwise, the only use of the peripheral suffixes outside the independent order is to mark the heads of conjunct and interrogative participles.

All conjunct sub-orders use the theme signs (position 2; §29.7), with |-i| TA th. 3 and |-eN| TA th. 4 prioritized over |-ekw| TA th. 2 (§29.7(e)); |-ni| obv. and |-waʾ| pl. (position 4; §29.8(a-b)); some or all of the conjunct order central pronominal suffixes (position 6; §29.10, 3.253); and one or more modal suffixes (position 5 and 7; §29.9(a-b) and 29.11(d-h)). Only the core conjunct and interrogative sub-orders use |-em| obv. (position 1; §29.6). Of the conjunct sub-orders, only the potential has |-waʾ| 2p (position 4), but this is also used in the injunctive component of the imperative order, in which all endings are formed in parallel fashion to those of the potential. In the prohibitive and potential sub-orders a combined pronominal and modal suffix is used in some pronominal categories, and in the other pronominal categories the core conjunct central pronominal suffix is used.

The basic pronominal suffixes of the conjunct order are the non-relational suffixes of the AI paradigm (3.253). (The two relational suffixes are used only in the core conjunct modes and, in the case of |-wet| X rel., the interrogative.) The AI suffixes are used in all AI, II, and TI endings. Distinct suffixes are used in the TA endings for certain subjects with third person, first plural exclusive, and second plural objects; these are used only in the core conjunct and interrogative sub-orders (and |-enakoʾw| 1s–2p is used only in the core conjunct). When a distinct TA suffix does not exist in the core conjunct and interrogative, or when an appropriate combined pronoun and mode suffix does not exist in the prohibitive or the potential, the corresponding suffix of the basic AI paradigm is used as a default.

In conjunct order TA endings that make pronominal reference to a first person and a second person, with either one the subject and the other the object, the central ending is selected according to the same rule of prioritization that applies in the independent order (3.312), assuming a classification as simply second plural for the suffix used for first singular on second plural (3.265, last line).

Core Conjunct Sub-order

30.7. The modes of the core conjunct sub-order use the theme signs on the conjunct order pattern (**§36**), the core conjunct central pronominal suffixes (all suffixes solely in position 6 that are not independent order suffixes), and the pronominal suffixes of positions 1 and 4. The modes are differentiated by the use of modal suffixes of position 7, initial change, and |e·h=| AOR. The participle uses the suffixes of position 8 instead of a modal suffix.

30.8. Plain conjunct. The plain conjunct mode (**§26.7**) uses the conjunct theme signs (**§36**), the core conjunct pronominal suffixes (**§37**), and the modal suffix |-i| conj. (**§29.11(f)**). The suffix |-i| conj. causes mutation of a preceding |t| (**§13.1**) and is replaced by *-e* after certain suffixes ending in |k| or |w| (listed in **§29.11(f)**). The inflections may be obtained from the paradigm of the aorist conjunct (3.316) by omitting the prefix |e·h=| AOR.

30.9. Aorist conjunct. The aorist conjunct mode (**§26.8**) uses the same endings as the plain conjunct (**§37.1**) combined with the aorist proclitic prefix |e·h=| AOR (**§29.1, 3**). The paradigm is given in full in (3.316), including forms for AI and II consonant stems and TA direct diminutives.

(The aorist conjunct paradigm is given on the next two pages.)

(3.316) Aorist conjunct paradigm

subject	AI and II	TI(1)	TA direct
1s	e·h=penoya·ni	e·h=pakatama·ni 1s–0	e·h=pakamaki 1s–3
	e·h=nepeya·ni		e·h=pakame·hiya·ni 1s–3 dim.
	e·h=šekišina·ni		
1s rel.	e·h=penowaki	e·h=pakatamowaki 1s–0 rel.	
2s	e·h=penoyani	e·h=pakatamani 2s–0	e·h=pakamači 2s–3
	e·h=nepeyani		e·h=pakame·hiyani 2s–3 dim.
	e·h=šekišinani		
1p	e·h=penoya·ke	e·h=pakatama·ke 1p–0	e·h=pakamakeči 1p–3
	e·h=nepeya·ke		e·h=pakame·hiya·ke 1p–3 dim.
	e·h=šekišina·ke		
12	e·h=penoyakwe	e·h=pakatamakwe 12–0	e·h=pakamakwe 12–3
	e·h=nepeyakwe		e·h=pakame·hiyakwe 12–3 dim.
	e·h=šekišinakwe		
2p	e·h=penoye·kwe	e·h=pakatame·kwe 2p–0	e·h=pakame·kwe 2p–3
	e·h=nepeye·kwe		e·h=pakame·hiye·kwe 2p–3 dim.
	e·h=šekišine·kwe		
3s	e·h=penoči	e·h=pakataki 3s–0	e·h=pakama·či 3s–3´
	e·h=nepeki		e·h=pakame·hiči 3s–3´ dim.
	e·h=šekišiki		
3p	e·h=penowa·či	e·h=pakatamowa·či 3p–0	e·h=pakama·wa·či 3p–3´
	e·h=nepowa·či		e·h=pakame·hiwa·či 3p–3´ dim.
	e·h=šekišinowa·či		
3´	e·h=penoniči,	e·h=pakataminiči 3´–0	e·h=pakama·niči 3´–3´´
	e·h=nepeniči		
	e·h=šekišiniči		
X	e·h=penoki	e·h=pakatameki X–0	e·h=pakameči X–3
	e·h=šekišineki		e·h=pakamemeči X–3´
	(see 3.262)		e·h=pakame·hiki X–3(´) dim.
X rel.	e·h=penoweči	e·h=pakatamoweči X–0 rel.	
0	e·h=ahte·ki		
	e·h=we·wenehki,		
	e·h=we·weneteki		
	e·h=wi·kaki		
0´	e·h=ahte·niki		
	e·h=we·weneteniki		
	e·h=wi·kaniki		

object	TA theme 2 and 2a obviative subject	inanimate subject
1s		_e·h=pakamekwiya ni_ 0–1s
2s		_e·h=pakamekwiyani_ 0–2s
1p		_e·h=pakamekwiya·ke_ 0–1p
12		_e·h=pakamekwiyakwe_ 0–12
2p		_e·h=pakamekwiye·kwe_ 0–2p
3s	_e·h=pakamekoči_ 3´–3s	_e·h=pakamekwiči_ 0–3s
3p	_e·h=pakamekowa·či_ 3´–3p	_e·h=pakamekwiwa·či_ 0–3p
3´	_e·h=pakamekoniči_ 3´´–3´	_e·h=pakamekwiniči_ 0–3´

subject	TA theme 3 1s object	1p object
2s	_e·h=pakamiyani_ 2s–1	
		e·h=pakamiya·ke 2–1p
2p	_e·h=pakamiye·kwe_ 2p–1s	
3s	_e·h=pakamiči_ 3s–1s	
3p	_e·h=pakamiwa·či_ 3p–1s	_e·h=pakamiyameči_ 3(´)–1p
3´	_e·h=pakaminiči_ 3´–1s	
X	_e·h=pakamiki_ X–1s	_e·h=pakami nameki_ X–1p
X rel.	_e·h=pakamiweči_ X–1s rel.	

subject	TA theme 4 2s object	2p object	12 object
1s	_e·h=pakamena ni_ 1s–2s	_e·h=pakamenako we_ 1s–2p	
1p		_e·h=pakamena ke_ 1p–2	
3	_e·h=pakamehki_ 3(´)–2s		
		e·h=pakamena·kwe	_e·h=pakamenakwe_
X	_e·h=pakameneki_ X–2s	3(´)–2p, X–2p	3(´)–12, X–12

30.10. Subjunctive. The subjunctive mode (§26.9) uses the core conjunct thematic and pronominal suffixes (§36-37) and the modal suffix |-e| subj. (§29.11(g)). The inflection is homophonous with that of the the plain conjunct for endings that end in the variant -e of |-i| conj. The endings that differ from those of the modes marked with |-i| conj. (3.316) are given in (3.317).

(3.317) Subjunctive paradigm (selected)

subject	AI and II	TI(1)	TA direct
1s	_penoya ne_	_pakatama ne_ 1s–0	_pakamake_ 1s–3s
2s	_penoyane_	_pakatamane_ 2s–0	_pakamate_ 2s–3s
1p	_penoya·ke_	_pakatama·ke_ 1p–0	_pakamakete_ 1p–3
3s	_penote_	_pakatake_ 3s–0	_pakama te_ 3s–3´
	nepeke		
	šekišike		
3p	_penowa te_	_pakatamowa te_ 3p–0	_pakama wa te_ 3p–3´

[Subjunctive paradigm (continued)]

subject	AI and II	TI(1)	TA direct
3´	*penonite,*	*pakataminite* 3´–0	*pakama nite* 3´–3´´
	nepenite		
	šekišinite		
X	*penoke*	*pakatameke* X–0	*pakamete* X–3
			pakamemete X–3´
0	*ahte·ke*		
0´	*ahte nike*		

TA theme 2 and 2a

object	obviative subject	inanimate subject
1s		*pakamekwiya ne* 0–1s
3s	*pakamekote* 3´–3s	*pakamekwite* 0–3s
3p	*pakamekowa te* 3´–3p	*pakamekwiwa te* 0–3p
3´	*pakamekonite* 3´´–3´	(unattested)

TA theme 3

subject	1s object	1p object
2s	*pakamiyane* 2s–1	
3s	*pakamite* 3s–1s	
3p	*pakamiwa te* 3p–1s	*pakamiyamete* 3(´)–1p
3´	*pakaminite* 3´–1s	
X	*pakamike* X–1s	*pakami nameke* X–1p

TA theme 4

subject	2s object
1s	*pakamena ne* 1s–2s
3	*pakamehke* 3(´)–2s
X	*pakameneke* X–2s

30.11. Changed conjunct. The changed conjunct mode (**§26.10**) uses the same endings as the plain conjunct and the aorist conjunct combined with initial change (**§29.4**).

(3.318) Contrast between modes marked with |-i| conj.

        Plain conjunct   *penoya ni* (← |peno-| AI 'go home', |–ya·ni| 1s/CONJ)

        Aorist conjunct   *e·h=penoya ni* (← |peno-| AI 'go home', |e·h=ya·ni| 1s/AOR)

        Changed conjunct   *pe noya ni* (← |peno-| AI 'go home', |IC–ya·ni| 1s/CC)

30.12. Negative. The negative mode (**§26.11**) uses the core conjunct thematic and pronominal suffixes (**§36-37**) and the modal suffix |-ini| neg.-iter. (**§29.11(h)**). The endings may be obtained from the paradigm of the aorist conjunct (3.316) by replacing the final vowel (*-i* or *-e*) by *-ini*, except that the ending for first singular on second plural does not add |-ini| neg.-iter. but has the shape |+enako·we| 1s–2p used in all core conjunct modes (**§29.10(b)**, end; 3.298). The negative forms with this ending are thus identical with the plain conjunct. The negative is always preceded in the sentence by the particle *a·kwi* 'not', though a single *a·kwi* occasionally serves for two successive negative verbs that are closely linked.

(3.319) Contrast between plain conjunct and negative (*a·kwi* 'not' omitted)

    (a)   Plain conjunct   *penoya·ni* (← |peno-| AI 'go home', |–ya·ni| 1s/CONJ)

            Negative   *penoya·nini* (|–ya·nini| 1s/NEG)

    (b)   Plain conjunct   *penoči* (|–či| 3s/CONJ)

            Negative   *penočini* (|–čini| 3s/NEG)

    (c)   Plain conjunct   *penoya·ke* (|–ya·ke| 1p/CONJ)

            Negative   *penoya·kini* (|–ya·kini| 1p/NEG)

30.13. Iterative. The iterative mode (**§26.12**) has the same endings as the negative (**§37.5**) combined with initial change (**§29.4**). The inflection for first singular on second plural is identical with that of the changed conjunct (3.299).

(3.320) Contrast between negative and iterative (*a·kwi* 'not' omitted)

    Negative   *penoya·nini* (← |peno-| AI 'go home', |–ya·nini| 1s/NEG)

    Iterative   *pe·noya·nini* (← |peno-| AI 'go home', |IC–ya·nini| 1s/ITER)

30.14. Conjunct participle. The conjunct participle (**§26.13**) uses the core conjunct thematic and pronominal suffixes (**§36-37**) combined with initial change (**§29.4**) or |e·h=| AOR (**§29.1, 3**). In place of a modal suffix, the conjunct participle has a peripheral pronominal suffix (position 8; **§29.12**, 3.302-304). The peripheral suffix marks the nominal category of the head of the participle, which is the head of the relative clause that the participle makes. Most participles have initial change, but those with locative or quasi-locative heads (2.251-267) have |e·h=| AOR (except on compound stems with |a·mi| PV POT; 2.270). The conjunct participle differs from the other core conjunct modes in the use of |-wa·| pl. (position 4), which does not appear where the other modes would use it if the head is marked by |-iki| ANpl. As in the other modes, the suffix for first singular on second plural is followed only by |-i| conj.|, realized as *-e*.

For each core conjunct pronominal inflection there are generally six participial endings. This number is increased to seven in second person forms (which may have |-e| VOC) and is further increased if rare first person participles are allowed for, and it is reduced to two in II proximate forms, which are constrained by the rules of obviation from having an animate head. With locative oblique heads there are also one or two additional inflections with |e·h=| AOR rather than initial change. It follows that every verb has potentially a vast number of distinct participial forms. The ten that potentially exist for one pronominal combination are illustrated in (3.321).

(3.321) Possible participles corresponding to *e·h=ašamena·ni* 'I fed you (sg.)'

        e·šamena·na 'that (anim.) which I fed you (sg.)'

        e·šamena·niki 'those (anim.) which I fed you (sg.)'

        e·šamena·ni 'that (inan.) which I fed you (sg.)'

        e·šamena·nini 'those (inan.) which I fed you (sg.)'

        e·šamena·nini 'that (obv.) which I fed you (sg.)'

        e·šamena·nihi 'those (obv.) which I fed you (sg.)'

        e·šamena·ni 'I who fed you (sg.)'

        e·šamena·ne 'O you (sg.) whom I fed'

        e·h=taši-ašamena·ni 'where I fed you (sg.)'

        e·h=taši-ašamena·nini 'the places where I fed you (sg.)'

For a TA verb with a third person proximate subject and a third person obviative object there are six participles with either the subject or the object as head:

(3.322) TA direct third person participles

ne·sa·ta 'the one (prox.) who killed him (obv.) or them (obv.)'

ne·sa·čiki 'the ones (prox.) who killed him (obv.) or them (obv.)'

ne·sa·čini 'the one (obv.) he (prox.) killed'

ne·sa·čihi 'the ones (obv.) he (prox.) killed'

ne·sa·wa·čini 'the one (obv.) they (prox.) killed'

ne·sa·wa·čihi 'the ones (obv.) they (prox.) killed'

There are another six participles, matching these, if the subject is obviative and the object is proximate.

Some speakers optionally use the participial forms with obviative singular *-ini* for obviative plural as well; these speakers have the same peculiarity in the demonstrative paradigms (§31.2).

30.15. Preterite modes. Five of the seven core conjunct modes have preterite counterparts made with the suffix |-ehe| pret. (§26.25, §29.11(e)). After |-ehe| pret. the modal suffixes |-i| conj., |-e| subj., and |-ini| neg.-iter. and the peripheral pronominal suffixes do not appear (except in two archaic participles that have a peripheral suffix; 3.294, 295). Thus the same inflectional endings are used in all five preterite modes. The subjunctive preterite and the negative preterite have only the ending (though the negative also has the particle *a·kwi* 'not'); the aorist preterite has |e·h=| AOR; and the changed preterite and the preterite participle have initial change and are identical.

The preterite endings may be formally derived from the corresponding subjunctive endings (or the core conjunct endings that have *-e*): replace the final *-e* by *-ehe*; if a sequence *-kwehe* results, replace it by *-koha*. A preterite form is not made if the inflection has |-ako·w| 1s–2p.

(3.323) Patterns of contrast between non-preterite and preterite endings

(a)	Plain conjunct	*peno<u>ya·ni</u>* (← |peno-| AI 'go home', |–ya·ni| 1s/CONJ)
	Subjunctive:	*peno<u>ya·ne</u>* (|–ya·ne| 1s/SUBJ)
	Subjunctive preterite:	*peno<u>ya·nehe</u>* (|–ya·nehe| 1s/SUBJ.PRET)
(b)	Plain conjunct	*peno<u>či</u>* (|–či| 3s/CONJ)
	Subjunctive:	*peno<u>te</u>* (|–te| 3s/SUBJ)
	Subjunctive preterite:	*peno<u>tehe</u>* (|–tehe| 3s/SUBJ.PRET)
(c)	Plain conjunct	*peno<u>ya·ke</u>* (|–ya·ke| 1p/CONJ)
	Subjunctive:	*peno<u>ya·ke</u>* (|–ya·ke| 1p/SUBJ)
	Subjunctive preterite:	*peno<u>ya·kehe</u>* (|–ya·kehe| 1p/SUBJ.PRET)
(d)	Plain conjunct:	*peno<u>ye·kwe</u>* (|–ye·kwe| 2p/CONJ)
	Subjunctive:	*peno<u>ye·kwe</u>* (|–ye·kwe| 2p/SUBJ)
	Subjunctive preterite:	*peno<u>ye·koha</u>* (|–ye·koha| 2p/SUBJ.PRET)

Interrogative Sub-order

30.16. The interrogative (§26.14-17) and prioritive (§26.18) modes of the interrogative sub-order use the same theme signs and pronominal suffixes as the core conjunct modes (§30.6), combined (sometimes irregularly) with the modal suffix |-w| irr. (position 5). There is also a modal suffix of position 7, which is |-e·ni| int. in the interrogative modes and |-e| subj. in the prioritive modes. Suffixes of position 8 are used in the interrogative modes, but not the prioritive, to pluralize third person animate central arguments, in addition to marking the heads of interrogative participles. The prioritive uses |-wa·| pl. (position 5) to pluralize a third person central argument; the interrogative uses this suffix only in the participle and then only optionally (3.212). No interrogative sub-order ending is made for first singular acting on second plural. The interrogative modes are differentiated by the use of initial change and |e·h=| AOR. The prioritive modes are differentiated by initial change but this is often invisible.

In the endings of the interrogative sub-order, |-w| irr. is overtly present as *-w* before a central pronominal suffix that begins with a vowel (3.324*ac*), with the variant *-ow* after retaining and deleting consonants (3.324*b*). Before this *-w* the direct theme sign |-a·| TA th. 1 appears overtly as *-a·*. Underlying |-w| irr. metathesizes with |-k| 3 (the replacement of |-t| 3 after a consonant [3.256]) or |-k| 0 to |-kw| 3,0 irr. (3.324*de*), and it contracts with |-ek| X to |-·k| X irr. (3.324*fg*). When |-w| irr. occurs with the suffixes for first plural exclusive object the combination is not concatenative but analogical. The interrogative equivalent of |-amet| 3–1p replicates the pattern of the third person animate (3.324*d*), giving (with the theme sign) |-i-y-amekw| 3–1p irr. (3.324*h*), and the interrogative equivalent of |-·namek| X–1p replicates the pattern of the indefinite subject (3.324*f*) suffixes, specifically those with a first singular object (3.324*g*), giving |-i-·nami·k| X–1p irr. (3.324*i*).

30.17. Interrogative modes. The plain, changed, and aorist interrogative have exactly the same endings. In addition, the changed interrogative has initial change, and the aorist interrogative has |e·h=| AOR. The interrogative participle has all the endings of the other interrogative modes and additional endings that indicate certain participial heads.

Some of the patterns of contrast between the general interrogative endings and corresponding subjunctive endings are shown in (3.324).

(3.324) Patterns of contrast between subjunctive and plain interrogative

(a)	Subjunctive:	*penoya ne* (← |peno-| AI 'go home', |–ya·ne| 1s/SUBJ)
	Plain interrogative:	*penowa ne ni* (|–wa·ne·ni| 1s/INT)
(b)	Subjunctive:	*nepeya ne* (← |nep-| AI 'die', |–ya·ne| 1s/SUBJ)
	Plain interrogative:	*nepowa ne ni* (|–wa·ne·ni| 1s/INT [connective *o*; **§8.3**])
(c)	Subjunctive:	*pakamakete* (← |pakam-| TA 'him', |–akete| 1p–3/SUBJ)
	Plain interrogative:	*pakama wakete ni* (|–a·wakete·ni| 1p–3/INT [|-a·|: 3.219])
(d)	Subjunctive:	*penote* (|–te| 3s/SUBJ)
	Plain interrogative:	*penokwe ni* (|–kwe·ni| 3s/INT ← |-w-k-e·ni| ← |-w-t-e·ni|)
(e)	Subjunctive:	*ahte ke* (|ahte·-| II 'be {somewhere}', |–ke| 0/SUBJ)
	Plain interrogative:	*ahte kwe ni* (|–kwe·ni| 0/INT ← |-w-k-e·ni|)
(f)	Subjunctive:	*penoke* (|-eke| X/SUBJ ← |-ek-e|)
	Plain interrogative:	*peno ke ni* (|-weke·ni| X/INT ← |-w-ek-e·ni|)
(g)	Subjunctive:	*pakamike* (|–ike| X–1s/SUBJ ← |-i-ek-e|)
	Plain interrogative:	*pakami ke ni* (|–i·ke| X–1s/INT ← |-i-w-ek-e·ni|)
(h)	Subjunctive:	*pakamiyamete* (|–iyamete| 3–1p/SUBJ)
	Plain interrogative:	*pakamiyamekwe ni* (|–iyamekwe·ni| 3–1p/INT) (cf. 3.324*d*)
(i)	Subjunctive:	*pakami nameke* (|–i·nameke| X–1p/SUBJ)
	Plain interrogative:	*pakami nami ke ni* (|–i·nami·ke·ni| X–1p/INT) (cf. 3.324*g*)

Paradigms of the plain interrogative are given in (3.325).

(3.325) Plain interrogative paradigm

subject	AI and II	TI(1)	TA direct
1s	*penowa ne ni* *nepowa ne ni* *šekišinowa ne ni*	*pakatamowa ne ni* 1s–0	*pakama wake ni* 1s–3
2s	*penowane ni* *nepowane ni* *šekišinowane ni*	*pakatamowane ni* 2s–0	*pakama wate ni* 2s–3
1p	*penowa·ke ni* *nepowa·ke ni* *šekišinowa·ke ni*	*pakatamowa·ke ni* 1p–0	*pakama wakete ni* 1p–3
12	*penowakwe ni* *nepowakwe ni* *šekišinowakwe ni*	*pakatamowakwe ni* 12–0	*pakama wakwe ni* 12–3
2p	*penowe·kwe ni* *nepowe·kwe ni* *šekišinowe·kwe ni*	*pakatamowe·kwe ni* 2p–0	*pakama we·kwe ni* 2p–3
3s	*penokwe ni* *nepokwe ni* *šekišinokwe ni*	*pakatamokwe ni* 3s–0	*pakama·kwe·hiki* 3s–3′
3p	*penokwe·hiki* *nepokwe·hiki* *šekišinokwe·hiki*	*pakatamokwe·hiki* 3p–0	*pakama·kwe·hiki* 3p–3′
3′	*penonikwe ni,* *nepenikwe ni* *šekišinikwe ni*	*pakataminikwe ni* 3′–0	*pakama nikwe ni* 3′–3″
X	*peno·ke ni* *šekišino·ke ni*	*pakatamo·ke ni* X–0	*pakama te ni* X–3 *pakamema te ni* X–3′
X rel.	*penowa te ni*	*pakatamowa te ni* X–0 rel.	(X–3′ rel.: see 3.255)
0	*ahte·kwe ni* *we·wenetokwe ni* *wi·kanokwe ni*		
0′	*ahte nikwe ni* *we·wenetenikwe ni* *wi·kanikwe ni*		

object	TA theme 2 and 2a obviative subject	inanimate subject
2s		*pakamekwiwane ni* 0–2s
1p		*pakamekwiwa·ke ni* 0–1p
12		*pakamekwiwakwe ni* 0–12
2p		*pakamekwiwe·kwe ni* 0–2p
3s	*pakamekokwe ni* 3′–3s	*pakamekwikwe ni* 0–3s
3p	*pakamekokwe·hiki* 3′–3p	*pakamekwikwe·hiki* 0–3p

TA theme 3

subject	1s object	1p object
2s	*pakami<u>wane ̇ni</u>* 2s–1	
		pakamiwa ̇ke ̇ni 2–1p
2p	*pakamiwe ̇kwe ̇ni* 2p–1s	
3s	*pakami<u>kwe ̇ni</u>* 3s–1s	
3p	*pakami<u>kwe ̇hiki</u>* 3p–1s	*pakami<u>yamekwe ̇ni</u>* 3(´)–1p
3´	*pakamini<u>kwe ̇ni</u>* 3´–1s	
X	*pakami ̇ke ̇ni* X–1s	*pakami ̇nami ̇ke ̇ni* X–1p

TA theme 4

subject	2s object	2p object	12 object
1s	*pakame<u>nowa ̇ne ̇ni</u>* 1s–2s	(no ending)	
1p		*pakame<u>nowa ̇ke ̇ni</u>*	
3	*pakame<u>nokwe ̇ni</u>* 3–2s	*pakame<u>nowa ̇kwe ̇ni</u>* 3–2p	*pakam<u>enowakwe ̇ni</u>* 3–12
X	*pakameno ̇ke ̇ni* X–2s		

30.18. Interrogative participle. In addition to the endings used in the other interrogative modes (3.325), the interrogative participle has endings that mark heads as animate or obviative, singular or plural. Where the general interrogative endings have *-e ̇ni*, these participial endings have *-e ̇na* anim. sg., *-e ̇hiki* anim. pl., *-e ̇hini* obv. sg., or *-e ̇hihi* obv. pl. (**§26.17**, 2.278-281; **§29.8(b)**, 3.212; **§29.11(d)**, 3.285, 288).

(3.326) Interrogative participles

(a) *ke ̇šawenamokwe ̇na* 'anyone who held it loosely' (O 139G)
(|ke·šawen-| TI(1) 'hold loosely', |IC–amokwe·na| 3s–0/INT.PPL(ANsg))

(b) *wi ̇h=na ̇ni ̇šiwa ̇kwe ̇hini* 'someone (obv.) who might be his companion' (K-Wap 44)
(|CV+| RED1, |ni·ši-| AI 'be two', |IC–wa·kwe·hini| 3p/INT.PPL(OBVsg))

(c) *wi ̇h=wi ̇te menokwe ̇hiki* 'whoever (pl.) is going to go with you (sg.)' (K-FASB 66)
(|wi·h=| FUT, |wi·te·m-| TA 'accompany', |IC–enokwe·hiki| 3–2s/INT.PPL(ANpl))

(d) *me ̇nwe netamawa ̇wake ̇hini* 'one (obv.) I approve of for her'
(|menwe·netamaw-| TA+O 'like O2 for',
|IC–a·wake·hini| 1s–3/INT.PPL(OBVsg))

(e) *taswi mi ̇na ̇kwe ̇hihi* 'as many (obv.) as he has given it to' (K-B 187)
(*taswi* 'as many as' [cf. 2.247];
|mi·N-| TA+O 'give O2 to', |IC–a·kwe·hihi| 3p–3´/INT.PPL(OBVpl))

30.19. Prioritive modes. The endings of both prioritive modes are identical, as the modes differ only by the presence or absence of initial change. The attested prioritive endings are those in (3.327). The forms are constructed with |me·hi| PV 'yet' (giving the meaning 'before'), their most common use, but with this the initial change is invisible.

(3.327) Prioritive paradigm

subject	AI and II	TI(1)	TA direct
1s	*me ̇h-penowa ̇ne*	*me ̇h-pakat<u>amowa ̇ne</u>*	*me ̇h-pakama ̇wake*
2s	*me ̇h-peno<u>wane</u>*	*me ̇h-pakat<u>amowane</u>*	
12	*me ̇h-peno<u>wakwe</u>*		
3s	*me ̇h-peno<u>kwe</u>*	*me ̇h-pakat<u>amokwe</u>*	*me ̇h-pakama ̇kwe* 3s–3´

[Prioritive paradigm, continued.]

3p	*meˑh-penowaˑkwe*	*meˑh-pakatamowaˑkwe*	*meˑh-pakamaˑwaˑkwe* 3p–3´
3´	*meˑh-penonikwe*		
X rel.	*meˑh-penowaˑte*		X: *meˑh-pakamaˑte* X–3
			(cf. MAE 854.1)

TA theme 2

object	obviative subject
3s	*meˑh-pakamekokwe* 3´–3s

TA theme 3

subject	1s object
X	*meˑh-pakamiˑke* X–1s

Prohibitive Sub-order

30.20. The prohibitive and future imperative modes of the prohibitive sub-order (**§26.19**) have the same theme signs as the core conjunct modes (**§30.6**) and a reduced set of pronominal suffixes: |-ni| obv. (**§29.8(a)**) and |-waˑ| pl. (**§29.8(b)**) of position 4; some of the core conjunct central pronominal suffixes of position 6 (3.186); and combined person and mode suffixes of positions 6 and 7 (**§29.10**, 3.265). All endings contain |-hk| proh. or |-hk| fut. imp. (**§29.9(bc)**), which combine differently with some theme signs (3.227). Some endings with |-hk| fut. imp. are used by some or all speakers in the function of the prohibitive mode (2.294, 302). In (3.328) the textually attested functions are given for the endings that are formally of the future imperative.

(3.328) Prohibitive paradigm and future imperative variants

subject	AI and II	TI(1)	TA direct
1s	*penohka*	*pakataka* 1s–0	*pakamiyeˑka* 1s–3
	nepehka		
	šekišika		
2s	*penohkani*	*pakatakani* 2s–0	*pakamiyeˑkani* 2s–3
	nepehkani	*pakatamoˑhkani*	*pakamaˑhkani* 2s–3 (fut. imp.)
	šekišikani	2s–0 (fut. imp.)	
1p	*penohkaˑke*	*pakatakaˑke* 1p–0	*pakamiyeˑkaˑke* 1p–3
	nepehkaˑke		
	šekišikaˑke		
12	*penohkakwe*	*pakatakakwe* 12–0	*pakamiyeˑkakwe* 12–3
	nepehkakwe		
	šekišikakwe		
2p	*penohkeˑko*	*pakatakeˑko* 2p–0	*pakamiyeˑkeˑko* 2p–3
	nepehkeˑko		*pakamaˑhkeˑko* 2p–3 (fut. imp.)
	šekišikeˑko		
3s	*penohkiče*	*pakatakiče* 3s–0	*pakamiyeˑkiče* 3s–3´
	nepehkiče		*pakamaˑhkiče* 3s–3´ (proh.)
	šekišikiče		

[Prohibitive paradigm, continued.]

3p	*penowa·hkiče*	*pakatamowa·hkiče* 3p–0	*pakamiye·wa·hkiče* 3p–3´
	nepowa·hkiče		*pakama·wa·hkiče* 3p–3´ (proh.)
	šekišinowa·hkiče		
3´	*penonihkiče,*	*pakataminihkiče* 3´–0	
	nepenihkiče		
	šekišinihkiče		
X	*penohki·ke*	*pakataki·ke* X–0	*pakamiye·ki·ke* X–3
	šekišiki·ke		
0	*ahte·hkiče*		
	we·wenetehkiče		
	wi·kakiče, wi·kahkiče		
0´	*ahte·nihkiče*		
	we·wenetenihkiče		
	wi·kanihkiče		

TA theme 2 and 2a

object	obviative subject	inanimate subject
1s		*pakamekwihka* 0–1s
2s		*pakamekwihkani* 0–2s
2p		*pakamekwihke·ko* 0–2p
3s	*pakamekohkiče* 3´–3s	(unattested)
3p	*pakamekowa·hkiče* 3´–3p	(unattested)

TA theme 3

subject	1s object	1p object
2s	*pakamihkani* 2s–1	
		pakamihka·ke 2–1p
2p	*pakamihke·ko* 2p–1s	
3s	*pakamihkiče* 3s–1s	
3p	*pakamiwa·hkiče* 3p–1s	*pakamiyamehkiče* 3(´)–1p
3´	*pakaminihkiče* 3´–1s	
X	*pakamihki·ke* X–1s	*pakami·namehki·ke* X–1p

TA theme 4

subject	2s object	2p object	12 object
1s	*pakamenaka* 1s–2s	*pakamenaka·wa* 1s–2p	
1p		*pakamenaka·ke* 1p–2	
3	*pakamenakiče* 3(´)–2s		
		pakamenaka·kwe	*pakamenakakwe*
X	*pakamenaki·ke* X–2s	3(´)–2p, X–2p	3(´)–12, X–12

Potential Sub-order

30.21. The potential sub-order comprises only the potential mode (**§26.20**). Like the prohibitive, it uses the same theme signs as the core conjunct modes (**§30.6**) and a reduced set of pronominal suffixes: |-ni| obv. (**§29.8(a)**), |-wa·| pl. (**§29.8(b)**), and |-wa·| 2p (**§29.8(c)**) of position 4; some of the core conjunct central pronominal suffixes of position 6 (3.186); and combined person and mode suffixes of positions 6 and 7 (**§29.10**, 3.265).

Potential endings fall into two sets. Those with a third person or indefinite subject have a suffix |-sa| 3,0 pot. or |-ene·ha| X pot., and the rest have |-hk| proh. For first singular, second singular. and first singular on second plural there are special potential suffixes of positions 6 and 7 that follow |-hk| pot.; otherwise |-hk| proh. is followed by the regular core conjunct central pronominal suffixes (position 6) together with |-ehe| pret. (position 7) in a modal function.

(3.329) Potential paradigm

subject	AI and II	TI(1)	TA direct
1s	*penohka·ha*	*pakataka·ha* 1s–0	*pakamiye·ka·ha* 1s–3
2s	*penohkapa*	*pakatakapa* 2s–0	*pakamiye·kapa* 2s–3
	nepehkapa		
	šekišikapa		
1p	*penohka·kehe*	*pakataka·kehe* 1p–0	*pakamiye·ka·kehe* 1p–3
12	*penohkakoha*	*pakatakakoha* 12–0	*pakamiye·kakoha* 12–3
2p	*penohke·koha*	*pakatake·koha* 2p–0	*pakamiye·ke·koha* 2p–3
3s	*penosa*	*pakatasa* 3s–0	*pakama·sa* 3s–3´
	nepesa		
	šekišisa		
3p	*penowa·sa*	*pakatamowa·sa* 3p–0	*pakama·wa·sa* 3p–3´
	nepowa·sa		
	šekišinowa·sa		
3´	*penonisa,*	*pakataminisa* 3´–0	
	nepenisa		
	šekišinisa		
X	*penone·ha*	*pakatane·ha* X–0	*pakamene·ha* X–3
	šekišinene·ha		*pakamemene·ha* X–3´
X rel.	*penowene·ha*		
0	*ahte·sa*		
	we·wenetesa		
	wi·kasa		
0´	*ahte·nisa*		
	we·wenetenisa		
	wi·kanisa		

	TA theme 2 and 2a	
object	obviative subject	inanimate subject
1s		*pakamekwihka·ha* 0–1s
2s		*pakamekwihkapa* 0–2s
2p		*pakamekwihke·koha* 0–2p
3s	*pakamekosa* 3´–3s	*pakamekwisa* 0–3s
3p	*pakamekowa·sa* 3´–3p	*pakamekwiwa·sa* 0–3p

	TA theme 3	
subject	1s object	1p object
2s	*pakamihkapa* 2s–1	
		pakamihka·kehe 2–1p
2p	*pakamihke·koha* 2p–1s	
3s	*pakamisa* 3s–1s	
3p	*pakamiwa·sa* 3p–1s	*pakamiyamesa* 3(´)–1p
3´	*pakaminisa* 3´–1s	
X	*pakamine·ha* X–1s	*pakami·namene·ha* X–1p

	TA theme 4		
subject	2s object	2p object	12 object
1s	*pakamenaka·ha* 1s–2s	*pakamenaka·wa·hi,* *pakamenaka·wa·ha* 1s–2p	
1p		*pakamenaka·kehe* 1p–2	
3	*pakamenesa* 3(´)–2s	*pakamenwa·sa* 3(´)–2p	*pakamenakosa* 3(´)–12
X	*pakamenene·ha* X–2s		

Imperative Order

30.22. The imperative order comprises two, non-contrastive sub-orders (**§26.21, §26.22**). The theme signs are used as in the conjunct order, except that there are no endings with |-ekw| TA th. 2. The imperative sub-order has the endings for second person or first person inclusive subject; these have combined suffixes of positions 6 and 7 that are unique to these endings (3.186). For the inclusive-subject suffixes, see (3.271). The injunctive sub-order has the endings for third person subject, animate or inanimate, which are formally of the conjunct type; in fact they exactly match the endings of the potential with |-če| 3,0 imp. substituted for |-sa| 3,0 pot.

(3.330) Imperative paradigm

subject	AI and II	TI(1)	TA direct
2s	*penono*	*pakatano* 2s–0	*pakami* 2s–3
	nepeno		
	šekišineno		
12	*penota we*,	*pakata ta we* 12–0	*pakama ta we* 12–3,
	penota ne,		*pakama ta ne*
	penota ke		
	nepeta we		
	šekišineta we		
2p	*penoko*	*pakatamoko* 2p–0	*pakamehko* 2p–3
3s	*penoče*	*pakatače* 3s–0	*pakama če* 3s–3´
	nepeče		
	šekišiče		
3p	*penowa če*	*pakatamowa če* 3p–0	*pakama wa če* 3p–3´
	nepowa če		
	šekišinowa če		
3´	*penoniče*,	*pakataminiče* 3´–0	
	nepeniče		
	šekišiniče		
0	*ahte če*		
	we weneteče		
	wi kače		
0´	*ahte niče*		
	we weneteniče		
	wi kaniče		

TA theme 3

subject	1s object	1p object
2s	*pakamino* 2s–1	
		pakamina ke 2–1p
2p	*pakamiko* 2p–1s	
3s	*pakamiče* 3s–1s	
		pakamiyameče 3–1p
3p	*pakamiwa če* 3p–1s	

TA theme 4

subject	2s object	2p object	12 object
3	*pakameneče* 3–2s	*pakamenwa če* 3–2p	*pakamenakoče* 3–12

PRONOUN INFLECTION

31. The different types of pronouns are inflected variously.

Emphatic Pronouns

31.1. The emphatic pronouns are listed in (2.11). They resemble the possessed forms of a dependent noun stem beginning with |i·|, except that the third person has *w-*, not *ow-* (cf. 3.49), and there is no suffix of core noun inflection (2.2, 3.2). (The final *-a*'s cannot be identified with |-a| ANsg.)

Demonstrative Pronouns

31.2. There are seven sets of demonstrative pronouns (§18.5; 3.331). They are inflected for the same nominal categories as nouns (§18.2), using several sets of similar suffixes. Some speakers, however, optionally use the obviative singular forms of demonstratives for obviative plural as well; these speakers have the same peculiarity in the inflection of participles (§30.14). The locatives are made with a suffix |-ahi| loc., but not all sets have this form.

(3.331) Paradigms of demonstrative pronouns

	'this'	'this other (near)'	'that (going away)'
anim. sg.	*mana*	*i·ya·ka*	*ma·hiya*
inan. sg.	*mani*	*i·ya·mani*	*ma·hiye*
anim. pl.	*ma·haki*	*i·ya·ma·haki*	*ma·hiye·ka*
inan. pl.	*ma·hani*	*i·ya·ma·hani*	*ma·hiye·ne*
obv. sg.	*ma·hani*	*i·ya·ma·hani*	*ma·hiye·ne*
obv. pl.	*ma·hahi*	*i·ya·ma·hahi*	*ma·hiye·ha*
loc.	*ayo·hi*	*i·ya·ma·hi*	

	'that'	'that other (away)'	'that (gone, before)'	'that (further on)'
anim. sg.	*i·na*	*i·na·ka*	*i·niya*	*anika·na·ka*
inan. sg.	*i·ni*	*i·na·mani*	*i·niye*	*anika·ne*
anim. pl.	*i·niki*	*i·na·ma·haki, i·ne·ke*	*i·niye·ka, i·niye·ke*	*anika·ne·ke*
inan. pl.	*i·nini*	*i·na·ma·hani*	*i·niye·na, i·niye·ne*	*anika·ne·ne*
obv. sg.	*i·nini*	(*i·na·ma·hani*), *i·ne·ne*	*i·niye·na, i·niye·ne*	*anika·ne·ne*
obv. pl.	*i·nihi*	(*i·na·ma·hahi*)	*i·niye·ha, i·niye·he*	*anika·ne·he*
loc.	*i·nahi*	*i·na·ma·hi*		*anika·na·hi*

(The parenthesized forms are not attested.)

31.3. *mana* 'this'. The *mana* set has three stems: |man-| in the animate and inanimate singular, |ma·h-| in the plural and obviative, and |ayo·-| in the locative. The regular noun suffixes of (3.2) are added to mark the nominal categories.

This is the basic proximal demonstrative. It prototypically refers or draws attention to someone or something that is physically near at hand. It is the equivalent of 'here' used when handing something to someone. In this function either animate *mana* or inanimate *mani* may be used for an object that would be named by an animate noun. By extension, the *mana* set may also refer to what is well known and perhaps felt as close, but not physically present. In narrative it may introduce or re-introduce a character. The inanimate singular *mani* 'this' may refer to the utterance or set of utterances it is in, or it may be used cataphorically to introduce the topic or segment of speech that immediately follows.

31.4. *i·na* 'that'. The *i·na* set has a stem |i·n-| inflected by suffixes identical with those that are used on verbs outside the independent indicative and which appear as a full set marking the heads of participles (§29.12).

This is the basic distal demonstrative, used for reference to things that are further away than those typically referred to by the *mani* set. When used alone in narrative it ordinarily refers not to a current character but to one mentioned just previously. It may also, however, be used as the determiner in a noun phrase referring to a character that is thereby placed in focus or removed from focus (defocussed), functioning at its weakest like a definite article. The inanimate singular *i·ni* 'that' may refer anaphorically to the topic or segment of speech that immediately precedes. In equational sentences a demonstrative of the *i·na* set may appear before the old (or given) term of the equation when this follows all or part of the new term of the equation, sometimes duplicating the demonstrative that it precedes (as in O 99F).

31.5. *i·ya·ka* 'this other (near)'. The *i·ya·ka* set, outside the animate singular and the locative, appears to be formed from a stem |i·ya·-| inflected by the full forms of the the *mana* set. The animate singular has a suffix |-ka| ANsg, and the locative suffixes |-ma·hi| to the stem |i·ya·-|.

This set is not common, being found in narratives only in quoted speech. It refers to someone or something, visible or invisible, which is relatively near but contrasted with something nearer:

(3.332)   *mana=ča·h nekoti, i·ya·ka na·hka.* (Jones 1907:50.20-21, 51)
           'Here is one, and there is another.'
               (*mana* 'this (anim.)'; |=ča·hi| 'so'; *nekoti* 'one';
               i·ya·ka 'that other (near) (anim.)'; *na·hka* 'also'.

31.6. *i·na·ka* 'that other (away)'. The *i·na·ka* set is formed like the *i·ya·ka* set except with a stem |i·na·-|, but it also has an older paradigm with a stem |i·ne·-| and absentative suffixes in |-e| (**§31.8**). In fact, the ostensibly older forms *i·ne·ke* anim. pl. and *i·ne·ne* obv. sg. are actually more common than the longer forms, and *i·ne·ne* is the only obviative form attested.

This set is also rare. In quoted speech it seems to be the distal counterpart of the *i·ya·ka* set. For example, *i·na ma·hani ana·hkanani* (A 62G) is used to refer generically to fiber mats (*ana·hkanani*), with the demonstrative apparently specifying 'like the ones you were making' or something similar. These pronouns may also be used in narrative with a force like 'meanwhile, those others', to shift the story back to characters last mentioned at a different location.

31.7. *ma·hiya* 'that going away'. Beside the animate singular, which appears to have a stem |ma·hiy-| and the suffix |-a| ANsg, there is an inanimate singular *ma·hiye*. This matches the stem |ma·hiye·-| found in the four-syllable forms, which have the absentative suffixes that are more fully attested in the *i·niya* set (**§31.8**). There is no locative.

The *ma·hiya* set is the proximal absentative demonstrative. It is used for someone or something that is seen going away, or is out of sight having recently left, or is absent but thought of as only recently departed. What it refers to need not be in motion, and *ma·hiye* is the demonstrative used for paths that extend away from the speaker.

31.8. *i·niya* 'that (gone, before)'. This set is inflected like *ma·hiya* and like it lacks a locative. Beside *i·niye* inan. sg. the longer, four-syllable forms have a stem |i·niye·-| that matches this followed by the absentative suffixes, which are found with either -a or -e: |-ke|, |-ka| anim. pl.; |-ne|, |-na| inan. pl.; |-ne|, |-na| obv. sg.; |-he|, |-ha| obv. pl. Not all of these suffixes are equally common, however. Most speakers have only those with -a in this paradigm, which is apparently the younger variant, and one speaker is known to have had only -e. Several speakers have a mixed paradigm with *i niye ka* anim. pl. beside *i niye ne* obv. sg., inan. pl., and *i niye he* obv. pl.

The *i niya* set is the distal absentative demonstrative. It specifies that which is absent, whether elsewhere, dead, or of an earlier time. In narrative it has the function of *i na* at a further remove, referring back to someone or something mentioned earlier than whatever is or might be specified with a pronoun of the *i na* set. Typically, for example, when pronouns of the *i na* set are used to switch between two characters, a pronoun of the *i niya* set is used to refer back to a third character.

31.9. ***anika na ka* 'that (further on)'.** Outside the animate singular this set has *anika ne* inan. sing. and in the longer forms a stem |anika·ne·-| with the variants of the absentative suffixes (**§31.8**) that end in -e and a locative on a stem |anika·na·-|. There are variants without the initial a-.

The demonstratives of this set refer to someone or something further on or further away. It is not used in narratives outside quoted speech and has no discourse function.

Interrogative Demonstrative

31.10. Functioning as the interrogative corresponding to the demonstrative pronouns is the set with *ta na* 'which one is he?; where is he?'. This is inflected like the *i na* set: *ta niki* 'which ones are they (anim.)?; where are they (anim.)?'.

Other Inflected Pronouns

31.11. The indefinite (**§18.6**), interrogative (**§18.7**), place-holder (**§18.8**), and alternative (**§18.9**) pronouns are inflected like noun stems, except that only the last two have locatives. The alternative pronoun has the locative *kotakeki* used with or without a noun, and an archaic locative *kotakenoki* (phonemics conjectured) 'elsewhere, in another place' used only by itself. The indefinite and interrogative locatives are suppletive: *nekotahi* 'somewhere, somewhere else'; *ta nahi* 'where?', *ta tepi* 'where to?; where from?'

Chapter 4.

§§32-58. Derivational Morphology

INTRODUCTION

Stem Components

32. The stems of words are derived from components. The components of primary stems are initials, medials, and finals. A secondary stem consists of a primary or secondary stem and, almost always, a final. The components of a stem may, in turn, be derived from stems or components. Initials, medials, and finals may be derived from noun stems or components, and initials and finals may also be derived from verb stems. Finals are specialized to one part of speech; they determine the status of the stem as a noun, verb, or particle, and for verbs they determine the inflectional category.

PRIMARY STEMS

Constituent Structure of Primary Stems

33. A primary stem consists of an initial alone, an initial and a final, or an initial, a medial, and a final. (In analyses of stem-derivation, the underlying forms of the different stem components are distinguished by giving initials with a trailing hyphen, finals with a leading hyphen, and medials with both.)

    (4.1) Stem = Initial
       (a)   *mahkwa* 'bear'
           (stem and initial |mahkw-| AN 'bear')
       (b)   *nepwa* 'he dies'
           (stem and initial |nep-| AI 'die')
    (4.2) Stem = Initial + Final
       (a)   *mesa·pe·wa* 'giant'
           (stem |mesa·pe·w-| ← |mes-| 'big' + |-a·pe·w| 'person')
       (b)   *wa·peškesiwa* 'he is white'
           (stem |wa·peškesi-| AI 'be white' ← |wa·pešk-| 'white' + |-esi| AI ABSTR)

    (c)   *nana·hika·pa·wa* 'he takes his place standing'
            (stem |nana·hika·pa·-| AI 'stand in position'
               ← |nana·h-| 'arranged, set' + |-i-ka·pa·| AI 'stand')

    (d)   *ki·škešwa* 'he cuts him apart'
            (stem |ki·škešw-| TA 'cut apart' ← |ki·šk-| 'severed' + |-ešw| TA 'cut')

(4.3) Stem = Initial + Medial + Final

    (a)   *wa·peškinameške·wa* 'he has white skin'
            (|wa·peškinameške·-| AI 'have white skin'
               ← |wa·pešk-| 'white' + |-inamešk-| 'skin' + |-e·| AI ABSTR)

    (b)   *maka·hkwatwi* 'it is a big stick, a tree with a large trunk'
            (|maka·hkwat-| II 'be a big tree, stick'
               ← |mak-| 'big', |-a·hkw-| 'tree, stick', |-at| II ABSTR)

    (c)   *matako·hkwe·šinwa* 'he lies with his head covered'
            (|matako·hkwe·šin-| AI 'lie with covered head'
               ← |matakw-| 'covered' + |-ehkwe·-| 'head' + |-išin| AI 'lie')

    (d)   *ki·škikwe·šwewa* 'he cuts off his head'
            (|ki·škikwe·šw-| TA 'cut off the head of'
               ← |ki·šk-| 'severed' + |-ikwe·-| 'neck' + |-ešw| TA 'cut')

Initials used as stems are specified for part of speech and inflectional category (4.1). Otherwise, the final determines the inflectional category of a stem. Finals may be abstract (4.2*a*, 4.3*ab*) or concrete (4.2*bc*, 4.3*cd*). In transitive stems like (4.2*c*, 4.3*d*) the final specifies the means or type of action that produces the resulting state or condition specified by the initial. The more concrete of such finals are referred to as instrumental finals. A fuller gloss of |-ešw| TA 'cut' would be 'act on animate by cutting edge (causing ..)', and a more explicit gloss of the stem in (4.2*c*) would be 'act on animate by cutting edge so as to cause to be cut up or apart'.

Derivation of Initials

34. Some initials are primary roots that have no internal structure and are not derived from anything else: |ki·šk-| 'severed' (4.2*c*, 4.3*c*). Commonly, however, initials are derived from nouns, verbs, or other initials.

34.1. Initials derived from nouns. Initials derived from most noun stems show no modification in shape. A stem-final postvocalic |w| is retained in some cases and dropped in others (4.4*c*). A stem-final post-consonantal |y| is dropped (4.4*d*; cf. 4.27). Initials derived from dependent nouns incorporate the third-person pronominal prefix (|o+| 3; §28) as a non-pronominal formative element (4.4*e*, 5.4*g*). The initials corresponding to *ohkone·hi* 'his blanket' and *oko·te·hi* 'her skirt' are *ohkone·-* (4.4) and *oko·te·-* (4.4), without the ostensible diminutive suffix. Initials may also be derived from compound nouns; in this case the original prenoun remains as a separate preword in whatever construction the derived initial is used in (4.4*j*).

(4.4) Initials derived from simple and compound noun stems

    (a)   Initial |mahkw-| 'bear' ← noun |mahkw-| 'bear' (4.1*a*):
            mahkwayi 'bearskin' (← |mahkw-| 'bear' + |-ay| 'skin').

    (b)   Initial |ahkan-| 'hard' ← noun |ahkan-| 'bone' (*ahkani* 'bone'):
            ahkanikome·samwa TI(1) 'he hardens its point in the fire'
               (← |ahkan-| 'hard' + |-i-kome·-| 'nose, tip' + |-es| TI(1) 'burn, heat')

(c)   Initial |okima·w-| ~ |okima·-| ← noun |okima·w-| AN (*okima wa* 'chief'):
        okima wika ni 'chief's house' (← |okima·w-| 'chief' + |-ika·n| IN 'structure')
        okima hkwe wa 'chief's female relative' (← |okima·-| 'chief' + |-ehkwe·w|
            'woman')
        okima neniwa 'male leader, officer' (← |okima·-| 'chief' + |-*i*-neniw| 'man')

(d)   Initial |asen-| 'rock' ← noun |aseny-| IN,AN (*aseni* 'rock', *asenya* 'sweatlodge
            rock'):
        asena pe neniwa 'rock spirit' (← |asen-| 'rock' + |-a·pe·-| 'person' + |-neniw|
            'man')

(e)   Initial |oči·kwan-| ← noun |-či·kwan| 'knee' (*oči kwani, keči kwani* 'his, your
            knee'):
        oči kwanapiwa 'he kneels' (← |oči·kwan-| 'knee' + |-api| AI 'sit')

(f)   Initial |oto·n-| ← noun |-to·n| 'mouth, rim' (*oto ni* 'his mouth'):
        oto na pi 'bail' (← |oto·n-| 'mouth, rim' + |-a·py| 'string, cord')

(g)   Initial |ohkon-| 'liver-colored' ← noun |-hkon| 'liver' (*ohkoni* 'his liver; a liver'):
        ohkoni kwe wa AI 'he has a black eye' (← |ohkon-| + |-*i*·kwe·| AI 'have (such)
            eye')

(h)   Initial |ohkone·-| ← noun |-hkone·h| 'blanket, robe' (*ohkone hi* 'his blanket, robe'):
        ohkone ka pa wa AI 'he stands in a robe' (← |ohkone·-| 'robe' + |-*i*-ka·pa·| AI
            'stand')
        ohkone škwa 'corn-husk' (← |ohkone·-| 'robe' + |-aškw| 'leaf, plant, medicine')

(i)   Initial |oko·te·-| ← noun |-ko·te·h| 'skirt' (*oko te hi* 'her skirt'):
        oko te pisowa AI 'she puts, has a skirt on' (← |oko·te·-| 'skirt' + |-apiso| AI 'be
            tied')

(j)   Prenoun |ketaki| 'spotted' + initial |nenosw-| 'bovine'
        ← compound noun |ketaki-nenosw-| 'spotted cow' (*ketaki-nenoswa* 'spotted
            cow'):
        ketaki-nenoswaško hani 'spotted cow medicines (dim.)' (K-Spot 274)
            (+ |-aškw| 'medicine', |-·h| DIM; |-ani| inan. pl.)

The loss of the stem-final |w| in cases like (4.4c) must be accounted for as part of the derivational process if it cannot be subsumed under the types of contraction recognized in inflection (**§11.7, 10**).

34.2. Initials derived from transitive stems. When initials are derived from transitive verb stems their specification for an object and hence their gender specialization are both lost. In some cases the initial derived from a TI stem in |t| adds |aw| or, with ostensible contraction, |o·| (4.5*d*). Another common modification is the replacement of the |-aw| of a TA stem by |-w| (4.5*e*).

(4.5) Initials derived from transitive verb stems
    (a)   Initial |mi·hkem-| 'court' ← |mi·hkem-| TA 'court' (*mi hkeme wa* 'he courts her'):
            mi hkemehkwe we wa AI 'he is courting women'
                (← |mi·hkem-| 'court' + |-ehkwe·w-| 'wife, girlfriend' + |-e·| AI ABSTR)
    (b)   Initial |pye·t-| 'bring; hither' ← |pye·t-| TI(2) 'bring' (*pye to wa* 'he brings it'):
            pye tehkwe we wa 'he brings home a wife'
                (← |pye·t-| 'bring; hither' + |-ehkwe·w-| 'wife, girlfriend' + |-e·| AI ABSTR)
            pye ta mowa 'he flees in this direction'
                (← |pye·t-| 'bring; hither' + |-a·mo| AI 'flee')

(c)   Initial |nemat-| 'upright' ← |nemat-| TI(2) 'stand up' (*nemato·wa* 'he stands it up'):
       nematapiwa 'he sits upright' (← |nemat-| 'upright' + |-api| AI 'sit')

(d)   Initial |na·kataw-| 'follow' ← |na·kat-| TI(1) 'follow' (*na·katamwa* 'he follows it'):
       na·katawe·neme·wa 'he keeps him in mind'
              (← |na·kataw-| 'follow' + |-e·nem| TA 'think about')
       na·kato·se·wa 'he runs along (it)' (← |na·kato·-| 'follow' + |-isa·| AI 'run, fly, fall')

(e)   Initial |mehkw-| 'find, happen upon, happen to'
              ← |mehkaw-| TA 'find, discover' (*mehkawe·wa* 'he found him'):
       mehkwi PV 'happen to' (← |mehkw-| 'happen to' + |-i| PF ABSTR):
              i·niki=ča·hi mehkwi-wi·čawiwate (K-Spot 126)
              'so if you (sg.) happen to marry one of those' (*i·niki* 'those (anim.)'; |=ča·hi| 'so';
              mehkwi PV 'happen to', |wi·čawiw-| TA 'be with, be married to',
              |-ate| 2s–3/SUBJ)
       mehkoškawe·wa 'he comes upon him; he finds him with his foot'
              (← |mehkw-| 'find, happen upon' + |-eškaw| TA 'act on by foot or body')

34.3. Initials derived from AI stems and objectless TI themes. Initials derived from AI

stems sometimes show no modification:

(4.6) Initials derived directly from AI verb stems

(a)   Initial |ša·šo·k-| 'whistle' ← |ša·šo·k-| AI 'whistle' (*ša·šo·kwa* 'he whistles'):
       ša·šo·kina·ke·wa 'he whistles a tune' (← |ša·šo·k-| 'whistle' + |-ina·ke·| AI 'sing')

(b)   Initial |ako·si·-| 'climbing' ← |ako·si·-| AI 'climb' (*ako·siwa* 'he climbs'):
       ako·si·nehkawe·wa 'he chases him up a tree'
              (← |ako·si·-| 'climbing' + |-inehkaw| TA 'chase, pursue')
       ako·si·pahowa 'he runs up (a tree)'
              (← |ako·si·-| 'climbing' + |-paho| AI 'run')
       ako·si·ya·mowa 'he flees up a tree'
              (← |ako·si·-| 'climbing' + |-a·mo| AI 'flee' [for -*y*-, see §10.1])

More commonly there are various adjustments in shape, for example the addition of |-w|
FORMTV. This purely formative element is like inflectional |-w| 3,0 in causing umlaut of
stem-final |a·| in most stems (3.244, 245; 4.7*b*), but it differs in that after a consonant it is
replaced by |-o·w| (4.7*c*), which is often heard in the younger pronunciation *ow*:

(4.7) Initials from AI verb stems with added |-w| FORMTV

(a)   Initial |ni·miw-| 'dance' ← |ni·mi-| AI 'dance' (*ni·miwa* 'he dances'):
       ni·miwahamwa 'he sings to accompany dancing'
              (← |ni·miw-| 'dance' + |-ah| TI(1)-O 'act on by tool', here 'sing')
       ni·miwisenwi 'it (song) is of the dancing variety'
              (← |ni·miw-| 'dance' + |-isen| II 'lie, be').

(b)   Initial |atame·w-| 'smoke' ← |atama·-| AI 'smoke' (*atame·wa* 'he smokes'):
       atame·wapiwa 'he sits and smokes, sits as a smoker (in a ceremony)'
              (← |atame·w-| 'smoke' + |-api| AI 'sit'; cf. *e·tame·ha* 'smoker')

(c)   Initial |a·mano·w-| 'sex' ← |a·man-| AI 'rut, have sex' (*a·manwa* 'he or she has sex'):
       a·mano·wite·he·wa 'he thinks about sex' (K-Words 58, AW)
              (← |a·mano·w-| 'sex' + |-*i*-te·he·| AI 'think')

The element |-w| FORMTV also derives initials from TI(1) themes; by definition, the theme differs
from the stem in including the theme sign |-am| TI(1) th. (§29.7(**f**)). When a verb that is used

transitively is incorporated as a verbal complement it may retain its valence for a primary object as a valence for a secondary object of the derived stem.

(4.8) Initial from TI(1) themes with added |-w| FORMTV

|a·hkwamatamo·w-| 'sick' ← |a·hkwamat-am-| TI(1)-O 'be sick'

(*a·hkwamatamwa* 'he's sick'):

(a) *kehči-a·hkwamatamo·wesiwa* 'he's like he's seriously sick' (K-FASB 49, AW)

(← *kehči* PV 'greatly', |a·kwamatamo·w-| 'sick' + |-esi| AI ABSTR)

(b) *a·hkwaha·hkwamatamowahkye·šinwa* (K-W 436, AW)

'he is lying there like someone who is sick'

(← |CVCV+| RED2,

|a·kwamatamo·w-| 'sick' + |-ahkye·-| '(on the) ground' + |-i-šin| AI 'lie')

The element |-w| FORMTV is used in the same way to derive the verbal component of incorporated complement clauses from AI stems and TA direct and TI(1) themes (**§70.3**).

Without the addition of |-w| FORMTV, a stem-final short |i| is deleted and a stem-final short |o| is replaced by |w|.

(4.9) Initials from AI verb stems in |i| and |o| without added |-w| FORMTV

(a) Initial |nepiw-| 'wet' ← |nepiwi-| AI,II 'be wet':

nepiwa·hkosiwa 'he is soaking wet'

(← |nepiw-| 'wet' + |-a·hkw-| CLSFR (4.26*b*) + |-esi| AI ABSTR)

(b) Initial |pekow-| 'dusty' ← |pekowi-| AI,II 'be dusty':

pekowi·kwe·šinwa 'he lies with dusty face'

(← |pekow-| 'dusty' + |-i·kw-e·-| 'eye, face' + |-išin| AI 'lie')

(c) Initial |nemasw-| 'stand' ← |nemaso-| AI 'stand' (*nemasowa* 'he is standing'):

nemaswise·wa 'he lands on his feet' (← |nemasw-| 'stand' + |-isa·| AI 'run, fly, fall')

nemasohoti·waki 'they have sex standing up'

(← |nemasw-| 'stand' + |-ahw| TA 'act on by tool' + |-eti·| AI RECIP)

Initials derived from most AI stems in |a·| have umlaut to |e·|. Stems in |a·| that do not have umlaut before inflectional |-w| 3,0 also lack umlaut in derived initials. Both kinds of stems in |a·| and stems in underlying |e·| sometimes have |-w| FORMTV and sometimes lack it; if contraction accounts for this it is not consistent.

(4.10) Initials from AI verb stems in |a·|

(a) Initial |nepe·-| 'sleep' ← |nepa·-| AI 'sleep' (*nepe·wa* 'he sleeps'):

nepe·škawe·wa 'his (prox.) powers put him (obv.) to sleep'

(← |nepe·-| 'sleep' + |-eškaw| TA 'act on by foot or body')

(b) Initial |mato·teše·w-| 'sweatbathing'

← |mato·teša·-| AI 'take a sweatbath' (*mato·teše·wa* 'he takes a sweatbath'):

mato·teše·wika·ni 'sweatlodge'

(← |mato·teše·w-| 'sweatbathing' + |-ika·n| IN 'structure')

(c) Initial |nepwa·hka·-| 'smart'

← |nepwa·hka·-| AI 'be smart' (*nepwa·hka·wa* 'he is smart'):

nepwa·hka·neniwa 'an intelligent man' (|-i-neniw| 'man')

(d) Initial |nepwa·hka·w-| 'smart' (cf. 4.10*c*):

nepwa·hka·wesiwa 'he is wise' (|-esi| AI ABSTR)

(4.11) Initials from AI verb stems in |e·|

(a) Initial |ata·we·-| 'trading' ← |ata·we·-| AI 'trade' (*ata·we·wa* 'he trades'):

ata·we·neniwa 'trader, merchant' (← |ata·we·-| 'trading' + |-i-neniw| 'man')

(b)   Initial |ame·-| 'reacting' ← |ame·-| AI 'react' (ame·wa 'he pays attention, reacts'):
      ame·na·kosiwa 'he appears to notice, shows a reaction on his face' (4.83)
            (← |ame·-| 'reacting' + |-ina·kosi| AI 'appear, seem')

(c)   Initial |mya·no·te·-| 'menstruating'
            ← |mya·no·te·-| AI 'menstruate' (mya·no·te·wa 'she menstruates'):
      mya·no·te·ka·ni 'menstrual hut'
            (← |mya·no·te·-| 'menstruating' + |-ika·n| IN 'structure')

(d)   Initial |a·hkwe·w-| 'angry' ← |a·hkwe·-| AI 'be angry' (a·hkwe·wa 'he is angry'):
      a·hkwe·wina·kosiwa 'he looks angry' (← |-ina·kosi| AI 'appear, seem')

Some initials are derived from intransitive stems by dropping the abstract final that is a component of a derived final. In such cases the derivation of the initial appears to depend on the derivational make-up of the final rather than that of the stem, since the abstract final that is dropped is not a constituent of the stem as a whole. For example, stems that incorporate the derived passive final pair |-ekosi| AI, |-ekwat| II (4.82-83) make initials by dropping the abstract final pair |-esi| AI, |-at| II, which forms these finals by combining with the inverse theme sign (|-ekw| TA th. 2).

(4.12) Initial derived by deletion of |-esi| AI, |-at| II

(a)   Initial |mena·kw-| 'stink' ← |mena·kosi-| AI, |mena·kwat-| II 'stink'
      (mena·kosiwa, mena·kwatwi 'he, it stinks'):
      menamena·kwini·kwe·wa 'he has stinky eyes'
            (← |CVCV+| RED2, |mena·kw-| 'stink' + |-ini·kw-| 'eye' + |-e·| AI ABSTR)

(b)   Initial |mo·wečiwiya·kw-| 'smell of excrement' ← |mo·wečiwiya·kwat-| II
      'smell of excrement' (mo·wečiwiya·kwatwi 'it smells of excrement';
            ← |mo·wečiw-| 'having excrement, dungy' + |-iya·kwat| II 'smell'):
      mo·wečiwiya·kotonwa 'his mouth smelled of excrement'
            (← |mo·wečiwiya·kw-| 'smelling of excrement' + |-eton-| 'mouth' +
      |-Ø| AI ABSTR)

The dropping of the final |-i| in the formation of initials from stems with |-iwi| AI,II 'be' (4.9ab; 4.237) could be analyzed the same way.

Initials derived from stems with |-išin| AI 'lie' (4.73a) replace this with an otherwise unused final |-išimo| AI 'lie', which lengthens |o| before |-w| FORMTV (cf. 4.196, 4.258).

(4.13) Initial |ma·wa·šimo·w-| 'gathering' ← |ma·wa·šin-| AI 'gather socially':
      ma·wa·šimo·wika·ni 'hotel' (← |ma·wa·šimo·w-| 'gathering' + |-ika·n| IN 'structure')

There are some other idiosyncratic patterns:

(4.14) Initial |pakikaw-| 'dripping' ← |pakika·-| AI,II (pakike·wa, pakike·wi 'he, it drips'):
      pa·hpakikawa·naki·kwe·htawe·wa 'he (prox.) lets his tears flow upon him (obv.)'
            (← |pa·hpakikawa·naki·kwe·-| AI 'his eyes drip tears' + |-·htaw| TA APPLIC;
      AI ← |Ca·h+| RED1, |pakikaw-| 'dripping' + |-a·naki·kw-| 'eye' + |-e·| AI ABSTR)

34.4. Initials derived from II verbs. Initials derived from II verbs do not ordinarily add |-w| FORMTV. II stems referring to time or weather that end in a vowel add |-n| in the derived initial; before this a short vowel is lengthened and one stem replaces |-Cwi| with |o·|. (There is no example for a stem in |i·|; see 4.16a.)

(4.15) Initials derived from II stems

(a)   Initial |ni·pen-| 'harvest' ← |ni·pen-| II 'be harvest' (ni·penwi 'it is harvest time'):
      ni·peni PN,PV 'harvest' (← |ni·pen-| 'harvest' + |-i| PF ABSTR):
            ni·peni-wi·seniweni 'garden crops' (wi·seniweni 'food')

(b)   Initial |wa·pan-| 'dawn' ← |wa·pan-| II 'be dawn' (*wa panwi* 'it is dawn'):
       wa panemiwa 'daylight overtakes him; he lives till dawn'
          (← |wa·pan-| 'dawn' + |-emi| AI 'be overtaken by time of day')

(c)   Initial |pehkote·n-| 'night' ← |pehkote·-| II 'be night' (*pehkote wi* 'it is night'):
       pehkote nemiwa 'he is overtaken by night'
          (← |pehkote·n-| 'night' + |-emi| AI 'be overtaken by time of day')

(d)   Initial |kemiya·n-| 'rain' ← |kemiya·-| II 'rain' (*kemiya wi* 'its is raining'):
       kemiya nešiwa 'he gets caught in the rain' (|-eši| AI 'be caught in the weather')

(e)   Initial |pepo·n-| 'winter' ← |pepo·-| II 'be winter' (*pepo wi* 'it is winter'):
       pepo ni PN,PV 'winter' (← |pepo·n-| 'winter' [cf. 5.19c] + |-i| PF ABSTR):
          pepo ni-ki wite wa 'he (bird) stays through the winter' (*ki wite wa* 'he stays')

(f)   Initial |ana·ko·n-| 'evening' ← |ana·kwi-| II 'be evening' (*ana kwiwi* 'it is
       evening'):
       ana ko nemiwa 'he is overtaken by evening'
          (← |ana·ko·n-| 'evening' + |-emi| AI 'be overtaken by time of day')

There are at least two II stems that ostensibly make a derived initial by adding |-w|; one ends
in |i·|, and the other ends in |o·| and also makes an initial with added |n|.

(4.16) Initials ostensibly derived from II stems with |w|

(a) |meno·hkami·w-| 'spring' (as if from |meno·hkami·-| II 'be spring')
       meno·hkami wi PV 'spring' (← |meno·hkami·w-| 'spring' + |-i| PF ABSTR; 5.13c):
       meno·hkami wi-ni miwaki 'they have a spring dance' (*ni miwaki* 'they dance')

(b) |pepo·w-| 'winter' (as if from |pepo·-| II 'be winter'; cf. 4.15e)
       pepo wi PV 'winter' (← |pepo·w-| 'winter' + |-i| PF ABSTR):
       Only in: |pepo·wi-ki·ke·no-| AI 'hold a winter clan feast' (O 12J; 5.13*f*)

Alternatively, however, these initials can be taken as regularly derived from identical noun stems
(**§31.1**) of the type that is made from II stems with the agentive noun final |-w| (**§46.1**). The
corpus does not appear to attest these particular nouns as such, but **meno·hkami wi* IN 'spring' is
also implied by the particle *meno·hkami we* 'last spring', and such nouns would have parallels in
the names of other seasons and the like.

34.5. Initials derived from components. An initial may be derived from two initials or
from an initial and a postradical, a formative element which may itself be derived from a medial.
The fusion of two initials into a new initial appears in some cases to reflect the restructuring of
stems in which the first element was originally a preverb formed with |-i| PF ABSTR. The second
initial was often a relative root that took the original preverb as its complement. These initials
are analyzed as having a connective |i| (4.17a) except when the second component begins with a
vowel (4.17*bcdef*).

(4.17) Initials derived from two initials

(a)   Initial |košima·t-| 'gingerly' ← |koS-| 'fear' + connective |i| + |ma·t-| 'move':
       košima tapiwa 'he sits gingerly' (|-api| AI 'sit') (K-W 126)
       košima tene wa 'he holds him gingerly' (|-en| TA 'act on by hand') (K-M 688o)

(b)   Initial |makinehp-| 'high' ← |mak-| 'big' + |inehp-| '{so} high' (**§22.4(b)**, 2.110):
       makinehpa·hki wi 'it is high ground' (|-a·hki·| II 'be higher ground, hill, rise')
       makinehpašiwa 'he has a load piled high on his back'
          (|-aši| AI 'have a back-load')

(c)   Initial |čakinehp-| 'low' ← |čak-| 'small' + |inehp-| '{so} high':
       čakinehpya·hiwi 'it is low' (|-ya·| II ABSTR; |-·hi| DIM)

(d)   Initial |no·te·hkw-| 'not far or long enough' ← |no·te·-| 'incomplete' + |ahkw-| '{so far}' (**§22.4(a)**): *no·te·hkwisenwi* 'it (pole) is too short' (|-isen| II 'lie, be')

(e)   Intial |te·pahkw-| 'reach' ← |te·p-| 'enough' + |ahkw-| '{so far}' (**§22.4(a)**): *te·pahkoškamwa* 'he attains it' (|-ešk| TI(1) 'act on by foot or body')

(f)   Initial |tepahkw-| 'measure' ← |tep-| 'match, own' + |ahkw-| '{so far}' (**§22.4(a)**): *tepahkwihto·wa* 'he measures it' (|-ht| TI(2) ABSTR)

34.6. Postradicals. Initials often include a post-radical extension, or postradical. A postradical is an added formative element and in some cases appears to be purely formal. For example, an initial may have variants with different postradicals specialized for use in different stems. Hence in many cases no clear-cut meaning can be assigned to these elements and they are left unglossed. Others are given a general label or tentative gloss. In a few cases the postradical has a fairly clear meaning, typically narrowing the application of the initial to a particular shape, configuration, abstract type of action, or the like. Postradicals and prefinals (**§37, §37.2**) appear to be essentially the same class of formatives, with a largely joint membership. They often show a preference for occurring both after particular initials and before particular finals, and hence the analysis of their role in some stems may be ambiguous. Their underlying forms are written like those of medials, with leading and trailing hyphens.

(4.18) Postradical |-at-|

(a) |pa·hkat-| 'break open' ← |pa·hk-| 'open' + |-at-|:
       pa·hkatenamwa 'he breaks it off or open where it closes or is attached, rips it at the seam, opens its cover' (|-en| TA,TI(1) 'act on by hand')
       (cf. *pa·hkenamwa* 'he opened it, uncovered it')

(b) |ši·pat-| 'stretch' ← |ši·p-| 'stretch, endure' + |-at-|:
       ši·patenamwa 'he stretched it' (|-en| TA,TI(1) 'act on by hand')
       (cf. *ši·papene·wa* 'he endures hunger' [|-apene·| AI 'be hungry'])

(c) |ma·wat-| 'gather, assemble' ← |ma·w-| + |-at-| (cf. |ma·wa·-| [4.20*a*]):
       ma·watenamwa 'he gathers it' (|-en| TA,TI(1) 'act on by hand')
       ma·wači·waki 'they assemble' (|-i·| AI ABSTR)

(4.19) Postradical |-ešk-|, |-eška·-| (intensifier)

(a) |wa·pešk-| 'white' ← |wa·p-| 'pale, gray; white (arch.)' + |-ešk-|:
       wa·peškya·wi 'it is white' (|-ya·| II ABSTR)
       (cf. *wa·pya·wi* 'it is light-colored' [← |wa·p-ya·-|])

(b) |ši·pešk-| 'drag on, protract' ← |ši·p-| 'stretch, endure' + |-ešk-|:
       ša·ši·peškowe·wa 'he speaks drawlingly, very slowly' (|-owe·| AI 'speak')
       ši·peškya·wi 'it stretches with difficulty' (|-ya·| II ABSTR)

(c) |peši·šk-| 'skin completely' ← |peši·-| 'skin' + |-ešk-|:
       peši·škene·wa 'he skinned him completely' (|-en| TA,TI(1) 'act on by hand')
       (cf. *peši·ne·wa* 'he skins him' [← |peši·-en-|])

(d) |peši·ška·-| 'skin completely' ← |peši·-| 'skin' + |-eška·-|:
       peši·ška·ne·wa 'he skinned him completely' (K-W 740; analysis as in 4.19*c*)

(e) |si·keška·-| (also |si·kaška·-|) 'empty out' ← |si·k-| 'pour, spill, empty' + |-eška·-|:
       si·keška·namwa 'he pours, spills, dumps it, them out' (|-en| TA,TI(1) 'act on by hand')
       (cf. *si·kenamwa* 'he pours it' [← |si·k-en-|])

(4.20) Postradical |-a·-|
  (a) |ma·wa·-| 'gather, assemble' ← |ma·w-| + |-a·-| (cf. |ma·wat-| [4.18c]):
       ma·wa·ške·waki 'they assemble' (|-eška·| AI,II 'move, become')
       ma·wa·ke·waki 'they camp together' (|-i-k-| 'dwelling', |-e·| AI ABSTR)
  (b) |si·ka·-| 'exhaust' ← |si·k-| 'pour, spill, empty' (4.19e) + |-a·-|:
       si·ka·nawe·wa 'he cleans him out, wins everything from him in gambling'
            (|-enaw| TA 'act on by missile or shot, gamble against')
       si·ka··hpwe·wa 'he smoked him (pipe) out completely' (|-hpw| TA 'act on by
            mouth')
  (c) |peka·-| 'crumbled' ← |pek-| 'crumbled, to pieces' (4.24a) + |-a·-|:
       peka·če·namwa 'he made it crumble when he grasped it'
            (|-eče·-| 'small body', |-en| TA,TI(1) 'act on by hand')

(4.21) Postradical |-e·-|
  (a) |a·nwe·-| 'not believing' ← |a·nw-| 'fail to' + |-e·-|:
       (in stems that are the antonyms of ones with |te·pwe·-| 'believing')
       a·nwe··htawe·wa 'he disbelieves him'
       a·nwe··še·wa 'he does not believe'
            (cf. *te·pwe··htawe·wa* 'he believes him', *te·pwe··še·wa* 'he believes')
  (b) |seswe·-| 'scatter, splash' ← |sesw-| 'spray' (4.90b) + |-e·-|:
       seswe··škamwa 'he makes it scatter or splash'
       seswe··hanwi 'it made a splash'

(4.22) Postradical |-i-| 'massively, blanketing'
  (a) |ahpi-| 'forcefully or massively down on top' ← |ahp-| 'on' + |-i-|:
       ahpihkye··hokowa AI 'he was pinned to the ground' (|-ahky-e·-| 'earth', |-ahoko| AI
            'be acted on by mass of water, weight, or falling object' [4.78a])
       ahpihokowa AI 'he has a mass fall down on top of him' (|-ahoko| AI 'be acted on
            by mass of water, weight, or falling object' [4.78a])
       ahpihwe·wa TA 'he piles {something} on top of him' (|-ahw| TA [4.95a])
       ahpiškamwa TI(1) 'he steps on it' (|-ešk| TI(1) [4.94b]))
  (b) |a·pi-| 'untie' (?): See 4.95e.
  (c) |kepi-| (?), |naki-| (?), |tepi-| (?): as these ostensible initials appear to be found only
       before |-eškaw| TA, |-ešk| TI(1) 'act on by foot or body', the stems that apparently
       contain them are analyzed as having |-iškaw| TA, |-išk| TI(1) 'act on by body mass
       or presence' (4.94c), with prefinal |-i-| 'mass, sheer presence'.
            (The postradical |-i-| 'massively, blanketing' is matched by the prefinal |-i-|
            'mass, sheer presence' [4.94c, 4.95e].)

(4.23) Postradical |-ik-| 'stick-like'
  (a) |ma·čik-| 'move in a stick-like fashion' ← |ma·t-| 'move' + |-ik-|:
       ma·čikanwe·wa 'he has an erection' (|-anw-| 'arrow, penis', |-e·| AI ABSTR)
            (cf. *ma·tapiwa* 'he moves in his seat' ← |ma·t-| 'move', |-api| AI 'sit')
  (b) |pepeškwik-| 'peel with stick-like configuration' ← |pepeškw-| 'shed, peel' + |-ik-|:
       pepeškwike·šamwa 'he peels it (a stick) with a knife' (|-eš| TI(1) 'cut')
            (cf. *pepeškoče··ške·wa* 'he's shedding' (|-eče·-| 'small body', |-eška·| AI 'move,
            become')

(4.24) Postradical |-ihk-| 'massively, totally'
   (a) |pekihk-| 'to small pieces' ← |pek-| 'crumbled, to pieces' + |-ihk-|:
          pekihkešamwa 'he cuts it to pieces' (|-eš| TI(1) 'cut')
          (cf. *pekeče·ya·senwi* 'it is turned to dust by the wind'
             [|-eče·-| 'small body', |-a·sen| II 'wind to blow; be blown by wind'];
             pekene·wa 'he shells him (corn)' [← |pek-| + |-en| TA,TI(1) 'act on by hand'])
   (b) |a·čihk-| 'segmented, having large repeating segments' ← |a·t-| 'back, again' + |-ihk-|:
          a·čihkya·wi 'it is in sections, is made up of segments' (|-ya·| II ABSTR)
          (cf. *a·čikenwi* 'it (as a design) repeats' [|-iken| II 'grow, happen, be'])
(4.25) Postradical |-w|, |-o·| (deriving initials of number and amount)
   (a) |ni·šw-|, |ni·šo·-| 'two' ← |ni·š-| + |-w|, |-o·|
          (cf. *ni·šiwaki* 'they are two', *ni·šenwi* 'twice'):
             ni·šwi 'two'
             ni·šwayaki 'two sets, pairs, tribes'
             ni·šwihe·wa 'he makes, gets, kills, has two of them (anim.)' (4.86a)
             ni·šo·hkwe·we·wa 'he has two wives'
                (|-ehkwe·w-| 'wife' [4.30]; contraction: 1.126)
             ni·šo·namo·ki 'they held, carried it together; they held, carried two of them (inan.)'
                (|-en| TI(1) 'act on by hand' [4.97])
             ni·šo·wose·waki 'the two of them walk together' (|-(w)ose·| AI 'walk')
   (b) |ča·ko·-| 'all' ← |ča·k-| + |-o·| (cf. *ča·ki* 'all'):
          ča·ko·ne·wa 'they all carried him' (|-en| TI(1) 'act on by hand' [4.97])
   (c) |ma·nw-|, |ma·no·-| 'much, many' ← |ma·n-| (cf. 4.99b)
          ma·nwikamikesiwaki 'they are of many households'
          ma·no·hpowaki 'they eat together as many'

Some medials appear also in postradical use. Compared to true medials, postradicals derived from medials have attenuated meanings; they modify the initial rather than functioning as an independent, semantically noun-like component; and they do not incorporate a postmedial (§35).

(4.26) Postradical |-a·hkw-| 'extended solid' (← medial |-a·hkw-| 'tree, stick' [4.3b])
   (a) |ši·pa·hkw-| 'stretch out' ← |ši·p-| 'stretch, endure' (4.18b, 4.19b) + |-a·hkw-|:
          ši·pa·hkwika·te·wa 'he stretches his legs in his stride' (|-ka·t-| 'leg, foot',
             |-e·| AI ABSTR)
   (b) |nepiwa·hkw-| 'wet all over' ← |nepiw-| 'wet' (4.9a) + |-a·hkw-|:
          nepiwa·hkosiwa 'he is soaking wet' (|-esi| AI ABSTR)
   (c) |meškwa·hkw-| 'all red' ← |meškw-| red' + |-a·hkw-|:
          meškwa·hkone·wa 'he painted him red, painted his body and limbs red'
          (cf. *meškone·wa* 'he painted something red on him, got red on him by touching')
The postradical made from the medial |-epy-| 'water' (noun |nepy-| 'water', *nepi*) drops the |y|:
(4.27) Postradical |-ep| 'watery' (← medial |-epy-| 'water'; cf. 4.4(d))
   (a) |wi·nep-| 'cruddy, slimy, filthy and wet' ← |wi·n-| 'filthy' + |-ep|:
          wi·nepinenye·hpwe·wa 'he made her breasts a cruddy, slimy mess with his mouth'
             (|-i-nenye·-| 'breast(s)', |-hpw| TA 'act on by mouth')
   (b) |meškop-| 'pink' ← |meškw-| 'red' + |-ep|:
          meškopa·te·wi 'it is pink' (|-a·te·| II 'be dyed or colored')

Derivation of Medials

35. Medials may be derived from noun stems or noun finals. One large class of medials is derived from dependent nouns. Often there is a noun final derived from a noun in the same way as the medial. Some medials that are not derived are the suppletive counterparts of nouns. Some medials diverge in meaning from the matching noun, calling into question the synchronic status of the derivation.

A medial may consist of a single, core medial, or it may include also a premedial or a postmedial, or both. As a consequence, medials typically fall into sets that have the same core medial and different selections of these added formative elements. Premedials often have no discernible meaning; in such cases the variants with or without a premedial are selected by the stems in which they are used. Often one of the variants seems to be rarer and recessive while the other is the one used productively. Other premedials, generally those that are themselves derived from medials, have a discernible semantic content and are selected to specify a more precise reference than what the basic medial alone would have. Postmedials, on the other hand, are always abstract formatives and are selected by the morphological context. They appear to be almost completely specialized, each being used before certain finals or classes of finals. The common postmedials are |-e·-| and |-ak-| (variant |-e·k-|); two medials have a postmedial |-amik-|.

The medials corresponding to dependent nouns often have variants in addition to those generated by the use of premedials and postmedials. One variant may have a shape identical or nearly identical to that of the noun, while the other variant may be more divergent. For the medials that have such variants, one may be used before a postmedial and the other before an abstract final. The distribution often does not conform to a rigid pattern, however, and stem doublets are found in which two variant medials are possible.

In the derivation of a medial from a noun there is sometimes a modification in shape, most commonly the replacement of the initial vowel or the dropping of the initial vowel, consonant (or *ow-*), or consonant-vowel syllable. It is generally an open question whether an ostensible connective |i| (|-*i*-|) used before a derived medial could rather be taken as added in the derivation of the medial (**§8.1**). A final post-consonantal |w| may be dropped. Long high vowels may be shortened, and other medial vowels may be replaced. In a few cases a medial derived from a dependent noun deletes an initial pre-consonantal |h| or |š| or adds an initial |a|. Nouns that are formally diminutive make medials from the non-diminutive counterpart of the stem.

A medial that is not followed by a concrete final is followed by an abstract final, commonly |-e·| AI ABSTR or |-esi| AI, |-at| II ABSTR but also |-a·| AI ABSTR, |-i·| AI ABSTR, |-∅| AI ABSTR, or |-N| AI ABSTR. Medials add no postmedial before |-e·| AI ABSTR and typically add the postmedial |-ak-| before |-esi| AI, |-at| II ABSTR.

The examples of medials in the following sections illustrate a number of patterns of derivation without being anywhere near exhaustive.

35.1. Medials derived from non-dependent nouns. Some medials are derived from noun stems with no modification other than perhaps the addition of a postmedial. In at least one case an unpossessed dependent noun is treated as a non-dependent noun and makes a medial with the prefix |me+| (3.19, 25) incorporated (4.28*c*). Although the existence of this stem and of rare nonce forms (4.28*d*) suggests that the derivation of medials from nouns is an active, synchronically accessible process, it is, in fact, not commonly used in the formation of new stems.

(4.28) Medials derived from nouns without modification

(a)   Medial |-pi·sehka·h-e·-| 'shirt' ← |pi·sehka·h-| (*pi·sehka·hi* 'shirt')
        kečipi·sehka·he·ne·wa 'he takes his (obv.) shirt off'
        (|ket-| 'out', |-i-pi·sehka·h-e·-| 'shirt', |-en| TA 'act on by hand')

(b)   Medial |-ahky-e·-| 'earth' ← |ahky-| (*ahki* 'earth, land')
        te·pahkye·hamwa 'he can touch bottom'
        (|te·p-| 'enough', |-ahky-e·-| 'earth', |-ah| TI(1) 'act on by tool')

(c)   Medial |-mi·nakay-| 'penis' ← |mi·nakay-| (*mi·nakayi* 'a penis'; *owi·nakayi* 'his —')
        makimi·nakaye·wa 'he has a large penis' (K-M 325i; reduplicated pl. K-OWM 29)
        (|mak-| 'big', |-i-mi·nakay-| 'penis', |-e·| AI ABSTR)
        (More commonly the medial is |-i-nakay-| 'penis' [cf. 4.54].)

(d)   Humorous nonce medial |-ki·kehčina·hkwapiso·n-e·-| 'full outfit worn around'
        ← virtual compound noun *ki·* (PV)PN 'around' +
        |kehčina·hkwapiso·n-| 'full outfit'
        ← |kehčina·hkwapiso-| AI 'be fully dressed, wear full costume' + |-en| NF (4.193):
        e·h=kekiki·kehčina·hkwapiso·ne·šino·hiniči. (S-IM 15)
        'She lay there with all the wraps she was traveling around in on.'
        (|kek-| 'having', |-i-ki·kehčina·hkwapiso·n-e·-| 'full outfit', |-šin| AI 'lie',
        |-o·hi| DIM)

Beside |-ahky-e·-| 'earth' (4.28b) there is also a medial with loss of the stem-final |y| (cf. 4.4d)
and a different postmedial.

(4.29) Medial |-ahk-amik-| 'earth; general activity or situation' ← |ahky-| (*ahki* 'earth, land')

(a)   *ahkwahkamikatwi* 'the world ends' (|ahkw-| 'end', |-ahk-amik-| 'earth', |-at| II ABSTR)

(b)   *se·kahkamikatwi* 'people are scared'
        (|se·k-| 'scared', |-ahk-amik-| 'general situation', |-at| II ABSTR)

Some medials show a semantic narrowing compared to the noun they are derived from:

(4.30) Medial |-ehkwe·w-| 'wife, girlfriend' ← |ihkwe·w-| (*ihkwe·wa* 'woman'; also 4.5ab)
        awatehkwe·we·wa 'he takes home a wife' (|awat-| 'take away'; |-e·| AI ABSTR)
        (|awat-| 'take away' ← |awat-| TI(2) 'take away': *awato·wa* 'he takes it away')

(4.31) Medial |-neniw| 'war captive' ← |neniw-| (*neniwa* 'man')
        pye·čineniwe·wa 'he brings home war captives or scalps'
        (|pye·t-| 'bring' (4.5b), |-i-neniw-| 'war captive', |-e·| AI ABSTR)

The medials for 'dish' (4.32) and 'root' (4.33) show the loss of initial vowels and the
derivation of variants with different postmedials.

(4.32) Medial |-na·kan-|, |-na·kan-e·-|, |-na·kan-ak-| 'dish, bowl' ← |ana·kan-| (*ana·kani* 'dish,
        plate')

(a)   Medial |-na·kan-| 'dish' before |-Ø| II ABSTR:
        ki·šina·kanwi 'it had already been dished into bowls' (K-W 300)
        (|ki·š-| PERF, |-i-na·kan-| 'dish', |-Ø| AI ABSTR)

(b)   Medial |-na·kan-e·-| 'dish' ← medial |-na·kan-| + postmedial |-e·-|:
        kekina·kane·senwi 'it is in a dish' (|kek-| 'with', |-i-na·kan-e·-| 'dish', |-sen| II 'lie, be')

(c)   Medial |-na·kan-ak-| 'dish' ← medial |-na·kan-| + postmedial |-ak-|:
        ma·nwina·kanakatwi 'there are many bowls of it'
        (|ma·nw-| 'many', |-i-na·kan-ak-| 'bowl', |-at| II ABSTR)

(4.33) Medial |-če·pihk-|, |-če·pihk-ak-| 'root' ← |oče·pihk-| (*oče pihki* 'root')

   (a)   *kečiče pihkisahto wa* 'he yanks it out by the roots'

           (|ket-| 'out', |-i-če·pihk-| 'root', |-saht| TI(2) 'cause by quick action')

   (b)   *pi·siče pihkakato·hiwi* 'it has fine roots'

           (|pi·s-| 'small, fine', |-i-če·pihk-ak-| 'root', |-at| II ABSTR, |-o·-hi| DIM)

The medials for 'water' (4.34), 'hole' (4.35), and 'game animal' (4.36) have the loss of the initial consonant of the noun.

  (4.34) Medial |-epy-|, |-epy-e·-|, |-epy-e·k-| 'water' ← |nepy-| (*nepi* 'water')

   (a)   *aškepye wa* 'he drowns' (|ašk-| 'tired', |-epy-| 'water', |-e·| AI ABSTR)

   (b)   *a·wasepye wa* 'he hauls sap' (|a·wat-| 'convey by loads', |-epy-| 'water',

           |-e·| AI ABSTR)

   (c)   *po·nepye wa* 'he quit drinking'

           (|po·n-| 'cease', |-epy-| 'water', |-e·| AI ABSTR [idiom: |-epy-e·-| AI 'drink alcohol'])

   (d)   *tahkepye·šinwa* 'he cools off by taking a swim'

           (|tahk-| 'cold', |-epy-e·-| 'water', |-išin| AI 'lie')

   (e)   *akwa·pye·ki wa* 'he swims ashore'

           (|akwa·-| 'out of medium', |-epy-e·k-| 'water', |-i·| ABSTR)

  (4.35) Medial |-a·nak-| 'hole' ← |wa·nakw-| (*wa·nakwi* 'hole')

           (|-a·nak-| is treated as if |-a·n-ak-|, with postmedial |-ak-|; and, in fact, comparative

           evidence shows that the noun was originally back-formed from the medial)

           maka·nakatwi 'it's a big hole, cave' (|mak-| 'big', |-a·nak-| 'hole', |-at| II ABSTR)

  (4.36) Medial |-o·sw-| 'game animal' ← |mo·sw-| (*mo·swa* 'moose' [presumably narrowed

           from an originally broader meaning])

   (a)   *a·ko·ho·swe wa* 'he hunts buffalo (esp. on foot, by driving)'

           (|a·ko·h-| 'walling off, driving', |-o·sw-| 'game animal', |-e·| AI ABSTR)

   (b)   *peši no·swe wa* 'he skins an animal' (e.g., a bear, a deer)

           (|peši·n-| 'skin' [← |peši·n-| TA 'skin'], |-o·sw-| 'game animal', |-e·| AI ABSTR)

The medials for 'moccasin' and 'leggin' show the removal of the ostensible diminutive suffix.

  (4.37) Medial |-mahkesen-| 'moccasin' ← |mahkese·h-| (*mahkese·hi* 'moccasin', archaic

           stem |mahkesen-| 2.36*b*)

           pi·wa·himahkesene wa 'he wears beaded moccasins'

           (|pi·wa·h-| 'beaded' [←*pi·wa·hi* 'bead'], |-i-mahkesen-| 'moccasin', |-e·| AI ABSTR)

  (4.38) Medial |-matet-e·-| 'leggin' ← |matete·h-| (*matete·hani* 'leggins')

           wa·wa·pimatete wa 'he's wearing white leggins'

           (|CV+| RED1, |wa·p-| 'white', |-i-matet-| 'leggin', |-e·| AI ABSTR)

The medials for 'firewood' and 'bag' have both the loss of the initial consonant and the removal of the diminutive suffix.

  (4.39) Medial |-es-| 'firewood' ← |mese·h-| (*mese·hi* 'piece of firewood'; the noun stem

           |mese·h-| is formally the diminutive of a stem |mes-|; cf. 3.89)

           manese wa 'he cuts firewood' (|man-| 'gather, take', |-es-| 'firewood', |-e·| AI ABSTR)

  (4.40) Medial |-aškimot-e·-| 'bag' ← |maškimote·h-| (*maškimote·hi* 'bag')

           ši·kwaškimote·namwa 'he left (it as) an empty bag'

           (|ši·kw-| 'empty, left over', |-aškimot-e·-| 'bag', |-en| TI(1) 'act on by hand')

One medial for 'head' has a rarer variant with the premedial |-a·-|.

(4.41) Medial |-tep-|, |-a·tep-| 'head' ← |otepy-| 'brain' (*otepi 'brain', oto·tepi·mi 'his brain')

    (a)   *ko·kitepe·wa* 'he (prox.) washed his (prox.) hair'

            (|ko·k-| 'wash', |-i-tep-| 'head', |-a·| AI ABSTR)

    (b)   *mi·kesa·tepe·wa* 'he has wampum strung in his hair'

            (|mi·kes-| 'wampum', |-a·tep-| 'head', |-e·| AI ABSTR)

The medial for 'snow' illustrates both premedial |-a·-| and vowel shortening:

(4.42) Medial |-a·kon-|, |-a·kon-e·-| 'snow' ← |ako·n-| (ako·na 'snow')

    (a)   *meškowa·koni·wi* 'there is blood on the snow'

            (|meškow-| 'bloody' [← |meškowi-| AI,II 'be bloody'], |-a·kon-| 'snow', |-i·| II ABSTR)

    (b)   *a·nwa·koni·wa* 'he struggles in the deep snow'

            (|a·nw-| 'unable', |-a·kon-| 'snow', |-i·| AI ABSTR [4.71])

    (c)   *matakwa·kone·wa* 'he covered himself with snow'

            (|matakw-| 'covered', |-a·kon-| 'snow', |-e·| AI ABSTR)

    (d)   *tawa·kone·škamwa* 'he cleared the snow from it with his feet'

            (|taw-| 'cleared, unblocked', |-a·kon-e·-| 'snow', |-ešk| TI(1) 'act on by foot or body')

Loss of initial syllables is found in the medials for 'bone' and 'blood'.

(4.43) Medial |-kan-|, |-kan-e·-| 'bone' ← |ahkan-| (ahkani 'bone')

    (a)   *pehkwikane·wa* 'he has a bone with a lump on it'

            (|pehkw-| 'lump', |-i-kan-| 'bone', |-e·| AI ABSTR)

    (b)   *po·hkwikane·sowa* 'he has a bone broken by gunshot'

            (|po·hkw-| 'break, snap', |-i-kan-e·-| 'bone', |-eso| AI 'be acted on by heat, gunshot')

(4.44) Medial |-škw-e·k-| 'blood' ← |meškw-| (meškwi 'blood')

    (a)   *sa·kiškwe·katwi* 'it is bleeding, showing blood'

            (|sa·k-| 'emergent, partly visible', |-i-škw-e·k-| 'blood', |-at| II ABSTR)

    (b)   *pye·čiškwe·kihto·wa* 'he leaves a trail of blood this way' (|pye·čiškwe·kiht-| TI(2)-O)

            (|pye·t-| 'coming', |-i-škw-e·k-| 'blood', |-i-ht| TI(2) ABSTR)

35.2. Medials derived from dependent nouns. Some medials have the same shape as the dependent noun they correspond to.

(4.45) Medial |-hka·hk-|, |-hka·hk-e·-| 'chest' ← |-hka·hk-| (nehka·hki 'my chest')

    (a)   *ketakihka·hke·wa* 'he (bird) has a speckled breast'

            (|ketak-| 'spotted, striped', |-i-hka·hk-| 'chest', |-e·| AI ABSTR)

    (b)   *kečihka·hke·piwa* 'he sits with his chest out'

            (|ket-| 'out', |-i-hka·hk-e·-| 'chest', |-api| AI 'sit')

(4.46) Medial |-kahkwan-| 'shin, leg' ← |-kahkwan-| (nekahkwani 'my shin')

        mehčikahkwanwa 'he has bare shins'

             (|meht-| 'bare', |-i-kahkwan-| 'shin', |-∅| AI ABSTR)

In some cases a dependent noun stem that begins with a cluster loses the |h| or |š| from the cluster in the medial:

(4.47) Medial |-kaš-| 'nail, hoof, claw' ← |-škašy| (neškaš(y)e·ki 'my nails')

        kaka·nwikaše·wa 'he has long nails, claws'

             (|Ca_a·+| RED1, |kenw-| 'long', |-i-kaš-| 'nail, claw', |-e·| AI ABSTR)

(4.48) Medial |-keten-| 'vagina' ← |-hketen-| (ohketenani 'her vagina')

        mešiketene·wa 'she has a large vagina' (|meš-| 'big', |-i-keten-| 'vagina',

        |-e·| AI ABSTR)

A stem-final |-ay| or |-kan| may also be deleted.

(4.49) Medial |-namešk-|, |-namešk-e·-| 'skin' ← |-nameškay| (*nenameškaya* 'my skin')

   (a)   *asa winameške wa* 'he has brown skin'
         (|asa·w-| 'yellow, brown', |-i-namešk-| 'skin', |-e·| AI ABSTR)

   (b)   *ka·hkihkinameške nawe wa* 'he scratches his (obv.) skin with a shot'
         (|ka·hkihk-| 'scratch', |-i-namešk-e·-| 'skin', |-enaw| TA 'shoot')

(4.50) Medial |-kw-e·-| 'neck' ← |-i-hkwe·kan| (*nehkwe·kani* 'my neck')

   sakikwe pine wa 'he (prox.) tied a cord around his (obv.) neck'
         (|sak-| 'hold', |-i-kw-e·-| 'neck', |-apiN| TA 'tie')

The medial |-kw-| 'neck' is used only before the postmedial |-e·-|. Other, longer medials for 'neck', one of which has the unmodified shape of the noun stem, are used before an abstract final as well as before postmedial |-e·-|.

(4.51) Medial |-hkwe·kan-|, |-hkwe·kan-e·-| 'neck' ← |-hkwe·kan| (*nehkwe·kani* 'my neck')

   (a)   *wa peškihkwe·kanwa* 'he has a white neck'
         (|wa·pešk-| 'white', |-i-hkwe·kan-| 'neck', |-0| AI ABSTR)

   (b)   *oče pihkihkwe·kane·ške wa* 'he made his neck tendons stand out'
         (|oče·pihk-| 'root, root-like', |-i-hkwe·kan-e·-| 'neck', |-eška·| AI 'become')

Similarly, the medial for 'foot' (archaically 'leg') has one shape before an abstract final and an irregular shorter form, with no postmedial, before most concrete finals. The longer, regular shape is used before |-ka·pa·| AI,II 'stand' and appears rarely before concrete finals in a few other stems.

(4.52) Medial |-ka·-|, |-ka·t-|, |-ka·t-e·-| 'foot' ← |-hka·t| (*nehka·či* 'my foot')

   (a)   *sakika ne wa* 'he grabs him by the leg'
         (|sak-| 'grab, hold', |-i-ka·-| 'foot, leg', |-en| TA 'act on by hand')

   (b)   *mehčika te wa* 'he has bare feet' (|meht-| 'bare', |-i-ka·t-| 'foot', |-e·| AI ABSTR)

   (c)   *se·sika te·ka pa wa* 'he stands with his foot on something'
         (|se·s-| 'placed or resting atop', |-i-ka·t-e·-| 'foot', |-ka·pa·| AI 'stand')

   (d)   *ša waša wano wika te·se waki* 'they do Shawnee Dance steps'
         (|CVCV+| RED2, |ša·wano·w-| 'Shawnee', |-i-ka·t-e·-| 'foot', |-isa·| AI 'run, fly, fall')

An |i·| at the beginning of a dependent noun stem is dropped from the corresponding medial; in most cases connective |i| appears instead, but the medial for 'tooth' has the premedial |-a·-| (cf. 4.41*b*, 42). Other long high vowels are shortened in several cases.

(4.53) Medial |-i·k-| 'dwelling', |-i·k-amik-| 'household' ← |-i·k-| (*ni ki* 'my house')

   (a)   *ki šike wa* 'he finished building a house' (|ki·š-| PERF, |-i·k-| 'dwelling',
         |-e·| AI ABSTR)

   (b)   *ma nwikamikesiwaki* 'there were many households of them'
         (|ma·nw-| 'many', |-i·k-amik-| 'household', |-esi| AI ABSTR)

(4.54) Medial |-win-|, |-win-e·-| 'horn, braid' ← |-i·wi·n| (*owi wi nani* 'his horn, braid')

   (a)   *me meškwiwine wa* 'he has red horns'
         (|CV+| RED1, |meškw-| 'red', |-i-win-| 'horn', |-e·| AI ABSTR)

   (b)   *kekiwine senwi* 'it has horns'
         (|kek-| 'having', |-i-win-e·-| 'horn', |-isen| II 'lie, be')

(4.55) Medial |-a·pit-|, |-a·pit-e·-| 'tooth' ← |-i·pit| (*ni piči* 'my tooth')

   (a)   *kaka nwa pite wa* 'he has long teeth'
         (|Ca_a·+| RED1, |kenw-| 'long', |-a·pit-| 'tooth', |-e·| AI ABSTR)

(b)   *pešepaˑpiteˑnamwa* 'he smears its blade'

   (|pešep-| 'lubricate, grease, smear', |-aˑpit-eˑ-| 'tooth', |-en| TI(1) 'act on by hand')

The medial for 'mouth' shortens |oˑ| and adds |e| at the beginning.

(4.56) Medial |-eton-|, |-eton-eˑ-| 'mouth, lips, rim, edge' ← |-toˑn| (*netoˑni* 'my mouth')

(a)   *pemiwetonwa* 'he has a greasy mouth'

   (|pemiw-| 'greasy', |-eton-| 'mouth', |-Ø| AI ABSTR)

(b)   *mešketoneˑkwaˑmwa* 'he sleeps with his mouth open'

   (|mešk-| '(spread) open, agape', |-eton-eˑ-| 'mouth', |-ekwaˑm| AI 'sleep')

Some dependent nouns have an added |a| in the corresponding medials; this may be considered a connective |a| (§8.5; 1.100). (These cases of |a| were historically part of the dependent noun stem and were lost when the nouns were regularized by replacing |n-a..|, for example, with |ne-| 1s.)

(4.57) Medial |-anow-|, |-anow-eˑ-| 'cheek' ← |-noway| (*nenowayi* 'my cheek')

(a)   *makwanoweˑwa* 'he has a swollen cheek'

   (|makw-| 'bump', |-anow-| 'cheek', |-eˑ| AI ABSTR)

(b)   *maˑmahkateˑwanoweˑpiwa* 'he sits with blackened cheeks'

   (|CV+| RED1, |mahkateˑw-| 'black', |-anow-eˑ-| 'cheek', |-api| AI 'sit')

(4.58) Medial |-apay-|, |-ap-eˑ-|, |-apay-eˑ-| 'thigh, femur' ← |-pay| (*nepaya* 'my thigh, femur')

(a)   *nasawapeˑpiwa* 'he sits astraddle' (|nasaw-| 'forked', |-ap-eˑ-| 'thigh', |-api| AI 'sit')

(b)   *šowapayeˑkwiˑčinwa* 'he floats with his thighs spread'

   (|šow-| 'spread apart', |-apay-eˑ-| 'thigh', |-akwiˑčin| AI 'be in water')

In contrast to the medial |-anow-eˑ-| 'cheek' (4.57), the |a| is not added to the prefinal |-now-eˑ-| 'cheek' (4.66c).

35.3. Premedials. Some medials, both primary and derived, incorporate a premedial. A premedial may be either primary or derived from a medial. In some cases a premedial is relatively abstract, either being an automatic component of a medial (4.42, 55) or making a synonymous doublet beside a medial (4.41b). In other cases a premedial narrows the semantic range of the simplex medial (4.59-61).

(4.59) Primary premedials

(a) |-iniˑkw-| 'eye' ← premedial |-in-| + |-iˑkw-| 'eye, face'

   paˑškiniˑkweˑwa 'he has a split eyeball'

   (|paˑšk-| 'burst', |-iniˑkw-| 'eye', |-eˑ| AI ABSTR)

   memekwiniˑkweˑnowa 'he rubs his eyes'

   (|memekw-| 'oscillating', |-iniˑkweˑ-| 'eye', |-eno| AI 'act on self by hand')

   (cf. *myaˑšiˑkweˑwa* 'he has poor eyesight')

(b) |-aˑnehkw-| 'hair of the head' ← premedial |-aˑn-| + |-ehkw-| 'head, hair'

   peneškaˑnehkweˑwa 'his hair is loose, undone'

   (|penešk-| 'down, undone, unclothed', |-aˑnehkw-| 'hair', |-eˑ| AI ABSTR)

   kakaˑnwaˑnehkweˑwa 'he has long hair'

   (|Caˑ_a+| RED1, |kenw-| 'long', |-aˑnehkw-| 'hair of the head', |-eˑ| AI ABSTR)

   (cf. *kakaˑnoˑhkweˑwa* 'he has long hair'; the usual word)

Some premedials are derived from medials. These derived premedials always seem to narrow the reference that the medial alone would otherwise have. They occur both with primary medials (4.60ab) and with medials derived from nouns (4.60c, 61). The set of these premedials has some overlap of membership with derived postradicals (4.26-27) and prefinals.

(4.60) Premedial |-a·nak-| 'hole' ← medial |-a·nak-| 'hole' (4.35)
   (a)   Medial |-a·nak-i·kw-| 'eye' ← |-a·nak-| 'hole' + |-i·kw-| 'eye, face' (4.9b, 62a)
      we wena·naki·kwe·wa 'he has pretty eyes'
        (← |we·wen-| 'pretty', |-a·naki·kw-| 'eye', |-e·| AI ABSTR)
   (b)   Medial |-a·nak-eše·-| 'ear, aural canal' ← |-a·nak-| 'hole' + |-eše·-| 'ear'
      pa·hka·nakeše·me·wa 'he opens his ears in speaking to him'
        (|pa·hk-| 'open', |-a·nak-eše·-| 'ear', |-m| TA 'act on by speaking')
   (c)   Medial |-a·nak-eton-| 'mouth' ← |-a·nak-| 'hole' + |-eton-| 'mouth, lips' (4.56)
      maka·naketonwa 'he has a large mouth'
        (|mak-| 'big', |-a·nak-eton-| 'mouth', |-∅| AI ABSTR)
(4.61) Premedial |-a·hkw-| 'extended solid' ← medial |-a·hkw-| 'tree, stick' (cf. 4.25)
      Medial |-a·hkw-i-win-| 'horn' ← |-a·hkw-| 'extended solid' + |-i-win-| 'horn, braid'
      kaka·nwa·hkwiwine·wa 'he has long horns'
        (|Ca_a·+| RED1, |kenw-| 'long', |-a·hkwiwin-| 'horn', |-e·| AI ABSTR)

35.4. Other variation in medials. In two sets of forms, medials that end in |e·| or would ordinarily have the postmedial |-e·-| replace or alter this.

Where the finals that indicate action by heat or fire (|-esw| TA, |-es| TI(1), |-eso| AI, |-ete·| II) would follow the |-e·-|, they have variants with |a(h)| instead of |e| (|-asw| TA, |-as| TI(1), |-aso| AI, |-ahte·| II), and the postmedial |-e·-| does not appear.

(4.62) Loss of |e·| in medials before finals for 'by heat, by fire'
   (a)   *pahki·kwasowa* 'smoke bothers his eyes'
      pahki·kwahte·wi 'it is so smoky it bothers the eyes'
        (|pahk-| '(?)', |-i·kw-e·-| 'eye, face', |-aso| AI. |-ahte·| II 'be acted on by heat, fire')
   (b)   *apečasowa* 'he warms his belly'
        (|ap-| 'warm', |-eče·-| 'belly', |-aso| AI 'be acted on by fire, heat')

The |-e·-| is retained before these finals after |Cy| (4.63a) and often elsewhere (4.43b, 63b); some stems have doublets with both treatments.

(4.63) Retention of |e·| in medials before finals for 'by heat, by fire'
   (a)   *kwa·škopye·hte·wi* 'it bubbles as it boils'
        (|kwa·škw-| 'splash, jump', |-epye·-| 'water', |-ahte·| II 'be acted on by fire, heat')
   (b)   *apinehke·sowa* 'he warms his hands'
        (|ap-| 'warm', |-i-nehk-e·-| 'hand', |-aso| AI 'be acted on by fire, heat')

Where the final |-ači| AI 'be cold', the final |-a·pata·ni| AI 'appear', or the prefinal |-aw-| (always in |-awišin| AI 'get wet') would follow postmedial |-e·-| (or the medial |-ka·-| 'foot'), a |w| is inserted between these elements, as if the medials had |-e·w-| (or |-ka·w-|).

(4.64) Added |w| before |-ači| AI 'be cold', |-a·pata·ni| AI 'appear', |-awišin| AI 'get wet'
   (a)   *nenye·hpinehke·wačiwa* 'his fingers were numb with cold'
        (|nenye·hp-| 'numb', |-i-nehk-e·-w-| 'hand', |-ači| AI 'be cold')
   (b)   *nepačika·wačiwa* 'his feet were cold'
        (|nepat-| 'cold' [← |nepači-| AI 'be cold'], |-i-ka·-w-| 'foot', |-ači| AI 'be cold')
   (c)   *meškwinameške·wa·pata·niwa* 'his skin looks like it is red'
        (|meškw-| 'red', |-i-namešk-e·-w-| 'skin', |-a·pata·ni| AI 'appear')
   (d)   *ko·kinameške·wawišinwa* 'his skin is washed clean in the water'
        (|ko·k-| 'wash, immerse', |-i-namešk-e·-w-| 'skin', |-awišin| AI 'get wet')
   (e)   *tahkika·wawišinwa* 'he cooled his feet in the water'
        (|tahk-| 'cold, cool', |-i-ka·-w-| 'foot', |-awišin| AI 'get wet')

Derivation of Noun Finals

36. Noun finals may be primary or derived, and primary finals may be concrete or abstract. Only a few concrete noun finals are not derived, at least synchronically. Otherwise, concrete noun finals are either derived from noun stems or from medials. Noun finals are generally derived from medials by the addition of an abstract noun final, though synchronically, at least, this may not be overt.

36.1. Noun finals derived from nouns. Stem-derived noun finals are derived from noun stems by some of the same processes that derive medials from nouns (**§35**). There may be no change, an initial vowel may be dropped or replaced, or an initial consonant or longer sequence may be dropped. Rarer modifications include the shortening of long high vowels. Derivational suffixes are not used. From some nouns there is both a medial and a noun final derived in the same way; in other cases the derived medial and noun final may differ.

(4.65) Stem-derived noun finals

(a) |-ehpwa·kan| 'pipe' ← |ahpwa·kan-| AN (*ahpwa·kana* 'pipe')
     meškohpwa·kana 'catlinite pipe' (|meškw-| 'red', |-ehpwa·kan| 'pipe')

(b) |-e·mehkwa·h| 'spoon' ← |e·mehkwa·h-| IN (*e·mehkwa·hi* 'spoon')
     mehtekwe·mehkwa·hi 'wooden spoon'
     (|mehtekw-| 'tree, stick, wood', |-e·mehkwa·h| 'spoon')

(c) |-ihkwe·w| 'woman' ← |ihkwe·w-| AN (*ihkwe·wa* 'woman'; cf. 4.30)
     naha·kanihkwe·wa 'co-resident daughter-in-law'
     (|naha·k(an)-| 'living with in-laws', |-ihkwe·w| 'woman')

(d) |-na·kan| 'dish' ← |ana·kan-| IN (*ana·kani* 'dish, plate'; cf. 4.32)
     mehtekwina·kani 'wooden dish' (|mehtekw-| 'tree, stick, wood',
     |-i-na·kan| 'dish')

(e) |-a·pikon| 'squash' ← |wa·pikon-| IN (*wa·pikoni* 'squash, pumpkin')
     ina·pikoni 'squash of {such} kind' (|iN-| '{so}', |-a·pikon| 'squash'):
     ča·ki=meko ina·pikonani 'squashes of every kind' (K-YC 8)
     (*ča·ki* 'all'; *=meko* EMPH; |-ani| INpl)

(f) |-i·škeno·h| 'bird' ← |wi·škeno·h| (*wi·škeno·ha* 'bird')
     meškwi·škeno·ha 'cardinal; scarlet tanager' (|meškw-| 'red', |-i·škeno·h| 'bird')

(g) |-kon| 'feather' ← |mi·kon-| AN (*mi·kona* 'long feather')
     ketiwikona 'eagle feather'
     (|ketiw-| 'eagle' [← *ketiwa* 'eagle, golden eagle'], |-i-kon| 'feather')

(h) |-šip| 'duck' ← |ši·ši·p-| AN (*ši·ši·pa* 'duck')
     mešiši·pa 'mallard' (|meS-| 'big', |-i-šip| 'duck')

(i) |-eto·w| 'manitou' ← |maneto·w-| (*maneto·wa* 'manitou, god')
     we·ne·heto·wa 'what manitou?' (|we·he·h-| [← *we·ne·ha* 'who?'],
     |-eto·w| 'manitou')

36.2. Noun finals derived from medials. Noun finals are derived from some medials without overt modification, but more commonly the medial adds an abstract noun final. The final may match the shape of a medial and abstract final followed by a suffix of secondary derivation; such finals must be recognized as primary in noun stems that are not derived by secondary derivation from a verb stem.

(4.66) Noun finals derived from medials

(a) |-aˑhkw| 'tree, stick' ← |-aˑhkw-| 'tree, stick' (cf. 4.26)
      pakaˑnaˑhkwi 'walnut tree' (|pakaˑn-| [← *pakaˑni* 'nut'], |-aˑhkw| 'tree')
      miˑšamaˑhkwi 'sacred-pack pole'
      (|miˑšaˑm-| [← *miˑšaˑmi* 'sacred pack'], |-aˑhkw-| 'stick')

(b) |-nečy| 'finger' ← |-neč-| 'hand, finger' + |-y| NF ABSTR
      aškweˑneči 'little finger', *netaškweˑnečyeˑni* 'my little fingers'
      (|aškweˑ-| 'last'; cf. *kesiˑnečeˑwa* 'he washes his hands' [4.69*a*])
      aˑwinoˑhikaneči 'index finger'; as if combined irregularly with the rarer variant
      aˑwinoˑhikani [JMo; acc. HWB] ← |aˑwinoˑhikeˑ-| AI 'point at things' [cf. 4.195])

(c) |-ity| 'rear end' ← |-itiy-| 'rear end'
      onoweˑti 'his buttocks', *onoweˑtiˑki* 'on his buttocks'
      (stem |-noweˑty| ← |-now-eˑ-| 'cheek' [cf. 4.57], |-ity| 'rear end')

(d) |-aˑpehkw| 'stone, metal' ← |-aˑpehk-| 'stone, metal' + |-w| NF ABSTR
      pasaˑpehkwa 'lump of coal' (|pas-| 'heat, heated', |-aˑpehkw| 'stone')
      (cf. *pemiwaˑpehkesiwa* 'he (pot) is greasy' [|pemiw-| 'greasy', |-esi| AI ABSTR])

(e) |-ikaˑn| 'dwelling, structure' ← |-ik-| 'dwelling' + |-eˑ| AI ABSTR, |-en| NF (**§45.1**)
      neˑkatoˑkašeˑhikaˑni 'stable' (|neˑkatoˑkašeˑh-| 'horse', |-ikaˑn| 'structure')

(f) |-yeˑkenw| 'cloth, hide' ← |-yeˑk-| 'cloth, hide' + |-enw| NF ABSTR
      aškipakyeˑkenwi 'green cloth' (|aškipak-| 'green', |-yeˑkenw| 'cloth')
      pahkyeˑkenwi 'buffalo robe' (|pahk-| '(?)', |-yeˑkenw| 'hide')

In cases like (4.66*a*), |-w| NF ABSTR (as in 4.66*d*) could be set up; this would be removed phonologically by a regular rule that simplifies |w-w| to |w| (**§9.3**).

Derivation of Verb Finals

37. Verb finals may be abstract or concrete and may be primary or derived. Abstract primary verb finals consist of a single element. The template for concrete primary verb finals comprises a prefinal and an abstract final, but these elements may fuse and, in fact, one of the two may be left with no overt shape.

Some concrete verb finals are secondary, being derived from verb stems. In these the verbal category is preserved, and the alterations in shape are a subset of those found in the derivation of noun finals (**§36.1**).

Because verb stems typically come in pairs, with different forms used depending on the gender of the intransitive subject or the primary object (**§18.3**), finals also tend to come in pairs. In some cases stems and finals are the same for both genders. Many intransitive verbs are unpaired; unpaired AI stems are generally those for actions performed only by living beings, and unpaired II stems are perhaps always impersonal verbs (2.82).

37.1. Abstract intransitive finals. Any vowel that can end an intransitive verb stem (all except short |e| and |a|) may be an abstract final in an unpaired AI or II verb. The residue of the stem before such a stem-final vowel may be non-recurring, making the segmentation opaque or questionable. In other stems the vowel is a clearly delimited recurring final added to recurring initials. AI stems have abstract |-∅| and |-N| after certain medials. Some unpaired II stems have ostensible abstract finals |-an|, |-en|, |-in|, or |-at|. Some stems have no final (4.1*b*).

A given final for one gender is not always paired with the same final for the other gender. Some pairings are used after large classes of initials or other elements, while others are found in only a few stems. Although no meaning can be assigned to abstract finals, there is a tendency for certain pairings to recur in stems with similar or opposite meanings. Truly synonymous stems differing only in the selection of the final are rare.

(4.67) Pairings of abstract intransitive finals

(a) |-esi| AI, |-ya·| II   After initials for colors and most other qualities.
     wa peškesiwa AI, *wa peškya wi* II 'he, it is white'
     meškosiwa AI, *meškwa wi* II 'he, it is red'
     kehpakesiwa AI, *kehpakya wi* II 'he, it is thick'
     nešiwana tesiwa AI, *nešiwana ča wi* II 'he, it is destroyed; it is destructive, ruinous'
     pana tesiwa AI, *pana ča wi* II 'he, it is ruined; he faints, loses his mind, perishes'
     inehpesiwa AI, *inehpya wi* II 'he, it is {so} high'

(b) |-esi| AI, |-at| II   After postmedial |-ak-| (|-e·k-|); certain medials; etc.
     ahpi ·hčiwanakesiwa AI, *ahpi ·hčiwanakatwi* II 'he, it weighs {so much}'
     ma nwayakesiwaki AI, *ma nwayakato ni* II 'there are many kinds of them'
     ahkwanahkesiwa AI, *ahkwanahkatwi* II 'he, it is {so} tall a tree'
     sanakesiwa AI, *sanakatwi* II 'he, it is easy, easy to get'
     we činowesiwa AI, *we činowatwi* II 'he, it is easy, easy to get'
     we nehpenesiwa AI, *we nehpenatwi, we nehpenya wi* II 'it is easy for him, to do it'

(c) |-eN| AI, |-an| II   In stems that describe tastes.
     wi kenwa AI, *wi kanwi* II 'he, it tastes good'
     wi škopenwa AI, *wi škopanwi* II 'he, it is sweet'

(d) |-i| AI, |-en| II   With numerals; after |h|, usually before |-(o)·hi| DIM; etc.
     ni šiwaki AI, *ni šeno ni* II 'there are two of them (anim., inan.)'
     ke ko ·hiwa AI, *ke ko ·henwi* II 'he, it is something' (used with a negative)
     pepehke ·he ·hiwa AI (|pepehke·hi-| AI + |-·h| DIM) 'he is light (in weight)',
        pepehke ·heno ·hiwi II (|pepehke·hen-| II + |-o·h| DIM) 'it is light (in weight)'
     ahkwiwa AI, *ahkonwi* II 'he, it is {so} long (in physical length)'
        Cf. *ahkwa wi* II (← |ahkw-|, |-ya·| II) 'it is {so} long (in duration)'.
     akiwa AI, *akenwi* II 'he, it disappears'
     pehkiwa AI, *pehkenwi* II 'he, it is different, of a different kind, another one'

(e) |-eši| AI, |-a·hen| II   Before |-(o)·hi| DIM. (Also *čaka ·henwi* II if negative.)
     čakeši ·hiwa AI, *čaka ·heno ·hiwi* II 'he, it is small'
     papi weši ·hiwaki AI, *papi wa ·heno ·hiwani* II 'they (anim., inan.) are small'

(f) |-esi| AI, |-et| II
     we wenesiwa AI, *we wenetwi* II 'he, it is good, good-looking'
     mya nesiwa AI, *mya netwi* II 'he, it is bad; he is ugly'

(g) |-aN| AI, |-an| II
     kosekwanwa AI, *kosekwanwi* II 'he, it is heavy'

(h) |-eN| AI, |-en| II
     aškenwa AI, *aškenwi* II 'he, it is raw'

(i) |-eN| AI, |-et| II
     anenwa AI, *anetwi* II 'he, it is rotten'

(j) |-∅| AI, |-et| II
     ma ne wa AI, *ma ne twi* II 'there is a lot of him, it' (cf. *ma ne* 'many')

Some intransitive pairs with stative meanings can be described as secondary derivatives made from the corresponding transitives (4.297-298), but two common pairs are made with abstract finals added to an initial derived from the TI stem:

(4.68) Statives with |-in| AI, |-e·| II

(a) *ako·činwa* AI, *ako·te·wi* II 'he, it hangs' (initial |ako·t-| ← stem |ako·t-| TI(2) 'hang': *ako·to·wa* TI(2) 'he hangs it up' [4.86*b*])

(b) *akwi·činwa* AI, *akwi·te·wi* II 'he, it is in water or other liquid, is floating' (initial |akwi·t-| ← stem |akwi·t-| TI(2) 'put, have in water': *akwi·to·wa* TI(2) 'he has it in water, soaks it' [4.86*i*])

When stems that contain a medial do not have a concrete final, the medial is followed by an abstract final; in most cases this abstract final is |-e·| ABSTR (4.12*a*, 14, 23*a*, 26*a*, 41*b*, 43*a*, 45*a*, 47, 48, 49*a*, 52*b*, 54*a*, 55*a*, 57*a*, 60*a*). After the medials that end in |n|, the final used is |-∅| AI,II ABSTR (4.12*b*, 32*a*, 46, 51*a*, 56*a*, 60*c*).

A few stems take |-a·| AI ABSTR (4.41*a*, 69); these denote external action by the subject on the body part.

(4.69) |-a·| AI ABSTR after body-part medials

(a) *kesi·neče·wa* 'he washes his hands' (*nekesi·neča* 'I wash my hands') (|kesi·-| 'wash', |-neč-| 'hand', |-a·| AI ABSTR)

(b) *kesi·kwe·wa* 'he washes his face' (*nekesi·kwa* 'I wash my face') (|kesi·-| 'wash', |-i·kw-| 'face', |-a·| AI ABSTR)

Medials referring to the head or face that end in |kw| have |-N| AI ABSTR after postmedial |-e·-| in stems that denote motion but have no concrete final.

(4.70) |-N| AI ABSTR after medials for 'head' and 'face'

(a) *pi·tehkwe·nwa* 'he stuck his head in' (|pi·t-| 'into', |-ehkw-e·-| 'head', |-N| AI ABSTR)

(b) *pa·hki·kwe·nwa* 'he opens his eyes, uncovers his eyes or face' (|pa·hk-| 'open, uncover', |-i·kw-e·-| 'eyes, face', |-N| AI ABSTR)

(c) *či·keškwe·nwa* 'he lifts his head' (|či·k-| 'stick up', |-eškw-e·-| 'head', |-N| AI ABSTR)

(d) *keteškwe·nwa* 'he stuck his head out, up' (|ket-| 'out', |-eškw-e·-| 'head', |-N| AI ABSTR)

In a few combinations in which a medial denotes an instrument or medium it is followed by |-i·| AI ABSTR (4.42*b*, 4.71*abcde*). Some impersonal stems also have |-i·| II ABSTR after a medial (4.42*ab*, 4.71*f*).

(4.71) |-i·| AI, II ABSTR after medials

(a) *akwa·pye·ki·wa* 'he comes ashore out of the water' (|akwa·-| 'out of medium', |-epye·k-| 'water', |-i·| AI ABSTR)

(b) *a·čikaši·wa* 'he uses his fingernails, putting pressure or weight on them' (|a·t-| 'repeat, reverse', |-i-kaš-| 'nail, claw', |-i·| AI ABSTR)

(c) *a·wahkikaši·wa* 'he claws, uses his nails or claws to grip' (|a·wahk-| 'with clawed hand', |-i-kaš-| 'nail, claw', |-i·| AI ABSTR)

(d) *aše·nawi·wa* 'he slides back' (|aše·-| 'back, backwards', |-naw-| 'body', |-i·| AI ABSTR)

(e) *kwa·škopye·nehki·wa* 'he splashes the water with his hands' (AW) (|kwa·škw-| 'splash', |-epye·-| 'water', |-nehki·| AI [← |-nehk-| 'hand', |-i·| AI ABSTR])

(f)   *na·witepehki·wi* 'it is midnight'
        (|na·w-| 'middle', |-*i*-tepehk-| 'night', |-*i*·| II ABSTR)

Stems with an ostensible medial followed by |-*i*·| AI,II ABSTR (4.71*abcef*) could also be analyzed as having a derived final in which the medial is used as a prefinal. This analysis appears to be required in cases like (4.71*e*), where there is also an ordinary medial.

37.2. Concrete intransitive finals. A number of abstract final pairs occur with prefinals to form concrete finals.

(4.72) Concrete finals with |-i| AI, |-en| II

(a) |-iki| AI (← |-*i*-k-i|), |-iken| II (← |-*i*-k-en|) 'grow, be, happen'
        kehčikiwa AI, *kehčikenwi* II 'he, it is old' (|keht-| 'great')
        sa·kiwa AI, *sa·kenwi* II 'he, it (a plant) sprouts, grows, grows up'
        ni·kiwa AI 'he is born'

(b) |-ači| AI (← |-at-i-|), |-aten| II (← |-at-en|) 'be cold'
        si·kačiwa AI, *si·katenwi* 'he, it froze' (|si·k-| 'empty out')

(c) |-ači| AI (← |-at-i-|), |-aten| II (← |-at-en|) 'be a hill'
        ki·škapehkačiwa AI, *ki·škapehkatenwi* II 'he, it is a steep cliff' (|ki·šk-| 'cut off')

(4.73) Concrete finals with |-in| AI, |-en| II

(a) |-išin| AI (← |-*i*-S-in|), |-isen| II (← |-*i*-S-en|) 'fall, lie, be'
        šekišinwa AI, *šekisenwi* 'he, it lies, is lying ({somewhere})'
        pakišinwa AI, *pakisenwi* II 'he, it lands, falls to earth ({somewhere})'

(b) |-ičin| AI (← |-*i*-t-in|), |-iten| II (← |-*i*-t-en|) 'encounter constraint on movement'
        ki·škičinwa AI, *ki·škitenwi* II 'he cut himself, it got ripped (as on a fence, nail)'
        no·ničinwa AI, *no·nitenwi* II 'he, it does not fit' (|no·n-| 'too much, many to fit')
        paši·škičinwa AI 'his foreskin is pushed back in copulating' (|paši·šk-| 'peel, skin')

(c) |-a·šin| AI, |-a·sen| II 'be acted on by wind, air'
        pi·ta·šinwa AI, *pi·ta·senwi* II 'he, it blows in, inside' (|pi·t-| 'into')

(4.74) Concrete finals with |-a·| AI, |-a·| II (umlauting)

(a) |-a·ška·| AI,II 'rush, fly, fall'
        we·pa·ške·wa AI, *we·pa·ške·wi* II 'he, it falls' (|we·p-| semantically empty,
            lit. 'begin')
        nowa·ške·wa AI, *nowa·ške·wi* II 'he, it rushes out' (|now-| 'exit')

(b) |-eška·| AI,II 'move, become'
        pa·seške·wa AI, *pa·seške·wi* II 'he, it swells up' (|pa·s-| 'swollen, bloated')
        ma·ta·naki·kwe·ške·wa AI 'he moves his eyes' (|ma·t-| 'move',
            |-a·naki·kw-e·-| 'eye')
        mama·ta·po·ške·wi II 'it flows' (|Ca+| RED1, |ma·t-| 'move', |-a·po·-| 'liquid')

(c) |-isa·| AI,II 'run, fly, fall'
        čapo·kise·wa AI, *čapo·kise·wi* II 'he, it falls in the water'
        pye·čise·wa AI, *pye·čise·wi* II 'he, it runs, flies this way; the time comes'

(4.75) Concrete final with |-a·| AI, |-a·| II (non-umlauting)

(a) |-ka·pa·| AI,II 'stand'
        sa·kika·pa·wa AI, *sa·kika·pa·wi* II 'he, it stands sticking out'

An AI final may also consist of a prefinal added to a concrete final. In the most straightforward cases the prefinal is derived from a medial; a prefinal may be added to a final that already incorporates a prefinal (4.76*d*).

(4.76) Finals derived from prefinal plus concrete final
  (a) |-ahkišin| AI 'lie, be prone or supine'
      (← |-ahky-| 'earth' + |-išin| AI 'fall, lie, be' [4.73*a*])
      kehtahkišinwa 'he lies down flat' (GBC-BDB 36 [2x])
      pe·wahkišinwa 'she lies back yielding' (S-IM 18)
  (b) |-a·ke·poso| AI, |-a·ke·pote·| II 'speed through the air'
      (← |-a·ke·-| 'wing' + |-poso| AI, |-pote·| II; 4.78*s*)
      pema·ke·posowa AI, *pema·ke·pote·wi* II 'he, it goes shooting through the air' (AW)
  (c) |-ka·wose·| AI 'step, take a step' (← |-ka·-| 'foot' + |-(w)ose·| AI 'walk')
      išika·wose·wa 'he steps {so}':
        če·wi-'šika·wose·waki 'they have the same way of walking' (K-W 103)
        sese·sika·wose·wa 'he walks with hurrying steps'
        we·pika·wose·wa 'he starts taking steps'
  (d) |-we·(we·)ya·ke·poso| AI, |-we·(we·)ya·ke·pote·| II 'go whizzing through the air'
      (← |-we·(we·)-| 'noise' + |-a·ke·poso| AI, |-a·ke·pote·| II [4.76*b*])
      aniwe·we·ya·ke·posowa AI 'he goes whizzing loudly through the air'
      anwe·we·ya·ke·posowa, anwe·ya·ke·posowa AI, *anwe·we·ya·ke·pote·wa,*
        anwe·ya·ke·pote·wa II 'he, it goes whizzing through the air'
  (e) |-ye·ki| AI, |-ye·ken| II 'grow' (|-ye·| [← |-ye·w| 'flesh, muscle'] +
      |-iki| AI, |-iken| II 'grow, be, happen' (4.72*a*)
      pemye·kiwa AI 'he grows (for a period)'
      we·pye·kenwi II 'it starts growing'

Some intransitive finals are combinations of two concrete finals. In most of these the second final adds a specification of speed or mode of locomotion to the first final. In at least one case a TI final appears as a prefinal (4.77*d*).

(4.77) Finals derived from two concrete finals
  (a) |-a·si·paho| AI 'climb rapidly' (← |-a·si·| AI 'climb' + |-paho| AI 'run'):
      pye·ta·si·pahowa AI 'he comes climbing rapidly'
      pena·si·pahowa AI 'he climbs down rapidly'
  (b) |-a·si·yo·te·| AI 'climb crawling' (← |-a·si·| AI 'climb' + |-o·te·| AI 'crawl'):
      ahkwita·si·yo·te·wa AI 'he climbs crawling up on top'
      keta·si·yo·te·wa AI 'he climbs down crawling'
  (c) |-a·ške·pote·| II 'speed through the air'
      (← |-a·ška·| AI,II 'speed' + |-pote·| II [4.78*s*]):
      ina·ške·pote·wi II 'it goes shooting off' (K-M 681g, of lies, collectively)
  (d) |-o·taši| AI 'carry a load on the back'
      (← |-o·t| TI(1) 'carry on the back' + |-aši| AI 'carry a backload'):
      pi·to·tašiwa AI 'he enters with a backload'
      pye·to·tašiwa AI 'he arrives with a backload'
  (e) |-o·te·paho| AI 'crawl rapidly' (← |-o·te·| AI 'crawl' + |-paho| AI 'run'):
      čapo·ko·te·pahowa AI 'he crawls rapidly into the water'
      tetepo·te·pahowa AI 'he crawls rapidly around in a circle'

A number of final pairs that refer to undergoing an action or process (passively or reflexively), or to the resulting state, have the abstract middle-reflexive finals |-o| AI and |-te·| II (**§52.4**) added to the respective transitive finals, often with various adjustments in shape. For example, before |-o| AI postconsonantal |w| drops and |N| is replaced by |s|, and before |-te·| II |s| and |t| are dropped. Some final pairs with this configuration do not incorporate otherwise identifiable transitive finals.

(4.78) Finals derived with |-o| AI, |-te·| II

(a) |-aho| AI 'paddle a canoe' (cf. |-ahw| TA 'act on by tool' [4.95a])
  kekenahowa 'he paddles fast'
  pye·tahowa 'he comes paddling'

(b) |-aho·so| AI, |-aho·te·| II 'be dragged or transported, drag self, crawl, ooze'
  (cf. |-aho·N| TA, |-aho·t| TI(2) 'drag')
  aškwaho·sowa AI 'he is left out of the vehicle'
  kehkaho·sowa AI, *kehkaho·te·wi* 'he, it left a mark from crawling or being dragged'
  ketaho·sowa AI, *ketaho·te·wi* II 'he, it slides or oozes out'

(c) |-ahkaso| AI, |-ahkate·| II 'be standing, stood up, stuck in the ground'
  (cf. |-ahkaN| TA, |-ahkat| TI(2) 'stand up, stick in the ground')
  aye·nahkasowa AI, *aye·nahkate·wi* II 'he, it is still standing'
  inahkasowa AI, *inahkate·wi* II 'he, it is standing {so}'

(d) |-aso| AI, |-ahte·| II 'be acted on by heat'
  sahkasowa AI, *sahkahte·wi* 'he, it caught fire'

(e) |-aso| AI, |-ate·| II 'be acted on by heat' (cf. |-asw| TA, |-as| TI(1) [4.96a])
  ahkasowa AI, *ahkate·wi* 'he, it burned up'

(f) |-aško·so|, |-eško·so| AI, |-aško·te·|, |-eško·te·| II 'be acted on by ingested food'
  (cf. |-eško·N| TA 'act on by feeding')
  inaško·sowa, *ineško·sowa* AI, *inaško·te·wi*, *ineško·te·wi* II 'he, it is, feels {so} after eating'
  mehkwinawe·ško·sowa AI 'he remembers after eating'
  wi·kowaško·sowa AI 'he is sleepy after eating'

(g) |-a·hkaso| AI, |-a·hkate·| II 'dry, be dried'
  (cf. |-a·hkasw| TA, |-a·hkas| TI(1) [4.96b])
  ki·ša·hkasowa AI, *ki·ša·hkate·wi* II 'he, it has finished drying'
  menwa·hkate·wi II 'it dries nicely'
  kaška·hkasowa AI, *kaška·hkate·wi* II 'he, it dries hard, with a crust'

(h) |-eso| AI, |-ete·| II 'be acted on by heat, gunshot'
  (cf. |-esw| TA, |-es| TI(1) [4.96c]; 4.296n, 4.297c)
  akosowa AI, *akote·wi* II 'he, it sticks from being heated or burned'
  aškesowa AI, *aškete·wi* II 'he, it boils dry'
  atosowa AI 'he burns himself'
  ki·šesowa AI, *ki·šete·wi* II 'he, it is cooked done'
  nekesowa AI, *nekete·wi* II 'he, it melts'
  pakesowa AI, *pakete·wi* II 'he, it explodes' (from any cause)
  po·hkosowa AI, *po·hkote·wi* II 'he (his bone), it is broken by gunshot'

(i) |-ešo| AI 'be cut' (cf. |-ešw| TA, |-eš| TI(1) 'cut' [4.96d]; 4.296k)
  pahkwe·šowa AI 'he cuts a piece off himself'
  pehtešowa AI 'he accidentally cuts himself'

(j) |-eˑnemo| AI 'think, act mentally' (cf. |-eˑnem| TA 'think about' [4.90c])

ahpe nemowa AI+O 'he relies on O2'

mečime nemowa AI 'he hesitates'

mi·ša·te nemowa AI 'he is glad, proud'

na·pe nemowa AI+O 'he regards O2 as a replacement'

pe·we nemowa AI 'he gives up'

(k) |-hpo| AI 'eat' (cf. |-hpw| TA 'act on by mouth, taste' [4.93ab])

ašihpowa AI 'he uses ({something} as) a sauce or dip'

ato·hpowa AI 'he eats from ({something} as) a dish or bowl'

ni·šo·hpowaki AI 'they eat together as a pair'

(l) |-ikwaˑso| AI, |-ikwaˑteˑ| II 'sew, be sewn'

(cf. |-ikwaˑN| TA, |-ikwaˑt| TI(1) 'sew' [4.88b])

ačikwaˑsowa AI 'she sews'

nahikwaˑsowa AI 'she knows how to sew'

se·nipa·hikwaˑsowa AI, se·nipa·hikwa·te·wi II 'she sews ribbon appliqué, it is

sewn with ribbon appliqué'

tahtakwikwa·te·wani II 'they (inan.) are sewn together'

(m) |-inaˑso| AI, |-inaˑhteˑ|, |-inaˑteˑ| II 'boil' (cf. |-inaˑsw| TA, |-inaˑs| TI(1) 'boil')

kwa·škwinaˑsowa AI, kwa·škwina·hte·wi, kwa·škwina·te·wi II 'he, it boils'

si·kina·hte·wi, si·kina·te·wi II 'it boils over'

(n) |-isaho| AI 'jump, fling self' (cf. |-isah| TA 'jerk, shove, yank, fling, grab, swish')

kwa·škwisahowa AI 'he jumps off, dismounts, disembarks'

šekisahowa AI 'he flings himself down'

(o) |-itehkaˑso| AI, |-itehkaˑteˑ| II 'be named, be called (as a name)'

(cf. |-itehkaˑN| TA, |-itehkaˑt| TI(1) 'name')

išitehkaˑsowa AI, išitehka·te·wi II 'he, it is named {so}'

(p) |-iyaˑso| AI, |-iyaˑhteˑ| II 'smell in cooking or burning'

(cf. |-iyaˑsw| TA, |-iyaˑs| TI(1) 'cause to smell by cooking, burning')

menwiyaˑsowa AI, menwiya·hte·wi II 'he, it smells good in cooking, burning'

ko·nači·hiya·hte·wi 'it smells of burning kinnikinnick'

(q) |-paho| AI, |-pahoˑteˑ| II 'run' (cf. |-pah| TA 'run from', |-pahtoˑ| TI(2)-O 'run')

ki·wipahowa AI, ki·wipaho·te·wi 'he, it runs about'

pemipahowa AI, pemipaho·te·wi II 'he, it runs along, by'

(r) |-piso|, |-apiso| AI, |-piteˑ|, |-apiteˑ| II 'be tied; tie on clothing; have spasms'

(cf. |-piN|, |-apiN| TA, |-pit|, |-apit| TI(2) 'tie' [4.89g])

akwa·hkwapisowa AI, akwa·hkwapite·wi II 'he, it is tied on, against'

či·hči·kwapisowa AI 'she hiked up her skirt'

ihpisowa AI, ihpite·wi II 'he, it is tied {so}'

nenekapisowa AI 'he trembles all over'

(s) |-poko| AI, |-pokoˑteˑ| II 'float, drift in water' (cf. |-pw|, |-hpw| TA 'act on variously

by mouth' [4.92b, 4.93ab] and 4.80, 81), apparently with a metaphorical meaning

'be sucked'

akwa·pokowa AI, akwa·poko·te·wi II 'he, it floats ashore'

pemipokowa AI, pemipoko·te·wi II 'he, it drifts along, by'

pye·hpoko·te·wi II 'comes drifting'

(t) |-poso| AI, |-pote·| II 'be subjected to a quick, hard stroke or strokes'
       (cf. |-poN| TA, |-pot| TI(2) 'subject to quick, hard strokes, saw, file, grind' [4.89*h*])
            aniwipote·wi II 'it (arrow) is highly effective'
            pa·sikipote·wi II 'it gets sawed up'
            šekwiposowa AI 'he (corn) is crushed up'

The derivational pattern in (4.78) is also found in secondary derivation, making stative stems from the corresponding transitive stems (4.296).

A number of finals that make verbs of undergoing are built on a TA final (or virtual final) followed by the inverse theme sign |-ekw| TA th. 2. (A virtual TA stem or final is one that has the shape of a TA but is not used before inflectional endings.) In one set of these finals, |-i| AI ABSTR or |-o| AI ABSTR is added to form a secondary final |-ekwi| AI PASSIVE or |-eko| AI PASSIVE, and there is no corresponding II. These derived finals are also used in secondary derivation (4.79*a*, end).

(4.79) Finals incorporating |-ekwi| AI ~ |-eko| AI PASSIVE

(a) |-o·mekwi| AI, |-o·meko| AI 'ride on horseback' (← |-o·m| 'carry on back' TA [4.98*e*])
            naho·mekwiwa, naho·mekowa 'he knows how to ride (a horse)'
            (cf. *no·mekwiwa, no·mekowa* 'he rides a horse' ← |no·m-| TA 'carry on back')

(b) |-paho·nekwi| AI, |-paho·neko| AI 'ride a horse at a gallop'
            ki·hka·paho·nekwiwa AI 'he circles around riding his horse at a gallop'
            ni·šo·paho·nekowaki AI 'they rode double at a gallop'
            pye·hpaho·nekwiwa AI 'he arrived on his horse at a gallop'

(c) |-aho·nekwi| AI, |-aho·neko| AI 'ride in a wagon'
            pemaho·nekwiwa, pemaho·nekowa 'he rides along in a wagon'

Other derived finals of undergoing have only |-eko| AI PASSIVE.

(4.80) Finals incorporating |-eko| AI PASSIVE

(a) |-eneko| AI 'thrash around, fool around' (|-en| TA,TI(1) 'act on by hand' [4.97])
            kekenekowa AI 'he has {something} with him in his activities'
            inenekowa AI 'he carries on {so}'
            tanenekowa AI 'he thrashes around, plays around, fools around'

(b) |-atahoko| 'go with a load' (|-atahw| TA 'act on by stick' [4.95*c*])
            ketatahokowa AI 'he emerges into the open carrying a load'
            pakamatahokowa AI 'he arrives with a load'
            pye·tatahokowa AI 'he comes carrying a load'

In the set in which |-eko| AI is added to |-ahw| TA 'act on by tool' (4.95*a*) the II, when present, has |-an| II ABSTR added to the corresponding TI, |-ah| TI(1).

(4.81) Finals incorporating |-eko| AI PASSIVE, |-an| II ABSTR

(a) |-ahoko| AI, |-ahan| II 'be acted on by mass of water, weight, or falling object'
            ahpihkye·hokowa AI 'he was pinned to the ground' (4.22*a*)
            ahpihokowa AI 'he has a mass fall down on top of him' (4.22*a*)
            ayi·hkwinehke·hokowa AI 'his arms get tired from the weight'
            a·ya·šo·ka·hokowa AI 'he staggers under the weight'
            ko·hka·hanwi II 'it (canoe) tips over, is overset'
            mehtahokowa AI 'he is hit by a falling object'; *mehtahanwi* II 'it is windswept'
            mo·škahokowa AI, *mo·škahanwi* II 'he, it is flooded, flooded out'
            paka·hokowa AI, *paka·hanwi* II 'he, it is completely submerged'

ni·sahanwi II 'it (trap) fell, clamped shut'

seswe·hanwi II 'it gets splashed'

si·keni·kwe·hokowa AI 'he gets squirted in the face'

Other verbs of undergoing have |-ekw| TA th. 2 followed by |-esi| AI ABSTR and |-at| II ABSTR. This combination makes an abstract passive final pair |-ekosi| AI, |-ekwat| II PASSIVE that derives stems (4.82) and finals (4.83) from certain transitive stems and finals, or virtual stems or finals. The virtual stems and finals used before this final pair either match an actual TA with an abstract final |-m| that is replaced by underlying |-w| (4.82*b*(2), 83*e*), or they match an actual TI in |-t| with the addition of underlying |-aw| (4.82*b*(3), 83*b*), or in one case |-a·m| (4.82*b*(1)). The TA stems and finals with actual or virtual underlying |-aw| or |-a·w| contract this to *a·* (4.82*b*(2,3), 4.83*bde*).

(4.82) Abstract passive finals

    (a) |-ekosi| AI, |-ekwat| II PASSIVE added to TA stem

      1)   *a·čimekosiwa* AI 'he is told about' (cf. |a·čim-| TA 'tell about' [4.90*d*])

      2)   *wa·wi·tekwatwi* II 'it (a name) is mentioned as famous, is used as a name'
             (cf. |wa·wi·t-| TA 'call by name'; note 4.82*b*(3))

    (b) |-ekosi| AI, |-ekwat| II PASSIVE added to virtual TA stem

      1)   *kohta·mekosiwa* 'he is feared' (cf. |koš-| TA, |koht-| TI(1) 'fear')

      2)   *mena·kosiwa* AI, *mena·kwatwi* II 'it smells, stinks'
             (as if from virtual |mena·w-| beside |mena·m-| TA 'smell' [4.86*f*])

      3)   *wa·wi·ta·kosiwa* AI 'he is mentioned as famous'
             (cf. |wa·wi·t-| TA 'call by name'; note 4.82*a*(2))

(4.83) Concrete passive finals made with |-ekosi| AI, |-ekwat| II PASSIVE (4.82)

    (a) |-a·čimekosi| AI, |-a·čimekwat| II 'be told of' (cf. |-a·čim| TA 'tell about' [4.98*b*])

         ina·čimekosiwa AI, *ina·čimekwatwi* II 'he, it is told of {so}'

         mena·na·čimekosiwa AI 'strange tales are told of him'

         mi·ša·ta·čimekosiwa AI, *mi·ša·ta·čimekwatwi* II 'he, it is mentioned with pride'

         pakama·čimekosiwa AI 'he is reported to arrive'

    (b) |-e·neta·kosi| AI, |-e·neta·kwat| II 'be thought of' (cf. |-e·nem| TA, |-e·net| TI(1) 'think about' [4.90*c*])

         kehke·neta·kosiwa AI, *kehke·neta·kwatwi* II 'he, it is known'

         tepe·neta·kosiwa AI, *tepe·neta·kwatwi* II 'he, it is owned'

         nenehke·neta·kosiwa AI, *nenehke·neta·kwatwi* II 'he, it is thought about'

    (c) |-(ih)pokosi| AI, |-(ih)pokwat| II 'taste, have a taste' (cf. |-ihpw| TA 'taste')

         âhkwihpokwatwi II 'it tastes sour, strong'

         ihpokosiwa, ihpokwatwi 'he, it tastes {so}'

         myâhpokosiwa, myâhpokwatwi 'he, it tastes bad'

         wi·kihpokosiwa, wi·kihpokwatwi 'he, it tastes good'

         wi·škopihpokosiwa 'he (as, corn) tastes sweet'

    (d) |-ina·kosi| AI, |-ina·kwat| II 'look, appear; have an expression on the face' (cf. |-inaw| TA 'regard, feel about' [4.94*g*])

         ame·na·kosiwa AI 'he shows a reaction on his face'

         išina·kosiwa AI, *išina·kwatwi* II 'he, it looks, appears {so}'

         ki·wa·čina·kosiwa AI, *ki·wa·čina·kwatwi* II 'he, it looks lonely'

         pehki·nina·kosiwa AI, *pehki·nina·kwatwi* II 'he, it looks different'

(e) |-iya·kosi| AI, |-iya·kwat| II 'be smelled, have an odor'
       (as if from virtual |-iya·w| beside |-iya·m| TA [4.90*e*])
            išiya·kosiwa AI, *išiya·kwatwi* II 'he, it smells {so}'
            mya·šiya·kosiwa AI, *mya·šiya·kwatwi* II 'he, it smells bad'

The passive final used in primary derivation (4.82) is not productive and makes stems that are
lexicalized and often irregularly formed; there are also passive finals used in secondary
derivation, which are highly productive and formally transparent (**§53.6**)

37.3. Intransitive finals derived from stems. Verb finals derived from stems may retain
their shape, if they begin with a vowel, or they may drop their initial vowel, consonant, or
syllable. Other kinds of modification are rare. The semantics may differ, with the derived final
often having a more general meaning.

(4.84) Stem-derived intransitive finals

(a) |-a·kwaso| AI, |-a·kwate·| II 'be sitting, lying, or piled (on the ground)'
       ← |a·kwaso-| AI, |a·kwate·-| II (*a·kwasowa, a·kwate·wi* 'he, it is piled up')
            ki·wa·kwasowa AI, *ki·wa·kwate·wi* II 'he, it lies around discarded, dead,
                 destroyed'
            kwa·pa·kwasowaki AI, *kwa·pa·kwate·wani* II 'they (anim., inan.) lie scattered'
            mama·ka·kwasowaki AI, *mama·ka·kwate·wani* II 'they (anim., inan.) are in big
                 piles'
            mehta·kwasowa AI 'he is sprawled on the ground naked'
            pehkwa·kwasowaki AI, *pehkwa·kwate·wani* 'they swarm, pile, or are piled
                 together'

(b) |-a·šowi·| AI 'wade' ← |a·šowi·-| (*a·šowi·wa* 'he wades')
            paka·ya·šowi·wa 'he wades into the water'
            akwa·ya·šowi·wa 'he wades out of the water'

(c) |-ako·čin| AI, |-ako·te·| II 'hang' ← |ako·čin-| AI, |ako·te·-| II
       (*ako·činwa* AI, *ako·te·wi* II 'he, it hangs'; 4.68*a*)
            a·ya·tesako·čino·ki AI, *a·ya·tesako·te·wani* II 'they (anim., inan.) hang
                 separately'
            kekako·činwa AI, *kekako·te·wi* II 'he, it hangs with {something} in or on him, it'
            inako·činwa AI, *inako·te·wi* II 'he, it hangs {so}'
            pehkwako·čino·ki AI, *pehkwako·te·wani* II 'they (anim., inan.) hang in a bunch'

(d) |-akwi·čin| AI, |-akwi·te·| II 'be in water, float' ← |akwi·čin-| AI, |akwi·te·-| II
       (*akwi·činwa* AI, *akwi·te·wi* II 'he, it is in water'; 4.68*b*)
            šekwakwi·činwa AI, *šekwakwi·te·wi* II 'he it decays, falls apart lying in water'
            te·hte·pakwi·činwa AI, *te·hte·pakwi·te·wi* II 'he, it is floating'

(e) |-atawa·pi| AI 'look' ← |natawa·pi-| AI (*natawa·piwa* 'he looks (around), tries to
       see')
            aniwatawa·piwa AI 'he looks around a lot'
            a·hkwatawa·piwa AI 'he keeps a sharp eye'

(f) |-o·še·| AI 'give birth, have children' ← |no·še·-| AI (*no·še·wa* 'she gives birth')
            mehpo·še·wa AI 'she passes on to her baby the effects of violating a pregnancy
                 taboo'
            tano·še·wa AI 'she gives birth, lays eggs {somewhere}'
            pemeno·še·wa AI 'he, she minds a baby' (|pemen-| TA,TI(1) 'take care of')

(g) |-aˑnehkeˑ| AI 'dig' ← |waˑnehkeˑ-| AI (*waˑnehkeˑwa* 'he digs a hole')
  konakwaˑnehkeˑwa AI 'he digs through an obstacle'
  poˑhkaˑnehkeˑwa AI 'he digs a hole through'
  pyeˑtaˑnehkeˑwa AI 'he digs coming this way'

(h) |-*i*-senyeˑ| AI 'eat' ← |wiˑseni-| AI (*wiˑseniwa* 'he eats')
  kiˑmisenyeˑwa AI 'he eats secretly'
  tahtakwisenyeˑwaki AI 'they all eat together'
  tašisenyeˑwa AI 'he eats {somewhere}'
  weˑpisenyeˑwa AI 'he begins eating'

(i) |-*i*ˑseni| AI 'eat' ← |wiˑseni-| AI (*wiˑseniwa* 'he eats')
  kiˑšiˑseniwa 'he finishes eating' (see 1.39)
  kehčiˑseniwa 'he eats a lot'

37.4. Transitive final pairs. There are three widespread patterns of contrast in transitive final pairs (4.85), and a few minor patterns. When the TI adds |t| to the TA (4.85*a*), there are other changes as well. An |-N| or |-m| always drops; a preceding |-či| in the TA final drops in one case, and a preceding |-ši| (< |-S-i|) in a TA final is replaced by either |-se| (< |-S-e|) or, in one stem pair, |-h|. An |-S| in the TA is replaced by |h| before the |-t|. A sequence |-hpw-t| becomes |-ht|, but otherwise |-Cw-t| becomes |-Cot| (< |-Cw-*e*-t|) or |-Cet|. If the TA has |-Caw|, or if it has |-Cw| and does not add |-t|, the TI drops the |-aw| or |-w|.

(4.85) Patterns of contrast in the shapes of transitive finals

  (a) TI adds |t| to TA (with adjustments)

|-h| TA	|-ht| TI(2)
|-N| TA	|-t| TI(1), |-t| TI(2), |-t| TI(3)
|-m| TA	|-t| TI(1)
|-šim| TA	|-set| TI(2), |-ht| TI(2)
|-pam| TA	|-pet| TI(1)
|-čim| TA	|-čit| TI(2), |-t| TI(2)
|-S| TA	|-ht| TI(1), |-ht| TI(2)
|-C-w| TA	|-C-ot| TI(1)
|-hpw| TA	|-hpet| TI(1), |-ht| TI(1)

  (b) TI subtracts |-aw| from TA

|-kaw| TA	|-k| TI(1)
|-kwaw| TA	|-kw| TI(1)
|-naw| TA	|-n| TI(1)
|-taw| TA	|-t| TI(1)

  (c) TI subtracts |-w| from TA

|-hw|	|-h| TI(1)
|-sw|	|-s| TI(1)
|-šw|	|-š| TI(1)

The common final |-en| TA,TI(1) 'act on by (holding or manipulating with the) hand (or fingers)' makes identical stems for objects of either gender. Two rare patterns are in (4.86*op*). One common verb shows suppletion: *amweˑwa* TA, *miˑčiwa* TI(3) 'he eats him, it'. Double-object stems (TA+O) systematically lack a TI: *miˑneˑwa* (|miˑN-| TA) 'he gives O2 to him', *kemoˑtemeˑwa* 'he steals O2 from him', *koˑkenamaweˑwa* 'he washes O2 for him'. Some TI stems are attested only with reflexive objects (2.43; e.g., 4.341*ac*) or as bases for secondary derivation (4.275-277).

37.5. Abstract transitive finals. The two most common abstract transitive final pairs (4.86*ab*) both indicate the most general transitive notions, usually causative but also applicative. Both are used in primary stems, in the derivation of concrete finals, and in secondary derivation. Other abstract final pairs are uncommon or rare. For many primary stems with abstract finals the residue of the stem is not found elsewhere, and stem segmentation is based on the contrast in the final pair and the recurrence of some finals. In other primary stems the abstract final is added to an identifiable initial.

(4.86) Abstract transitive finals

(a) |-h| TA, |-ht| TI(2)   Typically with identifiable initials.
      akihe·wa TA, *akihto·wa* TI(2) 'he loses him, it' (|ak-| 'lost, disappear')
      anihe·wa TA, *anihto·wa* TI(2)-O 'he defeats him, wins the game or contest'
      apwi·he·wa TA, *apwi·hto·wa* TI(2) 'he waits for him, it' (initial only here)
      ašihe·wa TA, *ašihto·wa* TI(2) 'he makes him, it' (|aN-| 'fixed, done')
      kaškihe·wa TA, *kaškihto·wa* TI(2) 'he can do, can get, buys him, it' (|kašk-| 'able')
      ni·šwihe·wa TA, *ni·šwihto·wa* TI(2) 'he makes, gets two of him, it' (|ni·šw-| 'two')
      pana·čihe·wa TA, *pana·čihto·wa* TI(2) 'he ruins him, it' (|pana·t-| 'ruined')
      so·kihe·wa TA, *so·kihto·wa* TI(2) 'he ties him, it' (|so·k-| 'held')
      te·pihe·wa TA, *te·pihto·wa* TI(2) 'he pleases him, it' (|te·p-| 'enough')
      wi·čihe·wa TA, *wi·čihto·wa* TI(2) 'he lives with him, it' (|wi·t-| 'with')
      |-h| TA, |-ht| TI(2) CAUS (**§54.9**), |-h| TA, |-ht| TI(2) APPLIC (**§55.10**)

(b) |-N| TA, |-t| TI(2)   Typically in unanalyzable stems.
      ako·ne·wa TA, *ako·to·wa* TI(2) 'he hangs him, it, places him, it aloft'
      apo·ne·wa TA 'he roasts {something} for him'
      awane·wa TA, *awato·wa* TI(2) 'he takes him, it away, home'
      a·wane·wa TA, *a·wato·wa* TI(2) 'he takes him, it in loads, multiple trips
      kahkine·wa TA, *kahkito·wa* TI(2) 'he hides him, it'
      nemane·wa TA, *nemato·wa* TI(2) 'he stands him, it up'
      ni·pine·wa TA, *ni·pito·wa* TI(2) 'he weaves him, it'
      |-N| TA, |-t| TI(2) CAUS (**§54.11**), |-N| TA, |-t| TI(2) ABSTR (**§54.12**)

(c) |-notaw| TA, |-not| TI(1) APPLIC.
      keša·činotawe·wa TA 'he is gentle towards him'
      ki·šinotamwa TI(1) 'he obtains it, secures it, procures it by effort'
      mesawinotawe·wa TA 'he envies him'
      se·kinotawe·wa TA, *se·kinotamwa* TI(1) 'he's afraid for him,
         frightened over him, it'
      |-·notaw| TA, |-·not| TI(1) APPLIC (**§54.6**)

(d) |-nohkataw| TA, |-nohkat| TI(1) APPLIC.
      nasata·winohkatawe·wa TA 'he acts crossly towards him'
      keša·činohkatawe·wa TA 'he is kind or friendly to him'
      |-nohkataw| TA, |-nohkat| TI(1) APPLIC (**§54.7**)

(e) |-i·htaw| TA, |-i·ht| TI(1) APPLIC.
      mawi·htawe·wa TA, *mawi·htamwa* TI(1) 'go for' (|maw-| 'go and')
      me·neši·htawe·wa TA, *me·neši·htamwa* TI(1) 'he is bashful, shy, embarrassed
         before him, ashamed of it' (|me·neS-| 'ashamed, embarrassed')
      mo·hki·htawe·wa TA, *mo·hki·htamwa* TI(1), TI(1)-O 'he rushes out to attack
         him, it; he attacks enemies' (|mo·hk-| 'into view')

oči·htawe wa TA 'he goes at him from{somewhere}' (|ot-| 'from {somewhere}')

otami·htawe wa TA 'he is busy with him' (|otam-| 'busy, occupied')

|-·htaw| TA, |-·ht| TI(1) APPLIC (§54.5)

(f) |-aw| TA, |-∅| TI(1)

anawe wa TA, *anamwa* TI(1) 'he resembles him, it'

nenawe wa TA, *nenamwa* TI(1) 'he recognizes him, it'

mehkawe wa TA, *mehkamwa* TI(1) 'he found him, it'

to·tawe wa TA, *to·tamwa* TI(1) 'he treats him, it {so}'

|-aw| TA, (rare) |-∅| TI APPLIC (§54.1)

|-hkaw| TA, |-hk| TI(1) APPLIC (§54.8)

(g) |-m| TA, |-t| TI(1)

kome wa TA, *kotamwa* TI(1) 'he swallows him, it'

mena·me wa TA, *mena·tamwa* TI(1) 'he smells him, it'

no·me wa TA, *no·tamwa* TI(1) 'he carries him, it on his back'

|-·m| TA, |-·t| TI(1) APPLIC (§54.4)

(h) |-am| TA, |-at| TI(1)   (Cf. 4.90(b))

pakame wa TA, *pakatamwa* TI(1) 'he hits him, it' (|pak-|, imitative)

wa·pame wa TA, *wa·patamwa* TI(1) 'he looks at him, it' (|wa·p-| 'visible')

(i) |-em| TA, |-et| TI(1)

mi·hkeme wa TA, *mi·hketamwa* TI(1) 'he courts her, picks him (e.g. apple), it'

(j) |-N| TA, |-t| TI(1)

anawine wa TA, *anawitamwa* TI(1) 'he creeps up on him, it'

anohka·ne wa TA, *anohka·tamwa* TI(1) 'he asks him, it to help with something'

ine wa TA, *itamwa* TI(1) 'he says {so} to or about him, it'

mane wa TA, *matamwa* TI(1) 'he copulates with her, it'

nakane wa TA, *nakatamwa* TI(1) 'he leaves him, it behind'

na·kane wa TA, *na·katamwa* TI(1) 'he follows the trail or route of him, it'

pakine wa TA, *pakitamwa* TI(1) 'he discards him, it'

wawi·nwa·ne wa TA, *wawi·nwa·tamwa* TI(1) 'he praises, brags about him, it'

(k) |-N| TA, |-t| TI(2)

akwi·ne wa TA, *akwi·to wa* TI(2) 'he has him, it in water, soaks him, it'

(l) |-N| TA, |-t| TI(3)

na·ne wa TA, *na·twa* TI(3) 'he goes after him, it, goes to get him, it'

(m) |-a·N| TA, |-a·t| TI(1)

aka·wa·ne wa TA, *aka·wa·tamwa* TI(1) 'he wants, craves, longs for him, it'

po·ta·ne wa TA, *po·ta·tamwa* TI(1) 'he blows on him, it' (|po·t-| 'blow, etc.')

tepa·ne wa TA, *tepa·tamwa* TI(1) 'he loves, cherishes him, it' (|tep-| 'match, own')

wi·kwa·ne wa TA, *wi·kwa·tamwa* TI(1) 'he pays attention to him, it'

(n) |-S| TA, |-ht| TI(1)

kose wa TA, *kohtamwa* TI(1) 'he fears him, it'

(o) |-S| TA, |-ht| TI(2)

ase wa TA, *ahto wa* TI(2) 'he has him, it, puts him, it {somewhere}'

nese wa TA, *nehto wa* TI(2) 'he kills him, it'

(p) |-w| TA, |-t| TI(1)

ne·we wa TA, *ne·tamwa* TI(1) 'he sees him, it'

(q) |-w| TA, |-yo·| TI(3)
           awe wa TA, *ayo wa* TI(3) 'he uses him, it'

37.6. Concrete transitive finals. Concrete transitive finals are sometimes called instrumental finals, since most of them specify a particular means or instrument of action. The most common concrete final pairs are given here, sorted into those that add |t| in the TI (4.87-93); those that subtract |-aw| (4.94); those that subtract |w| (4.95-96); and one with no change (4.97).

In some cases these finals have the shape of causatives made by adding |-h| TA, |-ht| TI(2) or |-N| TA, |-t| TI(2) to AI finals, with replacement of |a·| or |e·| by |a| (**§54.9, 11**).

(4.87) Concrete transitive finals with |-h| TA, |-ht| TI(2)

(a) |-isah| TA, |-isaht| TI(2) 'act on swiftly' (cf. |-isa·| AI,II 'run, fly, fall')
           ata·hpisahe wa TA, *ata·hpisahto wa* TI(2) 'he grabs him, it, jerks him, it away'
           čapo·kisahe wa TA, *čapo·kisahto wa* TI(2) 'he flings him, it into water'
           komisahe wa TA, *komisahto wa* TI(2) 'he swallows him, it whole'
           pawisahe wa TA, *pawisahto wa* TI(2) 'he gives him, it a shake'
           ka·čisahe wa TA, *ka·čisahto wa* TI(2) 'he shoves him, it'

(4.88) Concrete transitive finals with |-N| TA, |-t| TI(1)

(a) |-ikwa·N| TA, |-ikwa·t| TI(1) 'act on by boring'
           nešiwana·čikwa·ne wa TA, *nešiwana·čikwa·tamwa* TI(1) 'he ruins it by boring'

(b) |-ikwa·N| TA, |-ikwa·t| TI(1) 'sew'
           ačikwa·ne wa TA, *ačikwa·tamwa* TI(1) 'he sews him, it'

(c) |-inaN| TA, |-inat| TI(1) 'assail' (cf. 4.89*e*)
           mawinane wa TA, *mawinatamwa* TI(1) 'he attacks, runs up to him, it'

(d) |-ihkaN| TA, |-ihkat| TI(1) 'leave behind, outrun'
           očihkane wa TA, *očihkatamwa* TI(1) 'he leaves him, it behind ({there})'

(e) |-pahwa·N| TA, |-pahwa·t| TI(1) 'run to'
           natwipahwa·ne wa TA 'he runs seeking him'
           na·čipahwa·tamwa TI(1) 'he runs to it'

(f) |-itehka·N| TA, |-itehka·t| TI(1) 'name'
           išitehka·ne wa TA, *išitehka·tamwa* TI(1) 'he names him, it {so}'

(4.89) Concrete transitive finals with |-N| TA, |-t| TI(2)

(a) |-ahkaN| TA, |-ahkat| TI(2) 'stick in the ground, etc., to stand'
           nana·hahkane wa TA, *nana·hahkato wa* TI(2) 'he sets him, it fixed in the ground'

(b) |-aho·N| TA, |-aho·t| TI(2) 'drag, convey by (paddling a) canoe'
           pemaho·ne wa TA, *pemaho·to wa* TI(2) 'he drags him, it, conveys him, it by canoe'

(c) |-aškenaN| TA, |-aškenat| TI(2) 'fill' (cf. |-aškene·| AI 'be filled, fill')
           anaškenane wa TA, *anaškenato wa* TI(2) 'he fills him (e.g., pipe), it, loads it (gun)'

(d) |-a·waN| TA, |-a·wat| TI(2) 'change the location of more than one of'
           ni·sa·wane wa TA, *ni·sa·wato wa* TI(2) 'he took them (anim., inan.) down, unloaded them'
           nowa·wane wa TA, *nowa·wato wa* TI(2) 'he takes, carries them (anim., inan.) out'

(e) |-inaN| TA, |-inat| TI(2) 'kill' (sometimes metaphorical) (cf. |-ine·| AI 'die'; cf. 4.88*c*)
           a·hpečinane wa TA, *a·hpečinato wa* TI(2) 'he kills him, it for good; he knocks him out cold'
           pašinato wa TI(2): *nepašinato ni·yawi* "I came near killing myself" (Jones 1907:116.22, 117)
           pi·ke·nane wa TA 'he beat him to death, wore him out'

(f) |-iweN| TA, |-iwet| TI(2) 'lead, convey'
    pakišiwene wa TA, *pakišiweto wa* TI(2) 'he took (and left) him, it {somewhere}'

(g) |-aˑhpenaN| TA, |-aˑhpenat| TI(2) 'use, treat' (cf. |-aˑhpene·| AI 'be ill, afflicted')
    inaˑhpenane wa TA, *inaˑhpenato wa* TI(2) 'he gets, uses him, it {so}'
    myaˑnaˑhpenane wa TA, *myaˑnaˑhpenato wa* TI(2) 'he mistreats him, it'
    |-hpenaN| TA, |-hpenat| TI(2) 'use, treat'
    aˑnoˑhpenane wa TA, *aˑnoˑhpenato wa* TI(2) 'he is unable to deal with, kill him, it'
    kaško ˑhpenane wa TA, *kaško ˑhpenato wa* TI(2) 'he is able to deal with, kill him, it'
    |-ipenaN| TA, |-ipenat| TI(2) 'use, treat'
    mya šipenane wa TA, *mya šipenato wa* TI(2) 'he treats him, it badly, harms him, it'
    |-penaN| TA, |-penat| TI(2) 'use, treat' (cf. |-pene·| AI 'be ill, afflicted')
    ihpenane wa TA, *ihpenato wa* TI(2) 'he does {so} to him, it'
    myaˑhpenane wa TA, *myaˑhpenato wa* TI(2) 'he cripples him, it'

(h) |-paho·N| TA, |-paho·t| TI(2) 'act on by running' (cf. |-paho| AI 'run')
    na čipaho ne wa TA, *na čipaho to wa* TI(2) 'he runs to get him, it'
    awačipaho ne wa TA, *awačipaho to wa* TI(2) 'he runs away with him, it'
    ihpaho ne wa TA 'he runs to him {somewhere}'
    sakinehke paho ne wa AI 'he runs holding his hand'

(i) |-piN| TA, |-pit| TI(2) 'tie' (AI, II: 4.78*q*)
    ihpine wa TA, *ihpito wa* TI(2) 'he ties him, it {so}'
    na pine wa TA, *na pito wa* TI(2) 'he has him, it around his neck'
    |-apiN| TA, |-apit| TI(2) 'tie' (AI, II: 4.78*q*)
    akwa ˑhkwapine wa TA, *akwa ˑhkwapito wa* TI(2) 'he ties him, it against
        something'
    inapine wa TA, *inapito wa* TI(2) 'he ties him, it {so}'
    sakapine wa TA, *sakapito wa* TI(2) 'he ties him, it to something'
    wi ˑke tapine wa TA, *wi ˑke tapito wa* TI(2) 'he ties him, it carefully'

(j) |-poN| TA, |-pot| TI(2) 'subject to quick, hard strokes, saw, file, grind'
    ki ˑškipone wa TA, *ki ˑškipoto wa* TI(2) 'he saws him (board), it off'
    pi ˑke pone waki TA 'they gang-rape her to death'
    po ˑhkipone wa TA 'he drills a hole in him (e.g., pipe)'
    šekwipone wa TA 'he crushes him (corn)'

(4.90) Concrete transitive finals with |-m| TA, |-t| TI(1)

(a) |-m| TA, |-t| TI(1) 'act on by vocalization'
    akime wa TA, *akitamwa* TI(1) 'he counts them (anim., inan.)'
    mawime wa TA, *mawitamwa* TI(1) 'he mourns, bewails him, it'
    wanime wa TA, *wanitamwa* TI(1) 'he deceives him, it'

(b) |-am| TA, |-at| TI(1) 'act on by mouth, teeth'
    ča kame wa TA, *ča katamwa* TI(1) 'he eats him, it all up'
    ni mame wa TA, *ni matamwa* TI(1) 'he holds it sticking out of his mouth'
    seswame wa TA, *seswatamwa* TI(1) 'he sprays {something} on him, it by
        mouth'
    otame wa TA, *otatamwa* TI(1) 'he bites him, it {somewhere}'

(c) |-e·nem| TA, |-e·net| TI(1) 'think about, regard, act on by mind or thought'
        kehke·neme·wa TA, *kehke·netamwa* TI(1) 'he knows him, it'
        ketema·ke·neme·wa TA, *ketema·ke·netamwa* TI(1) 'he has compassion for him, it'
        mata·kwe·neme·wa TA, *mata·kwe·netamwa* TI(1) 'he enjoys him, it'
        mehkwe·neme·wa TA, *mehkwe·netamwa* TI(1) 'he thinks of, remembers him, it'
        menwe·neme·wa TA, *menwe·netamwa* TI(1) 'he likes him, it'
        mese·neme·wa TA, *mese·netamwa* TI(1) 'he benefits from him, it'
        nahe·neme·wa TA, *nahe·netamwa* TI(1) 'he thinks him, it fit, proper, right'
        nana·he·neme·wa TA, *nana·he·netamwa* TI(1) 'he has authority over him, it'
        tepe·neme·wa TA, *tepe·netamwa* TI(1) 'he owns him, it'

(d) |-im| TA, |-ot| TI(1) 'speak to, about' (|-im| TA treated as if |-em| after |Cw|)
        a·čime·wa TA, *a·totamwa* TI(1) 'he tells about him, it'
        a·šime·wa TA, *a·šotamwa* TI(1) 'he urges him, it'
        nahkome·wa TA, *nahkotamwa* TI(1) 'he agrees with him, it, accepts his proposal'
        natome·wa TA, *natotamwa* TI(1) 'he calls, asks for him, it'
        mama·tome·wa TA, *mama·totamwa* TI(1) 'he prays to him, it'
        me·nešime·wa TA, *me·nešotamwa* TI(1) 'he shames him, it by speech'
        nenehkime·wa TA, *nenehkotamwa* TI(1) 'he mentions him, it'
        wa(·)pašime·wa TA, *wa(·)pašotamwa, wapasotamwa* TI(1) 'he makes fun of
            him, it'

(e) |-iya·m| TA, |-iya·t| TI(1) 'smell'
        kočiya·me·wa TA, *kočiya·tamwa* TI(1) 'he sniffs at him, it'
        menwiya·me·wa TA, *menwiya·tamwa* TI(1) 'he likes the smell of him, it'

(f)   Body-part medial as prefinal + |-a·m| TA, |-a·t| TI(1) 'act on by (body part)'
  1) |-etona·m| TA 'act on by mouth, talk' (← |-eton-| 'mouth')
        nešiwetona·me·wa TA 'he overpowered him with talk'
  2) |-ikaša·t| TI(1) 'act on by nail, claw' (← |-ikaš-| 'nail, claw')
        pahkwe·kaša·tamwa TI(1) 'he cuts off a piece of it with his fingernail'
  3) |-itiya·m| TA 'act on by anus' (← |-itiy-| 'rear end')
        pakišitiya·me·wa TA 'he releases him from his anus'
  4) |-neča·m| TA, |-neča·t| TI(1) 'act on by hand'; also metaphorical (← |-neč-| 'hand')
        mya·nawineča·me·wa TA 'he overpowers him using his hands'
        nana·hineča·me·wa TA, *nana·hineča·tamwa* TI(1) 'he takes charge of him, it'

(4.91) Concrete transitive finals with |-m| TA, |-t| TI(2)

(a) |-čim| TA, |-čito·| TI(2) 'snag, resist the motion of' (AI, II: 4.73*b*)
        paši·škičime·wa TA 'she pushes his foreskin back in copulating'
        patahkičime·wa TA 'he impales him, lets him impale himself, on {something}'
        paškwa·hkwičito·wa TI(2) 'he rips it off by getting it snagged'

(b) |-ešim| TA, |-ešit| TI(1) 'flee'
        na·hkatešime·wa TA, *na·hkatešitamwa* TI(1) 'he abandons him, it in flight'

(c) |-šim| TA, |-set| (in one stem |-ht| [after a long vowel]) TI(2) 'place' (AI, II: 4.73*a*)
        ahkwa·wišime·wa TA, *ahkwa·wiseto·wa* TI(2) 'he fills him, it, fills {something}
            with him, it'
        kohkišime·wa TA, *kohkiseto·wa* TI(2) 'he changes his, its position'
        nana·hišime·wa TA, *nana·hiseto·wa* TI(2) 'he sets him, it in place'

neneškišime wa TA, *neneškiseto wa* TI(2) 'he spreads him, it out'

paka·šime wa TA, *paka·hto wa* TI(2) 'he boils him, it' (|paka·-| 'into water')

(d) |-pam| TA, |-pet| TI(1) 'taste'

mya·hpame wa TA, *mya·hpetamwa* TI(1) 'he dislikes his, its taste' (|mya·N-| 'bad')

(4.92) Concrete transitive finals with |-w| TA, |-ot| TI(1) after consonant

(a) |-w| TA, |-ot| TI(1) 'shoot'

mešwe wa TA, *mešotamwa* TI(1) 'he shoots and hits him, it'

pemwe wa TA, *pemotamwa* TI(1) 'he shoots (at) him, it'

(b) |-pw| TA, |-pot| TI(1) 'act on by teeth'

sakipwe wa TA, *sakipotamwa* TI(1) 'he bites him, it'

(4.93) Concrete transitive finals with |-w| TA, |-(e)t| TI(1) after consonant

(a) |-hpw| TA, |-hpet| TI(1) 'taste'

wi·kihpwe wa TA, *wi·kihpetamwa* TI(1) 'he likes his, its taste'

a·nawihpetamwa TI(1) 'he tastes it and doesn't like it'

(b) |-hpw| TA, |-ht| TI(1) 'act on by mouth'

no·škwa·hpwe wa TA, *no·škwa·htamwa* TI(1) 'he licks him, it'

po·tetone·hpwe wa TA 'he or she kisses him or her'

saketone·htamwa TI(1) 'he bites its rim, holds it with his mouth by the rim'

(4.94) Concrete transitive finals with |-Caw| TA, |-C| TI(1)

(a) |-ehkaw| TA, |-ehk| TI(1) 'act on by foot or body'

na·sehkawe wa TA, *na·sehkamwa* TI(1) 'he goes up to him, it'

ni·škehkawe wa TA 'he crowds him, is in his way'

pesehkawe wa TA, *pesehkamwa* TI(1) 'he puts on, wears him, it (hat, footwear)'

pi·sehkawe wa TA, *pi·sehkamwa* TI(1) 'he puts him, it on (as a shirt)'

(b) |-eškaw| TA, |-ešk| TI(1) 'act on by foot or body'

kepoškawe wa TA, *kepoškamwa* TI(1) 'he boxes him in, closes it using his foot'
(|kepw-| 'shut, block', variant of |kep-| [4.94c])

ki·weškawe wa TA, *ki·weškamwa* TI(1) 'he wears him, it as clothing, has him, it on'

ni·škeškawe wa TA 'he messes things up for him (e.g., a ceremony or a bed)'

maya·škawe wa TA, *maya·škamwa* TI(1) 'he comes directly to him, it'

takeškawe wa TA, *takeškamwa* TI(1) 'he kicks him, it'

(c) |-iškaw| TA, |-išk| TI(1) 'act on by body mass or presence'
(← prefinal |-i-| 'mass, sheer presence' + |-eškaw| TA, |-ešk| TI(1) [4.94b])

kepiškawe wa TA, *kepiškamwa* TI(1) 'he blocks, inhibits him, it (by being there)'
(|kep-| 'shut, block')

nakiškawe wa TA 'he goes to meet him' (|nak-| 'stop')

tepiškawe wa TA 'he replaces him by being ceremonially adopted for him'
(|tep-| 'match, own')

(For *ahpiškamwa* TI(1) 'he steps on it', see 4.22.)

(d) |-i·hkaw| TA, |-i·hk| TI(1) (~ |-o·hkaw| TA, |-o·hk| TI(1)) 'deal with, be occupied with'

ča·ko·hkawe wa TA 'they all deal with him together'

nana·hi·hkawe wa TA, *nana·hi·hkamwa* TI(1) 'he attends to him, it'

ni·šo·hkawe wa TA, *ni·šo·hkamwa* TI(1) 'the two of them deal with him, it
together'

ma·no·hkawe wa TA 'the large number of them deal with him together'

[continued →]

wiʼkeʼčiʼhkawewa TA, *wiʼkeʼčiʼhkamwa* TI(1) 'he deals carefully with him, it'
wiʼtoʼhkawewa TA, *wiʼtoʼhkamwa* TI(1) 'he cooperates, joins in, goes along
    with him, allows him; he takes part in it'

(e) |-ekwaw| TA, |-ekw| TI(1) 'act on by (the power of) dream'
      mehkokwawewa TA 'he learns of him in a dream'
      natokwawewa TA, *natokwamwa* TI(1) 'he seeks him, it in a dream'

(f) |-enaw| TA, |-en| TI(1) 'act on by missile or shot, gamble against'
      čaʼkenawewa TA, *čaʼkenamwa* TI 'he hits all of them (anim., inan.) with a
        shot; he wins everything from him in gambling'
      peškonawewa 'he misses him with his shot'

(g) |-inaw| TA, |-in| TI(1) 'regard, feel about'
      keteminawewa TA, *keteminamwa* TI(1) 'he pities, blesses him, it'
      mačinawewa TA, *mačinamwa* TI(1) 'he dares against him, it, challenges him, it'
      mesawinawewa TA, *mesawinamwa* TI(1) 'he regards him, it as a tempting morsel'
      neškinawewa TA, *neškinamwa* TI(1) 'he hates him, it'
      pehkiʼnawewa TA, *pehkiʼnamwa* TI(1) 'he thinks he, it looks strange or
        different, doesn't recognize him, it'

(h) |-ehtaw| TA, |-eht| TI(1) 'hear, listen to'
      kaʼškehtawewa TA, *kaʼškehtamwa* TI(1) 'he hears him, it'
      menohtawewa TA, *menohtamwa* TI(1) 'he likes hearing him, it'
      nenohtawewa TA, *nenohtamwa* TI(1) 'he understands him, it'
      teʼpweʼhtawewa TA, *teʼpweʼhtamwa* TI(1) 'he believes him, it'

(i) |-etaw| TA, |-et| TI(1) 'pay attention or regard to' (only these two stems)
      kosetawewa TA, *kosetamwa* TI(1) 'he fears him, it, respectfully defers to him'
      pesetawewa TA, *pesetamwa* TI(1) 'he listens to him, it'

(4.95) Concrete transitive finals with |-hw| TA, |-h| TI(1)

(a) |-ahw| TA, |-ah| TI(1) 'act on by (hand-held) tool'; also metaphorical
      kaškahwewa TA, *kaškahamwa* TI(1) 'he manages to deal with him, it by tool;
        he brings her to climax (by copulation or masturbation)'
      kehkahwewa TA, *kehkahamwa* TI(1) 'he designates him, it'
      niʼmahwewa TA, *niʼmahamwa* TI(1) 'he sets, carries him, it on a stick'
      panahwewa TA, *panahamwa* TI(1) 'he misses hitting him, it with hand-held tool'
      patahkahwewa TA, *patahkahamwa* TI(1) 'he pierces, impales him, it'
      piʼtahwewa TA, *piʼtahamwa* TI(1) 'he buries him, it'
      sahkahwewa TA, *sahkahamwa* TI(1) 'he sets fire to him, it'
      siʼkahwewa TA, *siʼkahamwa* TI(1) 'he pours him, it out'

(b) |-ačihw| TA, |-ačih| TI(1) 'act on by solid mass (?)'
      (← prefinal |-at-| + |-ihw| TA, |-ih| TI(1) [4.86*f*])
      kepačihwewa TA, *kepačihamwa* TI(1) 'he plugs his hole (trapping him), plugs it'
      nekwačihwewa TA, *nekwačihamwa* TI(1) 'he hoes, weeds, hills him (as, corn), it'

(c) |-atahw| TA, |-atah| TI(1) 'act on by (striking with a) stick, copulating'
      (← prefinal |-at-| + |-ahw| TA, |-ah| TI(1) [4.86*a*])
      čaʼkatahwewa TA, *čaʼkatahamwa* TI(1) 'he clubs them, it (village) all (to death)'
      kiʼškatahwewa TA, *kiʼškatahamwa* 'he whips him, it'
      šekwatahwewa TA, *šekwatahamwa* TI(1) 'he smashes him (e.g., ice), it to pieces'
      šiʼkwatahwewa TA 'he wears her out copulating with her'

(d) |-ešihw| TA, |-eših| TI(1) 'chase'; |-eših| TI(1)-O 'go on a hunt'
       mi wešihwe wa TA, **mi wešihamwa* TI(1) 'he drives, chases, orders him, it away'
       pemešihwe wa TA 'he goes chasing after him'
       mahkwešihamwa TI(1)-O 'he goes on a bear hunt'
       we pešihamwa TI(1)-O 'he sets off on a hunt'

(e) |-ihw| TA, |-ih| TI(1) 'act on the whole of by tool (?)'
       (← prefinal |-i-| 'mass, sheer presence' + |-ahw| TA, |-ah| TI(1) [4.86a])
       a pihwe wa TA, *a pihamwa* TI(1) 'he unties him, it' (|a·p-| 'untie')
       (For *ahpihwe wa* TA 'he piles {something} on top of him', see 4.22.)

(f) |-ikahw| TA, |-ikah| TI(1) 'act on by axe, chop, hew'
       papaka škikahwe wa TA, *papaka škikahamwa* 'he chops him, it into slabs'
       pi kikahwe wa TA 'he chops him (e.g., ice) to pieces'
       wa nehkwikahamwa TI(1) 'he hollows it out with an axe'

(g) |-i·hw| TA, |-i·h| TI(1) 'act on by fencing'
       kepi hwe wa TA, *kepi hamwa* TI(1) 'he fences him, it in'

(4.96) Other concrete transitive finals with |-Cw| TA, |-C| TI(1)

(a) |-asw| TA, |-as| TI(1) 'act on by fire' (cf. 4.78d)
       ahkaswe wa TA, *ahkasamwa* TI(1) 'he burns him, it (up)'

(b) |-a·hkasw| TA, |-a·hkas| TI(1) 'dry with heat' (cf. 4.78f)
       ki ša hkaswe wa TA, *ki ša hkasamwa* 'he finishes drying him, it'

(c) |-esw| TA, |-es| TI(1) 'act on by fire, heat, cooking, shooting with a firearm,
       smoking tobacco, boiling medicine' (cf. 4.78g)
       akoswe wa TA, **akosamwa* TI 'he makes him, it stick by heating or burning'
       ka hkeswe wa TA, *ka hkesamwa* TI(1) 'he dries him, it by the fire, in the sun'
       ki šeswe wa TA, *ki šesamwa* TI(1) 'he cooks him, it done'
       nekeswe wa TA, *nekesamwa* TI(1) 'he melts him, it'
       pakeswe wa TA, *pakesamwa* TI(1) 'he explodes him, it (by heating or otherwise)'
       pa škeswe wa TA 'he shot him with a firearm; he struck him with lightning'
       si seswe wa TA, *si sesamwa* TI(1) 'he pokes, singes him, it with a burning stick'
       si swe wa TA, *si samwa* TI(1) 'he fries him, it'
       wi škopeswe wa TA, *wi škopesamwa* TI(1) 'he adds sugar in cooking him, it'
       na teswe wa TA 'he tries to make him come by burning tobacco'
       ša poswe wa TA 'he gives him a laxative'

(d) |-ešw| TA, |-eš| TI(1) 'act on by cutting edge'
       ki škešwe wa TA, *ki škešamwa* TI(1) 'he cuts him, it off'
       pekihkešwe wa TA, *pekihkešamwa* TI(1) 'he cuts him, it to bits'
       po hkešwe wa TA, *po hkešamwa* TI(1) 'he cuts a hole in him, it'

(4.97) Concrete transitive final pair with with identical TA and TI(1)
       |-en| TA, TI(1) 'act on by (holding or handling with) hand, fingers'; also metaphorical
       aškone wa TA, *aškonamwa* TI(1) 'he saves him, it, doesn't give away or use him, it'
       ata hpene wa TA, *ata hpenamwa* TI(1) 'he takes him, it'
       a piškone wa TA, *a piškonamwa* TI(1) 'he unties him, it'
       čapo kenamwa TA, *čapo kenamwa* TI(1) 'he dips him, it in water, liquid'
       kekye nene wa TA, *kekye nenamwa* TI(1) 'he holds him, it firmly'
       ko kene wa TA, *ko kenamwa* TI(1) 'he washes him, it'
       [continued →]

ma·watene·wa TA, *ma·watenamwa* TI(1) 'he gathers him, it, them (anim., inan.)'
mešene·wa TA, *mešenamwa* TI(1) 'he catches, grabs him, it'
mo·ne·wa TA 'he plucks him (bird)'
nahkone·wa TA, *nahkonamwa* TI(1) 'he takes in his hand, accepts, catches him, it'
ni·me·ne·wa TA, *ni·me·namwa* TI(1) 'he lifts him, it in the air'
ni·'sene·wa TA, *ni·'senamwa* TI(1) 'he lowers him, it, takes, sets him, it down'
pa·hkene·wa TA, *pa·hkenamwa* TI(1) 'he uncovers him, it, opens (door for) him, it'
pemene·wa TA, *pemenamwa* TI(1) 'he takes care of him, it'
po·hkone·wa TA, *po·hkonamwa* TI(1) 'he breaks, snaps him, it in two'
so·'kene·wa TA, *so·'kenamwa* TI(1) 'he holds him, it in his hand'
otehtene·wa TA, *otehtenamwa* TI(1) 'he gets, obtains him, it'
wi·šikene·wa TA, *wi·šikenamwa* TI(1) 'he holds him, it tight'
wi·wene·wa TA, *wi·wenamwa* TI(1) 'he wraps him, it'

37.7. Transitive finals derived from stems. In the derivation of verb finals from transitive stems the same kinds of changes in shape are found as in the case of intransitives (**§37.3**).

(4.98) Stem-derived transitive finals

(a) |-ako·N| TA, |-ako·t| TI(2) 'hang' ← |ako·N-| TA, |ako·t-| TI(2)
     (*ako·ne·wa* TA, *ako·to·wa* TI(2) 'he hangs him, it, places him, it aloft' [4.86*b*])
     ačitawa·nakwako·ne·wa TA 'he hangs him upside-down'
     nana·hako·to·wa TI(2) 'he hangs it in place'
     paškitako·ne·wa TA, *paškitako·to·wa* TI(2) 'he hangs him, it over'
     takwako·ne·wa TA, *takwako·to·wa* TI(2) 'he hangs him, it in addition'
     wi·ke·tako·to·wa TI(2) 'he hangs it carefully'

(b) |-a·čim| TA, |-a·tot| TI(1) 'tell about' ← |a·čim-| TA, |a·tot-| TI(1)
     (*a·čime·wa* TA, *a·totamwa* TI(1) 'he tells about him, it' [4.90*d*])
     ahkwa·čime·wa TA, *ahkwa·totamwa* TI(1) 'he tells of him, it {so far}'
     tana·čime·wa TA, *tana·totamwa* TI(1) 'he tells of him, it being {somewhere}'

(c) |-a·čimoh| TA 'tell, inform' ← |a·čimoh-| TA
     (*a·čimohe·wa* 'he tells, informs him' [cf. **§54.10**])
     ahkwa·čimohe·wa TA 'he stopped telling him'
     ina·čimohe·wa TA 'he tells, informs him {so}'
     tana·čimohe·wa TA 'he tells him {somewhere}; he is (engaged in) instructing him'

(d) |-a·pam| TA, |-a·pat| TI(1) 'look at, see' ← |wa·pam-| TA, |wa·pat-| TI(1) 'look at'
     (*wa·pame·wa* TA, *wa·patamwa* TI(1) 'he looks at him, it' [4.86*g*])
     mawa·pame·wa TA, *mawa·patamwa* TI(1) 'he goes to see him, it'
     mečima·pame·wa TA 'he stares at him'
     mehtose·neniwa·pame·wa TA 'looking at him he thinks he's a human being'
     osa·pame·wa TA, *osa·patamwa* TI(1) 'he observes him, it from {somewhere}'
     pana·pame·wa TA, *pana·patamwa* TI(1) 'he loses sight of him, it'

(e) |-a·pam| TA, |-a·pat| TI(1) 'select' ← |wa·pam-| TA, |wa·pat-| TI(1) + |CV+| (**§39.2**)
     (*wa·wa·pame·wa* TA, *wa·wa·patamwa* TI(1) 'he selects him, it' [4.147*e*])
     ki·ša·pame·wa 'he has already picked him out' (K-MHTW 36)

(f) |-o·m| TA, |-o·t| TI(1) 'carry on back' ← |no·m-| TA, |no·t-| TI(1)
     (*no·me·wa* TA, *no·tamwa* TI(1) 'he carries him, it on his back' [4.86*f*])
     awato·me·wa TA, *awato·tamwa* TI(1) 'he carries him, it off on his back'

po·no·me·wa TA, po·no·tamwa TI(1) 'he sets him, it down from his back'
pye·to·me·wa TA, pye·to·tamwa TI(1) 'he brings him, it on his back'

(g) |-apwi·h|, |-pwi·h| TA 'wait for' ← |apwi·h-| TA
    (apwi·he·wa TA 'he waits for him' [4.86a])
        aškačipwi·he·wa TA 'he gets impatient waiting for him'
        tanapwi·he·wa TA 'he waits for him {somewhere}'

Particle Finals

38. Many particles consist solely of an unanalyzable stem (e.g., a·neta 'some', na·hka, na·hkači 'also', =ke·hi 'moreover', ki·hpene 'in the event that, once it happens that', mo·hči 'even').

Some internally unanalyzable particles are derived from initials or stems.

(4.99) Derived unanalyzable particles

(a) no·ta P 'too soon' ← |no·te·-| 'incomplete, falling short, not succeeding'
    (e.g. no·te·kiwa 'he is not full grown'; no·te·čime·wa 'he gives out in swimming')

(b) ma·ne P 'much, many' ← |ma·ne·-| (in |ma·ne·-| AI, |ma·ne·t-| II 'be much,
    many': ma·ne·wa AI, ma·ne·twi II 'there is much of him, it' [4.67j])

(c) ki·hka P 'all around' ← |ki·hka·-| 'circling around'
    (e.g., ki·hka·wose·wa 'he walks around in a circle')

Distinct from these are initials that are derived from particles, which are not used freely but rather serve to incorporate the particle into verb stems, for example as a semantic verbal complement or in a verb of being.

(4.100) Initial derived from particle

(a) Initial |ke·htena·h-| ← particle ke·htena 'truly, it is true that':
        ke·htena·he·netamwa 'he thinks it true' (|-e·net| TI(1) 'think about')
        ke·htena·hiwi 'it is true' (|-i| II ABSTR)

(b) Initial |i·nina·h-| ← particle i·nina·hi '(at) that time':
        i·nina·hiwiwi 'it is that time' (|-iwi| II ABSTR)

38.1. Particles with |-i|. Many particles are formed from initials by the abstract particle final |-i| PF ABSTR.

(4.101) Particles derived from initials with |-i| PF ABSTR

(a) aya·pami P 'back (to previous location)' ← |aya·pam-|
        (cf. aya·pami·wa 'he went back'):
        aya·pami·pye·ya·wa·či 'when they arrived back' (O 163A)
        e·h=na·kwa·či aya·pami. 'And she went back home.' (K-M 42c)

(b) iši P '{so}; in {some} way; to {somewhere}' ← |iN-|:
        peteki-'ši '(going) back' (A 1D); tepina·hi-'ši '(up) straight' (A 113H)

(c) kekeni P 'quickly' ← |keken-| 'quick' (cf. 4.78a):
        kekeni=mekoho e·h=ahkani·hiči. 'He rapidly became very thin.' (K-M 153d)

(d) ki·hki·hki P 'just the same, regardless, defiantly' ← |ki·hki·hk-|
        (cf. ki·hki·hkesiwa 'he is contrary'; ki·hki·hkime·wa 'he bids him against his will'):
        me·šeni ki·hki·hki. 'Touch them (anim.) anyway.' (K-M 569i)

(e)   *ni·šwi* P 'two' ← |ni·šw-| (← |ni·š-| [4.67*d*]):
       ni·šwi wi·kiyapye·ni 'two houses' (K-M 593n)
       ni·šwi keki·šihapetoke 'you probably made two (anim.)' (K-M 380c)

(f)   *pi·neši* P 'acting on one's own, unprovoked' ← |pi·neS-| 'on one's own'
       (cf. *pi·nesahkamiki* '(in the) remote wilderness';
           pi·nese·netisowa 'he thinks of himself spontaneously'):
       pi·neši=mekoho ki·h=mi·winehke. (K-M 938r)
       'Your hand will move away of its own accord.'

38.2. Prewords with |-i|. Prewords (prenouns, preverbs, and preparticles) are also commonly formed from initials by |-i| PF ABSTR. The derivation of prewords from noun stems (4.102*f*, 4.103*fghi*) and verb stems (4.102*e*, 4.103*c*) is via initials formed from the stems by the usual processes (4.4, 7).

(4.102) Preverbs derived from initials with |-i| PF ABSTR

(a)   *iši* PV '{so}; in {some} way; to {somewhere}' ← |iN-| (so all relative roots [**§22.4**]):
       a·kwi ke·ko·hi iši-mya·netekini 'it is not evil in any way' (O 73C)
       we·ta paniki iši-meškineče·či 'he would hold his hand open to the east' (O 41A)

(b)   *kehči* PV 'greatly' ← |keht-| (cf. 4.103*b*):
       e·h=kehči-wi·če·nomaki 'I played with them a lot' (A 12A)
       e·h=kehči-wa·pamekoči 'he (obv.) stared at him intently' (O 65A)

(c)   *ki·ši* PV PERF ← |ki·š-| 'finish, have already':
       ki·ši-na·kwa·či 'after he (had) left' (S-RL 74)

(d)   *ki·wi* PV 'around, about, in places' ← |ki·w-|:
       e·h=ki·wi-wi·hkowe·či 'he went around inviting people' (K-BD 22)

(e)   *nepo·wi* PV '(of) dying' ← initial |nepo·w-| (cf. 4.7c) ← |nep-| AI 'die':
       e·h=nepo·wi-mama·tomawa·či 'they made death-bed prayers to her' (K-WF 64)

(f)   *okima·wi* PV '(of) chief' ← initial |okima·w-| ← |okima·w-| AN (*okima·wa* 'chief'):
       e·h=okima·wi-nehta·we·mikahki 'it has slain a chief' (K-B 280)

(g)   *pye·či* PV 'coming, moving or oriented this way' ← |pye·t-|:
       pye·či-mya·hkesiniwahi 'they (obv.) came back crippled' (O 18E)

(h)   *taši* PN '{somewhere}; be engaged in' ← |taN-|:
       i·nahi e·taši-nakamočiki 'the ones who sang there' (O 11I)
       taši-mayo·waki 'they were crying' (O 9C)

(4.103) Prenouns derived from initials with |-i| PF ABSTR

(a)   *iši* PV 'of {some} kind' ← |iN-| (cf. 4.102*a*):
       meše=meko ='nahi iši-nakamo·ni 'any kind of song' (K-Fish 82)

(b)   *kehči* PN 'great' ← |keht-| (cf. 4.102*b*);
       kekye·hči PN 'great (pl.)' ← |kekye·ht-| (4.129*a*):
       kehči-ni·ča·pa 'a doll larger than the others' (A 1G)
       kekye·hči-pene·waki 'great big turkeys' (K-TO 12)
       kekye·hči-we·ta·se·waki 'great warriors' (K-MWL 15)

(c)   *ki·ke·nowi* PN '(of) clan feast' ← |ki·ke·now-| (4.7a) ← |ki·ke·no-| AI 'hold clan feast':
       ki·ke·nowi-nakamo·ni 'clan-feast song'

(d)   *meši* PN 'big' ← |meS-|; *memye·ši* PN 'big (pl.)' ← |memye·S-|:
       meši-nepisi 'large lake' (K-MFS 23)
       memye·ši-mahkwaki 'large bears' (K-FC 305)

(e)   *meškwi* PN 'red' ← |meškw-| 'red':

      meškwi-pene·wa 'red turkey' (K-B 319)

(f)   *na·tawino·ni* PN '(of) medicine' ← initial |na·tawino·n-| ← |na·tawino·n-| IN

      (*na·tawino·ni* 'medicine'):

      na·tawino·ni-nakamo·nani 'medicine songs' (O 26B)

(g)   *nenoswi* PN '(of) buffalo' ← initial |nenosw-| ← |nenosw-| AN (*nenoswa* 'buffalo'):

      nenoswi-oškaše·ki 'buffalo hoofs' (K-SBSB 17)

      nenoswi-aša·ti·hi 'buffalo(-hunting) arrow' (K-PLA 12)

(h)   *okima·wi* PN '(of) chief' ← initial |okima·w-| ← |okima·w-| AN 'chief' (cf. 4.102*f*):

      okima·wi-nenoswa 'buffalo chief, chief of the buffalos' (K-B 15)

      okima·wi-oškinawe·ha 'youth from a chiefly family, chief's son'

(i)   *pi·ša·kani* PN '(of) buckskin' ← initial |pi·ša·kan-| ← |pi·ša·kan-| IN

      (*pi·ša·kani* 'rawhide, leather'):

      pi·ša·kani-pi·sehka·hi 'buckskin shirt'

(j)   *taši* PN '(of) {somewhere}' ← |taN-|:

      na·mahkamiki taši-maneto·waki 'the spirits of the underworld' (K-FC 411)

(4.104) Preparticles derived from initials with |-i| PF ABSTR

(a)   *ahkwiči* PP 'on top' ← |ahkwit-|:

      ahkwiči-asenye, ahkwič-asenye 'on top of a, the rock' (K-B 199, K-PKM 7)

(b)   *či·ki* PP 'by the side of, next to' ← |či·k-|:

      či·ki-si·po·we 'by a, the river' (S-RSW 38)

      či·ki-ki·ška·pehkatenwe 'at the base or edge of a, the cliff' (K-ULG 7, K-WPGB 1)

(c)   *iši* PP 'of {some} kind' ← |iN-| (cf. 4.102*a*, 103*a*):

      i·ni iši-nye·wenwi. 'Just those four times.' (O 20G; cf. 2.246)

(d)   *keki* PP 'with, having along' ← |kek-| 'with, having'):

      keki-apeno·he, kek-apeno·he 'with (their) children' (K-BH 4, K-WarD 27)

(e)   *ma·wači* PP 'gathering; (most) of all':

      ma·wač-ahkowi 'last of all, furthest in the rear' (O 55A) (*ahkowi* 'behind')

(f)   *ni·šwi* PP 'two' ← |ni·šw-| (cf. 4.101*e*):

      ni·šwi-še·šketo·he 'two kettles of it' (K-B 238)

38.3. Homophonous particles and prewords. The formation of free particles, preverbs, prenouns, and preparticles by suffixing |-i| PF ABSTR to many of the same initials results in numerous cases in which words with the same shape and the same or similar meaning appear in these distinct grammatical functions. In fact, all the free particles in (4.101) are also used as preverbs, for the most part with exactly the same meanings:

(4.105) Preverbs that are also synonymous free particles

(a)   *aya·pami* PV 'back (to previous location)' (cf. 4.101*a*):

      wi·h=aya·pami-pi·tike·wa·či 'for them to come back in' (O 8C)

(b)   *kekeni* PV 'quickly' (cf. 4.101*c*):

      wi·h=kekeni-pahkinwiye·či 'so his umbilical cord will fall off quickly' (A 116A)

(c)   *ki·hki·hki* PV 'just the same, regardless, defiantly' (cf. 4.101*d*):

      e·h=ki·hki·hki-=meko·-kehke·netaki 'he had insistent memories of it' (K-Wap 159I)

(d)   *pi·neši* PV 'acting on one's own, unprovoked' (cf. 4.101*f*):

      nepi·neši-mehtose·neniwipena·toke=·h=we·na. (JP-KT 46)

        'I guess we (exc.) came to life spontaneously.'

In texts it can be uncertain whether a word of this kind is a preverb or a free particle when it precedes a verb form that has no inflectional prefixes.

When *ni·šwi* 'two' or *neswi* 'three' is used as a preverb it has the added meaning of 'together, as a group' and may refer to either the subject or the object.

(4.106) Use of *ni·šwi* PV 'both (together), as a pair, jointly' (cf. 4.101*e*)

(a)   *e·h=ni·šwi-ki·šihto·wa·či mi·ša·mi.* (K-Spot 1; tr. HP)
       "They both took part in making the sacred pack."

(b)   *e·h=ni·šwi-pemenekowa·či* 'she (obv.) raised the two of them together' (K-W 34)
The preverb corresponding to *nekoti* 'one' modifies the meaning of the head verb rather than enumerating one of its arguments:

(4.107) Use of *nekoti* PV 'in one go, once and for all'

(a)   *wi·h=nekoti-menwi-ona·pe·miyani* (A 74B)
       'for you (sg.) to be happily married once and for all'

(b)   *e·h=nekoti-=mekoho·-ča·ka·mi·wa·či.* 'They all moved at the same time.' (K-FC 745)
This homophony among particles and prewords is, however, an artifact of parallel derivational processes and does not reflect an inherent categorial plasticity or an automatic interchangeability between form classes. Many particles cannot be used as prewords at all (4.99), and many prewords are used in only one type of stem (noun, verb, or particle). The individual properties of the specific initial (including its class membership) determine the possible function or functions of a word shape derived from it by adding |-i| PF ABSTR. Some preverbs have no homophone in any other function: e.g., *a·mi* PV POT, *ki·* PV 'around', *ki·h* PV PERF, *pwa·wi* (*pa·wi*) PV 'not' (4.110*b*). Many preparticles also are matched in no other function: e.g., *či·ki* PP 'next to' (103*b*), *nehkani, nahkani* PP 'during all of'. The initial in *nawe·ni* PN 'pretty, handsome' (*e·nowe·ni* in Jones 1907) only makes this prenoun and has no other use. The initials referring to colors, like |meškw-| 'red', freely form prenouns, like *meškwi* PN 'red' (4.103*e*), but they do not form free particles or preparticles and do not make preverbs except in limited circumstances, when they modify a nominal notion in the head verb. Some other initials for qualities follow the same pattern, e.g., *meši* PN 'big' (4.103*d*). The nearly synonymous *kehči* 'great, greatly', in contrast, is a preverb (4.102*b*) as well as a prenoun (4.103*b*). The initials that are relative roots generally also form only free particles (2.19; 4.101*b*) and preverbs (2.93-121, *passim*; 4.102*h*), but *taši* '{somewhere}' is also a prenoun (4.103*j*), and *iši* '{so}; in {some} way; to {somewhere}' is found in all four functions (4.101*b*, 102*a*, 103*a*, 104*c*). All numerals occur as free particles (4.101*e*); some are also preparticles (4.104*f*); *nekoti* 'one', *ni·šwi* 'two', and *neswi* 'three' are also preverbs, but with narrowed meaning (4.106, 107).

Despite the occurrence of many crosscutting formal relationships, then, homophonous particles and prewords are, for the most part, best taken as formed independently by a separate derivation for each form class. Prewords have a formal resemblance to particles, but they are not particles syntactically; they are components of compound stems. Also, within the same word class the semantic relationship between a preword and the compounds it forms (**§60**) is the same as that between the initial the preword is derived from and the stems that it appears in. The homophony of many particles, preverbs, prenouns, and preparticles is the formal consequence of the use of the same morphological process in more than one grammatical category.

38.4. Shifts of prewords and particles to a different form class. Distinct from the systemic homophony that arises from parallel formal derivation are cases in which a derivational process converts a particle into a preword or the reverse, or converts a preword into one of a different type. Transfers in category of this kind are quite limited in number.

One type of categorial shift occurs when a compound is the basis for secondary derivation (**§40**). If a compound noun makes a derived verb the prenoun becomes a preverb in the surface structure of the resulting compound verb (4.108, 4.238*efgh*), and conversely when nouns are derived from compound verbs the preverbs become prenouns (4.109).

(4.108) Prenoun used as preverb

(a) *nawe ni-še·škesi·he·hiwa* 'she is a pretty girl'
    (*nawe ni* (PN)PV 'pretty', |še·škesi·he·hi-| AI 'be a girl (dim.)')
    ← |nawe·ni-še·škesi·he·h-| AN 'pretty girl' + |-i| AI ABSTR
    (*nawe ni* PN 'pretty', |še·škesi·he·h-| AN 'girl (dim.)')

(b) *wi·h=maneto wi-ote·hiči* (K-SGG 101)
    'so that he would have a manitou heart'
    (|wi·h=| FUT, *maneto wi* (PN)PV 'of manitou';
    |ote·hi-| AI 'have a heart', |e·h=–či| 3s/AOR)
    (Cf. *maneto wi-ohpikayi* 'manitou rib' [*maneto wi* PN ← *maneto wa* 'manitou'])

(4.109) Preverb used as prenoun

(a) *menwi-mehtose·neniwiweni* 'healthy life' (O 6D)
    (*menwi* (PV)PN 'good', *mehtose neniwiweni* 'life, health')
    ← |menwi-mehtose·neniwi-| AI 'have good health, lead a healthy life' (O 41G)
    (*menwi* PV 'well', |mehtose·neniwi-| AI 'live, be alive')

(b) *pwa wi-menwi-pema·tesiweni* 'health that is not good' (O 112E)
    (*pwa wi* (PV)PN 'non-', *menwi* (PV)PN 'good', *pema·tesiweni* 'health')
    ← |pwa·wi-menwi-pema·tesi-| AI 'not be in good health, not feel well' (K-M 934d)
    (*pwa wi* PV 'not', *menwi* PV 'well', |pema·tesi-| AI 'live, feel (so)')

(c) *pwa wi-=mekoho ke·ko·hi -ketemina·ti·weni* 'a complete non-blessing' (K-Wpn 241)
    (*pwa wi* (PV)PN 'non-', *ketemina·ti·weni* 'blessing'; =*mekoho* EMPH;
    ke·ko·hi 'something, anything; [not] in any way')
    ← |pwa·wi-ketemina·ti·-| AI 'not bless each other'

(d) *anemi-menwi-wi·če·noti·weni* (K-GBuff 124)
    'continued pleasant association with others'
    (*anemi* (PV)PN 'going on', *menwi* (PV)PN 'good'; *wi·če·noti·weni* 'association')
    ← |anemi-menwi-wi·če·noti·-| AI 'go on associating, playing with each other nicely')

Analyzing cases like those in (4.108, 109) as having prewords that have been transferred from one category to another in secondary derivation accounts for why, for example, *nawe ni* PN 'pretty' appears as an ostensible preverb only in stems derived from compound nouns, and why *menwi* PV 'well', *pwa wi* PV 'not', and *anemi* PV 'go on' appear as ostensible prenouns only in stems derived from compound verbs, with marginal exceptions (see below for *anemi* (PV)PN).

Similarly, when compound nouns enter into the formation of exocentric particle compounds the prenouns are recategorized as preparticles (**§60.3**)

In somewhat the same way a free particle that only has an adverbial function may appear as the prenoun to a noun that is derived from a verb:

(4.110) Free particle used as prenoun
    kenwe·ši-mehtose·neniwiweni 'long life' (O 140H)
    (*kenwe·ši* (P)PN 'long', *mehtose neniwiweni* 'life')
    ← *kenwe·ši* P 'for a long time', |mehtose·neniwi-| AI 'live'

A free particle that is used freely as a preverb might be considered to be recategorized as a prenoun when it modifies a prenoun, but as in the examples in (5.36*bcd*) proof may be lacking.

Also, a few non-derived free particles are used as prenouns or preparticles.

(4.111) Particle used as prenoun or preparticle

    (a)   *ke·hta* PN 'former, old' ← *ke·hta* P 'formerly':
        ke·hta-ki·ke·na·wa 'former prisoner of war' (K-YF 27)
        oke·hta-owi·wahi 'his former wives' (K-HS 31)

    (b)   *iše, aše, še* PN 'mere, minor, ordinary' ← *iše, aše* P 'just, not seriously'
        še-neme·si·ha (or *šeneme·si·ha*) 'minnow' (cf. *neme·si·ha* 'little fish')
        aše-wa·pikone·hi 'little speckled squash' (cf. *wa·pikoni* 'squash, pumpkin')
        iš-anikwa 'graysquirrel' (cf. *anikwa* 'squirrel') (F.T. Siebert, Jr., p.c. 1963)

    (c)   *našawaye, ašawaye* PN 'of ancient times' ← *našawaye, ašawaye* P 'long ago'
        našawaye-mehtose·neniwaki 'people of ancient times' (K-PBLA 1)
        ašawaye-mehtose·neniwaki 'people of ancient times' (SP-FSSW 51)

    (d)   *meše* PP ← *meše* P 'freely, any, in some or any way'
        meše-na·hina·hi 'a little ways off' (O 72F) (*na·hina·hi* 'time, distance')
        meš-a·ya·nina·hi 'at intervals, spaced apart' (Jones 1907:166.18-19)

The prenouns and preparticles in the non-derived compounds in (4.111) are different from the prenouns and preverbs of transferred category in (4.108-110), since the compounds in (4.111) are not derived from constructions in which the prewords are free particles. Some ostensible compound particles of this kind are best regarded as lexicalized as single words: e.g., *menwinehki* 'for a good little while' (← |menwi| 'good' + |nehki| '{so} long'), *menwitaswi* 'a fair number or amount, a few' (← |menwi| 'good' + |taswi| '{so} much, many'). A few common collocations often appear to be treated phonotactically like compounds despite including a first element that is not categorially a preword (such as a demonstrative pronoun) and in some cases arguably straddling a syntactic boundary: e.g., *i·ni-nehki* (written as one word) 'that long' (O 15I), 'that's how long' (O 16B).

    Another type of categorial shift is found when certain preverbs appear after the head verb for emphasis.

(4.112) Preverb postposed as free particle

    (a)   *a·kwi wi·h=nesena·kwini kaški.* 'They will not succeed in killing you (pl.)' (K-B 243)
        (*a·kwi* 'not'; |wi·h=| FUT, |neS-| TA 'kill', |-ena·kwini| 3–2p/NEG;
        kaški (PV)P 'be able to')

    (b)   *wi·h=ne·se·wa·čini katawi* 'whenever they were nearly recovered' (O 45G)
        (|wi·h=| FUT, |ne·se·-| AI 'live on', |IC–wa·čini| 3p/ITER; *katawi* (PV)P 'almost')

    (c)   *e·h=mešketoki kehči* 'he opened his mouth wide' (K-Apay 95)
        (|mešketon-| AI 'open one's mouth', |e·h=–ki| 3s/AOR; *kehči* (PV)P 'greatly')

    (d)   *nene·se·ha·wa=mekoho ki·ši.* 'I already have made him well.' (K-M 842i)
        (|ne·se·h-| TA 'cure', |ne–a·wa| 1s–3s/IND; =*mekoho* EMPH; *ki·ši* (PV)P PERF)

    (e)   *menwawihkapa koči* 'you'd make an attempt to be good' (A 132E)
        (|menwawi-| AI 'be good', |–hkapa| 2s/POT; *koči* (PV)P 'try to')
        wi·h=nese·wa koči 'he's going to try to kill him' (K-MAE 635f)
        (|wi·h=| FUT, |neS-| TA 'kill', |–e·wa| 3s–3′/IND; *koči* (PV)P 'try to')

    (f)   *penaha·hkwa·no natawi* 'you'd better comb your hair' (K-Apay 91).
        (|penaha·hkwa·-| AI 'comb one's hair', |–no| 2s/IMP; *natawi* (PV)P 'seek to')
        i·ni=ča·h=wi·h=nakamoyakwe natawi. (K-ECRP 153; tr. TB)
        "We had now better start to sing"

        (*i·ni* 'now'; |=ča·hi| 'so'; |wi·h=| FUT, |nakamo-| AI 'sing', |e·h=–yakwe| 12/AOR;
        natawi (PV)P 'seek to')

  (g)   *či·kakohamoko mani nawači wi·kiya·pi.* 'First sweep out this house.' (JP-SD 91)
        (|či·kakoh-| TI(1) 'sweep', |–amoko| 2p/IMP; *mani* 'this (inan.)';
        nawači (PV)P 'first, stop to'; *wi·kiya·pi* 'house')

       e·h=ni·miha·či nawači. "he would first make them dance." (K-Wap 169; tr. TB)
        (|ni·mih-| TA 'make dance', |e·h=–a·či| 3s–3´/AOR; *nawači* (PV)P 'first')

  (h)   *e·h=mačina·ti wa·či we·pi* 'they started in to challenge each other' (K-Koch 23)
        (|mačina·ti·-| AI 'challenge each other', |e·h=–wa·či| 3p/AOR; *we·pi* (PV)P 'start to')

  (i)   *e·h=mya·nesiči=meko ma·wači* 'he was the ugliest of all' (K-JM 15A)
        (|mya·nesi-| AI 'be ugly'; |e·h=–či| 3s/AOR; =*meko* EMPH;
        ma·wači (PV)P '(most) of all')

The post-verbal particles in (4.112) have exactly the same function that the homophonous preverbs have and never appear as ostensible free particles except when they follow the verb they modify, usually with no full words intervening. The occasional appearance of such words after the verb is thus best explained as the optional postposition of a preverb. Other preverbs that may be postposed include: *aye·ši* 'staying' (K-M 155b), *nano·či* 'persisting to the end' (O 152J), *ni·ka·ni* 'leading' (O 107D), *pi·htawi* 'additionally' (O 100F), *pye·či* 'coming' (C-YS 4), and *wa·wotami* 'taking time' (O 137G). Postverbal occurrences of *ki·ša·koči* 'extremely' (e.g. O 61D) may be interpreted the same way, although this word is also used preverbally as a free particle with the same meaning (5.68).

Less systematic shifts of category in prewords are idiomatic features of specific lexical items and combinations. For example, in the common expression *anemi-mehtose·neniwa* 'the-People-to-Be, the People-to-Come, the future human race, future generations' (*anemi* (PV)PN 'going on', *mehtose·neniwa* 'person') the anomalous preverb as prenoun is the equivalent of the preverb in the explicit participial expression *ni·ka·ni wi·h=anemi-mehtose·neniwičiki* 'those who will go on to live in the future' (K-M 527c) (*ni·ka·ni* 'in the future'; |wi·h=| FUT, |anemi| PV 'go on', |mehtose·neniwi-| AI 'live' [← |mehtose·neniw-| 'person', |-i| AI ABSTR], |IC–čiki| PPL/3(ANpl)).

38.5. Particles with |-e|. Some particles end in an *-e* that is part of the stem: *aše*, *iše* 'just, not seriously'; =*iyo·we*, *iyo·we* PAST; *kapo·twe* 'at some point'; *me·kwe·he* 'I believe'; *nama·nike* 'unprecedentedly'. Other particles in *-e* have an abstract final |-e| PF EXO or |-e| PF ABSTR.

The particle final |-e| EXO makes particles with an exocentric semantic structure and enumerative particles that serve as numeral quantifiers in noun phrases. These exocentric particles are often equivalent to a prepositional phrase or an adverbial noun phrase in English. The second element in an enumerative particle may indicate a numeral classifier, an order of magnitude, or a unit of measure. In these particles the final |-e| EXO either follows a medial (which may be derived from a noun) (4.113), or it combines with the stem of a noun or intransitive verb to form the second member of a particle compound (**§60.4**). When added after a |k|, |-e| EXO is realized as *-i* (4.113*hm*), except after medials that take |-e·| AI ABSTR (4.113*f*). In the case of medials from noun stems in |-e·w|, the sequence |-e·w| + |-e| EXO is realized as simply *-e* (4.113*dj*).

  (4.113) Particles with |-e| PF EXO

  (a)   *ahkwita·kone* 'on top of the snow'
        (← |ahkwit-| 'on top', |-a·kon-| 'snow' [4.42], |-e| EXO)
        [continued →]

(b)   *a·pehtaweče* 'up to the waist' (← |a·pehtaw-| 'half', |-eč-| 'body', |-e| EXO)

(c)   *či·ka·hkwe* 'next to a tree' (O 13B)
      (← |či·k-| 'by the side of', |-a·hkw-| 'tree, stick', |-e| EXO)

(d)   *či·ke·škote* 'at the edge of the prairie' (← |či·ke·-| [← |či·k-| 'by the side of' (cf. 4.21)],
      |-aškote·w| 'prairie' [← |maškote·w-| IN], |-e| EXO)

(e)   *kekikane* 'along with the bones, bones and all' (K-W 192, C-WH 31)
      (← |kek-| 'with, having', |-i·kan-| 'bone' [4.43], |-e| EXO)

(f)   *maya·wihka·hke* 'in the middle of the chest' (S-YMSG 67)
      (← |maya·w-| 'in the main (part of)', |-i·hka·hk-| 'chest', |-e| EXO
      [cf. |-e·| AI ABSTR])

(g)   *nehkaniki·šekwe, nahkaniki·šekwe* 'all day long'
      (← |nehkan-|, |nahkan-| 'for all of', |-i·ki·šekw| 'day', |-e| EXO)

(h)   *na·mepye·ki* 'under the water' (← |na·m-| 'under', |-epye·k-| 'water' [4.34],
      |-e| EXO)

(i)   *na·waka·me* 'midway across the water or lodge'
      (← |na·w-| 'in the middle of', |-aka·m-| 'opposite side', |-e| EXO)

(j)   *na·waškote* 'in the fire'
      (← |na·w-| 'in the middle of', |-aškote·w| 'fire' [← |aškote·w-| IN], |-e| EXO)

(k)   *na·wawahi·me* 'in the middle'
      (← |na·w-| 'in the middle of', |-awahi·m-| 'whatchamacallit' [§18.8], |-e| EXO)

(l)   *neswa·hkwe* 'three hundred' (← |nesw-| 'three', |-a·hkw-| 'tree; hundred', |-e| EXO)

(m)   *ni·šwa·pitaki* 'twenty'
      (← |ni·šw-| 'two', |-a·pitak-| '-ty' [← |-a·pit-| 'tooth', postmedial |-ak-|], |-e| EXO)

(n)   *nye·wawahi·me* 'for four years'
      (← |nye·w-| 'four', |-awahi·m-| 'year' [← 'whatchamacallit'; §18.8], |-e| EXO)

There is a set of six particles ending in a segmentable |-e| PF ABSTR that is not analyzable as |-e| EXO (4.113). These all end in *-e·we* and have doublets with |-i| PF ABSTR (hence *-e·wi*) that appear as preverbs (and at least one prenoun), but for some speakers this distinction in shape is not made consistently. Either shape may be used as a free particle, and at least one speaker uses several of the variants in *-e·we* as preverbs.

(4.114) Particles and prewords with |-e| PF ABSTR ~ |-i| PF ABSTR

(a)   *meso·te·we* P,PN,PV, *meso·te·wi* P,PN,PV 'all over, universal(ly)'

1)   *meso·te·we* P:
     meso·te·we=mekoho e·h=ka·škehtawa·wa·či. 'they heard him all over' (O 107A)

2)   *meso·te·wi* P:
     meso·te·wi=meko nepe·hpe·šoko·pi. 'I was scarified all over.' (A 56D)

3)   *meso·te·we* PN:
     nemeso·te·we-ni·hka·netike 'my friends, I say to you all' (K-FC 504)

4)   *meso·te·wi* PN:
     kemeso·te·wi-kemešo·mesena·naki 'the grandfathers of all of us' (K-GBuff 216)

5)   *meso·te·we* PV:
     e·h=meso·te·we-=meko -a·čimoheči 'everyone was told' (K-WKG 31)

6)   *meso·te·wi* PV:
     e·h=meso·te·wi-atama·wa·či 'they all smoked' (O 29B)

   (b)   *a·hpene·we* P,PV, *a·hpene·wi* P,PV 'only, nothing but' (cf. *a·hpene* 'all alike')

    1)   *a·hpene·we* P:

       a·hpene·we=mekoho me·nwikeniki 'nothing except what is good' (K-FC 677)

    2)   *a·hpene·wi* P:

       a·hpene·wi=ča·h=mekoho e·ši-menwikeki 'so only the good way' (K-Spot 199)

    3)   *a·hpene·we* PV:

       ki·h=a·hpene·we-=meko -nesa·pwa. (K-TG 54)

       'You (pl.) will only kill thém. (Théy won't kill [any of] yóu.)'

    4)   *a·hpene·wi* PV:

       wi·h=a·hpene·wi-we·wene·netaki 'that only *he* would be in control' (C-FS 27)

The other particles with the same variation in shape, although not in all cases the same range of attested uses, are: *kwe·hkwe·we* 'too far', *we·te·we* '(not) in the least', *no·make·we* 'for a short time' (also *no·make*), and *kehčine·we* 'personally, in person' (cf. *kehčine* 'nearby').

38.6. Particles with |-eki| LOC. Some particles appear to incorporate |-eki| LOC, the locative suffix used on nouns (**§24**).

   (4.115) Particles with |-eki| LOC

    (a)   *ahkiki* 'down below' (cf. 1.151)

    (b)   *ahkwita·hki·ki* 'on top of the hill, ridge, bank'

    (c)   *ahpemeki* 'up aloft'

    (d)   *aka·mete·ki* 'on the other side of the lodge'

    (e)   *apate·hki·ki* 'on the side of the hill'

    (f)   *mehči·ki* 'down, down on the ground'

    (g)   *nanakote·ki* 'in the center of the lodge'

    (h)   *na·mahki·ki* 'deep under ground'

    (i)   *na·meki* 'on the inside; under, underneath'

    (j)   *pasihki·ki, pasehki·ki* 'at the foot of the hill'

38.7. Particles in segmentable *-hka*. Some particles appear to attest an abstract particle final |-hka| (|-i-hka|; |-ehka| with contraction), but the analysis of these is often not clear.

   (4.116) Particles with |-hka| PF ABSTR

    (a)   *ayi·ne·hka* 'persisting inappropriately' (← |ayi·N-|, |aye·N-| 'persisting')

    (b)   *a·ya·šo·hka* 'back and forth' (← |a·šow-| 'across')

    (c)   *me·mešihka* 'maybe, perhaps, for example, as one possibility' (cf. *meše* 'or', etc.)

    (d)   *nešihka* 'alone, by himself, by themselves' (← |neS-| 'alone')

    (e)   *wa·natohka* 'unconcernedly, as if nothing was wrong' (← |wa·n-| 'at ease')

REDUPLICATION

Types of Reduplication

39. Reduplication operates at the beginning of words, deriving reduplicated forms from unreduplicated forms. There are two general types, one-syllable reduplication (glossed RED1) and two-syllable reduplication (glossed RED2). Reduplication applies to the initial, but the application of two-syllable reduplication may necessarily include the whole stem and even part or all of the inflectional ending, and the semantic scope of the reduplication is the entire stem. Reduplicated forms indicate various kinds of plurality, repetition, and multiplicity.

Reduplication is common on verbs and certain particles and prenouns; it is rare on noun stems and pronouns. Two-syllable reduplication may apply to a stem that already has one-syllable reduplication. One-syllable reduplication may be iterated, but in most such cases the first or innermost application is lexicalized. A stem with two-syllable reduplication never has further reduplication.

Reduplicated initials or stems may be lexicalized with narrowed meanings. Most initials have only one pattern of one-syllable reduplication; where two patterns are found it is more common for one to be lexicalized in certain stems than for the variation to be non-contrastive. The functions of the two types of reduplication overlap, and in some cases the meaning of an initial with one-syllable reduplication is not sharply distinct from that of the unreduplicated form. Some initials and stems never have one-syllable reduplication, and in a few cases neither type of reduplication is possible. Many initials are found only with what is evidently a reduplicated shape.

One-syllable Reduplication

39.1. One-syllable reduplication marks repetition or plurality. On a verb it may indicate that the action is repeated on the same or different occasions, for example if a plural subject or object acts or is acted on separately or if a medial has a plural reference, or it may indicate that the action or state itself has repetitive components or is extended or kept up. With numeral initials and some others and with some particles it also has a distributive or reciprocal meaning.

One-syllable reduplication has a number of different formal realizations. All patterns include a vowel (which may or may not copy the vowel of the initial), and this is always preceded by a copy of the stem-initial consonant if there is one. In some patterns there is also a consonant after the vowel. In others there are also changes in the vowel of the initial syllable of the stem. Stem-initial |kw-| is treated in reduplication as a single consonant (4.117e, 4.125a). Other stem-initial clusters of a true consonant and a semivowel (|CY-|) may copy only the true consonant or the entire cluster; most speakers seem to prefer either one pattern or the other, but some use both.

39.2. The one-syllable default pattern. The normal, default pattern of one-syllable reduplication is given formulaically as |CV+|. The initial consonant, if any, is copied as the |C| in the reduplication. The vowel in the reduplication (|V|) is most generally |a·| (4.117a-m), but it is |e·| if the vowel in the first syllable of the stem is |e| or |e·| (4.117n-r). If there is no stem-initial consonant a |y| is inserted between the reduplication and the stem-initial vowel, which is either |a| or |a·| in all attested cases (4.117abcd). The only other stem-initial vowel that undergoes normal one-syllable reduplication is o-, but it is treated as if it were |wo-| (4.117m).

(4.117) Normal one-syllable reduplication

    (a)   *a·yahkwahte·či* 'as far as his arrows went' (K-W 909)

          ← |ahkwahte·-| AI 'shoot arrow (or arrows) {so far}'

    (b)   *ki·ši-wi·seniya·ne, i·ni wi·h=a·ya·čimoya·ni.* (K-FC 293)

          'After I have eaten I will tell the story.'

          ← |a·čimo-| AI 'tell, report, make one's report, tell what happened'

(c)   *wi·h=a·ya·čimohenako·we* 'I'm going to be instructing you' (O 62A)
    ← |a·čimoh-| TA 'inform'

(d)   *a·ya·teši* 'separately from each other' (JB-WMD 13) ← *a·teši* 'in a separate place'

(e)   *e·h=kwa·kwa·koho·ma·wa·či* 'they kept shouting at them' (JP- GTF 21)
    ← |kwa·koho·m-| TA 'shout at'

(f)   *e·h=we·pi-ma·mahkate·wi·či* 'he began (the practice of) fasting' (O 60C)
    ← |mahkate·wi·-| AI 'fast'

(g)   *ma·mi·čiwa·či* 'what they would eat (on those occasions)' (O 44B)
    ← |mi·či-| TI(3) 'eat'

(h)   *wi·h=anemi-na·nakamowa* 'he will continue to sing (on different occasions)'
    (O 133F)
    ← |nakamo-| AI 'sing'

(i)   *na·na·kwa·ko* 'leave (you pl.; going to separate destinations)' (O 64B)
    ← |na·kwa·-| AI 'leave, depart'

(j)   *e·h=na·ni·šo·hkwe·we·wa·či* 'they had two wives each' (K-YF 33)
    ← |ni·šo·hkwe·we·-| AI 'have two wives'
    e·h=na·ni·šo·ma·niči 'they (obv.) each carried two (obv.) on their backs' (K-F 222)
    ← |ni·šo·m-| TA 'carry two on the back'
    e·h=na·ni·šo·piwa·či 'they sat in pairs' (K-WarD 10)
    ← |ni·šo·pi-| AI 'sit together, sit as a pair'

(k)   *e·h=anemi-na·nowi·niči* 'they (obv.) went out (separately)' (JP-GTF 17)
    ← |nowi·-| AI 'exit, go out'

(l)   *e·h=sa·so·kena·wa·či* 'they constantly hold them' (A 118C) ← |so·ken-| TA 'hold'

(m)   *wa·wotami* 'spending, taking time' (O 137B; A 107D) ← *otami* 'be occupied doing'

(n)   *ne·nekotenwi* 'once each, once each time' (O 43H; K-M 440e) ← *nekotenwi* 'once'

(o)   *ne·ne·htawi* 'separately from each other' (O 32C) ← *ne·htawi* 'separately'

(p)   *a·kwi .. pe·pehki·na·towe·yakwini.* 'We don't speak different languages.' (A 83C):
    |pe·pehki·n-| 'different from each other' ← |pehki·n-| 'different'

(q)   *pe·peno·či* 'far each time, far from each other' (K-Kin 61; K-YC 11) ← *peno·či* 'far'

(r)   *te·te·pihekwiye·kwe* 'what had good effects on you (pl.)' (O 120D)
    ← |te·pih-| TA 'please, do good for'

The stem |pya·-| AI 'come, come back, arrive {somewhere}' has normal reduplication, with
pe·- (or *pye·-*) when the |a·| is umlauted to *e·* (4.118*ab*; cf. 3.244). When the stem is realized as
pya·- the reduplication is sometimes the expected *pa·-* (4.118*cd*) but more commonly *pe·-*
(4.118*ef*).

(4.118) One-syllable reduplication of |pya·-| AI 'come'

(a)   *pe·pye·waki* 'they (always) come' (K-BLI 3)

(b)   *pye·pye·waki* 'they (sometimes) come' (S-IM 11)

(c)   *e·h=pa·pya·ya·ni* 'when I come (at different times)' (K-MLF 84)

(d)   *e·h=pa·pya·wa·či* 'they (habitually) come' (K-SSP 54)

(e)   *e·h=pe·pya·ya·ni* 'that I (habitually) come' (S-Apay 27L)

(f)   *e·h=pe·pya·wa·či* 'they came back (separately)' (JB-Tiger 57)

The reduplication of |nekot-| 'one' is usually regularly *ne·-*, but some speakers reduplicate this
initial in at least some stems with *na·-*. There seems to be no difference of meaning between the
two kinds of reduplication and no evidence for this irregularity with other numeral initials.

(4.119) One-syllable reduplication of |nekot-| 'one'
- (a) *ne·nekoti* 'one apiece, one each' (O 52D); 'one here and there' (K-ECRP 59); 'singly' (K-WarD 4), 'one by one' (K-HS 30D, K-MHTW 27)
- (b) *na·nekoti* 'one apiece' (Jones 1907:196.21; JB-M 16; Sh-Elm 35, 42, 48; X2-SAR 170); 'one here and there' (JP-KT 43); 'one by one' (Jones 1907:168.3; JB-BP 36, 47), 'one at a time' (JB-MD 17, 19)
- (c) *e·h=ne·nekoto·hpo·hiwa·či* 'they each ate from a separate bowl' (O 4H) (← *nekoto·hpo·hiwa* 'he eats alone')
- (d) *e·h=na·nekoto·hpwa·či* 'she nibbled them (anim.) one by one' (Jones 1907:318.2)
- (e) *ne·nekotwa·hkwe* 'one hundred each' (K-MAE 244a)
- (f) *na·nekotwa·hkwe* 'one hundred each' (JB-Tiger 78)

39.3. Less common variants of one-syllable reduplication. Other variants of one-syllable reduplication have various short and long vowels, and some add a consonant (|h| or |š|) after the vowel; in two patterns with a short vowel there is also modification of the first vowel of the stem.

Many initials reduplicate with short |a|, which may be followed by |h| before a stop; reduplication with |e| is apparently found only with a few stems that have |e| as the first vowel. Only initials beginning with consonants have short-vowel reduplication.

(4.120) Reduplication |Ca+|
- (a) |kakano·N-| TA, |kakano·t-| TI(1) 'speak at length to, say words over' ← |kano·N-| TA, |kano·t-| Ti(1) 'speak to': *nekakano·neko·pena* 'we (exc.) were spoken to at length' (O 65J) *e·h=we·pi-kakano·neči* 'one starts saying words over them' (A 172C) *e·h=kakano·taki* 'he said words over it' (O 38G)
- (b) |mamahk-| ← |mahk-| 'remove' *wi·h=wi·ke·či·=meko·-mamahkete·wi* 'every bit of it will burn away' (K-W 1044) *e·h=mamahkeše·šoči* 'his ears were cut off' (K-CM 6) *ohtawakayani=na·hka e·h=mamahkeša·mawoči* 'and his ears were cut off' (K-KK 10)
- (c) |mamakw-| ← |makw-| 'lump, bump, swell' *mamakwa·hkiwiwi* 'the terrain has hills' (K-MAE 1166b) *po·si·=mekoho·-mamakwipehkwakiki* (K-Auto 155) '(turtles) with the largest bumps on their backs'
- (d) |mama·t-| ← |ma·t-| 'move' *po·ni-mama·tapo·sa·niki nepi* 'when the water stopped moving' (K-Fish 41) *ki·ši-we·pi-mama·či·wa·čini* 'after they (babies) start to move' (A 103E)
- (e) |mami·na·w-| ← |mi·na·w-| 'in detail, in all particulars' *e·h=we·pi-mami·na·wite·he·či* 'he began thinking seriously' (K-FC 704) *e·h=anemi-mami·na·wite·he·či* 'on the way he thought it over' (K-Wap 106)
- (f) |nanak-| ← |nak-| 'stop': *e·h=pa·wi-nanakesiči* 'because he stops at nothing' (C-WH 13)
- (g) |nana·niškw-| ← |na·niškw-| '(slipping) loose' *e·h=nana·niškwinehke·či* 'he pulled his hands loose' (K-M 108h)
- (h) |nani·šw-| ← |ni·šw-| 'two' *e·h=ki·-nani·šoše·škači* 'he had his ears perking up' (JP-YMPE 56)

(i) |papahk-| ← |pahk-| 'sever (string-like)'

    na·htaswi oče·pihkani e·h=papahkeškaminitehe (K-SSP 63)

      'he (obv.) had broken several roots with the force of his feet'

    e·h=we·pi-papahkataminiči so·kisoči. (K-SSP 155)

      'she (obv.) began biting through the cords that bound him'

(j) |papahkw-| ← |pahkw-| 'pull out, off'

    papahkonapahkwe·waki 'they removed their lodge-coverings' (K-GBuff 15)

    e·h=papahkwačiwe·ya·seniki (K-B 299)

      'they (inan. obv.) were uprooted by the wind'

(k) |papahkwe·-| 'remove pieces' ← |pahkwe·-| 'remove a piece'

    e·h=papahkwe·šwa·či 'he cut pieces off of him' (K-FC 346)

(l) |papaši·šk-| ← |paši·šk-| 'peel'

    e·h=papaši·škite·hte·kwe·niči 'her (obv.) temples were skinned' (K-BLM 8)

(m) |papa·sik-| ← |pa·sik-| 'split'

    papa·siki 'half and half, a half each, in two pieces' (K-BLI 9; K-W 192; JP-KT 41)

    e·h=papa·sikahaki 'she chopped it to pieces' (S-Apay 8)

    papa·sika·senokwe·ni 'they (trees) had been split apart by the wind' (K-B 311)

(n) |papi·w-| 'small (pl.)' ← |pi·w-| 'small' (4.159*f*)

    pe·pi·wikeno·hiki 'small articles (of clothing)' (A 15B)

    papi·wi-pe·škiti·hani 'small baskets' (A 59D)

(o) |papo·hkw-| ← |po·hkw-| 'break (stick-like) in two'

    papo·hkosonisa 'they (obv.) would have fractures caused by gunshots' (O 40B)

    e·h=papo·hkwa·seniki mehteko·ni. 'Trees were snapped off by the wind.' (JB-M 11)

(p) |papas-| ← |pas-| 'slapping, brushing, grazing, glancing, skimming'

    e·h=pye·či-papasipahoyani 'when you came skipping along' (K-PMW 5)

    ki·wi-papasinekwe·ška·ti·waki 'their wings were grazing each other' (K-M 768j)

    e·h=papasinowe·tiye·hwa·či 'he spanked him' (S-Apay 53)

(q) |papa·hkat-| ← |pa·hkat-| 'break open' (4.18*a*)

    e·h=katawi-papa·hkasehka·niki onakeši 'his gut almost burst' (K-M 429j)

(r) |tata·tw-| ← |ta·tw-| 'tear'

    e·h=tata·toče·saha·či 'he (eagle) tore up his (deer's) belly' (K-Wap 37)

    e·h=anemi-tata·twa·wakeškaki ahki 'he tore up the earth as he ran' (K-WLBS 15)

(s) |tato·k-| ← |to·k-| 'spreading open, apart'

    tato·kikome·wa 'his nostrils flare open' (Jones 1911:796)

    e·h=nana·hi-tato·kika·piniči 'he (obv.) sat with his legs spread apart' (JP-Apay 68)

(t) |wawa·s(e·)-| 'glitter, sparkle' ← |wa·s(e·)-| 'shine'

    pye·či-wawa·se·ške·wi 'it glittered as it came' (K-ECRP 100)

    i·ni we·wa·sete·niki 'those sparks (obv.)' (K-OKUT 9)

    we·wa·sanote·ki 'something sparkling' (K-WD 37)

(4.121) Reduplication |Cah+|

    (a) |kahki·w-| 'tightly wrapped' (← |ki·w-| 'around'); only in one stem:

      kahki·wišineno·='nahi. 'Now lie wrapped up tight!' (K-EGC 7)

    (b) |pahpaw-| ← |paw-| 'shake'

      e·h=pahpawisaheči 'he was shaken' (K-MHTW 18)

      e·h=pahpawinawi·niči 'he (bird, obv.) flapped his wings' (K-M 636e)

(c) |tahtakw-| 'all together, together with each other' ← |takw-| 'together with'
        awita tahtakwiseto wa·sa 'they wouldn't put them with each other' (K-MortF 21)
        e·h=tahtakwi-po·ni wa·či 'they (two families) camped together' (O 67I)

(d) |kahka·hkihk-| ← |ka·hkihk-| 'scratch' (cf. 4.125c)
        kahka·hkihki·kwe·wa 'she has scratches on her face' (C-FS 13 [AW])

(4.122) Reduplication |Ce+|

(a) |pepeškw-| 'shed, peel' ← |peškw-| 'fall off'
        wi·h=pepeškwikeša·te·wi 'it (stick) must have the bark shaved off it' (X2-SAR 85)
        e·h=pepeškwa·waki·niki 'it was bare ground (obv.)' (K-M 502e)
        pepeškwitepe·waki 'their heads are shaved' (C-FRS 4)
        e·h=pepeškoče·niči 'he (dog, obv.) had no hair' (K-WTS 4)

(b) |šešekw-| ← |šekw-| 'crush'
        ahkanani šešekohamoko 'crush the bones to pieces (you pl.)' (K-WC 19)
        šešekote·ke=ke·hi kekahkwanwa·wi (K-Spot 285)
        'moreover, if your (pl.) shin is pulverized by a bullet'
        e·h=ča·ki-šešekwataki 'he chewed it all to pieces' (S-Apay 13)

A few initials reduplicate with |i·| or |o·|, or with |a·|, |i·|, or |o·| followed by |h|. The patterns
with and without |h| cannot be distinguished if |h| cannot form a cluster with the initial consonant.

(4.123) Reduplication |Ci·+|

(a) |ki·ki·p-| ← |ki·p-| 'fall' (cf. 4.126d)
        pye·či-ki·ki·pise·wa 'he keeps falling as he comes' (X6-OS 33)

(b) |ki·ki·w-| ← |ki·w-| 'around, about'
        nye·wawahi·ne neki·ki·wita 'I stayed around (unmarried) for four years' (A 186D)
        e·h=ki·ki·wa·pye·niki asapa·pye·ni 'ropes (obv.) were strung about' (K-RYL 18)

(c) |pi·pemw-| TA, |pi·pemot-| TI(1) ← |pemw-| TA, |pemot-| TI(1) 'shoot (at)'
        e·h=pi·pemwa·či 'he shot several arrows at it' (K-Wap 37)

(d) |si·si·s-| ← |si·s-| 'nip, pinch, squeeze'
        si·si·satahote 'if glancing blows are struck at them' (K-Wap 51)
        si·si·samatače 'let him have sharp pains' (K-M 840i)
        si·si·si-menono 'drink a tiny bit at a time' (K-WF 45; song)
        wi·h=si·si·si-kesi·ya·wi 'let it be bitingly cold' (K-FC 338)

(4.124) Reduplication |Co·+|

        |so·so·p-| ← |so·p-| 'savor'
        ki·wi-so·so·patamo·ki 'they were sucking away at it' (K-W 995)

(4.125) Reduplication |Ca·h+|

(a) |ka·hka·k-| ← |ka·hk-| 'barehanded, empty-handed'
        keki·wi-ka·hka·hka·mopena 'we (inc.) fled about empty-handed' (K-Wewi 15)

(b) |ka·hka·hk-| 'scorch, unbearably hot' ← |ka·hk-| 'dry'
        e·h=ki·ša·koči-=meko-ka·hka·hkesoči (K-WKG 44)
        'it was made as unbearably hot as could be for them'
        e·h=we·pi-ka·hka·hkete·ki 'it began to get stifling hot' (K-M 131b)

(c) |ka·hka·hkihk-| ← |ka·hkihk-| 'scratch' (cf. 4.121d)
        ka·hka·hkihki·kwe·wa 'she has scratches on her face' (C-FS 13 [EK])

(d) |kwa·hkwa·p-| ← |kwa·p-| 'scatter'
        kwa·hkwa·pa·hke·wa 'he throws, scatters it in different directions' (K-Words 27)

(e) |pa·hpak-| ← |pak-| 'drip'
    pa·hpakike wi 'it is dripping' (AW); see also 4.143

(f) |pa·hpa·k-| ← |pa·k-| 'slap, pat'
    nepi e·h=pa·hpa·kepye·haminiči (Jones 1907:68.12-13, with [pāpāg-])
      'she (obv.) began to pat the water with the palms of her hands'
    e·h=pa·hpa·kahwa·či 'she patted him (horse)' (S-Pit 17)

(g) |pa·hpa·šk-| ← |pa·šk-| 'split'
    no make we e·h=pa·hpa·škahaki 'he cracked (the nuts) for a short time' (K-FC 48)

(h) |ta·hta·po·-| ← |ta·po·-| 'side by side'
    ta·hta·po·šimeči 'they would be placed side by side' (O 15C)

(i) |ta·hta·k-| ← |ta·k-| 'touch'
    ča·kenwi=meko wi·h=ta·hta·kenaki. 'So that I can touch him everywhere.' (C-YS 8)

(4.126) Reduplication |Ci·h+|

(a) |či·hči·k-| ← |či·k-| 'stick out, stick up'
    či·hči·kitiye·sahohčike·wa 'he's riding a bucking bronco' (K-Words 6)
    e·h=či·hči·kaškenike·či 'he stirred up the grass and leaves' (K-TM 7)
    e·h=či·hči·kenamawoči 'it was held out (tauntingly) to them' (SP-TF 89)

(b) |či·hči·kw-| ← |či·kw-| 'moved out of place, having part(s) removed'
    e·h=či·hči·kwapisowa·či 'they hiked up their skirts' (K-WLB 12)
    ki·ši-či·hči·kwataki 'after he had gnawed it clean' (JP-OPLA 14)

(c) |či·hči·p-| ← |či·p-| 'make a small, quick movement'
    taswi či·hči·pini·kwe·yakwe 'all of us (inc.) that blink with our eyes' (O 129D)
    e·h=či·hči·panowe·pisoniči 'their (obv.) cheeks would quiver' (K-SGG 104)
    e·h=či·hči·pisikiwe·hwa·či (K-EGC 34)
      'he poked him more than once in the back (with something)'

(d) |ki·hki·p-| ← |ki·p-| 'fall' (cf. 4.123*a*)
    e·taši-ki·hki·pehkwe·sa·čiki 'those whose heads are nodding' (C-WH 14)

(e) |ki·hki·šk-| ← |ki·šk-| 'cut off' (cf. 4.128*c*)
    e·h=ki·hki·ška·hkiwe·hiniki 'where there were small cuts in the ridge' (JP-OPLA 3)

(4.127) Reduplication |Co·h+|

(a) |ko·hko·hka·-| ← |ko·hka·-| 'overset'
    ko·hko·hka·ya·wi 'it's tippy' (K-Words 6)

(b) |po·hpo·hk-| ← |po·hk-| 'poked through, hole'
    e·h=po·hpo·hkya·niki 'it (obv.) had holes' (K-M 201d)
    e·h=po·hpo·hkešamowa·či 'they cut holes in them' (JB-RE 5)

The four initials with |k-| and a long vowel followed by |šk| reduplicate with |kVš+|, copying the vowel and both consonants. One initial with |šk| after a short vowel follows the same pattern.

(4.128) Reduplication |kVš+| (|ka·š+|, |ki·š+|, |koš+|, |kwa·š+|)

(a) |ka·ška·šk-| ← |ka·šk-| 'perceive'
    neka·ška·škehtawa·wa 'I could hear him' (K-K 8)

(b) |ka·ška·šk-| ← |ka·šk-| 'scrape'
    e·h=ka·ška·škahwa·či 'he scraped (the singed hair off) them' (K-CGB 12)

(c) |ki·ški·šk-| ← |ki·šk-| 'cut off' (cf. 4.126*e*)
    ki·ški·škeške·wi 'it tears to shreds' (K-Words 28)
    e·h=ki·ški·škikwe·šwa·či 'he cut their heads off' (SP-BPCS 18)
    wi·h=anemi-ki·ški·ška·pehkatenwi 'let there be cliffs' (K-M 1166k)

(d) |koškoškoškw-| ← |koškoškw-| 'dangerous'
      kekoškoškoškwi·hta·pena 'we (inc.) are doing dangerous things' (JB-LR 29)

(e) |kwa·škwa·škw-| (|kwa·škwa·škwe·-|) ← |kwa·škw-| (|kwa·škwe·-|) 'jump off, pop out'
      kwa·škwa·škwatame·kwe 'if you (pl.) let some drop as you eat it' (K-B 104)
      kwa·škwa·škwe·hwa·čini (C-WH 12)
      'whenever they (corn, anim. pl.) popped out (of a mortar) as she pounded them'

Some initials that have a short vowel have reduplication with a short vowel and also modification of the vowel in the stem itself: |Ce-| or |Ca-| reduplicates as |CeCye·+|, and |ko-| reduplicates as |kokwe·+|.

(4.129) Reduplication |CV_Ye·+|

(a) |kekye·hči| PN 'great, large (pl.)' ← |kehči| PN 'great, large' (4.159*bc*)
      kekye·hči-we·ta·se·waki 'great warriors' (K-MWL 15)
      kekye·hči-mehteko·ni 'great trees' (K-MGW 2)

(b) *kekye·hčine* P 'near each other' (K-AIG 5); 'nearer and nearer' (K-PLA 22)
      ← *kehčine* P 'near, nearby'

(c) |kekye·hk-| ← |kehk-| 'know'
      kekye·hkinawa·či P 'indicatively (pl.), there are indications' (O 112D)
      ki·h=kekye·hkahwa·wa 'you will designate him (each time)' (K-MP 19)

(d) |kekye·t-| ← |ket-| 'out'
      ki·ši-kekye·tenaki 'after he took them out' (K-Wap 192)
      e·h=ča·ki-kekye·ta·ška·wa·či 'they all fell out of their places' (K-WLBS 15)

(e) |kekye·tešk-| ← |ketešk-| 'get loose, loosen'
      wi·h=kekye·teškikome·ške·wani 'their ends will come loose' (K-WF 75)
      e·h=kekye·teškineče·saheči 'his hands were jerked away' (K-M 6h)

(f) |memye·s-| ← |mes-| 'all, whole'
      e·h=ki·wi-memye·sisahto·či 'he was swallowing them whole' (K-WB 2)

(g) |memye·ši| PN 'big (pl.)' ← |meši| PN 'big' (4.159*d*; cf. 4.131))
      memye·ši-mahkwaki 'large bears' (K-FC 305)
      memye·ši-wi·teko·wi-ma·tesani 'large arrowheads' (*lit.*, 'owl knives') (K-PLA 6)

(h) |nenye·maso-| AI, |nenye·mate·-| II, initial |nenye·mataw-| (cf. 4.5*d*) ← |nemaso-| AI, |nemate·-| II, |nemat-| TI(2) 'stand'
      e·h=nenye·masoči 'he stood there' (K-Wap 106)
      i·ni=mekoho e·h=nenye·mate·ki 'that's where it remains standing' (K-FC 582)
      nenye·mato·kanepiwa 'he sits with his knees up':
        ašikani e·h=nenye·mato·kanepiči 'he sat with one knee up' (K-RP 2)

(i) |pepye·n-| ← |pan-| 'lose grip'
      e·h=anemi-pepye·nena·či 'he kept losing his grip on him' (JP-Apay 50)

(j) |pepye·sakw-| ← |pasakw-| 'sticky'
      e·h=pepye·sakwiminaka·po·seniki 'it (liquid, obv.) had sticky lumps' (K-M 934f)

(k) |pepye·tekw-| ← |petekw-| 'bent over'
      e·h=pepye·tekwapisoči 'she was tied in a ball' (K-JM 21)
      e·h=pepye·tekwikwayawe·na·či 'he pushed their necks down' (K-WKG 38)

(l) |pepye·tašk-| ← |patašk-| 'spattered on, plastered against'
      e·h=pepye·taškiseniki 'it (obv.) was spattered (on something)' (K-BLI 26)

(m) |kokwe·hk-| ← |kohk-| 'turn, change'

　　　e·h=ki·wi-kokwe·hkišiki 'he kept turning over as he lay' (SP-MortB 13)

　　　e·h=anemi-kokwe·hka pata·niniki (O 133F)

　　　'it (obv.) continues to change its appearance'

(n) |kokwe·nakw-| ← |konakw-| 'through obstacle'

　　　e·h=kokwe·nakwihčiwe·šwa·či (JB-MAF 15)

　　　'he cut holes through his (obv.) arm muscles'

(o) |kokwe·nep-| ← |konep-| 'turn over, turn around'

　　　kokwe·nepa pamiko 'look all around at me (you pl.)' (K-B 146; song)

　　　e·h=taši-kokwe·nepeče·na·či 'he would roll him over' (JP-OPLA 14)

(p) |kokwe·t-| ← |kot-| 'try'

　　　nekokwe·tenekwa 'he felt me' (K-WPGB 4)

　　　nekokwe·tepye·hike 'I'm trying to write something' (C-Hist 22)

　　　e·h=kokwe·ta·šohwe·či 'he practiced shooting' (K-FC 86)

(q) |kokwe·taw-| ← |kotaw-| 'into water or earth'

　　　e·h=kokwe·tawiškiwe·sa·niči 'they sank into the mud' (C-PD 7)

A few initials beginning with |Ce·|, |Cye·|, or |kwe·| have a reduplicated shape that matches the output templates in (4.129), with |CeCye·-| or |kokwe·-|.

　(4.130) Reduplication |CV_Ye·+| on initials with |e·|

(a) |kekye·htena·m-| ← |ke·htena·m-| 'seriously'

　　　e·h=kekye·htena·mehtawoči 'what she said was taken seriously' (O 67G)

(b) |kokwe·hta·n-| ← |kwe·hta·n-| 'frightfully'

　　　kokwe·hta·ni P, PV 'frightfully' (K-FC 516; K-Spot 22)

(c) |pepye·m-| ← |pye·m-| 'twist'

　　　e·h=pepye·metone·pisoniči 'their (obv.) mouths would twist up' (K-SGG 104)

One stem with |Ce-| reduplicates with |CeCe·+| (cf. 4.129g, 4.159d), and several initials with |Ca-|, |Ce-|, and |i-| reduplicate with |CaCa·+|, or |aya·+| with inserted |y|.

　(4.131) Reduplication |Ce_e·+|

(a) |meme·ša·-| II 'be big (pl.)' ← |meša·-| II 'be big'

　　　meme·ša·hiwani 'they (inan.) were larger' (A 59E)

　　　me·me·ša·kini ana·kanani 'large bowls' (K-Auto 276)

　(4.132) Reduplication |Ca_a·+|

(a) |čača·hkw-| ← |čahkw-| 'short'

　　　e·h=čača·hko·hkwe·hiči 'he had short hair' (K-SGG 95)

(b) |aya·nekiN-| AI ← |inekiN-| AI 'be {so} big'

　　　|aya·nekihkw-| ← |inekihkw-| '{so} big'

　　　mani=ke·hi e·ya·nekino·hiya·ke 'And this is how big we are.' (K-FC 66)

　　　e·ya·nekihkwihkawe·niči 'how big his (obv.) tracks were' (X10-PBW 63)

(c) |kaka·nw-| ← |kenw-| 'long'

　　　mani e·ši-kaka·nwa·nikini 'ones (inan. obv.) this long' (K-PLA 7)

　　　e·h=kaka·no·hkwe·či 'he had long hair' (K-SGG 94)

(d) |mama·k-| ← |mak-| 'big'

　　　e·h=mama·kekino·hiniči 'they (anim. obv.) got bigger' (K-K 18)

　　　e·h=mama·kipwa·me·či 'she had large thighs' (K-ORF 6)

　　　[continued →]

(e) |papa·m-| ← |pem-| 'along, by, sequentially'
       e·h=wa·se·ya·ki nepapa·mehka 'I travel in daytime' (K-PBLA 5)
       e·h=ki·wi-papa·mwe·taki 'they went around announcing' (C-SD 9)
       e·h=papa·mipenoniči 'they (anim. obv.) took off running' (K-MIM 18)

(f) |papa·mit-| ← |pemit-| 'crosswise, at the side'
       papa·mita·hkwika·ni 'log cabin'
       e·h=ki·wi-papa·mitose·wa·či 'they were walking back and forth' (K-RGC 27)
       e·h=papa·miteka·či 'She went on sometimes dancing sideways.' (K-W 159)

The stems and initials that have the reduplication |aya·+| (4.132b) more commonly have |a·ya·+|, and for some stems of this class, including all with basic short |a-|, only this shape is attested.

(4.133) Reduplication |Ca·_a·+|

(a)   *a·ya·nehki·hi* 'a little each' (Jones 1907:12.5, 7) ← *anehki·hi* 'a little'
(b)   *a·ya·nike·me·hi* 'a little further each time' (K-FC 649) ← *anike·me·hi* 'a little further'
(c) |a·ya·ni·hw-| TA ← |ani·hw-| TA 'compete against, try to outdo or beat'
       e·h=a·ya·ni·hoti·wa·či=meko 'they were having a contest with each other' (K-B169)
(d) |a·ya·nehp-| ← |inehp-| '{so} tall'
       nano·pehka=mekoho e·h=a·ya·nehpapiniči 'they sat enormously tall' (K-FC 102)
(e) |a·ya·nekiN-| AI ← |inekiN-| AI 'be {so} big' (cf. 4.132b)
       |a·ya·nekihkw-| ← |inekihkw-| '{so} big' (cf. 4.132b)
       a·ya·nekinowa·tehe 'the size they had been' (K-WYB 76)
       kene·ne·ta·pena a·ya·nekihkwa·ki. 'We see how big they (inan.) are.' (K-Spot 133)
       a·ya·nekihkwihto·wa·či 'the size they made it (inan. sg.)' (K-FC 105)

Two-syllable Reduplication

39.4. Two-syllable reduplication marks an action or state as repeated either on the same or different occasions. It is sometimes used for actions that continue without sharp internal segmentation. It does not always have a meaning distinct from that of one-syllable reduplication, and with initials that do not take one-syllable reduplication it may even mark simple plurality. Two-syllable reduplication always has the template |CVCV+| with a short second vowel; the non-syllabic components (|C|) may be any allowable consonant sequences. The inflectional ending or its umlaut effect is included in the reduplication if the stem alone is not long enough for the application of the two-syllable template. If the sequence to be reduplicated begins with a vowel, an |h| is inserted before it. If a prefix or initial change is present, reduplication takes place as if it were absent, and the prefix or initial change attaches or applies to the reduplication normally. There are two subtypes in free variation. One type repeats the second vowel of the stem, shortening it if it is long; the other type replaces the second vowel with |a|. In both types a post-consonantal semivowel in the second syllable is sometimes not copied.

(4.134) Reduplication |CVCV+|

(a)   Stem beginning with two short-vowel syllables:
       matamatakwišineno 'keep lying covered up' (A 39F) (|matakwišin-| AI)
       e·h=we·pi-menomenowa·či 'they began drinking it (again)' (O 47A)
       (|meno-| AI+O)

(b)   Stem with the long vowel in the second syllable shortened:

    ki·saki·sa tesonisa (O 40C) (|ki·sateso-| AI)

      'they (obv.) would have received serious gunshot wounds'

    wi·h=anemi-takwi-mamamama tome·kwiki (O 101B) (|mama·tom-| TA)

      'ones you must also include in your prayers on into the future'

    we·či- .. -wa wawa wa kahamowa·či (O 118D) (|wa·wa·kah-| TI(1)-O)

      'why they (always) give war whoops'

    po·hkipo·hki·kwa·ta 'one who is one of the One-Eyes' (C-WH 3, SP-WH 3)

      (|po·hki·kwe·-| AI 'have one eye'; cf. *po·hkipo·hki·kwa·čiki* 'the One-Eyes' and
the note to **§28.19**, 3.131)

(c)   Reduplicated stem with prefix:

    nešekišekišine 'I was lying down' (A 108B) (|šekišin-| AI)

(d)   Stem with umlaut of |a·| to |e·| (cf. 3.244):

    nekotahi e·h=nepanepa·či 'he was sleeping someplace' (K-ECRP 14) (|nepa·-| AI)

    mehtahkamiki nepenepe·wa 'he's sleeping on the ground' (K-Fish 12)

    nahkaniki·šekwe=meko='pi·='na nepenepe·wa. (S-TO 2)

      'He slept and slept, all day long, they say.'

(e)   With part of the ending reduplicated:

    meše=meko·='nahi ki·h=mi·nami·na·pwa. (K-Spot 217)

      'You (pl.) may give them to anyone.'

      (|wi·h=| FUT, |CVCV+| RED2, |mi·N-| TA+O 'give O2 to', |ke–a·pwa| 2p–3/IND)

    anemi-mi·nemi·nema·pi owi·yawi. (K-M 218m)

      'She was given away to them (obv.), time after time.' (|anemi| PV 'away',
|CVCV+| red2, |mi·N-| TA+O 'give O2 to', |–ema·pi| X–3´/IND)

(4.135) Reduplication |CVCa+|

(a)   Stem beginning with two short-vowel syllables:

    e·h=manamanese·wa·či (K-MFS 2) (|manese·-| AI)

      'they (always) gathered firewood'

    manamaneto·wiwaki (C-Hist 17) (|maneto·wi-| AI|)

      'they used to have spiritual power'

    e·h=pakapakesoniči 'they (obv.) exploded continually' (S-Apay 37) (|pakeso-| AI)

(b)   Stem with a long vowel and a short vowel:

    wi·h=anemi-sa·kasa·kenwi 'it will continue to grow' (K-M 1184m) (|sa·ken-| II)

    e·h=na·pana·pehkwe·hwa·wa·či (K-ICH 4) (|na·pehkwe·hw-| TA)

      'they used to lasso them around the neck'

(c)   Stem with long |e·| reduplicated as |a|

    e·h=panapane·netamo·hiči (C-RS 32) (|pane·net-| TI(1)-O)

      'he kept losing consciousness slightly'

(d)   With |e| or |e·| of ending reduplicated as |a|

    ki·ši-manamanekočiki (K-M 814h) (|maN-| TA, |IC–ekočiki| 3´–3/PPL(ANpl))

      'the ones they (obv.) have been copulating with'

    pe·pye·či-manamane·wa (K-M 511m) (|maN-| TA, |–e·wa| 3s–3´/IND)

      'he came often to copulate with them (obv.)'

(4.136) Reduplication |VCVh+|

(a)   Stem with two short vowels:

    e·h=anehanemehka·či 'he kept walking on' (K-FC 322) (|anemehka·-| AI)

ᴇ·ʰ=asihasipo·hpowa·či 'when they ate together in groups' (O 4B) (|asipo·hpo-| AI)

wi·ʰ=išahišawiyakwe 'what we are to keep on doing' (A 104E) (|išawi-| AI)

(b)   Stem with a long and a short vowel:

ki·ʰ=a·čiha·čimo (O 153B) 'you (sg.) must tell your story (repeatedly)' (|a·čimo-| AI)

e·nihe·nikehtawate 'if you always laugh at what they say' (A 50F) (|e·nikehtaw-| TA)

(c)   Stem with a long second vowel shortened:

ka·ta .. owihowi·weti·ʰke·ko 'don't marry each other' (O 90C) (|owi·weti·-| AI)

e·ʰ=we·pi-onihoni·ča·nesiya·ni 'I began to have children' (A 194B) (|oni·ča·nesi-| AI)

wi·ʰ=anemi-inahina·čimohe·kwe (O 82B) (|ina·čimoh-| TA) 'how you (pl.) will go on instructing them'

opyehopye·ni P 'taking his time' (X6-MM 35; also PL, MM) (cf. 4.136d, 4.137f) ← opye·ni P 'slowly'

(d)   With a second vowel reduplicated but a preceding semivowel not reduplicated:

e·ʰ=we·pi-amahamwa·wa·či (K-SGG 113) (|amw-| TA, |e·ʰ=–a·wa·či| 3p–3′/AOR) 'they started eating them (anim.)'

opehopye·ni P 'taking his time' (K-M 720k, 1136n; also S) (cf. 4.136c)

(e)   With initial change:

e·nahina·čimohena·kwe (O 161EF) (|ina·čimoh-| TA) 'what he used to instruct you (pl.) to do'

e·šahišawiči 'things he did, things that happened to him' (O 149C) (|išawi-| AI)

e·yohayo·či 'what he used to wear' (A 90B) (|ayo·-| TI(3))

(f)   With a prefix:

netanohanohka·neko·pi ke·ko·hi (A 62C) (|anohka·N-| TA) 'I kept being asked to make things'

netanahanahtaki·pena 'we used to braid strings' (A 48C) (|anahtaki·-| AI)

(g)   With part or all of the ending reduplicated:

maškimote·heki ahtohahto·pi 'it was placed in yarn bags' (A 93A) (|CVCV+| RED2, |aht-| TI(2) 'put {somewhere}', |+o·pi| X–0/IND)

a·mi-amwehamwe·kwiki 'the things (anim.) you (pl.) would eat' (K-B 318) (|a·mi| PV POT, |CVCV+| RED2, |amw-| TA 'eat', |IC–e·kwiki| 2p–3/PPL(ANpl))

iwahiwa=ʾpi "she used to say" (K-M 779n; tr. HP) (|CVCV+| RED2, |i-| AI 'say {so}', |+wa| 3s/IND; |=ipi| HRSY)

"a·kwi," wi·ʰ=taši-iyahiya·ni 'for me to be saying "no"' (K-M 485c) (|wi·ʰ=| FUT, |taši| PV 'engage in', |CVCV+| RED2, |i-| AI 'say {so}', |+ya·ni| 1s/AOR)

i·ni wi·ʰ=iyehiye·kwe 'that's what you (pl.) will always say' (K-BHD 128) (|wi·ʰ=| FUT, |i-| AI 'say {so}', |+ye·kwe| 2p/PPL(obl))

"...," e·ʰ=iyohiyowa·č=a·pehe ' "...," they would always say' (C-IW 3) (|i-| AI 'say {so}' [§8.3, 1.93], |+wa·či| 3p/AOR)

"...," e·ʰ=išihišiči. "... he use to say to me." (X2-SAR 189; tr. anon.) (|CVCV+| RED2, |iN-| TA 'say {so} to', |e·ʰ=–iči| 3s–1s/AOR)

"...," e·ʰ=ikohikoči ' "...," he (obv.) would always tell him' (O 60B) (|CVCV+| RED2, |iN-| ~ |0-| TA 'say {so} to', |e·ʰ=–ekoči| 3′–3s/AOR)

(4.137) Reduplication |VCah+|

(a)   With |e| reduplicated as |a|
       e·h=anahanemehka·či 'he kept walking on' (K-PBLA 9)
       e·h=we·pi-anahanenwi·či 'she began taking baths' (K-FC 565)
       e·nahinehta·ke·ya·ni (K-WarD 32; S-YMSG 51) (|inehta·ke·-| AI)
          'what I always hear told'
       e·nahineka·wa·či 'they way they dance' (K-BD 29) (|ineka·-| AI)

(b)   With connective |e| reduplicated as |a|
       wi·h=itahiteyakwe 'what will happen to each of us (inc.)' (O 130B) (|it-| AI; 3.175*a*)

(c)   With |e·| reduplicated as |a|
       wi·h=inahine·nečike·wa·či (K-Mes 22) (|ine·nečike·-| AI)
          'how they would always think about people'

(d)   With |o| reduplicated as |a|
       e·nahinowe·kwe·ni 'whatever she says' (C-G 2) (|inowe·-| AI)
       apeno·heki ketenahinowe 'you're talking like a child' (K-BS 2)

(e)   With |e·| of the ending reduplicated as |a|
       wi·h=amwahamwe·kwe (K-MWG 44) (|amw-| TA, |+e·kwe| 2p conj.)
          'so that you (pl.) would (habitually) eat them (anim.)'
       e·mwahamwe·hiya·na (K-FW 11)
       (|amw-| TA, |IC–e·hiya·na| 1s–3/DIM/PPL(ANsg))
          'the one (anim.) I eat a little of from time to time'
       e·nahine·koha=·yo·we (K-SD 55) (|iN-| TA, |IC–e·koha| 2p–3/PPL(obl))
          'what you (pl.) used to say to them'

(f)   With |e·| reduplicated as |a| and a preceding semivowel not reduplicated:
       opahopye·ni 'taking his time' (K-MLF 4, K-S 14; C-PD 22; JB-BP 2) (cf. 4.136*cd*)
       amahamwe·waki (C-O 44) (|amw-| TA, |–e·waki| 3p–3´/IND)
          'they (customarily) eat them (anim.)'
       a·kwi=na·hka wi·h=amahamwe·kwini (C-O 46) (|amw-| TA, |–e·kwini| 2p–3/NEG)
          'you (pl.) will never eat them again'

Irregularities and Special Cases

39.5. Initials and stems with irregular reduplication. A few initials and stems are reduplicated as if they had a different shape from the one that otherwise occurs.

The relative roots that begin with |t-| are usually reduplicated as if they began with |it-| (cf. 3.167-175), regardless of whether or not they have an oblique complement. This irregular treatment is found with either one-syllable reduplication (as |Ca_a·+| [4.132] or |Ca·_a·+| [4.133]) or two-syllable reduplication, but never with both types from the same stem. In some cases regular reduplication is also made, which for one initial may be of either type.

(4.138) Relative root with |t-| and reduplication |Ca_a·+|
(a) |taso·hka·ke·-| AI '{so many} are after X' → |aya·taso·hka·ke·-|:
          e·ya·taso·hka·ke·wa·či 'how many were after each' (K-M 299c)
(b) |taso·ke·-| AI '{so many} dwell together' → |aya·taso·ke·-|:
          e·ya·taso·ke·wa·či 'everyone living in each lodge' (O 111B)

(c) |taswih-| TA 'have, kill {so many}') → |aya·taswih-|:
         e·ya·taswiha·we·kwe·ni (K-Spot 137)
         'as many of them (anim.) as you may each possess'
(4.139) Relative root with |t-| and reduplication |Ca·_a·+|
   (a) |tasokoni·h-| TA 'cause to fast for {so many} days'
         a·ya·tasokoni·heči 'how many days they were each made to fast' (K-BB 39)
   (b) |taswi| PV '{so many}'
         na·htaswa·hkwe=meko a·ya·taswi-pepo·nwa·čiki (K-WYB 65) (3.181)
         'those who were several hundred years of age'
(4.140) Relative roots with |t-| and two-syllable reduplication
   (a) |tanwe·kesi-| AI 'be (engaged in) crying'
         netahitanwe·kesi 'I was crying' (A 37C)
   (b) |tana·čimoh-| TA 'be (engaged in) instructing'
         netahitana·čimohekwa 'she was (always) giving me instructions' (A 55D)
   (c) |tana·ye·net-| TI(1) 'be laughing at'
         we·kone·hi .. e·tahitana·ye·netamani 'what are you laughing at?' (K-GF 5)
   (d) |tanekwa·mo·hi-| AI 'be sleeping {somewhere} (dim.)'
         keye·hapa .. i·nah=meko e·tahitanekwa·mo·hiyanehe. (K-WYB 31)
         'It turns out you were sleeping right there.'
   (e) |to·taw-| TA 'treat {so}'
         e·tohito·tawa·či 'the different things he did to them' (K-Kin 71)
         ke·ko·he·hi=meko ki·h=tohito·ta·kwipwa. (K-WYB 171)
         'they (inan.) will keep plaguing you (pl.)', *lit.* 'doing little things to you'
In contrast to the pattern in (4.140), when the relative root |taN-| '{somewhere}; be engaged in'
occurs before |i|, giving the sequence *taši-*, it reduplicates regularly. The two types of
reduplication are partially differentiated. The reduplicated shape *ta·taši(-)* (with |CV+| RED1) is
used as a preverb and as an initial, but only when the meaning is '{somewhere}'. (This is also
the shape used in semantically specialized stems that begin with *taši-* but no longer contain the
relative root |taN-| synchronically.) The reduplicated shape *tašitaši-* (with |CVCV+| RED2) is
used only as an initial but with either meaning.
(4.141) Reduplication of *taši-*
   (a)   *ta·taši(-)* (← |taN-| '{somewhere}')
         e·h=ta·taši-wača·hotehe 'where she used to cook' (K-TO 29)
         e·h=ta·tašisenye·ničini 'the places where they (obv.) eat' (K-SGG 118)
   (b)   *ta·taši-* in frozen stems
         ta·tašima·pi 'she is the topic of gossip' (A 141A)
         mani .. wi·h=ta·taši·hkamani 'this is for you (sg.) to play with' (C-WH 1)
         neta·taši·hka·kwa 'she's always after me' (C-Ston 29)
   (c)   *tašitaši-* (← |taN-i-| 'be engaged in')
         e·h=tašitašisenye·či 'he was eating away' (K-FC 96, K-TO 27)
         e·h=tašitašite·he·šiki 'he lay in bed thinking' (K-ORF 1)
         meše=mekoho e·h=tašitašina·ke·niči. (K-FC 143)
         'They kept on singing for some time.'

(d)   *tašitaši-* (← |taN-i-| '{somewhere}')

       ayo ʰ=mekoho ahpene ʼči ki ʰ=pe pye ʼči-tašitašisenye. (K-FC 523)

       'You must come and eat here all the time.'

       i ʼnahi e ʼtašitašina ʼka ʼta 'the one who was singing there' (K-SD 16)

The stem |to·taw-| TA (4.140*e*) also has regular two-syllable reduplication:

    (4.142) Regular reduplication of |to·taw-| TA 'treat {so}'

(a)   *ke ʼko ʰi to ʼtato ʼta ʼkwa* (K-M 701b)

       'he (obv.) is having sex with her (habitually)', *lit.*, 'doing something to her'

(b)   *e ʰ=taši- ke ʼko ʰi -to ʼtoto ʼto ʰki* (K-WKG 6)

       'he was having sex with you (sg.) (on those occasions)'

The stem |iha·-| (~ |a·-|) AI 'go {somewhere}' does not take one-syllable reduplication. There are two attestations of regular two-syllable reduplication (4.143*a*), but much more often the reduplication of this stem is |ayahaya·-| AI, as if the stem were *|aya·-| AI (4.143*b*), or optionally |ayehaye·-| when the |a·| is umlauted to |e·| (4.143*c*). Since the changed form of this stem could also be seen as implying a stem *|aya·-| AI (3.159), the formal relationship between reduplicated and unreduplicated stems with change conforms to a regular pattern.

    (4.143) Reduplication of |iha·-| AI 'go {somewhere}'

(a)   Regular two-syllable reduplication (|ihahiha·-|)

       a ʼkwi= ʼpi=meko nešihka nekotahi ihahiha ʼčini (K-Koch 68)

       'They say she never went anywhere by herself.'

       a ʼkwi meše=meko ʼ= ʼnahi ihahiha wa ʼčini 'they do not wander around' (K-M 716b)

(b)   Irregular two-syllable reduplication (|ayahaya·-|)

       nanawi e ʼyahaya ʼta 'one who goes to remote areas' (K-Kin 34)

       wi ʼtamawino e ʼyahaya wane ʼni 'tell me where you've been going' (K-BD 26)

(c)   Irregular two-syllable reduplication with umlaut (|ayehaye·-|, |ayahaye·-|)

       nekotahi ayehaye ʼtoke ʰhiki 'they must always go someplace' (K-M 854h)

       i ʼtepi ayahaye waki 'they used to go there' (SP-Fish 19)

Secondary derivatives of this stem reduplicate the same way (4.143*d*).

    (4.144) Reduplication of a secondary derivative of |iha·-| AI 'go {somewhere}'

       e ʰ=ahte ʼniki netayahaye ʰha wa 'I allow her to go where it (obv.) is' (K-M 166e)

The stem |pya·-| AI 'come' makes the changed reduplicated form of the stem as if it first underwent initial change (to |pye·ya·-|; 3.158) and then was reduplicated.

    (4.145) Reduplication of |pya·-| AI 'come' with initial change

(a)   *i ʼniki pe pye ʼya ʼčiki* 'the ones that keep coming' (K-Mes 17)

(b)   *i ʼna ʰhi pe pye ʼya ʼkwe ʼna* 'whoever keeps going over there' (JP-Apay 62)

In one text the changed form of |wa·wot-|, the reduplication of |ot-| 'from {somewhere}', is twice made as if on |owa·wot-| AI:

    (4.146) Optional irregular initial change with reduplication of |ot-| 'from {somewhere}'

       we wa woʼčiwenowa ʼkwe ʼni ayahaya ʼko. (C-WH 27 [with ⟨ke⟩ written for ⟨ko⟩])

       'Go back to the various places you were taken from, wherever they may be.'

The prefixed forms of |i-| AI 'say {so}' (with an ostensible stem |si-|; 3.145) do not reduplicate.

39.6. Lexicalized reduplication. Some initials and stems with reduplication are lexicalized: either they do not have an unreduplicated counterpart, or they differ from it in having a distinct, more specialized meaning that is not accounted for by the reduplication alone.

(4.147) Some lexicalized stems with one-syllable reduplication

    (a) |kakano·neti·-| AI 'converse'

             e·h=kakano·neti·wa·či 'they conversed' (K-SGG 48)

             Cf. *kano·neti·waki* 'they speak to each other, one of them speaks to the other'.

    (b)   *pe·hki=meko ni·h=ma·mata·kwa·čimo·='noki.* (JP-MWM 1)

             'Today I'm going to tell a really interesting and entertaining story.'

             Cf. *e·h=mata·kwe·netamowa·či* 'they were delighted about it' (K-SPCF 46))

    (c) |na·nawasoti·-| AI 'race'

             wi·h=mawi-na·nawasoti·ya·ni. 'I'm going to go race.' (S-IM 6)

             e·h=na·nawasoti·heči. 'They were made to race.' (K-TM 10)

             Cf. *nawaswe·wa* 'he overtakes him', *nawasohkye·wa* 'he wins the race'.

    (d) |pa·pakam-| TA 'club to death'

             ki·h=pa·pakamene 'I'll club you to death' (K-SBSB 2)

             Cf. *pakame·wa* 'he hit him (by striking or by throwing something)'.

    (e) |wa·wa·pam-| TA, |wa·wa·pat-| TI(1) 'pick out, select'

             e·h=wa·wa·pama·či=meko wi·h=owi·wičini še·škesi·he·hani. (K-E 9)

             'He selected the girl he wanted to marry.'

             Cf. *wa·pame·wa* 'he looks at him'.

(4.148) Some lexicalized stems with two-syllable reduplication

    (a) |kanakanawi-| AI 'give a speech, say words'

             e·h=kanakanawiči 'he began his speech' (O 5H)

             Cf. *kanawiwa* 'he speaks'.

    (b) |apahapane·ni-| AI 'laugh'

             apahapane·niwa 'she laughed' (A 58D)

             Cf. *apane·niwa* 'he smiles'.

Some initials are found in certain stems or before certain medials only with reduplication.

(4.149) Stems occurring only with reduplication

    (a) |kekye·hkim-| TA 'teach'

             e·h=kekye·hkima·či 'he taught them'

             Cf. |kekye·hk-| ← |kehk-| 'know' (4.129c).

    (b)   Stems with |kekye·n-| ← |ken-| 'restrain'

             kekye·nene·wa 'he held on to him (obv.) (so he (obv.) wouldn't fall)' (K-SGG 35)

             nekekye·nenama·hkwi 'I'm holding on (for support)' (K-HS 29)

             a·kwi .. wi·h=ki·ši-kekye·napisoničini. (K-FC 582)

               'they (obv.) will not have been tied fast'

             Cf. *kenaho·čikani* 'prisoner tie' (K-Kin 27) (|-aho·t| TI(2) 'drag')

    (c)   Stems with |kekye·p-| ← |kep-| 'close, block'

             ke·kye·pi·kwa·čiki 'those who are blind' (O 112B)

             e·h=kekye·pi·kwe·šiki 'he lay with his eyes closed' (K-ECRP 69)

             kekye·peše·wa 'he's deaf' (K-Med 56)

             ke·kye·pa·tesita 'one who is stupid, retarded' (K-Kin 40)

    (d)   Stems with |kekye·škat-|, |kekye·škataw-| 'begrudging' ← |kaškat-| 'reluctant'

             nekekye·škatawe·nemekwa (K-Words 1)

               'he begrudged me (something), resented (something about) me'

a·kwi=ča·h=a·pehe owiye·ha nahi-kekye·škatenawakini. (K-TO 11)
> 'I never rebuff a challenge to gamble from anyone.'

Cf. *kekye·škatesiwa* 'he is disobliging' (K-Wapes 27),
> beside *e·h=kaškatesiči* 'he held back, was suddenly reluctant'
> (Jones 1907:212.23).

(e)   Stems with |nana·tw-| 'ask questions' ← |natw-| (~ |nataw-|) 'seek'
> *nana·tohtawe·wa* 'he asks him a question'
> *nana·tome·wa* TA 'he asks after him, asks questions about him'

Cf. *natome·wa* 'he asks him to come, summons him, invites him'.

Many initials, stems, and particles occur only in what is ostensibly a reduplicated shape: e.g., *a·yahpi·hčina·hi* 'every once in a while', *čačawi·hi* 'sometimes', |kaka·t-| 'joking', |ki·hki·hk-| 'contrarily, defiantly', |ko·ko·k-| 'jiggle', |koškoškw-| 'dangerous', |mamahk-| 'bumpy', |mama·tw-| 'pray, worship', *ma·mahka·či* 'necessarily, without fail', |ma·mata·n-| 'fun', |me·menat-| TI(1)-O 'vomit', |memye·šk-| 'troubled, messy', |memekw-| 'move rapidly back and forth (shaking or rubbing)', *me·mečine·hi* 'for the last time', *me·mešihka* 'maybe, perhaps (for example)', |me·me·čik-| 'certain, positive', *me·mye·hči* 'unavoidably', |nanakw-| 'in the middle, between', |nana·h-| 'arranged, in place, ready, controlled', |nana·hp-| 'with something (extraneous) at the same time', *na·na·kači* '(tracking) exactly', |nenehk-| 'regarding, about', |nenek-| 'tremble', |nenye·hp-| 'weak, numb', |nenye·škw-| 'disperse', |papak-|, |papaka·šk-| 'flat', *pe·pye·hči* 'it must be, it is required that', |pi·hpi·šk-| 'soft, cushiony', |sasak-| 'tangled', |sasa·k-| 'fastidious', |ša·ša·kw-| 'crush', |te·hte·p-| 'bobbing, moving rhythmically up and down', |tetep-| 'circling', |wa·wan-| 'bad, failing', |wa·wana·t-| 'confusedly', |wa·wa·t-| 'reciprocally, mutually', |wa·wi·sw-| TA 'singe the hair off', |wa·wi·t-| TA 'name, call by name', *wa·wosa·hi* 'it is expected, unsurprisingly; even, unexpectedly', |we·we·p-| 'rock, swing'.

39.7. Diversity and overlap of types. The two types of reduplication do not have contrastive meanings that are used consistently with every initial or stem. Several factors work against the existence of such an ideal system.

Some initials have more than one kind of one-syllable reduplication. In some cases in which an initial appears to reduplicate differently from the norm it can be recognized as part of a lexicalized stem that does not contain the initial synchronically.

(4.150) Reduplication of |pem-| 'along, by' and homophones

(a) |papa·m-| ← |pem-| 'along, by' (4.132*e*)

(b) |pe·pem-| ← |pem-| only in |pemen-| TA, TI 'take care of':
> *wi·h=anemi-pe·pemenakiki* 'those who will take care of it in succession' (O 78D)

(c) |pi·pem-| ← |pem-| only in |pemw-| TA, |pemot-| TI(1) 'shoot (at)' (4.123*b*)

The initial |natw-| (~ |nataw-|) 'seek' reduplicates as |nana·tw-| in stems referring to asking questions, which lack unreduplicated counterparts (4.149*e*, 4.151*a*), and in a few others (4.151*bcd*), but otherwise it reduplicates with |na·+| (4.152).

(4.151) Reduplication of |natw-| 'seek' as |nana·tw-|

(a)   *nana·tome·wa* TA 'he asks after him, asks questions about him' (4.149*e*)

(b)   *nano·škwe=meko maneto·wahi e·h=ki·wi-nana·twe·we·ma·či* (K-MLF 65 [AW])
> 'he went about aimlessly trying to draw the manitous with his wailing'

(c)   *e·h=nana·toče·naki* 'she felt around for it' (K-K 12)

(d)   *e·h=nana·toče·hokoči* 'she (obv.) tried to hit him with it' (K-M 946o)

(4.152) Reduplication of |natw-| 'seek' as |na·natw-|

    (a)   *e·h=we·pi-na·natoma·či neniwahi* 'he began to invite men to meals' (K-SGG 109)

    (b)   *ki·h=na·natota·sa·pena mehtose·neniwiweni* (K-FC 399)

                 'we are to (always) pray to them for life'

In some cases two patterns of reduplication are attested for an initial without there being a clear distinction between them. Idiomatic differences between stems and variation between speakers are both possible. In this category are the reduplication of |ki·p-| 'fall' as both |ki·ki·p-| (4.123*a*) and |ki·hki·p-| (4.126*d*) and the rare reduplication of |ki·šk-| 'cut off' as |ki·hki·šk-| (4.126*e*) beside usual |ki·ški·šk-| (4.128*c*).

    Some initials and stems lack one-syllable reduplication entirely; systematic examples include many initials and stems beginning with |a-| and all stems containing |iN-| '{so}' (except if this is a component of a derived initial or of |inekiN-| AI 'be {so} big' [4,132*b*, 133*e*]). For others one-syllable reduplication may be lexicalized with a specialized meaning (4.147). In these cases two-syllable reduplication may be used in functions that one-syllable reduplication has with other stems, such as marking simple plurality.

(4.153) Initials and stems taking only two-syllable reduplication

    (a)   *e·h=asahasa·wa·naki·kwe·niči* 'he had brown eyes' (K-TO 7)

    (b)   *asahasa·mi-wi·šate·niwani* 'they (winter lodges, inan. obv.) are too hot' (K-PLA 27)

    (c)   *'na·ki·ša·koči=meko e·h=išihišina·kosiwa·či če·wi·šwi* (K-TO 13)

                 'they both looked extremely beautiful'

    (d)   *ki·ša·koči-=mekoho -mačimačina·kosiwaki* (K-FC 33)

                 'they are extremely ugly looking'

The overlap in the functions of the two types of reduplication is seen in verbs that refer to inherently durative states; some of these indicate the extended, unsegmented duration of the state with one type of reduplication, others with the other.

(4.154) Two types of reduplication used for continuous state

            One-syllable reduplication (also 4.156*a*):

    (a)   *e·h=ki·ki·wita·či.* 'He (just) stayed there.' (K-PBLA 1)

            e·h=ka·ki·wita·wa·či. 'They (just) stayed there.' (JP-Apay 35)

    (b)   *e·h=nenye·masoči* 'He (just) stood there.' (K-Mes 15)

            Two-syllable reduplication (also 4.156*a*):

    (c)   *e·h=apihapiči.* 'He (just) sat there.' (K-MGL 6)

    (d)   *mehto·či mya·no·ta·ta e·h=išihišika·pa·či* (K-Wap 106)

                 'he just stood there like a menstruant'

    (e)   *e·h=meškwimeškwi·kwe·šiki* 'he just lay there with his red face' (K-FC 695)

    (f)   *e·h=šekišekišiki.* 'He (just) lay there.' (K-TO 9)

(4.155) Two types of reduplication used for multiple acts

    (a)   *e·h=na·na·kwa·wa·či.* 'They left, going to their separate homes.' (K-FC 414)

    (b)   *e·h=penopenowa·či.* 'They went away to their respective homes.' (K-FC 127)

The stem |na·kwa·-| AI 'leave, depart' (4.155*a*) occurs less commonly with two-syllable reduplication; |peno-| AI 'go away, go home' (4.155*b*) never has one-syllable reduplication, and the reduplicated stem |penopeno-| AI is also used for departures by one person on different occasions.

    For some stems the two types of reduplication are used interchangeably in the same or parallel expressions.

(4.156) Stems using both types of reduplication equivalently

   (a)   *e·h=a·ya·hpeta naki·kwe piči* 'he sat there staring blankly' (K-FC 557)

        e·h=a·hpeha·hpeta naki·kwe piči 'he sat there staring blankly' (X10-Met 44)

   (b)   *e·h=ka·ki·ša·kočina·kosiwa·či* 'they looked very beautiful' (K-RFB 11)

        e·h=ki·šaki·ša·kočina·kosiniči 'they (obv.) looked very beautiful' (K-M 98.l)

   (c)   *ni·h=po·ni--'pi -ma·mahkate·wi.* 'I'm supposed to stop fasting.' (K-MLF 26)

        ni·h=po·ni--'pi -mahkamahkate·wi. 'I'm supposed to stop fasting.' (K-Wap 44K)

   (d)   *asa·mi=mekoho me·menwina·kwatwi* 'it's all just too beautiful' (K-M 562n)

        e·h=menwimenwina·kwateniki 'it all looked beautiful' (K-M 61f)

   (e)   *ahpene·či=meko ·='noki ayo·h=oči-we·pi ki·h=me·menwi-pema·tesi.* (K-WD 96)

        'From this time on you will always have good health.'

        a·kwi=ke·hi·='nahi wi·h=taši-menwimenwi-pema·tesiyanini. (K-Auto 45)

        'And if you do that you will never be well.'

39.8. Double reduplication. Stems with one-syllable reduplication may sometimes be reduplicated again with either one-syllable or two-syllable reduplication. In such cases the inner reduplication characterizes an inherent aspect of the action and may be lexicalized or in effect treated as lexicalized, and the outer reduplication indicates that this complex action is repeated. There are, however, cases where the inner reduplicated stem is unlikely to be lexicalized (4.157*efij*, 4.158*e*).

(4.157) One-syllable reduplication on reduplicated stems

   (a)   *e·h=taši-ka·kakano·neti·či* 'he engaged her in conversation' (K-RFB 10) (4.147*a*)

   (b)   *e·h=ke·kekye·hkima·či* 'he would teach them' (JP-BAB 72) (4.149*a*)

   (c)   *e·h=ke·kekye·pi·kwe·piniči* (K-ECRP 141) (4.149*c*)

        'they (obv.) sat there with their eyes closed'

   (d)   *e·h=ma·ma·mata·kwa·čimoči.* (K-Wap 161) (4.147*b*)

        'His stories were always very entertaining.'

        nema·ma·mata·kwi-peseše 'I always listened with great interest' (K-Auto 79)

   (e)   *meše=meko e·h=taši-ma·mama·ne·hto·wa·či.* (K-TCB 3)

        'They (just) went along making lots of them each time.'

   (f)   *e·h=we·pi-ma·mama·sehka·niki mi·ša·mi.* (K-FC 724) (4.120*d*)

        'The sacred pack began moving.'

   (g)   *e·h=na·na·nawasoti·wa·či* 'they ran races' (K-Koch 4) (4.147*c*, 4.158*d*)

   (h)   *e·h=pa·pa·pakama·či* 'he clubbed them all to death' (K-FC 407) (4.147*d*)

   (i)   *wi·škeno·he·hahi e·h=pa·pi·pemwa·či* (S-Apay 22)

        'he would shoot birds on such occasions'

   (j)   *onehkeki pa·papahkahama·kwa* (BL-RL 25)

        'it (obv.) pecked trough the bonds on her hands'

(4.158) Two-syllable reduplication on reduplicated stems

   (a)   *ki·ši-a·yaha·ya·čimoniči* 'after she (obv.) finished her account' (K-FC 286) (4.117*b*)

   (b)   *mehto·či=mekoho ke·hčikita netaši-a·yaha·ya·čimohekwa.* (K-FC 80) (4.117*c*)

        'It was just as if a grown-up was instructing me.'

   (c)   *ki·ši-we·pi-takwatakwaniki, e·h=we·pi-a·yaha·ya·teso·hke·či.* (K-Auto 163)

        'After there began to be frost he started telling winter stories.'

   (d)   *e·h=na·nana·nawasoti·wa·či* 'they ran races' (K-Koch 4) (4.157*g*)

(e)   *e·h=mya·ši-=meko -papapapahkwe·no·hiči.* (X6-MF 20) (4.120*k*)
          'he kept sort of pulling pieces off himself'

(f)   *pepyepepye·tekoče·ške·wa* 'he doubled up with each stride' (K-W 728) (4.129*k*)

39.9. Reduplication on nouns and pronouns. Reduplication is sometimes present on nouns and, rarely, pronouns, but it does not occur systematically with these classes of words.

There is a small set of prenouns with reduplicated variants that mark plurality, and compound nouns with these prenouns are freely reduplicated. The same treatment is also found when the place-holder pronoun is used as a default noun final after these elements (2.15).

(4.159) Prenouns (and a fused prenoun [4.159*c*]) with reduplication

(a)   *čača·ki-mehtose·neni·hahi* 'little people' (JB-LR 35) (← |čak-| 'small')

(b)   *kekye·hči-pene·waki* 'large turkeys' (K-TO 12) (4.129*a*)
          kekye·hči-mi·ša·mani 'major sacred packs' (K-CDWP 2)

(c)   *kekye·hčawahi·naki* 'important people, community leaders' (LL-Auto 16)

(d)   *memye·ši-mehteko·ni* 'large trees' (K-CDWP 7) (4.129*g*)
          memye·ši-kohpiči-nenoso·hi 'large buffalos (obv.)' (K-FC 383)

(e)   *na·nawe·ni-še·škesi·he·hahi* 'pretty young girls (obv.)' (K-Pach) (← |nawe·n-|)
          na·nawe·ni-=meko -oškinawe·he·haki 'handsome young men, indeed' (K- 15)

(f)   *papi·wi-we·ta·se·he·haki* 'lesser warriors' (K-WarD 9) (4.120*n*)
          papi·wi-mi·ša·me·hani 'minor sacred packs' (K-BB 58)
          papi·wi-še·šketo·he·hahi 'small cooking pots (obv.)' (K-B 39)

Many nouns are derived from verb stems that incorporate reduplication. In some nouns of this type the underlying verb comes with lexicalized reduplication, but in others the reduplication has the same transparent function it would have in the underlying verb. The distinction may depend on accidents of attestation.

(4.160) Agent nouns from verb stems with one-syllable reduplication

(a)   *ki·ški·ška·pehkateno·ni* 'steep bluffs, cliffs' (HL)

(b)   *mamakwahki·ki* 'in the hills' (X5-RL 3, 2x)

(c)   *me·mešenahkye·ha* 'law-enforcement officer' (K-W 198, K-GCF 2)

(d)   *na·na·pitiye·ška·ke·ha* (K-Med 44)
          'snake sp.', *lit.*, 'the one that crawls up people's rectums'

(e)   *pa·pakeso·hahi* '(kernels of) popcorn (obv. pl.)' (K-F 2)

(4.161) Abstract and instrumental nouns from verb stems with one-syllable reduplication

(a)   *a·ya·čimo·ni* 'story' (C-Hist 19; JP-GTF 1, SP-SM 1)
          ke·ht-a·ya·čimo·ni (i.e., *ke·hta-a·ya·čimo·ni*) 'old story' (C-UAN cover)

(b)   *a·ya·teso·hka·kanaki* 'winter stories' (JP-TO 53)

(c)   *anemi-kokwe·hka·piweni* 'seeing the changes of seasons on into the future' (K-B 307)

(d)   *ma·mata·kwa·čimo·ni, ma·mata·kwa·čimoweni* 'entertaining story' (SP-Stories 1)

(e)   *pa·pakačikani* 'hammer, club' (O 49C)

A number of abstract nouns are found that incorporate a two-syllable reduplication of the underlying verb; the reduplication is not lexicalized but has its usual verbal function.

(4.162) Abstract and instrumental nouns from verb stems with two-syllable reduplication

(a)   *a·maha·mano·wa·čimoweni* 'talk about sexual topics' (K-FC 301)

(b)   *ma·ne·.. e·nihe·nikowa·kani* 'a lot of jokes' (K-Auto 81)

(c)   *(i·)ni·.. inahina·čimo·ni* 'that kind of speaking' (K-FC 561)

(d)   *netenahinehta·ke·wen=a·pehe* 'the way I always hear (the story)' (K-GF 28)

(e)   *ki·h=a ya čimohene inehineška ·ti weni* (K-M 353k) (cf. 4.215)
       'I'm going to teach you about positions.'

(f)   *inehine neti weni* 'people's attitudes towards each other' (K-M 1022d) (cf. 4.215)

(g)   *kanakanawi ·ni* 'the speaking; the homilies and prayers' (K-B 87, K-ECRP 104)
       (cf. 4.192*c*)

(h)   *menamena ·škono ·ni* 'eating meat' (JP-HLOS 69) (cf. 4.193*d*)

(i)   *mi šami ·ša miweni* 'the doings of the sacred pack' (K-ECRP 89, 2x)

(j)   *onahona pe miweni* 'marriage (by women), getting married' (K-M 324.l) (cf. 4.207*u*)

(4.163) Noun derived from a doubly reduplicated verb stem

       mani a čipanakiči iši-a yaha ya čimo ·ni 'these various stories' (K-Auto 90)

Nouns with the prenoun *iši* reduplicated as *išihiši* are used to refer to different kinds, similarly to the use of oblique participles centering on the corresponding preverb.

(4.164) *išihiši* PN 'of {such} kinds'

       meše=meko išihiši-na ·tawino ne·hi 'all different kinds of medicines' (K-Auto 260)

In the noun for 'log cabin' (4.132*f*), which is not derived from a verb stem, the reduplication nevertheless applies to the verbal component of the stem rather than to the noun as a whole.

The one pronoun that has reduplication is the animate interrogative pronoun; it is attested with two variants of two-syllable reduplication:

(4.165) Reduplication of *we ne·ha* 'who?'

(a)   *we newe ne·haki=ča·hi ayo·hi ki wita čiki.* 'So, what kinds of creatures are here?'
       (K-M 765b)
       we newe ne·haki=yá pi i ya·h=e wičiki. 'Well, who else lives there?' (K-MFS 14)

(b)   *we nawe ne·haki·='niki.* 'Who are they?' (FE-Lang 27)

SECONDARY STEMS

General Characteristics

40. A secondary stem is one derived from another stem, which may be either primary or secondary and either a simple stem or a compound. Almost all secondary derivation is by the addition of a suffix to a stem, but some derived nouns also have initial change. Most secondary derivation makes a stem of a different formal category from that of the stem it is derived from. Diminutive suffixes behave differently; they modify stems semantically but do not change their formal category and thus differ from both secondary finals and inflectional suffixes. There is some overlap in the morphology used in primary and secondary stem derivation.

Secondary stems are often made from other secondary stems. All the intermediate secondary stems of a complex derivation may not be attested, however, and some intermediate stems implied by further derivatives are, in fact, unlikely to be independently usable. The intermediate stages in secondary derivation that are not attested as stems can be considered virtual stems. Alternatively, in some cases combinations of secondary finals may be taken to function as a single secondary final that makes derivatives directly, without intermediate stages.

SECONDARY STEMS: NOUNS FORMED FROM NOUNS

Diminutives (§41)

41.1. Diminutives of nouns. Diminutives (§25) can be formed from most nouns.
Diminutive noun stems always end in a long vowel followed by |h|. The few pronouns that make
diminutives do so like nouns.

The default suffix marking diminutives on nouns is |-e·h| (which is always -e·h- and does not
underlie the suffixes with ostensible contraction [4.168ff.). This suffix may be added to a
diminutive suffix of another shape. Both genders form diminutives the same way.

    (4.166) Diminutive nouns with |-e·h| DIM

      (a) |-kwise·h-| 'son (dim.)' ← |-kwis-| 'son'

          okwise·hani 'his little, dear, or pitiful son' (cf. *okwisani* 'his son')

      (b) |mi·ša·me·h-| 'sacred pack (dim.)' ← |mi·ša·m-| 'sacred pack'

          mi·ša·me·hi 'minor sacred pack' (cf. *mi·ša·mi* 'sacred pack')

The use of the diminutive is ordinarily optional, but it is obligatory on compound nouns that have
one of the prenouns that explicitly specify small size (*čaki* 'small'; *papi·wi* and *čača·ki* 'small
(pl.)'; *pi·si* 'tiny') or the prenoun *nawe·ni* 'pretty, handsome' (4.159*aef*, 4.167).

    (4.167) Obligatory diminutives with certain prenouns

      (a)   *čaki-nepise·hi* 'small lake' (*nepisi* 'lake')

          čaki-wi·kiya·pe·hi 'small house' (*wi·kiya·pi* 'house')

      (b) *papi·wi-še·šketo·he·haki* 'small kettles' (*še·šketo·ha* 'unlidded kettle')

      (c) *pi·si-mi·čipe·he·haki* 'small game' (*mi·čipe·ha* 'game animal')

          pi·si-aškote·hi 'tiny (bits of) fire' (i.e., sparks) (K-CGB 6) (*aškote·wi* 'fire')

      (d) *nawe·ni-oškinawe·he·hani* 'a handsome young man (obv.)' (K-MLF 8)

      (e) *nawe·ni-še·škesi·he·hani* 'a pretty young girl (obv.)' (K-MBGS 18)

Stems ending in |-Cw| make diminutives in |-Co·h|; the default suffix is sometimes added
after this.

    (4.168) Diminutives in |-Co·h| from stems in |-Cw|

      (a) *anake·hko·ha* 'small piece of a bark wall' (*anake·hkwa* 'bark (on a house)')

      (b) *mahkahko·hi* 'pail' (*mahkahkwi* 'box')

      (c) *mahko·ha* 'bear cub' (*mahkwa* 'bear')

      (d) *mehteko·hi* 'small tree, small stick' (*mehtekwi* 'tree, stick')

      (e) *pepikwe·ško·hi* 'small whistle' (*pepikwe·škwi* 'whistle')

    (4.169) Diminutives in |-Co·he·h| from stems in |-Cw|

      (a) *mešikene·piko·he·ha* 'young underwater bear' (*mešikene·pikwa* 'underwater bear')

      (b) *šeka·ko·he·ha* 'kitten skunk' (*šeka·kwa* 'skunk')

In some cases diminutives without the added |-e·h| appear to be lexicalized (e.g., 4.168*bc*), but in
other cases there is no reason to think this. There is also a lexicalized diminutive from *šeka·kwa*
'skunk' (4.169*b*): *šeka·ko·ha* 'onion'; the diminutive of this is likewise *šeka·ko·he·ha* 'little
onion'. There is, however, no competing or ambiguous form beside *mešikene·piko·he·ha* 'young
underwater bear' (4.149*a*), the name of a water monster which is found in the diminutive only
once.

Stems ending in |-Cy| make diminutives in |-Ci·h|. A few nouns that do not end in |-Cy| also take this suffix.

(4.170) Diminutives in |-Ci·h| from stems in |-Cy|

    (a)   *ahpeni ha* 'wild potato (*Apios tuberosa*)' (*ahpenya* 'potato', earlier 'wild potato')

    (b)   *asaye ya pi hi* 'buckskin string' (|-e·ya·py| NF 'cord')

    (c)   *aseni hani* 'small stones' (*aseni* 'stone', pl. *asenye ni*)

    (d)   *tahkepi hi* 'little spring' (*tahkepi* 'spring of water; well')

(4.171) Diminutive in |-Ci·h| from stems in |-C|

    (a)   *neme ·si ha* 'little fish' (*neme ·sa* 'fish')

            neme ·si he ha 'little fish'

            šeneme ·si ha 'minnow' (← *iše* 'mere' + *neme ·si ha*; 4.111*b*)

    (b)   *oče pihki hi* 'small root' (K-W 887) (*oče pihki* 'root', pl. *oče pihkani*)

Beside the form in (4.171*b*) there is also regular *oče pihke hi* 'small root' (JB-M 37, pl. [2x]).

Most stems in |-Vw| have obligatory double marking in diminutives; the first suffix contracts with the stem to -*V·h*, and |-e·h| DIM is added to this. Other stems, especially inanimates, do not add |-e·h| DIM; animates with this shorter stem shape are perhaps always lexicalized (e.g., 4.179*c*).

(4.172) Diminutives in |-V·h| and |-V·he·h| from stems in |-Vw|

    (a)   *ihkwe he ha* 'young woman' (*ihkwe wa* 'woman')

    (b)   *kekye hči-neni he haki* 'older men' (*kekye hči* 'old (pl.)'; *neniwa* 'man')

    (c)   *anehki hi aškote hi* 'a little fire' (K-M 1092*c*) (*aškote wi* 'fire') (also 4.167*c*)

    (c)   *ta twa hki hi* 'small ravine' (*ta twa hkiwi* 'ravine')

    (d)   *owi nani he hi* 'little tongue' (*owi naniwi* 'tongue')

Many stems of several types ending in |-n| contract with the diminutive suffix to -*a·h*. This is the regular treatment of stems with the primary final |-ika·n| 'structure' and the secondary finals |-ikan|, making nouns of instrument and the like (4.145; §45.2-4), and |-wen|, which makes verbal abstracts (§45.7), and it is also found with some other stems ending in |-an|, |-a·n|, and |-wen|.

(4.173) Diminutives in |-a·h| from stems in |-n|

            With |-ika·n| 'structure':

    (a)   *pehkwika hi* 'a small dome-shaped lodge' (*pehkwika ni* 'dome-shaped lodge')

    (b)   *mato teše wika hi* 'a small sweatlodge' (*mato teše wika ni* 'sweatlodge')

            With |-ikan| (instrument):

    (c)   *ša posika hi* 'a little laxative' (*ša posikani* 'laxative')

    (d)   *ki škitepe hika hi* 'a small stump' (*ki škitepe hikani* 'tree stump')

    (e)   *penaha ka hi* 'a little comb' (*penaha kani* 'comb')

            With |-wen| (verbal abstract):

    (f)   *wi ·seniwa hi* 'a little food' (*wi ·seniweni* 'food, meal')

    (g)   *mi ša tesiwa hi* 'a bit of finery' (*mi ša tesiweni* 'finery')

            Others:

    (h)   *ana ka hi* 'a small bowl' (*ana kani* 'bowl')

    (i)   *pi ša ka hi* 'a buckskin thong' (*pi ša kani* 'piece of rawhide')

    (j)   *pi tanwa ha* 'a little quiver' (*pi tanwa na* 'quiver')

    (k)   *anake wa hi* 'a small birchbark canoe' (*anake weni* 'birchbark canoe')

    (l)   *mehkone wa hi* 'a little blanket' (*mehkone weni* 'blanket')

    (m)   *meko te wa hi* 'a little skirt, dress' (*meko te weni* 'skirt, dress')

There are other nouns in |-an| and |-a·n| that take the default suffix |-e·h| DIM. Nouns in |-i·n| and |-o·n| and personified abstracts in |-wen| also take |-e·h| DIM:

(4.174) Diminutives with |-e·h| DIM from stems in |-n|

    (a)   *ahkane̱·hani* 'small (or pitiful) bones' (*ahkani* 'bone')

    (b)   *paka·ne̱·hani* 'small nuts' (*paka·ni* 'nut')

    (c)   *owi·wi·ne̱·ha* 'a small horn' (*owi·wi·na* 'horn')

    (d)   *na·tawino·ne̱·hi* 'kind of medicine' (*na·tawino·ni* 'medicine')

    (e)   *ahpene·wene̱·ha* '(the Spirit of) Disease' (*ahpene·weni* 'disease, epidemic')

Noun stems ending in |-ay| have three treatments. Body-part terms apparently have diminutives with |-a·h| replacing |-ay|, though only one is attested.

(4.175) Diminutive of body-part term in |-ay|

        owi·naka·hi 'his little penis', *mi·naka·hani* 'little penises' (*owi·nakayi* 'his penis')

The dependent noun *netaya* 'my pet, esp. my dog, my horse' adds |-i·h| DIM, as if it were a stem in |-Cy| (4.170; cf. §11.4, 1.148).

(4.176) Diminutive of *netaya* 'my pet'

        netayi·ha 'my pet (dim.)'

Nouns that comprise an initial that is derived from a noun stem and |-ay| NF 'skin, hide' replace the initial with one derived from the corresponding diminutive (4.177*abcd*). Some other nouns ending in the sequence |-ay| make their diminutives the same way, with the material preceding the |-ay| treated as a virtual noun stem (4.177*efg*).

(4.177) Diminutives of nouns with stem-final |-ay|

        Initial derived from a noun; |-ay| NF 'skin, hide'

    (a)   *ašaško̱·haya* 'little muskrat skin' (*ašaškwaya* 'muskrat skin')

    (b)   *e·sepa̱·haya* 'little raccoonskin' (*e·sepanaya* 'raccoonskin')

    (c)   *nenoso̱·hayi* 'small buffalo robe' (*nenoswayi* 'buffalo robe')

    (d)   *owiye·he̱·haya* 'small animal skin' (*owiye·haya* 'animal skin')

        Initial not derived from a noun

    (e)   *apahko̱·haya* 'small cattail-reed mat' (A 23B) (*apahkwaya* 'cattail-reed mat')

    (f)   *owi·šehko̱·hayi*, *mi·šehko̱·hayi* 'small, pitiful scalp' (*owi·šehkwayi*, *mi·šehkwayi* 'scalp')

    (g)   *omakohko̱·hayi* 'his little hat' (*makohkwayi* 'hat')

41.2. Diminutives of pronouns. Some indefinite (§18.6) and interrogative (§18.7) pronouns have diminutive forms made with |-e·h| DIM.

(4.178) Diminutives of indefinite and interrogative pronouns

    (a)   *we·ne·he·ha* 'who (is the little one)?' (*we·ne·ha* 'who?')

    (b)   *ke·ko·he·hi* 'any little thing, in any little way'

The homophonous nouns derived from the indefinite pronouns also make diminutives in the regular way (§18.6).

41.3. Formal diminutives. Many nouns have the shape of a diminutive but do not have an explicit diminutive meaning. Some of these formal diminutives seem to have an inherent flavor of endearment or relatively small size, but others do not. Some nouns have both a non-diminutive shape and a formal diminutive that are used interchangeably with no apparent difference in meaning (4.179*fg*). In such cases an explicit diminutive meaning is indicated by adding |-e·h| DIM to the formal diminutive variant. Stems in |-Vw| may have a formal diminutive in |-V·h| (cf. 4.172).

(4.179) Formal diminutives.

- (a) *anemo‧ha* 'dog' (*anemwa* only in insults and names; *anemo‧he‧ha* 'puppy')
- (b) *kwi‧yese‧ha* 'boy' (cf. *kwi‧yese‧he‧ha* 'little boy')
- (c) *mači-maneto‧ha* 'evil spirit, monster; the Devil' (*maneto‧wa* 'spirit, god, monster')
- (d) *mahkese‧hi* 'moccasin' (cf. *apeno‧hi-mahkese‧he‧hani* 'children's moccasins')
- (e) *maškimote‧hi* 'bag' (cf. *čaki-maškimote‧he‧hi* 'a little bag' [A 21C])
- (f) *e‧sepana, e‧sepa‧ha* 'raccoon' (cf. *i‧ni iši-nekoti e‧sepa‧he‧ha* 'just that one raccoon': *i‧ni* 'that', *iši* '{so}', *nekoti* 'one' [cf. 2.246])
- (g) *ašaškwa, ašaško‧ha* 'muskrat' (cf. *ašaško‧he‧ha* 'baby muskrat')

41.4. Hypocoristic diminutives. A large class of formal diminutive stems show hypocoristic (that is, nickname-like) shortening. Before a suffix |-‧h| DIM, the final consonant or consonant cluster of the stem is dropped, together with, in many cases, one or more preceding |CV| syllables. The full form of the stem may or may not be attested. Names are often found in hypocoristic form. (See also 4.232.)

(4.180) Hypocoristic formal diminutives

- (a) *ahpwa‧kanimo‧ha* (K) 'tobacco bag' (also *ahpwa‧kanimote‧ha* [C, LL])
- (b) *ka‧hkimo‧hi* (K) 'fiber bag' (also *ka‧hkimote‧hi* [Jones 1907:96.14; K])
- (c) *ka‧wipo‧hi* (AW, LYB) 'file' (cf. *ka‧wipočikani* 'file' [Jones 1911:813])
- (d) *kehči‧pi‧hi* 'belt' (cf. *kehči‧piso‧ni-neniwaki* 'belt-men' [in drum ceremony])
- (e) *kepe‧yo‧ha* 'Kapayou' (cf. *kepe‧yo‧ma‧wa*, a man's name)
- (f) *mi‧šimo‧hi* (C), *omi‧šimo‧hi* (K) 'paunch, rumen' (cf. *mi‧šimote‧hi* [Jones 1911:812])

In some cases the variants are used by different speakers (4.180*a*). For other stems the hypocoristic form may be either less common (4.180*b*) or more common (4.180*cdef*) than the full form. In the cases noted Jones has the full form, sometimes uniquely (4.180*bcf*).

41.5. Hypocoristic shortening of compound nouns. A particular pattern of hypocoristic shortening is applied to compound nouns. The second member of the compound is dropped completely, and the suffix |-i| PF ABSTR that forms the prenoun is replaced by an ostensible noun final |-i‧h|. The full compound is often not attested.

(4.181) Hypocoristically shortened compound nouns

- (a) *asayi‧hani* 'buckskin ones' ← *asayi* PN 'of buckskin' (← *asaya* 'skin'): *mahkese‧hani, asayi‧hani* 'moccasins, buckskin ones' (K-MortF 21)
- (b) *ki‧weške‧wi‧hi* 'passenger train' ← **ki‧weške‧wi* PN 'of travelers' (cf. *ki‧weška‧ta* 'traveler')
- (c) *kohpiči‧ha* 'buffalo' ← *kohpiči-nenoswa* (*kohpiči* 'up-country', *nenoswa* 'bovine')
- (d) *neno‧te‧wi‧ha* 'Indian tobacco' ← *neno‧te‧wi-ase‧ma‧wa*
- (e) *pi‧ša‧kani‧hi* 'buckskin coat' ← *pi‧ša‧kani* PN 'of buckskin'
- (f) *pi‧wa‧pehkwi‧hi* 'steel trap' ← *pi‧wa‧pehkwi-ni‧samo‧hi, lit.* 'metal deadfall'

41.6. Formal diminutives of kinship terms. Some kinship terms make normal diminutives (4.166*a*), and some appear to have no diminutive form (e.g., *nekya* 'my mother', *no‧sa* 'my father, father's brother'). (What would be the diminutive of 'mother' is lexicalized as *neki‧ha* 'my mother's sister, my step-mother', a separate term.) But for most kinship terms, while there may be formal diminutives made by suffixation or hypocoristic shortening, these are lexicalized with at best only a slight affective flavor.

(4.182) Kinship terms with hypocoristic shortening
- (a)   *nemešoʹha* 'my grandfather' (usual form) (also *nemešo mesa* 'my grandfather')
- (b)   *nenekwaʹha* 'my cross-nephew' (usual form) (also *nenekwanesa* 'my cross-nephew')

Four kinship terms have alternate short stems without the usual formal |-e·h| DIM that are used at least optionally with some possessors by some speakers. Two of these have a form with |-eʹh| DIM if the possessor is first or second singular and an optional form without |-eʹh| DIM if the possessor is third singular (4.183*ab*). (There is only one example of a short stem with a plural possessor, but kinterms with plural possessors are relatively uncommon.) Another has both variants also with a first singular possessor (4.183*c*) and in secondary derivation (4.311*i*). The fourth one is like the first two but with the short stem also attested in the plural with a first singular possessor (4.183*d*). The kinship terms with this variation tend to generalize the forms with |-eʹh| DIM; the speakers that use the short forms also use the long forms, and most speakers use only the long forms.

(4.183) Kinship terms used with and without formal |-e·h| DIM
- (a)   *nemiseʹha* 'my elder sister', *kemiseʹha* 'your (sg.) elder sister'
        omisani (JP), *omiseʹhani* (JP, others) 'his, her elder sister'
- (b)   *neseseʹha* 'my elder brother', *keseseʹha* 'your (sg.) elder brother'
        osesani 'his elder brother' (C, X10), *oseseʹhani* (C, X10, others) 'his elder brother'
- (c)   *nesiʹma* (K, C, X10), *nesiʹmeʹha* (K, C, X10, others) 'my younger brother', *kesiʹmeʹha* 'your (sg.) younger brother'
        osiʹmani (C, LL, X10), *osiʹmeʹhani* (C, LL, others) 'his, her younger brother'
        → |osiʹmem-|, |osiʹmeʹhem-| TA 'have as younger sibling' (4.311*i*)
- (d)   *nešiseʹha* 'my (maternal) uncle', *kešiseʹha* 'your (sg.) uncle'
        nešisaki (SP), *nešiseʹhaki* (K, JP, JB) 'my (maternal) uncles'
        ošisani (C, JP), *ošiseʹhani* (C, others) 'his uncle'
        kešisenaʹna (C), *kešiseʹhenaʹna* (C, others) 'our (inc.) uncle'

The vocative singulars (§28.17) of these nouns end in *-e*, which would be regular from either the short stem or the long stem. Several vocative singulars of other kinship terms have hypocoristic shortening (3.116-121) as well as other anomalies. Three nouns referring to in-laws and having stems in |-v·w| make their vocatives as if from formal diminutives derived by replacing this |-v·w| by |-v·h| (3.123-124).

41.7. Sound symbolism in diminutives. There are a few traces of sound-symbolic consonant replacement in diminutives. This process is completely lexicalized. The relic cases show |š| replacing |s| and |šk| replacing |hk|.

(4.184) Sound symbolism in diminutives

nešemisa, nešemiʹha 'my cross-niece' ← *nesemya* 'my daughter-in-law' (4.186*d*)
Another example is in (4.187*b*).

41.8. Possessed diminutives. Although the many lexically specific peculiarities of diminutives make it clear that they are made by stem derivation and not inflection, there is one circumstance in which the diminutive is marked among the inflectional suffixes. When a diminutive noun is possessed, the possessed-theme marker |-em| (§28.5), if it is used, is suffixed to the stem before the diminutive ending |-e·h| DIM, in the position it would have if the stem were not diminutive.

(4.185) Possessed diminutive nouns

   (a) *keše ʾšketo ʾheme ʾhena ʾna* 'our (inc.) little kettle' ← *še ʾšketo ʾhe ʾha* 'little kettle'
       (Cf. *neše šketo ʾhema* 'my kettle' ← *še šketo ʾha* 'kettle')

   (b) *ketapeno ʾheme ʾhwa waki* 'your (pl.) children (dim.)' ← *apeno ʾhe ʾha* 'child (dim.)'
       (Cf. *ketapeno ʾhemaki* 'your (sg.) children' ← *apeno ʾha* 'child')

   (c) *neki ʾšete me ʾhena ʾni* 'our little offering of cooked food' (cf. *ki ʾšete wi* 'cooked food')

One noun makes a possessed form on a stem which is otherwise always hypocoristically shortened; this is lexicalized in a narrowed meaning (3.92).

Archaic Diminutives (§42)

42. A suffix |-es| NF appears to derive some kinship terms from others and is also part of some underived noun stems. Since it is not productive its function is not synchronically salient, but it often occurs in nouns that also incorporate a formal diminutive |-e·h|. It makes some personal names from common nouns. Comparative evidence confirms that this is an archaic diminutive suffix.

(4.186) Derivation of kinship terms with |-es| NF DIM

   (a) *nemešo mesa* 'my grandfather' (cf. 4.182a) ← *nemešo ma* 'my father-in-law'
   (b) *nenekwanesa* 'my cross-nephew' (cf. 4.182b) ← *nenekwana* 'my son-in-law'
   (c) *no ʾhkomesa* 'my grandmother' ← *no ʾhkoma* 'my mother-in-law'
   (d) *nešemisa* 'my cross-niece' ← *nesemya* 'my daughter-in-law' (4.184)

Presumably the diminutive form of these consanguineal terms reflects the fact that they designate relatives a person would ordinarily have at an earlier age than the corresponding in-laws.

(4.187) Other nouns with |-es| NF DIM

   (a) *a yamowe ʾsa* (man's name) ← *a yamowe wa* 'cannibal giant' (Sauk)
   (b) *iškwe ʾse ʾha* 'girl' (← *ihkwe wa* 'woman') (cf. §41.7)
   (c) *maneto ʾse ʾha* 'worm' (← *maneto wa* 'snake')
   (d) *mekesi ʾsa* (man's name) ← *mekesiwa* 'bald eagle'
   (e) *mi ʾkesa* 'wampum bead' (cf. *pi ʾsimi ʾkaki* 'wampum beads')
   (f) *neni ʾča nesa* 'my child', dim. *neni ʾča nese ʾha*
   (g) *okima ʾhkwe ʾsa* (woman's name) ← *okima ʾhkwe wa* 'chief's female relative'
   (h) *neta nesa* 'my daughter', dim. *neta nese ʾha*

Some nouns end in |-eš|. The synchronic status of this is unclear, but historically these nouns are mostly borrowings of Ojibwe words that had the diminutive and pejorative suffix |-išš|.

(4.188) Nouns with |-eš| NF

   (a) *me ʾmehta neša* 'sheep' (cf. Ojibwe *maanishtaanish*)
   (b) *šama ʾkaneša* 'soldier' (cf. *šama ʾkani* 'spear'; Ojibwe *zhimaaganish* 'soldier')

Secondary Final |-esiw| *NF added to nouns* (§43)

43. The secondary noun final |-esiw| NF is semantically vague, but in the clearest cases it derives nouns from other nouns with similar meanings. A number of names are made from nouns with this. In some nouns with ostensible |-esiw| NF the formation of the base stem includes other elements (4.189c).

(4.189) Nouns with |-esiw| NF
- (a)   *pene ˙siwa* 'raptor' (cf. *pene wa* 'turkey')
- (b)   *ketate ˙siwa* (man's name) ← *ketate wa* 'otter'
- (c)   *aškote ne ˙siwa* 'Spirit of Fire' ← *aškote wi* 'fire' + |-ene·-| II 'blaze' + |-w| NF (§46.1)

Names of creatures with ostensible |-(·)si·h| NF added to an AI verb stem are probably agent nouns in |-w| NF (§46.1) with suffixed |-esiw| NF (which would contract to |-·siw|) plus the diminutive (contracting with this to |-·si·h|; 4.172). They may or may not have initial change.

(4.190) Agent nouns with |-(·)si·h| NF
- (a)   *ke ˙kye pi ˙kwe ˙si ˙ha* (duck with small eyes) (cf. *kekye pi ˙kwe wa* 'he's blind')
- (b)   *mano ˙minehke ˙si ˙ha* (bird sp.) (cf. *mano ˙minehke wa* 'he gathers wild rice')

Collective Nouns (§44)

44. Two suffixes make inanimate collective nouns on inanimate (4.191a) or animate (4.191b) noun stems. These are rarely found without locative inflection (2.151ab) or further secondary derivation (4.235gh).

(4.191) Collective nouns
- (a) |-ihkiw| IN (general collective):
  wi ˙kiya pihkiwi 'collection of houses' (K-Med 54) (← *wi ˙kiya pi* 'house')
  wi ˙kiya pihki ˙ki 'among the houses, in the settlement' (← |-eki| LOC)
  matepwihkiwi 'group of abandoned lodge-frames' (K-Kin 39):
  matepwihki ˙ki 'among abandoned lodge-frames' (K-T 10; C-UAN 2; S-OWA 1)
  ayo ˙hi o ˙te wenihki ˙ki 'among these towns' (K-TYFB 19)
- (b) |-ina·w| IN 'the land or collectivity of'
  aša ˙hina wi 'the Sioux country' (K-FC 337) (← *aša ˙ha* 'Sioux')
  aša ˙hina ˙ki 'in Sioux country'
  po ˙hki ˙kwe ˙hina wi (C-WH 9) 'the land of the One-Eyes'
  mo ˙hkoma ˙nina ˙ki 'among the White people' (K-Auto 251)
  me ˙ta ˙so pi ˙hina ˙ki 'among Federal officials' (C-Hist 24; JB-MF 14)
  maneto ˙na ˙ki 'among the manitous' (K-Wap 23) (← |maneto·w-|; §11.10, 1.183)
  ne ˙kato ˙kaše ˙hina ˙ki 'in the horse country, where horses were' (K-ICH 9, 10)
  neni ˙na ˙ki oči 'through males, by patrilineal descent' (K-Kin 5) (cf. 1.182, 2.151b)

SECONDARY STEMS: NOUNS FORMED FROM VERBS

Abstract Nouns (§45)

45. Some abstract nouns designate the state or activity denoted by a verb, while others label an instrument, product, or undergoer that is characteristically used, produced, or affected in the performance of the verbal action. The secondary finals that form abstract nouns all end in |-en|. The primary and secondary stems from which abstract nouns are derived are often not attested as verbs.

45.1. Nouns with |-en| NF. The secondary final |-en| NF makes nouns from AI stems. Before this, stem-final |i| and |o| are lengthened, and stem final |e·| is umlauted to long |a·| or (in stems with |-ike·| AI DETRANS [§53.2) replaced by short |a|.

(4.192) AI stem in |-i| + |-en| NF

  (a) *ahpapi ni* 'chair' (← |ahpapi-| AI 'sit on {something}')

  (b) *ahpitiye pi ni* 'afterbirth' (|ahpitiye·pi-| AI 'sit with rear end on {something}')

  (c) *kanawi ni* 'words' (← |kanawi-| AI 'speak'; cf. 4.148a, 4.162g, 4.210e)

(4.193) AI stem in |-o| + |-en| NF

  (a) *a čimo ni* 'story' (← |a·čimo-| AI 'tell, report, make one's report, tell what happened')

  (b) *ki ke no ni* 'clan feast; clan-feast food' (← |ki·ke·no-| AI 'hold a clan feast')

  (c) *mama tomo ni* 'worship, religion' (← |mama·tomo-| AI 'worship')

  (d) *mena škono ni* 'fresh meat' (← |mena·škono-| AI 'eat fresh meat')

  (e) *mo šo ni* 'scalp-lock' (← |mo·šo-| AI 'get a haircut')

  (f) *nakamo ni* '(ceremonial) song' (← |nakamo-| AI 'sing')

  (g) *wa pamo ni* 'mirror' (← |wa·pamo-| AI 'look at one's reflection')

  (h) *we ši ho ni* 'paint' (← |we·ši·ho-| AI 'paint one's face')

  (i) *we we piso ni* 'swing' (← |we·we·piso-| AI 'swing (on a swing, in a hammock)')

  (j) *kepiškwa tawe ho ni* 'door-flap'
      (as if ← *|kepiškwa·tawe·ho-| AI 'close one's doorway by tool')

(4.194) AI stem in |-e·| + |-en| NF

  (a) *aškote hka ni* 'match, firesteel' (← |aškote·hke·-| AI 'make fire')

  (b) *ihkwe wanohkya ni* 'women's products'
      (as if ← *|ihkwe·wanohkye·-| AI 'do women's work')

  (c) *ma wa ka ni* 'town' (← |ma·wa·ke·-| AI 'have a town together')

  (d) |pehtawa·n-| IN 'hearth' (← |pehtawe·-| AI 'make a fire'):
      keto kima mena na opehtawa ni 'our chief's town' (ritual metaphor)
      (K-BHD2 208)

  (e) *wi hkwe wanehka ni* 'backload bundle'
      (← |wi·hkwe·wanehke·-| AI 'make a backload bundle')

(4.195) AI stem in |-ike·| AI DETRANS + |-en| NF

  (a) *apwa čikani* 'roasting scaffold, roasting spit'
      (← |apwa·čike·-| AI 'roast meat on a roasting scaffold or roasting spit')

  (b) *ine nečikani* '(a god's) plan, blessing' (← |ine·nečike·-| AI 'plan {so}')

  (c) *kepi hikani* 'fence' (Jones 1911:813) (← |kepi·hike·-| AI 'make an enclosure')

  (d) *kohkahikani* 'bridge' (← |kohkahike·-| AI 'make a bridge' [Jones 1911:749])

  (e) *kwa pahikani* 'dipper' (← |kwa·pahike·-| AI 'dip up, scoop up')

  (f) *nasa hkohikani* 'roasting spit' (← |nasa·hkohike·-| AI 'roast on spits')

  (g) *pahkwe šikani* 'wheat flour' < *'bread' (← |pahkwe·šike·-| AI 'cut off a slice')

  (h) *pa pakačikani* 'hammer' (← |CV+| RED1 + |pakačike·-| AI 'strike')

  (i) *pa škesikani* 'firearm' (← |pa·škesike·-| AI 'shoot a firearm')

  (j) *pehkwapičikani* 'bundle' ← TI(2) (← |pehkwapičike·-| AI 'tie things into bundles; give presents')

  (k) *saka pye nikani* 'halter' (← |saka·pye·nike·-| AI 'lead a horse on a rope')

Stems in |-išin| AI 'lie' make nouns on the virtual final |-išimo| (cf. 4.13, 258):

(4.196) Stem in |-išin| AI 'lie' + |-en| NF

    (a)   *ahpišimo·na* 'mattress' (as if ← *|ahpišin-| AI 'lie on {something}')

    (b)   *apehkwe·šimo·na* 'pillow' (← |apehkwe·šin-| AI 'lie with head supported')

45.2. Nouns with |-kan| NF derived from transitive stems. For the majority of nouns in |-kan| there is no corresponding verb in |-ike·| AI DETRANSITIVIZER that is attested, as is the case for the nouns in (4.195). Although this AI is probably formable in almost all cases, such nouns can alternatively be derived directly from the underlying transitive verb. Most of these nouns can be described as derived directly from attested TI stems by a secondary final |-ikan| NF (4.197). In some cases only a TA exists, but the noun is formed by suffixing |-ikan| NF to what the corresponding TI would be if it were not unidiomatic (4.198). For other nouns in |-ikan|, not even the ostensible transitive stems are attested. While lack of attestation in such cases could be accidental (4.199), some nouns in |-kan| NF are formed from virtual transitive stems that are probably not used as verbs (4.200).

(4.197) TI stem + |-ikan| NF

    (a)   *ako·čikani* 'pothook' (← |ako·t-| TI(2) 'hang, place aloft')

    (b)   *ota·hkwe·nečikanani* 'his beloved' (← |a·hkwe·net-| TI(1) 'think a great deal of')

    (c)   *ka·wipočikani* 'file' (Jones 1911:813) (← *|ka·wipot-| TI(2) 'file')

    (d)   *kepačihikani* 'stopper, cork' (← |kepačih-| TI(1) 'stop up as or in a hole')

    (e)   *kepanohikani* 'lid' (← |kepanoh-| TI(1) 'shut in')

    (f)   *ni·miwahikani* 'dancing song' (← |ni·miwah-| TI(1)-O 'sing a dancing song')

    (g)   *patahkahikani* 'meat spear' (← |patahkah-| TI(1) 'spear')

    (h)   *wi·hkwe·pičikani* 'bundle' (← *|wi·hkwe·pit-| TI(2) 'bundle up')

(4.198) Unused TI stem + |-ikan| NF (TA attested)

    (a)   *pasitiye·hikani* 'quirt' (cf. |pasitiye·hw-| TA 'spank')

    (b)   *saketone·pičikani* 'bridle' (cf. |saketone·piN-| TA 'bridle, put a bridle on')

(4.199) Unattested TI stem + |-ikan| NF

    (a)   *ša·ponikani* 'needle' (← *|ša·pon-| TI(1))

    (b)   *si·pye·hikani* 'soap' (← *|si·pye·h-| TI(1))

    (c)   *te·we·hikana* 'drum' (← *|te·we·h-| TI(1))

(4.200) Virtual TI stem + |-ikan| NF

    (a)   *kešihka·pye·hikani* 'fork'

    (b)   *mesenahikani, mesanahikani* 'document, letter, piece of writing'

    (c)   *nasikani* 'roasting spit (archaic)'

45.3. Nouns with |-kan| NF derived from AI stems. Some nouns are derived from AI stems in |-a·| or |-e·| by |-kan| NF, before which stem-final |-e·| is replaced by |-a·|. At least one consonant-final stem is treated like a stem in |-e·| before this final (4.203; cf. 4.204*d*).

(4.201) AI stem in |-a·| + |-kan| NF

    (a)   *ahtwa·kani* 'poultice' (← |ahtwa·-| AI 'apply a poultice')

    (b)   *nepa·kani* 'bed' (← |nepa·-| AI 'sleep')

(4.202) AI stem in |-e·| + |-kan| NF

    (a)   *a·teso·hka·kana* 'myth, "winter story" ' (← |a·teso·hke·-| AI 'tell myths')

    (b)   *či·ška·kani* 'fart' (← |či·ške·-| AI 'fart')

    (c)   *ina·towa·kani* 'language' (← |ina·towe·-| AI 'speak {such} a language')

    (d)   *inowa·kani* 'word' (← |inowe·-| AI 'state {so} to X')

    (e)   *išite·ha·kani* 'thought, plan' (← |išite·he·-| AI 'think, plan {so}')

(f)   *ketemaˑkiteˑhaˑkani* 'feeling of wretchedness'
        (← |ketemaˑkiteˑheˑ-| AI 'feel wretched')
(g)   *meˑnešiteˑhaˑkani* 'shame' (← |meˑnešiteˑheˑ-| AI 'be ashamed')
(h)   *moˑšowaˑkani* 'scissors' (as if ← *|moˑšowe-| AI 'cut X's hair')
(i)   *naˑpitaˑwaˑkani* 'necklace' (← |naˑpitaˑweˑ-| AI 'have things around the neck')

(4.203) AI stem in consonant + |-kan| NF

(a)   *noˑnaˑkani* 'breast' (as if ← *|noˑne-| ← |noˑn-| AI 'nurse, suck at the breast')

Stems with a body-part medial and |-eˑ| AI ABSTR, or |-Ø| AI ABSTR (4.204d; cf. 4.203), make nouns in this way. In some cases a body-part medial followed by |-aˑkan| might be considered a derived primary noun final. In one noun this formation is based on a medial followed by the postmedial |-eˑ-| treated as an AI final (4.204a).

(4.204) Noun with body-part medial + |-eˑ| AI ABSTR (or postmedial |-eˑ-|) + |-kan| NF

(a)   *ahtoˑmyaˑkani* 'saddle' (as if ← |ahtoˑmyeˑ-| AI
        ← |aht-| [← |aht-| TI(2) 'put {somewhere}'] + |-oˑmy-e·-| 'on the back')
(b)   *ašaˑšinameškaˑkani* '(fish's) skin slime' (← |ašaˑšinameške-| AI 'have slippery skin')
(c)   *meniwisikiwaˑkani* 'back sores' (as if ← *|meniwisikiweˑ-| AI 'have sores on back')
(d)   *miˑsetonaˑkani* 'moustache' (← |miˑseton-| AI 'have a moustache')
(e)   *niˑkaˑninehkaˑkani* 'front hoof or paw'
        (as if ← *|niˑkaˑninehkeˑ-| AI 'have a front hand')
(f)   *niˑsiˑpinečaˑkani* 'finger' (as if ← *|niˑsiˑpinečeˑ-| AI 'have a fringe of fingers')
(g)   *noˑhkipiwaˑkanaki* 'down' (as if ← *|noˑhkipiweˑ-| AI 'have soft feathers')
(h)   *pehkwikanaˑkani* 'ankle' (← |pehkwikaneˑ-| AI 'have a lumpy bone')
(i)   *poˑhkitepaˑkani* 'fontanelle' (← |poˑhkitepeˑ-| AI 'have a hole in the head')
(j)   *šoˑniyaˑhaˑnowaˑkani* 'silver tail' (as if ← *|šoˑniyaˑhaˑnoweˑ-| AI 'have a silver tail')

45.4. Nouns with |-aˑkan| NF derived from transitive stems. A few nouns are made with a suffix |-aˑkan| NF added to a transitive stem. The |-aˑ-| in this suffix can be identified with the theme signs |-aˑ| TA th. 1 (**§29.7a**) and |-am| TI(1) th. (**§29.7f**). The transitive stem may not be attested as a verb stem.

(4.205) TI(1) stem + |-aˑkan| NF

(a)   *kotaˑkani* 'throat' (← |kot-| TI(1) 'swallow')
(b)   *kemeˑnawaˑtaˑkana* 'your lover'
        (← unused TI(1) *|meˑnawaˑt-| to |meˑnawaˑN-| TA 'love, admire, adore')
(c)   *ošehkiˑtaˑkani* 'clothing' (← |ošehkiˑt-| TI(1) 'wear as clothing')
(d)   *penahaˑkani* 'comb' (as if ← *|penah-| TI(1);
        cf. the derived initial |penah-| in |penahaˑhkwaˑ-| AI 'comb one's hair')
(e)   *šekitaˑkani* 'urine (on something?)' (← |šekit-| TI(1) 'urinate on')

(4.206) TA stem + |-aˑkan| NF

tehkinaˑkani 'cradleboard' (← |tehkiN-| TA 'tie to cradleboard')

45.5. Nouns with |-aˑn| NF derived from TI(1) stems. A few nouns have |-aˑn| NF added to a TI(1) stem to designate an undergoer or product of the action.

(4.207) TI(1) stem + |-aˑn| NF

(a)   *takwahaˑni* 'corn mush' (← |takwah-| TI(1) 'grind up')

  (b) *ketasa·ni* 'nocake (parched corn ground fine); nocake mush'
     (← *|ketas-| TI(1); cf. |ketasw-| TA 'make (corn) into *ketasa·ni*')

  (c) *no·hkaha·ni* 'pemmican' (← |no·hkah-| TI(1) 'pound soft')

  (d) *pa·hpa·ša·nani* inan. pl. 'thin slices of dried meat'
     (← *|pa·hpa·š-| TI(1) 'prepare (meat) as *pa·hpa·ša·nani*')

  (e) *|pi·sehka·n-| (← |pi·sehk-| TI(1) 'put on (as a shirt or dress)')
     → formal diminutive (**§41.3**): *pi·sehka·hi* 'shirt'

45.6. Nouns with |-a·w| NF derived from TA stems. The equivalent to |-a·n| NF (**§45.5**) for animates is a secondary final |-a·w| NF that is added to TA stems to make a small number of nouns that designate undergoers. Although the verbal origin of these nouns is clear, the underlying verb may not be in use. This formation furnishes unpossessed kinship terms, though only a few are textually attested; plural forms are given here if that is all that is found.

  (4.208) TA stem + |-a·w| NF

  (a) *|aškipwa·w-| (← *|aškipw-| TA 'eat raw')
     → formal diminutive (**§41.3**): *aškipwa·ha* "sweet potato"

  (b) *ki·ke·na·wa* 'captive, prisoner of war' (← *|ki·ke·n-| TA)

  (c) *meškwa·swa·wa* 'yarn belt' (← *|meškwa·sw-| TA 'dye red')

  (d) *okwisema·wa* 'the son' (K-BD 32, A 75E) (← |okwisem-| TA 'have as a son')

  (e) *oni·ča·nesema·waki* 'the children (in the family or families)'
     (← |oni·ča·nesem-| TA 'have as one's child')

  (f) *osi·mema·waki* (C-G 4, X10-PBW 78), *osi·me·hema·waki* (X6-OS 29) 'the
     younger siblings' (← |osi·mem-| TA 'have as a younger sibling')

  (g) *ota·nesema·wa* 'the daughter' (Jones 1907:102.15)
     (← |ota·nesem-| TA 'have as a daughter')

  (h) *papakena·wa* 'corncake' (← *|papaken-| TA 'make flat by hand')

45.7. Nouns with |-wen| NF. The suffix |-wen| NF is added to AI and TI(3) stems and to TI(1) and TI(2) themes to make abstract and concrete nouns. The abstract nouns of this type are verbal nouns that designate the state or activity denoted by the verb. The concrete nouns designate the characteristic or generic means whose employment or existence constitutes the verbal action or state, or the characteristic observable result. The TI themes are in most cases objectless or in objectless use, but derivation from a fully transitive theme is possible, with the valence for the object retained and the object appearing syntactically as a nominal adjunct. The treatment of the stem before |-wen| NF is the same as before |-w| FORMTV (**§34.3**).

  (4.209) Abstract nouns from AI + |-wen| NF

  (a) **ahpanehki·weni* 'step, pace' (← |ahpanehki·-| AI 'step {somewhere}')
     (cf. *ni·šwi-ahpanehki·wene* 'two paces'; 4.377*b*)

  (b) *ahpi·htesiweni* 'age' (← |ahpi·htesi-| AI 'be {so} old')

  (c) **aneškenačike·weni* 'pipeful' (← |aneškenačike·-| AI 'fill things')
     (cf. *nekoti-aneškenačike·wene* 'one pipeful'; 4.377*a*)

  (d) *kehkye·weni* 'old age' (← |kehkya·-| AI 'be old')

  (e) *kemo·toweni* 'stealing, theft' (← |kemo·t-| AI 'steal')

  (f) *keša·tesiweni* 'kindness' (← |keša·tesi-| AI 'be kind')

  (g) *ketema·kesiweni* 'misery' (← |ketema·kesi-| AI 'be miserable, poor')

  (h) *keteminawesiweni* 'blessing' (← |keteminawesi-| AI 'receive a blessing')
     (*oketeminawesiweni* 'the blessing he received; the blessing he bestowed')

(i) *ki·ke·noweni* 'the celebration of the clan feast, the clan feast (generic)'
       (← |ki·ke·no-| AI 'hold a clan feast'; cf. 4.211*b*)

(j) *mahkate·wi·weni* 'fasting' (← |mahkate·wi·-| AI 'fast')

(k) *mama·tomoweni* 'worshipping' (← |mama·tomo-| AI 'worship')

(l) *mi·hkeče·wi·weni* 'work' (← |mi·hkeče·wi·-| AI 'work')

(m) *mi·ka·ti·weni* 'warfare, mortal combat' (← |mi·ka·ti·-| AI 'fight')

(n) *mehtose·neniwiweni* 'life' (← |mehtose·neniwi-| AI 'live')

(o) *nana·hkawesiweni* 'witchcraft, black magic' (← |nana·hkawesi-| 'practice witchcraft')

(p) *natawa·piweni* 'vision, eyesight' (← |natawa·pi-| 'look, seek to see')

(q) *nepo·weni* 'death' (← |nep-| AI 'die' [1.99])

(r) *nešiwana·tesiweni* 'destruction' (← |nešiwana·tesi-| AI 'be destroyed')

(s) *ne·se·weni* 'cure, recovery' (← |ne·se·-| AI 'recover, be cured or saved, live (not die)')

(t) *ona·pe·miweni* 'marriage (of a woman)' (← |ona·pe·mi-| AI 'have a husband')

(4.210) Abstract nouns of observable result from AI + |-wen| NF

(a) *či·pe·hkohkwe·weni* 'memorial feast, "ghost feast" '
       (← |či·pe·hkohkwe·-| AI 'celebrate a memorial feast')

(b) *išawiweni* 'ceremony of {such} sort' (← |išawi-| AI 'do {so}')

(c) *iše·wi·weni* 'custom' (← |iše·wi·-| AI 'perform {such} work or activity')

(d) *iyoweni* 'what is said, expression used' (← |iyo-| for |i-| AI 'say {so}'; cf. 1.93)

(e) *kanawiweni* 'speeches, words spoken formally' (← |kanawi-| AI 'speak') (cf. 4.192*c*)

(f) *ne·moweni* 'breath' (← |ne·mo-| AI 'breathe')

(4.211) Concrete nouns from AI + |-wen| NF

(a) *aša·šinameške·weni* 'slime, the stuff that makes the (fish's) skin slippery'
       (← |aša·šinameške·-| AI 'have slippery skin'; cf. 4.204*b*)

(b) *ki·ke·noweni* 'food offered in the clan feast' (cf. 4.209*i*)
       (← |ki·ke·no-| AI+O 'hold a clan feast serving O2')

(c) *mi·ša·tesiweni* 'finery' (← |mi·ša·tesi-| AI 'wear finery, dress up')

(d) *sehkwiweni* 'spittle' (← |sehkwi-| AI 'spit')

(e) *šekiweni* 'urine' (← |šeki-| AI 'urinate')

(f) *taši·hka·noweni* 'toy' (← |taši·hka·no-| AI 'play')

(g) *wi·seniweni* 'meal, food for meal or feast' (← |wi·seni-| AI 'eat, eat a meal')

(4.212) Nouns from TI(1) theme + |-wen| NF

(a) *a·hkwamatamo·weni* 'sickness' (← |a·hkwamat-| TI(1)-O)

(b) *inehinesamo·weni owi·ya·si* 'the different ways of cooking meat' (K-OKUT 42)
       (← |CVCV+| RED2 + |ines-| TI(1) 'cook {so}')

(c) *kotake·netamo·weni* 'suffering' (← |kotake·net-| TI(1)-O 'suffer')

(d) *pakitamo·weni* 'adoption ceremony' (← |pakit-| TI(1)-O 'hold an adoption')

(e) *wi·sakamatamo·weni* 'painful thing' (← |wi·sakamat-| TI(1)-O 'feel pain')

(4.213) Nouns from TI(2) theme + |-wen| NF

(a) *panesihto·weni* 'war honors' (← |panesiht-| TI(2)-O 'win war honors')

(b) *sanakihto·weni* 'hard thing' (← |sanakiht-| TI(2)-O 'have a hard time')

(c) *takwaho·to·weni* 'trapping' (← |takwaho·t-| TI(2)-O 'trap')

(d) *teso·to·weni* 'trapping (archaic)' (← *|teso·t-| TI(2)-O 'trap';
       cf. |teso·taw-| TA 'set a trap for (archaic)')

(4.214) Nouns from TI(3) + |-wen| NF

   (a)   *ayo·weni* 'tool' (← |ayo·-| TI(3) 'use')

   (b)   *mi·čiweni* 'food' (← |mi·či-| TI(3) 'eat')

Some large sets of abstract nouns with |-wen| NF are formed in parallel fashion from secondary derivatives of the same class. Verbal nouns are made for TA verbs via the intermediate-stage reciprocal stem with |-(e)ti·| AI RECIP (§53.7) (also 4.162*ef*). These nouns do not necessarily imply reciprocal acts and are sometimes clearly active or passive.

(4.215) Nouns from TA + |-(e)ti·| AI RECIP + |-wen| NF

   (a)   *apwi·heti·weni* 'waiting' (← |apwi·h-| TA 'wait for')

   (b)   *či·nawe·ti·weni* 'kinship, kin' (← |či·nawe·m-| TA 'be related to')

   (c)   *ina·ko·ti·weni* 'kinship relationships' (← |ina·ko·m-| TA 'be related {so} to')

   (d)   *iti·weni* 'popular saying' (← |iti·-| AI 'say {so} to each other' ← |iN-| TA 'say {so} to')

   (e)   *kaka·čiti·weni* 'teasing' (← |kaka·čim-| TA 'tease verbally')

   (f)   *ka·htwe·neti·weni* 'sympathizing' (← |ka·htwe·nem-| TA 'grieve for')

   (g)   *keša·te·neti·weni* 'kind thoughts' (← |keša·te·nem-| TA 'think kindly of')

   (h)   *ketemina·ti·weni* 'blessing (received)' (← |keteminaw-| TA 'bless')

   (i)   *mi·hketi·weni* 'courtship' (← |mi·hkem-| TA 'court')

   (j)   *neseti·weni* 'killing' (← |neS-| TA 'kill')

   (k)   *owi·weti·weni* 'married life' (← |owi·wem-| TA 'have as wife')

   (l)   *tanwe·we·ti·weni* 'arguing' (← |tanwe·we·m-| TA 'argue with')

   (m)   *tepa·neti·weni* 'love' (← |tepa·N-| TA 'love')

   (n)   *wača·heti·weni* 'ceremonial feasting', *lit.* 'cooking for each other' (← |wača·h-| TA 'cook for')

Verbal nouns denoting ceremonies and conditions are sometimes made from AI verbs of being derived from noun stems.

(4.216) Nouns from noun stem + |-i| AI 'be' + |-wen| NF

   (a)   *aškihkwe·wiweni* 'menarche, becoming a woman' (← |aškihkwe·wi-| AI 'have first menstruation')

   (b)   *e·he·wiweni* 'Swan (Dance) Ceremony' (← |e·he·wi-| AI 'be a swan')

   (c)   *ihkwe·wiweni* 'womanhood' (← |ihkwe·wi-| AI 'be a woman')

   (d)   *ki·wakamo·hiweni* 'Singing-Around Rite' (← |ki·wakamo·hi-| AI 'be a Singing-Around Rite member, celebrate the Singing-Around Rite')

   (e)   *maneto·wiweni* 'spiritual power' (← |maneto·wi-| AI 'be a manitou')

   (f)   *mete·wiweni* 'Grand Medicine Rite, Midewin' (← |mete·wi-| AI 'be a Grand Medicine member, celebrate the Grand Medicine Rite')

   (g)   *neniwiweni* 'being a man; men (indefinite)' (← |neniwi-| AI 'be a man'): *e·šite·he·ki neniwiweni* 'the way men like it to be' (K-Kin 30)

   (h)   *neno·te·wiweni* 'the Indian way of life' (← |neno·te·wi-| AI 'be an Indian')

   (i)   *okima·wiweni* 'being chief, chieftainship' (← |okima·wi-| AI 'be a chief')

   (j)   *mačowiye·hiweni* 'meanness' (← |mačowiye·hi-| AI 'be a mean person')

   (k)   *pašito·hiweni* 'being old men' (← |pašito·hi-| AI 'be an old man'): *ki·na·na pašito·hiweni* 'we (inc.) old men' (K-FC 374)

   (l)   *pešekwa·hiweni* 'divorce' (← |pešekwa·hi-| AI 'be a divorced person')

   (m)   *ši·ka·wiweni* 'strict mourning after the death of a spouse' (← |ši·ka·wi-| AI 'be a widow or widower in strict mourning')

    (n)   *wa·pano·wiweni* 'Wapano ceremony' (← |wa·pano·wi-| AI 'be a Wapano member')

    (o)   *wa·waneška·hiweni* 'wickedness' (← |wa·waneška·hi-| AI 'be a bad person')

    (p)   *we·ta·se·wiweni* 'being a warrior, status as a warrior'

            (← |we·ta·se·wi-| AI 'be a warrior')

Abstract nouns are derived from some particles and particle phrases using |-wen| NF. If they end in |-V·hi| they are treated like an AI verb stem and add |-wen| directly; otherwise they are formed as if from a verb of being made by lengthening the final vowel of the particle and adding |-hi| AI.

    (4.217) Nouns from particles with |-wen| NF on virtual AI stems

    (a)   *hawo·hiweni* 'saying "yes," the word "yes" ' (cf. *hawo·ʔ* 'yes (agreeing)')

    (b)   *mahkwa·či·hiweni* 'quietness, the quiet life' (cf. *mahkwa·či* 'calmly, quietly')

    (c)   *mešemeko·hiweni* "priviledge to do as they please" (K-W 184; tr. HP)

          (cf. *meše=meko* 'freely, any way (he) wants')

    (d)   *me·mečine·hiweni* 'end of life' (cf. *me·mečine·hi* 'for the last time')

    (e)   *no·či·hiweni* 'saying *no·či*' (cf. *no·či*, the sacred vocable in prayers)

For some nouns in ostensible |-wen| NF an underlying verb is not in use:

    (4.218) Nouns in |-wen| NF from unused verbs

    (a)   *ahpene·weni* 'disease'

    (b)   *mehkone·weni* 'blanket'

    (c)   *meko·te·weni* 'dress'

    (d)   *mi·wašiweni, mi·wešiweni* 'bundle, pack'

    (e)   *o·te·weni* 'town'

The nouns for 'blanket' and 'dress' (4.218*bc*) supply the indefinite-possessed forms to the dependent nouns *ohkone·hi* 'his blanket' and *oko·te·hi* 'her dress'.

Agent Nouns (**§46**)

46. An agent noun derives from an intransitive verb the designation of someone or something that characteristically does, undergoes, or is what the verb denotes.

46.1. Nouns with |-w| NF. The secondary final |-w| NF makes a few agent nouns from AI and II stems and from TI(1) and TI(2) themes. It is not used productively; a special function for such a noun is in (2.78). With TI(1) themes it appears to be found only when there is further derivation: either a formal diminutive |-·h| NF (**§41.3**) is added (4.219*ae*), or the stem forms a derived initial before a concrete noun final (4.219*b*).

    (4.219) Agent nouns with |-w| NF from AI stems and TI(1) and TI(2) themes

    (a) |či·niškatamw-| (← |či·niškat-| TI(1)) 'suck the juice out of by biting':

          či·niškatamo·ha 'katydid'

    (b) |ki·we·tamw-| (← |ki·we·t-| TI(1)-O 'go about shouting'):

          ki·we·tamohkwe·ha (woman's name, Thunder Clan) (|-ehkwe·h| 'woman')

    (c)   *ne·nawihto·wa* 'camp policeman' (← *|ne·nawiht-| TI(2))

    (d)   *nana·hkawesiwa* 'witch' (← |nana·hkawesi-| AI 'be a witch, practice witchcraft')

    (e) |pa·škatamw-| (← |pa·škat-| TI(1) 'crack open by biting'): *pa·škatamo·ha* 'parrot'

    (4.220) Agent nouns with |-w| NF from II stems

    (a)   *awanwi* 'thick fog (archaic)' (← |awan-| II: *awanwi* 'there is thick fog' [archaic])

    (b)   *kehčikami·wi* 'sea' (as if ← *|kehčikami·-| II 'be a large body of water')
          (cf. *wa·hkamikami·wi* 'water (in a river, lake) is clear' [|-kami·| II 'be a body of
          water'])
    (c)   *no·tenwi* 'wind' (← |no·ten-| II 'wind to blow': *no·tenwi* 'the wind blows')
    (d)   *pekeše·wi* 'fog' (K-W 705, tr. HP) (← |pekeše·-| II 'be smoke, smoky; be fog,
          foggy')

A few agent nouns in |-w| have initial change (cf. 4.191):

    (4.221) Agent nouns with |-w| NF and initial change
    (a)   *ka·ka·nwikaše·wa* 'grizzly bear' (← |kaka·nwikaše·-| AI 'have long claws'
          [cf. 3.178])
    (b)   *ke·nwa·sowe·wa* 'mountain lion' (← *|kenwa·sowe·-| AI 'have a long tail')

46.2. Nouns with |-h| NF. The secondary final |-h| NF, combined with initial change, freely makes agent nouns from AI and II stems; a few agent nouns are also made in this way from TA inverse themes (4.229*a*) and TI themes. Before this final some stem-final vowels are replaced: |a·| is sometimes umlauted to long |e·| (4.222) and sometimes retained (4.223); |-i| AI in verbs of possession (§48) is replaced by |-e·| (4.226*b-e*), except if the verb stem ends in |-ki|; short |i| in other stems (and in verbs of possession in |-ki|) is lengthened to |i·| (4.225, 4.226*a*); short |o| is lengthened to |o·| (4.228). After a consonant |o·| is ordinarily inserted (4.229*acdef*), but at least one stem adds |e·| (4.229*b*), and |-am| TI(1) th. is replaced by |-a·| (4.230). The stems in |a·| that do not have umlaut to |e·| before |-h| NF are |nepwa·hka·-| AI 'be smart' (also with umlaut), |kehkya·-| 'be old', and those with the finals |-ehka·| AI 'go', |-eška·| AI,II 'move, become', |-isa·| AI,II 'run, fly, fall', |-i·hta·| AI 'be clothed' (also with umlaut), and |-ya·| II. The one example from a stem in |-ka·pa·| AI 'stand' shows an irregular replacement of |a·| by |o·| (4.231).

    (4.222) Agent nouns with |-h| NF and initial change: stems with umlauting |-a·|
    (a)   *e·tame·ha* 'smoker (at a ceremony)' (← |atama·-| AI 'smoke')
    (b)   *me·hkate·wi·hte·ha* 'nun' (← |mahkate·wi·hta·-| AI 'wear black clothing'; cf.4.223*c*)
    (4.223) Agent nouns with |-h| NF and initial change: stems with retained |-a·|
    (a)   *ke·hkya·haki* 'old folks' (← |kehkya·-| AI 'be old (person)')
    (b)   *ke·pya·hi* 'thimble' (← *|kepya·-| II 'block')
    (c)   *ke·takišehki·hta·ha* 'clown'
          (← |ketakišehki·hta·-| AI 'wear striped or spotted clothing'; cf. 4.222*b*)
    (d)   *me·hkikwe·ška·ha* (species of insect) (← |mahkikwe·ška·-| AI 'have the head fall
          off')
    (e)   *me·me·ša·hani* 'big beads' (← |meme·ša·-| II 'be big (pl.)'
          < |Ce_e·+| RED1, |meS-ya·-| II)
    (f)   *na·me·ya·hkwisa·ha* (species of large bird that flies through the woods, perhaps
          goshawk)
          (← *|na·me·ya·hkwisa·-| AI 'fly through the woods')
    (g)   *ne·pwa·hka·ha* 'wise one' (← |nepwa·hka·-| AI 'be smart') (also *ne·pwa·hke·ha*)
    (h)   *ne·sawa·hi* 'forked support pole' (← |nasawa·-| II 'be forked' < |nasaw-ya·-| II)
    (i)   *te·tepisa·ha* 'wheel' (← |tetepisa·-| AI 'turn, spin')
    (4.224) Agent nouns with |-h| NF and initial change: stems with |e·|
    (a)   *ke·kye·hkwe·ha* 'teacher; brown thrasher' (← |kekye·hkwe·-| AI 'teach')
    (b)   *ke·no·te·hi* 'long lodge' (← |keno·te·-| II 'be a long lodge')
    (c)   *ma·ma·keše·ha, me·ma·keše·ha* 'mule' (← |mama·keše·-| AI 'have big ears')

(d)   *ma ma twe·ha, me ma twe·ha* 'catbird' (← |mama·twe·-| AI 'moan')

(e)   *me mešenahkye·ha* 'law-enforcement officer'
        (← |CV+| RED1, |mešenahkye·-| AI 'arrest X')

(f)   *me na koče·ha* 'daddy-longlegs' (← |mena·koče·-| AI 'have a stinky body')

(g)   *me škwitepe·ha* 'red-headed woodpecker' (← |meškwitepe·-| AI 'have a red head')

(h)   *mi seče·ha* 'peach' (← |mi·seče·-| AI 'have a fuzzy body')

(i)   *mo na ne·ha* 'woodchuck' (← *|mo·na·ne·-| AI 'dig a hole')

(j)   *na nahkonike·ha* 'catcher (in baseball)'
        (← |CV+| RED1, |nahkonike·-| AI 'catch things')

(k)   *ne mate·hi* 'upright pole' (← |nemate·-| II 'stand')

(l)   *ne sawihkeče·ha* (species of bird) (← |nasawihkeče·-| AI 'have a forked tail')

(4.225) Agent nouns with |-h| NF and initial change: stems with |-i|

(a)   *e hkawa pi·ha* 'guard' (← |ahkawa·pi-| AI 'watch as a watchman, guard')

(b)   *mi či·ha* 'eater of (it)' (← |mi·či-| TI(3) 'eat'):
        In *owi nenwi-mi či·ha* 'meadowlark' (*lit.*, 'fat-eater'; imitative of its call)

(c)   *ma mi či·hi* 'peyote' (← |CV+| RED1, |mi·či-| TI(3) 'eat')

(d)   *ne na hkawesi·ha* 'witch' (← |nana·hkawesi-| AI 'be a witch, practice witchcraft')

(e)   *pe hkosi·ha* 'boil (on skin), gland' (← |pehkosi-| AI 'be a lump')

(4.226) Agent nouns with |-h| NF and initial change: verbs of possession with |-i|

(a)   *we pehkwa hki·ha* 'Ball-Player' (← |opehkwa·hki-| AI 'have a ball')

(b)   *we pene me·ha* 'Turkey-Owner' (← |opene·mi-| AI 'have turkeys')

(c)   *we to seni me·ha* 'Has-A-Rock' (← |oto·seni·mi-| AI 'have a rock')

(d)   *we wi še·ha* 'Rolling-Skull' (← |owi·ši-| AI 'have a head')

(e)   *we yo se·ha* 'Indian agent' (← |o·si-| AI, AI+O 'have (O2 as) father'; called this as
        the representative of the President, who was traditionally addressed as 'father')

(4.227) Agent nouns with |-h| NF and initial change (virtual in these two): stems with |-i·|

(a)   *mi simi si·ha* 'jerusalem artichoke' (← |CVCV+| RED2, |mi·si·-| AI 'defecate')

(b)   *ki wa ni·ha* 'bird sp.' (← |ki·wa·ni·-| AI 'lose one's way')

(4.228) Agent nouns with |-h| NF and initial change: stems in |-o|

(a)   *e nepye ha so·ha* 'pictured person, being, or creature'
        (← |anepye·ha·so-| AI 'be depicted')

(b)   *e nwe we ha so·ha* 'drum' (← |anwe·we·ha·so-| AI 'be sounded by beating')

(c)   *ki wakamo·ha* 'member of the Singing-Around rite'
        (← *|ki·wakamo-| AI 'go around singing')

(d)   *me šena so·ha* 'prisoner, convict' (← |mešena·so-| AI 'be arrested')

(e)   *pi neši-pe mipaho·ha* 'automobile' (*pi neši* 'spontaneously', |pemipaho-| AI 'run';
        5.15e)

(f)   *we ča ho·ha* 'cook' (← |wača·ho-| AI 'cook')

(4.229) Agent nouns with |-h| NF and initial change: |o·| or |e·| inserted after consonant

(a)   *a čimeko·ha* 'one told about, well-known story character, hero of the tale'
        (*keta čimeko·ha* 'the one you talk about')
        (← |a·čim-| TA 'tell about', |-ekw| TA th. 2)

(b)   *a mane·ha* 'whore' (← |a·maN-| AI 'breed, rut, have sex, have sexual
        inclinations')

(c)   *ke mo to·ha* 'thief' (← |kemo·t-| AI 'steal')

(d)   *ne po·ha* 'carcass' (← |nep-| AI 'die')

(e)   *ša·šo·ko·ha* (species of small duck; *lit.* 'whistler') (← |ša·šo·k-| AI 'whistle')
(f)   *wi·sakeno·ha* 'Bitter' (a dog's name in a story, wrongly translated "Hold-Tight" [Jones 1907:73], as if 'biter'; the name of a star) (← |wi·sakeN-| AI 'taste bitter')

(4.230) Agent noun with |-h| NF: TI(1) theme |-am| replaced by |-a·h|
(a)   *ne·na·hota·ha* 'director of a ceremony' (← |nana·hot-| TI(1) 'direct (a ceremony)')
(b)   *wa·pata·ha* 'one that looks at (it)' (← |wa·pat-| TI(1) 'look at'):
       ki·šekwi-wa·pata·ha 'least bittern', *lit.*, 'the one that looks at the sky' (A 101G)
(c)   *pwa·wi-kehke·neta·ha* 'ignoramus' (← |pwa·wi| PV NEG, |kehke·net-| TI(1) 'know')

(4.231) Agent noun with |-h| NF from stem in |-ka·pa·| AI 'stand'
       na·ni·sika·po·haki 'split-feather headdress'
          (← |CV+| RED1, *|ni·sika·pa·-| AI 'stand dipping')

Some nouns are evidently the hypocoristic formal diminutives (§41.4) of agent nouns made with initial change.

(4.232) Agent nouns with initial change and hypocoristic shortening
(a)   *ke·kineši·ha* 'bull' (← *|kekinešiwe·-| AI 'have testicles')
(b)   *ne·nye·hpe·ha* 'cripple' (← |nenye·hpesi-| AI 'lose coordination, lose use of limbs')
(c)   *ne·topa·ha* 'member of a war party' (← |natopani-| AI 'go on the warpath')
(d)   *še·šketo·ha* 'unlidded cooking pot, cauldron' (← *|še·šketon-| AI 'have a plain rim')
(e)   *we·mi·ko·ha* 'Thunder Clan member' (← |omi·koni-| AI 'have feathers')

Agent nouns for sets of relatives or the like that are derived from reciprocal stems in |-ti·| AI have |-h| NF without initial change:

(4.233) Agent nouns with |-h| NF and no initial change
(a)   *owi·weti·haki* 'the married couple, the man and his wife (or wives)'
          (← |owi·weti·-| AI 'be married')
(b)   *owi·hka·neti·haki* 'the friends' (← |owi·hka·neti·-| AI 'be friends')

46.3. Nouns derived by initial change. Initial change also appears in a few names that are derived from common nouns. The examples are river names derived from compound nouns.

(4.234) Names derived from nouns by initial change
(a)   *me·sisi·po·wi, me·šisi·po·wi* 'Mississippi River' (← *meši* PN 'big' + *si·po·wi* 'river')
(b)   *me·škwisi·po·wi* 'Red River (Oklahoma)' (← *meškwi* PN 'red' + *si·po·wi* 'river')

SECONDARY STEMS: VERBS FORMED FROM NOUNS

47. Several categories of verbs are formed from noun stems.

Verbs of Being (§47.1-2)

47.1. Verbs of being and becoming. Verbs of being or becoming are freely made from noun stems with the final |-iwi| AI,II 'be'. This takes the shape |-i| AI,II 'be' after a stem in |-Vw| and often after stems in other consonants, usually as as a free variant but for some nouns as the only shape attested for the final. A stem in |-Cw| combines with |-iwi| AI,II as |-Cowi| (§11.3, 1.140) and combines with the variant |-i| AI,II as |-Cwi|.

(4.235) Verbs of being with |-iwi| AI,II 'be'

    (a)   *aseniwiwa* AI 'he is, becomes a rock, turns to stone' (← |aseny-| IN 'stone')

    (b)   *kohkoseniwiwa* AI 'he is a granite boulder' (← |kohkoseny-| IN 'granite boulder')

    (c)   *meškwa·hkowiwa* AI 'he is a cedar' (← |meškwa·wa·hkw-| AN 'cedar';
           ni·h=meškwa·wa·hkowi 'I shall be a cedar' [K-YC 5])

    (d)   *paka·na·hkowiwa* AI 'he is a walnut tree' (← |paka·na·hkw-| IN 'walnut tree';
           nepaka·na·hkowi "I am a walnut" [Jones 1907:126.10 [-ūwʲ]])

    (e)   *šama·kanešiwiwa* AI 'he is, becomes a soldier' (← |šama·kaneš-| AN 'soldier')

(4.236) Verbs of being with |-i| AI,II 'be'

    (a)   *asena·mišiwa* AI 'he is a hard maple' (← |asena·mišy-| IN 'hard maple';
           Jones 1907:128.1 [1s])

    (b)   *ihkwe·wiwa* AI 'she is a woman' (← |ihkwe·w-| AN 'woman')

    (c)   *mahkwiwa* AI 'he is, becomes a bear' (← |mahkw-| AN 'bear')

    (d)   *maneto·wiwa* AI 'he is a manitou, has the nature of a manitou'
           (← |maneto·w-| AN 'manitou')

    (e)   *mehtose·neniwiwa* 'he is a person, he is or becomes alive'
           (← |mehtose·neniw-| 'person')

    (f)   *okima·wiwa* AI 'he is a chief' (← |okima·w-| AN 'chief')

    (g) |wi·kiya·pihkiwi-| II 'be a collection of houses' (← |wi·kiya·pihkiw-| IN [4.191*a*])

    (h) |aša·hina·wi-| II 'be the Sioux country' (← |aša·hina·w-| IN [4.191*b*])

(4.237) Verbs of being with |-i| AI,II 'be' or |-iwi| AI,II 'be'

    (a)   *mehtekomišiwa* AI (Jones 1907:126.5), *mehtekomišiwiwa* AI (K-RYL 8) 'he is an
           oak' (← |mehtekomišy-| IN 'oak')

    (b)   *mi·ša·miwi* II (K-FC 104, etc.), *mi·ša·miwiwi* II (K-FC 126, etc.) 'it is a sacred
           pack' (← |mi·ša·m-| IN 'sacred pack')

    (c)   *name·siwa* AI (Jones 1907:182.T), *neme·siwa* AI (K-E 3, SP-Fish 17,
           JB-MAF 31), *name·siwiwa* AI (Jones 1907:182.11), *neme·siwiwa* AI (K-Wap
           177, SP-Fish 17, JB-MAF 28) 'he is a fish' (← |name·s-|, |neme·s-| AN 'fish')

    (d)   *oškinawe·hiwa* AI, *oškinawe·hiwiwa* AI 'he is, becomes a young man, is a bachelor'
           (← |oškinawe·h-| AN 'youth, teen-age boy; never-married boy or man'

    (e)   *še·škesi·hiwa* AI, *še·škesi·hiwiwa* AI 'she is, becomes a maiden, is a virgin'
           (← |še·škesi·h-| AN 'teen-age girl; never-married girl or woman; virgin')

    (f)   *we·pesi·hiwa* AI, *we·pesi·hiwiwa* AI 'he is crazy' (← |we·pesi·h-| AN 'crazy person')

    (g)   *wi·kiya·piwi* II (K-SSP 72), *wi·kiya·piwiwi* II (K-SSP 184) 'it is a house'
           (← |wi·kiya·p-| 'house')

47.2. Verbs of having as an attribute in |-iwi| AI,II. A special category of verbs of being has |-iwi| AI,II 'have (noun) as an attribute; be covered, dusted, or smeared with (noun); have some (noun) on him, it'; in this use the final has no shorter variant.

    (4.238) Verbs of being that denote having an attribute, with |-iwi| AI,II

    (a)   *kehkye·weniwiwa* AI 'he is aged' (← |kehkye·wen-| IN 'old age')

    (b)   *mi·koniwiwa* AI, *mi·koniwiwi* II 'he, it has feathers, is feathered'
           (← |mi·kon-| AN 'feather')

    (c)   *mi·ša·tesiweniwiwa* AI 'he wears his finery' (K-FC 335)
           (← |mi·ša·tesiwen-| IN 'finery, fancy clothes'

    (d)   *nepiwiwa* AI, *nepiwiwi* II 'he, it is wet, has some water on him, it'
           (← |nepy-| IN 'water')

(e)   *onamaškayiwiwa* AI (← *onamaškaya* 'skin' [3.37]):
       še ˈški=meko e ˈh=onamaškayiwiči 'there was nothing left of him but skin'
       (K-M 153e)
(f)   *owi ˈšiwiwi* II 'it has a head on it, a head part' (← *owi ˈši* 'head' [3.26]):
       e ˈh=owi ˈšiwiki 'its head, the head part of it', *lit.*, 'where it has a head' (K-HS 28)
(g)   *papakye ˈhiwiwa* AI 'he (a pipe) is axe-bladed' (← |papakye·h-| IN 'axe')
(h)   *pekowiwa* AI, *pekowiwi* II 'he, it is dusty' (← |pekw-| IN 'dust, ashes')
(i)   *sasa ˈhkwe ˈweniwiwa* AI, *sasa ˈhkwe ˈweniwiwi* II 'he, it is restricted by taboo,
       forbidden'
       (← *sasa ˈhkwe ˈweni* 'something forbidden or taboo')
(j)   *saya ˈwita ˈmihkanasoweniwiwi* II 'it has a sour taste' (K-SGG 20)
       (← unattested noun in |-wen| [4.210] ← unattested |saya·wita·mihkanaso-| AI
       'has a tingly or shuddery feeling in the jaw from heat')

Verbs of Possession (§48)

48. Verbs of possession are made freely from nouns and furnish the usual way of stating the simple notion 'have'. The final |-i| AI ABSTR is added to the third-person-possessed theme, which is the form for a noun with a third-person singular possessor minus the core inflectional suffix for nominal category (3.1). The derived verb thus incorporates the third-person prefix (with any irregularities it may have), as well as the thematic suffix |-em| if the noun requires this. Verbs of possession are made from the third-person-possessed theme of compound nouns with the prefix |o+| 3 before either the prenoun or the head noun or both, the same patterns as in the inflection of compound nouns (§28.8).

AI verbs of possession are freely used with a secondary object (§22.3), especially if the object is third person. Overtly transitive stems may be derived from these AI stems (§53.2).

(4.239) AI verbs of possession
(a)   *oni ˈča ˈnesiwa* AI(+O) 'he has (O2 as) a child' (← *oni ˈča ˈnesani* 'his child')
(b)   *ošo ˈniya ˈhemiwa* AI 'he has money'
       (← *ošo ˈniya ˈhemi* 'his money' ← *šo ˈniya ˈhi* 'money')
(c)   *otayo ˈweniwa* AI(+O) 'he has (O2 as) a tool'
       (← *otayo ˈweni* 'his tool' ← *ayo ˈweni* 'tool')
(d)   *oto ˈhpwa ˈkanimo ˈhiwa* AI 'he has a tobacco pouch' (← *oto ˈhpwa ˈkanimo ˈhani*
       'his tobacco pouch' ← *ahpwa ˈkanimo ˈha* 'tobacco pouch')
(e)   *opi ˈša ˈkani-pi ˈsehka ˈhe ˈhiwa* AI 'he has a little buckskin shirt' (K-Auto 1)
       (← *opi ˈša ˈkani-pi ˈsehka ˈhi* 'his buckskin shirt'
       ← *pi ˈša ˈkani* PN 'of buckskin' [← *pi ˈša ˈkani* IN 'buckskin'] + *pi ˈsehka ˈhi* 'shirt')
(f)   *meškwahki ˈhi-ona ˈpe ˈmiwa* AI 'she has a Meskwaki husband' (K-Koch 92)
       (← *meškwahki ˈhi-ona ˈpe ˈmani* 'her Meskwaki husband' [X5-EBE 21; 3.54]
       ← *meškwahki ˈhi* PN [← *meškwahki ˈha* 'Meskwaki'] + *ona ˈpe ˈmani* 'her husband')
(g)   *oni ˈka ˈni-omami ˈši ˈhemiwa* AI+O (K-Bene 101)
       'he has O2 as his lead ceremonial attendant'
       (← **oni ˈka ˈni-omami ˈši ˈhemani* 'his lead ceremonial attendant'
       ← *ni ˈka ˈni* PN 'leading' + *mami ˈši ˈha* 'ceremonial attendant')

   (h)   *onehpeni-oˑšisemiwa* AI+O 'he has O2 as a step-grandchild' (K-Kin 1)

          (← *onehpeni-oˑšisemani* 'his step-grandchild'

          ← *nehpeni* PV 'step' + *oˑšisemani* 'his grandchild')

In verbs of possession the third-person prefix is a derivational element that is part of the stem. The pronominal prefixes are used before it as with any verb:

   (4.240) Verb of possession with inflectional prefix

         ketowiˑyawipwa 'you (pl.) have O2 as your body' (O 83E) (< |ke-*t*-owiˑyawi-pwa|)

         (|owiˑyawi-| AI+O 'have O2 as a body' [← *owiˑyawi* 'his body']; |ke–pwa| 2p/IND)

   Just as nouns can only be inflected for animate possessors, only AI verbs of possession can be derived from nouns. Possession by an inanimate may, however, be specified by an II verb that adds |-ˑmikat| II ABSTR (§52.1) to the AI verb. A participle made from this II verb furnishes the equivalent of a noun possessed by an inanimate.

   (4.241) II derivative for indicating inanimate possession

     (a)   *maˑhani=čaˑhi nakamoˑnani iˑniˑnaˑtawino ni eˑh=onakamoˑniˑmikahki.* (K-Spot 220)

         'And these songs are the songs of that medicine.'

         (|onakamoˑniˑmikat-| II 'have (as) a song' ← |onakamoˑniˑ-| AI 'have (as) a song')

     (b)   *weˑwiˑpiči mikahki* (C-Ston 27) 'its tooth, the tooth of the inanimate thing', *lit.*

         'that which it has as its tooth'

         (|owiˑpiči·mikat-| II 'have (as) a tooth' ← |owiˑpiči-| AI 'have (as) a tooth, teeth')

As these examples show, II stems derived with |-ˑmikat| II ABSTR retain the valences of the stem they are derived from and may take a secondary object as an argument. II verbs of possession are rare examples of an II+O verbal type, which also includes II's derived from TI's (4.267).

   Another construction that can be used to indicate possession by an inanimate is exemplified in (4.238*f*).

Verbs of Making and Related Derivatives (§49)

49.1. Verbs of making in |-ehkeˑ| AI. Verbs of making are derived from nouns to indicate making, gathering, or otherwise actively obtaining an item in the usual manner. The final |-ehkeˑ| AI 'make' is added to the noun stem. Verbs made this way are probably to be considered lexicalized despite being, for the most part, semantically transparent. The recessive contraction to |i| rather than |iˑ| (§11.4, 1.152) is found when stems in |-Cy| combine with this final (4.242*ck*), some formally diminutive nouns appear as non-diminutive stems before it (4.242*fg*), and one stem has the archaic contraction of |ay-e| to |eˑ| (4.242*d*).

   (4.242) Verbs of making with |-ehkeˑ| AI 'make'

     (a)   *ahteˑhiminehkeˑwa* 'he picks strawberries' (← *ahteˑhimini* 'strawberry')

     (b)   *apahkwaˑhkeˑwa* 'she makes cattail-reed mats'

         (← *apahkwaya* 'cattail reed (*Typha spp.*), cattail-reed mat')

     (c)   *asapihkeˑwa* 'she gathers Indian hemp'

         (← *asapya* 'plant or fiber of Indian hemp (*Apocynum spp.*)')

     (d)   *aseˑhkeˑwa* 'she tans, prepares hides' (← *asayi* 'skin, buckskin')

     (e)   *aškoteˑhkeˑwa* 'he makes fire' (← *aškoteˑwi* 'fire')

     (f)   *mahkesenehkeˑwa* 'she makes moccasins' (← |mahkesen-| for *mahkeseˑhi*

         'moccasin')

(g)   *maškimote·hke wa* 'she makes a bag' (← |maškimote·-| for *maškimote·hi* 'bag')
(h)   *meškwa·swa·hke wa* 'she makes a yarn belt' (← *meškwa·swa wa* 'yarn belt')
(i)   *nenosohke wa* 'he hunts buffalo' (← *nenoswa* 'buffalo')
(j)   *pene·hke wa* 'he hunts turkeys' (← *pene wa* 'turkey')
(k)   *wi·kopihke wa* 'she gathers basswood inner bark' (← *wi·kopi* 'strip or fiber of
       basswood (*Tilia americana*) inner bark', pl. *wi·kopye ni*)

For one noun the attested verb of making is formed from a variant of the final |-ehka·so| AI, as if
'make for oneself' (← |-ehka·N| TA [cf. 4.342] + |-o| AI [§53.5]; cf. 4.247); before this the noun
stem irregularly adds |y|.

    (4.243) Verb of making with |-ehka·so| AI 'make'
        nepo·pihka·sowa 'he makes soup' (← |nepo·p-y-| ← |nepo·p-| 'soup')
        (Cf. *nepo·pi* 'soup', *keki-nepo·pe* 'broth and all'.)

The final |-ehke·| AI 'make' is also present in primary finals:

    (4.244) Primary finals containing |-ehke·| AI 'make'
(a) |-iwanehke·| AI, AI+O 'make a pack, backload' (cf. |-iwan-| 'load')
       ašiwanehke wa 'AI, AI+O 'he makes a bundle (of O2) for a backload'
       a·pihiwanehke wa AI 'he unties a pack'
(b) |-a·po·hke·| AI+O 'boil liquid' (cf. |-a·pow-| 'liquid')
       ana·po·hke wa AI+O 'he boils O2'
       ki·ša·po·hke wa AI+O 'he finishes boiling O2'

49.2. Possessed theme + |-ehkaw| TA. The secondary final |-ehkaw| TA, a transitivized
form of |-ehke·| AI 'make' (← |-ehke·| AI + |-aw| TA [§54.1]), is added to a third-person-
possessed theme to make a verb that denotes giving or ascribing someone or something to be (or
to function as) the thing designated by the possessed theme. In the common use with kinship
terms these verbs denote the ascription of an imagined, imputed, or falsely ascribed relationship.
The attested examples take as a secondary object the person about whom the claim or assertion is
made.

    (4.245) Verbs from possessed theme + |-ehkaw| TA
(a)   *ona·pe·mehkawe wa* 'he made O2 out to be her (obv.) husband' (S-TO 19)
(b)   *oni·ča·nesehkawe wa* 'he claims that O2 is his (obv.) son' (C-Hist 43)
(c)   *oši·ši·kwanehkawe wa* 'he gives O2 to him to be his rattle':
       wi·h=oši·ši·kwanehko na niki 'those (anim.) I will give you as rattles' (K-TCSB 80)
(d)   *owi·wehkawe wa* 'he claims O2 is his (obv.) wife' (K-WYB 156)

49.3. Possessed theme + |-ehka·so| AI, AI+O. Corresponding to verbs derived from
possessed nouns with |-ehkaw| (§49.2) there are derived reflexive stems made with |-ehka·so| AI,
AI+O. These are most commonly used with a secondary object. In most cases these stems refer
to the treatment of a person as one's relative of the designated sort, especially if the arrangement
is informal, assumed, or irregular. Such a verb may also indicate pretended or imaginary
relationship or possession.

    (4.246) Verbs from possessed theme + |-ehka·so| AI, AI+O
(a)   *okwisehka·sowa* AI+O 'he claims him as his son' (K-WYB 3; X11-BG 53)
(b)   *omešo·mesehka·sowa* AI+O 'he treats him as his grandfather' (K-M 1172b)
(c)   *omi·ša·mehka·sowa* AI+O 'he claims that it is his sacred pack' (K-SSP 248)
(d)   *ona·pe·mehka·sowa* AI+O 'she makes O2 her husband' (K-K 16)
(e)   *oni·ča·nesehka·sowa* AI+O 'he treats O2 as his own child' (K-SPC 13)

(f) *owiˑnakeˑhkaˑsowa* AI+O 'he uses O2 as his penis' (← |owiˑnakay-| (cf. 4.242*d*);
     K-M 222*b*)
(g) *owiˑwehkaˑsowa* AI 'he pretends to have a wife' (K-OWM 38; X6-OS 4)
(h) *oˑhkomesehkaˑsowa* AI+O 'he treats O2 like a grandmother' (K-BBWM 3D)
(i) *oˑsehkaˑsowa* AI+O 'he treats O2 like a father' (X11-BG 56)
(j) *oˑšisemehkaˑsowa* AI+O 'he treats O2 like a grandchild' (K-BBWM 3)

49.4. Noun + |-ehkaˑso| AI. The suffix |-ehkaˑso| AI (< |-ehkeˑ| AI 'make' + |-N| TA [**§54.12**]
+ |-o| AI [**§53.5**]; cf. 4.242) has a reflexive meaning with a few nouns ('make oneself into').

     (4.247) Noun + |-ehkaˑso| AI (contraction: **§11.6**)
(a) *manetoˑhkaˑso* AI 'he conjures, makes himself into a manitou'
        (← |manetoˑw-| 'manitou')
(b) *okimaˑhkaˑsowa* AI "he pretends to be chief" (only Michelson 1925:289)
        (← |okimaˑw-| 'chief')

These derivatives differ formally from the usual verbs of pretending (**§51**, 4.260), which are not
derived from nouns directly but from the verbs of being derived from them with |-i| AI 'be'
(4.235).

SECONDARY STEMS: VERBS FORMED FROM VERBS

A number of secondary finals make verbs from verb stems; more than one such final often
appears serially in the same form. Most of these finals change the valence of the verb, adding or
subtracting verbal arguments, but those here treated first do not (**§50-52**). Some secondary finals
appear also as abstract finals in the formation of primary finals.

Diminutive Verbs (**§50**)

50. Verbs very commonly contain a diminutive suffix (**§25**). The diminutive morpheme,
which always has an |h| preceded by a long vowel, is typically used if the state or action denoted
by the verb is inherently or situationally attenuated in some way, or if someone or something
small is involved. With verbs that have a scalar adjectival meaning the diminutive may have the
force of a comparative ('more'). It also may have scope over one or more of the verbal
arguments, indicating smallness or, more typically, an attitude of sympathy or endearment.

50.1. Diminutive of intransitive verbs. With intransitive verbs the suffix is |-ˑhi| DIM,
which directly follows the stem. A stem-final short vowel is lengthened, with |i| replaced by |eˑ|
in the finals that make AI and II verbs of being (**§47, 47.1**; also **§53.6**, 4.306-308), AI verbs of
possession (**§48**), and stems that incorporate |-ˑhi| DIM. A consonant-final stem inserts |oˑ|, and
|i-| AI 'say {so}' uses the stem variant |iyo-| (**§8.3**, 1.93). One set of II stems has |-hen|, usually
with the suffix added a second time to give |-henoˑhi| II dim. (4.249*i*; cf. 4.249*c*).

     (4.248) Diminutive AI verbs
(a) *atehčiˑmeˑhi eˑyaˑhičiki* 'those who had gone a little ways off' (O 151G)
(b) *čakešiˑheˑhiwa* 'he is small' (← |čakešiˑhi-| AI 'be small')
(c) *čaki-kiˑkeˑnoˑhiyeˑkwe* 'when you hold a small clan feast' (O 81B) (← |kiˑkeˑno-| AI)
(d) *kiˑnaˑna, 'waˑpanwi,' eˑh=iyoˑhiyakwe* (K-WC 48; AW)
        'in what we lesser creatures call "morning"'

(e)   *keˑhtesi hičiki* 'older people' (O 7K) (← |kehtesi-| AI 'be old')

(f)   *eˑh=mehtoseˑneniweˑhiyakwe* 'we poor mortals' (O 144E)
      (← |mehtoseˑneniwi-| AI ← |mehtoseˑneniw-| 'person' + |-i| AI 'be')

(g)   *metemoˑheˑhiwa* 'she is an old woman'
      (← |metemoˑhi-| AI 'be an old woman' ← |metemoˑh-| 'old woman'
      + |-i| AI 'be')

(h)   *naheseˑhkweˑhiwa* 'he knows how to cook a little' (← |naheseˑhkweˑ-| AI)

(i)   *nepoˑhiwa* 'he did' (← |nep-| AI 'die')

(j)   *eˑh=neˑnekotoˑhpoˑhiwaˑči* 'they each ate from a separate bowl' (O 4H)
      (← |CV+| RED1, |nekotoˑhpo-| AI 'eat singly'; 4.119c)

(k)   *iˑni=meko eˑšiˑniˑšiˑhiwaˑči.* 'Those were the only two there were.' (O 44E)
      (← |niˑši-| AI 'be two' [idiom: cf. 2.241, 246])

(l)   *netoniˑčaˑneseˑhipena* 'we (exc.) had a baby' (A 157B) (← |oniˑčaˑnesi-| AI [§48])

(m)   *eˑh=owiˑkeˑhiyakwe* 'our camp' (A 9B) (← |owiˑki-| AI 'dwell, have a home
      {somewhere}' ← |owiˑk-| [← *ow-iˑk-i* 'his dwelling'] + |-i| AI ABSTR [§48])

(n)   *teˑpesiˑhiˑtokeˑhiki* 'they must be somewhat thankful' (O 123A)
      (← |teˑpesi-| AI 'be thankful')

(4.249) Diminutive II verbs

With |-ˑhi| DIM:

(a)   *eˑnaˑkwiˑhiki* 'early that evening' (A 40E) (← |anaˑkwi-| II 'be evening')

(b)   *aˑmi-čahkwiˑtemyaˑhiniki* 'where the water (obv.) would be shallow' (O 54E)
      (← |čahkwiˑtemyaˑ-| II 'be shallow water')

(c)   *papakyeˑheˑhi čeˑkaˑhenoˑhiki* 'a little hatchet' (A 19E)
      (← |čakaˑhen-| II 'be small' [once as a negative and once describing a lake])

(d)   *memeˑšaˑhiwani* 'they (inan.) were larger' (A 59E) (← |memeˑšaˑ-| 'be big' II)

(e)   *eˑh=aški-menoˑhkamiˑhiniki* 'in the early spring (obv.)' (O 1H)
      (← |aški| PV 'first', |menoˑhkamiˑ-| II 'be spring')

(f)   *naˑhtasokonakatoˑhikini* 'after a few days (each time)' (A 8F)
      (← |naˑhtasokonakat-| II 'be a few days')

(g)   *piˑsičeˑpihkakatoˑhiniki* 'one (obv.) with fine roots' (O 46G)
      (← |piˑsičeˑpihkakat-| II 'have fine roots')

(h)   *keˑsipi .. tawaˑhiwi* 'there was only (so much) space' (A 41F)
      (← |tawaˑ-| II 'be space'; *keˑsipi* 'only')

With |-ˑhen(oˑhi)| DIM:

(i)   *inekihkwaˑhenwi* II, *inekihkwaˑhenoˑhiwi* II 'it is {so} large (dim.)'
      (← |inekihkwaˑ-| II 'be {so} large')

50.2. Diminutive of transitive verbs. The diminutive forms of transitive verbs have the diminutive suffix after the theme sign and before other inflectional suffixes (3.186). If the inflection contains |-aˑ| TA th. 1, the diminutive suffix is |-eˑhi| and the theme sign has the variant |-∅| before this (3.192). A form with this secondary suffix |-eˑhi| TA th. 1 dim. takes AI inflections; hence, in the independent indicative the number of the object is not distinguished even with a first or second singular subject. The diminutive suffix does not appear after |-eN| TA th. 4. The diminutive combines with the other theme signs and with TI(3) stems as it would with intransitive stems of the same shape, with |i| lengthened to |iˑ| and |oˑ| inserted after a consonant. Forms with the secondary suffix |-ekoˑhi| TA th. 2 dim. take regular transitive pronominal inflections; this suffix has the shape |-ekoˑh| before |-enaˑn| 1p,12 and |-waˑw| 2p.

(4.250) Diminutive TA with |-e·hi| TA th. 1 dim.

    (a)   *nemenwe neme·hi* 'I like the dear one or dear ones'

    (b)   *nešihka wi čihe·hiwa* 'he lived alone with her' (K-SSP 253)

    (c)   *mya·ši-·· -kose·hipi* 'he was sort of feared' (X6-MF 21)

    (d)   *ne we·hiya·nini* 'every time I merely saw her' (A 45F)

    (e)   *i·ni e ne·hiya·niki* 'the only ones I told to do that' (K-W 180)

    (f)   *ne·se·hiyana* 'your victim, the poor thing you killed' (K-WYB 43)

    (g)   *či nawe me·hiye·kwiki* 'your (pl.) dear relatives' (O 122F)

    (h)   *i·niki .. e nohka ne·hikiki* 'those (few) that had been sent' (K-B 276)

    (i)   *we·ši·he·hihke·koha* 'you (pl.) should paint them (children) up' (K-WC 48)

    (j)   *awita .. ne neškime·hihkapa* 'you (sg.) should not scold him (baby)' (K-WYB 104)

    (k)   *mawi-komisahe·hino* 'you (sg., the youngest child) go swallow him up' (K-W 268)

(4.251) Diminutive TA with |-eko·hi| (~ |-eko·h|) TA th. 2 dim.

    (a)   *netanwe we meko·hiwa* 'he spoke to me rather angrily' (K-FC 28)

    (b)   *še·ški=ke·h=wi na neketemina·ko·hiwaki ni·na.*
       'I was only blessed by them, that was all.' (K-BHD 34)

    (c)   *mehteno·h=koh=mek=a pehe anemo·haki nepe·pye či-wa pameko·hiwaki*
       'only the dogs ever came to see me' (K-Spot 20)

    (d)   *nekwi nomeko·hena·na* 'the poor thing misses us (exc.)' (AW)

    (e)   *kekwi·nomeko·hwa·wa* 'the poor thing misses you (pl.)' (AW)

    (f)   *netanemi-tepahoko·hipi šo·niya·he·haki*
       'I used to get paid a little money' (K-Auto 250)

    (g)   *e·h=anehki·hiniči=mekoho i·nihi pye·nota·ko·hiwa či·hi.*
       "there were few who came to them" (K-FC 475; tr. HP)

(4.252) Diminutive TA with |-ekwi·hi| TA th. 2a dim.

    (a)   *wi·h=nenenhke nemekwi·hiwa=wi na=meko* 'still it will think of him, too' (K-B 100)

    (b)   *wi·h=anemi- .. -asemihekwi·hiye·kwe* 'so that it will be of aid to you (pl.)'
       (K-SSP 214)

(4.253) Diminutive TA with |-i·hi| TA th. 3 dim.

    (a)   *na·hina·h=ni·hka pye·či-nepe·wi·hiyani.*
       'This is the first time you ever came and stayed overnight with me.' (K-Wap 102)

    (c)   *ni·na wi čihi·hiyanehe* 'if you had lived with me, you poor thing' (K-Auto 90)

    (d)   *a·kwi=mekoho owiye·ha wi čihi·hičini.* 'No one lives with me.' (K-FC 11)

(4.254) Diminutive TI(1)

    (a)   *e·ši-kehke netamo·hiya·ni* 'how I understand things to be, to the extent I do'
       (A 141D)

    (b)   *wi·h=ošehki tamo·hiya·ni* '(a few) things for me to wear' (A 128C)

    (c)   *awita=mekoho ki na ke·ko·h=mekoho iši-kehke netamo·hihkapa* (K-FC 418; tr. HP)
       "perhaps you do not know what to do"

(4.255) Diminutive TI(2)

    (a)   *taswi ne·hihto·hiya·ni* 'everything I may know how to make' (A 78D)

    (b)   *a·kwi=mekoho ke·ko·hi wi·h=paši-=mekoho -ahto·hiyanini.* (K-FC 35)
       'You (sg.) will have nothing at all.'

(4.256) Diminutive TI(3)

       wi·h=mi·či·hiči taši·hkamwa (K-BB 69)
       'she occupies herself with (getting) something to eat'

Verbs of Pretending to and Acting Like (§51)

51. AI verbs may be made from AI stems or TI(1) themes to denote a state or action that resembles that of the simple verb. These add secondary suffixes preceded by |-w| FORMTV (~ |-o(·)w| [§8.4]; cf. §34.3, 4.7, 4.8); a long |a·| that is subject to umlaut is replaced by |e·|.

Verbs of pretending are made from AI and TI verbs with a secondary suffix |-ehka·no| AI 'pretend' or |-ehka·so| AI 'pretend'. The vowel before the |-w| FORMTV that precedes this contracts with the following |-w-e-|, leaving a long vowel. These verbs usually indicate feigning, dissembling, or acting out in play or fantasy, but they sometimes have the meaning 'act like, make as if to, set about trying to'. To express the notion of pretending, there is also a periphrastic construction with |iši·hka·no-| AI or |išiwe·pi·hka·no-| AI 'pretend {so}' and a verbal complement (5.141a).

Verbs for actions that are like what the simple verb denotes but do not involve pretending are made with the secondary suffixes |-esi| AI (which does not contract) and |-a·tesi| AI.

Verbs of both these types may be derived from compound stems (**§70.2**).

51.1. Verbs of pretending from AI verbs. The more frequent of the two suffixes that make verbs of pretending is |-ehka·no| AI 'pretend'. It is used after AI stems ending in a vowel (4.257a-m, 4.262a), including umlauting |-a·| (4.257n-p), or a consonant (4.257q).

(4.257) AI + |-ehka·no| AI 'pretend'

  (a) *anwe·we·kome·hka·nowa* 'he pretends to snore' (← |anwe·we·kome·-| AI)
  (b) *apeno·ha·towe·hka·nowa* 'he pretends to talk like a child' (← |apeno·ha·towe·-| AI)
  (c) |inetone·mo·hka·no-| AI (← |inetone·mo-| AI 'speak {so}'):
         i ni=ča·hi we·či-inehinetone·mo·hka·noya·ni. (K-FC 186; tr. HP)
         "So that is why I am trying to make a speech."
  (d) *išišimo·hka·nowa* 'he pretends to speak with {such} a voice' (← |išišimo-| AI)
  (e) *kanakanawi·hka·nowa* 'he makes as if to give a speech' (K-SBSB 18, K-FC 228)
         (← |kanakanawi-| AI 'give a speech, say (formal) words')
  (f) *mayo·hka·nowa* 'he pretends to cry' (← |mayo·-| AI 'weep')
  (g) *mya·no·te·hka·nowa* 'she pretends to be menstruating' (← |mya·no·te·-| AI)
  (h) *no·tehkwe·we·hka·nowa* (← |no·tehkwe·we·-| AI 'sneak in with a girl'):
         e·h=ki·wi- .. -na·no·tehkwe·we·hka·nowa·či. (K-TYFB 7)
         'they went around making as if they were sneaking in with girls'
  (i) *tepowe·hka·nowa* 'he plays at holding a council' (K-W 167)
         (← |tepowe·-| AI 'deliberate, hold a council')
  (j) *wača·ho·hka·nowa* 'he pretends to cook' (A 2C) (← |wača·ho-| AI)
  (k) *wa·wana·si·hka·nowa* 'he pretends not to know how to climb' (← |wa·wana·si·-| AI)
  (l) *we·pesi·hi·hka·nowa* 'he pretends to be crazy' (← |we·pesi·hi-| AI 'be crazy')
  (m) |wi·seni·hka·no·hi-| AI dim. ← |wi·seni·hka·no-| AI (← |wi·seni-| AI 'eat'):
         wi·seni·hka·no·hino=wi na=meko. 'Make like you're eating (you sg.)!' (K-Wap 46)
         (Men's conventional invitation to start eating.)
  (n) *neneka·pye·hka·nowa* 'he pretends to have chills' (← |neneka·pya·-| AI)
  (o) *nepe·hka·nowa* 'he pretends to sleep' (← |nepa·-| AI)
  (p) *ši·še·hka·nowa* 'he pretends to hunt' (← |ši·ša·-| AI)
  (q) *nepo·hka·nowa* 'he pretends to be dead' (← |nep-| AI 'die, be dead')

Stems in |-išin| AI 'lie' (4.74*a*) replace this with the virtual final |-išimo| AI (cf. 4.13, 4.196).

(4.258) AI in |-išin| AI 'lie' + |-ehka·no| AI 'pretend'

mehkawišimo·hka·nowa 'he pretends to stumble' (C-MWP 10)
(← |mehkawišin-| AI 'stumble')

51.2. Verbs of pretending from TI verbs. The suffix |-ehka·no| AI 'pretend' is also the usual one used with TI(1) verbs. It is added to the theme of the verb, including |-am| TI(1) th., which has the same treatment as a consonant-final AI stem, inserting formative |-o·w| with contraction. (The other TI classes are not attested in this construction.) These AI derivatives may be made from ordinary TI's or objectless TI's.

(4.259) TI(1) + |-ehka·no| AI 'pretend'

(a) *pehtatahamo·hka·nowaki* AI 'they (thunderers) pretend to strike by accident'
(K-D 26) (← |pehtatah-| TI(1) 'strike accidentally')

(b) *a·hkwamatamo·hka·nowa* AI 'he pretends to be sick' (K-T 12, K-MFS 37;
S-RSW 36) (← |a·hkwamat-| TI(1)-O 'be sick')

(c) *wa·wane·netamo·hka·nowa* AI 'he pretends not to know' (K-SF 25)
(← |wa·wane·net-| TI(1), TI(1)-O 'fail to know')

An AI verb of pretending derived from a TI theme may also be used as a transitivized verb (AI+O) with an object of either gender (5.147*bc*).

51.3. Verbs of pretending with |-ehka·so| AI. Less commonly, verbs of pretending are made from AI stems and TI(1) themes with the variant suffix |-ehka·so| AI 'pretend'.

(4.260) AI or TI(1) + |-ehka·so| AI 'pretend'

(a) *owi·wi·hka·sowa* 'he pretends to be married' (K-Words 32)

(b) *a·hkwamatamo·hka·sowa* 'he pretends to be sick' (JP-GTF 45) (cf. 4.259*a*)

This is, however, the variant of the suffix that is strongly favored in the formation of the verbs of pretending that are freely made from nouns, which are based on the derived verb of being made with |-i| AI 'be' (§47, 4.235, 236); it is identical with the suffix added directly to nouns and possessed themes in semantically similar derivatives (§49.3, 4.246; §49.4, 4.247).

(4.261) Verb of being + |-ehka·so| AI 'pretend'

(a) *e·škiki·hi·hka·sowa* 'he pretends to be a young person'

(b) *kehčineniwi·hka·sowa* 'he acts as though he is a great man' (K-BHD 131)

(c) *metemo·hi·hka·sowa* 'he pretends to be an old woman'

(d) *pašito·hi·hka·sowa* 'he pretends to be an old man'

(e) *pešekwa·hi·hka·sowa* 'he pretends to be divorced' (K-MFS 19)

(f) *še·škesi·hi·hka·sowa* 'she pretends to be a virgin'

(4.262) Verb of being + |-ehka·no| AI 'pretend'

(a) *pešekesiwi·hka·nowa* 'he pretends to be a deer' (K-JM 20)

Presumably |we·pesi·hi·hka·no-| AI 'pretend to be crazy' (4.257*l*) has |-ehka·no| AI because the underlying AI has been lexicalized as 'be crazy' rather than 'be a crazy person' (*we·pesi·ha*), which is explicitly *we·pesi·hiwiwa*.

51.4. Verbs of similar state or action with |-esi| AI or |-a·tesi| AI. The secondary finals |-esi| AI and |-a·tesi| AI make derivatives of AI stems and TI(1) themes that have the added meaning 'be or act as if, be the kind that, have the nature or manner of' (4.263). First person diminutive forms with these finals appear to have a self-deprecating flavor (4.264*ab*).

(4.263) AI or TI(1) + |-esi| AI or |-a·tesi| AI meaning 'be or act as if', etc.

(a) *kekye·peše·wesiwa* 'he's like he's deaf' (K-SSP 36; AW)
(← |kekye·peše·-| AI 'be deaf')

(b) *ke·hči-a·hkwamatamo·wesita* 'one who is like he is seriously sick' (K-FASB 49)
      (← *kehči* PV 'greatly', |a·hkwamat-| TI(1)-O 'be sick')

(c) *kekye·peše·wa·tesiwa* 'he's like he's deaf' (AW; given as synonymous with 4.262*a*);
      mya·ši_kekye·peše·wa·tesiwa 'he is sort of hard of hearing' (K-Med 1.56R)

(d) *e·h=opiškwe·če·wa·tesiči=meko·po·si.* (K-MOR 11)
      'Her swollen belly put her in an advanced condition.'

(e) *apina=meko e·h=patapatakwa·naki·kwe·wa·tesiniči.* 'He was even one with
      dreamy, half-closed eyes.' (K- 7N)

(f) *ki·nwa·wa=wi·na nana·ši ki·h=po·nwe·we·ti·wesipwa!?* (K-W 525)
      'You two will NEVER stop bickering!'

(4.264) AI + |-esi| AI or |-a·tesi| AI and |-·hi| DIM

(a) *aše=koh=meko nenatonehkwe·we·wesi·hipena* 'we're just looking for women'
      (K-IML 4)
      (← |natonehkwe·we·-| AI 'seek women')

(b) *aše=meko_ni·h=kokwe·tepye·hike·wa·tesi·hi.* 'I just want to try and write a little.'
      (EJ diary) (← |kokwe·tepye·hike·-| AI 'try to write'.

(c) *e·h=anemi-=meko -tanwe·we·ti·wesi·hiwa·či.* (K-SF 79A)
      'And they were as if quarreling on the way.' (← |tanwe·we·ti·-| AI 'quarrel')

Derived Verbs for Inanimate and Non-Controlling Subjects (§52)

52. Some derivatives furnish stems for use with inanimate or non-sentient arguments that are
not provided for by the ordinary inflections of an appropriate primary verb.

52.1. II stems derived from AI stems. AI stems that lack an II counterpart may derive a
stem for use with an inanimate subject. These are verbs that prototypically have a human being
or at least a sentient being as subject. Occasionally, however, this derivative may also be made
from an AI that is matched by an II if the inanimate subject is the transformation of a person or
represents a person metaphorically or by synecdoche, or to indicate that an inanimate subject is
affected the way a person would be. For most stems this derived stem is made with the
secondary final |-·mikat| II ABSTR (4.265), but stems that have a medial followed by |-e·| AI
ABSTR add |-ya·| II ABSTR (2.266*abcfgh*), and stems with a medial followed by |-Ø| AI ABSTR add
|-e·ya·| II ABSTR (4.266*de*).

Before |-·mikat| II ABSTR a short vowel is lengthened, |o·| is inserted after a consonant, and
umlauting |a·| is replaced by |e·|; the stem |i-| AI 'say {so}' is replaced by |iyo·-|.

(4.265) Stems derived from AI's with |-·mikat| II ABSTR

(a) *ahkwa·čimo·mikatwi* II 'the story goes {so far}' (← |ahkwa·čimo-| AI)

(b) *ako·si·paho·mikatwi* II 'it runs up (the tree)' (Jones 1907:96.19; of a head)
      (← |ako·si·paho-| AI 'climb at a run')

(c) *anakwi·mikatwi* II 'it has fat on it' (Jones 1907:176.11) (← |anakwi-| AI 'be fat')

(d) *aniwise·mikatwi* II 'it goes fast' (S-Shak 38, of a boat) (← |aniwisa·-| AI 'run fast')

(e) *a·ya·nehko·ti·mikato·ni* II 'each of them (inan.) comes after another'
      (← |a·ya·nehko·ti·-| AI 'they follow each other')

(f) *ihe·mikatwi* II 'it goes {somewhere}' (← |iha·| AI)

(g) *ihketo·mikatwi* II 'it says {so}' (← |ihketo-| AI)

(h)   *išiso mikatwi* II 'its name is {so}' (← |išiso-| AI)

(i)   *iyo mikatwi* II 'it says {so}' (← |i-| AI)

(j)   *ki·kesi mikatwi* II 'it becomes strong' (K-MP4 67)
      (← |ki·kesi-| AI 'be vigorous, have stamina, regain one's strength)

(k)   *ki·wa·tesi mikatwi* II 'it is lonesome' (K-FC 509; a sacred pack after the owners'
      deaths)
      (← |ki·wa·tesi-| AI 'be lonely'; cf. |ki·wa·ča·-| II 'it (as a place) is lonely')

(l)   *ki·wite mikatwi* II 'it stays' (← |ki·wita·-| AI)

(m)   *maneto·wi mikatwi* II 'it has manitou power' (← |maneto·wi-| AI)

(n)   *mayo mikatwi* II 'it weeps' (← |mayo·-| AI)
      (Cf. *mayo·wi* II 'it weeps' in ritual songs.)

(o)   *mi·ša·te·nemo mikatwi* II 'it is proud, glad' (← |mi·ša·te·nemo-| AI)

(p)   *mi·škawesi mikatwi* II 'it is strong' (← |mi·škawesi-| AI 'be strong'; cf. |mi·škawa·-| II)

(q)   *naki mikatwi* II 'it stops' (Jones 1907:362.9, of rising water)

(r)   *nasata·wesi mikaywi* II 'it is intolerant, exclusionary'
      (← |nasata·esi-| AI 'be unfriendly, standoffish';
      cf. |nasata·wa·-| II 'be unfriendly')

(s)   *nehta·we mikatwi* II 'it makes a killing' (← |nehta·we·-| AI; 4.282*b*):
      e·h=okima·wi-nehta·we mikahki 'it has slain a chief' (K-B 280)

(t)   *nemaso mikatwi* II 'it stands' (← |nemaso-| AI 'stand'; cf. |nemate·-| II 'stand'):
      aseni=či·hi e·h=nemaso mikateniki 'they found a stone standing there' (K-BS 6;
      the stone is the transformation of a boy)

(u)   *nepo mikatwi* II 'it died' (← |nep-| AI 'die')

(v)   *ne·se mikatwi* II 'it survives' (← |ne·se·-| AI 'be cured, survive')

(w)   *pana·tesi mikatwi* II 'it is destroyed, lost' (← |pana·tesi-| AI 'lose one's life, one's
      mind, consciousness'; cf. |pana·ča·-| II 'be ruined, be broken'):
      nekoti mi·so·ni e·h=pana·tesi mikatokwe·ni. (SP-MortB 45) 'One name has been
      lost.' (Great Spirit's announcement of a person's death.)
      e·h=pana·tesi mikateniki omehtose·neniwiwenwa·wi (JoP-MortH 1)
      'when their lives are lost' (ritual periphrasis for 'when they die')

(x)   *peno mikatwi* II 'it goes away' (← |peno-| AI)

(y)   *pye mikatwi* II 'it comes' (← |pya·-| AI)

(z)   *se·kesi mikatwi* II 'it is frightened' (← |se·kesi-| AI)

(aa) *šawesi mikatwi* II 'it is hungry' (K-OKUT 13, of fire) (← |šawesi-| AI)

(bb) *te·pwe mikatwi* II 'it is true' (← |te·pwe·-| AI 'speak the truth')

(cc) *wi·seni mikatwi* II 'it eats' (← |wi·seni-| AI)

(dd) *wi·šikesi mikatwi* II 'it is powerful' (K-FC 142, of a protective sacred pack;
      K-FC 153, of medicine with powers derived from a sacred pack)
      (← |wi·šikesi-| AI 'be strong, powerful'; cf. |wi·šikya·-| II 'be powerful, tough')

(4.266) Stems derived from AI's with |-ya·| II ABSTR

(a)   *asa·wikane·ya·wi* II 'it is a yellow bone' (cf. |wa·kikane·-| AI 'have a crooked bone')

(b)   *mama·kikane·ya·wani* II 'they are big bones'

(c)   *meškwataye·ya·wi* II 'it has a red front' (C-RS 5, of a coat)
      (← |meškwataye·-| AI 'have a red belly')

(d) *mi·sa·hkoniwipehkwane·ya·wi* II 'it has a mossy roof'
     (cf. |mamakwipehkwan-| AI 'have a lumpy back')

(e) *pekeše·wa·naketone·ya·wi* II 'it is a smoky hole'
     (cf. |pemiwa·naketon-| AI 'have a greasy mouth')

(f) *pi·ya·pehkowika·te·ya·wi* II 'it has iron legs' (JB-Tiger 17, of chairs)
     (cf. |šo·škika·te·-| AI 'straighten one's leg')

(g) *wa·siki·nikome·ya·wi* II 'it has a sharp point'
     (← |wa·siki·nikome·-| AI 'have a sharp nose, beak')

(h) *wa·siki·nitepe·ya·wi* II 'it has a sharp-pointed top' (K-FW 9, of a church steeple)
     (cf. |makitepe·-| AI 'have a big head')

52.2. II stems derived from TI themes. The suffix |-·mikat| II ABSTR is also added to TI themes to make verbs with inanimate subjects.

(4.267) Stems derived from TI themes with |-·mikat| II ABSTR

(a) *aka·wa·tamo·mikatwi* II 'it desires' (K-FC 207, with a sentential complement)

(b) *a·hkwamatamo·mikatwi* II 'it is sick' (K-FC 364)

(c) *kehke·netamo·mikatwi* II 'it has consciousness' (K-B 246, K-WYB 107)

(d) *menwe·netamo·mikatwi* II 'it is pleased' (K-FC 160)

(e) *tahka·hkoškamo·mikatwi* II 'it casts a shadow' (X2-SAR 53)

(f) *we·te·wihto·mikatwi* II (← |we·te·wiht-| TI(2) [only with a negative]):
     e·h=pwa·wi-=meko -we·te·wihto·mikateniki 'it didn't even make a dent' (K-RL 23)

(g) *wi·sakamatamo·mikatwi* II 'it feels pain' (K-FC 364)

The II stems derived from TI's are generally objectless, or ambiguously transitive (4.267*af*), but some forms of this type have clear syntactic objects (4.268), making them rare examples of the II+O verbal type (cf. 4.241). As with objectless TI's that can be transitivized (TI-O+O; 2.87-88), the object may be of either gender. These derivatives thus furnish a way to describe an inanimate acting on an inanimate or a non-sentient animate, combinations of arguments that are not provided for in the inflectional paradigms of transitive verbs.

(4.268) TI theme with |-·mikat| II ABSTR and animate syntactic object
     no·nane·htamo·mikatwi II+O 'its mouth is stuffed full of O2'
        (← |no·nane·ht-| TI(1)):
     na·hina·hi no·nane·htamo·mikahki asapye·hi. (C-Ston 32)
        'when it couldn't get any more Indian hemp (obv. pl.) in its mouth'

52.3. AI stems for subjects not in control. The AI suffix |-·mikesi| AI ABSTR makes verbs that indicate that an action that is usually actively controlled by a sentient subject is performed without the subject being in control, either because it is non-sentient (but grammatically animate) or because what it does is directly controlled by higher powers. These verbs are uncommon. Before this suffix stems are treated as before the TI counterpart (§52.1).

(4.269) Stems derived from AI's with |-·mikesi| AI ABSTR

(a) *ihe·mikesiwa* AI 'he (thing) goes {somewhere}' (S-RSW 25)

(b) *pemehke·mikesiwa* AI 'he (person) is carried past, along' (JP-WMD 28)

(c) *peno·mikesiwa* AI 'he (thing) departs' (K-Auto 169),
     'he (person) is borne away, departs this earth' (K-WYB 200; 2.8)

52.4. II stems from two-gender stems. A few intransitive stems may be used with a subject of either gender but optionally add |-·mikat| to make an explicit II stem. The attested examples are |(i)t(o)-| 'be {so}, fare {so}' (*itwa* AI, *towi* II) and stems with the final |-ika·pa·| AI,II 'stand'.

(4.270) Explicit II derived from undifferentiated intransitive stems

    (a)   *itoˑmikatwi* II 'it is {so}':

          wiˑh=itoˑmikahki kiˑyaˑnaˑni 'how our lives are to be' (SP-MortB 25)

    (b)   *kiˑwikaˑpaˑmikatwi* II 'it stands about' (K-BHD 71, K-Spot 174, 181)

The final |-isaˑ| AI,II is widely used with a subject of either gender, but in at least a few stems it is found only with added |-ˑmikat| if the subject is inanimate (4.265*d*).

52.5. Causatives from stems in |-ˑmikesi| AI, |-ˑmikat| II. The regular formation of TA and TI(2) causatives from AI stems (§54.9) extends also to stems derived with |-ˑmikesi| AI, |-ˑmikat| II ABSTR (4.334-335). In this derivation the abstract final |-esi| AI, |-at| II drops (cf. 4.12), and these causatives may thus be analyzed as made specifically from the AI stem, in conformity with the regular pattern.

Intransitives Derived from Transitives (§53)

53. Several kinds of intransitive stems are derived from transitive stems. In some cases an AI is derived from a TA, or an intransitive pair is derived from a transitive pair. In other cases an AI or an intransitive pair is derived from a TI stem or a virtual TI stem that substitutes for the TA stem.

53.1. Detransitive verbs. Transitive verbs make three kinds of detransitivized counterparts, which lose the valence for a primary object. General detransitives refer to performing the action as such, considered as an activity of the subject affecting unspecified people or things in general. Indefinite detransitives refer to action on an indefinite person (X; §18.4), which may have a specific cross-reference to an indefinite person referred to inflectionally in the same context (e.g., A 16E, 52C). There is also a small class of specialized detransitives that imply action on a characteristic object of animate gender.

53.2. General detransitives. All general detransitives are made from TI stems. If the corresponding TA stem does not end in |-N| or |-aw|, the general detransitive is made in most cases by suffixing |-ikeˑ| AI DETRANS to the TI stem; before this, |t| has the regular mutation to |č| (§13.1). Some final pairs with a TA in |-N| also follow this pattern (4.271*o*). In the examples that follow, the TI stem that the AI derivative is made on may be deduced by subtracting *-ikeˑ*; if this suffix is preceded by *č*, the primary stem is written out and specified as TI(1) or TI(2).

    (4.271) General detransitives with |-ikeˑ| AI DETRANS

        (a)   *apwaˑčikeˑwa* 'he roasts on a scaffold' (← |apwaˑt-| TI(1) 'roast')

        (b)   *anweˑweˑsikeˑwa* 'he fires a shot'

        (c)   *čiˑkakohikeˑwa* 'he sweeps'

        (d)   *kehkahikeˑwa* 'he designates'

        (e)   *kepiˑhikeˑwa* 'he fences, encloses an area with a fence'

        (f)   *koˑkenikeˑwa* 'he washes, does washing'

        (g)   *kwaˑškwačikeˑwa* 'he drops food from his mouth' (← |kwaˑškwat-| TI(1))

        (h)   *nasaˑhkohikeˑwa* 'he roasts meat on a spit'

        (i)   *naˑkataweˑnečikeˑwa* 'he watches over things' (← |naˑkataweˑnet-| TI(1))

        (j)   *naˑčineˑhikeˑwa* 'he buys'

        (k)   *nekwačihikeˑwa* 'he hills (crops)'

        (l)   *paˑškesikeˑwa* 'he shoots a firearm'

(m) *si·kahike·wa* 'he serves (food)'
(n) *si·kina·sike·wa* 'he lets the pot boil over'
(o) *so·kihčike·wa* 'he ties things' (← |so·kiht-| TI(2))
(p) *tanwe·we·počike·wa* 'he can be heard filing or sawing' (← |tanwe·we·pot-| TI(2))
(q) *tawenike·wa* 'he clears things away, does the clearing, clears a space'
(r) *wa·wa·pačike·wa* 'he makes a choice, chooses' (← |wa·wa·pat-| TI(1) 'choose')
(s) *wi·škopanohike·wa* 'he sweetens food, uses sugar'

TI's in |t| that are matched by a TA in |N| usually add |-kye·| AI DETRANS, before which the stem-final |t| is replaced by |h| (cf. **§9.1**). The same pattern of derivation is found with the many TA's in |N| that have no idiomatic TI beside them; these may be analyzed as having a virtual TI as the basis of the detransitive derivative.

(4.272) General detransitives with |-kye·| AI DETRANS
(a) *anahpihkye·wa* 'she gives wedding garments to a new bride' (K-ManMa 2)
   (cf. |anahpiN-| TA 'dress (a new bride) in wedding garments')
(b) *anohka·hkye·wa* 'he gives orders' (cf. |anohka·N-| TA)
(c) *ihkye·wa* 'he says {so}' (← |iN-| TA, |it-| TI(1) 'say {so} to')
(d) *kano·hkye·wa* 'he speaks' (← |kano·N-| TA, |kano·t-| TI(1) 'speak to')
(e) *matahkye·wa* 'he caught up' (← |mataN-| TA, |matat-| TI(1) 'overtake, catch up to')
(f) *mečiminahkye·wa* 'he commits murder' (cf. |mečiminaN-| TA 'murder')
(g) *mi·hkye·wa* AI+O 'he gives O2 away' (cf. |mi·N-| TA+O 'give O2 to')
(h) *wa·pato·hkye·wa* AI(+O) 'he shows something, O2' (cf. |wa·pato·N-| TA 'show to')

In at least one case a TA in |N| that refers to speaking optionally adds |-mo| AI 'speak, make sound orally' after |-kye·| AI DETRANS, making |-kye·mo| AI DETRANS.

(4.273) General detransitive with |-kye·mo| AI DETRANS
kano·hkye·mowa 'he speaks' (← |kano·N-| 'speak to'; cf. 4.272d) (K-B 61)

In some cases the detransitive stem specifies action on a semantically nominal element that is present in the primary stem as a derived initial or a medial.

(4.274) General detransitives in |-ike·| AI DETRANS with internal object
(a) *e·mehkwa·nahike·wa* 'he uses a spoon' (|e·mehkwa·n-| 'spoon')
(b) *kečiče·pihkahike·wa* 'he pulls a stump' (|-če·pihk-| 'root')
(c) *mo·naškahike·wa* 'he digs weeds' (|-ašk-| 'grass, weed')
(d) *no·hka·mehkonike·wa* 'he digs to make soft earth' (|-a·mehkw-| 'earth surface')
(e) *pakapahkwe·hike·wa* 'he knocks on the wall' (|-apahkwe·-| 'wall of house')
(f) *wi·ke·čihkeše·we·nike·wa* 'he carefully stirs the fire' (|-hkeše·we·-| 'coals')

Some detransitives have an idiomatic meaning.

(4.275) General detransitives in |-ike·| AI DETRANS with idiomatic meanings
(a) *ahčike·wa* AI, AI+O 'he plants (O2)' (cf. |aht-| TI(2) 'have; put {somewhere}')
(b) *kota·hkohike·wa* AI, AI+O 'he practices shooting (using O2 as a target)'
   (← |kot-| 'try', |-a·hkw-| 'extended solid' [4.61], |-ah| TI(1) 'act on by tool')
(c) *mawinačike·wa* 'he goes and grabs things' (cf. |mawinat-| TI(1) 'run at')
(d) *sakanahkenike·wa* 'he signs his name', *lit.* 'touches the tip (of the pen)'

In many cases the action is one that can be performed only on animate objects, and the TI stem used in the derivation has only a virtual existence and is never found inflected as such. The implied objects in such cases may be people, horses, or anything else referred to by a grammatically animate noun.

(4.276) General detransitives in |-ike·| AI DETRANS with people as implied object

    (a)   *ki·škikwe·šike·wa* 'he cuts off heads' (X2-SAR 170)

    (b)   *ni·mihčike·wa* 'he gives a dance'

    (c)   *no·še·hčike·wa* 'she serves as a midwife'

    (d)   *wa·wa·pačike·wa* 'he chooses a wife' (K-MortE 47) (cf. 4.271*r*)

    (e)   *wi·swihčike·wa* 'he does the naming' (GBC-Wapan 48)

(4.277) General detransitives in |-ike·| AI DETRANS with a horse as implied object

    (a)   *ki·ški·škahike·wa* 'he whips his horse'

    (b)   *nakehkwe·nike·wa* 'he reins in his horse'

    (c)   *saka·pye·nike·wa* 'he leads a horse'

    (d)   *sakapičike·wa* 'he ties up his horse'

    (e)   *tanahkye·hčike·wa* 'he puts his horse to pasture'

(4.278) General detransitives in |-ike·| AI DETRANS with other animates as implied object

    (a)   *anaho·čike·wa* 'he readies a drum for use (filling with water or tying on drumhead)'
        (cf. |anaho·N-| TA 'fill, fill a container with; tie drumhead on (drum)')

    (b)   *anwe·we·hike·wa* 'he drums' (< |anwe·we·h-| TI(1); cf. |anwe·we·hw-| TA)

    (c)   *asa·we·kisike·wa* 'she tans hides' (cf. |asa·we·kisw-| TA 'tan')

    (d)   *mo·nike·wa* 'he plucks fowl' (cf. |mo·n-| TA)

    (e)   *pahte·hčike·wa* 'he puffs on a pipe to start it'
        (as if < *|pahte·ht-| TI(1); cf. |pahte·hpw-| TA 'puff on him (a pipe)')

The prototypical (or only) undergoers of the verbal actions in (4.278) are things referred to by nouns of animate gender: drums, hides, birds, and pipes. In the case of (4.278*b*) the AI and its underlying TI can be used when a bowl or something else of inanimate gender is used as a drum, but an actual drum, which would ordinarily be the implied undergoer of the AI, is always animate.

For many stems that have the shape of general detransitives in |-ike·| AI DETRANS there is no attested primary transitive stem.

(4.279) General detransitives in |-ike·| AI DETRANS with no transitive stem attested

    (a)   *ahpaškinanišike·wa* 'he butchers on leaves' (Jones 1907:74.1)
        (cf. |ahpaškinanih-| TA 'butcher on leaves')

    (b)   *kohkahike·wa* 'he makes a bridge' (Jones 1911:749)

    (c)   *pema·sike·wa* 'he (sun) goes shining': *pe·ma·sika·ta* 'the Sun'

    (d)   *peškone·nawačike·wa* 'he gets the fire started with something'

    (e)   *tepatohačike·wa* AI+O 'he follows his advice and example'

    (f)   *wa·sesike·wa* 'he (sun) lights things up'

Some combinations of TI final and |-ike·| AI DETRANS can or must be considered lexicalized as derived primary finals with specialized meanings.

(4.280) Stems with |-esike·| AI 'cook' (← |-es| TI(1) [4.96*c*; p. 276] + |-ike·| AI DETRANS)

    (a)   *ki·šesike·wa* 'he's through cooking'

    (b)   *nana·hesike·wa* 'he attends to the cooking'

(4.281) Stems with |-hčike·| AI 'do things' (← |-ht| TI(2) [4.86*a*] + |-ike·| AI DETRANS)

    (a)   *išihčike·wa* 'he does things {so}'
        (|išiht-| TI(2) 'make {so}' has a different meaning)

    (b)   *menwihčike·wa* 'he does things well' (no TI attested)

    (c)   *pešikwihčike·wa* 'he does the right thing' (no TI attested)

(4.282) Stems with |-a·hkonike·| AI 'make, impose law, rules'

> (← |-a·hkw-| 'extended solid' [4.61], |-en| TI(1) [4.97] + |-ike·| AI DETRANS)

    (a)   *menwa·hkonike·wa* 'he has a good rule, law'

    (b)   *sanaka·hkonike·wa* 'he sets difficult rules'

The ostensible final |-esike·| AI 'cook' (4.280) is synonymous with |-ese·hkwe·| AI 'cook', a derived primary final that also incorporates, with the same semantic narrowing, the primary final |-es| TI(1) 'act on by fire, heat, cooking, shooting with a firearm, smoking tobacco, boiling medicine'.

For a few verbs a general detransitive is made with the suffix |-a·we·| AI DETRANS (4.283*a-c*) or |-a·nawe·| AI DETRANS (4.283*d-f*).

(4.283) General detransitives with |-a·we·| AI DETRANS and |-a·nawe·| AI DETRANS.

    (a)   *na·pita·we·wa* 'he has something around his neck'
> (← |na·pit-| TI(2) 'have around the neck')

    (b)   *nehta·we·wa* 'he kills something, makes a killing' (← |neht-| TI(2) 'kill')

    (c)   *nekoška·we·wa* 'he occupies territory' (← |nekošk-| TI(1) 'cover by foot or body')

    (d)   *ahkoška·nawe·wa* 'he wears out clothes' (← |ahkošk-| TI(1) 'wear out')

    (e)   *kaškihta·nawe·wa* 'he buys things' (← |kaškiht-| TI(2) 'buy')

    (f)   *tawa·kone·ška·nawe·wa* 'he clears the ground of snow with his feet' (taw-| 'clear' + |-a·kone·-| 'snow' + |-ešk| TI(1) 'act on by foot or body') (K-MWL 17)

The verb |apwi·h-| TA, |apwi·ht-| TI(2) 'wait for' and the finals derived from it add |-esi| AI to the TI stem.

(4.284) General detransitives with |-esi| AI DETRANS

    (a)   *a·nawapwi·htesiwa* 'he gave up waiting' (← |a·nawapwi·ht-| TI(2))

    (b)   *tanapwi·htesiwa* 'he was waiting ({somewhere})' (← |tanapwi·ht-| TI(2))

There is no consistent pattern for forming a general detransitive if the TA of a stem pair ends in |-aw|. Stems with the final |-i·hkaw| TA, |-i·hk| TI(1) 'deal with' (4.94*d*) and the stem |wi·to·hkaw-| TA, |wi·to·hk-| TI(1) (4.285*j*) regularly make general detransitives as if with a suffix |-a·so| AI DETRANS added to the TI. A few stems and finals that do not have a TA in |-aw| also make a general detransitive with |-a·so|; one verb adds |-a·so| after the TA stem (4.285*g*).

(4.285) General detransitive stems with |-a·so| AI DETRANS

    (a)   *ahta·sowa* 'he puts something away' (← |aht-| TI(2) 'put {somewhere}')

    (b)   *akita·sowa* 'he counts' (← |akim-| TA, |akit-| TI(1) 'count')

    (c)   *kaški·hka·sowa* 'he persuades, gets permission' (cf. |kaški·hkaw-| TA 'persuade')

    (d)   *kehči·hka·sowa* 'he is stubborn, refuses'
> (cf. |kehči·hkaw-| TA 'persist with, keep after, devote all efforts to')

    (e)   *koči·hka·sowa* 'he tries to persuade, tries to be allowed'
> (cf. |koči·hkaw-| TA 'try to persuade')

    (f)   *ma·či·hka·sowa* 'he pesters, presses hard' (cf. |ma·či·hkaw-| TA 'press hard')

    (g)   *mehkawa·sowa* 'he finds something, things' (← |mehkaw-| TA 'find')

    (h)   *pemaho·ta·sowa* 'he drags a load along, carries a load along in a vehicle'
> (← |pemaho·t-| TI(2) 'drag along')

    (i)   *pi·taha·sowa* AI 'he buries things in a storage pit' (← |pi·tah-| TI(1) 'bury')

    (j)   *wi·to·hka·sowa* 'he joins in, takes part' (cf. |wi·to·hkaw-| TA 'cooperate with' [4.94*d*])

Two stems with |-inaw| TA, |-in| TI(1) 'regard, feel about' (4.94*g*) make a general detransitive as if with a suffix |-ehkwe·| AI DETRANS added to the TA, contracting to |-ina·hkwe·| AI (4.286*ab*). The stem |pat-| TA 'singe the hair off in a fire' uniquely has |-ahkwe·| AI DETRANS (4.286*c*).

(4.286) General detransitive stems with |-ehkwe·| AI and |-ahkwe·| AI

    (a)   *ketemina·hkwe wa* 'he bestows a blessing' (← |keteminaw-| TA 'pity, bless')

    (b)   *mačina·hkwe wa* 'he challenges' (← |mačinaw-| TA 'dare against, challenge')

    (c)   *patahkwe wa* 'he singes the hair off in a fire' (← |pat-| TA 'singe the hair off')

For some transitive verbs the equivalent of a corresponding detransitive is formed with a primary final that is suppletive to the transitive final pair. For example, beside stems with |-ehtaw| TA, |-eht| TI(1) 'hear, listen to' (like *nenohtawe wa* TA, *nenohtamwa* TI(1) 'he understands him, it'; 4.94*h*) and the stem *pesetawe wa* TA, *pesetamwa* TI(1) 'he listens to him, it' (with |-etaw| TA, |-et| TI(1) 'pay attention or regard to'; 4.94*i*) there are stems with |-eše·| AI 'hear, listen': *nenoše wa* AI 'he understands', *peseše wa* AI 'he listens'. In other cases the derivation is simply irregular: *ašatwa* 'he feeds people' (usually 'he gives a "return" feast (for the family ceremonially adopting him to replace their deceased relative)') (← |ašam-| TA 'feed'); *wi·če we wa* 'he goes along (on the trip, journey)' (← |wi·te·m-| TA 'accompany, go with').

A general detransitive may take a secondary object (**§22.3**) or an instrumental oblique (**§22.4(g)**). A detransitive is commonly used with a secondary object if it is lexicalized with a narrowed meaning, and also in some cases with an apparent implication that there is a general activity, that can be named as such, which affects the object.

(4.287) General detransitive with secondary object

    (a)   *wa pikonani si·kahike no* 'dish out the pumpkins!' (K-ECRP 147)
                (|si·kahike·-| AI+O 'serve as food' ← |si·kah-| TI(1) 'dish out, ladle, spill' [4.270*m*])

    (b)   *ča·ki=meko ·='ni a·mihtahi pa·hpa·hkenike yakwe ota·hwi nemwa wani.* (C-O 10)
           'We should then ransack *all* their stuff.'
                (|pa·hpa·hkenike·-| AI+O 'ransack' ← |CV+| RED1, |pa·hkenike·-| AI 'open, uncover things' ← |pa·hken-| TI(1) 'open, uncover')

    (c)   *e·h=pahkwe šike niči owi neno ni* 'she (obv.) cut off a piece of fat' (K-WWB 6)
                (|pahkwe·šike·-| AI 'cut piece(s) off thing(s)' ← |pahkwe·š-| TI(1) 'cut a piece off')

(4.288) General detransitive with instrumental oblique

    (a)   *meškwa·swa waki so·kiso·kihčike pi* (A 93B) 'they were tied with yarn-belts'
                (|CVCV+| RED2, |so·kihčike·-| AI 'tie things' ← |so·kiht-| TI(2) 'tie')

53.3. Indefinite detransitives. Indefinite detransitives are formed with several secondary finals, all ending in |e·|. The selection of the final is largely determined by the shape of the TA stem, but for some stems the selection is determined lexically, and some doublets are attested. For many transitive stems no derivative of this kind is found. In the following examples the indefinite object is glossed 'X'; translations may omit this or may use 'people', 'one', 'you', or 'us' in an indefinite sense.

The most general of these suffixes is |-iwe·| AI DETRANS, which may be considered the default suffix. After a stem in |-w| the |i| of this suffix is treated like |e| and the suffix appears as *-owe·* (**§11.3**, 1.139).

(4.289) Indefinite detransitives with |-iwe·| AI DETRANS

    (a)   *išiwe wa* 'he says {so} to X' (← |iN-| TA 'say {so} to')

    (b)   *kano·šiwe wa* 'he speaks to X' (← |kano·N-| TA 'speak to')

    (c)   *mi·hkečihiwe wa* 'he doctors X' (← |mi·hkečih-| TA 'doctor')

    (d)   *mi·šiwe wa* AI+O 'he gives O2 to X' (← |mi·N-| TA+O 'give O2 to')

    (e)   *nepe wowe wa* 'he spends the night, stays overnight with X'
                (← |nepe·w-| TA 'sleep at the house of')

(f)   *nešiwe·wa* 'he kills X' (← |neS-| TA 'kill'; cf. 4.290*d*)

(g)   *ne·wowe·wa* 'he sees X' (← |ne·w-| TA 'see')

(h)   *pemowe·wa* 'he shoots X' (← |pemw-| TA 'shoot with an arrow')

(i)   *sakipowe·wa* 'he bites X' (← |sakipw-| TA 'bite')

(j)   *tepa·šiwe·wa* 'he loves X' (← |tepa·N-| TA 'love')

Some TA stems ending in |N| that derive a general detransitive with |-kye·| AI DETRANS (4.272) use this as an indefinite detransitive as well.

(4.290) Indefinite detransitives with |-kye·| AI DETRANS

(a)   *anohka·hkye·wa* 'he gives orders to X' (← |anohka·N-| TA) (cf. 4.272*b*):

   1)   *ki·h=anohka·hkye wi·h=natone·hamo·neki.* (K-FC 34)

       'You can order people to look for some for you.'

   2)   *e·h=anohka·hkye·či wi·h=natomemeči.* (K-MMB 9)

       'He ordered someone to summon him (obv.).'

(b)   *kano·hkye·wa* 'he speaks to X' (← |kano·N-| 'speak to') (cf. 4.272*d*):

A few stems make an indefinite detransitive with |-ehkye·| AI DETRANS or in at least one case |-ahkye·| AI DETRANS.

(4.291) Indefinite detransitives with |-ehkye·|, -ahkye·| AI DETRANS

(a)   *kosehkye·wa* 'he fears X, gets frightened' (← |koS-| TA 'fear')

(b)   *mešenahkye·wa* 'he arrests, captures X' (← |mešen-| TA 'arrest, capture')

(c)   *nawasohkye·wa* 'he wins the race, outruns the others' (← |nawasw-| TA 'outrun')

(d)   *nesehkye·wa* 'he kills X' (← |neS-| TA 'kill'; cf. 4.288*f*)

Some TA stems in |m| make their indefinite detransitive with |-ke·| AI DETRANS, before which the |m| drops (cf. §9.1). Most of these, including all verbs of speaking or thinking, add |-mo| AI 'speak, make sound orally' to this, giving |-ke·mo| AI DETRANS.

(4.292) Indefinite detransitives with |-ke·| AI DETRANS

(a)   *wa·pake·wa* 'he watches others, looks on' (← |wa·pam-| 'look at')

(b)   *wi·če·noke·wa* 'he enjoys life with others' (← |wi·če·nom-| TA 'socialize, play with')

(c)   *wi·či-mehtose·neni·ke·wa* 'he lives with others'

     (← |wi·či-mehtose·neni·m-| 'live with')

(d)   *wi·hpoke·wa* 'he eats with others' (← |wi·hpom-| TA 'eat (the same meal) with')

(e)   *wi·tapi·ke·wa* 'he sits with others' (← |wi·tapi·m-| TA 'sit with')

(4.293) Indefinite detransitives with |-ke·mo| AI DETRANS

(a)   *ašake·mowa* 'he feeds X' (← |ašam-| TA 'feed')

(b)   *menwe·neke·mowa* 'he likes X' (← |menwe·nem-| TA 'like')

(c)   *me·nešike·mowa* 'he shames X by speech' (← |me·nešim-| TA 'shame by speech')

(d)   *nahkoke·mowa* 'he agrees, says yes to X' (← |nahkom-| TA 'declare agreement with')

(e)   *natoke·mowa* 'he summons X' (← |natom-| TA 'call, call for')

(f)   *na·katawe·neke·mowa* 'he watches over X' (← |na·katawe·nem-| TA 'keep track of')

(g)   *neškike·mowa* 'he admonishes, forbids X' (← |neškim-| 'admonish, forbid')

(h)   *pahkike·mowa* 'he assigns food to X in a ceremony' (← |pahkim-| TA 'assign duty to')

TA stems in |-aw| have indefinite detransitives with |-a·ke·| replacing this; these can be analyzed as adding *|-eke·| AI DETRANS to the TA stem, with regular contraction (cf. §11.7).

(4.294) Indefinite detransitives with *|-eke·| AI DETRANS

(a)   *anehka·ke·wa* 'he is friendly with X' (← |anehkaw-| TA 'be acquainted with')

(b) *ketemina·ke·wa* 'he blesses X' (|keteminaw-| TA 'pity, bless')

(c) *mayo·hta·ke·wa* 'he makes O2 cry for or of X'
     (← |mayo·htaw-| TA+O 'make O2 cry of or for')

(d) *neškina·ke·wa* 'he hates X' (← |neškinaw-| TA 'hate')

(e) *no·ta·ke·wa* 'he hears X, hears it said' (← |no·taw-| TA 'hear (it said by)')

(f) *peminehka·ke·wa* 'he chases X' (← |peminehkaw-| TA 'chase')

(g) *wa·patama·ke·wa* 'he looks into O2 for X' (← |wa·patamaw-| TA+O 'look at O2
     for')

TA stems that end in |-im| TA 'act on by speaking' (and |ata·m-| TA 'sell to', |wi·hkom-| TA 'invite to eat') make indefinite detransitives by replacing |-im| (|-m|) with |-we·|, |-owe·| AI DETRANS. Although the selection of the variants |-we·| AI and |-owe·| AI may have originally been phonologically conditioned it is no longer predictable. Some stems in |-im| TA 'act on by speaking' also make an indefinite intransitive with |-ke·mo| AI DETRANS (4.293).

(4.295) Indefinite detransitives with |-(o)we·| AI DETRANS

(a) *ata·we·wa* AI+O 'he sells it' (← |ata·m-| TA+O 'sell O2 to')

(b) *a·yači·twe·wa* 'he gives X strict instructions'
     (← |a·yači·čim-| TA 'give strict instructions to' ← |a·yači·t-im-|)

(c) *inowe·wa* 'he declares {so} to X' (← |išim-| TA 'declare {so} to' ← |iN-im-|)

(d) *kekye·hkwe·wa* 'he teaches' (← |kekye·hkim-| TA 'teach')

(e) *ki·šowe·wa* 'he promises X' (← |ki·šim-| TA 'promise, declare decision to')

(f) *pahkowe·wa* 'he declares to X (as a decision), decides'
     (← |pahkim-| TA 'assign duty or honor to, dedicate to'; cf. 292*h*)

(g) *wi·hkowe·wa* 'he invites X to eat' (← |wi·hkom-| TA 'invite to eat')

53.4. Specialized detransitives. Specialized detransitives are made with a suffix |-a·| AI DETRANS added to a TA stem. These derivatives are made only in a few specific cases where the TA has a prototypical object and refer to action on that object. They are not formally distinct from the TA direct (with |-a·| TA th. 1) in all inflectional forms (and cf. 2.89).

(4.296) Specialized detransitive with |-a·| AI DETRANS

     |ketahwa·-| AI 'dig Indian potatoes' (← |ketahw-| TA 'dig up'):

     e·h=ketahwa·yani 'when you were digging Indian potatoes' (JP-GTF 32)

53.5. Middle reflexives. Middle reflexives are intransitives with a passive or reflexive meaning; in some cases they have a classical middle-voice meaning, indicating a reflexive action that is indirect or attenuated. AI middle reflexives are derived from TA stems by the addition of the abstract final |-o| AI. When a TA stem adds |-o| AI, a stem-final |N| is replaced by |s|, and a stem-final |Cw| drops the |w|. Middle reflexives with passive meanings and stems ending in |-so| AI may have inanimate counterparts in |-te·| II. Some middle reflexive stems are analyzed as primary formations with finals that are derived from transitive finals by the same processes that derive stems from stems (4.78). Many stems and finals with the shape of middle reflexives have no transitive counterpart.

(4.297) Middle reflexives with |-o| AI MID-REF

(a) *apo·sowa* 'he roasts for himself' (← |apo·N-| TA 'roast for')

(b) *a·čimowa* 'he tells his story, makes his report' (← |a·čim-| TA 'tell about')

(c) *a·teso·hka·sowa* 'legends are told of him' (← |a·teso·hka·N-| TA 'tell legends about')

(d) *kahkisowa* 'he hides' (← |kahkiN-| TA 'hide')

(e) *ka·si·kwe·howa* 'he wipes his (own) face' (← |ka·si·kwe·hw-| TA 'wipe the face of')

(f)   keši·penowa 'he scratches' (← |keši·pen-| TA 'scratch')

(g)   ki·šihowa 'he makes himself (the way he is)' (← |ki·ših-| TA 'make')

(h)   mahkate·wa·hkonowa 'he paints himself black; he is painted black'
       (← |mahkate·wa·hkon-| TA 'paint black') (Jones 1907:198.22; K-TCSB 35)

(i)   mama·tomowa 'he prays, worships' (← |mama·tom-| TA 'pray to, worship')

(j)   mehčinawe·nowa 'he undresses' (← |mehčinawe·n-| TA 'undress')

(k)   mo·šowa 'he gets a haircut' (← |mo·šw-| TA 'cut the hair of')

(l)   natota·sowa 'he begs, prays' (← |natota·S-| TA 'beg, pray to')

(m)   na·tawihowa 'he doctors himself' (← |na·tawih-| TA 'doctor')

(n)   no·sowa 'he fumigates himself' (← |no·sw-| TA, |no·s-| TI(1) 'fumigate with smoke')

(o)   pakisowa 'he ducked, dodged' (← |pakiN-| TA 'cast away')

(p)   pehtawasowa 'he makes a fire for himself' (← |pehtawaN-| TA 'make fire for')

(q)   sakikwe·pisowa 'he is tied by the neck, hanged' (← |sakikwe·piN-| 'tie by neck,
       hang')

(r)   ša·kwe·nemowa 'he is unwilling' (← |ša·kwe·nem-| TA 'be unwilling for O (to)')

(r)   te·pe·nemowa 'he is satisfied' (← |te·pe·nem-| TA 'think O got what they
       deserved')

(t)   wača·howa AI(+O) 'he cooks (O2)' (← |wača·h-| TA(+O) 'cook (O2) for')

(u)   wani·hka·sowa AI 'he forgets' (← |wani·hka·N-| TA 'forget')

(v)   we·we·pisowa 'he swings (on a swing, in a hammock)' (← |we·we·piN-| TA
       'swing')

(w)   wi·wenowa 'he clothes himself' (← |wi·wen-| TA 'wrap')

(4.298) Middle reflexives with |-o| AI, |-te·| II MID-REF

(a)   inakimowa AI, inakite·wi II 'he, it is valued {so}' (cf. |akim-| TA, |akit-| TI(1)
       'count')

(b)   nemasowa AI, nemate·wi II 'he, it stands' (← |nemaN-| TA, |nemat-| TI(2) 'stand')

(c)   pakesowa AI, pakete·wi II 'he, it blows up' (← |pakesw-| TA, |pakes-| TI(1) 'blow
       up')

Two AI stems with |-i-h| TA ABSTR have the TA treated as if it ended in |-iN|:

(4.299) Irregular middle reflexives with |-o| AI, |-te·| II MID-REF

(a)   akisowa AI, akihte·wi II 'he, it is lost' (← |akih-| TA, |akiht-| TI(2) 'lose')

(b)   so·kisowa AI, so·kihte·wi II 'he, it is tied' (← |so·kih-| TA, |so·kiht-| TI(2) 'tie')

There is some evidence for the formation of the middle reflexive to a TA stem in |-aw| by
replacing the stem-final |aw| with umlauting |a·|:

(4.300) Middle reflexive with |-a·| AI beside |-aw| TA

(a)   a·šito·nike·wa AI 'he trades' (|a·šito·nika·-| AI ← |a·šito·nikaw-| TA 'trade with')

(b)   penaha·hkwe·wa AI 'he combs his hair' (|penaha·hkwa·-| AI
       ← |penaha·hkwaw-| TA 'comb the hair of')

Most cases of this pattern, however, appear to be synchronically opaque: for example, |-ehka·| AI
'go, walk' beside |-ehkaw| TA 'act on by foot or body'; |-eška·| AI, II 'become' beside |-eškaw|
TA 'act on by foot or body'. The productive formation, though it is not frequently attested,
appears to replace |-aw| TA with |-a·so| AI MID-REF.

(4.301) Middle reflexive with |-a·so| AI beside |-aw| TA

       kehke·netama·sowa AI+O 'he knows O2 about himself'
       (← |kehke·netamaw-| TA+O)

Another minor pattern has a middle reflexive in |-oʻso| AI beside |-aw| TA:

(4.302) Middle reflexive with |-oʻso| AI beside |-aw| TA

mayaʻškoʻsowa AI+O 'he encounters O2 (affecting himself)'

(← |mayaʻškaw-| TA 'encounter, come directly to'):

wiʻh=poʻni-mayaʻškoʻsoyaʻke nepoʻweni (JoP-MortH 4)

'so that we may cease to encounter death'

The last two types could perhaps be considered indirect reflexives (**§53.9**), but there are not enough examples to establish the generality of the formations.

53.6. Derived passives. Derived passives are freely made from transitive stems with the endings |-aʻso| AI, |-aʻteʻ| II PASSIVE and have an explicitly passive meaning. If the TA of a stem pair ends in |Cw| both passive suffixes are added to the TI stem in |C|. Some stem pairs with a TA in |N| add both passive suffixes to the TI in |t|, but others add |-aʻso| AI to the TA in |N|, in some cases where there is no matching TI stem but in other cases where there is one. Otherwise |-aʻso| AI PASSIVE is added to the TA stem, and |-aʻteʻ| II PASSIVE is added to the TI stem. Some formations with |-aʻso| AI PASSIVE (4.303) are homophonous with formations with |-aʻso| AI DETRANS (4.285), and at least one stem is attested with both meanings (4.285*i*, 4.304*i*).

(4.303) Derived passives with |-aʻso| AI PASSIVE added to TA

  (a) *ahkawaʻpamaʻsowa* AI 'he is watched over' (← |ahkawaʻpam-| TA 'guard')

  (b) *kanoʻnaʻsowa* 'he is addressed' (← |kanoʻN-| TA 'speak to'; cf. |kanoʻt-| TI(1))

  (c) *kiʻškamaʻsowa* AI 'he is bitten off' (← |kiʻškam-| TA 'bite off'):

    kiʻškamaʻsota 'chewing tobacco'

  (d) *mašahkwaʻnaʻsowa* AI 'he is scalped' (← |mašahkwaʻN-| TA 'scalp')

  (e) *mehkweʻnemaʻsowa* AI 'he is remembered' (← |mehkweʻnem-| TA 'remember')

  (f) *menesaʻsowa* AI 'he (hide) is stretched' (← |meneS-| TA 'stretch (a hide)')

  (g) *miʻhkemaʻsowa* AI 'she is courted' (← |miʻhkem-| TA 'court, pick')

  (h) *miʻnaʻsowa* AI+O 'he was given O2; O2 was given to him'

    (← |miʻN-| TA+O 'give O2 to'; no TI)

  (i) *nesaʻsowa* AI 'he is put to death' (← |neS-| TA 'kill')

  (j) *tehkinaʻsowa* AI 'he is tied to a cradleboard' (← |tehkiN-| TA; no TI)

(4.304) Derived passives with |-aʻso| AI, |-aʻteʻ| II PASSIVE added to TI

  (a) *anahoʻtaʻsowa* AI 'he (drum) has the drumhead tied on, (water drum) is filled'

    (cf. |anahoʻN-| TA 'fill, fill a container with; tie drumhead on (drum)'; cf. 4.278*a*)

  (b) *anešaʻsowa* AI 'his image is incised' (← |aneš-| TI(1) 'cut out, incise';

    cf. |anešw-| TA)

  (c) *anweʻweʻhaʻsowa* AI 'he (drum) is beaten'

    (← |anweʻweʻh-| TI 'make sound by beating' [|-ah|, 4.95*a*];

    cf. |anweʻweʻhw-| TA)

  (d) *asaʻweʻkisaʻsowa* AI 'he (hide) is tanned' (cf. |asaʻweʻkisw-| TA 'tan')

  (e) *čaʻkeškaʻteʻwi* II 'it is trampled to pieces'

    (← |čaʻkešk-| TI(1) 'degrade by foot or body, wear out')

  (f) *kehkahaʻsowa* AI, *kehkahaʻteʻwi* II 'he, it is designated'

    (← |kehkah-| TI(1) 'designate'; cf. |kehkahw-| TA)

  (g) *menwiʻhkaʻsowa* AI, *menwiʻhkaʻteʻwi* II 'he, it is well taken care of'

    (← |menwiʻhkaw-| TA, |menwiʻhk-| TI(1) 'take good care of')

  (h) *nanaʻhiʻhkaʻsowa* AI 'he is attended to; an adoption is held form him (deceased)'

    (← |nanaʻhiʻhkaw-| TA, |nanaʻhiʻhk-| TI(1) 'attend to; hold adoption for')

(i)   *pi·taha·sowa* AI 'he is buried' (← |pi·tah-| TI(1) 'bury'; cf. |pi·tahw-| TA)

(4.305) Derived passives with |-a·so| AI PASSIVE added to TA, |-a·te·| II PASSIVE added to TI

(a)   *ki·šiha·sowa* AI, *ki·šihta·te·wi* II 'he, it is made'
          (← |ki·ših-| TA, |ki·šiht-| TI(2) 'make')
(b)   *pemena·sowa* AI, *pemena·te·wi* II 'he, it is taken care of'
          (← |pemen-| TA, TI(1) 'take care of')
(c)   *tepa·na·sowa* AI, *tepa·ta·te·wi* 'he, it is loved, cherished'
          (← |tepa·N-| TA, |tepa·t-| TI(1) 'love, cherish')
(d)   *tepe·nema·sowa* AI, *tepe·neta·te·wi* II 'he, it is owned, controlled'
          (← |tepe·nem-| TA, |tepe·net-| TI(1) 'own, have control of')
(e)   *wa·pama·sowa* AI, *wa·pata·te·wi* II 'he, it is looked at'
          (← |wa·pam-| TA, |wa·pat-| TI(1) 'look at')

One stem pair with a TI(3) of unique shape is irregular:

(4.306) Derived passives from the verb 'to use'

          awa·sowa AI, *ayo·te·wi*, *ayo·ta·te·wi* II 'he, it is used' (← |aw-| TA, |ayo·-| TI(3) 'use')

With some finals the derived passives are primary formations made with the corresponding abstract passive final (4.81-83). In addition, there are several derived passive formations that are characteristic of high-register language. Most of these have the shape of a derived abstract noun (§45) suffixed by |-iwi| AI,II 'be' (§47), but the implied intermediate-stage nouns are generally not in use. The one case in which the noun does exist is included here for comparison (4.308e). Several stems are attested with more than one of these suffixes.

(4.307) Derived passives with |-a·kaniwi| AI PASSIVE added to TA

(a)   *a·čimoha·kaniwiwa* AI 'he is informed' (← |a·čimoh-| TA 'inform')
(b)   *išima·kaniwiwa* AI 'he is told {so}' (← |išim-| TA 'declare {so} to')
(c)   *ketema·kiha·kaniwiwa* AI 'he is persecuted' (← |ketema·kih-| TA 'persecute')
(d)   *kosa·kaniwiwa* AI 'he is feared' (← |koS-| TA 'fear')
(e)   *mešwa·kaniwiwa* AI 'he is struck by an arrow' (← |mešw-| TA 'hit with an arrow')
(f)   *natoma·kaniwiwa* AI 'he is summoned' (← |natom-| TA 'summon')
(g)   *neškima·kaniwiwa* AI 'he is forbidden' (← |neškim-| TA 'forbid')
(h)   *pemena·kaniwiwa* AI 'he is taken care of' (← |pemen-| TA 'take care of')
(i)   *takona·kaniwiwa* AI 'he is included' (← |takon-| TA 'include')
(j)   *wi·hkoma·kaniwiwa* AI 'he is invited to eat' (← |wi·hkom-| TA 'invite to eat')

(4.308) Derived passives with |-a·kaniwi| AI PASSIVE added to TI

(a)   *ine·neta·kaniwiwa* AI 'he is considered to be or do {so}'
          (← |ine·net-| TI(1) 'think of {so}'; cf. |ine·nem-| TA)
(b)   *koseta·kaniwiwa* 'he is not freely approached, is given respectful distance'
          (← |koset-| TI(1); cf. |kosetaw-| TA 'be shy towards, be afraid to approach')
(c)   *kya·wata·kaniwiwa* AI 'he is the object of jealousy'
          (← |kya·wat-| TI(1) 'be jealous about'; cf. |kya·wam-| TA 'be jealous of')
(d)   *mawita·kaniwiwa* AI 'he is mourned' (← |mawit-| TI(1) 'mourn'; cf. |mawim-| TA)
(e)   *me·nawa·ta·kaniwiwa* AI 'he is admired, liked'
          (cf. *keme·nawa·ta·kana* 'your lover' beside |me·nawa·N-| TA 'adore' [4.205b])
(f)   *neškina·kaniwiwa* AI 'he is hated' (← |neškin-| TI(1) 'hate'; cf. |neškinaw-| TA)
(g)   *šekwataha·kaniwiwa* AI 'he is smashed up'
          (← |šekwatah-| TI(1) 'smash up'; cf. |šekwatahw-| TA)

    (h)   *ši·kwe·neta·kaniwiwa* 'he is considered second-best'
          (← |ši·kwe·net-| TI(1) 'consider second-best'; cf. |ši·kwe·nem-| TA)
    (i)   *te·pwe·hta·kaniwiwa* AI 'he is heeded'
          (← |te·pwe·ht-| TI(1); cf. |te·pwe·htaw-| TA 'believe')

(4.309) Derived passives with |-e·weniwi| AI PASSIVE added to TA

    (a)   *ahkawa·pame·weniwiwa* AI 'he is guarded'
    (b)   *anohka·ne·weniwiwa* AI 'he is given a task'
    (c)   *ase·weniwiwa* AI 'he is placed {somewhere}'
    (d)   *awe·weniwiwa* AI 'he is used'
    (e)   *a·čime·weniwiwa* AI 'he is told about'
    (f)   *a·čimohe·weniwiwa* AI 'he is instructed'
    (g)   *a·nwe·htawe·weniwiwa* AI 'he is not believed'
    (h)   *ine·weniwiwa* AI 'he is told (to do) {so}; he is called {so}'
    (i)   *išime·weniwiwa* AI 'he is told {so}'
    (j)   *kano·ne·weniwiwa* AI 'he is spoken to'
    (k)   *kehkahwe·weniwiwa* AI 'he is named'
    (l)   *mama·tome·weniwiwa* AI 'he is worshipped'
    (m)   *mawime·weniwiwa* AI 'he is mourned'
    (n)   *nana·hapihe·weniwiwa* AI 'he is installed in office'
    (o)   *natome·weniwiwa* AI 'he is summoned, called for'
    (p)   *nawasehkawe·weniwiwa* AI 'he is picked up on the way, taken along'
    (q)   *nenehke·neme·weniwiwa* AI 'he is thought about'
    (r)   *neškehtawe·weniwiwa* AI 'he is ignored as he speaks'
    (s)   *pahkime·weniwiwa* AI 'he is given the right or duty'
    (t)   *pemene·weniwiwa* AI 'he is taken care of'
    (u)   *takone·weniwiwa* AI 'he is included'
    (v)   *tašihe·weniwiwa* AI 'he is killed {somewhere}'
    (w)   *to·tawe·weniwiwa* AI 'he is treated {so}'
    (x)   *wa·wi·te·weniwiwa* AI 'he is given a name'
    (y)   *wi·saka·hpenane·weniwiwa* AI 'he is cruelly put to death'

(4.310) Other derived passives

With |-e·wesi| AI PASSIVE added to TA

    (a)   *kano·ne·wesiwa* AI 'he is spoken to' (← |kano·N-| TA 'speak to')
    (b)   *natome·wesiwa* AI 'he is summoned' (← |natom-| TA 'call, summon')

With |-eti·| AI RECIP (§53.7) + |-wen| NF (4.209) + |-iwi| II (§47.2) added to TA

    (c)   *koseta·ti·weniwiwa* AI 'one is afraid to approach him (e.g., tobacco)' (K-Auto 220)
          (← |kosetaw-| TA 'avoid from reserve or respect') (cf. 4.322*f*)
    (d)   *me·nešiti·weniwiwa* AI 'he suffers embarrassment'
          (← |me·nešim-| TA 'embarrass by speech'):
               a·kwi=ma·hi·='ni me·nešiti·weniwikini i·ni e·h=išawiki. 'One is not made to feel
               embarrassed for doing that (i.e., fasting).' (K-MLF 82)

53.7. Reciprocals. Reciprocals are formed from TA stems with the suffix |-eti·| AI RECIP.
Before this, some stems drop a stem-final |-m| and elide the |e|; some stems ending in |m| retain it,
and from some stems there are doublets. The stem |iN-| TA 'say {so} to' drops entirely before
|-eti·| AI RECIP and the |e| is replaced by |i| (4.311*e*). Stems in |-w| contract as before |-ekw| TA th. 2.

Reciprocal stems are prototypically used for actions performed reciprocally and symmetrically by both or all actors on each other, but they are also used for partly reciprocal or joint activities. They often refer to a joint activity in which the specific actions undertaken and undergone are complementary rather than symmetrical, and they are sometimes used when the undergoer is only one or a subset of the active participants. With an indefinite subject or as a base in some secondary derivatives a reciprocal stem usually has a passive meaning, with no implication of reciprocal or joint activity (but a non-passive reciprocal use is at A 136C). Though conventionally cited with plural inflection, reciprocals may also be used with singular subjects; in such cases the subject may be a representative singular, or the reference may be to the involvement of the subject in a joint activity.

(4.311) Formation of stems with |-eti·| AI RECIP

(a) *asemiheti waki* AI 'they help each other' (← |asemih-| TA 'help')

(b) *ašati waki* AI 'they feed each other' (K, JP), *ašameti waki* (Jones 1907:272.7)
     (← |ašam-| TA 'feed')

(c) *a·šiti waki, a·šimeti waki* AI 'they encourage, urge, coax each other' (← |a·šim-| TA)

(d) *išiti waki* AI 'they tell each other {so}', *išimeti waki* (← |išim-| TA; cf. 4.314c)

(e) *iti waki* AI 'they said {so} to each other' (← |iN-| TA; cf. 4.314d)

(f) *kehke·neti waki* AI 'they are intimate with each other', *lit.* 'they know each other,'
     (K-M 548h), *kehke·nemeti waki* (K-M 549h) (← |kehke·nem-| TA 'know')

(g) *keša·čiheti waki* AI 'they are kind to each other' (← |keša·čih-| TA)

(h) *keša·te·neti waki* AI 'they think kindly of each other' (← |keša·te·nem-| TA)

(i) *ki·šiti waki* AI 'they agree on a plan, promise each other' (A 69A)
     (← |ki·šim-| TA 'declare one's plan for, promise')

(j) *ki·winehka·ti waki* AI 'they chase each other around' (K-B 210)
     (← |ki·winehkaw-| TA 'chase around')

(k) *natoti waki* AI 'they invite each other' (← |natom-| TA 'call for')

(l) *nena·ti waki* AI 'they recognize each other' (← |nenaw-| TA)

(m) *neškiti waki* AI 'they admonish each other', |neškimeti·-|
     (← |neškim-| TA; cf. 4.314g)

(n) *ne·woti waki* AI 'they see each other, they meet' (← |ne·w-| TA 'see')

(o) *pemeneti waki* AI 'they take care of each other' (← |pemen-| TA)

(p) *pemoti waki* AI 'they shoot at each other' (← |pemw-| TA)

(q) *tepa·neti waki* AI 'they love each other' (← |tepa·N-| TA)

(r) *wi·hpe·ti waki, wi·hpe·meti waki* AI 'they sleep together' (← |wi·hpe·m-| TA)

(s) *wa·pati waki* AI 'they look at each other' (← |wa·pam-| TA)

(t) *wi·čawi·ti waki* AI 'they are together, they are married' (← |wi·čawiw-| TA)

(u) *wi·či·so·ti waki* AI 'they are fellow clan-members'
     (← |wi·či·so·m-| TA; also |wi·či wi·so·m-| TA)

(4.312) Stems with |-eti·| AI RECIP for complementary or only partly reciprocal actions

(a) *ahko·ti waki* AI 'they follow one after the other'
     (← |ahko·w-| TA 'follow, come behind, come next after')

(b) *išisaheti waki* AI 'they push each other {so}, to {there}' (← |išisah-| TA):
     wi·h=pwa wi- aškote·ki -išisaheti wa·či (K-MP1 51)
     'so they do not push each other into the fire'

(c) *iti waki* AI '{so} said one to the other' (← |iN-| TA) (cf. 4.311e)

(d) |kehkahama·ti·-| AI: *ki mo·či-kehkahama·ti·waki* AI (K-B 189)
      'it was secretly revealed by one to the other'

(e) |kehkahoti·-| AI: *ki·h=kehkahoti·pwa* (K-FC 755)
      'you (pl.) must name one of your number'

(f)   *maneti·waki* AI 'they copulate' (← |maN-| TA '(male) to copulate with')

(g)   *mi·hketi·waki* AI 'they court', |mi·hkemeti·-| (4.312*e*)
      (← |mi·hkem-| TA '(man) to court')

(h)   *nana·hišiti·waki* AI 'they lay each other to rest' (← |nana·hišim-| TA)

(i)   *osi·meti·waki, osi·me·heti·waki* AI 'they are brothers'
      (← |osi·mem-|, |osi·me·hem-| TA 'have as younger sibling' [4.325*h*])

(j)   *otehkwe·meti·waki* AI 'they are brother and sister'
      (← |otehkwe·mem-| TA '(male) to have as sister')

(k)   *owi·weti·waki* AI 'they are married, get married'
      (← |owi·wem-| TA 'take as a wife')

(l)   *we·po·ti·waki* AI (← |we·po·m-| TA 'start carrying on one's back')
      'they start off, one carrying the other on his back'

(m)   *wi·hkoti·waki* AI 'one of them invites others to eat'
      (← |wi·hkom-| TA 'invite to eat')

(4.313) Stems with |-eti·| AI RECIP and singular subject

(a) |ine·neti·-| AI (← |ine·nem-| TA 'think about {so}'):
      a·hpene=meko ine·neti·no·i·ya·hi. (K-B 83; tr. HP)
      "think of each other equally alike down there [you sg.]"

(b) |iti·-| AI (← |iN-| TA 'say {so} to':
      i·ni=koh=e·ti·či·mehtose·neniwa. (JB-MortL 6)
      'That's certainly what people tell each other.'

(c)   *ki·mi·hka·ti·wa* AI 'she is having a secret affair with another man'
      (Jones 1907:142.1)

(d) |mačina·ti·-| AI 'challenge each other' (← |mačinaw-| TA 'challenge, dare against'):
      e·h=mačina·ti·či. 'He offered a challenge.'

(e) |mi·hketi·-|, |mi·hkemeti·-| AI (← |mi·hkem-| TA '(man) to court; pick') (cf. 4.311*g*):
      mi·hketi·wa 'she's seeing someone' (K-JM 10)
      ihkwe·wa ne·hi-mi·hketi·ta meše=meko·='nahi neniwahi (K-Kin 11)
      'a woman who makes a practice of taking up with any and all men'
      wi·h=mi·hkemeti·yani (K-M 41e; K-FC 108)
      'when you (sg.) want to court, for you (sg.) to court'

(f) |pemeneti·-| AI (← |pemen-| TA 'take care of'):
      me·nwi-pemeneti·ta ..=·yo·we 'one whose marriage had been one in which he
      and his (late) wife had taken good care of each other' (K-MortE 4)

(g)   *tepa·neti·wa* AI 'they love each other' (C-PD 27h)
      (Follows *ča·ki .. e·na·towa·ta* 'every tribe', *lit.* 'he who speaks every language'.)

(4.314) Stems with |-eti·| AI RECIP and indefinite subject

(a) |anepye·hoti·-| AI (← |anepye·hw-| TA 'draw; write down'):
      e·h=anepye·hoti·ki 'there was an enrollment' (Jones 1907:34.9)

(b) |išikiheti·-| AI (← |išikih-| TA 'make (the body of) grow or be {so}'):
      išikiheti·pi 'we (women, indefinite) are made to be {so}' (A 38A, 146F)

(c) |išiti·-|, |išimeti·-| AI (← |išim-| TA 'tell {so}'; cf. 311*d*):
       e·šiti·kini=koči i·ni e·šawiki. (K-ECRP 107; cf. A 100G)
       'Of course, one should do the things one is told to do.'
       ateškawi anemi-išimeti·ke 'if one is told one thing after another' (K-SSP 168)

(d) |iti·-| AI (← |iN-| TA 'say {so} to' (cf. 4.311*e*, 4.312*c*):
       we·či-iti·ki 'the reason why we (women, indefinite) are told {so}' (A 34E)

(e) |mi·neti·-| AI+O (← |mi·N-| TA+O 'give O2 to'):
       a·šitami mi·neti·pi ke·ko·hi. 'One is given things in return.' (A 63C)

(f) |neseti·-| AI (← |neS-| TA 'kill'):
       a·kwi=koči a·hpeči-neseti·kini e·h=neseti·ki. (X2-SAR 31)
       'Of course, when we (game, indefinite) are killed, we are not killed for good.'

(g) |neškiti·-|, |neškimeti·-| AI (← |neškim-| TA 'admonish, forbid'; 4.311*m*):
       we·či-neškiti·ki 'the reason why we (indefinite) are forbidden' (A 67G)
       neškimeti·pi 'one is admonished' (K-BB 44)

(h) |se·kiti·-| AI (← |se·kim-| TA 'frighten by words'):
       e·h=se·kiti·ki 'because we (indefinite) are frightened (by what is said)' (A 100E)

For some AI verbs a formal reciprocal made on a causative stem derived with |-h| TA ABSTR (**§59.4**) designates the collective activity of a large group. These are sometimes found with singular subjects, in which case they appear to differ little from the underlying AI but reflect the fact that the activity is prototypically undertaken in a group.

(4.315) Verbs of collective activity with |-h| TA ABSTR + |-eti·| AI RECIP

(a)   *atame·heti·waki* AI 'they all have a smoke together' (O 3F) (← |atama·-| AI 'smoke')

(b)   *a·mi·heti·waki* AI 'they all move camp together' (← |a·mi·-| AI 'move, camp')
       Also: *e·h=a·mi·heti·či* 'he moved (by himself)' (K-MKD 4)

(c)   *ni·miheti·waki* AI 'they all have a dance together' (← |ni·mi-| AI 'dance')

(d)   *po·ni·heti·waki* AI 'they all camp together' (← |po·ni·-| AI 'camp')
       Also: *e·h=po·ni·heti·či* 'he camped (by himself)' (K-WB 4)

Some stems ostensibly in |-eti·| are not synchronically derived from TA stems and are not reciprocals. There are also some stems that appear to be synchronically derived with |-eti·| AI RECIP but nevertheless do not function as reciprocals but as AI or AI+O stems.

(4.316) Non-reciprocal verbs incorporating |-eti·| AI RECIP

(a)   *mi·ka·ti·wa* AI 'he fights, engages in mortal combat'

(b)   *we·peneti·wa* AI 'he starts to fight'
       (and all stems with |-eneti·| AI 'fight' [as if ← |-en| TA (4.97) + |-eti·| AI RECIP])

(c)   *kakano·neti·wa* AI(+O) 'he converses (with O2)'
       (← |Ca+| RED1, |kano·N-| TA 'speak to')

(d)   *nowa·waneti·waki* AI 'the mob of them went out'
       mehtose·neniwa wi·h=pye·či-pi·ta·waneti·wa (K-FC 475)
       'the people (representative singular) will come trooping in'
       (and all stems with |-a·waneti·| AI 'go in numbers') (cf. 4.89*d*)

Reciprocals that occasionally have the syntax of verbs like *kakano·neti·wa* AI+O (4.316c), with a secondary object instead of a conjoined subject, are analyzed as true reciprocals that optionally take this construction, rather than as lexicalized AI+O's.

(4.317) Reciprocal verb with the syntax of an AI+O
       |ne·woti·-| AI 'see each other' (4.310*n*):
       ki·h-ki·ši-ne·woti·či owi·hka·nani 'after he had met with his friend' (K-Wap 104)

53.8. Reflexives. Explicit reflexives are made from TA stems with the suffix |-etiso| AI REFL. Stems combine with this exactly as with |-eti·| AI RECIP (**§53.7**).

(4.318) Reflexives with |-etiso| AI REFL

    (a)   *a·čimetisowa* (K, AW), *a·čitisowa* (AW) 'he tells about himself'
          (← |a·čim-| TA 'tell about')

    (b)   *a·teso·hka·tisowa* AI 'he tells winter stories to himself' (K-Auto 236)
          (← |a·teso·hkaw-| TA [4.323*e*])

    (c)   *ina·čitisowa* AI 'he tells {so} about himself' (K-WD 18) (← |ina·čim-| TA)

    (d)   *itesowa* AI 'he says {so} to himself' (Jones 1907:286.22) (← |iN-| TA)

    (e)   *kehke·netama·tisowa* AI(+O) 'he knows (O2) about himself' (K-TG 92, K-FC 3, 490)
          (← |kehke·netamaw-| TA(+O) ← |kehke·net-| TI(1), TI(1)-O)

    (f)   *kehke·netisowa* AI 'he knows (about) himself' (K-ORF 4, K-WT 1, K-OBES 32)
          (← |kehke·nem-| TA)

    (g)   *ko·kenetisowa* AI 'he washes himself' (K-Med 29) (← |ko·ken-| TA)

    (h)   *mawitisowa, mawimetisowa* AI 'he weeps for himself' (K-B 72, K-CWB 11)
          (← |mawim-| TA)

    (i)   *menwinawe·metisowa* AI 'he pleases himself by speaking' (K-M 1086i)
          (← |menwinawe·m-| TA)

    (j)   *pakatisowa* AI 'he hits himself' (Jones 1911:845) (← |pakam-| TA)

    (k)   *pehki·na·ko·tisowa* AI 'he feels a difference in himself' (A 36B)
          (← |pehki·na·ko·m-| TA)

    (l)   *pemenetisowa* AI 'he takes care of himself' (A 24D, 28G) (← |pemen-| TA)

    (m)   *pemotisowa* AI 'he shot himself' (K-MIM 43, C-Hist 42, SP-SM 12)
          (← |pemw-| TA)

    (n)   *pye·netisowa* AI 'he brought himself' (K-B 208) (← |pye·N-| TA)

    (o)   *šahkamo·netisowa* AI 'he feeds himself' (K-Kin 50) (← |šahkamo·N-| TA)

    (p)   *tepa·netisowa* AI 'she protects herself from physical advances' (K-M 690k)
          (← |tepa·N-| TA 'love, cherish, keep for oneself')

    (q)   *wa·patisowa* AI 'he looks at himself; he considers his life' (K-YF 5, K-WYB 141)
          (← |wa·pam-| TA)

Idiomatically a few verbs formed with |-etiso| AI REFL are not semantically reflexive and are like reciprocals in taking a second object referring to a joint actor:

(4.319) Reflexive with second object

        kakano·netisowa AI(+O) 'he conducts a conversation (with O2), says his (formal) words to O2' (K-WYB 101, K-MLF 20)

53.9. Indirect reflexives. Some transitive verbs make a derivative that indicates that the action is for the benefit of the subject. These add a suffix |-eso| AI to the TI stem or |-eteso| AI to the TA stem; these suffixes have the shape of middle reflexives made from the causative suffix |-eN|, |-eteN| TA (**§54.13**).

(4.320) Indirect reflexives with |-eso| INDIR.REFL

    (a)   *akwa·hesowa* 'he ladles food from the pot for himself'
          (← |akwa·h-| TI(1) 'remove from water or fire by tool')

    (b)   *akwa·pye·hesowa* 'he ladles food from the pot for himself'
          (← |akwa·pye·h-| TI(1) 'pull out of water or fire by tool, ladle out')

    (c)   *a·pihesowa* 'he does untying for himself, unties his sacred bundle' (K-IFSB 2)
          (← |a·pih-| TI(1) 'untie')

(d) *kakano·tesowa* 'he addresses his words; he converses' (K-WKG 33, LL-LH 1)
     (← |ka+| RED1, |kano·t-| TI(1) 'speak to')

(e) *kekye·hkahesowa* 'he named his choices' (S-YMSG 42)
     (← |kekye·hkah-| TI(1) 'designate (multiple times)')

(f) |kepa·hkoheso-| AI (cf. |kepa·hkohw-| TA 'emprison'):
     ke·pa·hkohesočiki 'the jailers' (SP-WH 17)

(g) *nasa·hkohesowa* 'he barbecues meat for himself'
     (← |nasa·hkoh-| TI(1) 'roast on sticks set next to the fire')

(h) *te·te·wa·hkohesowa* 'he does some pounding on a tree' (K-WWB 22)
     (← |te·te·wa·hkoh-| TI(1) 'pound repeatedly as a solid')

(i) *po·hkahesowa* 'he makes a hole for himself, pokes through (copulating)' (K-S 31)
     (← |po·hkah-| TI(1) 'make a hole in by tool')

(j) *po·tahesowa* 'he pounds in a mortar' (cf. |po·tahw-| TA 'pound (corn) in a mortar')

(4.321) Indirect reflexives with |-eteso| AI INDIR.REFL
     nana·hi·hka·tesowa 'he gets things set for himself, prepares for the future'
     (← |nana·hi·hkaw-| TA 'attend to' + |-eteso| AI INDIR.REFL) (K-Auto 43)

The minor middle reflexive patterns in (4.301) and (4.302) could be considered indirect reflexives.

53.10. Derived impersonal II verbs. Resembling the passive stems derived from transitives (**§53.6**), there are impersonal II verbs derived from AI stems by a suffix |-weniwi| II IMPERS; such derivatives have the shape of verbs of being in |-iwi| II (**§47**) made on nouns in |-wen| (**§45.7**). These impersonal verbs may be made from TI stems by first adding the general detransitive suffix |-ike·| AI DETRANS (4.271).

(4.322) Derived impersonal verbs with |-weniwi| II IMPERS
     (a) *ahkihke·weniwiwi* II 'the garden crops are planted'
          (← |ahkihke·-| AI(+O) 'plant (O2)')

     (b) |išawiweniwi-| II (← |išawi-| AI 'do {so}'):
          pehki ni-išawiweniwiwi 'it is done differently'
          e·šawiweniwiki 'how it is done'

     (c) *išihčike·weniwiwi* II 'it is done {so}' (← |išihčike·-| AI 'do things {so}'; 4.281*a*)

     (d) *išite·he·weniwiwi* II 'the opinion is {so}' (K-Auto 185)

     (e) *iše·wi·weniwiwi* II 'the custom is {so}' (A 174G) (← |iše·wi·-| AI 'do {so}')

     (f) |iti·weniwi-| II (← |iti·-| AI; 4.311*e*):
          e·ti·weniwiki 'what is said' (C-RS 12)

     (g) |kanawiweniwi-| II (← |kanawi-| AI 'speak'):
          e·ši-kanawiweniwiki 'how the speeches are spoken' (C-SD 4)

     (h) |kehkye·weniwi-| II (← |kehkya·-| AI 'be old'):
          e·h=kehkye·weniwiki 'old age'

     (i) |keta·si·weniwi-| II (← |keta·si·-| AI 'climb down'):
          we·či-keta·si·weniwiki 'the way down' (C-MWP 17)

     (j) *me·meta·teke·weniwiwi* II 'there is an entertaining dance'

     (k) *me·meta·tose·weniwiwi* II 'a good time is had walking around' (K-M 274b)

     (l) *nekwačihike·weniwiwi* II 'the corn is hilled' (← |nekwačihike·-| AI 'hill corn')

     (m) |pi·tike·weniwi-| II (← |pi·tike·-| AI 'enter'):
          we·či-pi·tike·weniwiki 'the entrance (of a building)' (K-M 578a)

(n)   *pašitoweʼweniwiwi* II 'it is a lie' (K-BB 86)

Another type of impersonal verb is made from the stems derived with |-h-eti·| AI (4.315) or incorporating |-eti·| AI RECIP by replacing |-eti·| with |-ete·| II IMPERS.

(4.323) Derived impersonal verbs with |-ete·| II IMPERS

(a)   *aʼmiʼheteʼwi* II 'camp is broken, everyone moves' (← |a·mi·-| AI 'move')

(b)   *niʼmiheteʼwi* II 'there is dancing' (← |ni·mi-| AI 'dance') (A 146C)

(c)   *poʼniʼheteʼwi* II 'camp is made, everyone camps' (← |po·ni·-| AI 'camp')

(e)   *nowaʼwaneteʼwi* II 'a large group (as, of people) goes out' (see 4.316*d*)

Transitives Derived from Intransitives (§54)

54. Transitive verbs are derived from intransitives according to two general patterns. Applicatives retain the same subject and add an object for the person or thing affected by the action. Causatives add a subject and change the syntactic role of the original intransitive subject to that of the object of the derived transitive. In a few cases causatives are also made from transitive stems.

54.1. Applicatives with |-aw| TA. The final |-aw| TA APPLIC makes applicatives from certain AI stems that end in |e·|, replacing this vowel. These applicatives are frequently made from AI stems in |-e·| AI ABSTR (after medials), |-ehke·| AI 'make' (**§49.1**), and |-ike·| AI DETRANS (4.271), or stems with finals that incorporate these elements. The single attested example of the corresponding TI has the deletion of the stem-final |e·| with no added suffix (4.325). If the source verb is an AI+O, the derived verb is a TA+O with the same secondary object.

(4.324) Applicatives with |-aw| TA APPLIC

(a)   *anaʼpoʼhkaweʼwa* TA+O 'he boils O2 for him' (← |ana·po·hke·-| AI+O 'boil O2')

(b)   *anepyeʼhikaweʼwa* TA 'he writes to him' (← |anepye·hike·-| AI 'write')

(c)   *ašikaweʼwa* TA 'he makes a house for him' (← |ašike·-| AI 'make a house')

(d)   *ašiwanehkaweʼwa* TA 'he makes up a pack for him' (← |ašiwanehke·-| AI; 4.244*a*)

(e)   *aʼtesoʼhkaweʼwa* TA 'he tells him a winter story' (← |a·teso·hke·-| AI)

(f)   *čiʼpeʼhkohkwaweʼwa* TA 'he has a memorial feast for him'
      (← |či·pe·hkohkwe·-| AI)

(g)   *inenikaweʼwa* TA 'he gestures, makes signs to him {so}' (← |inenike·-| AI)

(h)   *kiʼšesehkwaweʼwa* TA 'he finished cooking for him' (← |ki·šesehkwe·-| AI)

(i)   *kokweʼčikwaʼsikaweʼwa* TA 'she practices sewing for him' (A 2F)
      (← |kokwe·čikwa·sike·-| AI 'practice sewing')

(j)   *menesaweʼwa* TA 'he cuts firewood for him'
      (← |menese·-| AI 'cut, gather firewood')

(k)   *menwapahkwaweʼwa* TA 'he makes a nice roof for him'
      (cf. |anapahkwe·-| AI 'make a roof')

(l)   *mesenahikaweʼwa* TA 'he owes him money'
      (← |mesenahike·-| AI 'he owes money')

(m)   *pahteʼhčikaweʼwa* TA 'he puffs to start a pipe for him'
      (← |pahte·hčike·-| AI; 4.278*e*)

(n)   *paʼškahikaweʼwa* TA 'he cracks nuts for him' (← |pa·škahike·-| AI 'crack nuts')

(o)   *po·ta·hkwawe·wa* TA+O 'he puts O2 in the pot for him' (← |po·ta·hkwe·-| AI+O)

(p)   *si·kahikawe·wa* TA 'he serves food to him' (← |si·kahike·-| AI; 4.271*m*)

(q)   *we·pa·hkawe·wa* TA+O 'he throws O2 to him' (← |we·pa·hke·-| AI+O)

(4.325) Applicative with |-aw| TA, |-∅| TI(1) APPLIC

       pi·tikawe·wa TA, 'he enters the place where he (obv.) is', *pi·tikamwa* TI(1)

       'he enters it' (K-M 830i) (← |pi·tike·-| AI 'enter')

54.2. Verbs of possession with |-em| TA, |-et|, |-emet| TI(1). AI verbs of possession with |-i| AI ABSTR (§48), including those derived from compound nouns, make applicatives by adding |-em| TA and |-et| or |-emet| TI(1) with loss of the stem-final |i|. If the underlying noun ends in |Cy| or is treated as such in inflection, it retains this underlying shape and treatment after the loss of the |i|, with contraction of |Cy-e| to |Ci| (4.326*aj*). The longer variant of the TI suffix (|-emet| TI(1)) may be used regardless of whether or not the underlying noun takes the possessed-theme marker |-em| (3.1, 19). Some TI verbs attest both shapes. One TI is attested that ends with |-iwet|, as if made from a verb in |-iwi| AI (4.326*i*).

AI verbs of possession are freely used as AI+O's with secondary objects, and this is the construction heavily preferred in simple statements with a third person object; the corresponding applicative TA's are more apt to be used if the object is not a third person proximate and in participles and other complex verbs. In many cases, however, the two possessive constructions are used interchangeably.

(4.326) Applicative verbs of possession with |-em| TA, |-et|, |-emet| TI(1) APPLIC

(a)   *okime·wa* TA 'he has her as his mother'
     (← |oki-| AI(+O) 'have (O2 as) a mother' ← |oky-i-| ← *okye·ni* 'his mother'):
     a·kwi=ma·h=ni·na okimena·nini. 'You're not my mother.' (K-WT 11)

(b)   *okwiseme·wa* TA 'he has him as a son' (← |okwisi-| AI(+O)):
     ketokwisemenepwa 'you (pl.) are my sons' (K-WT 11)
     o·sani='pi kehke·nemekwa wi·h=okwisemekoči. (K-B 1)
     'His father (obv.) knew beforehand that he (prox.) would be his son.'
     kehke·nemikwe·ni wi·h=okwisemiči (K-B 186)
     'he seems to have known beforehand that I would be his son'

(c)   *omehte·heme·wa* TA 'he has him (bow) as his bow' (← |omehte·hi-| AI(+O)):
     wi·h=omehte·hemaka 'what will be my bow' (K-B 16)

(d)   *omi·ša·metamwa, omi·ša·memetamwa* TI(1) 'he has it as his sacred pack'
     (← |omi·ša·mi-| AI(+O)):
     ketomi·ša·meta·pwa 'it's our sacred pack' (K-YC 17)
     i·ni we·mi·ša·metaka 'the one who owned that sacred pack' (K-B 300)
     mani wi·h=omi·ša·metamani mi·ša·mi. (K-SSP 214; tr. HP)
     "You will claim this sacred pack as your sacred pack."
     a·kwi .. ni·na·na nešihka omi·ša·memetama·kini. (O 126I)
     'it's not the sacred pack of us (exc.) alone'

(e)   *onakamo·netamwa, onakamo·nemetamwa* TI(1) 'he has it as his song'
     (← |onakamo·ni-| AI(+O)):
     wi·h=onakamo·netamanini 'the songs you (sg.) are going to have' (K-ECRP 115)
     wi·h=onakamo·nemetamanini 'the songs you (sg.) are going to have' (K-B 72)

(f)   *ona·pe·meme·wa* TA, *ona·pe·metamwa* TI(1) 'she has or takes him, it as husband'
        (← |ona·pe·mi-| AI(+O)):
        ona·pe·mena·ke 'if we marry you' (K-ILM 23)
        mači-maneto·hani=mekoho wi·h=ona·pe·meme·wa 'she will marry the Devil'
          (K-FC 526)
        nekoti=meko kehči-ma·wa·ka·ni neča·ki-ona·pe·meta. (K-Wewi 3)
          'I married a whole big town.'

(g)   *oni·ča·neseme·wa* TA 'he or she has him or her as a child'
        (← |oni·ča·nesi-| AI(+O)):
        na·hina·h=meko we·ni·ča·nesema·wate·ni (K-WYB 6)
          'just at the time you become his mother'
        wi·h=oni·ča·nesemakwa 'the one who will be our (inc.) child' (K-WYB 53)
        kekehke·nemene wi·h=oni·ča·nesemena·ni (K-FC 498)
          'I knew beforehand that you would be my child'

(h)   *osi·me·heme·wa* TA 'he or she has him or her as a younger sibling'
        (← |osi·me·hi-| AI(+O)):
        ahpene·či=meko osi·me·hema·pi 'they are always younger siblings' (K-CWB 19)
        ketosi·me·hemene 'you are my younger brother' (K-RYL 7, S-RSW 34)
        we·si·me·hemeta 'the younger brother' (K-MLF 66)

(i)   *otato·hposo·niwetamwa* TI(1) 'he claims it as his tablecloth' (K-WC 21)
        (as if ← *|otato·hposo·niwi-| AI(+O) ← *otato·hposo·ni* 'his tablecloth')

(j)   *otayime·wa* TA 'he has him as a pet'
        (← |otayi-| AI(+O) ← *otaye·ni* 'his pet' [1.148]):
        ki·h=otayimekona naki mehto·či. 'It will be as if they own us as slaves.' (K-B 188)
        e·h=otayimeči 'they were kept as pets' (K-WKG 45)

(k)   *owi·hta·weme·wa* TA 'he has him as a brother-in-law' (← |owi·hta·wi-| AI(+O)):
        kemenwe·nemene wi·h=owi·hta·wemena·ni 'I'd like you to be my
        brother-in-law' (K-B 292)

(l)   *owi·weme·wa* TA 'he has or takes her as his wife' (← |owi·wi-| AI(+O)):
        e·h=owi·wemena·ni 'and you are my wife' (K-D 14)
        ki·h=owi·wemi 'you may marry me' (K-MLF 96)
        i·niye·ne·pe·ši-owi·wema·čini 'the one he had almost married' (K-SSP 257)

(m)   *otaša·ti·hemetamwa* 'he has it as his headed arrow' (← |otaša·ti·hi-| AI(+O)):
        wi·h=otaša·ti·hemetama·nini 'the ones that will be my headed arrows' (K-B 16)

(n)   *o·šisememe·wa* TA, *o·šisemetamwa*, *o·šisememetamwa* TI(1)
        'he or she has him or her, it as a grandchild' (← |o·šisemi-| AI(+O)):
        wi·h=o·šisememaketa 'the one who will be our (exc.) grandchild' (K-MortF 37)
        o·ni·ni·na·na·mi·ša·mani e·h=ča·ki-=mekoho -o·šisememetama·ke. (K-FC 402)
          "And we are the grandfathers to all sacred bundles." (tr. HP)

(o) |oki·ke·nowi-nakamo·net-| TI(1) 'have as clan feast song' (K-GBuff 91):
        wi·h=oki·ke·nowi-nakamo·netamowa·čini 'those that will be their clan-feast
        songs'
        |oki·ke·nowi-onakamo·net-| TI(1) 'have as clan feast song' (K-Spot 221):
        ki·h=oki·ke·nowi-onakamo·neta·pwa 'you will have them as your clan-feast
        songs'

54.3. Applicatives with |-em| TA, |-et| TI(1). A few AI verbs add an applicative |-em| TA; the corresponding TI's with added |-et| TI(1) are rare outside of stems that are a base for further derivation (e.g. 4.308c). Before this suffix pair, |e·| is replaced by |a| and |i| drops, with contraction of |Cw-e| to |Co|.

(4.327) Applicatives with |-em| TA, |-et| TI(1) APPLIC

(a)   *aša·ha·towame·wa* TA 'he speaks Sioux to him' (← |aša·ha·towe·-| AI)

(b)   *ina·towame·wa* TA 'he speaks {such a} language to him' (← |ina·towe·-| AI)

(c)   *kemo·teme·wa* TA+O 'he steals O2 from him' (← |kemo·t-| AI(+O) 'steal (O2)')

(d)   *kya·kome·wa* TA 'she is jealous of her (as a sexual rival)'
        (← |kya·kwi-| AI '(woman) to be (sexually) jealous')

(e)   *kya·wame·wa* TA, *kya·watamwa* 'he is jealous of him (as a sexual rival), about it'
        (← |kya·we·-| AI 'be (sexually) jealous', in older usage '(man) to be jealous')

(f)   *metawame·wa* TA 'he takes offense at him' (← |metawe·-| 'sulk, pout' AI)

54.4. Applicatives of joint action with |-·m| TA, |-·t| TI(1). Verbs referring to joint action are made from AI stems by adding the preverb *wi·či* PV and the derivational suffix |-·m| TA APPLIC; there are a few corresponding TI's with |-·t| TI(1). Before this final pair short vowels are lengthened and |a·| is replaced by |e·|; in one stem |iwi| is replaced by |i·| (4.328b).

(4.328) Applicatives with |-·m| TA, |-·t| TI(1) APPLIC (compound stems)

(a)   *wi·či-nesapi·me·wa* 'he stays home with him' (O 15F) (← |nesapi-| AI)

(b)   *wi·či-mehtose·neni·me·wa* TA, *wi·či-mehtose·neni·tamwa* TI(1) 'he lives with him,
        it (at the same time and place)' (← |mehtose·neniwi-| AI)

(c)   *wi·či-te·pesi·me·wa* TA 'he is happy together with him' (← |te·pesi-| AI)

(d)   *wi·či-kehkye·me·wa* TA 'he grows old with him' (← |kehkya·-| AI)

(e)   *wi·či-ki·ke·no·me·wa* TA 'he joins him in giving a clan feast' (← |ki·ke·no-| AI)

The same formation is also found with concrete finals. The initial |wi·t-| 'with' is used, and the final pair |-·m| TA, |-·t| TI(1) APPLIC is added as in the compound stems that have *wi·či* PV 'with'. The final |e·| of |-i-te·he·-| AI 'think' is optionally replaced by |a|; |-i-ka·pa·| AI 'stand' is replaced by the virtual final |-i-ka·pawi| (which undergoes the regular vowel-lengthening). Apparently only one of these applicatives has beside it an intransitive stem from which it could be regularly derived, and this stem is a synchronically opaque combination of the initial |wi·t-| 'with' and an otherwise non-occurring final (4.329d). Thus, although applicatives derived from finals must be secondary derivatives, since they end in a sequence of two finals, they must be derived from AI stems containing |wi·t-| that have only a virtual existence (marked in the analysis with an asterisk).

(4.329) Applicatives with |-·m| TA, |-·t| TI(1) APPLIC (simplex stems)

(a)   *wi·čikamikesi·me·wa* TA 'he lives in the same village as he does'
        (← *|wi·čikamikesi-| AI 'live jointly')

(b)   *wi·čika·pawi·me·wa* TA 'he stands with him' (C-Hist 9) (← *|wi·čika·pa·-| AI)
        (Also: *wi·čika·pawi·htawe·wa* TA [§54.5],
         wi·čika·pawinohkatawe·wa TA [§54.7])

(c)   *wi·čite·hame·wa*, *wi·čite·he·me·wa*, TA, *wi·čite·hatamwa* TI(1) 'he is with him, it in
        thought, joins his thoughts with him, it'
        (← *|wi·čite·he·-| AI 'think jointly')

(d)   *wi·hpe·me·wa* TA, *wi·hpe·tamwa* TI(1) 'he sleeps with him, it'
        (← |wi·hpe·-| AI 'sleep with someone')

- (e) *witapi me wa* TA 'he sits with him' (← *|witapi-| AI 'sit jointly')
- (f) *witeke me wa* TA 'he dances along with him' (← *|witeka·-| AI 'dance jointly')
- (g) *witeneko me wa* TA 'he is in with him' (← *|witeneko-| AI 'thrash around jointly')

54.5. Applicatives with |-·htaw| TA, |-·ht| TI(1). The most general applicative suffix pair is |-·htaw| TA, |-·ht| TI(1) APPLIC. Before this final pair a short vowel is lengthened, but stems in |-mo| replace the |o| by |wi| or retain it as |o|, in either case without lengthening. Also, stems in |-ka·pa·| AI 'stand' are replaced by virtual stems in |-ka·pawi|, and |ka·škanaso-| AI 'whisper' is replaced by a virtual stem |ka·škanaci-|; the applicative final pair is added to these virtual stems with the regular lengthening. This final pair is also used in primary stems in the shape |-i·htaw| TA, |-i·ht| TI(1) (4.86c).

(4.330) Applicatives with |-·htaw| TA, |-·ht| TI(1) APPLIC

- (a) *api·htawe wa* TA, *api·htamwa* TI(1) 'he sits by him, it, where he, it is' (← |api-| AI)
- (b) *a·čimwihtawe wa* TA 'he reports on his behalf' (← |a·čimo-| AI)
- (c) *a·hkwe·htawe wa* TA, *a·hkwe·htamwa* TI(1) 'he is angry at him, it' (← |a·hkwe·-| AI)
- (d) *e·niki·kwe·htawe wa* TA 'he smiles at him' (← |e·niki·kwe·-| AI)
- (e) *kahkiso·htawe wa* TA 'he hides from him' (← |kahkiso-| AI)
- (f) *ka·škanači·htawe wa* TA 'he whispers to him' (← |ka·škanaso-| AI)
- (g) *mama·činawi·htawe wa* TA 'he moves about before him' (← |ma·činawi·-| AI)
- (h) *meškineče·htawe wa* TA 'he holds his hand open to him' (← |meškineče·-| AI)
- (j) *nakamwihtawe wa* TA 'he sings for him' (← |nakamo-| AI)
- (k) *ni·mi·htamwa* TI(1) 'he dances on it' (← |ni·mi-| AI)
- (l) *pakamika·pawi·htawe wa* TA 'he arrives and stands before him' (← |pakamika·pa·-| AI 'stand arrived')
- (m) *sa·kinaniwe·htawe wa* TA 'he sticks out his tongue at him' (← |sa·kinaniwe·-| AI)
- (n) *wi·seni·htawe wa* TA 'he eats for him' (song) (← |wi·seni-| AI)

54.6. Applicatives with |-·notaw| TA, |-·not| TI(1). Another applicative secondary final is |-·notaw| TA, |-·not| TI(1). Before this suffix pair, short vowels are lengthened (4.331hk); an |a·| that umlauts (3.244) is replaced by |e·| (4.331bj); an |o| (lengthened to |o·|) is inserted after a consonant except |N| (4.331e); in one stem |iwi| is replaced by |i·| (4.331d); and |-ka·pa·| AI 'stand' is replaced by |-ka·pawi|, which undergoes the regular vowel-lengthening (4.331g). After a stem in |N| the suffixes are |-otaw| TA, |-ot| TI(1) (4.331c). The corresponding primary suffix pair is |-notaw| TA, |-not| TI(1), which is preceded by short /i/ as a connective vowel (4.86c).

(4.331) Applicatives with |-·notaw| TA, |-·not| TI(1) APPLIC

- (a) *ašičike·notawe wa* TA 'he lives close to him' (← *|ašičike·-| AI)
- (b) *ihe·notawe wa* TA 'he goes {somewhere} to him' (← |iha·-| AI 'go {somewhere}')
- (c) *keteškwe·notawe wa* TA, *keteškwe·notamwa* TI(1) 'he sticks his head out to see him, it' (← |keteškwe·N-| AI 'stick one's head out, stick one's head in')
- (d) *mehtose·neni·notawe wa* TA, *mehtose·neni·notamwa* TI(1) 'he lives with him, it' (← |mehtose·neniwi-| AI 'live, be or become a person')
- (e) *nepo·notamwa* TI(1) 'he died from it' (← |nep-| AI 'die')
- (f) *nepwa·hka·notawe wa* TA, *nepwa·hka·notamwa* TI(1) 'he has the cleverness to get him, it' (← |nepwa·hka·-| AI 'be smart'; 3.246)
- (g) *pakamika·pawi·notawe wa* TA 'he arrives and stands before him' (← |pakamika·pa·-| AI 'stand arrived')
- (h) *pema·tesi·notamwa* TI(1) 'he lives from it, by it' (← |pema·tesi-| AI 'live, be in health')

(i)   *po ni notawe wa* TA, *po ni notamwa* TI(1) 'he camps in with him, it' (← |po·ni·-| AI)

(j)   *pye notawe wa* TA, *pye notamwa* TI(1) 'he comes to him, it' (← |pya·-| AI}

(k)   *te pesi notawe wa* TA, *te pesi notamwa* TI(1) 'he is pleased with him, it'
        (← |te·pesi-| AI)

54.7. Applicatives with |-nohkataw| TA, |-nohkat| TI(1). Some stems make applicatives
with |-nohkataw| TA, |-nohkat| TI(1) APPLIC. Before this final pair short vowels are not
lengthened and |a·| is not attested. After a stem in |N| |-nohkataw| TA APPLIC appears as
|-ohkataw| TA (4.332c) or |-ahkataw| TA (4.332f), and after a stem in |-ni| it is |-hkataw| TA
(4.332e); the TI counterparts of these shortened variants are not attested. The finals |-nohkataw|
TA, |-nohkat| TI(1) APPLIC are also used in primary stem derivation (4.86d).

(4.332) Applicatives with |-nohkataw| TA, |-nohkat| TI(1)

(a)   *anwa či nohkatawe wa* TA, *anwa či nohkatamwa* TI(1) 'he is willing toward him,
        it' (← |anwa·či·-| AI 'be willing')

(b)   *ašinawe nohkatawe wa* TA 'he is glad at his (obv.) return' (← |ašinawe·-| AI)

(c)   *a manohkatawe wa* TA 'he has sex with her' (← |a·maN-| AI 'be lustful, have sex')

(d)   *mi ša te nemonohkatawe wa* TA 'he is glad to see him'
        (← |mi·ša·te·nemo-| AI 'be glad')

(e)   *natopanihkatawe wa* TA 'he goes on the warpath against him'
        (← |natopani-| AI 'go on the warpath')

(f)   *no nahkatawe wa* TA 'he sucks at her breast' (← |no·N-| AI 'suck at the breast')

(g)   *pakamika pawinohkatawe wa* TA 'he arrives and stands before him'
        (← |pakamika·pa·-| AI 'stand arrived')

(h)   *pye tašinohkatawe wa* TA 'he brings a load of game to him' (← |pye·taši-| AI)

(i)   *okima winohkatawe wa* TA 'he is chief over them' (← |okima·wi-| AI 'be chief')

(j)   *pemetone monohkatawe wa* TA 'he speaks for him' (← |pemetone·-mo-| AI)

(k)   *ša kwe nemonohkatawe wa* TA, *ša kwe nemonohkatamwa* TI(1) 'he is unwilling
        towards him, it' (← |ša·kwe·nemo-| AI 'be unwilling')

(l)   *wana pe winohkatawe wa* TA, *wana pe winohkatamwa* TI(1) 'he meets him, it
        bravely' (← |wana·pe·wi-| AI 'be brave'; ritual terms for having the courage to fast)

54.8. Applicative with |-hkaw| TA, |-hk| TI(1). One common word has a unique applicative
formation, adding |-hkaw| TA, |-hk| TI(1) APPLIC.

(4.333) Applicative with |-hkaw| TA, |-hk| TI(1)

        ni mihkawe wa TA, *ni mihkamwa* TI(1) 'he dances for, over, to him, it'
        (← |ni·mi-| AI)

54.9. Causatives with |-h| TA, |-ht| TI(2). Causatives are commonly made from AI stems
with the final pair |-h| TA, |-ht| TI(2) CAUS. Before this in a few stems an |a·| or |e·| is replaced by
|a| (4.334ht), but an |a·| that is subject to umlaut is usually replaced by |e·| (4.334cgt); |o| is
unchanged (4.334j,bb) or replaced by |o·| (4.334bb) or |wi| (4.334bnr,dd,gg), or in single cases |a|
(4.334m) or |wa·| (4.334p); |-ka·pa·| AI 'stand' is replaced by |-ka·pawi| (4.334x).

The stem on which the causative is formed may retain verbal syntax as an incorporated
secondary predicate (§70.1).

(4.334) Causatives with |-h| TA, |-ht| TI(2)

(a)   *ahkawa pihe wa* TA, *ahkawa pihto wa* TI(2) 'he makes him, it a guard'
        (← |ahkawa·pi-| AI 'be a lookout, guard')

(b)   *ana swihe wa* TA 'he makes him fight'
        (← |ana·so-| AI 'wrestle, tussle') (also 4.341a)

(c)   *atameˑheˑwa* TA 'he gives him a smoke' (← |atamaˑ-| AI 'smoke')

(d)   *ayiˑhkwiheˑwa* TA 'he tires him out' (← |ayiˑhkwi-| AI 'be tired')

(e)   *aˑhkweˑheˑwa* TA 'he makes him angry' (← |aˑhkweˑ-| AI 'be angry')

(f)   *čiˑtapiheˑwa* TA 'he makes him sit upright' (← |čiˑtapi-| AI 'sit upright')

(g)   *iheˑheˑwa* TA 'he has him go {somewhere}' (← |ihaˑ-| 'go {somewhere}')

(h)   *kiˑyosaheˑwa* TA 'he makes him walk around' (← |kiˑyoseˑ-| AI 'walk around')

(i)   *mamaˑčiˑheˑwa* TA 'he makes him move, gives him life'
        (← |mamaˑčiˑ-| AI ← |Ca+| RED1, |maˑčiˑ-| AI 'move')

(j)   *mamaˑtomoheˑwa* TA 'he makes him worship' (← |mamaˑtomo-| AI 'pray')

(k)   *mayoˑheˑwa* TA 'he makes him weep' (← |mayoˑ-| AI 'weep')

(l)   *mehtoseˑneniwiheˑwa* TA 'he makes him live' (← |mehtoseˑneniwi-| AI 'live')

(m)   *menaheˑwa* TA(+O) 'he gives him a drink (of O2)' (← |meno-| AI(+O) 'drink (O2)')

(n)   *miˑšaˑteˑnemwiheˑwa* TA, *miˑšaˑteˑnemwihtoˑwa* TI(2) 'he makes him, it glad'
        (← |miˑšaˑteˑnemo-| AI 'be glad')

(o)   *nanaˑhiˑhteˑheˑwa* TA 'he dresses, clothes him' (← |nanaˑhiˑhtaˑ-| AI 'get dressed')

(p)   *nawahpwaˑheˑwa* TA 'he sends food for the journey with him'
        (← |nawahpo-| AI 'he takes food for the journey')

(q)   *naˑnawasotiˑheˑwa* TA 'he has them race, races them'
        (← |naˑnawasotiˑ-| AI 'race against each other')

(r)   *nemaswiheˑwa* TA 'he makes him stand' (← |nemaso-| AI 'stand')

(s)   *neniwiheˑwa* TA 'he makes him a man' (← |neniwi-| AI 'be a man')

(t)   *nepaheˑwa* TA 'he puts him to bed, gives him a place to sleep'
        (← |nepaˑ-| AI 'sleep')
        nepeˑheˑwa TA 'he lets or has him sleep, gets or puts him to sleep'

(u)   *nepwaˑhkaˑheˑwa* TA 'he makes him wise' (← |nepwaˑhkaˑ-| AI 'be smart'; 3.246)

(v)   *neˑseˑheˑwa* TA 'he cures him' (← |neˑseˑ-| AI 'recover, be cured, be saved')

(w)   *niˑmiheˑwa* TA 'he has him dance, gives a dance for him' (← |niˑmi-| AI 'dance')

(x)   *niˑšoˑkaˑpawiheˑwa* TA 'he has them stand together as a pair'
        (← |niˑšoˑkaˑpaˑ-| AI 'stand together as a pair')

(y)   *noˑšeˑheˑwa* TA 'she helps her give birth' (← |noˑšeˑ-| AI 'give birth')

(z)   *okimaˑwiheˑwa* TA 'he makes him chief' (← |okimaˑwi-| AI 'be chief')

(aa) *pehčameˑheˑwa* TA 'he deceives him' (← |pehčameˑ-| AI 'be mistaken, misled')

(bb) *penoheˑwa, penoˑheˑwa* TA 'he sends him back home'
        (← |peno-| AI 'depart, go home')

(cc) *šeˑškiˑkweˑheˑwa* TA 'he lets him go with unblackened face'
        (← |šeˑškiˑkweˑ-| AI 'have the face unblackened (by charcoal), not be fasting')

(dd) *teˑpeˑnemwiheˑwa* TA 'he satisfies him' (← |teˑpeˑnemo-| AI 'be satisfied')

(ee) *teˑpweˑheˑwa* TA 'he believes him' (← |teˑpweˑ-| AI 'speak the truth')

(ff) *wiˑhkoweˑheˑwa* TA 'he has him invite people' (← |wiˑhkoweˑ-| AI 'invite'; 4.294g)

(gg) *wiˑˑswiheˑwa* TA, *wiˑˑswihtoˑwa* TI(2) 'he names him, it'
        (← |wiˑso-| AI 'be named, have a name or clan')

When a causative has an inanimate object it is sometimes made not from the AI but from the derived II with |-ˑmikat| II (**§52**). The abstract component of this suffix (|-at| II) is dropped and |-i-ht| TI(2) is added directly to the element |-ˑmik|, which is otherwise not used independently.

(4.335) Causatives on II stems in |-·mikat| II with |-ht| TI(2) CAUS
- (a)   *mi·hkeče·wi mikihto·wa* TI 'he makes it work' (← |mi·hkeče·wi·-| AI)
- (b)   *mi·ša·te·nemo mikihto·wa* TI 'he makes it glad'
    (← |mi·ša·te·nemo·mikat-| II; 4.265*o*)
- (c)   *nesapi mikihto·wa* TI 'he leaves it out' (K-MWS 60, about a song)
    (← |nesapi-| AI 'stay home'; cf. |nesapih-| TA 'leave behind, leave at home')
- (d) |ni·ka·ni·mikiht-| TI 'make be the leading one' + |-aw| TA (§55.2) →
    ni·ka·ni mikihtawe·wa TI 'he makes O2 be the leading one for him'
    (← |ni·ka·ni·mikat-| II 'be the leading one, be in the lead')
- (e)   *nowi mikihto·wa* TI 'he sends it forth' (K-Wapes 28, of a blessing)
    (← |nowi·-| AI 'go out, exit')
- (f)   *peno mikihto·wa* TI 'he made it go' (← |peno·mikat-| II [4.264*x*])
- (g)   *pye mikihto·wa* TI 'he makes it come' (← |pye·mikat-| II [4.264*y*])
- (h)   *wi·seni mikihto·wa* TI 'he makes it eat' (← wi·seni·mikat-| II [4.264*cc*])

The same construction is also attested once with a non-sentient animate object for which an AI in |-·mikesi| AI (4.268) would be appropriate; again the abstract component (|-esi| AI) drops.

(4.336) Causative on AI stem in |-·mikesi| with |-h| TA CAUS
    keči mikihe·wa TA 'he makes him come out' (K-M 44b, of corn)
    (← *|keči·mikesi-| AI 'emerge' ← |keči·-| AI 'come into the open')

Since the abstract finals |-esi| AI and |-at| II are dropped in these causatives, both the TA and the TI can, in fact, be derived formally from stems with |-·mikesi| AI, which would conform to the derivation of other TA and TI causatives both from AI stems (e.g., 4.334*a*).

The suffix |-h| TA CAUS also makes causatives from TI themes; in these derivatives |-am| TI(1) th, is replaced by |-a| or |-amwi| and |-o·| TI(2) th. is replaced by |a·|. The one stem in |-en| TI(1) attested in this formation adds |-at| before the theme sign (4.337*e*).

(4.337) Causatives on TI(1) themes with |-h| TA (|-am| TI(1) th. → |-a|)
- (a)   *awato·tahe·wa* TA+O 'he has him carry O2 off on his back' (← |awato·t-| TI(1))
- (b)   *kočiya·tahe·wa* TA+O 'he has him smell O2' (← |kočiya·t-| TI(1))
- (c)   *nana·heškahe·wa* TA+O 'he has him wear O2' (← |nana·hešk-| TI(1) 'don')
- (d)   *ni·matahe·wa* TA+O 'he has him hold O2 in his mouth' (← |ni·mat-| TI(1))
- (e)   *so·kenatahe·wa* TA+O 'he has him hold O2 in his hand' (← |so·ken-| TI(1))
- (f)   *wi·hpe·tahe·wa* TA+O 'he has him sleep with O2' (← |wi·hpe·t-| TI(1); 4.329*d*)

(4.338) Causatives on TI(1) themes with |-h| TA (|-am| TI(1) th. → |-amwi|)
- (a)   *kehke·netamwihe·wa* TA+O 'he lets him know O2, gives him knowledge of O2'
    (← |kehke·net-| TI(1) 'know')
- (b)   *me·šenamwihe·wa* TA+O 'he has him touch O2'
- (c)   *nahkotamwihe·wa* TA 'he gets him to agree' (← |nahkot-| TI(1)-O)
- (d)   *nenehke·netamwihe·wa* TA+O 'he makes him think about O2'
- (e)   *ne·tamwihe·wa* TA+O 'he has him see O2'
- (f)   *si·hpwe·netamwihe·wa* TA 'he makes him suffer'
    (← |si·hpwe·net-| TI(1)-O 'suffer')
- (g)   *tepe·netamwihe·wa* TA+O 'he dedicates O2 to him' (← |tepe·net-| TI(1) 'own')
- (h)   *we·pi·hkamwihe·wa* TA+O 'he has him take up O2'
- (i)   *we·we·ne·netamwihe·wa* TA+O 'he puts him in charge of O2'

(4.339) Causatives on TI(2) themes with |-h| TA (|-o·| TI(2) th. → |-a·|)

    (a)   *awata·he wa* TA+O 'he has, makes him take O2 with him, sends O2 with him'
           (← |awat-| TI(2) 'take away, take home')

    (b)   *na·pita·he wa* TA+O 'he puts O2 around his (obv.) neck'
           (← |na·pit-| TI(2) 'put around one's neck')

A few causatives are found made from II stems with |-ht| TI(2) CAUS. The II stems are reshaped or extended in different ways.

(4.340) Causatives from II stems

    (a)   *kemiya·nwihto wa* TI(2)-O 'he makes it rain' (← |kemiya·-| II 'rain')

    (b) |mehpo·niht-| TI(2)-O 'make it snow' (← |mehpo-| II 'snow') + |-aw| TA (**§55.2**)
           → *mehpo·nihtawe wa* TA 'he makes it snow on, for them' (K-W 1062)

    (c)   *pehkote·nemwihto wa* TI(2)-O 'he waits for nightfall', *lit.*, 'lets it become night'
           (← |pehkote·-| II 'be dark, night')

54.10. Applicatives with |-h| TA, |-ht| TI(2). In some stems the final pair |-h| TA, |-ht| TI(2) is added to an AI stem with an applicative force. The treatment of stem-final vowels is probably the same as in the common patterns before these finals in causative use (**§54.9**), but only the replacement of |o| by |wi| is attested. In a few cases the finals have either a causative or an applicative function.

(4.341) Applicatives with |-h| TA, |-ht| TI(2)

    (a)   *ana·swihe wa* TA, *ana·swihto wa* TI(2) 'he wrestles, tussles, teases, toys with him, it'
           (← |ana·so-| AI 'wrestle, tussle') (also 4.334*b*)

    (b)   *a·čimwihe wa* TA, *a·čimwihto wa* TI(2) 'he tells him, talks to or about it'
           (← |a·čimo-| AI 'he tells, reports, tells his story')

    (c)   *kakano·neti·he wa* TA 'he converses with him'
           (← |kakano·neti·-| AI 'converse'; 4.316*c*)

    (d)   *keteški·he wa* TA 'he escapes from him' (← |keteški·-| AI 'get free, escape')

    (e)   *ki·ke·nwihe wa* TA 'he holds a clan feast over him'
           (← |ki·ke·no-| AI 'hold a clan feast')

    (f)   *mi·ka·ti·he wa* TA 'he fights him' (← |mi·ka·ti·-| AI 'fight'; 4.315*a*)

    (g)   *nakamwihe wa* TA, *nakamwihto wa* TI(2) 'he sings for, over him, it'
           (← |nakamo-| AI sing')

The derivatives in (4.341*b*) are rare. Usual is |a·čimoh-| TA 'tell, inform', here analyzed as a lexicalized primary stem.

54.11. Causatives with |-N| TA, |-t| TI(2). A smaller set of stems makes causatives with |-N| TA, |-t| TI(2). Before this causative suffix pair an |e·| is replaced by |a| (4.342*aef*); |o| is unchanged (4.342*b*) or replaced by |o·| (4.342*eh*); and one stem replaces |a·| with |awa| (4.342*d*; cf. 4.344*ef*).

(4.342) Causatives with |-N| TA, |-t| TI(2)

    (a)   *aškepyane wa* TA, *aškepyato wa* TI(2) 'he drowns him, it'
           (← |aškepye·-| AI 'drown')

    (b)   *ato·hpone wa* TA+O 'he lets him use O2 as his dish'
           (← |ato·hpo-| AI+O 'use O2 as a dish')

    (c)   *mahkate·wi·ne wa* TA, *mahkate·wi·to wa* TI(2) 'make fast, supervise the fasting of'
           (← |mahkate·wi·-| AI 'fast')

    (d)   *mato·tešawane wa* TA 'he gives him a sweatbath'
           (← |mato·teša·-| AI 'take a sweatbath')

(e)   *nahpamoʾneʾwa* TA 'he puts something in his (obv.) food' (← AI *|nahpamo-|)

(f)   *otaʾpyaneʾwa* TA, *otaʾpyatoʾwa* TI(2) 'he strings, ropes him, it to {somewhere}'
       (← |otaʾpyeʾ-| AI 'be tied, linked to, from {somewhere}'

(g)   *piʾtikaneʾwa* TA, *piʾtikatoʾwa* TI(2) 'he brings or takes him, it in' (← |piʾtikeʾ-| AI)

(h)   *šahkamoʾneʾwa* TA 'he hand-feeds him' (← |šahkamo-| AI 'put food in one's mouth')

54.12. Applicatives with |-N| TA, |-t| TI(1) or |-t| TI(2). In applicative use the final |-N| TA is matched by either |-t| TI(1) or |-t| TI(2). Before these applicative final pairs stem-final |eʾ| is replaced by |aʾ| (4.343*bcdef*, 4.344*acd*, 4.345*abc*), except that stems in |-aweʾ| referring to fire or its effects replace |eʾ| with |a| (4.344*ef*).

(4.343) Applicatives with |-N| TA, |-t| TI(1)

(a)   *anaʾhpawaʾneʾwa* TA, *anaʾhpawaʾtamwa* TI(2) 'he invokes the power of his blessing
       by reciting his dream of him, it' (← |anaʾhpawaʾ-| AI 'recite one's blessing dream')

(b)   *aʾtesoʾhkaʾneʾwa* TA 'he tells a winter story about him' (← |aʾtesoʾhkeʾ-| AI)

(c)   *čiʾškaʾneʾwa* TA, *čiʾškaʾtamwa* TI(1) 'he farts at, on him, it' (← |čiʾškeʾ-| AI)

(d)   *noʾšaʾneʾwa* TA, *noʾšaʾtamwa* TI(1) 'she gives birth to him, it' (← |noʾšeʾ-| AI)

(e)   *tepowaʾneʾwa* TA, *tepowaʾtamwa* TI(1) 'he deliberates, holds council over him, it'
       (← |tepoweʾ-| AI 'hold council')

(f)   *waniʾhkaʾneʾwa* TA, *waniʾhkaʾtamwa* TI(1) 'he forgets him, it'
       (← |waniʾhkeʾ-| AI(+O) 'forget (O2)')

(4.344) Applicatives with |-N| TA, |-t| TI(2)

(a)   *ašiwanehkaʾtoʾwa* TI(2) 'he makes it into a bundle for a backload'
       (← |ašiwanehkeʾ-| AI 'make up a bundle for a backload')

(b)   *aʾhpawaʾneʾwa* TA, *aʾhpawaʾtoʾwa* TI(2) 'he dreams of him, it'
       (← |aʾhpawaʾ-| AI 'dream')

(c)   *išihčikaʾneʾwa* TA, *išihčikaʾtoʾwa* TI(2) 'he makes, constructs him, it to be {so}'
       (← |išihčikeʾ-| AI 'do things {so}'; 4.281*a*)

(d)   *nanaʾhihčikaʾtoʾwa* TI(2) 'he prepares it, puts it together' (← *|nanaʾhihčikeʾ-| AI)

(e)   *pehtawaneʾwa* TA, *pehtawatoʾwa* TI(2), TI(2)-O 'he makes a fire for him, stokes
       it, keeps it burning; he stokes the fire' (← |pehtaweʾ-| AI 'make a fire')

(f)   *pekešawaneʾwa* TA, *pekešawatoʾwa* TI(2) 'he smokes him, it, causes him, it to
       smoke' (← |pekešaweʾ-| AI 'make smoke')

(4.345) Applicative with |-N| TA, |-t| TI(1) and TI(2)

(a)   *mehkwaʾnehkaʾneʾwa* TA, *mehkwaʾnehkaʾtoʾwa* TI(2) 'he finds him, it by digging'
       (cf. |-aʾnehkeʾ| AI 'dig' and 4.345*bc*); TI(1) not attested.

(b)   *pyeʾtaʾnehkaʾneʾwa* TA, *pyeʾtaʾnehkaʾtamwa* TI(1) (AW), *pyeʾtaʾnehkaʾtoʾwa* TI(2)
       (JP) 'he comes digging towards him, it or to dig him, it out'
       (← |pyeʾtaʾnehkeʾ-| AI 'dig a hole hither')

(c)   *waʾnehkaʾneʾwa* TA, *waʾnehkaʾtamwa* TI(1), *waʾnehkaʾtoʾwa* TI(2) 'he digs (a
       hole in) him, it' (← |waʾnehkeʾ-| AI 'dig').

54.13. Causatives and applicatives with |-eN| TA and |-eteN| TA. There are also small sets of causatives and applicatives made from TI stems with |-eN| TA and |-eteN| TA. Some stems are found with non-mutating |n|. Corresponding TI's are not attested. These suffixes can be described as added either to the TI stem or to the TI stem extended by |-aw| (cf. §34.2, 4.5*d*; §37.2, 4.83*b*), which here contracts to |oʾ|. One stem of this kind is derived from a TA double-object stem in |-amaw| (§55.1) which is lexicalized in an idiomatic meaning as a TA (4.349).

(4.346) Causatives with |-eN|, |-en| TA

    (a)   *ahtene wa* TA(+O) 'he blames him (for O2)'

          (|ahteN-| TA(+O) ← |aht-| TI(2) 'have, put {somewhere}')

    (b)   *wa·pato·ne wa* TA+O 'he shows O2 to'

          (|wa·pato·N-| TA+O ← |wa·pat-aw-| ← |wa·pat-| TI(1) 'look at')

    (c)   *wi·hpe·tene wa* TA 'he puts O2 in his (obv.) bed'

          (|wi·hpe·ten-| ← |wi·hpe·t-| TI(1) 'sleep with'; |n| shown by e·h=wi·hpe·tenikehe

          'it must have been put in bed with me' [K-Auto 84])

(4.347) Causative with |-eteN|, |-eten| (?) TA from TI(1) (extended by |-aw|).

    (a)   *kekeško·tene wa* TA+O 'he gives O2 to him to have with him'

          (← |kekešk-| TI(1) 'have on or in oneself')

    (b)   *ni·maškaho·tene wa* TA 'he fastens something in his (obv.) hair'

          (|ni·maškaho·teN-| ← |ni·maškah-| TI(1) 'fasten, wear in one's hair')

(4.348) Applicative with |-eteN| TA from TI3.

    ayo·tene wa TA+O 'he uses O2 on him' (|ayo·teN-| [AW] ← |ayo·-| TI3 'use')

(4.349) Causative with |-eteN| (or |-eten|?) TA from stem in |-amaw| TA (**§55.1**).

    sahkahamo·tene wa TA 'he has him offer tobacco'

          (← |sahkahamaw-| TA 'he offers tobacco to him')

54.14. Reflexive causatives. For a few transitive verbs, reflexive causatives are formed. These have the shape of middle reflexive derivatives with |-o| from secondary TA stems in |-n| (**§53.5**), but the putative intermediate-stage TA's are not attested, though some parallel formations are found. There are two patterns of formation, each with a different internal semantic structure. In one pattern, there are three stems that end in *-eno*; one of these adds |-eteno| AI to the TA; one adds |-eteno| AI to the TI extended by |-aw|; and the third adds |-eno| AI to the |-t| of the TI(1). These denote that the secondary object is caused to perform the action of the verb on the subject.

    (4.350) Reflexive causatives with |-eteno|, |-eno| AI

        (a)   *ne·wotenowa* AI+O 'he shows himself to O2' (← |ne·w-| TA 'see')

        (b)   *nakiško·tenowa* AI+O 'he causes O2 to meet up with him'

             (← |nakišk-| TI(1) 'meet')

        (c)   *wi·hpe·tenowa* AI+O 'he gets into the bed of O2' (← |wi·hpe·t-| TI(1) 'sleep with')

In another pattern, a stem in |-h| TA ostensibly adds |-o·no|. These derivatives denote that the subject actively causes himself to perform or undergo the normally passive or involuntary action of the underlying verb.

    (4.351) Reflexive causatives with |-o·no| AI

        (a)   *išihkawe·ho·nowa* AI 'he purposely makes footprints {so}'

             (cf. |išihkawe·-| AI 'one's tracks are {so}', |ki·wihkawe·ho-| AI 'make tracks

             around')

        (b)   *kohkikiho·nowa* AI 'he transforms himself, makes himself take on another form'

             (← *|kohkikih-| TA 'make change form' ← |kohkiki-| AI 'change form')

        (c)   *na·kwiho·nowa* AI 'he changes his appearance'

             (← *|na·kwih-| TA 'change the appearance of'; cf. |na·kosi-| AI 'appear, show up')

        (d)   *neno·te·wikiho·nowa* AI 'he takes on human form' (← |neno·te·wiki-| AI 'be

             human')

Transitives Derived from Transitives (§55)

55. From simple transitive stems double-object TA stems (TA+O) are freely derived. In a double-object stem a valence for a semantic indirect object is added to an ordinary transitive; the semantic indirect object is the primary object of the double-object verb, and the original primary object is the secondary object. Double-object verbs are always formed from a TI stem (or a virtual TI stem) but the secondary object may be of either gender. A TA that is not matched by a TI forms a double-object verb from a virtual stem that has a shape appropriate to a matching TI. Double-object verbs with inanimate primary objects do not exist, however.

55.1. Double-object TA's from TI(1) stems. TI(1) stems make the double-object form by adding |-amaw| TA to the stem; this derivation can also be described as the addition of |-aw| to the TI(1) theme, incorporating |-am| TI(1) th.

(4.352) Double-object TA in |-amaw| from TI(1)

   (a)   *inakitamawe wa* TA+O 'he prices O2 {so} for him'
       (← |inakit-| TI(1) 'price {so}')

   (b)   *kakano·tamawe wa* TA+O 'he speaks to O2 for him' (← |kakano·t-| TI(1))

   (c)   *kehkahamawe wa* TA+O 'he designates O2 for him' (← |kehkah-| TI(1))

   (d)   *kehke·netamawe wa* TA+O 'he knows O2 of him' (← |kehke·net-| TI(1))

   (e)   *ketenamawe wa* TA+O 'he takes O2 out of him' (← |keten-| TI(1))

   (f)   *kya·tamawe wa* TA+O 'he keeps O2 a secret from him' (← |kya·t-| TI(1))

   (g)   *mi·hketamawe wa* TA+O 'he courts O2 of his' (cf. |mi·hkem-| TA 'court')

   (h)   *natotamawe wa* TA+O 'he asks him for O2' (← |natot-| TI(1) 'ask about')

   (i)   *ne·konamawe wa* TA+O 'he shoves O2 into him' (← |ne·kon-| TI(1))

   (j)   *ne·tamawe wa* TA+O 'he sees him with, having O2' (← |ne·t-| TI(1) 'see')

   (k)   *neškinamawe wa* TA+O 'he hates O2 for him' (← |neškin-| TI(1) 'hate')

   (l)   *nehkenamawe wa* TA+O 'he pushes O2 into his mouth'
       (← |nehken-| TI(1) 'put out of sight by hand')

   (m)   *no·tamawe wa* TA+O 'he hears O2 of his' (← |no·t-| TI(1) 'hear (as words)')

   (n)   *ota·hi·nemetamawe wa* TA+O 'he has O2 as his property from him'
       (← |ota·hi·nemet-| TI(1) 'have as property')

Some TA stems in |-amaw| are not double-object verbs. Some of these are derived from objectless stems (4.353e), and others correspond to no TI that is in use.

(4.353) Other TA stems in |-amaw|

   (a)   *kehkino·hamawe wa* TA 'he teaches him'

   (b)   *mami·šamawe wa* TA 'he serves as his ceremonial attendant'

   (c)   *nahkohamawe wa* TA 'he assists him in singing'

   (d)   *natonamawe wa* TA 'he seeks lice on him'

   (e)   *ni·miwahamawe wa* TA 'he sings for him to dance'
       (← |ni·miwah-| TI(1)-O 'sing dancing songs')

   (f)   *sanaka·hkonamawe wa* TA 'he sets difficult rules for him'

   (g)   *ši·še·notamawe wa* TA 'he hunts game for him'
       (cf. |ši·ša·-| AI 'hunt'; |-·not| TI(1) APPLIC)

   (h)   *wi·tamawe wa* TA 'he tells him (what is so)'

55.2. Double-object TA's from TI(2) and TI(3) stems. TI(2) stems and TI(3) stems ending in a consonant make the double-object form by adding |-aw| TA to the stem.

(4.354) Double-object TA in |-aw| from TI(2)

(a) *anemihe·mikihtawe·wa* TA+O 'he makes O2 go {some} way for him' (O 73E)
　　(← |anemihe·mikiht-| TI(2) [4.335, 336] ← |anemihe·mikat-| II [4.264]
　　← |anemiha·-| AI 'go {some} way')

(b) *akwi·tawe·wa* TA+O 'he soaks O2 for him' (← |akwi·t-| TI(2))

(c) *anemiwetawe·wa* TA+O 'he carries O2 off for him' (← |anemiwet-| TI(2))

(d) *awatawe·wa* TA+O 'he takes O2 of his away, takes O2 to him' (← |awat-| TI(2))

(e) *ča·kihtawe·wa* TA+O 'he kills all of O2 for him' (cf. |ča·kih-| TA 'kill all of')

(f) *kahkitawe·wa* TA+O 'he hides O2 from him' (← |kahkit-| TI(2))

(g) *ki·šihtawe·wa* TA+O 'he finishes O2 for him' (← |ki·šiht-| TI(2))

(h) *meškisetawe·wa* TA+O 'he spreads O2 for him' (← |meškiset-| TI(2))

(i) *na·tawe·wa* TA+O 'he goes after O2 for him' (← |na·t-| TI(3) 'go after, go to get')

(j) *pehkwapitawe·wa* TA+O 'he ties O2 into a bundle for him' (← |pehkwapit-| TI(2))

(k) *pi·tikatawe·wa* TA+O 'he brings O2 in for him' (← |pi·tikat-| TI(2))

(l) *wa·pašihtawe·wa* TA+O 'he wastes O2 of his' (← |wa·pašiht-| TI(2))

Very few stems are attested with irregular double-object forms. The verb |neht-| TI(2) 'kill' has the unique irregularity of adding |-amaw| to a TI(2) (4.355*a*). The verb |amw-| TA 'eat', for which the TI is the suppletive stem |mi·či-| TI(3), makes this form on a virtual stem *|amot-| TI(1) derived from the TA by the addition of |-et| TI(1) (**§54.3**) in a purely abstract function (4.355*b*).

(4.355) Irregular double-object stems

(a) *nehtamawe·wa* TA+O 'he kills O2 for him' (← |neht-| TI(2) 'kill')

(b) *amotamawe·wa* TA+O 'he eats O2 of his' (← *|amot-| TI(1) ← |amw-| TA 'eat').

Instrumental Oblique Added to Intransitives (**§56**)

56. Stems derived with |-ike·| AI DETRANS (**§53.2**, 4.271) may be marked to take an instrumental oblique (**§22.4(g)**) by the addition of the suffix |-we·| AI 'with {something}, using {something}'.

(4.356) Instrumental oblique added with |-we·| AI 'with, using {something}'

(a) *ašihčike·we·wa* AI(+O) 'he makes things with, of {something}'
　　(← |ašihčike·-| AI 'make things' [← |ašiht-| TI(2) 'make' + |-ike·| AI DETRANS] +
　　|-we·| AI 'with, using {something}'):

1) *ni·yawi ki·h=ašihčike·we·pwa* (O 74B)
　　'you must use my body to make what you make' (*ni·yawi* 'my body')

2) *i·nihi a·mi-ašihčike·we·kini* (K-MortF 21)
　　'(leggins, inan. pl.) that would be made of those (deer, obv. pl.)'

3) *wi·h=ašihčike·we·wa='pi ahki ni·yawi.* (K-M 1116b)
　　'He's going to make the Earth out of me, he says.'
　　(*ahki* 'earth'; *ni·yawi* 'my body')

(b)   *mi·ša·čihčike·we·wa* AI(+O) 'he decorates things with {something}'
      (← |mi·ša·čihčike·-| AI 'decorate things'):
          ma·hani .. ki·h=mi·ša·čihčike·we·pwa (K-B 40)
              'you must use these things to decorate with, as ornaments for things'
              (*ma·hani* 'these (inan.)')

SECONDARY STEMS IN PARTICLES

   The secondary derivation of particles involves some of the processes found in noun
derivation (**§36**) and some of the morphology used in the primary derivation of particles (**§38**).
The processes described here are the ones particularly germane to particles.

Diminutives (**§57**)

   57. Particles form diminutives on a number of different patterns, but all diminutive suffixes
include an |h| preceded by a long vowel. Diminutive particles indicate attenuation or comparison.
   57.1. Diminutive of particles in -*i*. Particles ending in -*i* most commonly make their
diminutive form by replacing this with -*i·me·hi*. One diminutive particle of this kind has a more
common variant with -*i·meki·hi* (4.357*c*).
   (4.357) Diminutives of particles: -*i* → -*i·me·hi*
      (a)   *ahkowi me·hi* 'a little bit behind' ← *ahkowi* 'behind'
      (c)   *aškači me·hi, aškači meki·hi* 'after a little while' ← *aškači* 'after a while'
      (d)   *a·sami me·hi* 'further upstream' ← *a·sami* 'upstream; west' (cf. 4.358*b*)
      (e)   *kaškiški me·hi* 'a bit up in front' ← *kaškiški* 'in the way ahead'
      (f)   *kenwe·ši me·hi* 'for quite a long time' ← *kenwe·ši* 'for a long time'
      (g)   *sa·kiči me·hi* 'a little outside' ← *sa·kiči* 'outside'
If a particle is the oblique complement of a particle formed from a relative root, which is always
postposed, the diminutive is added to the second word.
   (4.358) Diminutive of particle phrase
      (a)   *anik=oči me·hi* 'a little further on, a little later'
              (← *anika* 'further on, away' + *oči* 'from or in the direction of {somewhere}')
      (b)   *a·sam=oči me·hi* 'a little towards the west'
              (← *a·sami* 'west', *oči* 'from or in the direction of {somewhere}'; cf. 4.357*d*)
Particles that ostensibly incorporate the nominal suffix |-eki| LOC (**§38.6**, 4.115) make their
diminutive in three different ways. One set behaves like true locative nouns: the virtual noun
stem that precedes |-eki| adds |-e·h| DIM (the regular diminutive suffix of nouns), and |-eki| LOC
follows this (4.359*a*). Another set drops the ostensible |-eki| LOC altogether and makes the
diminutive on the residue, treated as a particle (4.359*b*). At least one particle with ostensible
|-eki| LOC is treated as unanalyzable and adds the usual diminutive suffix of particles after this
(4.359*c*).

(4.359) Diminutives of particles having ostensible |-eki| LOC

    (a)   *ahpeme ˙heki* 'a little bit above' ← *ahpemeki* 'up above' (4.115*c*)

    (b)   *na ˙mahki ˙me ˙hi* 'just below the ground'
            ← *na ˙mahki ˙ki* 'below the ground' (4.115*h*)

    (c)   *ahkiki ˙me ˙hi* 'just below' ← *ahkiki* 'down below' (4.115*a*)

Much less commonly a particle in *-i* makes a diminutive in *-i ˙hi*.

    (4.360) Diminutive of particle: *-i* → *-i ˙hi*

        i ˙ni taswi ˙hi 'that's only how many' ← *i ˙ni taswi* 'that's how many' (*i ˙ni* 'that')

57.2. Diminutive of particles in -e. Particles in *-e* make their diminutives by replacing this with *-e ˙me ˙hi* or *-e ˙he*.

    (4.361) Diminutive of particles: *-e* → *-e ˙me ˙hi*

    (a)   *i ˙ye ˙me ˙hi* 'a little while back, not so long ago'
            ← *i ˙ye* 'in the past' (< '*back then')

    (b)   *pemičinawe ˙me ˙hi* 'a little to one side' ← *pemičinawe* 'to one side'

    (c)   *ašawe ˙me ˙hi* 'quite a while ago' ← *ašawaye* (before enclitic: *ašawe=*) 'long ago'

    (4.362) Diminutive of particles: *-e* → *-e ˙he*

    (a)   *kehčine ˙he* 'nearer, fairly near' ← *kehčine* 'near'

    (b)   *ma ˙ne ˙he* 'quite a few, fairly many' ← *ma ˙ne* 'many'

    (c)   *či ˙ke ˙škote ˙he* 'almost at the edge of the prairie'
            ← *či ˙ke ˙škote* 'at the edge of the prairie'

    (d)   *na ˙waka ˙me ˙he meše=na ˙hina ˙hi* 'a little ways out in the water'
            ← *na ˙waka ˙me* 'out in the middle of the water'; *meše=na ˙hina ˙hi* 'at a short
            distance'

57.3. Diminutive of particles in -a. Particles in *-a* attest three ways of making diminutives: three are found that replace *-a* with *-e ˙wi ˙me ˙hi*, one has *-a ˙ha*, and one has *-e ˙me ˙hi*.

    (4.363) Diminutive of particles: *-a* → *-e ˙wi ˙me ˙hi*

    (a)   *no ˙te ˙wi ˙me ˙hi* 'a bit before' ← *no ˙ta* 'too soon' (cf. preverb *no ˙te ˙wi*)

    (b)   *ma ˙maye ˙wi ˙me ˙hi* 'sooner, after a shorter interval' ← *ma ˙maya* 'early'

    (c)   *menehte ˙wi ˙me ˙hi* 'first by a bit, a little ahead of the other'
            ← *menehta* 'first' (cf. initial *menehta m-*)

    (4.364) Diminutive of particle: *-a* → *-a ˙ha*

        anemya ˙ka ˙ha 'further downstream' ← *anemya ˙ka* 'downstream'

    (4.365) Diminutive of particle: *-a* → *-e ˙me ˙hi*

        anike ˙me ˙hi 'a bit further on, away, later' ← *anika* 'further on, further off'

Head Particles of Particle Compounds (**§58**)

58. In exocentric and enumerative particle compounds the head particle is derived from a noun or verb stem in the same way that single-word exocentric and enumerative compounds are derived (**§38.5**, 4.113). Although these derived head particles are separate phonological words, they have no independent existence outside particle compounds. Examples are in **§60.5** (exocentric compounds) and **§60.6** (enumerative compounds).

Chapter 5.

§§59-71. Sentence Structure

INTRODUCTION

59. Meskwaki sentences are of several types. VERBAL SENTENCES are those that contain a verbal predication. Those without a verbal predication are EQUATIONAL, SUBSTANTIVE, and GAPPED sentences if they are nevertheless predications, and SENTENCE FRAGMENTS if they are not predications.

Sentences are composed of one or more words arranged in a linear order. Some words are compounds (**§60**), which comprise more than one phonological word; there are COMPOUND NOUNS, COMPOUND VERBS, and PARTICLE COMPOUNDS. Words constitute functional modules that make up the structure of the sentence (**§61**). The component modules of a sentence are NOUN PHRASES (**§62**), VERB PHRASES (**§63**), and PARTICLE PHRASES (**§64**).

Sentences may combine as the clauses of a larger sentence. The central predication of such a sentence is the MAIN CLAUSE and its verb is the main verb. The clause of any verb that is nominalized is treated syntactically as a noun phrase. Clauses besides the main clause that are not nominalized are SUBORDINATE clauses, and a sentence with one or more subordinate clauses is a COMPLEX sentence (**§69**).

The overt linear order and adjacency of words may play a role in defining the structure of a sentence and communicating its meaning, but a pair or set of words may also function as a module within the sentence or as a compound without regard to their adjacency or, in some cases, their linear order. In particular, it is extremely common for the components of a module or a compound to be DISCONTINUOUS (**§71**), that is, separated in the sentence by words that are not constituent parts of the module or compound. Modules and compounds of different kinds differ in the extent to which they may be discontinuous. A module may be part of a higher-level module within the organization of the sentence.

The word order and modular structure of a sentence play no role in distinguishing subjects and objects. The functional categories of subject, primary object, and secondary object are determined by the derivation and inflection of the nouns and verbs in the sentence. (Word order may indicate the ranking of two obviatives, which may effectively determine their syntactic function; see the discussion in **§73.11**.) Where a particular word order is not obligatory (or highly favored), the position of words in a sentence may have a DISCOURSE function, indicating relative prominence of various kinds. Recurring patterns allow several sentence POSITIONS to be defined (**§65**).

COMPOUNDS

60. Compound words comprise two or more phonological words and therefore contain one or more word boundaries, but they behave like single words for purposes of inflection and within the functional structure of the larger sentence. The different kinds of compounds differ somewhat in the manner and degree of their treatment as units.

Each compound has a single head word (a HEAD NOUN, HEAD VERB, or HEAD PARTICLE) preceded by one or more prewords (PRENOUNS, PREVERBS, or PREPARTICLES). In most cases prewords are derived from initials by |-i| PF ABSTR (**§38.2**). The initials the prewords are formally based on may be derived from noun stems (**§34.1**; 5.2, 12), intransitive verb stems (**§34.3-4**; 5.3*abc*, 11), or TI themes (5.3*d*). A preword may not be made directly from a TA stem, but the equivalent is formally made from the AI reciprocal that is derived productively from a TA (**§53.7**; 5.3*c*).

Prewords are not distinct parts of speech and do not correspond to separate grammatical categories: a preword is a kind of morpheme that makes part of a word, exactly like the initial of a simple stem (**§18.11**). In particular, prewords are not particles (**§38.3**).

Compound Nouns

60.1. A compound noun consists of one or more prenouns and a head noun. A prenoun modifies its head noun in the manner of an adjective or attributive. The prenouns always precede the head noun, but the components of a compound noun may be separated in the sentence by words that are not part of the compound (**§71.1**, 5.153).

(5.1) Prenouns derived from primary initials
- (a) *ni·ka·ni-mami·ši·ha* 'head ceremonial attendant' (O 5E)
  (*ni·ka·ni* PN 'leading' ← |ni·ka·n-| 'leading, ahead')
- (b) *kehči-maneto·wa* 'the great manitou, God' (O 25F)
  (*kehči* PN 'great' ← |keht-| 'great, greatly')

(5.2) Prenouns derived from noun stems
- (a) *wi·teko·wi-mi·ša·mi* 'the Owl Sacred Pack' (O 1B)
  (*wi·teko·wi* PN 'of owl' ← |wi·teko·w-| AN [→ *wi·teko·wa* 'owl'])
- (b) *mi·ša·mi-a·teso·hka·kana* 'sacred pack legend ("winter story")'
  (*mi·ša·mi* PN 'of sacred pack' ← |mi·ša·m-| IN [→ *mi·ša·mi* 'sacred pack'])

(5.3) Prenouns derived from verb stems or themes
- (a) *ni·miwi-nakamo·ni* 'dancing song' (O 10D)
  (*ni·miwi* PN 'of dancing' [cf. 5.14*c*] ← |ni·miw-| [4.7*a*] ← |ni·mi-| AI 'dance')
- (b) *ki·ke·nowi-ana·kani* 'clan-feast dish' (K-WSB 32)
  (*ki·ke·nowi* PN 'of clan feast' [cf. 5.14*a*] ← |ki·ke·now-| [as in 4.7]
  ← |ki·ke·no-| AI 'hold a clan feast')
- (c) *neseti·wi-na·tawino·ni* 'people-slaying medicine' (K-MP 27)
  (*neseti·wi* PN 'of slaying people' ← |neseti·w-|
  [as in 4.7; cf. *neseti·weni* 'killing, murder'] ← |neseti·-| AI 'kill each other')
- (d) *pakitamo·wi-kanakanawi·ni* 'adoption ceremony speeches' (K-Auto 244)
  (*pakitamo·wi* PN 'of adoption ceremony' ← |pakitamo·w-| [cf. *pakitamo·weni*
  'adoption ceremony'] ← |pakit-| TI(1) 'release' + |-am| TI(1) th. + |-o·w| [**§34.3**])

Prenouns ostensibly derived from verb stems or themes (5.3) could also be taken as derived from the corresponding abstract nouns made with |-wen| NF (5.3*cd*, 5.14*ac*) by the suppression of the stem-final |-en|, as in the case of the homophonous preverbs (5.14).

Multiple prenouns may reflect three distinct constructions. A prenoun may be added to a noun that is already a compound noun, either lexicalized (5.4*a*) or not (3.62, 63), a process that may be repeated (5.4*b*). In other cases, two prenouns may form a sort of compound prenoun (PN-PN), either because they are derived as a unit from a compound noun, which is typically lexicalized (5.4*cdef*), or because the first prenoun modifies the second in the manner of a particle compound or particle phrase (3.64, 5.4*h*; cf. 5.36*cd*). These constructions may also be iterated or occur together (5.4*f*).

(5.4) Double and triple prenouns

(a) *wa peški-kohpiči-nenoswa* 'white buffalo' (K-B 11)
(*wa peški* PN 'white' + *kohpiči-nenoswa* 'buffalo';
kohpiči-nenoswa 'buffalo' ← *kohpiči* PN 'upland, wild' + *nenoswa* 'bovine')

(b) *wa peški-kehči-kohpiči-nenoswa* 'great white buffalo' (K-CWB 33)
(*wa peški* PN 'white' + *kehči* PN 'great' + *kohpiči-nenoswa* 'buffalo')

(c) *kohpiči-nenoswi-opehkwanani* 'buffalo backs' (K-Kin 32)
(*kohpiči-nenoswi* PN 'of buffalo' [← |kohpiči-nenosw-| AN
(→ *kohpiči-nenoswa* 'buffalo'; 5.4*a*)] + *opehkwanani* 'backs')

(d) *mahkwi-mi ša mi-ni miweni* (K-BBD 1)
'The dance of the Bear(-Clan) sacred pack.' (Title.)
(← *mahkwi-mi ša mi* PN 'of the Bear sacred pack' + *ni miweni* 'dance';
← *mahkwi* PN [← *mahkwa* 'bear']; *mi ša mi* PN [← *mi ša mi* 'sacred pack'])

(e) *ki šekwi-mi ša mi-a teso hka kani* (K-SSP 1)
'the (written) legend of the Sky Sacred Pack'
(*ki šekwi-mi ša mi* PN 'of the Sky Sacred Pack'
+ *a teso hka kani* '(written) legend';
← *ki šekwi* PN [← *ki šekwi* 'sky'] + *mi ša mi* PN [← *mi ša mi* 'sacred pack'])

(f) *ana kwi-mahkwi-mi ša mi-a čimo ni* (K-SBSB 1)
'the story of the Star Bear Sacred Pack'
(← *ana kwi* PN [← *ana kwa* 'star'] + *mahkwi* PN [← *mahkwa* 'bear']
+ *mi ša mi* PN [← *mi ša mi* 'sacred pack'] + *a čimo ni* 'story')

(g) *wa pi-nenoswi-onemači n-ohka či-mi ša mi* (K-MP1 5)
'the White Buffalo Left Rear Foot Sacred Pack'
(*wa pi-nenoswi-onemači ni-ohka či* PN 'of white buffalo left rear foot',
mi ša mi 'sacred pack'
[← *wa pi-nenoswi* PN 'of white buffalo' (← *wa pi-nenoswa* 'white buffalo
[← *wa pi* PN 'white', *nenoswa* 'buffalo']) + *onemači ni-ohka či* PN 'of left foot'
(← *onemači ni* PN 'left' [← *onemači neki* 'on his left, on the left' minus |-eki| loc.]
+ *ohka či* PN 'of foot' [← *ohka či* 'his foot; an animal's foot'; cf. **§34.1**, 4.4*e*])])

(h) *ma wači-=meko -kehči-we ta se wa* 'the greatest warrior' (K-BB 21)
(← *ma wači-kehči* PN-PN 'greatest' [← *ma wači* P,PN 'of all' + *kehči* PN 'great'];
=*meko* EMPH; *we ta se wa* 'warrior')

Compound Verbs

60.2. A compound verb consists of one or more preverbs and a head verb; compound verbs have all the syntactic properties of plain, uncompounded verbs. The preverbs always precede the head verb, but the components of a compound verb are often separated by other words (**§71.2**, 5.154-157). (When a preverb is postposed for emphasis it becomes a free particle [4.112].) Preverbs have a wide range of functions: they may act as aspectuals or modals (5.5), negatives (5.6), directionals (5.7), and adverbials of degree or manner in the broadest sense, which may modify either the head verb (5.8) or another preverb (5.8*i*); they may bear a valence for an oblique or an instrumental oblique (5.9; **§22.4**), or they may be the oblique complement of a relative root (5.10); and they may act as a higher predicate (5.11). These are not discrete functional categories, and some preverbs have meanings that range over more than one of them.

(5.5) Aspectual and modal preverbs

   (a)   *ki·ši-mehtena·pi.* 'He's already been unwrapped.' (O 108F)
          (*ki·ši* PV PERF, |mehten-| TA 'unpack', |-a·pi| X–3/IND)

   (b)   *nye·wokoni nepemi-we·ši·ho* 'I painted my face for four days' (K-Auto 16)
          (*nye·wokoni* 'for four days';
          pemi PV 'along' [cf. 5.7*c*], |we·ši·ho-| AI 'paint one's face', |ne–∅| 1s/IND)
          e·h=pemi-nowi·či "He steped out." (K-TCSB 99; tr. TB)
          pemi PV 'along', |nowi·-| AI 'exit', |e·h=–či| 3s/AOR)
          e·h=pemi-nowi·niči "[he] (obv.) walked out" (K-BHD 52; tr. TB)
          pemi PV 'along', |nowi·-| AI 'exit', |e·h=–niči| 3'/AOR)

   (c)   *mani kekehke·neta pye·či-'šima·kaniwiyani* (K-B 69)
          'you know all the instructions you have been receiving'
          (*mani* 'this (inan.)'; |kehke·net-| TI(1) 'know', |ke–a| 2s–0/IND;
          pye·či PV 'have been up to now, in the preceding stretch of time' (cf. 5.7*d*),
          |išima·kaniwi-| AI 'be told {so}', |IC–yani| 2s/PPL(obl))
          pye·či-iši-menwawitehe 'the nice way he had been acting earlier' (A 119B)
          (*pye·či* PV 'have been up to now, in the preceding stretch of time',
          iši PV '{so}' [5.9*e*], |menwawi-| AI 'do well', |IC–tehe| 3s/PRET.PPL(obl))

   (d)   *taši-wapaši-kano·nena·kwe* 'if they're poking fun at you (pl.)' (O 89A)
          (*taši* PV 'be engaged in' [cf. 5.9*j*], |wapaši| PV 'mockingly',
          |kano·N-| TA 'speak to', |–ena·kwe| 3–2p/SUBJ)
          taši-pemeniye·kapa 'you'd be taking care of him' (A 76B)
          (*taši* PV 'be engaged in', |pemen-| TA 'take care of', |–iye·kapa| 2s–3/POT)

   (e)   *e·h=we·pi-kanakanawiči* 'he began his speech' (O 5I)
          (*we·pi* PV 'begin', |CVCV+| RED2, |kanawi-| AI 'speak', |e·h=–či| 3s/AOR)

   (f)   *a·mi-ayo·či* 'the one he would use' (O 16C)
          (*a·mi* PV POT, |ayo·-| TI(3) 'use', |IC–či| 3s–0/PPL(INsg))

(5.6) Negative preverbs

   (a)   *e·h=pwa·wi-ki·hki·twe·wa·či* 'because they are not cry-babies' (A 118B)
          (*pwa·wi* PV 'not', |ki·hki·twe·-| AI 'be a cry-baby', |e·h=–wa·či| 3p/AOR)
          a·kwi wi·h=pwa·wi-ne·se·he·kwini. 'You (pl.) will not fail to heal him.' (O 77D)
          (*a·kwi* 'not'; |wi·h=| FUT, |pwa·wi| PV 'not', |ne·se·h-| TA 'cure',
          |–e·kwini| 2p–3/NEG)

(b)   *e·h=po·ni-nowi wa·či* 'they stopped going out' (O 8F)
       (*po·ni* PV 'cease, no longer', |nowi·-| AI 'go out', |e·h=–wa·či| 3p/AOR)

(5.7) Preverbs indicating direction and spatial extent

(a)   *wi·h=anemi-menwi-pema·tesiwa* 'he will go away in good health' (O 91D)
       (|wi·h=| FUT, |anemi| PV 'going, continuing on', |menwi| PV 'well' [5.8*i*],
       |pema·tesi-| AI 'live, be healthy', |–wa| 3s/IND)

(b)   *e·h=ki·wi-pi·pemwa·či* 'he went around shooting them' (K-TO 4)
       (*ki·wi* PV 'around, in places',
       |Ci·+| RED1, |pemw-| TA 'shoot', |e·h=–a·či 3s–3′/IND)

(c)   *e·h=pemi-ki·ya·kwate·kini ahkanani* (C-O 35)
       'the successive places where there are bones lying around'
       (*pemi* PV 'serially, one after the other' [cf. 5.5*b*],
       |ki·ya·kwate·-| II 'lie around', |e·h=–kini| 0/PPL(loc.obl.pl); *ahkanani* 'bones')

(d)   *pye·či-mya·hkesiniwahi* 'they (obv.) came back crippled' (O 18E)
       (*pye·či* PV 'coming' [cf. 5.5*c*], |mya·hkesi-| AI 'be crippled', |–niwahi| 3′p/IND)

(5.8) Adverbial preverbs of degree or manner

(a)   *e·h=aški-oni·ča·nesiwa·či* 'when they have their first child' (K-Kin 13)
       (*aški* PV 'newly, for the first time', |oni·ča·nesi-| AI 'have a child',
       |e·h=–wa·či| 3p/AOR)

(b)   *e·h=a·či-we·ši·heči* 'he was freshly painted' (O 2F)
       (*a·či* PV 'over again', |we·ši·h-| TA 'paint', |e·h=–eči| X–3/AOR)

(c)   *e·h=a·hkowi-nepo·hiwa·či* 'since they died each time' (A 157E)
       (*a·hkowi* PV 'every time', |nepo·hi-| AI 'die', |e·h=–wa·či| 3p/AOR)

(d)   *e·h=a·hpeči-apane·niniči* 'he (obv.) was always smiling' (K-RMDW 2)
       (*a·hpeči* PV 'permanently', |apane·-| AI 'smile', |e·h=–niči| 3′/AOR)
       e·h=a·hpeči-pi·tike·niči '(he saw) them (obv.) go in and not come out' (JB-BP 21)
       (*a·hpeči* PV 'permanently', |pi·tike·-| AI 'enter', |e·h=–niči| 3′/AOR)

(e)   *keča·ki-owi·wemenepwa* 'I have all of you as my wives' (K-MMDR 6)
       (*ča·ki* PV 'all', |owi·wem-| TA '(man to) marry', |ke–enepwa| 1s–2p/IND)
       keča·ki-kehke·nemeko·toke·hiki 'presumably they all know about you (sg.)' (K-FC 6)
       (*ča·ki* PV 'all', |kehke·nem-| TA 'know', |ke–eko·toke·hiki| 3p–2s/DUB)

(f)   *katawi-nepo·hite* 'if he is almost dead' (K-Kin 60)
       (*katawi* PV 'almost', |nepo·hi-| AI 'die', |–te| 3s/SUBJ)

(g)   *e·h=kehči-wa·pamekoči* 'he (obv.) stared at him intently' (O 65A)
       (*kehči* PV 'greatly', |wa·pam-| TA 'look at', |e·h=–ekoči| 3′–3s/AOR)

(h)   *neki·ša·koči-se·kesi.* 'I was terribly frightened.' (A 36F)
       (*ki·ša·koči* PV 'extremely', |se·kesi-| AI 'be frightened', |ne–Ø| 1s/IND)

(i)   *e·h=ki·ša·koči-wa·hkami-nenoše·či* 'he could hear very clearly' (K-SSP 13-14)
       (*ki·ša·koči* PV 'extremely', *wa·hkami* PV 'clearly',
       |nenoše·-| AI 'hear', |e·h=–či| 3s/AOR)

(j)   *e·h=mehči-=mekoho·-kano·šiyameči.* 'And he spoke to us quite openly.' (O 123C)
       (*mehči* PV 'openly'; =*mekoho* EMPH;
       |kano·N-| TA 'speak to', |e·h=–iyameči| 3–1p/AOR)

(k)   *wi·h=menwi-pye·waki* 'they will come back in good shape' (O 93B)
       (|wi·h=| FUT, |menwi| PV 'well', |pya·-| AI 'come', |–waki| 3p/IND)

(l)   *e·h=meso·te·wi-atama·wa·či* 'they all smoked' (O 29B)
       (*meso·te·wi* PV 'wholly, universally', |atama·-| AI 'smoke', |e·h=–wa·či| 3p/AOR)

(m)   *nawači-a·čimowa* 'before proceeding he spoke' (O 25A)
       (*nawači* PV 'first, stop to', |a·čimo-| AI 'narrate', |–wa| 3s/IND)

(n)   *neni·šwi-keteminawesipena* 'we received a blessing together' (O 70A)
       (*ni·šwi* PV 'as a pair', |keteminawesi-| AI 'be blessed', |ne–pena| 1p/IND)

(o)   *a·kwi=meko wi·h=paši-te·pwe·hto·na·nini.* (A 134B)
       'I'm just not going to believe you at all.'
          (*a·kwi* 'not'; =*meko* EMPH; |wi·h=| FUT, |paši| PV 'almost', (with neg.) 'at all',
          |te·pwe·htaw-| TA 'believe', |–ena·nini| 1s–2s/NEG)
       nepaši-pana·čihto·ni·yawi. (Jones 1907:116.18-19, 117)
       "I came near bringing ruin upon myself."
          (|paši| PV 'almost', |pana·čiht-| TI(2) 'ruin', |ne–o| 1s–0/IND ; *ni·yawi* 'myself')

(p)   *e·h=po·si-=meko -sasakanikini* 'in the very thickest parts of the brush' (A 173D)
       (*po·si* PV 'very, moreso' [cf. as P (5.16g(1)), PP (5.16h), PN (A 7C)];
          =*meko* EMPH; |sasakan-| II 'be thicket', |e·h=–nikini| 0´/PPL(loc.obl.pl)

(q)   *po·so·te·wi-keša·čiheti·waki* 'they were extremely kind to each other' (A 69C)
       (*po·so·te·wi* PV 'extremely', |keša·čiheti·-| AI 'be kind to each other',
          |–waki| 3p/IND)

(r)   *e·h=wawa·či-apane·neti·wa·či* 'when they smile at each other' (K-Kin 30)
       (*wawa·či* PV 'mutually' [cf. 5.9k], |apane·neti·-| AI 'smile at each other',
          |e·h=–wa·či| 3p/AOR)

(5.9) Preverbs with oblique or instrumental oblique valences (cf. 2.93-134)

(a)   *peno·či=mekoho wi·h=ahkwi-kohtaminiwahi* (K-FC 21)
       'they (obv.) will fear it from a long ways off'
          (*peno·či* 'far'; =*mekoho* EMPH;
          |wi·h=| FUT, |ahkwi| PV '{so far}', |koht-| TI(1) 'fear', |–aminiwahi 3´p/IND)
       še·ški=meko po·hkwi e·h=ahkwi-ne·ne·woti·wa·či (K-Bene 33)
       'they didn't see each other more than partially'
          (*še·ški* 'not more than'; =*meko* EMPH; *po·hkwi* 'partly, half';
          |ahkwi| PV '{so far}',
          |CV+| RED1, |ne·woti·-| AI 'see each other', |e·h=–wa·či| 3p/AOR)

(b)   *a·wasi·me·h=meko ki·h=ahpi·hči-tepa·neko·ki* (K-ECRP 21)
       'they will love you (sg.) all the more'
          (|a·wasi·me·hi| 'more'; =*meko* EMPH; |wi·h=| FUT,
          |ahpi·hči| PV 'to {such} a degree', |tepa·N-| TA 'love', |ke–eko·ki| 3p–2s/IND)
       aye·niwe=ke·h=meko e·h=ahpi·hči-wawa·sete·niki. (K-B 158)
       'what's more, it (obv.) kept sparkling with undiminished intensity'
          (*aye·niwe* 'always the same'; |=ke·hi| 'moreover'; =*meko* EMPH;
          |ahpi·hči| PV 'to {such} a degree', |wawa·sete·-| II 'sparkle', |e·h=–niki| 0´/AOR)

(c)   *nano·pehka=meko e·h=inehpi-kawiše·seniki* (K-Koch 8)
       'there was a big pile of it (obv.)'
          (*nano·pehka* 'to a great extent'; =*meko* EMPH;
          inehpi PV '{so} high', |kawiše·sen-| II 'lie fallen', |e·h=–niki| 0´/AOR)

(d)   *meše=meko e·h=inekihkwi-wa·šesiniči* (K-Auto 278)
       'when anyone (obv.) has a good-sized open wound'
          (*meše* 'freely, middlingly'; *=meko* EMPH;
          inekihkwi PV 'of {such} extent', |wa·šesi-| AI 'have a hole', |e·h=–niči| 3´/AOR)

(e)   *a·wasi neteši-nenehke·nema·wa* 'I thought about him more (than the other)' (A 81C)
          (*a·wasi* 'more';
          |iši| PV '{so}', |nenehke·nem-| TA 'think about', |ne–a·wa| 1s–3s/IND)
       we·ta·paniki e·h=iši-we·pose·wa·či 'they start walking to the east' (A 173B)
          (*we·ta·paniki* 'east (obv.)';
          iši PV 'to {somewhere}', |we·pose·-| AI 'start walking', |e·h=–wa·či| 3p/AOR)

(f)   *e·h=keki-nowi·či wa·hkone·wani* 'he went out with Indian tobacco' (JP-KT 47)
          (|keki| PV 'having {something}', |nowi·-| AI 'exit', |e·h=–či| 3s/AOR;
          wa·hkone·wani 'Indian tobacco (obv.)')

(g)   *i·nah=mekoho e·h=oči-we·piseniki mye·wi* (K-FC 18)
       'a road (obv.) started from right there'
          (|i·nahi| 'there'; *=mekoho* EMPH; *oči* PV 'from {somewhere}',
          |we·pisen-| II 'begin', |e·h=–niki| 0´/AOR; *mye·wi* 'road')
       omi·ša·meki=mekoho e·h=oči-kehke·nema·či (K-FC 330)
       'because of (the power of) his sacred pack he knew about him'
          (*omi·ša·meki* 'his sacred bundle (loc.)'; *=mekoho* EMPH;
          oči 'because of {something}', |kehke·nem-| |e·h=–a·či| 3s–3´/AOR)
       wa·wi·tawi e·h=oči-pehtawe·ki 'a fire was built on both sides' (K-CDWP 7)
          (*wa·wi·tawi* 'on both sides';
          oči PV 'oriented {so}', |pehtawe·-| AI 'make fire', |e·h=–eki| X/AOR)
       ki·šekwi e·h=po·hkya·niki e·h=oči-pi·čiweneči (K-FC 18)
       'he was taken in through a hole in the sky (obv.)'
          (*ki·šekwi* 'sky'; |po·hkya·-| II 'be, have a hole', |e·h=–niki| 0´/PPL(loc.obl);
          oči PV 'through {some hole}', |pi·čiweN-| 'lead in', |e·h=–eči| X–3/AOR)

(h)   *o·ni·=·na we·na·pe·mičini e·h=takwi-mešeneči.* (X12 in X11-MRW 49)
       'She was captured along with the husband she had acquired.'
          (|o·ni| 'and then'; |i·na| 'that (anim.)'; *we·na·pe·mičini* 'the one (obv.) she married';
          takwi PV 'along with {something}', |mešen-| TA 'capture', |e·h=–eči| X–3/AOR)

(i)   *i·ni=mani ša·ka e·h=taswi-pepo·nwe·yani.* (K-Auto 150, with ⟨swi.pe⟩; tr. IP)
       "you are now nine years old"
          (*i·ni* 'that (inan.)'; now, then'; *=mani* 'as it is now'; *ša·ka* 'nine';
          taswi PV '{so many}', |pepo·nwe·-| 'be .. years old', |e·h=–yani| 2s/AOR)
          (NOTE: more commonly |taswipepo·nwe·-| AI 'be {so many} years old')

(j)   *sa·kiči e·h=taši-kakano·neti·wa·či* 'they talked outside' (O 71B)
          (*sa·kiči* 'outside'; *taši* PV '{somewhere}' [cf. 5.5*d*],
          |kakano·neti·-| AI 'converse', |e·h=–wa·či| 3p/AOR)

(k)   *e·h=wa·wa·či-kečisa·či nekoti neniwani.* (K-TO 7)
       'He ran out into the open (to see) another man coming towards him.'
          (*wa·wa·či* PV 'mutually with {something}' [cf. 5.8*l*],
          |kečisa·-| AI 'emerge running', |e·h=–či| 3s/AOR;
          nekoti 'one'; *neniwani* 'man (obv.)')

(5.10) Preverbs as complements of oblique valences on head verbs

    (a)   *e·h=če·wi-=mekoho·-inekineniči.* (K-FC 64; tr. HP)

        "And they were both [obv.] exactly the same size."

        (*če·wi* PV 'same (as each other)', |inekiN-| AI 'be {so} big', |-niči| 3´/AOR;

        =*mekoho* EMPH)

    (b)   *nekekye·htena·mi-inehtawa·pena* 'we took what she said seriously' (O 68F)

        (*kekye·htena·mi* PV 'seriously', |inehtaw-| TA 'listen to {so}',

        |ne–a·pena| 1p–3/IND)

    (c)   *ka·ta kwi·natawi-išinawe·hiye·ka·ke* 'don't let us make them feel uneasy' (O 114F)

        (*ka·ta* 'don't'; *kwi·natawi* PV 'at a loss',

        |išinawe·h-| TA 'make feel {so}', |–iye·ka·ke| 1p–3/PROH)

    (d)   *če·w-ahpi·hčikičihi* 'those (obv.) of the same age as he was' (K-B 9)

        (*če·wi* PV 'same (as each other)',

        |ahpi·hčiki-| AI 'be {so} old', |IC–čihi| 3s/PPL(OBVpl))

(5.11) Preverbs acting as higher predicates

    (a)   *e·h=kaški-pehtawe·wa·či* 'they were able to make a fire' (K-TYFB 52)

        (*kaški* PV 'be able to', |pehtawe·-| AI 'make a fire', |e·h–wa·či| 3p/AOR)

        a·kwi kaški-nepa·ya·nini 'I couldn't sleep' (A 164E)

        (*a·kwi* 'not'; *kaški* PV 'be able to', |nepa·-| AI 'sleep', |–ya·nini| 1s/NEG)

        ki·ši-pwa·wi-kaški-pya·niči (Sh-Apay 12)

        'after it proved impossible to get him (obv.) to come'

        (*ki·ši* PV PERF, *pwa·wi* PV 'not', *kaški* PV 'be able to',

        |pya·-| AI 'come', |IC–niči| 3´/CC)

    (b)   *e·h=koči-so·nepye·hwa·či nepi* 'he tried flicking water on her' (K-MMD 4)

        (*koči* PV 'try to',

        |so·nepye·hw-| TA 'flick water on by tool', |e·h–a·či| 3s–3´/AOR; *nepi* 'water')

        e·h=koči-mi·hkemehkwe·we·či 'he tried to court women' (K-SGG 127)

        (*koči* PV 'try to', |mi·hkemehkwe·we·-| AI 'court women', |e·h–či| 3s/AOR)

    (c)   *peno·či mawi-po·ni·te* 'if he went to camp far away' (O 56E)

        (*peno·či* 'far away';

        mawi PV 'go and', |po·ni·-| AI 'camp {somewhere}', |–te| 3s/SUBJ)

        atehči·me·hi e·h=mawi-pakitameki (O 13B)

        'they (inan.) were taken a little ways off and thrown away'

        (*atehči·me·hi* 'a little ways away';

        mawi PV 'go and', |pakit-| TI(1) 'discard', |e·h–ameki| X–0/AOR)

    (d)   *ne·tawi-nesena·kwini* 'whenever they are seeking to kill you (pl.)' (O 94E)

        (|natawi| PV 'seek to', |neS-| TA 'kill', |IC–ena·kwini| 3–2p/ITER)

        a·kwi=ma·hi natawi-na·kwa·ya·nini. 'I'm not planning to go home.' (K-FC 76J)

        (*a·kwi* 'not'; =*ma·hi* 'you see';

        natawi PV 'seek to', |na·kwa·-| AI 'leave', |–ya·nini| 1s/NEG)

        natawi-we·pina·ke·ko "it is time for you [pl.] to begin singing" (K-FC 557; tr. HP)

        (*natawi* PV 'seek to', |we·pina·ke·-| AI 'start singing', |–ko| 2p/IMP)

The aspectual preverb *we·pi* PV 'begin' (5.5*e*), the negative preverb |po·ni| PV 'cease, no longer' (5.6*b*), and perhaps some others could also be considered to function as higher verbs.

Some preverbs that are ostensibly derived from verbs retain their verbal character, rather than being nominalizations (cf. 5.14). Some of these can be construed as manner adverbials, but others seem to function essentially as subordinate verbs.

(5.12) Preverbs ostensibly derived from verb stems and retaining verbal function

   (a)   *wi·h=a·hkwe·wi-nowi·ya·ni* 'that I would go out angry' (K-B 310)
         (|wi·h=| FUT, |a·hkwe·wi| PV 'being angry' [← |a·hkwe·-| AI 'be angry'],
         |nowi·-| AI 'go out', |e·h=—ya·ni| 1s/AOR)

   (b)   *ki·h=meškwi·kite·wi-=meko='pi -anahanenwi·pwa.* (K-FC 517)
         'It will be tedious indeed, how much you must bathe.'
         (|wi·h=| FUT, *meškwi·kite·wi* PV 'tediously'
         [← |meškwi·kite·-| AI 'be exasperated'],
         | CVCV+| RED2, |anenwi·-| AI 'swim, bathe', |ke–pwa| 2p/IND;
         =*meko* EMPH; |=ipi| HRSY)

   (c)   *e·h=to·hki-mayo·či* 'he woke up crying' (K-FC 625)
         (|to·hki| PV 'waking up' [← |to·hki·-| AI 'wake up'],
         |mayo·-| AI 'weep', |e·h=—či| 3s/AOR)

It is likely, however, that all such preverbs can be derived from an initial that either forms the matching AI stem or is derived from it.

Some preverbs are derived from nouns, but their use is restricted. Probably all such preverbs are also used as prenouns. In some cases the head verbs they appear with as preverbs make derived abstract nouns that occur with the same or similar prewords as prenouns.

(5.13) Preverbs derived from nouns

   (a)   *e·h=nahi-asayi-mi·hkeče·wi·či.* 'She knew how to make things of buckskin.'
         (K-WD 70)
            (*nahi* PV 'given to', *asayi* PV 'of hide', |mi·hkeče·wi·-| AI 'work',
            |e·h=—či| 3s/AOR)
            (Implying **asayi-mi·hkeče·wi·weni* 'buckskin work, products'
            ← *asayi* PN '(of) buckskin' + *mi·hkeče·wi·weni* 'work, products'.)

   (b)   *nenenemehkiwi-ki·ke·nopena.* 'We are holding a Thunder Clan feast.'
         (K-TCSB 91)
            (*nenemehkiwi* PV 'of thunder', |ki·ke·no-| AI 'hold clan feast', |ne–pena| 1p/IND)
            (Implying **nenemehkiwi-ki·ke·no·ni* 'Thunder (Clan) clan feast'
            ← *nenemehkiwi* PN 'of thunder' + *ki·ke·no·ni* 'clan feast'.)
         nenemehkiwi-owi·so·niwaki 'they have Thunder (Clan) names' (JP-KT 8)
            (*nenemehkiwi* PV 'of thunder', |owi·so·ni-| AI 'have a name', |–waki| 3p/IND)
            (Cf. *mahkwi-mi·so·ni* 'Bear (Clan) name' [JP-KT 24] ←
            mahkwi PN 'of bear' [← *mahkwa* 'bear']
            + *mi·so·ni* 'name' [*owi·so·ni* 'his name'])

   (c)   *wi·h=meno·hkami·wi-ni·mihčike·yani* 'you must give a spring dance' (K-WSB 56)
            (|wi·h=| FUT, *meno·hkami·wi* PV 'of spring',
            |ni·mihčike·-| AI 'give a dance' (4.275*b*), |e·h=—yani| 2s/AOR)
            (This and similar compound verbs [4.16*a*] imply **meno·hkami·wi-ni·miweni*
            'spring dance', with *meno·hkami·wi* PN 'of spring')

(d)   *e·h=ta·taši-nenoswi-ni·miwa·či* 'where they have buffalo dances' (K-BD 2C)
       (|CV+| RED1, |taši| PV '{somewhere}',
         |nenoswi| PV 'of buffalo', |ni·mi-| AI 'dance', |e·h=–wa·či| 3p/PPL(loc.obl))
       (Cf. |nenoswi| PN 'of buffalo'.)

(e)   *e·h=okima·wi-nehta·we·mikahki* 'it made a killing of a chief' (K-B 280)
       (*okima·wi* PV 'of chief', |nehta·we·mikat-| II 'make a killing', |e·h=–ki| 0/AOR)
       (Cf. |okima·wi| PN 'of chief' [4.102*f*].)

(f)   *e·h=pepo·wi-ki·ke·noki* 'in a winter clan feast' (O 12J)
       (*pepo·wi* PV 'of winter' [as if from unattested |pepo·w-| IN 'winter'; 4.16*b*],
         |ki·ke·no-| AI 'hold a clan feast', |e·h=–eki| X/AOR)

(g)   *e·h=maneto·wi-ošinetaminiči* (K-MMD 23)
       'that she [obv.] had married among manitous'
       (*maneto·wi* PV 'of manitou' [← *maneto·wa* 'manitou, god, snake'],
         |ošinet-| TI(1)-O 'have relatives by marriage', |e·h=–aminiči| 3s(-O)/AOR)
       e·h=maneto·wi-kehkinawa·čihčika·soyani (K-DSB 23; tr. EK)
       "you were marked as being godly"
       (*maneto·wi* PV 'of manitou',
         |kehkinawa·čihčika·so-| AI 'be distinctively marked', |e·h=–yani| 2s/AOR)
       e·h=aški-we·pi-manemaneto·wi-kanawiči (K-CWB 14)
       'when he first begins the religious talks'
       (*aški* PV 'first', *we·pi* PV 'begin', |CVCV+| RED2, *maneto·wi* PV 'of manitou',
         |kanawi-| AI 'speak', |e·h=–či| 3s/AOR)
       e·h=maneto·wi-ketakikaniki (K-HS 21)
       'it (obv.) was striped like a snake'
       (*maneto·wi* PV 'of manitou', |ketakikan-| 'be striped stick', |e·h=–niki| 0´/AOR)

Abstract nouns made productively with |-wen| NF regularly make derived prewords with |-i|
PF replacing the |-en|, as if directly from the underlying verb (cf. 4.7, 102). These are used as
both preverbs (cf. 5.3) and prenouns.

(5.14) Prewords corresponding to abstract nouns in |-wen| NF

(a)   *nahi-ki·ke·nowi-kanakanawite* 'if he's good at giving clan feast speeches'
       (K-BB 54)
       (*nahi* PV 'given to',
         ki·ke·nowi (PN)PV 'of clan feast' [← |ki·ke·nowen-|, |ki·ke·no·n-| IN 'clan feast'
           ← |ki·ke·no-| AI 'give clan feast'],
         |CVCV+| RED2, |kanawi-| AI 'speak', |–te| 3s/SUBJ)
       (Cf. *ki·ke·nowi-kanakanawi·ni* 'clan feast speeches, prayers' [K-Auto 243],
         with *ki·ke·nowi* PN 'of clan feast' [5.3*b*].)

(b)   *wi·h=mi·ka·ti·wi-ayo·yani* 'that you (sg.) would use it for warfare' (K-WD 143G)
       (|wi·h=| FUT, *mi·ka·ti·wi* (PN)PV 'of war' [← |mi·ka·ti·wen-| IN 'war, mortal
         combat' ← |mi·ka·ti·-| AI 'fight'], |ayo·-| TI(3) 'use', |e·h=–yani| 2s/AOR)
       (Cf. *mi·ka·ti·wi-ayo·weni* 'battle weaponry' [O 49A], with *mi·ka·ti·wi* PN 'of
         war'.)
       wi·h=mi·ka·ti·wi-ni·miwaki 'they shall dance the war dance' (K-WarD 11)
       (|wi·h=| FUT, *mi·ka·ti·wi* PV 'of war', |ni·mi-| AI 'dance', |–waki| 3p/IND)
       (Cf. *mi·ka·ti·wi-ni·miweni* 'war dance' [K-WarD 1].)

(c)   *wiˑh=ni miwi-nakamo niwiwani* 'they will be dancing songs' (K-Spot 222)
       (|wiˑh=| FUT, *ni miwi* (PN)PV 'of dancing' [← |niˑmiwen-| IN 'dance' ←
       |niˑmi-| AI 'dance'], |nakamoˑniwi-| II 'be a song', |–wani| 0p/IND)
       (Cf. *ni miwi-nakamo nani* 'dancing songs' [O 10D]
       ← *ni miwi* PN 'of dancing' + *nakamo nani* 'songs'.)

There are no prewords made directly from the noun stems |kiˑkeˑnowen-|, |kiˑkeˑnoˑn-| IN 'clan feast' or |miˑkaˑtiˑwen-| IN 'war', without suppression of the derivational ending. In the case of *ni miwi* PN,PV 'of dancing', there is beside this usual form a single possible attestation of *ni miweni* PN: *ni miweni-nakamo nani* 'dancing songs' (K-Spot 316). Presumably this could as well be taken as *ni miweni nakamo nani*, with *ni miweni* as an adjunct noun (**§22.5**).

Ostensible preverbs in lexicalized combinations with participles and agent nouns in |-h| NF (**§46.2**), which are used especially as male names, apparently must be taken as prenouns added to the participle or derived noun and not as preverbs with the underlying verb stem, since initial change is found only on the second element, not on the preword (contrast 4.230*c*). Other expressions that appear to have this construction may also be lexicalized (5.15*f*).

(5.15) Prewords on participles and agent nouns

(a)   *ahki-ne masotaˑha* "He-who-makes-the-Earth-rise-at-his-Call" (Jones 1907:12.13)
       (|ahki| PN 'of earth'; *|nemasot-| TI(1) 'make stand by calling', |IC–aˑh-|
       [cf. 4.230])

(b)   *ahki-niˑkaˑnisaˑta* (Swan Clan man)
       (|ahki| PN 'of earth'; |niˑkaˑnisaˑ-| AI 'fly in the lead', |IC–ta| 3/PPL(ANsg))

(c)   *mehtekwi-peˑkataˑha* (Brown Bear Clan man)
       (|mehtekwi| PN 'of tree, stick'; |pakat-| TI(1) 'hit', |IC–aˑh-| [cf. 4.230*bc*])

(e)   *piˑneši-peˑmipahoˑha* 'automobile' (*piˑneši* 'spontaneously', |pemipaho-| AI 'run')

(f)   *keˑhta-wiˑčawiwaka* 'my former husband' (A 148D; cf. 5.121*a*(2))
       (*keˑhta* PN 'old, former'; |wiˑčawiw-| TA 'be with', |IC–aka| 1s–3/PPL(ANsg))

Particle Compounds

60.3. A particle compound consists of a preparticle and a head particle. In addition to simple particle compounds with the same internal syntax as compound nouns and verbs (5.16), there are exocentric (5.17-19) and enumerative (5.21) particle compounds.

In a simple particle compound the head particle is a free particle (**§18.10**), which may be used by itself, and the preparticle modifies it in the same way that a prenoun or preverb modifies a head noun or head verb. In fact, the preparticles used in simple particle compounds are typically matched by identical preverbs. The distinction between particle compounds and particle phrases (**§64**) is not sharp; there is no morphological test for discriminating them as there is in the case of compound verbs and verbs modified by free particles. It seems reasonable to take as particle compounds those with a first element that is bound as an ostensible proclitic (5.16*a*), is not used alone (5.16*b*), is semantically empty (5.16*c*), or always shows elision where possible (5.16*defgh*). Enclitics may usually be added either to the preparticle (but not to *ana* [5.16*a*; and see Note]) or to the head particle. Ostensible particle compounds that are found without an internal word-divider have sometimes been transcribed as if restructured as single words, but the distinction can often not be tested and has not been consistently made.

(5.16) Simple particle compounds

  (a) |ana| (intensifier with certain particles):

   1) *ana=nešiwi, 'na=nešiwi* (A 167) 'as terribly as can be, terrific, awful' (*nešiwi* 'terribly')

   2) *ana=kiˑšaˑkoči, 'na=kiˑšaˑkoči* 'as extremely as possible' (*kiˑšaˑkoči* 'extremely')

  (b) *piˑkeˑwi* 'to exhaustion':

   1) *piˑkeˑw-aškači* 'after a very long time' (C-FS 14; SP-Pich1 85)
       piˑkeˑwi-aškači (K-W 228; SP-Pich1 86)

   2) *ana=kiˑšaˑkoči .. piˑkeˑwi-ašawaye* 'way, way long ago' (K-M 929b)
       ana-piˑkeˑwi-ašawaye "ever so long before" (K-Wap 161; tr. TB)

  (c) *iši* '{so}' (idiom: 2.246):

   1) *iši-nyeˑwi: iˑni=meko iši-nyeˑwi* 'those were the only four' (O 37E)

   2) *iši-nyeˑwenwi: iˑni iši-nyeˑwenwi* 'just those four times' (O 20G)
       (*iˑni* 'that (inan.)'; *=meko* EMPH; *nyeˑwi* 'four'; *nyeˑwenwi* 'four times')

  (d) *katawi* 'almost':

   1) *kataw-aškweˑyawi* 'almost at the end of the row'
       (*aškweˑyawi* 'at the end of the row')

  (e) *kehči* 'greatly':

   1) *kehč-ahkowi* 'long afterwards' (K-YC 32) (*ahkowi* 'behind')

   2) *kehč-ahpemeki* 'way up high' (K-RYL 4; C-PD 2) (*ahpemeki* 'up, above')

   3) *kehč-anemyaˑka* 'far downstream' (K-MIM 10) (*anemyaˑka* 'downstream')

   4) *kehč-ataˑnahka=meko* "very far over this way" (K-Wap 72; tr. TB)
       (*ataˑnahka* 'over this way'; *=meko* EMPH)

   5) *kehč-aˑwasi* 'a lot more' (K-Wap 90; X6-MF 15) (*aˑwasi* 'more'; *=meko* EMPH)
       kehči-=meko -aˑwasi 'a great deal more' (SP-BSAB 49)

   6) *kehči-=meko -penoˑči* "very far off indeed" (K-Wap 71; tr. TB)
       (*penoˑči* 'far away'; *=meko* EMPH)

  (f) *maˑwači* 'of all' (making superlatives):

   1) *maˑwač-ahkowi* 'last of all' (usual expression);
       maˑwači-ahkowi apenoˑha 'the youngest child of the family' (only K-Kin 13)
       maˑwač-ahkowi=meko, maˑwači-=meko -ahkowi 'last of all' (*ahkowi* 'behind')

   2) *maˑwač-ahpemeki* 'highest up of all' (*ahpemeki* 'up, above, in the air or sky')

   3) *maˑwači-menehta* "first of all" (K-FC 386; tr. HP)
       maˑwači-mehtami 'first of all' (BL-RL 3)
       maˑwači-=mekoho -menehta "the very first" (K-FC 620; tr. HP)

  (g) *meči* 'quite' (cf. 5.117*h*):

   1) *meč-aškači* 'after quite a long time' (K-M 662b)

   2) *meči-poˑsi* 'the worst' (K-OKUT 29):
       (*aˑkwi*) *meči-poˑsi* '(not) very much' (K-M 240i, 434d)

   3) (*aˑkwi*) *meči-kwiˑyena* '(not) quite right' (A 65E, 81B, 119B; K-FC 593):
       ayoˑh=wiˑna aˑkwi meči-kwiˑyena. (K-M 490e; tr. HP)
       "It is not a very good thing to do that here."

  (h) *poˑsi* 'moreso, to an extreme':

   1) *poˑs-ahpemeki* 'even higher, (even) further up'
       poˑsi-=meko -ahpemeki "still higher" (K-W 194; tr. HP)
       (*ahpemeki* 'up, above, in the air'; *=meko* EMPH)

2) *po·s-anehki·hi* 'even less (than before)' (*anehki·hi* 'a little bit')

3) *po·s-ašiči* 'closer' (LL in LLJB-Ksh 4);
   po·si-=meko -ašiči 'even closer' (K-MMB 18)
      (*ašiči* 'close'; *=meko* EMPH)

4) *po·s-aškači* 'much later' (K-WWB 17);
   po·si-=meko -aškači me·hi 'a good while afterwards' (K-Wap 53)
      (*aškači* 'later'; *aškači me·hi* 'later (dim.)'; *=meko* EMPH)

5) *po·s-a·wasi, po·s-a·wasi me·hi* 'even more (than before)'
      (*a·wasi* 'more', *a·wasi me·hi* 'more (dim.)')

6) *po·si-kehčine* 'nearer' (K-FASB 7);
   po·si-kehčine=meko (K-S 8), *po·si-kehčine·he=meko* (K-Wap 119) '(even) nearer';
   po·si-=meko -kehčine (K-HS 27),
    po·si-=meko -kehčine·he (K-FC 369) '(even) nearer'
      (*kehčine* 'near', *kehčine·he* 'near (dim.)'; *=meko* EMPH)

7) *po·si-na·meki* 'further under' (K-CBFB 23) (*na·meki* 'underneath')

8) *po·si-na·waka·me=meko* 'further out in the stream' (K-K 11)
      (*na·waka·me* 'in midstream'; *=meko* EMPH)

9) *po·si-=meko -peno·či* 'even further away' (K-BS 3)
      (*peno·či* 'far away'; *=meko* EMPH)

(i) *tepi* 'exactly, full number of':

1) *tepi-nye·wenwi* 'exactly four times' (K-BHD2 95)

2) *tepi-nye·wokoni* 'the full four days' (JP-YMPE 84)

3) *a·kwi=·'pi tepi-meta·sokoni* 'not the full ten days' (SP-Mak 22)

60.4. Exocentric and enumerative compounds. Exocentric and enumerative particle compounds have the same formal and semantic structure as single-word exocentric and enumerative particles (**§38.5**, 4.113) but have the form of compounds. They differ from simple particle compounds in that the head particle, although a separate phonological word, cannot be used except in compounds of these types. As a distinct word the head particle is referred to as an exocentric compound member (ECM), but this is a morphological label of convenience rather than a distinct part of speech.

In these particle compounds the preparticle is derived from an initial with |-i| PF ABSTR (**§38.2**, 4.104), and the head particle is derived from the stem of a noun (or virtual noun) or of an intransitive verb by suffixing |-e| PF EXO, which combines irregularly with stems of certain types. After |k|, |-e| EXO is usually replaced by -*i* (5.18*b*(1), *c*(9)) but may sometimes be retained as -*e* (5.17*f*(9)). When an AI or II stem in |-e·| adds |-e| EXO the outcome is a single -*e* (5.18*b*(2)-(5)). Some AI and II verbs with an abstract final (|-i| AI,II, |-at| II, |-en| II) drop the final and add |-e| EXO (5.18*b*(6), *c*(1)-(3), (5)-(6), (9), 5.19*ab*), but those with |-ya·| II ABSTR retain this as -*ye* (5.18*b*(7)). Often, however, |-e| EXO is added rather to a noun stem (or virtual noun stem) derived from the II by the addition of |-w| NF (**§46.1**, 4.220; 5.18*c*(4), (7), (10)-(13)). The verb |pepo·-| II 'be winter' makes *pepo·nwe* ECM 'winter, year' (5.19*c*, 21*a*(4), 21*e*), as if the verb were *|pepo·n-| II (cf. **§34.4**, 4.15*e*), which comparative evidence supports (see 5.19*c*).

Prevocalic elision of the final vowel of the first member of the compound is common. Compounds that are not attested without elision or with a written word divider may be taken to be restructured as single words (and are so written in 5.18*b*). Even in such cases, however, an enclitic may attach to the preparticle (5.18*b*(4)).

When head particles are derived from the head nouns of compound nouns (5.17*e*(4), *h*(2)), the prenouns are ostensibly recategorized as preparticles (cf. §**38.4**).

60.5. Exocentric compounds. Exocentric particle compounds are often equivalent to English prepositional phrases or adverbial noun phrases. The head particle is made from a noun stem or, less commonly, from an intransitive verb stem:

(5.17) Exocentric particle compounds with head particles derived from nouns

(a) *ahkwiči* PP 'on top of' (← |ahkwit-| + |-i| PF ABSTR; 4.104*a*):

1) *ahkwiči-ki·škitepe·hikane* 'on top of a stump' (K-FW 14, K-Pich 39)
   (*ki·škitepe·hikane* ECM ← |ki·škitepe·hikan-| IN 'stump' + |-e| PF EXO)

2) *ahkwiči-mese* 'on top of the woodpile' (SP-HL 36)
   (*mese* ECM ← |mese·h-|, |-mes-| [cf. 3.89] 'piece of firewood')

3) *ahkwiči-pemitasakatwe* 'on top of a log' (K-W 190)
   (← *pemitasakatwi* 'fallen log')

4) *ahkwiči-penekwa·hkiwe* 'on top of an overhanging bank' (SP-KCB 20)
   (← *penekwa·hkiwi* 'overhanging bank')

5) *ahkwiči-šowanakeše* 'on top of vines' (K-SGG 15) (← *šowanakeši* 'vine')

(b) *aka·mi* PP 'on the other side of':

1) *aka·mi-kehčikami·we* 'on the other side of the sea, ocean' (K-Pich 1, JP-MWM 17)
   (← *kehčikami·wi* 'sea, ocean')

2) *aka·mi-pi·kihtanwe* 'on the other side of the Missouri River' (SP-Wet 1)
   (← *pi·kihtanwi* 'Missouri River')

(c) *a·pehtawi* PP 'half, halfway':

1) *a·pehtawi-pena·we* 'for half the summer' (K-MLF 64, K-FC 91)
   (*pena·we* ECM [← |pena·wi-| II 'be the warm months of the year' + |-e| PF EXO])

2) *a·pehtawi-ki·šekwe* 'halfway to the sky' (Jones 1907:62.17, K-FC 257, JB-Tiger 33)
   (← *ki·šekwi* 'sky')

(d) *a·šowi* PP 'across, on or to the other side'; *a·ya·šowi* PP (← |CV+| RED1, *a·šowi* PP):

1) *a·šowi-kehčikami·we* 'across the sea, ocean' (K-W 671) (cf. 5.17*b*(1))

2) *a·šowi-kepi·hikane* 'on the other side of the fence' (SP-Mak 15)
   (← *kepi·hikani* 'fence')

3) *a·šowi-očini·kwe .. oški·šekwi* 'his other eye' (K-W 52)
   (*očini·kwe* ECM ← *|očini·kwe·-| AI 'have an eye oriented {so}')

4) *a·šowi-si·ke·ya·we* 'around the (next) bend (of the river)' (K-W 937, K-Wap 154)
   (*si·ke·ya·we* ECM ← *|si·ke·ya·w-| IN 'river bend'
   ← |si·ke·ya·-| II 'be, have a river bend')

5) *a·ya·šowi-pehkwa·hkwa·we* 'back and forth across the grove of trees' (JP-MC8D 19))
   (← *pehkwa·hkwa·wi* 'grove')

6) *a·ya·šowi-wa·panwe* 'every other day' (K-Spot 42) (← *wa·panwi* 'day')

(e) *či·ki* PP 'by the side of, next to' (4.104*b*):

1) *či·ki-kehčikami·we* 'at the edge of the sea' (K-GBuff 55, K-W 112) (cf. 5.17*b*(1))

2) *či·ki-pemitasakatwe* 'next to a log' (JB-SB 10, K-W 568) (cf. 5.17*a*(3))

3) *či·ki-wi·kiya·pihkiwe* 'near the settlement' (K-GB 35, K-JM 22, K-M 306*j*)
   (← *wi·kiya·pihkiwi* 'collection of houses' [2.150])

4) *či·ki-=meko -kohpiči-nenoswi-ki·ška·pehkatenwe* 'right next to the buffalo cliff'
   (K-MLF 78) (← *kohpiči-nenoswi-ki·ška·pehkatenwi* 'buffalo cliff (where buffalo
   manitous live)')

(f) *keki* PP 'with, having along':

1) *keki-čiˑmaˑne* 'with the canoe, canoe and all' (K-B 27, K-W 269)
   (← *čiˑmaˑni* 'canoe')

2) *keki-apenoˑhe, kek-apenoˑhe* 'with children, accompanied by their children, with their children in tow' (← *apenoˑha* 'child') (K-ECRP 55; K-Wap 18) (4.104*d*);
   keki-=mekoho -apenoˑhe "including all the children" (K-FC 177; tr. HP)

3) *keki-ihkweˑwe, keki-ˑhkweˑwe* 'including the women' (← *ihkweˑwa* 'woman') (K-GBuff 213; K-FASB 59, K-FC 315, K-IFSB 1, etc.)

4) *keki-mahkesene* 'with moccasins on' (← |mahkesen-| for |mahkeseˑh-| IN 'moccasin') (K-M 176)

5) *keki-maškimoteˑhe* 'with the bag, bag and all' (C-YBB 8) (← *maškimoteˑhi* 'bag')

6) *keki-meškwe* 'while still bloody' (K-OKUT 2)
   (*meškwe* ECM ← |meškw-| IN 'blood' + |-e| EXO)

7) *keki-nepoˑpe* 'with the broth, broth and all' (K-FC 94) (← |nepoˑp-| IN 'soup')

8) *keki-=meko -nepye* 'together with the water' (K-MFS 30) (← |nepy-| IN 'water')

9) *kek-očeˑpihke* 'with the roots' (S-W 31) (← *očeˑpihki* 'root')

10) *keki-onešiwe* 'along with the testicles' (cf. *onešiwahi* 'his testicles'):
    owiˑnaka wa wani keki-onešiwe (Jones 1907:196.16)
    'their penises with the testicles attached'

11) *keki-=mekoho -pešekesiwe* 'including the deer' (K-Spot 82) (← *pešekesiwa* 'deer')

12) *keki-piˑsehkaˑhe* 'wearing a shirt' (← *piˑsehkaˑhi* 'shirt') (K-TCSB 103)

13) *keki-tehkinaˑkane* 'with the cradleboard' (C-RS 24, SP-BKWM 80)
    (← *tehkinaˑkani* 'cradleboard')

14) *keki-wiˑkiyaˑpe* 'along with the house' (AW) (← |wiˑkiyaˑp-| IN 'house'; 3.97):
    keki-wiˑkiyaˑpe=meko (K-WYB 197)

15) *keki-wiˑsaye* 'with the hair on' (K-OKUT 2) (cf. *owiˑsayi* 'a hair')

(g) *naˑmi* PP 'underneath, within':

1) *naˑmi-anaˑhkane* 'under the mat' (K-FC 356)
   (← *anaˑhkani* 'mat')

2) *naˑmi-asenye* 'under a rock' (← |aseny-| IN 'stone'; *aseni*) (K-M 459*c*, 1195*g*)

3) *naˑmi-kehtikaˑne* 'somewhere in the cornfield' (SP-P 32, SP-KFK 33)
   (← *kehtikaˑni* '(planted) field')

(h) *naˑwi* PP 'in the middle of, amidst':

1) *naˑwi-=mekoho -asenye* 'right in the middle of the rock' (K-SSP 28)
   (← |aseny-| IN 'stone'; =*mekoho* EMPH)

2) *naˑwi-=mekoho -ašaˑhi-maˑwaˑkaˑne* (K-FC 334)
   'smack in the middle of a Sioux village'
   (← *ašaˑhi-maˑwaˑkaˑni* 'Sioux village' ← *ašaˑhi* PN 'of Sioux', *maˑwaˑkaˑni* 'village')

3) *naˑwi-kiˑškaˑpehkatenwe* 'in the middle of a cliff' (K-Apay 101, FASB 84):
   naˑwi-=meko -kiˑškaˑpehkatenwe 'right in the middle of a precipice' (K-BHD 5)
   (← *kiˑškaˑpehkatenwi* 'cliff' ← |kiˑškaˑpehkaten-| II 'be a cliff')
   naˑwi-kiˑškiˑškaˑpehkatenwe 'amid cliffs':
   naˑwi-=meko -kiˑškiˑškaˑpehkatenwe 'right among the cliffs' (K-FC 568)
   (as if ← *|kiˑškiˑškaˑpehkatenw-| IN ← |kiˑškiˑškaˑpehkaten-| II 'be cliffs')

4) *na·wi-=meko=na·hka -nepise* 'right back into the middle of the lake' (JP-MC8D 22)
     (← *nepisi* 'lake'; =*meko* EMPH; *na·hka* 'again')

5) *na·wi-nepye* 'in the midst of the water' (K-Auto 41) (← |nepy-| IN 'water')

6) *na·wi-pekeše·we* 'through the mist' (K-M 8b; HP "amidst the smoke")
     (*pekeše·we* ECM ← *pekeše·wi* IN 'smoke'; cf. 5.18*c*(8))

7) *na·wi-=mekoho -šepwa·hkiwe* 'right in the middle of the valley' (K-M 698k)
     (← *|šepwa·hkiw-|* IN 'valley')

8) *na·wi-wa·pikonimišihkiwe* 'in the middle of a pumpkin patch' (SP-MBW 58)
     (← *|wa·pikonimišihkiw-|* IN 'pumpkin patch')

9) *na·wi-=mekoho -wi·kiya·pihkiwe* 'in the very midst of the houses' (K-FC 782)
     (cf. 5.17*e*(3))

(i) *pi·či* PP 'inside':

1) *pi·či-mahkahkwe* 'in the box' (Voorhis 1971:67)
     (← *mahkahkwi* 'box')

2) *pi·či-wa·nata·kane* 'in the hollow of the mound' (K-Spot 309)
     (← *wa·nata·kani* 'depression on ceremonial mound')

(5.18) Exocentric particle compounds with head particles derived from verbs

(a) *a·ya·šowi* PP (← |CV+| RED1, *a·šowi* PP; cf. 5.16*d*):
     a·ya·šowi-pehkote 'every other night' (K-SGG 214)
     (*pehkote* ECM ← |pehkote·-| II 'be night')

(b) *keki* PP 'with, having along':

1) *kekaški* (or *kek-aški*) 'raw, while still raw' (AW, Jones 1907:166.3, BL-OS 6,
     K-GB 46, K-SF 36, K-SGG 91, K-W 424; always written as one word)
     (← |keki| PP 'with, having' + *aški* ECM [← |ašken-| II 'be raw' + |-e| EXO])

2) *keki-=meko -meškwano·te* 'while still red-hot' (K-MMGW 10)
     (*meškwano·te* ECM ← |meškwano·te·-| II 'be red hot' + |-e| EXO)

3) *keki-mya·no·te* 'while menstruating' (K-Wewe 8)
     (*mya·no·te* ECM ← |mya·no·te·-| AI 'menstruate' + |-e| EXO)

4) *kekine·se* 'alive, while still alive' (*ne·se* ECM ← |ne·se·-| AI 'be still alive' + |-e| EXO)
     (O 50D. NOTE: this is never written with a word divider in syllabic texts.)
     keki-=ke·h=-ne·se=meko 'what's more even while still alive' (JB in LLJB-KSH 16)

5) *kekipasete* 'while still hot' (K-EGC 19, K-TCSB 65)
     (*pasete* ECM ← |pasete·-| II 'be hot (e.g., food)' + |-e| EXO)

6) *kekiši·ka·we* 'while still in strict mourning for a spouse' (K-MortE 46, K-SGG 79)
     (*ši·ka·we* ECM ← |ši·ka·wi-| AI 'be widow, widower in strict mourning' + |-e| EXO)

7) *kekitahkye* 'while still cold' (K-TM 2)
     (*tahkye* ECM ← |tahkya·-| II 'be cold' + |-e| EXO)

(c) *na·wi* PP 'in the middle of, amidst':

1) *na·wi-=meko -aša·hahkiwe* 'right in the middle of a bunch of Siouxs' (K-MDLA 11)
     (← *|aša·hahkiwi-|* II 'be ground covered with Siouxs' [← |aša·h-| AN 'Sioux'];
     cf. |mešise·wahkiwi-| II 'be a lek, a place where prairie chickens gather')

2) *na·wi-ihkwe·wahkiwe* 'in the middle of the women' (K-WLB 13)
     (← *|ihkwe·wahkiwi-|* II 'be ground covered with women')

?   3) *na·wi-kepiwahkiwe* 'in the middle of some brushwood' ()
     (← *|kepiwahkiwi-|* II 'be ground covered with brush')

4) *na·wi-ki·wa·ča·we* 'in the middle of a lonely place' (K-Auto 143, K-M 326i)
(*ki·wa·ča·we* ECM ← |ki·wa·ča·w-| [← |ki·wa·ča·-| II 'be lonely', |-w| NF] + |-e| EXO)

5) *na·wi-=mekoho·-mahkwa·tahkiwe* 'in a quiet or holy place' (K-M 496k, 503j)
(← *|mahkwa·tahkiwi-| II 'be a quiet place' [← |mahkwa·t-| 'quiet'];
cf. |wa·waneška·hahkiwi-| II 'be a wicked place, a place of bad behavior')

6) *na·wi-=meko·-nenoswahkiwe* 'right in the middle of a herd of buffalo' (K-B 2)
(← *|nenoswahkiwi-| II 'be ground covered with buffalos')

7) *na·wi-=mekoho·-nešiwatwe* 'right in the middle of a dangerous place' (K-ECRP 59A)
(*nešiwatwe* ← |nešiwatw-| [← |nešiwat- II 'be a danger' + |-w| NF + |-e| EXO)

8) *na·wi-pekeše* 'amidst the smoke or fog' (K-SGG 210, K-FC 231, K-OKUT 45, etc.)
na·wi-=meko·-pekeše 'completely cloaked in fog' (K-SGG 212)
(*pekeše* ECM ← |pekeše·-| II 'be smoky, be foggy'; cf. 5.17*h*(6))

9) *na·wi-pi·kwaški* 'in the middle of thick weeds' (K-CBFB 20; A 40C)
(*pi·kwaški* ECM ← |pi·kwašk-| [← |pi·kw-ašk-at-| II 'be thick weeds'] + |-e| EXO)

10) *na·wi-pi·kwa·we* 'in the middle of a thicket' (A 37B)
(*pi·kwa·we* ECM ← *|pi·kwa·w-| [← pi·kwa·-| II 'be a thicket'] + |-w| NF + |-e| EXO)

11) *na·wi-=mekoho·-sanakatwe* 'right in the most difficult places' (K-FC 785)
(*sanakatwe* ECM
← *|sanakatw-| [← sanakat-| II 'be difficult'] + |-w| NF] + |-e| EXO)

12) *na·wi-sasakanwe* 'in the middle of the brush' (A 173C),
na·wi-=mekoho·-sasakanwe 'right in the midst of a thicket' (K-SSP 250)
(*sasakanwe* ECM ← *|sasakanw-| [← sasakan-| II 'be brush'] + |-w| NF | + |-e| EXO)

13) *na·wi-='yo=ke·h=meko·-mehta·hte·we* 'now, right out in the hot sun' (K-MBT 3)
(*mehta·hte·we* ECM
← |mehta·hte·w-| [← |mehta·hte·-| II 'be hot sun'] + |-w| NF + |-e| EXO)

(5.19) Exocentric compounds with |nehkani|, |nahkani| PP 'throughout, the length of time of, the whole (period) long' and head particles derived from verbs or nouns:

(a) *nehkani-ana·kwe* 'all through the evening' (Jones 1907:210.9)
(*ana·kwe* ECM ← |ana·kw-| [← |ana·kwi-| II 'be evening'] + |-e| EXO)

(b) *nehkani-pena·we* 'all summer long'; 'in the course of the warm season' (O 9G, 90F)
(*pena·we* ECM ← |pena·w-| [← |pena·wi-| II 'be the warm season'] + |-e| EXO)

(c) *nehkani-pepo·nwe* 'all winter long' (K-SPC 23, K-Wap 164, K-WMB 22)
(*pepo·nwe* ECM ← |pepo·nw-| [irregularly ← |pepo·-| II 'be winter' (cf. 4.15e),
which replaces *pepo·n- II; cf. Menominee *pepo·n* '(it is) winter'] + |-e| EXO)

(d) *nehkani-tepehkwe* 'all night long' (K-MM 10)
(*tepehkwe* ECM ← |tepehkw-| [← *tepehkwi* 'night'])

The compounds in (5.19*bcd*) are attested with medial word dividers written in the syllabic texts cited, but most constructions with with |nehkani|, |nahkani| PP are treated as single words: *nehkaniki·šekwe* (K, X6), *nahkaniki·šekwe* (C, S, SP, JP, JB, LL, X10) 'all day long' (4.113*g*; 5.112*c*); *nehkanitepehkwe* (K, X6), *nahkanitepehkwe* (C, S, SP, JP, JB, LL, X10) 'all night long' (5.112*e*).

In some cases an exocentric compound exists beside a single-word exocentric particle in which the final is derived from the noun that the head particle of the compound is made from (5.20*a*). Another equivalent construction is a particle phrase (5.71) consisting of the particle corresponding to the preparticle of the compound followed by the locative form of the noun from which the head particle is derived (5.20*b*).

(5.20) Alternate constructions

(a) *ahkwič-atasane* (S-RL 56) 'on top of the platform' (← *atasani* 'platform')
ahkwičitasane (K-M 175k) 'on top of the platform'
(← |ahkwit-| 'on top' + |-i-tasane| [← |atasan-| IN 'platform'])

(b) *ahkwiči-asenye* 'on top of the rock' (K-B 199, K-WYB 198),
ahkwič-asenye (K-PKM 7) (4.104*a*)
ahkwiči aseni·ki, aseni·ki ahkwiči 'on top of the rock' (5.71*a*)

60.6. Enumerative compounds. The preparticle in an enumerative compound is a numeral or numeral substitute (e.g., *ke·swi* 'how much, many?', *na·htaswi* 'several, a few', *taswi* '{so much, many}'). The second component is derived from a noun (but may not be attested as such).

(5.21) Enumerative compounds

(a) *nekoti* PP 'one':

1) *nekoti-aneškenačike·wene* 'one pipeful' (K-B 80) (cf. 4.209*c*)
2) *nekoti-ki·šeswe* 'in, for one month' (Jones 1907:140.16, K-W 412)
(← |ki·šesw-| AN 'month; sun, moon')
3) *nekoti-pehkwineče* 'one fistful' (C-WH 12)
4) *nekoti-pepo·nwe* 'in, for one year' (K-BB 30, K-MESB 49) (cf. 5.19*c*)
5) *nekoti-te·tepeče·ha·te·he* 'one barrelful' (K-MKD 7) (← *te·tepeče·ha·te·hi* 'barrel')
6) *nekoti-wa·se·ya·we* 'in, for one day' (K-CGB, K-M 214k [with word divider];
K-BBWM 6, K-BD 6 [no word-divider]) (← |wa·se·ya·w-| IN 'daylight, day')

(b) *ni·šwi* PP 'two':

1) *ni·šwi-ahpanehki·wene* 'two paces' (SP-PD1 2) (cf. 4.209*a*)
2) *ni·šwi-si·niti·he .. menihki* 'two pails of milk' (K-Pich 9)
3) *ni·šwi-še·šketo·he* 'two kettlefuls' (K-B 238) (← *še·šketo·ha* 'kettle')
4) *ni·šwi-te·tepeče·ha·te·he* 'two barrelfuls' (cf. 5.21*a*(5)):
na ni·šwi-te·tepeče·ha·te·he kwe·ke·ši 'two barrels of crackers each' (S-YMSG 19)

(c) *nye·wi* PP 'four':

1) *nye·wi-ki·šeswe* 'for four months' (K-B 204, K-M 768a) (cf. 5.21*a*(2))
2) *nye·wi-mahkahkwe* 'four thousand' (JB-Tiger 65) (← |mahkahkw-| IN 'box')
3) *nye·wi-wa·se·ya·we* 'for four days' (K-PBLA 3, C-L 352) (cf. 5.21*a*(6))

(d) *ke·swi* PP 'how much?':

ke·swi-šo·niya·he 'how much money?' (← |šo·niya·h-| IN 'money')

(e) *na·htaswi* PP 'several':

1) *na·htaswi-pena·we* "for several seasons" (K-Auto 15; tr. IP) (cf. 5.19*b*)
2) *na·htaswi-pepo·nwe* 'for several years' (K-Auto 136) (cf. 5.19*c*)
3) *na·htaswi-tepehkwe* 'for several nights' (cf. 5.21*c*(3):
a·kwi=ke·hi na·htaswi-tepehkwe 'not for just a few nights' (K-Auto 80)

(f) *taswi* PP '{so many}':

1) *5 taswi-ahpanehki·wene* 'at five paces' (SP-KFC 29)
2) *nekotwa·hkwe tasw-ahpanehki·wene* 'one hundred paces' (JB-WMD 2)

Enumerative compounds occur with adjunct nouns (5.21*b*(2,4)). It is noteworthy that the numeral preparticles in enumerative compounds have the literal meanings of the corresponding free numeral particles (*nekoti* P 'one', *ni·šwi* P 'two', etc.), unlike the homophonous preverbs, which have collective and idiomatic meanings (4.106-107).

As with some exocentric compounds (5.20*a*), some enumerative compounds exist beside single-word particles with a final derived from the noun or virtual noun that the head particle is made from (e.g., *nekoti-tepehkwe* beside *nekotitepehkwe* 'for one night'), but the distinction is not consistently made (5.21a(6)), and the examples in 5.21 are normalized as compounds.

The system of numbers and counting is illustrated in Goddard and Thomason (2014:404-407) and in Jones (1911:857-865).

MODULES

61. The constituent modules of sentences are noun phrases (**§62**), verb phrases (**§63**), and particle phrases (**§64**). A module is an abstract structural unit consisting of one or more words. The words that make up a module need not occur as a contiguous sequence but may be separated by other modules or parts of other modules. The internal structure of a module is part of the structure of the sentence, and a single component in a module may be semantically or syntactically linked to another module.

Noun Phrases

62. A prototypical noun phrase may be thought of as consisting of a noun and words that modify or depend on the noun. A noun phrase may, however, comprise only a noun or a pronoun, or, conversely, it may consist of one or more noun modifiers without a noun (**§62.1**). A noun phrase may be linked to the rest of a sentence in four basic ways: by the agreement function of the pronominal reference made by an inflected verb or possessed noun (**§22**); as the complement of the oblique valence of another word (**§22.4**); as an adjunct (**§22.5**); or as one of the terms of an equational sentence (**§66.1**). Noun phrases may also contain adnominal particles (5.28, 5.36, 5.47, 5.51, 5.56*bc*, 5.57*a*).

In a locative noun phrase a noun, or a determiner used without a noun, is in the locative form (**§§24, 28.15, 31.2**), but a determiner used with a noun is optionally either locative (2.153, 5.32*e*) or not (5.32*d*). A locative noun phrase may be part of a particle phrase of location (5.71).

More than one noun phrase may combine to form a higher order noun phrase. In such cases the additional noun phrase may be conjoined, with or without a particle meaning 'and'; it may be in apposition, having the same referent; it may be a possessor noun phrase referred to by the pronominal inflection of a possessed noun in its agreement function; or it may be an adjunct. Conjoined and appositional nouns may agree or differ in obviation; if one is proximate and the other obviative the combined noun phrase is construed as proximate (**§62.4**).

A noun phrase may consist of or contain a participle (**§26.13, 17**), a verb form that functions as a noun or noun modifier, and it may thus include all the parts of the clause that centers on the participle in its verbal function. Other kinds of nominalized verbs may also be the components of noun phrases (5.40*ef*, 5.73*a*).

A noun phrase may contain a determiner or a quantifier, or both. The determiners are the demonstrative, place-holder, and alternative pronouns (**§18.5, 8, 9**); these adopt the gender of the noun they modify or substitute for and agree with the noun in nominal category (**§18.2**). A demonstrative may be used with the alternative pronoun (5.25). The quantifiers are numerals and other particles and hence show no agreement for nominal categories. A numeral quantifier specifying a higher number may be a particle phrase consisting of many words (5.76*d*). A determiner usually precedes the noun but occasionally follows it (5.32-33). Quantifiers most often precede the noun but frequently come after it (5.34-35). In possessive noun phrases the possessor may precede or follow the possessed noun (5.41-42), but it always precedes if it is itself a possessed noun (5.41*b*) or if the noun phrase is discontinuous (5.162).

A noun phrase may consist of or contain an emphatic, interrogative, or indefinite pronoun (**§18.4, 6, 7**). A noun phrase with an emphatic pronoun may also contain a quantifier (5.27, 5.30*d*) or a modifying particle (5.28*a*), or both, and an emphatic pronoun may appear in apposition with a noun (4.216*k*, 5.39*e*) or in construction with a modifying verb (5.40*f*). As in verbal agreement (**§22**, 2.66), a plural emphatic pronoun may be in construction with a noun that specifies only one of the components of the conjoined set being referred to (5.39*f*).

The following sections give examples of types of noun phrases. Simple noun phrases of one or two words are given first, followed by three-word noun phrases and a few examples of even longer ones.

62.1. Noun phrases of one or two words without a noun or participle.
A.) One word.
    (5.22) Determiner alone
        (a)   *mana* "this person" (K-FC 274; tr. HP)
        (b)   *i·niki* "them" (K-FC 289; tr. HP)
    (5.23) Quantifier alone
        (a)   *a·neta* 'some (of them)' (O 18D)
        (b)   *ma·ne* 'many of them' (O 154F)
        (c)   *ni·šwi* 'two': *ni·šwi ne·sa·čiki* 'the ones that killed two' (K-WarD 11)
             (|neS-| TA 'kill', |IC–a·čiki| 3–3´/PPL(ANpl))
    (5.24) Other pronoun alone
        (a)   *ki·na* 'you (sg.)' (A 174C)
        (b)   *ki·na·na* 'us (inc.)' (O 138F)
        (c)   *owiye·ha* 'someone' (O 85C), 'anyone' (O 35A)
        (d)   *we·ne·ha* 'who?' (K-FC 59, 114)
        (e)   *ta·na* 'which one?' (K-M 241a)
B.) Two words (single noun phrase).
    (5.25) Two determiners alone
        ma·haki kotakaki 'these others' (K-SGG 124)
    (5.26) Determiner + quantifier
        (a)   *i·niki ni·šwi* 'those other two, those two' (S-RL 66; SP-MBS 90)
        (b)   *i·na=nekoti, i·na nekoti* 'that (other) one' (K-GF 27; K-ManMa 8)
    (5.27) Emphatic pronoun + quantifier
        (a)   *ni·na·na ni·šwi* 'we (exc.) two, the two of us' (SP-KFC 25)
        (b)   *ki·nwa·wa če·wi·šwi* 'both of you' (K-M 830k)
    (5.28) Quantifier, determiner, or other pronoun with modifying particle
        (a)   *mo·hči=ni·na* 'even I' (O 70C, 85G)
        (b)   *ne·h=ki·na* (A 26G), *ki·na=ne·hi* (A 59C) 'you, too' (cf. 5.121*e*)
        (c)   *mehteno·h=a·neta* 'only some' (O 124A) (cf. 5.36*c*, 5.72*e*)
            mehteno·hi ayo·hi 'only here' (K-FC 88)
        (d)   *i·niki=mekoho* 'those same ones' (K-FC 163)

C.) Two words (noun phrase and adjunct noun phrase).

(5.29) Quantifier + adjunct determiner

- (a) *a·neta=ma·haki* "some of these" (K-ECRP 72 2x; tr. TB)
- (b) *ni·šwi·='niki* 'two of them' (JB-LR 6)

(5.30) Adjunct determiner or emphatic pronoun + quantifier

- (a) *mana a·neta* 'some of these (representative singular)' (O 79F)
- (b) *ma·haki a·neta* 'some of these (people)' (O 113A)
- (c) *i·niki a·neta* 'some of them' (C-Hist 24)
- (d) *wi·nwa·wa a·neta* 'some of them' (JP-KT 45B)

62.2. Noun phrases of one or two words containing a noun or participle.

A.) One word.

(5.31) Noun or participle alone

- (a) *ni·ča·paki* 'dolls' (A 1E)
- (b) *neni·ča·paki* 'my dolls' (A 2F)
- (c) *osekwisani* 'her paternal aunt (obv.)' (A 46B)
- (d) *wi·teko wi-mi·ša·mi* 'the Owl Sacred Pack' (O 1B)
- (e) *no·hkomeseki* 'at my grandmother's (loc.)' (K-MLF 84)
- (f) *wi·čawiwaka* 'my husband' (A 94B) (cf. 5.32*f*)
         (|wi·čawiw-| TA 'be with', |IC–aka| 1s–3/PPL(ANsg))

B.) Two words: single noun phrase.

(5.32) Determiner + noun (or participle)

- (a) *i·niki neniwaki* 'those men' (O 1F)
- (b) *kotakani neniwani* 'another man (obv.)' (K-Kin 63)
- (c) *i·ni ni·miheti wi-nakamo·ni* 'that dance song' (O 21G)
- (d) *mani ki·ke·no·neki* 'in this clan feast' (JP-KT 4)
         (*mani* 'this (inan.)'; *ki·ke·no·neki* 'clan feast (loc.)')
- (e) *i·nahi mi·ša·meki* 'in that sacred pack' (K-FC 725)
            (*i·nahi* 'that (loc.); there'; *mi·ša·meki* 'sacred pack (loc.)')
- (f) *i·niya wi·čawiwaka* 'my late wife' (A 145E) (cf. 5.31*f*)
         With obviative singular demonstrative for obviative plural (**§21**):
- (g) *ma·hani meškwahki·hahi* 'these Meskwakis (obv.)' (C-Hist 20)
- (h) *i·nini mahwe·wahi* 'those wolves (obv.)' (LL in LLJB-Ksh 3)

(5.33) Noun + determiner

- (a) *mi·ša·mi=mani* "this sacred pack" (K-SSP 213; tr. HP)
- (b) *mehtose·neniwa=kotaka* "the other people" (K-FASB 62; tr. HP)
- (c) *neta·hwi·hemena·nani ma·hani* 'these possessions of ours (exc.)' (A 164G)
- (d) *kemešo·hena·na·='niya* 'our (inc.) late grandfather' (C-KO 15)
- (e) *ma·tesi mani awato·no.* 'Take this knife.' (K-EGC 1)
         (*ma·tesi* 'knife'; *mani* 'this (inan.)'; |awat-| TI(2) 'take', |–o·no| 2s–0/IMP)

(5.34) Quantifier + noun

- (a) *ni·šwi neniwaki* 'two men' (O 1E)
- (b) *ni·šwi mehteko·ni* 'two sticks' (K-FC 345)
- (c) *a·neta neniwa* 'some men (representative singular)' (K-BB 48)
- (d) *a·neta neniwaki* 'some men' (K-OWM 29)
- (e) *ča·ki maneto·waki* 'all the spirits' (K-OWM 20)
- (f) *ča·ki ke·ko·hi* 'everything' (K-MWG 22, K-GB 10; usually without a divider)

(5.35) Noun + quantifier

- (a)   *mahkwaki niˑšwi* 'two bears' (K-FC 306)
- (b)   *miˑkaˑtiˑwi-miˑšaˑmani nyeˑwi* 'four war bundles' (K-MFWB 1)
- (c)   *apenoˑhaki aˑneta* 'some children' (K-BH 9)

(5.36) Noun and modifying particle

- (a)   *noˑsa=taˑtaki* 'my father's brother' (K-Auto 167)
     (*noˑsa* 'my father, my father's brother'; *=taˑtaki* 'sort of, as it were')
- (b)   *kiˑšaˑkoči=meko memyeˑši-manetoˑwahi* 'extremely large snakes (obv.)'
     (K-Fish 125)
     (*kiˑšaˑkoči* 'extremely'; *=meko* EMPH;
     memyeˑši PN 'large (pl.)', *manetoˑwahi* 'snakes (obv.)')
- (c)   *kiˑšaˑkoči meši-keˑnwaˑsoweˑwani* 'an extremely large cougar (obv.)'
     (K-TYFB 25-26)
     (*kiˑšaˑkoči* 'extremely'; *meši* PN 'large', *keˑnwaˑsoweˑwani* 'mountain lion (obv.)')
- (d)   *kiˑšaˑkoči naweˑni-wiˑkiyaˑpeˑhi* '(it was) an extremely fine-looking house'
     (K-Mes 13)
     (*kiˑšaˑkoči* 'extremely'; *naweˑni* PN 'handsome', *wiˑkiyaˑpeˑhi* 'house (dim.)')
- (e)   *siˑsepaˑhkwi mehtenoˑhi* 'only sugar' (K-FC 204)
     (*siˑsepaˑhkwi* 'sugar'; *mehtenoˑhi* 'only' [also 5.28c, 5.72e])
- (f)   *aˑhpene=meko kemešoˑmesenaˑnaki* 'grandfathers of all of us alike' (O 124F)
     (*aˑhpene* 'all alike'; *=meko* EMPH; *kemešoˑmesenaˑnaki* 'our (inc.) grandfathers')

Some particles in noun phrases modify prenouns (5.36bcd); at least some of these can also be taken as particles that have been recategorized as prenouns in the surface structure of the compound noun (§38.4; §60.1, 5.4h).

(5.37) Noun and oblique

- (a)   *iˑnahi taši-ihkweˑwahi* 'the women (obv.) there' (K-MMD 15)
     (*iˑnahi* 'there'; *taši* PN '{somewhere}', *ihkweˑwahi* 'women (obv.)')
- (b)   *iˑni=meko iši neniwaki* 'men of that same kind' (K-WKG 45)
     (*iˑni* 'that (inan.)'; *=meko* EMPH; *iši neniwaki* 'men of {such} kind')

C.) Two words: coordinate noun phrases.

(5.38) Conjoined nouns

- (a)   *ihkweˑwa neniwa* 'a woman (prox.) and a man (prox.)':
     ihkweˑwa neniwa aˑhkwamatamowaˑte (K-Kin 66)
     'if a woman or a man is sick'
     (|aˑhkwamat-| TI(1)-O 'be sick', |-amowaˑte| 3p(-0)/SUBJ)
- (b)   *ihkweˑwa neniwani* 'a woman (prox.) and a man (obv.)':
     ihkweˑwa neniwani eˑh=taši-kaˑškanasowaˑči. (S-YMSG 15)
     'A woman and a man were whispering.'
     (|taši| PV 'be engaged in', |kaˑškanaso-| AI 'whisper', |eˑh=—waˑči| 3p/AOR)

(5.39) Nouns or noun and pronoun in apposition

- (a)   *weˑpeneˑmeˑha neniwa* 'The man (called) Turkey-Owner.' (K-TO 1, title)
- (b)   *neˑtopaˑhaki neniwaki* 'men on the warpath' (K-MMWP 1)
     (*neˑtopaˑhaki* 'war party (anim. pl.)'; *neniwaki* 'men')
- (c)   *kiˑyamoweˑwani ihkweˑwani* 'a female giant (obv.)' (K-MMGW 1)
     (*kiˑyamoweˑwani* 'cannibal giant (obv.)'; *ihkweˑwani* 'woman (obv.)')

(d)   *a·pehtawesi·hi-neno·te·wa me·mehteko·ši·ha a·neta* (K-GCF 1)

       'a half-French halfbreed Indian'

       (*a·pehtawesi·hi* PN 'halfbreed' [← *a·pehtawesi·ha* 'halfbreed'],

        neno·te·wa 'Indian';

        me·mehteko·ši·ha 'Frenchman', *a·neta* P 'some', here 'partly, the other part')

(e)   *wi·nwa·wa ko·šisemena·naki* 'our grandchildren themselves' (O 85B)

       (*wi·nwa·wa* 3p/EMPH; *ko·šisemena·naki* 'our (inc.) grandchildren')

(f)   *wi·nwa·wa ošemi·hani* 'he and his niece (by) themselves' (O 150C) (Cf. 5.101*c*.)

       (*wi·nwa·wa* 3p/EMPH; *ošemi·hani* 'his niece')

(5.40) Noun or pronoun in construction with modifying participle (**§26.13**) or aorist (**§26.8**)

  (a)   *ki·wa·ni·ta neniwa* 'The man who got lost.' (K-MGL 1, title)

  (b)   *ni·mičiki ihkwe·waki* 'the women who dance' (K-BD 7)

  (c)   *metemo·ha we·ta·nesita* 'the old woman who had (her as) a daughter' (K-TG 11)

  (d)   *oškinawe·ha me·hkate·wi·ta* 'The young man who fasted.' (S-YF 1, title)

  (e)   *mato·teše·wika·ni e·h=meša·niki* 'a big sweatlodge' (K-B 322) (Cf. 2.177.)

  (f)   *ki·na·na e·h=mehtose·neniwe·hiyakwe* 'we poor mortals' (O 144E)

       (*ki·na·na* 12/EMPH;

       |mehtose·neniwe·hi-| AI 'be a person (dim.)', |e·h=–yakwe| 12/AOR)

D.) Two words: one the possessor of the other.

  (5.41) Possessor + possessed noun

    (a)   *owiye·he·haki ohka·twa·wani* 'animals' feet' (A 99G)

    (b)   *omešo·hani oto·te·mani* 'his grandfather's brother' (K-FC 332)

    (c)   *ihkwe·wa oči·kwaneki* 'to the woman's knees' (O 54F)

  (5.42) Possessed noun + possessor

    (a)   *o·sani neniwa* "the man's father" (K-FC 82; tr. HP)

    (b)   *otahkimi keše·maneto·wani* "the Great Manitou's [obv.] land" (K-M 280e; tr. HP)

E.) Two words: one an adjunct to the other.

  (5.43) Quantifier or indefinite pronoun + adjunct noun

    (a)   *a·neta neniwahi* "some of the / men [obv.]" (K-FC 277-278; tr. HP)

    (b)   *ni·šwi osi·me·hwa·wahi* 'two of their younger brothers' (K-G 5)

    (c)   *owiye·ha ki·či·škwe·haki* 'any (sg.) of your (sg.) enemies' (K-MFWB 83)

  (5.44) Adjunct noun + quantifier

    (a)   *neto·kima·mena·naki ni·šwi* 'two of our (exc.) chiefs' (K-Auto 286)

    (b)   *kemi·ši·kwa·kanani nye·wi* 'four of your whiskers' (JB in LLJB-K 21)

    (c)   *one·moweni a·neta* 'some of his breath' (Sh-Apay 4)

  (5.45) Noun and adjunct noun or participle.

    (a)   *nakamo·nani ki·ke·no·ni* 'clan-feast songs' (O 78F)

        (*nakamo·nani* 'songs'; *ki·ke·no·ni* 'clan feast [adjunct]')

    (b)   *anene·wi wi·kiya·pi* 'the smokehole of a house' (SP-PD2 89)

        (*anene·wi* 'smokehole'; *wi·kiya·pi* 'house [adjunct]')

    (c)   *iši-mi·hkeče·wi·weni ihkwe·wiweni.* 'the types of work done by women' (A 127C)

        (*iši* PN '{so}'; *mi·hkeče·wi·weni* 'work'; *ihkwe·wiweni* 'womanhood [adjunct]')

    (d)   *i·ni mi·ša·mi ke·teminawesiničini* (K-FC 784; tr. HP)

       "the sacred bundle which belong[s] to the person who was blessed [obv.]"

        (*i·ni* 'that (inan.)'; *mi·ša·mi* 'sacred pack';

        |keteminawesi-| AI 'be blessed', |IC–ničini| 3′/PPL(OBVsg) [adjunct participle])

(e) *aša·ti·hani asenye·ni* 'stone arrowheads', *lit.*, 'stones of headed arrows' (K-FC 33)
　　(*aša·ti·hani* 'arrows having arrowheads [adjunct]'; *asenye·ni* 'stones')

(f) *nenoswi-owi·wi·naki na·tawino·ni* 'Buffalo-horn medicine.' (K-BH 1, title)
　　(*nenoswi* PN 'of buffalo'; *owi·wi·naki* 'horns [adjunct]';
　　na·tawino·ni 'medicine')

(5.46) Noun and adjunct locative noun or pronoun.

(a) *ohka·či onemači·neki* 'his left (rear) hoof' (K-MP1 14)
　　(*ohka·či* 'his foot'; *onemači·neki* 'on his left side (loc.) [adjunct]')

(b) *i·ya·h=owiye·he·hani* 'the animals (obv. sg.) up there' (K-WD 151)
　　(*i·ya·hi* 'yonder [adjunct]'; *owiye·he·hani* 'animal (obv. sg.)')

A particle that modifies a following noun may be taken as an adjunct particle (5.47), but in some combinations such ostensible particles must be taken as prenouns derived from particles (4.111*a*), and this analysis may thus be preferable in all such cases (4.111*bc*).

(5.47) Noun with adjunct particle (alternative analysis)

(a) *ašawaye kanawi·ni* 'archaic vocabulary' (K-Kin 1)
　　(*ašawaye* 'long ago [adjunct]'; *kanawi·ni* 'words')

(b) *našawaye neno·te·wa* 'an Indian of long ago' (also 5.56*c*, 5.57*a*; cf. 5.110*c*)

62.3. Noun phrases of more than two words.

A.) Three words: single noun phrase.

(5.48) Two determiners + noun

(a) *mana kotaka mehtose·neniwa* "the other people" (K-Wap 17; tr. TB)
　　(*mana* 'this (anim.)'; *kotaka* 'other (anim.)'; *mehtose·neniwa* 'person')

(b) *kotaka mana mehtose·neniwa* "the other people" (K-FC 248; tr. HP)

(c) *i·niki kotakaki neniwaki* 'those other men' (S-TMSG 10)
　　(*i·niki* 'those (anim.)'; *kotakaki* 'others (anim.)'; *neniwaki* 'men')

(5.49) Determiner + quantifier + noun; quantifier + determiner + noun

(a) *mana nekoti maneto·wa* 'this one particular manitou' (K-OKUT 37)
　　(*mana* 'this (anim.)'; *nekoti* 'one'; *maneto·wa* 'manitou')

(b) *i·niki nye·wi neniwaki* 'those four men' (X6-MM 25)
　　(*i·niki* 'those (anim.)'; *nye·wi* 'four'; *neniwaki* 'men')

(c) *nye·wi=·'nihi mahkwahi* 'those four bears (obv.)' (C-YBB 3)
　　(*nye·wi* 'four'; *i·nihi* 'those (obv.)'; *mahkwahi* 'bears (obv.)')

(5.50) Determiner (+ enclitic particle) + noun + quantifier

(a) *kotakaki še·škesi·he·haki ni·šwi* 'two other young girls' (K-W 31)
　　(*kotakaki* 'others (anim.)'; *še·škesi·he·haki* 'young girls'; *ni·šwi* 'two')

(b) *i·niki=·'nahi mami·ši·haki ni·šwi* 'including those two attendants' (K-SSP 273)
　　(*i·niki* 'those (anim.)'; *=i·nahi* 'with that'; *mami·ši·haki* 'attendants';
　　ni·šwi 'two')

(5.51) With modifying particle or locative

(a) *kotakeki no·seki=ta·taki* 'at my other paternal uncle's' (K-Auto 210)
　　(*kotakeki* 'other (loc.)'; *no·seki* 'my father (loc.)'; *=ta·taki* 'sort of')

(b) *ayo·h=mani meneseki* 'here on this island' (K-Wap 16)
　　(|ayo·hi| 'here'; *mani* 'this (inan.)'; *meneseki* 'island (loc.)')

(c) *we·ta·se·waki=meko mo·šaki* 'warriors alone' (K-WarD 8)
　　(*we·ta·se·waki* 'warriors'; *=meko* EMPH; *mo·šaki* 'alone' [cf. O 11I])

   (d)   *wi ˙nwa wa=meko ne ˙htawi* 'only they' (K-WarD 8)

         (*wi ˙nwa wa* 3p/EMPH; *=meko* EMPH; *ne ˙htawi* 'separately, exclusively')

   (e)   *ne ˙htawi=meko neniwaki* 'only men, exclusively men' (K-MMB 18)

         (*ne ˙htawi* 'separately, exclusively'; *=meko* EMPH; *neniwaki* 'men')

   (f)   *wi na=mekoho kehčine wi one moweni* 'his own personal breath' (O 84A)

         (*wi na* 3s/EMPH; *=mekoho* EMPH; *kehčine wi* 'personally'; *one moweni* 'his breath')

B.) Three words: two noun phrases.

  (5.52) Conjoined nouns with conjunction

   (a)   *še ˙škesi ˙haki o ni neniwaki* 'Maidens and Men.' (K-MM 1, title)

         (*še ˙škesi ˙haki* 'teenage girls, virgins'; *o ni* 'and (then)'; *neniwaki* 'men')

   (b)   *ihkwe wa anemo ˙hani ˙= 'nahi* 'The woman and the dog (obv.).'

        (Jones 1907:38, title)

         (*ihkwe wa* 'woman (prox.)'; *anemo ˙hani* 'dog (obv.)'; *=i nahi* 'with that')

   (c)   *mahkwani kaho ni ke ˙nwa ˙sowe wani* (JB-LR 8)

        'a bear (obv.) and a mountain lion (obv.)'

         (*mahkwani* 'bear (obv.)'; *kaho ni* 'and (then)';

         ke ˙nwa ˙sowe wani 'cougar (obv.)')

   (d)   *ihkwe waki na ˙hkači neniwaki* 'women as well as men' (O 1C)

  (5.53) Including a participle

   (a)   *nye wi me ˙me ˙ša nikini ana ˙kanani* 'four large bowls (obv.)' (O 4B)

         (*nye wi* 'four'; |Ce_e·+| RED1, |meša·-| II 'be big', |IC–nikini| 0´/PPL(INpl);

         ana ˙kanani 'bowls')

   (b)   *i ˙nini nye wi ke ˙ka ˙no ˙te nikini* 'those four longhouses (obv.)' (K-YF 17)

         (*i ˙nini* 'those (inan.)'; *nye wi* 'four';

         |Ca_a·+| RED1, |keno·te·-| II 'be a long room', |IC–nikini| 0´/PPL(INpl))

   (c)   *ma ˙haki ne ˙sa čiki neniwani* 'these (people) who killed the man' (JP-MDAT 33)

         (*ma ˙haki* 'these (anim.)'; |neS-| TA 'kill', |IC–a·čiki| 3–3´/PPL(ANpl);

         neniwani 'man (obv.)')

   (d)   *metemo ˙ha ota ˙nesani we ˙na ˙pe minita* (K-TG 11)

        'the old woman whose daughter had gotten married'

         (*metemo ˙ha* 'old woman (prox.)'; *ota ˙nesani* 'her daughter (obv.)';

         |ona·pe·mi-| AI 'have a husband', |IC–nita| 3´/PPL(ANsg). The head of the

         participle is the proximate possessor of the obviative subject.)

   (e)   *neno ˙te wa neniwa ne ˙nemehkiwita.* (K-MBT 1, title)

        'The Indian man who became a thunderer.' (*neno ˙te wa* 'Indian'; *neniwa* 'man';

        |nenemehkiwi-| AI 'be a thunderer', |IC–ta| 3/PPL(ANsg))

  (5.54) Possessive noun phrases

   (a)   *no ˙sa ˙= 'niya oto ˙te mani* 'my late father's brother' (K-Auto 157)

         (*no ˙sa* 'my father'; *i ˙niya* 'that (anim. abs.)'; *oto ˙te mani* 'his brother')

   (b)   *i ˙niya oškinawe ˙ha o ˙sani* "the young man's father" (K-FC 56: tr. HP)

         (*i ˙niya* 'that (anim. abs.)'; *oškinawe ˙ha* 'young man'; *o ˙sani* 'his father')

   (c)   *o ˙sani i na kwi yese ˙ha* "the boy's father" (K-FC 100; tr. HP)

         (*o ˙sani* 'his father'; *i na* 'that (anim.)'; *kwi yese ˙ha* 'boy')

   (d)   *neniwa otehkwe mani oni ˙ča ˙nesani* 'a man's sister's child' (K-Kin 1)

         (*neniwa* 'man'; *otehkwe mani* 'his sister'; *oni ˙ča ˙nesani* 'his or her child')

(5.55) With two-word adjunct noun phrase

(a) *i·ni=·šawiweni mama·tomo·ni* "that kind of worship" (K-MP1 18; tr. TM)
   (*i·ni* 'that (inan.)'; |išawiweni| 'procedure, way of performing ceremony
   [adjunct]'; *mama·tomo·ni* 'worship')

(b) *ma·haki=wi·na a·teso·hka·kanaki a·neta* "So some of these legends"
   (K-Auto 150; tr. IP)
   (*ma·haki* 'these (anim.)'; *=wi·na* 'but'; *a·teso·hka·kanaki* 'legends [adjunct]';
   a·neta 'some')

(c) *ma·haki a·neta mi·čipe·he·haki* "some of these little game" (K-Wap 15; tr. TB)
   (*ma·haki* 'these (anim.)'; *a·neta* 'some'; *mi·čipe·he·haki* 'small game')

(d) *ke·tema·kesita iškwe·se·he·ha a·teso·hka·kana.* (K-ULG 1)
   'The winter story of the unfortunate little girl.' (Title.)
   (|ketema·kesi-| AI 'be poor', |IC-ta| 3/PPL(ANsg);
   iškwe·se·he·ha 'little girl [adjunct]'; *a·teso·hka·kana* 'legend')

C.) Longer noun phrases.

(5.56) With one participle

(a) *me·hkate·wi·čiki oškinawe·haki ni·šwi osi·meti·haki.* (K-TYFB 1)
   'The two young brothers who fasted.' (Title.)
   (|mahkate·wi·-| AI 'fast'; |IC–čiki| 3/PPL(ANpl); *oškinawe·haki* 'youths';
   ni·šwi 'two'; *osi·meti·haki* 'brothers')

(b) *waša·šahi ne·sa·ta nešihka=meko nekoti neniwa.* (K-MKOS 1)
   'A certain man who killed Osages single-handed.' (Title.)
   (*waša·šahi* 'Osages (obv.)'; |neS-| TA 'kill', |IC–a·ta| 3–3´/PPL(ANsg);
   nešihka 'alone'; *=meko* EMPH; *nekoti* 'one'; *neniwa* 'man')

(c) *ka·ka·nwikaše·wani pe·minehka·kota ihkwe·wa našawaye neno·te·wa.* (K-WPGB 1)
   'The Indian woman of long ago who was pursued by a grizzly bear.' (Title.)
   (*ka·ka·nwikaše·wani* 'grizzly bear (obv.)';
   |peminehkaw-| TA 'pursue', |IC–ekota| 3´–3/PPL(ANsg); *ihkwe·wa* 'woman';
   našawaye 'long ago' [5.47]; *neno·te·wa* 'Indian')

(5.57) With two participles

(a) *ihkwe·wa me·hkate·wi·ta wi·sahke·hani ke·temina·kota našawaye neno·te·wa.*
   'The Indian woman of long ago who fasted and was blessed by Wîsahkêha.'
   (K-IWF 1, title)
   (*ihkwe·wa* 'woman'; |mahkate·wi·-| AI 'fast', |IC–ta| 3/PPL(ANsg);
   wi·sahke·hani 'Wîsahkêha (obv.)'; |keteminaw-| TA 'bless',
   |IC–ekota| 3´–3/PPL(ANsg); *našawaye* 'long ago' [5.47]; *neno·te·wa* 'Indian')

(b) *mani e·yo·ta ayo·hi e·hte·niki mi·ša·meki* (O 42C)
   'one who used this which is in this sacred pack'
   (*mani* 'this (inan.)'; |ayo·-| TI(3) 'use', |IC–ta| 3–0/PPL(ANsg); *ayo·hi* 'this (loc.)';
   |ahte·-| II 'be {somewh.}', |IC–niki| 0´/PPL(INsg); *mi·ša·meki* 'sacred pack (loc.)')

62.4. Determiner with conjoined nouns. When a determiner is used with two conjoined
nouns, one of which is proximate and the other obviative, the determiner is proximate.

(5.58) Determiner + two nouns

(a) *ma·haki=na·hkači mešihke·ha mahkwa·hke·hani* (O 2I)
   'also this snapping turtle (prox.) and mud turtle (obv.)' (*ma·haki* 'these (prox.)')

(b)   *i niki kwi yese ha omeso ta nahi* "the boy and his parents" (K-FC 282; tr. HP)
        (*i niki* 'those (prox.)'; *kwi yese ha* 'boy (prox.)'; *omeso ta nahi* 'his parents (obv.)')

62.5. Possessor noun phrase as adjunct to pronominal inflection. A noun phrase may be the possessor of the pronominal subject of a verb (5.59). Noun phrases of this sort can be considered a type of adjunct linked to the inflectional pronoun.

(5.59) Possessor noun phrase as adjunct to pronominal inflection

(a)   *ni na=ke hi a kwi=ke ko hi ašenokini.* (K-B 216; tr. HP)
        "Nothing of mine, is missing."
            (*ni na* 1s/EMPH; *=ke hi* 'moreover'; *a kwi* 'not'; *ke ko hi* 'something, anything';
            |ašeno-| AI,II 'be gone', |–kini| 0/NEG)

(b)   *na hka ='na oškinawe ha i nahi e h=ahte niki.* (K-Bene 106; tr. TB)
        "And the young-man's things were also there." ("Things" = 'fancy clothing'.)
            (|na hka| 'also'; |i na| 'that (anim.)'; *oškinawe ha* 'young man'; *i nahi* 'there';
            |ahte -| II 'be {somewhere}', |e h=–niki 0´/AOR)

(c)   *kotaka mehtose neniwa e h=pwa wi ki šikeniki.* (K-FC 214; tr. HP)
        "All the other people's things did not bear." ("Things" = 'planted crops'.)
            (*kotaka* 'other (anim.)'; *mehtose neniwa* 'person (representative singular)';
            pwa wi PV 'not', |ki šiken-| II 'ripen, bear (fruit)', |e h=–niki| 0´/AOR)

(d)   *a kwi=ke hi owiye ha a wasi me hi ahpi hča nikini.* (K-Spot 286)
        'No one's (sacred pack, obv.) is more powerful than the others.'
            (*a kwi* 'not'; *=ke hi* 'moreover'; *owiye ha* 'anyone'; *a wasi me hi* 'more';
            |ahpi hča -| II 'be {so} powerful', |–nikini| 0´/NEG)

(e)   *kesese hena na mači hkiwesa ma wač=ahpemeki wi h=ahte niwi= 'pi.* (C-G 4)
        'Our elder brother's (scalp, obv.) is supposedly going to be at the top.'
            (*kesese hena na* 'our older brother', *mači hkiwesa* 'Elder Brother';
            |ma wači| '(most) of all', *ahpemeki* 'up';
            |wi h=| FUT, |ahte -| 'be {somewhere}', |–niwi| 0´s/IND; |=ipi| HRSY)

Verb Phrases

63. A verb phrase is an inflected verb together with any particles that directly modify the verb, which may be contiguous or separated by other words. No sharp line can be drawn between adverbial particles (**§63.1-6**), which modify verbs, and clausal particles (**§67.2**), whose scope is the whole clause. In this account, a free particle with no other syntactic link is taken to be an adverbial particle if it modifies a preverb, or if there is concrete evidence from morphology that it is part of the verbal complex (**§63.3-4**); in the absence of such evidence it is taken to be a sentence particle. Similarly, the arguments of a verb are taken as components of the sentence, including most complements of oblique valences borne by relative roots (**§22.4**) that are part of verb stems. An oblique complement is considered part of the verb phrase only if it is itself a preverb (5.10), or if it is the complement of a semantically empty place-holder and corresponds to the initial in simplex stems that are closely related paradigmatically (**§63.6**). A verb may have more than one modifier, but multiple modifiers do not form verb phrases of different kinds.

Verbal modifiers may themselves be modified, especially by *=meko, =mekoho* EMPH.

NOTE: the verb phrase as defined here for Meskwaki is entirely distinct from the verb phrase recognized by some syntactic theories in, for example, English, which does not exist in Meskwaki (Goddard and Dahlstrom 2022).

63.1. Negative particles. Negative verbs occur with different negative particles depending on the mode: *a·kwi* 'not' (rarely *kwi*) is used with the negative mode (§26.11), *ka·ta* 'don't' with the prohibitive (§26.19), and *awita* 'not (pot.)' with the potential (§26.20). A potential verb sometimes has *a·kwi* instead of *awita* (2.315-316), but this is rare in the texts. The irregular enclitic |=ihi| NEG is used with the independent indicative or the potential (§4.4; 2.206-208). With other modes simple negation is indicated by the preverb *pwa·wi, pa·wi* PV 'not' (§26.11).

The negative particles may occur with *nana·ši*, which changes their meaning from 'not' to 'never'. This usually directly follows the negative particle (except when an enclitic intervenes), but for extra emphasis it may come after the verb in sentence-final position.

(5.60) Use of *nana·ši* with negative particles
- (a)   *a·kwi=nana·ši še·ški·kwe·hečini* (O 58F)
  'he was never allowed to have his face unblackened [and go the day without fasting]'
  (*a·kwi* 'not'; *nana·ši* '(ever)';
  |še·ški·kwe·h-| TA 'allow to have face unblackened', |–ečini| X–3/NEG)
- (b)   *a·kwi wi·h=nešiwana·ča·kini nana·ši* (K-FC 126; tr. HP)
  "it will never spoil in any way at all"
  (*a·kwi* 'not'; |wi·h=| FUT, |nešiwana·ča·-| II 'spoil', |–kini| 0/NEG; *nana·ši* '(ever)')
- (c)   *ka·ta=meko nana·ši wani·hke·hkani* 'never forget it' (A 176C)
  (*ka·ta* 'don't'; =meko EMPH; *nana·ši* '(ever)';
  |wani·hke·-| AI+O 'forget O2', |–hkani| 2s/PROH)
- (d)   *ka·ta ša·kwe·nemohkani nana·ši.* 'Don't ever be unwilling.' (K-SPC 9)
  (*ka·ta* 'don't'; |ša·kwe·nemo-| AI 'be unwilling', |–hkani| 2s/PROH; *nana·ši* '(ever)')
- (e)   *awita=·pi nana·ši ahkwima·či wa·sa* 'they would never run out of breath' (O 53A)
  (*awita* 'not (pot.)'; |=ipi| HRSY; *nana·ši* '(ever)';
  |ahkwima·či·-| AI 'be exhausted from running', |–wa·sa| 3p/POT)

The particle *a·kwi* 'not' (and also *pwa·wi, pa·wi* PV 'not') may be made emphatic with the particle phrase *paši-we·te·we, paši-we·te·wi* (5.69a), which gives the meaning 'in no way at all, not even close':

(5.61)   *a·kwi paši-we·te·we e·šikenikehe išawiwa·čini* (K-MP2 75)
  'they don't come anywhere near doing it the way it used to be done'
  (*a·kwi* 'not'; *paši-we·te·we* 'in any way at all'; |išiken-| II 'be done {so}',
  |IC–nikehe| 0´/PRET.PPL; |išawi-| AI 'do {so}', |–wa·čini| 3p/NEG)

63.2. Particles making temporal clauses. The particle *na·hina·hi* 'time, the first time, distance' is used with verbs in various modes to specify a temporal reference (§26). It most commonly precedes the verb but may also follow it.

(5.62) Verb phrases with *na·hina·hi* 'time'
- (a)   *na·hina·hi ona·pe·miyane* "when I am married" (K-FC; tr. HP)
  (*na·hina·hi* 'time'; |ona·pe·mi-| AI '(woman) to get, be married', |–yane| 2s/SUBJ)
- (b)   *mesa·hkwahi e·h=ki·šikiniči na·hina·hi* (O 2A)
  'at the time (of year) when the ears of corn were ripe'
  (*mesa·hkwahi* 'ears of corn (obv.)'; |ki·šiki-| AI 'be ripe', |e·h=–niči| 3´/AOR;
  na·hina·hi 'time')

Similarly, the particle *i·nina·hi* '(at) that time' is used with a following verb to form a verb phrase that acts with deictic force or as a predicate nominal, for example as the second term of an equational sentence (**§66.1**, 5.94) correlative with a verb phrase containing *na·hina·hi*.

(5.63) Verb phrase with *i·nina·hi* 'that time'

    (a)   *i·nina·h=we·na=·še ahkwahkamikahke* (K-ECRP 78)

        'at that time when the world ends, that is'

            (|i·nina·hi| 'that time'; |=we·na| 'rather'; |iše| 'just';

            |ahkwahkamikat-| II 'be the end of the world', |–ke| 0/SUBJ)

    (b)   *na·hina·h=meko ne·wakwini i·nina·h=meko ne·sakwe* (K-SGG 169)

        'At whatever time we (inc.) see them, (is the time when) we kill them.'

            (|na·hina·hi| 'time'; =*meko* EMPH; |ne·w-| TA 'see', |IC–akwini| 12–3/ITER;

            |i·nina·hi| 'that time'; =*meko* EMPH; |neS-| TA 'kill', |IC–akwe| 12–3/CC)

63.3. Particle making potential verbs. In sentences in which *i·ni* 'then' or *o·ni* 'and then' would ordinarily be followed by an aorist verb (**§26.8**, 2.174), the potential mode is expressed by a particle *a·mihtahi* and a verb in the plain conjunct (2.169). Since the potential is otherwise marked by inflection or by the preverb *a·mi* POT (2.269-270), *a·mihtahi* POT is taken as part of the verb phrase, although it usually occurs among the sentence-initial particles rather than immediately before the verb. The formal relationship between *a·mi* PV POT and *a·mihtahi* P POT is unique.

63.4. Particles with oblique valences. Some particles bear the oblique valence whose complement is relativized as the head of a participle but do not form part of the verb stem as preverbs. These almost always precede the verb, but in rare instances they are found postposed.

(5.64) Particles bearing an oblique valence for a participle

    (a)   *nehki pe·mi-a·hkwamatamowa·či.* 'for as long as they were still injured' (O 45F)

            (*nehki* 'for {so} long'; |pemi| PV 'along',

            |a·hkwamat-| TI(1)-O 'be sick', |IC–amowa·či| IC–3p(-0)/PPL(obl))

    (b)   *taswi pi·tike e·piwa·či* 'as many as were seated inside' (O 29B)

            (*taswi* '{so many}'; *pi·tike* 'inside';

            |api-| AI 'sit {somewhere}'; |IC–wa·či| 3p/PPL(obl))

    (c)   *wi·te·mekoči taswi* 'as many as went with him' (O 17J)

            (|wi·te·m-| TA 'accompany', |IC–ekoči| 3´–3s/PPL(obl); *taswi* '{so many}')

63.5. Particles related to verb-forming initials. Some free particles are derived from initials that may also appear in verb stems and preverbs and thus typically have the same shape as a synonymous preverb. This formal affinity is taken as evidence that the free particle is closely linked to the verb as an adverbial modifier. Also, in some cases it is evident that the free particle specifically modifies just one component of the verb stem, such as a preverb.

(5.65) Particles related to verb stems and preverbs

    (a)   *aya·pami e·h=pye·či-pi·tike·niči* 'they came back in' (K-SF 51)

            (*aya·pami* P 'back'; *pye·či* PV 'coming', |pi·tike·-| AI 'go in', |e·h=–niči| 3´/AOR)

            (Cf. *aya·pami* PV 'back' [O 8C, 154G]; |aya·pami·-| AI 'go back'.)

    (b)   *ki·ša·koči=meko e·h=nešiwi-tašiniči owi·či·škwe·hani.* (K-FC 112; tr. TB)

        "there was an extremely massive number indeed of their enemies"

            (*ki·ša·koči* P 'extremely'; =*meko* EMPH; *nešiwi* PV 'terribly',

            |taši-| AI 'be {so many}', |e·h=–niči| 3´/AOR; *owi·či·škwe·hani* 'his enemy (obv.)')

            (Cf. *ki·ša·koči* PV 'extremely'; 5.68.)

63.6. Oblique complements of empty valence-bearers. A particle is considered part of a verb phrase if it is the complement of a semantically empty oblique valence borne by a verb, and if it corresponds to the concrete initial in verbs that are paradigmatically closely linked. This is the case with enumerative obliques that are the complement of |taši-| AI, |tasen-| II 'be {so much, so many}' (initial |tasw-|, |taso·-|). The fact that numbers may be indicated by an initial combined with a residual particle phrase (5.66*bc*) further supports taking bound and free enumerative elements as having the same syntactic status.

(5.66) Enumerative oblique or residue as part of verb phrase

    (a)   *šwa·šika tašiwaki* 'there are eight of them' (2.128)

          (*šwa·šika* 'eight'; |taši-| AI 'be {so many}', |–waki| 3p/IND)

          (Cf. *ni·šiwaki* 'there are two of them' (← |ni·ši-| AI 'be two').)

    (b)   *e·h=meta·šiwa či=ke·h=wi·nwa·wa neswini·siwe.* (JP-YMPE 73)

        'And there were altogether thirteen of them.'

          (|meta·ši-| AI 'be ten', |e·h–wa·či| 3p/AOR; |=ke·hi| 'moreover';

          wi·nwa·wa 3p/EMPH; *neswini·siwe* '(ten, etc.) plus three')

    (c)   *e·h=meta·šiwa či=ča·h=nekoti·='nahi.* 'So there were eleven of them.' (JB-FS 1)

          (|meta·ši-| AI 'be ten', |e·h–wa·či| 3p/AOR; |=ča·hi| 'so';

          |nekoti| 'one'; |=i·nahi| 'with that, and')

It is possible that some manner obliques that are the complement of |iN-| '{so}' (*iši* PV) should also be analyzed as parts of the verb phrase.

(5.67) Particle joined to verb by |iN-| '{so}'

    (a)   *ki·ša·koči=meko e·h=iši-menwamataki.* 'It felt extremely nice to her.' (K-K 12)

          (*ki·ša·koči* P 'extremely'; *=meko* EMPH; |iši| PV '{so}',

          |menwamat-| TI(1)-O 'have a nice sensation', |e·h–aki| 3s(-0)/AOR)

    (b)   *kena·či=meko e·h=išihtaniki.* '... and they (obv.) flowed slowly.' (K-M 72a)

          (*kena·či* 'slowly'; *=meko* EMPH; |išihtan-| II 'flow {so}', |e·h–niki| 0'/AOR)

The parallelism of constructions with *ki·ša·koči* 'extremely' as a free particle (before or after the verb), a free particle linked by *iši* PV '{so}', and a preverb suggests that these are syntactically equivalent.

(5.68) Three (or four) constructions with *ki·ša·koči* 'extremely' as verbal modifier

    (a)   *ki·ša·koči=meko e·h=wi·kaniki.* 'It (obv.) tasted extremely good.' (K-WTS 9)

          (*ki·ša·koči* P 'extremely'; *=meko* EMPH; |wi·kan-| II 'taste good', |e·h–niki| 0'/AOR)

    (b)   *e·h=wi·ša·pene·wa·či=ke·hi ki·ša·koči.* (O 61D)

        'Moreover, they were as hungry as they could be.'

          (|wi·ša·pene·-| AI 'be hungry', |e·h–wa·či| 3p/AOR; *=ke·hi* 'moreover';

          ki·ša·koči P [or (PV)P (4.112)] 'extremely')

    (c)   *ki·ša·koči=meko e·h=iši-wi·keneniči i·nini* (K-SGG 112)

        'it (anim. obv.) tasted extremely good'

          (*ki·ša·koči* P 'extremely'; *=meko* EMPH;

          |iši| PV '{so}', |wi·keN-| AI 'taste good', |e·h–niči| 3'/AOR); *i·nini* 'that (obv.)')

    (d)   *e·h=ki·ša·koči-wi·kaniki.* 'it (obv.) tasted extremely good' (K-RYL 2)

          (*ki·ša·koči* PV 'extremely'; |wi·kan-| II 'taste good', |e·h–niki| 0'/AOR)

Examples of *ki·ša·koči* P as a particle modifier are in (5.72*a*).

Particle Phrases

64. A particle phrase is a phrase headed by a particle. It may comprise particles used together idiomatically; a particle in apposition with another particle or with a locative noun or pronoun; a particle and its modifier; or a particle and its complement, which may be another particle, a locative oblique or instrumental oblique noun, or a verb. It may also include modifiers of the components, from enclitic particles to one or more locative participles. The distinction between particle phrases that include one particle modifying another and particle compounds is not sharp (**§60.3**). Some particle phrases are usually written without a word divider, and particle phrases are often written in the editions like particle compounds, with linking hyphens. Some particle phrases, like some particles, may function syntactically as noun phrases (**§62**).

(5.69) Idiomatic combinations of two particles

    (a)   *paši-we·te·we, paši-we·te·wi* 'in any way at all' (intensifier with *a·kwi* 'not'; 5.61)
            (*paši* 'at all' PP [also PV 5.8o]; *we·te·we, we·te·wi* 'in any way, to any extent')

    (b)   *kehči-menwa·hi, kehči-=meko menwa·hi* 'rather, quite well, quite enough'
            (*kehči* 'greatly' [also PN 5.1b, PV 5.8g]; *menwa·hi* [only after *kehči*];
            =*meko* EMPH)

    (c)   *a·kwi kana·kwa* 'it's impossible' (5.102g); also edited as *a·kwi-kana·kwa*

    (d)   *a·kwi nana·ši* 'never' (5.60)

    (e)   *neši-ša·pwe·ši* 'as the only one of all' (divider never written)
            (*neši* 'alone' PP [also PV 5.147a], *ša·pwe·ši* 'as the only one')

(5.70) Particles in apposition

    (a)   *atehči či·ka·hkwe* 'away next to a tree' (K-BH 11)
            (*atehči* 'away'; *či·ka·hkwe* 'next to a tree')

    (b)   *manahka peno·či* 'far away' (K-TO 35)
            (*manahka* 'at a distance'; *peno·či* 'far away')

    (c)   *peno·či=meko ki·hka* 'in a long circuit' (K-Wap 48)
            (*peno·či* 'far away'; =*meko* EMPH; *ki·hka* '(circling) around')

(5.71) Particle and locative noun or pronoun

    (a)   *ahkwiči aseni·ki* 'on top of the rock' (K-Wap 195; S-YMSG 28)
           aseni·ki ahkwiči 'on top of the rock' (K-ECRP 114; JB-Tiger 29)
            (*ahkwiči* 'on top'; *aseni·ki* 'rock (loc.)' [cf. 5.20b])

    (b)   *i·nahi ahkwiči* (K-SSP 29), *i·nah=ahkwiči* (K-CWB 9) 'on top of it'
            (*i·nahi* 'that (loc.), there'; *ahkwiči* 'on top')

    (c)   *omi·ša·meki na·meki* 'inside his sacred pack' (K-B 312)
           na·meki mi·ša·meki 'inside the sacred pack' (K-FC 724)
            (*(o)mi·ša·meki* '(his) sacred pack (loc.)'; *na·meki* 'inside, underneath')

    (d)   *nepi·ki=ke·hi ahkwitepye·ki* 'and on the surface of the water' (K-SGG 57)
            (*nepi·ki* 'water (loc.)'; |=ke·hi| 'moreover'; *ahkwitepye·ki* 'on top of the water')
           i·ya·hi ahkwitepye·ki 'down to the surface of the water' (K-M 818c)
            (*i·ya·hi* 'over there, down here'; *ahkwitepye·ki* 'on top of the water')

    (e)   *i·nah=ahkwiči-mehtekwe* 'on top of that log' (JP-OPLA 4)
            (*i·nahi* 'that (loc.), there'; *ahkwiči-mehtekwe* 'on top of the log')

(5.72) Modifier + particle

(a) *asa·mi* 'too (much)':

   1)   *asa·mi ašawaye* 'too long ago' (K-SPC 67)

       asa·mi=mekoho ašawaye 'too long ago' (K-M 956f)

   2)   *asa·mi kehčine* 'too close' (K-M 73g, with no divider)

   3)   *asa·mi kenwe·ši* 'too long a time' (A 134D, with divider; K-M 190c, no divider)

(b) *ča·ki* 'all':

   1)   *ča·ki na·mahkamiki* 'everywhere under the earth' (K-M 909q)

       ča·ki=meko na·mahkamiki 'all over under the earth' (SP-RL 37)

   2)   *ča·ki=meko ahkwitahkamiki* 'all over the earth' (JP-Apay 34)

(c) *ki·ša·koči* 'extremely, as much as possible':

   1)   *ki·ša·koči ahpemeki* 'very far up' (K-M 257.l)

       ki·ša·koči=meko kehč-ahpemeki 'extremely high up' (K-SGG 147)

          (*ahpemeki* 'up, above, in the air or sky'; *kehč-ahpemeki* 'way high up' [5.16e(2)])

   2)   *ki·ša·koči anasa·ki* 'extremely exceptional' (K-Apay 9)

          (*anasa·ki* 'outstanding, exceptional')

   3)   *ki·ša·koči aškači* 'after a very long interval' (K-FC 582), 'very late' (K-M 1058b)

       ki·ša·koči=meko aškači 'much later on' (K-Fish 65)

       ki·ša·koči aškači=meko "it will be a very long time yet" (K-M 978b; tr. HP)

          (*aškači* 'a long time later')

   4)   *ki·ša·koči kenwe·ši* 'for an extremely long time' (*kenwe·ši* 'for a long time')

   5)   *ki·ša·koči ma·ne* 'a great many' (*ma·ne* 'many')

   6)   *ki·ša·koči no·make* 'for an extremely short time' (*no·make* 'for a short time)

   7)   *ki·ša·koči peno·či* 'extremely far away' (*peno·či* 'far away')

(d) *kwi·yena* 'exactly'

   1)   *kwi·yena=ke·hi·='nina·h* 'And by the way, right then ...' (A 37D)

          (|=ke·hi| 'moreover'; |i·nina·hi| 'at that time')

(e) *mehteno·hi* 'only'

   1)   *mehteno·hi tepehki* 'only at night' (K-FC 176)

(f) *nešiwi* 'frightfully, terribly'

   1)   *nešiwi kenwe·ši* 'for a frightfully long time' (SP-Kishk 86)

   2)   *nešiwi=meko ma·ne* 'frightfully many' (K-MKOS 8)

       nešiwi ma·ne=mekoho 'frightfully much' (K-FC 215; no divider)

          (*ma·ne* 'many, much'; *=meko, =mekoho* EMPH)

(g) *pe·hki* 'really'

   1)   *pe·hki=meko peno·či* 'really far away' (K-Kin 62)

          (*=meko* EMPH; *peno·či* 'far away')

(5.73) Particle containing a relative root with its complement

(a) *ahkwi* '{so} far, {so} long' (**§22.4(a)**):

       na·witepehki·ke ahkwi 'until midnight' (K-Bene 102)

          (|na·witepehki·-| II 'be midnight', |-ke| 0/SUBJ)

(b) *ahpi·hči* 'to {such} a degree, extent' (**§22.4(b)**)

       menw-ahpi·hči 'just right, not too hard' (K-M 739g)

       menw-ahpi·hči=mekoho 'to just the right extent' (K-M 652c)

          (*menwi* 'well, nicely')

(c) |iši| '{so}, {some} way, to {somewhere}' (**§22.4(c)**)

   1) *peteki=·'ši* 'back (in space or time)' (A 1D)

       (*peteki* 'back')

   2) *i·tepi=·'ši* 'to there' (K-Kin 39)

       (*i·tepi* '(to) there, thither'; |iši| 'to {somewhere}')

   3) *a·čipanakiči=·'ši* 'in all kinds of ways' (K-Kin 71)

       (*a·čipanakiči* 'all different kinds'; |iši| '{some} way')

   4) *wi·kiya·peki iši* (K-FC 211), *wi·kiya·peki=·ši* (JP-Apay 35) 'to the house'

       (*wi·kiya·peki* 'house (loc.)'; |iši| 'to {somewhere}')

(d) *išiwe·pi* 'signifying {so}'

     With aorist clause as complement: (A 178E)

(e) *nehki* 'for {so} long a time' (cf. 2.242)

   1) *asa·mi nehki* 'for too long a time' (K-FC 421; no divider)

   2) *asa·m=a·ya nehki* 'for too long a time each time' (K-WD 119)

(f) *oči* 'from {somewhere}, oriented {so}, through {some hole}' (**§22.4(d)**)

   1) *wa·wi·tawi=meko oči* 'on all sides' (K-PBLA 26)

       (*wa·wi·tawi* 'on both sides')

   2) *onemači·neki oči* 'from the left, with his left hand' (K-FM 27)

       (*onemači·neki* 'his left (loc.)')

   3) *we·či-kesi·ya·niki oči* 'on the north side' (K-FC 102)

       (*we·či-kesi·ya·niki* 'north (obv.)')

   4) *anene·ki oči* 'through the smoke-hole' (K-SF 95)

       (*anene·wi* 'smoke-hole': *anene·ki* 'smoke-hole (loc.)')

(g) *ota·hkiwe* 'from {some} side of the hill' (cf. 2.113)

     we·ta·paniki ota·hkiwe 'from, on the east side of the hill' (K-WKG 26)

       (*we·ta·paniki* 'east (obv.)')

(h) *taši* '{somewhere}' (**§22.4(e)**)

   1) *i·nahi taši* 'in that place' (K-WYB 183)

       (*i·nahi* 'there')

   2) *ištwi·teki taši* 'in the street' (SP-SM 12)

       (*ištwi·teki* 'street (loc.)'; *taši* '{somewhere}')

   3) *na·ma·kone taši* 'down under the snow' (SP-PD1 5)

       (*na·ma·kone* 'under the snow' [or na·mako·ne]; *taši* '{somewhere}')

   4) *sa·kiči taši* 'outdoors, outside' (A 57F)

       (*sa·kiči* 'outside'; *taši* '{somewhere}')

(i) *taswi* '{so much, so many}' (**§22.4(f)**)

   1) *nešiwi taswi* 'a frightfully large number' (K-TO 29)

       (*nešiwi* 'frightfully, terribly')

   2) *meše taswi* 'of a fair extent' (JB-LR 74)

     meše taswi·hi 'a fair amount' (BL-Myths 7) (cf. 4.359)

(5.74) Particle and instrumental oblique

   (a) *keki=meko oni·ča·neswa·wahi* 'including their children' (LL-Auto 16)

       (*keki* 'with, having along'; *oni·ča·neswa·wahi* 'their children')

(b)   *keki꞊meko ma maneto winičihi na·hka maneto wahi* (K-Mes 19)
      'including those who had manitou power (obv.) and manitous (obv.)'
          (*keki* 'with, having along'; *꞊meko* EMPH; |CV+| RED1,
          |maneto·wi-| AI 'be a manitou, have godlike power', |IC–ničihi| 3′/PPL(OBVpl);
          na·hka 'also'; *maneto wahi* 'manitous (obv.)')

(c)   *takwi꞊meko owi·wa·wahi* 'together with their wives' (K-WKG 46)
          (*takwi* 'together with'; *꞊meko* EMPH; *owi·wa·wahi* 'their wives (obv.)')

(5.75) Particle modified by *na·hina·hi* 'time, distance'

(a)   *meše-na·hina·hi* 'a little ways off' (K-WWB 13, divider; K-FC 558, no divider)
          (*meše* 'freely, middlingly', *na·hina·hi* 'time, distance');
          meše꞊meko na·hina·hi, meše꞊mekoho na·hina·hi (K-FC 331)
      me meše-na na·hina·hi 'each a little ways off' (K-FC 168, no divider)

(b)   *te·pi-na·hina·hi* 'for quite a while' (K-W 1107; no divider)
          (*te·pi* 'enough'; *na·hina·hi* 'time, distance')

(c)   *a·hpene na·hina·hi* "at regular, set times" (K-FASB 94; tr. HP)
          (*a·hpene* 'all the same'; *na·hina·hi* 'time, distance')

(d)   *ahpi·hči-na·hina·hi* 'at {such} a distance' (K-W 314)
          (*ahpi·hči* 'to {such} degree'; *na·hina·hi* 'time, distance'

(5.76) Complex quantifier

(a)   *ni·šwa pitaki no·hika* 'twenty-seven' (SP-PK 1)

(b)   *ni·šwa pitaki nya·nanwi* 'twenty-five' (A 126B)
      ni·šwa pitaki nya·nanwinesiwe 'twenty-five' (SP-MC8D 26)

(c)   *no·hika taswa·hkwe* 'seven hundred' (SP-KFC 29)
          (*no·hika* 'seven'; *taswa·hkwe* '{so many} hundred')

(d)   *nekotwa·hkwe nya·nanwi꞊·'nahi taswimahkahkwe* (C-Hist 3)
      'one hundred and five thousand'
          (*nekotwa·hkwe* 'one hundred'; |nya·nanwi| 'five'; |꞊i·nahi| 'with that, and';
          taswimahkahkwe '{so many} thousand')

(5.77) Other complex particle phrases

(a)   *peno·či꞊meko iši-ni·ka·ni* 'way far off in the future' (K-Wap 1)
          (*peno·či* 'far away'; *꞊meko* EMPH; *iši* PP '{so}'; *ni·ka·ni* 'ahead, in the future')

(b)   *kehči꞊meko a·wasi-taswi* 'a great amount more' (SP-BSAB 49)
          (*kehči* 'greatly'; *꞊meko* EMPH; *a·wasi* 'more'; *taswi* '{so much, so many}')

(c)   *meše꞊meko inekihkwi ki·hka* 'a good-sized area around' (K-TYFB 17)
          (*meše* 'middlingly'; *꞊meko* EMPH; *inekihkwi* 'to, of {such} extent';
          ki·hka 'around')

(d)   *ki·ša·koči na·hina·hi iši-peno·či nanawi* (K-Kin 34)
      'at an extremely great distance far out in the wilderness'
          (*ki·ša·koči* 'extremely'; *na·hina·hi* 'time, distance'; *iši* '{so}'; *peno·či* 'far';
          nanawi 'in the middle of nowhere')

(e)   *mehtekomiši·ki či·ka·hkwe we·či-kesi·ya·ki ota·hkwe we·či-pwa·wi-ki·šesowiki*
      (O 13B)
          'next to a black oak on the north side where the sun did not strike'

POSITIONS

POSITIONS

65. The words and phrases in a verbal sentence (**§59**) occur in positions that can be defined in relation to the beginning and the end of the sentence, the verb, and each other (Dahlstrom 1993, 1995, 2005). Before (that is, to the left of) the verb there are, from left to right, essentially three potential positions with discourse functions: TOPIC, NEGATIVE, and FOCUS; and one position with a syntactic function: OBLIQUE. Adverbial clauses may also occur after the Topic position, and the focus position may occur more than once. After (or to the right of) the verb there are no rigidly ordered positions; subjects, primary objects, secondary objects, and verbal complements follow the verb in no fixed order. Clausal particles (**§67.2**) and subordinate clauses (**§69**) may come before or after the verb. One or more interjections may precede the entire sentence.

Topic

65.1. The Topic position stands outside the syntax of the rest of the sentence. The material that comes after the Topic position is in every way a complete sentence by itself, except that it never has a second Topic position. A Topic is a noun phrase that states what the sentence that comes after it relates to or is about; its function can be generically glossed 'as for' or 'in the case of'. A sentence-conjoining particle (**§67.1**, **§68.2**) is the only component of a sentence that may occur with the Topic; if this is a free particle it is placed at the beginning of the sentence, preceding the Topic, and if it is an enclitic the Topic (or its first component) serves as its host.

(5.78) Topic position

(a) *mani=ke·hi mi·ša·mi, a·kwi=ke·ko·hi wi·h=iši-wa·wani-išawiyanini.* (K-ECRP 94)
'And when it comes to this sacred pack, you will not do anything incorrectly.'
(*mani* 'this (inan.)'; =*ke·hi* 'moreover'; *mi·ša·mi* 'sacred pack'; *a·kwi* 'not';
ke·ko·hi 'something, anything'; |wi·h=| FUT; *iši* PV '{so}',
wa·wani PV 'inadequately, incorrectly', |išawi-| AI 'do {so}'; |–yanini| 2s/NEG)

(b) *pa·wi-=meko -nakesita, i·na·='na·='na wi·šiki-mehtose·neniwa.* (O 145D)
'As for the one who isn't backward, she will be the one with a good, strong life.'
(|pa·wi| PV 'not', |nakesi-| AI 'be hesitant', |IC–ta| 3/PPL(ANsg); =*meko* EMPH;
|i·na| 'that (anim.)' (3x); *wi·šiki* (PV)PN 'strong'; *mehtose·neniwa* 'person')

(c) *i·ni='yo, 'hawo,' inenaka·ha=koh=meko.* (K-FC 350)
'For in that case I would certainly have said yes.'
(*i·ni* 'that (inan.)'; |=iyo| 'for'; *hawo* 'alright';
|iN–| TA 'say {so} to', |–enaka·ha| 1s–2s/POT; |=kohi| 'certainly'; =*meko* EMPH)

(d) *o·ni pepikwe·škwi, ...* 'And as for the whistle, ...' (O 80C)
(*o·ni* 'and then'; *pepikwe·škwi* 'whistle')

Negative

65.2. The Negative position may be filled by any one of the negative particles: *a·kwi* 'not', *ka·ta* 'don't', *awita* 'not (pot.)'.

(5.79) Negative position

(a) *a·kwi ke·ko·hi wi·h=mi·čiye·kwini.* 'You will not eat anything.' (K-YC 20)
(*a·kwi* 'not'; *ke·ko·hi* 'something, anything';
|wi·h=| FUT, |mi·či-| TI(3) 'eat', |–ye·kwini| 2p–0/NEG)

(b) *ka·ta ke·ko·hi mani taswi e·nenako·we wi·h=kya·tamawe·kwe ine·nemiye·ke·ko.*
(O 82C)
'Don't think of keeping secret from them any part of all that I'm telling you now.'
(*ka·ta* 'don't'; *ke·ko·hi* 'something, anything'; *mani* 'this (inan.)'; *taswi* '{so much}'; *e·nenako·we* 'what I tell you (pl.)';
wi·h=kya·tamawe·kwe 'that you (pl.) conceal it from them';
|ine·nem-| TA 'think about {so}', |–iye·ke·ko| 2p–3/PROH)

(c) *awita='pi nana·ši ihkwe·wa oči·kwaneki ahkomi·sa.* (O 54F)
'They say the woman would never be in water up to her knees.'
(*awita* 'not (pot.)'; |=ipi| HRSY; *nana·ši* '(ever)'; *ihkwe·wa* 'woman';
oči·kwaneki 'her knees (loc.)'; |ahkomi·-| AI 'be {so} far in water', |–sa| 3s,0/POT)

The negative particles may also pattern like any clausal particle, occurring before the Oblique position that immediately precedes the verb. A negative particle sometimes occurs twice with the same verb, both in the Negative position and in a later pre-verbal position; this is not unusual when a direct discourse quote intervenes (5.87*b*) but otherwise rare.

(5.80) Negative particle like clausal particle

(a) *mani=na·hka pepikwe·škwi a·kwi anwe·we·htamowa·čini.* (O 10H)
'And also they did not blow this whistle.'
(*mani* 'this (inan.)'; *na·hka* 'also'; *pepikwe·škwi* 'whistle';
a·kwi 'not'; |anwe·we·ht-| TI(1) 'blow audibly', |–amowa·čini| 3p–0/NEG)

(b) *i·niki=ke·hi ihkwe·waki ki·ke·nočiki a·kwi i·nahi awiwa·čini* (O 11H)
'what's more, the women who were hosts of the clan feast were not present'
(*i·niki* 'those (anim.)'; |=ke·hi| 'moreover'; *ihkwe·waki* 'women';
|ki·ke·no-| AI 'hold clan feast', |IC–čiki| 3/PPL(ANpl); *a·kwi* 'not';
i·nahi 'there'; |awi-| AI 'be {somewhere}', |–wa·čini| 3p/NEG)

Negative preverbs are sometimes separated from their head verb in much the same way that the negative particles are (5.81), but they may be preceded by other preverbs (5.81*bcd*).

(5.81) Separation of negative preverb

(a) *e·h=pwa·wi-=meko taswi no·ta·koči -a·nwe·hta·koči.* (K-SGG 69)
'As many as heard him did not fail to believe him.'
(|pwa·wi| PV 'not', |a·nwe·htaw-| TA 'disbelieve', |e·h=–ekoči| 3'–3s/AOR;
=*meko* EMPH;
taswi '{so many}'; |no·taw-| TA 'hear talk', |IC–ekoči| 3'–3s/PPL(obl))

(b) *e·hpi·hči-pwa·wi- e·škote·wi·hi -peno·mikahki* (Jones 1907:224.7-8)
'until the steamboat departed' (*lit.*, 'for as long as it did not depart')
(|ahpi·hči| PV 'be in the process of' [2.100, 200], |pwa·wi| PV 'not',
|peno·mikat-| II 'depart', |IC–ki| 0/CC; *e·škote·wi·hi* 'steamboat')

(c) *natawi-po·ni- mani kehkeše·wi -we·šiwe·ši·hono.* (K-Wap 44)
'It's time that you ceased painting your face with this charcoal.'
(*natawi* PV 'seek to', *po·ni* PV 'cease'; *mani* 'this (inan.)'; *kehkeše·wi*
'charcoal'; |CVCV+| RED2, |we·ši·ho-| AI 'paint one's face', |–no| 2s/IMP)

(d)   *i ˙ni we ˙či-kwayahkwi-=mekoho -pwa ˙wi- owiye ˙ha -sa ˙ka ˙totamawaki* (K-FC 355)
      'That's why I take the precaution not to reveal anything about it to anyone.'
          (*i ˙ni* 'that (inan.)'; |oči| PV 'from {something}', *kwayahkwi* PV 'prudently';
          =mekoho EMPH; *pwa ˙wi* PV 'not'; *owiye ˙ha* 'anyone';
          |sa ˙ka ˙totamaw-| TA+O 'tell about part of O2 to', |IC–aki| 1s–3+O/PPL(obl))

Since non-negative compound verbs may be discontinuous (**§71.2**), it is not clear that separated negative preverbs must be recognized as a distinct type.

Focus

65.3. Noun phrases in the Focus position are weakly emphatic or contrastive. They may have any syntactic role. There are often two noun phrases in Focus position, and at least one rare case of three Focus noun phrases is found. When an oblique complement occurs before the Focus position rather than before the verb (**§65.5**), it can be taken to be in the first of two Focus positions (5.83*fg*, 5.161*a*).

(5.82) Focus position

(a)   *wi ˙teko wa e ˙h=ketoči nanakote ˙ki.* (O 106F)
      'An owl hooted in the middle of the lodge.'
          (*wi ˙teko wa* 'owl'; |keto-| AI 'hoot', |e ˙h=–či 3s/AOR;
          nanakote ˙ki 'in the middle of the lodge')

(b)   *oči ma ˙ni ˙= 'na pašito ˙ha e ˙h=ahte ˙niki.* 'The old man's canoe was there.' (JB-BP 11)
          (|oči ˙ma ˙ni| 'his canoe'; |i ˙na| 'that (anim.)'; *pašito ˙ha* 'old man';
          |ahte ˙-| II 'exist, be {somewhere}', |e ˙h=–niki| 0´/AOR)

(c)   *ni ˙šwi meše we ˙wahi e ˙h=nesa ˙či.* 'He killed two elk.' (SP-Fish 23)
          (*ni ˙šwi* 'two'; *meše we ˙wahi* 'elk (obv. pl.)';
          |neS-| TA 'kill', |e ˙h=–a ˙či| 3s–3´/AOR)

(d)   *mo ˙hči=nekoti owi ˙pi e ˙h=pwa ˙wi-mehkaki.* (X8-Apay 12)
      'He did not find even one of his arrows.'
          (*mo ˙hči* 'even' [5.28*a*, 5.119*q*, 5.122*a*]; *nekoti* 'one'; *owi ˙pi* 'his arrow';
          pwa ˙wi PV 'not'; |mehk-| TI(1) 'find', |e ˙h=–aki| 3s–0/AOR)

(e)   *o ˙ni=wi ˙na neniwa e ˙h=a ˙čimoha ˙či okye ˙ni.* (K-B 261)
      'And then for his part the man informed his mother.'
          (*o ˙ni* 'and then'; *wi ˙na* 3s/EMPH; *neniwa* 'man';
          |a ˙čimoh-| TA 'inform', |e ˙h=–a ˙či| 3s–3´/AOR; *okye ˙ni* 'his mother (obv.)')

(5.83) Two Focus positions

(a)   *owiye ˙ha ke ˙ko ˙hi ašama ˙te* 'if anyone gives them something to eat' (K-Kin 43)
          (*owiye ˙ha* 'someone, anyone'; *ke ˙ko ˙hi* 'something, anything';
          |ašam-| TA+O 'feed O2 to', |–a ˙te| 3s–3´/SUBJ)

(b)   *ahkowi pe ˙mehka ˙ta otehkwe ˙mani nemi ˙nekwa wi ˙h=owi ˙wiya ˙ni.* (K-EGC 3)
      'The one walking in the rear gave me his sister to marry.'
          (*ahkowi* 'behind'; |pemehka ˙-| 'walk along', |IC–ta| 3/PPL(ANsg);
          otehkwe ˙mani 'his sister (obv.)';
          |mi ˙N-| TA+O 'give O2 to', |ne–ekwa| 3s–1s/IND;
          |wi ˙h=| FUT, |owi ˙wi-| AI+O '(man to) marry O2', |e ˙h=–ya ˙ni| 1s/AOR)

(c)   *e·h=pwa·wi-=meko owiye·ha ke·ko·hi -akihto·či.* 'No one lost anything.' (K-B 214)
       (*pwa·wi* PV 'not', |akiht-| TI(2) 'lose', |e·h=–o·či| 3s–0/AOR;
       =meko EMPH; *owiye·ha* 'anyone'; *ke·ko·hi* 'something, anything')

(d)   *nahi·´, mani aškote·wi ihkwe·waki a·kwi wi·h=wa·patamowa·čini.* (K-FC 516; tr. HP)
       "Now, the women shall not look at this fire."
       (*nahi·´* 'Alright!'; *mani* 'this (inan.)'; *aškote·wi* 'fire'; *ihkwe·waki* 'women';
       a·kwi 'not'; |wi·h–| FUT, |wa·pat-| TI(1) 'look at', |–amowa·čini| 3p–0/NEG)

(e)   *o·ni ki·ško·ha nye·wi wi·h=nana·hapina·či* (K-TCSB 70; tr. TB)
       "And a K. will tie four of them up"
       (*o·ni* 'and then'; *ki·ško·ha* 'Kishko division member'; *nye·wi* 'four';
       |wi·h–| FUT, |nana·hapiN-| TA 'tie up', |e·h=–a·či| 3s–3′/AOR)

(f)   *wa·pake ayo·h=meko kekimesi ki·h=nepa·pena.* (K-WYB 160; tr. TB)
       "To-morrow night everyone of us indeed must sleep here"
       (*wa·pake* 'tomorrow'; |ayo·hi| 'here'; *=meko* EMPH; *kekimesi* 'every';
       |wi·h–| FUT, |nepa·-| AI 'sleep {somewhere}', |ke–pena| 12/IND)

(g)   *na·hkači i·nah=meko i·na pašito·he·ha oto·te·mani e·h=apihapiniči.*
       "And that old-man's brother was also sitting in there." (AK-WYB 190; tr. TB)
       (*na·hkači* 'also'; |i·nahi| 'there'; *=meko* EMPH;
       i·na 'that (anim.)', *pašito·he·ha* 'old man', *oto·te·mani* 'his brother (obv.)';
       |CVCV+| RED2, |api-| AI 'sit {somewhere}', |e·h=–niči| 3′/AOR)

(5.84) Three Focus positions
       wi·sahke·ha mahwe·wahi a·mo·wahi e·h=ašama·či. (K-WB 1)
       'When Wîsahkêha Fed Bees to the Wolves.' (Title.)
       (*wi·sahke·ha* (name); *mahwe·wahi* 'wolves (obv.)'; *a·mo·wahi* 'bees (obv.)';
       |ašam-| TA+O 'feed O2 to', |e·h=–a·či| 3s–3′/AOR)

65.4. Focus before and after Negative. A variant word order is sometimes found with a negative particle between two preverbal noun phrases. In the cases noted the first noun phrase is an emphatic pronoun (5.85*abc*) or, less commonly, a noun (5.85*d*), and the second one is an indefinite pronoun.

(5.85) Negative particle between focus noun phrases
       (a)   *ki·na=ke·h=ne·hi a·kwi owiye·ha wi·h=nahi-ne·wohkini.* (K-SSP 24; tr. HP)
              (Your house will be invisible.) "And no one will be able to see you[, either]."
              (*ki·na* 2s/EMPH; |=ke·hi| 'moreover'; |ne·hi| 'too'; *a·kwi* 'not'; *owiye·ha* 'anyone';
              |wi·h–| FUT, |nahi| PV 'be given to', |ne·w-| TA 'see', |–ehkini| 3–2s/NEG)

       (b)   *ni·na=·yo a·kwi owiye·ha pana·pamakini.* (K-SSP 101; tr. HP)
              (The Sun is speaking.) "I never fail to see any one."
              (*ni·na* 1s/EMPH; |=iyo| 'for'; *a·kwi* 'not'; *owiye·ha* 'anyone';
              |pana·pam-| TA 'miss seeing', |–akini| 1s–3/NEG)

       (c)   *ni·na=ke·hi a·kwi owiye·ha me·h-kehke·nemičini.* (K-WYB 144; tr. TB)
              "There isn't anyone that knows me yet." (= 'No manitou has blessed me yet.')
              (*ni·na* 1s/EMPH; |=ke·hi| 'moreover'; *a·kwi* 'not'; *owiye·ha* 'anyone';
              |me·hi| PV 'yet', |kehke·nem-| TA 'know', |–ičini| 3s–1s/NEG)

       (d)   *ata·pya·nani a·kwi owiye·ha wi·h=pemaho·na·čini.* (C-IW 19)
              'No creature will pull the vehicle (obv.) along.'
              (*ata·pya·nani* 'wagon (obv.)'; *a·kwi* 'not'; *owiye·ha* 'anyone';
              |wi·h–| FUT, |pemaho·N-| TA 'drag along', |–a·čini| 3s–3′/NEG)

The translations by native speakers of the examples in (5.85) are against taking the sentence-initial pronouns as Topics, and only in (5.85*c*) might the context lend support to such an analysis. The noun in (5.85*d*) is clearly not a Topic.

Oblique

65.5. When a verb incorporates an overt or virtual relative root (**§22.4**, with more examples) the preferred site for its oblique complement is the Oblique position, directly before the verb.

    (5.86) Oblique position

        (a)   *či·kepye·ki e·h=a·či.* 'He went to the edge of the water.' (K-TO 17)
            (*či·kepye·ki* 'at, to the water's edge'; |iha·-| AI 'go {somewhere}', |e·h=–či| 3s/AOR)

        (b)   *i·tepi e·h=iši-we·pose·či.* 'He started walking there.' (K-TO 44)
            (*i·tepi* '(to) there'; |iši| PV '{so}', |we·pose·-| AI 'start walking', |e·h=–či| 3s/AOR)

        (c)   *nešihka=ke·h=mekoho ihkwe·wa i·nahi e·h=awiči.* (K-SSP 70; tr. HP)
           "The woman was there all alone."
            (*nešihka* 'alone'; |=ke·hi| 'moreover'; |=mekoho| EMPH, *ihkwe·wa* 'woman';
            i·nahi 'there'; |awi-| AI 'be {somewhere}', |e·h=–či| 3s/AOR)

        (d)   *a·kwi, "mahkate·wi·no," išikini* 'I wasn't told to fast' (K-Auto 94)
            (*a·kwi* 'not'; |mahkate·wi·-| AI 'fast', |–no| 2s/IMP;
            |iN-| TA 'say {so} to', |–ikini| X–1s/NEG)

        (e)   *a·kwi e·škikita i·nahi awičini.* 'There are no young people there.' (K-BB 1)
            (*a·kwi* 'not'; |aškiki-| 'be young', |IC–ta| 3/PPL(ANsg); *i·nahi* 'there';
            |awi-| AI 'be {somewhere}', |–čini| 3s/NEG)

        (f)   *"ašihtawino," e·h=inaki nekya.* ' "Make it for me," I said to my mother.' (A 3C)
            (|ašihtaw-| TA+O 'make O2 for', |–ino| 2s–1s/IMP;
            |iN-| TA 'say {so} to', |e·h=–aki| 1s–3/AOR; *nekya* 'my mother')

65.6. Words after oblique quote, before verb. When the oblique complement is speech or thought quoted as direct discourse, the presence of any material between this and the higher verb that bears the oblique valence is rare, except that it is fairly common for a negative particle (**§63.1**) to appear in this position, either singly (5.87*a*) or repeated from before the quote (5.87*b*).

    (5.87) Words between oblique quote and following verb
        Negative particle alone:

        (a)   *"meči='hi='yo=ni·na," ka·ta išite·he·hke·ko.* (K-Spot 301)
           'Don't think, "It's none of my business." '
            (*meči* 'quite'; |=ihi| NEG; |=iyo| 'for'; *ni·na* 1s/EMPH; *ka·ta* 'don't';
            |išite·he·hke·-| 'think {so}', |–ko| 2p/IMP)

        (b)   *a·kwi=ke·hi, "a·kwi-kana·kwa," a·kwi išiyamečini.* (K-B 227)
           'He didn't even tell us (exc.), "It's impossible." '
            (*a·kwi* 'not'; |=ke·hi| 'moreover'; *a·kwi-kana·kwa* 'it's impossible';
            a·kwi 'not', |iN-| TA 'say {so} to', |–iyamečini| 3–1p/NEG)

        Other words:

        (c)   *'mi·ša·mi ki·h=ašihto·pwa,' ni·na='yo·we ketenepwa.* (O 72I)
           ' "The two of you shall make a sacred pack," I told you.'
            (*mi·ša·mi* 'sacred bundle'; |wi·h=| FUT, |ašiht-| TI(2) 'make', |ke–o·pwa| 2p–0/IND;
            ni·na 1s/EMPH; |=iyo·we| PAST; |iN-| TA , |ke–enepwa 1s–2p/IND)

(d)　*šewe·na ki·h=nawači-=meko -ne·se·ha·wa,' i·ni=na·hka e·h=išiči nemešo·mesa.*
'And then my grandfather said to me, "But you will cure him first."' (K-MESB 32)
(*šewe·na* 'but'; |wi·h=| FUT; *nawači* PV 'first'; =*meko* EMPH;
|ne·se·h-| TA 'cure', |ke–a·wa| 2s–3s/IND; *i·ni* 'then'; *na·hka* 'also';
|iN-| TA 'say {so} to', |e·h=–iči| 3s–1s/AOR; *nemešo·mesa* 'my grandfather')

65.7. Other positions for oblique complements. In some cases the oblique complement of a verb does not occur in the Oblique position. The oblique complement of a relative root (or virtual relative root) may occur after the verb, but this is infrequent. In (5.88) the postverbal position adds emphasis.

(5.88) Postverbal oblique complement

(a)　*e·h=ina·hpawa·wa·či a·hpene=meko.* (K-WD 3)
'They both dreamt exactly the same thing.'
(|ina·hpawa·-| AI 'dream {so}', |e·h=–wa·či| 3p/AOR;
a·hpene 'both or all the same'; =*meko* EMPH)

(b)　*o·ni=ki·nwa·wa, ki·ško·ha ki·ke·nota wi·h=ota·kwapiči we·či-pakišimoniki,*
o·ni tohka·na ‖ we·ta·paniki. (K-TCSB 67-68)
'And of you, the Kishko hosts must sit on the west, and the Tohkans on the east.'
(*o·ni* 'and'; *ki·nwa·wa* 2p/EMPH; *ki·ško·ha* 'Kishko division member';
ki·ke·nota 'host of clan feast'; |wi·h=| FUT, |ota·kwapi-| AI 'sit in {such}
direction', |–či| 3s/AOR; *we·či-pakišimoniki* 'in the west (obv.)';
tohka·na 'Tohkan division member'; *we·ta·paniki* 'in the east')

A postverbal position is, however, the preferred site for locative adjuncts (§22.5) that function as obliques to verbs that do not contain a relative root to which they are linked.

(5.89) Postverbal oblique as locative adjunct without relative root

(a)　*ahpene·či=meko='pi e·h=ma·ne·wa·či i·nahi.* (K-FC 216)
'There were always a lot of them there.'
(*ahpene·či* 'every time'; =*meko* EMPH; |=ipi| HRSY;
|ma·ne·-| AI 'be many', |e·h=–wa·či| 3p/AOR; *i·nahi* 'there')

(b)　*e·h=na·kwa·či i·tepi* 'And she left for there.' (K-M 195a)
(|na·kwa·-| AI 'leave', |e·h=–či| 3s/AOR; *i·tepi* '(to) there')

(c)　*na·hina·h=ča·hi ne·topaniwe·kwe·ni i·tepi, ...* (K-GBuff 261; tr. TB)
"Whenever you go on the war-path over there ..."
(|na·hina·hi| 'time'; =*ča·hi* 'so';
|natopani-| AI 'go on the warpath', |IC–we·kwe·ni| 2p/CH.INT; *i·tepi* '(to) there')

(d)　*ke·tawi-na·wahkwe·niki e·h=pya·či i·ya·hi pehkwa·hkwa·ki* (K-KK 5)
'Almost at noon he arrived over at the grove.'
(*katawi* PV 'almost', |na·wahkwe·-| II 'be noon', |IC–niki| 0´/CC;
|pya·-| AI 'arrive', |e·h=–či| 3s/AOR; *i·ya·hi* 'yonder';
pehkwa·hkwa·ki 'grove (loc.)')

(e)　*e·h=na·kwa·či wi·sahke·ha o·hkomese·heki.* (K-SF 97)
'Wîsahkêha left to go to his grandmother's.'
(|na·kwa·-| AI 'leave'; *wi·sahke·ha* (name);
o·hkomese·heki 'his grandmother's (loc.)')

In another similar construction, there is a postverbal particle phrase consisting of a particle formed from a relative root and its oblique complement (5.73):

(5.90) Postverbal particle phrase with oblique

   (a)   *e·h=na·kwa·či i·tepi=·ši.* 'And he left for there.' (S-FYF 2)
         (Verb as in 5.89b; *i·tepi* '(to) there'; |iši| 'to {somewhere}')

   (b)   *e·h=a·čimohekoči i·nah=taši.* 'And he (obv.) instructed him there.' (K-SSB 5)
         (|a·čimoh-| TA 'instruct', |e·h=—ekoči| 3´–3s/AOR;
         |i·nahi| 'there'; *taši* '{somewhere}')

Word Order after the Verb

65.8. Following the verb there are no fixed positions to which words or phrases of particular categories or functions are assigned. An animate subject and object may occur in either order, regardless of which one is the obviative (5.91a-d), or which one is a demonstrative (5.91ef), and a secondary object may precede or follow a primary object (5.91gh). Sentence-final position is, however, a weakly emphatic site for particles and noun phrases. Subordinate clauses occur with a similarly free word order.

(5.91) Free word order among the noun phrases after the verb

   (a)   *e·h=mo·šiha·či=ke·hi meškwahki·ha mo·hkoma·nani.* (K-CDWP 13)
       'And the Meskwaki had a vision of the American (obv.).'
         (|mo·ših-| TA 'have a vision of', |e·h=—a·či| 3s–3´/AOR; =ke·hi| 'moreover';
         meškwahki·ha 'Meskwaki'; *mo·hkoma·nani* 'American (obv.)')

   (b)   *e·h=pakina·či oto·hpwa·kanimote·hani kwi·yese·ha, . . .* (C-G 19)
       'the boy threw down his tobacco bag (obv.)'
         (|pakiN-| TA 'throw down', |e·h=—a·či| 3s–3´/AOR;
         oto·hpwa·kanimote·hani 'his tobacco bag (obv.)'; *kwi·yese·ha* 'boy')

   (c)   *taka·wi=meko e·h=na·no·te·hkwamekoči ihkwe·wa anemo·hani.* (JP-GTF 43)
       'The dog (obv.) was barely missing the woman with its bites.'
         (*taka·wi* 'a little'; =*meko* EMPH; |CV+| RED1, |no·te·hkwam-| TA 'miss biting',
         |e·h=—ekoči| 3´–3s/AOR; *ihkwe·wa* 'woman'; *anemo·hani* 'dog (obv.)')

   (d)   *. . . e·h=ki·ma·hekoči aša·hahi neniwa.* (K-IML 2)
       'some Siouxs (obv.) spied on the man'
         (|ki·ma·h-| TA 'watch unseen', |e·h=—ekoči| 3´–3s/AOR;
         aša·hahi 'Siouxs (obv. pl.)'; *neniwa* 'man')

   (e)   *kapo·twe e·h=kehke·nema·či wi··sahke·ha i·nini.* (K-M 912e)
       'At some point Wîsahkêha knew that it was her (obv.).'
         (*kapo·twe* 'at some point'; |kehke·nem-| TA 'know', |e·h=—a·či| 3s–3´/AOR;
         wi··sahke·ha (name); *i·nini* 'that (obv.)')

   (f)   *wi·na=na·hkači e·h=kehke·nema·či=mekoho i·nini*
        masahkamikohkwe·wa. (K-M 912f)
       'And Masahkamikohkwêwa was also fully aware that it was him (obv.).'
         (*wi·na* 3s/EMPH; *na·hkači* 'also'; |kehke·nem-| TA 'know', |e·h=—a·či| 3s–3´/AOR;
         =*mekoho* EMPH; *i·nini* 'that (obv.)';
         masahkamikohkwe·wa 'Masahkamikohkwêwa')

(g)   *e·h=anemi-mi·na·či mekosani o·hkomesahi.* (C-O 47)
'He gave the awls to his grandmothers (obv.) on his way.'
(*anemi* PV 'continue on', |mi·N-| TA+O 'give O2 to', |e·h=–a·či| 3s–3´/AOR;
mekosani 'awls'; *o·hkomesahi* 'his grandmothers (obv.)')

(h)   . . . *e·h=mi·na·či ihkwe·wani nya·nanwi.* (JP-MC8D 27)
'he gave the woman (obv.) five'
(|mi·N-| TA+O 'give O2 to', |e·h=–a·či| 3s–3´/AOR;
ihkwe·wani 'woman (obv.)'; *nya·nanwi* 'five')

(i)   . . . *i·ni=wi·na e·h=mi·na·či ona·pe·mani oto·šehki·ta·kani ihkwe·wa.* (K-FM 30)
'then the woman gave <u>her</u> clothing to her husband (obv.)'
(*i·ni* 'then'; *wi·na* 3s/EMPH; |mi·N-| TA+O 'give O2 to', |e·h=–a·či| 3s–3´/AOR;
ona·pe·mani 'her husband (obv.)'; *oto·šehki·ta·kani* 'her clothing';
ihkwe·wa 'woman')

As the examples suggest, any emphasis or other effect that may be signaled by the different orderings of the noun phrases after the verb is evidently quite subtle. One function that can be identified for sentence-final position, however, is to mark the end of a segment of the narrative in which the character the noun refers to has been the most prominent. For example, *mahkate·w-anakwe·wa* 'Black Rainbow (prox.)' occurs at the end of a sentence after an obviative participle in (O 155E). In the next sentence another character (his Sioux prisoner) takes center stage as a new proximate, and Black Rainbow is relegated to obviative status (O 155F).

VERBLESS SENTENCES

66. Equational sentences (**§66.1**), substantive sentences (**§66.2**), and gapped sentences (**§66.3**) are predications that lack a verbal predicate. They may, however, contain verbs as participles or other nominalizations, or in subordinate clauses. Sentence fragments (**§66.4**) are verbless sentences that are not predications.

Equational Sentences

66.1. An equational sentence identifies a NEW entity by reference to a GIVEN entity. (In an interrogative sentence the identification is asked for or questioned, and in a negative sentence it is denied.) The two terms of the equation are noun phrases or function as such, and there is no linking verb. The New term may represent either completely new information or familiar information that is recalled, while the Given term refers to an entity that is taken to be known from previous or current information or experience, or that is a familiar or more or less generic concept. The equational sentence states that what is referred to by the New term is identical with or an instance of what is referred to by the Given term. Equational sentences in which one or both terms are participles (including oblique participles) are common. An oblique participle with two relative roots may be equated to a single Given term (5.92*i*). If the Given term is a demonstrative pronoun, the New term is sometimes not directly identified with this but rather has a meaning like that of an adjunct noun: 'about, pertaining to' (5.92*l*).

The Given term precedes the New term (5.92) when the New term is definite or a definition, or if it refers to a member or members of a specific class, in which case its reference may be non-specific (5.93*d*). In the song text in (5.92*m*) the Given term is discontinuous, straddling the New term. In this construction the New term may be preceded by a pleonastic demonstrative pronoun of the *i·ni* 'that' set (5.78*b*, 5.93).

(5.92) Equational sentences: Given + New

(a) *manaha neto·te mena·na* 'this is our (exc.) brother' (K-FC 113)
    (*manaha* 'this (anim.)'; *neto·te mena·na* 'our (exc.) sibling')

(b) *mani aškote·wi tepowe·wi-aškote·wi.* "This fire is a council fire." (K-M 1084; tr. HP)
    (*mani* 'this (inan.)'; *aškote·wi* 'fire'; *tepowe·wi* PN 'of council')

(c) *ma·hahi ne·nesa·čihi.* 'These are the ones he killed.' (K-M 138.l)
    (*ma·hahi* 'these (obv.)';
    |CV+| RED1; |neS-| TA 'kill', |IC–a·čihi| 3s–3´/PPL(OBVpl))

(d) *wi·sahke·ha ayo·hi wi·h=taši-nana·he·netaka.* (K-FC 267)
    'Wîsahkêha is to be the one who rules here.'
    (*wi·sahke·ha* (name); *ayo·hi* 'here'; |wi·h=| FUT; *taši* PV '{somewhere}',
    |nana·he·net-| TI(1)-O 'rule, be the ruler' |IC–aka| 3s(–0)/PPL(ANsg))

(e) *ma·haki=koči neniwaki wi·h=nakamočiki.* (K-FC 146; tr. HP)
    "As these men folks are the ones to do the singing."
    (*ma·haki* 'these (anim.)'; *=koči* 'of course'; *neniwaki* 'men (obv.)';
    |wi·h=| FUT; |nakamo-| AI 'sing', |IC–čiki| 3p/PPL(ANpl))

(f) *o=ši·ši·paki=wi·na pe·hki wi·h=a·hkwe·nemakečiki.* (K-FC 152)
    'But ducks are the ones we especially prefer.'
    (*o* 'or'; *ši·ši·paki* 'ducks'; *=wi·na* 'but'; *pe·hki* 'really';
    |wi·h=| FUT; |a·hkwe·nem-| TA 'think a lot of', |IC–akečiki| 1p–3/PPL(ANpl))

(g) *i·ni e·šawiwa·či* 'that was what they did' (O 1H)
    (*i·ni* 'that (inan.)'; |išawi-| AI 'do {so}'; |IC–wa·či| 3p/PPL(obl))

(h) *i·ni=ča·h=meko e·nenako·we.* "So this is all I have to say to you." (K-FC 508; tr. HP)
    (*i·ni* 'that (inan.)'; |=ča·hi| 'so'; *=meko* EMPH;
    |iN-| TA 'say {so} to', |IC–enako·we| 1s–2p/PPL(obl))

(i) *mani=kohi we·či-išawiya·ni.* (K-FC 563)
    'This is the reason why I'm acting the way I am.'
    (*mani* 'this (inan.)'; *=kohi* 'certainly';
    |oči| PV 'from {somewhere}', |išawi-| AI 'be {so}', |IC–ya·ni| 1s/PPL(obl))

(j) *o=mani=koh=mekoho me·nwikeki mehteno·hi.* (K-FC 257; tr. HP)
    "This is the only good thing."
    (*o* 'or'; *mani* 'this (inan.)'; |=kohi| 'certainly'; *=mekoho* EMPH; |menwiken-| II 'be
    good', |IC–ki| 0/PPL(INsg); *mehteno·hi* 'only' [5.28*c*, 5.36*c*, 5.72*e*])

(k) *ma·haki ·kohpiči-nenoso·haki e·nakwiki a·kwi=wi·na·=·niki.* (K-FC 399)
    'The ones that we call mere buffalos here are not what they are.'
    (*ma·haki* 'these (anim.)'; *kohpiči-nenoso·haki* 'buffalos (dim.)';
    |iN-| TA 'say {so} to', |IC–akwiki| 12–3/PPL(ANpl);
    a·kwi 'not'; |=wi·na| 'but'; |i·niki| 'those (anim.)')

(l) *i·niki kemeso·ta·naki=·yo·we.* (K-MFWB 36) (cf. 5.96*b*)
    'Those [flowers with faces] were your late parents.'
    (*i·niki* 'those (anim.)'; *kemeso·ta·naki* 'your parents'; *=iyo·we* PAST)

(m) *mehto·či manaha ni·na·na=mekoho.* 'It's as if he is one of our own.' (K-FC 113)
    (*mehto·či* 'like'; *manaha* 'this (anim.)'; *ni·na·na* 1p/EMPH; *=mekoho* EMPH)

(n) *ča·ki nemešo·mesaki ki·yo·te·neniwaki.*
'All serpents are my grandfathers.' (song; K-SSB 44)
(*ča·ki* 'all'; *nemešo·mesaki* 'my grandfathers'; *ki·yo·te·neniwaki* 'serpents')

(5.93) Equational sentences: Given + *i·ni*-set pronoun + New
(a) *mani·=’ni·=’ni na·tawino·ni.* 'This is that medicine.' (O 99G)
(|mani| 'this (inan.)'; |i·ni| 'that (inan.)' (2x); *na·tawino·ni* 'medicine')
(b) *ni·na=ča·hi·=’ni·=’ni.* "I was the one." (K-M 361m; tr. HP) (See 2.25.)
(*ni·na* 1s/EMPH; |=ča·hi| 'so'; |i·ni| 'that (inan.)' (2x))
(c) *mehteno·h=mekoho owiye·ha me·hkate·wi·ta i·na wi·h=kehke·netaka.* (K-FC 165)
'Only someone who fasts will know them.'
("The only person that will know them all is the one who fasts" [tr. HP])
(|mehteno·hi| 'only'; *=mekoho* EMPH; *owiye·ha* 'someone';
|mahkate·wi·-| AI 'fast', |IC–ta| 3/PPL(ANsg); *i·na* 'that (anim.)';
|wi·h=| FUT, |kehke·net-| TI(1) 'know', |IC–aka| 3–0/PPL(ANsg))

The equation of two temporal clauses has a substantivized clause with *na·hina·hi* 'time' as the Given term followed by a substantivized clause with *i·nina·hi* 'that time' (equivalent to *i·ni* 'that (inan.)' + *na·hina·hi* 'time') as the New term (**§63.2**, 5.63*b*, 5.94*ab*; cf. **§69.5**, 5.128). The mode in the first clause may be any mode that can be used in a conditional temporal clause (**§26**), and the mode in the second clause is a changed conjunct in its absolute rather than relative function (**§26.10**). In this construction, |wi·h=| FUT may occur with the changed conjunct in the second clause, which is not the case when the changed conjunct indicates completion before something else (2.194). This anomaly can be explained by taking the verb in the second clause as a sort of temporal participle (Thomason 2001).

(5.94) Equational sentences of time: *na·hina·hi* (Given) + *i·nina·hi* (New)
(a) *na·hina·h=meko ki·ši-nahisenye·hite, i·nina·hi wi·h=nesehki aša·haki.* (K-Wap 25)
"at the time when it has learned to eat, then the Sioux will kill you" (tr. TB)
(|na·hina·hi| 'time'; *=meko* EMPH; *ki·ši* PV PERF,
|nahisenye·hi-| AI 'know how to eat (dim.)', |–te| 3s/SUBJ; *i·nina·hi* 'that time';
|wi·h=| FUT, |neS-| TA 'kill', |IC–ehki| 3–2s/CC; *aša·haki* 'Siouxs')
(b) *na·hina·h=mekoho we·wi·wiwane·ni i·nina·hi wi·h=oni·ča·nesiyani.* (K-FC 13)
'Just as soon as you take a wife will be the time when you have the (foretold) child.' ("Just as soon as you have a wife then you will have the child." [tr. HP])
(|na·hina·hi| 'time'; *=mekoho* EMPH;
|owi·wi-| AI 'take, have a wife', |IC–wane·ni| 2s/CH.INT; *i·nina·hi* 'that time';
|wi·h=| FUT, |oni·ča·nesi-| AI(+O) 'have (O2 as) a child', |IC–yani| 2s/CC)

Equational sentences of time may have *i·nina·hi* in the New clause without *na·hina·hi* in the Given clause. These border on being non-equational conditional sentences.

(5.95) Equational sentences of time: (Given) + *i·nina·hi* (New)
(a) *e·h=katawi-=meko -kawisa·niki i·nina·hi e·h=po·nikahaki.* (C-PD 25)
'Just at the point when (the tree) was about to fall, he stopped chopping on it.'
(*katawi* PV 'almost', |kawisa·-| II 'fall over', |e·h=–niki| 0´/AOR; *=meko* EMPH;
i·nina·hi 'that time'; |po·nikah-| TI(1) 'cease chopping', |e·h=–aki| 3s–0/AOR)
(b) *takwa·kike=meko i·nina·hi wi·h=penopenoye·kwe.* (K-BLI 15)
'Next fall will be the time when you can all go home.'
(|takwa·ki-| II 'be fall', |–ke| 0/SUBJ; *=meko* EMPH; *i·nina·hi* 'that time';
|wi·h=| FUT, |CVCV+| RED2, |peno-| AI 'go home', |IC–ye·kwe| 2p/CC)

If the New term is indefinite or completely new information it precedes the Given term.

(5.96) Equational sentences: New + Given

(a) *mesa pe waki ma·haki.* 'These are giants.' (= 'This is about giants.') (C-G 1)
　　(*mesa pe waki* 'giants'; *ma·haki* 'these (anim.)')

(b) *kemeso ta naki=´yo we i·niki.* (K-MFWB 27) (cf. 5.92*l*)
　　'Those [flowers with faces] were your parents.'
　　(Or: 'Your parents are what those were.')
　　(*kemeso ta naki* 'your parents'; =*iyo we* PAST; *i·niki* 'those (anim.)')

(c) *maneto wa=ma·h=ye toke·=´na.* "He is probably a Spirit" (K-WSB 39; tr. HP)
　　(*maneto wa* 'manitou'; |=ma·hi| 'you see'; |=ye·toke| 'it seems'; |i·na| 'that (anim.)')

(d) *me nwikeki=koči=mani* "this is a good thing" (K-FC 204; tr. HP)
　　(|menwiken-| II 'be good', |IC–ki| 0/PPL(INsg); =*koči* 'of course';
　　mani 'this (inan.)')

(e) *ki yo te neniwa nemešo mesa.* 'My grandfather is a serpent.' (song; K-SSB 43)
　　(*ki yo te neniwa* 'serpent'; *nemešo mesa* 'my grandfather')

(f) *mehto či=koh=mekoho keto te mena naki i·niki wa·koše·haki.* (K-FC 748; tr. HP)
　　"because the foxes are just the same as our brothers."
　　(*mehto či* 'like'; |=kohi| 'certainly'; =*mekoho* EMPH; *keto te mena naki*
　　'our (inc.) siblings'; *i·niki* 'those (anim.)'; *wa·koše·haki* 'foxes')

(g) *neniwani=či·hi i·niye ne ketiwani* (K-MESB 28)
　　'he saw that the one who had been an eagle had turned into a man'
　　("behold the one who was an eagle changed to a man." [tr. TB])
　　(*neniwani* 'man (obv.)'; =*či·hi* 'it was discovered';
　　i·niye ne 'that (gone, before; obv.)'; *ketiwani* 'eagle, golden eagle')

(h) *neno te·hkwe wa we wi·wiya·na.* (C-PB 2)
　　'The one I'm married to is an Indian woman.'
　　(*neno te·hkwe wa* 'Indian woman';
　　|owi·wi-| AI+O 'marry O2'+ |IC–ya·na| 1s/PPL(ANsg))
　　neno te·hkwe wa·=´na we wi·wiya·na. (C-PB 3): same, with *i·na* 'that (anim.)'

In (5.92*a*) the New term (*neto te mena na* 'our brother') comes second, because it refers to a definite person ('the one who is our brother'), but in (5.96*f*) the New term (*keto te mena naki* 'our (inc.) siblings') comes first, because it refers to a general class and not to specific individuals. In other cases this distinction may be subtle or non-existent (as between 5.92*l* and 5.96*b*).

Questions with the question words *we ne·ha* 'who?', *we·kone·hi* 'what?', *ta ni* 'how?', *ta nahi* 'where?', *ta·tepi* 'whither?', and *ta na, ta ni* 'which one is, where is (he, it)?' (§18.7; 2.153; §31.10-11) are equational sentences. The question word is treated as the New term and is almost always sentence-initial; the verb appears as a participle acting as the Given term.

(5.97) Equational sentences with question words

(a) *we ne·ha=ča·hi wi·h=owi·wiyana.* 'So who are you going to marry?' (K-FC 59)
　　(*we ne·ha* 'who?'; |=ča·hi| 'so';
　　|wi·h=| FUT, |owi·wi-| AI+O '(man to) marry O2', |IC–yana| 2s/PPL(ANsg))

(b) *we ne·ha=ye toke mehtose neniwa wi·h=ne waka.* (JP-YMPE 46)
　　'What person am I going to see, I wonder?'
　　(*we ne·ha* 'who?'; =*ye toke* 'perhaps'; *mehtose neniwa* 'person';
　　|wi·h=| FUT, |ne·w-| TA 'see', |IC–aka| 1s–3/PPL(ANsg))

(c)   *we ne ha=ča h=če wina h=ni kiya na.* (SP-MRD 34)
'Who was born at the same time I was?'
(*we ne ha* 'who?'; |=ča hi| 'so'; |če wina hi| 'at the same time';
|ni ki-| AI 'be born', |IC–ya na| 1s/PPL(ANsg))

(d)   *we kone hi= 'yo=mani.* 'What is this?' (K-M 462k)
(*we kone hi* 'what?'; |=iyo| 'for'; *mani* 'this (inan.)')

(e)   *we kone h=ya pi=ni na ne hpatama ni.* (K-FC 288)
'O.K. now, what was in my food that I ate?'
(|we kone hi| 'what?'; =*ya pi* 'O.K. now!'; *ni na* 1s/EMPH;
|nahpat-| TI(1) 'eat accidentally in one's food', |IC–ama ni| 1s–0/PPL(INsg))

(f)   *we kone h=ye toke we či-ma wačimi nameki.* (K-FC 793)
'Why have we been called together, I wonder?' (*Lit.*: 'from what, for what reason?')
(|we kone hi| 'what?'; =*ye toke* 'perhaps'; |oči| PV 'from {something}',
|ma wačim-| TA 'call together', |IC–i nameki| X–1p/PPL(obl))

(g)   *mana masahkamikohkwe wa we kone hi we čihači* (K-M 361f; tr. HP)
"Why do you try [with] M[asahkamikohkwêwa] ..?"
(*mana* 'this (anim.)', *masahkamikohkwe wa* (name); *we kone hi* 'what?';
|očih-| TA 'act on for {some} reason', |IC–ači| 2s–3/PPL(obl))

(h)   *ta ni=ye toke a mi- šawiči* 'what could he possibly do?' (A 147A)
(*ta ni* 'how?'; =*ye toke* 'it seems';
a mi PV POT, |išawi-| AI 'do {so}', |IC–či| 3s/PPL(obl))

(i)   *ta nah=ya pi e h=awiwa či ki waki.* "Where are your wives?" (K-WYB 163; tr. TB)
(|ta nahi| 'where?'; =*ya pi* 'O.K. now!';
|awi-| AI 'be {somewhere}', |e h=–wa či| 3p/PPL(loc.obl); *ki waki* 'your wives')

(j)   *ta nahi= 'yo wa woči-menoye kwe.* 'Where have you been drinking?' (JB-Tiger 71)
(*ta nahi* 'where?'; |=iyo| 'for'; |CV+| RED1, |oči| PV 'from {somewhere}',
|meno-| AI 'drink', |IC–ye kwe| 2p/PPL(obl))

(k)   *ta nah=ya pi e h=ne wači.* 'Where did you see him?' (K-TO 4) (Cf. 2.124.)
(*ta nahi* 'where?'; =*ya pi* 'O.K. now!';
|ne w-| TA 'see', |e h=–ači| 2s–3/PPL(loc.obl))

(l)   *ta tepi e ya yakwe.* 'Where are we (inc.) going?' (K-MTHB 5)
(*ta tepi* 'whither?'; |iha -| AI 'go {somewhere}', |IC–yakwe| 12/PPL(obl))

(m)   *ta tepi=ča hi we či ye kwe.* 'Where did you (pl.) come from?' (K-FC 640)
(*ta tepi* 'whither?'; =*ča hi* 'so';
|oči -| 'come from {somewhere}', |IC–ye kwe| 2p/PPL(obl))

(n)   *ta na=ya pi ketaya.* 'Where is your pet?' (JB-FS 34)
(*ta na* 'which one (anim.)? where is (anim.)?'; =*ya pi* 'O.K. now!';
ketaya 'your pet')

(o)   *ta na=ča hi wi h=owi wiyana.* 'Who do you want to marry?' (K-FM 6)
(*ta na* 'which one (anim.)?'; =*ča hi* 'so';
|wi h=| FUT, |owi wi-| AI+O '(man to) marry O2', |IC–yana| 2s/PPL(ANsg))

(p)   *ta niki=ča hi '-'niki '-'niki pe ši-nesehkiki.* (K-Koch 92)
'Which are the ones (you referred to) that almost killed you?'
(*ta niki* 'which ones (anim.)?'; |=ča hi| 'so'; |i niki| 'those (anim.)' (2x);
|paši| PV 'almost', |neS-| TA 'kill', |IC–ehkiki| 3–2s/PPL(ANpl))

Questions with *ta·nina·hi* 'when?' have the same general structure; the verb is in the changed conjunct, designating a time in an absolute sense (§26.10, 2.196-198), but this ostensibly functions as a sort of temporal participle (Thomason 2001). As in equational sentences of time (5.94), |wi·h=| FUT may occur with the changed conjunct in this construction.

(5.98) Ostensible equational sentences with *ta·nina·hi* 'when?'

(a) *ta·nina·h=ya·pi wi·h=pya·či.* "When is he coming?" (K-FC 555; tr. HP)
   (|ta·nina·hi| 'when?'; *=ya·pi* 'O.K. now!';
   |wi·h=| FUT, |pya·-| AI 'come', |IC–či| 3s/CC)

(b) *ta·nina·h=ča·h·ke škimači.* 'When did you persuade her?' (K-FC 432)
   (|ta·nina·hi| 'when?'; |=ča·hi| 'so'; |kaškim-| TA 'persuade', |IC–ači| 2s–3/CC)

(c) *ta·nina·h=ča·hi a·mi-kočawiyakwe i·ni='ši.* (K-FC 432; tr. HP)
   "When could we try that?"
   (|ta·nina·hi| 'when?'; |=ča·hi| 'so';
   a·mi PV POT, |kočawi-| AI 'try', |IC–yakwe| 12/CC; *i·ni* 'that (inan.)'; |iši| '{so}')

(d) *ni·na ta·nina·hi wi·h=nepo·hiya·ni.* "When am I going to die" (K-FC 721; tr. HP)
   (*ni·na* 1s/EMPH; *ta·nina·hi* 'when?';
   |wi·h=| FUT, |nepo·hi-| AI 'die', |IC–ya·ni| 1s/CC)

(e) *me·kwe·h=ča·hi ta·nina·hi wi·h=po·nahkate·wi yani.* (K-FC 31; tr. HP)
   "when do you think you'll quit fasting?"
   (|me·kwe·he| 'I believe; it is thought likely'; *=ča·hi* 'so'; *ta·nina·hi* 'when?';
   |wi·h=| FUT, |po·nahkate·wi·-| AI 'cease fasting', |IC–yani| 2s/CC)

Equational sentences in which a direct quotation is the New term and an oblique-headed participle of the quotative verb is the Given term appear, at least some of the time, to carry the implication that the veracity of what was said is in question.

(5.99) Quotation (New) + quotative verb as participle (Given)

(a) *"ehe·he," e·či='p=a·pehe.* (K-MLF 61)
   ' "Yes," is what he would always say (unconvincingly).'
   (*ehe·he* 'yes'; |i-| AI 'say {so}', |IC–či| 3s/PPL(obl); |=ipi| HRSY; |a·pehe| 'usually')

(b) *"neki·ši-=kohi·-kaškowe wi·h=owi·wiya·ni," e·na·či='pi*
   (K-M 257i; tr. HP, expanded)
   " 'I have been accepted to marry her,' [is what] he told [them (mistakenly)]."
   (*ki·ši* PV PERF, |kaškowe·-| AI 'persuade X', |ne–∅| 1s/IND; *=kohi* 'certainly';
   |wi·h=| FUT, |owi·wi-| AI+O '(man to) marry (O2)', |e·h=–ya·ni| 1s/AOR;
   |iN-| TA 'say {so} to', |IC–a·či| 3s–3´/PPL(obl); |=ipi| HRSY)

(c) *"mawi-=ča·hi·-pako·ši-pehtawe·wa," e·na·či.* (JP-TO 103)
   ' "Well, he went to get a fire ready," is the (lying) reply she made to her.'
   (*mawi* PV 'go and', *pako·ši* PV 'ahead of time',
   |pehtawe·-| AI 'make a fire', |–wa| 3s/IND; |=ča·hi| 'so'; *e·na·či* [5.99b])

Substantive Sentences

66.2. Substantive sentences state the existence or being of an entity or condition without reference to another entity and without the use of a verbal predicate. There are also interrogative and negative sentences of this type. A negative sentence has *a·kwi*, and this may serve as a higher predicate with a complement clause in the future aorist (5.102*deh*).

(5.100) Substantive sentences: with demonstratives

(a)   *i·ni.* 'That's it.' (K-TO 46); "That's all." (K-FC 142; tr. HP); 'That's enough.'
      (*i·ni* 'that (inan.)')

(b)   *i·ni?* 'Is that it?'; 'All set?' (C-YBB 7)
      (*i·ni* 'that (inan.)'; *?* Q)

(c)   *i·ni=čá·hi.* 'There it is.' (O 101G)
      (*i·ni* 'that (inan.)'; *=ča·hi* 'so'; *΄* EMPH)

(d)   *o·΄, mana=čá·hi, ano·se.* 'Oh, here it is, Father.' (K-FC 357)
      (*o·΄* 'Oh!'; *mana* 'this (anim.)'; *=ča·hi* 'so'; *΄* EMPH; *ano·se* 'father (voc.)')

(e)   *o·ni=na·hkači mani·* . . . 'And there's also this (as follows): . . .' (K-Wap 78)
      (*o·ni* 'and then'; *na·hkači* 'also'; *mani* 'this (inan.)')

(f)   *ta·na=ča·hi.* 'Which one is he?' (K-PKM 6); *ta·na=ča·h.* 'Where is he?' (C-O 20)
      (*ta·na* 'which one (anim.)? where is (anim.)?'; |=ča·hi| 'so')

(g)   *mani=mekoho na·na·kači.* 'It will be this same way exactly.' (O 141H)
      (*mani* 'this (inan.)'; *=mekoho* EMPH; *na·na·kači* 'exactly')

(5.101) Substantive sentences: with noun phrases

(a)   *kašina·hi, papi·wi·ata·mine·haki.* (K-M 51e; tr. HP)
      "Why, say, this is very small corn."
      (*kašina·hi* 'well?'; *papi·wi* PN 'tiny (pl.)', *ata·mine·haki* 'corn (dim.)')

(b)   *nenoso·ni=či·hi; a·kwi=wi·na kohpiči·hani, ketaki-nenoso·ni.* (K-Spot 164; tr. HP)
      "It was a cow, not a buffalo, but a spotted cow."
      (*nenoso·ni* 'cow; buffalo (obv.)'; *=či·hi* 'it was discovered'; *a·kwi* 'not';
      =wi·na 'but'; *kohpiči·hani* 'buffalo (obv.)'; *ketaki* PN 'spotted',
      nenoso·ni 'cow; buffalo (obv.)')

(c)   *o·ni=wi·nwa·wa ošemi·hani nešihka.* (O 150C) (Cf. 5.39*f*.)
      'And then it was only him and his niece.'
      (*o·ni* 'and then'; *wi·nwa·wa* 3p/EMPH; *ošemi·hani* 'his niece'; *nešihka* 'alone')

(5.102) Substantive sentences: with *a·kwi* 'not'

(a)   *a·kwi.* 'It won't happen, it won't be a problem.' (O 97E)
      (*a·kwi* 'not'; cf. 5.106*a*)

(b)   *ni·na·na a·kwi.* "We have nothing to do with it." (K-FC 220; tr. HP)
      (*ni·na·na* 1p/EMPH; *a·kwi* 'not')

(c)   *ni·na a·kwi=mekoho ke·ko·hi* "its nothing to me" (K-FC 668; tr. HP)
      (*ni·na* 1s/EMPH; *a·kwi* 'not'; *=mekoho* EMPH; *ke·ko·hi* 'something, anything')

(d)   *a·kwi=ke·h=ma·mahka·či wi·h=pana·ča niki.* (O 14F)
      'Moreover, it would not necessarily be that it (obv.) was damaged.'
      (*a·kwi* 'not'; |=ke·hi| 'moreover'; *ma·mahka·či* 'necessarily';
      |wi·h=| FUT, |pana·ča·-| II 'be ruined', |e·h=–niki| 0΄/AOR)

(e)   *wi·h=če·če·kesoniči=ke·hi a·kwi.* (K-FC 347)
      'And he would not scream out from being burned.'
      (|wi·h=| FUT, |če·če·keso-| 'be made to scream by being burned',
      |e·h=–niči| 3΄/AOR; *=ke·hi* 'moreover'; *a·kwi* 'not')

(f)   *a·kwi=ke·ko·hi še·ški wi·čiwi·čihite owiye·ha.* (K-FC 524; tr. HP)
"it would be alright if some one lives with me." (Just as a house-mate.)
    (*a·kwi* 'not'; *ke·ko·hi* 'something'; *še·ški* 'only';
    |CV+| RED2, |wi·čih-| TA 'live with', |–ite| 3s–1s/SUBJ; *owiye·ha* 'someone')

(g)   *a·kwi-kana·kwa* (5.69*c*, 5.87*b*), *a·kwi=meko kana·kwa*
'it's impossible; I can't do it; it's no use; it can't be helped; it makes no difference'
    (*a·kwi* 'not', *kana·kwa* (only in this idiom); *=meko* EMPH)
NOTE: *kana·kwa* alone is a reduced form of this and has the same negative meaning (A 123D, 127A, 134A).

(h)   *a·kwi-kana·kwa no·ta nepi wi·h=menowa·či* (O 45F)
'it was not allowed for them to drink water too soon'
    (*a·kwi-kana·kwa* 'it's not possible'; *no·ta* 'too soon'; *nepi* 'water';
    |wi·h=| FUT, |meno-| AI+O 'drink O2', |e·h=–wa·či 3p/AOR)

Gapped Sentences

66.3. Gapped sentences are verbless sentences for which a verbal predicate may be supplied from the preceding context. They can be understood as, in effect, verbal sentences that have been reduced by the omission of the verb and sometimes other words. For example, in (5.103*ab*) the second lines are gapped sentences that are understood as having the same verbs as in the first lines; in (5.103*b*) the understood verb would have a different inflection. The relative root in a gapped verb may remain behind as a particle (5.103*f*).

    (5.103) Gapped verbs

(a)   *ki·h=ma·wačiweto·pwa mena·škono·ni,*
meše=we·=meko·='nahi ke·ko·hi. (FC 170; tr. HP)
"And you must bring some meat or anything else."
    (|wi·h=| FUT, |ma·wačiwet-| TI(2) 'bring together', |ke–o·pwa| 2p–0/IND;
    mena·škono·ni 'fresh meat'; *meše=meko·='nahi* 'any'; *|=we·na|* 'in fact';
    ke·ko·hi 'something, anything')

(b)   *me·mešihka=mekoho ki·h=ki·ša·koči-=mekoho -se·kesipwa.*
ni·na=ke·hi a·kwi. (K-FC 140)
'Maybe you (pl.) will be extremely frightened, but I will not be.'
    (*me·mešihka* 'perhaps'; *=mekoho* EMPH (2x);
    |wi·h=| FUT, *ki·ša·koči* PV 'extremely', |se·kesi-| AI 'be scared', |ke–pwa| 2p/IND;
    ni·na 1s/EMPH; *=ke·hi* 'moreover'; *a·kwi* 'not')

(c)   *i·noki a·kwi.* 'Not now.' (K-FC 597) (= 'You should not remind her of it now.')
    (*i·noki* 'now'; *a·kwi* 'not')

(d)   A: *ki·ši-pye·hpahowa?* 'Has he come running?'
B: *we·ne·ha.* 'Who?' (= 'Has who come running?') (S-Shak 5)
    (*ki·ši* PV PERF, |pye·hpaho-| AI 'come running', |–wa| 3s/IND; ? Q;
    we·ne·ha 'who?')

(e)   *ki·hka·na=ča·h we·ne·hani.* 'And who (did) your <u>friend</u> (marry)?' (K-MHTW 14)
    (*ki·hka·na* 'your friend'; |=ča·hi| 'so'; *we·ne·hani* 'who (obv.)?')

(f)   *o·sani we·či-omaya·wi·či e·h=otapiniči, okye·ni onemači·neki oči.* (K-MFWB 47)
       'His father sat on his right hand, and his mother on his left.'
          (*o·sani* 'his father'; |oči| PV 'oriented {so}',
          |omaya·wi·-| AI 'use right hand'; |IC–či| 3s/PPL(obl);
          |otapi-| AI 'sit oriented {so}', |e·h=–niči| 3´/AOR;
          okye·ni 'his mother'; *onemači·neki* 'on his left'; *oči* P 'oriented {so}')

In (5.103*f*), the verb stem |otapi-| 'sit oriented {so}' (in the first clause) is, in effect, repeated without its verbal final (|-api-| AI 'sit') in the second clause, leaving behind only the initial |ot-| 'oriented {so}' (**§22.4(d)**) in the form of the particle *oči* 'oriented {so}'.

Some idiomatic structures have the form of gapped sentences, without the omitted predicate necessarily being present in the context. This is the case when there is no higher verb or predicate particle in construction with an aorist conjunct (2.178), subjunctive (2.186-188, 5.122*t*(1); cf. 5.120*c*(3)), interrogative participle (2.282; 5.122*i*(6), 5.122*t*(3)), or future aorist conjunct (2.337). In some cases there is a more explicit form of the idiom with the predicate present.

(5.104) Idiom with optional gapping of the higher verb
   (a)   *meše=meko e·h=tahpene·wa·ne·ni ni·h=tahpene.* (JP-GTF 5, 7);
          e·h=tahpene·wa·ne·ni ni·h=tahpene. (JP-GTF 4)
          'I'll die wherever I die!' ('I don't care! Let whatever happens to me happen!')
             (*meše* 'freely' [5.17*j*]; =*meko* EMPH; |tahpene·-| AI 'die {somewhere}',
             |e·h=–wa·ne·ni| 1s/INT.PPL(loc.obl); (same verb), |wi·h=| FUT, |ne–∅| 1s/IND)
   (b)   *meše=meko e·h=tahpene·wa·ne·ni.* (JP-GTF 5, 14)
          'I'll die wherever I die!' (*Lit.*: 'Wherever I may die.')

The sentence in (5.104*b*) has exactly the same idiomatic meaning as those in (5.104*a*) from the same text, even though the matrix verb is omitted.

Sentence Fragments

66.4. A word or sequence of words that is not part of a sentence and not a predication is a sentence fragment. Common sentence fragments are titles (5.4*b*, 5.39*a*, 5.40*ad*, 5.45*c*, 5.52*ab*, 5.53*e*, 5.55*c*, 5.56*abc*, 5.57*a*, 5.84), labels on drawings, words cited by themselves, and interjections and other free-standing particles. Answers to content questions may be taken as sentence fragments or as gapped sentences. Certain particles used with an imperative force may be considered sentence fragments when there is no obvious gapped verb that can be supplied from the context.

(5.105) Interjections
   (a)   *ehe·he., ehę·he.* 'Yes (that's right).'
   (b)   *hao·ʔ.* 'O.K. (I'll do so)'; 'Yes (I will).'; 'Hello!' (or *hawo·ʔ*, transcribing ⟨a wo⟩;
          normalized as /hawo/ in the edition of *Masahkamikohkwêwa* and elsewhere)
   (c)   *o·ho·ʹ., ǫ·hǫ·ʹ.* 'So <u>that's</u> it.'; 'I see.'
   (d)   *či·hče·ʹ* 'Will you look at that!'; 'How cute!'; 'How odd!'
   (e)   *kašina·kwa.* 'Well?'; 'What gives?'

(5.106) Particles and particle phrases
    (a)   *a·kwi.* 'No.' (Cf. 5.102*a*.)
    (b)   *mahkwa·či.* "Be quiet." (K-FC 429; tr. HP)
    (c)   *a·peči·´, pena·´, kekeni.* "Come on now, quickly." (K-Wap 183; tr. TB)
    (d)   *sese·si.* 'Hurry!' (K-RYL 2)
(5.107) Cited names and labels
    (a)   *mešihke·ha.* 'Turtle.' (Answer to: 'What is your name?') (K-T 3)
    (b)   *ana·kwa.* 'Star.' (Caption next to a drawing of a star.) (K-SGG 218)
    (c)   *aškote·wi.* 'Fire.' (Label on the diagram of a ceremony.) (K-TG 63)
    (d)   *metemo·ha e·h=či·tapiči.* (Label next to "W" [i.e., West] on a diagram.) (K-FM 23)
            'Where the old woman sits.'

SENTENCE PARTICLES

67. A sentence particle is a free particle which is not part of a module (**§61**) but rather has a syntactic and semantic link to the sentence as a whole. Particles that modify the verbal notion or are oblique complements of verbs are considered to be sentence particles unless they fall into the specific categories of adverbial particles that are part of verb phrases (**§63.1-6**). In general, sentence particles have the same freedom of word order as adverbial particles (5.68*ab*), though some patterns and preferences can be identified. In the following sections an attempt has been made to give a full range of examples of different kinds of particles.

Sentence Conjunctions

67.1. A sentence conjunction occurs sentence-initially and links a sentence to what immediately precedes it. Some are occasionally repeated after the first clause of the sentence (5.108*a*(3)), and as a rare stylistic variant some may occur only after the first word or phrase (5.108*a*(4)). The words that have been identified as used as sentence conjunctions are in (5.108). Of these *na·hka* (variant *na·hkači*) 'also, and also, and' is also used as a free particle with essentially the same meaning (5.119*r*); this is its use in (5.108*c*).

(5.108) Sentence conjunctions
    (a)   *o·ni* 'and, and then'
      1)   *o·ni pe·hki e·h=we·pwe·we·hoči.* 'And then it began to be beaten in earnest.' (O 20J)
                (*o·ni* 'and then'; *pe·hki* 'really';
                |we·pwe·we·hw-| TA 'begin beating audibly', |e·h=—eči| X–3/AOR)
      2)   *o·ni pepikwe·škwi, . . .* 'And as for the whistle, . . .' (O 80C)
                (*o·ni* 'and then'; *pepikwe·škwi* 'whistle')
      3)   *o·ni aškwisa·ke, o·ni sa·kiči wi·h=iši-wi·hkowe·ye·kwe.* (K-BHD 106)
             'And then, if there is any left, you may go outside and invite (others) to eat.'
             (*o·ni* 'and then' (2x); |aškwisa·-| II 'be left over', |–ke| 0/SUBJ;
             sa·kiči 'outside'; |wi·h=| FUT, |iši| PV 'to {somewhere}',
             |wi·hkowe·-| AI 'invite people to eat', |e·h=—ye·kwe| 2p/AOR)

4)   *i·tepi e·h=a·či o·ni='pi e·ši-kehkahamawoči.* (K-MFWB 59)

       'And then, they say, he went where he had been told to go.'

       (*i·tepi* 'thither'; |iha·-| AI 'go {somewhere}', |e·h=—či| 3s/AOR;

       o·ni 'and then'; |=ipi| HRSY;

       |iši| PV '{so}', |kehkahamaw-| TA+O 'designate O2 for', |IC—eči| X-3/PPL(obl))

(b) *na·hka, na·hkači* 'also, and also, and'

   1)   .., *na·hka a·kwi anwe·we·htamekini pepikwe·škwi.* (O 25B)

       '.., and the whistle was not blown.'

       (*na·hka* 'and'; *a·kwi* 'not';

       |anwe·we·ht-| TI(1) 'blow audibly', |—amekini| X-0/NEG; *pepikwe·škwi* 'whistle')

   2)   *na·hkači ni·h=nawahpwa·ha·wa.* (O 156I)

       'And I'm also going to give him food for his journey.'

       (*na·hkači* 'and also';

       |wi·h=| FUT, |nawahpwa·h-| TA 'send food with', |ne–a·wa| 1s-3s/IND)

(c) *kaho·ni* 'and then, so then'

       kaho·ni na·hka e·h=a·čimohiki. 'So then I was again given instructions.' (A 98C)

       (*kaho·ni* 'and then'; *na·hka* 'again'; |a·čimoh-| TA 'inform', |e·h=—iki| 3s-1s/AOR)

(d) *o* 'or' (never followed by a phonological word boundary or an enclitic)

   1)   .., *o=meše=ke·hi ahpene·wenehka·sa.* '.., or maybe he would get a disease.' (O 56F)

       (*o* 'or'; *meše* 'freely'; *=ke·hi* 'moreover';

       |ahpene·wenehka·-| AI 'get a disease', |—sa| 3s/POT)

   2)   *o=kapo·twe we·pi-mya·ši-to·tawake,* ... (A 137A)

       'And if, on the other hand, I began at some point to treat her badly, ...'

       (*o* 'or'; *kapo·twe* 'at some point';

       we·pi PV 'begin', *mya·ši* 'badly', |to·taw-| TA 'treat {so}', |—ake| 1s-3/SUBJ)

   3)   *o=wa·waneška·hiyane=ke·h,* ... 'But if you turn <u>bad</u>, ...' (A 28A)

       (*o* 'or'; |wa·waneška·hi-| AI 'be bad', |—yane| 2s/SUBJ; *=ke·hi* 'moreover')

(e) *šewe·na* (*šewe·=*), *išewe·na* (*išewe·=*), *ašewe·na* (*ašewe·=*) 'but, still'

   1)   *šewe·na ki·h=koši-mekoho.* 'But you must keep well away from me.' (O 157D)

       (*šewe·na* 'but'; |wi·h=| FUT, |koS-| TA 'fear', |ke–i| 2s-1s/IND; *=mekoho* EMPH)

   2)   *šewe·=pe·hki nemya·še·wi.* 'But I did a really poor job of it.' (A 3A)

       (*šewe·na* 'but'; *pe·hki* 'really'; |mya·še·wi| AI 'do the task badly', |ne–∅| 1s/IND)

(f) *koči·hi* 'although (granted), even though'

   1)   *wi·h=pwawi-a·noha·no·tame·kwe, koči·h kekimesi=meko ki·h=owi·wašipwa.*

       (K-B 210)

       'So that you won't be overloaded, though all of you will have loads on your

      backs.'

       (|wi·h=| FUT, *pwawi* , |CVCV+| RED2, |a·no·t-| TI(1)-O 'fail to carry on back',

       |e·h=—ame·kwe| 2p(-0)/AOR; |koči·hi| 'although'; *kekimesi* 'everyone';

       =meko EMPH; |wi·h=| FUT, |owi·waši-| AI 'have load on back', |ke–pwa| 2p/IND)

   2)   .., *koči·h osekwisani menwi-to·ta·kwa* (A 46B)

       '.., even though, of course, her aunt treated her well'

       (|koči·hi| 'although'; *osekwisani* 'her father's sister';

       |menwi| PV 'well', |to·taw-| 'treat {so}', |—ekwa| 3´-3s/IND)

A sentence beginning with *koči·hi* 'although' (5.108*f*) is often followed by one beginning with *šewe·na* 'but', or a variant of this (5.108*e*); these particles then link the two sentences together with the meaning 'Even though .., still ...' (A 142CD; O 80FG, 84H-85A, 85HI).

Clausal Particles

67.2. A clausal particle qualifies the statement made by a clause. In some cases a particle may ostensibly qualify only the verb, but because scope is variable for some particles and can be difficult to determine objectively, no distinction is made between clausal particles in a strict sense and verb-modifying particles that do not form verb phrases (**§63**). Clausal particles may occur before or after the verb, with the position after the verb generally implying a greater degree of emphasis or narrative salience. Functionally, a clausal particle may specify time (when or how long), location, manner, degree, or logical status. Particles of location, manner, and degree may be the complements of relative roots (**§22.4**). Some particles of logical status may have the semantic force of a higher verb.

A temporal particle may indicate a specific time or a time relative to another event (or to the speech event), or it may specify frequency or duration. Some exocentric compounds function as temporal particles (5.17*c*(1)).

(5.109) Particles indicating specific time

(a) *ana·kowe* 'yesterday' (K-MIM 30, C-RP 1, S-Pit 8)

(b) *aškačitepehki* 'late at night' (A 64E)

(c) *kekišeye·pa* 'in the morning' (Jones 1907:108.5, 146.11, 212.3)

(d) *ma·maya* 'early in the morning' (O 13E) (cf. 5.110*r*)

(e) *no·te·tepehkwe* 'before the night was out' (A 150E)

(f) *še·pa·ye* 'early this morning (earlier today)' (K-FR 10, C-UAN 14, S-RSW 10)

(g) *tepehki* 'at night' (A 107E, 158B; O 98B)

(5.110) Particles indicating relative time

(a) *ača·hmeko* 'only then, for the first time' (A 18D, 36G, 43F, 191B; O 56A, 118E)

(b) *ahkowi* 'afterwards, later, second' (A 172E, 182D; O 111F) (cf. 5.114*b*)
    ahkowi·me·hi 'a little later' (K-FC 497)

(c) *ašawaye* (*ašawe=*) 'long ago' (K-B 47; S-OWA 1; SP-FSSW 48; JP-MTC 1; JB-SB 1):
    ašawaye=meko (K-CDWP 6), *ašawe=meko* (K-B 152; SP-FW 78; X10-PBW)
    ašawaye='pihi (SP-MCEA 46), *ašawe='pi* (K-CM 1)
    našawaye (*našawe=*) 'long ago' (O 69G; C-SD 14; SP-MRD 1; JP-MTC 2)
    našawaye=meko (K-Wap 1), *našawe=meko* (K-ILM 32; SP-MRD 28; LL-LH 14)
    našawaye='pi (K-ICH 1), *našawe='pi* (K-CM 1)
    anašawaye (K-M 171g, 474b, K-MOR 13, etc.)

(d) *ašitahi* (with negative) '(not) for a long time' (A 50A)

(e) *aškači* 'much later' (A 177E; O 67I)
    aškači·meki·hi 'after a little while (dim.)' (A 37F; K-Kin 60)
    aškači·me·hi 'a little later (dim.)' (A 125D; O 66G)

(f) *aškiča·hi* 'at first' (A 22E; O 68E)

(g)   *če·wina·hi* 'at the same time' (O 61B)

(h)   *i·noki* 'now, today, this time' (A 17C, 47D; O 63H, 126C, 143E)

(i)   *i·nina·hi* 'at that time, by now' (A 18G, 23B, 31D, 120F, 188E; O 2G, 70B)

(j)   *i·ye·me·hi* 'a while back, not so long ago' (A 79D)

(k)   *kapo·twe* 'at some point' (A 11A, 16A, 16E; O 60D, 60H, 62E)

(l)   *kawi·ša·ni* 'before'; "beforehand" (K-FASB 7; tr. HP)

(m)   *ka·hkami* 'from the start' (A 116F, 171B)

(n)   *kehčine·he* "for a short time"; "a little while" (K-FC 252, 497; tr. HP) (cf. 5.114*i*)

(o)   *keye·či·hi* 'recently, a short time ago' (K-M 904d);
       'soon, soon after, in a short while' (O 92C)
      keye·či·he 'recently' (K-SGG 45, K-M 940h); 'soon' (K-M 575i)
      kaye·či·hi 'recently' (K-M 131e), *kaye·či·h=* (K-M 956h)

(p)   *ke·keya·hi* 'finally, eventually, in time' (A 3D, 20E, 31A; O 150A, 154H; C, S, SP, JP)
      ke·kaya·hi (S, X6)

(q)   *ke·waki* 'still' (A 14C, 183D)

(r)   *ma·maya* 'early, earlier than otherwise' (A 169H, 173F) (cf. 5.109*d*)

(s)   *menehta* 'first' (A 154E, 172D; O 3H, 4A, 5I, 20B; SP-MRD 3)
      menehtami (K-WSB 81; C-FS 7; S-RSW 8; JB-M 16; X10-PBW 66)
      mehtami (K-RYL 7; C-SD 14; S-RP 4; SP-HL 40; JP-MWM 34)

(t)   *ni·ka·ni* 'in the future' (O 94C); 'ahead of time'

(u)   *no·ta* 'too soon' (O 2G, 7FG, 35G, 38B, 45F)

(v)   *pa·no·hi* 'not until (then)' (A 106B)

(w)   *pa·pekwa* 'right away' (A 8F, 71F, 162D, 183B)

(x)   *pa·ši* 'continuing, continuing until':

   1) *pa·ši=ča·h=mekoho ayo·nina·hi ki·h=ahkwi-a·ya·tota.* (K-M 895i)
      'You must tell about it (= your life) right up to the present time.'
      (|=ča·hi| 'so'; =*mekoho* EMPH; *ayo·nina·hi* 'now'; |wi·h=| FUT,
      |ahkwi| PV '{so} far', |CV+| RED1, |a·tot-| TI(1) 'tell about', |ke–a| 2s–0/IND)

   2) *pa·ši='pi=mekoho nehkanitepehkwe* 'continuing all night long' (K-FC 745)
      (|=ipi| HRSY; =*mekoho* EMPH; *nehkanitepehkwe* 'all night long')

   3) *pa·ši=mekoho e·h=kwi·yese·he·hiyani očipye·či* (K-M 1075o; tr. HP)
      "right from the time when you were a little boy"
      (=*mekoho* EMPH; |kwi·yese·he·hi-| AI 'be a boy (dim.)', |e·h=–yani| 2s/AOR;
      očipye·či 'since {some time}')

   4) *pa·ši=mekoho e·h=kehkye·weniwiki* 'until a very old age' (K-FC 328)
      (=*mekoho* EMPH; |kehkye·weniwi-| II 'be old age', |e·h=–ki| 0/AOR)

(y)   *peteki* 'back' (A 1D, 27E, 78A, 138B, 182B; O 59C) (cf. 5.114*n*)
      peteki·me·hi 'a short while back' (K-FC 192)

(5.111) Particles indicating frequency

(a)   *ahpene·či* 'every time' (A 4F, 19C; O 4D)

(b)   *a·yahpi·hčina·hi* 'every once in a while' (A 65G, 115G; O 52F, 153A)

(c)   *a·yaškači* 'at long intervals, not too often' (A 9E, 148C, 151A)

(d)   *čačawi·hi* 'sometimes' (A 97C, 151F; O 9C, 14D)

(e)   *me·menwina·hi* 'every now and then' (O 157A)

(f)   *na·hka, na·hkači* 'again' (5.108*c*, 5.117*n*)

(g)   *sekihkatami* 'constantly, all the time' (K-MP2 28)

    aˑkwi sekihkatami "seldom" (K-Spot 294; tr. HP) (*aˑkwi* 'not')

(5.112) Particles indicating duration

(a)   *kenweˑši* 'for a long time' (A 50E, 61C, 89H; O 36F, 45A, 59B)

    kenweˑši meˑhi 'for quite a long time (dim.)' (A 94B, 182D; O 141B, 147F)

(b)   *menwinehki* 'for some time' (K-BHD 30)

(c)   *nehkanikiˑšekwe* (O 7E), *nahkanikiˑšekwe* (C-IW 20) 'all day long'

(d)   *nehkanipepoˑnwe* (O 58G), *nahkanipepoˑnwe* (C-SD 17) 'all winter long'

(e)   *nehkanitepehkwe* (O 35C), *nahkanitepehkwe* (C-FS 1) 'all night long' (cf. 5.19*d*)

(f)   *noˑmake* 'in, for a short time' (A 109B, 150G; O 7A)

    noˑmakeˑwe (O 37A) 'for a short time'

Locative particles may indicate a specific or relative location. Those designating a relative location with a scalar value usually also have a diminutive form (**§57**). The locative forms of nouns and pronouns (**§§24, 28.15, 31.2**; cf. **§38.6**) and exocentric locative compounds (exx. in 4.113, 5.17) also function as particles of location. Particles may also form various kinds of particle phrases having a locative function (5.71, 5.72*b*, 5.72*c*(1), 5.72*c*(7), 5.72*g*(1), 5.73*cfgh*).

(5.113) Particles indicating specific location

(a)   *čiˑkaˑhkwe* 'next to a tree' (O 13B)

(b)   *čiˑkepyeˑki* 'at the edge of the water' (O 56D)

(c)   *mehči* 'to, on the ground' (K-FC 494, 584, K-ORF 3, K-Apay 39) (cf. 5.115*q*, 118*e*)

(d)   *nanakoteˑki* 'in the middle of the lodge' (O 106F, 120E)

(e)   *nanawi* 'in some lonely place, out in the wilderness' (K-TCSB 42, 57) (cf. 5.115*w*)

(f)   See 4.113*acdfhijk*.

(5.114) Particles indicating relative location

(a)   *ahkiki* 'down, down below' (A 56E, 102B)

    ahkiki meˑhi 'just below' (K-M 87h, 665e)

(b)   *ahkowi* 'behind' (O 15D, 104H) (cf. 5.110*b*)

    ahkowi meˑhi 'a little bit behind' (K-FC 242, 497)

(c)   *ahkwiči* 'on top' (A 172B)

(d)   *ahpemeki* 'up, up above, in the sky' (A 102A, 109F; O 80G, 150K)

    ahpemeˑheki 'a little bit above' (K-FC 393)

(e)   *ašiči* 'near, nearby' (A 5C; O 67C, 104I, 160D)

(f)   *atehči* 'away someplace, off someplace' (A 151F, 166F)

    atehči meˑhi 'a little ways off (dim.)' (O 13B, 39F, 71H, 151G)

(g)   *aˑsami* 'upstream; up the line (of the railroad); west' (K-MLF 3, K-BKTE 1)

    aˑsami meˑhi 'further upstream' (K-FC 288)

(h)   *kaškiški* 'in the path, so as to head (someone) off' (K-Wap 39; SP-BKWM 86)

    kaškiški meˑhi 'almost in the path (dim.)' (K-GF 16, K-WB 10)

(i)   *kehčine* 'nearby' (A 20E)

    kehčineˑhe "close by" (K-FC 49, 147; tr. HP); "nearer" (K-FC 444; tr. HP)

(j)   *kiˑhka* 'round about' (O 94E)

(k)   *mehči* 'down, on the ground' (K-FC 494, 584)

(l)   *mehčiˑki* 'down, downward, down below, on the ground' (K-FC 20, K-M 84i, K-WTS 7)

(m)   *penoˑči* 'far, far away' (A 173G; O 56E, 65F, 80F)

    penoˑči meˑhi 'pretty far away (dim.)' (A 167A)

(n)   *peteki* 'back' (A 173E) (cf. 5.110*y*)
    peteki me·hi 'further back' (K-M 911f)

(o)   *pi·tike* 'inside' (A 58A; O 2D. 12A, 29B, 36B, 136A)

(p)   *sa·kiči* 'outside, outdoors' (A 32A, 57F; O 71B)
    sa·kiči me·hi 'a little ways outside (dim.)' (A 41G)

(q)   *tepina·hi* 'directly above or opposite' (A 110D, 112G)

(r)   *waninawe* 'on all sides' (A 137G)

(s)   *wa·wi·tawi* 'on both sides, ends' (K-FC 168; S-YMSG 27; SP-MBS 88)
    wi·tawi 'on both sides, ends' (K-MIM 28; C-RS 5; SP-KFC 23)

Particles broadly classified as indicating manner include a wide range of types.

(5.115) Particles indicating manner

(a)   *aše* 'just' (O 81G, 91A, 114C, 121E, 130B, 145B, 156A);
    iše 'just' (A 6D, 13D, 38D, 38E, 39C, 47F, 68F, 78A, 85C, 104E, 121A, 129D,
    131G, 145D, 146F, 189B, 193E)

(b)   *ahkwa·wi* 'full, to the full amount' (A 93E)

(c)   *ayi·ne·hka* 'persistingly' (O 8G)

(d)   *a·ya·kwači* 'in piles' (A 41E)

(e)   *a·ya·šo·hka* 'alternately, taking turns' (O 1F)

(f)   *išiwe·pi* 'signifying {so}' (A 178E; 5.73*d*)

(g)   *kakišaši·pye* 'reluctantly, with reservations, barely having the courage or restraint';
    kekišaši·pye (JB-SB 16, X6-OS 16)
  1)   "against their feelings" (K-FC 429; tr. HP); "half willingly" (K-FC 474; tr. HP)
  2)   *aše=mekoho kakišaši·pye a·kwi nesa·čini.* (K-FC 513; tr. HP)
    "It is about all he can do not to kill them"
    (*aše* 'just'; =*mekoho* EMPH; *a·kwi* 'not'; |neS-| TA 'kill', |–a·čini| 3s–3´/NEG)

(h)   *kehčine·we* 'in person, personally' (O 88H, 121F);
    kehčine·wi (S-TO 22; cf. 5.51*f*)

(i)   *kehpetawi* 'as the complete set, amount, or number':
  1)   *nye·wawahi·me=meko kehpetawi* 'for four full years' (K-WSB 22)
  2)   *a·kwi me·mešahkwahkini mana mi·ha kehpetawi=meko.* (C-Hist 30)
    'The weather was never clear this whole month of May.'
    (*a·kwi* 'not'; |CV+| RED1, |mešahkwat-| II 'be a clear day', |–kini| 0/NEG;
    mana 'this (anim.)', *mi·ha* 'May (adjunct)'; =*meko* EMPH)

(j)   *kekeni* 'quickly' (A 72F)

(k)   *kekine·se* 'alive, while still alive' (O 50D)

(l)   *kena·či* 'slowly, gradually, lightly, easily, softly' (O 89H, 150K; cf. 5.67*b*)
  1)   *kena·či=mekoho ki·h=anwe·we·hta·pwa* 'you (pl.) must blow it softly' (O 82A)
    (|wi·h=| FUT, |anwe·we·ht-| TI(1) 'blow audibly', |ke–a·pwa| 2p–0/IND)

(m)   *ki·mo·či* 'secretly'; 'on the sly' (K-TCSB 47):
  1)   *ki·mo·či=ke·h=meko i·ni e·h=išite·he·či.* (TCSB 18; tr. TB)
    "She indeed thought about them to herself alone and in a quiet way"
    (|=ke·hi| 'moreover'; =*meko* EMPH; *i·ni* 'that (inan.)';
    |išite·he·-| 'think {so}', |e·h=–či| 3s/AOR)

(n)   *ki·na·kwi* 'confidently, have the confidence to, comfortably' (A 24D, 128F;
    O 87A)

(o) *kwi·yena* 'exactly' (O 106D)

(p) *mahkwa·či* 'quietly, calmly' (A 28G, 51D, 70C, 84A, 132F; O 9B, 77A, 78A, 98B)

(q) *mehči* "by hand," like *mehta·hkwi* (K-FASB 58; tr. HP) (cf. 5.113*c*, 118*e*)

(r) *mehta·hkwi* 'without the usual instrumentality, without anything else, unwrapped, a capella, barehanded, empty-handed' (O 29D, 101F; K-FC 211, 251, 791)

(s) *memye·ški* 'messily, carelessly, haphazardly':

1) *memye·ški=mekoho nekepa·hkoha pena ni·ke·hena·ni.* (K-BHD 125; tr. TB)
   "Indeed we did not close up our house very good."
   (=*mekoho* EMPH; |kepa·hkoh-| TI(1) 'close up', |ne–a·pena| 1p–0/IND;
   ni·ke·hena·ni 'our house (dim.)')

(t) *me·me·kwe·šawe* 'speaking out of turn, butting in' (K-Wap 49; S-Apay 4);
   me·me·kwe·šawi (K-Wap 100, K-Fish 61)

(u) *nahe·ka* 'slowly' (O 19D, 19H; JB-RB 10; X6-MM 17);
   nahe·kaše 'slowly, quietly, gently' (K-W 140)

(v) *nano·nemi* 'without saying a word, silently, on the quiet':

1) *nano·nemi=meko wi·h=taši-mami·ši·hiniči* (K-MP3 26)
   'that they (obv.) be serving as ceremonial attendants in silence'
   (=*meko*, =*mekoho* EMPH; |wi·h=| FUT, *taši* PV 'be engaged in',
   |mami·ši·hi-| AI 'be ceremonial attendant', |e·h=–niči| 3′/AOR)

2) *nano·nemi=mekoho e·h=taši-ašihašihto·či.* (K-FC 92)
   'He had been making them without saying anything about it.'
   ([see v(1)]; CVCV+| RED2, |ašiht-| TI(2) 'make', |e·h=–o·či| 3s–0/AOR)

(w) *nanawi* 'worthlessly, uselessly, badly, in vain' (cf. 5.113*e*)

1) *a·kwi nanawi išawiya·nini.* (K-FC 570N; tr. HP) "I was not a bad character."
   (*a·kwi* 'not'; |išawi-| AI 'be, fare, do {so}', |–ya·nini| 1s/NEG)

2) *a·kwi owiye·ha nanawi ine·nemehkini.* (K-B 81; tr. HP)
   "no one thinks of you out of the way"
   (*a·kwi* 'not'; *owiye·ha* 'anyone';
   |ine·nem-| TA 'think {so} about', |–ehkini| 3–2s/NEG)

3) *nanawi=mekoho ketene·neta‿ki·yawi.* (K-M 587b; tr. HP)
   "You have wasted your thoughts about it [= your life]."
   (=*mekoho* EMPH; |ine·net-| TI(1) 'think {so} about', |ket–a| 2s–0/IND;
   ki·yawi 'yourself, your life')

(x) *nano·škwe* 'blindly, not knowing if it would be correct or effective' (K-FC 337, 760)

(y) *na·mo·či* 'in one's mind, (thinking) to oneself'

1) *pašito·ha e·h=a·hkwe·wite·he·či na·mo·či* (K-FC 8; tr. HP)
   "the old man felt rather angry down in his heart"
   (*pašito·ha* 'old man'; |a·hkwe·wite·he·-| AI 'feel angry', |e·h=–či| 3s/AOR)

(z) *na·na·kači* '(tracking, repeating) exactly' (O 64D, 64F, 65B; also 4.100g)

(aa) *pi·neši* 'of one's own accord, unprovoked' (A 133A)

(bb) *pi·no·ši* 'innovating, doing or being something new and different':

1) *pi·no·ši=meko e·h=we·weneteniki.* 'it was unique and beautiful' (K-M 395c; HP
   "a fancy new kind") (|we·wenet-| II 'be good, pretty', |e·h=–niki| 0′/AOR)

2) *pi·no·ši=meko e·h=išihišihto·či.* (K-Bene 68)
   'She was always making something new and different.'
   (|CVCV+| RED2, |išiht-| 'make {so}', |e·h=–o·či| 3s–0/AOR)

(cc) *sese·si* 'hurriedly' (A 111E)

(dd) *šešeka·či* 'jokingly, toyingly, frivolously, casually' (K-Spot 193);
    šešeka·hi (5.122e(7); K-Wapan 80)

(ee) *še·še·hkami* 'freely, readily, unrestrained, without good reason' (K-FC 165, 362, 483)

(ff) *tepiki·ški* 'abruptly' (O 8I)

(gg) *wanimo·škwe* 'at will, of one's own free will, simply as one wishes' (with negative):
  1)   *a·kwi wanimo·škwe wi·h=anemi-ina·čimočini.* (K-FC 391)
      'He will not be telling what he himself thinks.' (But what I think.)
      (*a·kwi* 'not'; |wi·h=| FUT, *anemi* PV 'go on',
      |ina·čimo-| AI 'tell, report {so}', |–čini 3s/NEG)
  2)   *a·kwi wanimo·škwe i·ni wi·h=išawiya·nini.* 'I'm not free to do that now.'
      (K-M 645h; translated as: 'I can do that only if things are right')
      (*a·kwi* 'not'; *i·ni* 'that (inan.)'; |wi·h=| FUT; |išawi-| AI 'do {so}', |–ya·nini| 1s/NEG)

(hh) *waye·či* 'effortlessly, without lifting a finger' (K-W 274; SP-MTS 8)

(ii) *wa·natohka* 'as if nothing were amiss or unusual; untroubled, coolly' (O 151H)

Some particles that indicate kind or degree as oblique complements or in other constructions are otherwise considered sentence particles rather than components of verb phrases (**§63.6**). Most of these are not matched by initials, but some are also used as preverbs.

(5.116) Particles indicating kind or degree

(a) *anehki·hi* 'a little bit' (A 30F; O 46H, 49F);
    a·ya·nehki·hi 'a little each, a little at a time' (O 55F)

(b) *anikaši* 'besides that, beyond that':
  1)   *i·ni=wi·na anikaši* 'but besides that, but otherwise' (K-WSB 82, K-FC 197)
      (*i·ni* 'that (inan.)'; =*wi·na* 'but')

(c) *asa·mi* 'too much' (cf. 5.72a; also PV):
  1)   *asa·mi=meko še·ški a·hpetose·wa.* (A 75F)
      'Too much of the time all he does is just constantly walk around.'
      (=*meko* EMPH; *še·ški* 'only', |a·hpetose·-| AI 'walk constantly', |–wa| 3s/IND)

(d) *atena·wi* 'less' (O 58B)

(e) *ateškawi* 'one thing after another, all sorts of things (e.g., as lies or excuses)':
  1)   *ateškawi=mek=a·pehe išikenwi* 'it would happen in all different ways' (K-M 323)
      (|=meko| EMPH; |=a·pehe| 'usually'; |išiken-| II 'be {so}', |–wi| 0s/IND)
  2)   *ateškawi=meko e·h=inowe·niči* (K-W 727; tr. HP)
      "They [obv.] made all sorts of excuses."
      (=*meko* EMPH; |inowe·-| AI 'tell X {so}', |e·h=–niči| 3'/AOR)
  3)   *me·mešihka=meko ateškawi=meko ki·h=inowe* (K-M 113; tr. HP)
      "you are sure to deny the facts"
      (*me·mešihka* 'perhaps'; =*meko* EMPH;
      |wi·h=| FUT, |inowe·-| AI 'tell X {so}', |ke–∅| IND)

(f) *a·hpene* 'all the same' (A 55A; O 82D, 82F, 83A, 83C, 97D, 115E, 118C)

(g) *a·wasi* 'more' (A 59A, 81C, 82C, 124AB, 127D, 187F);
    a·wasi·me·hi 'more, a little more' (A 22B, 64B, 125D; O 58B, 127A)

(h) *aye·niwe* 'staying the same, in the same place' (O 16A, 140E; C, S, SP, JB, LL);
    e·ye·niwe (A 51F, 162A; K, C, JP, X6, X8, X10)

(i) *a·čipanaki·či* 'all different kinds' (A 47C, 50C; O 117A, 145G, 146C)

(j)   *e·škami* 'increasingly'; 'more and more' (A 109H, 157A) (also PV):

  1)   *e·škami=mekoho e·h=inehponiki.* 'it snowed more and more.' (K-FC 314)

        (=*mekoho* EMPH; |inehpo-| II 'snow {so}', |e·h=–niki| 0´/AOR)

  2)   *e·h=makekineniči=mekoho e·škami.* "It grew larger and larger" (K-FC 515; tr. HP)

        (|makekiN-| AI 'be big', |e·h=–niči| 3´/AOR; =*mekoho* EMPH)

  3)   *e·škami=mekoho e·h=aniwa·ška·niči.* 'He (obv.) went faster and faster.'
       (K-FC 630; "It gradually speed faster." [tr. HP])

        (=*mekoho* EMPH; |aniwa·ška·-| AI 'go fast', |e·h=–niči| 3´/AOR)

(k)   *ke·sipi* 'only (that, those)' (also PV):

  1)   *ki·na·na=meko ke·sipi* 'only you and I' (A 88B)

        (*ki·na·na* 12/EMPH; =*meko* EMPH)

  2)   *ke·sipi=meko e·h=owi·ke·hiya·ni tawa·hiwi* (A 41F)
       'there was only just enough room for my little house'

        (=*meko* EMPH; |owi·ke·hi-| AI 'dwell {somewhere} (dim.)',
        |e·h=–ya·ni| 1s/PPL(loc.obl); |tawa·hi-| II 'be space (dim.)', |–wi| 0s/IND)

(l)   *nešihka* 'alone' (A 43B, 96A, 138D; O 44D, 74D, 150C):

  1)   *a·kwi=ni·na·na nešihka omi·ša·miya·kini.* (O 126D)
       'It's not the sacred pack of us alone.'

        (*a·kwi* 'not'; *ni·na·na* 1p/EMPH;
        |omi·ša·mi-| AI+O 'have O2 as sacred pack',|–ya·kini| 1p/NEG)

(m)   *ne·htawi* 'separately, all of one kind together' (O 115I) (also PV);
     ne·ne·htawi 'apart from each other' (O 32C)

(n)   *ne·ya·pi* 'same as before' (O 55D, 116D) (also PV)

(o)   *taka·wi* 'a little bit' (A 108F; O 42E, 47I, 48G, 51IJ)

Many particles qualify a clause in a relatively abstract way, though the distinction between these and the more concrete manner particles is not sharp. The uses of some of these are often highly idiomatic, as can be seen from the examples referred to.

(5.117) Abstract qualifying particles

  (a)   *a·hpene·we* 'nothing but, without exception' (O 91D, 137A)

  (b)   *a·šita* 'in turn, in return' (O 73G);
       a·šitami (A 63AC)

  (c)   *ka·pa·čiči* 'barely managing, barely succeeding' (Jones 1907:56.8, 134.18)

  (d)   *ke·kya·ta* 'nearly' (O 151E)

  (e)   *masa·či* 'barely' (O 65F)

  (f)   *ma·mahka·či* 'necessarily, without fail' (A 133C; O 11F, 14F, 15H, 36D, 38AC, 97F,
       129AH); (as a negative, presumably with expressive-negative intonation;
       5.122*d*, NOTE; see 1.52) 'it is not necessary', 'why did it have to be?'
       (K-M 320g, JP-GTF 8)

  (g)   *meči* 'quite' (5.16*g*):

  1)   *meči=ke·h=mekoho e·h=wa·wanetone moniči.* (K-SSP 15; tr. HP)
       "He [obv.] .. could hardly talk"

        (*meči* 'quite'; |=ke·hi| 'moreover'; =*mekoho* EMPH;
        |wa·wanetone·mo-| AI 'be unable to talk', |e·h=–niči| 3´/AOR)

  2)   *meči=meko nemi·ša·te·nemo.* "I was somewhat glad" (K-Auto 65; tr. IP)
        (*meči* 'quite'; =*meko* EMPH; |mi·ša·te·nemo-| AI 'be happy', |ne–∅| 1s/IND)

3)   *meči=mekoho keta·nwe·hto·ne.* "I rather doubt your words" (K-M 906b; tr. HP)
       (*meči* 'quite'; =*mekoho* EMPH; |a·nwe·htaw-| TA 'disbelieve', |ke–ene| 1s–2s/IND)

4)   *meči=koh=mek=a·peh=ni·na newa wanawi=pe·hki.* (C-FS 20; tr. EK)
      "I never was much good at this."
       (*meči* 'quite'; |=kohi| 'certainly'; |=meko| EMPH; |=a·pehe| 'usually';
       ni·na 1s/EMPH; |wa·wanawi-| AI 'not know how', |ne–ø| 1s/IND; *pe·hki* 'really')

meči + |=ihi| NEG (5.122*d*):

5)   *meči=·'h(i)* + !? EN: 'it's hardly the case that' (A 131F, 183F, 192D; O 103E,
      142CF).

6)   *ni·na=·'h=we·=ke·h=mani*[/?] *meči neteneniwi!?* (K-M 424b; tr. HP)
      "I myself am not a man"
       (*ni·na* 1s/EMPH; |=ihi| NEG; |=we·na| 'in fact'; |=ke·hi| 'moreover';
       |=mani| 'as it is now'; *meči* 'quite'; |ineniwi-| AI 'be a man', |ne–ø| 1s/IND; !? EN)

7)   *meči=·'=ča·hi·=·'nahi neniwiwa!?* "she is not a man" (K-M 681c; tr. HP)
       (*meči* 'quite'; |=ihi| NEG [**§4.4**; **§6.3**, 1.55]; |=ča·hi| 'so'; |i·nahi| 'with that';
       |neniwi-| AI 'be a man', |–wa| 3s/IND; !? EN)

(h) *meso·te·we* 'universally' (O 54C, 55F, 80D, 84B, 88E, 107A, 129D, 159B)
     meso·te·wi 'universally' (A 54D, 135J; O 82D)

(i) *meše* 'freely; maybe, perhaps' (A 148A; O 11E, 15A, 32G, 56F, 59B, 66A, 76E,
     126H, 129F):
     meše=meko 'as you wish, as he wishes' (A 39E, 151B; O 148D);
     meše·=·'nahi 'as may be, at will, maybe, may, might, being allowed to' (A 64D,
     113F, 118A, 142A, 151F, 172E, 180G, 187B, 194E; O 7K, 39B, 47A, 49B,
     50D, 57BC, 59E, 87B, 120G, 125H, 136F, 148F, 159F)

(j) *me·mečine·hi* 'for the last time, as the last one' (A 178E; O 158C)

(k) *me·mye·hči* 'unavoidably' (O 48H); *me·mye·hči!?* 'it's not necessary' (K-M 223.1)

(l) *naye·nenwi* 'of or affecting oneself or one's own group'

  1) *a·kwi ni·na·na=mekoho naye·nenwi ki·šihta·tisoya·kini.* (K-FC 180; tr. HP)
      "we never made this for ourselves"
       (*a·kwi* 'not'; *ni·na·na* 1p/EMPH; =*mekoho* EMPH;
       |ki·šihta·tiso-| AI 'make O2 for oneself', |–ya·kini| 1p/NEG)

  2) *naye·nenwi=·'yo=ke·h=mekoho e·h=pi·tahwa·niči.* (K-FC 430; tr. HP)
      "as they were burying them [=their children] themselves"
       (|=iyo| + |=ke·hi| [5.123*e*]; =*mekoho* EMPH;
       |pi·tahw-| TA 'bury', |e·h–a·niči| 3´–3´´/AOR)

(m) *pe·hki* 'really, in earnest, fully, completely, successfully' (A 3A, 13AB, 58F, 81E,
     89A, 188DG; O 20J, 40C, 50D)

(n) *pe·pye·hči* 'it must be, it is required that' (A 39B):

  1) *šewe·na pe·pye·hči=meko nye·wenwi=na·hka·=·'ni i·h=išawiči.* (K-MP4 57)
      "Still, he had to do that over four times." (Michelson 1925:277)
       (*šewe·na* 'still'; =*meko* ; *nye·wenwi* 'four times'; |na·hka| 'again';
       |i·ni| 'that (inan.)'; |i·h=| FUT, |išawi-| AI 'do {so}', |e·h=–či| 3s/AOR)

(o) *še·ški* 'only; all that happened was that' (A 6E, 8D, 17D, 30A; O 10BGIJ, 11D, 24Q)

(p) *ta·taki* 'sort of, basically, usually' (A 1F, 2B, 93D, 125C, 141D, 145A, 163B,
     178E, 186E, 191F; O 96G)

Also used to mark a future aorist as a purpose clause:

1)   *wi·h=ne womeči ta·taki i·nini neniwani.* (K-FC 642)

    'to make it so that that man would be seen'

    (|wi·h=| FUT, |ne·w-| TA 'see', |–emeči| X–3´/AOR;

    i·nini neniwani 'that man (obv.)')

Some particles characterize the logical status of a clause, with or without a conceptual link to the preceding or assumed context. These typically provide a qualification or indication of significance that frames the entire clause.

(5.118) Particles indicating logical status in the abstract

(a)   *kehkinawa·či* 'indicatively, significantly, as a sign, you can tell' (O 41D; C-UAN 4)

    kekye·hkinawa·či 'indicatively, significantly, there are signs' (O 112D; JB-WMD 9):

1)   *kekye·hkinawa·či=ke·h menwe·nemehke ki wi-mečima·pamenesa.* (JB-WMD 9)

    'If she likes you (you'd be able to tell because) she'd always stare at you.'

    (|=ke·hi| 'moreover'; |menwe·nem-| TA 'like', |–ehke| 3–2s/SUBJ;

    ki wi PV 'around', |mečima·pam-| TA 'stare at', |–enesa| 3–2s/POT)

    †*keye·hkinawa·či* 'indicatively, as a sign' (S-Pit 1)

(b)   *ki·hpene* 'in the event, once (it happens)' (A 5C, 77C, 169G; O 7DG, 144H, 153F)

1)   *ki·hpene=meko nwe·wi wa·čini* 'once they went out' (O 8B)

2)   *ki·hpene=meko aše·ya·monite* 'once they (obv.) retreated' (O 52G)

3)   *we·pipahonite ki·hpene* 'once they (obv.) started running' (O 52I)

(c)   *ki·ša·či* 'it is too bad, tough luck, a great bother':

1)   *ki·ša·či=mekoho pano·mekote.* "it will be awful if she falls off." (K-FC 613; tr. HP)

    (=*mekoho* EMPH; |pano·meko-| AI 'fall off while riding', |–te| 3s/SUBJ)

2)   *ki·ša·či=mekoho wi·nwa·wa kehkaha·sowaki* (K-FC 709; tr. HP)

    "They have been troubled to be called upon"

    (=*mekoho* EMPH; *wi·nwa·wa* 3p/EMPH;

    |kehkaha·so-| AI 'be designated', |–waki| 3p/IND)

(d)   *kwayahkwi* 'taking the prudent course, deciding to go ahead':

1)   "*o·´, po·ne·nemi=meko kwayahkwi keta·nesa.* (K-M 125m; tr. HP)

    "You had better just stop thinking about [your daughter.]"

    (|po·ne·nemi| TA 'cease thinking of'; =*meko* EMPH; *keta·nesa* 'your daughter')

2)   *i·ni=·pi kwayahkwi=mekoho pe·hki e·h=na·kana·wa·či i·nini neniwani.*

    "Then they decided to follow the man." (K-SSP 65; tr. HP)

    (*i·ni* 'then'; |=ipi| HRSY; =*mekoho* EMPH; *pe·hki* 'really';

    |na·kaN-| TA 'follow', |e·h=–a·wa·či| 3p–3´/AOR;

    i·nini neniwani 'that man (obv.)')

3)   *kwayahkwi=meko e·h=a·čimowa·či* (K-FASB 63; tr. HP)

    "[they] thought it was no use, so they made up their minds to tell"

    (=*meko* EMPH; |a·čimo-| AI 'tell, report', |e·h=–wa·či| 3p/AOR)

4)   *o·ni e·h=owi·wiya·ni=mekoho kwayahkwi.* (K-M 837p; tr. HP)

    "so I just married them and was done with it."

    (*o·ni* 'and then';

    |owi·wi-| AI+O '(man to) marry O2', |e·h=–ya·ni| 1s/AOR; =*mekoho* EMPH)

(e) *mehči* 'openly, ostensibly; frankly, to put it bluntly' (cf. 5.113*c*, 115*q*):

  1)   *aʼkwi=ʼpi=mekoho mehči kehči-asemihekowa ʼčini mehtose ʼneniwahi.*
       (K-FC 334)
       "and the people did not seem to help them." (tr. HP)
       (*aʼkwi* 'not'; |=ipi| HRSY; =*mekoho* EMPH; *kehči* PV 'greatly',
       |asemih-| TA 'help', |–ekowaʼčini| 3´–3p/NEG; *mehtose ʼneniwahi* 'people (obv.)')

  2)   *mehči=niʼhka ketaʼnweʼhto nepwa* 'I frankly don't believe you' (C-Ston 22)
       (=*niʼhka* MAN'S.EXPL; |aʼnwe·htaw-| TA 'disbelieve', |ke–enepwa| 1s–2p/IND)

(f) *mehtoʼči* 'like, it is as if' (5.92*k*, 5.96*d*; A 120A, 125A, 141B, 167B, 168C;
       O 35E, 46C, 58A, 83E, 88D, 94G, 96H, 110E, 128F, 133B, 136A)

(g) *menaʼni* 'it is peculiar, unexplainable, weird' (K-W 178)

(h) *meʼkweʼhe* 'I believe' (A 1B, 2F, 98E, 107C, 125B, 140A, 171B, 174C; O 51A, 87B);
       'it is thought likely' (5.98*e*)

(i) *meʼmesoʼsi* 'doing an incredible or extraordinary thing':

  1)   *meʼmesoʼsi=meko=manihi kemeʼmehči-=mekoho -neʼwipena.* (K-SSP 171; tr. HP)
       "it is an unusual thing for you to be able to see us personally."
       (=*meko(ho)* EMPH; =*manihi* 'as it is now'; |CV+| RED1, |mehči| PV 'openly';
       |ne·w-| TA 'see', |ke–ipena| 2–1p/IND)

(j) *meʼmešihka* 'perhaps, for example; quite likely' (A 138A;
       O 76D, 122F, 123A, 139H)

(k) *meʼmeʼčiki* 'being sure; I have no doubt' (A 144E; O 88B, 125J, 134E, 147F)

(l) *namaʼnike* 'unprecedentedly' (A 135F)

(m) *natawaʼči* 'resolving accordingly, with resignation' (A 72F, 81A, 131B, 157D)

(n) *naʼpi* 'for the better' (A 50E, 58G, 107H, 145B, 192C, 193I)

(o) *wanimoʼči* 'perchance' (A 140B; O 59A, 114B):

  1)   *wanimoʼči menehta nepoʼhiyaʼne* 'if I should happen to die first' (A 189E)
       (*menehta* 'first'; |nepo·hi-| AI 'die', |–ya·ne| 1s/SUBJ)

  2)   *oniʼčaʼneseʼhiyane wanimoʼči* 'should you happen to have a baby' (K-WYB 104)
       (|oni·ča·nese·hi-| AI 'have a baby', |–yane| 2s/SUBJ)

  3)   *wanimoʼči nesaʼhkiče kaški.* (K-WYB 140; tr. TB)
       "someone might be able to kill him"
       (|neS-| TA 'kill', |–a·hkiče| 3s–3´/PROH, *kaški* (PV)P 'be able to')

(p) *waʼšipaka, waʼwaʼšipaka* 'the wrong one instead of the other,
       the wrong way around':

  1)   *waʼšipaka=meko=kiʼna taši-pemeniyeʼkapa* (A 76B)
       <u>You'd</u> be the one taking care of <u>him</u>'
       (=*meko* EMPH; *kiʼna* 2s/EMPH; *taši* PV 'be engaged in',
       |pemen-| TA 'take care of', |–iye·kapa| 2s–3/POT)

  2)   *waʼwaʼšipaka=yeʼtoke wiʼh=teʼpweʼhtoʼnaʼni.* (K-W 1075)
       'It would seem to be the wrong way around for <u>me</u> to follow what <u>you</u> say.'
       (=*yeʼtoke* 'it seems';
       |wi·h=| FUT, |te·pwe·htaw-| TA 'believe', |e·h=–ena·ni| 1s–2s/AOR)

(q) *wa·wosa·hi* (with or without an overt negative) 'it is to be expected, unsurprisingly'
(A 139D, 190D, 192D; O 102D, 131A); (as if with negative; 5.122*d*, NOTE)
'unexpectedly, it is not to be expected, surprisingly'; 'even' (A 163G);
wa·wasa·hi (K-B 192; C-RS 18)

With no negative:

1) *wa·wosa·h=ča·h=meko i·noki=ye·toke i·ni*
e·h=ki·ši--mekoho -mehkwinawe·mena·ni. (K-ECRP 24; tr. TB)
"It certainly must be that I have now reminded you of things."
(|=ča·hi| 'so'; =*meko(ho)* EMPH; *i·noki* 'now'; =*ye·toke* 'it seems'; *i·ni* 'now';
ki·ši PV PERF, |mehkwinawe·m-| TA 'remind', |e·h=-ena·ni| 1s–2s/AOR)

With overt negative:

2) *a·kwi wa·wosa·hi wi·h=nesekwiye·kwini.* (K-FASB 53; tr. HP)
"You are not going as far as to be killed by it."
(*a·kwi* 'not'; |wi·h=| FUT, |neS-| TA 'kill', |–ekwiye·kwini| 0–2p/NEG)

With = '= NEG (from |=ihi| [5.122*d*]) shown by the retention of the |-i| in *wa·wosa·hi*:

3) *wa·wosa·hi='=ča·hi ki·h=we·pi‿wa·waneška·hi.* (A 139D)
'So it wouldn't be expected that you would start being badly behaved.'
(=*ča·hi* 'so';
|wi·h=| FUT, *we·pi* PV 'begin', |wa·waneška·hi-| AI 'be bad', |ke–∅| 2s/IND)

As if with negative:

4) *wa·wosa·h=ča·hi·='nahi ki·h=a·nwe·hta·pwa.* (K-FC 517; tr. HP)
"so no doubt you will not disbelieve it."
(|=ča·hi| 'so'; |=i·nahi| 'in that case';
|wi·h=| FUT, |a·nwe·ht-| TI(1) 'disbelieve', |ke–a·pwa| 2p–0/IND)

5) *a·neta wa·wosa·h=mekoho e·h=kano·nekoči* (K-FC 523; tr. HP)
"Some would even tell him"
(*a·neta* 'some'; =*mekoho* EMPH; |kano·N-| TA 'speak to', |e·h=–ekoči| 3´–3s/AOR)

(r) *wi·ša·wi* 'maybe, perhaps' (A 155F)

(5.119) Particles indicating logical status in context

(a) *ahkwiya·či* 'especially, all the more':

1) *ahkwiya·či ki·ke·noyakwini* 'especially whenever we have clan feasts' (K-FC 299)
ahkwiya·hi 'especially, all the more' (A 54F, 161D; K-ECRP 106; C-G 9I; S-RL 84):

2) *ahkwiya·h aškiča·h* 'especially at first' (A 156B)

(b) *aniwe·wi* 'contrariwise, in contrast, unlike the other(s), oddly' (A 158E; C, S);
aniwe·we (K-FASB 86)

(c) *apina* 'even (to the point of)' (A 17E, 144C, 164E, 167C):

1) *apina nenenekapiso* 'I was even trembling' (A 65C [verb emended])

2) *e·h=po·ni--meko -ši·ša·nič=apina.* 'He (obv.) even stopped hunting.'
(X10-TAN 74)
(*po·ni* PV 'cease to', |ši·ša·-| AI 'hunt', |e·h=–niči| 3´/AOR; =*meko* EMPH)

(d) *a·hpene·we* 'nothing but, without exception' (O 91D, 137A):

1) *a·hpene·we=mekoho me·nwikeniki nenehke·netasa.* (K-FC 677)
'He should think of nothing but what is good.'
(=*mekoho* EMPH; |menwiken-| II 'be good', |IC–niki 0´/PPL(INsg);
|nenehke·net-| TI(1) 'think about', |–asa| 3s–0/POT)

2)   *ki·na=meko a·hpene·we ki·h=ne·wa·wa.* (K-SSP 55)
     'You will just be able to see him.' (He won't be able to see you.)
     (*ki·na* 2s/EMPH; *=meko* EMPH; |wi·h=| FUT, |ne·w-| TA 'see', |ke–a·wa| 2s–3s/IND)

(e) *a·wa·či* 'even' (A 129C):
1)   *atehči a·wa·či e·h=awi·hiyakwe* 'even when we're off by ourselves' (K-M 810k)
     (*atehči* 'away'; |awi·hi-| AI 'be {somewhere} (dim.)', |e·h=–yakwe| 12/AOR)
2)   *e·h=pwa·wi-a·wa·či-wi·siki·hiniči* 'she (obv.) didn't even have a scar' (K-M 268g)
     (*pwa·wi* PV 'not', |wi·siki·hi-| AI 'have a scar (dim.)', |e·h=–niči| 3′/AOR)

(f) *a·ya·pye·či* 'on top of everything else, even going so far as to':
1)   *a·ya·pye·či=meko e·h=ša·ša·kohamawoči oto·hkaneme·hani.* (K-ECRP 39; tr. HP)
     "Indeed they even went as far as to smash his bones up."
     (*=meko* EMPH; |ša·ša·kohamaw-| TA+O 'smash up O2 for', |e·h=–eči| X–3/AOR;
     oto·hkaneme·hani 'his bones (dim.)')

(g) *e·yi·ki* 'as well' (A 13B, 15A, 48G, 63B, 91H, 100B; O 59E, 64J, 75D, 84G, 133E)
(h) *kakata·ni* 'when it would be expected to be (or have been) the other(s)':
1)   *neniwa kakata·ni atena·wi e·h=a·ya·tasokoni·či, kakata·ni.* (K-Wap 25; tr. TB)
     "It ought to have been the other way but the man fasted the least number of
     days." (In contrast to the woman.)
     (*neniwa* 'man'; *atena·wi* 'less';
     |CV+| RED1, |tasokoni·-| AI 'go {so many} days in fasting', |e·h=–či| 3s/AOR)
2)   *a·kwi='pi kakata·ni pašito·hahi nahi-=mekoho -pi·tipi·tika·kowa·čini.* (K-FC 212)
     "None of the old men ever visited them." (Only the young men did.) (tr. HP)
     (*a·kwi* 'not'; |=ipi| HRSY; *pašito·hahi* 'old men (obv.)'; *nahi* PV 'be given to',
     |CVCV+|RED2, |pi·tikaw-| TA 'visit', |–ekowa·čini| 3′–3p/NEG; *=mekoho* EMPH)

(i) *kana·hi* 'at least' (A 141F; O 140B)
(j) *kahkino·hi* 'now we'll see!'; 'I'll bet it won't happen that':
1)   *kahkino·hi·='nahi ki·h=kehke·nemi* (K-SSP 14; tr. HP)
     "I bet you'll not know a thing about me"
     (|=i·nahi| 'with that'; |wi·h=| FUT, |kehke·nem-| TA 'know', |ke–i| 2s–1s/IND)
2)   *kahkino·h ni·h=mi·si.* (Jones 1907:274.15, 275)
     "Now see if I really shall ease myself!" (Said after eating a self-touting laxative.)
     (|wi·h=| FUT, |mi·si·-| AI 'defecate', |ne–∅| 1s/IND)

(k) *kete·='nahi* 'by reversal, by a change of mind or fortune' (cf. 5.121*b*) (A 138D):
1)   *kete·='nahi pe·hki=meko e·h=mayake·netamowa·či ohkiwanwa·wani.*
     (K-FASB 42)
     "After it was too late they thought very strange of their noses" (tr. HP)
     (*pe·hki* 'really'; *=meko* EMPH; |mayake·net-| TI(1) 'think odd',
     |e·h=–amowa·či| 3p–0/AOR; *ohkiwanwa·wani* 'their noses')
2)   *kete·='nahi i·nah=meko e·h=apihapiči e·h=taši-pakamemeči omešo·mesani.*
     (K-TCSB 41)
     'With second thoughts he sat right where his grandfather (the water monster
     that blessed him) had been struck (by the Thunderers).'
     (|i·nahi| 'there'; *=meko* EMPH;
     |CVCV+| RED2, |api-| AI 'sit {somewhere}', |e·h=–či| 3s/AOR;
     |taši| PV '{somewhere}', |pakam-| TA 'hit', |e·h=–emeči| X–3′/PPL(loc.obl);
     omešo·mesani 'his grandfather (obv.)')

3)   *kete·='nahi='pi e·h=keše mowa·či.* (K-WKG 13)
    'With a complete change of attitude, the story goes, they fawned over them (the children they had earlier abandoned).'

(l)   *ke·htena* 'truly, it's true, sure enough (as had been stated)' (A 10D, 12AE, 15C, 16A, 35F; O 14E, 50BC, 41FG, 63B, 70H, 73A, 88E, 103A, 112D, 119AB, 135I, 153I)

(m)   *ki·hki·hki* 'nevertheless, going ahead anyway' (A 111G, 130F; O 41E)

(n)   *kočike·hkwi* '(although) of course':

1)   *kočike·hkwi=ke·h=i·ni=mekoho wi·h=aški-ki·ke·noyani.* (K-ECRP 118; tr. TB)
    "Although that will be the first time you ever gave a clan feast."
    (|=ke·hi| 'moreover'; |=wi·na| 'but'; *i·ni* 'that (inan.)'; *=mekoho* EMPH;
    |wi·h=| FUT, |aški| PV 'first', |ki·ke·no-| AI 'give clan feast', |e·h=–yani| 2s/AOR)

2)   *i·ni=ke·h=wi·na wi·h=oči-pwa wi-nenohta·ti wa·či kočike·hkwi* (K-Wap 13)
    'and that will be why they will not understand each other, of course'
    (*i·ni* 'that (inan.)'; |=ke·hi| 'moreover'; |=wi·na| 'but';
    |wi·h=| FUT, |oči| PV 'from {something}', |pwa·wi| PV 'not',
    |nenohta·ti·-| AI 'understand each other', |IC–wa·či| 3p/PPL(obl))

(o)   *kwaye·ši* 'that way' (A 25A, 60C, 118A);
    "It will help" (K-Spot 283; tr. HP); "so you can" (K-FC 406; tr. HP)

(p)   *mi·škota* 'what's more, what's worse' (A 123F)

(q)   *mo·hči* 'even' (A 17E. 47F, 88A, 106A, 120C, 144CD, 146A, 158B; O 3D, 8J, 45A, 48F, 70C, 75HJ, 80G, 85G, 89A, 94H, 99D) (cf. 5.28a, 5.82d,

(r)   *na·hka* 'also' (A 7A, 30B; O 10E) (cf. 5.108b); also cliticized (A 2A, 18H; O 10H)
    na·hkači 'also' (O 2B, 6B); also cliticized (O 2I)

(s)   *ne·pehe* 'say!; oh I forgot to say; or rather; or I should have said'
    (Used when the speaker realizes having forgotten or misstated something.)
    (O 69G, 70A; K-Apay 18, K-FC 132, K-ILM 32, K-M 161k, 241d;
    C-Ston 3d, 4m); also cliticized (O 69H; C-Ston 4s).

(t)   *we·nahi* 'I see now; oh, here it is' (A 26E; O 59C, 62E, 63A, 99BH)

1)   *we·nahi* "but I see now that" (K-FC 471; tr. HP)

2)   *we·nahi·='ni* "O Yes, thats it" (K-FC 711; tr. HP);
    "Well, that must be the way" (K-TCSB 13; tr. TB)

3)   *kašina·hi, we·nah=mani* 'Well, now, look at this' (K-WSB 23)

Some particles may function as higher verbs, though this seems to be optional. The selection of moods in the lower clauses of these sentences tends to be idiosyncratic and variable.

(5.120) Particles functioning as higher verbs

(a)   *keye·hapa* 'as it turned out; it turns (turned) out that, actually, I later realized'
    Without verbal predicate: A 15E, 42C, 155D.
    With changed preterite (2.353): A 13D, 26C, 69A, 119C.
    With aorist preterite (2.355).

(b)   *šepawi·hta* 'fortunately' (K-RYL 6, SGG 14); 'it's fortunate' (O 122F)
    With independent or negative in a single clause:

1)   *šepawi·hta='yo we aša·hki waki nekehč-amwa waki.* (K-RYL 6)
    'Fortunately I ate a huge number of crawfishes earlier.'
    (|=iyo·we| PAST; *aša·hki waki* 'crawfishes';
    |kehči| PV 'greatly', |amw-| TA 'eat', |ne–a·waki| 1s–3p/IND)

2)   *šepawiˑhta aˑkwi kaškoˑhpenašiyamečini* (K-M 435b; tr. HP)
       "But it was luck that [he] could not kill any of us"
       (*aˑkwi* 'not'; |kaškoˑhpenaN-| TA 'be able to kill', |–iyamečini| 3–1p/NEG)
   With changed conjunct:

3)   *šepawiˑhta=wiˑna pyeˑyaˑči.* 'But it's a good thing he came.' (C-PD 28)
       (|=wiˑna| 'but'; |pyaˑ-| AI 'come', |IC–či| 3s/CC)

4)   *šepawiˑhta eˑsamiˑnepwaˑhkayaˑni.* 'It's a good thing I'm so smart.' (C-RS 9)
       (|asaˑmi| PV 'too much', |nepwaˑhkaˑ-| AI 'be smart', |IC–yaˑni| 1s/CC)
   With changed preterite:

5)   *šepawiˑhta ayoˑhi eˑwiyanehe* (K-M 17j; tr. HP)
       "It is a good thing that you are here."
       (*ayoˑhi* 'here'; |awi-| AI 'be {somewhere}', |IC–yanehe| 2s/CH.PRET)

6)   *šepawiˑhta=yeˑtoke pwaˑwi-nepoˑhiyanehe.* (K-SGG 87)
       'I guess you're lucky you didn't die.'
       (|=yeˑtoke| 'it seems';
       |pwaˑwi| PV 'not', |nepoˑhi-| AI 'die', |IC–yanehe| 2s/CH.PRET)

(c)   *kehkeˑnemaˑpi* 'I don't know' (K-Wap 9; C-UAN 13; also S, SP, JP, JB, LL, X10);
       keˑnemaˑpi 'I don't know' (O 72GJ, 93E; C-UAN 13; S-Pit 10)
   With interrogative participle:

1)   *keˑnemaˑpi eˑyahayaˑkweˑni.* (K-M 229.l; tr. HP)
       "We don't know where he went."
       (|CVCV+| RED2, |ihaˑ-| AI 'go', |IC–kweˑni| 3s/INT.PPL(obl))
   With future aorist conjunct:

2)   *keˑnemaˑpi wiˑh=teˑpweˑči.* (K-M 366i; tr. HP)
       "I don't know if she was telling the truth."
       (|wiˑh=| FUT, |teˑpweˑ-| AI 'say what is true', |eˑh=–či| 3s/AOR)
   With subjunctive:

3)   *keˑnemaˑpi=čaˑhi manahka ihaˑte keki šekomenaˑki.* (K-M 123d; tr. HP)
       "I wonder if she went to our skies."
       (|=čaˑhi| 'so'; *manahka* 'at a distance'; |ihaˑ-| AI 'go {somewhere}',
       |–te| 3s/SUBJ; *keki šekomenaˑki* 'our (inc.) skies (loc.)')

ENCLITICS

68. Enclitics are words of two or three syllables that cannot be the first word in a sentence, clause, or breath group and are always joined without an intervening pause to a preceding word (**§4.1**), the HOST of the enclitic, which may itself be an enclitic. In syllabary writings enclitics are not preceded by a written word divider; the very rare exceptions are writing errors (1.263-267). Before an enclitic that is not followed by another enclitic, the host has a demarcative stress (**§5**). An enclitic with a compound, module, or other syntactically linked phrase may attach to either the first word or the last. Syntactically enclitics are PHRASE ENCLITICS (**§68.1**) or SENTENCE ENCLITICS (**§68.2**); most are either one or the other, but some are used in both ways.

Words of two or three syllables that are not enclitics may be cliticized. Such cliticized words are treated exactly like enclitics phonologically.

Sequences of enclitics or cliticized words, or of both together, are common. As a general rule in such sequences, any sentence enclitics come first, the phrase enclitics are next, and the cliticized words, with their associated phrase enclitics, are last. Because, however, some words ostensibly fall into more than one of these categories, and some simply have their own lexically specific behavior, there is some variation in the sequential order of these words. Examples of a sentence enclitic inserted between a phrase enclitic and the word that would otherwise be its host are in (5.122*f*(4), *j*(13), *l*(3), *p*(1), *u*(1), *v*(4,6), *w*(8,10); 5.123*d*(1); 5.147*a*); in (5.122*u*(4)) the sentence enclitic is inserted in the middle of an idiomatic phrase.

Enclitics typically have abstract meanings and often idiomatic uses. The conventional glosses used for them are thus little more than mnemonics. In (5.121) and (5.122) additional sample translations are given after the conventional gloss.

Phrase Enclitics

68.1. Phrase enclitics modify words or modules (**§61**).

(5.121) Phrase enclitics

(a) |=iyo·we| PAST; 'former' (cf. 5.122*h*):

1) *kena pe ma=·yo we* 'your former husband' (K-SGG 236)

2) *oke ·hta-ona pe mani=·yo we* 'her former husband' (K-Kin 13)

3) *owi wa wahi=·yo we* 'their former wives' (K-RFB 14)

    owi wa wahi iyo we 'their former wives' (K-RFB 14; see **§68.2**)

(b) |=i·nahi| 'with that'; 'and' (cf. 5.122*i*):

1) *o ·hkomesani, omešo ·hani ·=·nahi* 'his grandmother and his grandfather' (K-KN 8)

2) *mehte ·hani, akahko ·hani ·=·nahi ni šwi* (K-Spot 28)

    'a bow (obv.) and two blunt arrows'

3) *nekoti ihkwe wani, neniwani ·=·nahi, kwi yese ·hani ·=·nahi* (K-Mes 9)

    'a woman (obv.) along with a man (obv.) and a boy (obv.)'

(c) |=ke·hi| 'moreover' (cf. 5.122*j*); 'as well as, including, or perhaps, in particular':

1) *ihkwe wa=ke ·hi* 'as well as women' (representative singular) (O 3D)

2) *nakamo nani=ke ·hi* 'including the songs' (O 163C)

3) *o=wa waneška ·hahi=ke ·hi, ...* 'But as for the bad actors, ...' (A 80B)

4) *kokwe ·čikwa ·sono pi wa ·hani, se nipa ·hi=ke ·hi.* (A 60A)

    'practice sewing beads, or ribbon appliqué'

    ("try to make bead work or fancy ribbon work"; tr. HP)

    (|kokwe·čikwa·so-| AI 'try to sew', |–no| 2s/IMP;

    pi wa ·hani 'beads'; *se nipa ·hi* 'ribbon')

5) *.. we či-kohtameki wi škopano ·hiki=ke ·h wi ·h=mi čiki.* (A 49A)

    '.. which is why they (indef.) are afraid to eat anything sweet, in particular.'

    (|oči| PV 'from {something}', |koht-| TI)1) 'fear', |IC–ameki| X–0/PPL(obl);

    |wi·škopano·hi-| II 'be sweet (dim.)', |IC–ki| 0/PPL(INsg);

    |wi·h=| FUT, |mi·či-| TI(3) 'eat', |e·h=–eki| X–0/AOR)

(d) |=meko| (|=mekoho|) EMPH (all-purpose weak emphatic particle)
  1)   *a·ya·šo·hka=meko* 'alternately' (O 1F; a manner particle in focus position)
  2)   *nekoti=meko si·pwa·kana* 'a single cornstalk' (O 2D)
  3)   *i·ni=meko* 'the same thing, the same one, the same way' (O 7E, 46D, 48D);
           'right then, right away, immediately' (O 7H, 8H, 17I)
  4)   *i·nina·h=mekoho* 'at that precise time' (K-Spot 59)
           ("positively at that time"; tr. HP)
  5)   *ki·h=wača·ho=mekoho.* "Go ahead and cook." (K-SSP 31; tr. HP)
  6)   *"hao·?´," e·h=iči=mekoho.* "'Alright,' he answered willingly." (K-FC 741; tr. HP)
           (*hao·?´* 'Alright'; |i-| AI 'say {so}', |e·h=–či| 3s/AOR)
  7)   *meše=meko·='nahi* 'any' (A 53D, 67B, 152A, 162E, 173C; O 11B, 32E. 54E, 148F)
           idiom: *meše* 'freely' (5.117*i*) + |=meko| EMPH + |=i·nahi| 'with that' (5.121*b*)
(e) |=ne·hi| 'too' (cf. **§62.1**, 5.28*b*; 5.122*q*):
           ki·na=ne·hi. 'You, too.' (A 59C)

The enclitic |=ne·hi| 'too' (5.121*e*) has the peculiarity that it may also be used as a free particle
with the pronoun it modifies cliticized after it (5.28*b*): *ne·h=mani* 'this (inan.) too' (K-FC 181);
ne·h=ni·na 'I also' (K-FC 382). This word order is preferred when the whole phrase is cliticized
(O 65H).

Sentence Enclitics

68.2. Sentence enclitics qualify a sentence or clause as a whole, or link it to the preceding
context. They are usually found in second position in the clause, cliticized to the first word or to
another enclitic. When there is more than one sentence enclitic, the order in which they occur is
largely but not entirely fixed. Some sentence enclitics may occur sentence-finally and may be
repeated in the same clause (notably |=ipi| HRSY and |=a·pehe| 'usually'), and |=ke·hi| 'moreover'
may be attached to a verb or verb phrase. Some sentence enclitics are used optionally as non-
enclitics: *a·pehe* 'usually' (K-BKTE 7; LL-Auto 28; X10-Tan 90); *iyo·we* PAST (K-SGG 164; cf.
5.121*a*(3)). These retain the syntax of enclitics, however, in that they can never appear sentence-
initially or after a pause.

  (5.122) Sentence enclitics
  (a) |=a·pehe| 'usually'; 'always, generally, would, sometimes':
    1)   *nema·ne·pen=a·pehe.* 'There would be a lot of us.' (A 5E)
    2)   *mo·hči=mek=a·pehe ni·na netaši–=mekoho -neškehtawa·wa.* (K-FC 237; tr. HP)
            "I get so tired of his talks some times."
            (*mo·hči* 'even'; |=meko|, =*mekoho* EMPH; *ni·na* 1s/EMPH;
            |taši| PV 'be engaged in', |neškehtaw-| TA 'hate to hear', |ne–a·wa| 1s–3s/IND)
  (b) |=ča·hi| 'so'; 'and, (and) consequently, that being so'; a logical link to the preceding
          discourse or to the pragmatic context; also used in questions and in answers.
          NOTE: |=ča·hi| 'so' may be used in two successive clauses or sentences to link
          both as a unit to the preceding context (O 65GH, 130EF); rarely, it is repeated
          after the verb, adding an expressive flavor (C-SD 26).
    1)   *i·ni=ča·h=nekoti ke·temino·nako·we.* 'So, that's one thing I bless you with.'
            (O 76H)

2) *o·sani=ke·hi e·h=nekotihekoči, e·h=tepa·nekoči=ča·hi.* (K-FC 1; tr. HP)
   "and she was the only child her father had and he loved her dearly."

3) *a·čimohi=ča·hi.* "So you tell them about it." (K-FC 463; tr. HP)

4) *ni·miko=ča·hi, ihkwe·tike.* "So dance[,] women." (K-FC 659; tr. HP)

5) *kaši=ča·h=ketešawi* "What is the matter with you .. ?" (K-FC 605; tr. HP)

6) *kaši=ča·h=e·h=teki.* 'So, how come?'; 'So, (tell me) what happened?'
   (K-M 1070g)

7) *e·ne·nemenokwe·ni=ča·hi.* "Now how did he bless you?" (K-FC; tr. HP)

8) A: *"'šina·kwa.* B: *"o·', neki·šike=ča·hi."* (K-M 483jk; tr. HP)
   A: "Well[?]" B: "Oh, I have made the wickiup."

9) A: *"kaši='yo ketešiwe·pi- ayo·hi -ki·wita."*
   B: *"'šina·kwa, nečapo·kisa=ča·hi."* (K-M 913pq)
   A: 'How did you come to be here?' B: 'Well, I fell into the water.'

10) *mana=ča·hi·='na·='na.* "Here is the one." (K-M 948p; tr. HP)

11) *ma·haki=ča·h!?* (Or: *ma·haki·='=ča·h!?*) 'What about these?' (EK; see §6.3, 1.55)
    (*ma·haki* 'these (anim.)'; |=ihi| NEG [§4.4; 5.122*d*]; !? EN)

12) *i·ni=čá·hi.* 'There it is!' (O 101G)
    (*i·ni* 'that (inan.)'; |=ča·hi| 'so'; ´ EMPH [§6.5])

(c) |=či·hi| 'it was discovered'; 'I (he, etc.) then (suddenly) found, realized, learned,
   saw that; the next thing I (he, etc.) knew; here (there) it (etc.) was':

1) *neniwa=či·h e·h=wa·pamaki.* 'I saw it was a man, when I looked at him.' (A 65A)

2) *pašito·he·hani=či·hi* "He saw that it was an old man [obv.]" (K-FC 23; tr. HP)

3) *e·h=aseniwiniči=či·hi* 'and they saw that he (obv.) had turned to stone' (O 160E)

4) *kaši·', newe·pi-=či·h -mi·ša·čiheko·pi.* (A 91E)
   'Why, to my surprise, I was soon being dressed in fancy clothes.'

5) *anemo·hahi=či·hi e·h=taši-ka·ška·škahomeči.* (K-FC 407; tr. HP)
   "they found the dogs [obv.] being scraped"

6) *ayo·h=či·hi e·h=nenye·masonitehe.* (K-M 9g; tr. HP)
   "Here he saw where he [obv.] had been standing."

7) *i·nah=či·hi nepisi e·h=ahte·niki.* (K-M 632k; tr. HP)
   "there they saw a lake [obv.]"

8) *i·nah=či·hi kepiškwa·te e·h=nemasoniči.* (K-M 972m; tr. HP)
   "there he [obv.] was, standing in the doorway."

9) *a·kwi=či·hi·='pi te·pwe·ničini o·šisemani.* (K-M 898k; tr. HP)
   "and [she] found out that her grandson [obv.] had not been telling the truth."

(d) |=ihi| NEG (expressive and idiomatic; §4.4, §6.3, 1.54, 55, 57); always followed by
   |=ča·hi| (5.122*b*(11)), |=iyo| (5.122*g*), |=ke·hi| (5.122*j*), |=we·na| (5.122*u*), or |=ya·pi|
   (5.122*w*).

   NOTE: In certain idiomatic combinations the zero variant of |=ihi| NEG before
   |=ča·hi| and |=ke·hi| may be written overtly as =·'= (5.118*q*(3), 5.122*b*(11)). The
   negative meaning that *ma·mahka·či* (5.117*f*) has before |=ča·hi| can be ascribed to
   such an elided |=ihi| NEG, but the same negative meaning may also be found where
   |=ihi| cannot be present (K-M 320g; 1.53). The presence of an elided |=ihi| NEG
   before a |=ča·hi| that follows *wa·wosa·hi, wa·wasa·hi* 'it is to be expected' (5.118*q*)
   may be shown by the otherwise irregular retention of the vowel after |h| before the

enclitic (5.118*q*(3); cf. **§4.2**), but this effect is usually leveled out, leaving no phonological trace. As a consequence *wa·wosa·hi, wa·wasa·hi* may be used with the negative value it would have if |=ihi| were present (5.118*q*(4-5)).

1) *meči=·hi=·yo=ni·na¹⁽?⁾ neteneniwi!?* 'Well, gee, I'm not a <u>man</u>, after all!' (O 103E)

2) *ki·h=pwa·wi-=·h=we·na ke·keya·hi -we·ta·se·wi.* (K-WYB 41; tr. TB)
    "You no doubt eventually will become a brave."

3) *ki·h=pwa·wi-=·h=we·=-ki·šiki* (K-BHD2 8; tr. HP)
    "[The] time will come when you will be grown up"

4) *wa·wane netamwa=·h=ya·pi e·h=nešiwana·ča·niki.* (K-Auto 225; tr. IP)
    "I guess he knows .. it is bad."

5) *nepo·hiwa=·h=we·na?* 'He isn't dead, is he?' (K-Wap 137)
    ("Is he dead?"; tr. TB)

6) *ke·ko·hiwa=·h=we·na·=·na kekwisa!?* (S-RL 16)
    'Your son doesn't amount to anything!' (Sarcastic.)

7) *wi·h=te·pwe·wa=·hi=·yo!?* "He couldn't be right!" (K-FC 250; tr. AW)
    ("O well he isn't telling the truth any way."; tr. HP)

(e) |=ipi| (|=ipihi|) HRSY; 'they say, it is said, supposedly; you're supposed to, let's say'. NOTE: Speakers vary greatly in the frequency with which this enclitic is used. When it appears more than once in a sentence the iteration does little more than demarcate breath groups. It may occur after a phrase enclitic, with the ostensible syntax of a second phrase enclitic (5.12*b*, 5.89*b*, 5.122*e*(2); O 7HK, 14E, 41F, 52I, 154H), or before a phrase enclitic, with the ostensible syntax of a sentence enclitic (5.110*x*(2), 5.141*d*; O 9E, 44G, 68C, 117D, 154E), even when it occurs more than once in a sentence.

1) *i·ni e·šawiči=·pi.* 'That's what they say he did.' (K-TO 26)

2) *našawaye=·pi še·ški-meko=·pi ki·šekwi e·h=ako·te·ki.* (K-M 1c; tr. HP)
    "it is said that a long, long time ago, the sky was supposed to be the only thing that hangs."

3) *ni·h=ineniwi=·pi.* "I will pretend to be a man." (K-M 354b; tr. HP)

4) *'kemya·na·ko·mekwa=·pi,' e·h=išiki.* (K-M 1089.1; tr. HP)
    "when I was told that you disliked me"

5) *ki·h=pi·tike=·pi.* "It is said for you to come in." (K-M 1188a; tr. HP)

6) *ki·h=nenoswi-ki·ke·nopwa=·pi.* (K-FC 404; tr. HP)
    "You are to hold a buffalo clan feast, it is said."

7) *šešeka·hi=·pi keto·če·ka·ma ki·h=anasa·wa.* (C-FS 20)
    'Make believe [cf. 5.115*dd*] you're anteing up your fisherskin, let's say.'

(f) |=iškwe| WOMAN'S EXPLETIVE (mild, usually untranslated):
1) *na·kwa·ta·we·=·škwe.* "Let us go home." (K-M 281e; tr. HP)

2) *mehči=·škwe=ni·na ma·haki nešahkwe·nema·waki.* (K-M 495g; HP differs)
    'It seems obvious to *me* that these women are listless.'

3) *kaši=·škwe nekya išawiwa.* (K-M 573h; tr. HP)
    "What is the matter with my mother?"

4) *pe·hki=·škwe=mekoho kemena·na·čimo.* (K-M 1141j; tr. HP)
    "Oh, but that's a funny story you told." ('Funny': i.e., 'strange, weird'.)

(g) |=iyo| 'for': 'after all, I say this because, in (this) case, for instance'; also to temper
a question ('by the way, I must ask you, tell me') or contradiction ('(no,)
actually'):

1) *ni na= 'yo a·kwi wi·h=kekye·hkimenako we.* 'For I won't be your teacher.' (O 99F)

2) *ma·hiya= 'yo wi·čawiwata netowi·hka·ni.* (A 188C)
'After all, your late husband was my friend.'

3) *netepa·na wa= 'yo* 'I say this since I love her' (A 190B)

4) *ni na= 'yo* 'Like me, ...' (A 17A, 25D, 83E, 132G, 171D)

5) *ni na= 'yo=wi na a·kwi wi·h=neškimena·nini.* (A 136B)
'Like me, for instance, I won't scold you.'

6) *kaši= 'yo ketešawi.* "What is the matter with you?" (K-M 924c; tr. HP)

7) *peno·či= 'yo=wi na·= 'niki awiwaki kešemi·ha.* (O 65F)
'But, your niece and her people live far away.'

(h) |=iyo·we| PAST (cf. 5.121*a*):

1) *ketene= 'yo we* 'I told you before' (A 73A)

2) *ni na= 'yo we wi·tamo·nako we.* 'It was I who told you things.' (O 72H)

3) *ki wi-ošehki tama·nini= 'yo we* 'the clothes I had been wearing' (A 57D)

4) *i·niya ihkwe·he·ha= 'yo we e·ye·h-pwa·wi-ona·pe·miya·ni ka·ki wi·-'te·maka*
(A 119C) 'that young woman I had gone around with before I got married'

(i) |=i·nahi| 'with that' (cf. 5.121*b*); 'withal, after that, in those circumstances, now
(you can)'; often idiomatic or part of an idiomatic phrase:

1) *na na·kwa·ko·= 'nahi* 'now go on your separate ways' (O 64B)

2) *kapo·twe·= 'nahi owi·wani e·h=matanemeči* (C-RP 6)
'soon after that his wife was overtaken'

3) *ke·htena·= 'nahi kapo·twe* 'sure enough, soon after that' (A 177F)

4) *a·kwi·= 'nahi ke·ko·hi ine·nema·čini.* (K-M 611i; tr. HP)
"Now he is not thinking of doing anything to them."

5) *ta·ni·= 'nahi* 'I wish, I hope' (A 81D, 147G; O 82G, 147F):
ta·ni·= 'nahi anwa·či·te. 'I hope she'll consent.' (A 84D; 2.187)

6) *a·mi-'šawiwa·ne·ni·= 'nah=mani* (A 127C)
'I wonder what would have become of me now'

(j) |=ke·hi| 'moreover' (5.121*c*); 'and, and here, and another thing (was), besides, also,
furthermore, meanwhile, for example, to be precise'; marks a clause of equal
importance with what precedes; sometimes the equivalent of = '*yo=ke·hi*:

1) *ki na=ke·hi* "As for you, ..." (K-MESB; tr. TB)

2) *wi na=ke·hi.* 'He did, too.' (K-BHD 1) ("He also (went)."; tr. TB)

3) *kana·h nekotawahi·ne, ni·šwawahi·ne=ke·h* (A 141F)
'for at least one year, if not two'

4) *i·ni=ke·hi* '(And) that was (also) when' (O 2F, 3A, 3G, 119E)

5) *i·ni=ke·h=meko* 'and then right away, immediately' (O 9E, 14A, 17E, 18B)

6) *o=ča·ki-=ke·h -kohtamakwe, ...* 'And besides, if we were all afraid of it, ...'
(A 104G)

7) *a·kwi=ke·hi= 'pi wi·h=a·hkwamataki* (O 158B)
'And, they say, it was not that he was sick, either.'

8) *a·kwi=ke·h=a·čimoya·nini.* 'But I didn't tell.' (A 108D)

With verb as host:

9) *šewe·na ahpene·či=mekoho ki·h=nenehke·nemipwa=ke·hi.* (O 75B)
'Still, you must in particular think of me always.'

10) *meči=·h=we·na keme·h-kehke·nema pena wi·h=nepo·hiči=ke·hi*
(K-ECRP 16; tr. TB) "we don't know yet for sure whether he is dead or not"

With verb as host and emphatic intonation (§6.5):

11) *kekehke·neta=ké·hi.* 'You <u>know</u> that.' (A 84B)

In second position and with verb:

12) *a·kwi=ke·h=wi·na=·pi nahi-mahkate·wi·hičini=ke·hi.* (K-FC 791; tr. HP)
(He relied only on the sacred bundle,) "and he never fasted either"

New subject:

13) *na·hina·hi we·pina·ke·yakwe, ki·h=wi·šiki-=ke·h=mekoho -kehkino·sopwa.*
"When the time comes for us to sing them you must indeed try hard to
remember them." (K-ECRP 131; tr. TB)

Equivalent of = *·yo=ke·hi* (5.123e):

14) *i·nini=ke·hi okwisani pe·hki=meko e·h=makekineniči* (K-WKG 9)
'Now, that son of hers was really big, ...'

15) *e·h=aniwisa·či=ke·hi, ...* 'Now, he was a fast runner, ...' (K-WKG 26)

(k) |=ki·na| 'see now, see what I told you':

1) *i·ni=ma·h=ki·na.* 'See what I was telling you.' (K-SSP 147) ("There now, .."; tr. HP)

2) *ki·ši-=ma·h=ki·na -pye·na·pi.* 'See now, she has been brought back.' (K-B 7)

(l) |=koči| 'you know'; 'I can tell you, believe me, incidentally, of course, that's all':

1) *keki·ši-=koči -kehke·neta* 'after all, you already know (it)' (A 29F)

2) *pe·hki=koči no·hkomesa neta·hpeči-a·ya·čimohekwa* (A 58C)
'You know, Grandmother really kept instructing me all the time'

3) *sanakatwi=koči=wi·na=meko pe·hki* 'But of course, it's really hard' (A 104A)

4) *ke·waki=koči=mani ketaškiki.* 'Remember, you're still young now.' (A 183D)

5) *ki·h=kehke·neta pwa=koči i·ni* 'and I guarantee you will know about that' (O 78G)

6) *mani=koči=mani e·šikeki pema·tesiweni.* (O 146E)
'Let me tell you how it is with life.'

7) *ni·h=kehke·nema pena=koči.* (K-FC 705; tr. HP)
"and we are bound to know about them"

8) *ki·h=owi wi=koči=wi·na nekotenwi, a·kwi ni·šenwi.* (K-FC 607; tr. HP)
"It is true that you will be married at least once, but not twice."

9) *i·ya·h=koči pya·yane, i·ni wi·h=kehke·netamani.* (K-FC 614; tr. HP)
"Of course when you get there .. you'll know what is required."

(m) |=kohi| 'certainly'; 'I assure you, make no mistake, you must know, without a doubt':

1) *sanakatwi=kohi mehtose·neniwiweni.* 'Life is definitely hard.' (O 58H)

2) *ketepa·nene=kohi.* "For I am truly fond of you." (Jones 1907:138.19, 139)

3) *maneto·wa=kohi kenenehke·nemeko·toke* (O 66C; tr. HP)
"the Manitou must have thought of you"

4) *netaneno·te wi=kohi.* "well I am an Indian to be sure" (K-FC 12)

5) *kese·kimeko·pi=kohi* (K-TCSB 42; tr. TB)
"You were told that only to be frightened"

6) *i·ni=kohi´.* 'That's just the thing!' (O 88G); "That's right" (K-B 163; tr. HP);
"That's the idea!" (K-M 376d; tr. HP)

(n) |=mani| 'as it is now'; 'now, as it is'; often reinforcing a synonymous word:

  1) *ke·waki=koči=mani ketaškiki.* 'Remember, you're still young now.' (A 183D)

  2) *i·noki=mani e·nena·ke* 'what we're now telling you' (A 180E)

  3) *i·ni=ke·h=mani e·h=ki·šikiya·ni.* 'And now here I'm grown up.' (O 69I)

(o) |=mata| 'alternatively'; 'instead, rather, but'

  1) *pepo·kehe=mata, sanakihto·hkapa.* (A 38H)
     'If it had been winter instead, you would have had a hard time.'

  2) *a·kwi, ni·na=mata meše=mekoho ni·h=taši-mehtomehtose·neniwi.* (O 129F)
     'Not so; in my case I'm going to happily go along being alive.'

  3) *ni·na=mata.* "Just let me have a turn." (Jones 1907:114.21, 115)

  4) *kemi·ša·mi=mata na·teyane, wi·h=te·pwe·hto·na·ni.* (Jones 1907:320.18)
     'Only if you go get your sacred bundle, <u>then</u> I'll do what you say.'

  5) *a·kwi-kana·kwa; pene·waki=mata.* 'I can't (eat it); I'd rather have turkeys.'
     (K-B 13)

  6) *mani=mata menwikenwi e·ne·nemena·ke.* (K-B 94; tr. HP)
     "But this is good, the way we bless you"

(p) |=ma·hi| 'you see'; 'mind you, you understand, I mean, obviously':

  1) *ki·na=ma·h=meko ki·h=ašihto.* 'You must make it yourself, remember.' (O 102F)

  2) *i·ni=ma·h we·či-a·pi-na·naki.* 'Well, you see, that's why I went to get her.' (A 58E)

  3) *.., ki·ke·nočiki=ma·hi.* '(I'm just talking about) the hosts, you understand.' (O 8D)

  4) *.., ki·nwa·wa=ma·hi e·hpi·hči-ne·se·ye·kwe.* (O 93C)
     '.. that is, as long as you (pl.) are still living'
     ("This will be while you are living."; tr. HP)

(q) |=ne·hi| 'too' (5.121*e*); highly idiomatic as a sentence enclitic:

  1) *ahpene·či=·yo=ne·hi=·pi·=·nini ašihto·wa·ka·hkimote·hani* (K-FC 42; tr. HP)
     "as she has been making the sacks right along"

  2) *"hao·ʔ·," e·h=ina·či=meko=ne·hi=·na.* (K-FC 56: tr. HP)
     " 'Alright' he answered her willingly."

  3) *ši··, a·hkwamatakani=wi·na=ne·hi.* 'Say, might you be having pains.' (A 108D)

  4) *ki·wa·tesihkani=wi·na=ne·hi.* "Are you lonesome?" (SSP 71; tr. HP)

(r) |=ni·hka| MAN'S EXPLETIVE (mild, usually untranslated):

  1) *pe·hki=ní·hka, nano·te·nemenowakwe·ni.* (A 144B)
     'Golly, he had it all wrong about us.' ("Gee"; tr. HP)

  2) *iši-pwa·wi-=ni·hka=·yo·we ni·na -kaškimenowa·ne·ni.* (A 154D)
     'Darn it, how come I couldn't win your consent, before?'

  3) *ši··, ta·ni=ča·h=ni·hka, nemešo.* (O 65G)
     'Hey, I know what I'm saying, Grandfather!'

(s) |=ta·ni| 'if you agree'; 'if you will, please; why don't I?':

  1) *ano·hko, mani=ča·h=ta·ni wi·h=išawiya·ni: ...* (K-DSB 36)
     'Well, Grandmother, here's what I'd like your permission to do: ...'
     (*ano·hko* 'grandmother (voc.)'; *mani* 'this (inan.)'; |=ča·hi| 'so';
     |wi·h=| FUT, |išawi-| AI 'do {so}', |IC–ya·ni| 2s/PPL(obl))

  2) *o··, ki·na=ta·ni e·h=owi·kiye·kwe ki·h=iši-wi·te·mene.* (A 83B)
     'Oh, then let me go with you to <u>your</u> family's house.'

  3) *ni·h=awana·wa=ta·ni.* 'Why don't I take him (a deer) home?' (K-Wewi 27)
     (|wi·h=| FUT, |awaN-| TA 'take away, take home', |ne–a·wa| 1s–3s/IND)

(t) |=tike| MAN'S EXPLETIVE (mild, usually untranslated):

1) *nawoˑteˑweˑyaˑne=tike.* (Jones 1907:260.3) 'I wonder if I could go visiting somewhere and get something to eat.' (Asking permission.)

2) *meše=tike!* 'Let's just forget about it!' (K-B 90)

3) *eˑšikenokwe ni=tike iˑniye miˑčiyaˑni.* (K-B 183; tr. HP)
    "I wonder how the food which I have eaten is"

(u) |=weˑna| 'at least, after all' (**§6.5**, end); tempering what has just been said: 'rather, or actually, but actually, or at least'; *=weˑ=* before most consonant-initial enclitics:

1) *iˑni=weˑ=meko peˑhki eˑh=kiˑšikiči nešiseˑha.* (O 71A)
    'right now my uncle is, in fact, fully grown up'

2) *iˑni eˑšiki, eˑšiyameči=wéˑna wiˑtekoˑwa.* (O 66I)
    'That's what I was told, or, actually, what an owl told the two of us.'

3) *niˑna=weˑn=aˑpehe eˑšiteˑheˑyaˑni.* 'At least it's what I always think.' (A 147D)

4) *meše=weˑ=mekoˑ=ʼnahi* 'in fact, any' (K-FC 17, 33, 37)
    (< *meše=mekoˑ=ʼnahi* 'any' (5.121*d*(7)) + |=weˑna|)

5) Examples after |=ihi| NEG: 5.122*d*(2-3, 5-6, 8), 5.122*i*(10).

(v) |=wiˑna| 'but'; 'however, though, contrary to what you might think':

1) *niˑna=wiˑna, ...* 'But as for me, ...' (A 6C)

2) *keyeˑhapa=keˑh=wiˑna ..* (A 13D, 15E, 26C, 69A)
    'Actually, though; I later realized, though; it turned out, however'

3) *šiˑʼ, koči-wačaˑhono=wiˑna=kiˑna kiˑšikihtoˑyani.* (A 12D)
    'Say, why don't you try and <u>cook</u> what you've raised, yourself?'

4) *naˑhka peˑhki=koči=wiˑna=meko nemiˑšaˑteˑnemo* (A 184D)
    'And furthermore, you know I'm really very pleased ..'

5) *aˑkwi=wiˑna=niˑna nahi-koˑkenakini.* (A 116C)
    'But it wasn't me that washed him.'

6) *o=keˑhtena=wiˑna=meko aˑkwi nahi-aˑhkweˑčini.* (A 191E)
    'And he really <u>did</u> never get angry.'

(w) |=yaˑpi| 'here I go, here we go, get ready, here's the deal' (**§6.5**, 1.60); after *iˑni* 'now' and the like with emphatic intonation ('Alright now ..'); in questions 'now tell me, let me get this straight' (A 145E):

1) *iˑni=yápi.* 'I'm off.' (K-WWB 23); 'Here we go; I'm ready.'

2) *iˑni=yápi peˑhki.* 'Now we'll really have a time!' (K-WWB 19)

3) *kaho ni=yápi wiˑh=aˑtotamaˑni eˑšawiyaˑni.* (A 1A)
    'So, now I shall tell the story of my life.'

4) *iˑni=yápi eˑh=naˑnenaˑni.* 'Alright now, I'm here to get you.' (A 40F)

5) *nahiˑ=ʼni=yápi wiˑh=mawi-anenwiˑyani.* (A 55F)
    'Alright, now it's time for you to go and bathe.'

6) *iˑni=yápi wiˑh=weˑpaˑhkeˑyaˑni kiˑyawi.* (O 150E)
    'Alright, I'm going to throw you now.'

7) *nahiˑ, ʼmešeˑ=ʼnahi kiˑh=kaˑkiˑkeˑnopwa,ʼ keteko pena=yaˑpi.*
    (K-FC 554, AW; tr. HP)
    "Now we were told to hold clan feasts whenever we want to."

8) *šiˑʼ, aˑkwi=yaˑpi=mekoho kanaˑkwa.* "Say, I can not possibly do it."
    (K-Spot 55A; tr. HP)

9) *i ni=yá pi e ʹh=ki ʹši-mehkokwawiki.*
"Just to let you know, I have already been seen in a dream." (K-Wap 88; tr. TB)

10) *nahi ʹ, kema ʹmata ʹkwi-=ya pi=meko -nesa pwa meši-mehtose ʹneniwa.*
"Now you have made the, if I may say, unusual killing of this large being."
(K-WYB 151; tr. TB)

11) *ane ʹhe, i ni=yá pi wi ʹh=anohka ʹnena ʹni.* (K-FC 223; tr. HP)
"Mother, I want to have you do an errand for me."

12) *a ʹkwi=ya pi owi ʹwiyanini?* 'Now tell me, you're not married?' (K-WWB 26)

(x) |=ye·hapa| 'it turns out' (§26.3):

1) *meše=meko ʹ= 'nahi iši-mi ʹčipe ʹha i nini=meko ne na ʹhe nemekočini=ye ʹhapa.*
"Just any kind of a game is after all taken care of by him [obv.]."
(K-Bene 89; tr. TB)

2) *mani e ʹši-kanakanawiki=ye ʹhapa e ʹh=ki ʹke ʹnoki.* (K-FC 802; tr. HP)
"I have found out and this was the correct way of speaking in clan feasts."

3) *i ni=ča ʹh=ye ʹhapa we ʹči-po ʹsite ʹhe yani.* (A 175E)
'So that now seems to explain why you feel so bad.'

4) *oni ʹča nesihkapa=meko=ye ʹhapa.* (A 193H)
'You could indeed have a child, as we now see.'

(y) |=ye·pani| 'mind you'; 'I really think that'; often in warnings and the like;
|=ya·pani| (younger variant) (§26.4):

1) *a ʹkwi=ye pani kekye ʹhkinawa ʹči*
me ʹhi- ke ʹko ʹhi -iši-wa waneška ʹhi ʹhka noya ʹnini.
"mind you, I never have done anything bad, yet" (K-M 874n; tr. HP)

2) *a ʹkwi=ye pani kehke ʹnetama ʹkini wi ʹh=išihišina ʹke wa ʹke ʹni.* (K-FC 374; tr. HP)
"We have not the least idea as to how we are to sing"

3) *a ʹkwi=ye pani menwawiyanini i ni e ʹšawiyani* (K-M 551g; tr. HP)
"you are not doing right"

4) *nahi ʹ, mani=ya pani wi ʹh=išikeki.* (SP-SBS 56)
'Alright, this is what is going to happen.'

(z) |=ye·toke| 'it seems'; 'probably, quite likely, I suppose' (2.171d, 346, 359, 360;
§26.2):

1) *ke ʹkeya ʹh=meko ʹ= 'ni ke ʹhtena e ʹh=te pwe ʹhtawa ʹtehe=ye ʹtoke.* (A 120E)
'Eventually, then, he actually seems to have believed her.'

2) *i ni=ča ʹh=ye ʹtoke we ʹči-pwa ʹwi-kohtamakwe.* (A 104F)
'So that's probably why we aren't afraid of it.'

3) *i ni=ke ʹh=ye ʹtoke=ne ʹh=ki ʹna e ʹne nemiyani.* (A 26G)
'What's more, that's quite likely what <u>you</u> think of <u>me</u>, too.'
("I suppose that's what you are thinking of me too." [tr. HP])

4) *i ni=ča ʹh=meko=ye ʹtoke e ʹna ʹkwate ʹki i ʹni* (K-BHD 125; tr. TB in B87:84)
"Very likely it is lying just as we left it"

68.3. Sentence enclitics sometimes combine idiomatically with meanings that are not simple concatenations of their basic meanings.

(5.123) Idiomatic combinations of sentence enclitics

(a)   = ʼh=weˑna 'rather, or rather' (correcting; normal intonation [**§6.5**]; cf. 5.122d(2,3,5,6))

1)   *iˑna neniwa, oškinaweˑha=ʼh=weˑna* 'that man, or rather youth' (K-JM 16)

2)   *kiˑna=ʼh=weˑna kewa waneška ˑhi.* 'It's rather <u>you</u> who are the rascal.' (C-UAN 17)

(b)   =keˑh=mani 'for, for instance' (giving the evidence)

1)   *meše ˑ=ʼnah=keˑh=mani eˑh=anemi-pakamekoči* (K-BHD 4; tr. TB) "for they would sometimes strike him"

(c)   =keˑh=wiˑna 'and for another thing, and in particular':

1)   *aˑkwi=keˑh=wiˑna niˑna menwe ˑnemakini.* 'And besides, I don't like him.' (A 130A)

2)   *mana=keˑh=wiˑna* "And this [other] one .." (K-SSP 67B; tr. HP)

3)   *kaˑta=keˑh=wiˑna=keˑhi owiyeˑha aˑčimohiyeˑkani.* (K-M 520m; tr. HP) "But don't you tell anyone."

(d)   =wiˑna=čaˑhi 'but at the same time, but even so' (O 11E)

1)   *eˑh=pwa wi-=wiˑna=čaˑh=meko keˑkoˑhi -inaˑhpawaˑči.* (K-WSB 22; tr. HP) "but [he] never had a dream of any kind"

(e)   = ʼyo=keˑhi 'as; now (I should say)' (marks parenthetical information that will soon be significant to the narrative); 'you understand (that)' (A 3C, 11C, 18C), 'remember' (A 36G, 40C), 'bear in mind' (A 39B, A 193D; K-WKG 22):

1)   *eˑh=mahkateˑwiˑwaˑči=ʼyo=keˑhi, ..* (O 61E) 'It should be explained that they were fasting, ..'

2)   *kepi nešihipwa=ʼyo=keˑhi.* (O 157J) 'For you people attacked me without provocation'

3)   *eˑh=poˑhkiˑkweˑči=ʼyo=keˑhi.* 'Now, remember, he only had one eye.' (K-FASB 85)

COMPLEX SENTENCES

69.   A complex sentence has a main clause and one or more subordinate clauses (**§59**). A subordinate clause is either an attributive clause or a complement clause. Conjoined sentences may be taken as the components of a compound sentence, but this is a category in the organization of discourse rather than one of syntax. Syntactically a compound sentence is simply two sentences.

Examples in this section are drawn mostly from the "Autobiography" and "Owl" texts, which should be consulted for the full contexts.

Attributive Clauses

69.1.   Attributive clauses include temporal clauses, conditional clauses, and purpose clauses. Temporal and conditional clauses are distinguished as a matter of descriptive convenience but are often marked with the same morphology.

69.2. Temporal clauses. Attributive temporal clauses have a verb in the aorist conjunct (§26.8), subjunctive (§26.9), changed conjunct (§26.10), iterative (§26.12), changed interrogative (§26.15), or aorist interrogative (§26.16) mode. The verb may occur in construction with *na·hina·hi* P 'time' to specify 'at the time or times when' (§63.2, 5.62; 2.174, 184, 198, 213, 275, 276, 278), and this particle is required for the changed interrogative to have a temporal meaning. Temporal clauses most often precede the main verb but, to varying degrees, they may alternatively come after the main clause: A 18B, 69D, O 133F (aorist); O 77E (subjunctive); O 5I, 9A (changed conjunct); O 42A (iterative).

(5.124) Temporal clauses

    (a)   *e·h=taši·hka·noya·ni* 'when I played' (A 1E)
        (|taši·hka·no-| AI 'play', |e·h=–ya·ni| 1s/AOR)

    (b)   *čaki-ki·ke·no·hiye·kwe* 'when you hold a small clan feast' (O 81B)
        (*čaki* PV 'small', |ki·ke·no·hi-| AI 'hold a clan feast (dim.)', |–ye·kwe| 2p/SUBJ)

    (c)   *ki·šetone·moniči* 'after he had finished speaking' (O 101D)
        (|ki·šetone·mo-| AI 'finish speaking', |IC–niči| 3´/CC)

    (d)   *ni·miwa·čini* 'whenever they dance' (O 118D)
        (|ni·mi-| AI 'dance', |IC–wa·čini| 3p/ITER)

A verb in the aorist conjunct may be weakly subordinated to a preceding clause with the meaning 'and, and then'. In third-person narrative, however, where main clauses generally have aorist conjunct verbs, the subordinate relationship may be less clear-cut.

(5.125) Aorists in clause-chaining

    (a)   *wi·kiya·pe·hani netašihašihto, ni·ča·paki e·h=owi·kihaki.* (A 2E)
        'I used to make little houses and had the dolls live in them.'
        (*wi·kiya·pe·hani* 'houses (dim.)';
        |CVCV+| RED2, |ašiht-| TI(2) 'make', |ne–o| 1s–0/IND; *ni·ča·paki* 'dolls';
        |owi·kih-| TA 'make dwell {somewhere}', |e·h=–aki| 1s–3/AOR

    (b)   *e·h=sakinekwe·na·či, e·h=we·pa·hke·či.* (O 150H)
        'He took her under the arm and threw her.'
        (Or: 'Taking her under the arm, he threw her.')
        (|sakinekwe·n-| TA 'take by the arm', |e·h=–a·či| 3s–3´/AOR;
        |we·pa·hke·-| AI+O 'throw O2', |e·h=–či| 3s/AOR)

    (c)   *e·h=sakakwa·piki e·h=wa·pameči* (A 101E)
        'when we (indef.) look at an angle in looking at them (corpses)'
        (Or: 'when we (indef.) look at them looking at an angle')
        (|sakakwa·pi-| AI 'look aslant', |e·h=–eki| X/AOR;
        |wa·pam-| TA 'look at', |e·h=–eči| X–3/AOR)

69.3. Conditional clauses. Conditional clauses have a verb in the aorist conjunct, subjunctive, or changed interrogative. They also have a preference for preceding the main verb but may follow the main clause: A 42F, 49E, 79C (aorist); A 8A, O 53D, 77E (subjunctive); A 112H, 113B (changed interrogative).

(5.126) Conditional clauses

    (a)   *e·h=se·kesiya·ni* 'since I was frightened' (A 42F)
        (|se·kesi-| AI 'be frightened', |e·h=–ya·ni| 1s/AOR)

    (b)   *e·h=wa·waneška·hiči* 'because of her wanton behavior' (A 121B)
        (|wa·waneška·hi-| AI 'be bad', |e·h=–či| 3s/AOR)

(c)   *mya·nowesiwa ona·pe·mani e·h=nepeniči* (A 168A)
      'she's been overcome by the death of her husband'
         (|mya·nowesi-| AI 'be overcome', |–wa| 3s/IND; *ona·pe·mani* 'her husband (obv.)';
         |nep-| AI 'die', |e·h=–niči| 3´/AOR)

(d)   *mi·ka·ti·wa·te* 'if they were fighting' (O 14B)
         (|mi·ka·ti·i| AI 'fight', |–wa·te| 3p/SUBJ)

(e)   *kwi·yese·hiwane·ni* 'if you're a boy' (A 112H)
         (|kwi·yese·hi-| AI 'be a boy', |IC–wane·ni| 2s/CH.INT)

A condition may also be expressed by a declarative main verb followed by a participle headed by the oblique complement of the relative root |ot-| 'because of {something}' (**§22.4(d)**). The main verb states the cause or circumstance, and the participle states the resulting state or action that is explained by this. The relative root in these participles (typically appearing as *we·či* PV) may be generically glossed 'which is (the reason) why' or, in a separate substantive sentence (**§66.2**), 'and that is why' (A 25E, 49A, 53F, 87H, 171E, 187E, 193F; O 56I, 66D, 103G).

69.4. Purpose clauses. The verb in a purpose clause has |wi·h=| FUT and aorist conjunct endings (**§26.24**, 2.331, 332). Purpose clauses ordinarily follow the main clause but may precede.

(5.127) Purpose clauses

(a)   *.., wi·h=sahkahamawa·wa·či i·nini wi·teko·wayani.* (O 7J)
      '.., in order to make a tobacco offering to that owl skin.'
         (|wi·h=| FUT, |sahkahamaw-| TA 'offer tobacco to', |e·h=–a·wa·či| 3p–3´/AOR;
         i·nini 'that (obv.)'; *wi·teko·wayani* 'owl skin (obv.)')

(b)   *wi·h=pwa·wi- kenwe·ši -taši-kotakihto·ki ..* (A 100F)
      'In order not to be suffering for a long time ..'
         (|wi·h=| FUT, *pwa·wi* PV 'not', *taši* PV 'be engaged in',
         |kotakiht-| TI(2)-O 'suffer', |e·h=–o·ki| X(-0)/AOR; *kenwe·ši* 'a long time')

69.5. Substantival attributive clauses. Beside attributive clauses that are subordinate to main-clause verbs (5.124, 126, 127), there are clauses with the same modes and equivalent meanings that are substantivized as components of equational or substantive sentences or as the complements of relative roots.

Substantival temporal clauses are marked by *na·hina·hi* P 'time' or *i·nina·hi* P 'the time, that time' (equivalent to *i·ni* 'that (inan.)' + *na·hina·hi*; **§63.2**, 5.63; 5.94-95, 128); less commonly a temporal clause in ostensible substantival function lacks one of these particles (2.277, 5.73*a*, 95, 128*b*). The subordinating and substantival uses of verbs in construction with *na·hina·hi* P 'time' intergrade.

(5.128) Substantival temporal clauses (equational sentences)

(a)   *mani·=·'nina·hi wi·h=ašenoya·ni.* 'This is the time when I will be gone.' (O 59F)
         (|mani| 'this (inan.)'; |i·nina·hi| 'that time';
         |wi·h=| FUT, |ašeno-| AI 'be absent', |e·h=–ya·ni| 1s/AOR)

(b)   *i·nina·h=meko mehteno·hi we·ši·heči.* (O 2G)
      'It was only at that time that it (anim.) was painted.'
         (*i·nina·hi* 'that time'; *=meko* EMPH; *mehteno·hi* 'only';
         |we·ši·h-| TA 'paint', |IC–eči| X–3/CC)

A substantival conditional or purpose clause is most often the New term in an equational construction preceding the oblique participle with |ot-| 'because of {something}' that constitutes the Given term (5.129*ab*, 5.130*b*). Other uses are illustrated in (5.130*acd*; cf. A 178E).

(5.129) Substantival conditional clauses

(a) *e·h=či nawe maki=ke·h we či-a·ya čimohaki* (A 46A)

'To be precise, because she was my relative was the reason why I instructed her.'

(|či·nawe·m-| TA 'be related to', |e·h=–aki| 1s–3/AOR; |=ke·hi| 'moreover';

|oči| PV 'from {something}', |pwa·wi| PV 'not',

|ašihtaw-| TA 'make O2 for', |IC–ena·ni| 1s–2s/PPL(obl))

(b) *e·h=mawi-mi·ka·ti niči i·ni='pi we či-mayo·wa·či.* (O 18C)

'Because the others (obv.) were going off to war was the reason why they cried.'

(|mawi| PV 'go and', |mi·ka·ti·-| AI 'fight', |e·h=–niči| 3´/AOR;

i·ni 'that (inan.)'; |=ipi| HRSY;

|oči| PV 'from {something}', |mayo·-| AI 'cry', |IC–wa·či| 3p/PPL(obl))

(c) *e·h=ona·pe·miči-ye·toke*!? *no·hkomesena·na*!? (K-MIM 18; !?: AW)

'Could it possibly be that it's because our grandmother got married!!'

(|ona·pe·mi-| AI 'have or get a husband', |e·h=–či| 3s/AOR; *=ye·toke* 'perhaps';

no·hkomesena·na 'our (exc.) grandmother'; !? EN)

(5.130) Substantival purpose clauses

(a) *a·kwi=ke·h wi·h=owi·wiwa·či oči-taši·hkawa·wa·čini.* (A 80C)

'They aren't after them in order to marry them.'

(*a·kwi* 'not'; |=ke·hi| 'moreover'; |wi·h=| FUT,

|owi·wi-| AI 'have O2 as wife', |e·h=–wa·či| 3p/aor; |oči| PV 'from {something}',

|taši·hkaw-| TA 'be dealing with', |–a·wa·čini| 3p–3´/NEG)

(b) *wi·h=nahikwa·soyani=ma·hi we či-pwa·wi-ašihto·na·ni.* (A 3E)

'The reason I don't do it for you is so you'll learn how to sew.'

(|wi·h=| FUT, |nahikwa·so-| AI 'know how to sew', |e·h=–yani| 2s/AOR;

=ma·hi 'you see'; |oči| PV 'from {something}', |pwa·wi| PV 'not',

|ašihtaw-| 'make O2 for', |IC–ena·ni| 1s–2s/PPL(obl))

(c) *wi·h=nahi-ko·kenike·yani* (A 16C)

'(that's why I treated you like that:) so you'd learn to do the washing'

(|wi·h=| FUT, |nahi| PV 'know how to',

|ko·kenike·-| AI 'do washing' |e·h=–yani 2s/AOR)

(d) *wi·h=ka·škehto·nakwe maneto·waki* (O 136C)

'(that's precisely why we sing:) so that the manitous will hear us'

(|wi·h=| FUT, |ka·škehtaw-| TA 'hear', |e·h=–enakwe| 3,X–12/AOR;

maneto·waki 'manitous')

Complement Clauses

69.6. A complement clause may be either a verbal complement, syntactically dependent on a verb stem, or an oblique complement, linked specifically to a relative root (**§22.4**). Verbal complements most commonly follow their verb, while oblique complements almost always occur in the oblique position before the verb (**§65.5**).

A particle containing a relative root may also be in construction with an oblique complement clause (5.73*a*; A 178E).

69.7. Verbal complement clauses. Verbal complements are of many kinds, corresponding to the range of meanings of the verbs that take this construction. The verb of the complement clause is ordinarily in the aorist conjunct, with |wi·h=| FUT used for occurrences later than the time of the main verb or treated as such.

(5.131) Verbal complements with aorist conjunct

    (a)   *aškiča·h=ke·h netanwa·či e·h=ašihto·ya·ni* (A 22E)
        'even though at first I had been quite willing to make them'
        (|aškiča·hi| 'at first'; |=ke·hi| 'moreover'; |anwa·či·-| AI 'consent', |ne–∅| 1s/IND;
        |ašiht-| TI(2) 'make', |e·h=–o·ya·ni| 1s-0/AOR)

    (b)   *ki·ša·koči-sanakatwi e·h=nepo·hke·ki* (A 123C)
        'it's the hardest thing there is to have a death in the family'
        (*ki·ša·koči* PV 'extremely', |sanakat-| II 'be difficult', |–wi| 0s/IND;
        |nepo·hke·-| AI 'have a death in the family', |e·h=–eki| X/AOR)

    (c)   *nemi·ša·te·nemo e·h=te·pwe·htawiyani* 'I'm pleased that you heeded me' (A 184D)
        (|mi·ša·te·nemo-| AI 'be pleased', |ne–∅| 1s/IND;
        |te·pwe·htaw-| TA 'believe', |e·h=–iyani| 2s-1s/AOR)

(5.132) Verbal complements with future aorist conjunct

    (a)   *nekekye·htena·mite·he=meko wi·h=wi·čawi·ti·yakwe mahkwa·či.* (A 84C)
        'I'm very serious that we should have a quiet marriage together.'
        (|kekye·htena·mite·he·-| AI 'think seriously', |ne–∅| 1s/IND; *=meko* EMPH;
        |wi·h=| FUT, |wi·čawi·ti·-| AI 'be with each other', |e·h=–yakwe| 12/AOR,
        mahkwa·či 'quietly, calmly')

    (b)   *a·kwi .. menwikekini ma·nenwi wi·h=ona·pe·miye·kwe* (A 140E)
        'it's not a good thing for you (women) to marry many times'
        (*a·kwi* 'not'; |menwiken-| II 'be good', |–kini| 0/NEG; *ma·nenwi* 'many times';
        |wi·h=| FUT, |ona·pe·mi-| AI 'have or get a husband', |e·h=–ye·kwe| 2p/AOR)

69.8. Objective sentential complements. Transitive verbs of knowing, desiring, and perceiving and certain others are used with two kinds of verbal complements. The construction with the simpler syntax has the subordinate clause as a sort of object; these clauses ordinarily have an aorist or future aorist verb and most often follow the higher verb:

(5.133) Clause as object

    (a)   *e·h=kehke·netaki=mekoho e·h=a·hpawa·či.* (K-FC 625; tr. HP)
        "He knew that he was dreaming."
        (|kehke·net-| TI(1) 'know', |e·h=–aki| 3s-0/AOR; *=mekoho* EMPH;
        |a·hpawa·-| AI 'dream', |e·h=–či| 3s/AOR)

    (b)   *ke·senwi .. keno·ta·ke i·niya wi·čawiwaka e·h=pakamaki* (A 145E)
        'how many times did you hear that I hit my late wife?'
        (*ke·senwi* 'how many times';
        |no·ta·ke·-| AI 'hear what people say', |ke–∅| 2s/IND;
        i·niya 'that (anim. abs.)', *wi·čawiwaka* 'my spouse';
        |pakam-| TA 'hit', |e·h=–aki| 1s-3/AOR)

    (c)   *e·h=aka·wa·tama·ni wi·h=oni·ča·nesiya·ni* 'that I wanted to have children'
        (A 192B)
        (|aka·wa·t-| TI(1) 'desire', |e·h=–ama·ni| 1s-0/AOR;
        |wi·h=| FUT, |oni·ča·nesi-| AI 'have child', |e·h=–ya·ni| 1s/AOR)

Alternatively, such verbs may copy the subject or object of the verb in the subordinate clause as an object and take the clause as a complement that is not syntactically an object. If the argument copied to be the object of the higher verb is the same as its subject, the higher verb is a reflexive.

(5.134) Clause as complement with an argument copied as object

    (a)   *kekehke nemeko pi e·h=ketema kihehki* (A 135J)
        'it's known (about you) that he treats you cruelly'
        (|kehke·nem-| TA 'know', |ke–eko·pi| X–2s/IND;
        |ketema·kih-| TA 'ill-treat', |e·h=–ehki| 3–2s/AOR)

    (b)   *ketaka wa nene wi·h=anwa·či yani* 'I want you to consent' (A 147F)
        (|aka·wa·N-| TA 'desire', |ke–ene| 1s–2s/IND;
        |wi·h=| FUT, |anwa·či·-| AI 'consent', |e·h=–yani| 2s/AOR)

    (c)   *kočawino wi·h=pwa wi-wani·hka naci wi čawiwata e·h=pana pamači* (A 183C)
        'try not to forget that you have lost sight of your husband (through death)'
        (|kočawi-| AI 'try', |–no| 2s/IMP;
        |wi·h=| FUT, *pwa wi* PV 'not', |wani·hka·N-| TA 'forget', |e·h=–ači| 2s–3/AOR;
        wi čawiwata 'your spouse'; |pana·pam-| TA 'lose sight of', |e·h=–ači| 2s–3/AOR

    (d)   *ki·ši-kehke netisokini e·h=ačihkwiki* (A 103B)
        'after we (indef.) learn that we're pregnant'
        (*ki·ši* PV PERF, |kehke·netiso-| AI 'know about self', |IC–ekini| X/ITER;
        |ačihkwi-| AI 'be pregnant', |e·h=–eki| X/AOR)

With an inanimate subject in the lower clause the two constructions cannot be distinguished:

(5.135) Complement with inanimate subject

        e·h=ne tamowa či ne·kwa nahkwateniki e·h=anema·seniki. (K-FC 168-169; tr. HP)
        "they saw a cloud drifting away"
        ('They saw that a cloud was drifting away.' Or: 'They saw a cloud as it drifted away.')
        (|ne·t-| TI(1) 'see', |e·h=–amowa·či| 3p–0/AOR;
        ne·kwa nahkwateniki 'cloud (obv., inan. ppl.)';
        |anema·sen-| II 'be blown away', |e·h=–niki| 0´/AOR)

The essential interchangeability of these two kinds of complements and the similarity of the constructions in which they appear indicate that they are both varieties of a single type of objective sentential complement.

69.9. Oblique participles as objective complements. Participles headed by an oblique argument are syntactically nouns, but they are sometimes treated like objective sentential complements. In particular a non-oblique argument of the participle is sometimes copied as the object of the higher verb, in the same way as in (5.134).

(5.136) Oblique-headed participle as object (cf. 5.133)

    (a)   *mani·=·noki kekehke neta e·to·to na·ni.* (K-FC 1; tr. HP)
        "You now know what I am doing with you"
        (|mani| 'this (inan.)', |i·noki| 'now'; |kehke·net-| 'know', |ke–a| 2s–0/IND;
        |to·taw-| TA 'treat {so}', |IC–ena·ni| 1s–2s/PPL(obl))

    (b)   *kekehke neta pwa e·hpi·hči-=mekoho -we newe nehpenihenakwe* (K-FC 178)
        'you know how easily they have always killed us'
        (|kehke·net-| TI(1) 'know', |ke–a·pwa| 2p–0/IND;
        |ahpi·hči| PV 'to {such} a degree'; |CVCV+| RED2,
        |we·nehpenih-| TA 'kill easily', |IC–enakwe| 3–12/PPL(obl); =*mekoho* EMPH)

(c)   *ka·ta wani·hke·hke·ko=mani e·ši-kanakanawiya·ni* (K-FC 810)
      'do not forget the way I have been giving the speeches'
         (*ka·ta* 'don't'; |wani·hke·-| AI+O 'forget O2', |–hke·ko| 2p/PROH;
         mani 'this (inan.)';
         |iši| PV '{so}', |CVCV+| RED2, |kanawi-| AI 'speak', |IC–ya·ni| 1s/PPL(obl))

(5.137) Oblique-headed participle with argument copied as object (cf. 5.134)

(a)   *nekya a·kwi te·pahkwi-kehke·nemakini e·šina·kosikwe·ni.* (A 17A)
      'I never got to know what my mother looked like'
         (*nekya* 'my mother'; *a·kwi* 'not'; *te·pahkwi* PV 'attain', |kehke·nem-| TA 'know',
         |–akini| 1s–3/NEG; |išina·kosi-| AI 'look {so}', |IC–kwe·ni| 3s,0/INT.PPL(obl))

(b)   *kewani·hka·nene e·šina·kosiwane·ni* 'I forgot how you looked' (K-M 817o)
         (|wani·hka·N-| TA 'forget', |ke–ene| 1s–2s/IND;
         |išina·kosi-| 'appear {so}', |IC–wane·ni| 2s/INT.PPL(obl))

69.10. Complements of subjunctive verbs. When the higher verb is in the subjunctive mode, an objective sentential complement in construction with it is also in the subjunctive.
    (5.138) Subjunctive complement of a subjunctive

(a)   *ki·ši-kehke·netame·kwe ke·htena nahikeke* (O 88E)
      'when you (pl.) have come to know that it is truly right'
         (*ki·ši* PV PERF, |kehke·net-| TI(1) 'know', |–ame·kwe| 2p–0/SUBJ;
         ke·htena 'truly'; |nahiken-| II 'be proper', |–ke| 0/SUBJ)

(b)   *ki·ši-=ke·h -nahikwa·soyane kehke·nemeneke* (A 60C)
      'and when people know that you have learned to sew'
         (|ki·ši| PV PERF, |nahikwa·so-| AI 'know how to sew', |–yane| 2s/SUBJ;
         |=ke·hi| 'moreover'; |kehke·nem-| TA 'know', |–eneke| X–2s/SUBJ)

(c)   *ne·tamakwe a·ya·kwate·ke* 'if we saw that there were piles of it' (O 147A)
         (|ne·t-| TI(1) 'see', |–amakwe| 12–0/SUBJ;
         |CV+| RED1, |a·kwate·-| II 'lie piled', |–ke| 0/SUBJ)

Another example is in (A 77C). The subjunctive may also be used in the objective complement of a future verb (2.191).

69.11. Oblique complement clauses. Oblique complement clauses are the complements of the relative roots in a variety of verbs. With verbs of saying or thinking the complement may be in either direct or indirect discourse.

69.12. Direct discourse in oblique complements. Direct discourse complements are islands; they do not interact with the syntax or obviation structure of the framing sentence, and they may be nested one inside another. (In the editions they are set off by quotation marks.)
    (5.139) Oblique complement clause in direct discourse

(a)   *"ašihtawino," e·h=inaki nekya* (A 3C)
      'when [i.e., whenever] I asked my mother to do it for me'
      (*Lit.*: 'when I said to my mother, "Make it for me" ')
         (|ašihtaw-| TA+O 'make O2 for', |–ino| 2s–1s/IMP;
         |iN-| TA 'say {so} to', |e·h=aki| 1s–3/AOR; *nekya* 'my mother')

(b)   *"we·ne·ha=ye·toke i·na," e·h=išite·he·či.* (K-FC 10)
      ' "I wonder who that is," he thought.'
         (*we·ne·ha* 'who?'; *=ye·toke* 'it seems'; *i·na* 'that (anim.)';
         |išite·he·-| AI 'think {so}', |e·h=–či| 3s/AOR)

(c)   " 'wi·h=wa pamaki,' ketekwa," e·h=išiwe·či pašito·he·ha. (K-FC 26)
      ' " 'I'd like to see him,' he says about you," the old man declared.'
      (Or: ' "He says he'd like to see you," the old man declared.')
         (|wi·h=| FUT, |wa·pam-| TA 'see', |e·h=–aki| 1s–3/AOR;
         |iN-| TA 'say {so} to, of', |ke–ekwa| 3s–2s/IND;
         |išiwe·-| AI 'say {so} to X', |e·h=–či| 3s/AOR; pašito·he·ha 'old man')

In naming constructions having a name or other designation as the complement of a verb of naming, the older construction treats the complement as an island (6.3); the noun in such a complement is proximate even if the entity referred to is obviative in the framing sentence (5.140ab). In the younger construction, the complement is not treated as an island, and the noun is assimilated to an obviative in the framing sentence that has the same reference (5.140c).

(5.140) Obviation in naming constructions

(a)   'mahkwa' e nemečini 'the one (star, obv.) called "the Bear (prox.)" ' (X10-Met 62)
      (mahkwa 'bear'; |iN-| TA 'say {so} to, of', |IC–emečini| X–3´/PPL(OBVsg))

(b)   o·ni='pi okye·ni, awahi·ma išisoniwani atehkwaya. (K-M 28f)
      'And as for her mother, her name was Atehkwaya.'
      (o·ni 'and (then)'; =ipi HRSY; okye·ni 'his or her mother';
      awahi·ma (placeholder, anim.; §18.8);
      |išiso-| AI 'be named {so}', |–niwani| 3´s/IND; atehkwaya (name))

(c)   'pa·pahkwa·hani' e nemečini ki·šeso·ni (JB-LR 30)
      'the month (obv.) called "Papahkwâha (obv.)" '
      (pa·pahkwa·hani 'Bark-Works-Out month (obv.)'; e nemečini (see (a));
      ki·šeso·ni 'month (obv.)')

69.13. Indirect discourse in oblique complements. When the complement is in indirect discourse, the verb is in the same mode as the higher verb if this is independent indicative (5.141) or aorist (5.142). (The commas between the clauses, as given here, are not present in all the editions.)

(5.141) Oblique complement clause in indirect discourse (with independent indicative)

(a)   nekwi·yese·he·hi, netešiwe·pi·hka·no. (K-BHD 58)
      'I pretended to be a little boy.' (Cf: nekwi·yese·he·hi. 'I am a little boy.')
         (|kwi·yese·he·hi-| AI 'be a little boy', |ne–∅| 1s/IND;
         |išiwe·pi·hka·no-| AI 'pretend {so}', |ne–∅| 1s/IND)

(b)   nekano·nekwa=nekoti, netena·hpawa. (K-BHD2 9; tr. HP)
      "I dream't that some one spoke to me."
      (Cf. nekano·nekwa=nekoti. 'Someone spoke to me.')
         (|kano·N-| TA 'speak to', |ne–ekwa| 3s–1s/IND; nekoti 'one';
         |ina·hpawa·-| AI 'dream {so}', |ne–∅| 1s/IND)

(c)   ketepa·ši=ke·hi mani, ketena·čimo. (K-OBES 171)
      'You love me even now, you say.' (Cf.: ketepa·ši. 'You love me.')
         (|tepa·N-| TA 'love', |ke–i| 2s–1s/IND; |=ke·hi| 'moreover';
         mani 'as it is now'; |ina·čimo-| AI 'narrate {so}', |ke–∅| 2s/IND)

(d)   mehto·či='pi=mekoho pemwa·pi, ahpi·hčawiwa. (O 46C)
      'They say he acted just as if he were shot.'
         (mehto·či 'like, as if'; |=ipi| HRSY; =mekoho EMPH;
         |pemw-| TA 'shoot', |–a·pi| X–3/IND;
         |ahpi·hčawi-| AI 'act {so}', |–wa| 3s/IND)

(e) *mehto·či=mekoho ihkwe·wani wi·čihe·wa, išina·kwateniwi e·h=owi·kiči.* (K-FC 523)
'His place looked as if he had a woman living there with him.'
(*mehto·či* 'like, as if'; *=mekoho* EMPH; *ihkwe·wani* 'woman (obv.)';
|wi·čih-| TA 'live with', |–e·wa| 3s–3´/IND;
|išina·kwat-| 'appear {so}' II, |–niwi| 0´/IND; *e·h=owi·kiči* 'where he lived')

(f) *kašketiwa, ina·čimowa.* 'He's constipated, he says.' (K-SF 32)
(|kašketi-| AI 'be constipated', |–wa| 3s/IND,
|ina·čimo-| AI 'narrate {so}', |–wa| 3s/IND)

(g) *o·šisemiwa=ke·hi, ina·ko·me·wa i·nini ona·pe·mani.* (K-M 976k; tr. HP)
"By [classificatory] relationship she is the grandmother of her husband."
(|o·šisemi-| AI+O 'have O2 as grandchild', |–wa| 3s/IND; *=ke·hi* 'moreover';
|ina·ko·m-| TA 'be related {so} to', |-e·wa| 3s–3´/IND; *i·nini* 'that (obv.)';
ona·pe·mani 'her husband (obv.)')

(5.142) Oblique complement clause in indirect discourse (with aorist)

(a) *mehto·či=meko i·nahi e·h=ki·wi-taši-wi·če·we·či, e·h=ahpi·hčawiči.* (K-TYFB 49)
'He acted as if he were going around there with others.'
(*mehto·či* 'like'; *=meko* EMPH; *i·nahi* 'there'; *ki·wi* PV 'around',
taši PV '{somewhere}', |wi·če·we·-| AI 'accompany X', |e·h=–či| 3s/AOR;
|ahpi·hčawi-| AI 'act {so}', |e·h=–či| 3s/AOR)

(b) *kapo·twe·='ni wi·h=owi·weti·ya·ke, e·h=išiči.* (A 188A)
'Then after a time he said to me that we should get married.'
(|kapo·twe| 'at some point'; |i·ni| 'then';
|wi·h=| FUT, |owi·weti·-| AI 'marry each other', |–ya·ke| 1p/AOR;
|iN-| TA 'say {so} to', |e·h=–iči| 3s–1s/AOR)

If the higher verb is in the subjunctive, the verb in the indirect discourse complement may be aorist (5.143; A 146E, 179F) or subjunctive (5.144).

(5.143) Future aorist in oblique complement of subjunctive

(a) *wi·h=ni·miči, išite·he·te* 'if she wants to dance' (K-SD 51)
(|wi·h=| NEG, |ni·mi-| AI 'dance', |e·h=–či| 3s/AOR;
|išite·he·-| AI 'think {so}', |–te| 3s/SUBJ)

(5.144) Subjunctive in oblique complement of subjunctive

(a) *ki·hpene wi·hpe·mate ina·hpawa·yane* (A 169G)
'if you ever dream that you're sleeping with him'
(*ki·hpene* 'in the event that'; |wi·hpe·m-| TA 'sleep with', |–ate| 2s–3/SUBJ;
|ina·hpawa·-| AI 'dream {so}', |–yane| 2s/SUBJ)

(b) *wi·h=kya·take, išite·he·te* 'if he intends to keep it a secret' (O 134F; 2.193)
(|wi·h=| FUT, |kya·t-| TI(1) 'keep secret', |–ake| 3s–0/SUBJ;
|išite·he·-| AI 'think {so}', |–te| 3s/SUBJ)

The absence of the usual non-temporal meaning of the ostensible future subjunctive in cases like (5.144b; contrast 2.339) reflects the fact that the subjunctive inflection appears here by attraction to the mode of the higher verb. Attraction into the subjunctive mode is also found in locative oblique participles (2.192). Attraction into the iterative is also found (2.212).

INCORPORATED COMPLEMENTS

70. Some of the mechanisms of stem derivation that derive initials and secondary stems from simple verb stems may also be used to incorporate a complement clause into the higher verb that governs it. The verb of the complement clause may be a plain verb (with no preverb) or a compound verb (with one or more preverbs). When the clause is incorporated, the derived plain verb or head verb is a single phonological word with an internal syntactic boundary; it contains two predicates, each of which may take arguments, preverbs, and modifiers. The final in the derived verb is the MATRIX PREDICATE and is preceded by the SECONDARY PREDICATE. In the interlinears of the Autobiography and Owl texts the glosses of the two component predicates are separated by a right square bracket (]).

Other cases of a mismatch between verbal structure and sentence structure involve preverbs that modify not the head verb but a free particle or particle phrase (**§70.5**).

Causative Verbs

70.1. The syntax of causative verbs made with |-h| TA, |-ht| TI(2) (**§54.9**) shows that they have an incorporated secondary predicate that may retain some of the properties of a verb in a complement clause. (It is likely, however, that some verbs derived with this final pair are lexicalized and lack this property.) The examples in (5.145) are analyzed according to their ostensible component parts, with the internal syntax and corresponding semantics discussed further below.

(5.145) Preverb modifying secondary predicate of causative

    (a)   *ki·h=ne ya pi-neno te wiha wa kemešo·ha.* (K-SSP 120; tr. HP)

        "Now you may turn your grandfather back to a human."

            (|wi·h=| FUT, *ne ya pi* PV 'back, as before', |neno·te·wih-| 'cause to be a human', |ke–a·wa| 2s–3s/IND; *kemešo·ha* 'your grandfather')

    (b)   *e·h=asa mi–ke·hi -čahkwi-mehtose neniwiha·či* (K-TG 57)

        'and because he made their lives too short'

            (*asa mi* PV 'too much', *čahkwi* PV 'short',
            |mehtose·neniwih-| TA 'cause to live', |e·h=–a·či| 3s–3´/AOR; |=ke·hi| 'moreover')

    (c)   *i ni e·h=ki ši-menwi-pema tesihaki.* (K-Bene 97; tr. TB)

        "I have now brought her to good-health"

            (*i ni* 'now'; *ki ši* PV PERF, *menwi* PV 'well',
            |pema·tesih-| TA 'cause to live', |e·h=–aki| 1s–3/AOR)

In (5.145*a*) the compound stem *ne ya pi neno te wih-* TA 'turn O back into a human being' is derived from the compound stem *ne ya pi neno te wi-* AI 'become a human being again, resume human form' (*ne ya pi* PV 'back, as before' + *neno te wi-* AI 'be human') plus the suffix |-h| TA CAUS. The preverb pertains only to the incorporated secondary predicate and not to the matrix predicate or to the head verb as a whole. In (5.145*b*) the compound stem *asa mi čahkwi mehtose neniwih-* TA 'make O's life too short' (*lit.* 'make O live too short') is derived from *čahkwi mehtose neniwi-* AI 'live a short life' (*čahkwi* PV 'short' + *mehtose neniwi-* AI 'live'); *asa mi* PV 'too much' modifies *čahkwi* PV 'short'. In (5.145*c*) *ki ši* PV PERF is associated with the matrix predicate (cf. A 112B; O 83D, 120A), while *menwi* PV 'well' is part of the secondary predicate only, combining with |pema·tesi-| AI 'live' to make the incorporated compound stem *menwi pema·tesi-* AI 'be in good health'.

Verbs of Pretending

70.2. Verbs of pretending made from AI stems and TI(1) themes with |-ehka·no| AI or |-ehka·so| AI (**§51**) may be derived from compound stems; the preverb in the derived verb then modifies only the incorporated secondary predicate. The phonological word boundary between the preverb and the head verb is retained, but the suffix |-ehka·no|, |-ehka·so| AI 'pretend' has semantic scope over the entire compound (**§70**).

(5.146) Compound stem + |-ehka·no| AI 'pretend'

(a)   *e·h=kehči-a·hkwamatamo·hka·noči* 'He pretended to be very sick.' (K-FC 559)
(|kehči a·hkwamatamo·hka·no-| AI 'pretend to be very sick'
[← |kehči| PV 'greatly', |a·hkwamat-am-| TI(1)-O 'be sick' + |-w| FORMTV (4.8)
+ |-ehka·no| AI 'pretend'], |e·h=–či| 3s/AOR) (Cf. 4.258a.)

(b)   *e·h=nahi-ki·ke·no·hka·noči.* (K-Bene 1)
'he pretended to be accomplished at giving clan feasts'
(|nahi ki·ke·no·hka·no-| AI 'pretend to be adept at giving a clan feast'
[← |nahi| PV 'be adept at', |ki·ke·no-| AI 'give clan feast' + |-w| FORMTV (4.7)
+ |-ehka·no| AI 'pretend'], |e·h=–či| 3s/AOR)

(c)   *e·h=pwa·wi-=mekoho·-nenoše·hka·noči.* 'he pretended to be deaf' (K-SSP 14)
(|pwa·wi nenoše·hka·no-| AI 'pretend not to (be able to) hear'
[← |pwa·wi| PV 'not', |nenoše·-| AI 'hear, understand' + |-w| FORMTV (4.7)
+ |-ehka·no| AI 'pretend'], |e·h=–či| 3s/AOR; =mekoho EMPH)

In the compound verbs with the preverb |pwa·wi| PV 'not' (5.146c, 5.147c) the negation has scope only over the head verb of the underlying compound; native speakers deny that it can have scope over the secondary final and say that, for example, (5.146c) cannot mean 'he did not pretend to understand', a meaning that can only be expressed by a periphrastic construction.

When a verb of pretending is made from a transitive verb, the TI theme (cf. 4.8), appears as the incorporated secondary predicate (5.147). The object of the TI is ostensibly retained as a secondary object of the derived AI, but the possible use also with an animate object (5.147b) suggests that the derived AI is made on an objectless TI theme and as such takes an optional secondary object in the usual way (cf. 2.87-88; 4.267).

(5.147) Verbs of pretending with objects

(a)   *wi·na=·pi=meko neši-tepe·netamo·hka·sowa i·ni šo·niya·hi.*
'She made like she alone owned that money all by herself.' (X6-Marks 10)
(*wi·na* 3s/EMPH; |=ipi| HRSY; =meko EMPH;
|neši tepe·netamo·hka·so-| AI+O 'pretend to own O2 alone'
[← (|neši| PV 'alone', |tepe·net-| TI(1) 'own' + |-am| TI(1) th.) + |-w| FORMTV
+ |-ehka·so-| AI 'pretend'], |-wa| 3s/IND; *i·ni* 'that (inan.)'; *šo·niya·hi* 'money')

(b)   *e·h=we·pi-peškopeškonamo·hka·soči* 'he pretended to start to miss him' (SP-F2 41)
(|we·pi peškopeškonamo·hka·so-| AI+O 'pretend to start missing O2'
[← (|we·pi| PV 'begin', |CVCV+| RED2, |peškon-| TI(1) 'miss shooting'
+ |-am| TI(1) th.) + |-w| FORMTV + |-ehka·so| AI 'pretend'], |e·h=–či| 3s/AOR)

(c) *e·h=pwa·wi-nenamo·hka·noniči owi·yawi.* (X6-Marks 31)

'He (obv.) pretended not to recognize him (prox.).'

(|pwa·wi nenamo·hka·no-| AI+O 'pretend not to recognize O2'

[← (|pwa·wi| PV 'not', |nen-| TI(1) 'recognize' + |-am| TI(1) th.) + |-w| FORMTV

+ |-ehka·no| AI 'pretend'], |e·h=–niči| 3'/AOR; *owi·yawi* IN 'his body, himself, him')

(5.147b) and (5.147c) illustrate two ways of handling the case with a pronominal animate object; in (5.147c) the secondary object is marked overtly with *owi·yawi* IN 'his body' used as a pronoun (2.43).

Incorporation in Verbs of Perception and Narration

70.3. Verbs may be incorporated as secondary predicates before the finals |-i-te·he·| AI 'think' (cf. 4.7c, 4.8b), |-e·nem| TA, |-e·net| TI(1) 'think about' (4.90c), and, less freely, |-a·čim| TA 'tell about' (4.98b). The incorporated verbs attested in this construction are AI stems, TA direct themes (with |-a·| TA th. 1), or TI(1) themes (with |-am| TI(1) th.). The incorporated stem or theme adds |-w| FORMTV, the same formal process that derives initials which do not function as incorporated predicates (§34.3) from AI stems (4.7) and objectless TI(1) themes (4.8). Before |-w| FORMTV, |-a·| TA th. 1 is umlauted to -e·, making -e·w (cf. 4.7b), and |-am| TI(1) th. inserts |o·| (often heard as |o|), making -amo(·)w; the verb |pya·-| AI 'come' takes the shape |pye·te·-|, which is not otherwise found (149d, 150c). The object of an incorporated transitive verb becomes the primary object of a transitive matrix verb or the secondary object of an intransitive matrix verb; if the object is animate the incorporated verb may be a TA or a TI.

(5.148) Incorporated complement + |-i-te·he·| AI 'think'

(a) *mi·hkemehkwe·we·wite·he·wa* (K-Med 58; cf. K-M 413i, S-TO 15)

'he is thinking about courting women'

(← |mi·hkemehkwe·we·w-| 'that S courts women'

[← |mi·hkemehkwe·we·-| AI 'court women' + |-w| FORMTV]

+ |-i-te·he·| AI 'think', |–wa| 3s/IND)

(b) *e·h=tepowe·wite·he·či* "[he] thought of having a council" (K-M 9a; tr. HP)

(← |tepowe·w-| 'that S has a council'

[← |tepowe·-| AI 'have a council' + |-w| FORMTV] + |-i-te·he·| AI 'think',

|e·h=–či| 3s/AOR)

(c) *e·h=ki·ši-=meko -ne·se·wite·he·niči* (K-B 228; tr. HP)

"[He (obv.)] already thought he was well."

(*ki·ši* PV PERF; *=meko* EMPH; |ne·se·w-| 'that S lives on'

[← |ne·se·-| AI 'live on' + FORMTV] + |-i-te·he·| AI 'think', |e·h=–niči|)

(d) *mehkamo·wite·he·wa* 'he thought he found it' (K-Words 17; AW)

(← |mehkamo·w-| 'that S finds O'

[← |mehk-| TI(1) 'find' + |-am| TI(1) th. + |-w| FORMTV]

+ |-i-te·he·| AI 'think', |–wa| 3s/IND)

(e) *tepe·netamo·wite·he·wa ki·yawi.* 'He thinks he owns you.' (K-M 1057b)

("he . . . thinks he owns your life"; tr. HP)

(← |tepe·netamo·w-| 'that S owns O'

[← |tepe·net-| TI(1) 'own' + |-am| TI(1) th. + |-w| FORMTV]

+ |-i-te·he·| AI 'think', |–wa| 3s/IND; *ki·yawi* 'yourself, you (sg., inan.)')

(f)   *meso·te·we=mekoho tepe·netamo·wite·he·sa owiye·hani.* (K-FC 677, AW; tr. HP)
       "He would feel as if he owned all the living things."
           (*meso·te·we* 'universally'; *=mekoho* EMPH;
           |tepe·netamo·w-| 'that S owns O' [as in 5.148*e*]
           + |-*i*-te·he·| AI 'think', |–sa| 3s/POT; *owiye·hani* 'creatures (obv. sg.)')

(g)   *oškinawe·haki mi·hkeme·wite·ha·čiki* (K-M 179a)
       'the young men who thought they were courting her'
           (*oškinawe·haki* 'young men'; |mi·hkeme·w-| 'that S courts O'
           [← mi·hkem-| TA 'court' + |-a·| TA th. 1 + |-w| FORMTV] + |-*i*-te·he·| AI 'think',
           |IC–čiki| 3/PPL(ANpl))

(5.149) Incorporated complement + |-e·nem| TA 'think about, consider' (4.90*c*)

(a)   *kese·kesiwe·nemene=meko.* (K-WYB 50; tr. TB)
       "I thought that you were indeed frightened."
           (← |se·kesiw-| 'that O is frightened' [← |se·kesi-| AI 'be frightened' +
           |-w| FORMTV] + |-e·nem| TA 'think about', |ke–ene| 1s–2s/IND; *=meko* EMPH)

(b)   *e·h=sese·sapene·we·nemaki* (K-WYB; tr. TB)
       "because I thought they were hurriedly getting hungry"
           (← |sese·sapene·w-| [|sese·sapene·-| AI 'get hungry rapidly' + |-w| FORMTV]
           + |-e·nem| TA 'think about', |e·h–=aki| 1s–3/AOR)

(c)   *kapo·twe=meko kenešiwana·čihčike·we·nemene.* (K-OMSP 17)
       'I'm beginning to think that you've wrecked things (i.e., ruined your blessing).'
           (*kapo·twe* 'at some point'; *=meko* EMPH;
           |nešiwana·čihčike·w-| 'that O wrecks things'
           [← |nešiwana·čihčike·-| AI 'ruin things, wreck things, do some wrecking'
           (← |nešiwana·čiht-| TI(2) 'ruin, wreck' + |-ike·| DETRANS [§53.2])
           + |-w| FORMTV] + |-e·nem| TA 'think about', |ke–ene| 1s–2s/IND)

(d)   *e·h=pye·te·we·nema·či=meko owiye·hani* (K-HS 13)
       'he was certain whoever it was was coming (to him)'
           (← |pye·te·w-| 'that O comes'
           [← |pya·-| AI 'come' (irreg.) + |-w| FORMTV] + |-e·nem| TA 'think about',
           |e·h–=a·či| 3s–3′/IND; *=meko* EMPH; *owiye·hani* 'someone (obv.)')

(e)   *ketanehkawe·we·nemekowa·toke owiye·ha* (K-W 104, AW; tr. HP)
       "Some one must think he is acquainted with you [pl.]"
           (|anehkawe·w-| 'that S is acquainted with O'
           [← |anehkaw-| TA 'be acquainted with' + |-a·| TA th. 1 + |-w| FORMTV]
           + |-e·nem| TA 'think about', |ke–ekowa·toke| 3s–2p/DUB; *owiye·ha* 'someone')

When compound verbs are incorporated, any preverb that becomes part of the derived verb modifies only the incorporated secondary predicate. (There are superficially similar cases in which it is not a compound verb that is incorporated, and a preverb occurring with the derived stem, not being part of the incorporated verb, modifies only the matrix verb [5.148*c*].)

(5.150) Incorporated compound verb + |-*i*-te·he·| AI 'think', |-e·nem| TA 'think about'

(a)   *a·wasi·me·hi wi·h=ahpi·hči-kehke·netamowite·he·wa owiye·ha* (K-B 148; tr. HP)
       "some one will think that he knows more about it"
           (*a·wasi·me·hi* 'more'; |wi·h=| FUT, |ahpi·hči| PA 'to {such} a degree',
           |kehke·netamo·w-| 'that S knows O'

[← |kehke·net-| TI(1) 'know' + |-am| TI(1) th. + |-w| FORMTV]

+ |-*i*-te·he·| AI 'think', |–wa| 3s/IND; *owiye·ha* 'someone')

(Cf. *kehke·netamwa* 'he knows it'.)

(b) *ne·hi-mi·hkeče·wi·we·nema·wate·na* (K-Fish 165)

'whoever you consider to be a good worker'

(|nahi mi·hkeče·wi·we·nem-| TA 'consider O to be a good worker'

[← |nahi mi·hkeče·wi·-| AI 'be a good worker', *lit.* 'know how to work'

(← *nahi* PV 'be adept at, know how to', |mi·hkeče·wi·-| AI 'work')

+ |-w| FORMTV + |-e·nem| TA 'think about'], |IC–a·wate·na| 2s–3/INT.PPL(ANsg)

(c) *ke·tawi-pye·te·we·nemačini* 'any time you think he's about to come back' (K-MS 10)

(|katawi pye·te·we·nem-| TA 'think that O is about to come back'

[|katawi pya·-| AI 'almost come' (← *katawi* PV 'almost', |pya·-| AI 'come')

+ |-w| FORMTV (cf. 5.149*d*) + |-e·nem| TA 'think about'], |IC–ačini| 2s–3/ITER)

(d) *o·ni ki·ši-ki·ke·nowe·nemaki* (K-B 195; an account of a dream experience)

'and then, when they were finished with the clan feast, as I imagined'

(*o·ni* 'and then'; |ki·ši ki·ke·nowe·nem-| TA 'think O to be finished celebrating c. f.'

[← |ki·ši ki·ke·no-| AI 'finish celebrating c. f.' (← *ki·ši* PV PERF, |ki·ke·no-| AI

'celebrate c. f.') + |-w| FORMTV + |-e·nem| TA 'think about'], |IC–aki| 1s–3/CC)

(e) *e·h=pwa·wi-=meko·-kehke·netamo·we·nema·či.* (K-FC 282; tr. HP)

"and [she] knew that he was out of his mind."

(← *pwa·wi-kehke·netamo·w-* 'that O is out of his mind'

[← *pwa·wi* PV 'not' + |kehke·net-| TI(1)-O 'know' + |-am| TI(1) th. + |-w| FORMTV]

+ |-e·nem| TA 'think about', |e·h=–a·či| 3s–3′/AOR; =*meko* EMPH)

(f) *pwa·wi-=ke·hi·-nenwamatamo·we·nemiye·kani.* (K-M 115m; tr. EK)

"It seems like you think he didn't feel it."

(*pwa·wi-nenwamatamo·w-* 'that O does not feel it'

[← *pwa·wi* PV 'not' + |nenwamat-| TI(1) 'feel' + |-am| TI(1) th. + |-w| FORMTV]

+ |-e·nem| TA 'think about', |–iye·kani| 2s–3/PROH; =*ke·hi* 'moreover')

A clausal particle (§67.2) or an oblique complement may also be associated only with the secondary predicate, as if an entire sentence was incorporated into the matrix predicate.

(5.151) Incorporated complement with clausal particle or oblique

(a) *masa·či e·h=konakwi·we·netaki metemo·ka owi·ya·wa·wi.* (K-Wap 155; tr. TB)

"the old lady thought that they barely passed through with their lives"

(*masa·či* 'barely'; |konakwi·we·net-| TI(1) 'think inan. O gets through'

[← |konakwi·-| AI 'get through (danger)' + |-w| FORMTV + |-e·net| TI(1) 'consider'],

|e·h=–aki| 3s–0/AOR; *metemo·ka* 'old woman'; *owi·ya·wa·wi* 'themselves')

(b) *a·kwi=me·kwe·he še·ški owi·hka·neti·we·nemena·kwini.* (K-M 1139j; tr. HP)

"I do not think that you two are thought of as being only friends."

(*a·kwi* 'not; =*me·kwe·he* 'I think'; *še·ški* 'only';

|owi·hka·neti·we·nem-| TA 'consider O to be friends'

[← owi·hka·neti·- AI 'be friends' + |-w| FORMTV + |-e·nem| TA 'consider'],

|–enakwini| X–12/NEG)

(c) *nekotahi ·= 'niye·ka oto·te·weniwa·čima·pi.* (K-B 225; tr. HP)
  "some where they have a town, so it is said of them"
  (|nekotahi| 'somewhere'; |i·niye·ka| 'those (anim., abs.)';
  |oto·te·weniwa·čim-| TA 'report O to have a town ({somewhere})'
  [← |oto·te·weni-| AI 'have a town ({somewhere})' + |-w| FORMTV
  + |-a·čim| TA 'tell about'], |-a·pi| X–3/IND)

In (5.151*a*) the clausal free particle *masa·či* 'barely' modifies only the incorporated secondary predicate |konakwi·-| AI 'get through'. In (5.151*b*) the clausal free particle *še·ški* 'only, as the only thing' modifies the incorporated secondary predicate |owi·hka·neti·-| AI 'be friends (with each other)'. In (5.151*c*) the locative particle *nekotahi* 'somewhere' is the oblique complement of the incorporated secondary predicate |oto·te·weni-| AI 'have a town ({somewhere})'; it refers to where the town was and not to where the report was made.

Initials Functioning as Incorporated Verbs

70.4. In some cases an ostensibly underived initial is associated with a preverb or free particle that does not go with the verb as a whole. Initials with this syntax can be taken as incorporated secondary predicates derived from intransitive verb stems by the deletion of an abstract final.

(5.152) Initial as incorporated verb

(a) *i·ni e·h=pye·či-ni·se·netama·ni ni·yawi.* (K-B 192)
  'Then I imagined myself coming down.'
  (*i·ni* 'then'; |pye·či·ni·se·net-| TI(1) 'think inan. O comes down'
  [← |pye·či| PV 'coming', |ni·se·net-| TI 'think inan. O descends'
  (← |ni·s-| 'down, descend, lower' [as if |ni·si·-| AI 'get down, descend'],
  |-e·net| TI(1) 'consider')], |e·h=—ama·ni| 1s–0/AOR; *ni·yawi* 'myself (inan.)')

(b) *i·nah=mekoho taši-ni·šwa·čimowa ošise·hani* (O 68D)
  'she told of being with her uncle in that same place'
  (*i·nahi* 'there'; *=mekoho* EMPH;
  |taši·ni·šwa·čimo-| AI 'report being with O2 {somewhere}'
  [← *taši* PV '{somewhere}', |ni·šwa·čimo-| AI 'report being with O2'
  (← |ni·šw-| 'two together' [as if |ni·ši-| AI 'be two, be together'] + |-a·čimo| AI
  'report (one's experiences)')], |-wa| 3s/IND; *ošise·hani* 'her uncle (obv.)')

(c) *manahka netana·čimo we·či-na·wahkwe·ki.* (SP-MortA 10; tr. HP)
  "Now I will tell the experience I had over south [=down south]."
  (*manahka* 'away'; |tana·čimo-| AI 'tell about one's experiences {somewhere}'
  [← |taN-| '{somewhere}' (as if |tanesi-| AI 'be {somewhere}')
  + |-a·čimo| AI 'tell about one's experiences'], |ne–0| 1s/IND;
  we·či-na·wahkwe·ki 'in the south')

(d) *i·nahi ni·či-neniwaki tana·čime·waki aka·sani.* (SP-MortA 10)
  'The other men I was with talked about a Kaw (being) there.'
  (*i·nahi* 'there'; *ni·či-neniwaki* 'my fellow men';
  |tana·čim-| TA 'talk about O1 (being) {somewhere}'
  [← |taN-| '{somewhere}' (as if |tanesi-| AI 'be {somewhere}')
  + |-a·čim| TA 'tell about'], |-e·waki| 3p–3´/IND; *aka·sani* 'Kaw (obv.)')

In (5.152*a*) the initial |ni·s-| 'down, descend, lower' functions as if it were the verb |ni·si·-| AI 'get down, descend' (← |ni·s-| 'down' + |-i·| AI ABSTR) in a compound stem with the preverb |pye·či| 'come, hither' that is incorporated as a secondary predicate. In (5.152*b*) the initial |ni·šw-| (usually 'two together, as a pair') has the meaning and syntax of the verb |ni·ši-| AI 'be two, be together', which is commonly used with a conjoined nominal and pronominal subject (cf. 2.66). Without the matrix verb the sentence would be: *i·nah=mekoho taši-ni·šiwaki ošise·hani.* 'She was with her uncle in that same place.' (*ni·šiwaki* 'they are two': |ni·ši-| AI 'be two', |–waki| 3p/IND.) With the incorporation as a secondary predicate, the preverb *taši* and its locative oblique complement *i·nahi* 'there' remain associated with this component alone, and the conjoined nominal subject *ošise·hani* 'her uncle' is left (as an adjunct in the surface syntax) with a syntactic relation only to the initial, which lacks any other characteristics of a verb. In (5.152*c*) 'down south' is not where the narration takes place but where the events being narrated took place. In effect, the initial |taN-| '{somewhere}' (**§22.4(e)**) functions like the verb |tanesi-| AI 'be {somewhere}' (← |taN-| '{somewhere}' + |-esi| AI ABSTR) and retains its (discontinuous) oblique locative complement when incorporated as a secondary predicate.

Preverbs Modifying Particles

70.5. Similar to incorporated complements in having a mismatch between the formal and semantic structure of verb stems are cases in which a preverb modifies not the head verb of the stem it is part of but rather a free particle or particle phrase.

(5.153) Preverb modifying free particle or particle phrase

(a) *nema·wači-=mekoho ahkiki -tane·netiso·hi.* (K-FC 387; tr. TB)
"I consider myself to be the lowest."
(*ma·wači* PV 'most of all', *=mekoho* EMPH; *ahkiki* 'down below'; |tane·netiso·hi-| AI 'consider self to be {somewhere} (dim.)', |ne–∅| 1s/IND)

(b) *e·h=ki·ša·koči-=či·h=meko na·hka na·wi-=meko -nenoswahkiwe -šekišiki.* (K-B 4)
'She found that she was again lying in the very center of a herd of buffalo.'
(*ki·ša·koči* PV 'as much as possible'; |=či·hi| 'it was discovered'; *=meko* EMPH; *na·hka* 'again'; *na·wi* PP 'in the middle', *nenoswahkiwe* ECM 'buffalo-herd'; |šekišin-| AI 'lie {somewhere}', |e·h=–ki| 3s/AOR)

In (5.153*a*) *ma·wači* PV 'gather (and); most of all', which is used productively to make superlatives, is the preverb in a compound stem |ma·wači tane·netiso-| AI, as shown by the fact that the inflectional prefix |ne-| 1 is added to it. Although formally a preverb, however, *ma·wači* does not modify the head verb but rather the included free locative particle |ahkiki| 'down below'. Similarly, in (5.153*b*) *ki·ša·koči* PV 'as much as possible' is formally the preverb in a compound stem |ki·ša·koči šekišin-|, but it does not modify the head verb |šekišin-| AI 'lie {somewhere}', and the compound verb is, in fact, meaningless taken by itself. Rather *ki·ša·koči-* PV modifies the preparticle *na·wi* 'in the middle' in the included locative oblique phrase *na·wi-nenoswahkiwe* 'in the middle of a buffalo herd'.

DISCONTINUOUS CONSTITUENTS

71. A pervasive feature of Meskwaki discourse of all varieties and levels of formality is the presence of compounds, modules, and other multi-word constituent parts of sentences that are discontinuous. In a discontinuous constituent words that are component parts of it are separated by words that are not part of it. Discontinuous constituents are not aberrant or imperfect realizations of constituents with contiguous components. They have an independent status in the organization of Meskwaki discourse, with important functions in the integration of sentences.

In the examples in this section the components of a discontinuous constituent are underlined and those of a second discontinuous constituent have double underlining. There are sometimes corresponding underlines in the translation.

Discontinuous Compound Nouns

71.1. A prenoun may be separated from its head noun by a phrase enclitic (**§68.1**; 5.154*a*) or by one or more sentence enclitics (**§68.2**; 5.154*bcd*), or by both (5.154*e*). A phrase enclitic in this position is part of the noun phrase and modifies either the prenoun or the compound as a whole. A sentence enclitic occurring in the middle of a compound noun, however, is not a constituent of the noun phrase.

(5.154) Discontinuous compound nouns

(a)   *šewe·na ni·ka·ni-=meko -mami·ši·hani i·ni e·h=ina·wa·či.* (K-MP3 41)
       'But they (the ceremonial attendants) had to tell the leading attendant about it.'
           (*šewe·na* 'but'; *ni·ka·ni* PN 'leading', *mami·ši·hani* 'attendant (obv.)';
           =*meko* EMPH; *i·ni* 'that (inan.)'; |iN-| TA 'say {so} to', |e·h=-a·wa·či| 3p–3´/AOR)

(b)   *owi·či-=či·h -nenoso·hi ni·šwi e·h=pya·niči, ihkwe·wahi.* (K-KN 1)
       'And here he [(a buffalo)] saw two other buffalos coming towards him, females.'
           (|-i·či| PN 'fellow', *nenoso·hi* 'buffalos (obv.)', |o–∅| 3s (possessor; 3.19, 49);
           |=či·hi| 'it was discovered' [5.122c]; *ni·šwi* 'two';
           |pya·-| AI 'come', |e·h=-niči| 3´/AOR; *ihkwe·wahi* 'women (obv.)')

(c)   *ki·či-=mata -neni·na·naki i·nah=awiwa·tehe* (K-PKM 4)
       'If, instead, the other men (those of our enemy) had been there'
           (|-i·či| PN 'fellow', |neniw-| 'man', |ke–ena·naki| 12(ANpl);
           =*mata* 'alternatively' [5.122o]; *i·nahi* 'there';
           |awi-| AI 'be {somewhere}', |–wa·tehe| 3p/SUBJ.PRET)

(d)   *ni·ka·ni-=ke·hi=·pi -mami·ši·ha ki·wi-ni·ka·ni·ta ...* (K-MP4 8)
       'And they say the leading attendant was the one who went around in the lead, ...'
           (*ni·ka·ni* PN 'leading', *mami·ši·ha* 'attendant'; |=ke·hi| 'moreover'; |=ipi| HRSY;
           |ki·wi| PV 'around', |ni·ka·ni·-| AI 'lead', |IC–ta| 3/PPL(ANsg))

(e)   *owi·či-=ke·h=wi·na=meko -mehtose·neniwahi i·nihi e·taši-ketemaha·čihi.* (X6-MF 3)
       'And what's more his own fellow people were the ones he was persecuting.'
           (|-i·či| PN 'fellow', *mehtose·neniwahi* 'people (obv.)', |o–∅| 3s (possessor);
           |=ke·hi| 'moreover' [5.122j]; |=wi·na| 'but' [5.122v, 5.123c];
           |=meko| EMPH [5.121d]; *i·nihi* 'those (obv.)';
           |taši| PV 'be engaged in', |ketemah-| TA 'abuse', |IC–a·čihi| 3–3´/PPL(OBVpl))

Discontinuous Compound Verbs

71.2. A preverb may be separated from its head verb not only by one or more enclitics (5.155), but also by independent words (5.81; 5.156), including participles (5.156*d*), and even by subordinate clauses (5.158). Particles, pronouns, nouns, and participles that are the oblique complements of the head verb often occur immediately before it after any preverbs (5.157). If there is more than one preverb it is most commonly just the first one that is separated from the rest of the compound verb stem, but especially in certain idioms two preverbs may be separated together (5.122*r*(2)), and a compound stem sometimes occurs in more than two discontinuous pieces (5.158*e*).

(5.155) Discontinuous compound verbs with included enclitics

(a) *ki ši-=meko -ki ke nokini* 'after the clan-feast was over' (O 12H)
(*ki ši* PV PERF, |ki·ke·no-| AI 'hold a clan feast', |IC–kini| X/ITER; *=meko* EMPH)

(b) *e h=ča ki-=meko -ne se ha či* 'he would heal all of them' (O 43D)
(*ča ki* PV 'all', |ne·se·h-| TA 'cure', |e·h=–a·či| 3s–3´/AOR; *=meko* EMPH)

(c) *ki h=pye či-=ča h=-natomipwa* 'so, you must come to call me' (O 159G)
(|wi·h=| FUT, *pye či* PV 'coming', |natom-| TA 'call for', |ke–ipwa| 2p–1s/IND;
|=ča·hi| 'so')

(d) *ki h=kekeni-=ča h=meko -ona pe mi* 'so, you'd better marry him quickly' (A 80D)
(|wi·h=| FUT, *kekeni* PV 'quickly',
|ona·pe·mi-| AI+O 'have O2 as husband', |ke–∅| 2s/IND; |=ča·hi| 'so'; *=meko* EMPH)

(5.156) Discontinuous compound verbs with included non-enclitic words

(a) *nepye či- keta nesa -wa pama pena.* (Jonas Poweshiek, sample sentences, 1914)
'We have come to look at your daughter.'
(*pye či* PV 'coming', |wa·pam-| TA 'look at', |ne–a·pena| 1p–3/IND;
keta nesa 'your daughter')

(b) *wi h=pwa wi- aša hahi -kehke nemekoči* (Jones 1907:224.8)
'so that the Siouxs would not know about her'
(|wi·h=| FUT, *pwa wi* PV 'not', |kehke·nem-| TA 'know', |e·h=–ekoči| 3´–3s/AOR;
aša hahi 'Siouxs (obv. pl.)')

(c) *wi h=anemi-=mekoho ma haki neniwaki -ma mi wepye namo ki owi šasowenwa wi.*
"Let the men here, wipe off their sweat." (K-FC 305; tr. HP)
(|wi·h=| FUT, *anemi* PV 'go on', |CV+| RED1,
|mi·wepye·n-| TI(1) 'wipe off (liquid)', |–amo·ki| IND; *=mekoho* EMPH;
ma haki 'these (anim.)', *neniwaki* 'men'; *owi šasowenwa wi* 'their sweat')

(d) *e h=ki ši-=ʼyo=ke hi=ʼpi me nwe nema čini -mi hkemekoči.* (K-SSP 44; tr HP)
"As the man whom she was stuck on was already courting her."
(*ki ši* PV PERF, |mi·hkem-| TA 'court', |e·h=–ekoči| 3´–3s/AOR;
|=iyo=ke·hi| [5.123*e*]; |=ipi| HRSY;
|menwe·nem-| TA 'like', |IC–a·čini| 3–3´/PPL(OBVsg))

(e) *wi h=ča ki-=wi na neto te maki -owi wiwane ni=ʼpi, ...* (K-MMDR 10)
'It is said that, if you want to marry all my sisters, ...'
(|wi·h=| FUT, *ča ki* PV 'all', |owi·wi-| AI+O 'have O2 as wife', |IC–wane·ni|
2s/CH.INT; |=ipi| HRSY; *=wi na* 'but'; *neto te maki* 'my same-sex siblings')

(5.157) Discontinuous compound verbs with included oblique complements

(a) *ki·ši- mehči·ki -ahte·ki* "after it settled down on the ground" (K-ECRP 100; tr. TB)
(*ki·ši* PV PERF, |ahte·-| II 'be {somewhere}', |IC–ki| 0/CC;
mehči·ki 'down on the ground')

(b) *wi·h=pwa·wi- nepo·pi ahki·ki -pakika·niki* (K-CWB 52)
'so that soup would not drip on the ground'
(|wi·h=|FUT, *pwa·wi* PV 'not', |pakika·-| II 'drip {somewhere}', |e·h=–niki| 0′/AOR;
nepo·pi 'soup'; *ahki·ki* 'on the ground')

(c) *e·h=pwa·wi-=ke·hi -nahi-anwa·či- e·h=owi·kiwa·či -taši-wi·seniči.*
(K-MESB 76; tr. TB) "He seldom ate at their own house."
(*pwa·wi* PV 'not', *nahi* PV 'be given to', *anwa·či* PV '[not] as much as before',
taši PV '{somewhere}', |wi·seni-| AI 'eat', |e·h=–či| 3s/AOR;
|=ke·hi| 'moreover';
|owi·ki-| AI 'dwell {somewhere}', |e·h=–wa·či| 3p/PPL(loc.obl))

(5.158) Discontinuous compound verbs with included subordinate clauses

(a) *anemi-=ne·h=ni·na ahpene·či ke·ko·hi e·nena·nini -te·pwe·htawiyane* (K-M 26j)
'if <u>you</u> always believe <u>me</u> every time I tell you something'
("if you believe what I am going to tell you from time to time"; tr. HP)
(*anemi* PV 'go on', |te·pwe·htaw-| TA 'believe', |–iyane| 2s–1s/SUBJ;
|=ne·hi| 'too'; *ni·na* 1s/EMPH; *ahpene·či* 'every time';
ke·ko·hi 'anything'; |iN-| TA 'say {so} to', |IC–ena·nini| 1s–2s/ITER)

(b) *i·ni we·či- ahpene·či ne·woti·wa·čini -mi·ka·ti·wa·či* (O 18G)
'that was the reason they always made war every time they encountered each other'
(*i·ni* 'that (inan.)';
|o·či| PV 'from {something}', |mi·ka·ti·-| AI 'fight', |IC–wa·či| 3p/PPL(obl);
ahpene·či 'every time'; |ne·woti·-| AI 'see each other', |IC–wa·čini| 3p/ITER)

(c) *e·h=pwa·wi- nana·ši nehki pe·mi-mahkate·wi·či -ne·wa·či kotakahi* (K-WD 127)
'he never saw any others for as long as he was fasting'
(*pwa·wi* PV 'not', *nana·ši* '[not] ever', |ne·w-| TA 'see', |e·h=–a·či| 3s–3′/AOR;
kotakahi 'others (obv.)'; *nehki* 'for {so} long', |pemi| PV 'along',
|mahkate·wi·-| AI 'fast', |IC–či| 3s/PPL(obl))

(d) *pwa·wi-='h=we·na ka·hkami, i·ni išite·he·ya·ne, i·ni -išahišawihka·ha* (K-FC 633)
'if I had wanted to do that, I would not have failed to do that right away each time'
(*pwa·wi* PV 'not', |CVCV+| RED2, |išawi-| AI 'do {so}', |–hka·ha| 1s/POT;
|=ihi| NEG; |=we·na| 'after all'; *ka·hkami* 'from the start';
i·ni 'that (inan.)' (2x); |išite·he·-| AI 'think {so}', |–ya·ne| 1s/SUBJ)

(e) *we·či- e·h=apeno·hiki -nawači-=mekoho nye·wokoni -mahkate·wi·ki* (K-Auto 46)
'the reason why one first fasts for four days when one is a child'
(|o·či| PV 'from {something}', *nawači* PV 'first',
|mahkate·wi·-| AI 'fast', |IC–ki| X/PPL(obl); =*mekoho* EMPH;
nye·wokoni 'for four days'; |apeno·hi-| AI 'be a child', |e·h=–ki| X/AOR)

Discontinuous Noun Phrases

71.3. Words constituting a single complex noun phrase are very commonly discontinuous. A determiner (5.159), quantifier (5.162), possessor noun phrase (5.163), nominal adjunct (5.164, 172*d*), or noun or pronoun in apposition (5.165) may be separated from the noun it is in construction with by one or more words that are not part of the complex noun phrase. Most commonly the parts of a discontinuous noun phrase are separated by a verb of which the noun phrase is an argument, or by a particle containing a relative root of which it is the oblique complement (5.159*fg*). In some cases, however, what is included between the separated parts of a noun phrase is an adnominal or clausal particle (5.170*ab*) or a noun phrase (5.170*cde*); in (5.170*fg*) postposed and recategorized preverbs serve as pegs for discontinuous noun phrases. Conjoined nouns may sometimes be discontinuous (A 51C), but the second term of such constructions can also be taken as a gapped sentence (**§66.3**).

A determiner in a discontinuous noun phrase is always the first component (5.159), but a quantifier or possessor may occur either earlier or later in the sentence than the noun it is separated from (5.162, 163). If there are two discontinuous noun phrases with separate syntactic links to the same verb, one seems always to be completely inside the other, so that both first parts are in one order and both second parts are in the opposite order (5.168). Two discontinuous noun phrases that are part of the same module, however, such as possessor and possessed noun phrases that together form a possessive noun phrase, may be interwoven, with the first and second parts of each in the same order (5.169); interwoven noun phrases may also be interrupted by material alien to both (5.169*b*).

A demonstrative pronoun may be repeated before the separated noun (5.160), or repeated without a noun (5.161); these are not repairs or expansions, and native speakers translate these constructions as if the demonstrative occurred only once.

One or both of the noun phrases in an equational sentence may be discontinuous (5.171-172), particularly if one or both include participles. The Given term occurs inside the New term.

In cases where word order has a function, the position of the first component of a discontinuous noun phrase always counts as the functional position of the phrase. For example, if a discontinuous noun phrase straddles a verb, it functions as if the entire noun phrase were before the verb, in the Focus position. And if both terms of an equational sentence are discontinuous, the first part of the Given term occurs between the two parts of the New term, where a one-word Given term would occur, with the rest of the Given term following the second part of the New term (5.172).

It is common for the second part of a discontinuous noun phrase to occur at the end of its clause, and for the first part to occur at the beginning of the clause, either as the first word or following the first word and any enclitics for which it serves as host. In such cases a discontinuous phrase furnishes the clause as a whole with a unifying structural framework. A less common pattern is in (5.159j).

    (5.159) Discontinuous noun phrase: determiner and noun

        (a)   *ma·haki menwihčike·waki wa·koše·haki* (K-FC 588; tr. HP)
                "<u>These Foxes</u> have done very good"
                    (*ma·haki* 'these'; |menwihčike·-| AI 'do well', |–waki| 3p/IND;
                    wa·koše·haki 'foxes')

(b)   *i·nihi=ke·hi e·h=taši-wača·hekowa·či ihkwe·wahi.* (K-ILM 18)
        'And in addition the women (obv.) were cooking something for them.'
            (*i·nihi* 'those (obv.)'; |=ke·hi| 'moreover'; *taši* PV 'be enganged in',
            |wača·h-| TA 'cook for', |e·h=—ekowa·či| 3´–3p/IND; *ihkwe·wahi* 'women (obv.)')

(c)   *mani maneto·wa anawitamwa o·te·weni.* (K-SGG 174)
        'A monster is sneaking up on this town.'
            (*mani* 'this (inan.)'; *maneto·wa* 'god, snake, monster';
            |anawit-| TI(1) 'sneak up on', |—amwa| 3s–0/IND; *o·te·weni* 'town')

(d)   *i·ni=ke·hi='pi ·='na e·h=ne·wa·či ota·nesani meškwiketiwa* (JB-RE 18)
        'and then Red Eagle saw his daughter'
            (*i·ni* 'then'; =ke·hi 'moreover'; |=ipi| HRSY; |i·na| 'that (anim.)'; |ne·w-| TA 'see',
            |e·h=—a·či| 3s–3´/AOR; *ota·nesani* 'his daughter'; *meškwiketiwa* 'Red-Eagle')

(e)   *i·nini e·h=mi·neči še·škesi·he·hani.* (K-F 12; tr. HP)
        "The young girl [obv.] was given to him [prox.]."
            (*i·nini* 'that (obv.)'; |mi·N-| TA 'give O2 to', |e·h=—eči| X–3/AOR;
            še·škesi·he·hani 'girl (obv.)')

(f)   *i·ni='pi i·nini e·h=apehkwe·šimeči mya·mi·wi-mi·šehkwayani.* (K-DSB 48)
        'Then he was laid with those Miami scalps under his head as a pillow.'
            (*i·ni* 'then'; |=ipi| ; *i·nini* 'those (inan.)';
            |apehkwe·šim-| TA 'lay with head supported {by someth.}', |e·h=—eči| X–3/AOR;
            mya·mi·wi-mi·šehkwayani 'Miami scalps')

(g)   *i·nahi='pi awiwaki wi·kiya·peki* 'they were in that house' (K-FC 217)
            (*i·nahi* 'that (loc.)'; |=ipi| HRSY; |awi-| AI 'be {somewhere}', |—waki| 3p/IND;
            wi·kiya·peki 'house (loc.)')

(h)   *ayo·h=taši nepi·ki* 'in this water' (SP-Fish 6)
            (|ayo·hi| 'here; this (loc.)'; *taši* '{somewhere}'; *nepi·ki* 'water (loc.)')

(i)   *ayo·hi ahkwiči ahki·ki* 'on this earth' (K-FC 461)
            (*ayo·hi* 'here; this (loc.)'; *ahkwiči* 'on top'; *ahki·ki* 'earth (loc.)')

(j)   *e·h=mama·toma·či i·nini metemo·he·ha ihkwe·wani kete·='nahi.* (K-WFBW 7J)
        'And now instead the old woman entreated aid from that woman.'
            (|mama·tom-| TA 'entreat aid from', |e·h=—a·či| 3s–3´/AOR; *i·nini* 'that (obv.)';
            metemo·he·ha 'old woman'; *ihkwe·wani* 'woman (obv.)'; *kete·='nahi* 'instead')

(5.160) Discontinuous noun phrase: repeated determiner and noun
(a)   .., *i·nihi e·h=ne·wa·či i·nihi kehčika·na·hahi,* .. 'she saw those chickadees'
        (S-Apay 11)
            (*i·nihi* 'those (obv.)' (2x); |ne·w-| TA 'see', |e·h=—a·či| 3s–3´/AOR;
            kehčika·na·hahi 'chickadees (obv.)')

(b)   *i·ni=ke·hi='pi ·='na e·h=penoči i·na piti·ša·ha.* (S-Pit 35)
        'And then Pitisha (Petit-Jean) went home.'
            (*i·ni* 'then'; |=ke·hi| 'moreover'; |=ipi| HRSY; |i·na| 'that (anim.)' (2x);
            |peno-| AI 'go off, go home', |e·h=—či| 3s/AOR; *piti·ša·ha* 'Pitisha (Petit-Jean)')

(c)   *o·ni='pi ·='niki e·h=a·hkwe·wa·či='pi i·niki e·ye·hkwe·waki.* (S-RSW 38)
        'And then those berdaches got mad.'
            (*o·ni* 'and then'; |=ipi| HRSY (2x); |i·niki| 'those (anim.)' (2x);
            |a·hkwe·-| AI 'be angry', |e·h=—wa·či 3p/AOR; *e·ye·hkwe·waki* 'berdaches')

(d) *i·ni=meko=·pi i·nihi 'amehkwaki' e·h=išitehka·na·wa·či*
    i·nihi pe·paka·ška·nowa·niči·hi.
    'In that moment they named <u>those flat-tailed creatures</u> "beavers." ' (K-SGG 112)
      (*i·ni* 'then'; *=meko* EMPH; |=ipi| HRSY; *i·nihi* 'those (obv.)' (2x);
      amehkwaki 'beavers (prox.)'; |išitehka·N-| TA 'name', |e·h=–a·wa·či| 3p–3´AOR;
      |papaka·ška·nowe·-| AI 'have a flat tail', |IC–niči·hi| 3´/PPL(OBVpl))

(e) *i·nahi·=·nihi i·nah=mi·ša·meki e·piniči·hi.* (K-MP1 15)
    'Those are the ones that are there in that sacred pack.'
      (*i·nahi* 'there, that (loc.)' (2x); *i·nihi* 'those (obv.)';
      mi·ša·meki 'sacred pack (loc.)';
      |api-| AI 'be {somewhere}', |IC–niči·hi| 3´/PPL(OBVpl)

(5.161) Discontinuous noun phrase: repeated determiner

(a) *pe·hki=ni·hka=meko ma·haki ma·mahkate·wesiwaki=ma·haki.* (JB-FS 13)
    'Boy, <u>these (kids)</u> are really black.'
      (*pe·hki* 'really'; |=ni·hka| MAN'S.EXPL; *=meko* EMPH; *ma·haki* 'these' (2x);
      |CV+| RED1, |mahkate·wesi-| AI 'be black', |–waki| 3p/IND)

(b) *i·ya·h=ke·h=a·peh=ma·haki neta·taši·wi·če noma·pena ma·haki.* (K-M 260)
    'We used to play with <u>these (creatures)</u> down there.'
    ("We used to play with the eagles down there." [tr. HP])
      (|i·ya·hi| 'yonder'; |=ke·hi| 'moreover'; |=a·pehe| 'usually'; *ma·haki* 'these' (2x);
      |CV+| RED1, *taši* PV '{somewhere}',
      |wi·če·nom-| TA 'play with', |ne–a·pena| 1p–3/IND)

(c) *i·ni=ča·hi=·pi·=·niki we·či-kehči-·ne·nema·wa·či=·pihi i·niki.* (S-Shak 36)
    'So that's why <u>those people</u> thought a great deal of him.
      (*i·ni* 'that (inan.)'; |=ča·hi| 'so'; |=ipi(hi)| HRSY; |i·niki| 'those (anim.)' (2x);
      |oči| PV 'from {something}', |kehči| PV 'greatly',
      |ine·nem-| TA 'think of {so}', |IC–a·wa·či| 3p–3´/PPL(obl))

(5.162) Discontinuous noun phrase: quantifier and noun

(a) *ayo·h=ča·h ni·šwi awiwaki mahkwaki.* (K-MWL 14)
    '<u>Two bears</u> live here.' (Referring to a large tree.)
      (|ayo·hi| 'here'; |=ča·hi| 'so';
      ni·šwi 'two'; |awi-| AI 'be {somewhere}', |–waki| 3p/IND; *mahkwaki* 'bears')

(b) *ma·ne·=·ni e·h=nesa·wa·či neniwaki mehtose·neniwahi.* (K-PKM 7)
    'Then the men killed <u>many people (obv.)</u>.'
      (|ma·ne| 'many'; |i·ni| 'then'; |neS-| TA 'kill', |e·h=–a·wa·či| 3p–3´/AOR;
      neniwaki 'men (prox.)'; *mehtose·neniwahi* 'people (obv.)')

(c) *kekimesi=mekoho i·na oškinawe·ha e·h=neškina·koči mehtose·neniwahi*
    (K-ECRP 111)
    "<u>Every one of the people</u> [obv.] hated this young-man" (tr. TB)
      (*kekimesi* 'every'; *=mekoho* EMPH; *i·na* 'that (anim.)',
      oškinawe·ha 'young man'; |neškinaw-| TA 'hate', |e·h=–ekoči| 3´–3s/AOR;
      mehtose·neniwahi 'people (obv.)')

(d)   *ayoꞏh=či ꞏh=wi ꞏna <u>ihkwe wahi</u> e ꞏh=taši-manese niči <u>niꞏšwi.</u>* (K-Wewi 22)
      'Suddenly here he saw <u>two women</u> [obv.] gathering firewood.'
          (|ayoꞏhi| 'here'; |=čiꞏhi| 'it was discovered'; *wiꞏna* 3s/EMPH;
          ihkwe wahi 'women (obv.)'; *taši* PV 'be engaged in',
          |maneseꞏ-| AI 'gather firewood', |eꞏh=–niči| 3'/AOR; *niꞏšwi* 'two')

(e)   *i niye ne=meko owi pani e ꞏh=we we pahte či <u>niꞏšwi</u>* (K-EGC 27)
      'he shot off <u>those same two arrows of his</u>'
          (*i niye ne* 'those (inan. abs.)'; *=meko* EMPH; *owi pani* 'his arrows'; |CV+| RED1,
          |we pahteꞏ-| AI+O 'shoot O2 as an arrow', |eꞏh=–či| 3s/AOR; *niꞏšwi* 'two')

(f)   *nepi <u>čaꞏki</u> wi ꞏh=pana čihto wa <u>si po wani, tahkepye ꞏni.</u>* (C-IW 21)
      'He will ruin the water <u>of all the rivers and springs.</u>'
          (*nepi* 'water'; |wiꞏh=| FUT, |pana čiht-| TI(2) 'destroy', |–o wa| 3s–0/IND;
          čaꞏki 'all', *si po wani* 'rivers', *tahkepye ni* 'springs' [adjunct noun phrase])

(5.163) Discontinuous noun phrase: possessor and possessed noun

(a)   *aškači <u>neno te wa</u> e ꞏh=oni ča nese hiniči <u>owi wani</u>* (K-MMDR 15)
      'Some time later the <u>Indian's wife</u> had a baby.'
          (*aškači* 'some time later'; *neno te wa* 'Indian';
          |oni ča neseꞏhi-| AI 'have a baby', |eꞏh=–niči| 3'/AOR; *owi wani* 'his wife')

(b)   *<u>mana</u>=ča ꞏhi meša ꞏniwi <u>owiꞏki.</u>* (K-FC 756; tr. HP)
      "<u>This person's</u> wickiup is large."
          (*mana* 'this (anim.)'; |=ča ꞏhi| 'so'; |mešaꞏ-| II 'be big', |–niwi| 0'/IND;
          owiꞏki 'his dwelling')

(c)   *<u>i niya</u>=ke ꞏhi ihkwe wa e ꞏh=wa wana či-mi ša te nemoniči <u>omeso ta nahi.</u>*
      (K-FC 639)
      "<u>The woman's parent[s]</u> were excited and so glad" (tr. HP)
          (*i niya* 'that (anim. abs.)'; *=ke ꞏhi* 'moreover'; *ihkwe wa* 'woman';
          wa wana či PV 'excitedly', |mi ša te nemo-| AI 'be glad', |eꞏh=–niči| 3'/AOR;
          omeso ta nahi 'her parents (obv.)')

(d)   *<u>i ꞏna</u>=na ꞏhkači omeso ta nahi e ꞏh=ča ꞏkihemeči še škesi ꞏha.* (K-SD 1)
      'And also the <u>girl's parents</u> had both been killed.'
          (*i ꞏna* 'that (anim.)'; *na ꞏhkači* 'also'; *omeso ta nahi* 'her parents (obv.)';
          |ča kih-| TA 'kill all of', |eꞏh=–emeči| X–3'/AOR; *še škesi ꞏha* 'teen-age girl')

(e)   *aškači <u>o ꞏsani</u> e ꞏh=pya niči <u>kwi yeseꞏha,</u> e ꞏh=pye tašiniči.* (K-Apay 23)
      'Some time later the <u>boy's father</u> (obv.) came back, carrying a load of game.'
          (*aškači* 'some time later'; *o ꞏsani* 'his father (obv.)';
          |pyaꞏ-| AI 'come', |eꞏh=–niči| 3'/AOR; *kwi yeseꞏha* 'boy';
          |pye taši-| AI 'come carrying a load of game', |eꞏh=–niči| 3'/AOR)

(5.164) Discontinuous noun phrase: nominal and adjunct nominal (also 5.172*d*)

(a)   *<u>kotaka</u>=mata ketemino ꞏhke <u>ma ꞏhaki</u>* (K-MFWB 42)
      'if <u>another of these</u> blesses you (sg.)'
          (*kotaka* 'another (anim.)'; *=mata* 'alternatively';
          |keteminaw-| TA 'bless', |–ehke| 3–2s/SUBJ; *ma ꞏhaki* 'these (anim.)' [adjunct])

(5.165) Discontinuous noun phrase: two nouns or a noun and a pronoun in apposition

(a) *kapo·twe=meko <u>omešo·mesani</u> e·h=mawinaneti niči ke·nwa·sowe·wani <u>šo·kesi·hani</u>*
'<u>his grandfather the giant lizard</u> presently attacked the mountain lion' (K-MMWP 6)
(*kapo·twe* 'at some point'; *=meko* EMPH; *omešo·mesani* 'his grandfather (obv.)';
|mawinaneti·-| AI 'attack each other, start fighting', |e·h=–niči| 3´/AOR;
ke·nwa·sowe·wani 'mountain lion (obv.)'; *šo·kesi·hani* 'giant lizard (obv.)')

(b) *<u>awahi·maki</u> ki·h=ašiha·waki <u>pešekesiwi-oškaše·ki</u>.* (K-TCSB 69)
"You will prepare <u>deer-hoofs</u>." (TB in Michelson 1930:146)
(*awahi·maki* (placeholder, anim. pl. [§18.8]); |wi·h=| FUT, |aših-| TA 'make',
|ke–a·waki| 2s–3p/IND; *pešekesiwi* PN 'of deer', *oškaše·ki* 'hoofs')

(c) *<u>wi·nwa·wa</u>='pi·='ni e·h=mayo·wa·či <u>ki·ke·na·waki</u>.* (O 152E)
'Then it was <u>the prisoners' turn</u> to weep, they say.'
(*wi·nwa·wa* 3p/EMPH; |=ipi| HRSY; |i·ni| 'then';
|mayo·-| AI 'weep', |e·h=–wa·či| 3p/AOR; *ki·ke·na·waki* 'prisoners of war')

(5.166) Discontinuous noun phrase: noun and participle

(a) *e·škikeniki=ke·h=meko ayo·pi <u>mo·šowa·kani</u>.* (A 115A)
'And another thing, a brand-<u>new pair of scissors</u> was used.'
(|aškiken-| II 'be new', |IC–niki| 0´/PPL(INsg); |=ke·hi| 'moreover'; *=meko* EMPH;
|ayo·-| TI(3) 'use', |–pi| X–0/IND; *mo·šowa·kani* 'pair of scissors')

(b) *<u>i·niye·ne</u> neniwani='pi·='yo·we·='ni awato·niwani <u>ne·semečini</u>.* (K-WSB 16)
"<u>This slain man</u> had taken it from there." (HP)
(*i·niye·ne* 'that (obv. abs.)', *neniwani* 'man (obv.)'; |=ipi| HRSY; |=iyo·we| PAST;
|i·ni| 'that (inan.)'; |awat-| TI(2) 'take away', |–o·niwani| 3´–0/IND;
|neS-| TA 'kill', |IC–emečini| X–3´/PPL(OBVsg))

(5.167) Discontinuous noun phrase that is an argument of a participle

<u>mani</u>=ča·h=ki·wawita pya·te <u>pepikwe·škwi</u> (O 14H)
'and if in such a case the one who had <u>this whistle</u> with him came'
(*mani* 'this (inan.)'; |=ča·hi| 'so';
|ki·wawi-| TI(3) 'go around having', |IC–ta| 3/PPL(ANsg);
|pya·-| AI 'come', |–te| 3s/SUBJ; *pepikwe·škwi* 'whistle')

(5.168) Two discontinuous noun phrases with one intervening verb

(a) *o·ni <u>i·na i·ni</u> e·h=kekika·pa·či <u>papakehko·hi</u> me·mi·šama·ka·ta.* (K-TCB 18)
'And then <u>that attendant</u> stood holding <u>that flat warclub</u>.'
(*o·ni* 'and then'; *i·na* 'that (anim.)'; *i·ni* 'that (inan.)';
|kekika·pa·-| AI 'stand having {something}', |e·h=–či| 3s/AOR;
papakehko·hi 'flat warclub'; *me·mi·šama·ka·ta* 'one who serves as attendant')

(b) *<u>nye·wi</u>='pi·='nah=e·h=akwa·hkwapite·niki <u>owi·wi·neki</u> mehteko·ni.*
'There were <u>four sticks</u> tied <u>to its horns</u>.' (SP-RL 28)
(*nye·wi* 'four'; |=ipi| HRSY; |i·nahi| 'that (loc.)'; |akwa·hkwapite·-| II 'be tied against',
|e·h=–niki| 0´/AOR; *owi·wi·neki* 'his horn(s) (loc.)'; *mehteko·ni* 'sticks')

(c) *<u>i·na</u>=wi·na <u>i·ya·h</u>=e·h=pya·či <u>otehkwe·meki</u> i·na me·meškwimatete·ha.*
'<u>Red-Leggins</u>, meanwhile, arrived <u>over at his sister's</u>.' (S-RL 87)
(*i·na* 'that (anim.)' (2x); *=wi·na* 'but'; |i·ya·hi| 'yonder'; |pya·-| AI 'come', |e·h=–či|
3s/AOR; *otehkwe·meki* 'his sister (loc.)'; *me·meškwimatete·ha* 'Red-Leggins')

(5.169) Intertwoven discontinuous noun phrases

(a)   *ayo·h*=*ma·hahi ahkwitahkimiki taši-mehtose·neniwahi*

      'these people here on earth' (SP-Under 64)

        (|ayo·hi| 'here'; *ma·hahi* 'these'; *ahkwitahkimiki* 'on earth';

        taši PN '{somewhere}', *mehtose·neniwahi* 'people (obv.)')

(b)   *kaši*=*'yo*=*tike i·niya*=*mani išikeni·toke ko·sena·na ohkone·hi.*

      (K-Apay 46)

      'So, what do you suppose gives with our absent father's blanket here?'

        (*kaši* 'what?'; |=iyo| 'for'; |=tike| MAN'S.EXPL; *i·niya* 'that (anim. abs.)';

        mani 'this (inan.)'; |išiken-| II 'be {so}', |–ni·toke| 0´s/DUB;

        ko·sena·na 'our (inc.) father'; *ohkone·hi* 'his blanket.)

(5.170) Discontinuous noun phrase without intervening verb

(a)   *manaha ahkwiya·či nekya pe·hki*=*mekoho kwe·setawaka.* (FC 353; tr. HP)

      "More so to my mother I really do reverence her."

      (*Lit.*: 'My mother especially is who I really revere.')

        (*manaha* 'this (anim.)', *nekya* 'my mother'; *ahkwiya·či* 'especially';

        pe·hki 'really'; =*mekoho* EMPH;

        |kosetaw-| TA 'respect, avoid', |IC–aka| 1s–3/PPL(ANsg))

(b)   *o·ni*=*ča·h e·h*=*pya·či i·niya*=*na·hka nešise·ha.* (A 181A)

      'So then my uncle came over for the second time.'

        (*o·ni* 'and then'; |=ča·hi| 'so'; |pya·-| AI 'come', |e·h–či| 3s/AOR;

        i·niya 'that (abs.)', *nešise·ha* 'my uncle'; *na·hka* 'again')

(c)   *mana owi·wahi me·meškwimateta·ta* (SP-RL 93)

      'Red-Leggins' wives (obv.)'

        (*mana* 'this (anim.)'; *owi·wahi* 'his wives'; *me·meškwimateta·ta* 'Red-Leggins')

(d)   *e·h*=*maniha·či*=*'na*=*'nini pene·wani ihkwe·wa.* (JP-TO 96)

      'The woman took the turkey (obv.) away from him (obv.).'

        (|manih-| TA 'take O2 from', |e·h–a·či| 3s–3´/AOR;

        |i·na| 'that', *ihkwe·wa* 'woman'; |i·nini| 'that (obv.)', *pene·wani* 'turkey (obv.)')

(e)   *nenanawakihta·koniwani mana nepakiwaya·hemi otaye·ni wa·waneška·ha.*

      (SP-Pich1 57; tr. HP)

      "This bad boy's pet has spoiled my good sheet."

        (|nanawakihtaw-| TA+O 'wastefully ruin O2 for', |ne–ekoniwani| 3´s–1s/IND;

        mana 'this (anim.)'; *nepakiwaya·hemi* 'my sheet'; *otaye·ni* 'his pet (obv.)';

        wa·waneška·ha 'rascal')

(f)   *nahi·´, či·kakohamoko mani nawači wi·kiya·pi.* (JP-SD 91)

      'Alright, first sweep up this house.'

        (*nahi·´* 'Alright!'; |či·kakoh-| TI(1) 'sweep', |–amoko| 2p–0/IMP;

        mani 'this (inan.)'; *nawači* (PV)P 'first, stop to' [4.112g]; *wi·kiya·pi* 'house')

(g)   *o·ni*=*'na ki·ši-pya·ta e·h*=*nana·tohtawa·či i·nini ki·mo·či pe·pye·či-wi·te·ma·ničini.*

      'And then the one who had come back secretly questioned the one (obv.) who had

      been accompanying him (second obv.).' (Sh-Elm 17)

        (*o·ni* 'and them'; |i·na| 'that (anim.)'; *ki·ši* PV PERF, |pya·-| AI 'come',

        |IC–ta| 3/PPL(ANsg); |nana·tohtaw-| TA 'ask', |e·h–a·či| 3s–3´/AOR;

        ki·mo·či (PV)P 'secretly'; *i·nini* 'that (obv.)', |CV+| RED1, *pye·či* PV 'coming',

        |wi·te·m-| TA 'accompany', |IC–a·ničini| 3´–3´´/PPL(OBVsg))

(5.171) Equational sentence with a discontinuous New term

(a) *ni·na=koči=manihi <u>neketeminawesiweni</u>.* (K-FC 206; tr. HP)
"This is <u>my blessing</u>."
  (*ni·na* 1s/EMPH; =*koči* 'of course'; *manihi* 'this';
  neketeminawesiweni 'my blessing')

(b) *koči·hi <u>ni·na</u> i·ni <u>newi·seniweni</u>.* (K-FC 220; tr. HP)
"although the food is mine." (*Lit.*: 'Although that is <u>my food</u>.')
  (*koči·hi* 'although'; *ni·na* 1s/EMPH; *i·ni* 'that (inan.)'; *newi·seniweni* 'my food')

(c) *i·niya nenoswa nekoti <u>ota·nesani</u>.* (K-TG 16; tr. Anon.)
"for one belongs to that Buffalo" (*Lit.*: 'One (of them) is <u>that buffalo's daughter</u>.')
  (*i·niya* 'that (anim. abs.)'; *nenoswa* 'buffalo'; *nekoti* 'one';
  ota·nesani 'his daughter')

(d) *i·niya kepašito·hemena·na i·ni <u>e·nahina·čimoči</u>.* (K-FC 779; tr. HP)
"that was <u>what our old man used to say</u>."
  (*i·niya* 'that (anim. abs.)', *kepašito·hemena·na* 'our old man'; *i·ni* 'that (inan.)';
  |CVCV+| RED2, |ina·čimo-| AI 'tell {so}', |IC–či| 3s/PPL(obl))

(e) *mani=koh=ni·hka e·hkawa·pamekwiyakwe <u>mi·ša·mi</u>.* (K-FC 240)
'It's <u>this sacred bundle</u> that watches over us.'
("This pack is the thing that watches us." [tr. HP])
  (*mani* 'this (inan.)'; |=kohi| 'certainly'; =*ni·hka* MAN'S.EXPL; |ahkawa·pam-| TA
  'guard', |IC–ekwiyakwe| 0–12/PPL(INsg); *mi·ša·mi* 'sacred pack')

(f) *mana=ča·hi e·ški-mehkwe·nemehka <u>mekesiwa</u>.* (K-ECRP 86)
'Well, it's <u>this eagle</u> that first thought of you.'
("This eagle is the one who first thought of you." [tr. TB])
  (*mana* 'this (anim.)'; =*ča·hi* 'so'; |aški| PV 'first',
  |mehkwe·nem-| TA 'remember', |IC–ehka| 3–2s/PPL(ANsg); *mekesiwa* 'eagle')

(g) *ma·hani=ke·hi maneto·wa a·hkwi-=mekoho -ka·škehtakini <u>ši·ši·kwanani</u>.* (K-TG 59)
'And <u>these gourd rattles</u> are the things that the manitou hears keenly.'
  (*ma·hani* 'these (inan.)'; =*ke·hi* 'moreover'; *maneto·wa* 'manitou';
  a·hkwi PV 'sharply'; =*mekoho* EMPH;
  |ka·škeht-| TI(1) 'hear', |IC–akini| 3s–0/PPL(INpl); *ši·ši·kwanani* 'gourd rattles')

(h) *šewe·na <u>mani=meko</u> e·na·towe·či <u>e·na·towe·yakwe</u>.* (K-MESB 30C; tr. TB)
"but he talked just the same language as we do."
(*Lit.*: 'But the language he spoke was <u>this same language that we speak</u>.')
  (*šewe·na* 'but'; *mani* 'this (inan.)'; =*meko* EMPH; |ina·towe·-| AI 'speak {some}
  language' (2x), |IC–či| 3s/PPL(obl); |IC–yakwe| 12/PPL(obl))

(i) *i·ni=meko wi·h=išawiyani <u>e·ne·nemena·ni</u>.* (K-SSP 104; tr. HP)
"you will be able to do it, <u>the way I bless you</u>."
  (*i·ni* 'that (inan.)'; =*meko* EMPH; |wi·h=| FUT, |išawi-| AI 'do {so}', |IC–yani|
  2s/PPL(obl); |ine·nem-| TA 'think of {so}', |IC–ena·ni| 1s–2s/PPL(obl))

(j) *nye·wi neniwaki pešekesiwi-owi·ši <u>mi·čiwa·či</u>.* (K-SD 78; instructions for a
ceremony)
'The deer head is eaten by four men.' ("4 men will eat the deer head" [tr. Anon.])
(*Lit.*: 'The [previously mentioned] deer head is <u>something that four men eat</u>.')
  (*nye·wi* 'four'; *neniwaki* 'men'; *pešekesiwi-owi·ši* 'deer head';
  |mi·či-| TI(3) 'eat', |IC–wa·či| 3p–0/PPL(INsg))

(5.172) Equational sentence with both New and Given terms discontinuous

(a) *mami·nateno·ha=ke·hi·='nihi otaye·hi ka·ka·nwikaše·wahi*. (K-WKG 22)
'Bear in mind, those grizzly bears are the pets of Maminatenoha.'
(*mami·nateno·ha* 'Maminatenoha'; |=ke·hi| 'moreover'; |i·nihi| 'those (obv.)';
otaye·hi 'his pets (obv.)'; *ka·ka·nwikaše·wahi* 'grizzly bears (obv.)')

(b) *kekimesi=koh=mekoho i·ni ki·kena·ni ni·kena·ni*. (K-FC 381)
'That house of ours (exc.) is the house of every one of us (inc.).'
(*kekimesi* 'every'; |=kohi| 'certainly'; =*mekoho* EMPH; *i·ni* 'that (inan.)';
ki·kena·ni 'our (inc.) house'; *ni·kena·ni* 'our (exc.) house')

(c) *ni·na·='na netawe·ma·wa ke·temino·hka*, ... (K-FASB 86; tr. HP)
"The one who had blessed you .. is my brother."
(|ni·na| 1s/EMPH; |i·na| 'that (anim.)'; *netawe·ma·wa* 'my (woman's) brother';
|keteminaw-| TA 'bless', |IC–ehka| 3–2s/PPL(ANsg))

(d) *mamahke·hi-metemo·ha='pi ma·hani ošekiweni wi·škopa·powi*. (K-Auto 37)
'The sap of these (trees) is Old Lady Toad's urine.'
(*mamahke·hi-metemo·ha* 'Old Lady Toad'; |=ipi| HRSY;
ma·hani 'these (inan.)' [adjunct]; *ošekiweni* 'her urine'; *wi·škopa·powi* 'sap')

Discontinuous Particle Phrases

71.4. All types of particle phrases may incorporate an enclitic (5.70c, 5.71d, 5.72, 5.73f(1), 5.74, 5.75a, 5.77), and some types may be discontinuous in the manner of discontinuous noun phrases, which they often contain.

(5.173) Discontinuous particle phrase

(a) *kapo·twe e·h=kano·nekoči opehkwaneki nekoti oči*. (K-MFWB 25)
'At some point someone spoke to him from behind.'
(*kapo·twe* 'at some point'; |kano·N-| TA 'speak to', |e·h–ekoči| 3´–3s/AOR;
opehkwaneki 'his back (loc.)'; *nekoti* 'one'; *oči* 'from {somewhere}')

(b) *ahkwiči·='nahi·='ni e·h=ahto·či ma·tesi ošehkeki*. (JP-Apay2 12)
'With that, she placed that knife on her belly.'
(|ahkwiči| 'on top'; |=i·nahi| 'with that' (5.122i); |i·ni| 'that (inan.)';
|aht-| TI(2) 'place {somewhere}', |e·h–o·či| 3s–0/AOR;
ma·tesi 'knife'; *ošehkeki* 'her belly (loc.)')

(c) *ni·šwa·pitaki=ke·hi·='nihi nye·wi e·h=tašiniči owi·wahi*. (K-HS 32)
'And twenty-four was the number of his wives.'
(*ni·šwa·pitaki* 'twenty'; |=ke·hi| 'moreover'; |i·nihi| 'those (obv.)'; *nye·wi* 'four';
|taši-| AI 'be {so many}', |e·h–niči| 3´/AOR; *owi·wahi* 'his wives (obv.)')

Discontinuous Clauses

71.5. Subordinate clauses are often discontinuous, with words that are part of the main clause occurring in their midst. Discontinuous clauses that are verbal or oblique complements or that center on a participle function in the larger sentence as types of discontinuous noun phrases. Other kinds of subordinate clauses, however, may also have discontinuous elements. In some cases a noun phrase that is functionally part of a subordinate clause is discontinuous across words that are part of the main clause, or even across the entire main clause. In other cases individual words that belong with the main clause occur within a subordinate clause. In fact, the words of the two clauses are sometimes thoroughly intertwined.

(5.174) Discontinuous temporal clause

(a) *o ni= ʼpi ki ši-a yaha ya čimohekowa či e ʼh=penopenowa či i nini wa ko ʼhani.*
(K-FC 704)
"Then <u>after Foxy finished instructing them</u>, then they went to their homes." (tr. HP)
(*o ni* 'and then'; |=ipi| HRSY; *ki ši* PV PERF,
|CVCV+| RED2, |CV+| RED1, |a-čimoh-| TA 'instruct', |IC–ekowa·či| 3´–3p/CC;
|CVCV+| RED2, |peno-| AI 'go home', |e·h=–wa·či| 3p/AOR;
i nini 'that (obv.)', *wa ko ʼhani* 'Fox (man's name, obv.)')

(b) *ke ko ʼh=e nowe čini i ni=meko e ʼh=išikeniki i na ihkwe wa.* (K-WM 12)
'<u>Whenever that woman said anything</u>, that very thing happened.'
(|ke·ko·hi| 'anything'; |inowe·-| AI 'say {so}', |IC–čini| 3s/CC;
i ni 'that (inan.)'; =meko EMPH; |išiken-| II 'happen {so}', |e·h=–niki| 0´/AOR;
i na 'that (anim.)', *ihkwe wa* 'woman')

(c) *e taswi-=meko -anwe we katenikini e ʼh=a ʼhtawa ʼsa wa či pa škesikanani.*
(K-PKM 4)
'<u>Every time the guns (obv.) fired</u>, some of them (anim.) fell over backwards.'
(|taswi| PV '{so much, so many}'; =meko EMPH;
|anwe·we·kat-| II 'make noise', |IC–nikini| 0´/ITER;
|a·htawa·sa·-| AI 'fall backwards', |e·h=–wa·či| 3p/AOR; *pa škesikanani* 'guns')

(d) *i niya=ča ʼh na ʼhina ʼhi ne po ʼhiči kekehkino ʼsopwa toke ni ʼhka na.* (K-MS 15)
'And you (pl.) probably observed carefully <u>at the time my friend died</u>.'
(*i niya* 'that (anim. abs.)'; |=ča·hi| 'so';
na ʼhina ʼhi 'time'; |nepo·hi-| AI 'die', |IC–či| 3s/CC;
|kehkino·so-| AI 'observe closely', |ke–pwa·toke| 2p/DUB; *ni ʼhka na* 'my friend')

(e) *anemo ʼhaki a ʼkwi menwi-pema ʼtesikini ki ši-amočini.* (K-FASB 93; tr. HP)
"<u>After eating these dogs</u> one does not feel good"
(*anemo ʼhaki* 'dogs';
a ʼkwi 'not'; *menwi* PV 'well', |pema·tesi-| AI 'live', |–kini| X/NEG;
ki ši PV PERF, |amw-| TA 'eat', |IC–ečini| X–3/CC)

(f) *ki ši-=ča ʼh=ni na -tahkana ʼkwike, i ni wi ʼh=na kwa ya ni.* (K-WSB 74; tr. HP)
"I'll go, <u>after it is cool in the evening</u>"
(*ki ši* PV PERF; |tahkana·kwi-| II 'be cool evening', |–ke| 0/SUBJ; *i ni* 'then';
|=ča·hi| 'so'; *ni na* 1s/EMPH; |wi·h=| FUT, |na·kwa·-| AI 'leave', |e·h=–ya·ni| 1s/AOR)

(5.175) Discontinuous conditional clauses

(a) *kehkinawa pamate=ča ʼh e šihto čini ke ko ʼh menwawihkapa kekya* (A 46D)
'<u>if you learn by watching whenever your mother makes anything</u>, you would do well'
(|kehkinawa·pam-| TA 'watch to learn', |–ate| 2s–3/SUBJ; |=ča·hi| 'so';
|ašiht-| TI(2) 'make', |IC–o·čini| 3s–0/ITER, |ke·ko·hi| 'anything';
|menwawi-| AI 'do well', |–hkapa| 2s/POT; *kekya* 'your mother')

(b)   *i·ni=mata ayo·h=meko pya·hkapa* <u>*ine·nemehke*</u>. (K-MFWB 42)
   '<u>If instead he blessed you to do that</u>, you could come here.'
     (*i·ni* 'that (inan.)'; =*mata* 'alternatively'; |*ayo·hi*| 'here'; =*meko* EMPH;
     |*pya·-*| AI 'come', |–*hkapa*| 2s/POT;
     |*ine·nem-*| TA 'think about {so}', |–*ehke*| 3–2s/SUBJ)

(c)   *kotakaki a·kwi wi·h=nahikenikini* <u>*anohka·ne·kwe*</u>. (K-FC 272; tr. HP)
   "It will not do <u>if you get some people out of their clan</u>." (Literally, 'other people'.)
     (*kotakaki* 'others (anim.)'; *a·kwi* 'not';
     |*wi·h=*| FUT, |*nahiken-*| II 'be proper', |–*nikini*| 0'/NEG;
     |*anohka·N-*| TA 'give task to', |–*e·kwe*| 2p–3/SUBJ)

(5.176) Discontinuous verbal complement clauses

(a)   <u>*we·či-na·wahkwe·niki*</u> *e·h=kehkahamawoči* <u>*ota·hkwe wi·h=a·wa·či*</u>. (K-WD 3)
   "They were both told <u>to go south</u>." (HP)
     (*we·či-na·wahkwe·niki* 'south (obv.)'; |*kehkahamaw-*| TA+O 'designate O2 to',
     |*e·h=–eči*| AOR; *ota·hkwe* 'in {such} direction';
     |*wi·h=*| FUT, |*iha·-*| AI 'go {somewhere}', |*e·h=–wa·či*| 3p/AOR)

(b)   <u>*nye·wokonakahke*</u> *ki·h=kehkahamawa·waki* <u>*wi·h=ma·wačiweto·wa·či*</u>
   <u>*ni·peni-wi·seniweni*</u>. (K-FC 270)
   'You must instruct them <u>to bring together garden foods in four days</u>.'
   (The people were then told right away to bring the food four days later.)
     (|*nye·wokonakat-*| II 'be four days', |–*ke*| 0/SUBJ;
     |*wi·h=*| FUT, |*kehkahamaw-*| TA+O 'designate O2 for', |*ke–a·waki*| 2s–3p/IND;
     |*wi·h=*| FUT, |*ma·wačiwet-*| TI(2) 'bring together', |*e·h=–o·wa·či*| 3p–0/AOR;
     ni·peni-wi·seniweni 'garden-crop food')

(c)   *i·ni=ke·hi=·pi·=·'nihi owi·či·škwe·hwa·wahi mami·ši·haki=meko e·h=anohka·neči*
   <u>*wi·h=pi·tahwa·wa·či*</u>. (K-Bene 114; tr. TB)
   "It is said that the ceremonial attendants were instructed <u>to bury their enimies</u>."
     (*i·ni* 'then'; =*ke·hi* 'moreover'; |=*ipi*| HRSY; |*i·nihi*| 'those (obv.)';
     owi·či·škwe·hwa·wahi 'their enemies (obv.)';
     mami·ši·haki 'ceremonial attendants'; =*meko* EMPH;
     |*anohka·N-*| TA 'give a task to', |*e·h=–eči*| X–3/AOR;
     |*wi·h=*| FUT, |*pi·tahw-*| TA 'bury', |*e·h=–a·wa·či*| 3p–3'/AOR)

(d)   <u>*e·h=tanehkwe·šinowa·či*</u> *ki·h=sasa·hkwe* <u>*wi·h=pakišinani*</u>. (K-BBWM 74)
   'It will be taboo to you for you <u>to alight at the head of their graves</u>.'
   ("You must forbid to light on the head end." [tr. HP])
     (|*tanehkwe·šin-*| AI 'lie with head {somewhere}', |*e·h=–wa·či*| 3p/PPL(loc.obl);
     |*wi·h=*| FUT, |*sasa·hkwe·-*| AI 'be restricted by taboo', |*ke–Ø*| 2s/IND;
     |*wi·h=*| FUT, |*pakišin-*| AI 'alight, land', |*e·h=–ani*| 2s/AOR)

(e)   *i·noki=ča·hi* <u>*mana kekwisa*</u> *ki·h=koči-asemihene* <u>*wi·h=po·ni-we·pesi·hiwiči*</u>.
   'So now I will try to help you <u>so your son will no longer be insane</u>.'
   (K-OBES 108)
     (*i·noki* 'now'; =*ča·hi* 'so'; *mana* 'this (anim.)'; *kekwisa* 'your son';
     |*wi·h=*| FUT, *koči* PV 'try to', |*asemih-*| TA 'help', |*ke–ene*| 1s–2s/IND;
     |*wi·h=*| FUT, *po·ni* PV 'cease', |*we·pesi·hiwi-*| AI 'be crazy', |*e·h=–či*| 3s/AOR)

(f)   *o ni=ʼpi iškweˑse ·hahi <u>we wenesi ·hiničihi</u> e ·h=anohanohka ʼnekoči*
       wi ·h=anemi-me mešenamawaˑči. (K-ECRP 12; tr. TB)
       "The girls would tell him <u>to catch the pretty ones for them</u>."
          (*o ni* 'and then', |=ipi| HRSY; *iškweˑse ·hahi* 'girls (obv.)';
          |we·wenesi·hi-| AI 'be pretty (dim.)', |IC–ničihi| 3´/PPL(OBVpl);
          |CVCV+| RED2, |anohka·N-| TA 'give task to', |e·h=–ekoči| 3´–3s/AOR;
          |wi·h=| FUT, *anemi* PV 'go on',
          |CV+| RED1, |mešenamaw-| TA+O 'catch O2 for', |e·h=–aˑči| 3s–3´/AOR)

(5.177) Discontinuous objective sentential complements

    (a)   *e ʼne ʼnema wate ni=kohi kepye či-nana ʼtohto ne <u>aškote neˑsiwa</u>.* (K-SF 96)
           'I came to ask you <u>what you think of the Spirit of Fire</u>.' (Complete utterance.)
              (|ine·nem-| TA 'think about {so}', |IC–a·wate·ni| 2s–3/INT.PPL(OBL);
              =*kohi* 'certainly';
              pyeˑči PV 'coming', |nana·tohtaw-| TA 'ask', |ke–ene| 1s–2s/IND;
              aškote neˑsiwa 'Spirit of Fire')

    (b)   *i ʼnihi=na ·hka aša ·hahi e ·h=aˑčimoči <u>e ·h=nepa ʼniči</u>.* (K-OMSP 6)
           'And he told <u>where those Siouxs were sleeping, also</u>.'
              (*i ʼnihi* 'those (obv.)'; *na ·hka* 'also'; *aša ·hahi* 'Siouxs (obv.)';
              |a·čimo-| AI 'tell', |e·h=–či| 3s/AOR; |nepa·-| AI 'sleep', |e·h=–niči| 3´/PPL(loc.obl))

    (c)   *sa ʼniti ·hinikini menwe ʼnetamwa <u>e ·h=ki ·ke ʼnoweči</u>.* (K-TCSB 108; tr. TB)
           "He likes it <u>when the clan feasts are given on Sundays</u>."
              (|sa·niti·hi-| II 'be Sunday', |IC–nikini| 0´/ITER;
              |menwe·net-| TI(1) 'like', |–amwa| 3s–0/IND;
              |ki·ke·no-| AI 'hold clan feast', |e·h=–weči| X/REL/AOR)

    (d)   *ča ·ki=meko tahka ·hkwi neto ·hkanemeki neka škihto me na ʼtama ni <u>e ·h=e ʼmikateki</u>.*
           'I felt <u>a shadow go all over in my bones</u> when I smelled that.' (K-BBD 39)
              (*ča ·ki* 'all'; =*meko* EMPH; *tahka ·hkwi* 'shadow';
              neto ·hkanemeki 'my bones (loc.)';
              |ka·škiht-| TI(2) 'sense, feel', |ne–o| 1s–0/IND;
              |mena·t-| TI(1) 'smell', |IC–ama·ni| 1s–0/CC;
              |ihe·mikat-| II 'go {somewhere}', |e·h=–eki| 0/AOR)

    (e)   *meso ʼte we=meko e ·h=aka wa ʼtamowa ·či wi ·h=ne ʼtamowa ·či <u>mi ·ša ʼmi</u>*
           <u>*mehtose·neniwaki*</u> *e ·šikenikweˑni.* (K-YC 16)
           '<u>All the people</u> wanted to see <u>what the sacred bundle was like</u>.'
              (*meso ʼte we* 'universally'; =*meko* EMPH;
              |aka·wa·t-| TI(1) 'desire', |e·h=–amowa·či| 3p–0/AOR;
              |wi·h=| FUT, |ne·t-| TI(1) 'see', |e·h=–amowa·či| 3p–0/AOR;
              mi ·ša ʼmi 'sacred pack';
              mehtose ʼneniwaki 'people'; |išiken-| II 'be {so}', |IC–nikwe·ni| 0´/INT.PPL(obl))

(5.178) Discontinuous oblique complement clause

    (a)   *mi ·čiči oči e ·h=ahte ʼniki.* (K-WSB 53; tr. HP [label on diagram])
           "The side <u>where his eatables were</u>"
              (|mi·či-| TI(3) 'eat', |IC–či| 3s–0/PPL(INsg); *oči* 'oriented {so}' (**§22.4(d)**);
              |ahte·-| II 'be {somewhere}', |e·h=–niki| 0´/PPL(loc.obl))

(b) *ka·ta=ke·hi <u>wi·h=kekye·škatawe·nemači</u> išite·he·hkani <u>owiye·ha</u>.*
(K-FC 609; tr. HP)
"And do not feel <u>stingy toward any one</u>."
(*ka·ta* 'don't'; *=ke·hi* 'moreover';
|wi·h=| FUT, |kekye·škatawe·nem-| TA 'resent, begrudge', |e·h=–ači| 2s–3/AOR;
|išite·he·-| AI 'think {so}', |–hkani| 2s/PROH; *owiye·ha* 'someone')

(c) *<u>wi·h=kehke·nema·či=meko</u> e·h=išite·he·či <u>'pene·sa' e·nema·te·hini</u>.* (Bene 72A)
'He wanted <u>to know who it was that was called Penesa</u>.'
(|wi·h=| FUT, |kehke·nem-| |e·h=–a·či| ; *=meko* EMPH;
|išite·he·-| AI 'think {so}', |e·h=–či| 3s/AOR; *pene·sa* 'Penesa';
|iN-| TA 'say {so} to, of', |IC–ema·te·hini| X–3′/INT.PPL(OBVsg))

(d) *ahkwiya·h=meko <u>nekotahi oči·yane</u> ine·netisoyane <u>maneto·na·ki</u>.* (K-ECRP 110)
"Especially if you think in your heart <u>that you came from some place in the realms of the Manitos</u>." (tr. TB)
(|ahkwiya·hi| 'especially'; *=meko* EMPH; *nekotahi* 'somewhere';
|oči·-| AI 'come from {somewhere}', |–yane| 2s/SUBJ;
ine·netiso-| AI 'think of oneself {so}', |–yane| 2s/SUBJ;
maneto·na·ki 'among the manitous')

(e) *<u>wi·h=nesa·či=ma·hi</u> e·h=inowe·či <u>nye·wi okima·wahi</u>* (K-FC 270; tr. HP)
"The reason for this is that he says he wants <u>to slay four chiefs</u>."
(|wi·h=| FUT, |neS-| TA 'kill', |e·h=–a·či| 3s–3′/AOR; *=ma·hi* 'you see';
|inowe·-| 'tell X {so}', |e·h=–či| 3s/AOR; *nye·wi* 'four'; *okima·wahi* 'chiefs (obv.)')

(f) *<u>e·h=ne·wa·či</u> e·h=ina·hpawa·či <u>otawe·ma·wahi</u>* (K-Wap 129; tr. TB)
".. when she dreamt <u>that she saw her brothers</u>."
(|ne·w-| TA 'see', |e·h=–a·či| 3s–3′/AOR;
|ina·hpawa·-| AI 'dream {so}', |e·h=–či| 3s/AOR;
otawe·ma·wahi 'her brothers (obv.)')

(g) *<u>nene·wa·wa=</u>'škwe netena·hpawa ke·kye·peša·ta.* (K-SSP 44)
'I dreamt <u>that I saw one who was deaf</u>.'
(|ne·w-| TA 'see', |ne–a·wa| 1s–3s/IND; |=iškwe| WOMAN'S EXPL;
|ina·hpawa·-| AI 'dream {so}', |ne–∅| 1s/IND;
|kekye·peše·-| AI 'be deaf', |IC–ta| 3/PPL(ANsg))

(h) *mehto·či=meko <u>pi·tike e·h=owi·kiwa·čini</u> ketašina·ke·pena <u>maneto·waki</u>.* (O 136A)
'It's just as if we were singing <u>inside the lodges where the manitous live</u>.'
(*mehto·či* 'as if'; *=meko* EMPH; *pi·tike* 'inside';
|owi·ki-| AI 'dwell {somewhere}', |e·h=–wa·čini| 3p/PPL(loc.obl.pl);
|tašina·ke·-| AI 'sing {somewhere}', |ke–pena| 12/IND; *maneto·waki* 'manitous')

(i) *kapo·twe <u>e·h=anwe·we·'seniki</u> e·h=tanehkwe·hiči <u>ke·ko·hi</u> e·h=pekeče·šiniči
a·mo·wahi <u>ihkwe·wa</u>.* (K-MGW 5)
'Later <u>there was a noise of something</u> at the woman's head
where the bees (in a beehive) cracked open when they fell.'
(*kapo·twe* 'at some point'; |anwe·we·sen-| II 'be noise', |e·h=–niki| 0′/AOR;
|tanehkwe·hi-| AI 'have head {somewhere}', |e·h=–či| 3s/PPL(loc.obl); *ke·ko·hi*
'something'; |pekeče·šin-| AI 'fall and crack open', |e·h=–niči| 3′/PPL(loc.obl);
a·mo·wahi 'bees (obv.)'; *ihkwe·wa* 'woman')

Chapter 6.

§§72-73. Discourse Structure

72. Some aspects of Meskwaki grammar can only be fully understood from how they are used in connected narratives containing complex sentences and sequences of sentences. This is because the organization and presentation of discourse has grammatical features as well as, naturally, conventional stylistic aspects. Where there is variation in the use of grammatical devices, depending typically on the speaker or the genre, these components interact. This chapter especially treats the grammatical aspects of the organization of discourse, but makes some references to stylistic features. Discourse features are documented by texts.

General Features of Texts

72.1. Kinds of texts. The texts on which this grammar is based are written versions of oral compositions. Most of them are the tellings of traditional winter stories, legendary tales, and historical accounts, including first-person narratives, reports, and descriptions of activity. William Jones's texts were taken down from dictation and edited with the aid of his father, but most writers wrote out versions of spoken texts that they had presumably heard and in many cases delivered orally themselves any number of times. Some writers attribute some texts to older family members.

The narrative texts range from brief tales a few pages long to legends and cycles of stories with many episodes filling hundreds of pages. In the traditional telling of winter stories they were strung together over many nights by means of deft expository transitions. This practice explains why many of the texts have component parts that in other tellings or other traditions are separate tales.

72.2. First-person texts. In ordinary conversation, first-person narratives (like the "Autobiography"), and generic descriptions (like the expository sections of the "Owl" text) main verbs are predominantly in the independent indicative mode (**§26.1**), with negative statements in the negative mode (**§26.11**) and other modes used as appropriate, including the potential mode (**§26.20**), the plain interrogative (**§26.14**), and the other modes of the independent order, especially the dubitative (**§26.2**). The aorist conjunct is used in clauses that function as main clauses after *kaho ni* 'so then', *o ni* 'and, then', and *i ni* 'then', and also in nominalizations in equational sentences with the force of '(was) the time when' (e.g. A 1B).

72.3. Third-person texts. In third-person narratives, like the bulk of the texts (including the narrative section of "Owl"), main clauses have the aorist conjunct mode (§26.8, 2.176) and are made negative by the preverb *pwa wi* (~ *pa wi*) 'not' (2.26, 3.289). Narratives may, however, include narrator's comments and explanations in the form of asides in the conversational style, using the independent indicative or the negative. The examples of such asides from Alfred Kiyana in (6.1) all characteristically have the hearsay enclitic *=ipi* or the full verb *ipi* '(indefinite) says {so}', although Kiyana uses these sparingly in his narrative prose. In (6.1*a*) the aorist form for 'they went' is reprised by the indicative form of the same verb.

(6.1) Parenthetical remarks without a narrative aorist

    (a)   *meše=meko nano škwe e·h=a wa či. (we či-=ʼpi -pakišimoniki ihe waki.)* (K-B 290)
             'They went in just any direction. (They went west, it is said.)'
             (*meše* 'freely'; *=meko* EMPH; *nano škwe* 'randomly';
             |iha·-| AI 'go {somewhere}', |e·h=–wa·či| 3p/AOR;
             we či-pakišimoniki 'west (obv.)'; *=ipi* HRSY;
             |iha·-| AI 'go {somewhere}', |–waki| 3p/IND

    (b)   *nakamo nani našawe akihte wani, ipi.* (K-Benesa 152; tr. TB)
             "The songs it is said have long since been lost."
             (*nakamo nani* 'songs'; *našawe* 'long ago'; |akihte·-| II 'be lost', |–wani| 0p/IND;
             |i-| AI 'say {so}, |–pi| X/IND)

    (c)   *ni šwihe wa=ke hi=ʼpi otehkwe mahi.* (K-BHD 22)
             'By the way, they say he had two sisters.'
             (|ni·šwih-| TA 'have two of', |–e·wa| 3s–3′/IND; *=ke hi* 'moreover'; *=ipi* HRSY;
             otehkwe mahi 'his sisters')

    (d)   *šewe na=ʼpi pe po nikini a kwi=nana ši še ški kwe hečini.* (O 58F)
             'But they say that in winter he was never allowed to have his face unblackened.'
             (*šewe na* 'but'; *=ipi* HRSY; |pepo·-| II 'be winter', |IC–nikini| 0′/ITER;
             a kwi 'not'; *nana ši* '(ever)';
             |še ški kwe h-| TA 'let have an unblackened face (i.e., allow not to be fasting)',
             |–ečini| X–3/NEG)

The flow of narrative may be interrupted in other ways. An important fact that is not relevant at the moment but will be as the story unfolds can be signaled or re-emphasized by the compound enclitic *=iyo=ke hi* 'by the way, bear in mind, remember, you understand' (*=iyo* 'for' + *=ke hi* 'moreover'; 5,123*e*), or sometimes by *=ke hi* 'moreover' alone (5.122*j*; cf. 6.1*c*). A simple self correction can be indicated by a following *=ʼh=we na* 'rather, or rather' (5.123*a*), and a correction or supplied omission may be preceded by *ne pehe*, which corresponds to 'or rather', 'I mean', 'I forgot to say', and the like (§14.2; 5.119*s*). The chronological sequence of events may be consciously scrambled by the use of overlay, when the narrator rushes ahead in the telling and then jumps back to fill in details, often with some repetition.

72.4. Direct and indirect discourse. Characteristic of all genres is the use of direct discourse, which in Meskwaki includes quoted speech and thought, or what is presented as such. All such quotations are like ordinary speech in the selection of verbal modes. But while some quotations are intended to report what someone actually said or thought, others, especially short ones, merely summarize the logical content (2.104, 5.139*a*, 6.2).

(6.2) Direct discourse not used for literal quotation

(a)   *'mi·ša mi='pi ni·h=ašihto,' iwa='yo·we.* (O 68B)
'He said that he was supposed to make a sacred pack.'
(*lit.*, 'He once said, "It is said I must make a sacred pack." ')
    (*mi·ša·mi* 'sacred pack'; *=ipi* HRSY;
    |wi·h=| FUT, |ašiht-| TI(2) 'make', |ne–o| 1s–0/IND;
    |i-| AI 'say {so}', |–wa| 3s/IND; *=iyo·we* PAST)

(b)   *'ni·h=wi·ke·tesa,' išite·he·wa·te* 'if they think they're going to cook it properly'
    (O 96I) (*lit.*, 'If they think, "I'm going to cook it carefully" ')
    (|wi·h=| FUT, |wi·ke·tes-| TI(1) 'cook carefully', |ne–a| 1s–0/IND;
    |išite·he·-| AI 'think {so}, |–wa·te| 3p/SUBJ)

(c)   *'ni·h=ki·ke·no,' išite·he·ye·kwe* 'If you wish to celebrate a clan feast, ...' (O 126G)
    (*lit.*, 'If you think, "I want to celebrate a clan feast,"...')
    (|wi·h=| FUT, |ki·ke·no-| AI 'hold a clan feast', |ne–| 1s/IND;
    |išite·he·-| AI 'think {so}, |–ye·kwe| 2p/SUBJ)

(d)   po·ni·hkawino, iši. 'Tell it to quit bothering me!' (K-CBFB 5M)
    (*lit.*, 'Tell it: Quit bothering me!' Not a quote.)
    (|po·ni·hkaw-| TA 'leave alone', |–ino| 2s–1s/IMP;
    |iN-| TA 'say {so} to', |–i| 2s–3/IMP)

Clauses in indirect discourse may also be complements of verbs with relative roots (examples in §69.13). A name or kinship term in a naming construction can be considered to be a complement in indirect discourse (5.140, 6.3).

(6.3) Naming constructions

(a)   *masahkamikohkwe·wa, wi·h=išisowa.* (K-M 2d)
'Masahkamikohkwêwa shall be her name.'
    (*masahkamikohkwe·wa* (name);
    |wi·h=| FUT, |išiso-| AI 'be named {so}', |–wa| 3s/IND)

(b)   *keme·šo·mesena·na=ča·h, ki·h=ina·ko·ma·pena wi·teko·waki.* (O 124D)
'So, "grandfather" is the term of relationship we shall all use for owls.'
    (*keme·šo·mesena·na* 'our (inc.) grandfather'; *=ča·hi* 'so';
    |wi·h=| FUT, |ina·ko·m-| TA 'be related to {so}', |ke–a·pena| 12–3/IND;
    wi·teko·waki 'owls')

At least in older usage, the complements in such constructions were islands unaffected by obviation (5.140*ab*), but the fact that these complements can be discontinuous (5.140*b*) and can be followed by an enclitic (6.3*b*) points to their being indirect discourse complements.

The Use of Nominals in Narrative

72.5. Nouns. Because Meskwaki verbs make pronominal reference to subjects and objects, sentences without demonstrative pronouns or nouns are possible, in fact commonplace. As a corollary of this circumstance, the use of overt nominals (demonstratives, nouns, and participles), while not unusual, can show particular patterns and functions in the organization of discourse. A story about a man will not refer to him repeatedly with the noun *neniwa* 'man', but will typically use this only if clarification is needed when there is more than one character, particularly after another character has just been mentioned. The use of a noun when it is not needed for clarification may be for defocusing, to indicate that the character is exiting the narrative.

72.6. Names. Many characters, even leading characters, are given no names. Characters are typically referred to simply by the appropriate term for their age and sex. These extremely frequent, highly topical nouns are: *apeno·ha* 'child', *kwi·yese·ha* 'boy', *iškwe·se·ha* 'girl'; *oškinawe·ha* 'unmarried teenage boy', *še·škesi·ha* 'unmarried teenage girl'; *neniwa* 'man', *ihkwe·wa* 'woman'; *pašito·ha* 'old man', *metemo·ha* 'old woman'. The first five of these terms also have diminutives for the younger age ranges in each case, and the last two have diminutives that tend to imply relatively older characters. Other highly topical nouns include *okima·wa* 'chief', *maneto·wa* 'manitou, god, spirit, monster', as well as ones appropriate to specific stories.

Even when a name is given it is typically used sparingly. For example, in Alfred Kiyana's 38-page story of *we·te·sepaneme·ha* (*lit.*, 'Raccoon-Owner') the main character's name is used only once, on p. 20, when he misses his raccoons after a four-year separation (see 6.20(c)). The title on page 1 has a gloss of this: *we·tayita·e·sepa·hahi* 'the one who had pet raccoons'. In Charley H. Chuck's 34-page story with the title *we·to·seni·me·h* (*lit.*, 'Rock-Owner,' rendered as 'Has-a-Rock'), he never uses this name, actually that of the hero's uncle, in his narrator's voice, but only in what the hero says the first time he refers to him. The hero's older brother, *ki·škesita* 'Cut-Off', appears on p. 1 but is not named until p. 21 (revealing a plot element), and then three more times (two straddling a quote), always correlating with a shift of location. In Sâkihtanohkwêha's 22-page story of the *pepo·natesi·hkwe·waki* (*lit.*, 'Winter-Spirit Women', rendered as 'Ice Maidens') they are mentioned on p. 11 and seen on p. 12, but they are not named until p. 16, when they arrive in the Ice World where they live, and only once after that, when the naming signals a defocusing at the end of the episode about them on p. 21. In Kiyana's 53-page story of *we·wi·pe·ha* ('Arrow-Owner') he uses the name only in the title.

72.7. Demonstrative pronouns. Some demonstrative pronouns (§§18.5, 31.2) have special functions when they refer to characters in narratives. Forms of *i·na* 'that' (§31.4) are used in several ways, such as to narrow the reference to one of a set, to reintroduce a major character in a new segment or episode, to defocus a character at the end of an episode, and in a basic grammatical function in equational expressions (2.227a, 5.78b). One common use is, not to continue reference to the current topic, but to refer back across that character to the next preceding potential topic, especially a central character.

(6.4) Use of *i·na* to shift reference back

    (a)   *i·n=a·mihtahi='pi anwe·we·htaki. / o·ni i·na ke·ko·h=meko išawisa.* (O 14IJ)

        '(If an enemy (obv.) was in a rage, ..) then he [the leader] would blow it [the whistle], they say. And then something would happen to <u>that one</u> [the enemy, not the leader].'

          (*i·ni* 'then'; *a·mihtahi* POT; =*ipi* HRSY;

          |anwe·we·ht-| TI(1) 'blow audibly', |–aki| 3s–0/CONJ;

          o·ni 'and, then'; *i·na* 'that (anim.)'; *ke·ko·hi* 'something'; =*meko* EMPH;

          |išawi-| AI 'do {so}', |–sa| 3s/POT)

    (b)   *meše=meko·='nahi e·ya·kwe·ni e·h=a·či='pihi. /*

        i·na=ke·hi·='hkwe·wa e·h=nekoto·ke·hiči='pi, e·h=nešike·či. /

        i·na=ke·h neniwa maškote·ki e·h=tahkami·či. (S-TO 6)

        (A man has set out on a journey from the house he shares with his sister to seek a wife.) 'He went wherever he was going. / And <u>that</u> woman stayed alone with the house to herself. / And <u>that</u> man crossed the open prairie.'

(*meše=meko˙=ʼnahi* 'any';

|iha·-| AI 'go {somewhere}', |IC–kwe·ni| 3s,0/INT.PPL(obl);

|iha·-| 'go {somewhere}', |e·h=–či| 3s/AOR; =*ipi(hi)* HRSY;

i·na 'that (anim.)'; =*ke·h(i)* 'moreover' 2x; *ihkwe·wa* 'woman';

|nekoto·ke·hi-| AI 'live alone (dim.)', |e·h=–či| 3s/AOR;   =*ipi(hi)* HRSY;

|nešike·-| AI 'have a house to oneself', |e·h=–či| 3s/AOR;

i·na 'that (anim.)'; =*ke·h(i)* 'moreover'; *neniwa* 'man';

maškote·ki 'prairie (loc.)'; |tahkami·-| AI 'cross open space', |e·h=–či| 3s/AOR)

Some speakers use *mana* 'this' (§31.3) the way others use *i·na*, for defocusing and for a reintroduced topic.

(6.5) Use of *mana* to defocus and to shift reference to a reintroduced topic (JB-Tiger 49)

(a)   *e·h=awatenamawoči, e·h=na·kwa·či=wi·na=mana. / mana=ke·hi·=ʼni*
        e·h=we·pinehkawa·či otaye·hi. / meše=na·hina·h=e·nemehka·či=mana, ...

        (The hero has traded his magic tablecloth to a stockman for a magic hat.) 'It was handed over to him, and this [hero] for his part left. / And then this [other] one began driving his animals. / And after this [hero] had gone a little ways, ...'

        (|na·kwa·-| AI 'leave', |e·h=–či| 3s/AOR, *wi·na* 3s/EMPH; *mana* 'this (anim.)' 3x;
        =*ke·hi* 'moreover'; *i·ni* 'then'; |we·pinehkaw-| TA 'drive', |e·h=a·či| 3s–3´/AOR;
        otaye·hi 'his animals (obv.)'; *meše=na·hina·hi* 'a little ways off';
        |anemehka·-| AI 'go on', |IC–či| 3s/CC)

A speaker who uses *mana* in this way may also use *i·na* in a more restricted function:

(6.6) Discourse use of *i·na* and *mana*

(a)   *kaho·ni˙=ʼna ihkwe·wa e·h=pi·tike·či. nepi e·h=kwa·pahaki ana·kaneki i·na*
        ihkwe·wa, e·h=kekapiči. / kaho·ni=mana oškinawe·ha e·h=na·kwa·či. ... /
        kaho·ni˙=ʼna, "[long quote]," e·h=ineči ihkwe·wa. (C-FS 4)

        'And then that woman came in. And that woman poured some water into a bowl and sat holding it. / And then this young man left ... / And then that woman was asked, "..."

        (*kaho·ni* 'and then' 3x; *i·na* 'that (anim.)' 3x; *ihkwe·wa* 'woman' 3x;
        |pi·tike·-| AI 'enter', |e·h=–či| 3s/AOR; *nepi* 'water';
        |kwa·pah-| TI(1) 'dip out', |e·h=–aki| 3s-0/AOR; *ana·kaneki* 'bowl (loc.)';
        |kekapi-| AI 'sit holding {something}', |e·h=–či| 3s/AOR; *mana* 'this (anim.)';
        oškinawe·ha 'young man'; |na·kwa·-| AI 'leave', |e·h=–či| 3s/AOR;
        |iN-| TA 'say {so} to', |e·h=–eči| X–3/AOR)

In (6.6) the arrival and foreshadowing behavior of the prospective future wife of the hero are highlighted by the double use of *i·na ihkwe·wa* 'that woman' in a chiastic structure (Subject Verb, Verb Subject). The young man is then referred to with *mana*, and the narrative shifts back to the young woman with *i·na* in a discontinuous noun phrase that straddles the long quote addressed to her by his sister.

The absentative demonstrative *i·niya* 'that (gone, before)' (§31.8) may be used to refer back to someone or something mentioned in a previous episode (6.7*ac*), or to refer back across two or more other potential topics (6.7*bc*).

(6.7) Discourse use of *i·niya*

   (a)   *pi·tike·niči, neniwani=či·hi <u>i·niye·ne</u> ketiwani.* (K-MESB 28)
          'When he (obv.) went in, he saw that the one (obv.) who had been an eagle was a man.'

              (|pi·tike·-| AI 'enter', |IC–niči| 3´/CC; *neniwani* 'man (obv.)';
              =či·hi 'it was discovered' (5.122c); *i·niye·ne* 'that (obv., abs.)';
              ketiwani 'eagle (obv.)')

   (b)   *"...," e·h=ina·či mehtose·neniwahi. / e·h=te·pesiwa·či. /*
          o·ni·=·'niya ni·ka·ni·ta, "..," e·h=ina·či. (K-B 207; tr. HP)
          "'[quote],' he [hero, prox.] told the people [obv.]. They [prox.] felt very happy over it. Then that leader [prox.; another man] again '[long quote],' he [prox.] told them [obv.]."

              (|iN-| TA 'say {so} to', |e·h=–a·či| 3s–3´/AOR; *mehtose·neniwahi* 'people (obv.)';
              |te·pesi-| AI 'be glad', |e·h=–wa·či| 3p/AOR; *o·ni* 'and then';
              i·niya 'that (anim., abs.); ni·ka·ni·-| AI 'lead', |IC–ta| 3/PPL(ANsg)); |iN-| TA ..)

   (c)   *o·ni <u>i·niya</u>| neniwa e·h=pye·nota·koči <u>i·niye·he</u> neniwahi.* (K-SSP 97; tr. HP)
          (The hero and a girl have pledged to marry. He tells her father he will come for her after he receives a further blessing. The girl dislikes a former suitor and turns away other young men.) "Then <u>the</u> man was visited by <u>the same</u> men [who had blessed him]."

              (*o·ni* 'and then'; *i·niya* 'that (anim., abs.)'; *neniwa* 'man';
              |pye·notaw-| TA 'come to', |e·h=–koči| 3´–3s/AOR;
              i·niye·he 'those (obv., abs.)'; *neniwahi* 'men (obv.)')

The specialized demonstrative *i·na·ka* 'that other (far away)' (§31.6) is used in narrative to shift the story back to a character or characters at a different location or acting separately. In this use it can often be translated as 'meanwhile, that other (one)', 'at the same time, that other (one)', or the like.

(6.8) Discourse use of *i·na·ka*

   (a)   <u>*i·na·ka*</u>*=ke·hi mami·ši·ha e·h=ki·yose·či.* (K-FC 555; tr. HP)
          (A man goes and instructs a ceremonial attendant ["waiter"] to invite clan members to come and host a clan feast. He returns home, and the women talk with him about the request of the one blessed to keep up the ceremonies during his eight-year absence.)
          "<u>At this time the</u> waiter was walking about."

              (*i·na·ka* 'that other (anim.)'; *=ke·hi* 'moreover'; *mami·ši·ha* 'attendant';
              |ki·yose·-| AI 'walk', |e·h=–či| 3s/AOR)

   (b)   <u>*i·ne·ke*</u>*=ke·hi=·'pi e·h=ki·ša·koči·=mekoho -se·kesiwa·či.* (K-FC 345; tr. HP)
          (A captive is tortured and dies.) "<u>The others</u> were terribly scared."

              (*i·ne·ke* 'those others (anim.)'; *=ke·hi* 'moreover'; *=ipi* HRSY; |ki·ša·koči| PV
              'extremely', |se·kesi-| AI 'be scared', |e·h=–wa·či| 3p/AOR; *=mekoho* EMPH)

OBVIATION

73. A pervasive feature of Meskwaki grammar and discourse is the system of obviation, which distinguishes two subtypes of third person, differentiating the more peripheral obviative from the more central proximate. The proximate has a higher pronominal rank and is the default category; when contrasted with an obviative, its use indicates that someone or something is, in some sense, of greater interest. While governed by grammatical constraints, the assignment of proximate and obviative status is, to a considerable extent, the result of a free choice by the speaker and can be used to structure and present the flow of information. The general principle is that if there are two animates in the same context only one can be proximate, but what counts as the same context is variable. There are systematic exceptions to this principle when two proximates are conjoined or semantically linked, or when they are treated facultatively as being in separate minimal contexts. Multiple obviatives may occur in the presence of a more central proximate. Inanimates occur as obviatives (indicated only by verbal inflection) in the presence of third person animates under the same conditions as animates, but an inanimate cannot outrank an animate and cause it to be obviative.

Morphological Aspects of the Obviative

73.1. Obligatory obviative inflection. Animate nouns and demonstratives and other pronouns that inflect for nominal categories have obviative forms and distinguish obviative singular and plural. Intransitive verbs have distinct obviative forms for both animate and inanimate subjects; in the independent indicative obviative singular and plural are distinguished (2.52*a*, 2.53*b*). Transitive verbs distinguish obviative singular and plural only for the subjects and inverse objects of some independent indicative forms (3.242*b*). In the conjunct order, TA forms with first, second, or indefinite person subjects add a suffix for an obviative object (3.187*cd*). Except in these cases, the inflection of forms that make pronominal reference to an obviative object (or inverse subject) does not contain a suffix that refers to this obviative (3.190*a*, 3.191*a*). Transitive animate verbs with indefinite subjects (TA passives) may mark obviative objects (3.187*ab*). An animate head of a participle may be marked as obviative singular or plural. Proximate and obviative possessors are not differentiated in nominal inflection.

An animate noun with a third-person possessor always has an obviative nominal suffix (3.37-38), unless this is displaced by a locative suffix (**§28.15**, 3.99). The possessor is always animate, and in fact is always a sentient animate being.

(6.9) Animate noun with third-person possessor

okwisani 'his or her son'	*okwisahi* 'his or her sons'
okwiswa wani 'their son'	*okwiswa wahi* 'their sons'

A verb can be inflected for only a single proximate. Hence a transitive animate verb with a third person subject and object can be inflected for a proximate subject and an obviative object (6.10*a*), and for an obviative subject and a proximate object (6.10*b*), but not for two proximates. The inflections for proximate acting on obviative include the direct theme sign |-a·| (**§29.7(a)**), and those for obviative on proximate have the inverse theme sign |-ekw| (**§29.7(b)**).

(6.10) TA verbs with proximate and obviative (aorist conjunct)
  (a) Direct   *e·h=tepa·na·či* 'he or she (prox.) loved him, her, or them (obv.)'
                e·h=tepa·na·wa·či 'they (prox.) loved him, her, or them (obv.)'
  (b) Inverse *e·h=tepa·nekoči* 'he, she, or they (obv.) loved him or her (prox.)'
                e·h=tepa·nekowa·či 'he, she, or they (obv.) loved them (prox.)'
A verb may, however, be inflected for two obviatives, but in this case also subject and object
must be ranked, with one higher than the other on the person hierarchy (3.189). Thus here also
there is a formal contrast between direct and inverse.
  (6.11) TA verbs with two obviatives (aorist conjunct)
    (a) Direct   *e·h=tepa·na·niči* 'he, she, or they (1ˢᵗ obv.) loved him, her, or them (2ⁿᵈ obv.)'
    (b) Inverse *e·h=tepa·nekoniči* 'he, she, or they (2ⁿᵈ obv.) loved him, her, or them (1ˢᵗ obv.)'
The distinction made by the two obviative-on-obviative inflections may be glossed as a contrast
between 'first (or nearer, or higher) obviative (3′) on second (or further, or lower) obviative (3″)'
(6.11a) and 'second obviative (3″) on first obviative (3′)' (6.11b). In both of these endings,
however, the underlying suffix |-nit| 3′ marks the first obviative; there is no suffix anywhere in
the language for a second or further obviative category.

Discourse Functions of Proximate and Obviative

73.2. Proximate. As a general rule, when there is more than one animate third person in a
context one of them must be selected as proximate and the other or others are then obviative.
The proximate is used for the character that is the main focus of attention at that point in the
narrative. This may be the hero of the tale or the main topic of an episode or a shorter span. The
proximate is apt to be of higher topicality, more apt to be what things are about and more apt to
be an agent and mover of the narrative. Hence humans are ordinarily the proximate when
interacting with animals, and they also tend strongly to be the proximate in encounters with
spirits. At the same time, proximate status may also flag someone or something of momentary
interest. In one passage, a sacred pipe is proximate in sentences in which human beings and the
spirit who gave the pipe are obviative (K-ECRP 74). Also, the proximate may be a character,
even a secondary one, from whose point of view things are described.
  73.3. Sustained proximate. The simplest way to present two characters that are interacting
is to make one an invariant proximate with the other therefore being an invariant obviative. In
the passage in (6.12), for example, a man is the proximate and a pursuing grizzly bear is the
obviative throughout. (Meskwaki has no way to simply contrast 'he' and 'it', of course.)
  (6.12) Sustained proximate and obviative.
          (A man (prox.) is being pursued by a grizzly bear (obv.) towards a river; K-MIM 6)
  .1   *i·ya·h=meko ašiči pe·hki e·h=a·nemihekoči i·nini ka·ka·nwikaše·wani.*
        'As he got near, the grizzly bear (obv.) really pressed him (prox.) hard.
  .2   *meše=meko menwina·hi e·h=pye·hpahoniči,*
        It (obv.) came running not far behind,
  .3   *šewe·na nepi e·h=wa·wani-'na·kwa·teniki=meko, si·po·wi.*
        but the water was still too far away, the stream.
  .4   *e·h=ki·ši-=wi·na=meko -pi·te·ya·hkwipahoči,*
        He (prox.) had already run in among the trees, however,

.5   *eˑh=neˑtaki pemitasakatwi eˑh=šaˑpwaˑnakateniki,*
        and he (prox.) saw a log that was hollow all the way through,

.6   *eˑh=kaškihkete ˑniki=keˑhi.*
        and what's more, it had dried hard.

.7   *eˑh=piˑto teˑsaˑči.*
        He (prox.) crawled inside.

.8   *eˑh=noˑnitepe ˑčiniči.*
        And it (obv.) couldn't get its head in.

.9   *wiˑna=keˑhi eˑh=meme ˑnawičiki=meko iˑnahi pemitasakatoki.*
        At the same time, he (prox.) had plenty of room in that log.

.10   *eˑh=taši-wa ˑwana ˑhpenanekoči=meko.*
        And it (obv.) was just not able to get at him (prox.).

.11   *aškači čeˑh=we ˑpi-tetepeče ˑnaminiči.*
        After a while it (obv.) began to roll it [i.e., the log].

.12   *aškači čiˑkepyeˑki eˑh=pyeˑto ˑniči.*
        And after a while it (obv.) got it to the edge of the water.

.13   *kwi ˑyena=meko eˑh=kenwi ˑtemya ˑniki eˑh=čapoˑkisahto ˑniči.*
        Right where the water was deep it (obv.) threw it in.

.14   *mani=meko eˑši-čapoˑkisa ˑniki, naˑmepyeˑki eˑh=taši-kečisahoči,*
        And just as soon as it [the log] went in, he (prox.) scampered out under the water

.15   *akaˑmeˑheki eˑh=inanaˑmoči.*
        and (prox.) swam underwater to the other side.'

At the beginning of this passage, the grizzly bear is named with an obviative noun (line 1), but after that neither the man nor the bear is referred to by a noun or pronoun. They are kept distinct by the inflections on the verbs, two TA verbs inflected for obviative on proximate (in lines 1 and 10), and AI and TI verbs with proximate inflection for the man and obviative inflection for his pursuer. There are also four II verbs with obviative inflection (in lines 3, 5, 6, 13, and 14).

73.4. Alternating proximates. The other way of presenting the actions of two characters is by shifting the focus from one to the other with alternating proximates. A change in which character is proximate is a PROXIMATE SHIFT; the new proximate may be a character that is reintroduced or completely new, and may previously have been proximate or obviative. There may also be a partial proximate shift, with a new proximate having been included in a previous plural proximate, or a new proximate plural including the previous proximate. In the passage in (6.13) proximate status shifts between the hero Black Rainbow and his Sioux enemies, and to different subsets of the Siouxs. In this and the following examples proximate shifts are indicated by a double bar (‖) and generally correspond to paragraphs in the edition. An exception is in line 15, where the new paragraph marks a break between episodes.

    (6.13) Multiple proximate shifts.

        (A group of Meskwaki captives are being burned alive by their enemies, until now only Black Rainbow and his niece remain.) (O 150H-152G)

.1   *eˑh=sakinekwe ˑnaˑči, eˑh=weˑpaˑhke ˑči.*
        He (prox.) took her (obv.) under the arm and threw her (obv.).

.2   ‖ *šeˑški ašaˑhaki aškoteˑwi eˑh=neˑtamowaˑči eˑh=anemaˑškaˑniki, iˑniyeˑne ihkweˑwani.*
        The Siouxs (prox.) only saw fire (obv.) flying away, which was that woman (obv.).

.3 ‖ *o·ni=wi·na e·h=mawinaneči, e·h=so·kiheči.*
And then it was his (prox.) turn to be set upon and tied.

.4 *kena·či=meko ahpemeki e·h=išiwena·či e·taši·hka·kočihi.*
Slowly he (prox.) took those (obv.) that were busy with him (prox.) up to the sky.

.5 *e·h=ma·no·hkawoči=ke·hi, šewe·na e·h=pwa·wi-=mekoho ·kaški·so·kiheči.*
There was actually a whole gang mobbing him (prox.), but still it was simply impossible to tie him (prox.) up.

.6 *ahpemeki=mekoho ki·ši-pye·na·či,*
And after he (prox.) had brought them (obv.) right up to the sky,

.7 *e·h=pekihkeška·niki e·h=awiwa·či.*
the spot where they (prox.) all were broke into pieces.

.8 ‖ *e·h=kwa·pa·škawa·či aša·haki.*
The Siouxs (prox.) fell all over the place.

.9 ‖ *ke·kya·ta=meko e·h=ča·kiha·či.*
And he (prox.) killed pretty nearly all of them (obv.).

.10 ‖ *mehteno·h=mekoho ši·ša·čiki e·h=aškwiheči,*
Only some hunters (prox.) escaped being killed,

.11 *na·hkači atehči me·hi e·ya·hičiki ihkwe·waki e·h=aškwiheči.*
and also some women (prox.) who had gone a little ways off were not killed.

.12 ‖ *wi·na=ke·h=wa·natohka mahkate·wi-anakwe·wa e·h=pemi-we·pose·či.*
But as for Black Rainbow (prox.), without giving it a further thought he (prox.) started walking.

.13 *aya·pami·pye·ya·či we·či·či,*
And when he (prox.) arrived back where he (prox.) had come from,

.14 *e·h=a·čimoči e·to·tawomeči owi·hka·nwa·wahi.*
he (prox.) reported how their companions (obv.) had been treated.

.15 *o·ni=·pi e·h=na·twe·we·kahwa·či.*
And then, they say, he (prox.) summoned them (obv.) with a drum.

.16 ‖ *ma·ne=meko e·h=pya·wa·či aša·haki,*
Many were the Siouxs (prox.) that came,

.17 *kekimesi=mekoho e·h=mešeneči.*
and every one of them (prox.) was captured.

.18 ‖ *i·ni=mekoho e·to·tawa·wa·či.*
They (prox.) treated *them* (obv.) the same way.

.19 ‖ *wi·nwa·wa=·pi·=·ni e·h=mayo·wa·či ki·ke·na·waki.*
Then it was the captives' (prox.) turn to weep, they say.

.20 *kekimesi=mekoho e·h=mayo·wa·či.*
Every last one of them (prox.) wept.

.21 *o·ni nekoti ihkwe·wa e·h=peno·heči.*
And then one woman (prox.) was sent home.

In (6.13) the hero Black Rainbow, who is who the story as a whole is about, is the dominant proximate (lines 1, 3-6, 9, 12-15). Plurals that include him and others (lines 7, 18) are also proximate. One correlate of his high topical rank is that proximate shifts to him need not be accompanied by an overt proximate nominal (lines 3, 9), though his name *is* used at the beginning of a major episode (line 12). There are proximate shifts that highlight the Sioux enemies (lines 2, 16-17), the Sioux captives (lines 19-20), and separate groups of Sioux minor players (lines 10, 11), and there is a proximate shift to the Sioux woman who will be the focus of the next episode (line 21). The proximate shift in line 8 takes place in two stages: first the proximate that encompasses only the hero expands to include the Siouxs (line 7), and then this composite proximate contracts to just the Siouxs (line 8). Passive verbs are common (lines 3, 5, 10, 11, 14, 17, 21); their use avoids a simultaneous switch of proximate and obviative, and this appears to be their intended function.

Frequent proximate shifts are naturally also characteristic of passages with multiple independently acting characters. The passage in (6.14) illustrates this and also shows how proximate assignment can be used to manipulate point of view and build narrative tension.

(6.14) Multiple proximate shifts among multiple characters.

(A married woman has taken up with another man while her husband is away and regrets his return, until he says he will leave again in four days.) (K-YMF 2-4)

.1   *nye wokonakateniki, e·h=na·kwa niči ona·pe mani.*
     After four days, her husband (obv.) left.

.2   *na·kwa niči, e·h=mayo·hka noči.*
     And when he (obv.) left, she (prox.) pretended to cry.

.3   *"mehto·či='škwe ke·htena," e·h=iči.*
     She (prox.) blurted out, "It looks like it's for real!"

.4   ‖ *"kaši=ni·hka išawiwa," e·h=išite he·či neniwa.*
     "What *is* the matter with her?" the man (prox.) thought.

.5   ‖ *i·na ka=ke·hi ihkwe·wa, i·ni=pe·hki.*
     And for the woman (prox.) back home, things then got serious.

.6   ‖ *e·h=pwa·wi-=ke·h=meko -kehke·nema wa·či ke·htesičiki.*
     Now, the old folks (prox.) were unaware of her (obv.) activities.

.7   ‖ *kapo·twe e·h=kehke·nema·či we·wi·hka·nita i·niye·ne ki·weška·ničini.*
     In time the friend (prox.) of that absent traveler (obv.) became aware of what she (obv.) was doing.

.8   ‖ *(ke·keya·h=meko='pi atehči we·pi-nepe·waki kotakani neniwani.)*
     (They say that eventually she (prox.) and the other man (obv.) had started sleeping away someplace.)

.9   ‖ *e·h =a·hkwe·či oškinawe·ha owi·hka·nani e·h=mi·hketamawomeči owi·wani.*
     The young man (prox.) was angry that his friend's (obv.) wife (obv.) was being made love to by another.

.10 *aškači e·h=pya·niči.*
     After some time he (obv.) [i.e., his friend (obv.)] returned.

.11 *te·kwa·kiniki, aya·pami e·h=pya·niči owi·hka·nani.*
     His friend (obv.) came back that fall.

.12 *aškači e·h=a·čimoha·či owi·hka·nani.*
     And after a time he (prox.) told his friend (obv.) what was happening.

.13 *"nahi´, ni·hka·ne, kaši·='h=to·tamani," e·h=ineči.*
     "Come on, my friend, why worry about it?" he (prox.) was told.

     [Four more expressions of unconcern framed by *e·h=ineči* 'he (prox.) was told'.]

.14 *a·kwi=meko kana·kwa.*
     It had *no* effect.

.15 ‖ *"kaši=ni·hka ketešawi e·h=pwa wi-=ye·toke·-kya·we·yani,"* *e·h=ineči we·wi·wita.*
"What's the matter with you that you seem not to be jealous?" the woman's husband (prox.) was asked.

.16 *"o·´, meše·='nah-we·=wi·na kya·we·hka·ha, wi·h=kya·we·ya·ni išite·he·ya·ne,"* *e·h=ina·či owi·hka·nani.*
"Oh, I *could* be jealous if I wanted to be jealous," he (prox.) told his friend (obv.).

.17 ‖ *"kaši=we·=ča·h=keteši-pwa·wi-kya·we,"* *e·h=ina·či.*
"So, why is it that you're not jealous?" he (prox.) asked him (obv.).

.18 *"o·´, ni·h=kya·we,"* *e·h=ineči.*
"Oh, *I'll* be jealous," he (prox.) was answered.

.19 *"o·´, i·ni=ma·h=ki·na,"* *e·h=išiwe·či.*
"Well, that's what I'm talking about!" he (prox.) declared.

.20 *o·ni=ye·toke e·h=anawiwa·či.*
And then it seems they (prox.) went on a hunt.

.21 ‖ *o·ni ihkwe·wa·na·hka e·h=ki·ši-=meko·-mehka·ti·či owi·hka·nani.*
And the woman (prox.) wasted no time in getting together with her friend (obv.) again.

.22 ‖ *o·ni i·ya·hi ki·ši-pya·wa·či peno·či·me·hi, i·tepi aya·pami e·h=a·či,*
And then, after they (prox.) [i.e., the hunters] had arrived quite far away, he (prox.) went back there,

.23 *e·h=nenoswiči.*
becoming a buffalo (prox.).

In (6.14) the man who is the center of attention is largely backgrounded as an obviative while his wife and friend are foregrounded as alternating proximates. The man is proximate for one line that gives his thoughts (line 4), and the woman's parents make a one-line appearance (line 6). The man is still not the proximate when his return is described from the perspective of his friend (line 10), and he seemingly expresses acceptance of an open marriage in a series of remarks that are framed by the passive quotative verb *e·h=ineči* 'he (i.e., the friend) was told' (lines 11-13 and five lines here omitted). Focus shifts to the man in line 14, which has only particles and hence no marking of proximate or obviative, and in lines 15 and 16 the man is briefly proximate. There is then a proximate shift back to the friend which continues as the two friends talk (lines 17-19), even when the man finally and portentously admits his jealousy in a yet another quote that is framed by a passive verb (line 18). This proximate expands to a plural that includes the man with his friend (line 20). Next there is a proximate shift to the wife back home (line 21). And then a proximate shift back to the two friends (line 22) immediately contracts, in the same sentence, to the man alone, without an overt nominal, and, with the unexpected, syntactically bare verb *e·h=nenoswiči* 'he became a buffalo', he embarks on his journey of revenge (line 23).

73.5. Possessed proximates. In the passages in 6.12-14 the proximates, obviatives, and proximate shifts are signaled by verbal inflections and occasional overt nominals. The use of obviative intransitive verbs and inverse transitives is supplemented by the frequent use of passives, which reduce the clutter of supernumerary obviatives. But the freedom to choose the relative ranking of subject and object has no parallel in the inflection of possessed nouns, which must be obviative when the possessor is third person. Nevertheless, there are ways of having the one possessed be proximate. The more formal way is to make the equivalent of a possessed proximate with the participle of a verb of possession (6.15.1b, 2b, 3b).

(6.15) Obviative possessed noun and equivalent proximate participle

.1a *ona·pe·mani* 'her husband (obv.)' (6.14.1)

.1b *we·wi·wita* 'the woman's husband (prox.), 'the husband (prox.) of' (6.14.15)
   (*lit.*, 'the one (prox.) who has (her [obv.] as) a wife')

.2a *owi·hka·nani* 'his friend (obv.)' (6.14.9, 11, 12, 16)

.2b *we·wi·hka·nita* 'his friend (prox.)', 'the friend (prox.) of' (6.14.7)
   (*lit.*, 'the one (prox.) who has (him [obv.] as) a friend')

.3a *okwisani* 'his or her son (obv.)'

.3b *we·yo·sita* 'his (obv.) son or daughter (prox.)'
   (*lit.*, 'the one (prox.) who has (him [obv.] as) a father')
   we·kita 'her (obv.) son or daughter (prox.)'
   (*lit.*, 'the one (prox.) who has (her [obv.] as) a mother')

The correspondence between the two ways of indicating possession can be seen when the one possessed becomes the focus of attention and shifts from obviative to proximate:

(6.16) Obviative possessed noun shifts to proximate participle
   (A woman has become lost on the prairie and is intensely searched for.) (K-B 5)
   ona·pe·mani apina=meko e·h=mahkate·wi·niči. ‖
   o·ni=·'pi we·wi·wita, "...," e·h=ineči.
   'Her husband (obv.) even fasted [to gain the pity of the spirits and a blessing]. ‖
   And then the woman's husband (prox.) was told [by a spirit], "..." '
      (*ona·pe·mani* 'her husband (obv.)'; *apina* 'even'; =*meko* EMPH;
      |mahkate·wi·-| AI 'fast', |e·h=–niči| 3'/AOR; *o·ni* 'and then'; =*ipi* HRSY;
      |owi·wi-| TA 'have (O2 as) a wife', |IC–ta| 3/PPL(ANsg);
      |iN-| TA 'say {so} to', |e·h=–eči| X–3/AOR)

73.6. "Honorary proximate." The more direct way to get a possessed noun to be proximate is simply to construe a possessed obviative noun as a proximate in cross-reference. In this fairly common construction an obviative is used as what has been nicknamed an "honorary proximate" (6.17*ab*). Even a possessed inanimate noun may be construed as proximate when the noun is highly salient or foregrounded as important, like a cinematic close-up (6.17*cd*). Some cases of this kind of disagreement might be analyzed as having a break in the construction, with proximate shifting to consistent obviative (6.17*e*). But this interpretation is not possible in cases where a possessed obviative noun is embedded within the discontinuous proximate noun phrase that it is in apposition with (6.17*f*).

(6.17) Obviative construed as proximate

(a) *ši·hwi·! wi·htwiya·ha okwisani aniweke·wa.* (SP-Pich1 102)
   'My! the blacksmith's son (obv.) dances (prox.) very well.'
      (*ši·hwi·!* 'My!'; *wi·htwiya·ha* 'blacksmith'; *okwisani* 'his son (obv.)';
      |aniweka·-| AI 'dance well', |-wa| 3s/IND)

(b) *nemešo·ha=mekoho oto·te·mani i·ni e·ne·nemita.* (K-FC 331; trans. HP)
   "it is my grandpa's brother [obv.], who [prox.] is thinking that way of me."
      (*nemešo·ha* 'my grandfather'; =*mekoho* EMPH; *oto·te·mani* 'his brother (obv.)';
      i·ni 'that (nan.)'; |ine·nem-| TA 'think about {so}', |IC–ita| 3–1s/PPL(ANsg))

(c) *'mahkwa' e·ne·kwiki ana·kwaki. / i·na=ča·hi otasa·mi wi·h=ni·sise·wi.* (K-SBSB 9)
(A bearskin will fall down from heaven.) 'It's the stars (prox.) you (pl.) call "the Bear (prox.)." That is, it's its (prox. anim.) skin (inan.) that will fall (prox.) [to earth].'
(*mahkwa* 'bear'; |iN-| TA 'say {so} to, about', |IC-e·kwiki| 2p–3/PPL(ANpl); *ana·kwaki* 'stars (anim.)'; *i·na* 'that (anim.)'; =*ča·hi* 'so'; *otasa·mi* 's.o.'s skin'; |wi·h=| FUT, |ni·sisa·-| AI,II |–wi| 0s/IND)

(d) *masa·či=meko e·h=kaški-keta·si·či, e·h=nepiwiki oko·te·hani.* (JB-RB 9)
(A woman carrying her baby flees from Sioux warriors and swims across a river.) 'She (prox.) was barely able to climb up the bank, as her (prox.) skirts were wet (prox.).'
(*masa·či* 'barely'; =*meko* EMPH; |kaški| PV 'be able to', |keta·si·-| AI 'climb a hill', |e·h=–či| 3s/AOR; |nepiwi-| II 'be wet', |e·h=–ki| 0/AOR; *oko·te·hani* 'her skirts (inan.)')

(e) *mani=wi·na ki·šihto·ta owi·hka·nani. ma·hani=ke·hi.* (K-ECRP 85; tr. TB)
(In a vision an eagle lets the one being blessed see God, who created one earth.) "[But] His friend [obv.] is the one [prox.] who made this one. And here he [obv.] is."
(*mani* 'this (inan.)' [= this earth]; =*wi·na* 'but'; |ki·šiht-| TI(2) 'make', |IC-o·ta| 3–0/PPL(ANsg); *owi·hka·nani* 'his friend (obv.)'; *ma·hani* 'this (obv.)'; =*ke·hi* 'moreover')

(f) *ma·haki ni·h=anohka·na·waki masahkamikohkwe·wa otaye·hi ketiwaki.*
"I shall hire M.'s [prox.] pet [obv.] eagles [prox.]." (K-M 437f; tr. HP)
(*ma·haki* 'these (prox.)'; |wi·h=| FUT, |anohka·N-| TA 'hire', |ne–a·waki| 1s–3p/IND; *masahkamikohkwe·wa* (name); *otaye·hi* 'her pets (obv.)'; *ketiwaki* 'eagles (prox.)')

73.7. Conjoined proximates. Speakers also have some freedom to violate the principle of one proximate in a context when nouns are conjoined. A noun conjoined with a proximate noun may be either proximate (6.18*ab*) or obviative (6.18*cd*). In all cases of conjoined proximate and obviative, however, demonstratives and verbs show agreement with a proximate plural (5.38*ab*, 5.58, 6.18).

(6.18) Proximate conjoined with proximate or obviative
Proximate and proximate:

(a) *o·ni=a·mihtahi če·wi·šwi wa·peška·hkoneči ihkwe·wa, neniwa.* (O 53G)
'And then both the man (prox.) and the woman (prox.) would be painted white.'
(*o·ni* 'and then'; *a·mihtahi* POT; *če·wi·šwi* 'both'; |wa·peška·hkon-| TA 'paint white', |–eči| X–3/CONJ; *ihkwe·wa* 'woman (prox.)'; *neniwa* 'man (prox.)')

(b) *e·h=aški-ne·woti·wa·či neno·te·wa, mo·hkoma·na.* (C-IW 1)
'When the Indian (prox.) and the American (prox.) first met (*lit.*, saw each other).'
(|aški| PV 'first', |ne·woti·-| AI 'see each other', |e·h=–wa·či| 3p/AOR; *neno·te·wa* 'Indian (prox.)'; *mo·hkoma·na* 'American (prox.)')

Proximate and obviative:

(c) *e·h=ni·šo·ka·wa·či i·nini še·škesi·hani, i·na neniwa.* (K-SD 9; tr. anon.)
"That maiden [obv.] and man [prox.] danced as a pair [prox. pl.]."
(|ni·šo·ka·-| AI 'dance as a pair', |e·h=–wa·či| 3p/AOR; *i·nini* 'that (obv.)', *še·škesi·hani* 'teenage girl (obv.)'; *i·na* 'that (anim. prox.)', *neniwa* 'man (prox.)')

(d) *e·h=aški-ne·woti·wa·či mo·hkoma·nani, neno·te·waki, meškwahki·ha.* (C-IW 1)
'When the American (obv.) and the Indians (prox.), the Meskwaki (prox.), first met.'
(|aški| PV 'first', |ne·woti·-| AI 'see each other', |e·h=–wa·či| 3p/AOR;
mo·hkoma·nani 'American (obv.)'; *neno·te·waki* 'Indians (prox.)';
meškwahki·ha 'Meskwaki (prox.)')

In the Owl text, the two turtles (i.e., turtle-shell rattles) are referred to four times with conjoined nouns that are the subject of passive verbs: in three cases the second noun is obviative (O 2I, 3G, 15C), while in one case both are proximate (O 51B).

It is possible that the conjoining of an obviative with a proximate is sometimes intended to suggest a lower rank on a scale of topicality or agency, comparable to that of a possessed noun or an obviative object. If so, however, the effect would seemingly be extremely subtle in cases like (6.18*cd*), where the contexts strongly suggest equal rank and agency. Such cases seem distinct from the nearly synonymous construction in (6.19), where the verb is singular and the obviative is an adjunct.

(6.19) Proximate subject and obviative adjunct
še·škesi·he·ha meše·='nah=meko pašito·he·hani wi·h=ni·šo·ke·wa. (K-SD 51F)
"a young girl [prox.] may dance with an old man [obv.]" (tr. anon.)
(*še·škesi·he·ha* 'teenage girl (dim.; prox.)'; *meše·='nah=meko* 'perhaps, may';
pašito·he·hani 'old man (dim.; obv.);
|wi·h=| FUT, |ni·šo·ka·-| AI 'dance as a pair', |–wa| 3s/IND)

73.8. Two proximates. Two proximates sometimes occur close enough together for one of them ordinarily to have to be an obviative. In some cases the proximate that occurs second is in a proximate island that provides a secondary highlight within a wider context dominated by the proximate that occurs first. A second proximate of this type is not only anomalous by being unexpectedly proximate, it is subject to being abruptly demoted to an obviative in a subsequent construction that explicitly includes the first proximate.

(6.20) Proximate island as highlighting
(a) *kehčine pye·ya·wa·či e·h=apiči='hkwe·wa, e·h=mawi-nana·hapiči.* (K-B 291)
(The chief invites the hero to go with him to where he and his sister live.)
"When they [prox.] came near where the woman [prox.] was sitting,
he [the chief, prox.] went over and sat there." (tr. HP)
(*kehčine* 'near'; |pya·-| AI 'come', |IC–wa·či| 3p/CC;
|api-| AI 'sit {somewhere}', |e·h=–či| 3s/PPL(loc.obl); *ihkwe·wa* 'woman (prox.)';
|mawi| PV 'go and', |nana·hapi-| AI 'sit down', |e·h=–či| 3s/AOR)
(b) *i·ni=ke·hi='pi·='niki e·h=pemi-anisa·wa·či mekesiwaki.* (K-ECRP 161; tr. TB)
nese·ma·wa e·h=ašenoči se·hkahamawoči·ni.
"It is said that those eagles [prox.] now flew off.
The tobacco [prox.] that [obv.] was burned for them [prox.] was now gone."
(*i·ni* 'then'; *=ke·hi* 'moreover'; *=ipi* HRSY; *i·niki* 'those (anim.)';
|pemi| PV 'set about', |anisa·-| AI 'fly up', |e·h=–wa·či| 3p/AOR;
mekesiwaki 'bald eagles (prox.)';
nese·ma·wa 'tobacco (prox.)'; |ašeno-| AI 'be gone', |e·h=–či| 3s/AOR;
|sahkahamaw-| TA 'offer tobacco to', |IC–ečini| X–3/PPL(OBVsg))

(c)   *ke·waki=či·hi e·h=apwi·hekoči.* (K-MOR 4)
       mehto·či e·h=mama·kanahkahki mehtekwi e·h=ina·pata·niki.
       waninawe e·h=nepa·niči ahpemeki.
       (A man (prox.) returns home to see the pet raccoons (obv.) he had left behind.)
       'He found they (obv.) were still waiting for him (prox.).
       There was a tree (inan.) that (prox.) looked like it (prox.) had thick branches.
       They (obv.) were sleeping all over in it.'
          (*ke·waki* 'still'; *=či·hi* 'it was surprisingly found that';
          |apwi·h-| TA 'wait for', |e·h=–ekoči| 3´–3s/AOR; *mehto·či* 'like';
          |mama·kanahkat-| II 'has large branches', |e·h=–ki| 0/AOR; *mehtekwi* 'tree';
          |ina·pata·ni-| II 'appear {so}', |e·h=–ki| 0/AOR; *waninawe* 'on all sides';
          |nepa·-| AI 'sleep {somewhere}', |e·h=–niči| 3´/AOR; *ahpemeki* 'aloft')

In (6.20*a*) the woman is becoming of central importance in the narrative at this point, as her brother, the chief, is trying to arrange a marriage between her and the hero. The reference to her as proximate, between two other proximates in the same sentence that include or refer to her brother, brings her to the fore as a major figure. The proximate status of the tobacco in (6.20*b*), similarly between references to the eagles as proximate, also highlights it and its disappearance. It is, however, then demoted to an obviative as the head of the passive participle of which the eagles are the proximate primary object. (Although the verb |sahkahamaw-| could literally be 'burn O2 for', as it was translated by TB, here it presumably has its idiomatic meaning 'offer tobacco to', since if it had been burned there would be no point in highlighting the fact that it had disappeared.) In (6.20*c*) the pet raccoons remain obviative when referred to explicitly, but their continued loyal presence is highlighted by the inanimate proximate reference to the appearance of the tree they are sleeping in.

In general, the abrupt appearance of a second proximate in the same sentence may highlight a central character or one higher in topicality, with or without the explicit demotion of another proximate.

(6.21) Abrupt proximate shift

(a)   *o·ni='pi i·niya e·h=kaški-=mekoho·-pya·či we·wi·wi·ne·hita,* (K-M 103f; tr. HP)
       wi·sahke·ha se·ka·nowe·saha·čini.
       e·h=ki·mo·či-=ke·h=mekoho·-pya·či.
       "And then the one [prox.] who had horns succeeded in coming,
       the one [obv.] W[isahkeha] [prox.] had grabbed by the tail.
       The one [prox.] with horns came stealthily." (HP supplies the specification of the subject in the last sentence.)
          (*o·ni* 'and then'; *=ipi* HRSY; *i·niya* 'that (anim., abs.)'; |kaški| PV 'be able',
          |pya·-| AI 'come', |e·h=–či| 3s/AOR (2x); *=mekoho* EMPH (2x);
          we·wi·wi·ne·hita 'one who has horns (prox.)';
          wi·sahke·ha (the Culture Hero; prox.);
          |saka·nowe·sah-| TA 'grab by the tail', |IC–a·čini| 3s–3´/PPL(OBVsg);
          ki·mo·či PV 'secretly'; *=ke·hi* 'moreover')

(b)   *e·h=ni·ka·nika·pa·wa·či so·kenakiki wi·sahke·ha mi·šiwe·čini mi·ša·mani.*
(K-W 1110)
"Those [prox.] stood first in line who [prox.] held in their hands sacred bundles
which W[isahkeha] [prox.] had given." (tr. HP)
   (|ni·ka·nika·pa·-| AI 'stand first', |e·h=—wa·či| 3p/AOR;
   |so·ken-| TI(1) 'hold in hand', |IC—akiki| 3–0/PPL(ANpl);
   wi·sahke·ha (the Culture Hero, prox.);
   |mi·šiwe·-| AI 'give O2', |IC–čini| 3s/PPL(INpl);
   mi·ša·mani 'sacred bundles (inan.)')

(c)   *o·´, ni·na=wi·na, mana me·šenaka,*
   a·kwi owiye·ha wi·h=we·we·ne·netamawičini. (K-MWL 34)
'Oh, as for me, this is the one [prox.] *I* captured.
No one [prox.] will have a say over him besides me,'
   (*o·´* 'Oh'; *ni·na* 1s/EMPH; *=wi·na* 'but'; *mana* 'this (anim.)';
   |mešen-| TA 'capture', |IC–aka| 1s–3/PPL(ANsg); *a·kwi* 'not';
   owiye·ha 'anyone (prox.)'; |wi·h=| FUT;
   |we·we·ne·netamaw-| TA+O 'be in charge of O2 of', |–ičini 3s–1s/NEG)

(d)   *me·mešenakiki no·hkomesa e·h=awatawaki.* (K-Auto 155)
'I took the ones (prox.) I caught to my grandmother (prox.).'
   (|CV+| RED1, |mešen-| TA 'catch', |IC–akiki| 1s–3/PPL(ANpl);
   no·hkomesa 'my grandmother';
   |awataw-| TA+O 'take O2 to', |e·h=–aki| 1s–3/AOR)

In (6.21*a*) a proximate is momentarily demoted to obviative, when an encounter with the Culture
Hero is recalled, but then immediately reset as a proximate. In (6.21*b*), (6.21*c*), and (6.21*d*) there
is no overt demotion of the proximate. The Culture Hero is again the second proximate in
(6.21*b*), his blessing being the highest there is; the use of the indefinite detransitive |mi·šiwe·-| AI
'give' (4.298*d*) rather than |mi·N-| TA 'give to' avoids having the first proximate briefly switch to
an obviative. The appearance of the minimally topical indefinite pronoun *owiye·ha* as a second
proximate in (6.21*c*) must reflect the fact that the indefinite others it refers to are Meskwakis,
who always outrank their enemies as a default; here it is the use of a ditransitive verb (TA+O),
which does not inflect for the secondary object, that avoids overtly switching the first proximate
to an obviative. The two proximates in the focus position in (6.21*d*) are the mud turtles that the
writer has described hunting and his grandmother, who is the newer focus and too highly ranked
to be subordinated as an obviative.

In some cases a second proximate in the same sentence is contrasted with or opposed to the
first, but they have the same apparent topical rank and do not directly interact.

(6.22) Abrupt proximate shift
   (a)   *tohka·na=na·hkači ma·nake·mote,* (K-TCSB 66-67; tr. TB)
      i·ni wi·h=maniheči ki·ško·haki.
      "Again, if a T. wins [an eating contest], then the K.'s food is taken away from him."
         (*tohka·na* 'member of the Tohkan division (prox.)'; *na·hkači* 'again';
         |ma·nake·mo-| AI 'beats others', |–te| 3s/SUBJ; *i·ni* 'then';
         |wi·h=| FUT, |manih-| TA 'rob', |(e·h=)–eči| X–3/AOR;
         ki·ško·haki 'members of the Kishko division (prox.)')

(b)   *ma·haki e·h=ki·ši-=mekoho me·me·čiki -kehke·nemači,*
       e·nehki i·niye·ka. (K-SSP 199)
       'Now you have positively found out about these (prox.),
       as those others (prox.) told you.'
           (*ma·haki* 'these (prox.)'; |ki·ši| PV PERF, |kehke·nem-| TA 'know',
           |e·h=–ači| 2s–3/AOR; =*mekoho* EMPH; *me·me·čiki* 'positively';
           |iN-| TA 'say {so} to', |IC–ehki| 3–2s/PPL(obl); *i·niye·ka* 'those (prox., abs.)')

(c)   *e·h=we·pi-a·ya·čimohiwa·či nehki pe·mi-pwa·wi-ne·woti ye·kwe=ye·toke*
       ne·nepo·hičiki. (K-FR 20)
       'And they (prox.) began to tell me about those (prox.) that had died since you (pl.)
       and they had, I suppose, last seen each other.'
           (|we·pi| PV 'begin', |CV+| RED1, |a·čimoh-| TA 'tell', |e·h=–iwa·či| 3p–1s/AOR;
           nehki 'for {so} long'; |pemi| PV 'along', |pwa·wi| PV 'not';
           |ne·woti·-| AI 'see each other', |IC–ye·kwe| 2p/PPL(obl); =*ye·toke* 'I suppose';
           |CV+| RED1, |nepo·hi-| 'die', |IC–čiki| 3/PPL(ANpl))

In (6.22c) the second proximate is syntactically an adjunct of the first verb, which has the first
proximate as subject, and also a component of the subject of the second verb, but it is probably
significant that the second verb separates it from the rest of the sentence.

Minor clauses with impersonal verbs commonly have the expected obviative inflection
(6.23a). In (6.23b) the obviative verb is the sole indication that the particles that make up the
idiomatic expression in the main clause imply a reference to a third person animate.

(6.23) Impersonal verb with inanimate obviative

(a)   *katawi-wa·panike i·ni wi·h=pya·wa·či ayo·hi.* (K-FC 343; tr. HP)
       "They [prox.] will arrive here when it is almost morning [obv.]."
           (*katawi* PV 'almost', |wa·pan-| II 'be morning', |–nike| 0ˊ/SUBJ; *i·ni* 'then';
           |wi·h=| FUT, |pya·-| AI 'come', |(e·h=)–wa·či| 3p/AOR; *ayo·hi* 'here')

(b)   *mani=na·hkači meno·hkami·nike, ča·ki-meko -ke·ko·hi.* (K-W 35; tr. HP)
       "This coming spring [obv.] we'll give them [prox.] all we can." (I.e., 'we'll give
       them everything we've got; we'll make a maximum effort against them'.)
           (*mani* 'this (inan.)'; *na·hkači* 'again';
           |meno·hkami·-| II 'be spring', |–nike| 0ˊ/SUBJ;
           ča·ki 'all'; =*meko* EMPH; *ke·ko·hi* '(some)thing')

But quite frequently, especially in quoted speech or thought, such verbs are inflected for an
inanimate proximate. In some cases these seem to be of low salience as virtual frozen forms
(6.24ab), but in other cases they may have relatively more significant, highlighted information
(6.24c).

(6.24) Impersonal verb with inanimate proximate

(a)   *ma·hani wi·h=mi·čičini neta·nesa wa·pake.* (K-FC 42)
       'My daughter (prox.) shall eat these tomorrow (prox.).'
       (A thought; literally, 'These are what my daughter will eat tomorrow.')
           (*ma·hani* 'these (inan.)'; |wi·h=| FUT, |mi·či-| TI(3) 'eat', |IC–čini| 3s/PPL(INpl);
           neta·nesa 'my daughter'; |wa·pan-| II 'be morning', |–ke| 0/SUBJ)

(b)   *wa·paki ma·ne·waki mehtose·neniwaki.* (K-Auto 75; tr. IP)
       "Next day [prox.]. throngs of people [prox.] came."
           (|wa·pan-| II 'be morning', |IC–ki| 0/CC;
           |ma·ne·-| AI 'be many', |–waki| 3p/IND; *mehtose·neniwaki* 'people (prox.)')

(c)   *ni·na=ke·hi keye·či·he;* (K-WTH 3; ed. LT)

      na·hina·hi e·h=ni·peki i·nina·hi e·h=kaškimaki.

      (A man reports that he successfully proposed to a woman in early spring; a second
      suitor says of her:) 'I did so more recently;

      during high summer (prox.) is when I persuaded her (prox.).'

          (*ni·na* 1s/EMPH; *=ke·hi* 'moreover'; *keye·či·he* 'recently';

          na·hina·hi 'at the time'; |ni·pen-| II 'be when crops ripen', |e·h=–ki| 0/AOR;

          i·nina·hi 'at that time'; |kaškim-| TA 'persuade', |e·h=–aki| 1s–3/AOR)

Sometimes when there are two inanimate subjects in the same sentence one is proximate and
the other obviative. In some cases there seems to be no difference in the salience or topicality of
the two inanimates (6.25*a*), but in other cases the obviative verb has ordinary incidental
information and the proximate one appears to be highlighted (6.25*bc*).

(6.25) Proximate and obviative inanimates together

    (a)   *wa·pake='pi na·wahkwe·nike i·ni wi·h=pya·či,* (K-BHD 54; tr. TB)

          "tomorrow [prox.] he [prox.] will come at noon [obv.]."

              (|wa·pan-| II 'be morning', |–ke| 0/SUBJ; *=ipi* HRSY;

              |na·wahkwe·-| II 'be noon', |–nike| 0´/SUBJ;

              i·ni 'then'; |wi·h=| FUT, |pya·-| AI 'come', |(e·h=)–či| 3s/AOR)

    (b)   *na·hina·h=mekoho na·wahkwe·niki, e·h=ma·ne·teki wi·seniweni.* (K-FC 244)

          (They [prox.] began bringing together the food for their clan feast.)

          'When noon came (obv.), there was lots (prox.) of food.'

              (*na·hina·hi* 'at the time'; *=mekoho* EMPH;

              |na·wahkwe·-| II 'be noon', |IC–niki| 0´/CC;

              |ma·ne·t-| II 'be much', |e·h=–eki| 0/AOR; *wi·seniweni* 'food')

    (c)   *meše·='nah=kapo·twe te·kwa·kiniki katawi,*

          na·hina·h=we·=meko e·h=we·pi- ne·nekoti -ki·pisa·ki ta·htapako·ni, ... (C-PB 1)

          'And one day when it was nearly autumn (obv.),

          just when single leaves were starting to fall (prox.), in fact, ...'

          (the hero, a young man [prox.], once again sees a mysterious woman [obv.].)

              (*meše·='nahi* 'about'; *kapo·twe* 'at some point';

              |takwa·ki-| II 'be fall', |IC–niki| 0´/CC; *katawi* 'almost' (PV)P;

              na·hina·hi 'at the time'; |=we·na| 'in fact'; *=meko* EMPH;

              |we·pi| PV 'begin', |ki·pisa·-| II 'fall', |e·h=–ki| 0/AOR; *ne·nekoti* 'one by one';

              ta·htapako·ni 'leaves (inan.)')

An impersonal II verb always retains proximate inflection when it has an animate proximate
as an adjunct (internal point-of-reference adjunct: 2.138).

(6.26) Proximate II with animate proximate adjunct

    (a)   *e·h=wi·škwe·we·kahki me·yo·čiki.* (O 160 and 12 other occurrences)

          'and there was a din (prox.) of people (prox.) weeping.'

              (|wi·škwe·we·kat-| II 'be loud noise', |e·h=–ki| 0/AOR;

              |mayo·-| AI 'weep'. |IC–čiki| 3/PPL(ANpl))

(b)   *e·h=pye·či-ka·hka·hkihkwe·ki= 'pi nenemehkiwaki e·h=pye·čisa·wa·či.*
       (S-RL2 14; ed. LT) 'There came the rattle (prox.) of the thunderers (prox.) as
       they (prox.) came flying.'
           (|pye·či| PV 'coming', |ka·hka·hkihkwe·-| II 'be a rattling sound', |e·h=-ki| 0/AOR;
           =*ipi* HRSY; *nenemehkiwaki* 'thunderers';
           |pye·čisa·-| AI 'come flying', |e·h=-wa·či| 3p/AOR)

(c)   *i·ya·ma·haki=wi·na e·h=po·ni·hete·ki a·mi·čiki= 'pihi.* (S-RL2 27)
       'Meanwhile, camp was made (prox.) by those others (prox.) who had moved.'
           (*i·ya·ma·haki* 'these others (anim., prox.)'; =*wi·na* 'but';
           |po·ni·hete·-| II 'camp (is) made', |e·h=-ki| 0/AOR;
           |a·mi·-| AI 'move camp', |IC–čiki| 3/PPL(ANpl); =*ipihi* HRSY)

(d)   *e·h=ma·wa·seki mehtose·neniwaki.* (SP-RL 20)
       'There was a village (prox.) of people (prox.).'
           (|ma·wa·sen-| II 'be a village ({somewhere})', |e·h=-ki| 0/AOR;
           mehtose·neniwaki 'people (prox.)')

These cases contrast with sentences in which an II is logically independent of an animate
proximate and syntactically separate:

(6.27) Obviative II syntactically separate from animate proximate

(a)   *ki·ša·koči=meko menwi-ki·šekateniwi me·nwite·ha·čiki.* (K-RC 21)
       For good-hearted people (prox.) the weather is extremely fine (obv.).'
           (*ki·ša·koči* 'extremely'; =*meko* EMPH;
           |menwi| PV 'well', |ki·šekat-| II 'be day', |–eniwi| 0'/IND;
           |menwite·he·-| AI 'be good-hearted', |IC–čiki| 3s/PPL(ANpl))

In (6.27) the animate plural participle is not an adjunct syntactically linked to the verb; rather, the
obviative inflection on the verb adds a notion similar to 'where *they* are' or 'when *they* are
present'.

   An II verb also retains proximate inflection in certain other cases where it is in construction
with a verb that has an animate proximate argument and does not refer to a distinct entity. For
example, the sentences in (6.28) have a locative oblique participle *e·h=tašiheči* 'where he (prox.)
was killed' that is the locative complement (6.28a) or subject (6.28b) of the higher II verb, which
is also proximate. (These are from a passage in which a manitou reveals to the one blessed a
vision of the killing of his parents by enemies.)

(6.28) Proximate II with animate proximate in a complement or subject

(a)   *o·= 'ni·= 'noki e·šiseki ahkanani e·h=tašiheči=ko·sa.* (K-MFWB 30)
       'Well, that's how the bones are (prox.) now at the place where your father (prox.)
       was killed.'
           (*o·´* 'oh'; *i·ni* 'that (inan.)'; *i·noki* 'now';
           |išisen-| II 'be (lying) {somewhere} {so}', |IC–ki| 0/PPL(obl); *ahkanani* 'bones';
           |taših-| TA 'kill {somewhere}', |e·h=-eči| X–3/PPL(loc.obl); *ko·sa* 'your father')

(b)   *e·šina·kwahki e·h=tašiheči=ko·sa.* (K-MFWB 30)
       'It's what the place where your father (prox.) was killed looks like (prox.).'
           (|išina·kwat-| II 'look {so}', |IC–ki| 0/PPL(obl);
           |taših-| TA 'kill {somewhere}', |e·h=-eči| X–3/PPL(loc.obl); *ko·sa* 'your father')

73.9. Obviative for external point of view. An animate third person may be obviative as a
way to indicate that there is an external observer, even when there is no proximate present.

Earlier in the same passage from which the sentences in (6.28) are taken, when the hero is shown the killings of his parents they are always referred to by obviative inflections (6.29*a*). This frames what he sees in his vision as being from his point of view. When the hero of the "White Buffalo" text returns from a journey to visit a manitou, reference to him shifts to the obviative to indicate that his return is experienced by someone else, specifically his father (6.29*b*).

(6.29) Obviative indicating external observer

(a)　　"*i·na=ko·sa*," *e·h=ineči.*
　　　kapo·twe e·h=nesemeči, e·h=ki·škikwe·šomeči.　(K-MFWB 30)
　　　' "That's your father," he was told.
　　　After a while he (obv.) was killed, and his (obv.) head was cut off.'
　　　　　(*i·na* 'that (anim.)'; *ko·sa* 'your father';
　　　　　|iN-| TA 'say {so} to', |e·h=—eči| X–3/AOR;
　　　　　kapo·twe 'at some point'; |neS-| TA 'kill', |e·h=—emeči| X–3´/AOR;
　　　　　|ki·škikwe·šw-| TA 'cut the head off of', |e·h=—emeči| X–3´/AOR)

(b)　　*e·h=pi·tikawa·či maneto·wani i·nahi e·winičini. /* (K-B 17)
　　　‖ *ke·htena=meko nye·wokonakateniki e·h=pya·niči.*
　　　(The hero [prox.] tells his father [obv.] that he will return in four days and goes to where water is shooting out of a cliff.)
　　　'He (prox.) went in to visit a manitou (obv.) who lived there.
　　　/ And true to his word, after four days (obv.) he (obv.) came back.'
　　　　　(|pi·tikaw-| TA 'enter to visit', |e·h=—a·či| 3s–3´/AOR;
　　　　　maneto·wani 'manitou (obv.)'; *i·nahi* 'there';
　　　　　|awi-| AI 'be {somewhere}', |IC–ničini| 3´/PPL(OBVsg);
　　　　　ke·htena 'truly'; *=meko* EMPH;
　　　　　|nye·wokonakat-| II 'be four days', |IC–eniki| 0´/CC;
　　　　　|pya·-| AI 'come', |e·h=—niči| 3´/AOR)

In the passage of Kiyana's "White Buffalo" text in which (6.29*b*) occurs the hero is initially proximate and his father obviative. The particle *ke·htena* 'truly', which here means 'sure enough' in the sense of 'as stated, predicted, or promised', shifts the point of view to the father, and even though the father is not referred to in any other way, the reference to the hero shifts into the obviative. In the same text, when the manitou shows the hero the White Buffalo ceremony in a dream, the manitous that perform it remain in the obviative for over 28 manuscript pages (which include lengthy song texts), except for two brief proximate shifts marking highlights (K-B 118-147).

In some cases in which the obviative indicates an external point of view, Meskwaki translators have supplied an explicit mention of the proximate observer.

(6.30) Obviative translated by supplying a proximate

(a)　　*waninawe e·h=sa·kahaniki me·me·ša·nikini asenye·ni.* (K-WD 128-129; tr. HP)
　　　"He [prox.] could see large rocks [obv.] sticking out of the water all around."
　　　　　(*waninawe* 'on all sides'; |sa·kahan-| II 'is exposed out of the water', |e·h=—niki|
　　　　　0´/AOR; |meme·ša·-| II 'be big (pl.)', |IC–nikini| 0´/PPL(INpl); *asenye·ni* 'rocks')

(b)   *kaši´, kapoˑtwe=ˀpihi eˑh=pyaˑniči.* (S-IM 12G)
      ‖ *keˑhtena ihkweˑwaki.*
      ‖ *eˑh=pyeˑčikawiniči=ˀpi, eˑh=poˑniˑheteˑniki=ˀpi.*
      (The hero is told that some women will come, among whom he should seek his wife.)
      'Why, soon (he saw) someone (obv.) coming. / Sure enough, it was some women (prox.). / (He saw) a bunch of them (obv.) coming and a camp being made (obv.).'
      (Translation dictated by HL to TM: "And then later he saw there were a lot of maids coming. ... And he saw there was a lot of girls coming again. Right at that place they stopped & camped.")
         (*kaši´* 'why!'; *kapoˑtwe* 'at some point'; *=ipi(hi)* HRSY 3x;
         |pyaˑ-| AI 'come', |eˑh=—niči| 3´/AOR;
         keˑhtena 'truly'; *ihkweˑwaki* 'women (prox.)';
         |pyeˑčikawi-| AI 'come as a group', |eˑh=niči| 3´/AOR;
         |poˑniˑheteˑ-| II 'camp is made', |eˑh=—niki| 0´/AOR)

73.10. Proximate and obviative. When the subject and the primary object are both expressed by nominals they may occur in either order relative to each other and in any order relative to the verb. For example, when both subject and object follow the verb, either one may occur first, regardless of which of them is proximate and which obviative. (The examples in 6.31 are repeated from 5.91.)

   (6.31) Proximate and obviative arguments both following the verb
   (a) Proximate subject + obviative object:
        eˑh=moˑšihaˑči=keˑhi meškwahkiˑha moˑhkomaˑnani. (K-CDWP 13)
        'And the Meskwaki (prox.) had a vision of the American (obv.).'
           (|moˑših-| TA 'have a vision of', |eˑh=—aˑči| 3s–3´/AOR; *=keˑhi* 'moreover';
           meškwahkiˑha 'Meskwaki (prox.)'; *moˑhkomaˑnani* 'American (obv.)')
   (b) Obviative object + proximate subject:
        eˑh=pakinaˑči otoˑhpwaˑkanimoteˑhani kwiˑyeseˑha, ... (C-G 19)
        'the boy (prox.) threw down his tobacco bag (obv.)'
           (|pakiN-| TA 'throw down', |eˑh=—aˑči| 3s–3´/AOR;
           otoˑhpwaˑkanimoteˑhani 'his tobacco bag (obv.)'; *kwiˑyeseˑha* 'boy (prox.)')
   (c) Proximate object + obviative subject:
        takaˑwi=meko eˑh=naˑnoˑteˑhkwamekoči ihkweˑwa anemoˑhani. (JP-GTF 43)
        'The dog (obv.) was barely missing the woman (prox.) with its bites.'
           (*takaˑwi* 'a little'; *=meko* EMPH; |CV+| RED1, |noˑteˑhkwam-| TA 'miss biting',
           |eˑh=—ekoči| 3´–3s/AOR; *ihkweˑwa* 'woman (prox.)'; *anemoˑhani* 'dog (obv.)')
   (d) Obviative subject + proximate object:
        ... eˑh=kiˑmaˑhekoči ašaˑhahi neniwa. (K-IML 2)
        '... some Siouxs (obv.) spied on the man (prox.).'
           (|kiˑmaˑh-| TA 'watch unseen', |eˑh=—ekoči| 3´–3s/AOR;
           ašaˑhahi 'Siouxs (obv.)'; *neniwa* 'man (prox.)')

The verbs in (6.32ab) have the direct theme sign (6.10a), here indicating that proximate is acting on obviative, and those in (6.32cd) have the inverse theme sign (6.10b), indicating obviative acting on proximate. The same range of possibilities exists with the verb in other positions, between the two noun phrases or after both of them.

73.11. Two obviatives. In sentences like those in (6.31), where the subject is proximate and the primary object is obviative, or the reverse, the inflection of the verb specifies the syntactic roles of the two arguments: one is unambiguously the subject and the other the object. If both subject and object are obviative, however, the specification of syntactic roles may be less clear-cut. The inflection of the verb distinguishes first obviative acting on second obviative (6.11*a*) from second obviative acting on first obviative (6.11*b*), but in some cases the ranking of the two obviatives as first (nearer, higher) and second (further, lower) may not be determined by linear order or by any other syntactic or inflectional means. In the large corpus of texts examined by Thomason (2004) there are three attested patterns for sentences in which the subject and primary object are both obviative nominals, or where one is an uninflected quantifier treated as obviative.

(6.32) Attested patterns with overt obviative noun phrases for both subject and object

    (a) Direct (6.11*a*)

          Subject (3´) + Object (3´´) (33 examples)

          Object (3´´) + Subject (3´) (10 examples)

    (b) Inverse (6.11*b*)

          Object (3´) + Subject (3´´) (10 examples)

For all three of these patterns the verb (V) may occur in any position, before, after, or between the subject (S) and object (O) noun phrases.

(6.33) Obviative subject + obviative object (with direct inflection)

    V + S (3´) + O (3´´) (3 exx.):

    (a) *e·h=anemi-pi·taho·na·niči mešemo·kani pešekisiwani.* (C-WH 14)

        '(He [prox.] watched as) the old lady (obv.) dragged the deer (obv.) off inside.'

          (*anemi* PV 'go on', |pi·taho·N-| TA 'drag in', |e·h=–a·niči| 3´–3´´/AOR;

          mešemo·kani 'old woman [humorous] (obv.)'; *pešekisiwani* 'deer (obv. sg.)')

    S (3´) + V + O (3´´) (25 exx.):

    (b) *nenemehkiwahi e·h=pakama·niči i·nini mači-maneto·he·hani.* (K-WYB 48; tr. TB)

        (The man [prox.] saw:) "The Thunderers [obv.] had struck that evil manitou [obv.]."

          (*nenemehkiwahi* 'thunderers (obv.)'; |pakam-| TA 'hit', |e·h=–a·niči| 3´–3´´/AOR;

          i·nini 'that (obv.)'; *mači-maneto·he·hani* 'evil manitou (obv.)')

    S (3´) + O (3´´) + V (6 exx.):

    (c) *osese·hani=ke·hi=·pi mehta·hkwi=meko mešwe·he·hahi e·h=pemo·ma·niči.*

        (X6-OS 31)

        'His older brother (obv.) was carrying some little rabbits (obv.) on his back with nothing else.'

          (*osese·hani* 'his or her older brother'; *=ke·hi* 'moreover'; *=ipi* HRSY;

          mehta·hkwi 'without anything'; *=meko* EMPH;

          mešwe·he·hahi 'rabbits (dim., obv.)';

          |pemo·m-| TA 'carry along on back', |e·h=–a·niči| 3´–3´´/AOR)

(d)   *i·nihi=ke·hi wi·či-ši·še·ma·čihi na·nano·pehka e·h=nesa·niči owiye·he·hahi.*
      (JB-MF 2)
      'The ones (obv.) he (prox.) was hunting with each killed a great many
      animals (obv.).'
           (*i·nihi* 'those (obv.)'; *=ke·hi* 'moreover'; |wi·či-ši·še·m-| TA 'hunt with',
           |IC–a·čihi| 3s–3´/PPL(OBVpl); |CV+| RED1, |nano·pehka| 'a great many';
           |neS-| TA 'kill', |e·h=–a·niči| 3´–3´´/AOR; *owiye·he·hahi* 'animals (obv.)')
           (Note: the discontinuous object noun phrase unambiguously follows the subject;
           it is counted as being before the verb because that is where its first component
           is.)

(6.34) Obviative object + obviative subject (with direct inflection)
      V + O (3´´) + S (3´) (5 exx.)

(a)   *e·h=anemi-no·ma·niči i·nini apeno·he·hani owi·wani.* (K-Fish 127)
      'His wife (obv.) went along with the baby (obv.) on her back.'
           (*anemi* PV 'go on', |no·m-| TA 'carry on back', |e·h=–a·niči| 3´–3´´/AOR;
           i·nini 'that (obv.)'; *apeno·he·hani* 'baby (obv.)'; *owi·wani* 'his wife (obv.)')

(b)   *e·h=we·pi-=či·hi=·pi -nasa·hkohwa·niči i·nini konwa·ške·hani=·nini.* (JP-Apay 65)
      'And to their surprise, (they [prox.] saw) him (obv.) set about roasting that frog
      (obv.) on a stick.'
           (*we·pi* PV 'start to',
           |nasa·hkohw-| TA 'roast on a stick', |e·h=–a·niči| 3´–3´´/AOR;
           =či·hi 'it was suddenly observed'; |=ipi| HRSY; *i·nini* 'that (obv.)';
           konwa·ške·hani 'frog (obv.)'; |i·nini| 'that (obv.)' [= 'him'])

      O (3´´) + V + S (3´) (4 exx.):

(c)   *če·wina·h=meko mešihke·he·hahi e·h=no·ša·na·niči owi·wahi.* (K-MMD 27)
      'At exactly the same time his wives (obv.) gave birth to baby snapping turtles
      (obv.).'
           (*če·wina·hi* 'both or all at the same time'; *=meko* EMPH;
           mešihke·he·hahi 'snapping turtles (dim., obv.)';
           |no·ša·N-| TA 'give birth to', |e·h=–a·niči| 3´–3´´/AOR;
           owi·wahi 'his wives (obv.)')

      O (3´´) + S (3´) + V (1 ex.):

(d)   *neniwa owi·wani ahpene·či kotakani neniwani manamana·nite, ...* (K-Kin 63)
      'If another man (obv.) is always screwing a man (prox.)'s wife (obv.), ...'
           (*neniwa* 'man'; *owi·wani* 'his wife (obv.)'; *ahpene·či* 'always';
           kotakani 'another (obv.)'; *neniwani* 'man (obv.)';
           |CVCV+| RED2, |maN-| TA '(man to) copulate with', |–a·nite| 3´–3´´/SUBJ)

(6.35) Obviative object + obviative subject (with inverse inflection)
      V + O (3´) + S (3´´) (1 ex.):

(a)   *na·hkači e·h=mya·hkeška·koniči ihkwe·wahi apeno·hani, ...* (K-Auto 279)
      'Also, when women (obv.) are injured by a child (obv.) (when giving birth), ...'
      ("And when the women are being made ill by the birth of a child, ..."; tr. IP)
           (*na·hkači* 'also';
           |mya·hkeškaw-| TA 'injure by foot or body', |e·h=–ekoniči| 3´´–3´/AOR);
           ihkwe·wahi 'women (obv.)'; *apeno·hani* 'child (obv.)')

O (3´) + V + S (3´´) (5 exx.):

(b) *kaho ni= 'pi owi·hka·nwa wani e·h=mawinanekoniči nenoso ni, ...* (SP-SH 20)

'And then one of their friends (obv.) was attacked by a buffalo (obv.), ...'

(*kaho ni* 'and then'; |=ipi| HRSY; *owi·hka·nwa wani* 'their friend (obv.)';
|mawinaN-| TA 'run at, attack', |e·h=–ekoniči| 3´´–3´/AOR;
nenoso ni 'buffalo (obv.)')

(c) *na·hka nekoti neniwa, a·kwi oškinawe·ha, owi·wani e·h=mešenekoniči aša·hahi.*
(K-SD1)

'And there was a certain man (prox.), no longer young, whose wife (obv.) was
captured by Siouxs (obv.).'

(*na·hka* 'also'; *nekoti* 'one'; *neniwa* 'man (prox.)'; *a·kwi* 'not';
oškinawe·ha 'young man (prox.)'; *owi·wani* 'his wife (obv.)';
|mešen-| TA 'capture', |e·h=–ekoniči| 3´´–3´/AOR; *aša·hahi* 'Siouxs (obv.)')

O (3´) + S (3´´) + V (4 exx.):

(d) *omeso ta nahi=ke·hi= 'pi aša·hahi nesekoniwahi.* (K-MFWB 1)

'And they say his parents (obv.) had been killed by Siouxs (obv.).'

(*omeso ta nahi* 'his parents (obv.)'; *=ke·hi* 'moreover'; |=ipi| HRSY;
aša·hahi 'Siouxs (obv.)'; |neS-| TA 'kill', |–ekoniwahi| 3´´–3´p/IND)

(e) *keye·hapa=ke·h=wi na·= 'na pye·či-tahkamiwenekočini nenemehkiwahi*
ne·sekonitehe. (BL-RL 21)

'As a matter of fact, the one (obv.) that brought him (prox.) across was killed by
thunderers (obv.).'

(*keye·hapa* 'in fact'; *=ke·hi* 'moreover'; *=wi na* 'but'; |i·na| 'that (anim., prox.)';
|pye·či| PV 'coming'; |tahkamiweN-| TA 'take across';
|IC–ekočini| 3´–3s/PPL(OBVsg); *nenemehkiwahi* 'thunderers (obv.)';
|neS-| TA 'kill', |IC–ekonitehe| 3´´–3´/CH.PRET)

The sentences with the subject preceding the object and direct inflection (6.33) or with the object preceding the subject and inverse inflection (6.35) conform to the default expectation, as the argument treated as the first obviative in the verbal inflection literally precedes the second obviative. Those with the object preceding the subject and direct inflection (6.34), however, cannot be interpreted according to the default, but in all cases the intended meaning is clear from semantic and logical considerations. Even in the unfamiliar situation described in (6.34c), it is evident that the women gave birth to the turtles and not the other way around. In fact, the available examples suggest that where ambiguity is conceivable, this freedom of word order is disfavored, and the first obviative in the verbal inflection then always seems to precede the second obviative (as in 6.33b and most of the examples in 6.35).

The absence of examples with a second obviative subject preceding a first obviative object presumably reflects not so much an impossible combination of discourse features as the rarity of the need for the somewhat discordant combination of discourse functions that this would imply: a subject selected as lower ranked by the inverse inflection but preceding the object. The clash appears to be less when a second obviative object precedes a first obviative subject (6.34), since the direct inflection is the default.

The order of a subject and object that are both obviative is either free or linked to obviation rank. Examples like those in (6.34) and (6.35) show that the order of subject and object is not determined by these syntactic roles, any more than it is when one of the two overt arguments is proximate (6.31). And examples like those in (6.34) also show that when there is only one logical possibility word order does not even determine obviation rank.

Appendix 1.

Notes

This appendix contains notes and commentary on the grammar, including historical and comparative information, alternative analyses, and references to additional examples in published analyzed texts and to discussions of theoretical matters. The text of the grammar is referred to by section number (in bold type after §) or example number (not-bolded), or both.

NOTES TO CHAPTER 1. PHONOLOGY

§1.1. Contemporary Meskwaki has borrowings with /l/, /r/, /f/, and /v/ in otherwise assimilated words (Voorhis 1971:63, Goddard 1991:158), but as these sounds cannot be written in the traditional Meskwaki writing system their occurrence cannot be documented in earlier texts. Some words that were at first borrowed in completely assimilated form later acquired pronunciations with English sounds substituted in the speech of bilingual speakers. Some speakers write some imitative words with final consonants, but others write only vowels word-finally, in conformity with Meskwaki spelling norms. *štwiˑtikaˑha* 'streetcar' and *štwiˑteki* 'in the street' add word-initial /štw/, but ⟨st-⟩ and ⟨tw-⟩ are also written for this.

§3. The colloquial or casual style is described by Voorhis (1971:75-76) and discussed in Goddard (1988:195-195), with additional examples in Goddard (1991:159).

§9.1, 1.106. The word in Jones (1907:306.14) is written ⟨myācigeˤkitcⁱ⟩; the preaspiration of the [k] is also indicated in Jones's manuscript (Jones 1902). The final /i/ seems unlikely, since Meskwaki and Sauk have only -*e* in the prohibitive endings, disagreeing with Kickapoo, which does have -*i*. Contemporary speakers confirm /hk/ in such forms.

§11. A comprehensive survey of contraction in Meskwaki, with comparative notes, is in Goddard (2001).

§11.4. The nouns with archaic contraction of |Cy-e| to short |i| were mentioned in Goddard (2001:185). The recorded forms are: *aseniki* 'on the stone' (Jones 1907:176.17, and the manuscript, Jones 1902, 1:7; the manuscript Jones 1902, 1:14 2x [but printed with /iˑ/ in Jones 1907:202.6 and 202.8]; Jones 1911:849); *netasenimi* 'my rock', etc. (Jones 1911:852 [6 forms]); *otasenimi*'his stone', *otasenimani*'his stones' (Jones 1911:833 [both 3x in constructed sentences]); oto·hkimi 'his land' (Jones 1911:755); ketahkimi 'your (sg.) land' and ketahkimwa·wi 'your (pl.) land' (Michelson 1925:78, l. 34, and 80, l. 38); and *nenepimi* 'my water' (Michelson 1930:118.25). The short |i| is regular for some nouns in Kickapoo (Voorhis 1974:39-40): *nepiki* 'in the water' (Jones and Michelson 1915:12, 25, 42.1, 50.2, 66.13, 78.25); *aθeniki* 'on, against a stone' (Jones and Michelson 1915:12.15, 74.13).

§11.4, 1.148. Cf. *ketayina·na* 'our horse' (Jones 1907:218.11), *ketayiwa·wa* 'your (pl.) dog'. (Jones 1907:178.1)

§11.5. The contraction of |y-a| to *ye·* occurred historically in other morphological contexts but is not otherwise synchronically active. For example, the medial |-epye·k-| 'water' was originally from |-epy-| 'water' plus postmedial |-ak-| (**§35**; see the note to this below), but synchronically it contains a new postmedial |-e·k-|. Meskwaki retains archaic |CyaC| stem-internally in one set of forms in which the |a| appears to be historically secondary (Goddard 2002:191-192).

§11.10, 1.185. The synchronic noun final |-ihka·h| comes from unattested *|-ihka·| II 'abound in' (cf. Ojibwe *-ikaa* II in this meaning) plus the agentive secondary final |-h|, which always occurs with initial change (**§46.2**).

§12.2. A more abstract analysis would set up the stems that begin with |i-| as beginning with an underlying |e-| which is replaced by *i-* in word-initial position; things would, however, have to be arranged so that the word-initial environment includes the position after the proclitic preverbs (**§29.3**) and after two-syllable reduplication (**§39.4**).

NOTES TO CHAPTER 2. GRAMMATICAL CATEGORIES

§18.2. The gloss of a morpheme or word is a conventional translation; it may include labels of grammatical or semantic categories and may not cover all possible uses of the form. It does not necessarily provide a translation that can automatically be used in colloquial English, and in particular it may not provide all possible English equivalents. For example the convention is adopted of glossing the Meskwaki animate singular as 'he' ('him', 'his'), except where this is clearly inappropriate for biological or cultural reasons; English translations might, however, be 'she' ('her'), 'it' ('its'), 'they' ('them', 'their'), or 'one', depending on the context. The gloss 'it' is reserved for the inanimate singular.

§18.4, 2.11. The inclusive is coded "12" (representing first person "I" or "we" plus second person "you"). Although its reference includes the second person, it is a first person plural category. Some Algonquianists code the inclusive as "21" and even claim that it is second person, but the status of the inclusive as a first person category is a fact of universal grammar and logic. Many languages are like English in having a single first person plural category for both the inclusive and the exclusive, but no language in the world has a single category that unites the inclusive and the second plural. The unsurprising fact that the Meskwaki first plural inclusive shares morphology with the second person as well as with the first person exclusive is a matter of morphological process (the mechanics of morpheme selection) and does not indicate that inclusive as a grammatical category is a second person.

§19.4, 2.35*b*. This interpretation of the inanimate gender of *a·teso·hka·kani* fits all three known attestations and is to be preferred to the explanation by contextual contraction given in Goddard (2002:212). The use of *mani* 'this (inan.)' to refer indexically to the written text in which it appears is characteristic of the usage of Bill Leaf (Thomason 2015:349).

§21 (obviative). The term "obviative" was coined by Jean-André Cuoq (1866:43), as French *obviatif*, and was first used in English by J. Hammond Trumbull (1877:150). Howse (1844:123-125) referred to the obviative inflection as the "*Possessive* or *Accessory* case" and (in verbs) "the *relative* form," explaining that "when two 'third' persons .. meet together, this relational form serves to distinguish the *accessory* or dependent, from the *principal* or leading 'third' person .. thus obviating .. the ambiguity which would otherwise arise from the meeting of several third persons in the sentence."

§22, 2.66*a*. This sentence was heard in spontaneous conversation, and the translation is the speaker's.

§22.1. People and animals seem regularly to take the possessed-theme marker |-em|, while most articles of clothing and the like do not. Most nouns in |-n| do not (but some do), and neither of the two nouns in |-m| takes it. A preliminary list of nouns that do not take |-em| is in Bloomfield (1925-1927, [2]:185).

§22.2 (comment on 2.83 and 2.84). *pakišimowi* II 'the sun sets, it is sunset' has the shape of an AI stem, but the final |-išimo| is otherwise used only as a base for secondary derivation (4.13, 196, 257). It may reflect an original construction with *ki·šeswa* 'sun' and |pakišin-| AI 'land, drop to the ground' transposed into an impersonal II.

§22.3. In one example a secondary object is attested for an II that is derived from an AI. The subject is virtually personified, and the inanimate object precedes the inanimate subject:
   ma·hani=ča·hi nakamo·nani i·ni na·tawino·ni e·h=onakamo·ni·mikahki. (K-Spot 220)
   'And these songs are the songs of that medicine.'
      (*ma·hani* 'these (inan.)'; *=ča·hi* 'so'; *nakamo·nani* 'songs'; *i·ni* 'that (inan.)';
      na·tawino·ni 'medicine'; |onakamo·ni·mikat-| II(+O) 'have (O2 as) song(s)', |e·h=―ki|
      0/AOR)

§22.4. Oblique. Dahlstrom (2009) discusses the theoretical significance of Meskwaki obliques within Lexical Functional Grammar.

§22.4 (relative root). The term "relative root" (Bloomfield 1946:120) derives from the terminology proposed by Joseph Howse (1844:132), who distinguished "Relative Verbs," which have a "*generic* attribute," from "Absolute Verbs," which have a "*specific* attribute."

§22.4(g) (instrumental obliques), 2.130. The verb |ahkwa·wišin-| AI, |ahkwa·wisen-| II is used either as 'be filled', with the container as subject and the contents as an instrumental oblique (as here), or as 'fill', with the contents as the subject and the container in the locative (K-SF 77, K-MHTW 9, K-WSB 23).

§22.4(g), 2.131. The underlying verb |atama·-| AI 'smoke' is analyzed as taking the tobacco as a secondary object and the pipe as an instrumental oblique.

§22.5, 2.136d (*mano ne·ha oškinawe·hani*). Another construction with the same meaning in the same text is: *(i·)na mano ne·hi-kwi yese·ha* (S-RL 66).

§22.5, 2.141b (*kotaka·='ni* A 155C). Not *kotakani* 'other (obv.)' (as edited in Michelson 1925:326.42), since the use of the obviative would not be correct either inside or outside the quote. And not *kotaka·='ni* inside the quote, since *i·ni* 'then' would make no sense and would require an aorist verb.

§22.5, 2.143d. The context rules out taking *neniwa* as a Topic: the man and the girls are the conjoined subject of the immediately preceding reciprocal verb. HP translates it as if it were an adjunct: "Later the man's young girls [=the girls the man lived with] were all married." (K-FC 529; tr. HP). While this can be accepted as documenting the possibility of a discontinuous adjunct it does not seem the best interpretation of this sentence.

§22.6 (relational). The form earlier interpreted as *e·na·wa·te·ni* (Goddard 1995:145, ex. 77), as if a relational form meaning 'anything he's told (to do)', should be read *e·na·wate·ni* 'whatever you (sg.) tell him to do' (K-OBES 111-112), following AW and EK.

§26.2. The enclitic *=ye·toke* 'it seems, apparently, presumably' is found in: O 62F, 93F, 130CD; A 13E, 26G, 37A, 37F, 97E, 108H.

§26.3. There are additional examples of *keye·hapa* in (A 13D, 15E, 42C, 69A, 119C, 155D).

§26.5. Another mode attested by only a very few forms is the imprecative (Goddard 1993:231-233, 1995:141; §30.5). The variable presence of a pronominal prefix makes it uncertain which order it is in.

§26.8, 2.180 (narrative aorist without |e·h=|). Discussed in Goddard (1988:197, 206) with references to some additional examples.

§26.13, 2.248c. This was rejected by EK, who insisted on *we·či-po·n-o·siyani*, with the same construction as in 2.248a.

§26.18. Outside the prioritive, |me·hi| PV is used in negative expressions meaning 'yet' (A 110G, 146G). In prioritive constructions |-w| irr. must also have originally been a negative morpheme, as its cognate is in the Eastern Algonquian languages (Goddard 2006:193-194). The meaning 'before' of the prioritive construction thus stems from an original literal meaning 'when not yet'.

§26.19, 2.302 (prohibitive). The manuscript texts have four examples of |–iye·kiče| 3s–3´/PROH (JP 2x, JB, Anon.); Jones (1907:292.3) has *a·piškoniye·kiče* 'it appears she might have let them loose' (translated "it is just as likely that my grandmother has now let them loose!" with the ending written ⟨-iyä·kitcⁱ⟩), but Jones (1912:824) gives the ending |–iye·kiče| 3s–3´/PROH with the spelling ⟨-iyägitce⟩.

One writer has (formally prohibitive) |–iye·wa·hkiče| 3p–3´/PROH (JB-FS 24K, JB-M 48) beside (formally future imperative) |–a·wa·hkiče| 3p–3´/PROH (JB-SB 23).

The claim of a consistent distinction between future imperative and prohibitive forms (Goddard 1985) cannot be maintained in the light of the additional examples in the texts. Jones's table of "potential, potential subjunctive, and prohibitive" endings includes potential, prohibitive, and formally future imperative endings, inconsistently sorted and labeled, as well as some endings that are apparently spurious.

§26.19, 2.304-306 (future imperative). Of a piece with the these second person forms is the inclusive future imperative elicited by Michelson: *a·čima·hkakwe* 'we had better report them', with the ending |–a·hkakwe| 12–3/FUT.IMP (Goddard 1985:420).

§26.24. An example of the conclusive mode with the future is in Goddard (1995:132, ex. 25). The assertive mode is not attested with the future.

§26.24, 2.343 (*wi·h=komino*). The same form occurs in the identical Sauk song given by Skinner (1928:151).

§26.25. Bloomfield (1925-1927, [2]:211) called the preterite forms the "unreal mode," describing them as referring to "occurrence not fulfilled, or, by way of modesty or quotation, viewed as unreal." This is not the basic meaning and is only found in some preterite forms.

§26.25, 2.346. Additional examples of the aorist preterite after *=ye toke*: O 130C (cf. O130E without the enclitic), A 37F, A 167F, A 120E.

§26.25, 2.348-349. Additional examples of the future aorist preterite: ('were to have, ought to have') K-FC 203, K-M 364ab; ('was supposed to') K-M 214ik; ('was or were going to, was just about to') K-M 52g, 219.1, 580f.

§26.25, 2.350ff. Additional examples of the subjunctive preterite: A 38H, A 92G, A 127D, A 144D, A 145B, A 155E, A 175F, A 187A. There are no examples in "Owl."

§26.25, 2.355. An additional example of a future changed preterite: K-M 106p.

§26.25, 2.358. Additional examples of the negative preterite: K-Auto 272; (with *=ye toke*) K-M 258a, 516g.

§26.25, 2.360. The interpretation as a question follows the dictation by HL (Michelson 1925:116.34). Michelson's translation from HP ('It is a good thing that you chanced not to see it (the bear).') wrongly includes the preceding separate sentence (*šepawi·hta·='nahi!* 'It's a good thing!').

§26.25, 2.362-363. The inflected preterite participles are discussed in Goddard (1995:133-134). The reconstruction of the modal suffix is revised in Goddard (2007:249).

NOTES TO CHAPTER 3. INFLECTION

§28.2, 3.5, 3.98. *pe·škiti* 'basket' is a loanword from English, assimilated as if containing |-ity| NF 'rear end' (4.66c).

§28.2, 3.7. The mutation of |N| (< Proto-Algonquian *θ) was leveled out in noun stems: *ni·ši* 'my head', *owi·šani* 'heads' (cf. Menominee *ne·s* 'my head', *we·nan* and *we·san* 'animal heads'); *anake·weni* 'bark canoe' (cf. Shawnee *holake·ši* 'boat', *holake·lali* 'boats', *holake·leki* 'in a boat').

§28.2, 3.25 ('heart'). Rare forms are: *oto·te·hemi* 'his heart' (K-W 418; **§28.2**, 3.33), as if the possessed form of a non-dependent noun *ote·hi* 'a heart'; and *ote·hani*, evidently meaning 'animal hearts', attested once in a lexical list (K-Med 55); compare Menominee *otɛ·h* 'his heart; an animal heart'.

§28.2, 3.30. The only attested possessed form of *wi·kiya·pi* 'house' would be *kewi·kiya·pina·ni* 'our (inc.) house' (Jones 1907:376.12, 14-15), but this is extremely doubtful. The first occurrence is Jones's substitution for the unpossessed *wi·kiya·pi* of his manuscript (Jones 1902, 2:104.4), and the second occurrence has no source at all in the manuscript and simply repeats the first. AW, asked to comment, thought it should be *kewi·kiya·pena·ni*.

§28.2, 3.31. Possessed forms of *anwi* in the meaning 'shot, wizard's missle' include: *otanomani* 'her missles' (K-Koch 30), *ketanomi* 'your shots' (K-Spot 210), *otanomi* 'his shot' (JB-SB 7).

§28.2, after 3.36 (*newi·šemeki*). The avoidance form *kewi·šemeki* 'on your (sg.) head' is also in use (AW).

§28.9, 3.65-66. For the archaic contraction to short |i|, see the note to **§11.4**, above.

§28.14, 3.92. *metemo·h-a* 'old woman' has the shape of a hypocoristic diminutive (**§41.4**) of a stem *metemos-*.

§28.15, 3.110. *nepaya* 'my thigh' was obtained from Alfred Kiyana by Michelson (written in syllabics), and *opaya* 'thigh' was given by EK. See also **§28.4** (after 3.15).

§28.19, 3.131 (*po·hkipo·hki·kwa·yane*). The reduplication reflects the fact that this is the singulative of what is basically a plural group name, something like 'you of the one-eyed tribe'. A third person singular participle on this stem is in 4.134(b).

§28.19, 3.136. The vocative *ne·nye·škwi·yane* was used at least seven times by JP and at least once by BL.

§29.1, 3.139, and **§29.3**. Dahlstrom (1996) presents arguments to support the analysis of the ostensible proclitic tense and mode markers as prefixes. The phonological evidence suggests that they are bound to a stem less closely than the pronominal prefixes but to about the same degree as two-syllable reduplication (see note to **§12.2**, above, and **§39.4**).

§29.2, 3.144. The derived applicative *ihe·notaw-* TA 'go {somewhere} to' (**§54.6**, 4.331*b*) is not attested after pronominal prefixes in texts; AW used *netehe·notawa·wa* 'I went to him'.

§29.4, 3.164-166 (|we·yo·-| for |IC+o·-|). It is as if IC applied to an underlying |owo·-| (cf. 3.50), with regular IC to |we·wo·-| and then replacement of |w| by |y| (**§13.5**), giving |we·yo·-|.

§29.4, 3.165 (*we·yo·šisememena·ne*). The manuscript has has ⟨weyosisememenane⟩.

§29.4, 3.167 (|taN-|). |taši·hka·no-| AI 'play' does not contain the relative root |taN-| synchronically and has regular initial change: *te·ši·hka·no·hikini* 'as if merely playing' (K-FC 251, K-M 543). Regular initial change is also found in a single example each of similar iteratives from |taši·hka·ti·-| AI 'try to persuade, court or be courted' (K-B 258) and |taši·hk-| TI(1) 'be dealing with' (K-SGG 23). More recent texts (GBC) also have examples of regularized initial change on |taN-| when it is used as a relative root.

§29.4, 3.176a. Jones (1907:138.18) has ⟨Kacitcā ä'teg^i⟩ in a sentence he added; the verb was incorrectly emended by Bloomfield (1925-1927, [2]:204) to ⟨ähtägi⟩ (i.e., *e·hte·ki*), as if a participle from |ahte·-| II 'be ({somewhere})'. Unlike *ta·ni* 'what?', which is used in an equational construction with a participle (3.176*b*, 5.97), *kaši* 'what?' is used as an oblique complement (cf. **§18.7**).

§29.4, 3.184. AW used *tohka·niwita* 'he who is a Tohkan'. *tohka·na* is the only Meskwaki stem with a first syllable that has a short |o| which is preceded by a consonant other than |k| and not followed by |w|. It is a loan from Ioway [túkala], the name of a society that was the rival of the [máwatani] in war, ceremonies, and lacrosse (Skinner 1915:697-700).

§29.5 (3.186 table). Some analysis of some of the fused suffixes can be suggested, but segmentation into pronominal suffix and modal suffix seems synchronically unjustified.

§29.6. Position 1 (|-em| obv.). The only attested appearance of this suffix in an interrogative ending is in an apparent nonce form; it is added after the first of two occurrences of |-a·w| TA th. 1 irr. (← |-a·| TA th. 1, |-w| irr.) as if this were the final part of a TA stem:

ahpene·či=meko wi·h=nenehke·netamwa wi·h=iši-nesa·woma·wakwe·ni (K-W 715; tr. HP) "each one must constantly study how we [inc.] can slay him [obv.]"

29.7. Position 2 (e), and 3.200. The morphologically governed variability in the use of the second (inverse), third, and fourth theme signs shows that inverse is not a grammatical category but merely a morpheme.

29.7. Position 2 (f), 3.201. The idiosyncratic treatment of |-am| TI(1) th. before further suffixes and the fact that it may be absent in derivation show that it is an inflectional ending and not part of the stem.

29.7. Position 2 (g), 3.202. Similarly, the fact that |-o·| TI(2) th. may drop in derivation shows that it is inflectional.

§29.8. Position 4 (a), 3.204. In the original prayer this line begins *o=naˑhka=noˑči* and every word is followed by the enclitic ritual vocable *=noˑči*. The syntax challenged Michelson's best translator, Thomas Brown (1926), who wrote: "Again .. we ask .. life .. for our chief .. and all who are spread out .. under him" (revised to "as he spreads us out (in a village)" [Michelson 1928:71]).

§29.8. Position 4 (b), 3.210 (|-waˑhkiče| 3p prohibitive). Jones (1911:824) has endings with |-waˑ| pl. following |-hk| proh. after a connective |-i-|: *-hkiwaˑče* 3p/PROH (written ⟨-tcⁱ⟩), *-akiwaˑče* 3p–0/PROH (⟨-tcⁱ⟩), *-ihkiwaˑče* 3p–1s/PROH (⟨-tce⟩), *-iyeˑkiwaˑče* 3p–3´/PROH (⟨-iyäˈkiwātce⟩), but these do not appear in texts. These appear to be Sauk endings; Sauk has *-hkiwaˑče* 3p and *-ihkiwaˑče* 3p–1s in what Whittaker (1996:388-389) calls the Sauk "permissive" mode. Chuck (C) has *pyeˑči-nešiwaˑhkiwaˑče* 'they might come and kill me' (C-PD 34), with |-waˑ| repeated; this is a nonce formation and perhaps simply an eror, as he has *amwiwaˑhkiče* 'they might eat me' on the same page.

§29.9. Position 5 (e), 3.234 (first plural exclusive passive, core conjunct and interrogative). Originally these endings had core conjunct *-inamek X–1p (|-i| TA th. 3 + |-enamek| X–1p) and interrogative *-iˑnamek (← |-i-w-enamek| ← |-i| TA th. 3 + |-w| irr. + |-enamek| X–1p). The formally opaque long *iˑ* of the theme sign in the interrogative ending was generalized to the core conjunct ending, giving the equivalent of the Kickapoo paradigm *-iinamek-* X–1p, *-iinamek-een-* X–1p/INT (Voorhis 1974:83, 95).

§29.10. Position 6 ("the assertive mode has its own non-third person suffixes"). The archaic and even rarer independent potential mode (**§30.5**) apparently used central suffixes similar to those of the assertive.

§29.10. Position 6 (a), 3.236. The absolute suffixes |-pena| 1p,12 and |-pwa| 2p can be analyzed as |-p-enaˑn| and |-p-waˑw|, assuming a formative element |-p| combined with the objective suffixes |-enaˑn| 1p,12 and |-waˑw| 2p, and assuming that consonants are dropped in word-final position, with regular vowel-shortening.

§29.10. Position 6 (a), 3.236 (|-naˑwaˑ| 2p ast.). Not attested in a central argument marker but only after TA th. 4.

§29.10. Position 6 (a) (objective suffixes after |-ekw| TA th. 2). Inverse forms are not attested for the assertive mode, but they presumably had special assertive mode pronominal suffixes.

§29.10. Position 6 (a), after 3.237 ("Consonant-final stems add |e| ..."). In a more abstract analysis, the suffix |-p| sg. could be set up everywhere |-∅| sg. occurs, with the |p| dropped word-finally by a phonological rule. The added |e| would then be automatic before the underlying |p|.

§29.10. Position 6 (a), 3.250. In full: *memešihka=mekoho nekiˑwaˑniˑpenaˑtoke* "we (exc.) have probably made a mistake" (K-FC 183; tr. HP).

§29.10. Position 6 (b), 3.264 (|–iˑnameneˑha| X–1p/POT). The ending *-iˑnameneˑha* is found in texts (K-BLI 14, K-M 524) and was used by HWB (in 1998) and EK (in 2003); this matches

Kickapoo (Voorhis 1974:101). EK also gave *-i namine ha*, and AW preferred *-i namine ha* and *-inamine ha*, shapes apparently influenced by the corresponding singular *-ine ha* X–1p/POT.

§29.10. Position 6 (b), end (interrogative ending for 1s–2p apparently lacking). The interrogative ending *-enowe kwe ni* cited in the paradigms in Goddard (1994:207) cannot be confirmed from texts and is probably not correct. Michelson's notes reveal unsuccessful attempts to elicit the interrogative ending for 1s–2p, and he left it blank in the table of interrogative endings in Michelson (1914:406). Ostensible textual occurrences of ⟨-nowekweni⟩ (K-FC 249, K-Spot 176, 191. K-Wap 291, 220 2x, K-WKB 28) are all shown by context to be writing errors for ⟨-nowakweni⟩, i.e. *-(e)nowa kwe ni* 3,X–2p, despite the fact that speakers faced with such spellings have sometimes quite reasonably thought that they must represent an ending for 1s–2p (HP, AW).

§29.10. Position 6 (c), after 3.266 (|-sa| 3,0 pot. and |-če| 3,0 imp.). For example, |-če| cannot be |-t| 3 + injunctive |-ye| (Bloomfield 1925-1927, [2]:204), since |-t| is not used for inanimates (as |-če| is|), and |-ye| is disproved by |-i·ke| X proh.

§29.10. Position 6 (c), 3.267 (*no neče* 'let him suckle'). The interpretation follows Bloomfield (1925-1927, [2]:211); Jones has ⟨nōnetcⁱ⟩ "let her suckle [him]," as if a TA passive.

§29.10. Position 6 (d), 3.269 (*šekišineno.* 'Lie down!'). Michelson (1925:318.3) prints [cegiꞌcinu], following the form in the phonetic (dictated) text, but the ms. has ⟨šekišineno⟩.

§29.10 Position 6 (d), 3.271 (hortative). Jones gives only endings with |-ta·we| in his grammar (Jones 1911:826), and the few forms in his texts have this (Bloomfield 1925-1927, [2]:200-201); a form *pema mota we* 'let's flee', apparently in the casual pronunciation [pema·motae], was transcribed as if it were /pema·motahe/ (Jones 1902, 3:59) and later wrongly edited as ⟨Pemāmuteꞌᵉ⟩ (Jones 1907:286.11). Voorhis (1971:68) recorded |-ta·ke| "consistently" in 1969; EK used only |-ta·ne| and rejected the other variants.

§29.10. Position 6 (d), after 3.271 (elicited forms have *-ene ha* after a deleting consonant stem): for example, *pemiwetonene ha* 'one would have a greasy mouth' (EK in 2003).

§29.11. Position 7 (a) (|-etoke| ~ |-etoke·h| dub.). In a more abstract analysis the dubitative suffix can be set up as |-etoke·h| everywhere, with this being subject to consonant loss and vowel shortening in word-final position.

§29.11. Position 7 (c), 3.282. The assertive inflection *ne–na pani* 1s/AST matches the Ojibwe preterite *ni–naaban* (Nichols 1980:276-277), and *ke–enena wa pani* 1s–2p/AST agrees with the Eastern Ojibwe preterite *g–naawaaban* 2p–0s (Valentine 2001:311).

§29.11. Position 7 (d), 3.288. |IC–kwe·hini| 0/INT.PPL(INpl) is attested in the same form *e šitehka te kwe hini* in a passage that also has the corresponding obviative |IC–nikwe·hini| 0´/INT.PPL(INpl) on the same verb (K-B 19).

Jones (1911:827) lists *e h=–kwe hini* and *wi h=–kwe hini* as inanimate plural intransitive inflections, but there are no textual examples of these. Voorhis (1971:70) reports that

*|-kwe·hini| 0p int. was rejected by speakers, and that "plural interrogative participles seem not to occur" (in the Meskwaki of 1968). The texts, however, have distinct interrogative participle endings for animate plural and obviative plural heads (§30.18).

§29.11. Position 7 (e) (|-ehe| pret.). This suffix could alternatively be set up as underlying |-eha| pret., with the |a| being assimilated to the |e| when the |e| is not removed by contraction to |o|. But such an assimilation rule would operate on only this one morpheme, and an analysis is preferred that describes the alternation in the final vowel as morphological.

§29.11. Position 7 (h), 3.299. The full context is given in Goddard (1995:130, ex. 17).

§30.4. Independent conclusive. Only one speaker (HWB) was found in the 1990's who appeared to control the full conclusive paradigm; from him the pattern of the formation of the endings was confirmed, but not every inflection was actually heard.

§30.17 Interrogative. The putative general interrogative endings |+enokwe·hiki| 3p–2s int. and |+enowa·kwe·hiki| 3p–2p int. (Goddard 1994:207), given by Bloomfield (1925-1927, [2]:218) from the table in Michelson (1914:406), are not attested by any examples. They probably exist only in participles with animate plural heads, a use attested for |IC–enokwe·hiki| 3p–2s/INT.PPl(ANpl) (K-FASB 66). The putative ending |+iyamekwe·hiki| 3p–1p int. in the same table was later retracted by Michelson as "probably an error" (Bloomfield 1925-1927, [2]:218); this is also the ending expected for the participle.

§30.18. Interrogative participle. Voorhis (1971:70) reports that "plural interrogative participles seem not to occur" (in the Meskwaki of 1968). The texts, however, have distinct interrogative participle endings for animate plural and obviative plural heads, as these examples show.

§30.19. Prioritive modes, 3.327. In *me·h-pakami·ke* 'before I was seen' the vowel length is conjectured; the ending would be written the same as the corresponding subjunctive (|+ike| X–1s/SUBJ), and in later usage the subjunctive generally replaces the prioritive.

§31.5-6. The *i·ya·ka* and *i·na·ka* demonstratives are no longer in use, and their meanings have been deduced from the few occurrences in the texts.
    Jones (1911:855) gives the paradigm *i·na·ka* anim. sg., *i·na·mani* inan. sg., *i·na·ma·haki* anim. pl., *i·na·ma·hani* inan. pl., glossed as 'yonder .. but not out of sight'. Other than *i·na·ka*, the only textually attested forms with *i·na·-* are *i·na·mani* (Jones 1907:120.16), *i·na·ma·haki* (Jones 1907:358.8), and the form here quoted from A 62G. The manuscript texts have only *i·na·ka* and (Alfred Kiyana only) *i·ne·ke* anim. pl. and *i·ne·ne* obv. sg.

§31.7. The lack of the same *-a* and *-e* variants for the plural and obviative forms of *ma·hiya* as for *i·niya* reflects the much sparser attestation of this set, which probably had the same pattern of variants.

NOTES TO CHAPTER 4. DERIVATIONAL MORPHOLOGY

§34.6, 4.19*cd* (|peši·šk(a·)-| 'skin completely'). There is also |paši·šk-| 'skin, peel' (4.72*b*2, 4.81*a*) and |pašo·šk-| (S [emended], JB; AW).

§35. The postmedial |-e·k-| arose phonologically from the use of the postmedial |-ak-| after medials ending in |Cy| (|-epye·k-| 'water' ← |-epy-| + |-ak-|; cf. **§11.5**), but its use has been extended to other contexts (e.g., 4.44).

§35.1, 4.34 (medial |-a·nak-| 'hole'). There is also a medial |-a·n-|, |-a·n-e·-| 'hole'; historically the noun *wa·nakwi* is derived from or reshaped on the medial |-a·n-ak-|.

§35.1, 4.41 (medial |-tep-|, |-a·tep-| 'head' ← |otepy-| 'brain'). This was historically a dependent noun that did not end in |y|.

4.41*b*. *mi·kesa·tepe·wa* 'he has wampum strung in his hair' was used by SP and an anonymous writer; C has *mi·kese·tepe·wa*, with vowel assimilation.

§35.2, 4.47 (*kaka·nwikaše·wa* 'he has long nails, claws'). Not "*kaka·nwihkaše·wa*" (Siebert 1967:55).

§35.2, 4.48 (medial |-keten-| 'vulva'). The /k/ is supported by the [k] in Jones (1907:46.9, 322.21), the second of these with [g] in the manuscript (Jones 1902, 3:12). HWB pronounced this word with /hk/ in 1998, showing the assimilation of the medial to the shape of the noun.

§35.2, 4.50 (medial |-kw-e·-| 'neck'). The medial |-kw-| before |-e·| AI ABSTR only has the meaning 'penis' (as in *meškikwe·wa* 'his foreskin is retracted'); perhaps this was originally a specialized use of 'neck', but synchronically it is presumably a different element.

§35.2, 4.51 (medial |-hkwe·kan(-e·)-|). Other medials for 'neck' are: |-kwayaw-| (|-kwayaw-e·-|) and |-škwe·kan-| (|-škwe·kan-e·-|).

§35.2, 4.53*a* (|-*i*-k-| 'dwelling'; also 4.20*a*). The range of meaning is against recognizing a final |-ike·| AI 'act on dwelling (?)'.

§36.2, 4.65*f* (|-i·škeno·h| NF 'bird'). Words ostensibly having finals beginning in |i·| derived from nouns with |wi·-| could result from contraction (**§4.3**), but where uncontracted forms are not found derivation is the preferable synchronic analysis.

§36.2, 4.66*b* (medial |-neč-| 'hand, finger'). Originally the medial was |-nečy-|, but synchronically the |y| is present only in the noun final.

§36.2, 4.66*c* (|-ity| NF 'rear end'). For the medial |-itiy-|, cf. *mehčitiye·ne·wa* 'he (prox.) uncovers his (obv.) bottom' (|meht-| 'bare', |-itiy-e·-| 'rear end', |-en| TA 'act on by hand').

§37.2, 4.72a. *sa·kiwa* AI, *sa·kenwi* II 'he, it (a plant) sprouts, grows, grows up' and *ni·kiwa* AI 'he is born' are probably the derivational sources of the initials |sa·k-| 'partially visible' and

|ni·k-| 'multiply, divide' (cf. 4.9), rather than derived from them, if there is indeed still a synchronic relationship.

§37.2, 4.78*f.* |-eško·N| TA has been found only in *kewa nneško nene* 'I satisfied your hunger (K-M 930).

§37.2, 44.82*a*(2). See also 4.12*a*.

§37.2, 4.76*a* (*kehtahkišinwa*). Michelson (B95:18.25-26 and 27, 37) has *ketahkišinwa*, but I take the initial to be the same as in the essentially synonymous stem *kehčišinwa*.

§37.3, 4.84*i* (*ki·ši·seniwa* 'he finishes eating'). Originally by contraction (§4.3) from *ki·ši-wi·seniwa* but lexicalized.

§37.5, 4.86*e* (*mawi·htawe·wa* TA, *mawi·htamwa* TI(1) 'go for'). Found only in Jones (1907).

§37.5, 4.86*e*. *mo·hki·htawe·wa* TA 'he rushes out to attack him' and *oči·htawe·wa* TA 'he goes at him from {somewhere}' might be taken as secondary derivatives of *mo·hki·wa* 'he emerges into view, comes to the surface' and *oči·wa* 'he comes from {somewhere}' (§54.5), but the meanings seem specialized in a way that would not be accounted for in secondary derivatives.

§37.5, 4.86*k*. *akwi·ne·wa* TA 'he has him in water, soaks him' (JP-TO 98, YB-SS 6); the apparently younger form *akwi·čime·wa* TA (AW) has not been found in texts.

§37.5, 4.86*k*. Historically *anawine·wa* TA, *anawitamwa* TI(1) 'he creeps up on him, it' is a secondary derivative from *anawiwa* AI 'he goes on a distant hunt' (§54.12), but the meanings now diverge.

§37.6, 4.88*ab*. The finals for 'act on by boring' and 'sew' were presumably the same in origin, but they are listed separately because of the sharp divergence in meaning.

§37.6, 4.88*b* (|-ikwa·N| TA, |-ikwa·t| TI(1) 'sew'). Some stems have |-ikw| TI(1) 'sew' and some have both this and |-ikwa·t| TI(1) 'sew'.

§37.6, 4.89*e* (|-inaN| TA, |-inat| TI(2) 'kill'). *a·hpečinato·wa* TI(2) is deduced from *a·hpečinatawe·wa* TA+O 'kill O2 permanently for': *wi·h=a·hpečinato·nako·we* 'that I would kill them of yours "dead for ever" ' (K-M 620-621; tr. HP).

§37.6, 4.89*i*. From *na·pine·wa* TA, *na·pito·wa* TI(2) 'he has him, it around his neck' (with unidentified initial |na·-|) was derived the initial |na·p-| 'through a (tight) loop, looping around' (e.g. *na·pehkwe·hwe·wa* 'he lassoes him around the neck').

§37.6, 4.91*b*. *na·hkatešitamwa* 'he abandons him, it in flight' is also attested as *a·hkatešitamwa* (agreeing with Kickapoo); "*nakatešitamwa*" (Goddard 1994:112) is an incorrect phonemicization of the same word.

§37.6, 4.93*ab*. The final finals |-hpet| TI(1) 'taste' (4.93*a*) and |-ht| TI(1) 'act on by mouth' (4.93*b*) were presumably originally allomorphs, with |-ht| a syncopated form used after long vowels, as the examples here suggest.

§37.6, 4.94*i* (|-etaw| TA, |-et| TI(1) 'pay attention or regard to'). The gloss is arbitrary, based on just these two stems. The finals are probably ultimately the same as |-ehtaw| TA, |-eht| TI(1) 'hear, listen to' (4.93*h*), extended secondarily to *kosetawe·wa* TA, *kosetamwa* TI(1) 'he fears him, it, respectfully defers to him'.

§37.6, 4.95*a* (*kehkahwe·wa* TA, *kehkahamwa* TI(1) 'he designates him, it'). The finals may point to an original meaning 'he puts a mark on him, it (using something)', but their use may be purely metaphorical.

§37.7, 4.98f. The final pair |-o·m| TA, |-o·t| TI(1) 'carry on the back' can be described as synchronically derived from |no·m-| TA, |no·t-| TI(1), but historically it is the stem |no·m-| TA, |no·t-| TI(1) that is secondary, the result of a verb *nay- TA, *naw- TI(3) 'carry on the back' (preserved with these shapes in Shawnee) being reshaped on the basis of the synonymous finals.

§38.4, 4.109*ab*. These examples of preverbs used as prenouns were discussed by Bloomfield (1925-1927, [2]:190), who claimed that as they were "deverbative nouns from compound verbs" they "do not contain prenominal particles," i.e. prenouns, and wrote them without internal hyphens.

§38.4, 109*c* (K-Wpn 241). Published in Michelson (1932:78.23-24).

§38.4, 4.112*e*. In the text of (A 132E) there is no word divider before ⟨koči⟩, but this is not the enclitic =*koči* 'of course'; it was pronounced as a separate word by Sh (in Michelson 1925:322.25) and also by EK (in 2002), whose translation I follow.

§39.2, 4.117*d* (*a·ya·teši*). JB (JB-BP 5) and FM had both this and the variant form *a·wa·teši*; presumably this is reanalysis (cf. **§3**) rather than an innovative pattern of reduplication.

§39.3, 4.120*h* (|nani·šw-| ← |ni·šw-| 'two'). Possible additional examples of this short-vowel reduplication of 'two': *e·h=nani·šo·piwa·či* 'the two of them were sitting there together' (K-SF 52; also K-BBWM 93E; K-TG 74 [dim. obv.]; K-EGC 15, 32 [obv.]; etc.). This reduplication was not recognized in the 1990's, but if these words are read with *na·-* the meaning is 'four or more acting two by two', which does not fit the cited contexts.

§39.3, 4.120*o*. Jones (1907:14.5, 7) has |papo·hkw-| and also, for the same incident, apparent |po·po·hkw-| or |po·hpo·hkw-| (written with plain ⟨-p-⟩; Jones 1907:24.22).

§39.3, 4.123*a*. |ki·ki·p-| was obtained from EK 1997, and |ki·hki·p-| (4.126*d*) was obtained from AW in 1994.

§39.3, 4.126*d*. See the previous note.

§39.3, 4.132*b*, 4.133. The vowel length in the reduplication |aya·-| ~ |a·ya·-| cannot be determined from the syllabary texts; in the edited texts long |a·-| is written everywhere, since it is already present in Jones's texts. In addition, the occurrence of *a ya·-* in many forms having initial change (4.133*e*) appears to show that *a ya·-* had become the pronunciation in all forms, despite the occurrence of archaic initial change with *e ya·-* (4.132b) in some forms.

§39.4, 4.136*g* (*e ·h=iyohiyowa ·či* 'they always said {so}'). The reduplication with *iyoh-* is only found where the unreduplicated stem would have *iyo-* (1.93). The verb in *e ·h=iyo ·hiyakwe* (K-WC 48) is *iyo ·hi-*, the diminutive form of |i-| AI 'say {so}' (4.248*d*), used to imply that the speakers are lesser creatures than the deities being addressed (AW).

§39.7, 4.155*b* (*e ·h=penopenowa ·či*). "And they all went away to their respective homes." (HP tr.)

§39.8. Already in Michelson's day speakers disfavored iterated one-syllable reduplication. It is often edited out of his texts and generally rejected by speakers today.

§39.8, 4.157*h* (*e ·h=pa ·pa ·pakama ·či* 'he clubbed them all to death'). The next sentence explains that every dog was killed with a single blow.

§39.9, 4.160*b* (*mamakwahki ·ki* 'in the hills'). The unreduplicated noun *makwahkiwi* 'large hill' attests the |-w| that shows that |mamakwahkiw-| is in origin an agent noun. The underlying verbs are found in Kickapoo (Voorhis 1988:61), but the Meskwaki verbs are now made from these old agent nouns: *makwahkiwiwi* 'it is a large hill', *mamakwahkiwiwi* 'there are large hills'.

§41.1, 4.168*e* (*pepikwe ·ško ·hi* 'small whistle'). The apparent form *pepikwe ·škwi ·hi* "(bone) fife" (Jones 1907:348.14, 349) is unique; it does not have the form of a diminutive and may not have been intended as such. The manuscript has the usual, non-diminutive shape *pepikwe ·škwi* (Jones 1902, 2:67).

§41.1, 4.171*a* (*neme ·si ·ha* 'little fish'). The same diminutive suffix is presumably present in *e ·si ·ha* 'mussel shell, mussel', but Meskwaki does not preserve the stem without this (cf. Ojibwe *es* 'clam, shell', pl. *esag*).

§41.1, 4.173*j* (*pi ·tanwa ·ha* 'a little quiver'). This is attested only in the derived verb of possession |opi ·tanwa ·hi-| AI 'have a little quiver': *netopi ·tanwa ·hi* 'I had a little quiver' (K-Auto 1).

§41.1, 4.173*k* (*anake ·wa ·hi* 'a small birchbark canoe'). This is attested only in the possessed form *oto ·nake ·wa ·hwa ·wi* 'their small birchbark canoe' (K-SGG 82).

§45.2, 4.200*b* (*mesenahikani, mesanahikani* 'document, letter, piece of writing'). The underlying verb now diverges in meaning: |mesenahike·-|, |mesanahike·-| AI 'buy things on credit, be in debt' (from the traders' practice of recording the supplies advanced to hunters).

§45.7, 4.209*e* (*kemo ·toweni* 'stealing, theft'). A long /o·/ might be expected, but only short /o/ was heard.

§45.7, 4.212 (nouns in *-amo·weni*). These are normalized as all having long /o·/, which was heard in 4.212*b* and sometimes in 4.212*a*.

§45.7, 4.217*c* (*mešemeko·hiweni*). Unknown in the 1990's; Geary's edition has short /o/.

§45.7, 4.218*d* (*mi·wašiweni, mi·wešiweni* 'bundle, pack'). Cf. |owi·waši-| AI 'carry a pack'.

§46.1, 4.220. A number of exocentric-particle finals have the shape of otherwise unattested agent nouns made from II stems by adding |-w| NF (examples in 5.18*c*). Compare the preverbs in (4.16).

§46.2, 4.223. Also non-umlauting is *|-ihka·| II 'abound in' (**§11.10**, 1.185 and note above), which is not attested in verb stems.
Possible examples without initial change are:
maškote·we·towe·ha 'curlew' (but in this form there is no underlying verb; cf. *me·škote·wa·towa·ta* 'curlew', *lit.* 'Peoria speaker').
natopa·ha 'African lion' (reported by AW as used by someone else); this might be a hypocoristic shortening.

§46.2, 4.223*d* (*me·hkikwe·ška·ha* 'species of insect'). Accepted by AW as *me·hki·kwe·ška·ha*, which seems less likely.

§46.2, 4.225*b* (*owi·nenwi-mi·či·ha* 'meadowlark'). Its song is interpreted as: *owi·nenwi mi·činó·u!* 'eat fat!'

§47.2, 4.238*c* (*mi·ša·tesiweniwiwa* AI 'he wears his finery'). There is also the regular verb of possession *omi·ša·tesiweniwa* AI (K-FC 748) and the ostensible hybrid form *omi·ša·tesiweniwiwa* AI, AI+O (K-FC 622 2x, K-OKUT 63).

§47.2, 4.238*g* (*papakye·hiwiwa* AI 'he (a pipe) is axe-bladed'). Jones (1907:26.23, 27) has *papakye·hiwiničin[i] ohpwa·kanan[i]* 'pipe tomahawk (obv.)', translated "axe-bladed pipes." The missing initial change (*pa-* for *pe·-*) and the translation as inanimate plural are errors of the redaction; the noun is construed as animate as the subject of this participle and of another verb. There is no manuscript version.

§48, 4.239*a* (*oni·ča·nesiwa* AI 'he or she has a child'). Note the meaning 'get, come to have' in: *na·hina·h=meko we·ni·ča·nesiwakwe·ni* 'right whenever our (inc.) child is born' (K-SF 35).

§49.2, 4.245*d* (*owi·wehkawe·wa* 'he claims O2 is his (obv.) wife'):
e·h=owihowi·wehkawiwa·či oškinawe·haki ki·ya·wa·wi "the young-men have claimed that you are my wives" (K-WYB 156, tr. TB).

§51.2, 4.259*b*. An example derived from a compound stem:
e·h=kehči-a·hkwamatamo·hka·noči "He pretended to be very sick." (K-FC 559, tr. HP).

§51.3, 4.261*b*: *wiˑnaˑ=keˑhi neniwa eˑh=kehčineniwiˑhkaˑsočiˑ=meko.* "That man acted as though he was a great man." (K-BHD 131; tr. TB in Michelson 1928:85).

§52.1, 4.265*p* (*miˑškawesiˑmikatwi* II 'it is strong'). In three successive sentences about a sacred pack this word is used twice and the regular II (|miˑškawaˑ-| II) is used once (K-FC 296).

§52.1, 4.266*de*. The analysis of stems with |-∅| AI ABSTR as adding |-eˑyaˑ| II ABSTR parallels the analysis of other AI stems as adding the secondary finals |-ˑmikat| II ABSTR and |-eˑyaˑ| II ABSTR. If this parallelism is abandoned, these could be described as primary II stems with medials ending in postmedial |-eˑ| and a final |-yaˑ| II. The advantages of this are unclear.

§53.5, 4.297*r*. In K-B 27 (Michelson 1925:58.16) apparent *eˑh=šaˑkweˑnemowaˑči* (as if 'they were unwilling') should presumably be emended to *eˑh=šaˑkweˑnemekowaˑči* '(obv.) was unwilling for them (to)': HP translates the manuscript as "they were not wanted to" to try to capture the required meaning.

§53.5, 4.300*a* (*aˑšitoˑnikeˑwa* 'he trades'). There are also the variants |aˑšoˑnikaˑ-| AI 'trade' and |aˑšoˑnikaw-| TA 'trade with'. All of these are commonly found with secondary objects.

§53.8, 4.318. Uncertain is *kanoˑnetisowa* AI 'he speaks to himself' (only in Jones 1907:284.3, an addition not in the manuscript); cf. *kakanoˑnetisowa* 'he has a conversation with O2' (4.319).

§54.4, 4.329*b*. *wiˑčikaˑpawiˑhtaweˑwa* TA and *wiˑčikaˑpawinohkataweˑwa* TA are attested only by the derived reciprocals (C-RS 12, C-RS 20).

§54.8, 4.334k. Although *mayoˑheˑwa* TA 'he makes him weep' is a secondary derivative from |mayoˑ-| AI 'weep', the otherwise parallel stem |mayoˑm-| TA 'make weep by speaking, singing, or weeping' must be taken as primary, as |-m| TA 'act on by vocalization' (4.90*a*) is only a primary final.

§54.9, 4.340b. |mehpoˑniht-| TI(2)-O 'make it snow' (← |mehpo-| II 'snow') + |-aw|. The long |oˑ| is from AW, who said *mehpoˑhtowa* herself; cf. the lengthening before |-n-emi| AI (4.15f).

§54.11, 4.342*d* (*matoˑtešawaneˑwa* TA 'he gives him a sweatbath'). Now *matoˑtešaˑneˑwa*; the vowel lengths are recoverable from this and from analysis.

§54.12, 4.343 (applicatives with |-N| TA, |-t| TI(1)). Also in the final pairs in 4.88.

§54.12, 4.344 (applicatives with |-N| TA, |-t| TI(2)). Also in the final pairs in 4.89.

§54.12, 4.345*c* (*waˑnehkaˑtamwa*). The simplex TI(1) stem is unattested but guaranteed by |waˑnehkaˑtamaw-| TA+O 'dig O2 for' (S-RSW).

§54.13, 4.347*a* (*kekeškoˑteneˑwa* TA+O). There is also *kekaškoˑteneˑwa* TA+O 'he places O2 within him (obv.)' (K-WD 97); this appears to be a variant influenced by the final pair in *inaško·sowa* AI, *inaško·te·wi* II (which have variants with *-ešk-*) 'he, it is, feels {so} after eating' (4.78*f*).

NOTES TO CHAPTER 5. SENTENCE STRUCTURE

§60.1. Compound nouns are treated extensively by Thomason (2005).

§60.1, 5.4*g* (*onemači·neki* 'on his left, on the left'). K uses this as a dependent noun of the type that takes *o-* when unpossessed (cf. 3.26). Other speakers use this as a non-dependent noun: *nemači·neki* 'on the left' (JB-FS 19); cf. *maya·wineki* 'on the right' (JB-FS 17, 19). There is also *nemači·nina·ki* 'on the left' (C-Hist 5) (cf. 4.191*b*).

§60.2. Dahlstrom (2000:69-73) discusses the formation of compound verbs of different types.

§60.2, 5.10*d*. This compound verb is also in (O 58A).

§60.2, 5.13*f*. |pepo·wi| PV 'of winter' is apparently from an otherwise unattested noun *pepo·wi* 'winter' derived from the verb *pepo·wi* 'it is winter' (4.220; cf. 4.16*b*).

§60.2, 5.16*a*(1). It may be better to take *ana=nešiwi* and *'na=nešiwi* as being restructured as *ananešiwi* and *nanešiwi*, given the assimilated variants *anenešiwi* and *nenešiwi*.

§60.3, 5.16*i* (*tepi*). Compare with *tepi* PV: *aškači e·h=tepi- nye·wenwi -čapo·keneči.* 'After a while the number of times he was pushed under the water was up to four.' (K-MMGW 13).

§60.5, 5.17*f*(4). |mahkesen-| is used as the equivalent of the noun *mahkese·hi* 'moccasin' in archaic use and in derivatives (2.36*b*; 4.37, 242*f*); this was the original form of the noun stem, |mahkese·h-| being a hypocoristic shortening (**§41.4**).

§60.5, 5.17*f*(14). The transcription of *keki-wi·kiya·pe* 'along with the house' follows AW, who wrote a medial word divider. The ostensible form *keki-wi·kiya·pi* (S-Apay 50) was not accepted by AW and is presumably a writing error influenced by the simplex noun.

§62.2, 5.36*cd*. Nominal expressions like these are analyzed by Thomason (2005:428) as having *ki·ša·koči* as a prenoun modifying the following prenoun, with the two prenouns constituting a compound prenoun: *ki·ša·koči-meši* PN-PN extremely large', *ki·ša·koči-nawe·ni* PN-PN 'extremely attractive'.

§62.2, 5.38*b*. In the example, *taši* is emended from manuscript ⟨ta⟩.

§62.5, 5.59*a* ("Nothing of mine is missing."). Dahlstrom (1995:7) takes *ni·na* as a Topic, but the other examples given in 5.59 and the native speaker translations available for three of them argue against taking these possessor noun phrases as being Topics, if Topic is defined as a noun phrase that stands outside the rest of the sentence and states what it is about (**§65.1**).

§63 (Verb phrases). In some theories of formal grammar a verb phrase (VP) is a verb together with its direct or primary object. There is no evidence for a verb phrase of this type in Meskwaki and good evidence against its existence (Dahlstrom 1986, 1993; Goddard and Dahlstrom 2022). In Meskwaki the structure within which subjects, objects, obliques, and complement clauses are linked to verbs is the sentence.

§65 (POSITIONS). Dahlstrom (2004) proposed that the noun phrase or noun phrases in Focus position should be recognized as having the distinct status of Internal Topics, and she relabeled Topic as External Topic.

§65.3 (*Focus*). Dahlstrom (2003) analyzes Meskwaki focus constructions of various kinds.

§66.1, 5.92*i* (oblique participle with two relative roots). Dahlstrom (2014) discusses such cases.

§67.1, 5.108*c*. *naʰka, naʰkači* is both a conjunction with the meaning 'and also' (5.108*b*) and a clausal particle meaning 'again' (5.117*n*) or 'also' (5.119*r*).

§67.2, 5.110*c*. *našawaye* 'long ago' is a shortened form of *anašawaye*, which incorporates the intensifying particle |ana| (5.16*a*), with elision.

§70 (Incorporated complements). Meskwaki incorporated complements pose problems for at least three widely held theoretical premises (Ackerman and Webelhuth 1998; Dahlstrom 2000):
 1) The Weak Lexicalist Hypothesis: it is fully derived stems that are lexical entries, with syntactic and semantic properties.
 2) The Lexical Integrity Hypothesis: the internal morphology of words (alternatively stems) is opaque to syntax.
 3) The principle of "Morphological Expression": the assumption that a single predicate is expressed by a single syntactic item.
 These scholars propose "that the lexicon must be much more complex and flexible than standardly assumed" (Dahlstrom 2000:63-64); specifically:
 4) Preverb-Verb combinations are words (units in the lexicon).
 5) A preverb and its corresponding initial are different categorial realizations of the same lexical item (cf. Goddard 1988:66-67, 1990b:478-479).
 6) Verbs that incorporate verbs have two argument-taking predicates: the main (matrix) PREDICATE takes the incorporated verb as one of its arguments; the incorporated verb is a SECONDARY PREDICATE.
 7) Secondary predicates are accessible to the syntax.

§70.1, 5.145*a*. There is also the synonymous *neʸapi mehtoseʾneniwih-* TA (FC 352), and *ayaʾpami mehtoseʾneniwih-* TA 'bring back to life' (K-SSB 11, X10-PBW 73).

§70.1, 5.145*c*. This compound verb stem is also found with the preverb discontinuous (K-FC 140, tr. HP; K-B 287).

§70.2, 5.146*c*. HP's translation is: "and he played as if he was deaf."

§70.4, 5.152c (|tana·čimo-| AI). This is also used as a primary stem:

e·h=apihapiči e·h=tana·čimoči. 'He gave his report from where he was sitting.' (K-WLB 25) (|CVCV+| RED2, |api-| AI 'sit {somewhere}', |e·h=–či 3s/PPL(loc.obl); |tana·čimo-| AI 'report one's experiences {somewhere}', |e·h=–či| 3s/AOR)

§70.4, 5.152d. *i·nahi* 'there' is anaphoric to the discontinuous locative oblique complement in the preceding sentence (given here as ex. 5.152c) and must refer to where the men were saying the Kaw was, rather than to where they were talking. The unusual construction was edited out of Michelson's redaction (Michelson 1925:382, l. 17) as "broken," but it is well formed.

§71.2. The occurrence of discontinuous compound verbs in Meskwaki was pointed out by Michelson (1914).

§71.2, 5.156a. This sentence was included by Jonas Poweshiek in a collection of sentences he wrote for Michelson in 1914 (in NAA ms. 2643), and Michelson annotated it as, "A sentence spoken by an old woman, heard by Jonas."); cited in Michelson (1914:405).

§71.5, 5.175a. It is actually the iterative temporal clause inside the subjunctive conditional clause that is discontinuous.

NOTES TO CHAPTER 6. DISCOURSE STRUCTURE

§73.8, 6.21d. This sentence is discussed by Thomason (2004:424).

§73.8, 6.22a. TB's translation is as given in Michelson (1930:145).

§73.8, 6.25a. TB's translation is as given in Michelson (1928:68).

§73.9, after 6.29. The passage in (K-B 118-147) is discussed in Goddard (1990a:326-328).

§73.10. Examples of all word orders of subject and object are given and discussed by Thomason (2003, §2.3.1.2.2). Statistics and examples for two, three, and four noun phrases co-occurring in a clause are given, with discussion, by Thomason (2004).

§73.11. The fact that word order has no part in assigning the syntactic roles of subject and object is consonant with the lack of evidence in Meskwaki for the existence of a syntactic structure which would link the verb more closely to the object than to the subject (the VP of classical theory); see the note to **§63**, above.

Appendix 2.

Analysis of Inflections

The inflectional prefixes and suffixes used in the texts "The Autobiography of a Meskwaki Woman" (Goddard 2006b) and "The Owl Sacred Pack" (Goddard 2007), and some additional inflections, are explained in this appendix. The analysis follows that in Goddard (2004), which has a full list of abbreviations (for which see also pp. xxi-xxiii).

1. *List of prefixes.*

The inflectional prefixes indicated in the interlinear analysis of the texts are listed here. The three pronominal prefixes, the prefix marking unpossessed dependent nouns, and the abstract representation of initial change (**IC**+) are listed with a following plus sign (+). These affixes fuse with the following stem, sometimes irregularly. In contrast, the aorist and future prefixes are listed and marked in words with a double hyphen (=); although they are not strictly proclitics, as the use of "=" might imply, they are phonologically more independent from the following stem than the prefixes marked with "+", and their demarcation by "=" increases the transparency of inflected forms and facilitates database searches.

The aorist prefix and initial change have grammatical functions but no specific meaning; hence *eʔh=* is simply provided with the label "aor.," and initial change is not glossed.

eʔh=	aor.: the aorist prefix, which marks aorist conjunct, aorist interrogative, and participles with locative oblique heads (except before *aʔmi* POT)
	NOTE: dropped before *wiʔh=* FUT. (But *eʔh=* sometimes appears with a preverb *wiʔhi* (often elided to *wiʔh*), which has some of the functions of *wiʔh=* FUT.)
IC+	initial change; marks the changed modes of the conjunct and interrogative orders (changed conjunct, changed interrogative, changed preterite, iterative, and the participles)
ke+	2: second person pronominal prefix
	→ *k-* before *i·* and *o·* in dependent stems and with *wiʔh* FUT
	→ *ket-* before other vowels
ne+	1: first person pronominal prefix
	→ *n-* before *i·* and *o·* in dependent stems and with *wiʔh* FUT
	→ *net-* before other vowels
me+	unposs.: unpossessed dependent noun
	→ *m-* before *i·* in dependent stems

o+   3: third person animate pronominal prefix
                                    → *ow-* before *i·* in dependent stems
                                    → Ø before *o·* in dependent stems
                                    → *ot-* before other vowels
wi·h=   FUT: future prefix
                                    ne- (1) + *wi·h=* FUT+ → *ni·h=*
                                    ke- (2) + *wi·h=* FUT+ → *ki·h=*

2. *List of endings.*

The inflectional endings (ending complexes) indicated in the interlinear analysis with a preceding plus sign (+) are here listed, glossed, and analyzed. Homophonous endings are given separately if at least one component suffix is different. For each ending, each distinctly glossed use in each combination with an associated prefix or initial change is noted, except that combinations with *wi·h=* FUT are omitted; such multiple uses of the same ending are ordered alphabetically by gloss. In the pronominal component of a gloss, categories that are not distinguished are separated by a comma with no space, except that systematically a third person is glossed only as a proximate in an ending that has no obviative counterpart. Thus "3,0" means 'third person animate (3) or inanimate (0)', and "3–2s" glosses endings for third person proximate (3) acting on second singular (2s) that are also used for action by third person obviative (3´). In a few cases an ending or use not found in the analyzed texts has been added because it is more basic than an attested use of the ending or otherwise fills out a paradigm. Still, this is by no means a complete list of all endings used in Meskwaki.

The endings are analyzed into their separate component suffixes as an aid to understanding the function of the forms. A template for the verbal suffixes arranged by position class is in Goddard (2004:104). Pronominal suffixes of position 6 and combined suffixes of positions 6 and 7 that are used after only one theme sign are glossed for both arguments. No claim is made about the synchronic viability of these elements; in reality much of this morphology is presumably inaccessible to speakers except as points of contrast within paradigms. In many cases analyses of different levels of abstraction are possible. The citation of elements in the interlinear analysis of the texts tends toward less abstract representations, ones that more nearly resemble the shape of elements in actual forms. The discussion of phonological rules in some cases presents rules that account for some segments in these less abstract forms.

The aorist prefix (*e·h=*) and the initial change vowel ablaut (IC) are included in the analytical affix complex even when they are not overtly present in the occurring forms. Specifically, *e·h=* aor. is specified here even for forms that lack it overtly because it is displaced by the future prefix (*wi·h=*); and initial change is specified, as in the interlinear glosses, even if the actual inflected form does not indicate it overtly because the first stem vowel is long.

The individual suffixes that make up the endings are also listed separately, together with information on irregular combinations with stems or other suffixes. The endings (ending complexes) are marked with "+" and in bold type; a suffix that is the unique component of an ending is given in italics as a subentry. Suffixes that are not also endings are listed separately in normal type, marked with a hyphen.

Glosses with numbers in parentheses are placed after the corresponding gloss without the parentheses. Endings beginning with a raised dot (·) are alphabetized by their first consonant. The endings with the shape -Ø (zero) are at the end of the list.

+a	ANsg: animate singular on nouns
	-a anim. sg.: animate singular in ending complexes
+a	*ne–a* 1s–0/IND: ne- (1) -am (TI(1) th.) -∅ (sg.)
	1s(-0)/IND: same on an objectless TI(1)
	ke–a 2s–0/IND: ke- (2) -am (TI(1) th.) -∅ (sg.)
	2s(-0)/IND: same on an objectless TI(1)
-a	1s proh.: first singular prohibitive
+ači	*e·h=–ači* 2s–3/AOR: e·h= (aor.) -∅ (TA th. 1) -at (2s–3) -i (conj.)
	IC–ači 2s–3/CC: IC+ -∅ (TA th. 1) -at (2s–3) -i (conj.)
+ači	*IC–ači* 2s–3/PPL(INsg,obl): IC+ -∅ (TA th. 1) -at (2s–3) -i (inan. sg.)
+ačiki	*IC–ačiki* 2s–3/PPL(ANpl): IC+ -∅ (TA th. 1) -at (2s–3) -iki (anim. pl.)
+ačini	*IC–ačini* 2s–3/ITER: IC+ -∅ (TA th. 1) -at (2s–3) -ini (neg.-iter.)
	–ačini 2s–3/NEG: -∅ (TA th. 1) -at (2s–3) -ini (neg.-iter.)
+ahi	OBVpl: obviative plural on nouns
	-ahi obv. pl.: obviative plural in ending complexes
-ak	1s–3: first singular acting on third animate, conjunct and interrogative
+aka	*IC–aka* 1s–3/PPL(ANsg): IC+ -∅ (TA th. 1) -ak (1s–3) -a (anim. sg.)
+aka	*IC–aka* 3–0/PPL(ANsg): IC+ -am (TI(1) th.) -k (3) -a (anim. sg.)
	3(-0)/PPL(ANsg): same on an objectless TI(1)
+akani	2s–0/PROH: -am (TI(1) th.) -hk (proh.) -an (2s) -i (conj.)
	2s(-0)/PROH: same on an objectless TI(1)
+ake	1s–3/SUBJ: -∅ (TA th. 1) -ak (1s–3) -e (subj.)
+ake	3s–0/SUBJ: -am (TI(1) th.) -k (3) -e (subj.)
	3s(-0)/SUBJ: same on an objectless TI(1)
+akeči	*e·h=–akeči* 1p–3/AOR: e·h= (aor.) -∅ (TA th. 1) -aket (1p–3) -i (conj.)
	IC–akeči 1p–3/CC: IC+ -∅ (TA th. 1) -aket (1p–3) -i (conj.)
+akeči	*IC–akeči* 1p–3/PPL(INsg,obl): IC+ -∅ (TA th. 1) -aket (1p–3) -i (inan. sg.)
+akečini	1p–3/NEG: -∅ (TA th. 1) -aket (1p–3) -ini (neg.-iter.)
+akehe	*IC–akehe* 1s–3/PRET.PPL(obl): IC+ -∅ (TA th. 1) -ak (1s–3) -ehe (pret.)
-aket	1p–3: first plural exclusive acting on third animate, conjunct and interrogative
+aketa	*IC–aketa* +1p–3/PPL(ANsg): IC+ -∅ (TA th. 1) -aket (1p–3) -a (anim. sg.)
+ake·ko	2p–0/PROH: -am (TI(1) th.) -hk (proh.) -e·ko (2p proh.)
+ake·koha	2p–0/POT: -am (TI(1) th.) -hk (proh.) -e·kw (2p) -ehe (pret.)
+aki	ANpl: animate plural on nouns
	-aki anim. pl.: animate plural in ending complexes
+aki	*e·h=–aki* 1s–3/AOR: e·h= (aor.) -∅ (TA th. 1) -ak (1s–3) -i (conj.)
	IC–aki 1s–3/CC: IC+ -∅ (TA th. 1) -ak (1s–3) -i (conj.)
	–aki 1s–3/CONJ: -∅ (TA th. 1) -ak (1s–3) -i (conj.)
+aki	*IC–aki* 1s–3/PPL(INsg,obl): IC+ -∅ (TA th. 1) -ak (1s–3) -i (inan. sg.)
+aki	*e·h=–aki* 3s–0/AOR: e·h= (aor.) -am (TI(1) th.) -k (3) -i (conj.)
	3s(-0)/AOR: same on an objectless TI(1)
	IC–aki 3s–0/CC: IC+ -am (TI(1) th.) -k (3) -i (conj.)
	3s(-0)/CC: same on an objectless TI(1)
	–aki 3s–0/CONJ: -am (TI(1) th.) -k (3) -i (conj.)
+aki	*IC–aki* 3s–0/PPL(INsg,obl): IC+ -am (TI(1) th.) -k (3) -i (inan. sg.)

+akiče   3s–0/PROH: -am (TI(1) th.) -hk (proh.) -če (3,0 imp.)
                3s(-0)/PROH: same on an objectless TI(1)

+akiki   *IC–akiki* 1s–3/PPL(ANpl): IC+ -Ø (TA th. 1) -ak (1s–3) -iki (anim. pl.)

+akiki   *IC–akiki* 3–0/PPL(ANpl): IC+ -am (TI(1) th.) -k (3) -iki (anim. pl.)
                3(-0)/PPL(ANpl): same on an objectless TI(1)

+akini   *IC–akini* 1s–3/ITER: IC+ -Ø (TA th. 1) -ak (1s–3) -ini (neg.-iter.)
        –akini 1s–3/NEG: -Ø (TA th. 1) -ak (1s–3) -ini (neg.-iter.)

+akini   *IC–akini* 3s–0/ITER: IC+ -am (TI(1) th.) -k (3) -ini (neg.-iter.)
        –akini 3s–0/NEG: -am (TI(1) th.) -k (3) -ini (neg.-iter.)
                3s(-0)/NEG: same on an objectless TI(1)

+akini   *IC–akini* 3s–0/PPL(INpl): IC+ -am (TI(1) th.) -k (3) -ini (inan. pl.)

-ako·w   1s–2p: first singular on second plural, conjunct
        NOTE: after *-ako·w* 1s–2p all suffixes are replaced by *-e* (< *-i* conj.)

-akw   12: first plural inclusive in conjunct, interrogative, potential, and prohibitive
        → *-yakw* after a vowel

+akwa   *IC–akwa* 12–3/PPL(ANsg): IC+ -Ø (TA th. 1) -akw (12) -a (anim. sg.)

+akwe   *e·h=–akwe* 12–3/AOR: e·h= (aor.) -Ø (TA th. 1) -akw (12) -i (conj.)
        IC–akwe 12–3/PPL(INsg,obl): IC+ -Ø (TA th. 1) -akw (12) -i (inan. sg.)

+akwe   *–akwe* 12–3/SUBJ: -Ø (TA th. 1) -akw (12) -e (subj.)

+akwiki   *IC–akwiki* 12–3/PPL(ANpl): IC+ -Ø (TA th. 1) -akw (12) -iki (anim. pl.)

+akwini   12–3/NEG: -Ø (TA th. 1) -akw (12) -ini (neg.-iter.)

-am   TI(1) th.: theme sign of TI class 1
        → *-a·* before *p* in independent
        → *-a* word-finally and before *-k, -hk, -n,* and *č.*

+amakwe   *e·h=–amakwe* 12–0/AOR: e·h= (aor.) -am (TI(1) th.) -akw (12) -i (conj.)
        IC–amakwe 12–0/PPL(INsg,obl): IC+ -am (TI(1) th.) -akw (12) -i (inan. sg.)

+amakwe   *–amakwe* 12–0/SUBJ: -am (TI(1) th.) -akw (12) -e (subj.)

+amakwini   12–0/NEG: -am (TI(1) th.) -akw (12) -ini (neg.-iter.)

+amane   2s–0/SUBJ: -am (TI(1) th.) -an (2s) -e (subj.)

+amani   *e·h=–amani* 2s–0/AOR: e·h= (aor.) -am (TI(1) th.) -an (2s) -i (conj.)
                2s(-0)/AOR: same on an objectless TI(1)

+amanini   *IC–amanini* 2s–0/ITER: IC+ -am (TI(1) th.) -an (2s) -ini (neg.-iter.)
                2s(-0)/ITER: same on an objectless TI(1)
        –amanini 2s–0/NEG: -am (TI(1) th.) -an (2s) -ini (neg.-iter.)

+ama·kini   1p–0/NEG: -am (TI(1) th.) -a·k (1p) -ini (neg.-iter.)

+ama·nehe   1s/PRET.SUBJ: -am (TI(1) th.) -a·n (1s) -ehe (pret.)

+ama·ni   *e·h=–ama·ni* 1s–0/AOR: e·h= (aor.) -am (TI(1) th.) -a·n (1s) -i (conj.)
                1s(-0)/AOR: same on an objectless TI(1)
        IC–ama·ni 1s–0/CC: IC+ -am (TI(1) th.) -a·n (1s) -i (conj.)
                1s(-0)/CC: same on an objectless TI(1)

+ama·ni   *e·h=–ama·ni* 1s–0/PPL(loc.obl): e·h= (aor.) -am (TI(1) th.) -a·n (1s) -i (inan. sg.)
                1s(-0)/PPL(loc.obl): same on an objectless TI(1)
        IC–ama·ni 1s–0/PPL(INsg,obl): IC+ -am (TI(1) th.) -a·n (1s) -i (inan. sg.)

+ama·nini   *IC–ama·nini* 1s–0/ITER: IC+ -am (TI(1) th.) -a·n (1s) -ini (neg.-iter.)
        –ama·nini 1s–0/NEG: -am (TI(1) th.) -a·n (1s) -ini (neg.-iter.)
                1s(-0)/NEG: same on an objectless TI(1)

+ama·nini   *IC–ama·nini* 1s–0/PPL(INpl): IC+ -am (TI(1) th.) -a·n (1s) -ini (inan. pl.)

+ameke   X–0/SUBJ: -am (TI(1) th.) -ek (X) -e (subj.)

+ameki   *e·h=–ameki* X–0/AOR: e·h= (aor.) -am (TI(1) th.) -ek (X) -i (conj.)
     X(-0)/AOR: same on an objectless TI(1)
     –ameki X–0/CONJ: -am (TI(1) th.) -ek (X) -i (conj.)

+ameki   *IC–ameki* X–0/PPL(INsg,obl): IC+ -am (TI(1) th.) -ek (X) -i (inan. sg.)
     X(-0)/PPL(obl): same on an objectless TI(1)

+amekini   *IC–amekini* X–0/ITER: IC+ -am (TI(1) th.) -ek (X) -ini (neg.-iter.)
     –amekini X–0/NEG: -am (TI(1) th.) -ek (X) -ini (neg.-iter.)

-amet   3–1p: first plural exclusive (as object of third person animate)
     → -*yamet* after a vowel (which is always the case)
     NOTE: combines with modal markers, sometimes after metathesis:
       -(y)amet (3–1p) + -*w* (irr.) → -*(y)amekw* (3–1p irr.)
       -(y)amet (3–1p) + -*hk* (proh.) + -*če* (3,0 imp.) → -*(y)amehkiče* (3–1p proh.)
       -(y)amet (3–1p) + -*sa* (3,0 pot.) → -*(y)amesa* (3–1p pot.)
       -(y)amet (3–1p) + -*če* (3,0 imp.) → -*(y)ameče* (3–1p imp.)

+ame·kwe   *e·h=–ame·kwe* 2p–0/AOR: e·h= (aor.) -am (TI(1) th.) -e·kw (2p) -i (conj.)

+ame·kwe   *IC–ame·kwe* 2p–0/PPL(INsg,obl): IC+ -am (TI(1) th.) -e·kw (2p) -i (inan. sg.)

+ame·kwe   *–ame·kwe* 2p–0/SUBJ: -am (TI(1) th.) -e·kw (2p) -e (subj.)

+ame·kwini   *IC–ame·kwini* 2p–0/ITER: IC+ -am (TI(1) th.) -e·kw (2p) -ini (neg.-iter.)
     –ame·kwini 2p–0/NEG: -am (TI(1) th.) -e·kw (2p) -ini (neg.-iter.)

+aminiči   *e·h=–aminiči* 3´–0/AOR: e·h= (aor.) -am (TI(1) th.) -ni (obv.) -t (3) -i (conj.)

+aminičihi   *IC–aminičihi* 3´–0/PPL(OBVpl): IC+ -am (TI(1) th.) -ni (obv.) -t (3)
     -ihi (obv. pl.)
     3´(-0)/PPL(OBVpl): same on an objectless TI(1)

+amoko   2p–0/IMP: -am (TI(1) th.) -ko (2p imp.)

+amokwe·na   *IC–amokwe·na* 3s–0/INT.PPL(ANsg): IC+ -am (TI(1) th.) -kw (3,0 irr.)
     -e·n (int.) -a (anim. sg.)

+amokwe·ni   *IC–amokwe·ni* 3s–0/CH.INT: IC+ -am (TI(1) th.) -kw (3,0 irr.) -e·n (int.) -i
     (conj.)
     3s(-0)/CH.INT: same on an objectless TI(1)

+amowa·či   *e·h=–amowa·či* 3p–0/AOR: e·h= (aor.) -am (TI(1) th.) -wa· (pl.) -t (3) -i (conj.)
     3p(-0)/AOR: same on an objectless TI(1)

+amowa·či   *IC–amowa·či* 3p–0/PPL(INsg,obl): IC+ -am (TI(1) th.) -wa· (pl.) -t (3) -i (inan.
     sg.)
     3p(-0)/PPL(obl): same on an objectless TI(1)

+amowa·čini   *IC–amowa·čini* 3p–0/ITER: IC+ -am (TI(1) th.) -wa· (pl.) -t (3) -ini (neg.-iter.)
     –amowa·čini 3p–0/NEG: -am (TI(1) th.) -wa· (pl.) -t (3) -ini (neg.-iter.)

+amowa·sa   3p–0/POT: -am (TI(1) th.) -wa· (pl.) -sa (3,0 pot.)

+amowečini   *IC–amowečini* X–0/REL/ITER: IC+ -am (TI(1) th.) -wet (X rel.) -ini (neg.-iter.)

+amowe·kwe·ni   *e·h=–amowe·kwe·ni* 2p–0/AOR.INT: e·h= (aor.) -am (TI(1) th.) -w (irr.)
     -e·kw (2p) -e·ni (int.)

+amo·hkani   2s–0/FUT.IMP: -am (TI(1) th.) -hk (fut. imp.) -an (2s) -i (conj.)

+amo·hiyakwe   *IC–amo·hiyakwe* 12–0/DIM/PPL(INsg): IC+ -am (TI(1) th.) -·hi (dim.) -akw (12)
     -i (inan. sg.)

+amo·hiya·ni   1s–0/DIM/PPL(INsg,obl): IC+ -am (TI(1) th.) -·hi (dim.) -a·n (1s) -i (inan. sg.)

+amo·hiye·kwe   *e·h=–amo·hiye·kwe* 2p–0/DIM/AOR: e·h= (aor.) -am (TI(1) th.) -·hi (dim.)
                     -e·kw (2p) -i (conj.)

+amo·ki   3p–0/IND: -am (TI(1) th.) -w (3,0) -aki (anim. pl.)

+amwa   3s–0/IND: -am (TI(1) th.) -w (3,0) -a (anim. sg.)
        3s(-0)/IND: same on an objectless TI(1)

-an   2s: second singular in conjunct, interrogative, and prohibitive
    → *-yan* after a vowel

+ane   2s/SUBJ: -an (2s) -e (subj.)

+ane·ha   X–0/POT: -am (TI(1) th.) -ene·ha (X pot.)

+ani   INpl: inanimate plural on nouns
    -ani inan. pl.: inanimate plural in ending complexes

+ani   OBVsg: obviative singular on nouns
    -ani obv. sg.: obviative singular in ending complexes

+ano   2s–0/IMP: -am (TI(1) th.) -no (2s imp.)

-apa   2s pot.: second singular, potential

+asa   3s–0/POT: -am (TI(1) th.) -sa (3,0 pot.)

-at   2s–3: second singular acting on third animate in conjunct

+ata   *IC–ata* 2s–3/PPL(ANsg): IC+ -∅ (TA th. 1) -at (2s–3) -a (anim. sg.)

+ate   2s–3/SUBJ: -∅ (TA th. 1) -at (2s–3) -e (subj.)

+atehe   *e·h=–atehe* 2s–3/AOR.PRET: e·h= (aor.) -at (2s–3) -ehe (pret.)

-a·   TA th. 1 (direct theme sign): action on an animate that is lower than the actor
        in the hierarchy: $1,2 > X > 3 > 3' > 3''$
    → ∅ before a vowel
    NOTE:
        -a· (TA th. 1) + *-w* (3,0) → *-e·w*, (with contraction) *-e·*
        -a· (TA th. 1) + *-ni* (obv.) + *-w* (3,0) → *-e·niw*
        -a· (TA th. 1) + *-·hi* (dim.) → *-e·hi*

+a·či   *e·h=–a·či* 3s–3′/AOR: e·h= (aor.) -a· (TA th. 1) -t (3) -i (conj.)
    IC–a·či 3s–3′/CC: IC+ -a· (TA th. 1) -t (3) -i (conj.)
    –a·či 3s–3′/CONJ: -a· (TA th. 1) -t (3) -i (conj.)
    IC–a·či 3s–3′/PPL(INsg,obl): IC+ -a· (TA th. 1) -t (3) -i (inan. sg.)

+a·čihi   *IC–a·čihi* 3s–3′/PPL(OBVpl): IC+ -a· (TA th. 1) -t (3) -ihi (obv. pl.)

+a·čiki   *IC–a·čiki* 3–3′/PPL(ANpl): IC+ -a· (TA th. 1) -t (3) -iki (anim. pl.)

+a·čini   *IC–a·čini* 3s–3′/ITER: IC+ -a· (TA th. 1) -t (3) -ini (neg.-iter.)
    –a·čini 3s–3′/NEG: -a· (TA th. 1) -t (3) -ini (neg.-iter.)

-a·ha   1s pot.: first singular potential

+a·hkani   2s–3/FUT.IMP: -a· (TA th. 1) -hk (fut. imp.) -an (2s) -i (conj.)

+a·hke·ko   2p–3/FUT.IMP: -a· (TA th. 1) -hk (fut. imp.) -e·ko (2p proh.)

+a·hkiče   3s–3′/FUT.IMP: -a· (TA th. 1) -hk (fut. imp.) -če (3,0 imp.)

-a·k   1p: first plural exclusive in conjunct, interrogative, potential, and prohibitive
    → *-ya·k* after a vowel

+a·ke   *IC–a·ke* 1p/PPL(INsg,obl): IC+ -a·k (1p) -i (inan. sg.)

-a·kw   3,X–2p: second plural as object of third person animate or indefinite, conjunct
        and interrogative

-a·n   1s: first singular, conjunct and interrogative
    → *-ya·n* after a vowel

+aˑni   *eˑh=–aˑni* 1s/AOR: eˑh= (aor.) -aˑn (1s) -i (conj.)

+aˑničihi   *IC–aˑničihi* 3′–3′′/PPL(OBVpl): IC+ -aˑ (TA th. 1) -ni (obv.) -t (3)
        -ihi (obv. pl.)

+aˑpena   *ne–aˑpena* 1p–3/IND: ne- (1) -aˑ (TA th. 1) -pena (1p,12)
        ke–aˑpena 12–3/IND: ke- (2) -aˑ (TA th. 1) -pena (1p,12)

+aˑpena   *ke–aˑpena* 12–0/IND: ke- (2) -am (TI(1) th.) -pena (1p,12)

+aˑpetoke   *ne–aˑpetoke* 1s–0/DUB: ne- (1) -am (TI(1) th.) -p (sg.) -etoke (dub.)
        ke–aˑpetoke 2s–0/DUB: ne- (2) -am (TI(1) th.) -p (sg.) -etoke (dub.)

+aˑpi   X–0/IND: -am (TI(1) th.) -pi (X)
        X(-0)/IND: same on an objectless TI(1)

+aˑpi   X–3/IND: -aˑ (TA th. 1) -pi (X)

+aˑpwa   *ke–aˑpwa* 2p–0/IND: ke- (2) -am (TI(1) th.) -pwa (2p)

+aˑpwa   *ke–aˑpwa* 2p–3/IND: ke- (2) -aˑ (TA th. 1) -pwa (2p)

+aˑsa   3s–3′/POT: -aˑ (TA th. 1) -sa (3,0 pot.)

+aˑta   *IC–aˑta* 3–3′/PPL(ANsg): IC+ -aˑ (TA th. 1) -t (3) -a (anim. sg.)

+aˑte   3s–3′/SUBJ: -aˑ (TA th. 1) -t (3) -e (subj.)

+aˑtehe   *eˑh=–aˑtehe* 3s–3′/AOR.PRET: eˑh= (aor.) -aˑ (TA th. 1) -t (3) -ehe (pret.)
        IC–aˑtehe 3s–3′/CH.PRET: IC+ -aˑ (TA th. 1) -t (3) -ehe (pret.)

+aˑteˑni   X–3/INT: -aˑ (TA th. 1) -w (irr.) -et (X–3) -eˑni (int.)

+aˑwa   *ne–aˑwa* 1s–3s/IND: ne- (1) -aˑ (TA th. 1) -w (sg.) -a (anim. sg.)
        ke–aˑwa 2s–3s/IND: ne- (2) -aˑ (TA th. 1) -w (sg.) -a (anim. sg.)

+aˑwaki   *ne–aˑwaki* 1s–3p/IND: ne- (1) -aˑ (TA th. 1) -w (sg.) -aki (anim. pl.)
        ke–aˑwaki 2s–3p/IND: ke- (2) -aˑ (TA th. 1) -w (sg.) -aki (anim. pl.)

+aˑwateˑna   2s–3/INT.PPL(ANsg): -aˑ (TA th. 1) -w (irr.) -at (2s–3) -eˑni (int.) -a (anim. sg.)

+aˑwaˑči   *eˑh=–aˑwaˑči* 3p–3′/AOR: eˑh= (aor.) -aˑ (TA th. 1) -waˑ (pl.) -t (3) -i (conj.)
        –aˑwaˑči 3p–3′/CONJ: -aˑ (TA th. 1) -waˑ (pl.) -t (3) -i (conj.)

+aˑwaˑči   *IC–aˑwaˑči* 3p–3′/PPL(INsg,obl): IC+ -aˑ (TA th. 1) -waˑ (pl.) -t (3) -i (inan. sg.)

+aˑwaˑčihi   3p–3′/PPL(OBVpl): IC+ -aˑ (TA th. 1) -waˑ (pl.) -t (3) -ihi (obv. pl.)

+aˑwaˑčini   *IC–aˑwaˑčini* 3p–3′/ITER: IC+ -aˑ (TA th. 1) -waˑ (pl.) -t (3) -ini (neg.-iter.)
        –aˑwaˑčini 3p–3′/NEG: -aˑ (TA th. 1) -waˑ (pl.) -t (3) -ini (neg.-iter.)

+aˑwaˑsa   3p–3′/POT: -aˑ (TA th. 1) -waˑ (pl.) -sa (3,0 pot.)

+če   3s,0/IMP: -če (3,0 imp.)
        -če 3,0 imp.: third person animate and inanimate, imperative; also in the
          prohibitive
        → -iče after -hk proh., fut. imp.

+či   *eˑh=–či* 3s/AOR: eˑh= (aor.) -t (3) -i (conj.)
         3s–0/AOR: same on a Class 3 TI
        IC–či 3s/CC: IC+ -t (3) -i (conj.)
        –či 3s/CONJ: -t (3) -i (conj.)

+či   *eˑh=–či* 3s/PPL(loc.obl): eˑh= (aor.) -t (3) -i (inan. sg.)

+či   *IC–či* 3s/PPL(INsg,obl): IC+ -t (3) -i (inan. sg.)
         3s–0/PPL(INsg): same on a Class 3 TI with inan. sg. or obl. head

+čiki   *IC–čiki* 3/PPL(ANpl): IC+ -t (3) -iki (anim. pl.)

+čini   *IC–čini* 3s/ITER: IC+ -t (3) -ini (neg.-iter.)
        –čini 3s/NEG: -t (3) -ini (neg.-iter.)

+čini   3s/PPL(INpl,obl.pl): IC+ -t (3) -ini (inan. pl.)
                             3s–0/PPL(INpl): same on a Class 3 TI
+e   VOCsg: vocative singular on nouns
-e   conj.: see -*i* conj.
-e   inan. sg.: see -*i* inan. sg.
-e   subj.: subjunctive mode
-e   voc.: vocative as head of participle; cf. **+e** VOCsg
+eči   *e·h=–eči* X–3/AOR: e·h= (aor.) -Ø (TA th. 1) -et (X–3) -i (conj.)
                         IC–eči X–3/CC: IC+ -Ø (TA th. 1) -et (X–3) -i (conj.)
                         –eči X–3/CONJ: -Ø (TA th. 1) -et (X–3) -i (conj.)
+eči   *IC–eči* X–3/PPL(INsg,obl): IC+ -Ø (TA th. 1) -et (X–3) -i (inan. sg.)
+ečiki   *IC–ečiki* X–3/PPL(ANpl): IC+ -Ø (TA th. 1) -et (X–3) -iki (anim. pl.)
+ečini   *IC–ečini* X–3/ITER: IC+ -Ø (TA th. 1) -et (X–3) -ini (neg.-iter.)
                         –ečini X–3/NEG: -Ø (TA th. 1) -et (X–3) -ini (neg.-iter.)
+ečini   *IC–ečini* X–3/PPL(INpl,obl.pl): IC+ -Ø (TA th. 1) -et (X–3) -ini (inan. pl.)
-ehapa   con.: conclusive mode
                         → -*ehapan* before -*iki* (anim. pl.)
-ehe   pret.: preterite of aorist, subjunctive, negative, and participle; also in some
                             potential endings
                         → -*eha* after -*kw*: -*kw-eha* → -*koha*
                         NOTE: Modal and participial suffixes do not appear after -*ehe* (pret.).
+ehka   *IC–ehka* 3–2s/PPL(ANsg): IC+ -eN (TA th. 4) -k (3) -a (anim. sg.)
+ehke   3–2s/SUBJ: -eN (TA th. 4) -k (3) -e (subj.)
+ehki   *e·h=–ehki* 3–2s/AOR: e·h= (aor.) -eN (TA th. 4) -k (3) -i (conj.)
+ehki   *IC–ehki* 3–2s/PPL(INsg,obl): IC+ -eN (TA th. 4) -k (3) -i (inan. sg.)
+ehkini   3–2s/NEG: -eN (TA th. 4) -k (3) -ini (neg.-iter.)
+ehko   2p–3/IMP: -Ø (TA th. 1) -ehko (2p–3 imp.)
                         -ehko 2p–3 imp.: second plural on third, imperative
-ek   X: indefinite subject in conjunct and interrogative
+eke   X/SUBJ: -ek (X) -e (subj.)
+eki   LOC: locative on nouns
                         -eki loc.: locative in ending complexes
+eki   *e·h=–eki* X/AOR: e·h= (aor.) -ek (X) -i (conj.)
                             X–0/AOR: same on a Class 3 TI
                         –eki X/CONJ: -ek (X) -i (conj.)
+eki   *IC–eki* X/PPL(INsg,obl): IC+ -ek (X) -i (inan. sg.)
                             X–0/PPL(INsg,obl): same on a Class 3 TI
+ekini   *IC–ekini* X/ITER: IC+ -ek (X) -ini (neg.-iter.)
                             X–0/ITER: same on a Class 3 TI
                         –ekini X/NEG: -ek (X) -ini (neg.-iter.)
                             X–0/NEG: same on a Class 3 TI
+ekini   *e·h=–ekini* X/PPL(loc.obl.pl): e·h= (aor.) -ek (X) -ini (inan. pl.)
                         IC–ekini X/PPL(INpl,obl.pl): IC+ -ek (X) -ini (inan. pl.)
+ekoči   *e·h=–ekoči* 3´–3s/AOR: e·h= (aor.) -ekw (TA th. 2) -t (3) -i (conj.)
+ekoči   *IC–ekoči* 3´–3s/PPL(INsg,obl): IC+ -ekw (TA th. 2) -t (3) -i (inan. sg.)
+ekočihi   *IC–ekočihi* 3´–3s/PPL(OBVpl): IC+ -ekw (TA th. 2) -t (3) -ihi (obv. pl.)

+ekočiki	*IC–ekočiki* 3´–3/PPL(ANpl): IC+ -ekw (TA th. 2) -t (3) -iki (anim. pl.)
+ekočini	3´–3s/NEG: -ekw (TA th. 2) -t (3) -ini (neg.-iter.)
+ekočini	*IC–ekočini* 3´–3s/PPL(OBVsg): IC+ -ekw (TA th. 2) -t (3) -ini (obv. sg.)
+ekona·na	*ne–ekona na* 3s–1p/IND: ne- (1) -ekw (TA th. 2) -ena·n (1p,12) -a (anim. sg.)
	ke–ekona na 3s–12/IND: ke- (2) -ekw (TA th. 2) -ena·n (1p,12) -a (anim. sg.)
+ekosa	3´–3s/POT: -ekw (TA th. 2) -sa (3,0 pot.)
+ekota	*IC–ekota* 3´–3/PPL(ANsg): IC+ -ekw (TA th. 2) -t (3) -a (anim. sg.)
+ekowa·či	*e·h=–ekowa či* 3´–3p/AOR: e·h= (aor.) -ekw (TA th. 2) -wa· (pl.) -t (3) -i (conj.)
+ekowa·či	*IC–ekowa či* 3´–3p/CC: IC+ -ekw (TA th. 2) -wa· (pl.) -t (3) -i (conj.)
+ekowa·či	*IC–ekowa či* 3´–3p/PPL(INsg,obl): IC+ -ekw (TA th. 2) -wa· (pl.) -t (3) -i (inan. sg.)
+ekowa·či	*e·h=–ekowa či* 3´–3p/PPL(loc.obl): e·h= (aor.) -ekw (TA th. 2) -wa· (pl.) -t (3) -i (inan. sg.)
+ekowa·čini	3´–3p/NEG: -ekw (TA th. 2) -wa· (pl.) -t (3) -ini (neg.-iter.)
+ekowa·sa	3´–3p/POT: -ekw (TA th. 2) -wa· (pl.) -sa (3,0 pot.)
+ekowa·wa	*ke–ekowa wa* 3s–2p/IND: ke- (2) -ekw (TA th. 2) -wa·w (2p,3p) -a (anim. sg.)
+eko·ki	*ne–eko ki* 3p–1s/IND: ne- (1) -ekw (TA th. 2) -w (sg.) -aki (anim. pl.)
	ke–eko ki 3p–2s/IND: ke- (2) -ekw (TA th. 2) -w (sg.) -aki (anim. pl.)
+eko·ki	*–eko ki* 3´–3p/IND: -ekw (TA th. 2) -w (3,0) -aki (anim. pl.)
+eko·pena	*ne–eko pena* X–1p/IND: ne- (1) -ekw (TA th. 2) -pena (1p,12)
+eko·pi	*ne–eko pi* X–1s/IND: ne- (1) -ekw (TA th. 2) -pi (X)
	ke–eko pi X–2s/IND: ke- (2) -ekw (TA th. 2) -pi (X)
+eko·pwa	*ke–eko pwa* X–2p/IND: ke- (2) -ekw (TA th. 2) -pwa (2p)
+eko·toke	*ke–eko toke* 3s–2s/DUB: ke- (2) -ekw (TA th. 2) -w (sg.) -etoke (dub.)
-ekw	TA th. 2 (inverse theme sign): action on an animate that is higher than the actor in the hierarchy: 1,2 > X > 3 > 3´ > 3´´ > 0
	NOTE: Selected by different combinations of subject and object in different orders.
	→ *-eko* before *t, s*
	→ *-eko·* before *p* (|-ekw-p| → |-ekwe-p| → *-eko p*) (indefinite subject, independent order)
	Variant:
	-ekwi (TA th. 2a): inanimate subject
+ekwa	*ne–ekwa* 3s–1s/IND: ne- (1) -ekw (TA th. 2) -w (sg.) -a (anim. sg.)
	ke–ekwa 3s–2s/IND: ke- (2) -ekw (TA th. 2) -w (sg.) -a (anim. sg.)
+ekwa	*–ekwa* 3´–3s/IND: -ekw (TA th. 2) -w (3,0) -a (anim. sg.)
-ekwi	TA th. 2a: see *-ekw* TA th. 2
+ekwičini	0–3s/NEG: -ekwi (TA th. 2a) -t (3) -ini (neg.-iter.)
+ekwihka·ha	0–1s/POT: -ekwi (TA th. 2a) -hk (proh.) -a·ha (1s pot.)
+ekwihke·koha	0–2p/POT: -ekwi (TA th. 2a) -hk (proh.) -e·kw (2p) -ehe (pret.)
+ekwipena	*ne–ekwipena* 0–1p/IND: ne- (1) -ekwi (TA th. 2a) -pena (1p,12)
+ekwita	*IC–ekwita* 0–3/PPL(ANsg): IC+ -ekwi (TA th. 2a) -t (3) -a (anim. sg.)
+ekwiwa·či	*IC–ekwiwa či* 0–3p/PPL(INsg): IC+ -ekwi (TA th. 2a) -wa· (pl.) -t (3) -i (inan. sg.)
+ekwiyakwe	*IC–ekwiyakwe* 0–12/PPL(INsg): IC+ -ekwi (TA th. 2a) -akw (12) -i (inan. sg.)

+ekwiye·kwe	*IC–ekwiye·kwe* 0–2p/PPL(INsg,obl): IC+ -ekwi (TA th. 2a) -e·kw (2p) -i (inan. sg.)
-em	obv.: marks object as obviative with first, second, or indefinite subject
-em	poss. th.: makes the possessed theme of some nouns
+ema	*ne–ema* 1s(ANsg): ne- (1) -em (poss. th.) -a (anim. sg.)
+emaki	*e·h=–emaki* 1s–3′/AOR: e·h= (aor.) -em (obv.) -Ø (TA th. 1) -ak (1s–3) -i (conj.)
+emakini	*IC–emakini* 1s–3′/PPL(OBVsg): IC+ -em (obv.) -Ø (TA th. 1) -ak (1s–3) -ini (obv. sg.)
+emani	*o–emani* 3s(INpl): o- (3) -em (poss. th.) -ani (inan. pl.)
+emani	*o–emani* 3s(OBVsg): o- (3) -em (poss. th.) -ani (obv. sg.)
+emeči	*e·h=–emeči* X–3′/AOR: e·h= (aor.) -em (obv.) -et (X–3) -i (conj.)
+emeči	*e·h=–emeči* X–3′/PPL(loc.obl): e·h= (aor.) -em (obv.) -et (X–3) -i (inan. sg.)
+emeči	*IC–emeči* X–3′/PPL(INsg,obl): IC+ -em (obv.) -et (X–3) -i (inan. sg.)
+emečini	*IC–emečini* X–3′/PPL(OBVsg): IC+ -em (obv.) -et (X–3) -ini (obv. sg.)
+emeki	*ne–emeki* 1s(LOC): ne- (1) -em (poss. th.) -eki (loc.)
+emena·na	*ne–emena·na* 1p(ANsg): ne- (1) -em (poss. th.) -ena·n (1p,12) -a (anim. sg.)
	ke–emena·na 12(ANsg): ke- (2) -em (poss. th.) -ena·n (1p,12) -a (anim. sg.)
+emena·ni	*ke–emena·ni* 12(INsg): ke- (2) -em (poss. th.) -ena·n (1p,12) -i (inan. sg.)
+emete	X–3′/SUBJ: -em (obv.) -et (X–3) -e (subj.)
+emi	*ne–emi* 1s(INsg): ne- (1) -em (poss. th.) -i (inan. sg.)
	o–emi 3s(INsg): o- (3) -em (poss. th.) -i (inan. sg.)
+eminawaki	*o–eminawaki* X(ANpl): o- (3) -em (poss. th.) -inaw (X) -aki (anim. pl.)
+emwa·wahi	*o–emwa·wahi* 3p(OBVpl): o- (3) -em (poss. th.) -wa·w (2p,3p) -ahi (obv. pl.)
+emwa·waki	*ke–emwa·waki* 2p(ANpl): ke- (2) -em (poss. th.) -wa·w (2p,3p) -aki (anim. pl.)
+emwa·wani	*o–emwa·wani* 3p(INpl): o- (3) -em (poss. th.) -wa·w (2p,3p) -ani (inan. pl.)
-eN	TA th. 4: action on second person or first person inclusive

NOTE: Selected by different combinations of subject and object in different orders.

→ -en except as follows:

→ -ene word-finally and before *p*, *s*

→ -eh before *-k*

+enaka·ha	1s–2s/POT: -eN (TA th. 4) -hk (proh.) -a·ha (1s pot.)
+enakiče	3–2s/PROH: -eN (TA th. 4) -hk (proh.) -če (3,0 imp.)
+enaki·ke	X–2s/PROH: -eN (TA th. 4) -hk (proh.) -i·ke (X proh.)
+enakoha	*e·h=–enakoha* 3,X–12/AOR.PRET: e·h= (aor.) -eN (TA th. 4) -akw (12) -ehe (pret.)
+enako·we	*e·h=–enako·we* 1s–2p/AOR: e·h= (aor.) -eN (TA th. 4) -ako·w (1s–2p) -i (conj.)
	IC–enako·we 1s–2p/CC: IC+ -eN (TA th. 4) -ako·w (1s–2p) -i (conj.)
	1s–2p/PPL(1s): same
	1s–2p/PPL(2p): same
	1s–2p/PPL(INsg,obl): same
	–enako·we 1s–2p/NEG: -eN (TA th. 4) -ako·w (1s–2p) -i (conj.)
+enakwa	*IC–enakwa* 3,X–12/PPL(ANsg): IC+ -eN (TA th. 4) -akw (12) -a (anim. sg.)
+enakwe	*e·h=–enakwe* 3,X–12/AOR: e·h= (aor.) -eN (TA th. 4) -akw (12) -i (conj.)
	IC–enakwe 3,X–12/PPL(INsg,obl): IC+ -eN (TA th. 4) -akw (12) -i (inan. sg.)
+enakwini	*IC–enakwini* 3,X–12/ITER: IC+ -eN (TA th. 4) -akw (12) -ini (neg.-iter.)
	–enakwini 3,X–12/NEG: -eN (TA th. 4) -akw (12) -ini (neg.-iter.)

+ena·ke	*e·h=–ena·ke* 1p–2/AOR: e·h= (aor.) -eN (TA th. 4) -a·k (1p) -i (conj.)
+ena·ke	*IC–ena·ke* 1p–2/PPL(INsg,obl): IC+ -eN (TA th. 4) -a·k (1p) -i (inan. sg.)
+ena·kini	*–ena·kini* 1p–2/NEG: -eN (TA th. 4) -a·k (1p) -ini (neg.-iter.)
+ena·kwa	*IC–ena·kwa* 3,X–2p/PPL(ANsg): IC+ -eN (TA th. 4) -a·kw (3,X–2p) -a (anim. sg.)
+ena·kwe	*e·h=–ena·kwe* 3,X–2p/AOR: e·h= (aor.) -eN (TA th. 4) -a·kw (3,X–2p) -i (conj.) *IC–ena·kwe* 3,X–2p/CC: IC+ -eN (TA th. 4) -a·kw (3,X–2p) -i (conj.)
+ena·kwe	*IC–ena·kwe* 3,X–2p/PPL(INsg,obl): IC+ -eN (TA th. 4) -a·kw (3,X–2p) -i (inan. sg.)
+ena·kwe	*–ena·kwe* 3,X–2p/SUBJ: -eN (TA th. 4) -a·kw (3,X–2p) -e (subj.)
+ena·kwiki	*IC–ena·kwiki* 3,X–2p/PPL(ANpl): IC+ -eN (TA th. 4) -a·kw (3,X–2p) -iki (anim. pl.)
+ena·kwini	*IC–ena·kwini* 3,X–2p/ITER: IC+ -eN (TA th. 4) -a·kw (3,X–2p) -ini (neg.-iter.)
+ena·kwini	*–ena·kwini* 3,X–2p/NEG: -eN (TA th. 4) -a·kw (3,X–2p) -ini (neg.-iter.)
-ena·n	1p,12: pluralizes the first person for possessors of nouns and for subjects of inverse verbs in the independent order; used with ne- (1) to mark first person exclusive, and with ke- (2) to mark first person inclusive. → -ena· before -eki loc. and -etoke dub.
+ena·na	*IC–ena·na* 1s–2s/PPL(ANsg): IC+ -eN (TA th. 4) -a·n (1s) -a (anim. sg.)
+ena·na	*ne–ena·na* 1p(ANsg): ne- (1) -ena·n (1p,12) -a (anim. sg.) *ke–ena·na* 12(ANsg): ke- (2) -ena·n (1p,12) -a (anim. sg.)
+ena·naki	*ne–ena·naki* 1p(ANpl): ne- (1) -ena·n (1p,12) -aki (anim. pl.) *ke–ena·naki* 12(ANpl): ke- (2) -ena·n (1p,12) -aki (anim. pl.)
+ena·nani	*ne–ena·nani* 1p(INpl): ne- (1) -ena·n (1p,12) -ani (inan. pl.) *ke–ena·nani* 12(INpl): ke- (2) -ena·n (1p,12) -ani (inan. pl.)
+ena·nani	*ke–ena·nani* 12(OBVsg): ke- (2) -ena·n (1p,12) -ani (obv. sg.)
+ena·ne	1s–2s/SUBJ: -eN (TA th. 4) -a·n (1s) -e (subj.)
+ena·nehe	*e·h=–ena·nehe* 1s–2s/AOR.PRET: e·h= (aor.) -eN (TA th. 4) -a·n (1s) -ehe (pret.) *IC–ena·nehe* 1s–2s/PRET.PPL(obl): IC+ -eN (TA th. 4) -a·n (1s) -ehe (pret.) *–ena·nehe* 1s–2s/SUBJ.PRET: -eN (TA th. 4) -a·n (1s) -ehe (pret.)
+ena·ni	*e·h=–ena·ni* 1s–2s/AOR: e·h= (aor.) -eN (TA th. 4) -a·n (1s) -i (conj.) *IC–ena·ni* 1s–2s/CC: IC+ -eN (TA th. 4) -a·n (1s) -i (conj.)
+ena·ni	*IC–ena·ni* 1s–2s/PPL(INsg,obl): IC+ -eN (TA th. 4) -a·n (1s) -i (inan. sg.)
+ena·ni	*ne–ena·ni* 1p(INsg): ne- (1) -ena·n (1p,12) -i (inan. sg.) *ke–ena·ni* 12(INsg): ke- (2) -ena·n (1p,12) -i (inan. sg.)
+ena·nini	*–ena·nini* 1s–2s/NEG: -eN (TA th. 4) -a·n (1s) -ini (neg.-iter.)
+ena·nini	*IC–ena·nini* 1s–2s/PPL(INpl): IC+ -eN (TA th. 4) -a·n (1s) -ini (inan. pl.) 1s–2s/PPL(obl.pl): same
+ene	*ke–ene* 1s–2s/IND: ke- (2) -eN (TA th. 4) -∅ (sg.)
+eneke	*–eneke* X–2s/SUBJ: -eN (TA th. 4) -ek (X) -e (subj.)
+enene·ha	X–2s/POT: -eN (TA th. 4) -ene·ha (X pot.)
+enepena	*ke–enepena* 1p–2/IND: ke- (2) -eN (TA th. 4) -pena (1p,12)
+enepwa	*ke–enepwa* 1s–2p/IND: ke- (2) -eN (TA th. 4) -pwa (2p)
+eneče	3–2s/IMP: -eN (TA th. 4) -če (3,0 imp.)

+enesa 3–2s/POT: -eN (TA th. 4) -sa (3,0 pot.)

+ene·ha X/POT: -ene·ha (X pot.)

-ene·ha X pot.: indefinite subject, potential

NOTE: -am (TI(1) th.) + -ene·ha (X pot.) → **+ane·ha** X–0/POT

+ene·ha X–3/POT: -∅ (TA th. 1) -ene·ha (X pot.)

+enokwe·ni IC–enokwe·ni 3s–2s/INT.PPL(obl): IC+ -eN (TA th. 4) -kw (3,0 irr.) -e·ni (int.)

+enowakwe·ni 3,X–12/INT: -eN (TA th. 4) -w (irr.) -akw (12) -e·ni (int.)

+enowakwe·ni IC–enowakwe·ni 3,X–12/INT.PPL(obl): IC+ -eN (TA th. 4) -w (irr.) -akw (12) -e·ni (int.)

+enowa·ne·ni 1s–2s/INT: -eN (TA th. 4) -w (irr.) -a·n (1s) -e·ni (int.)

+eno·ke·ni X–2s/INT: -eN (TA th. 4) -w (irr.) -ek (X) -e·ni (int.)

+enwa·če 3–2p/IMP: -eN (TA th. 4) -wa· (2p) + -če (3,0 imp.)

+enwa·sa 3–2p/POT: -eN (TA th. 4) -wa· (2p) + -sa (3,0 pot.)

-epani ast.: assertive mode

-et X–3: indefinite acting on third animate, conjunct

+eta IC–eta X–3/PPL(ANsg): IC+ -∅ (TA th. 1) -et (X–3) -a (anim. sg.)

+ete X–3/SUBJ: -∅ (TA th. 1) -et (X–3) -e (subj.)

+etike VOCpl: vocative plural on noun

-etoke dub.: dubitative mode

→ -etoke·h before -iki (anim. pl.), -ini (inan. pl.)

+e·hiyakwa IC–e·hiyakwa 12–3.DIM/PPL(ANsg): IC+ -a· (TA th. 1) -·hi (dim.) -akw (12) -a (anim. sg.)

+e·hiyakwiki IC–e·hiyakwiki 12–3.DIM/PPL(ANpl): IC+ -a· (TA th. 1) -·hi (dim.) -akw (12) -iki (anim. pl.)

+e·hiya·nini IC–e·hiya·nini 1s–3/DIM/ITER: IC+ -a· (TA th. 1) -·hi (dim.) -a·n (1s) -ini (neg.-iter.)

+e·hiye·kwiki IC–e·hiye·kwiki 2p–3.DIM/PPL(ANpl): IC+ -a· (TA th. 1) -·hi (dim.) -iki (anim. pl.)

-e·ko 2p proh.: second plural, prohibitive

Compare -e·kw (2p) and -ko (2p imp.).

-e·kw 2p: second plural in the conjunct, interrogative, and potential

→ -ye·kw after a vowel

+e·kwe e·h=-e·kwe 2p–3/AOR: e·h= (aor.) -∅ (TA th. 1) -e·kw (2p) -i (conj.)

IC–e·kwe 2p–3/PPL(INsg,obl): IC+ -∅ (TA th. 1) -e·kw (2p) -i (inan. sg.)

+e·kwe 2p–3/SUBJ: -∅ (TA th. 1) -e·kw (2p) -e (subj.)

+e·kwiki IC–e·kwiki 2p–3/PPL(ANpl): IC+ -∅ (TA th. 1) -e·kw (2p) -iki (anim. pl.)

+e·kwini IC–e·kwini 2p–3/ITER: IC+ -∅ (TA th. 1) -e·kw (2p) -ini (neg.-iter.)

–e·kwini 2p–3/NEG: -e·kw (2p) -ini (neg.-iter.)

-e·ni interrog.: interrogative mode

→ -e·n before -a anim. sg.

→ -e·h before -iki anim. pl., -ini obv. sg., -ihi obv. pl.

NOTE: -e·ni (int.) + -i (inan. sg.), -ini (inan. pl.) → -e·ni

+e·toke 3s–3′/DUB: -a· (TA th. 1) -w (3,0) -etoke (dub.)

+e·wa 3s–3′/IND: -a· (TA th. 1) -w (3,0) -a (anim. sg.)

+e·waki 3p–3′/IND: -a· (TA th. 1) -w (3,0) -aki (anim. pl.)

-·hi	dim.: diminutive in verbs
	→ -o·hi after a consonant
	→ -o·h before -ena·n (1p,12) and -wa·w (2p,3p)
-hk	proh.: in all endings of the prohibitive mode and some endings of the potential
	→ -k after a deleting n in an AI stem, and optionally after n in an II stem
	NOTE (contrast -hk fut. imp.):
	-am (TI(1) th.) + -hk (proh.) → -ak
	-a· (TA th. 1) + -hk (proh.) → -iye·k
	-eN (TA th. 4) + -hk (proh.) → -enak
-hk	fut. imp.: makes distinct future imperative forms with two theme signs
	NOTE (contrast -hk proh.):
	-am (TI(1) th.) + -hk (fut. imp.) → -amo·hk
	-a· (TA th. 1) + -hk (fut. imp.) → -a·hk
+hka	1s/PROH: -hk (proh.) -a (1s proh.)
+hkakoha	12/POT: -hk (proh.) -akw (12) -ehe (pret.)
+hkani	2s/PROH: -hk (proh.) -an (2s) -i (conj.)
+hkapa	2s/POT: -hk (proh.) -apa (2s pot.)
+hka·ha	1s/POT: -hk (proh.) -a·ha (1s pot.)
+hke·ko	2p/PROH: -hk (proh.) -e·ko (2p proh.)
+hke·koha	2p/POT: -hk (proh.) -e·kw (2p) -ehe (pret.)
+hkiče	0/PROH: -hk (proh.) -če (3,0 imp.)
	3s/PROH: same
+i	ke–i 2s–1s/IND: ke- (2) -i (TA th. 3) -∅ (sg.)
+i	2s–3/IMP: -∅ (TA th. 1) -i (2s–3 imp.)
	-i 2s–3 imp.: second singular acting on third, imperative
+i	INsg: inanimate singular on nouns
	-i inan. sg.: inanimate singular in endings; marks inanimate singular or oblique singular head of participle
	→ -e (after first plural and second plural suffixes except the two-syllable first exclusive suffixes, -aket, -amet, and -ɳamek)
-i	TA th. 3: action on first person singular or first plural exclusive
	NOTE: Selected by different combinations of subject and object in different orders.
-i	conj.: used in conjunct modes not marked by a specific modal suffix; also in other modes after pronominal suffixes that are identical to those of the conjunct
	→ -e (after first plural and second plural suffixes except the two-syllable first plural exclusive suffixes -aket, -amet, and -ɳamek)
+iči	e·h=–iči 3s–1s/AOR: e·h= (aor.) -i (TA th. 3) -t (3) -i (conj.)
	IC–iči 3s–1s/CC: IC+ -i (TA th. 3) -t (3) -i (conj.)
+iči	IC–iči 3s–1s/PPL(INsg,obl): IC+ -i (TA th. 3) -t (3) -i (inan. sg.)
+ičiki	IC–ičiki 3–1s/PPL(ANpl): IC+ -i (TA th. 3) -t (3) -iki (anim. pl.)
+ičini	IC–ičini 3s–1s/ITER: IC+ -i (TA th. 3) -t (3) -ini (neg.-iter.)
	–ičini 3s–1s/NEG: -i (TA th. 3) -t (3) -ini (neg.-iter.)
-ihi	obv. pl.: obviative plural (head of participle)

+ihkapa	2s–1s/POT: -i (TA th. 3) -hk (proh.) -apa (2s pot.)
+ihka·ke	2–1p/PROH: -i (TA th. 3) -hk (proh.) -a·k (1p) -i (conj.)
+ihke·ko	2p–1s/PROH: -i (TA th. 3) -hk (proh.) -e·ko (2p proh.)
+ihki·ke	X–1s/PROH: -i (TA th. 3) -hk (proh.) -i·ke (X proh.)
+ika	*IC–ika* X–1s/PPL(ANsg): IC+ -i (TA th. 3) -ek (X) -a (anim. sg.)
+ikehe	*IC–ikehe* X–1s/CH.PRET: IC+ -i (TA th. 3) -ek (X) -ehe (pret.)
	X–1s/PRET.PPL(obl): same
+ikini	*IC–ikini* X–1s/ITER: IC+ -i (TA th. 3) -ek (X) -ini (neg.-iter.)
	–ikini X–1s/NEG: -i (TA th. 3) -ek (X) -ini (neg.-iter.)
+ikini	*IC–ikini* X–1s/PPL(obl.pl): IC+ -i (TA th. 3) -ek (X) -ini (inan. pl.)
+iki	*e·h=–iki* X–1s/AOR: e·h= (aor.) -i (TA th. 3) -ek (X) -i (conj.)
	IC–iki X–1s/CC: IC+ -i (TA th. 3) -ek (X) -i (conj.)
+iki	*IC–iki* X–1s/PPL(INsg,obl): IC+ -i (TA th. 3) -ek (X) -i (inan. sg.)
-iki	anim. pl.: animate plural (head of participle and in the assertive, conclusive, dubitative, and interrogative modes)
+iko	2p–1s/IMP: -i (TA th. 3) -ko (2p imp.)
+ikwe·na	*IC–ikwe·na* 3s–1s/INT.PPL(ANsg): IC+ -i (TA th. 3) -kw (3,0 irr.) -e·ni (int.) -a (anim. sg.)
+ikwe·ni	*–ikwe·ni* 3s–1s/INT: -i (TA th. 3) -kw (3,0 irr.) -e·ni (int.)
	IC–ikwe·ni 3s–1s/CH.INT: IC+ -i (TA th. 3) -kw (3,0 irr.) -e·ni (int.)
-inaw	X: indefinite possessor
+inawaki	*o–inawaki* X(ANpl): o- (3) -inaw (X) -aki (anim. pl.)
+inawani	*o–inawani* X(INpl): o- (3) -inaw (X) -ani (inan. pl.)
+inawi	*o–inawi* X(INsg): o- (3) -inaw (X) -i (inan. sg.)
+ine·ha	X–1s/POT: -i (TA th. 3) -ene·ha (X pot.)
-ini	inan. pl.: inanimate plural (head of participle and in dubitative mode)
-ini	neg.-iter.: negative and iterative modes
-ini	obv. sg.: obviative singular (head of participle)
+iniči	*e·h=–iniči* 3′–1s/AOR: e·h= (aor.) -i (TA th. 3) -ni (obv.) -t (3) -i (conj.)
+ino	2s–1s/IMP: -i (TA th. 3) -no (2s imp.)
+ipena	*ke–ipena* 2–1p/IND: -i (TA th. 3) -pena (1p,12)
+ipwa	*ke–ipwa* 2p–1s/IND: -i (TA th. 3) -pwa (2p)
+isa	3s–1s/POT: -i (TA th. 3) -sa (3,0 pot.)
+ita	*IC–ita* 3–1s/PPL(ANsg): IC+ -i (TA th. 3) -t (3) -a (anim. sg.)
+ite	3s–1s/SUBJ: -i (TA th. 3) -t (3) -e (subj.)
+itehe	*e·h=–itehe* 3s–1s/AOR.PRET -i (TA th. 3) -t (3) -ehe (pret.)
	IC–itehe 3s–1s/CH.PRET: IC+ -i (TA th. 3) -t (3) -ehe (pret.)
	3s–1s/PRET.PPL(obl): same
	–itehe 3s–1s/SUBJ.PRET: -i (TA th. 3) -t (3) -ehe (pret.)
+iwa·či	*e·h=–iwa·či* 3p–1s/AOR: e·h= (aor.) -i (TA th. 3) -wa· (pl.) -t (3) -i (conj.)
+iwa·čini	*IC–iwa·čini* 3p–1s/ITER: IC+ -i (TA th. 3) -wa· (pl.) -t (3) -wa· (pl.) -t (3) -ini (neg.-iter.)
+iyameči	*e·h=–iyameči* 3–1p/AOR: e·h= (aor.) -i (TA th. 3) -amet (3–1p) -i (conj.)
	IC–iyameči 3–1p/CC: IC+ -i (TA th. 3) -amet (3–1p) -i (conj.)
+iyameči	*IC–iyameči* 3–1p/PPL(INsg,obl): IC+ -i (TA th. 3) -amet (3–1p) -i (inan. sg.)
+iyamečini	3–1p/NEG: -i (TA th. 3) -amet (3–1p) -ini (neg.-iter.)

+iyamehkiče	3–1p/PROH: -i (TA th. 3) -amet (3–1p) -hk (proh.) + -če (3,0 imp.)
+iyamekweˑni	3–1p/: -i (TA th. 3) -amet (3–1p) -w (irr.) -eˑni (int.)
+iyamesa	3–1p/POT: -i (TA th. 3) -amet (3–1p) -sa (3,0 pot.)
+iyameta	*IC–iyameta* 3–1p/PPL(ANsg): IC+ -i (TA th. 3) -amet (3–1p) -a (anim. sg.)
+iyane	2s–1s/SUBJ: -i (TA th. 3) -an (2s) -e (subj.)
+iyani	*eˑh=–iyani* 2s–1s/AOR: eˑh= (aor.) -i (TA th. 3) -an (2s) -i (conj.)
+iyani	*IC–iyani* 2s–1s/PPL(INsg,obl): IC+ -i (TA th. 3) -an (2s) -i (inan. sg.)
+iyanini	*IC–iyanini* 2s–1s/ITER: IC+ -i (TA th. 3) -an (2s) -ini (neg.-iter.)
	–iyanini 2s–1s/NEG: -i (TA th. 3) -an (2s) -ini (neg.-iter.)
+iyanini	*IC–iyanini* 2s–1s/PPL(obl.pl): IC+ -i (TA th. 3) -an (2s) -ini (inan. pl.)
-iyeˑk	TA th. 1 proh.: -aˑ (TA th. 1) -hk (proh.) → -iyeˑk
+iyeˑkani	2s–3/PROH: -aˑ (TA th. 1) -hk (proh.) -an (2s) -i (conj.)
+iyeˑkapa	2s–3/POT: -aˑ (TA th. 1) -hk (proh.) -apa (2s pot.)
+iyeˑkaˑha	1s–3/POT: -aˑ (TA th. 1) -hk (proh.) -aˑha (1s pot.)
+iyeˑkaˑke	1p–3/PROH: -aˑ (TA th. 1) -hk (proh.) -aˑk (1p) -i (conj.)
+iyeˑkeˑko	2p–3/PROH: -aˑ (TA th. 1) -hk (proh.) -eˑko (2p proh.)
+iyeˑkwe	*eˑh=–iyeˑkwe* 2p–1s/AOR: eˑh= (aor.) -i (TA th. 3) -eˑkw (2p) -i (conj.)
+iyeˑkwini	2p–1s/NEG: -i (TA th. 3) -eˑkw (2p) -ini (neg.-iter.)
-iˑke	X proh.: indefinite subject in prohibitive
+iˑkeˑni	*IC–iˑkeˑni* X–1s/INT.PPL(obl): IC+ -i (TA th. 3) -w (irr.) -ek (X) -eˑni (int.)
+iˑnameki	*IC–iˑnameki* X–1p/PPL(INsg,obl): IC+ -i (TA th. 3) -ˑnamek (X–1p) -i (inan. sg.)
+iˑnamiˑkeˑni	X–1p/INT: -i (TA th. 3) -ˑnamek (X–1p) + -w (irr.) -eˑni (int.)
+iˑnamehkiˑke	X–1p/PROH: -i (TA th. 3) -ˑnamek (X–1p) + -hk (proh.) -iˑke (X proh.)
+iˑnameneˑha	X–1p/POT: -i (TA th. 3) -ˑnamek (X–1p) + -eneˑha (X pot.)
-k	0: inanimate in conjunct modes
-k	3: replaces -*t* (3) after a consonant
	NOTE: retaining consonant stems select -*k* (3) and insert -*e*-
-ˑk	X irr.: indefinite subject, irrealis (interrogative and prioritive)
	Analyzed as: -*w* (irr.) + -*ek* (X).
+ka	*IC–ka* 3/PPL(ANsg): IC+ -k (3) -a (anim. sg.)
+ke	0/SUBJ: -k (0) -e (subj.)
+kehe	*eˑh=–kehe* 0/AOR.PRET: eˑh= (aor.) -k (0) -ehe (pret.)
	–kehe 0/SUBJ.PRET: -k (0) -ehe (pret.)
+ki	*eˑh=–ki* 0/AOR: eˑh= (aor.) -k (0) -i (conj.)
	IC–ki 0/CC: IC+ -k (0) -i (conj.)
+ki	*IC–ki* 0/PPL(INsg,obl): IC+ -k (0) -i (inan. sg.)
	eˑh=–ki 0/PPL(loc.obl): eˑh= (aor.) -k (0) -i (inan. sg.)
+ki	*eˑh=–ki* 3s/AOR: eˑh= (aor.) -k (3) -i (conj.)
	IC–ki 3s/CC: IC+ -k (3) -i (conj.)
+kiki	*IC–kiki* 3/PPL(ANpl): IC+ -k (3) -iki (anim. pl.)
+kini	*IC–kini* 0/ITER: IC+ -k (0) -ini (neg.-iter.)
	–kini 0/NEG: -k (0) -ini (neg.-iter.)
+kini	*IC–kini* 0/PPL(INpl): IC+ -k (0) -ini (inan. pl.)
+kini	3s/NEG: -k (3) -ini (neg.-iter.)

+ko
2p/IMP: second plural, imperative
-*ko* 2p imp.: second plural imperative in endings
→ **+oko**, -*oko* after a consonant

-kw
3,0 irr.: equivalent to -*w* (irr.) + -*k* < -*t* (3) and -*w* (irr.) + -*k* (0)
→ -*okw* after a consonant

+kwe·hiki
IC–kwe·hiki 3p/INT.PPL(obl): IC+ -kw (3,0 irr.) -e·ni (int.) -iki (anim. pl.)

+kwe·na
IC–kwe·na 3s/INT.PPL(ANsg): IC+ -kw (3,0 irr.) -e·ni (int.) -a (anim. sg.)

+kwe·ni
e·h=–kwe·ni 3s,0/AOR.INT: e·h= (aor.) -kw (3,0 irr.) -e·ni (int.)
–*kwe·ni* 3s,0/INT: -kw (3,0 irr.) -e·ni (int.)

+kwe·ni
IC–kwe·ni 3s,0/INT.PPL(IN,obl): IC+ -kw (3,0 irr.) -e·ni (int.)
e·h=–kwe·ni 3,0/INT.PPL(loc.obl): e·h= (aor.) -kw (3,0 irr.) -e·ni (int.)

-·namek
X–1p: indefite acting on first plural exclusive
-*i* (TA th. 3) + -*namek* (X–1p) → -*i·namek* (X–1p)
NOTE: combines with modal markers, sometimes after metathesis:
-*i-·namek* (X–1p) + -*w* (irr.) → -*i-·nami·k* (X–1p irr.)
-*i-·namek* (X–1p) + -*hk* (proh.) → -*i-·namehk* (X–1p proh.)
-*i-·namek* (X–1p) + -*ene·ha* (X pot.) → -*i-·namene·ha* (X–1p pot.)

-ni
obv.: obviative animate or inanimate central participant in verbal endings
→ -*ini* after -*am* (TI(1) th.)

+niči
e·h=–niči 3´/AOR: e·h= (aor.) -ni (obv.) -t (3) -i (conj.)
IC–niči 3´/CC: IC+ -ni (obv.) -t (3) -i (conj.)

+niči
e·h=–niči 3´/PPL(loc.obl): e·h= (aor.) -ni (obv.) -t (3) -i (inan. sg.)
IC–niči 3´/PPL(INsg,obl): IC+ -ni (obv.) -t (3) -i (inan. sg.)

+ničihi
IC–ničihi 3´/PPL(OBVpl): IC+ -ni (obv.) -t (3) -ihi (obv. pl.)

+ničini
IC–ničini 3´/ITER: IC+ -ni (obv.) -t (3) -ini (neg.-iter.)
–*ničini* 3´/NEG: -ni (obv.) -t (3) -ini (neg.-iter.)

+ničini
IC–ničini 3´/PPL(OBVsg): IC+ -ni (obv.) -t (3) -ini (obv. sg.)

+ničini
e·h=–ničini 3´/PPL(loc.obl.pl): e·h= (aor.) -ni (obv.) -t (3) -ini (inan. pl.)

+nike
0´/SUBJ: -ni (obv.) -k (0) -e (subj.)

+nikehe
IC–nikehe 0´/PRET.PPL(obl): IC+ -ni (obv.) -k (0) -ehe (pret.)

+niki
e·h=–niki 0´/AOR: e·h= (aor.) -ni (obv.) -k (0) -i (conj.)

+niki
IC–niki 0´/CC: IC+ -ni (obv.) -k (0) -i (conj.)

+niki
–*niki* 0´/CONJ: -ni (obv.) -k (0) -i (conj.)

+niki
IC–niki 0´/PPL(INsg,obl): IC+ -ni (obv.) -k (0) -i (inan. sg.)
e·h=–niki 0´/PPL(loc.obl): e·h= (aor.) -ni (obv.) -k (0) -i (inan. sg.)

+nikiki
IC–nikiki 0´/PPL(ANpl): IC+ -ni (obv.) -k (0) -iki (anim. pl.)

+nikini
IC–nikini 0´/ITER: IC+ -ni (obv.) -k (0) -ini (neg.-iter.)

+nikini
–*nikini* 0´/NEG: -ni (obv.) -k (0) -ini (neg.-iter.)

+nikini
IC–nikini 0´/PPL(INpl): IC+ -ni (obv.) -k (0) -ini (inan. pl.)

+nikini
e·h=–nikini 0´/PPL(loc.obl.pl): e·h= (aor.) -ni (obv.) -k (0) -ini (inan. pl.)

+nikwe
IC–nikwe 3´/CH.PRI: IC+ -ni (obv.) -kw (3,0 irr.) -e (subj.)

+nikwe·ni
e·h=–nikwe·ni 0´/INT.PPL(loc.obl): e·h= (aor.) -ni (obv.) -kw (3,0 irr.) -e·ni (int.)

+nikwe·ni
IC–nikwe·ni 0´/INT.PPL(obl): IC+ -ni (obv.) -kw (3,0 irr.) -e·ni (int.)
3´/INT.PPL(obl): same

+nisa
3´,0´/POT: -ni (obv.) -sa (3,0 pot.)

+nite
3´/SUBJ: -ni (obv.) -t (3) -e (subj.)

+nitehe	*e·h=–nitehe* 3´/PRET.PPL(loc.obl): e·h= (aor.) -ni (obv.) -t (3) -ehe (pret.)
+niwahi	3´p/IND: -ni (obv.) -w (3,0) -ahi (obv. pl.)
+niwani	0´p/IND: -ni (obv.) -w (3,0) -ani (inan. sg.)
+niwani	3´s/IND: -ni (obv.) -w (3,0) -ani (obv. sg.)
+niwi	0´s/IND: -ni (obv.) -w (3,0) -i (inan. sg.)
+no	2s/IMP: second singular, imperative
	-no 2s imp.: second singular imperative in endings
+o	*ne–o* 1s–0/IND: ne- (1) -o· (TI(2) th.) -∅ (sg.)
	ke–o 2s–0/IND: ke- (2) -o· (TI(2) th.) -∅ (sg.)
-oko	2p imp.: see **+ko** 2p/IMP
-owa·	pl.: see -*wa·* pl.
-owa·w	2p,3p: see -*wa·w* 2p,3p
-owet	X rel.: see -*wet* X rel.
-o·	TI(2) th.: theme sign of Class 2 TI
+o·či	*e·h=–o·či* 3s–0/AOR: e·h= (aor.) -o· (TI(2) th.) -t (3) -i (conj.)
	3s(-0)/AOR; same on an objectless TI(2)
	IC–o·či 3s–0/CC: IC+ -o· (TI(2) th.) -t (3) -i (conj.)
+o·či	*IC–o·či* 3s–0/PPL(INsg,obl): IC+ -o· (TI(2) th.) -t (3) -i (inan. sg.)
+o·čiki	*IC–o·čiki* 3–0/PPL(ANpl): IC+ -o· (TI(2) th.) -t (3)
	3(-0)/PPL(ANpl): same on an objectless TI(2)
+o·čini	*IC–o·čini* 3s–0/ITER: IC+ -o· (TI(2) th.) -t (3) -ini (neg.-iter.)
+o·hiya·ni	*IC–o·hiya·ni* 1s–0/DIM/PPL(INsg,obl): IC+ -o· (TI(2) th.) -·hi (dim.) -a·n (1s) -i (inan. sg.)
+o·hkapa	2s–0/POT: -o· (TI(2) th.) -hk (proh.) -apa (2s pot.)
	2s(-0)/POT: same on an objectless TI(2)
+o·hke·koha	2p–0/POT: -o· (TI(2) th.) -hk (proh.) -e·kw (2p) -ehe (pret.)
+o·ke	X–0/SUBJ: -o· (TI(2) th.) -ek (X) -e (subj.)
+o·kini	X–0/NEG: -o· (TI(2) th.) -ek (X) -ini (neg.-iter.)
+o·kini	*IC–o·kini* X–0/PPL(INpl): IC+ -o· (TI(2) th.) -ek (X) -ini (inan. pl.)
+o·ki	*e·h=–o·ki* X–0/AOR: e·h= (aor.) -o· (TI(2) th.) -ek (X) -i (conj.)
	X(-0)/AOR: same on an objectless TI(2)
+o·ki	*IC–o·ki* X–0/CC: IC+ -o· (TI(2) th.) -ek (X) -i (conj.)
+o·ki	*IC–o·ki* X–0/PPL(INsg,obl): IC+ -o· (TI(2) th.) -ek (X) -i (inan. sg.)
+o·ko	2p–0/IMP: -o· (TI(2) th.) -ko (2p imp.)
+o·kwe·ni	3s–0/INT: -o· (TI(2) th.) -kw (3,0 irr.) -e·ni (int.)
+o·ne·ha	X–0/POT: -o· (TI(2) th.) -ene·ha (X pot.)
+o·ničini	*IC–o·ničini* 3´–0/PPL(OBVsg): IC+ -o· (TI(2) th.) -ni (obv.) -t (3) -ini (obv. sg.)
+o·no	2s–0/IMP: -o· (TI(2) th.) -no (2s imp.)
+o·pena	*ne–o·pena* 1p–0/IND: ne- (1) -o· (TI(2) th.) -pena (1p,12)
	ke–o·pena 12–0/IND: ke- (2) -o· (TI(2) th.) -pwa (2p)
	12(-0)/IND: same on an objectless TI(2)
+o·pi	X–0/IND: -o· (TI(2) th.) -pi (X)
+o·pwa	*ke–o·pwa* 2p–0/IND: ke- (2) -o· (TI(2) th.) -pwa (2p)
+o·ta	*IC–o·ta* 3–0/PPL(ANsg): IC+ -o· (TI(2) th.) -t (3) -a (anim. sg.)
+o·te	3s–0/SUBJ: -o· (TI(2) th.) -t (3) -e (subj.)

+o·wa   3s–0/IND: -o· (TI(2) th.) -w (3,0) -a (anim. sg.)

+o·waki   3p–0/IND: -o· (TI(2) th.) -w (3,0) -aki (anim. pl.)

+o·wane·ni   *IC–o wane ni* 2s–0/INT.PPL(obl): IC+ -o· (TI(2) th.) -w (irr.) -an (2s)
                      -e·ni (int.)

+o·wa·či   *e·h=–o wa či* 3p–0/AOR: e·h= (aor.) -o· (TI(2) th.) -wa· (pl.) -t (3) -i (conj.)

+o·wa·čini   3p–0/NEG: -o· (TI(2) th.) -wa· (pl.) -t (3) -ini (neg.-iter.)

+o·wa·ne·ni *IC–o wa ne ni* 1s–0/INT.PPL(obl): IC+ -o· (TI(2) th.) -w (irr.) -a·n (1s)
                      -e·ni (int.)

+o·wa·sa   3p–0/POT: -o· (TI(2) th.) -wa· (pl.) -sa (3,0 pot.)
               3p(-0)/POT: same on an objectless TI(2)

+o·wa·te   3p–0/SUBJ: -o· (TI(2) th.) -wa· (pl.) -t (3) -e (subj.)

+oweči   *IC–o weči* X–0/REL/PPL(obl): IC+ -o· (TI(2) th.) -wet (X rel.) -i (inan. sg.)

+o·yakwe   12–0/SUBJ: -o· (TI(2) th.) -akw (12) -e (subj.)

+o·yane   2s–0/SUBJ: -o· (TI(2) th.) -an (2s) -e (subj.)

+oyani   *e·h=–o yani* 2s–0/AOR: e·h= (aor.) -o· (TI(2) th.) -an (2s) -i (conj.)

+oyani   *IC–o yani* 2s–0/PPL(INsg,obl): IC+ -o· (TI(2) th.) -an (2s) -i (inan. sg.)

+oyanini   2s–0/NEG: -o· (TI(2) th.) -an (2s) -ini (neg.-iter.)
               2s(-0)/NEG: same on an objectless TI(2)

+o·ya·ke   *e·h=–o ya ke* 1p–0/AOR: e·h= (aor.) -o· (TI(2) th.) -a·k (1p) -i (conj.)
            IC–o ya ke 1p–0/CC: IC+ -o· (TI(2) th.) -a·k (1p) -i (conj.)

+o·ya·kini   1p–0/NEG: -o· (TI(2) th.) -a·k (1p) -ini (neg.-iter.)

+o·ya·ni   *e·h=–o ya ni* 1s–0/AOR: e·h= (aor.) -o· (TI(2) th.) -a·n (1s) -i (conj.)
               1s(-0)/AOR: same on an objectless TI(2)
            IC–o ya ni 1s–0/CC: IC+ -o· (TI(2) th.) -a·n (1s) -i (conj.)

+o·ya·ni   *IC–o ya ni* 1s–0/PPL(INsg,obl): IC+ -o· (TI(2) th.) -a·n (1s) -i (inan. sg.)

+o·ya·nini *IC–o ya nini* 1s–0/ITER: IC+ -o· (TI(2) th.) -a·n (1s) -ini (neg.-iter.)

+o·ya·nini *IC–o ya nini* 1s–0/PPL(INpl): IC+ -o· (TI(2) th.) -a·n (1s) -ini (inan. pl.)

+o·ye·kwe *e·h=–o ye kwe* 2p–0/AOR: e·h= (aor.) -o· (TI(2) th.) -e·kw (2p) -i (conj.)

+o·ye·kwe *IC–o ye kwe* 2p–0/PPL(INsg,obl): IC+ -o· (TI(2) th.) -e·kw (2p) -i (inan. sg.)

-p   sg.: first and second singular in the dubitative and conclusive
             NOTE: -p (sg.) appears as -Ø (sg.) word-finally.

+pena   *ne–pena* 1p/IND: ne- (1) -pena (1p,12)
             ke–pena 12/IND: ke- (2) -pena (1p,12)
                 12–0/IND: same with Class 3 TI
             -pena 1p,12: first plural exclusive and inclusive in the independent order
             → *-pena·* before modal suffixes

+petoke   *ke–petoke* 2s/DUB: ke- (2) -p (sg.) -etoke (dub.)

+pi   X/IND: -pi (X)
                 X–0/IND: same with Class 3 TI
             -pi X: indefinite subject in the independent order
             → *-p* before dubitative and conclusive modal suffixes

+pwa   *ke–pwa* 2p/IND: ke- (2) -pwa (2p)
             -pwa 2p: second plural in the independent order.
             → *-pwa·* before modal suffixes

+sa	3s,0/POT: -sa (3,0 pot.)
	-sa 3,0 pot.: third person animate or inanimate subject, potential mode
	NOTE: As if -t (3), -k (3), -k (0) + -sa (pot.) → -sa (3,0 pot.)
-t	3: third person animate in the conjunct
	→ -k after a consonant-final stem or suffix
-t	X–3 irr.: indefinite acting on third animate, irrealis (interrogative and prioritive)
	Analyzed as: -w (irr.) + -et (X–3).
+ta	IC–ta 3/PPL(ANsg): IC+ -t (3) -a (anim. sg.)
	3–0/PPL(ANsg): same with Class 3 TI
+te	3s/SUBJ: -t (3) -e (subj.)
+tehe	e·h=–tehe 3s/AOR.PRET: e·h= (aor.) -t (3) -ehe (pret.)
	IC–tehe 3s/PRET.PPL(obl): IC+ -t (3) -ehe (pret.)
-w	3,0: third person animate and inanimate in the independent order
	NOTE: -w 3,0 umlauts stem-final a· or TA Theme 1 a· to e· (except in -ka·pa· 'stand' and the older inflection of nepwa·hka·- 'be smart')
	NOTE: -w 3,0 contracts leaving a long vowel in the dubitative, assertive, and conclusive; after a consonant, -w 3,0 contracts with nonfinal -a- and -e- to -o·-
-w	irr.: irrealis; marks interrogative and prioritive modes
	→ -ow after a consonant
	Contracts with -e- leaving a long vowel:
	$\quad$ -w (irr.) + -et (X–3) → -t (X–3 irr.)
	$\quad$ -w (irr.) + -ek (X) → -·k (X irr.)
	NOTE: some combinations show metathesis and fusion:
	$\quad$ -w (irr.) + -k<-t (3), -k (0) → -kw (3,0 irr.)
	$\quad$ -w (irr.) + -amet (3–1p) → -amet (1p) + -w (irr.) → -amekw (3–1p irr.)
	$\quad$ -w (irr.) + -namek (X–1p) → -namek (1p) + -w (irr.) → -nami·k (X–1p irr.)
-w	sg.: first and second singular on TA themes 1 and 2 in the independent indicative
	→ -∅ after -ekw TA th. 2
	NOTE: not used in direct diminutive forms
+wa	3s/IND: -w (3,0) -a (anim. sg.)
	3s–0/IND: same with Class 3 TI
+waki	3p/IND: -w (3,0) -aki (anim. pl.)
+wakwe·ni	e·h=–wakwe·ni 12/AOR.INT: e·h= (aor.) -w (irr.) -akw (12) -e·ni (int.)
+wakwe·ni	IC–wakwe·ni 12/INT.PPL(obl): IC+ -w (irr.) -akw (12) -e·ni (int.)
+wane	IC–wane 2s/CH.PRI: IC+ -w (irr.) -an (2s) -e (subj.)
+wane·na	IC–wane·na 2s/INT.PPL(ANsg): IC+ -w (irr.) -an (2s) -e·ni (int.) -a (anim. sg.)
+wane·ni	e·h=–wane·ni 2s/AOR.INT: e·h= (aor.) -w (irr.) -an (2s) -e·ni (int.)
	IC–wane·ni 2s/CH.INT: IC+ -w (irr.) -an (2s) -e·ni (int.)
+wane·ni	e·h=–wane·ni 2s/INT.PPL(loc.obl): e·h= (aor.) -w (irr.) -an (2s) -e·ni (int.)
	IC–wane·ni 2s/INT.PPL(obl): IC+ -w (irr.) -an (2s) -e·ni (int.)
+wani	0p/IND: -w (3,0) -ani (inan. pl.)

-wa·	pl.: pluralizes the animate third person proximate in the conjunct, potential, and prohibitive, and in some forms of the interrogative participle → -owa· after a consonant stem or after a consonant-final theme NOTE: not used in conjunct participles with -iki anim. pl.
-wa·	2p: pluralizes certain second person objects in the potential and imperative
+wa·či	*e·h=—wa·či* 3p/AOR: e·h= (aor.) -wa· (pl.) -t (3) -i (conj.) 3p–0/AOR: same with Class 3 TI *IC—wa·či* 3p/CC: IC+ -wa· (pl.) -t (3) -i (conj.) *—wa·či* 3p/CONJ: -wa· (pl.) -t (3) -i (conj.)
+wa·či	*e·h=—wa·či* 3p/PPL(loc.obl): e·h= (aor.) -wa· (pl.) -t (3) -i (inan. sg.) *IC—wa·či* 3p/PPL(INsg,obl): IC+ -wa· (pl.) -t (3) -i (inan. sg.) 3p–0/PPL(INsg,obl): same with Class 3 TI
+wa·čini	*IC—wa·čini* 3p/ITER: IC+ -wa· (pl.) -t (3) -ini (neg.-iter.) *—wa·čini* 3p/NEG: -wa· (pl.) -t (3) -ini (neg.-iter.) 3p–0/NEG: same with Class 3 TI
+wa·čini	*e·h=—wa·čini* 3p/PPL(loc.obl.pl): e·h= (aor.) -wa· (pl.) -t (3) -ini (inan. pl.) *IC—wa·čini* 3p/PPL(obl.pl): IC+ -wa· (pl.) -t (3) -ini (inan. pl.) 3p–0/PPL(INpl): same with Class 3 TI and inanimate plural head
+wa·čini	*IC—wa·čini* 3p/PPL(OBVsg): IC+ -wa· (pl.) -t (3) -ini (obv. sg.)
+wa·ke·ni	*IC—wa·ke·ni* 1p/INT.PPL(obl): IC+ -w (irr.) -a·k (1p) -e·ni (int.)
+wa·ki	*o—wa·ki* 3p(LOC): o- (3) -wa·w (2p,3p) -eki (loc.)
+wa·ne·ni	*IC—wa·ne·ni* 1s/INT.PPL(obl): IC+ -w (irr.) -a·n (1s) -e·ni (int.)
-wa·t	X rel. irr.: indefinite subject, relational, irrealis (interrogative and prioritive) Analyzed as: -w (irr.) + -wet (X rel.).
+wa·če	3p/IMP: -wa· (pl.) -če (3,0 imp.)
+wa·sa	3p/POT: -wa· (pl.) -sa (3,0 pot.)
+wa·te	3p/SUBJ: -wa· (pl.) -t (3) -e (subj.)
+wa·tehe	*IC—wa·tehe* 3p/CH.PRET: IC+ -wa· (pl.) -t (3) -ehe (pret.) 3p/PRET.PPL(obl): same
+wa·te·ni	X/REL/INT: -w (irr.) -wet (X rel.) -e·ni (int.)
-wa·w	2p,3p: pluralizes second- and third-person possessors of nouns, and second-person subjects of inverse verbs in the independent order → -owa·w after stems and themes in -Cw → -(o)wa· before -eki loc. and -etoke dub.
+wa·wa	*ke—wa·wa* 2p(ANsg): ke- (2) -wa·w (2p,3p) -a (anim. sg.)
+wa·wahi	*o—wa·wahi* 3p(OBVpl): o- (3) -wa·w (2p,3p) -ahi (obv. pl.)
+wa·waki	*ke—wa·waki* 2p(ANpl): ke- (2) -wa·w (2p,3p) -aki (anim. pl.)
+wa·wani	*o—wa·wani* 3p(INpl): o- (3) -wa·w (2p,3p) -ani (inan. pl.)
+wa·wani	*o—wa·wani* 3p(OBVsg): o- (3) -wa·w (2p,3p) -ani (obv. sg.)
+wa·wi	*ke—wa·wi* 2p(INsg): ke- (2) -wa·w (2p,3p) -i (inan. sg.) *o—wa·wi* 3p(INsg): o- (3) -wa·w (2p,3p) -i (inan. sg.)
+weči	*e·h=—weči* X/REL/AOR: e·h= (aor.) -wet (X rel.) -i (conj.) *IC—weči* X/REL/CC: IC+ -wet (X rel.) -i (conj.)
+weči	*IC—weči* X/REL/PPL(INsg,obl): IC+ -wet (X rel.) -i (inan. sg.) *e·h=—weči* X/REL/PPL(loc.obl): e·h= (aor.) -wet (X rel.) -i (inan. sg.)
+wečini	*IC—wečini* X/REL/ITER: IC+ -wet (X rel.) -ini (neg.-iter.)

+wehapa	3s,0s/CON: -w (3,0) -ehapa (con.)
+wehapaniki	3p/CON: -w (3,0) -ehapa (con.) -iki (anim. pl.)
+wepani	3s,0s/AST: -w (3,0) -epani (ast.)
+wepaniki	3p/AST: -w (3,0) -epani (ast.) -iki (anim. pl.)
-wet	X rel.: indefinite subject, relational
	→ *-owet* after a consonant
	NOTE: -w (irr.) + *-wet* (X rel.) þ|□-*wa ɨ* (X rel. irr.)
+wete	X/REL/SUBJ: -wet (X rel.) -e (subj.)
+wetoke	3s,0s/DUB: -w (3,0) -etoke (dub.)
+wetoke·hiki	3p/DUB: -w (3,0) -etoke (dub.): -iki (anim. pl.)
+we·kwe·ni	*IC–we·kwe·ni* 2p/CH.INT: IC+ -w (irr.) -e·kw (2p) -e·ni (int.)
+we·kwe·ni	*IC–we·kwe·ni* 2p/INT.PPL(obl): IC+ -w (irr.) -e·kw (2p) -e·ni (int.)
+wi	0s/IND: -w (3,0) -i (inan. sg.)
+yakwe	*e·h–yakwe* 12/AOR: e·h= (aor.) -akw (12) -i (conj.)
+yakwe	*e·h–yakwe* 12/PPL(loc.obl): e·h= (aor.) -akw (12) -i (inan. sg.)
	IC–yakwe 12/PPL(INsg,obl): IC+ -akw (12) -i (inan. sg.)
+yakwe	12/SUBJ: -akw (12) -e (subj.)
+yakwini	*IC–yakwini* 12/ITER: IC+ -akw (12) -ini (neg.-iter.)
	–yakwini 12/NEG: -akw (12) -ini (neg.-iter.)
+yakwini	*IC–yakwini* 12/PPL(INpl): IC+ -akw (12) -ini (inan. pl.)
	12/PPL(obl.pl): same
+yana	*IC–yana* 2s/PPL(ANsg): IC+ -an (2s) -a (anim. sg.)
+yane	2s/SUBJ: -an (2s) -e (subj.)
+yanehe	2s/SUBJ.PRET: -an (2s) -ehe (pret.)
+yani	*e·h–yani* 2s/AOR: e·h= (aor.) -an (2s) -i (conj.)
	2s–0/AOR: same with Class 3 TI
+yani	*IC–yani* 2s/PPL(INsg,obl): IC+ -an (2s) -i (inan. sg.)
	e·h–yani 2s/PPL(loc.obl): e·h= (aor.) -an (2s) -i (inan. sg.)
+yanini	*IC–yanini* 2s/ITER: IC+ -an (2s) -ini (neg.-iter.)
	–yanini 2s/NEG: -an (2s) -ini (neg.-iter.)
+yanini	*IC–yanini* 2s–0/PPL(INpl): IC+ -an (2s) -ini (inan. pl.)
+ya·ke	*e·h–ya·ke* 1p/AOR: e·h= (aor.) -a·k (1p) -i (conj.)
	IC–ya·ke 1p/CC: IC+ -a·k (1p) -i (conj.)
+ya·ke	*IC–ya·ke* 1p/PPL(INsg,obl): IC+ -a·k (1p) -i (inan. sg.)
	e·h–ya·ke 1p/PPL(loc.obl): e·h= (aor.) -a·k (1p) -i (inan. sg.)
+ya·kini	*IC–ya·kini* 1p/ITER: IC+ -a·k (1p) -ini (neg.-iter.)
	–ya·kini 1p/NEG: -a·k (1p) -ini (neg.-iter.)
+ya·kini	*e·h–ya·kini* 1p/PPL(loc.obl.pl): e·h= (aor.) -a·k (1p) -ini (inan. pl.)
+ya·na	*IC–ya·na* 1s/PPL(ANsg): IC+ -a·n (1s) -a (anim. sg.)
+ya·ne	1s/SUBJ: -a·n (1s) -e (subj.)
+ya·nehe	1s/SUBJ.PRET: -a·n (1s) -ehe (pret.)
+ya·ni	*e·h–ya·ni* 1s/AOR: e·h= (aor.) -a·n (1s) -i (conj.)
	IC–ya·ni 1s/CC: IC+ -a·n (1s) -i (conj.)
+ya·ni	*IC–ya·ni* 1s/PPL(INsg,obl): IC+ -a·n (1s) -i (inan. sg.)
	e·h–ya·ni 1s/PPL(loc.obl): e·h= (aor.) -a·n (1s) -i (inan. sg.)

+ya·nini	*IC–ya·nini* 1s/ITER: IC+ -a·n (1s) -ini (neg.-iter.)
	–ya·nini 1s/NEG: -a·n (1s) -ini (neg.-iter.)
+ya·nini	*IC–ya·nini* 1s/PPL(INpl): IC+ -a·n (1s) -ini (inan. pl.)
+ye·kwe	*e·h=–ye·kwe* 2p/AOR: e·h= (aor.) -e·kw (2p) -i (conj.)
+ye·kwe	*e·h=–ye·kwe* 2p/PPL(loc.obl): e·h= (aor.) -e·kw (2p) -i (inan. sg.)
	IC–ye·kwe 2p/PPL(INsg,obl): IC+ -e·kw (2p) -i (inan. sg.)
	IC–ye·kwe 2p/PPL(loc.obl): IC+ -e·kw (2p) -i (inan. sg.) (With *a·mi* PV.)
+ye·kwe	2p/SUBJ: -e·kw (2p) -e (subj.)
+ye·kwini	*IC–ye·kwini* 2p/ITER: IC+ -e·kw (2p) -ini (neg.-iter.)
	–ye·kwini 2p/NEG: -e·kw (2p) -ini (neg.-iter.)
+∅	*ne–∅* 1s/IND: ne- (1) -∅ (sg.)
	ke–∅ 2s/IND: ke- (2) -∅ (sg.)
	2s–0/IND: same with Class 3 TI
	NOTE: -∅ (sg.) appears as -p (sg.) before a modal suffix.
+∅	VOCsg: vocative singular on nouns
	NOTE: indicated after stems in -*h* and with irregular kinship terms
-∅	sg.: first and second singular in the independent
	NOTE: not indicated for singular possessors of nouns
-∅	TA th. 1: see -a· (TA th. 1)

www.ingramcontent.com/pod-product-compliance
Lightning Source LLC
Chambersburg PA
CBHW080835120626
46553CB00009B/2433